Rules and Guidance for Pharmaceutical Manufacturers and Distributors 2022

Rules and Guidance for Pharmaceutical Manufacturers and Distributors 2022

Compiled by the Medicines and Healthcare products Regulatory Agency

Pharmaceutical Press

Published by Pharmaceutical Press

66–68 East Smithfield, London E1W 1AW, UK

© Crown Copyright 2022

Medicines & Healthcare products Regulatory Agency

Medicines and Healthcare products Regulatory Agency
10 South Colonnade,
Canary Wharf,
London E14 4PU.
Stay connected: mhra.gov.uk/stayconnected
Information on re-use of crown copyright information can be found on the MHRA
website: www.mhra.gov.uk

Designed and published by Pharmaceutical Press 2022

(**P.P**) is a trade mark of Pharmaceutical Press

Pharmaceutical Press is the publishing division of the Royal Pharmaceutical Society

First edition published in 1971 as the *Guide to Good Pharmaceutical Manufacturing Practice*, second edition in 1977, third edition 1983, fourth edition as the *Rules and Guidance for Pharmaceutical Manufacturers* in 1993, fifth edition as the *Rules and Guidance for Pharmaceutical Manufacturers and Distributors* in 1997, sixth edition in 2002, seventh edition in 2007, eighth edition in 2014, ninth edition in 2015, tenth edition in 2017, eleventh edition in 2022, reprinted in 2023

Index by Lyn Nesbitt-Smith of LNSIndexing, Brighton, UK

Typeset by Newgen Knowledge Works, Chennai, India

Printed in Great Britain by TJ Books Limited, Padstow, Cornwall

ISBN 978 0 85711 439 6 (print)

Contents

4 UK Guidance on the Manufacture, Importation and Distribution of Active Substances — 633

Future UK rules and guidance

The UK left the EU on 31 January 2020. EU legislation was carried forward during the transition period to provide stability to industry as well as time to implement necessary mitigations. After the transition period expired on 31 December 2020, Northern Ireland (NI) continues to comply with EU law as per the Northern Ireland Protocol (NIP) whilst GB (England, Scotland and Wales) does not.

The EU published (in December 2021) a package of measures designed to remove barriers to NI supply of medicines. The package includes an extension to the existing grace period to provide time to put in place long term legislative solutions and new legislative proposals which seek to resolve NI issues permanently to come into effect in 2022.

The extension to the grace period means that existing flexibilities for medicines supplied to NI will remain in place until the permanent solutions can be legislated for.

The Medicines and Healthcare products Regulatory Agency (MHRA) has published guidance online which is regularly updated and can be accessed here: https://www.gov.uk/government/collections/new-guidance-and-information-for-industry-from-the-mhra#importing-and-exporting.

Preface to the 2022 edition

This is the 2022 edition of Rules and Guidance for Pharmaceutical Manufacturers and Distributors (the "Orange Guide"). Now in its 11th edition the guide has been updated with revised sections on:

- Medicines and Healthcare products Regulatory Agency (MHRA) (Overview of the MHRA, Compliance Teams, Applications and Registrations, Defective Medicines Report Centre, Importing unlicensed medicines – import notifications, Criminal Enforcement Unit, and Compliance Management and Inspection Action Group)
- amended extracts from the Human Medicines Regulations 2012 relating to:
  - manufacture, importation and assembly,
  - wholesale dealing,
  - brokering medicine, and
  - manufacturing, importing and distributing active substances.
- the Code of Practice for Qualified Persons in Chapter 3, Guidance on Manufacture and Importation.
- UK guidance on complying with the guidelines on Good Distribution Practice for wholesale distributors and brokers of medicines and manufacturers, importers and distributors of active substances.
- UK guidance on:
  - risk-based inspections,
  - conditions of holding a manufacturer's licence, wholesale dealer's licence, a broker registration and an active substance registration, and
  - controls on certain medicinal products.

Extracts from the Medicines for Human Use (Clinical Trials) Regulations 2004 relating to manufacture, importation and assembly of investigational medicinal products have been added.

There is new guidance on:

- conditions of holding a manufacturing authorisation for investigational medicinal products,
- importing guidance for investigational medicinal products from countries on a list to Great Britain,

- Pharmaceutical Quality System expectations and Authorisation requirements for investigational medicinal products importation oversight,
- list of approved countries for import,
- pharmacovigilance for wholesalers,
- the naming of sites on a wholesale dealer's licence,
- self-inspection for wholesale dealers and the responsible person for import.

This revised edition brings together in one chapter Good Distribution Practice guidance and the MHRA's expectations for compliance.

There is also a new flowchart for the registration of handling active substance.

The 2022 version is available online, as part of "Medicines Complete" – a subscription-based database of leading medicines and healthcare references – and in e-reader formats.

The *Orange Guide* 2022

I am pleased to introduce the 11th edition of the Rules and Guidance for Pharmaceutical Manufacturers and Distributors known as the Orange Guide issued by the Medicines and Healthcare products Regulatory Agency (MHRA). This updates the 2017 edition and as with the previous publications it brings together existing and revised material concerning the manufacture, importation, distribution and brokering of human medicines and matters relating to the manufacture, importation and distribution of active substances.

We have introduced extracts from the Medicines for Human Use (Clinical Trials) Regulations 2004 and new guidance on conditions of holding a manufacturing authorisation for investigational medicinal products, guidance for importing investigational medicinal products from countries on a list to Great Britain, Pharmaceutical Quality System expectations and Authorisation requirements for investigational medicinal products importation oversight and list of approved countries for import. There is also new guidance on pharmacovigilance for wholesalers, the naming of sites on a wholesale dealer's licence, and self-inspection for wholesale dealers and the responsible person for import.

General updates have been provided including overview of the MHRA, Compliance Teams, Applications and Registrations, Defective Medicines Report Centre, Importing unlicensed medicines and import notifications, Criminal Enforcement Unit, Compliance Management and Inspection Action Group, the Code of Practice for Qualified Persons and guidance on manufacture and importation.

The amended extracts from the Human Medicines Regulations 2012 relate to manufacture, importation and assembly wholesale dealing, brokering medicine, manufacturing importing and distributing active substances, risk-based inspections, conditions of holding a manufacturer's licence, wholesale dealer's licence, a broker registration or an active substance registration.

Although much of the text in this book is available in its original form in other places, including various websites, I am pleased that the Orange Guide continues to satisfy a demand for information in one authoritative and convenient place. Also available is a separate updated GDP Guide for the wholesale dealing market.

I hope that this revised edition in its existing formats will continue to be useful, but the publication team very much welcome feedback so we can continue to improve this, and our other publications. See section on Feedback for details.

Dr Laura Squire OBE Chief Healthcare Quality and Access Officer
January 2022

Acknowledgements

To the European Commission for permission to reproduce the rules governing medicinal products in the EC. Vol IV. Good Manufacturing Practice for medicinal products (http://ec.europa.eu/health/documents/eudralex/vol-4/index_en.htm) © European Union, the text of the Directives (only European Union legislation printed in the paper edition of the *Official Journal of the European Union* [OJ] is deemed authentic), Regulations and Guidelines.

To the Royal Society of Biology, the Royal Pharmaceutical Society and the Royal Society of Chemistry for permission to reproduce the texts of the Code of Practice for Qualified Persons.

To the Heads of Medicines Agencies for permission to reproduce the names and addresses of other human and veterinary medicines authorities in Europe.

To Cogent for permission to reproduce the new Gold Standard role profile for the Responsible Person.

To HMSO and the Queen's Printer for Scotland for permission to reproduce extracts from the Human Medicines Regulations 2012 [SI 2012/1916] as amended and from the Medicines for Human Use (Clinical Trials) Regulations 2004 [SI 2004 No 1031]. Contains public sector information licensed under the Open Government Licence v3.0.

Feedback

Comments on the content or presentation of the Orange Guide are encouraged and will be used to develop further editions. Your views are valued and both the MHRA and Pharmaceutical Press would appreciate you taking the time to contact us. Please visit the feedback page at http://www.pharmpress.com/orangeguide-feedback or send your feedback to the address below:

"The Orange Guide"
Customer Services
Medicines and Healthcare products Regulatory Agency
10 South Colonnade,
Canary Wharf,
London E14 4PU
United Kingdom
Tel.: +44 (0)20 3080 6000
Fax: +44 (0)20 3118 9803

Introduction

This publication brings together the main pharmaceutical regulations, and guidance that manufacturers, wholesalers and brokers of human medicines are expected to follow when making, distributing or being involved in the supply of medicinal products. It also covers the main guidance which affects manufacturers, importers and distributors of active substances. It is of particular relevance to all holders of manufacturer's licences and wholesale dealer's licences and to their Qualified Persons (QPs) and Responsible Persons (RPs), and persons registered to broker finished medicinal products or manufacture, import or distribute active substances within the UK. All these players have a responsibility for ensuring compliance with many of these regulatory requirements.

The obligation on UK government to ensure that pharmaceutical manufacturers are authorised is stated in the Human Medicines Regulation 2012 [SI 2012/1916] ("the Regulations"). This Regulation is also the source of requirements for compliance with Good Manufacturing Practice (GMP), employment of QPs and repeated inspections by the MHRA. The Regulations also require importers, manufacturers and distributors of active substances who are established to register their activity with the MHRA.

The Regulations require all wholesale distributors to be authorised, to have available RPs or RPi and comply with the guidelines on Good Distribution Practice (GDP). The Regulations also require brokers of medicines to be registered with the MHRA and to comply with appropriate GDP requirements.

Manufacturers are required to name a QP on their manufacturer's licence. No batch of medicinal product may be released to the market unless a nominated QP has certified that it has been manufactured and checked in compliance with the laws in force. Guidance to QPs in fulfilling their responsibilities is given in the Regulations and in the Code of Practice[1] for Qualified Persons which they are expected to follow. In similar spirit,

---

[1] The Royal Society of Biology, The Royal Pharmaceutical Society, The Royal Society of Chemistry. Code of Practice for Qualified Persons. In: Register of Qualified Persons. London: The Royal Society of Biology, The Royal Pharmaceutical Society, The Royal Society of Chemistry 2009, revised August 2015.

wholesalers are required to appoint an RP or RPi who has the knowledge and responsibility to ensure that correct procedures are followed during distribution. Notes on the qualifications and duties of RPs and RPi are given to assist this.

The distribution network for medicinal products has become complex and involves many players. Revised guidelines for GDP assist wholesale distributors in conducting their activities and to prevent falsified medicines from entering the legal supply chain. The guidance also provides specific rules for persons involved in activities in relation to the sale or purchase of medicinal products while not conducting a wholesale activity, i.e. brokers of licensed human medicines.

The manufacture of active substances for use in a licensed medicinal product must be in compliance with the relevant GMP. Active substances imported from outside the EEA must have been manufactured in accordance with standards of GMP.

There are principles and guidelines for GMP for active substances, GDP guidelines for active substances, and guidelines for the formal risk assessment process for excipients.

The aim of GMP and GDP is to assure the quality of the medicinal product for the safety, well-being and protection of the patient. In achieving this aim it is impossible to over-emphasise the importance of people, at all levels, in the assurance of the quality of medicinal products.

The great majority of reported defective medicinal products has resulted from human error or carelessness, not from failures in technology. All the people involved with the production, Quality Control or distribution of medicinal products, whether key personnel, production or control or warehouse staff, inspectors of a regulatory authority or others involved in the many activities that lead to a patient taking a medicine, should bear this constantly in mind when performing their duties.

Glossary of UK Legislation

UK Legislation

THE HUMAN MEDICINES REGULATIONS 2012 [SI 2012/1916]

The Regulations set out a comprehensive regime for the authorisation of medicinal products for human use; for the manufacture, import, distribution, sale and supply of those products; for their labelling and advertising; and for pharmacovigilance.

For the most part the Regulations implement Directive 2001/83/EC of the European Parliament and of the Council of 6 November 2001 on the community code relating to medicinal products for human use (as amended). They also provide for the enforcement in the United Kingdom of Regulation (EC) No 726/2004 laying down Community procedures for the authorisation and supervision of medicinal products for human and veterinary use and establishing a European Medicines Agency.

THE MEDICINES (PRODUCTS FOR HUMAN USE) (FEES) REGULATIONS 2016 [SI 2016/190]

These Regulations make provision for the fees payable under the Medicines Act 1971 and other fees payable in respect of EU obligations including those relating to authorisations, licences, certificates and registrations in respect of medicinal products for human use.

THE MEDICINES FOR HUMAN USE (CLINICAL TRIALS) REGULATIONS 2004 [SI 2004/1031] AS AMENDED

These Regulations implement Directive 2001/20/EC on the approximation of laws, regulations and administrative provisions of the Member States relating to the implementation of good clinical practice in the conduct of clinical trials on medicinal products for human use.

THE UNLICENSED MEDICINAL PRODUCTS FOR HUMAN USE (TRANSMISSIBLE SPONGIFORM ENCEPHALOPATHIES) (SAFETY) REGULATIONS 2003 [SI 2003/1680]

These regulate the importation and marketing of unlicensed medicinal products for human use in order to minimise the risk of the transmission of transmissible spongiform encephalopathies via those products.

Medicines and Healthcare products Regulatory Agency

Medicines and Healthcare products Regulatory Agency

Contents

Medicines and Healthcare products Regulatory Agency

The Medicines and Healthcare products Regulatory Agency regulates medicines, medical devices and blood components for transfusion in the UK.

About the Medicines and Healthcare products Regulatory Agency

Our purpose is clear: to protect and improve patient health by enabling the earliest access to, and high-quality supply of, safe, effective and innovative medical products through proportionate, data-driven assessment of risks and benefits.

We aspire to be a leading global example of delivering excellence in public health and patient safety, enabled through regulation and at the forefront of innovation. Delivering our vision relies on our ability to act as one agency and to relentlessly pursue the delivery of meaningful outcomes for the patients we serve.

This means drawing together our scientific rigour and regulatory expertise to address the challenges faced by the life sciences sector and health service; how best to develop new regulatory frameworks and quickly realise the benefits that new therapies, artificial intelligence and innovative healthcare products can bring to patients, while still ensuring the right levels of safety, quality and efficacy. It also means more systematic engagement with patients and putting patient outcomes at the heart of what we do.

How We Operate

We are a government body that regulates medicines, medical devices and blood products for transfusion in the UK, underpinned by science and research.

We do this by making sure that the products we regulate — from painkillers to pacemakers — work properly and are acceptably safe; and by responding quickly and effectively when new concerns come to light.

No product is completely free of risk, but by using an array of evidence, we provide a critical appraisal of whether a healthcare product's benefits outweigh its risks and is suitable for use in the UK. Where some lower-risk medical devices are regulated by third party organisations, we set the regulatory requirements that define when those products can be approved for use in the UK.

To help the life sciences industry to develop effective and innovative healthcare products, we also engage proactively in the early stages of development.

We advise on the designs of clinical trials to ensure patient involvement and patient safety, and we advise on the evidence of safety and impact that developers will need to demonstrate for each product, to help products reach patients as quickly as possible while maintaining high levels of safety and quality.

Following our appraisal decision, we work with manufacturers to help them to comply with expectations of quality for their product to ensure they are safe to use.

We also monitor trends in data from a wide range of different sources, which enables us to quickly identify safety concerns.

Where these arise, we investigate and take a decision, using independent expertise, on the best course of action which could lead to products being removed from the UK market.

Our Responsibilities

The Medicines and Healthcare products Regulatory Agency is responsible for:

- ensuring that medicines, medical devices and blood components for transfusion meet applicable standards of safety, quality and efficacy;
- ensuring that the supply chain for medicines, medical devices and blood components is safe and secure;
- promoting international standardisation and harmonisation to assure the effectiveness and safety of biological medicines;
- helping to educate the public and healthcare professionals about the risks and benefits of medicines, medical devices and blood components, leading to safer and more effective use;
- supporting innovation and research and development that's beneficial to public health; and
- influencing UK, EU and international regulatory frameworks so that they are risk proportionate and effective at protecting public health.

All licensed human medicines available in the UK are subject to rigorous scrutiny by the MHRA before they can be used by patients. This ensures that human medicines meet acceptable standards on safety, quality and efficacy. It is the responsibility of the MHRA and the expert advisory bodies set up by the Human Medicines Regulations 2012 [SI 2012/1916] to ensure that the sometimes difficult balance between safety and effectiveness is achieved. MHRA experts assess all applications for new human medicines to ensure that they meet the required standards. This is followed up by a system of inspection and testing that continues throughout the lifetime of the medicine.

As the UK government's public health body that brings together the regulation of human medicines and medical devices, science and research, the roles of the MHRA are to:

- license medicines, manufacturers and distributors;
- register brokers of finished medicines and manufacturers, importers and distributors of active substances;
- register websites that offer medicines for sale or supply to the public;
- regulate medical devices;
- approve UK clinical trials;
- monitor medicines and medical devices after licensing;

- ensure the safety and quality of blood;
- tackle illegal activity involving medicines, medical devices and blood;
- promote an understanding of the benefits and risks;
- facilitate the development of new medicines;
- support innovation in medicines and medical devices;
- be a leading provider of data and data services for healthcare research;
- work with international partners on issues; and
- provide a national voice for the benefits and risks of medicines, medical devices and medical technologies.

Our priorities are outlined in our Delivery Plan Delivery Plan 2021-2023: Putting patients first: a new era for our agency. The plan ensures we keep a constant focus on delivering meaningful outcomes for patients, protecting public health through excellence in regulation and science and becoming a truly world-leading, enabling regulator. The plan sets out 14 objectives grouped into 6 central themes:

- Scientific innovation
- Healthcare access
- Patient safety
- Dynamic organisation
- Collaborative partnerships
- Financial sustainability

You can find the Delivery Plan 2021-2023 on our website: www.gov.uk/mhra

Compliance

The MHRA is responsible for ensuring compliance with the standards that apply to the manufacture and supply of medicines on the UK market. This is achieved by licensing, inspection and enforcement across the full lifecycle of medicines, including manufacturers, wholesale dealers and importers of medicines, and by inspecting clinical trials, toxicology laboratories and pharmacovigilance systems.

Compliance Teams and Applications and Registrations

Compliance Teams

Compliance comprises of dedicated teams of Inspectors for Good Manufacturing Practice (GMP), Good Distribution Practice (GDP), Good Laboratory Practice (GLP), Good Clinical Practice (GCP) and Good Pharmacovigilance Practice (GPvP).

Good Manufacturing Practice (GMP)

GMP Inspectors conduct inspections of pharmaceutical manufacturers and other organisations to assess compliance with EU guidance on Good Manufacturing Practice (GMP) and the relevant details contained in marketing authorisations and Clinical Trials Authorisations. They ensure that medicines supplied to the UK and its mutual recognition partners meet consistent high standards of quality, safety and efficacy. Overseas manufacturing sites to be named on UK marketing authorisations are also required to pass an inspection prior to approval of the marketing authorisation application. Following approval, a risk-based inspection programme maintains on-going surveillance of UK and overseas manufacturing site compliance with EU GMP.

GMP Inspectors are responsible for inspecting and authorising a range of manufacturers of sterile and non-sterile dosage forms, biological products, investigational medicinal products, herbal products and active pharmaceutical ingredients, in addition to certain analytical laboratories. The manufacture of unlicensed medicines by holders of Manufacturer "Specials" Licences in the UK NHS and commercial sector is also inspected on a routine basis to assess compliance with relevant legislation and GMP.

The safety and quality of human blood for transfusion, or for further manufacture into blood-derived medicines, are ensured through inspections of relevant collection, processing, testing and storage activities at Blood Establishments and UK Hospital Blood Banks. These inspections assess compliance with specific UK regulatory requirements, which take into account the detailed principles of GMP.

GMP Inspectors serve on a number of UK and international technical and standards committees and provide help and advice to senior managers, Ministers and colleagues across the Agency, as necessary. Support and expertise are also provided to the inspection programmes of the European Directorate for Quality of Medicines (EDQM) and the World Health Organization (WHO).

Good Manufacturing Practice: gmpinspectorate@mhra.gov.uk

Good Distribution Practice

GDP Inspectors conduct inspections of sites of wholesale dealers to assess compliance with EU Guidelines on Good Distribution Practice (GDP) and the conditions of a wholesale dealer's licence set out in the Human Medicines Regulations 2012 [SI 2012/1916].

Inspectors will ensure that medicinal products are handled, stored and transported under conditions as prescribed by the marketing authorisation or product specification.

Inspections are undertaken of new applicants and then subsequently on a routine schedule based on a risk assessment of the site.

Good Distribution Practice: GDP.Inspectorate@mhra.gov.uk

Good Laboratory Practice

Good Laboratory Practice (GLP) Inspectors conduct inspections of UK facilities that carry out non-clinical studies for submission to domestic and international regulatory authorities to assess the safety of new chemicals to humans, animals and the environment. These inspections are designed to assure that studies are performed in accordance with relevant regulation and the Organisation for Economic Co-operation and Development (OECD) principles as required by OECD Council acts relating to the Mutual Acceptance of Data. The range of test facilities to be monitored include those involved in the testing of human and veterinary pharmaceuticals, agrochemicals, food and feed additives, industrial chemicals and cosmetics.

Good Laboratory Practice: gxplabs@mhra.gov.uk

Good Clinical Practice

The GCP Inspectorate is responsible for inspecting clinical trials for compliance with Good Clinical Practice (GCP). Compliance with this good practice provides assurance that the rights, safety and well-being of trial subjects are protected, and that the results of the clinical trials are reliable.

The function of the GCP Inspectorate is to assess the compliance of organisations with UK legislation relating to the conduct of clinical trials in investigational medicinal products. This is achieved through carrying out inspections of sponsor organisations that hold Clinical Trial Authorisations (CTAs), organisations that provide services to clinical trial sponsors or investigator sites.

Clinical Practice: ctdhelpline@mhra.gov.uk

Good Pharmacovigilance Practice

Good Pharmacovigilance Practice (GPvP) is the minimum standard for monitoring the safety of medicines on sale to the public in the UK. The MHRA's Pharmacovigilance Inspectorate conducts inspections of marketing authorisation holders (MAHs) to determine whether they comply with pharmacovigilance obligations established within the UK. GPvP inspections are scheduled as part of the MHRA's national inspection programme according to a risk-based approach, largely founded on the risk factors listed in EU statutory guidance (Good Vigilance Practice [GVP] Module III), as modified by the Exceptions and modifications to EU guidance on good pharmacovigilance practices that apply to UK MAHs and the licensing authority.

Good Pharmacovigilance Practice: gpvpinspectors@mhra.gov.uk

Applications and Registrations

Manufacturer's and wholesale dealer's licence/authorisations

Manufacture of and wholesale dealing in medicinal products are licensable activities under UK legislation. These licences are referred to as process licences and include a wide range of licences covering the diverse activities listed below:

- Licences for the manufacture/importation of licensed medicinal products for human use, commonly abbreviated to MIA.
- "Specials" licences for the manufacture/importation of unlicensed medicinal products for human use, commonly abbreviated to MS.
- Authorisations for the manufacture/importation of Investigational Medicinal Products for human use, commonly abbreviated to MIA(IMP).
- Authorisations for the manufacture/importation of licensed medicinal products for veterinary use, commonly abbreviated to ManA.
- "Specials" licences for the manufacture of unlicensed medicinal products for veterinary use, commonly abbreviated to ManSA.
- Authorisation for the manufacture of Exempt Advanced Therapy Medicinal Products, commonly abbreviated to MeAT.
- Licences for the wholesale dealing of medicinal products for human use, commonly abbreviated to WDA(H).
- Licences for the wholesale dealing/importation of medicinal products for veterinary use, commonly abbreviated to WDA(V).
- Blood Establishment Authorisations, commonly abbreviated to BEA.

The MHRA make use of computer technology to process all applications for new licences, variations to existing licences, changes of ownership, terminations, and cancellations, as well as suspensions and revocations on the instructions of the Inspection Action Group (IAG). They are also responsible for issuing Certificates of Good Manufacturing Practice (GMP) and Good Distribution Practice (GDP) on behalf of the GMP and GDP Compliance Teams.

Registrations

The Human Medicines Regulations 2012 set out requirements that certain activities require registration and that a minimum of information be published on a publicly accessible register. These activities include the following:

- Brokering of finished human medicines.
- Manufacture, importation and distribution of active substances.
- Internet sales of medicine in Northern Ireland to the public.

MHRA process all applications for registration, variations to existing registrations, annual compliance reports, terminations, cancellations, suspensions and revocations, making extensive use of computer technology to do so.

Export certificates

The MHRA is also responsible for issuing certificates in support of the World Health Organization (WHO) scheme on the quality of pharmaceutical products moving in international commerce (often referred to as export certificates):

- Certificate of a pharmaceutical product (CPP): the certificate shows details including:
  - the marketing authorisation holder;
  - the active ingredients and excipients;
  - the manufacturing, packaging and batch release sites;
  - whether or not the product is on the market in the UK.
- Certificate of licensing status (CLS): the certificate of licensing status is for importing agents who must screen bids made by an international tender for licensed or unlicensed products (excluding specials). The certificate has a limit of ten products and one country for each certificate. The product name, dosage form, active ingredients and amounts should be the same as the medicine's product licence (if it's licensed).
- Certificate of a pharmaceutical product (unlicensed): the drug must have been manufactured in the UK and you must have a manufacturer licence for the drug.
- Certificate of manufacturing status (CMS): the certificate confirms that the named sites on a specified manufacturer licence meet good manufacturing practice requirements. All or any of the sites named on the manufacture licence can be listed on the certificate. The certificate won't show any product specific information.

- Certificate for the importation of a pharmaceutical constituent (CPC): the specific active ingredient or excipient must be in either:
  - a current licensed human medicine; or
  - a national or international pharmacopoeia (official standards for pharmaceutical substances and medicines).

  The manufacturing site must hold a valid certificate of inspection from the MHRA. The certificate is country and ingredient specific. A certificate can be for only one site function, e.g. manufacture, packaging or batch release. You can apply for a certificate for each function.

Defective Medicines Report Centre

The role of the Defective Medicines Report Centre (DMRC) is to minimise the hazard to patients arising from the distribution of defective medicines by providing an emergency assessment and communication system across manufacturers, distributors, regulatory authorities and users.

It achieves this aim by:

- receiving and assessing reports of suspected defective medicinal products for human use.
- advising and monitoring necessary actions by the responsible Licence Holder.
- communicating the details of this action to relevant parties as necessary.

The DMRC is staffed by suitably trained and experienced personnel with backgrounds in pharmaceutical quality assurance and good manufacturing practice in hospital pharmacy and/or the pharmaceutical industry.

The pharmaceutical assessors are supported by administrative staff. Experts in specialist areas can be consulted when needed, e.g. experts in biological products, medical risk assessments or specific manufacturing techniques such as freeze-drying.

The DMRC operates a telephone line (020 3080 6574) from 08:45 to 16:45, Monday to Friday, except for public holidays, and can also be contacted directly via email at DMRC@mhra.gov.uk. Outside normal working hours, in an emergency, a MHRA Duty Officer (DO) can be contacted (07795 641 532). If needed the DO will contact the relevant professional (pharmaceutical or medical) for further advice.

Where a medicinal product recall is required, the decision is taken in consultation with the relevant Licence Holder. It is the Licence Holder's responsibility to ensure that a recall is carried out effectively throughout the distribution chain to the appropriate level. If necessary, the DMRC will issue a Recall Notification to support action taken by the Licence Holder.

Medicines Recall Notifications are issued by the DMRC to a number of contacts for onward cascade to healthcare professionals in the public and private sectors.

Medicines Recall Notifications are also copied to various professional and trade organisations and journals. Medicines Recall Notifications are published on the MHRA website usually within one working day of issue. A cumulative list of Licence Holder led recalls of UK licensed products and Medicines Recall Notifications is maintained on the MHRA website.

All existing centrally authorised product marketing authorisations (MAs) have been automatically converted into United Kingdom MAs, effective in Great Britain (only) and issued with a UK MA number on 1 January 2021. These UK MAs are referred to as "converted EU MAs". As a result of the implementation of the Northern Ireland Protocol, existing centrally authorised products will remain valid for marketing products in Northern Ireland.

For existing centrally authorised products the Licence Holder should inform the European Medicines Agency (EMA), in conjunction with the DMRC, if the medicinal product has been manufactured or distributed in the UK. Subsequent action may be delegated to the DMRC or progressed by the EMA. If the Licence Holder is unsure, the DMRC should be the first point of contact for all issues.

Recalling defective medicinal products – the responsibilities of distributors

To accord with the requirements of the Human Medicines Regulations 2012 [SI 2012/1916], the holder of a wholesale dealer's licence must comply with the guidelines on good distribution practice. In the case of a Licence Holder in Great Britain, these guidelines would be published under, or that apply by virtue of, Regulation C17 or, in the case of a Licence Holder in Northern Ireland, published by the European Commission in accordance with Article 84 of the 2001 Directive. The holder must maintain an emergency plan to ensure effective implementation of the recall from the market of a medicinal product where recall is either ordered by the licensing authority (or the competent authority of any EEA State in the case of Northern Ireland), or carried out in cooperation with the manufacturer of, or the holder of the marketing authorisation of, the product. The holder must also keep documents relating to the sale or supply of medicinal products under the licence that may facilitate the withdrawal or recall from sale of medicinal products in accordance with their emergency plan (Regulation 43(7) of the Human Medicines Regulations 2012 [SI 2012/1916]).

The holder of the wholesale dealer's licence should have in place detailed procedures that describe the action to be taken when a recall notice is received and must take appropriate steps to inform all customers who may have received stock of the batch(es) and medicinal product(s) that are affected by a recall.

Wholesalers should be aware that not all recalls will be accompanied by a Medicines Recall Notification issued by the MHRA and may be instituted at the request of a manufacturer or Licence Holder. In all cases the MHRA should have been notified of a recall in advance.

If a wholesaler has any doubts about a recall, they should contact the DMRC for advice.

Where a wholesaler receives a complaint regarding a suspected defective medicinal product, it should be referred to the relevant Licence Holder, manufacturer and/or the DMRC.

Note: Manufacturers' Licence Holders are by their nature carrying out wholesale distribution activities and must comply with the guidelines on good distribution practice in the case of a Licence Holder in Great Britain, published under, or that apply by virtue of, Regulation C17 or, in the case of a Licence Holder in Northern Ireland, published by the European Commission in accordance with Article 84 of the 2001 Directive, as if the Licence Holder were the holder of a wholesale dealer's licence (Regulation 39(8) of the Human Medicines Regulation 2012 [SI 2012/1916]). These guidelines also support the process of medicinal product recalls.

Importing unlicensed medicines – import notifications

Under Regulation 46 of the Human Medicines Regulations 2012 [SI 2012/1916], a medicine must have a marketing authorisation (includes Product Licences) unless exempt. One of these exemptions, which is in Regulation 167 of these regulations, is for the supply of unlicensed medicinal products for the special clinical needs of individual patients. Prospective importers must hold a relevant licence and must notify the MHRA of their intention to import:

- for import from a country on the approved country for import list (currently EU and EEA members) or within the EEA for Northern Ireland, a Wholesale Dealer's Licence valid for import and handling of unlicensed medicinal products;
- for import from a country outside the approved country for import list (currently non-EU and non-EEA members) or for Northern Ireland outside the EEA, a Manufacturer's "Specials" Licence valid for import.

Notifications of intent to import are processed by the Import Notification System (INS). The MHRA enters the information into the system and issues the Acknowledgement letters. The Pharmaceutical Assessment team assesses the notification taking into account the special need identified, the target population, the product and the manufacturer. The pharmaceutical assessor issues a letter objecting or not to the importation.

Criminal Enforcement Unit

Medicines legislation contains statutory provisions to enforce the requirements of the Human Medicines Regulations 2012 [SI 2012/1916] and the remaining provisions of the 1968 Medicines Act.

This enforcement role is carried out by the MHRA's Criminal Enforcement Unit, which comprises of Criminal Enforcement Intelligence and Criminal Enforcement Investigation sections.

The legislation confers certain powers, including rights of entry, powers of inspection, seizure, sampling and production of documents. Duly authorised Investigation Officers investigate cases using these powers and, where appropriate, criminal prosecutions are brought by the Crown Prosecution Service (CPS). The MHRA investigators also investigate offences under other legislation such as the Fraud Act, Trademarks Act and Offences Against the Person Act.

All reported breaches of medicines legislation are investigated. Reports are processed and risk assessed before a course of action is agreed in line with our published Enforcement Strategy.

The aim of the Intelligence Unit is to drive forward the implementation of intelligence-led enforcement and enable a more proactive approach to the acquisition and development of information. The Unit acts as a coordination point for all information-gathering activities and works in conjunction with a wide network of public and professional bodies and trade associations, e.g. UK Border Force, Customs, Department of Health and Social Care, Trading Standards and Port Health Authorities, the Police Service, and professional organisations such as the General Pharmaceutical Council (GPhC), General Medical Council and the Association of the British Pharmaceutical Industry (ABPI). Additionally, there is a network of other regulatory agencies and law enforcement bodies within the European Community and in other countries through which the Criminal Enforcement Unit can exchange information and follow trends in crime involving medicines and medical devices.

The Criminal Enforcement Unit coordinates initiatives to counteract and disrupt criminal activity involving the regulated and illegal supply chains. There is a protocol for dealing with falsified medicines infiltrating the licensed medicines supply chain.

Compliance Management and Inspection Action Group

Compliance management process

Compliance management is a non-statutory process providing oversight and monitoring of on-going corrective action plans in response to poor compliance that does not yet meet the threshold for consideration of adverse regulatory action. The process is managed via the Compliance Management Team (CMT) – a non-statutory group of senior GMDP inspectors, selected on the basis of their experience, who coordinate and advise on compliance management activities arising from chronic or significant GMP deficiencies.

> *Chronic GMP non-compliance: where major deficiencies are identified over a series of inspection cycles, which the company has not effectively addressed. There is no immediate potential for patient harm, but requires attention to avoid adverse regulatory action.*
>
> *Significant GMP non-compliance: where multiple major deficiencies are found at inspection, with no immediate potential for patient harm, which cannot be managed through the Risk-based Inspection (RBI) process but require quick attention to avoid adverse regulatory action.*

The main aim of the compliance management process is to re-focus companies towards a state of compliance, thus avoiding the need for regulatory action and the potential adverse impact to patient health through lack of availability of medicines as a result of action against an authorisation, as well as ensuring risk-based decision-making and efficient use of inspectorate resources.

The specific Compliance inspection case issues are considered by the CMT, who make decisions in conjunction with the inspector regarding the proportionate inspection and non-inspection compliance management actions required. This may include making recommendations on close monitoring of compliance improvements, recommendations for additional internal or external support or resources required, or reductions in capacity to facilitate compliance actions, ensuring that the compliance action plan remains on track, communicating with company senior management alerting them to any additional compliance concerns, and clearly outlining the consequences of continued non-compliance.

Chronic or significant GMP non-compliance are first identified at the inspection and communicated to the CMT who will collectively decide on an appropriate course of action based on the Inspector's recommendations. Decisions on compliance management actions are communicated to the company, following consideration of any written responses to a post-inspection letter, if relevant. The site inspector(s) and CMT will continue to monitor the effectiveness of these actions. The CMT process may also be initiated by the Inspection Action Group (IAG) following referral for significant or serious GMP deficiencies. In cases where consideration of adverse licensing action is no longer required due to improvements or mitigating actions, IAG may close their case referral and request that the CMT maintain compliance management oversight until completion of the remediation plans. Upon satisfactory conclusion of the remediation work, the company will be returned to the routine RBI programme; however, referral for consideration of regulatory action may still occur if the required improvements are not achieved in a timely manner.

Conversely, failure to address GMP non-compliance issues when a company is at the CMT may result in an upward referral to IAG so that formal actions against the licence, personnel named on the license or marketing authorisation holder can be taken.

Referral to the Inspection Action Group (IAG)

Critical findings at inspection are routinely referred to the MHRA's Inspection Action Group (IAG). The group considers referrals involving serious/critical GMP deficiencies.

Serious GMP non-compliance: where regulatory actions should be considered to remove a potential or actual risk to public health or patients, or subjects in a clinical trial.

The primary objective of IAG is to protect public health by ensuring that licensable activities meet the required regulatory standards.

The IAG is a non-statutory, multidisciplinary group constituted to advise the Chief Healthcare Quality and Access Officer on any recommendation for regulatory or adverse licensing action appropriate to the relevant good practice Division. There are two distinct groups:

- IAG1 considers issues related to Good Manufacturing Practice, Good Distribution Practice and Blood Establishment Authorisations (GMP/GDP/BEA) and has 24 scheduled meetings per year, usually the first and third Tuesdays of each month;
- IAG2 considers issues related to Good Clinical and Good Pharmacovigilance Practices (GCP/GPvP) and has 12 scheduled meetings per year, usually the fourth Tuesday of each month.

Where an urgent issue arises an emergency ad-hoc meeting can be held. The following attend both IAG1 and IAG2 meetings:

- the nominated Chair;
- at least one MHRA medical assessor;
- at least one MHRA pharmaceutical assessor;
- a solicitor from the Government Legal Services;
- at least one member of the IAG Secretariat;
- any inspector making a referral to the IAG;
- a representative from MHRA Criminal Enforcement Unit (if required); and
- members of the MHRA staff who may also attend for training purposes.

In addition, the following will attend IAG1:

- an expert/lead senior/senior GMP inspector;
- an expert/lead senior/senior GDP inspector;
- if required, a representative from the Veterinary Medicines Directorate https://www.gov.uk/government/organisations/veterinary-medicines-directorate; and
- an expert in blood and blood products (if required).

In addition, the following will attend IAG2:

- an expert/senior GCP inspector;
- an expert/senior GPvP inspector;
- the Clinical Trials Unit manager or deputy; and
- the Pharmacovigilance Risk Management Group manager or deputy.

REASONS FOR REFERRAL

This will usually happen if, during the inspection process, the inspector has identified one or more critical "deficiencies" as a result of a Good Practice Standards (GxP) inspection. However, a referral may also be made as a result of a licence variation, the failure to contact an organisation, the refusal of an organisation to accept an inspection, the outcome of enforcement activity, the outcome of a product recall or a person named on the licence as Production/Quality Control (QC)/Qualified Person not fulfilling their legal responsibilities.

The company will normally be informed during the closing meeting at inspection that a referral to IAG will be made. This will be further confirmed in the post-inspection letter and, from that point onwards, correspondence from the company should be directed to the IAG Secretariat copying in the site inspector.

How the process works:

- An inspection reveals serious (critical) deficiencies and the company is told it will be referred to IAG.
- A post-inspection letter is issued to company signed by a senior Inspector accredited in that area or a responsible operations manager/lead inspector.
- IAG discusses the case at its next available meeting (if necessary an emergency meeting can be called).
- IAG discusses any proposed action.
- The referred company is informed of any IAG actions and next steps.
- Actions are followed up at subsequent meetings until the situation is resolved.
- The matter is kept on the agenda until the IAG is satisfied that the referral can be closed.

IAG POSSIBLE ACTIONS

IAG1 (GMP/GDP/BEA)

- Refusal to grant a licence or a variation;
- Proposal to suspend the licence for a stated period or vary the licence;
- Notification of immediate suspension of the licence for a stated period (no longer than three months);
- Proposal to revoke the licence;
- Notice of suspension, variation or revocation;
- Action to remove a Qualified Person/Responsible Person (QP/RP) from the licence;
- Issue a Cease and Desist order in relation to a Blood Establishment Authorisation;
- Issue a warning letter to the company/individual;
- Request a written justification for actions of a QP/RP;
- Referral of a QP to their professional body;
- Increased inspection frequency;
- Statement of non-compliance with GMP or GDP;
- Restricted GMP and GDP certificates;
- Impose a production capacity restriction;
- Require engagement of external support for the remediation plan;
- Request the company/individual attend a meeting at the Agency; or
- Refer to MHRA Criminal Enforcement Unit for further consideration.

IAG2 (GCP/GPvP)

- Issue an infringement notice in relation to a clinical trial;
- Suspend or revoke a clinical trial authorisation;
- Further follow-up inspections or triggered inspections at related organisations (e.g. issues in GCP may trigger a GMP inspection);
- Referral to CHMP (Committee for Medicinal Products for Human Use) for consideration for or against a marketing authorisation (e.g. suspended, varied or revoked);
- Liaison and coordinated action with EMA (European Medicines Agency) and other Member States regarding concerns;
- Refer the case to the EMA for consideration of the use of the EU Infringement Regulation (which could result in a fine);
- Request a written justification for action of a QPPV (Qualified Person responsible for pharmacovigilance);
- Request the company/individual attend a meeting at the Agency; or
- Refer to the MHRA Criminal Enforcement Unit for further consideration.

In the case of inspections in third countries:

- a refusal to name a site on a marketing authorisation;
- a recommendation that a site be removed from a marketing authorisation;
- the issuing of a GMP non-compliance statement;
- in the case of an adverse (voluntary or triggered) active pharmaceutical ingredients (API) inspection, this could result in the removal of the API site from the marketing authorisation; or
- in the case of an adverse (voluntary or triggered) investigational medicinal products (IMP) inspection, this could result in the suspension of a clinical trial.

In all cases, an action could result in the withdrawal of product (API, IMP, medicinal product, etc.) from the market. This specific action is, however, handled by the Defective Medicines Reporting Centre (DMRC) rather than directly by the IAG.

CRITICAL PRODUCTS

The possible actions that the IAG may take involves consideration of the risk-benefit to patients and the supply situation where critical medicines are involved after consultation with the Department of Health and Social Care (DHSC), and for overseas products potentially with other national competent authorities.

A critical medicine is defined as one where there is no therapeutic alternative available or where other manufacturers do not have the available capacity to replace the demand when there is disruption to the existing supply chain.

LEGAL BASIS FOR THIS ACTION

The legal basis for licensing action is contained in:

- The Human Medicines Regulations 2012;
- The Medicines for Human Use (Clinical Trials) Regulations 2004; and
- The Blood Safety and Quality Regulations 2005.

WHAT A LICENCE HOLDER SHOULD DO IF REFERRED TO THE IAG

In the first instance, a referral should be treated as a requirement to immediately correct the deficiencies identified during the inspection and report completed actions to the IAG Secretariat/Inspectorate as soon as possible.

If, due to safety concerns, the referral results in an immediate suspension of a manufacturing/wholesale dealer's licence, this will be for a duration of three months, and during this time a company should be focused on correcting the inspection deficiencies.

If the referral results in a proposed suspension, variation or revocation of a licence, a company will have the following appeal options prior to a decision being made:

- may make written representations to the licensing authority (MHRA); or
- may appear before and be heard by a person appointed for the purpose by the licensing authority (a fee of £10,000 will be charged for a person-appointed request).

If a company submits written representations within the specified time period, the licensing authority shall take those representations into account before determining the matter. In practice, this means that any proposed action will not be progressed until the written representations have been reviewed and considered by the IAG and a recommendation made to the Divisional Director on whether to proceed with the action.

If a company submits a request for a Person-Appointed Hearing, this will be taken forward by the MHRA Panel Secretariat. Any proposed action will not be progressed until the Person-Appointed Hearing has taken place.

It should be noted that a Person-Appointed Hearing will offer its opinion only on whether a licence condition has been contravened. A final decision on whether to suspend or revoke a licence will still rest with the licensing authority, which will take the report of the Person-Appointed Hearing into account.

Follow-up actions that may be taken:

- a re-inspection to ensure that corrective actions are implemented;
- a request for regular updates on the corrective action plan;
- the issue of a short dated GMP certificate;
- a recommended increase of inspection frequency;
- a continued monitoring of the company by IAG via inspectorate updates; or
- if serious and persistent non-compliance continues, a referral for consideration of criminal prosecution.

Contact for further information: IAGSecretariat@mhra.gov.uk or IAG2Secretariat@mhra.gov.uk

CHARGING FOR COMPLIANCE MANAGEMENT COSTS

The Medicines (Products for Human Use) (Fees) Regulations 2016 section 30(b)(i) permits the MHRA to charge for the additional cost of inspector's time to review reports, CAPA and responses for companies that have been referred to the CMT or IAG. See Compliance Team blog "It pays to be compliant" for more details: https://mhrainspectorate.blog.gov.uk/2019/01/11/it-pays-to-be-compliant

Advice

The MHRA publishes a series of Guidance Notes relating to its statutory functions. Those of particular interest to manufacturers and wholesale dealers include:

GN 5   Notes for applicants and holders of a manufacturer's licence;
GN 6   Notes for applicants and holders of a wholesale dealer's licence (WDA(H)) or broker registration;
GN 8   A guide to what is a medicinal product;
GN 14   The supply of unlicensed medicinal products "Specials".

Contact details are as follows:

Address:
Customer Services, Medicines and Healthcare products Regulatory Agency, 10 South Colonnade London E14 4PU United Kingdom.
Telephone: +44 (0)20 3080 6000 (weekdays 09:00–17:00)
Fax: +44 (0)20 3118 9803
E-mail: info@mhra.gov.uk
Website: Medicines and Healthcare products Regulatory Agency – GOV.UK (www.gov.uk)

Guidance on Good Manufacturing Practice (GMP)

EU Guidance on Good Manufacturing Practice

PART I: Basic Requirements for Medicinal Products

Editor's note	The Introduction (below) to the EU Guidance on GMP which was written by the Commission makes reference to a "glossary" of some terms used in the Guide for GMP. This glossary appears immediately after the annexes.

In addition to this glossary a number of the annexes themselves also contain a glossary of some of the terms used in the particular annex to which they are attached. Part II of the EU Guidance on GMP contains a further glossary of terms used in that Part.

In this publication the Introduction (below) to the EU Guidance on GMP, the annexes, glossaries and Parts II and III have been presented as the Commission intended.

Contents of Part I

Contents continued

Contents continued

EU GMP GUIDE PART I

Contents continued

Contents continued

EU GMP GUIDE PART I

Contents continued

Contents continued

EU GMP GUIDE PART I INTRODUCTION

Introduction

The pharmaceutical industry of the EU maintains high standards of Quality Management in the development, manufacture and control of medicinal products. A system of marketing authorisations ensures that all medicinal products are assessed by a competent authority to ensure compliance with contemporary requirements of safety, quality and efficacy. A system of manufacturing authorisations ensures that all products authorised on the European market are manufactured/imported only by authorised manufacturers, whose activities are regularly inspected by the competent authorities, using Quality Risk Management principles. Manufacturing authorisations are required by all pharmaceutical manufacturers in the EU whether the products are sold within or outside of the Union.

Two directives laying down principles and guidelines of good manufacturing practice (GMP) for medicinal products were adopted by the Commission. Directive 2003/94/EC applies to medicinal products for human use and Directive 91/412/EEC for veterinary use. Detailed guidelines in accordance with those principles are published in the Guide to Good Manufacturing Practice, which will be used in assessing applications for manufacturing authorisations and as a basis for inspection of manufacturers of medicinal products.

The principles of GMP and the detailed guidelines are applicable to all operations that require the authorisations referred to in Article 40 of Directive 2001/83/EC, Article 44 of Directive 2001/82/EC and Article 13 of Directive 2001/20/EC, as amended. They are also relevant for pharmaceutical manufacturing processes, such as that undertaken in hospitals.

All Member States and the industry agreed that the GMP requirements applicable to the manufacture of veterinary medicinal products are the same as those applicable to the manufacture of medicinal products for human use. Certain detailed adjustments to the GMP guidelines are set out in two annexes specific to veterinary medicinal products and to immunological veterinary medicinal products.

The Guide is presented in three parts and supplemented by a series of annexes. Part I covers GMP principles for the manufacture of medicinal products. Part II covers GMP for active substances used as starting materials. Part III contains GMP related documents, which clarify regulatory expectations.

Chapters of Part I on "basic requirements" are headed by principles as defined in Directives 2003/94/EC and 91/412/EEC. Chapter 1 on Quality Management outlines the fundamental concept of quality management as applied to the manufacture of medicinal products. Thereafter, each chapter has a principle outlining the quality management objectives of that chapter and a text that provides sufficient detail for manufacturers to be made aware of the essential matters to be considered when implementing the principle.

According to the revised Article 47 and Article 51, respectively, of Directive 2001/83/EC and Directive 2001/82/EC, as amended, detailed guidelines on the principles of GMP for active substances used as starting materials shall be adopted and published by the Commission.

Part II was established on the basis of a guideline developed on the level of ICH and published as ICH Q7A on "active pharmaceutical ingredients". It has an extended application both for the human and the veterinary sector.

In addition to the general matters of Good Manufacturing Practice outlined in Parts I and II, a series of annexes providing detail about specific areas of activity is included. For some manufacturing processes, different annexes will apply simultaneously (e.g. annex on sterile preparations and on radiopharmaceuticals and/or on biological medicinal products).

A glossary of some terms used in the Guide has been incorporated after the annexes. Part III is intended to host a collection of GMP-related documents, which are not detailed guidelines on the principles of GMP laid down in Directives 2003/94/EC and 91/412/EC. The aim of Part III is to clarify regulatory expectations and it should be viewed as a source of information on current best practices. Details on the applicability are described separately in each document.

The Guide is not intended to cover safety aspects for the personnel engaged in manufacture. This may be particularly important in the manufacture of certain medicinal products such as highly active, biological and radioactive medicinal products. However, those aspects are governed by other provisions of Union or national law.

Throughout the Guide, it is assumed that the requirements of the Marketing Authorisation relating to the safety, quality and efficacy of the products are systematically incorporated into all the manufacturing, control and release for sale arrangements of the holder of the Manufacturing Authorisation.

For many years, the manufacture of medicinal products has taken place in accordance with guidelines for Good Manufacturing Practice and the manufacture of medicinal products is not governed by CEN/ISO standards. The CEN/ISO standards have been considered but the terminology of these standards has not been implemented in this edition.

It is recognised that there are acceptable methods, other than those described in the Guide, that are capable of achieving the principles of Quality Management. The Guide is not intended to place any restraint upon the development of any new concepts or new technologies that have been validated and provide a level of Quality Management at least equivalent to those set out in this Guide.

The GMP Guide will be regularly revised in order to reflect continual improvement of best practices in the field of Quality. Revisions will be made publicly available on the website of the European Commission: (http://ec.europa.eu/health/documents/eudralex/vol-4/index_en.htm).

EU GMP GUIDE PART I INTRODUCTION

1   PHARMACEUTICAL QUALITY SYSTEM

Principle

The holder of a Manufacturing Authorisation must manufacture medicinal products so as to ensure that they are fit for their intended use, comply with the requirements of the Marketing Authorisation or Clinical Trial Authorisation, as appropriate, and do not place patients at risk due to inadequate safety, quality or efficacy. The attainment of this quality objective is the responsibility of senior management, and requires the participation and commitment by staff in many different departments and at all levels within the company, by the company's suppliers and its distributors. To achieve this quality objective reliably there must be a comprehensively designed and correctly implemented Pharmaceutical Quality System[1] incorporating Good Manufacturing Practice and Quality Risk Management. It should be fully documented and its effectiveness monitored. All parts of the Pharmaceutical Quality System should be adequately resourced with competent personnel, and suitable and sufficient premises, equipment and facilities. There are additional legal responsibilities for the holder of the Manufacturing Authorisation and for the Qualified Person(s).

The basic concepts of Quality Management, Good Manufacturing Practice and Quality Risk Management are inter-related. They are described here in order to emphasise their relationships and their fundamental importance to the production and control of medicinal products.

Pharmaceutical Quality System[1]

1.1   Quality Management is a wide-ranging concept, which covers all matters that individually or collectively influence the quality of a product. It is the sum total of the organised arrangements made with the objective of ensuring that medicinal products are of the quality required for their intended use. Quality Management therefore incorporates Good Manufacturing Practice.

1.2   GMP applies to the lifecycle stages from the manufacture of investigational medicinal products, technology transfer, commercial manufacturing through to product discontinuation. However, the Pharmaceutical

---

[1]   Art 6 of Directives 2003/94/EC and 91/412/EEC requires manufacturers to establish and implement an effective pharmaceutical quality assurance system. The term "Pharmaceutical Quality System" is used in this chapter in the interests of consistency with ICH Q10 terminology. For the purposes of this chapter, these terms can be considered to be interchangeable.

Quality System can extend to the pharmaceutical development lifecycle stage as described in ICH Q10, which, although optional, should facilitate innovation and continual improvement and strengthen the link between pharmaceutical development and manufacturing activities. ICH Q10 is reproduced in Part III of the Guide and can be used to supplement the contents of this chapter.

1.3 The size and complexity of the company's activities should be taken into consideration when developing a new Pharmaceutical Quality System or modifying an existing one. The design of the system should incorporate appropriate risk management principles including the use of appropriate tools. Although some aspects of the system can be company wide and others site specific, the effectiveness of the system is normally demonstrated at the site level.

1.4 A Pharmaceutical Quality System appropriate for the manufacture of medicinal products should ensure that:

(i) Product realisation is achieved by designing, planning, implementing, maintaining and continuously improving a system that allows the consistent delivery of products with appropriate quality attributes;

(ii) Product and process knowledge is managed throughout all lifecycle stages;

(iii) Medicinal products are designed and developed in a way that takes account of the requirements of Good Manufacturing Practice;

(iv) Production and control operations are clearly specified and Good Manufacturing Practice adopted;

(v) Managerial responsibilities are clearly specified;

(vi) Arrangements are made for the manufacture, supply and use of the correct starting and packaging materials, the selection and monitoring of suppliers and for verifying that each delivery is from the approved supply chain;

(vii) Processes are in place to assure the management of outsourced activities;

(viii) A state of control is established and maintained by developing and using effective monitoring and control systems for process performance and product quality;

(ix) The results of product and processes monitoring are taken into account in batch release, in the investigation of deviations, and with a view to taking preventive action to avoid potential deviations occurring in the future;

(x) All necessary controls on intermediate products, and any other in-process controls and validations are carried out;

(xi) Continual improvement is facilitated through the implementation of quality improvements appropriate to the current level of process and product knowledge;

(xii)   Arrangements are in place for the prospective evaluation of planned changes and their approval prior to implementation taking into account regulatory notification and approval where required;

(xiii)   After implementation of any change, an evaluation is undertaken to confirm that the quality objectives were achieved and there was no unintended deleterious impact on product quality;

(xiv)   An appropriate level of root cause analysis should be applied during the investigation of deviations, suspected product defects and other problems. This can be determined using Quality Risk Management principles. In cases where the true root cause(s) of the issue cannot be determined, consideration should be given to identifying the most likely root cause(s) and to addressing those. Where human error is suspected or identified as the cause, this should be justified having taken care to ensure that process, procedural or system-based errors or problems have not been overlooked, if present. Appropriate corrective actions and/or preventive actions (CAPAs) should be identified and taken in response to investigations. The effectiveness of such actions should be monitored and assessed, in line with Quality Risk Management principles;

(xv)   Medicinal products are not sold or supplied before a Qualified Person has certified that each production batch has been produced and controlled in accordance with the requirements of the Marketing Authorisation and any other regulations relevant to the production, control and release of medicinal products;

(xvi)   Satisfactory arrangements exist to ensure, as far as possible, that the medicinal products are stored, distributed and subsequently handled so that quality is maintained throughout their shelf-life;

(xvii)   There is a process for self-inspection and/or quality audit, which regularly appraises the effectiveness and applicability of the Pharmaceutical Quality System.

1.5   Senior management has the ultimate responsibility to ensure an effective Pharmaceutical Quality System is in place, adequately resourced and that roles, responsibilities and authorities are defined, communicated and implemented throughout the organisation. Senior management's leadership and active participation in the Pharmaceutical Quality System are essential. This leadership should ensure the support and commitment of staff at all levels and sites within the organisation to the Pharmaceutical Quality System.

1.6   There should be periodic management review, with the involvement of senior management, of the operation of the Pharmaceutical Quality System to identify opportunities for continual improvement of products, processes and the system itself.

1.7   The Pharmaceutical Quality System should be defined and documented. A Quality Manual or equivalent documentation should be established and should contain a description of the quality management system including management responsibilities.

Good Manufacturing Practice for Medicinal Products

1.8   Good Manufacturing Practice is that part of Quality Management that ensures that products are consistently produced and controlled to the quality standards appropriate to their intended use and as required by the Marketing Authorisation, Clinical Trial Authorisation or product specification.

Good Manufacturing Practice is concerned with both production and quality control. The basic requirements of GMP are that:

(i)   all manufacturing processes are clearly defined, systematically reviewed in the light of experience and shown to be capable of consistently manufacturing medicinal products of the required quality and complying with their specifications;

(ii)   critical steps of manufacturing processes and significant changes to the process are validated;

(iii)   all necessary facilities for GMP are provided including:
- appropriately qualified and trained personnel;
- adequate premises and space;
- suitable equipment and services;
- correct materials, containers and labels;
- approved procedures and instructions, in accordance with the Pharmaceutical Quality System;
- suitable storage and transport;

(iv)   instructions and procedures are written in an instructional form in clear and unambiguous language, specifically applicable to the facilities provided;

(v)   procedures are carried out correctly and operators are trained to do so;

(vi)   records are made, manually and/or by recording instruments, during manufacture which demonstrate that all the steps required by the defined procedures and instructions were in fact taken and that the quantity and quality of the product was as expected;

(vii)   Any significant deviations are fully recorded, investigated with the objective of determining the root cause and appropriate corrective and preventive action implemented;

(viii)   records of manufacture including distribution which enable the complete history of a batch to be traced are retained in a comprehensible and accessible form;

(ix) the distribution of the products minimises any risk to their quality and takes account of Good Distribution Practice;

(x) a system is available to recall any batch of product, from sale or supply;

(xi) complaints about products are examined, the causes of quality defects investigated and appropriate measures taken in respect of the defective products and to prevent reoccurrence.

Quality Control

1.9 Quality Control is that part of Good Manufacturing Practice that is concerned with sampling, specifications and testing, and with the organisation, documentation and release procedures, which ensure that the necessary and relevant tests are actually carried out and that materials are not released for use, nor products released for sale or supply, until their quality has been judged to be satisfactory.

The basic requirements of Quality Control are that:

(i) adequate facilities, trained personnel and approved procedures are available for sampling and testing starting materials, packaging materials, intermediate, bulk and finished products, and where appropriate for monitoring environmental conditions for GMP purposes;

(ii) samples of starting materials, packaging materials, intermediate products, bulk products and finished products are taken by approved personnel and methods;

(iii) test methods are validated;

(iv) records are made, manually and/or by recording instruments, that demonstrate that all the required sampling, inspecting and testing procedures were actually carried out. Any deviations are fully recorded and investigated;

(v) the finished products contain active ingredients complying with the qualitative and quantitative composition of the Marketing Authorisation or Clinical Trial Authorisation, are of the purity required, and are enclosed within their proper containers and correctly labelled;

(vi) records are made of the results of inspection and that testing of materials, intermediate, bulk and finished products, is formally assessed against specification. Product assessment includes a review and evaluation of relevant production documentation and an assessment of deviations from specified procedures;

(vii) no batch of product is released for sale or supply prior to certification by a Qualified Person that it is in accordance with the requirements of the relevant authorisations in accordance with Annex 16;

EU GMP GUIDE PART I CHAPTER 1 PHARMACEUTICAL QUALITY SYSTEM

(viii) sufficient reference samples of starting materials and products are retained in accordance with Annex 19 to permit future examination of the product if necessary and that the sample is retained in the final pack.

Product Quality Review

1.10 Regular periodic or rolling quality reviews of all authorised medicinal products, including export only products, should be conducted with the objective of verifying the consistency of the existing process, the appropriateness of current specifications for both starting materials and finished product to highlight any trends and to identify product and process improvements. Such reviews should normally be conducted and documented annually, taking into account previous reviews, and should include at least:

(i) A review of starting materials including packaging materials used in the product, especially those from new sources and in particular the review of supply chain traceability of active substances;

(ii) A review of critical in-process controls and finished product results;

(iii) A review of all batches that failed to meet established specification(s) and their investigation;

(iv) A review of all significant deviations or non-conformances, their related investigations, and the effectiveness of resultant corrective and preventive actions taken;

(v) A review of all changes carried out to the processes or analytical methods;

(vi) A review of Marketing Authorisation variations submitted, granted or refused, including those for third country (export only) dossiers;

(vii) A review of the results of the stability monitoring programme and any adverse trends;

(viii) A review of all quality-related returns, complaints and recalls and the investigations performed at the time;

(ix) A review of adequacy of any other previous product process or equipment corrective actions;

(x) For new marketing authorisations and variations to marketing authorisations, a review of post-marketing commitments;

(xi) The qualification status of relevant equipment and utilities, e.g. HVAC, water, compressed gases, etc;

(xii) A review of any contractual arrangements as defined in Chapter 7 to ensure that they are up to date.

1.11 The manufacturer and, where different, marketing authorisation holder should evaluate the results of the review and an assessment made as to whether corrective and preventive action or any revalidation should be undertaken under the Pharmaceutical Quality System. There should be management procedures for the on-going management and review of these actions and the effectiveness of these procedures verified during self-inspection. Quality reviews may be grouped by product type, e.g. solid dosage forms, liquid dosage forms, sterile products, etc. where scientifically justified.

Where the marketing authorisation holder is not the manufacturer, there should be a technical agreement in place between the various parties that defines their respective responsibilities in producing the product quality review.

Quality Risk Management

1.12   Quality risk management is a systematic process for the assessment, control, communication and review of risks to the quality of the medicinal product. It can be applied both proactively and retrospectively.

1.13   The principles of quality risk management are that:

(i)   The evaluation of the risk to quality is based on scientific knowledge, experience with the process and ultimately links to the protection of the patient;

(ii)   The level of effort, formality and documentation of the quality risk management process is commensurate with the level of risk.

Examples of the processes and applications of quality risk management can be found inter alia in ICH Q9, which is reproduced in Part III of the Guide.

2 PERSONNEL

Principle

The correct manufacture of medicinal products relies upon people. For this reason there must be sufficient qualified personnel to carry out all the tasks that are the responsibility of the manufacturer. Individual responsibilities should be clearly understood by the individuals and recorded. All personnel should be aware of the principles of Good Manufacturing Practice that affect them and receive initial and continuing training, including hygiene instructions, relevant to their needs.

General

2.1 The manufacturer should have an adequate number of personnel with the necessary qualifications and practical experience. Senior management should determine and provide adequate and appropriate resources (human, financial, materials, facilities and equipment) to implement and maintain the quality management system and continually improve its effectiveness. The responsibilities placed on any one individual should not be so extensive as to present any risk to quality.

2.2 The manufacturer must have an organisation chart in which the interrelationships of the heads of Production, Quality Control and where applicable Head of Quality Assurance or Quality Unit referred to in point 2.5 and the position of the Qualified Person(s) are clearly shown in the managerial hierarchy.

2.3 People in responsible positions should have specific duties recorded in written job descriptions and adequate authority to carry out their responsibilities. Their duties may be delegated to designated deputies of a satisfactory qualification level. There should be no gaps or unexplained overlaps in the responsibilities of those personnel concerned with the application of Good Manufacturing Practice.

2.4 Senior management has the ultimate responsibility to ensure that an effective quality management system is in place to achieve the *quality objectives*, and that roles, responsibilities and authorities are defined, communicated and implemented throughout the organisation. Senior management should establish a quality policy that describes the overall intentions and direction of the company related to quality and should ensure continuing suitability and effectiveness of the quality management system and GMP compliance through participation in management review.

Key Personnel

2.5   Senior Management should appoint Key Management Personnel including the Head of Production, the Head of Quality Control and, if at least one of these persons is not responsible for the duties described in Article 51 of Directive 2001/83/EC[1], an adequate number, but at least one, Qualified Person(s) designated for the purpose. Normally, key posts should be occupied by full-time personnel. The heads of Production and Quality Control must be independent from each other. In large organisations, it may be necessary to delegate some of the functions listed in 2.6 and 2.7. Additionally, depending on the size and organisational structure of the company, a separate Head of Quality Assurance or Head of the Quality Unit may be appointed. Where such a function exists, usually some of the responsibilities described in 2.6, 2.7 and 2.8 are shared with the Head of Quality Control and Head of Production, and senior management should therefore take care that roles, responsibilities and authorities are defined.

2.6   The duties of the Qualified Person(s) are described in Article 51 of Directive 2001/83/EC and can be summarised as follows:

(a) for medicinal products manufactured within the European Union, a Qualified Person must ensure that each batch has been manufactured and checked in compliance with the laws in force in that Member State and in accordance with the requirements of the marketing authorisation[2];

(b) in the case of medicinal products coming from third countries, irrespective of whether the product has been manufactured in the European Union a Qualified Person must ensure that each production batch has undergone, in a Member State, a full qualitative analysis, a quantitative analysis of at least all the active substances, and all the other tests or checks necessary to ensure the quality of medicinal products in accordance with the requirements of the Marketing Authorisation. The Qualified Person must certify in a register or equivalent document, as operations are carried out and before any release, that each production batch satisfies the provisions of Article 51.

---

[1] Article 55 of Directive 2001/82/EC.

[2] According to Article 51 paragraph 1 of Directive (2001/83/EC), the batches of medicinal products that have undergone such controls in a Member State shall be exempt from the controls if they are marketed in another Member State, accompanied by the control reports signed by the qualified person.

The persons responsible for these duties must meet the qualification requirements laid down in Article 49[3] of the same Directive, they shall be permanently and continuously at the disposal of the holder of the Manufacturing Authorisation to carry out their responsibilities.

The responsibilities of a Qualified Person may be delegated, but only to other Qualified Person(s).

Guidance on the role of the Qualified Person is elaborated in Annex 16.

2.7 The Head of the Production Department generally has the following responsibilities:

(i) To ensure that products are produced and stored according to the appropriate documentation in order to obtain the required quality;

(ii) To approve the instructions relating to production operations and to ensure their strict implementation;

(iii) To ensure that the production records are evaluated and signed by an authorised person;

(iv) To ensure the qualification and maintenance of their department, premises and equipment;

(v) To ensure that the appropriate validations are done;

(vi) To ensure that the required initial and continuing training of their department personnel is carried out and adapted according to need.

2.8 The Head of the Quality Control Department generally has the following responsibilities:

(i) To approve or reject, as they see fit, starting materials, packaging materials, and intermediate, bulk and finished products;

(ii) To ensure that all necessary testing is carried out and the associated records evaluated;

(iii) To approve specifications, sampling instructions, test methods and other Quality Control procedures;

(iv) To approve and monitor any contract analysts;

(v) To ensure the qualification and maintenance of their department, premises and equipment;

(vi) To ensure that the appropriate validations are done;

(vii) To ensure that the required initial and continuing training of their department personnel is carried out and adapted according to need.

2.9 The Head of Production and Head of Quality Control and, where relevant, Head of Quality Assurance or Head of Quality Unit generally have some shared, or jointly exercised, responsibilities relating to quality including, in particular, the design, effective implementation, monitoring

---

[3] Article 53 of Directive 2001/82/EC.

and maintenance of the quality management system. These may include, subject to any national regulations:

(i)   The authorisation of written procedures and other documents, including amendments;

(ii)   The monitoring and control of the manufacturing environment;

(iii)   Plant hygiene;

(iv)   Process validation;

(v)   Training;

(vi)   The approval and monitoring of suppliers of materials;

(vii)   The approval and monitoring of contract manufacturers and providers of other GMP-related outsourced activities;

(viii) The designation and monitoring of storage conditions for materials and products;

(ix)   The retention of records;

(x)   The monitoring of compliance with the requirements of Good Manufacturing Practice;

(xi)   The inspection, investigation and taking of samples, in order to monitor factors that may affect product quality;

(xii) Participation in management reviews of process performance, product quality and the quality management system, and advocating continual improvement;

(xiii) Ensuring that a timely and effective communication and escalation process exists to raise quality issues to the appropriate levels of management.

Training

2.10   The manufacturer should provide training for all the personnel whose duties take them into production and storage areas or into control laboratories (including the technical, maintenance and cleaning personnel), and for other personnel whose activities could affect the quality of the product.

2.11   Besides the basic training on the theory and practice of Good Manufacturing Practice, newly recruited personnel should receive training appropriate to the duties assigned to them. Continuing training should also be given, and its practical effectiveness should be periodically assessed. Training programmes should be available, approved by either the Head of Production or the Head of Quality Control, as appropriate. Training records should be kept.

2.12 Personnel working in areas where contamination is a hazard, e.g. clean areas or areas where highly active, toxic, infectious or sensitising materials are handled, should be given specific training.

2.13 Visitors or untrained personnel should, preferably, not be taken into the Production and Quality Control areas. If this is unavoidable, they should be given information in advance, particularly about personal hygiene and the prescribed protective clothing. They should be closely supervised.

2.14 The pharmaceutical quality system and all the measures capable of improving its understanding and implementation should be fully discussed during the training sessions.

Personnel Hygiene

2.15 Detailed hygiene programmes should be established and adapted to the different needs within the factory. They should include procedures relating to the health, hygiene practices and clothing of personnel. These procedures should be understood and followed in a very strict way by every person whose duties take them into the production and control areas. Hygiene programmes should be promoted by management and widely discussed during training sessions.

2.16 All personnel should receive medical examination upon recruitment. It must be the manufacturer's responsibility that there are instructions ensuring that health conditions that could be of relevance to the quality of products come to the manufacturer's knowledge. After the first medical examination, examinations should be carried out when necessary for the work and personal health.

2.17 Steps should be taken to ensure as far as is practicable that no person affected by an infectious disease or having open lesions on the exposed surface of the body is engaged in the manufacture of medicinal products.

2.18 Every person entering the manufacturing areas should wear protective garments appropriate to the operations to be carried out.

2.19 Eating, drinking, chewing or smoking, or the storage of food, drink, smoking materials or personal medication in the production and storage areas, should be prohibited. In general, any unhygienic practice within the manufacturing areas or in any other area where the product might be adversely affected should be forbidden.

2.20   Direct contact should be avoided between the operator's hands and the exposed product, as well as with any part of the equipment that comes into contact with the products.

2.21   Personnel should be instructed to use the hand-washing facilities.

2.22   Any specific requirements for the manufacture of special groups of products, e.g. sterile preparations, are covered in the annexes.

Consultants

2.23   Consultants should have adequate education, training and experience, or any combination thereof, to advise on the subject for which they are retained. Records should be maintained stating the name, address, qualifications and type of service provided by these consultants.

3   PREMISES AND EQUIPMENT

Editor's note   Section 3.6 of Chapter 3, Part I of the GMP Guide has been revised as part of the improved guidance on prevention of cross-contamination, also involving Chapter 5. The revised text came into operation on 1 March 2015.

EU GMP GUIDE PART I CHAPTER 3
PREMISES AND EQUIPMENT

Principle

Premises and equipment must be located, designed, constructed, adapted and maintained to suit the operations to be carried out. Their layout and design must aim to minimise the risk of errors and permit effective cleaning and maintenance in order to avoid cross-contamination, build-up of dust or dirt and, in general, any adverse effect on the quality of products.

Premises

General

3.1   Premises should be situated in an environment which, when considered together with measures to protect the manufacture, presents minimal risk of causing contamination of materials or products.

3.2   Premises should be carefully maintained, ensuring that repair and maintenance operations do not present any hazard to the quality of products. They should be cleaned and, where applicable, disinfected according to detailed written procedures.

3.3   Lighting, temperature, humidity and ventilation should be appropriate and such that they do not adversely affect, directly or indirectly, either the medicinal products during their manufacture and storage, or the accurate functioning of equipment.

3.4   Premises should be designed and equipped so as to afford maximum protection against the entry of insects or other animals.

3.5   Steps should be taken in order to prevent the entry of unauthorised people. Production, storage and quality control areas should not be used as a right of way by personnel who do not work in them.

Production area

3.6   Cross-contamination should be prevented for all products by appropriate design and operation of manufacturing facilities. The measures to prevent cross-contamination should be commensurate with the risks. Quality Risk Management principles should be used to assess and control the risks.

Depending on the level of risk, it may be necessary to dedicate premises and equipment for manufacturing and/or packaging operations to control the risk presented by some medicinal products.

Dedicated facilities are required for manufacturing when a medicinal product presents a risk because:

(i)   the risk cannot be adequately controlled by operational and/or technical measures,

(ii)   scientific data from the toxicological evaluation does not support a controllable risk (e.g. allergenic potential from highly sensitising materials such as beta-lactams), or

(iii)   relevant residue limits, derived from the toxicological evaluation, cannot be satisfactorily determined by a validated analytical method.

Further guidance can be found in Chapter 5 and in Annexes 2, 3, 4, 5 and 6.

3.7   Premises should preferably be laid out in such a way as to allow the production to take place in areas connected in a logical order corresponding to the sequence of the operations and to the requisite cleanliness levels.

3.8   The adequacy of the working and in-process storage space should permit the orderly and logical positioning of equipment and materials so as to minimise the risk of confusion between different medicinal products or their components, to avoid cross-contamination and to minimise the risk of omission or wrong application of any of the manufacturing or control steps.

3.9   Where starting and primary packaging materials, or intermediate or bulk products are exposed to the environment, interior surfaces (walls, floors and ceilings) should be smooth, free from cracks and open joints, should not shed particulate matter and should permit easy and effective cleaning and, if necessary, disinfection.

3.10   Pipework, light fittings, ventilation points and other services should be designed and sited to avoid the creation of recesses that are difficult to clean. As far as possible, for maintenance purposes, they should be accessible from outside the manufacturing areas.

3.11   Drains should be of adequate size and have trapped gullies. Open channels should be avoided where possible, but, if necessary, they should be shallow to facilitate cleaning and disinfection.

3.12   Production areas should be effectively ventilated, with air control facilities (including temperature and, where necessary, humidity and filtration) appropriate to the products handled, the operations undertaken within them and the external environment.

3.13   Weighing of starting materials should usually be carried out in a separate weighing room designed for such use.

3.14   In cases where dust is generated (e.g. during sampling, weighing, mixing and processing operations, packaging of dry products), specific provisions should be taken to avoid cross-contamination and facilitate cleaning.

3.15   Premises for the packaging of medicinal products should be specifically designed and laid out so as to avoid mix-ups or cross-contamination.

3.16   Production areas should be well lit, particularly where visual on-line controls are carried out.

3.17   In-process controls may be carried out within the production area provided that they do not carry any risk to production.

Storage areas

3.18   Storage areas should be of sufficient capacity to allow orderly storage of the various categories of materials and products: starting and packaging materials, intermediate, bulk and finished products, products in quarantine, released, rejected, returned or recalled.

3.19   Storage areas should be designed or adapted to ensure good storage conditions. In particular, they should be clean and dry and maintained within acceptable temperature limits. Where special storage conditions are required (e.g. temperature, humidity) these should be provided, checked and monitored.

3.20   Receiving and dispatch bays should protect materials and products from the weather. Reception areas should be designed and equipped to allow containers of incoming materials to be cleaned where necessary before storage.

3.21   Where quarantine status is ensured by storage in separate areas, these areas must be clearly marked and their access restricted to authorised personnel. Any system replacing the physical quarantine should give equivalent security.

3.22   There should normally be a separate sampling area for starting materials. If sampling is performed in the storage area, it should be conducted in such a way as to prevent contamination or cross-contamination.

3.23   Segregated areas should be provided for the storage of rejected, recalled or returned materials or products.

3.24   Highly active materials or products should be stored in safe and secure areas.

3.25   Printed packaging materials are considered to be critical to the conformity of the medicinal product and special attention should be paid to the safe and secure storage of these materials.

Quality control areas

3.26   Normally, Quality Control laboratories should be separated from production areas. This is particularly important for laboratories for the control of biologicals, microbiologicals and radioisotopes, which should also be separated from each other.

3.27   Control laboratories should be designed to suit the operations to be carried out in them. Sufficient space should be given to avoid mix-ups and cross-contamination. There should be adequate suitable storage space for samples and records.

3.28   Separate rooms may be necessary to protect sensitive instruments from vibration, electrical interference, humidity, etc.

3.29   Special requirements are needed in laboratories handling particular substances, such as biological or radioactive samples.

Ancillary areas

3.30   Rest and refreshment rooms should be separate from other areas.

3.31   Facilities for changing clothes, and for washing and toilet purposes, should be easily accessible and appropriate for the number of users. Toilets should not directly communicate with production or storage areas.

3.32   Maintenance workshops should as far as possible be separated from production areas. Whenever parts and tools are stored in the production area, they should be kept in rooms or lockers reserved for that use.

3.33   Animal houses should be well isolated from other areas, with a separate entrance (animal access) and air-handling facilities.

Equipment

3.34   Manufacturing equipment should be designed, located and maintained to suit its intended purpose.

3.35   Repair and maintenance operations should not present any hazard to the quality of the products.

3.36   Manufacturing equipment should be designed so that it can be easily and thoroughly cleaned. It should be cleaned according to detailed and written procedures and stored only in a clean and dry condition.

3.37   Washing and cleaning equipment should be chosen and used in order not to be a source of contamination.

3.38   Equipment should be installed in such a way as to prevent any risk of error or contamination.

3.39   Production equipment should not present any hazard to products. Parts of the production equipment that come into contact with the product must not be reactive, additive or absorptive to such an extent that it will affect the quality of the product, and thus present any hazard.

3.40   Balances and measuring equipment of an appropriate range and precision should be available for production and control operations.

3.41   Measuring, weighing, recording and control equipment should be calibrated and checked at defined intervals by appropriate methods. Adequate records of such tests should be maintained.

3.42   Fixed pipework should be clearly labelled to indicate the contents and, where applicable, the direction of flow.

3.43   Distilled, deionised and, where appropriate, other water pipes should be sanitised according to written procedures that detail the action limits for microbiological contamination and the measures to be taken.

3.44   Defective equipment should, if possible, be removed from production and Quality Control areas, or at least be clearly labelled as defective.

4   DOCUMENTATION

Principle

Good documentation constitutes an essential part of the quality assurance system and is key to operating in compliance with GMP requirements. The various types of documents and media used should be fully defined in the manufacturer's Quality Management System.

Documentation may exist in a variety of forms, including paper-based, electronic or photographic media. The main objective of the system of documentation utilized must be to establish, control, monitor and record all activities that directly or indirectly impact on all aspects of the quality of medicinal products. The Quality Management System should include sufficient instructional detail to facilitate a common understanding of the requirements, in addition to providing for sufficient recording of the various processes and evaluation of any observations, so that on-going application of the requirements may be demonstrated.

There are two primary types of documentation used to manage and record GMP compliance: instructions (directions, requirements) and records/reports. Appropriate good documentation practice should be applied with respect to the type of document.

Suitable controls should be implemented to ensure the accuracy, integrity, availability and legibility of documents. Instruction documents should be free from errors and available in writing. The term "written" means recorded, or documented on media from which data may be rendered in a human readable form.

Required GMP Documentation (by type):

Site Master File: A document describing the GMP-related activities of the manufacturer.

Instructions (directions, or requirements) type:

Specifications: Describe in detail the requirements with which the products or materials used or obtained during manufacture have to conform. They serve as a basis for quality evaluation.

Manufacturing Formulae, Processing, Packaging and Testing Instructions:

Provide detail of all the starting materials, equipment and computerised systems (if any) to be used and specify all processing, packaging, sampling and testing instructions. In-process controls and process analytical technologies to be employed should be specified where relevant, together with acceptance criteria.

Procedures: (Otherwise known as Standard Operating Procedures, or SOPs), give directions for performing certain operations.

Protocols: Give instructions for performing and recording certain discrete operations. Technical Agreements: Are agreed between contract givers and acceptors for outsourced activities.

Record/Report type:

Records: Provide evidence of various actions taken to demonstrate compliance with instructions, e.g. activities, events, investigations and, in the case of manufactured batches, a history of each batch of product, including its distribution. Records include the raw data that is used to generate other records. For electronic records regulated users should define which data is to be used as raw data. At least, all data on which quality decisions are based should be defined as raw data.

Certificates of Analysis: Provide a summary of testing results on samples of products or materials[1] together with the evaluation for compliance to a stated specification.

Reports: Document the conduct of particular exercises, projects or investigations, together with results, conclusions and recommendations.

Generation and Control of Documentation

4.1   All types of document should be defined and adhered to. The requirements apply equally to all forms of document media types. Complex systems need to be understood, well documented and validated, and adequate controls should be in place. Many documents (instructions and/or records) may exist in hybrid forms, i.e. some elements as electronic and others as paper based. Relationships and control measures for master documents, official copies, data handling and records need to be stated for both hybrid and homogeneous systems. Appropriate controls for electronic documents such as templates, forms and master documents should be implemented. Appropriate controls should be in place to ensure the integrity of the record throughout the retention period.

4.2   Documents should be designed, prepared, reviewed and distributed with care. They should comply with the relevant parts of Product Specification Files, Manufacturing and Marketing Authorisation dossiers, as appropriate. The reproduction of working documents from master documents should not allow any error to be introduced through the reproduction process.

---

[1] Alternatively the certification may be based, in whole or in part, on the assessment of real-time data (summaries and exception reports) from batch-related process analytical technology (PAT), parameters or metrics as per the approved Marketing Authorisation dossier.

4.3 Documents containing instructions should be approved, signed and dated by appropriate and authorised persons. Documents should have unambiguous contents and be uniquely identifiable. The effective date should be defined.

4.4 Documents containing instructions should be laid out in an orderly fashion and easy to check. The style and language of documents should fit with their intended use. Standard Operating Procedures, Work Instructions and Methods should be written in an imperative mandatory style.

4.5 Documents within the Quality Management System should be regularly reviewed and kept up to date.

4.6 Documents should not be handwritten, although, where documents require the entry of data, sufficient space should be provided for such entries.

Good Documentation Practices

4.7 Handwritten entries should be made in a clear, legible, indelible way.

4.8 Records should be made or completed at the time each action is taken and in such a way that all significant activities concerning the manufacture of medicinal products are traceable.

4.9 Any alteration made to the entry on a document should be signed and dated; the alteration should permit the reading of the original information. Where appropriate, the reason for the alteration should be recorded.

Retention of Documents

4.10 It should be clearly defined which record is related to each manufacturing activity and where this record is located. Secure controls must be in place to ensure the integrity of the record throughout the retention period and validated where appropriate.

4.11 Specific requirements apply to batch documentation that must be kept for one year after expiry of the batch to which it relates or at least five years after certification of the batch by the Qualified Person, whichever is the longer. For investigational medicinal products, the batch documentation must be kept for at least five years after the completion or formal discontinuation of the last clinical trial in which the batch was used. Other requirements for retention of documentation may be described in legislation in relation to specific types of product (e.g. Advanced Therapy Medicinal Products) and specify that longer retention periods be applied to certain documents.

4.12   For other types of documentation, the retention period will depend on the business activity that the documentation supports. Critical documentation, including raw data (for example, relating to validation or stability), that supports information in the Marketing Authorisation should be retained while the authorization remains in force. It may be considered acceptable to retire certain documentation (e.g. raw data supporting validation reports or stability reports) where the data has been superseded by a full set of new data. Justification for this should be documented and take into account the requirements for retention of batch documentation, e.g. in the case of process validation data, the accompanying raw data should be retained for a period at least as long as the records for all batches whose release has been supported on the basis of that validation exercise.

    The following section gives some examples of required documents. The quality management system should describe all documents required to ensure product quality and patient safety.

Specifications

4.13   There should be appropriately authorised and dated specifications for starting and packaging materials, and finished products.

Specifications for starting and packaging materials

4.14   Specifications for starting and primary or printed packaging materials should include or provide reference to, if applicable:

(a) A description of the materials including:
- the designated name and the internal code reference;
- the reference, if any, to a pharmacopoeial monograph;
- the approved suppliers and, if reasonable, the original producer of the material;
- a specimen of printed materials;

(b) Directions for sampling and testing;

(c) Qualitative and quantitative requirements with acceptance limits;

(d) Storage conditions and precautions;

(e) The maximum period of storage before re-examination.

Specifications for intermediate and bulk products

4.15   Specifications for intermediate and bulk products should be available for critical steps or if these are purchased or dispatched. The specifications should be similar to specifications for starting materials or for finished products, as appropriate.

Specifications for finished products

4.16   Specifications for finished products should include or provide reference to:

(a) The designated name of the product and the code reference where applicable;
(b) The formula;
(c) A description of the pharmaceutical form and package details;
(d) Directions for sampling and testing;
(e) The qualitative and quantitative requirements, with the acceptance limits;
(f) The storage conditions and any special handling precautions, where applicable;
(g) The shelf-life.

Manufacturing Formula and Processing Instructions

Approved, written Manufacturing Formula and Processing Instructions should exist for each product and batch size to be manufactured.

4.17   The Manufacturing Formula should include:

(a) The name of the product, with a product reference code relating to its specification;
(b) A description of the pharmaceutical form, strength of the product and batch size;
(c) A list of all starting materials to be used, with the amount of each, described; mention should be made of any substance that may disappear in the course of processing;
(d) A statement of the expected final yield with the acceptable limits, and of relevant intermediate yields, where applicable.

4.18   The Processing Instructions should include:

(a) A statement of the processing location and the principal equipment to be used;
(b) The methods, or reference to the methods, to be used for preparing the critical equipment (e.g. cleaning, assembling, calibrating, sterilising);
(c) Checks that the equipment and work station are clear of previous products, documents or materials not required for the planned process, and that equipment is clean and suitable for use;

(d) Detailed stepwise processing instructions (e.g. checks on materials, pre-treatments, sequence for adding materials, critical process parameters [time, temp., etc.]);

(e) The instructions for any in-process controls with their limits;

(f) Where necessary, the requirements for bulk storage of the products, including the container, labelling and special storage conditions where applicable;

(g) Any special precautions to be observed.

Packaging instructions

4.19 Approved packaging instructions for each product, pack size and type should exist. These should include, or have a reference to, the following:

(a) Name of the product, including the batch number of bulk and finished product;

(b) Description of its pharmaceutical form, and strength where applicable;

(c) The pack size expressed in terms of the number, weight or volume of the product in the final container;

(d) A complete list of all the packaging materials required, including quantities, sizes and types, with the code or reference number relating to the specifications of each packaging material;

(e) Where appropriate, an example or reproduction of the relevant printed packaging materials, and specimens indicating where to apply batch number references, and shelf-life of the product;

(f) Checks that the equipment and work station are clear of previous products, documents or materials not required for the planned packaging operations (line clearance), and that equipment is clean and suitable for use;

(g) Special precautions to be observed, including a careful examination of the area and equipment in order to ascertain the line clearance before operations begin;

(h) A description of the packaging operation, including any significant subsidiary operations and equipment to be used;

(i) Details of in-process controls with instructions for sampling and acceptance limits.

Batch processing record

4.20 A batch processing record should be kept for each batch processed. It should be based on the relevant parts of the currently approved

Manufacturing Formula and Processing Instructions, and should contain the following information:

(a) The name and batch number of the product;
(b) Dates and times of commencement, significant intermediate stages and completion of production;
(c) Identification (initials) of the operator(s) who performed each significant step of the process and, where appropriate, the name of any person who checked these operations;
(d) The batch number and/or analytical control number as well as the quantities of each starting material actually weighed (including the batch number and amount of any recovered or reprocessed material added);
(e) Any relevant processing operation or event and major equipment used;
(f) A record of the in-process controls and the initials of the person(s) carrying them out, and the results obtained;
(g) The product yield obtained at different and pertinent stages of manufacture;
(h) Notes on special problems including details, with signed authorisation for any deviation from the Manufacturing Formula and Processing Instructions;
(i) Approval by the person responsible for the processing operations.

Note: Where a validated process is continuously monitored and controlled, then automatically generated reports may be limited to compliance summaries and exception/out-of-specification (OOS) data reports.

Batch packaging record

4.21   A batch packaging record should be kept for each batch or part batch processed. It should be based on the relevant parts of the packaging instructions. The batch packaging record should contain the following information:

(a) The name and batch number of the product,
(b) The date(s) and times of the packaging operations;
(c) Identification (initials) of the operator(s) who performed each significant step of the process and, where appropriate, the name of any person who checked these operations;
(d) Records of checks for identity and conformity with the packaging instructions, including the results of in-process controls;
(e) Details of the packaging operations carried out, including references to equipment and the packaging lines used;

(f) Whenever possible, samples of printed packaging materials used, including specimens of the batch coding, expiry dating and any additional overprinting;

(g) Notes on any special problems or unusual events including details, with signed authorisation for any deviation from the Packaging Instructions;

(h) The quantities and reference number or identification of all printed packaging materials and bulk product issued, used, destroyed or returned to stock, and the quantities of obtained product, in order to provide for an adequate reconciliation. Where there are robust electronic controls in place during packaging there may be justification for not including this information;

(i) Approval by the person responsible for the packaging operations.

Procedures and Records

Receipt

4.22 There should be written procedures and records for the receipt of each delivery of each starting material (including bulk, intermediate or finished goods), primary, secondary and printed packaging materials.

4.23 The records of the receipts should include:

(a) The name of the material on the delivery note and the containers;
(b) The "in-house" name and/or code of material (if different from a);
(c) Date of receipt;
(d) Supplier's name and manufacturer's name;
(e) Manufacturer's batch or reference number;
(f) Total quantity and number of containers received;
(g) The batch number assigned after receipt;
(h) Any relevant comment.

4.24 There should be written procedures for the internal labelling, quarantine and storage of starting materials, packaging materials and other materials, as appropriate.

Sampling

4.25 There should be written procedures for sampling, which include the methods and equipment to be used, the amounts to be taken, and any precautions to be observed to avoid contamination of the material or any deterioration in its quality.

Testing

4.26   There should be written procedures for testing materials and products at different stages of manufacture, describing the methods and equipment to be used. The tests performed should be recorded.

Other

4.27   Written release and rejection procedures should be available for materials and products, and in particular for the certification for sale of the finished product by the Qualified Person(s). All records should be available to the Qualified Person(s). A system should be in place to indicate special observations and any changes to critical data.

4.28   Records should be maintained for the distribution of each batch of a product in order to facilitate recall of any batch, if necessary.

4.29   There should be written policies, procedures, protocols, reports and the associated records of actions taken or conclusions reached, where appropriate, for the following examples:

- Validation and qualification of processes, equipment and systems;
- Equipment assembly and calibration;
- Technology transfer;
- Maintenance, cleaning and sanitation;
- Personnel matters including signature lists, training in GMP and technical matters, clothing and hygiene, and verification of the effectiveness of training;
- Environmental monitoring;
- Pest control;
- Complaints;
- Recalls;
- Returns;
- Change control;
- Investigations into deviations and non-conformances;
- Internal quality/GMP compliance audits;
- Summaries of records where appropriate (e.g. product quality review);
- Supplier audits.

4.30   Clear operating procedures should be available for major items of manufacturing and test equipment.

4.31   Logbooks should be kept for major or critical analytical testing, production equipment and areas where product has been processed. They should be used to record in chronological order, as appropriate, any use of the area, equipment/method, calibrations, maintenance, cleaning or repair operations, including the dates and identity of people who carried these operations out.

4.32   An inventory of documents within the Quality Management System should be maintained.

5   PRODUCTION

Editor's   Chapter 5 of Part I of the GMP Guide has been revised. Changes have
note   been made to paragraphs 5.17 to 5.22, including adding a new section, to
          improve the guidance on prevention of cross-contamination and to refer to
          toxicological assessment. Changes were also introduced in paragraphs 5.27
          to 5.30, including adding a new section, on the qualification of suppliers in
          order to reflect the legal obligation of Manufacturing Authorisation holders
          to ensure that active substances are produced in accordance with GMP.
          The changes include supply chain traceability. New paragraphs 5.35 and
          5.36 are inserted to clarify and harmonise expectations of manufacturers
          regarding the testing of starting materials while paragraph 5.71 introduces
          guidance on notification of restrictions in supply.
              The revised text came into operation on 1 March 2015.

Principle

Production operations must follow clearly defined procedures; they must comply with the principles of Good Manufacturing Practice in order to obtain products of the requisite quality, and be in accordance with the relevant Manufacturing and Marketing Authorisations.

General

5.1   Production should be performed and supervised by competent people.

5.2   All handling of materials and products, such as receipt and quarantine, sampling, storage, labelling, dispensing, processing, packaging and distribution should be done in accordance with written procedures or instructions and, where necessary, recorded.

5.3   All incoming materials should be checked to ensure that the consignment corresponds to the order. Containers should be cleaned where necessary and labelled with the prescribed data.

5.4   Damage to containers and any other problem that might adversely affect the quality of a material should be investigated, recorded and reported to the Quality Control Department.

5.5 Incoming materials and finished products should be physically or administratively quarantined immediately after receipt or processing, until they have been released for use or distribution.

5.6 Intermediate and bulk products purchased as such should be handled on receipt as though they were starting materials.

5.7 All materials and products should be stored under the appropriate conditions established by the manufacturer and in an orderly fashion to permit batch segregation and stock rotation.

5.8 Checks on yields, and reconciliation of quantities, should be carried out as necessary to ensure that there are no discrepancies outside acceptable limits.

5.9 Operations on different products should not be carried out simultaneously or consecutively in the same room unless there is no risk of mix-up or cross-contamination.

5.10 At every stage of processing, products and materials should be protected from microbial and other contamination.

5.11 When working with dry materials and products, special precautions should be taken to prevent the generation and dissemination of dust. This applies particularly to the handling of highly active or sensitising materials.

5.12 At all times during processing, all materials, bulk containers, major items of equipment and, where appropriate, rooms used should be labelled or otherwise identified with an indication of the product or material being processed, its strength (where applicable) and batch number. Where applicable, this indication should also mention the stage of production.

5.13 Labels applied to containers, equipment or premises should be clear, unambiguous and in the company's agreed format. It is often helpful, in addition to the wording on the labels, to use colours to indicate status (e.g. quarantined, accepted, rejected, clean).

5.14 Checks should be carried out to ensure that pipelines and other pieces of equipment used for the transportation of products from one area to another are connected in a correct manner.

5.15 Any deviation from instructions or procedures should be avoided as far as possible. If a deviation occurs, it should be approved in writing by a competent person, with the involvement of the Quality Control Department when appropriate.

5.16 Access to production premises should be restricted to authorised personnel.

Prevention of Cross-contamination in Production

5.17 Normally, the production of non-medicinal products should be avoided in areas and with equipment destined for the production of medicinal products but, where justified, could be allowed where the measures to prevent cross-contamination with medicinal products described below and in Chapter 3 can be applied. The production and/or storage of technical poisons, such as pesticides (except where these are used for manufacture of medicinal products) and herbicides, should not be allowed in areas used for the manufacture and/or storage of medicinal products.

5.18 Contamination of a starting material or of a product by another material or product should be prevented. This risk of accidental cross-contamination resulting from the uncontrolled release of dust, gases, vapours, aerosols, genetic material or organisms from active substances, other starting materials and products in process, from residues on equipment and from operators' clothing should be assessed. The significance of this risk varies with the nature of the contaminant and that of the product being contaminated. Products in which cross-contamination is likely to be most significant are those administered by injection and those given over a long time. However, contamination of all products poses a risk to patient safety dependent on the nature and extent of contamination.

5.19 Cross-contamination should be prevented by attention to the design of the premises and equipment as described in Chapter 3. This should be supported by attention to process design and implementation of any relevant technical or organizational measures, including effective and reproducible cleaning processes to control risk of cross-contamination.

5.20 A Quality Risk Management process, which includes a potency and toxicological evaluation, should be used to assess and control the cross-contamination risks presented by the products manufactured. Factors, including facility/equipment design and use, personnel and material flow, microbiological controls, physicochemical characteristics of the active substance, process characteristics, cleaning processes and analytical capabilities relative to the relevant limits established from the evaluation of the products, should also be taken into account. The outcome of the Quality Risk Management process should be the basis for determining the necessity for and extent to which premises and equipment should be dedicated to a particular product or product family. This may include dedicating specific product contact parts or dedication of the entire manufacturing facility. It may be acceptable to confine manufacturing activities to a segregated, self-contained production area within a multi-product facility, where justified.

5.21   The outcome of the Quality Risk Management process should be the basis for determining the extent of technical and organisational measures required to control risks for cross-contamination. These could include, but are not limited to, the following:

Technical measures

(i)   Dedicated manufacturing facility (premises and equipment);

(ii)   Self-contained production areas having separate processing equipment and separate heating, ventilation and air-conditioning (HVAC) systems. It may also be desirable to isolate certain utilities from those used in other areas;

(iii)   Design of manufacturing process, premises and equipment to minimize opportunities for cross-contamination during processing, maintenance and cleaning;

(iv)   Use of "closed systems" for processing and material/product transfer between equipment;

(v)   Use of physical barrier systems, including isolators, as containment measures;

(vi)   Controlled removal of dust close to source of the contaminant, e.g. through localised extraction;

(vii)   Dedication of equipment, dedication of product contact parts or selected parts that are harder to clean (e.g. filters), dedication of maintenance tools;

(viii)   Use of single-use disposable technologies;

(ix)   Use of equipment designed for ease of cleaning;

(x)   Appropriate use of air-locks and pressure cascade to confine potential airborne contaminant within a specified area;

(xi)   Minimising the risk of contamination caused by recirculation or re-entry of untreated or insufficiently treated air;

(xii)   Use of automatic clean in place systems of validated effectiveness;

(xiii)   For common general wash areas, separation of equipment washing, drying and storage areas.

Organisational measures

(i)   Dedicating the whole manufacturing facility or a self-contained production area on a campaign basis (dedicated by separation in time), followed by a cleaning process of validated effectiveness;

(ii)   Keeping specific protective clothing inside areas where products with high risk of cross-contamination are processed;

(iii)   Cleaning verification after each product campaign should be considered as a detectability tool to support the effectiveness of the Quality Risk Management approach for products deemed to present higher risk;

(iv)   Depending on the contamination risk, verification of cleaning of non-product contact surfaces and monitoring of air within the manufacturing area and/or adjoining areas in order to demonstrate effectiveness of control measures against airborne contamination or contamination by mechanical transfer;

(v)   Specific measures for waste handling, contaminated rinsing water and soiled gowning;

(vi)   Recording of spills, accidental events or deviations from procedures;

(vii)   Design of cleaning processes for premises and equipment such that the cleaning processes in themselves do not present a cross-contamination risk;

(viii)   Design of detailed records for cleaning processes to assure completion of cleaning in accordance with approved procedures and use of cleaning status labels on equipment and manufacturing areas;

(ix)   Use of common general wash areas on a campaign basis;

(x)   Supervision of working behaviour to ensure training effectiveness and compliance with the relevant procedural controls.

5.22   Measures to prevent cross-contamination and their effectiveness should be reviewed periodically according to set procedures.

Validation

5.23   Validation studies should reinforce Good Manufacturing Practice and be conducted in accordance with defined procedures. Results and conclusions should be recorded.

5.24   When any new manufacturing formula or method of preparation is adopted, steps should be taken to demonstrate its suitability for routine processing. The defined process, using the materials and equipment specified, should be shown to yield a product consistently of the required quality.

5.25   Significant amendments to the manufacturing process, including any change in equipment or materials, that may affect product quality and/or the reproducibility of the process should be validated.

5.26   Processes and procedures should undergo periodic critical re-validation to ensure that they remain capable of achieving the intended results.

Starting Materials

5.27   The selection, qualification, approval and maintenance of suppliers of starting materials, together with their purchase and acceptance, should be documented as part of the pharmaceutical quality system. The level of supervision should be proportionate to the risks posed by the individual materials, taking account of their source, manufacturing process, supply chain complexity and the final use to which the material is put in the medicinal product. The supporting evidence for each supplier/material approval should be maintained. Staff involved in these activities should have a current knowledge of the suppliers, the supply chain and the associated risks involved. Where possible, starting materials should be purchased directly from the manufacturer of the starting material.

5.28   The quality requirements established by the manufacturer for the starting materials should be discussed and agreed with the suppliers. Appropriate aspects of the production, testing and control, including handling, labelling, packaging and distribution requirements, complaints, recalls and rejection procedures, should be documented in a formal quality agreement or specification.

5.29   For the approval and maintenance of suppliers of active substances and excipients, the following is required:

Active substances[1]

Supply chain traceability should be established and the associated risks, from active substance starting materials to the finished medicinal product, should be formally assessed and periodically verified. Appropriate measures should be put in place to reduce risks to the quality of the active substance.

The supply chain and traceability records for each active substance (including active substance starting materials) should be available and be retained by the EEA-based manufacturer or importer of the medicinal product.

Audits should be carried out at the manufacturers and distributors of active substances to confirm that they comply with the relevant Good Manufacturing Practice and Good Distribution Practice requirements. The holder of the Manufacturing Authorisation shall verify such compliance either by themselves or through an entity acting on their behalf under a contract. For veterinary medicinal products, audits should be conducted based on risk.

---

[1] Specific requirements apply to the importation of active substances to be used in the manufacture of medicinal products for human use in Article 46b of Directive 2001/83/EC.

Audits should be of an appropriate duration and scope to ensure that a full and clear assessment of GMP is made; consideration should be given to potential cross-contamination from other materials on site. The report should fully reflect what was done and seen on the audit with any deficiencies clearly identified. Any required corrective and preventive actions should be implemented.

Further audits should be undertaken at intervals defined by the quality risk management process to ensure the maintenance of standards and continued use of the approved supply chain.

Excipients

Excipients and excipient suppliers should be controlled appropriately based on the results of a formalised quality risk assessment in accordance with the European Commission "Guidelines on the formalised risk assessment for ascertaining the appropriate Good Manufacturing Practice for excipients of medicinal products for human use".

5.30 For each delivery of starting material the containers should be checked for integrity of package, including tamper-evident seal where relevant, and for correspondence across the delivery note, the purchase order, the supplier's labels, and approved manufacturer and supplier information maintained by the medicinal product manufacturer. The receiving checks on each delivery should be documented.

5.31 If one material delivery is made up of different batches, each batch must be considered as separate for sampling, testing and release.

5.32 Starting materials in the storage area should be appropriately labelled (see section 13). Labels should bear at least the following information:

(i) The designated name of the product and the internal code reference where applicable;
(ii) A batch number given at receipt;
(iii) Where appropriate, the status of the contents (e.g. in quarantine, on test, released, rejected);
(iv) Where appropriate, an expiry date or a date beyond which retesting is necessary.

When fully computerised storage systems are used, all the above information need not necessarily be in a legible form on the label.

5.33 There should be appropriate procedures or measures to assure the identity of the contents of each container of starting material. Bulk containers from which samples have been drawn should be identified (see Chapter 6).

5.34   Only starting materials that have been released by the Quality Control Department and are within their retest period should be used.

5.35   Manufacturers of finished products are responsible for any testing of starting materials[2] as described in the Marketing Authorisation dossier. They can utilise partial or full test results from the approved starting material manufacturer but must, as a minimum, perform identification testing[3] of each batch according to Annex 8.

5.36   The rationale for the outsourcing of this testing should be justified and documented and the following requirements should be fulfilled:

(i)   Special attention should be paid to the distribution controls (transport, wholesaling, storage and delivery) in order to maintain the quality characteristics of the starting materials and to ensure that test results remain applicable to the delivered material;

(ii)   The medicinal product manufacturer should perform audits, either itself or via third parties, at appropriate intervals based on risk at the site(s) carrying out the testing (including sampling) of the starting materials in order to assure compliance with Good Manufacturing Practice and with the specifications and testing methods described in the Marketing Authorisation dossier;

(iii) The certificate of analysis provided by the starting material manufacturer/supplier should be signed by a designated person with appropriate qualifications and experience. The signature assures that each batch has been checked for compliance with the agreed product specification unless this assurance is provided separately;

(iv)   The medicinal product manufacturer should have appropriate experience in dealing with the starting material manufacturer (including experience via a supplier).

5.37   Starting materials should be dispensed only by designated persons, following a written procedure, to ensure that the correct materials are accurately weighed or measured into clean and properly labelled containers.

5.38   Each dispensed material and its weight or volume should be independently checked and the check recorded.

5.39   Materials dispensed for each batch should be kept together and conspicuously labelled as such.

---

[2] A similar approach should apply to packaging materials as stated in section 5.42.

[3] Identity testing of starting materials should be performed according to the methods and the specifications of the relevant Marketing Authorisation dossier.

Processing Operations: Intermediate and Bulk Products

5.40   Before any processing operation is started, steps should be taken to ensure that the work area and equipment are clean and free from any starting materials, products, product residues or documents not required for the current operation.

5.41   Intermediate and bulk products should be kept under appropriate conditions.

5.42   Critical processes should be validated (see "Validation" in this Chapter).

5.43   Any necessary in-process controls and environmental controls should be carried out and recorded.

5.44   Any significant deviation from the expected yield should be recorded and investigated.

Packaging Materials

5.45   The selection, qualification, approval and maintenance of suppliers of primary and printed packaging materials shall be accorded attention similar to that given to starting materials.

5.46   Particular attention should be paid to printed materials. They should be stored in adequately secure conditions such as to exclude unauthorised access. Cut labels and other loose printed materials should be stored and transported in separate closed containers so as to avoid mix-ups. Packaging materials should be issued for use only by authorised personnel, following an approved and documented procedure.

5.47   Each delivery or batch of printed or primary packaging material should be given a specific reference number or identification mark.

5.48   Outdated or obsolete primary packaging material or printed packaging material should be destroyed and this disposal recorded.

Packaging Operations

5.49   When setting up a programme for the packaging operations, particular attention should be given to minimising the risk of cross-contamination, mix-ups or substitutions. Different products should not be packaged in close proximity unless there is physical segregation.

5.50   Before packaging operations are begun, steps should be taken to ensure that the work area, packaging lines, printing machines and other equipment are clean and free from any products, materials or documents previously used, if these are not required for the current operation. The line clearance should be performed according to an appropriate check-list.

5.51 The name and batch number of the product being handled should be displayed at each packaging station or line.

5.52 All products and packaging materials to be used should be checked on delivery to the packaging department for quantity, identity and conformity with the Packaging Instructions.

5.53 Containers for filling should be clean before filling. Attention should be given to avoid and remove any contaminants such as glass fragments and metal particles.

5.54 Normally, filling and sealing should be followed as quickly as possible by labelling. If this is not the case, appropriate procedures should be applied to ensure that no mix-ups or mislabelling can occur.

5.55 The correct performance of any printing operation (e.g. code numbers, expiry dates) to be done separately or in the course of the packaging should be checked and recorded. Attention should be paid to printing by hand, which should be re-checked at regular intervals.

5.56 Special care should be taken when using cut-labels and when over-printing is carried out off-line. Roll-feed labels are normally preferable to cut-labels, in helping to avoid mix-ups.

5.57 Checks should be made to ensure that any electronic code readers, label counters or similar devices are operating correctly.

5.58 Printed and embossed information on packaging materials should be distinct and resistant to fading or erasing.

5.59 On-line control of the product during packaging should include at least checking the following:

(i)   General appearance of the packages;
(ii)   Whether the packages are complete;
(iii) Whether the correct products and packaging materials are used;
(iv)   Whether any over-printing is correct;
(v)   Correct functioning of line monitors.

Samples taken away from the packaging line should not be returned.

5.60 Products that have been involved in an unusual event should be reintroduced into the process only after special inspection, investigation and approval by authorised personnel. A detailed record should be kept of this operation.

5.61   Any significant or unusual discrepancy observed during reconciliation of the amount of bulk product and printed packaging materials and the number of units produced should be investigated and satisfactorily accounted for before release.

5.62   Upon completion of a packaging operation, any unused batch-coded packaging materials should be destroyed and the destruction recorded. A documented procedure should be followed if un-coded printed materials are returned to stock.

Finished Products

5.63   Finished products should be held in quarantine until their final release under conditions established by the manufacturer.

5.64   The evaluation of finished products and documentation that is necessary before release of product for sale is described in Chapter 6 (Quality Control).

5.65   After release, finished products should be stored as usable stock under conditions established by the manufacturer.

Rejected, Recovered and Returned Materials

5.66   Rejected materials and products should be clearly marked as such and stored separately in restricted areas. They should either be returned to the suppliers or, where appropriate, reprocessed or destroyed. Whatever action is taken should be approved and recorded by authorised personnel.

5.67   The reprocessing of rejected products should be exceptional. It is permitted only if the quality of the final product is not affected, the specifications are met and it is done in accordance with a defined and authorised procedure after evaluation of the risks involved. A record should be kept of the reprocessing.

5.68   The recovery of all or part of earlier batches that conform to the required quality by incorporation into a batch of the same product at a defined stage of manufacture should be authorised beforehand. This recovery should be carried out in accordance with a defined procedure after evaluation of the risks involved, including any possible effect on shelf-life. The recovery should be recorded.

5.69   The need for additional testing of any finished product that has been reprocessed, or into which a recovered product has been incorporated, should be considered by the Quality Control Department.

5.70   Products returned from the market and that have left the control of the manufacturer should be destroyed unless without doubt their quality is satisfactory; they may be considered for re-sale, re-labelling or recovery in a subsequent batch only after they have been critically assessed by the Quality Control Department in accordance with a written procedure. The nature of the product, any special storage conditions it requires, its condition and history, and the time elapsed since it was issued should all be taken into account in this assessment. Where any doubt arises over the quality of the product, it should not be considered suitable for re-issue or re-use, although basic chemical reprocessing to recover active ingredient may be possible. Any action taken should be appropriately recorded.

Product Shortage Due to Manufacturing Constraints

5.71   The manufacturer should report to the Marketing Authorisation holder (MAH) any constraints in manufacturing operations that may result in abnormal restriction in the supply. This should be done in a timely manner to facilitate reporting of the restriction in supply by the MAH, to the relevant competent authorities, in accordance with its legal obligations[4].

EU GMP GUIDE PART I CHAPTER 5 PRODUCTION

---

[4] Articles 23a and 81 of Directive 2001/83/EC.

6   QUALITY CONTROL

Principle

This chapter should be read in conjunction with all relevant sections of the GMP Guide.

Quality Control is concerned with sampling, specifications and testing as well as the organisation, documentation and release procedures that ensure that the necessary and relevant tests are carried out, and that materials are not released for use, nor products released for sale or supply, until their quality has been judged satisfactory. Quality Control is not confined to laboratory operations, but must be involved in all decisions that may concern the quality of the product. The independence of Quality Control from Production is considered fundamental to the satisfactory operation of Quality Control.

General

6.1   Each holder of a Manufacturing Authorisation should have a Quality Control Department. This department should be independent from other departments, and under the authority of a person with appropriate qualifications and experience, who has one or several control laboratories at their disposal. Adequate resources must be available to ensure that all the Quality Control arrangements are effectively and reliably carried out.

6.2   The principal duties of the Head of Quality Control are summarised in Chapter 2. The Quality Control Department as a whole will also have other duties, such as to establish, validate and implement all Quality Control procedures, oversee the control of the reference and/or retention samples of materials and products when applicable, ensure the correct labelling of containers of materials and products, ensure the monitoring of the stability of the products, participate in the investigation of complaints related to the quality of the product, etc. All these operations should be carried out in accordance with written procedures and, where necessary, recorded.

6.3   Finished product assessment should embrace all relevant factors, including production conditions, results of in-process testing, a review of manufacturing (including packaging) documentation, compliance with Finished Product Specification and examination of the final finished pack.

6.4   Quality Control personnel should have access to production areas for sampling and investigation as appropriate.

Good Quality Control Laboratory Practice

6.5   Control laboratory premises and equipment should meet the general and specific requirements for Quality Control areas given in Chapter 3. Laboratory equipment should not be routinely moved between high risk areas to avoid accidental cross-contamination. In particular, the microbiological laboratory should be arranged so as to minimize the risk of cross-contamination.

6.6   The personnel, premises and equipment in the laboratories should be appropriate to the tasks imposed by the nature and scale of the manufacturing operations. The use of outside laboratories, in conformity with the principles detailed in Chapter 7, Contract Analysis, can be accepted for particular reasons, but this should be stated in the Quality Control records.

Documentation

6.7   Laboratory documentation should follow the principles given in Chapter 4. An important part of this documentation deals with Quality Control and the following details should be readily available to the Quality Control Department:

(i)   Specifications;

(ii)   Procedures describing sampling, testing, records (including test worksheets and/or laboratory notebooks), recording and verifying;

(iii)   Procedures for and records of the calibration/qualification of instruments and maintenance of equipment;

(iv)   A procedure for the investigation of Out of Specification (OOS) and Out of Trend (OOT) results;

(v)   Testing reports and/or certificates of analysis;

(vi)   Data from environmental (air, water and other utilities) monitoring, where required;

(vii) Validation records of test methods, where applicable.

6.8   Any Quality Control documentation relating to a batch record should be retained following the principles given in Chapter 4 on retention of batch documentation.

6.9   Some kinds of data (e.g. tests results, yields, environmental controls) should be recorded in a manner permitting trend evaluation. Any OOT or OOS data should be addressed and subject to investigation.

EU GMP GUIDE PART I CHAPTER 6 QUALITY CONTROL

6.10　In addition to the information that is part of the batch documentation, other raw data such as laboratory notebooks and/or records should be retained and readily available.

Sampling

6.11　The sample taking should be done and recorded in accordance with approved written procedures that describe:

(i)　The equipment to be used;
(ii)　The amount of the sample to be taken;
(iii)　Instructions for any required subdivision of the sample;
(iv)　The type and condition of the sample container to be used;
(v)　The identification of containers sampled;
(vi)　Any special precautions to be observed, especially with regard to the sampling of sterile or noxious materials;
(vii)　The storage conditions;
(viii)　Instructions for the cleaning and storage of sampling equipment.

6.12　Samples should be representative of the batch of materials or products from which they are taken. Other samples may also be taken to monitor the most stressed part of a process (e.g. beginning or end of a process). The sampling plan used should be appropriately justified and based on a risk management approach.

6.13　Sample containers should bear a label indicating the contents, with the batch number, the date of sampling and the containers from which samples have been drawn. They should be managed in a manner to minimize the risk of mix-up and to protect the samples from adverse storage conditions.

6.14　Further guidance on reference and retention samples is given in Annex 19.

Testing

6.15　Testing methods should be validated. A laboratory that is using a testing method and did not perform the original validation should verify the appropriateness of the testing method. All testing operations described in the Marketing Authorisation or technical dossier should be carried out according to the approved methods.

6.16　The results obtained should be recorded. Results of parameters identified as quality attribute or critical should be trended and checked to make sure that they are consistent with each other. Any calculations should be critically examined.

6.17 The tests performed should be recorded and the records should include at least the following data:

(i)   Name of the material or product and, where applicable, dosage form;

(ii)   Batch number and, where appropriate, the manufacturer and/or supplier;

(iii)   References to the relevant specifications and testing procedures;

(iv)   Test results, including observations and calculations, and reference to any certificates of analysis;

(v)   Dates of testing;

(vi)   Initials of the persons who performed the testing;

(vii)   Initials of the persons who verified the testing and the calculations, where appropriate;

(viii) A clear statement of approval or rejection (or other status decision) and the dated signature of the designated responsible person;

(ix)   Reference to the equipment used.

6.18 All the in-process controls, including those made in the production area by production personnel, should be performed according to methods approved by Quality Control and the results recorded.

6.19 Special attention should be given to the quality of laboratory reagents, solutions, glassware, reference standards and culture media. They should be prepared and controlled in accordance with written procedures. The level of controls should be commensurate to their use and to the available stability data.

6.20 Reference standards should be established as suitable for their intended use. Their qualification and certification as such should be clearly stated and documented. Whenever compendial reference standards from an officially recognised source exist, these should preferably be used as primary reference standards unless fully justified (the use of secondary standards is permitted once their traceability to primary standards has been demonstrated and is documented). These compendial materials should be used for the purpose described in the appropriate monograph unless otherwise authorised by the National Competent Authority.

6.21 Laboratory reagents, solutions, reference standards and culture media should be marked with the preparation and opening date and the signature of the person who prepared them. The expiry date of reagents and culture media should be indicated on the label, together with specific storage conditions. In addition, for volumetric solutions, the last date of standardisation and the last current factor should be indicated.

6.22   Where necessary, the date of receipt of any substance used for testing operations (e.g. reagents, solutions and reference standards) should be indicated
on the container. Instructions for use and storage should be followed. In
certain cases it may be necessary to carry out an identification test and/or
other testing of reagent materials upon receipt or before use.

6.23   Culture media should be prepared in accordance with the media manufacturer's requirements unless scientifically justified. The performance of all
culture media should be verified prior to use.

6.24   Used microbiological media and strains should be decontaminated according to a standard procedure and disposed of in a manner to prevent the
cross-contamination and retention of residues. The in-use shelf-life of
microbiological media should be established, documented and scientifically justified.

6.25   Animals used for testing components, materials or products should, where
appropriate, be quarantined before use. They should be maintained and
controlled in a manner that assures their suitability for the intended use.
They should be identified, and adequate records should be maintained,
showing the history of their use.

On-going stability programme

6.26   After marketing, the stability of the medicinal product should be monitored according to a continuous appropriate programme that will permit
the detection of any stability issue (e.g. changes in levels of impurities
or dissolution profile) associated with the formulation in the marketed
package.

6.27   The purpose of the on-going stability programme is to monitor the product over its shelf-life and to determine that the product remains, and can
be expected to remain, within specifications under the labelled storage
conditions.

6.28   This mainly applies to the medicinal product in the package in which it
is sold, but consideration should also be given to the inclusion in the programme of bulk product. For example, when the bulk product is stored for
a long period before being packaged and/or shipped from a manufacturing
site to a packaging site, the impact on the stability of the packaged product should be evaluated and studied under ambient conditions. In addition, consideration should be given to intermediates that are stored and
used over prolonged periods. Stability studies on reconstituted product

are performed during product development and need not be monitored on an on-going basis. However, when relevant, the stability of reconstituted product can also be monitored.

6.29 The on-going stability programme should be described in a written protocol following the general rules of Chapter 4 and results formalised as a report. The equipment used for the on-going stability programme (stability chambers among others) should be qualified and maintained following the general rules of Chapter 3 and Annex 15.

6.30 The protocol for an on-going stability programme should extend to the end of the shelf-life period and should include, but not be limited to, the following parameters:

(i) Number of batch(es) per strength and different batch sizes, if applicable;

(ii) Relevant physical, chemical, microbiological and biological test methods;

(iii) Acceptance criteria;

(iv) Reference to test methods;

(v) Description of the container closure system(s);

(vi) Testing intervals (time points);

(vii) Description of the conditions of storage (standardised ICH/VICH conditions for long-term testing, consistent with the product labelling, should be used);

(viii) Other applicable parameters specific to the medicinal product.

6.31 The protocol for the on-going stability programme can be different from that of the initial long-term stability study as submitted in the Marketing Authorisation dossier provided that this is justified and documented in the protocol (e.g. the frequency of testing, or when updating to ICH/VICH recommendations).

6.32 The number of batches and frequency of testing should provide a sufficient amount of data to allow for trend analysis. Unless otherwise justified, at least one batch per year of product manufactured in every strength and every primary packaging type, if relevant, should be included in the stability programme (unless none is produced during that year). For products where on-going stability monitoring would normally require testing using animals and no appropriate alternative, validated techniques are available, the frequency of testing may take account of a risk–benefit approach. The principle of bracketing and matrixing designs may be applied if scientifically justified in the protocol.

6.33 In certain situations, additional batches should be included in the on-going stability programme, e.g. an on-going stability study should be conducted after any significant change or significant deviation to the process or package. Any reworking, reprocessing or recovery operation should also be considered for inclusion.

6.34   Results of on-going stability studies should be made available to key personnel and, in particular, to the Qualified Person(s). Where on-going stability studies are carried out at a site other than the site of manufacture of the bulk or finished product, there should be a written agreement between the parties concerned. Results of on-going stability studies should be available at the site of manufacture for review by the competent authority.

6.35   Out-of-specification or significant atypical trends should be investigated. Any confirmed out-of-specification result, or significant negative trend, affecting product batches released on the market, should be reported to the relevant competent authorities. The possible impact on batches on the market should be considered in accordance with Chapter 8 of the GMP Guide and in consultation with the relevant competent authorities.

6.36   A summary of all the data generated, including any interim conclusions on the programme, should be written and maintained. This summary should be subjected to periodic review.

Technical transfer of testing methods

6.37   Prior to transferring a test method, the transferring site should verify that the test method(s) comply with those as described in the Marketing Authorisation or the relevant technical dossier. The original validation of the test method(s) should be reviewed to ensure compliance with current ICH/VICH requirements. A gap analysis should be performed and documented to identify any supplementary validation that should be performed prior to commencing the technical transfer process.

6.38   The transfer of testing methods from one laboratory (transferring laboratory) to another laboratory (receiving laboratory) should be described in a detailed protocol.

6.39   The transfer protocol should include, but not be limited to, the following parameters:

(i)   Identification of the testing to be performed and the relevant test method(s) undergoing transfer;
(ii)   Identification of the additional training requirements;
(iii)   Identification of standards and samples to be tested;
(iv)   Identification of any special transport and storage conditions of test items;

(v) The acceptance criteria that should be based upon the current validation study of the methodology and with respect to ICH/VICH requirements.

6.40 Deviations from the protocol should be investigated prior to closure of the technical transfer process. The technical transfer report should document the comparative outcome of the process and should identify areas requiring further test method revalidation, if applicable.

6.41 Where appropriate, specific requirements described in other European Guidelines, should be addressed for the transfer of particular testing methods (e.g. Near Infrared Spectroscopy).

7   OUTSOURCED ACTIVITIES

Principle

Any activity covered by the GMP Guide that is outsourced should be appropriately defined, agreed and controlled in order to avoid misunderstandings that could result in a product or operation of unsatisfactory quality. There must be a written Contract between the Contract Giver and the Contract Acceptor, which clearly establishes the duties of each party. The Quality Management System of the Contract Giver must clearly state the way that the Qualified Person certifying each batch of product for release exercises their full responsibility.

> **Note:** *This chapter deals with the responsibilities of manufacturers towards the Competent Authorities of the Member States with respect to the granting of marketing and manufacturing authorizations. It is not intended in any way to affect the respective liability of Contract Acceptors and Contract Givers to consumers; this is governed by other provisions of Community and national law.*

General

7.1   There should be a written Contract covering the outsourced activities, the products or operations to which they are related, and any technical arrangements made in connection with it.

7.2   All arrangements for the outsourced activities, including any proposed changes in technical or other arrangements, should be in accordance with regulations in force, and the Marketing Authorisation for the product concerned, where applicable.

7.3   Where the marketing authorization holder and the manufacturer are not the same, appropriate arrangements should be in place, taking into account the principles described in this chapter.

The Contract Giver

7.4   The pharmaceutical quality system of the Contract Giver should include the control and review of any outsourced activities. The Contract Giver is ultimately responsible for ensuring processes are in place to assure the control of outsourced activities. These processes should incorporate quality risk management principles and notably include the following.

7.5   Prior to outsourcing activities, the Contract Giver is responsible for assessing the legality, suitability and competence of the Contract Acceptor to carry out the outsourced activities successfully. The Contract Giver is also responsible for ensuring, by means of the Contract, that the principles and guidelines of GMP as interpreted in this Guide are followed.

7.6   The Contract Giver should provide the Contract Acceptor with all the information and knowledge necessary to carry out the contracted operations correctly in accordance with regulations in force, and the Marketing Authorisation for the product concerned. The Contract Giver should ensure that the Contract Acceptor is fully aware of any problems associated with the product or the work that might pose a hazard to their premises, equipment, personnel, other materials or other products.

7.7   The Contract Giver should monitor and review the performance of the Contract Acceptor and the identification and implementation of any needed improvement.

7.8   The Contract Giver should be responsible for reviewing and assessing the records and the results related to the outsourced activities. They should also ensure, either by themselves, or based on the confirmation of the Contract Acceptor's Qualified Person, that all products and materials delivered to them by the Contract Acceptor have been processed in accordance with GMP and the marketing authorisation.

The Contract Acceptor

7.9   The Contract Acceptor must be able to carry out satisfactorily the work ordered by the Contract Giver such as having adequate premises, equipment, knowledge, experience and competent personnel.

7.10   The Contract Acceptor should ensure that all products, materials and knowledge delivered to them are suitable for their intended purpose.

7.11   The Contract Acceptor should not subcontract to a third party any of the work entrusted to them under the Contract without the Contract Giver's prior evaluation and approval of the arrangements. Arrangements made between the Contract Acceptor and any third party should ensure that information and knowledge, including those from assessments of the suitability of the third party, are made available in the same way as between the original Contract Giver and Contract Acceptor.

7.12   The Contract Acceptor should not make unauthorized changes outside the terms of the Contract that may adversely affect the quality of the outsourced activities for the Contract Giver.

7.13   The Contract Acceptor should understand that outsourced activities, including contract analysis, may be subject to inspection by the competent authorities.

The Contract

7.14   A Contract should be drawn up between the Contract Giver and the Contract Acceptor that specifies their respective responsibilities and communication processes relating to the outsourced activities. Technical aspects of the Contract should be drawn up by competent persons who are suitably knowledgeable in related outsourced activities and Good Manufacturing Practice. All arrangements for outsourced activities must be in accordance with regulations in force and the Marketing Authorisation for the product concerned, and agreed by both parties.

7.15   The Contract should describe clearly who undertakes each step of the outsourced activity, e.g. knowledge management, technology transfer, supply chain, subcontracting, quality and purchasing of materials, testing and releasing materials, undertaking production and quality controls (including in-process controls, sampling and analysis).

7.16   All records related to the outsourced activities, e.g. manufacturing, analytical and distribution records, and reference samples, should be kept by, or be available to, the Contract Giver. Any records relevant to assessing the quality of a product in the event of complaints or a suspected defect or to investigating in the case of a suspected falsified product must be accessible and specified in the relevant procedures of the Contract Giver.

7.17   The Contract should permit the Contract Giver to audit outsourced activities, performed by the Contract Acceptor or their mutually agreed subcontractors.

8 COMPLAINTS, QUALITY DEFECTS AND PRODUCT RECALLS

> **Editor's note**
>
> Extensive changes have been made to this chapter, which now reflects that Quality Risk Management principles should be applied when investigating quality defects or complaints and when making decisions in relation to product recalls or other risk-mitigating actions. It emphasises the need for the cause(s) of quality defects or complaints to be investigated and determined, and that appropriate preventive actions are put in place to guard against a recurrence of the issue, and clarifies expectations and responsibilities in relation to the reporting of quality defects to the Competent Authorities.

Principle

In order to protect public and animal health, a system and appropriate procedures should be in place to record, assess, investigate and review complaints including potential quality defects and, if necessary, to effectively and promptly recall medicinal products for human or veterinary use and investigational medicinal products from the distribution network. Quality Risk Management principles should be applied to the investigation and assessment of quality defects and to the decision-making process in relation to corrective and preventive actions of product recalls and other risk-reducing actions. Guidance in relation to these principles is provided in Chapter 1.

All concerned competent authorities should be informed in a timely manner in case of a confirmed quality defect (faulty manufacture, product deterioration, detection of falsification, non-compliance with the Marketing Authorisation or product specification file, or any other serious quality problems) with a medicinal or investigational medicinal product, which may result in the recall of the product or an abnormal restriction in the supply. In situations where product on the market is found to be non-compliant with the Marketing Authorisation, there is no requirement to notify concerned competent authorities provided that the degree of non-compliance satisfies the Annex 16 restrictions regarding the handling of unplanned deviations.

In case of outsourced activities, a Contract should describe the role and responsibilities of the manufacturer, the Marketing Authorisation holder and/or sponsor and any other relevant third parties in relation to assessment, decision-making, and dissemination of information and implementation of risk-reducing actions relating to a defective product.

Guidance in relation to contracts is provided in Chapter 7. Such Contracts should also address how to contact those responsible at each party for the management of quality defect and recall issues.

Personnel and Organisation

8.1 Appropriately trained and experienced personnel should be responsible for managing complaint and quality defect investigations and for deciding the measures to be taken to manage any potential risk(s) presented by those issues, including recalls. These persons should be independent of the sales and marketing organisation, unless otherwise justified. If these persons do not include the Qualified Person involved in the certification for release of the concerned batch or batches, the latter should be made formally aware of any investigations, risk-reducing actions and recall operations, in a timely manner.

8.2 Sufficient trained personnel and resources should be made available for the handling, assessment, investigation and review of complaints and quality defects, and for implementing any risk-reducing actions. Sufficient trained personnel and resources should also be available for the management of interactions with competent authorities.

8.3 The use of interdisciplinary teams should be considered, including appropriately trained Quality Management personnel.

8.4 In situations in which complaint and quality defect handling is managed centrally within an organisation, the relative roles and responsibilities of the concerned parties should be documented. Central management should not, however, result in delays in the investigation and management of the issue.

Procedures for Handling and Investigating Complaints including Possible Quality Defects

8.5 There should be written procedures describing the actions to be taken upon receipt of a complaint. All complaints should be documented and assessed to establish if they represent a potential quality defect or other issue.

8.6 Special attention should be given to establishing whether a complaint or suspected quality defect relates to falsification.

8.7 As not all complaints received by a company may represent actual quality defects, complaints which do not indicate a potential quality defect should be documented appropriately and communicated to the relevant group or person responsible for the investigation and management of complaints of that nature, such as suspected adverse events.

8.8   There should be procedures in place to facilitate a request to investigate the quality of a batch of a medicinal product in order to support an investigation into a reported suspected adverse event.

8.9   When a quality defect investigation is initiated, procedures should be in place to address at least the following:

(i)   The description of the reported quality defect.

(ii)   The determination of the extent of the quality defect. The checking or testing of reference and/or retention samples should be considered as part of this, and in certain cases, a review of the batch production record, the batch certification record and the batch distribution records (especially for temperature-sensitive products) should be performed.

(iii)   The need to request a sample, or the return, of the defective product from the complainant and, where a sample is provided, the need for an appropriate evaluation to be carried out.

(iv)   The assessment of the risk(s) posed by the quality defect, based on the severity and extent of the quality defect.

(v)   The decision-making process that is to be used concerning the potential need for risk-reducing actions to be taken in the distribution network, such as batch or product recalls, or other actions.

(vi)   The assessment of the impact that any recall action may have on the availability of the medicinal product to patients/animals in any affected market, and the need to notify the relevant authorities of such impact.

(vii)   The internal and external communications that should be made in relation to a quality defect and its investigation.

(viii) The identification of the potential root cause(s) of the quality defect.

(ix)   The need for appropriate Corrective and Preventative Actions (CAPAs) to be identified and implemented for the issue, and for the assessment of the effectiveness of those CAPAs.

Investigation and Decision-making

8.10   The information reported in relation to possible quality defects should be recorded, including all the original details. The validity and extent of all reported quality defects should be documented and assessed in accordance with Quality Risk Management principles in order to support decisions regarding the degree of investigation and action taken.

8.11   If a quality defect is discovered or suspected in a batch, consideration should be given to checking other batches and in some cases other products, in order to determine whether they are also affected. In particular, other batches which may contain portions of the defective batch or defective components should be investigated.

8.12   Quality defect investigations should include a review of previous quality defect reports or any other relevant information for any indication of specific or recurring problems requiring attention and possibly further regulatory action.

8.13   The decisions that are made during and following quality defect investigations should reflect the level of risk that is presented by the quality defect as well as the seriousness of any non-compliance with respect to the requirements of the marketing authorisation/product specification file or GMP. Such decisions should be timely to ensure that patient and animal safety is maintained, in a way that is commensurate with the level of risk that is presented by those issues.

8.14   As comprehensive information on the nature and extent of the quality defect may not always be available at the early stages of an investigation, the decision-making processes should still ensure that appropriate risk-reducing actions are taken at an appropriate time-point during such investigations. All the decisions and measures taken as a result of a quality defect should be documented.

8.15   Quality defects should be reported in a timely manner by the manufacturer to the marketing authorisation holder/sponsor and all concerned Competent Authorities in cases where the quality defect may result in the recall of the product or in an abnormal restriction in the supply of the product.

Root Cause Analysis and Corrective and Preventative Actions

8.16   An appropriate level of root cause analysis work should be applied during the investigation of quality defects. In cases where the true root cause(s) of the quality defect cannot be determined, consideration should be given to identifying the most likely root cause(s) and to addressing those.

8.17   Where human error is suspected or identified as the cause of a quality defect, this should be formally justified and care should be exercised so as to ensure that process, procedural or system-based errors or problems are not overlooked, if present.

8.18   Appropriate CAPAs should be identified and taken in response to a quality defect. The effectiveness of such actions should be monitored and assessed.

8.19   Quality defect records should be reviewed and trend analyses should be performed regularly for any indication of specific or recurring problems requiring attention.

Product Recalls and Other Potential Risk-reducing Actions

8.20   There should be established written procedures, regularly reviewed and updated when necessary, in order to undertake any recall activity or implement any other risk-reducing actions.

8.21   After a product has been placed on the market, any retrieval of it from the distribution network as a result of a quality defect should be regarded and managed as a recall. (This provision does not apply to the retrieval (or return) of samples of the product from the distribution network to facilitate an investigation into a quality defect issue/report.)

8.22   Recall operations should be capable of being initiated promptly and at any time. In certain cases recall operations may need to be initiated to protect public or animal health prior to establishing the root cause(s) and full extent of the quality defect.

8.23   The batch/product distribution records should be readily available to the persons responsible for recalls, and should contain sufficient information on wholesalers and directly supplied customers (with addresses, phone and/or fax numbers inside and outside working hours, batches and amounts delivered), including those for exported products and medical samples.

8.24   In the case of investigational medicinal products, all trial sites should be identified and the countries of destination should be indicated. In the case of an investigational medicinal product for which a marketing authorisation has been issued, the manufacturer of the investigational medicinal product should, in cooperation with the sponsor, inform the marketing authorisation holder of any quality defect that could be related to the authorised medicinal product. The sponsor should implement a procedure for the rapid unblinding of blinded products, where this is necessary for a prompt recall. The sponsor should ensure that the procedure discloses the identity of the blinded product only in so far as is necessary.

8.25   Consideration should be given following consultation with the concerned Competent Authorities, as to how far into the distribution network a recall action should extend, taking into account the potential risk to public or animal health and any impact that the proposed recall action may have. The Competent Authorities should also be informed in situations in which no recall action is being proposed for a defective batch because the batch has expired (such as with short shelf-life products).

8.26   All concerned Competent Authorities should be informed in advance in cases where products are intended to be recalled. For very serious issues (i.e. those with the potential to seriously impact upon patient or animal health), rapid risk-reducing actions (such as a product recall) may have to be taken in advance of notifying the Competent Authorities. Wherever possible, attempts should be made to agree these in advance of their execution with the concerned Competent Authorities.

8.27   It should also be considered whether the proposed recall action may affect different markets in different ways, and if this is the case, appropriate market-specific risk-reducing actions should be developed and discussed with the concerned Competent Authorities. Taking account of its therapeutic use the risk of shortage of a medicinal product which has no authorised alternative should be considered before deciding on a risk-reducing action such as a recall. Any decisions not to execute a risk-reducing action which would otherwise be required should be agreed with the Competent Authority in advance.

8.28   Recalled products should be identified and stored separately in a secure area while awaiting a decision on their fate. A formal disposition of all recalled batches should be made and documented. The rationale for any decision to rework recalled products should be documented and discussed with the relevant competent authority. The extent of shelf-life remaining for any reworked batches that are being considered for placement onto the market should also be considered.

8.29   The progress of the recall process should be recorded until closure and a final report issued, including a reconciliation between the delivered and recovered quantities of the concerned products/batches.

8.30   The effectiveness of the arrangements in place for recalls should be periodically evaluated to confirm that they remain robust and fit for use. Such evaluations should extend to both within office-hour situations as well as out-of-office hour situations and, when performing such evaluations, consideration should be given as to whether mock-recall actions should be performed. This evaluation should be documented and justified.

8.31   In addition to recalls, there are other potential risk-reducing actions that may be considered in order to manage the risks presented by quality defects. Such actions may include the issuance of cautionary communications to healthcare professionals in relation to their use of a batch that is potentially defective. These should be considered on a case-by-case basis and discussed with the concerned Competent Authorities.

9 SELF-INSPECTION

Principle

Self inspections should be conducted in order to monitor the implementation and compliance with Good Manufacturing Practice principles and to propose necessary corrective measures.

9.1 Personnel matters, premises, equipment, documentation, production, quality control, distribution of the medicinal products, arrangements for dealing with complaints and recalls, and self inspection should be examined at intervals following a prearranged programme in order to verify their conformity with the principles of Quality Assurance.

9.2 Self inspections should be conducted in an independent and detailed way by designated competent person(s) from the company. Independent audits by external experts may also be useful.

9.3 All self inspections should be recorded. Reports should contain all the observations made during the inspections and, where applicable, proposals for corrective measures. Statements on the actions subsequently taken should also be recorded.

ANNEX 1 MANUFACTURE OF STERILE MEDICINAL PRODUCTS

Principle

The manufacture of sterile products is subject to special requirements in order to minimise risks of microbiological contamination, and of particulate and pyrogen contamination. Much depends on the skill, training and attitudes of the personnel involved. Quality Assurance is particularly important, and this type of manufacture must strictly follow carefully established and validated methods of preparation and procedure. Sole reliance for sterility or other quality aspects must not be placed on any terminal process or finished product test.

> **Note:** *This guidance does not lay down detailed methods for determining the microbiological and particulate cleanliness of air, surfaces, etc. Reference should be made to other documents such as the EN/ISO Standards.*

General

1   The manufacture of sterile products should be carried out in clean areas, entry to which should be through airlocks for personnel and/or for equipment and materials. Clean areas should be maintained to an appropriate cleanliness standard and supplied with air that has passed through filters of an appropriate efficiency.

2   The various operations of component preparation, product preparation and filling should be carried out in separate areas within the clean area. Manufacturing operations are divided into two categories: firstly, those where the product is terminally sterilised and, second, those that are conducted aseptically at some or all stages.

3   Clean areas for the manufacture of sterile products are classified according to the required characteristics of the environment. Each manufacturing operation requires an appropriate environmental cleanliness level in the operational state in order to minimise the risks of particulate or microbial contamination of the product or materials being handled.

In order to meet "in operation" conditions these areas should be designed to reach certain specified air-cleanliness levels in the "at-rest" occupancy state. The "at-rest" state is the condition where the installation is installed and operating, complete with production equipment but with no operating personnel present. The "in-operation" state is the condition where the installation is functioning in the defined operating mode with the specified number of personnel working.

The "in-operation" and "at-rest" states should be defined for each clean room or suite of clean rooms.

For the manufacture of sterile medicinal products 4 grades can be distinguished:

Grade A: The local zone for high-risk operations, e.g. filling zone, stopper bowls, open ampoules and vials, making aseptic connections. Normally such conditions are provided by a laminar airflow work station. Laminar airflow systems should provide a homogeneous air speed in a range of 0.36–0.54 m/s (guidance value) at the working position in open clean-room applications. The maintenance of laminarity should be demonstrated and validated.

A uni-directional airflow and lower velocities may be used in closed isolators and glove boxes.

Grade B: For aseptic preparation and filling, this is the background environment for the Grade A zone.

Grades C and D: Clean areas for carrying out less critical stages in the manufacture of sterile products.

Clean Room and Clean Air Device Classification

4   Clean rooms and clean air devices should be classified in accordance with EN/ISO 14644-1. Classification should be clearly differentiated from operational process and environmental monitoring. The maximum permitted airborne particle concentration for each grade is given in the following table.

	Maximum permitted number of particles per m³ equal to or greater than the tabulated size			
	At rest		**In operation**	
Grade	0.5 µm	5.0 µm	0.5 µm	5.0 µm
A	3 520	20	3 520	20
B	3 520	29	352 000	2 900
C	352 000	2 900	3 520 000	29 000
D	3 520 000	29 000	Not defined	Not defined

5   For classification purposes in Grade A zones, a minimum sample volume of 1 m³ should be taken per sample location. For Grade A the airborne

particle classification is ISO 4.8 dictated by the limit for particles ≥5.0 μm. For Grade B (at rest) the airborne particle classification is ISO 5 for both considered particle sizes. For Grade C (at rest & in operation) the airborne particle classification is ISO 7 and ISO 8, respectively. For Grade D (at rest) the airborne particle classification is ISO 8. For classification purposes EN/ISO 14644-1 methodology defines both the minimum number of sample locations and the sample size based on the class limit of the largest considered particle size and the method of evaluation of the data collected.

6   Portable particle counters with a short length of sample tubing should be used for classification purposes because of the relatively higher rate of precipitation of particles ≥5.0 μm in remote sampling systems with long lengths of tubing. Isokinetic sample heads shall be used in unidirectional airflow systems.

7   "In-operation" classification may be demonstrated during normal operations, simulated operations or during media fills because worst-case simulation is required for this. EN/ISO 14644-2 provides information on testing to demonstrate continued compliance with the assigned cleanliness classifications.

Clean Room and Clean Air Device Monitoring

8   Clean rooms and clean air devices should be routinely monitored in operation and the monitoring locations based on a formal risk analysis study and the results obtained during the classification of rooms and/or clean air devices.

9   For Grade A zones, particle monitoring should be undertaken for the full duration of critical processing, including equipment assembly, except where justified by contaminants in the process that would damage the particle counter or present a hazard, e.g. live organisms and radiological hazards. In such cases monitoring during routine equipment set-up operations should be undertaken prior to exposure to the risk. Monitoring during simulated operations should also be performed. The Grade A zone should be monitored at such a frequency and with suitable sample size that all interventions, transient events and any system deterioration would be captured and alarms triggered if alert limits are exceeded. It is accepted that it may not always be possible to demonstrate low levels of ≥5.0 μm particles at the point of fill when filling is in progress, due to the generation of particles or droplets from the product itself.

10 It is recommended that a similar system be used for Grade B zones, although the sample frequency may be decreased. The importance of the particle monitoring system should be determined by the effectiveness of the segregation between the adjacent Grade A and B zones. The Grade B zone should be monitored at such a frequency and with suitable sample size that changes in levels of contamination, and any system deterioration would be captured and alarms triggered if alert limits are exceeded.

11 Airborne particle monitoring systems may consist of independent particle counters, a network of sequentially accessed sampling points connected by manifold to a single particle counter, or a combination of the two. The system selected must be appropriate for the particle size considered. Where remote sampling systems are used, the length of tubing and the radii of any bends in the tubing must be considered in the context of particle losses in the tubing. The selection of the monitoring system should take account of any risk presented by the materials used in the manufacturing operation, e.g. those involving live organisms or radiopharmaceuticals.

12 The sample sizes taken for monitoring purposes using automated systems will usually be a function of the sampling rate of the system used. It is not necessary for the sample volume to be the same as that used for formal classification of clean rooms and clean air devices.

13 In Grade A and B zones, the monitoring of the ≥ 5.0 µm particle concentration count takes on a particular significance because it is an important diagnostic tool for early detection of failure. The occasional indication of ≥ 5.0 µm particle counts may be false counts due to electronic noise, stray light, coincidence, etc. However, consecutive or regular counting of low levels is an indicator of a possible contamination event and should be investigated. Such events may indicate early failure of the HVAC system or filling equipment failure, or may also be diagnostic of poor practices during machine set-up and routine operation.

14 The particle limits given in the table for the "at-rest" state should be achieved after a short "clean-up" period of 15–20 minutes (guidance value) in an unmanned state after completion of operations.

15 The monitoring of Grade C and D areas in operation should be performed in accordance with the principles of quality risk management. The requirements and alert/action limits will depend on the nature of the operations carried out, but the recommended "clean-up period" should be attained.

EU GMP GUIDE PART I ANNEX 1 MANUFACTURE OF STERILE MEDICINAL PRODUCTS

16   Other characteristics such as temperature and relative humidity depend on the product and nature of the operations carried out. These parameters should not interfere with the defined cleanliness standard.

17   Examples of operations to be carried out in the various grades are given in the table below (see also paragraphs 28 and 35).

Grade	Examples of operations for terminally sterilised products (see paragraphs 28–30)
A	Filling of products, when unusually at risk
C	Preparation of solutions, when unusually at risk. Filling of products
D	Preparation of solutions and components for subsequent filling
Grade	Examples of operations for aseptic preparations (see paragraphs 31–35)
A	Aseptic preparation and filling
C	Preparation of solutions to be filtered
D	Handling of components after washing

18   Where aseptic operations are performed, monitoring should be frequent using methods such as settle plates, volumetric air and surface sampling (e.g. swabs and contact plates). Sampling methods used in operation should not interfere with zone protection. Results from monitoring should be considered when reviewing batch documentation for finished product release. Surfaces and personnel should be monitored after critical operations. Additional microbiological monitoring is also required outside production operations, e.g. after validation of systems, cleaning and sanitisation.

19   Recommended limits for microbiological monitoring of clean areas during operation:

	Recommended limits for microbial contamination			
Grade	Air sample cfu/m³	Settle plates (diameter 90 mm), cfu/4 hours	Contact plates (diameter 55 mm), cfu/plate	Glove print 5 fingers, cfu/glove
A	<1	<1	<1	<1
B	10	5	5	5
C	100	50	25	–
D	200	100	50	–

Notes:
(a) These are average values.
(b) Individual settle plates may be exposed for less than 4 hours.

20   Appropriate alert and action limits should be set for the results of particulate and microbiological monitoring. If these limits are exceeded operating procedures should prescribe corrective action.

Isolator Technology

21   The utilisation of isolator technology to minimize human interventions in processing areas may result in a significant decrease in the risk of microbiological contamination of aseptically manufactured products from the environment. There are many possible designs of isolators and transfer devices. The isolator and the background environment should be designed so that the required air quality for the respective zones can be realised. Isolators are constructed of various materials more or less prone to puncture and leakage. Transfer devices may vary from a single door to double door designs to fully sealed systems incorporating sterilisation mechanisms.

22   The transfer of materials into and out of the unit is one of the greatest potential sources of contamination. In general the area inside the isolator is the local zone for high-risk manipulations, although it is recognised that laminar airflow may not exist in the working zone of all such devices.

23   The air classification required for the background environment depends on the design of the isolator and its application. It should be controlled and for aseptic processing it should be at least Grade D.

24   Isolators should be introduced only after appropriate validation. Validation should take into account all critical factors of isolator technology, e.g. the quality of the air inside and outside (background) the isolator, sanitisation of the isolator, the transfer process and isolator integrity.

25   Monitoring should be carried out routinely and should include frequent leak testing of the isolator and glove/sleeve system.

Blow/Fill/Seal Technology

26   Blow/fill/seal units are purpose-built machines in which, in one continuous operation, containers are formed from a thermoplastic granulate, filled and then sealed, all by the one automatic machine. Blow/fill/seal equipment used for aseptic production which is fitted with an effective Grade A air shower may be installed in at least a Grade C environment, provided that Grade A/B clothing is used. The environment should comply with the viable and non-viable limits at rest and the viable limit only when in operation. Blow/fill/seal equipment used for the production of products that are terminally sterilised should be installed in at least a Grade D environment.

27   Because of this special technology particular attention should be paid to, at least the following:

- equipment design and qualification,
- validation and reproducibility of cleaning in place and sterilisation in place,
- background cleanroom environment in which the equipment is located,
- operator training and clothing,
- interventions in the critical zone of the equipment, including any aseptic assembly prior to the commencement of filling.

Terminally Sterilised Products

28   Preparation of components and most products should be done in at least a Grade D environment in order to give a low risk of microbial and particulate contamination, suitable for filtration and sterilisation. Where the product is at a high or unusual risk of microbial contamination (e.g. because the product actively supports microbial growth or must be held for a long period before sterilisation or is necessarily processed not mainly in closed vessels), then preparation should be carried out in a Grade C environment.

29   Filling of products for terminal sterilisation should be carried out in at least a Grade C environment.

30   Where the product is at unusual risk of contamination from the environment, e.g. because the filling operation is slow or the containers are wide-necked or necessarily exposed for more than a few seconds before sealing, the filling should be done in a Grade A zone with at least a Grade C background. Preparation and filling of ointments, creams, suspensions and emulsions should generally be carried out in a Grade C environment before terminal sterilisation.

Aseptic Preparation

31   Components after washing should be handled in at least a Grade D environment. Handling of sterile starting materials and components, unless subjected to sterilisation or filtration through a microorganism-retaining filter later in the process, should be done in a Grade A environment with Grade B background.

32   Preparation of solutions that are to be sterile filtered during the process should be done in a Grade C environment; if not filtered, the preparation

of materials and products should be done in a Grade A environment with a Grade B background.

33 Handling and filling of aseptically prepared products should be done in a Grade A environment with a Grade B background.

34 Prior to the completion of stoppering, transfer of partially closed containers, as used in freeze drying, should be done either in a Grade A environment with Grade B background or in sealed transfer trays in a Grade B environment.

35 Preparation and filling of sterile ointments, creams, suspensions and emulsions should be done in a Grade A environment, with a Grade B background, when the product is exposed and not subsequently filtered.

Personnel

36 Only the minimum number of personnel required should be present in clean areas; this is particularly important during aseptic processing. Inspections and controls should be conducted outside the clean areas as far as possible.

37 All personnel (including those concerned with cleaning and maintenance) employed in such areas should receive regular training in disciplines relevant to the correct manufacture of sterile products. This training should include reference to hygiene and to the basic elements of microbiology. When outside staff who have not received such training (e.g. building or maintenance contractors) need to be brought in, particular care should be taken over their instruction and supervision.

38 Staff who have been engaged in the processing of animal tissue materials or of cultures of microorganisms other than those used in the current manufacturing process should not enter sterile-product areas unless rigorous and clearly defined entry procedures have been followed.

39 High standards of personal hygiene and cleanliness are essential. Personnel involved in the manufacture of sterile preparations should be instructed to report any condition that may cause the shedding of abnormal numbers or types of contaminants; periodic health checks for such conditions are desirable. Actions to be taken about personnel who could be introducing undue microbiological hazard should be decided by a designated competent person.

40 Wristwatches, make-up and jewellery should not be worn in clean areas.

41   Changing and washing should follow a written procedure designed to minimize contamination of clean area clothing or carry-through of contaminants to the clean areas.

42   The clothing and its quality should be appropriate for the process and the grade of the working area. It should be worn in such a way as to protect the product from contamination.

43   The description of clothing required for each grade is given below:

- **Grade D:**   Hair and, where relevant, beard should be covered. A general protective suit and appropriate shoes or overshoes should be worn. Appropriate measures should be taken to avoid any contamination coming from outside the clean area.
- **Grade C:**   Hair and, where relevant, beard and moustache should be covered. A single or two-piece trouser suit, gathered at the wrists and with high neck and appropriate shoes or overshoes should be worn. They should shed virtually no fibres or particulate matter.
- **Grade A/B:**   Headgear should totally enclose hair and, where relevant, beard and moustache; it should be tucked into the neck of the suit; a facemask should be worn to prevent the shedding of droplets. Appropriate sterilised, non-powdered rubber or plastic gloves and sterilised or disinfected footwear should be worn. Trouser legs should be tucked inside the footwear and garment sleeves into the gloves. The protective clothing should shed virtually no fibres or particulate matter and retain particles shed by the body.

44   Outdoor clothing should not be brought into changing rooms leading to Grade B and C rooms. For every worker in a Grade A/B area, clean sterile (sterilised or adequately sanitised) protective garments should be provided at each work session. Gloves should be regularly disinfected during operations. Masks and gloves should be changed at least for every working session.

45   Clean area clothing should be cleaned and handled in such a way that it does not gather additional contaminants that can later be shed. These operations should follow written procedures. Separate laundry facilities for such clothing are desirable. Inappropriate treatment of clothing will damage fibres and may increase the risk of shedding of particles.

Premises

46 In clean areas, all exposed surfaces should be smooth, impervious and unbroken in order to minimize the shedding or accumulation of particles or microorganisms, and to permit the repeated application of cleaning agents and disinfectants where used.

47 To reduce accumulation of dust and to facilitate cleaning there should be no uncleanable recesses and a minimum of projecting ledges, shelves, cupboards and equipment. Doors should be designed to avoid those uncleanable recesses; sliding doors may be undesirable for this reason.

48 False ceilings should be sealed to prevent contamination from the space above them.

49 Pipes and ducts and other utilities should be installed so that they do not create recesses, unsealed openings and surfaces that are difficult to clean.

50 Sinks and drains should be prohibited in Grade A/B areas used for aseptic manufacture. In other areas air breaks should be fitted between the machine or sink and the drains. Floor drains in lower-grade clean rooms should be fitted with traps or water seals to prevent back-flow.

51 Changing rooms should be designed as airlocks and used to provide physical separation of the different stages of changing and so minimize microbial and particulate contamination of protective clothing. They should be flushed effectively with filtered air. The final stage of the changing room should, in the at-rest state, be the same grade as the area into which it leads. The use of separate changing rooms for entering and leaving clean areas is sometimes desirable. In general hand-washing facilities should be provided only in the first stage of the changing rooms.

52 Both airlock doors should not be opened simultaneously. An interlocking system or a visual and/or audible warning system should be operated to prevent the opening of more than one door at a time.

53 A filtered air supply should maintain a positive pressure and an airflow relative to surrounding areas of a lower grade under all operational conditions and should flush the area effectively. Adjacent rooms of different grades should have a pressure differential of 10–15 Pascals (guidance values). Particular attention should be paid to the protection of the zone of greatest risk, that is the immediate environment to which a product and cleaned components that contact the product are exposed. The various recommendations regarding air supplies and pressure differentials may need to be modified where it becomes necessary to contain some materials, e.g. pathogenic, highly toxic, radioactive, or live viral or bacterial materials or

products. Decontamination of facilities and treatment of air leaving a clean area may be necessary for some operations.

54   It should be demonstrated that airflow patterns do not present a contamination risk, e.g. care should be taken to ensure that airflows do not distribute particles from a particle-generating person, operation or machine to a zone of higher product risk.

55   A warning system should be provided to indicate failure in the air supply. Indicators of pressure differences should be fitted between areas where these differences are important. These pressure differences should be recorded regularly or otherwise documented.

Equipment

56   A conveyor belt should not pass through a partition between a Grade A or B area and a processing area of lower air cleanliness, unless the belt itself is continually sterilised (e.g. in a sterilising tunnel).

57   As far as practicable, equipment, fittings and services should be designed and installed so that operations, maintenance and repairs can be carried out outside the clean area. If sterilisation is required, it should be carried out, wherever possible, after complete reassembly.

58   When equipment maintenance has been carried out within the clean area, the area should be cleaned, disinfected and/or sterilised where appropriate, before processing recommences if the required standards of cleanliness and/or asepsis have not been maintained during the work.

59   Water treatment plants and distribution systems should be designed, constructed and maintained so as to ensure a reliable source of water of an appropriate quality. They should not be operated beyond their designed capacity. Water for injections should be produced, stored and distributed in a manner that prevents microbial growth, e.g. by constant circulation at a temperature above 70°C.

60   All equipment, such as sterilisers, air handling and filtration systems, air vent and gas filters, water treatment, generation, storage and distribution systems, should be subject to validation and planned maintenance; their return to use should be approved.

Sanitation

61   The sanitation of clean areas is particularly important. They should be cleaned thoroughly in accordance with a written programme. Where

disinfectants are used, more than one type should be employed. Monitoring should be undertaken regularly in order to detect the development of resistant strains.

62 Disinfectants and detergents should be monitored for microbial contamination; dilutions should be kept in previously cleaned containers and should be stored only for defined periods unless sterilised. Disinfectants and detergents used in Grade A and B areas should be sterile prior to use.

63 Fumigation of clean areas may be useful for reducing microbiological contamination in inaccessible places.

Processing

64 Precautions to minimize contamination should be taken during all processing stages, including the stages before sterilisation.

65 Preparations of microbiological origin should not be made or filled in areas used for the processing of other medicinal products; however, vaccines of dead organisms or of bacterial extracts may be filled, after inactivation, in the same premises as other sterile medicinal products.

66 Validation of aseptic processing should include a process simulation test using a nutrient medium (media fill). Selection of the nutrient medium should be made based on dosage form of the product and selectivity, clarity, concentration and suitability for sterilisation of the nutrient medium.

67 The process simulation test should imitate as closely as possible the routine aseptic manufacturing process and include all the critical subsequent manufacturing steps. It should also take into account various interventions known to occur during normal production as well as worst-case situations.

68 Process simulation tests should be performed as initial validation with three consecutive satisfactory simulation tests per shift and repeated at defined intervals and after any significant modification to the HVAC system, equipment, process and number of shifts. Normally process simulation tests should be repeated twice a year per shift and process.

69 The number of containers used for media fills should be sufficient to enable a valid evaluation. For small batches, the number of containers for media fills should at least equal the size of the product batch. The target should be zero growth and the following should apply:

- When filling fewer than 5,000 units, no contaminated units should be detected.

- When filling 5,000 to 10,000 units:
  - (a) one (1) contaminated unit should result in an investigation, including consideration of a repeat media fill;
  - (b) two (2) contaminated units are considered cause for revalidation, following investigation.
- When filling more than 10,000 units:
  - (a) one (1) contaminated unit should result in an investigation;
  - (b) two (2) contaminated units are considered cause for revalidation, following investigation.

70   For any run size, intermittent incidents of microbial contamination may be indicative of low-level contamination that should be investigated. Investigation of gross failures should include the potential impact on the sterility assurance of batches manufactured since the last successful media fill.

71   Care should be taken that any validation does not compromise the processes.

72   Water sources, water treatment equipment and treated water should be monitored regularly for chemical and biological contamination and, as appropriate, for endotoxins. Records should be maintained of the results of the monitoring and of any action taken.

73   Activities in clean areas and especially when aseptic operations are in progress should be kept to a minimum, and movement of personnel should be controlled and methodical, to avoid excessive shedding of particles and organisms due to over-vigorous activity. The ambient temperature and humidity should not be uncomfortably high because of the nature of the garments worn.

74   Microbiological contamination of starting materials should be minimal. Specifications should include requirements for microbiological quality, when the need for this has been indicated by monitoring.

75   Containers and materials liable to generate fibres should be minimised in clean areas.

76   Where appropriate, measures should be taken to minimize the particulate contamination of the end product.

77   Components, containers and equipment should be handled after the final cleaning process in such a way that they are not re-contaminated.

78   The interval between the washing and drying and the sterilisation of components, containers and equipment, as well as between their sterilisation and use, should be minimised and subject to a time limit appropriate to the storage conditions.

79   The time between the start of the preparation of a solution and its sterilisation or filtration through a microorganism-retaining filter should be minimised. There should be a set maximum permissible time for each product that takes into account its composition and the prescribed method of storage.

80   The bioburden should be monitored before sterilisation. There should be working limits on contamination immediately before sterilisation, which are related to the efficiency of the method to be used. Bioburden assay should be performed on each batch for both aseptically filled product and terminally sterilised products. Where overkill sterilisation parameters are set for terminally sterilised products, bioburden might be monitored only at suitable scheduled intervals. For parametric release systems, bioburden assay should be performed on each batch and considered as an in-process test. Where appropriate the level of endotoxins should be monitored. All solutions, in particular large-volume infusion fluids, should be passed through a microorganism-retaining filter, if possible sited immediately before filling.

81   Components, containers, equipment and any other article required in a clean area where aseptic work takes place should be sterilised and passed into the area through double-ended sterilisers sealed into the wall, or by a procedure that achieves the same objective of not introducing contamination. Non-combustible gases should be passed through microorganism-retentive filters.

82   The efficacy of any new procedure should be validated, and the validation verified at scheduled intervals based on performance history or when any significant change is made in the process or equipment.

Sterilisation

83   All sterilisation processes should be validated. Particular attention should be given when the adopted sterilisation method is not described in the current edition of the *European Pharmacopoeia*, or when it is used for a product that is not a simple aqueous or oily solution. Where possible, heat sterilisation is the method of choice. In any case, the sterilisation process must be in accordance with the marketing and manufacturing authorisations.

84   Before any sterilisation process is adopted its suitability for the product, and its efficacy in achieving the desired sterilising conditions in all parts of each type of load to be processed, should be demonstrated by physical measurements and biological indicators where appropriate. The validity of the process should be verified at scheduled intervals, at least annually,

and whenever significant modifications have been made to the equipment. Records should be kept of the results.

85   For effective sterilisation, the whole of the material must be subjected to the required treatment and the process should be designed to ensure that this is achieved.

86   Validated loading patterns should be established for all sterilisation processes.

87   Biological indicators should be considered as an additional method for monitoring the sterilisation. They should be stored and used according to the manufacturer's instructions, and their quality checked by positive controls. If biological indicators are used, strict precautions should be taken to avoid transferring microbial contamination from them.

88   There should be a clear means of differentiating products that have not been sterilised from those that have. Each basket, tray or other carrier of products or components should be clearly labelled with the material name, its batch number and an indication of whether or not it has been sterilised. Indicators such as autoclave tape may be used, where appropriate, to indicate whether or not a batch (or sub-batch) has passed through a sterilisation process, but they do not give a reliable indication that the lot is, in fact, sterile.

89   Sterilisation records should be available for each sterilisation run. They should be approved as part of the batch release procedure.

Sterilisation by Heat

90   Each heat sterilisation cycle should be recorded on a time/temperature chart with a sufficiently large scale or by other appropriate equipment with suitable accuracy and precision. The position of the temperature probes used for controlling and/or recording should have been determined during the validation and, where applicable, also checked against a second independent temperature probe located at the same position.

91   Chemical or biological indicators may also be used, but should not take the place of physical measurements.

92   Sufficient time must be allowed for the whole of the load to reach the required temperature before measurement of the sterilising time period is commenced. This time must be determined for each type of load to be processed.

93   After the high-temperature phase of a heat sterilisation cycle, precautions should be taken against contamination of a sterilised load during cooling.

Any cooling fluid or gas in contact with the product should be sterilised unless it can be shown that any leaking container would not be approved for use.

Moist Heat

94   Both temperature and pressure should be used to monitor the process. Control instrumentation should normally be independent of monitoring instrumentation and recording charts. Where automated control and monitoring systems are used for these applications, they should be validated to ensure that critical process requirements are met. System and cycle faults should be registered by the system and observed by the operator. The reading of the independent temperature indicator should be routinely checked against the chart recorder during the sterilisation period. For sterilisers fitted with a drain at the bottom of the chamber, it may also be necessary to record the temperature at this position, throughout the sterilisation period. There should be frequent leak tests on the chamber when a vacuum phase is part of the cycle.

95   The items to be sterilised, other than products in sealed containers, should be wrapped in a material that allows removal of air and penetration of steam, but which prevents recontamination after sterilisation. All parts of the load should be in contact with the sterilizing agent at the required temperature for the required time.

96   Care should be taken to ensure that steam used for sterilisation is of a suitable quality and does not contain additives at a level that could cause contamination of product or equipment.

Dry Heat

97   The process used should include air circulation within the chamber and the maintenance of a positive pressure to prevent the entry of non-sterile air. Any air admitted should be passed through a HEPA filter. Where this process is also intended to remove pyrogens, challenge tests using endotoxins should be used as part of the validation.

Sterilisation by Radiation

98   Radiation sterilisation is used mainly for the sterilisation of heat-sensitive materials and products. Many medicinal products and some packaging materials are radiation sensitive, so this method is permissible only when

the absence of deleterious effects on the product has been confirmed exper-
imentally. Ultraviolet irradiation is not normally an acceptable method of
sterilisation.

99   During the sterilisation procedure the radiation dose should be measured.
For this purpose, dosimetry indicators which are independent of dose rate
should be used, giving a quantitative measurement of the dose received
by the product itself. Dosimeters should be inserted in the load in sufficient number and close enough together to ensure that there is always a
dosimeter in the irradiator. Where plastic dosimeters are used, they should
be used within the time limit of their calibration. Dosimeter absorbances
should be read within a short period after exposure to radiation.

100   Biological indicators may be used as an additional control.

101   Validation procedures should ensure that the effects of variations in density of the packages are considered.

102   Materials handling procedures should prevent mix-up between irradiated
and non-irradiated materials. Radiation sensitive colour discs should also
be used on each package to differentiate between packages which have
been subjected to irradiation and those that have not.

103   The total radiation dose should be administered within a predetermined
time span.

Sterilisation with Ethylene Oxide

104   This method should only be used when no other method is practicable.
During process validation, it should be shown that there is no damaging effect on the product, and that the conditions and time allowed for
degassing are such as to reduce any residual gas and reaction products to
defined acceptable limits for the type of product or material.

105   Direct contact between gas and microbial cells is essential; precautions
should be taken to avoid the presence of organisms likely to be enclosed
in material such as crystals or dried protein. The nature and quantity of
packaging materials can significantly affect the process.

106   Before exposure to the gas, materials should be brought into equilibrium
with the humidity and temperature required by the process. The time
required for this should be balanced against the opposing need to minimize
the time before sterilisation.

107   Each sterilisation cycle should be monitored with suitable biological
indicators, using the appropriate number of test pieces distributed throughout the load. The information so obtained should form part of the batch
record.

108 For each sterilisation cycle, records should be made of the time taken to complete the cycle, the pressure, temperature and humidity within the chamber during the process, and the gas concentration and total amount of gas used. The pressure and temperature should be recorded throughout the cycle on a chart. The record(s) should form part of the batch record.

109 After sterilisation, the load should be stored in a controlled manner under ventilated conditions to allow residual gas and reaction products to reduce to the defined level. This process should be validated.

Filtration of Medicinal Products that cannot be Sterilised in their Final Container

110 Filtration alone is not considered sufficient when sterilisation in the final container is possible. With regard to methods currently available, steam sterilisation is to be preferred. If the product cannot be sterilised in the final container, solutions or liquids can be filtered through a sterile filter of nominal pore size of 0.22 micron (or less), or with at least equivalent microorganism-retaining properties, into a previously sterilised container. Such filters can remove most bacteria and moulds, but not all viruses or mycoplasmas. Consideration should be given to complementing the filtration process with some degree of heat treatment.

111 Due to the potential additional risks of the filtration method, compared with other sterilization processes, a second filtration via a further sterilised micro-organism retaining filter, immediately prior to filling, may be advisable. The final sterile filtration should be carried out as close as possible to the filling point.

112 Fibre-shedding characteristics of filters should be minimal.

113 The integrity of the sterilised filter should be verified before use and should be confirmed immediately after use by an appropriate method such as a bubble point, diffusive flow or pressure hold test. The time taken to filter a known volume of bulk solution and the pressure difference to be used across the filter should be determined during validation and any significant differences from this during routine manufacturing should be noted and investigated. Results of these checks should be included in the batch record. The integrity of critical gas and air vent filters should be confirmed after use. The integrity of other filters should be confirmed at appropriate intervals.

114 The same filter should not be used for more than one working day unless such use has been validated.

115   The filter should not affect the product by removal of ingredients from it or by release of substances into it.

Finishing of Sterile Products

116   Partially stoppered freeze-drying vials should be maintained under Grade A conditions at all times until the stopper is fully inserted.

117   Containers should be closed by appropriately validated methods. Containers closed by fusion, e.g. glass or plastic ampoules, should be subject to 100% integrity testing. Samples of other containers should be checked for integrity according to appropriate procedures.

118   The container closure system for aseptically filled vials is not fully integral until the aluminium cap has been crimped into place on the stoppered vial. Crimping of the cap should therefore be performed as soon as possible after stopper insertion.

119   As the equipment used to crimp vial caps can generate large quantities of non-viable particulates, the equipment should be located at a separate station equipped with adequate air extraction.

120   Vial capping can be undertaken as an aseptic process using sterilised caps or as a clean process outside the aseptic core. Where this latter approach is adopted, vials should be protected by Grade A conditions up to the point of leaving the aseptic processing area; thereafter stoppered vials should be protected with a Grade A air supply until the cap has been crimped.

121   Vials with missing or displaced stoppers should be rejected prior to capping. Where human intervention is required at the capping station, appropriate technology should be used to prevent direct contact with the vials and to minimise microbial contamination.

122   Restricted access barriers and isolators may be beneficial in assuring the required conditions and minimising direct human interventions into the capping operation.

123   Containers sealed under vacuum should be tested for maintenance of that vacuum after an appropriate, predetermined period.

124   Filled containers of parenteral products should be inspected individually for extraneous contamination or other defects. When inspection is done visually, it should be done under suitable and controlled conditions of illumination and background. Operators doing the inspection should pass regular eyesight checks, with spectacles if worn, and be allowed frequent breaks from inspection. Where other methods of inspection are used,

the process should be validated and the performance of the equipment checked at intervals. Results should be recorded.

Quality Control

125 The sterility test applied to the finished product should be regarded only as the last in a series of control measures by which sterility is assured. The test should be validated for the product(s) concerned.

126 In those cases where parametric release has been authorised, special attention should be paid to the validation and the monitoring of the entire manufacturing process.

127 Samples taken for sterility testing should be representative of the whole of the batch, but should in particular include samples taken from parts of the batch considered to be most at risk of contamination, e.g.:

(a) for products that have been filled aseptically, samples should include containers filled at the beginning and end of the batch and after any significant intervention,

(b) or products that have been heat sterilised in their final containers, consideration should be given to taking samples from the potentially coolest part of the load.

ANNEX 2 MANUFACTURE OF BIOLOGICAL ACTIVE SUBSTANCES AND MEDICINAL PRODUCTS FOR HUMAN USE

Editor's note: Annex 2 of the GMP Guide has been revised as a consequence of the adoption of the Guidelines on Good Manufacturing Practice specific to Advanced Therapy Medicinal Products pursuant to Article 5 of Regulation (EC) 1394/2007 of the European Parliament and of the Council of 13 November 2007 on advanced therapy medicinal products and amending Directive 2001/83/EC and Regulation (EC) No 726/2004.
Came into operation on 26 June 2018.

Scope

The methods employed in the manufacture of biological active substances and biological medicinal products for human use ("biological active substances and medicinal products") are a critical factor in shaping the appropriate regulatory control. Biologically active substances and medicinal products can therefore be defined largely by reference to their method of manufacture. This annex provides guidance on the full range of active substances and medicinal products defined as biological, with the exception of Advanced Therapy Medicinal Products ("ATMPs"), as defined in Article 1(1) of Regulation (EC) No 1394/2007[1]. The ATMPs are not covered by the present guideline. Manufacturers of ATMPs should refer to the Guidelines on Good Manufacturing Practice specific to Advanced Therapy Medicinal Products referred to in Article 5 of the above quoted Regulation.

This annex is divided into two main parts:

(a) Part A contains supplementary guidance on the manufacture of biological active substances and medicinal products, from control over seed lots and cell banks through to finishing activities and testing.

(b) Part B contains further guidance on selected types of biological active substances and medicinal products.

---

[1] Regulation (EC) No 1394 of the European Parliament and of the Council of 13 November 2007 on advanced therapy medicinal products and amending Directive 2001/83/EC and Regulation (EC) No 726/2004, OJ L 324, 10.12.2007, p. 121.

This annex, along with several other annexes of the Guide to GMP in EudraLex, Volume 4, provides guidance that supplements that in Parts I and II of that Guide. There are two aspects to the scope of this annex:

(a) Stage of manufacture: for biological active substances to the point immediately prior to their being rendered sterile, the primary guidance source is Part II. Guidance for the subsequent manufacturing steps of biological products is covered in Part I.

(b) Type of product: this annex provides guidance on the full range of medicinal products defined as biological, with the exception of ATMPs.

These two aspects are shown in Table 1; it should be noted that this table is illustrative only and not meant to describe the precise scope. It should also be understood that in line with the corresponding table in Part II of EudraLex, Volume 4, the level of GMP increases in detail from early to later steps in the manufacture of biological active substances but GMP principles should always be adhered to. The inclusion of some early steps of manufacture within the scope of this Annex does not imply that those steps will be routinely subject to inspection by the authorities.

Antibiotics are not defined as biological medicinal products; however, where biological stage 49 of manufacture occurs, guidance in this Annex may be used. Guidance for medicinal products derived from fractionated human blood or plasma is covered in Annex 14 of EudraLex, Volume 4, and for non-transgenic plant products in Annex 7.

In certain cases, other legislation is applicable to the starting materials. For example,

(a) Tissue and cells used as starting materials for medicinal products: Directive 2004/23/EC of the European Parliament and of the Council of 31 March 2004 on setting standards of quality and safety for the donation, procurement, testing, processing, preservation, storage and distribution of human tissues and cells[2], and Commission Directive 2006/17/EC of 8 February 2006 implementing Directive 2004/23/EC of the European Parliament and the Council, as regards certain technical requirements for the donation, procurement and testing of human tissues and cells[3], cover only their donation, procurement and testing. Such tissues and cells may provide the active substances for some biological medicinal product within the scope of this annex at

---

[2] OJ L 102, 7.4.2004, p. 48.
[3] OJ L 38, 9.2.2006, p. 40.

which point GMP and other medicinal product legislation requirements apply.

(b) Where blood or blood components used as starting materials for medicinal products: Directive 2002/98/EC of the European Parliament and the Council of 27 January 2003 setting standards of quality and safety for the collection, testing, processing, storage and distribution of human blood and blood components and amending Directive 2001/83/EC[4] and its Commission Directives provides the technical requirements[5] for the selection of donors and the collection and testing of blood and blood components.

Additionally, the manufacture and control of genetically modified organisms needs to comply with local and national requirements. In accordance with Directive 2009/41/EC of the European Parliament and the Council of 6 May 2009 on the contained use of genetically modified microorganisms[6], appropriate containment and other protective measures shall be established and maintained in facilities where any genetically modified microorganisms are handled. Advice should be obtained according to national legislation in order to establish and maintain the appropriate Biological Safety Level. There should be no conflicts with GMP requirements.

---

[4] OJ L 33, 8.2.2003, p. 30.
[5] Directive 2004/33/EC of 22 March 2004 implementing Directive 2002/98/EC of the European Parliament and the Council as regards certain technical requirements for blood and blood components and Good Practice Guidelines for blood establishments as referenced in Directive 2016/1214, amending Directive 2005/62/EC.
[6] OJ L 125, 21.5.2009, p. 75.

Table 1 Illustrative guide to manufacturing activities within the scope of Annex 2

Type and source of material	Example product	Application of this guide to manufacturing steps shown in grey			
1. Animal or plant sources: non-trans-genic	Heparins, insulin, enzymes, pro-teins, allergen extract, immu-nosera	Collection of plant, organ, animal material or fluid[7]	Cutting, mixing, and /or initial processing	Isolation and purification	Formulation, filling
2. Virus or bacteria/fer-mentation/cell culture	Viral or bacterial vaccines; enzymes, proteins	Establishment and maintenance of MCB[8], WCB, MVS, WVS	Cell culture and/or fer-mentation	Inactivation when applica-ble, isolation and purifica-tion	Formulation, filling
3. Biotech-nology: fermentation/ cell culture	Recombinant products, MAb, allergens, vaccines	Establishment and mainte-nance of MCB and WCB, MSL, WSL	Cell culture and/or fer-mentation	Isolation, purification, modification	Formulation, filling
4. Animal sources: transgenic	Recombinant proteins	Master and working trans-genic bank	Collection, cutting, mixing, and/ or initial processing	Isolation, pu-rification and modification	Formulation, filling
5. Plant sources: transgenic	Recombinant proteins, vac-cines, allergen	Master and working trans-genic bank	Growing, harvesting[9]	Initial ex-traction, isolation, purification, modification	Formulation, filling
6. Human sources	Urine-derived enzymes, hormones	Collection of fluid[10]	Mixing and/ or initial processing	Isolation and purification	Formulation, filling
7. Human sources	Products from cells tissues	Donation, procurement and testing of starting tissue/ cells[11]	Initial processing, isolation and purification.	Cell isolation, culture, puri-fication, com-bination with non-cellular components	Formulation, combination, filling

➡ **Increasing GMP requirements**

Note. See Glossary for explanation of acronyms.

[7] See section B1 for the extent to which GMP principles apply.

[8] See section on "Seed lot and cell bank system" for the extent to which GMP applies.

[9] HMPC guideline on Good Agricultural and Collection Practice – EMEA/HMPC/246816/2005.

[10] Principles of GMP apply; see explanatory text in "Scope".

[11] Human tissues and cells must comply with Directive 2004/23/EC and implementing Directives at these stages.

Principle

The manufacture of biological medicinally active substances and products involves certain specific considerations arising from the nature of the products and the processes. The ways in which biological medicinal products are manufactured, controlled and administered make some particular precautions necessary.

Unlike conventional medicinal products, which are manufactured using chemical and physical techniques capable of a high degree of consistency, the manufacture of biological active substances and medicinal products involves biological processes and materials, such as cultivation of cells or extraction from living organisms. These biological processes may display inherent variability, so that the range and nature of by-products may be variable. As a result, quality risk management (QRM) principles are particularly important for this class of materials and should be used to develop the control strategy across all stages of manufacture, so as to minimise variability and to reduce the opportunity for contamination and cross-contamination.

Since materials and processing conditions used in cultivation processes are designed to provide conditions for the growth of specific cells and microorganisms, this provides extraneous microbial contaminants the opportunity to grow. In addition, some products may be limited in their ability to withstand a wide range of purification techniques, particularly those designed to inactivate or remove adventitious viral contaminants. The design of the processes, equipment, facilities, utilities, the conditions of preparation and addition of buffers and reagents, and sampling and training of the operators are key considerations to minimise such contamination events.

Specifications related to products (such as those in Pharmacopoeial monographs, Marketing Authorisation [MA] and Clinical Trial Authorisation [CTA]) will dictate whether and to what stage substances and materials can have a defined level of bioburden or need to be sterile. Similarly, manufacturing must be consistent with other specifications set out in the MA or CTA guidance (e.g. number of generations [doublings, passages] between the seed lot or cell bank).

For biological materials that cannot be sterilized (e.g. by filtration), processing must be conducted aseptically to minimise the introduction of contaminants. Where they exist, CHMP guidance documents should be consulted on the validation of specific manufacturing methods, e.g. virus removal or inactivation. The application of appropriate environmental controls and monitoring and, wherever feasible, *in situ* cleaning and sterilization systems, together with the use of closed systems, can significantly reduce the risk of accidental contamination and cross-contamination.

Control usually involves biological analytical techniques, which typically have a greater variability than physicochemical determinations. A robust manufacturing process is therefore crucial and in-process controls take on a particular importance in the manufacture of biological active substances and medicinal products.

Biological medicinal products that incorporate human tissues or cells must take into account the requirements of Directive 2004/23/EC and Commission Directive 2006/17/EC. In line with Commission Directive 2006/86/EC of 24 October 2006, implementing Directive 2004/23/EC of the European Parliament and the Council as regards traceability requirements, notification of serious adverse reactions and events and certain technical requirements for the coding, processing, preservation, storage and distribution of human tissues and cells[12], collection and testing must be done in accordance with an appropriate quality system for which standards and specifications are defined in its Annex.

Biologically active substances and medicinal products must comply with the latest version of the Note for Guidance on Minimising the Risk of Transmitting Animal Spongiform Encephalopathy (TSE) Agents via Human and Veterinary Medicinal Products.

Part A. General Guidance

Personnel

1　Personnel (including those concerned with cleaning, maintenance or quality control) employed in areas where biological active substances and products are manufactured and tested should receive training, and periodic retraining, specific to the products manufactured in their work, including any specific security measures to protect product, personnel and the environment.

2　The health status of personnel should be taken into consideration for product safety. Where necessary, personnel engaged in production, maintenance, testing and animal care (and inspections) should be vaccinated with appropriate specific vaccines and have regular health checks.

3　Any changes in the health status of personnel, which could adversely affect the quality of the product, should preclude work in the production area and appropriate records kept. Production of BCG vaccine and tuberculin products should be restricted to staff who are carefully monitored by regular checks of immunological status or chest X-ray. Health monitoring of staff should be commensurate with the risk; medical advice should be sought for personnel involved with hazardous organisms.

---

[12] OJ L 294, 25.10.2006, p. 32.

4   Where required to minimise the opportunity for cross-contamination, restrictions on the movement of all personnel (including quality control [QC], maintenance and cleaning staff) should be controlled on the basis of QRM principles. In general, personnel should not pass from areas where there is exposure to live microorganisms, genetically modified organisms, toxins or animals to areas where other products, inactivated products or different organisms are handled. If such passage is unavoidable, the contamination control measures should be based on QRM principles.

Premises and equipment

5   As part of the control strategy, the degree of environmental control of particulate and microbial contamination of the production premises should be adapted to the active substance, intermediate or finished product and the production step, bearing in mind the potential level of contamination of the starting materials and the risks to the product. The environmental monitoring programme should be supplemented by the inclusion of methods to detect the presence of specific microorganisms (i.e. host organism, yeast, moulds, anaerobes, etc.) where indicated by the QRM process.

6   Manufacturing and storage facilities, processes and environmental classifications should be designed to prevent the extraneous contamination of products. Prevention of contamination is more appropriate than detection and removal, although contamination is likely to become evident during processes such as fermentation and cell culture. Where processes are not closed and there is therefore exposure of the product to the immediate room environment (e.g. during additions of supplements, media, buffers, gasses) control measures should be put in place, including engineering and environmental controls on the basis of QRM principles. These QRM principles should take into account the principles and guidance from the appropriate sections of Annex 1[13] to EudraLex, Volume 4, when selecting environmental classification cascades and associated controls.

7   Dedicated production areas should be used for the handling of live cells capable of persistence in the manufacturing environment. Dedicated production areas should be used for the manufacture of pathogenic organisms (i.e. Biosafety level 3 or 4).

---

[13] Although the title of Annex 1 refers to the manufacture of sterile medicinal products, it is not the intention to force the manufacture of sterile product at a stage when a low bioburden is appropriate and authorised. Its use is because it is the only EU GMP source of guidance on all of the classified manufacturing areas including the lower Grades D and C.

8 Manufacture in a multi-product facility may be acceptable where the following, or equivalent (as appropriate to the product types involved), considerations and measures are part of an effective control strategy to prevent cross-contamination:

(a) Knowledge of key characteristics of all cells, organisms and any adventitious agents (e.g. pathogenicity, detectability, persistence, susceptibility to inactivation) within the same facility;

(b) Where production is characterised by multiple small batches from different starting materials factors such as the health status of donors and the risk of total loss of product should be taken into account when considering the acceptance of concurrent working during development of the control strategy;

(c) Live organisms and spores are prevented from entering non-related areas or equipment by addressing all potential routes of cross-contamination and utilizing single-use components and engineering measures such as closed systems;

(d) Control measures to remove the organisms and spores before the subsequent manufacture of other products; these control measures should also take the heating, ventilation and air conditioning (HVAC) system into account. Cleaning and decontamination for the organisms and spores should be validated;

(e) Environmental monitoring specific for the microorganism being manufactured, where the microorganisms are capable of persistence in the manufacturing environment and where methods are available, is conducted in adjacent areas during manufacture and after completion of cleaning and decontamination. Attention should also be given to risks arising with use of certain monitoring equipment (e.g. airborne particle monitoring) in areas handling live and/or spore-forming organisms;

(f) Products, equipment, ancillary equipment (e.g. for calibration and validation) and disposable items are only moved within and removed from such areas in a manner that prevents contamination of other areas, other products and different product stages (e.g. prevent contamination of inactivated or toxoided products with non-inactivated products);

(g) Campaign-based manufacturing.

9 For finishing (secondary) operations[14], the need for dedicated facilities will depend on consideration of the above, together with additional considerations such as the specific needs of the biological medicinal product and the characteristics of other products, including any non-biological products,

---

[14] Formulation, filling and packaging.

in the same facility. Other control measures for finishing operations may include the need for specific addition sequences, mixing speeds, time and temperature controls, limits on exposure to light, and containment and cleaning procedures in the event of spillages.

10   The measures and procedures necessary for containment (i.e. for environment and operator safety) should not conflict with those for product quality.

11   Air-handling units should be designed, constructed and maintained to minimise the risk of cross-contamination between different manufacturing areas, and may need to be specific for an area. Consideration, based on QRM principles, should be given to the use of single-pass air systems.

12   Positive pressure areas should be used to process sterile products, but negative pressure in specific areas at the point of exposure of pathogens is acceptable for containment reasons. Where negative pressure areas or safety cabinets are used for aseptic processing of materials with particular risks (e.g. pathogens), they should be surrounded by a positive-pressure clean zone of appropriate grade. These pressure cascades should be clearly defined and continuously monitored with appropriate alarm settings.

13   Equipment used during handling of live organisms and cells, including those for sampling, should be designed to prevent any contamination during processing.

14   Primary containment[15] should be designed and periodically tested to ensure the prevention of escape of biological agents into the immediate working environment.

15   The use of "clean in place" and "steam in place" ("sterilisation in place") systems should be used where possible. Valves on fermentation vessels should be completely steam sterilisable.

16   Air-vent filters should be hydrophobic and validated for their scheduled lifespan with integrity testing at appropriate intervals based on appropriate QRM principles.

17   Drainage systems must be designed so that effluents can be effectively neutralised or decontaminated to minimise the risk of cross-contamination. Local regulation must be complied with to minimise the risk of contamination of the external environment, according to the risk associated with the biohazardous nature of waste materials.

---

[15] See main GMP Glossary on "Containment".

18   Due to the variability of biological products or manufacturing processes, relevant/critical raw materials (such as culture media and buffers) have to be measured or weighed during the production process. In these cases, small stocks of these raw materials may be kept in the production area for a specified duration, based on defined criteria such as for the duration of manufacture of the batch or of the campaign.

Animals

19   A wide range of animal species are used in the manufacture of a number of biological medicinal products. These can be divided into two broad types of sources:

(a) Live groups, herds, flocks: examples include polio vaccine (monkeys), immunosera to snake venoms and tetanus (horses, sheep and goats), allergens (cats), rabies vaccine (rabbits, mice and hamsters), transgenic products (goats, cattle);

(b) Animal materials derived post mortem and from establishments such as abattoirs: examples include abattoir sources for enzymes, anticoagulants and hormones (sheep and pigs).

In addition, animals may also be used in quality control either in generic assays, e.g. pyrogenicity, or specific potency assays, e.g. pertussis vaccine (mice), pyrogenicity (rabbits), BCG vaccine (guinea-pigs).

20   In addition to compliance with TSE regulations, other adventitious agents that are of concern (zoonotic diseases, diseases of source animals) should be monitored by an on-going health programme and recorded. Specialist advice should be obtained in establishing such programmes. Instances of ill-health occurring in the source/donor animals should be investigated with respect to their suitability and the suitability of in-contact animals for continued use (in manufacture, as sources of starting and raw materials, in quality control and safety testing); the decisions must be documented. A look-back procedure should be in place, which informs the decision-making process on the continued suitability of the biological active substance or medicinal product in which the animal-sourced starting or raw materials have been used or incorporated. This decision-making process may include the re-testing of retained samples from previous collections from the same donor animal (where applicable) to establish the last negative donation. The withdrawal period of therapeutic agents used to treat source/donor animals must be documented and used to determine the removal of those animals from the programme for defined periods.

21   Particular care should be taken to prevent and monitor infections in the source/donor animals. Measures should include the sourcing, facilities,

husbandry, biosecurity procedures, testing regimes, control of bedding and feed materials. This is of special relevance to specified pathogen-free animals where Ph.Eur. monograph requirements must be met. Housing and health monitoring should be defined for other categories of animals (e.g. healthy flocks or herds).

22   For products manufactured from transgenic animals, traceability should be maintained in the creation of such animals from the source animals.

23   Note should be taken of Directive 2010/63/EU on the protection of animals used for scientific purposes[16]. Housing for animals used in production and control of biological active substances and medicinal products should be separated from production and control areas.

24   For different animal species, key criteria should be defined, monitored and recorded. These may include age, weight and health status of the animals.

25   Animals, biological agents and tests carried out should be the subject of an identification system to prevent any risk of confusion and to control all identified hazards.

Documentation

26   Starting and raw materials may need additional documentation on the source, origin, distribution chain, method of manufacture and controls applied, to assure an appropriate level of control including their microbiological quality.

27   Some product types may require specific definition of what materials constitute a batch, particularly cells. For autologous and donor-matched situations, the manufactured product should be viewed as a batch.

28   Where human cell or tissue donors are used, full traceability is required from starting and raw materials, including all substances coming into contact with the cells or tissues through to confirmation of the receipt of the products at the point of use while maintaining the privacy of individuals and confidentiality of health-related information. Traceability records must be retained for 30 years after the expiry date of the medicinal product. Particular care should be taken to maintain the traceability of medicinal products for special use cases, such as donor-matched cells. Directives 2002/98/EC and Commission Directive 2005/61/EC of

---

[16] Directive 2010/63/EU of the European Parliament and the Council of 22 September 2010 on the protection of animals used for scientific purposes, OJ L 276, 10.10.2010, p. 33.

30 September 2005, implementing Directive 2002/98/EC of the European Parliament and the Council as regards, traceability requirements and notification of serious adverse reactions and events[17], apply to blood components when they are used as starting or raw materials in the manufacturing process of medicinal products.

Production

29 Given the variability inherent in many biological active substances and medicinal products, steps to increase process robustness, thereby reducing process variability and enhancing reproducibility at the different stages of the product lifecycle such as process design, should be reassessed during Product Quality Reviews.

30 As cultivation conditions, media and reagents are designed to promote the growth of cells or microbial organisms, typically in an axenic state, particular attention should be paid in the control strategy to ensure that there are robust steps that prevent or minimise the occurrence of unwanted bioburden and associated metabolites and endotoxins. For medicinal products from cells and tissues where production batches are frequently small, the risk of cross-contamination between cell preparations from different donors with various health statuses should be controlled under defined procedures and requirements.

Starting and raw materials

31 The source, origin and suitability of biological starting and raw materials (e.g. cryoprotectants, feeder cells, reagents, culture media, buffers, sera, enzymes, cytokines, growth factors) should be clearly defined. Where the necessary tests take a long time, it may be permissible to process starting materials before the results of the tests are available, the risk of using a potentially failed material and its potential impact on other batches should be clearly understood and assessed under the principles of QRM. In such cases, release of a finished product is conditional on satisfactory results of these tests. The identification of all starting materials should be in compliance with the requirements appropriate to its stage of manufacture. For biological medicinal products, further guidance can be found in Part I and Annex 8 and for biological active substances in Part II.

---

[17] OJ L 256, 1.10.2005, p. 32.

EU GMP GUIDE PART I ANNEX 2 MANUFACTURE OF BIOLOGICAL ACTIVE SUBSTANCES AND MEDICINAL PRODUCTS FOR HUMAN USE

32   The risk of contamination of starting and raw materials during their passage along the supply chain must be assessed, with particular emphasis on TSE. Materials that come into direct contact with manufacturing equipment or the product (such as media used in media-fill experiments and lubricants that may contact the product) must also be taken into account.

33   Given that the risks from the introduction of contamination and the consequences to the finished product is the same irrespective of the stage of manufacture, establishment of a control strategy to protect the product and the preparation of solutions, buffers and other additions should be based on the principles and guidance contained in the appropriate sections of Annex 1. The controls required for the quality of starting and raw materials and on the aseptic manufacturing process assume greater importance, particularly for products in respect of which final sterilisation is not possible. Where an MA or CTA provides for an allowable type and level of bioburden, e.g. at active substance stage, the control strategy should address the means by which this is maintained within the specified limits.

34   Where sterilization of starting and raw materials is required, it should be carried out where possible by heat. Where necessary, other appropriate methods may also be used for inactivation of biological materials (e.g. irradiation and filtration).

35   Reduction in bioburden associated with procurement of living tissues and cells may require the use of other measures such as antibiotics at early manufacturing stages. This should be avoided, but where it is necessary their use should be justified; they should be removed from the manufacturing process at the stage specified in the MA or CTA.

36   The donation, procurement and testing of human tissues and cells used as starting or raw materials should be in accordance with Directive 2004/23/EC[18]. Traceability for human tissues and cells used as starting materials for biological medicinal products should be maintained from the donor to the batch of a finished medicinal product. Appropriate arrangements should be made between the manufacturer and the supplier of tissues and cells regarding the transfer of health donor information that may become available after the supply of the starting material and may have an impact on the quality or safety of the medicinal product manufactured therefrom.

     (a) Their procurement, donation and testing in the EU is regulated under Directive 2004/23/EC and its implementing Commission directives.

---

[18] For blood-derived cells, compliance with Directive 2002/98 regarding donation, procurement and testing is likewise acceptable.

Such EU supply sites must hold appropriate approvals from the national competent authority(ies) under this Directive, which should be verified as part of starting material supplier management.

(b) Where such human cells or tissues are imported from third countries they must meet equivalent Community standards of quality and safety equivalent to those laid down in Directive 2004/23/EC. The traceability and serious adverse reaction and serious adverse event notification requirements are set out in Directive 2006/86/EC.

(c) There may be some instances where processing of cells and tissues used as starting materials for biological medicinal products will be conducted at tissue establishments. Such processing steps, e.g. freezing, are under the scope of Directive 2004/23/EC, which provides for the need of a Responsible Person (RP).

(d) Tissue and cells are released by the RP in the tissue establishment before shipment to the medicinal product manufacturer, after which normal medicinal product starting material controls apply. The test results of all tissues/cells supplied by the tissue establishment should be available to the manufacturer of the medicinal product. Such information must be used to make appropriate material segregation and storage decisions. In cases where manufacturing must be initiated prior to receiving test results from the tissue establishment, tissue and cells may be shipped to the medicinal product manufacturer, provided that controls are in place to prevent cross-contamination with tissue and cells that have been released by the RP in the tissue establishment.

(e) The transport of human tissues and cells to the manufacturing site must be controlled by a written agreement between the responsible parties. The manufacturing sites should have documentary evidence of adherence to the specified storage and transport conditions.

(f) Continuation of traceability requirements started at tissue establishments, through to the recipient(s), and vice versa, including materials in contact with the cells or tissues, should be maintained.

(g) A technical agreement should be in place between the responsible parties (e.g. manufacturers, tissue establishment, sponsors, MA holder) which defines the tasks of each party, including the RP and Qualified Person.

38 Where human or animal cells are used in the manufacturing process as feeder cells, appropriate controls over the sourcing, testing, transport and storage should be in place, including control of compliance with donation, procurement and testing standards equivalent to ones set in the Directive 2004/23.

EU GMP GUIDE PART I ANNEX 2 MANUFACTURE OF BIOLOGICAL ACTIVE SUBSTANCES AND MEDICINAL PRODUCTS FOR HUMAN USE

Seed lot and cell bank system

39   In order to prevent the unwanted drift of properties that might ensue from repeated subcultures or multiple generations, the production of biological medicinal substances and products obtained by microbial culture, cell culture or propagation in embryos and animals should be based on a system of master and working virus seed lots and/or cell banks.

40   The number of generations (doublings, passages) between the seed lot or cell bank, the active biological substance and the finished product should be consistent with specifications in the MA or CTA.

41   As part of product lifecycle management, establishment of seed lots and cell banks, including master and working generations, should be performed under circumstances that are demonstrably appropriate. This should include an appropriately controlled environment to protect the seed lot and cell bank, and the personnel handling it. During the establishment of the seed lot and cell bank, no other living or infectious material (e.g. virus, cell lines or cell strains) should be handled simultaneously in the same area or by the same persons. For stages prior to the master seed or cell bank generation, where only the principles of GMP may be applied, documentation should be available to support traceability, including issues related to components used during development with potential impact on product safety (e.g. reagents of biological origin) from initial sourcing and genetic development if applicable. For vaccines the requirements of Ph.Eur. monograph 2005:153 "Vaccines for human use" will apply.

42   Following the establishment of master and working cell banks, and master and working seed lots, quarantine and release procedures should be followed. This should include adequate characterization and testing for contaminants. Their on-going suitability for use should be further demonstrated by the consistency of the characteristics and quality of the successive batches of product. Evidence of the stability and recovery of the seeds and banks should be documented and records should be kept in a manner permitting trend evaluation.

43   Seed lots and cell banks should be stored and used in such a way as to minimize the risks of contamination (e.g. stored in the vapour phase of liquid nitrogen in sealed containers) or alteration. Control measures for the storage of different seeds and/or cells in the same area or equipment should prevent mix-up and take into account the infectious nature of the materials to prevent cross-contamination.

45   Storage containers should be sealed, clearly labelled and kept at an appropriate temperature. A stock inventory must be kept. The storage

temperature should be recorded continuously and, where used, the liquid nitrogen level monitored. Deviation from set limits and corrective and preventive action taken should be recorded.

46   It is desirable to split stocks and to store the split stocks at different locations so as to minimize the risks of total loss. The controls at such locations should provide the assurances outlined in the preceding paragraphs.

47   The storage and handling conditions for stocks should be managed according to the same procedures and parameters. Once containers are removed from the seed lot/cell bank management system, the containers should not be returned to stock.

Operating principles

48   Change management should, on a periodic basis, take into account the effects, including cumulative effects of changes (e.g. to the process), on the quality, safety and efficacy of the finished product.

49   Critical operational (process) parameters, or other input parameters that affect product quality, need to be identified, validated, documented and shown to be maintained within requirements.

50   A control strategy for the entry of articles and materials into production areas should be based on QRM principles. For aseptic processes, heat-stable articles and materials entering a clean area or clean/contained area should preferably do so through a double-ended autoclave or oven. Heat-labile articles and materials should enter through an airlock with interlocked doors where they are subject to effective surface sanitisation procedures. Sterilisation of articles and materials elsewhere is acceptable provided that there are multiple wrappings, as appropriate to the number of stages of entry to the clean area, and that they enter through an airlock with the appropriate surface sanitisation precautions.

51   The growth promoting properties of culture media should be demonstrated to be suitable for its intended use. If possible, media should be sterilized in situ. In-line sterilizing filters for routine addition of gases, media, acids or alkalis, anti-foaming agents, etc. to fermenters should be used where possible.

52   Addition of materials or cultures to fermenters and other vessels and sampling should be carried out under carefully controlled conditions to prevent contamination. Care should be taken to ensure that vessels are correctly connected when addition or sampling takes place.

53   Continuous monitoring of some production processes (e.g. fermentation) may be necessary; such data should form part of the batch record. Where continuous culture is used, special consideration should be given to the quality control requirements arising from this type of production method.

54   Centrifugation and blending of products can lead to aerosol formation and containment of such activities to minimise cross-contamination if necessary.

55   Accidental spillages, especially of live organisms, must be dealt with quickly and safely. Qualified decontamination measures should be available for each organism or groups of related organisms. Where different strains of single bacterial species or very similar viruses are involved, the decontamination process may be validated with one representative strain, unless there is reason to believe that they may vary significantly in their resistance to the agent(s) involved.

56   If obviously contaminated, such as by spills or aerosols, or if a potential hazardous organism is involved, production and control materials, including paperwork, must be adequately disinfected, or the information transferred out by other means.

57   In cases where a virus inactivation or removal process is performed during manufacture, measures should be taken to avoid the risk of recontamination of treated products by non-treated products.

58   For products that are inactivated by the addition of a reagent (e.g. microorganisms in the course of vaccine manufacture), the process should ensure the complete inactivation of live organism. In addition to the thorough mixing of culture and inactivant, consideration should be given to contact of all product-contact surfaces exposed to live culture and, where required, the transfer to a second vessel.

59   A wide variety of equipment is used for chromatography. QRM principles should be used to devise the control strategy on matrices, housings and associated equipment when used in campaign manufacture and in multi-product environments. The re-use of the same matrix at different stages of processing is discouraged. Acceptance criteria, operating conditions, regeneration methods, lifespan and sanitization or sterilization methods of columns should be defined.

60   Where irradiated equipment and materials are used, Annex 12 to EudraLex, Volume 4, should be consulted for further guidance.

61   There should be a system to assure the integrity and closure of containers after filling where the final products or intermediates represent a special risk and procedures to deal with any leaks or spillages. Filling and

packaging operations need to have procedures in place to maintain the product within any specified limits, e.g. time and/or temperature.

62 Activities in handling vials containing live biological agents must be performed in such a way as to prevent the contamination of other products or egress of the live agents into the work or external environment. The viability of such organisms and their biological classification should be taken into consideration as part of the management of such risks.

63 Care should be taken in the preparation, printing, storage and application of labels, including any specific text for patient-specific product of the contents on the immediate and outer packaging.

In the case of autologous products, the unique patient identifier and the statement "for autologous use only" should be indicated on the outer packaging or, where there is no outer packaging, on the immediate packaging.

64 The compatibility of labels with ultra-low storage temperatures, where such temperatures are used, should be verified.

65 Where donor (human or animal) health information becomes available after procurement, which affects product quality, it should be taken into account in recall procedures.

Quality control

66 In-process controls have a greater importance in ensuring the consistency of the quality of biological active substance and medicinal products than for conventional products. In-process control testing should be performed at appropriate stages of production to control those conditions that are important for the quality of the finished product.

67 Where intermediates can be stored for extended periods of time (days, weeks or longer), consideration should be given to the inclusion of finished product batches made from materials held for their maximum in-process periods in the on-going stability programme.

68 Certain types of cells (e.g. autologous cells) may be available in limited quantities and, where allowed in the MA, a modified testing and sample retention strategy may be developed and documented.

69 For cellular products, sterility tests should be conducted on antibiotic-free cultures of cells or cell banks to provide evidence for absence of bacterial and fungal contamination, and to be able to detect fastidious organisms where appropriate.

70   For biological medicinal products with a short shelf-life, which for the purposes of the annex is taken to mean a period of 14 days or less, and which need batch certification before completion of all end-product quality control tests (e.g. sterility tests), a suitable control strategy must be in place. Such controls need to be built on enhanced understanding of product and process performance and take into account the controls and attributes of starting and raw materials. The exact and detailed description of the entire release procedure, including the responsibilities of the different personnel involved in assessment of production and analytical data, is essential. A continuous assessment of the effectiveness of the quality assurance system must be in place including records kept in a manner that permits trend evaluation.

Where end-product tests are not available due to their short shelf-life, alternative methods of obtaining equivalent data to permit initial batch certification should be considered (e.g. rapid microbiological methods). The procedure for batch certification and release may be carried out in two or more stages-:

(a) Assessment by designated person(s) of batch-processing records, results from environmental monitoring (where available), which should cover production conditions, all deviations from normal procedures and the available analytical results for review in preparation for the initial certification by the Qualified Person;

(b) Assessment of the final analytical tests and other information available for final certification by the Qualified Person. A procedure should be in place to describe the measures to be taken (including liaison with clinical staff) where out-of-specification test results are obtained. Such events should be fully investigated and the relevant corrective and preventive actions taken to prevent recurrence documented.

PART B. SPECIFIC GUIDANCE ON SELECTED PRODUCT TYPES

B1. ANIMAL-SOURCED PRODUCTS[19]

This guidance applies to animal materials that include materials from establishments such as abattoirs. As the supply chains can be extensive and complex, controls based on QRM principles need to be applied (see also requirements of Ph.Eur. monographs, including the need for specific tests at defined stages). Documentation to demonstrate the supply chain

---

[19] See also Ph.Eur. monograph requirements, 0333.

traceability[20] and clear roles of participants in the supply chain, typically including a sufficiently detailed and current process map, should be in place.

1 Monitoring programmes should be in place for animal diseases that are of concern to human health. Organisations should take into account reports from trustworthy sources on national disease prevalence when compiling their assessment of risk and mitigation factors. Such organisations include the World Organisation for Animal Health (OIE, Office International des Epizooties[21]). This should be supplemented by information on health-monitoring and control programme(s) at national and local levels, the latter to include the sources (e.g. farm or feedlot) from which the animals are drawn and the control measures in place during transport to the abattoirs.

2 Where abattoirs are used to source animal tissues, they should be shown to operate to standards equivalent to those used in the EU. Account should be taken of reports from organisations such as the Food and Veterinary Office[22] who verify compliance with the requirements of food safety and quality, and veterinary and plant health legislation within the EU and third countries exporting to the EU.

3 Control measures for starting or raw materials at establishments such as abattoirs should include appropriate elements of a Quality Management System to assure a satisfactory level of operator training, materials traceability, control and consistency. These measures may be drawn from sources outside EU GMP but should be shown to provide equivalent levels of control.

4 Control measures for starting or raw materials should be in place to prevent interventions that may affect the quality of materials, or that at least provide evidence of such activities, during their progression through the manufacturing and supply chain. This includes the movement of material between sites of initial collection, partial and final purification(s), storage sites, hubs, consolidators and brokers. Details of such arrangements should be recorded within the traceability system and any breaches recorded and investigated, and actions taken.

5 Regular audits of the starting or raw material supplier should be undertaken that verify compliance with controls for materials at the different stages of manufacture.

Issues must be investigated to a depth appropriate to their significance, for which full documentation should be available. Systems should also

---

[20] See Chapter 5 in EudraLex, Volume 4.

[21] http://www.oie.int/eng/en_index.htm.

[22] http://ec.europa.eu/food/fvo/index_en.htm.

be in place to ensure that effective corrective and preventive actions are taken.

B2. ALLERGEN PRODUCTS

Materials may be manufactured by extraction from natural sources or manufactured by recombinant DNA technology.

1   Source materials should be described in sufficient detail to ensure consistency in their supply, e.g. common and scientific name, origin, nature, contaminant limits, method of collection. Those derived from animals should be from healthy sources. Appropriate biosecurity controls should be in place for colonies (e.g. mites, animals) used for the extraction of allergens. Allergen products should be stored under defined conditions to minimise deterioration.

2   The production process steps, including pre-treatment, extraction, filtration, dialysis, concentration or freeze-drying steps, should be described in detail and validated.

3   The modification processes to manufacture modified allergen extracts (e.g. allergoids, conjugates) should be described. Intermediates in the manufacturing process should be identified and controlled.

4   Allergen extract mixtures should be prepared from individual extracts from single-source materials. Each individual extract should be considered as one active substance.

B3. ANIMAL IMMUNOSERA PRODUCTS

1   Particular care should be exercised over the control of antigens of biological origin to assure their quality, consistency and freedom from adventitious agents. The preparation of materials used to immunise the source animals (e.g. antigens, hapten carriers, adjuvants, stabilising agents), and the storage of such material immediately prior to immunisation should be in accordance with documented procedures.

2   The immunisation, test bleed and harvest bleed schedules should conform to those approved in the CTA or MA.

3   The manufacturing conditions for the preparation of antibody sub-fragments (e.g. Fab or F(ab')2) and any further modifications must be in

accordance with validated and approved parameters. Where such enzymes are made up of several components, their consistency should be assured.

B4. VACCINES

1. Where eggs are used, the health status of all source flocks used in the production of eggs (whether specified pathogen-free or healthy flocks) should be assured.

2. The integrity of containers used to store intermediate products and the hold times must be validated.

3. Vessels containing inactivated products should not be opened or sampled in areas containing live biological agents.

4. The sequence of addition of active ingredients, adjuvants and excipients during the formulation of an intermediate or final product must be in compliance with specifications.

5. Where organisms with a higher biological safety level (e.g. pandemic vaccine strains) are to be used in manufacture or testing, appropriate containment arrangements must be in place. The approval of such arrangements should be obtained from the appropriate national authority(ies) and the approval documents be available for verification.

B5. RECOMBINANT PRODUCTS

1. Process condition during cell growth, protein expression and purification must be maintained within validated parameters to assure a consistent product with a defined range of impurities that is within the capability of the process to reduce to acceptable levels. The type of cell used in production may require increased measures to be taken to assure freedom from viruses. For production involving multiple harvests, the period of continuous cultivation should be within specified limits.

2. The purification processes to remove unwanted host cell proteins, nucleic acids, carbohydrates, viruses and other impurities should be within defined validated limits.

B6. MONOCLONAL ANTIBODY PRODUCTS

1. Monoclonal antibodies may be manufactured from murine hybridomas or human hybridomas or by recombinant DNA technology. Control meas-

ures appropriate to the different source cells (including feeder cells if used) and materials used to establish the hybridoma/cell line should be in place to assure the safety and quality of the product. It should be verified that these are within approved limits. Freedom from viruses should be given particular emphasis. It should be noted that data originating from products generated by the same manufacturing technology platform may be acceptable to demonstrate suitability.

2   Criteria to be monitored at the end of a production cycle and for early termination of production cycles should verify that these are within approved limits.

3   The manufacturing conditions for the preparation of antibody sub-fragment (e.g. Fab, F(ab')2, scFv) and any further modifications (e.g. radiolabelling, conjugation, chemical linking) must be in accordance with validated parameters.

B7. TRANSGENIC ANIMAL PRODUCTS

Consistency of starting material from a transgenic source is likely to be more problematic than is normally the case for non-transgenic biotechnology sources. Consequently, there is an increased requirement to demonstrate batch-to-batch consistency of product in all respects.

1   A range of species may be used to produce biological medicinal products, which may be expressed into body fluids (e.g. milk) for collection and purification. Animals should be clearly and uniquely identified and backup arrangements should be put in place in the event of loss of the primary marker.

2   The arrangements for housing and care of the animals should be defined such that they minimise the exposure of the animals to pathogenic and zoonotic agents. Appropriate measures to protect the external environment should be established. A health-monitoring programme should be established and all results documented; any incident should be investigated and its impact on the continuation of the animal and on previous batches of product should be determined. Care should be taken to ensure that any therapeutic products used to treat the animals do not contaminate the product.

3   The genealogy of the founder animals through to production animals must be documented. As a transgenic line will be derived from a single genetic founder animal, materials from different transgenic lines should not be mixed.

4 The conditions under which the product is harvested should be in accordance with MA or CTA conditions. The harvest schedule and conditions under which animals may be removed from production should be performed according to approved procedures and acceptance limits.

B8. TRANSGENIC PLANT PRODUCTS

Consistency of starting material from a transgenic source is likely to be more problematic than is normally the case for non-transgenic biotechnology sources. Consequently, there is an increased requirement to demonstrate batch-to-batch consistency of product in all respects.

1 Additional measures, over and above those given in Part A, may be required to prevent contamination of master and working transgenic banks by extraneous plant materials and relevant adventitious agents. The stability of the gene within defined generation numbers should be monitored.

2 Plants should be clearly and uniquely identified; the presence of key plant features, including health status, across the crop should be verified at defined intervals through the cultivation period to assure consistency of yield between crops.

3 Security arrangements for the protection of crops should be defined, wherever possible, such that they minimise the exposure to contamination by microbiological agents and cross-contamination with non-related plants. Measures should be in place to prevent materials such as pesticides and fertilisers from contaminating the product. A monitoring programme should be established and all results documented; any incident should be investigated and its impact on the continuation of the crop in the production programme should be determined.

4 Conditions under which plants may be removed from production should be defined. Acceptance limits should be set for materials (e.g. host proteins) that may interfere with the purification process. It should be verified that the results are within approved limits.

5 Environmental conditions (temperature, rain), which may affect the quality attributes and yield of the recombinant protein from time of planting, through cultivation to harvest and interim storage of harvested materials should be documented. The principles in documents such as "Guideline on Good Agricultural and Collection Practice for Starting Materials of Herbal origin"[23] of the Committee of Herbal Medicinal Products should be taken into account when drawing up such criteria.

---

[23] Doc. Ref. EMEA/HMPC/246816/2005.

EU GMP GUIDE PART I ANNEX 2 MANUFACTURE OF BIOLOGICAL ACTIVE SUBSTANCES AND MEDICINAL PRODUCTS FOR HUMAN USE

GLOSSARY TO ANNEX 2

Entries are included only where the terms are used in Annex 2 and require further explanation. Definitions that already exist in legislation or other sources are cross-referenced. In addition to this glossary, the GMP glossary in EudraLex, Volume 4[24] applies, unless indicated otherwise.

ACTIVE SUBSTANCE

See Article 1(3a) of Directive 2001/83/EC.

ADJUVANT

A chemical or biological substance that enhances the immune response against an antigen.

ALLERGOIDS

Allergens that are chemically modified to reduce IgE reactivity.

ANTIGENS

Substances (e.g. toxins, foreign proteins, bacteria, tissue cells) capable of inducing specific immune responses.

ANTIBODY

Proteins produced by the B-lymphocytes that bind to specific antigens. Antibodies may divided into two main types based on key differences in their method of manufacture:

Monoclonal antibodies (MAb):—homogeneous antibody population obtained from a single clone of lymphocytes or by recombinant technology and which bind to a single epitope.

Polyclonal antibodies:—derived from a range of lymphocyte clones, produced in human and animals in response to the epitopes on most "non-self" molecules.

AREA

A specific set of rooms within a building associated with the manufacturing of any one product or multiple products that has a common air-handling unit.

BIOBURDEN

The level and type (i.e. objectionable or not) of micro-organism present in raw materials, media, biological substances, intermediates or products.

---

[24] http://ec.europa.eu/health/files/eudralex/vol-4/pdfs-en/glos4en200408_en.pdf

Regarded as contamination when the level and/or type exceed specifications.

BIOLOGICAL MEDICINAL PRODUCT

See third paragraph of point 3.2.1.1.b. of Part I of Annex I to Directive 2001/83/EC.

BIOSAFETY LEVEL (BSL)

The containment conditions required to safely handle organisms of different hazards, ranging from BSL1 (lowest risk, unlikely to cause human disease) to BSL4 (highest risk, cause severe disease, likely to spread and no effective prophylaxis or treatment available).

CAMPAIGNED MANUFACTURE

The manufacture of a series of batches of the same product in sequence in a given period of time, followed by strict adherence to accepted control measures before transfer to another product. The products are not run at the same time but may be run on the same equipment.

CELL BANK

A collection of appropriate containers, the contents of which are of uniform composition, stored under defined conditions. Each container represents an aliquot of a single pool of cells.

CELL STOCK

Primary cells expanded to a given number of cells to be aliquoted and used as starting material for production of a limited number of lots of a cell-based medicinal product.

CLOSED SYSTEM

Where a drug substance or product is not exposed to the immediate room environment during manufacture.

CONTAINED USE

See Article 2(c) of Directive 2009/41/EC for all genetically modified organisms.

DELIBERATE RELEASE

See Article 2(3) of Directive 2001/18/EC of the European Parliament and the Council of 12 March 2001 on the deliberate release into the environment of genetically modified organisms and repealing Council Directive 90/220/EEC.

EXCIPIENT

See Article 1(3b) of Directive 2001/83/EC.

EX VIVO

Where procedures are conducted on tissues or cells outside the living body and returned to the living body.

FEEDER CELLS

Cells used in co-culture to maintain pluripotent stem cells. For human embryonic stem cell culture, typical feeder layers include mouse embryonic fibroblasts (MEFs) or human embryonic fibroblasts that have been treated to prevent them from dividing.

GENE

A sequence of DNA that codes for one (or more) protein(s).

GENETICALLY MODIFIED ORGANISM (GMO)

See Article 2(2) of Directive 2001/18/EC.

HAPTEN

A low-molecular-mass molecule that is not in itself antigenic unless conjugated to a "carrier" molecule.

HYBRIDOMA

An immortalised cell line that secretes desired (monoclonal) antibodies and is typically derived by fusing B-lymphocytes with tumour cells.

INTERMEDIATE PRODUCT

See definitions in GMP Glossary and Part II.

IN VIVO

Procedures conducted in living organisms.

LOOK-BACK

Documented procedure to trace biological medicinal substances or products that may be adversely affected by the use or incorporation of animal or human materials when either such materials fail release tests due to the presence of contaminating agent(s), or when conditions of concern become apparent in the source animal or human.

MASTER CELL BANK (MCB)

An aliquot of a single pool of cells which has generally been prepared from the selected cell clone under defined conditions, dispensed into multiple containers and stored under defined conditions. The MCB is used to derive all working cell banks.

MASTER VIRUS SEED (MVS)

As above, but in relation to viruses.

MASTER TRANSGENIC BANK

As above but for transgenic plants or animals.

MONOSEPSIS (AXENIC)

A single organism in culture that is not contaminated with any other organism.

MULTI-PRODUCT FACILITY

A facility that manufactures, either concurrently or in campaign mode, a range of different biological medicinal substances and products, and within which equipment train(s) may or may not be dedicated to specific substances or products.

PLASMID

A plasmid is a piece of DNA usually present in a bacterial cell as a circular entity separated from the cell chromosome; it can be modified by molecular biology techniques, purified out of the bacterial cell and used to transfer its DNA to another cell.

RAW MATERIALS

See 4th paragraph of point 3.2.1.1.b. of Part I of Annex I to Directive 2001/83/EC.

RESPONSIBLE PERSON (RP)

The person designated in accordance with Article 17 of Directive 2004/23/EC.

SCAFFOLD

A support, delivery vehicle or matrix that may provide structure for or facilitate the migration, binding or transport of cells and/or bioactive molecules.

SOMATIC CELLS

Cells, other than reproductive (germline) cells, which make up the body of a human or animal. These cells may be autologous (from the patient), allogeneic (from another human being) or xenogeneic (from animals) somatic living cells that have been manipulated or altered ex vivo, to be administered in humans to obtain a therapeutic, diagnostic or preventive effect.

SPECIFIED PATHOGEN FREE (SPF)

Animal materials (e.g. chickens, embryos or cell cultures) used for the production or quality control of biological medicinal products derived from groups (e.g. flocks or herds) of animals free from specified pathogens. Such flocks or herds are defined as animals sharing a common environment and having their own caretakers who have no contact with non-SPF groups.

STARTING MATERIALS

See the first and second paragraphs of point 3.2.1.1.b of Part I of Annex I to Directive 2001/83/EC.

TRANSGENIC

An organism that contains a foreign gene in its normal genetic component for the expression of biological pharmaceutical materials.

WORKING CELL BANK (WCB)

A homogeneous pool of microorganisms or cells that are distributed uniformly into a number of containers derived from an MCB, and which are stored in such a way as to ensure stability and for use in production.

WORKING VIRUS SEED (WVS)

As above but in relation to viruses.

WORKING TRANSGENIC BANK

As above but for transgenic plants or animals.

ZOONOSIS

Animal diseases that can be transmitted to humans.

ANNEX 3 MANUFACTURE OF RADIOPHARMACEUTICALS

EU GMP GUIDE PART I ANNEX 3 MANUFACTURE OF RADIOPHARMACEUTICALS

> **Editor's note** All radiopharmacies subject to a Manufacturer's "Specials" Licence will be expected to comply with these requirements.

Principle

The manufacture of radiopharmaceuticals shall be undertaken in accordance with the principles of Good Manufacturing Practice for Medicinal Products, Parts I and II. This annex specifically addresses some of the practices, which may be specific for radiopharmaceuticals.

> **Note i.** Preparation of radiopharmaceuticals in radiopharmacies (hospitals or certain pharmacies), using Generators and Kits with a Marketing Authorisation or a national licence, is not covered by this guideline, unless covered by national requirement.
>
> **Note ii.** According to radiation protection regulations it should be ensured that any medical exposure is under the clinical responsibility of a practitioner. In diagnostic and therapeutic nuclear medicine practices, a medical physics expert shall be available.
>
> **Note iii.** This annex is also applicable to radiopharmaceuticals used in clinical trials.
>
> **Note iv.** Transport of radiopharmaceuticals is regulated by the International Atomic Energy Association (IAEA) and radiation protection requirements.
>
> **Note v.** It is recognised that there are acceptable methods, other than those described in this annex, that are capable of achieving the principles of Quality Assurance. Other methods should be validated and provide a level of Quality Assurance at least equivalent to those set out in this annex.

Introduction

1 The manufacturing and handling of radiopharmaceuticals is potentially hazardous. The level of risk depends in particular upon the types of radiation, the energy of radiation and the half-lives of the radioactive isotopes. Particular attention must be paid to the prevention of cross-contamination, the retention of radionuclide contaminants and waste disposal.

2 Due to short shelf-life of their radionuclides, some radiopharmaceuticals may be released before completion of all quality control tests. In this case, the exact and detailed description of the whole release procedure, including the responsibilities of the involved personnel and the continuous assessment of the effectiveness of the quality assurance system, is essential.

3 This guideline is applicable to manufacturing procedures employed by industrial manufacturers, Nuclear Centres/Institutes and PET Centres for the production and quality control of the following types of products:

- Radiopharmaceuticals,
- Positron-emitting (PET) radiopharmaceuticals,
- Radioactive precursors for radiopharmaceutical production,
- Radionuclide generators.

Type of manufacture	Non-GMP*	GMP Part II & I (Increasing), including relevant annexes			
Radiopharmaceuticals, PET radiopharmaceuticals, radioactive precursors	Reactor/ cyclotron production	Chemical synthesis	Purifica-tion steps	Processing, formulation and dispensing	Aseptic or final sterilization
Radionuclide generators	Reactor/ cyclotron production	Processing			

* Target and transfer system from cyclotron to synthesis rig may be considered as the first step of active substance manufacture.

4 The manufacturer of the final radiopharmaceutical should describe and justify the steps for manufacture of the active substance and the final medicinal product and which GMP (Part I or II) applies for the specific process/manufacturing steps.

5 Preparation of radiopharmaceuticals involves adherence to regulations on radiation protection.

6 Radiopharmaceuticals to be administered parenterally should comply with sterility requirements for parenterals and, where relevant, aseptic working conditions for the manufacture of sterile medicinal products, which are covered in Eudralex, Volume 4, Annex 1.

7 Specifications and quality control testing procedures for the most commonly used radiopharmaceuticals are specified in the European Pharmacopoeia or in the Marketing Authorisation.

Clinical trials

8   Radiopharmaceuticals intended for use in clinical trials as investigational medicinal products should, in addition, be produced in accordance with the principles in Eudralex, Volume 4, Annex 13.

Quality Assurance

9   Quality Assurance is of even greater importance in the manufacture of radiopharmaceuticals because of their particular characteristics, low volumes and, in some circumstances, the need to administer the product before testing is complete.

10   As with all pharmaceuticals, the products must be well protected against contamination and cross-contamination. However, the environment and the operators must also be protected against radiation. This means that the role of an effective quality assurance system is of the utmost importance.

11   It is important that the data generated by the monitoring of premises and processes is rigorously recorded and evaluated as part of the release process.

12   The principles of qualification and validation should be applied to the manufacturing of radiopharmaceuticals and a risk management approach should be used to determine the extent of qualification/validation, focusing on a combination of Good Manufacturing Practice and Radiation Protection.

Personnel

13   All manufacturing operations should be carried out under the responsibility of personnel with additional competence in radiation protection. Personnel involved in production, analytical control and release of radiopharmaceuticals should be appropriately trained in radiopharmaceutical specific aspects of the quality management system. The Qualified Person (QP) should have the overall responsibility for release of the products.

14   All personnel (including those concerned with cleaning and maintenance) employed in areas where radioactive products are manufactured should receive appropriate additional training specific to these types of procedures and products.

15   Where production facilities are shared with research institutions, the research personnel must be adequately trained in GMP regulations and the

Quality Assurance (QA) function must review and approve the research activities to ensure that they do not pose any hazard to the manufacturing of radiopharmaceuticals.

Premises and Equipment

General

16   Radioactive products should be manufactured in controlled (environmental and radioactive) areas. All manufacturing steps should take place in self-contained facilities dedicated to radiopharmaceuticals.

17   Measures should be established and implemented to prevent cross-contamination from personnel, materials, radionuclides, etc. Closed or contained equipment should be used whenever appropriate. Where open equipment is used, or equipment is opened, precautions should be taken to minimize the risk of contamination. The risk assessment should demonstrate that the environmental cleanliness level proposed is suitable for the type of product being manufactured.

18   Access to the manufacturing areas should be via a gowning area and should be restricted to authorised personnel.

19   Workstations and their environment should be monitored with respect to radioactivity, particulate and microbiological quality as established during performance qualification (PQ).

20   Preventive maintenance, calibration and qualification programmes should be operated to ensure that all facilities and equipment used in the manufacture of radiopharmaceutical are suitable and qualified. These activities should be carried out by competent personnel and records, and logs should be maintained.

21   Precautions should be taken to avoid radioactive contamination within the facility. Appropriate controls should be in place to detect any radioactive contamination, either directly through the use of radiation detectors or indirectly through a swabbing routine.

22   Equipment should be constructed so that surfaces that come into contact with the product are not reactive, additive or absorptive so as to alter the quality of the radiopharmaceutical.

23   Re-circulation of air extracted from the area where radioactive products are handled should be avoided unless justified. Air outlets should be designed to minimize environmental contamination by radioactive particles and gases, and appropriate measures should be taken to protect the controlled areas from particulate and microbial contamination.

24 In order to contain radioactive particles, it may be necessary for the air pressure to be lower where products are exposed, compared with the surrounding areas. However, it is still necessary to protect the product from environmental contamination. This may be achieved by, for example, using barrier technology or airlocks, acting as pressure sinks.

Sterile production

25 Sterile radiopharmaceuticals may be divided into those that are manufactured aseptically and those that are terminally sterilised. The facility should maintain the appropriate level of environmental cleanliness for the type of operation being performed. For manufacture of sterile products the working zone where products or containers may be exposed to the environment, the cleanliness requirements should comply with the requirements described in Eudralex, Volume 4, Annex 1.

26 For manufacture of radiopharmaceuticals a risk assessment may be applied to determine the appropriate pressure differences, airflow direction and air quality.

27 In case of use of closed and automated systems (chemical synthesis, purification, on-line sterile filtration) a Grade C environment (usually "Hot-cell") will be suitable. Hot-cells should meet a high degree of air cleanliness, with filtered feed air, when closed. Aseptic activities must be carried out in a Grade A area.

28 Prior to the start of manufacturing, assembly of sterilised equipment and consumables (tubing, sterilised filters, and sterile closed and sealed vials to a sealed fluid path) must be performed under aseptic conditions.

Documentation

29 All documents related to the manufacture of radiopharmaceuticals should be prepared, reviewed, approved and distributed according to written procedures.

30 Specifications should be established and documented for raw materials, labelling and packaging materials, critical intermediates and the finished radiopharmaceutical. Specifications should also be in place for any other critical items used in the manufacturing process, such as process aids, gaskets or sterile filtering kits that could critically impact on quality.

31 Acceptance criteria should be established for the radiopharmaceutical including criteria for release and shelf-life specifications (examples: chemical identity of the isotope, radioactive concentration, purity, and specific activity).

32   Records of major equipment use, cleaning, sanitisation or sterilisation and maintenance should show the product name and batch number, where appropriate, in addition to the date and time and signature of the persons involved in these activities.

33   Records should be retained for at least 3 years unless another timeframe is specified in national requirements.

Production

34   Production of different radioactive products in the same working area (i.e. hot-cell, LAF unit), at the same time should be avoided in order to minimise the risk of radioactive cross-contamination or mix-up.

35   Special attention should be paid to validation including validation of computerised systems, which should be carried out in accordance with EudraLex, Volume 4, Annex 11. New manufacturing processes should be validated prospectively.

36   The critical parameters should normally be identified before or during validation and the ranges necessary for reproducible operation should be defined.

37   Integrity testing of the membrane filter should be performed for aseptically filled products, taking into account the need for radiation protection and maintenance of filter sterility.

38   Due to radiation exposure, it is accepted that most of the labelling of the direct container is done prior to manufacturing. Sterile empty closed vials may be labelled with partial information prior to filling, provided that this procedure does not compromise sterility or prevent visual control of the filled vial.

Quality Control

39   Some radiopharmaceuticals may have to be distributed and used on the basis of an assessment of batch documentation and before all chemical and microbiology tests have been completed. Radiopharmaceutical product release may be carried out in two or more stages, before and after full analytical testing:

(a) Assessment by a designated person of batch processing records, which should cover production conditions and analytical testing performed thus far, before allowing transportation of the radiopharmaceutical under quarantine status to the clinical department;

(b) Assessment of the final analytical data, ensuring all deviations from normal procedures are documented, justified and appropriately released prior to documented certification by the Qualified Person. Where certain test results are not available before use of the product, the Qualified Person should conditionally certify the product before it is used and should finally certify the product after all the test results have been obtained.

40　Most radiopharmaceuticals are intended for use within a short time and the period of validity with regard to the radioactive shelf-life must be clearly stated.

41　Radiopharmaceuticals having radionuclides with long half-lives should be tested to show that they meet all relevant acceptance criteria before release and certification by the QP.

42　Before testing performed samples can be stored to allow sufficient radio-activity decay. All tests including the sterility test should be performed as soon as possible.

43　A written procedure detailing the assessment of production and analytical data, which should be considered before the batch is dispatched, should be established.

44　Products that fail to meet acceptance criteria should be rejected. If the material is reprocessed, pre-established procedures should be followed and the finished product should meet acceptance criteria before release. Returned products may not be reprocessed and must be stored as radioactive waste.

45　A procedure should also describe the measures to be taken by the Qualified Person if unsatisfactory test results (Out-of-Specification) are obtained after dispatch and before expiry. Such events should be investigated to include the relevant corrective and preventive actions taken to prevent future events. This process must be documented.

46　Information should be given to the clinical responsible persons, if necessary. To facilitate this, a traceability system should be implemented for radiopharmaceuticals.

47　A system to verify the quality of starting materials should be in place. Supplier approval should include an evaluation that provides adequate assurance that the material consistently meets specifications. The starting materials, packaging materials and critical process aids should be purchased from approved suppliers.

Reference and Retention Samples

48   For radiopharmaceuticals sufficient samples of each batch of bulk-formulated product shall be retained for at least six months after expiry of the finished medicinal product unless otherwise justified through risk management.

49   Samples of starting materials, other than solvents gases or water used in the manufacturing process, shall be retained for at least two years after the release of the product. That period may be shortened if the period of stability of the material, as indicated in the relevant specification, is shorter.

50   Other conditions may be defined by agreement with the competent authority, for the sampling and retaining of starting materials and products manufactured individually or in small quantities or when their storage could raise special problems.

Distribution

51   Distribution of the finished product under controlled conditions, before all appropriate test results are available, is acceptable for radiopharmaceuticals, provided that the product is not administered by the receiving institute until satisfactory test results have been received and assessed by a designated person.

Glossary

PREPARATION

Handling and radiolabelling of kits with radionuclide eluted from generators or radioactive precursors within a hospital. Kits, generators and precursors should have a Marketing Authorisation or a national licence.

MANUFACTURING

Production, quality control and release and delivery of radiopharmaceuticals from the active substance and starting materials.

HOT–CELLS

Shielded workstations for manufacture and handling of radioactive materials. Hot-cells are not necessarily designed as an isolator.

QUALIFIED PERSON (QP)

QP as described in Directives 2001/83/EC and 2001/82/EC. QP responsibilities are elaborated in EudraLex, Volume 4, Annex 16.

ANNEX 4 MANUFACTURE OF VETERINARY MEDICINAL PRODUCTS OTHER THAN IMMUNOLOGICAL VETERINARY MEDICINAL PRODUCTS

> **Note:** This annex applies to all veterinary medicinal products falling within the scope of *Directive 2001/82/EC other than immunological veterinary medicinal products, which are the subject of a separate annex.*

Manufacture of Premixes for Medicated Feedingstuffs

For the purposes of these paragraphs:

- A *medicated feedingstuff* is any mixture of a veterinary medicinal product or products and feed or feeds that is ready prepared for marketing and intended to be fed to animals without further processing because of its curative or preventive properties or other properties as a medicinal product covered by Article 1 (2) of Directive 2001/82/EC;
- A *pre-mix for medicated feedingstuffs* is any veterinary medicinal product prepared in advance with a view to the subsequent manufacture of medicated feedingstuffs.

1　The manufacture of premixes for medicated feedingstuffs requires the use of large quantities of vegetable matter, which is likely to attract insects and rodents. Premises should be designed, equipped and operated to minimise this risk (point 3.4) and should also be subject to a regular pest control programme.

2　Because of the large volume of dust generated during the production of bulk material for premixes, specific attention should be given to the need to avoid cross-contamination and facilitate cleaning (point 3.14), e.g. through the installation of sealed transport systems and dust extraction, whenever possible. The installation of such systems does not, however, eliminate the need for regular cleaning of production areas.

3　Parts of the process likely to have a significant adverse influence on the stability of the active ingredient(s) (e.g. use of steam in pellet manufacture) should be carried out in a uniform manner from batch to batch.

4　Consideration should be given to undertaking the manufacture of premixes in dedicated areas that, if at all possible, do not form part of a main manufacturing plant. Alternatively, such dedicated areas should be surrounded by a buffer zone in order to minimise the risk of contamination of other manufacturing areas.

Manufacture of Ectoparasiticides

5   In derogation from point 3.6, ectoparasiticides for external application to animals, which are veterinary medicinal products and subject to Marketing Authorisation, may be produced and filled on a campaign basis in pesticide specific areas. However, other categories of veterinary medicinal products should not be produced in such areas.

6   Adequate validated cleaning procedures should be employed to prevent cross-contamination, and steps should be taken to ensure the secure storage of the veterinary medicinal product in accordance with the guide.

Manufacture of Veterinary Medicinal Products Containing Penicillins

7   The use of penicillins in veterinary medicine does not present the same risks of hypersensitivity in animals as in humans. Although incidents of hypersensitivity have been recorded in horses and dogs, there are other materials that are toxic to certain species, e.g. the ionophore antibiotics in horses. Although desirable, the requirements that such products be manufactured in dedicated, self-contained facilities (point 3.6) may be dispensed with in the case of facilities dedicated to the manufacture of veterinary medicinal products only. However, all necessary measures should be taken to avoid cross-contamination and any risk to operator safety in accordance with the guide. In such circumstances, penicillin-containing products should be manufactured on a campaign basis and should be followed by appropriate, validated decontamination and cleaning procedures.

Retention of Samples (point 1.4, viii and point 6.14)

8   It is recognised that, because of the large volume of certain veterinary medicinal products in their final packaging, in particular premixes, it may not be feasible for manufacturers to retain samples from each batch in its final packaging. However, manufacturers should ensure that sufficient representative samples of each batch are retained and stored in accordance with the guide.

9   In all cases, the container used for storage should be composed of the same material as the market primary container in which the product is marketed.

Sterile Veterinary Medicinal Products

10   Where this has been accepted by the competent authorities, terminally sterilised veterinary medicinal products may be manufactured in a clean area of a lower grade than the grade required in the annex on "Sterile preparations", but at least in a grade D environment.

ANNEX 5 MANUFACTURE OF IMMUNOLOGICAL VETERINARY MEDICINAL PRODUCTS

Principle

The manufacture of immunological veterinary medicinal products has special characteristics, which should be taken into consideration when implementing and assessing the quality assurance system.

Due to the large number of animal species and related pathogenic agents, the variety of products manufactured is very wide and the volume of manufacture is often low; hence, work on a campaign basis is common. Moreover, because of the very nature of this manufacture (cultivation steps, lack of terminal sterilisation, etc.), the products must be particularly well protected against contamination and cross-contamination. The environment also must be protected, especially when the manufacture involves the use of pathogenic or exotic biological agents and the worker must be particularly well protected when the manufacture involves the use of biological agents pathogenic to humans.

These factors, together with the inherent variability of immunological products and the relative inefficiency in particular of final product quality control tests in providing adequate information about products, mean that the role of the quality assurance system is of the utmost importance. The need to maintain control over all of the following aspects of GMP, as well as those outlined in this Guide, cannot be overemphasised. In particular, it is important that the data generated by the monitoring of the various aspects of GMP (equipment, premises, product, etc.) is rigorously assessed and informed decisions, leading to appropriate action, are made and recorded.

Personnel

1   All personnel (including those concerned with cleaning and maintenance) employed in areas where immunological products are manufactured should be given training in and information on hygiene and microbiology. They should receive additional training specific to the products with which they work.

2   Responsible personnel should be formally trained in some or all of the following fields: bacteriology, biology, biometry, chemistry, immunology, medicine, parasitology, pharmacy, pharmacology, virology and veterinary medicine, and should also have an adequate knowledge of environmental protection measures.

3   Personnel should be protected against possible infection with the biological agents used in manufacture. In the case of biological agents known to cause disease in humans, adequate measures should be taken to prevent infection of personnel working with the agent or with experimental animals.

Where relevant, the personnel should be vaccinated and subject to medical examination.

4   Adequate measures should be taken to prevent biological agents being taken outside the manufacturing plant by personnel acting as a carrier. Dependent on the type of biological agent, such measures may include complete change of clothes and compulsory showering before leaving the production area.

5   For immunological products, the risk of contamination or cross-contamination by personnel is particularly important.

Prevention of contamination by personnel should be achieved by a set of measures and procedures to ensure that appropriate protective clothing is used during the different stages of the production process.

Prevention of *cross-contamination* by personnel involved in production should be achieved by a set of measures and procedures to ensure that they do not pass from one area to another unless they have taken appropriate measures to eliminate the risk of contamination. In the course of a working day, personnel should not pass from areas where contamination with live microorganisms is likely or where animals are housed to premises where other products or organisms are handled. If such passage is unavoidable, clearly defined decontamination procedures, including change of clothing and shoes and, where necessary, showering, should be followed by staff involved in any such production.

Personnel entering a contained area where organisms had not been handled in open circuit operations in the previous twelve hours to check on cultures in sealed, surface-decontaminated flasks would not be regarded as being at risk of contamination, unless the organism involved was an exotic.

Premises

6   Premises should be designed in such a way as to control both the risk to the product and to the environment.

This can be achieved by the use of containment, clean, clean/contained or controlled areas.

7   Live biological agents should be handled in contained areas. The level of containment should depend on the pathogenicity of the microorganism

and whether it has been classified as exotic. (Other relevant legislation, such as Directives 90/219/EEC[1] and 90/220/EEC[2], also applies.)

8   Inactivated biological agents should be handled in clean areas. Clean areas should also be used when handling non-infected cells isolated from multi-cellular organisms and, in some cases, filtration-sterilised media.

9   Open circuit operations involving products or components not subsequently sterilised should be carried out within a laminar airflow work station (grade A) in a grade B area.

10   Other operations where live biological agents are handled (quality control, research and diagnostic services, etc.) should be appropriately contained and separated if production operations are carried out in the same building. The level of containment should depend on the pathogenicity of the biological agent and whether they have been classified as exotic. Whenever diagnostic activities are carried out, there is the risk of introducing highly pathogenic organisms. Therefore, the level of containment should be adequate to cope with all such risks. Containment may also be required if quality control or other activities are carried out in buildings in close proximity to those used for production.

11   Containment premises should be easily disinfected and should have the following characteristics:

(a) the absence of direct venting to the outside;
(b) a ventilation with air at negative pressure. Air should be extracted through HEPA filters and not be re-circulated except to the same area, and provided that further HEPA filtration is used (normally this condition would be met by routing the re-circulated air through the normal supply HEPAs for that area). However, recycling of air between areas may be permissible provided that it passes through two exhaust HEPAs, the first of which is continuously monitored for integrity, and there are adequate measures for safe venting of exhaust air should this filter fail;
(c) air from manufacturing areas used for the handling of exotic organisms should be vented through 2 sets of HEPA filters in series, and that from production areas not re-circulated;

---

[1] Council Directive 98/81/EC of 26 October 1998 amending Directive 90/219/ EEC on the contained use of genetically modified microorganisms (OJ L 330, 05.12.1998, pp. 13–31).
[2] Directive 2001/18/EC of the European Parliament and the Council of 12 March 2001 on the deliberate release into the environment of genetically modified organisms and repealing Council Directive 90/220/EEC – Commission Declaration (OJ L 106, 17.04.2001, pp. 1–39).

(d) a system for the collection and disinfection of liquid effluents including contaminated condensate from sterilizers, biogenerators, etc. Solid wastes, including animal carcasses, should be disinfected, sterilized or incinerated as appropriate. Contaminated filters should be removed using a safe method;

(e) changing rooms designed and used as airlocks, and equipped with washing and showering facilities if appropriate. Air pressure differentials should be such that there is no flow of air between the work area and the external environment or risk of contamination of outer clothing worn outside the area;

(f) an airlock system for the passage of equipment, which is constructed so that there is no flow of contaminated air between the work area and the external environment or risk of contamination of equipment within the lock. The airlock should be of a size that enables the effective surface decontamination of materials being passed through it. Consideration should be given to having a timing device on the door interlock to allow sufficient time for the decontamination process to be effective;

(g) in many instances, a barrier double-door autoclave for the secure removal of waste materials and introduction of sterile items.

12 Equipment passes and changing rooms should have an interlock mechanism or other appropriate system to prevent the opening of more than one door at a time. Changing rooms should be supplied with air filtered to the same standard as that for the work area, and equipped with air-extraction facilities to produce an adequate air circulation independent of that of the work area. Equipment passes should normally be ventilated in the same way, but unventilated passes, or those equipped with supply air only, may be acceptable.

13 Production operations such as cell maintenance, media preparation, virus culture, etc. likely to cause contamination should be performed in separate areas. Animals and animal products should be handled with appropriate precautions.

14 Production areas where biological agents particularly resistant to disinfection (e.g. spore-forming bacteria) are handled should be separated and dedicated to that particular purpose until the biological agents have been inactivated.

15 With the exception of blending and subsequent filling operations, one biological agent only should be handled at a time within an area.

16 Production areas should be designed to permit disinfection between campaigns, using validated methods.

17   Production of biological agents may take place in controlled areas provided that it is carried out in totally enclosed and heat-sterilised equipment, all connections also being heat sterilised after making and before breaking. It may be acceptable for connections to be made under local laminar airflow provided that these are few in number and proper aseptic techniques are used and there is no risk of leakage. The sterilisation parameters used before breaking the connections must be validated for the organisms being used. Different products may be placed in different biogenerators, within the same area, provided that there is no risk of accidental cross-contamination. However, organisms generally subject to special requirements for containment should be in areas dedicated to such products.

18   Animal houses where animals intended or used for production are accommodated should be provided with the appropriate containment and/or clean area measures, and should be separate from other animal accommodation.

      Animal houses where animals used for quality control, involving the use of pathogenic biological agents, are accommodated should be adequately contained.

19   Access to manufacturing areas should be restricted to authorised personnel. Clear and concise written procedures should be posted as appropriate.

20   Documentation relating to the premises should be readily available in a plant master file.

      The manufacturing site and buildings should be described in sufficient detail (by means of plans and written explanations) so that the designation and conditions of use of all the rooms are correctly identified as well as the biological agents that are handled in them. The flow of people and product should also be clearly marked.

      The animal species accommodated in the animal houses or otherwise on the site should be identified.

      The activities carried out in the vicinity of the site should also be indicated.

      Plans of contained and/or clean area premises should describe the ventilation system, indicating inlets and outlets, filters and their specifications, the number of air changes per hour and pressure gradients. They should indicate which pressure gradients are monitored by pressure indicator.

Equipment

21   The equipment used should be designed and constructed so that it meets the particular requirements for the manufacture of each product.

      Before being put into operation the equipment should be qualified and validated, and subsequently be regularly maintained and validated.

22   Where appropriate, the equipment should ensure satisfactory primary containment of the biological agents.

     Where appropriate, the equipment should be designed and constructed so as to allow easy and effective decontamination and/or sterilisation.

23   Closed equipment used for the primary containment of the biological agents should be designed and constructed so as to prevent any leakage or the formation of droplets and acrosols.

     Inlets and outlets for gases should be protected so as to achieve adequate containment, e.g. by the use of sterilising hydrophobic filters.

     The introduction or removal of material should take place using a sterilisable closed system, or possibly in an appropriate laminar air flow.

24   Equipment, where necessary, should be properly sterilised before use, preferably by pressurised dry steam. Other methods can be accepted if steam sterilisation cannot be used because of the nature of the equipment. It is important not to overlook such individual items as bench centrifuges and water baths.

     Equipment used for purification, separation or concentration should be sterilised or disinfected at least between uses for different products. The effect of the sterilisation methods on the effectiveness and validity of the equipment should be studied in order to determine the lifespan of the equipment.

     All sterilisation procedures should be validated.

25   Equipment should be designed so as to prevent any mix-up between different organisms or products. Pipes, valves and filters should be identified as to their function.

     Separate incubators should be used for infected and non-infected containers, and also generally for different organisms or cells. Incubators containing more than one organism or cell type will be acceptable only if adequate steps are taken to seal, surface decontaminate and segregate the containers. Culture vessels, etc. should be individually labelled. The cleaning and disinfection of the items can be particularly difficult and should receive special attention.

     Equipment used for the storage of biological agents or products should be designed and used in such a manner as to prevent any possible mix-up. All stored items should be clearly and unambiguously labelled and in leak-proof containers. Items such as seed stock of cells and organisms should be stored in dedicated equipment.

26   Relevant equipment, such as that requiring temperature control, should be fitted with recording and/or alarm systems.

     To avoid breakdowns, a system of preventive maintenance, together with trend analysis of recorded data, should be implemented.

EU GMP GUIDE PART I ANNEX 5 MANUFACTURE OF IMMUNOLOGICAL VETERINARY MEDICINAL PRODUCTS

27   The loading of freeze dryers requires an appropriate clean/contained area.
Unloading freeze dryers contaminates the immediate environment. Therefore, for single-ended freeze dryers, the clean room should be decontaminated before a further manufacturing batch is introduced into the area, unless this contains the same organisms, and double-door freeze dryers should be sterilised after each cycle, unless opened in a clean area.
Sterilisation of freeze dryers should be done in accordance with point 24. In case of campaign working, they should be sterilised at least after each campaign.

Animals and Animal Houses

28   General requirements for animal quarters, care and quarantine are laid down in Directive 86/609/EEC[3].

29   Animal houses should be separated from the other production premises and suitably designed.

30   The sanitary status of the animals used for production should be defined, monitored and recorded. Some animals should be handled as defined in specific monographs (e.g. specific pathogen-free [SPF] flocks).

31   Animals, biological agents and tests carried out should be the subject of an identification system so as to prevent any risk of confusion and to control all possible hazards.

Disinfection–Waste Disposal

32   Disinfection and/or wastes and effluents disposal may be particularly important in the case of manufacture of immunological products. Careful consideration should therefore be given to procedures and equipment aiming at avoiding environmental contamination, as well as to their validation or qualification.

---

[3] Directive 2003/65/EC of the European Parliament and the Council of 22 July 2003 amending Council Directive 86/609/EEC on the approximation of laws, regulations and administrative provisions of the Member States regarding the protection of animals used for experimental and other scientific purposes (OJ L 230, 16.09.2003, pp. 32–33).

Production

33　As a result of the wide variety of products, the frequently large number of stages involved in the manufacture of immunological veterinary medicinal products and the nature of the biological processes, careful attention must be paid to adherence to validated operating procedures, the constant monitoring of production at all stages and in-process controls.

　　Additionally, special consideration should be given to starting materials, media and the use of a seed lot system.

Starting Materials

34　The suitability of starting materials should be clearly defined in written specifications. These should include details of the supplier, the method of manufacture, the geographical origin and the animal species from which the materials are derived. The controls to be applied to starting materials must be included. Microbiological controls are particularly important.

35　The results of tests on starting materials must comply with the specifications. Where the tests take a long time (e.g. eggs from SPF flocks), it may be necessary to process starting materials before the results of analytical controls are available. In such cases, the release of a finished product is conditional upon satisfactory results of the tests on starting materials.

36　Special attention should be paid to knowledge of the supplier's quality assurance system in assessing the suitability of a source and the extent of quality control testing required.

37　Where possible, heat is the preferred method for sterilising starting materials. If necessary, other validated methods, such as irradiation, may be used.

Media

38　The ability of media to support the desired growth should be properly validated in advance.

39　Media should preferably be sterilised in situ or in line. Heat is the preferred method. Gases, media, acids, alkalis, defoaming agents and other materials introduced into sterile biogenerators should themselves be sterile.

Seed lot and cell bank system

40　In order to prevent the unwanted drift of properties that might ensue from repeated subcultures or multiple generations, the production of immunological veterinary medicinal products obtained by microbial, cell or tissue culture, or propagation in embryos and animals, should be based on a system of seed lots or cell banks.

41   The number of generations (doublings, passages) between the seed lot or cell bank and the finished product should be consistent with the dossier of authorisation for marketing.

42   Seed lots and cell banks should be adequately characterised and tested for contaminants. Acceptance criteria for new seed lots should be established. Seed lots and cell banks shall be established, stored and used in such a way as to minimise the risks of contamination, or any alteration. During the establishment of the seed lot and cell bank, no other living or infectious material (e.g. virus or cell lines) shall be handled simultaneously in the same area or by the same person.

43   Establishment of the seed lot and cell bank should be performed in a suitable environment to protect the seed lot and the cell bank and, if applicable, the personnel handling it and the external environment.

44   The origin, form and storage conditions of seed material should be described in full. Evidence of the stability and recovery of the seeds and cells should be provided. Storage containers should be hermetically sealed, clearly labelled and stored at an appropriate temperature. Storage conditions shall be properly monitored. An inventory should be kept and each container accounted for.

45   Only authorised personnel should be allowed to handle the material and this handling should be done under the supervision of a responsible person. Different seed lots or cell banks shall be stored in such a way as to avoid confusion or cross-contamination errors. It is desirable to split the seed lots and cell banks and to store the parts at different locations, to minimise the risk of total loss.

Operating principles

46   The formation of droplets and the production of foam should be avoided or minimised during manufacturing processes. Centrifugation and blending procedures that can lead to droplet formation should be carried out in appropriate contained or clean/contained areas to prevent transfer of live organisms.

47   Accidental spillages, especially of live organisms, must be dealt with quickly and safely. Validated decontamination measures should be available for each organism. Where different strains of single bacterial species or very similar viruses are involved, the process must be validated against

only one of them, unless there is reason to believe that they may vary significantly in their resistance to the agent(s) involved.

48 Operations involving the transfer of materials such as sterile media, cultures or product should be carried out in pre-sterilised closed systems wherever possible. Where this is not possible, transfer operations must be protected by laminar airflow workstations.

49 Addition of media or cultures to biogenerators and other vessels should be carried out under carefully controlled conditions to ensure that contamination is not introduced. Care must be taken to ensure that vessels are correctly connected when the addition of cultures takes place.

50 Where necessary, for instance when two or more fermenters are within a single area, sampling and addition ports, and connectors (after connection, before the flow of product, and again before disconnection) should be sterilised with steam. In other circumstances, chemical disinfection of ports and laminar airflow protection of connections may be acceptable.

51 Equipment, glassware, the external surfaces of product containers and other such materials must be disinfected before transfer from a contained area using a validated method (see point 47 above). Batch documentation can be a particular problem. Only the absolute minimum required to allow operations to GMP standards should enter and leave the area. If obviously contaminated, such as by spills or aerosols, or if the organism involved is an exotic, the paperwork must be adequately disinfected through an equipment pass, or the information transferred out by such means as photocopy or fax.

52 Liquid or solid wastes, such as the debris after harvesting eggs, disposable culture bottles, unwanted cultures or biological agents, are best sterilised or disinfected before transfer from a contained area. However, alternatives such as sealed containers or piping may be appropriate in some cases.

53 Articles and materials, including documentation, entering a production room should be carefully controlled to ensure that only articles and materials concerned with production are introduced. There should be a system that ensures that articles and materials entering a room are reconciled with those leaving so that their accumulation within the room does not occur.

54 Heat-stable articles and materials entering a clean area or clean/contained area should do so through a double-ended autoclave or oven. Heat-labile articles and materials should enter through an airlock with interlocked doors where they are disinfected. Sterilisation of articles and materials elsewhere is acceptable provided that they are double wrapped and enter through an airlock with the appropriate precautions.

55   Precautions must be taken to avoid contamination or confusion during incubation. There should be a cleaning and disinfection procedure for incubators. Containers in incubators should be carefully and clearly labelled.

56   With the exception of blending and subsequent filling operations (or when totally enclosed systems are used), only one live biological agent may be handled within a production room at any given time. Production rooms must be effectively disinfected between the handling of different live biological agents.

57   Products should be inactivated by the addition of inactivant accompanied by sufficient agitation. The mixture should then be transferred to a second sterile vessel, unless the container is of such a size and shape as to be easily inverted and shaken so as to wet all internal surfaces with the final culture/inactivant mixture.

58   Vessels containing inactivated products should not be opened or sampled in areas containing live biological agents. All subsequent processing of inactivated products should take place in clean areas Grades A and B or enclosed equipment dedicated to inactivated products.

59   Careful consideration should be given to the validation of methods for sterilisation, disinfection, virus removal and inactivation.

60   Filling should be carried out as soon as possible after production. Containers of bulk product prior to filling should be sealed, appropriately labelled and stored under specified conditions of temperature.

61   There should be a system to assure the integrity and closure of containers after filling.

62   The capping of vials containing live biological agents must be performed in such a way as to ensure that contamination of other products or escape of the live agents into other areas or the external environment does not occur.

63   For various reasons there may be a delay between the filling of final containers and their labelling and packaging. Procedures should be specified for the storage of unlabelled containers in order to prevent confusion and to ensure satisfactory storage conditions. Special attention should be paid to the storage of heat-labile or photosensitive products. Storage temperatures should be specified.

64   For each stage of production, the yield of product should be reconciled with that expected from that process. Any significant discrepancies should be investigated.

Quality Control

65 In-process controls play a especially important role in ensuring the consistency of the quality of biological medicinal products. Those controls that are crucial for the quality (e.g. virus removal), but cannot be carried out on the finished product, should be performed at an appropriate stage of production.

66 It may be necessary to retain samples of intermediate products in sufficient amount and under appropriate storage conditions to allow repetition or confirmation of a batch control.

67 There may be a requirement for the continuous monitoring of data during a production process, e.g. monitoring of physical parameters during fermentation.

68 Continuous culture of biological products is a common practice and special consideration needs to be given to the quality control requirements arising from this type of production method.

ANNEX 6 MANUFACTURE OF MEDICINAL GASES

Principle

Gases which fulfil the definition of medicinal product of Directive 2001/83/EC or Directive 2001/82/EC (hereinafter, medicinal gases) are subject to the requirements laid down in these Directives, including the requirements on manufacturing. In this regard, this Annex deals with the manufacture of active substance gases and with the manufacture of medicinal gases.

The delineation between the manufacture of the active substance and the manufacture of the medicinal product should be clearly defined in each Marketing Authorisation dossier. Normally, the production and purification steps of the gas belong to the field of manufacture of active substances. Gases enter the pharmaceutical field from the first storage of gas intended for such use.

Manufacture of active substance gases should comply with the Basic Requirements of this guide (Part II), the relevant part of this Annex and the other Annexes of the guide if relevant.

Manufacture of medicinal gases should comply with the Basic Requirements of this guide (Part I), the relevant part of this Annex and the other Annexes of the guide if relevant.

In the exceptional cases of continuous processes, where no intermediate storage of gas between the manufacture of the active substance and the manufacture of the medicinal product is possible, the whole process (from starting materials of active substance to medicinal finished product) should be considered as belonging to the pharmaceutical field. This should be clearly stated in the Marketing Authorisation dossier.

The Annex does not cover the manufacture and handling of medicinal gases in hospitals unless this is considered to be industrial preparation or manufacturing. However, relevant parts of this Annex may be used as a basis for such activities.

Manufacture of Active Substance Gases

Active substance gases can be prepared by chemical synthesis or be obtained from natural sources followed by purification steps, if necessary (as, for example, in an air separation plant).

1   The processes corresponding to these two methods of manufacturing active substance gases should comply with Part II of the Basic Requirements. However:

(a) the requirements regarding starting materials for active substances (Part II, Chapter 7) do not apply to the production of active substance gases by air separation (however, the manufacturer should ensure that the quality of ambient air is suitable for the established process and any changes in the quality of ambient air do not affect the quality of the active substance gas);

(b) the requirements regarding on-going stability studies (Part II, Chapter 11.5), which are used to confirm storage conditions and expiry/retest dates (Part II, Chapter 11.6), do not apply in case initial stability studies have been replaced by bibliographic data (see Note for Guidance CPMP/QWP/1719/00); and

(c) the requirements regarding reserve/retention samples (Part II, Chapter 11.7) do not apply to active substance gases, unless otherwise specified.

2   The production of active substance gases through a continuous process (e.g. air separation) should be continuously monitored for quality. The results of this monitoring should be kept in a manner permitting trend evaluation.

3   In addition:

(a) transfers and deliveries of active substance gases in bulk should comply with the same requirements as those mentioned below for the medicinal gases (sections 19 to 21 of this Annex);

(b) filling of active substance gases into cylinders or into mobile cryogenic vessels should comply with the same requirements as those mentioned below for the medicinal gases (sections 22 to 37 of this Annex) as well as Part II, Chapter 9.

Manufacture of Medicinal Gases

Manufacture of medicinal gases is generally carried out in closed equipment. Consequently, environmental contamination of the product is minimal. However, risks of contamination (or cross-contamination with other gases) may arise, in particular because of the reuse of containers.

4   Requirements applying to cylinders should also apply to cylinders bundles (except storage and transportation under cover).

Personnel

5   All personnel involved in manufacture and distribution of medicinal gases should receive an appropriate GMP training specifically applying to this type of products. They should be aware of the critically important aspects and potential hazards for patients from these products. The training programmes should include the tanker lorries drivers.

6 Personnel of subcontractors that could influence the quality of medicinal gases (such as personnel in charge of maintenance of cylinders or valves) should be appropriately trained.

Premises and equipment

PREMISES

7 Cylinders and mobile cryogenic vessels should be checked, prepared, filled and stored in separate areas from non-medicinal gases, and there should be no exchange of cylinders/mobile cryogenic vessels between these areas. However, it could be accepted to check, prepare, fill and store other gases in the same areas, provided they comply with the specifications of medicinal gases and that the manufacturing operations are performed according to GMP standards.

8 Premises should provide sufficient space for manufacturing, testing and storage operations in order to prevent any risk of mix-up. Premises should be designed to provide:

(a) separate marked areas for different gases;
(b) clear identification and segregation of cylinders/mobile cryogenic vessels at various stages of processing (e.g. "waiting checking" "awaiting filling", "quarantine", "certified", "rejected" "prepared deliveries").

The method used to achieve these various levels of segregation will depend on the nature, extent and complexity of the overall operation. Marked-out floor areas, partitions, barriers, signs, labels or other appropriate means could be used.

9 Empty cylinders/home cryogenic vessels after sorting or maintenance, and filled cylinders/home cryogenic vessels should be stored under cover, and protected from adverse weather conditions. Filled cylinders/mobile cryogenic vessels should be stored in a manner that ensures that they will be delivered in a clean state, compatible with the environment in which they will be used.

10 Specific storage conditions should be provided as required by the Marketing Authorisation (e.g. for gas mixtures where phase separation occurs on freezing).

EQUIPMENT

11 Equipment should be designed to ensure the correct gas is filled into the correct container. There should normally be no cross-connections between pipelines carrying different gases. If cross-connections are needed (e.g. filling equipment of mixtures), qualification should ensure that there is no risk of cross-contamination between the different gases. In addition, the manifolds should be equipped with specific connections. These connections may be subject to national or international standards. The use of connections meeting different standards at the same filling site should be carefully controlled, as well as the use of adaptors needed in some situations to bypass the specific fill connection systems.

12   Tanks and tankers should be dedicated to a single and defined quality of gas. However, medicinal gases may be stored or transported in the same tanks, other containers used for intermediate storage or tankers as the same non-medicinal gas, provided that the quality of the latter is at least equal to the quality of the medicinal gas and that GMP standards are maintained. In such cases, quality risk management should be performed and documented.

13   A common system supplying gas to medicinal and non-medicinal gas manifolds is acceptable only if there is a validated method to prevent backflow from the non-medicinal gas line to the medicinal gas line.

14   Filling manifolds should be dedicated to a single medicinal gas or to a given mixture of medicinal gases. In exceptional cases, filling gases used for other medical purposes on manifolds dedicated to medicinal gases may be acceptable if justified and performed under control. In these cases, the quality of the non-medicinal gas should be at least equal to the required quality of the medicinal gas and GMP standards should be maintained. Filling should then be carried out by campaigns.

15   Repair and maintenance operations (including cleaning and purging) of equipment, should not adversely affect the quality of medicinal gases. In particular, procedures should describe the measures to be taken after repair and maintenance operations involving breaches of the system's integrity. Specifically it should be demonstrated that the equipment is free from any contamination that may adversely affect the quality of the finished product before releasing it for use. Records should be maintained.

16   A procedure should describe the measures to be taken when a tanker is back into medicinal gas service (after transporting non-medicinal gas in the conditions mentioned in section 12, or after a maintenance operation). This should include analytical testing.

Documentation

17   Data included in the records for each batch of cylinders/mobile cryogenic vessels must ensure that each filled container is traceable to significant

aspects of the relevant filling operations. As appropriate, the following should be entered:

(a) name of the product;
(b) batch number;
(c) date and time of the filling operation;
(d) identification of the person(s) carrying out each significant step (e.g. line clearance, receipt, preparation before filling, filling, etc.);
(e) batch(es) reference(s) for the gas(es) used for the filling operation as referred to in section 22, including status;
(f) equipment used (e.g. filling manifold);
(g) quantity of cylinders/mobile cryogenic vessels before filling, including individual identification references and water capacity(ies);
(h) pre-filling operations performed (see section 30);
(i) key parameters that are needed to ensure correct filling at standard conditions;
(j) results of appropriate checks to ensure the cylinders/mobile cryogenic vessels have been filled;
(k) a sample of the batch label;
(l) specification of the finished product and results of quality control tests (including reference to the calibration status of the test equipment);
(m) quantity of rejected cylinders/mobile cryogenic vessels, with individual identification references and reasons for rejections;
(n) details of any problems or unusual events, and signed authorisation for any deviation from filling instructions; and
(o) certification statement by the Qualified Person, date and signature.

18   Records should be maintained for each batch of gas that is intended for delivery into hospital tanks. These records should, as appropriate, include the following (items to be recorded may vary depending on local legislation):

(a) name of the product;
(b) batch number;
(c) identification reference for the tank (tanker) in which the batch is certified;
(d) date and time of the filling operation;
(e) identification of the person(s) carrying out the filling of the tank (tanker);
(f) reference to the supplying tanker (tank), reference to the source gas as applicable;
(g) relevant details concerning the filling operation;
(h) specification of the finished product and results of quality control tests (including reference to the calibration status of the test equipment);

(i) details of any problems or unusual events, and signed authorisation for any deviation from filling instructions; and

(j) certification statement by the Qualified Person, date and signature.

Production

TRANSFERS AND DELIVERIES OF CRYOGENIC AND LIQUEFIED GAS

19   The transfers of cryogenic or liquefied gases from primary storage, including controls before transfers, should be in accordance with validated procedures designed to avoid the possibility of contamination. Transfer lines should be equipped with non-return valves or other suitable alternatives. Flexible connections, coupling hoses and connectors should be flushed with the relevant gas before use.

20   The transfer hoses used to fill tanks and tankers should be equipped with product-specific connections. The use of adaptors allowing the connection of tanks and tankers not dedicated to the same gases should be adequately controlled.

21   Deliveries of gas may be added to tanks containing the same defined quality of gas provided that a sample is tested to ensure that the quality of the delivered gas is acceptable. This sample may be taken from the gas to be delivered or from the receiving tank after delivery.

FILLING AND LABELLING OF CYLINDERS AND MOBILE CRYOGENIC VESSELS

22   Before filling cylinders and mobile cryogenic vessels, a batch(es) of gas(es) should be determined, controlled according to specifications and approved for filling.

23   In the case of continuous processes as those mentioned under "Principle", there should be adequate in-process controls to ensure that the gas complies with specifications.

24   Cylinders, mobile cryogenic vessels and valves should conform to appropriate technical specifications and any relevant requirements of the Marketing Authorisation. They should be dedicated to a single medicinal gas or to a given mixture of medicinal gases. Cylinders should be colour coded according to relevant standards. They should preferably be fitted with minimum pressure retention valves with a non-return mechanism in order to provide adequate protection against contamination.

25   Cylinders, mobile cryogenic vessels and valves should be checked before first use in production, and should be properly maintained. Where CE-marked medical devices are used, the maintenance should address the medical device manufacturer's instructions.

26   Checks and maintenance operations should not affect the quality and safety of the medicinal product. The water used for the hydrostatic pressure testing carried out on cylinders should be at least of drinking quality.

27   As part of the checks and maintenance operations, cylinders should be subject to an internal visual inspection before fitting the valve, to make sure they are not contaminated with water or other contaminants. This should be done:

   • when they are new and initially put into medicinal gas service;
   • following any hydrostatic statutory pressure test or equivalent test where the valve is removed;
   • whenever the valve is replaced.

   After fitting, the valve should be kept closed to prevent any contamination from entering the cylinder. If there is any doubt about the internal condition of the cylinder, the valve should be removed and the cylinder internally inspected to ensure that it has not been contaminated.

28   Maintenance and repair operations of cylinders, mobile cryogenic vessels and valves are the responsibility of the manufacturer of the medicinal product. If subcontracted, they should be carried out only by approved subcontractors, and contracts including technical agreements should be established. Subcontractors should be audited to ensure that appropriate standards are maintained.

29   There should be a system to ensure the traceability of cylinders, mobile cryogenic vessels and valves.

30   Checks to be performed before filling should include:

   (a) in the case of cylinders, a check, carried out according to defined procedure, to ensure that there is a positive residual pressure in each cylinder:
      • if the cylinder is fitted with a minimum pressure retention valve, when there is no signal indicating that there is a positive residual pressure, the correct functioning of the valve should be checked, and if the valve is shown not to function properly the cylinder should be sent to maintenance,
      • if the cylinder is not fitted with a minimum pressure retention valve, when there is no positive residual pressure the cylinder should be put aside for additional measures, to make sure that it is not contaminated with water or other contaminants; additional measures

could consist of internal visual inspection followed by cleaning using a validated method;

(b) a check to ensure that all previous batch labels have been removed;

(c) a check that any damaged product labels have been removed and replaced;

(d) a visual external inspection of each cylinder, mobile cryogenic vessel and valve for dents, arc burns, debris, other damage and contamination with oil or grease; cleaning should be done if necessary;

(e) a check of each cylinder or mobile cryogenic vessel outlet connection to determine that it is the proper type for the particular gas involved;

(f) a check of the date of the next test to be performed on the valve (in the case of valves that need to be periodically tested);

(g) a check of the cylinders or mobile cryogenic vessels to ensure that any tests required by national or international regulations (e.g. hydrostatic pressure test or equivalent for cylinders) have been conducted and are still valid; and

(h) a check to determine that each cylinder is colour-coded as specified in the Marketing Authorisation (colour-coding of the relevant national/international standards).

31　A batch should be defined for filling operations.

32　Cylinders that have been returned for refilling should be prepared with care in order to minimise the risks of contamination, in line with the procedures defined in the Marketing Authorisation. These procedures, which should include evacuation and/or purging operations, should be validated.

33　Mobile cryogenic vessels that have been returned for refilling should be prepared with care in order to minimise the risks of contamination, in line with the procedures defined in the Marketing Authorisation. In particular, mobile vessels with no residual pressure should be prepared using a validated method.

34　There should be appropriate checks to ensure that each cylinder/mobile cryogenic vessel has been properly filled.

35　Each filled cylinder should be tested for leaks using an appropriate method, prior to fitting the tamper-evident seal (see section 36). The test method should not introduce any contaminant into the valve outlet and, if applicable, should be performed after any quality sample is taken.

36　After filling, cylinders valves should be fitted with covers to protect the outlets from contamination. Cylinders and mobile cryogenic vessels should be fitted with tamper-evident seals.

37　Each cylinder or mobile cryogenic vessel should be labelled. The batch number and the expiry date may be on a separate label.

38   In the case of medicinal gases produced by mixing two or more different gases (in-line before filling or directly into the cylinders), the mixing process should be validated to ensure that the gases are properly mixed in every cylinder and that the mixture is homogeneous.

Quality control

39   Each batch of medicinal gas (cylinders, mobile cryogenic vessels, hospital tanks) should be tested in accordance with the requirements of the Marketing Authorisation and certified.

40   Unless different provisions are required in the Marketing Authorisation, the sampling plan and the analysis to be performed should comply, in the case of cylinders with the following requirements:

(a) In the case of a single medicinal gas filled into cylinders via a multi-cylinder manifold, the gas from at least one cylinder from each manifold filling cycle should be tested for identity and assay each time the cylinders are changed on the manifold;

(b) In the case of a single medicinal gas filled into cylinders one at a time, the gas from at least one cylinder of each uninterrupted filling cycle should be tested for identity and assay. An example of an uninterrupted filling cycle is one shift's production using the same personnel, equipment and batch of gas to be filled;

(c) In the case of a medicinal gas produced by mixing two or more gases in a cylinder from the same manifold, the gas from every cylinder should be tested for assay and identity of each component gas. For excipients, if any, testing on identity could be performed on one cylinder per manifold filling cycle (or per uninterrupted filling cycle in case of cylinders filled one at a time). Fewer cylinders may be tested in case of validated automated filling system;

(d) Premixed gases should follow the same principles as single gases when continuous in-line testing of the mixture to be filled is performed.

Premixed gases should follow the same principle as medicinal gases produced by mixing gases in the cylinders when there is no continuous in-line testing of the mixture to be filled.

Testing for water content should be performed unless otherwise justified. Other sampling and testing procedures that provide at least equivalent level of quality assurance may be justified.

41   Unless different provisions are required in the Marketing Authorisation, final testing on mobile cryogenic vessels should include a test for assay and identity on each vessel. Testing by batches should be carried out only if it has been demonstrated that the critical attributes of the gas remaining in each vessel before refilling have been maintained.

42 Cryogenic vessels retained by customers (hospital tanks or home cryogenic vessels), which are refilled in place from dedicated tankers, do not need to be sampled after filling provided that a certificate of analysis on the contents of the tanker accompanies the delivery. However, it should be demonstrated that the specification of the gas in the vessels is maintained over the successive re-fillings.

43 Reference and retention samples are not required, unless otherwise specified.

44 On-going stability studies are not required in case initial stability studies have been replaced by bibliographic data (see Note for Guidance CPMP/ QWP/1719/00).

Transportation of packaged gases

45 Filled gas cylinders and home cryogenic vessels should be protected during transportation, so that, in particular, they are delivered to customers in a clean state compatible with the environment in which they will be used.

Glossary

ACTIVE SUBSTANCE GAS
Any gas intended to be an active substance for a medicinal product.

AIR SEPARATION
Separation of atmospheric air into its constituent gases using fractional distillation at cryogenic temperatures.

COMPRESSED GAS
Gas which, when packaged under pressure for transport, is entirely gaseous at all temperatures above $-50°C$.

CONTAINER
A container is a cryogenic vessel (tank, tanker or other type of mobile cryogenic vessel), a cylinder, a cylinder bundle or any other package that is in direct contact with the gas.

CRYOGENIC GAS
A gas that liquefies at 1.013 bar at temperatures below $-150°C$.

CYLINDER

Container, usually cylindrical, suited for compressed, liquefied or dissolved gas, fitted with a device to regulate the spontaneous outflow of gas at atmospheric pressure and room temperature.

CYLINDER BUNDLE

An assembly of cylinders that are fastened together, interconnected by a manifold and transported and used as a unit.

EVACUATE

To remove the residual gas from a container/system to a pressure less than 1.013 bar, using a vacuum system.

GAS

Any substance that is completely gaseous at 1.013 bar and +20°C or has a vapour pressure exceeding 3 bar at +50°C.

HOME CRYOGENIC VESSEL

Mobile cryogenic vessel designed to hold liquid oxygen and dispense gaseous oxygen at patient's home.

HYDROSTATIC PRESSURE TEST

Test performed as required by national or international regulations, in order to ensure that pressure containers are able to withstand pressures up to the container's design pressure.

LIQUEFIED GAS

A gas that, when packaged for transport, is partially liquid (or solid) at a temperature above −50°C.

MANIFOLD

Equipment or apparatus designed to enable one or more gas containers to be emptied and filled at the same time.

MAXIMUM THEORETICAL RESIDUAL IMPURITY

Gaseous impurity from a possible backflow that remains after the cylinder pre-treatment process before filling. The calculation of the maximum theoretical residual impurity is relevant only for compressed gases and assumes that the gases behave as perfect gases.

MEDICINAL GAS

Any gas or mixture of gases classified as a medicinal product (as defined in Directives 2001/83/EC and 2001/82/EC).

MINIMUM PRESSURE RETENTION VALVE

A cylinder valve that maintains a positive pressure above atmospheric pressure in a gas cylinder after use, in order to prevent internal contamination of the cylinder.

MOBILE CRYOGENIC VESSEL

Mobile thermally insulated container designed to maintain the contents in a liquid state. In the Annex, this term does not include the tankers.

NON-RETURN VALVE

Valve that permits flow in one direction only.

PURGE

To remove the residual gas from a container/system by first pressurising and then venting the gas used for purging to 1.013 bar.

TANK

Static thermally insulated container designed for the storage of liquefied or cryogenic gas. They are also called "Fixed cryogenic vessels".

TANKER

In the context of the Annex, thermally insulated container fixed on a vehicle for the transport of liquefied or cryogenic gas.

VALVE

Device for opening and closing containers.

VENT

To remove the residual gas from a container/system down to 1.013 bar, by opening the container/system to the atmosphere.

ANNEX 7 MANUFACTURE OF HERBAL MEDICINAL PRODUCTS

Principle

Because of their often complex and variable nature, control of starting materials, storage and processing assume particular importance in the manufacture of herbal medicinal products.

The "starting material" in the manufacture of a herbal medicinal product[1] can be a medicinal plant, a herbal substance[2] or a herbal preparation[1]. The herbal substance shall be of suitable quality and supporting data should be provided to the manufacturer of the herbal preparation/herbal medicinal product. Ensuring consistent quality of the herbal substance may require more detailed information on its agricultural production. The selection of seeds, cultivation and harvesting conditions represent important aspects of the quality of the herbal substance and can influence the consistency of the finished product. Recommendations on an appropriate quality assurance system for good agricultural and collection practice are provided in the HMPC guidance document: "Guideline on Good Agricultural and Collection Practice for starting materials of herbal origin".

This Annex applies to all herbal starting materials: medicinal plants, herbal substances or herbal preparations.

---

[1] Throughout the annex and unless otherwise specified, the term "herbal medicinal product/preparation" includes "traditional herbal medicinal product/preparation".

[2] The terms herbal substance and herbal preparation, as defined in Directive 2004/24/EC, are considered to be equivalent to the Ph.Eur. terms herbal drug and herbal drug preparation respectively.

Table I llustrating the application of Good Practices to the manufacture of herbal medicinal products[3]

Activity	Good Agricultural and Collection Practice (GACP)[4]	Part II of the GMP Guide[†]	Part I of the GMP Guide[†]
Cultivation, collection and harvesting of plants, algae, fungi and lichens, and collection of exudates			
Cutting, and drying of plants, algae, fungi, lichens and exudates*			
Expression from plants and distillation**			
Comminution, processing of exudates, extraction from plants, fractionation, purification, concentration or fermentation of herbal substances			
Further processing into a dosage form including packaging as a medicinal product			

†Explanatory Note. The GMP classification of the herbal material is dependent upon the use made of it by the Manufacturing Authorisation holder. The material may be classified as an active substance, or an intermediate or a finished product. It is the responsibility of the manufacturer of the medicinal product to ensure that the appropriate GMP classification is applied.

*Manufacturers should ensure that these steps are carried out in accordance with the Marketing Authorisation/registration. For those initial steps that take place in the field, as justified in the Marketing Authorisation/registration, the standards of Good Agricultural and Collection Practice for starting materials of herbal origin (GACP) is applicable. GMP is applicable to further cutting and drying steps.

**Regarding the expression from plants and distillation, if it is necessary for these activities to be an integral part of harvesting to maintain the quality of the product within the approved specifications, it is acceptable that they are performed in the field, provided that the cultivation is in compliance with GACP. These circumstances should be regarded as exceptional and justified in the relevant Marketing Authorisation/registration documentation. For activities carried out in the field, appropriate documentation, control and validation according to the GMP principles should be assured. Regulatory authorities may carry out GMP inspections of these activities in order to assess compliance.

EU GMP GUIDE PART I ANNEX 7 MANUFACTURE OF HERBAL MEDICINAL PRODUCTS

---

[3] This table expands in detail the herbal section of Table 1 in Part II of the GMP Guide.

[4] As published by the European Medicines Agency (EMEA).

Premises and Equipment

Storage areas

1   Herbal substances should be stored in separate areas. The storage area should be equipped in such a way as to give protection against the entry of insects or other animals, especially rodents. Effective measures should be taken to prevent the spread of any such animals and micro-organisms brought in with the herbal substance, to prevent fermentation or mould growth and cross-contamination. Different enclosed areas should be used to quarantine incoming herbal substances and for the approved herbal substances.

2   The storage area should be well aerated and the containers should be located in such a way as to allow free circulation of air.

3   Special attention should be paid to the cleanliness and maintenance of the storage areas, particularly when dust is generated.

4   Storage of herbal substances and herbal preparations may require special conditions of humidity, temperature or light protection; these conditions should be provided and monitored.

Production area

5   Specific provisions should be made during sampling, weighing, mixing and processing operations of herbal substances and herbal preparations whenever dust is generated, to facilitate cleaning and to avoid cross-contamination, for example, dust extraction, dedicated premises, etc.

Equipment

6   The equipment, filtering materials, etc. used in the manufacturing process must be compatible with the extraction solvent, in order to prevent any release or undesirable absorption of substance that could affect the product.

Documentation

Specifications for starting materials

7   Herbal medicinal product manufacturers must ensure that they use only herbal starting materials manufactured in accordance with GMP and the Marketing Authorisation dossier. Comprehensive documentation on

audits of the herbal starting material suppliers carried out by, or on behalf of, the herbal medicinal product manufacturer should be made available. Audit trails for the active substance are fundamental to the quality of the starting material. The manufacturer should ensure that the suppliers of the herbal substance/preparation are in compliance with Good Agricultural and Collection Practice.

8   To fulfil the specification requirements described in the basic requirements of the Guide (Chapter 4), documentation for herbal substances/preparations should include:

- the binomial scientific name of plant (genus, species, subspecies/variety and author (e.g. Linnaeus); other relevant information such as the cultivar name and the chemotype should also be provided, as appropriate;
- details of the source of the plant (country or region of origin and, where applicable, cultivation, time of harvesting, collection procedures, possible pesticides used, possible radioactive contamination, etc.);
- which part(s) of the plant is(are) used;
- when a dried plant is used, the drying system should be specified;
- a description of the herbal substance and its macro- and microscopic examination;
- suitable identification tests including, where appropriate, identification tests for constituents with known therapeutic activity or markers. Specific distinctive tests are required where a herbal substance is liable to be adulterated/substituted. A reference authentic specimen should be available for identification purposes;
- the water content for herbal substances, determined in accordance with the European Pharmacopoeia;
- assay of constituents of known therapeutic activity or, where appropriate, of markers;
- the methods suitable to determine possible pesticide contamination and limits accepted in accordance with European Pharmacopoeia methods or, in absence thereof, with an appropriate validated method, unless otherwise justified;
- tests to determine fungal and/or microbial contamination, including aflatoxins, other mycotoxins, pest infestations and limits accepted, as appropriate;
- tests for toxic metals and likely contaminants and adulterants, as appropriate;
- tests for foreign materials, as appropriate.
- any other additional test according to the European Pharmacopoeia general monograph on herbal substances or to the specific monograph of the herbal substance, as appropriate.

Any treatment used to reduce fungal/microbial contamination or other infestation should be documented. Specifications and procedures should be available and include details of process, tests and limits for residues.

Processing instructions

9   The processing instructions should describe the different operations carried out upon the herbal substance such as cleaning, drying, crushing and sifting, and include drying time and temperatures, and methods used to control cut size or particle size.

10   In particular, there should be written instructions and records, which ensure that each container of herbal substance is carefully examined to detect any adulteration/substitution or presence of foreign matter, such as metal or glass pieces, animal parts or excrement, stones, sand, etc., or rot and signs of decay.

11   The processing instructions should also describe security sieving or other methods of removing foreign materials and appropriate procedures for cleaning/selection of plant material before the storage of the approved herbal substance or before the start of manufacturing.

12   For the production of an herbal preparation, instructions should include details of solvent, time and temperature of extraction, details of any concentration stages and methods used.

Quality Control

Sampling

13   Due to the fact that medicinal plant/herbal substances are heterogeneous in nature, their sampling should be carried out with special care by personnel with particular expertise. Each batch should be identified by its own documentation.

14   A reference sample of the plant material is necessary, especially in those cases where the herbal substance is not described in the European Pharmacopoeia or in another Pharmacopoeia of a Member State. Samples of unmilled plant material are required if powders are used.

15   Quality Control personnel should have particular expertise and experience in herbal substances, herbal preparations and/or herbal medicinal products in order to be able to carry out identification tests and recognise

adulteration, the presence of fungal growth, infestations, non-uniformity within a delivery of crude material, etc.

16 The identity and quality of herbal substances, herbal preparations and herbal medicinal products should be determined in accordance with the relevant current European guidance on quality and specifications of herbal medicinal products and traditional herbal medicinal products and, where relevant, to the specific Ph.Eur. Monographs.

ANNEX 8 SAMPLING OF STARTING AND PACKAGING MATERIALS

Principle

Sampling is an important operation in which only a small fraction of a batch is taken. Valid conclusions on the whole cannot be based on tests that have been carried out on non-representative samples. Correct sampling is thus an essential part of a system of Quality Assurance.

Note: Sampling is dealt with in Chapter 6 of the Guide, items 6.11–6.14. This Annex gives additional guidance on the sampling of starting and packaging materials.

Personnel

1   Personnel who take samples should receive initial and on-going regular training in the disciplines relevant to correct sampling. This training should include:

- sampling plans;
- written sampling procedures;
- the techniques and equipment for sampling;
- the risks of cross-contamination;
- the precautions to be taken with regard to unstable and/or sterile substances;
- the importance of considering the visual appearance of materials, containers and labels;
- the importance of recording any unexpected or unusual circumstances.

Starting Materials

2   The identity of a complete batch of starting materials can normally be ensured only if individual samples are taken from all the containers and an identity test performed on each sample. It is permissible to sample only a proportion of the containers where a validated procedure has been established to ensure that no single container of starting material has been incorrectly labelled.

3   This validation should take account of at least the following aspects:

- the nature and status of the manufacturer and of the supplier and their understanding of the GMP requirements of the Pharmaceutical Industry;

- the Quality Assurance system of the manufacturer of the starting material;
- the manufacturing conditions under which the starting material is produced and controlled;
- the nature of the starting material and the medicinal products in which it will be used.

Under such a system, it is possible that a validated procedure exempting identity testing of each incoming container of starting material could be accepted for:

- starting materials coming from a single product manufacturer or plant;
- starting materials coming directly from a manufacturer or in the manufacturer's sealed container where there is a history of reliability and regular audits of the manufacturer's Quality Assurance system are conducted by the purchaser (the manufacturer of the medicinal product) or an officially accredited body.

It is improbable that a procedure could be satisfactorily validated for:

- starting materials supplied by intermediaries such as brokers where the source of manufacture is unknown or not audited;
- starting materials for use in parenteral products.

4 The quality of a batch of starting materials may be assessed by taking and testing a representative sample. The samples taken for identity testing could be used for this purpose. The number of samples taken for the preparation of a representative sample should be determined statistically and specified in a sampling plan. The number of individual samples that may be blended to form a composite sample should also be defined, taking into account the nature of the material, knowledge of the supplier and the homogeneity of the composite sample.

Packaging Material

5 The sampling plan for packaging materials should take account of at least the following: the quantity received, the quality required, the nature of the material (e.g. primary packaging materials and/or printed packaging materials), the production methods and what is known of the Quality Assurance system of the packaging materials' manufacturer based on audits. The number of samples taken should be determined statistically and specified in a sampling plan.

ANNEX 9 MANUFACTURE OF LIQUIDS, CREAMS AND OINTMENTS

Principle

Liquids, creams and ointments may be particularly susceptible to microbial and other contamination during manufacture. Therefore special measures must be taken to prevent any contamination.

Premises and Equipment

1   The use of closed systems for processing and transfer is recommended in order to protect the product from contamination. Production areas where the products or open clean containers are exposed should normally be effectively ventilated with filtered air.

2   Tanks, containers, pipework and pumps should be designed and installed so that they may be readily cleaned and, if necessary, sanitised. In particular, equipment design should include a minimum of dead-legs or sites where residues can accumulate and promote microbial proliferation.

3   The use of glass apparatus should be avoided wherever possible. High-quality stainless steel is often the material of choice for parts coming into contact with product.

Production

4   The chemical and microbiological quality of water used in production should be specified and monitored. Care should be taken in the maintenance of water systems in order to avoid the risk of microbial proliferation. After any chemical sanitisation of the water systems, a validated flushing procedure should be followed to ensure that the sanitising agent has been effectively removed.

5   The quality of materials received in bulk tankers should be checked before they are transferred to bulk storage tanks.

6   Care should be taken when transferring materials via pipelines to ensure that they are delivered to their correct destination.

7   Materials likely to shed fibres or other contaminants, such as cardboard or wooden pallets, should not enter the areas where products or clean containers are exposed.

8   Care should be taken to maintain the homogeneity of mixtures, suspensions, etc. during filling. Mixing and filling processes should be validated.

Special care should be taken at the beginning of a filling process, after stoppages and at the end of the process to ensure that homogeneity is maintained.

9   When the finished product is not immediately packaged, the maximum period of storage and the storage conditions should be specified and adhered to.

ANNEX 10 MANUFACTURE OF PRESSURISED METERED DOSE AEROSOL PREPARATIONS FOR INHALATION

Principle

The manufacture of pressurised aerosol products for inhalation with metering valves requires special consideration because of the particular nature of this form of product. It should be done under conditions that minimise microbial and particulate contamination. Assurance of the quality of the valve components and, in the case of suspensions, of uniformity is also of particular importance.

General

1   There are presently two common manufacturing and filling methods as follows:

(a) Two-shot system (pressure filling). The active ingredient is suspended in a high boiling point propellant, the dose is put into the container, the valve is crimped on and the lower boiling point propellant is injected through the valve stem to make up the finished product. The suspension of active ingredient in propellant is kept cool to reduce evaporation loss.

(b) One-shot process (cold filling). The active ingredient is suspended in a mixture of propellants and held either under high pressure or at a low temperature, or both. The suspension is then filled directly into the container in one shot.

Premises and Equipment

2   Manufacture and filling should be carried out as far as possible in a closed system.

3   Where products or clean components are exposed, the area should be fed with filtered air, should comply with the requirements of at least a Grade D environment and should be entered through airlocks.

Production and Quality Control

4   Metering valves for aerosols are more complex pieces of engineering than most items used in pharmaceutical production. Their specifications, sampling and testing should recognise this. Auditing the Quality Assurance system of the valve manufacturer is of particular importance.

5   All fluids (e.g. liquid or gaseous propellants) should be filtered to remove particles greater than 0.2 micron. An additional filtration, where possible immediately before filling, is desirable.

6   Containers and valves should be cleaned using a validated procedure appropriate to the use of the product to ensure the absence of any contaminants such as fabrication aids (e.g. lubricants) or undue microbiological contaminants. After cleaning, valves should be kept in clean, closed containers and precautions taken not to introduce contamination during subsequent handling, e.g. taking samples. Containers should be fed to the filling line in a clean condition or cleaned on line immediately before filling.

7   Precautions should be taken to ensure uniformity of suspensions at the point of fill throughout the filling process.

8   When a two-shot filling process is used, it is necessary to ensure that both shots are of the correct weight in order to achieve the correct composition. For this purpose, 100% weight checking at each stage is often desirable.

9   Controls, after filling, should ensure the absence of undue leakage. Any leakage test should be performed in a way that avoids microbial contamination or residual moisture.

ANNEX 11 COMPUTERISED SYSTEMS

Principle

This annex applies to all forms of computerised systems used as part of GMP-regulated activities. A computerised system is a set of software and hardware components that together fulfil certain functionalities.

The application should be validated; IT infrastructure should be qualified.

Where a computerised system replaces a manual operation, there should be no resultant decrease in product quality, process control or quality assurance. There should be no increase in the overall risk of the process.

General

1   Risk management

Risk management should be applied throughout the lifecycle of the computerised system taking into account patient safety, data integrity and product quality. As part of a risk management system, decisions on the extent of validation and data integrity controls should be based on a justified and documented risk assessment of the computerised system.

2   Personnel

There should be close cooperation between all relevant personnel such as Process Owner, System Owner, Qualified Persons and IT. All personnel should have appropriate qualifications, level of access and defined responsibilities to carry out their assigned duties.

3   Suppliers and service providers

3.1   When third parties (e.g. suppliers, service providers) are used, e.g. to provide, install, configure, integrate, validate, maintain (e.g. via remote access), modify or retain a computerised system or related service or for data processing, formal agreements must exist between the manufacturer and any third parties, and these agreements should include clear statements of the responsibilities of the third party. IT departments should be considered analogous.

3.2   The competence and reliability of a supplier are key factors when selecting a product or service provider. The need for an audit should be based on a risk assessment.

3.3 Documentation supplied with commercial off-the-shelf products should be reviewed by regulated users to check that user requirements are fulfilled.

3.4 Quality system and audit information relating to suppliers or developers of software and implemented systems should be made available to inspectors on request.

Project Phase

4   Validation

4.1 The validation documentation and reports should cover the relevant steps of the lifecycle. Manufacturers should be able to justify their standards, protocols, acceptance criteria, procedures and records based on their risk assessment.

4.2 Validation documentation should include change control records (if applicable) and reports on any deviations observed during the validation process.

4.3 An up-to-date listing of all relevant systems and their GMP functionality (inventory) should be available.
   For critical systems an up-to-date system description detailing the physical and logical arrangements, data flows and interfaces with other systems or processes, any hardware and software prerequisites and security measures should be available.

4.4 User Requirements Specifications should describe the required functions of the computerised system and be based on documented risk assessment and GMP impact. User requirements should be traceable throughout the life cycle.

4.5 The regulated user should take all reasonable steps, to ensure that the system has been developed in accordance with an appropriate quality management system. The supplier should be assessed appropriately.

4.6 For the validation of bespoke or customised computerised systems there should be a process in place that ensures the formal assessment and reporting of quality and performance measures for all the lifecycle stages of the system.

4.7 Evidence of appropriate test methods and test scenarios should be demonstrated. In particular, system (process) parameter limits, data limits and error handling should be considered. Automated testing tools and test environments should have documented assessments for their adequacy.

4.8   If data are transferred to another data format or system, validation should include checks that data is not altered in value and/or meaning during this migration process.

Operational Phase

5   Data

Computerised systems exchanging data electronically with other systems should include appropriate built-in checks for the correct and secure entry and processing of data, in order to minimize the risks.

6   Accuracy checks

For critical data entered manually, there should be an additional check on the accuracy of the data. This check may be done by a second operator or by validated electronic means. The criticality and the potential consequences of erroneous or incorrectly entered data to a system should be covered by risk management.

7   Data storage

7.1   Data should be secured by both physical and electronic means against damage. Stored data should be checked for accessibility, readability and accuracy. Access to data should be ensured throughout the retention period.

7.2   Regular backups of all relevant data should be done. Integrity and accuracy of backup data and the ability to restore the data should be checked during validation and monitored periodically.

8   Printouts

8.1   It should be possible to obtain clear printed copies of electronically stored data.

8.2   For records supporting batch release it should be possible to generate printouts indicating if any of the data has been changed since the original entry.

9   Audit trails

Consideration should be given, based on a risk assessment, to building into the system the creation of a record of all GMP-relevant changes and deletions (a system-generated "audit trail"). For change or deletion of GMP-relevant data the reason should be documented. Audit trails need to be available and convertible to a generally intelligible form and regularly reviewed.

10   Change and configuration management

Any changes to a computerised system including system configurations should be made only in a controlled manner in accordance with a defined procedure.

11   Periodic evaluation

Computerised systems should be periodically evaluated to confirm that they remain in a valid state and are compliant with GMP. Such evaluations should include, where appropriate, the current range of functionality, deviation records, incidents, problems, upgrade history, performance, reliability, security and validation status reports.

12   Security

12.1   Physical and/or logical controls should be in place to restrict access to the computerised system to authorised persons. Suitable methods of preventing unauthorised entry to the system may include the use of keys, pass cards, personal codes with passwords, biometrics, restricted access to computer equipment and data storage areas.

12.2   The extent of security controls depends on the criticality of the computerised system.

12.3   Creation, change and cancellation of access authorisations should be recorded.

12.4   Management systems for data and for documents should be designed to record the identity of operators entering, changing, confirming or deleting data, including date and time.

13   Incident management

All incidents, not only system failures and data errors, should be reported and assessed. The root cause of a critical incident should be identified and should form the basis of corrective and preventive actions.

14   Electronic signature

Electronic records may be signed electronically. Electronic signatures are expected to:

(a) have the same impact as hand-written signatures within the boundaries of the company,

(b) be permanently linked to their respective record,

(c) include the time and date that they were applied.

15   Batch release

When a computerised system is used for recording certification and batch release, the system should allow only Qualified Persons to certify the release of the batches, and it should clearly identify and record the person releasing or certifying the batches. This should be performed using an electronic signature.

16   Business continuity

For the availability of computerised systems supporting critical processes, provisions should be made to ensure continuity of support for those processes in the event of a system breakdown (e.g. a manual or alternative system). The time required to bring the alternative arrangements into use should be based on risk and appropriate for a particular system and the business process it supports. These arrangements should be adequately documented and tested.

17   Archiving

Data may be archived. This data should be checked for accessibility, readability and integrity. If relevant changes are to be made to the system (e.g. computer equipment or programs), then the ability to retrieve the data should be ensured and tested.

Glossary

APPLICATION

Software installed on a defined platform/hardware providing specific functionality.

BESPOKE/CUSTOMIZED COMPUTERISED SYSTEM

A computerised system individually designed to suit a specific business process.

COMMERCIAL OFF-THE-SHELF SOFTWARE

Software commercially available, the fitness of which for use is demonstrated by a broad spectrum of users.

IT INFRASTRUCTURE

The hardware and software, such as networking software and operation systems, which make it possible for the application to function.

LIFECYCLE

All phases in the life of the system from initial requirements until retirement, including design, specification, programming, testing, installation, operation and maintenance.

PROCESS OWNER

The person responsible for the business process.

SYSTEM OWNER

The person responsible for the availability and maintenance of a computerised system, and for the security of the data residing on that system.

THIRD PARTY

Parties not directly managed by the holder of the manufacturing and/or import authorisation.

EU GMP GUIDE PART I ANNEX 11
COMPUTERISED SYSTEMS

ANNEX 12 USE OF IONISING RADIATION IN THE MANUFACTURE OF MEDICINAL PRODUCTS

> **Note:** *The holder of, or applicant for, a marketing authorisation for a product that includes irradiation as part of its processing should also refer to the note produced by the Committee for Proprietary Medicinal Products giving guidance on "Ionising radiation in the manufacture of medicinal products".*

Introduction

Ionising radiation may be used during the manufacturing process for various purposes, including the reduction of bioburden and the sterilisation of starting materials, packaging components or products, and the treatment of blood products.

There are two types of irradiation process: gamma irradiation from a radioactive source and high-energy electron irradiation (beta radiation) from an accelerator.

Gamma irradiation: two different processing modes may be employed:

(i) Batch mode: the product is arranged at fixed locations around the radiation source and cannot be loaded or unloaded while the radiation source is exposed.

(ii) Continuous mode: an automatic system conveys the products into the radiation cell, past the exposed radiation source along a defined path and at an appropriate speed, and out of the cell.

Electron Irradiation: the product is conveyed past a continuous or pulsed beam of high-energy electrons (beta radiation) which is scanned back and forth across the product pathway.

Responsibilities

1 Treatment by irradiation may be carried out by the pharmaceutical manufacturer or an operator of a radiation facility under contract (a "contract manufacturer"), both of whom must hold an appropriate Manufacturing Authorisation.

2 The pharmaceutical manufacturer bears responsibility for the quality of the product including the attainment of the objective of irradiation. The contract operator of the radiation facility bears responsibility for ensuring

that the dose of radiation required by the manufacturer is delivered to the irradiation container (i.e. the outermost container in which the products are irradiated).

3   The required dose, including justified limits, will be stated in the Marketing Authorisation for the product.

Dosimetry

4   Dosimetry is defined as the measurement of the absorbed dose by the use of dosimeters. Both understanding and correct use of the technique are essential for the validation, commissioning and control of the process.

5   The calibration of each batch of routine dosimeters should be traceable to a national or international standard. The period of validity of the calibration should be stated, justified and adhered to.

6   The same instrument should normally be used to establish the calibration curve of the routine dosimeters and to measure the change in their absorbance after irradiation. If a different instrument is used, the absolute absorbance of each instrument should be established.

7   Depending on the type of dosimeter used, due account should be taken of possible causes of inaccuracy, including the change in moisture content, change in temperature, time elapsed between irradiation and measurement, and the dose rate.

8   The wavelength of the instrument used to measure the change in absorbance of dosimeters and the instrument used to measure their thickness should be subject to regular checks of calibration at intervals established on the basis of stability, purpose and usage.

Validation of the Process

9   Validation is the action of proving that the process, i.e. the delivery of the intended absorbed dose to the product, will achieve the expected results. The requirements for validation are given more fully in the note for guidance on "the use of ionising radiation in the manufacture of medicinal products".

10   Validation should include dose mapping to establish the distribution of absorbed dose within the irradiation container when packed with product in a defined configuration.

11   An irradiation process specification should include at least the following:

(a) details of the packaging of the product;
(b) the loading pattern(s) of product within the irradiation container. Particular care needs to be taken, when a mixture of products is allowed in the irradiation container, that there is no under-dosing of dense product or shadowing of other products by dense product. Each mixed product arrangement must be specified and validated;
(c) the loading pattern of irradiation containers around the source (batch mode) or the pathway through the cell (continuous mode);
(d) maximum and minimum limits of absorbed dose to the product (and associated routine dosimetry);
(e) maximum and minimum limits of absorbed dose to the irradiation container and associated routine dosimetry to monitor this absorbed dose;
(f) other process parameters, including dose rate, maximum time of exposure, number of exposures, etc.

When irradiation is supplied under contract at least parts (d) and (e) of the irradiation process specification should form part of that contract.

Commissioning of the Plant

General

12   Commissioning is the exercise of obtaining and documenting evidence that the irradiation plant will perform consistently within predetermined limits when operated according to the process specification. In the context of this annex, predetermined limits are the maximum and minimum doses designed to be absorbed by the irradiation container. It must not be possible for variations to occur in the operation of the plant that give a dose to the container outside these limits without the knowledge of the operator.

13   Commissioning should include the following elements:

(a) design;
(b) dose mapping;
(c) documentation;
(d) requirement for re-commissioning.

Gamma irradiators

DESIGN

14   The absorbed dose received by a particular part of an irradiation container at any specific point in the irradiator depends primarily on the following factors:

(a) the activity and geometry of the source;

(b) the distance from source to container;

(c) the duration of irradiation controlled by the timer setting or conveyor speed;

(d) the composition and density of material, including other products, between the source and the particular part of the container.

15   The total absorbed dose will in addition depend on the path of containers through a continuous irradiator or the loading pattern in a batch irradiator, and on the number of exposure cycles.

16   For a continuous irradiator with a fixed path or a batch irradiator with a fixed loading pattern, and a given source strength and type of product, the key plant parameter controlled by the operator is conveyor speed or timer setting.

DOSE MAPPING

17   For the dose mapping procedure, the irradiator should be filled with irradiation containers packed with dummy products or a representative product of uniform density. Dosimeters should be placed throughout a minimum of three loaded irradiation containers that are passed through the irradiator, surrounded by similar containers or dummy products. If the product is not uniformly packed, dosimeters should be placed in a larger number of containers.

18   The positioning of dosimeters will depend on the size of the irradiation container. For example, for containers up to $1 \times 1 \times 0.5$ m, a three-dimensional 20 cm grid throughout the container, including the outside surfaces, might be suitable. If the expected positions of the minimum and maximum dose are known from a previous irradiator performance characterisation, some dosimeters could be removed from regions of average dose and replaced to form a 10 cm grid in the regions of extreme dose.

19   The results of this procedure will give minimum and maximum absorbed doses in the product and on the container surface for a given set of plant parameters, product density and loading pattern.

20   Ideally, reference dosimeters should be used for the dose-mapping exercise because of their greater precision. Routine dosimeters are permissible, but it is advisable to place reference dosimeters beside them at the expected positions of minimum and maximum dose, and at the routine monitoring position in each of the replicate irradiation containers. The observed values of dose will have an associated random uncertainty that can be estimated from the variations in replicate measurements.

21   The minimum observed dose, as measured by the routine dosimeters, necessary to ensure that all irradiation containers receive the minimum required dose will be set in the knowledge of the random variability of the routine dosimeters used.

22   Irradiator parameters should be kept constant, monitored and recorded during dose mapping. The records, together with the dosimetry results and all other records generated, should be retained.

Electron beam irradiators

DESIGN

23   The absorbed dose received by a particular portion of an irradiated product depends primarily on the following factors:

(a) the characteristics of the beam, which are: electron energy, average beam current, scan width and scan uniformity;
(b) the conveyor speed;
(c) the product composition and density;
(d) the composition, density and thickness of material between the output window and the particular portion of product;
(e) the output window-to-container distance.

24   Key parameters controlled by the operator are the characteristics of the beam and the conveyor speed.

DOSE MAPPING

25   For the dose-mapping procedure, dosimeters should be placed between layers of homogeneous absorber sheets making up a dummy product, or between layers of representative products of uniform density, such that at least ten measurements can be made within the maximum range of the electrons. Reference should also be made to sections 18 to 21.

26   Irradiator parameters should be kept constant, monitored and recorded during dose mapping. The records, together with the dosimetry results and all other records generated, should be retained.

Re-commissioning

27   Commissioning should be repeated if there is a change to the process or the irradiator that could affect the dose distribution to the irradiation container (e.g. change of source pencils). The extent of re-commissioning

depends on the extent of the change in the irradiator or the load that has taken place. If in doubt, re-commission.

Premises

28   Premises should be designed and operated to segregate irradiated from non-irradiated containers to avoid their cross-contamination. Where materials are handled within closed irradiation containers, it may not be necessary to segregate pharmaceutical from non-pharmaceutical materials, provided that there is no risk of the former being contaminated by the latter.

Any possibility of contamination of the products by a radionuclide from the source must be excluded.

Processing

29   Irradiation containers should be packed in accordance with the specified loading pattern(s) established during validation.

30   During the process, the radiation dose to the irradiation containers should be monitored using validated dosimetry procedures. The relationship between this dose and the dose absorbed by the product inside the container must have been established during process validation and plant commissioning.

31   Radiation indicators should be used as an aid to differentiating irradiated from non-irradiated containers. They should not be used as the sole means of differentiation or as an indication of satisfactory processing.

32   Processing of mixed loads of containers within the irradiation cell should be done only when it is known from commissioning trials or other evidence that the radiation dose received by individual containers remains within the limits specified.

33   When the required radiation dose is, by design, given during more than one exposure or passage through the plant, this should be with the agreement of the holder of the Marketing Authorisation and occur within a predetermined time period. Unplanned interruptions during irradiation should be notified to the holder of the Marketing Authorisation if this extends the irradiation process beyond a previously agreed period.

34   Non-irradiated products must be segregated from irradiated products at all times. Methods of doing this include the use of radiation indicators (item 31) and appropriate design of premises (item 28).

Gamma irradiators

35 For continuous processing modes, dosimeters should be placed so that at least two are exposed in the irradiation at all times.

36 For batch modes, at least two dosimeters should be exposed in positions related to the minimum dose position.

37 For continuous process modes, there should be a positive indication of the correct position of the source and an interlock between source position and conveyor movement. Conveyor speed should be monitored continuously and recorded.

38 For batch process modes, source movement and exposure times for each batch should be monitored and recorded.

39 For a given desired dose, the timer setting or conveyor speed requires adjustment for source decay and source additions. The period of validity of the setting or speed should be recorded and adhered to.

Electron beam irradiators

40 A dosimeter should be placed on every container.

41 There should be continuous recording of average beam current, electron energy, scan width and conveyor speed. These variables, other than conveyor speed, need to be controlled within the defined limits established during commissioning because they are liable to instantaneous change.

Documentation

42 The numbers of containers received, irradiated and dispatched should be reconciled with each other and with the associated documentation. Any discrepancy should be reported and resolved.

43 The irradiation plant operator should certify in writing the range of doses received by each irradiated container within a batch or delivery.

44 Process and control records for each irradiation batch should be checked and signed by a nominated responsible person and retained. The method and place of retention should be agreed between the plant operator and the holder of the Marketing Authorisation.

45 The documentation associated with the validation and commissioning of the plant should be retained for one year after the expiry date or at

least five years after the release of the last product processed by the plant, whichever is the longer.

Microbiological Monitoring

46 Microbiological monitoring is the responsibility of the pharmaceutical manufacturer. It may include environmental monitoring where product is manufactured and pre-irradiation monitoring of the product as specified in the Marketing Authorisation.

ANNEX 13 INVESTIGATIONAL MEDICINAL PRODUCTS

Principle

Investigational medicinal products should be produced in accordance with the principles and the detailed guidelines of Good Manufacturing Practice for Medicinal Products (The Rules Governing Medicinal Products in The European Community, Volume IV). Other guidelines published by the European Commission should be taken into account where relevant and as appropriate to the stage of development of the product. Procedures need to be flexible to provide for changes as knowledge of the process increases, and appropriate to the stage of development of the product.

In clinical trials there may be added risk to participating subjects compared to patients treated with marketed products. The application of GMP to the manufacture of investigational medicinal products is intended to ensure that trial subjects are not placed at risk, and that the results of clinical trials are unaffected by inadequate safety, quality or efficacy arising from unsatisfactory manufacture. Equally, it is intended to ensure that there is consistency between batches of the same investigational medicinal product used in the same or different clinical trials, and that changes during the development of an investigational medicinal product are adequately documented and justified.

The production of investigational medicinal products involves added complexity in comparison to marketed products by virtue of the lack of fixed routines, variety of clinical trial designs, consequent packaging designs, and the need, often, for randomisation and blinding and increased risk of product cross-contamination and mix up. Furthermore, there may be incomplete knowledge of the potency and toxicity of the product and a lack of full process validation, or, marketed products may be used which have been re-packaged or modified in some way. These challenges require personnel with a thorough understanding of, and training in, the application of GMP to investigational medicinal products. Co-operation is required with trial sponsors who undertake the ultimate responsibility for all aspects of the clinical trial including the quality of investigational medicinal products. The increased complexity in manufacturing operations requires a highly effective quality system.

The Annex also includes guidance on ordering, shipping, and returning clinical supplies, which are at the interface with, and complementary to, guidelines on Good Clinical Practice.

Notes

NON-INVESTIGATIONAL MEDICINAL PRODUCT[1]

Products other than the test product, placebo or comparator may be supplied to subjects participating in a trial. Such products may be used as support or escape medication for preventative, diagnostic or therapeutic reasons and/or needed to ensure that adequate medical care is provided for the subject. They may also be used in accordance with the protocol to induce a physiological response. These products do not fall within the definition of investigational medicinal products and may be supplied by the sponsor, or the investigator. The sponsor should ensure that they are in accordance with the notification/request for authorisation to conduct the trial and that they are of appropriate quality for the purposes of the trial taking into account the source of the materials, whether or not they are the subject of a marketing authorisation and whether they have been repackaged. The advice and involvement of a Qualified Person is recommended in this task.

MANUFACTURING AUTHORISATION AND RECONSTITUTION

Both the total and partial manufacture of investigational medicinal products, as well as the various processes of dividing up, packaging or presentation, is subject to the authorisation referred to in Article 13(1) Directive 2001/20/EC, cf. Article 9(1) Directive 2005/28/EC. This authorisation, however, shall not be required for reconstitution under the conditions set out in Article 9(2) Directive 2005/28/EC. For the purpose of this provision, reconstitution shall be understood as a simple process of:

- dissolving or dispersing the investigational medicinal product for administration of the product to a trial subject,
- or, diluting or mixing the investigational medicinal product(s) with some other substance(s) used as a vehicle for the purposes of administering it,

Reconstitution is not mixing several ingredients, including the active substance, together to produce the investigational medicinal product.

An investigational medicinal product must exist before a process can be defined as reconstitution.

The process of reconstitution has to be undertaken as soon as practicable before administration.

This process has to be defined in the clinical trial application / IMP dossier and clinical trial protocol, or related document, available at the site.

---

[1] Further information can be found in the European Commission's Guidance on Investigational Medicinal Products (IMPs) and other Medicinal Products used in Clinical Trials

Glossary

BLINDING

A procedure in which one or more parties to the trial are kept unaware of the treatment assignment(s). Single-blinding usually refers to the subject(s) being unaware, and double-blinding usually refers to the subject(s), investigator(s), monitor, and, in some cases, data analyst(s) being unaware of the treatment assignment(s). In relation to an investigational medicinal product, blinding shall mean the deliberate disguising of the identity of the product in accordance with the instructions of the sponsor. Unblinding shall mean the disclosure of the identity of blinded products.

CLINICAL TRIAL

Any investigation in human subjects intended to discover or verify the clinical, pharmacological and/or other pharmacodynamic effects of an investigational product(s) and/or to identify any adverse reactions to an investigational product(s), and/or to study absorption, distribution, metabolism, and excretion of one or more investigational medicinal product(s) with the object of ascertaining its/their safety and/or efficacy.

COMPARATOR PRODUCT

An investigational or marketed product (i.e. active control), or placebo, used as a reference in a clinical trial.

INVESTIGATIONAL MEDICINAL PRODUCT

A pharmaceutical form of an active substance or placebo being tested or used as a reference in a clinical trial, including a product with a marketing authorisation when used or assembled (formulated or packaged) in a way different from the authorised form, or when used for an unauthorised indication, or when used to gain further information about the authorised form.

INVESTIGATOR

A person responsible for the conduct of the clinical trial at a trial site. If a trial is conducted by a team of individuals at a trial site, the investigator is the responsible leader of the team and may be called the principal investigator.

MANUFACTURER/IMPORTER OF INVESTIGATIONAL MEDICINAL PRODUCTS

Any person engaged in activities for which the authorisation referred to in Article 13(1) of Directive 2001/20/EC is required.

ORDER

Instruction to process, package and/or ship a certain number of units of investigational medicinal product(s).

PRODUCT SPECIFICATION FILE

A reference file containing, or referring to files containing, all the information necessary to draft the detailed written instructions on processing, packaging, quality control testing, batch release and shipping of an investigational medicinal product.

RANDOMISATION

The process of assigning trial subjects to treatment or control groups using an element of chance to determine the assignments in order to reduce bias.

RANDOMISATION CODE

A listing in which the treatment assigned to each subject from the randomisation process is identified.

SHIPPING

The operation of packaging for shipment and sending of ordered medicinal products for clinical trials.

SPONSOR

An individual, company, institution or organisation which takes responsibility for the initiation, management and/or financing of a clinical trial.

Quality Management

1 The Quality System, designed, set up and verified by the manufacturer or importer, should be described in written procedures available to the sponsor, taking into account the GMP principles and guidelines applicable to investigational medicinal products.

2 The product specifications and manufacturing instructions may be changed during development but full control and traceability of the changes should be maintained.

Personnel

3 All personnel involved with investigational medicinal products should be appropriately trained in the requirements specific to these types of product.
　Even in cases where the number of staff involved is small, there should be, for each batch, separate people responsible for production and quality control.

4 The Qualified Person should ensure that there are systems in place that meet the requirements of GMP and should have a broad knowledge of

pharmaceutical development and clinical trial processes. Guidance for the Qualified Person in connection with the certification of investigational medicinal products is given in paragraphs 38 to 41.

Premises and Equipment

5   The toxicity, potency and sensitising potential may not be fully understood for investigational medicinal products and this reinforces the need to minimise all risks of cross-contamination. The design of equipment and premises, inspection / test methods and acceptance limits to be used after cleaning should reflect the nature of these risks. Consideration should be given to campaign working where appropriate. Account should be taken of the solubility of the product in decisions about the choice of cleaning solvent.

Documentation

Specifications and instructions

6   Specifications (for starting materials, primary packaging materials, intermediate, bulk products and finished products), manufacturing formulae and processing and packaging instructions should be as comprehensive as possible given the current state of knowledge. They should be periodically re-assessed during development and updated as necessary. Each new version should take into account the latest data, current technology used, regulatory and pharmacopoeial requirements, and should allow traceability to the previous document. Any changes should be carried out according to a written procedure, which should address any implications for product quality such as stability and bio equivalence.

7   Rationales for changes should be recorded and the consequences of a change on product quality and on any on-going clinical trials should be investigated and documented2.

Order

8   The order should request the processing and/or packaging of a certain number of units and/or their shipping and be given by or on behalf of the sponsor to the manufacturer. It should be in writing (though it may be transmitted by electronic means), and precise enough to avoid any ambiguity. It should be formally authorised and refer to the Product Specification File and the relevant clinical trial protocol as appropriate.

Product Specification File

9 The Product Specification File (see glossary) should be continually updated as development of the product proceeds, ensuring appropriate traceability to the previous versions. It should include, or refer to, the following documents:

- Specifications and analytical methods for starting materials, packaging materials;
- Intermediate, bulk and finished product;
- Manufacturing methods;
- In-process testing and methods;
- Approved label copy;
- Relevant clinical trial protocols and randomisation codes, as appropriate;
- Relevant technical agreements with contract givers, as appropriate;
- Stability data;
- Storage and shipment conditions.

The above listing is not intended to be exclusive or exhaustive. The contents will vary depending on the product and stage of development. The information should form the basis for assessment of the suitability for certification and release of a particular batch by the Qualified Person and should therefore be accessible to him/her. Where different manufacturing steps are carried out at different locations under the responsibility of different Qualified Persons, it is acceptable to maintain separate files limited to information of relevance to the activities at the respective locations.

Manufacturing Formulae and Processing Instructions

10 For every manufacturing operation or supply there should be clear and adequate written instructions and written records. Where an operation is not repetitive it may not be necessary to produce Master Formulae and Processing Instructions. Records are particularly important for the preparation of the final version of the documents to be used in routine manufacture once the marketing authorisation is granted.

11 The information in the Product Specification File should be used to produce the detailed written instructions on processing, packaging, quality control testing, storage conditions and shipping.

---

[2] Guidance on changes that require the request of a substantial amendment to the IMP dossier submitted to the Competent Authorities is given in the CHMP guideline on the Requirements to the Chemical and Pharmaceutical Quality Documentation Concerning Investigational Medicinal Products in Clinical Trials

Packaging Instructions

12   Investigational medicinal products are normally packed in an individual way for each subject included in the clinical trial. The number of units to be packaged should be specified prior to the start of the packaging operations, including units necessary for carrying out quality control and any retention samples to be kept. Sufficient reconciliations should take place to ensure the correct quantity of each product required has been accounted for at each stage of processing.

Processing, testing and packaging batch records

13   Batch records should be kept in sufficient detail for the sequence of operations to be accurately determined. These records should contain any relevant remarks which justify the procedures used and any changes made, enhance knowledge of the product and develop the manufacturing operations.

14   Batch manufacturing records should be retained at least for the periods specified in Directive 2003/94/EC.

Production

Packaging materials

15   Specifications and quality control checks should include measures to guard against unintentional unblinding due to changes in appearance between different batches of packaging materials.

Manufacturing operations

16   During development critical parameters should be identified and in-process controls primarily used to control the process. Provisional production parameters and in-process controls may be deduced from prior experience, including that gained from earlier development work. Careful consideration by key personnel is called for in order to formulate the necessary instructions and to adapt them continually to the experience gained in production. Parameters identified and controlled should be justifiable based on knowledge available at the time.

17   Production processes for investigational medicinal products are not expected to be validated to the extent necessary for routine production but

premises and equipment are expected to be qualified. For sterile products, the validation of sterilising processes should be of the same standard as for products authorised for marketing. Likewise, when required, virus inactivation/removal and that of other impurities of biological origin should be demonstrated, to assure the safety of biotechnologically derived products, by following the scientific principles and techniques defined in the available guidance in this area.

18 Validation of aseptic processes presents special problems when the batch size is small; in these cases the number of units filled may be the maximum number filled in production. If practicable, and otherwise consistent with simulating the process, a larger number of units should be filled with media to provide greater confidence in the results obtained. Filling and sealing is often a manual or semi-automated operation presenting great challenges to sterility so enhanced attention should be given to operator training, and validating the aseptic technique of individual operators.

Principles applicable to comparator product

19 If a product is modified, data should be available (e.g. stability, comparative dissolution, bioavailability) to demonstrate that these changes do not significantly alter the original quality characteristics of the product.

20 The expiry date stated for the comparator product in its original packaging might not be applicable to the product where it has been repackaged in a different container that may not offer equivalent protection, or be compatible with the product. A suitable use-by date, taking into account the nature of the product, the characteristics of the container and the storage conditions to which the article may be subjected, should be determined by or on behalf of the sponsor. Such a date should be justified and must not be later than the expiry date of the original package. There should be compatibility of expiry dating and clinical trial duration.

Blinding operations

21 Where products are blinded, systems should be in place to ensure that the blind is achieved and maintained while allowing for identification of "blinded" products when necessary, including the batch numbers of the products before the blinding operation. Rapid identification of product should also be possible in an emergency.

EU GMP GUIDE PART I ANNEX 13 INVESTIGATIONAL MEDICINAL PRODUCTS

Randomisation code

22   Procedures should describe the generation, security, distribution, handling and retention of any randomisation code used for packaging investigational products, and code-break mechanisms. Appropriate records should be maintained.

Packaging

23   During packaging of investigational medicinal products, it may be necessary to handle different products on the same packaging line at the same time. The risk of product mix up must be minimised by using appropriate procedures and/or, specialised equipment as appropriate and relevant staff training.

24   Packaging and labelling of investigational medicinal products are likely to be more complex and more liable to errors (which are also harder to detect) than for marketed products, particularly when "blinded" products with similar appearance are used. Precautions against mis-labelling such as label reconciliation, line clearance, in process control checks by appropriately trained staff should accordingly be intensified.

25   The packaging must ensure that the investigational medicinal product remains in good condition during transport and storage at intermediate destinations. Any opening or tampering of the outer packaging during transport should be readily discernible.

Labelling

26   Table 1 summarises the contents of Articles 26-30 that follow. Labelling should comply with the requirements of Directive 2003/94/EC. The following information should be included on labels, unless its absence can be justified, e.g. use of a centralised electronic randomisation system:

    (a) name, address and telephone number of the sponsor, contract research organisation or investigator (the main contact for information on the product, clinical trial and emergency unblinding);

    (b) pharmaceutical dosage form, route of administration, quantity of dosage units, and in the case of open trials, the name/identifier and strength/potency;

    (c) the batch and/or code number to identify the contents and packaging operation;

    (d) a trial reference code allowing identification of the trial, site, investigator and sponsor if not given elsewhere;

(e) the trial subject identification number/treatment number and where relevant, the visit number;

(f) the name of the investigator (if not included in (a) or (d));

(g) directions for use (reference may be made to a leaflet or other explanatory document intended for the trial subject or person administering the product);

(h) "For clinical trial use only" or similar wording;

(i) the storage conditions;

(j) period of use (use-by date, expiry date or re-test date as applicable), in month/year format and in a manner that avoids any ambiguity.

(k) "keep out of reach of children" except when the product is for use in trials where the product is not taken home by subjects.

27 The address and telephone number of the main contact for information on the product, clinical trial and for emergency unblinding need not appear on the label where the subject has been given a leaflet or card which provides these details and has been instructed to keep this in their possession at all times.

28 Particulars should appear in the official language(s) of the country in which the investigational medicinal product is to be used. The particulars listed in Article 26 should appear on the primary packaging and on the secondary packaging (except for the cases described in Articles 29 and 30). The requirements with respect to the contents of the label on the primary and outer packaging are summarised in Table 1. Other languages may be included.

29 When the product is to be provided to the trial subject or the person administering the medication within a primary package together with secondary packaging that is intended to remain together, and the secondary packaging carries the particulars listed in Paragraph 26, the following information shall be included on the label of the primary package (or any sealed dosing device that contains the primary packaging):

(a) name of sponsor, contract research organisation or investigator;

(b) pharmaceutical dosage form, route of administration (may be excluded for oral solid dose forms), quantity of dosage units and in the case of open label trials, the name/identifier and strength/potency;

(c) batch and/or code number to identify the contents and packaging operation;

(d) a trial reference code allowing identification of the trial, site, investigator and sponsor if not given elsewhere;

(e) the trial subject identification number/treatment number and where relevant, the visit number.

30 If the primary packaging takes the form of blister packs or small units such as ampoules on which the particulars required in Paragraph 26 cannot be

displayed, secondary packaging should be provided bearing a label with those particulars. The primary packaging should nevertheless contain the following:

(a) name of sponsor, contract research organisation or investigator;

(b) route of administration (may be excluded for oral solid dose forms) and in the case of open label trials, the name/identifier and strength/potency;

(c) batch and/or code number to identify the contents and packaging operation;

(d) a trial reference code allowing identification of the trial, site, investigator and sponsor if not given elsewhere;

(e) the trial subject identification number/treatment number and where relevant, the visit number;

31 Symbols or pictograms may be included to clarify certain information mentioned above. Additional information, warnings and/or handling instructions may be displayed.

32 For clinical trials with the characteristics identified in Article 14 of Directive 2001/20/EC, the following particulars should be added to the original container but should not obscure the original labelling:

(i)   name of sponsor, contract research organisation or investigator;

(ii)   trial reference code allowing identification of the trial site, investigator and trial subject.

33 If it becomes necessary to change the use-by date, an additional label should be affixed to the investigational medicinal product. This additional label should state the new use-by date and repeat the batch number. It may be superimposed on the old use-by date, but for quality control reasons, not on the original batch number. This operation should be performed at an appropriately authorised manufacturing site. However, when justified, it may be performed at the investigational site by or under the supervision of the clinical trial site pharmacist, or other health care professional in accordance with national regulations. Where this is not possible, it may be performed by the clinical trial monitor(s) who should be appropriately trained. The operation should be performed in accordance with GMP principles, specific and standard operating procedures and under contract, if applicable, and should be checked by a second person. This additional labelling should be properly documented in both the trial documentation and in the batch records.

Quality Control

34 As processes may not be standardised or fully validated, testing takes on more importance in ensuring that each batch meets its specification.

35   Quality control should be performed in accordance with the Product Specification File and in accordance with the information notified pursuant to Article 9(2) of Directive 2001/20/EC. Verification of the effectiveness of blinding should be performed and recorded.

36   Samples are retained to fulfill two purposes; firstly to provide a sample for analytical testing and secondly to provide a specimen of the finished product. Samples may therefore fall into two categories:

    Reference sample: a sample of a batch of starting material, packaging material, product contained in its primary packaging or finished product which is stored for the purpose of being analysed should the need arise. Where stability permits, reference samples from critical intermediate stages (e.g. those requiring analytical testing and release) or intermediates, which are transported outside of the manufacturer's control, should be kept.

    Retention sample: a sample of a packaged unit from a batch of finished product for each packaging run/trial period. It is stored for identification purposes. For example, presentation, packaging, labeling, leaflet, batch number, expiry date should the need arise.

    In many instances the reference and retention samples will be presented identically, i.e. as fully packaged units. In such circumstances, reference and retention samples may be regarded as interchangeable.Reference and retention samples of investigational medicinal product, including blinded product should be kept for at least two years after completion or formal discontinuation of the last clinical trial in which the batch was used, whichever period is the longer.

    Consideration should be given to keeping retention samples until the clinical report has been prepared to enable confirmation of product identity in the event of, and as part of an investigation into inconsistent trial results.

37   The storage location of Reference and Retention samples should be defined in a Technical Agreement between the sponsor and manufacturer(s) and should allow timely access by the competent authorities.

    Reference samples of finished product should be stored within the EEA or in a third country where appropriate arrangements have been made by the Community with the exporting country to ensure that the manufacturer of the investigational medicinal product applies standards of good manufacturing practice at least equivalent to those laid down by the Community. In exceptional circumstances the reference samples of the finished product may be stored by the manufacturer in another third country, in which case this should be justified, and documented in a technical agreement between the sponsor, importer in the EEA and that third country manufacturer.

    The reference sample should be of sufficient size to permit the carrying out, on, at least, two occasions, of the full analytical controls on the batch in accordance with the IMP dossier submitted for authorisation to conduct the clinical trial.

In the case of *retention samples*, it is acceptable to store information related to the final packaging as written or electronic records if such records provide sufficient information. In the case of the latter, the system should comply with the requirements of Annex 11.

Release of Batches

38   Release of investigational medicinal products (see paragraph 43) should not occur until after the Qualified Person has certified that the requirements of Article 13.3 of Directive 2001/20/EC have been met (see paragraph 39). The Qualified Person should take into account the elements listed in paragraph 40 as appropriate.

39   The duties of the Qualified Person in relation to investigational medicinal products are affected by the different circumstances that can arise and are referred to below. Table 2 summarises the elements that need to be considered for the most common circumstances:

(a) i) Product manufactured within EU but not subject to an EU marketing authorisation: the duties are laid down in article 13.3(a) of Directive 2001/20/EC.

(b) ii) Product sourced from the open market within EU in accordance with Article 80(b) of Directive 2001/83/EC and subject to an EU marketing authorisation, regardless of manufacturing origin: the duties are as described above, however, the scope of certification can be limited to assuring that the products are in accordance with the notification/request for authorisation to conduct the trial and any subsequent processing for the purpose of blinding, trial-specific packaging and labelling. The Product Specification File will be similarly restricted in scope (see 9).

(c) Product imported directly from a 3rd country: the duties are laid down in article 13.3(b) of Directive 2001/20/EC. Where investigational medicinal products are imported from a 3rd country and they are subject to arrangements concluded between the Community and that country, such as a Mutual Recognition Agreement (MRA), equivalent standards of Good Manufacturing Practice apply provided any such agreement is relevant to the product in question. In the absence of an MRA, the Qualified Person should determine that equivalent standards of Good Manufacturing Practice apply through knowledge of the quality system employed at the manufacturer. This knowledge is normally acquired through audit of the manufacturer's quality systems. In either case, the Qualified Person may then certify on the basis of documentation supplied by the 3rd country manufacturer (see 40).

(d) For imported comparator products where adequate assurance cannot be obtained in order to certify that each batch has been manufactured to equivalent standards of Good Manufacturing Practice, the duty of the Qualified Person is defined in article 13.3(c) of Directive 2001/20/EC.

40   Assessment of each batch for certification prior to release may include as appropriate:

- batch records, including control reports, in-process test reports and release reports demonstrating compliance with the product specification file, the order, protocol and randomisation code. These records should include all deviations or planned changes, and any consequent additional checks or tests, and should be completed and endorsed by the staff authorised to do so according to the quality system;
- production conditions;
- the validation status of facilities, processes and methods;
- examination of finished packs;
- where relevant, the results of any analyses or tests performed after importation;
- stability reports;
- the source and verification of conditions of storage and shipment;
- audit reports concerning the quality system of the manufacturer;
- Documents certifying that the manufacturer is authorised to manufacture investigational medicinal products or comparators for export by the appropriate authorities in the country of export;
- where relevant, regulatory requirements for marketing authorisation, GMP standards applicable and any official verification of GMP compliance;
- all other factors of which the QP is aware that are relevant to the quality of the batch.

The relevance of the above elements is affected by the country of origin of the product, the manufacturer, and the marketed status of the product (with or without a marketing authorisation, in the EU or in a third country) and its phase of development. The sponsor should ensure that the elements taken into account by the qualified person when certifying the batch are consistent with the information notified pursuant to Article 9(2) of Directive 2001/20/EC. See also section 44.

41   Where investigational medicinal products are manufactured and packaged at different sites under the supervision of different Qualified Persons, the recommendations listed in Annex 16 to the GMP Guide should be followed as applicable.

42   Where, permitted in accordance with local regulations, packaging or labelling is carried out at the investigator site by, or under the supervision of a clinical trials pharmacist, or other health care professional as allowed in those regulations, the Qualified Person is not required to certify the activ-

ity in question. The sponsor is nevertheless responsible for ensuring that the activity is adequately documented and carried out in accordance with the principles of GMP and should seek the advice of the Qualified Person in this regard.

Shipping

43   Investigational medicinal products should remain under the control of the sponsor until after completion of a two-step procedure: certification by the Qualified Person; and release by the sponsor for use in a clinical trial following fulfillment of the requirements of Article 9 (Commencement of a clinical trial) of Directive 2001/20/EC. Both steps should be recorded[3] and retained in the relevant trial files held by or on behalf of the sponsor. The Sponsor should ensure that the details set out in the clinical trial application and considered by the Qualified Person are consistent with what is finally accepted by the Competent Authorities. Suitable arrangements to meet this requirement should be established. In practical terms, this can best be achieved through a change control process for the Product Specification File and defined in a Technical Agreement between the QP and the Sponsor.

44   Shipping of investigational products should be conducted according to instructions given by or on behalf of the sponsor in the shipping order.

45   De-coding arrangements should be available to the appropriate responsible personnel before investigational medicinal products are shipped to the investigator site.

46   A detailed inventory of the shipments made by the manufacturer or importer should be maintained. It should particularly mention the addressees' identification.

47   Transfers of investigational medicinal products from one trial site to another should remain the exception. Such transfers should be covered by standard operating procedures. The product history while outside of the control of the manufacturer, through for example, trial monitoring reports and records of storage conditions at the original trial site should be reviewed as part of the assessment of the product's suitability for transfer and the advice of the Qualified person should be sought. The product should be returned to the manufacturer, or another authorised manufacturer, for re-labelling, if necessary, and certification by a Qualified Person. Records should be retained and full traceability ensured.

---

[3] A harmonised format for batch certification to facilitate movement between Member States is provided in attachment 3.

Complaints

48   The conclusions of any investigation carried out in relation to a complaint which could arise from the quality of the product should be discussed between the manufacturer or importer and the sponsor (if different). This should involve the Qualified Person and those responsible for the relevant clinical trial in order to assess any potential impact on the trial, product development and on subjects.

Recalls and Returns

Recalls

49   Procedures for retrieving investigational medicinal products and documenting this retrieval should be agreed by the sponsor, in collaboration with the manufacturer or importer where different. The investigator and monitor need to understand their obligations under the retrieval procedure.

50   The Sponsor should ensure that the supplier of any comparator or other medication to be used in a clinical trial has a system for communicating to the Sponsor the need to recall any product supplied.

Returns

51   Investigational medicinal products should be returned on agreed conditions defined by the sponsor, specified in approved written procedures.

52   Returned investigational medicinal products should be clearly identified and stored in an appropriately controlled, dedicated area. Inventory records of the returned medicinal products should be kept.

Destruction

53   The Sponsor is responsible for the destruction of unused and/or returned investigational medicinal products. Investigational medicinal products should therefore not be destroyed without prior written authorisation by the Sponsor.

54   The delivered, used and recovered quantities of product should be recorded, reconciled and verified by or on behalf of the sponsor for each trial site and each trial period. Destruction of unused investigational medicinal products should be carried out for a given trial site or a given trial period only

after any discrepancies have been investigated and satisfactorily explained and the reconciliation has been accepted. Recording of destruction operations should be carried out in such a manner that all operations may be accounted for. The records should be kept by the Sponsor.

55   When destruction of investigational medicinal products takes place a dated certificate of, or receipt for destruction, should be provided to the sponsor. These documents should clearly identify, or allow traceability to, the batches and/or patient numbers involved and the actual quantities destroyed.

Table 1: Summary of Labelling Details (§26 To 30)

a) name, address and telephone number of the sponsor, contract research organisation or investigator (the main contact for information on the product, clinical trial and emergency unblinding);

(b) pharmaceutical dosage form, route of administration, quantity of dosage units, and in the case of open trials, the name/identifier and strength/potency;

(c) the batch and/or code number to identify the contents and packaging operation;

(d) a trial reference code allowing identification of the trial, site, investigator and sponsor if not given elsewhere;

(e) the trial subject identification number/treatment number and where relevant, the visit number;

(f) the name of the investigator (if not included in (a) or (d);

(g) directions for use (reference may be made to a leaflet or other explanatory document intended for the trial subject or person administering the product

(h) "for clinical trial use only" or similar wording;

(i) the storage conditions;

(j) period of use (use-by date, expiry date or re-test date as applicable), in month/year format and in a manner that avoids any ambiguity.

(k) "keep out of reach of children" except when the product is for use in trials where the product is not taken home by subjects.

GENERAL CASE
For both the primary and secondary packaging (§26)

> Particulars a[4] to k

PRIMARY PACKAGE
Where primary and secondary packaging remain together throughout (§29)[5]

> a[6] b[7] c d e

PRIMARY PACKAGE
Blisters or small packaging units (§30)[5]

> a[6] b[7,8] c d e

---

[4] The address and telephone number of the main contact for information on the product, clinical trial and for emergency unblinding need not appear on the label where the subject has been given a leaflet or card which provides these details and has been instructed to keep this in their possession at all times (§ 27).

[5] When the outer packaging carries the particulars listed in Article 26.

[6] The address and telephone number of the main contact for information on the product, clinical trial and for emergency unblinding need not be included.

[7] Route of administration may be excluded for oral solid dose forms.

[8] The pharmaceutical dosage form and quantity of dosage units may be omitted.

Table 2: Batch Release of Products

ELEMENTS TO BE TAKEN INTO ACCOUNT(3)	PRODUCT AVAILABLE IN THE EU		PRODUCT IMPORTED FROM THIRD COUNTRIES		
	Product manufactured in EU without MA	Product with MA and available on EU market	Product without any EU MA	Product with a EU MA	Comparator where documentation certifying that each batch has been manufactured in conditions at least equivalent to those laid down in Directive 2003/94/EC cannot be obtained
BEFORE CLINICAL TRIAL PROCESSING					
a) Shipping and storage conditions	Yes				
b) All relevant factors (1) showing that each batch has been manufactured and released in accordance with: Directive 2003/94/EC, or GMP standards at least equivalent to those laid down in Directive 2003/94/EC.	Yes -		Yes (2)		
c) Documentation showing that each batch has been released within the EU according to EU GMP requirements (see Directive 2001/83/EC, article 51), or documentation showing that the product is available on the EU market and has been procured in accordance with article 80(b) of Directive 2001/83/EC.		Yes			
d) Documentation showing that the product is available on the local market and documentation to establish confidence in the local regulatory requirements for marketing authorisation and release for local use.					Yes
e) Results of all analysis, tests and checks performed to assess the quality of the imported batch according to:					
the requirements of the MA (see Directive 2001/83/EC, article 51b), or			-	Yes	-
the Product Specification File, the Order, article 9.2 submission to the regulatory authorities.			Yes	-	Yes
Where these analyses and tests are not performed in the EU, this should be justified and the QP must certify that they have been carried out in accordance with GMP standards at least equivalent to those laid down in Directive 2003/94/EC.			Yes	Yes	Yes
AFTER CLINICAL TRIAL PROCESSING					
f) In addition to the assessment before clinical trial processing, all further relevant factors (1) showing that each batch has been processed for the purposes of blinding, trial-specific packaging, labelling and testing in accordance with: Directive 2003/94/EC, or GMP standards at least equivalent to those laid down in Directive 2003/94/EC.	Yes -		Yes (2)		

Attachment 3

[LETTERHEAD OF MANUFACTURER]

Content of the Batch Certificate

Referred to in Art. 13.3 Directive 2001/20/EC

(1)   Name(s) of product(s)/product identifier(s) as referred to in the clinical trial application, where applicable.

(2)   EudraCT No(s) and sponsor protocol code number, when available.

(3)   Strength

   Identity (name) and amount per unit dose for all active substance(s) for each IMP (including placebo). The manner in which this information is provided should not unblind the study.

(4)   Dosage form (pharmaceutical form)

(5)   Package size (contents of container) and type (e.g. vials, bottles, blisters).

(6)   Lot/batch number

(7)   Expiry/retest/use by date

(8)   Name and address of manufacturer where the Qualified Person issuing the certificate is located.

(9)   Manufacturing Authorisation number for the site listed under item 8.

(10)   Comments/remarks

(11)   Any additional information considered relevant by the QP.

(12)   Certification statement.

(13)   "I hereby certify that this batch complies with the requirements of Article 13.3 of Directive 2001/20/EC "

(14)   Name of the QP signing the certificate

(15)   Signature

(16)   Date of signature

Explanatory Note

Investigational medicinal products may not be used in a clinical trial in a member state of the European Economic Area until the completion of the two-step procedure referred to in section 43 of this Annex. The first step is the certification of each batch by the Qualified Person of the manufacturer or importer that the provisions of Article 13.3(a), (b) or (c) of Directive 2001/20/EC have been complied with and documented in accordance with Art. 13.4 of the same Directive. According to Directive 2001/20/EC a batch of investigational medicinal product shall not have to undergo further checks in relation to the provisions of article 13.3(a), (b) or (c) of the same directive when it moves between Member States accompanied by batch certification signed by the Qualified Person. In order to facilitate the free movement of investigational medicinal products between Member States the content of these certificates should be in accordance with the above harmonised format. This format may also be used to certify batches destined for use within the Member State of the manufacturer or importer.

ANNEX 13 INVESTIGATIONAL MEDICINAL PRODUCTS

Detailed Commission guidelines on Good Manufacturing Practice for investigational medicinal products for human use, pursuant to the second subparagraph of Article 63(1) of Regulation (EU) No. 536/2014.

Editor's note:	These guidelines lay down appropriate tools to address specific issues concerning investigational medicinal products with regard to Good Manufacturing Practice. The tools are flexible to provide for changes as knowledge of the process increases and appropriate to the stage of development of the product (applicable from the date of entry into application of Regulation (EU) No. 536/2014 on Clinical Trials).

Introduction

These guidelines are based on the second subparagraph of Article 63(1) of Regulation (EU) No 536/2014[1].

These guidelines complement Commission Delegated Regulation (EU) 2017/1569 of 23 May 2017 supplementing Regulation (EU) No. 536/2014 on the Good Manufacturing Practice for investigational medicinal products for human use and arrangements for inspections[2] that have as their legal basis the first subparagraph of Article 63(1) of Regulation (EU) No. 536/2014.

These guidelines lay down appropriate tools to address specific issues concerning investigational medicinal products with regard to Good Manufacturing Practice. The tools are flexible to provide for changes as knowledge of the process increases and appropriate to the stage of development of the product.

An investigational medicinal product is defined in Article 2(5) of Regulation (EU) No. 536/2014 as a medicinal product that is being tested or

---

[1] Regulation (EU) No 536/2014 of the European Parliament and the Council of 16 April 2014 on clinical trials on medicinal products for human use, and repealing Directive 2001/20/EC (OJ L 158, 27.5.2014, p. 1).

[2] Commission Delegated Regulation (EU) 2017/1569 of 23 May 2017 supplementing Regulation (EU) No. 536/2014 of the European Parliament and the Council by specifying principles of and guidelines for Good Manufacturing Practice for investigational medicinal products for human use and arrangements for inspections (OJ L 238/12, 16.09.2017).

used as a reference, including as a placebo, in a clinical trial, and manufacturing is defined as total and partial manufacture, as well as the various processes of dividing up, packaging and labelling (including blinding) in Article 2(24) of that Regulation.

Article 63(1) of Regulation (EU) No. 536/2014 provides that investigational medicinal products shall be manufactured by applying manufacturing practice that ensures the quality of such medicinal products in order to safeguard the safety of the subject and the reliability and robustness of clinical data generated in the clinical trial ("Good Manufacturing Practice").

Good manufacturing practice for investigational medicinal products is set out in Commission Delegated Regulation (EU) No. 2017/1569 and in these guidelines.

Furthermore, where applicable, the manufacturers and the competent authorities should also take into account the detailed guidelines referred to in the second paragraph of Article 47 of Directive 2001/83/EC[3], published by the Commission in the "Guide to good manufacturing practice for medicinal products and for investigational medicinal products" (EudraLex, Volume 4). Examples of applicable parts of EudraLex, Volume 4 to investigational medicinal products, not specifically mentioned in these guidelines, are Part I, Chapters 2 and 6, and Part III.

With regard to EudraLex, Volume 4, Part II, it should be noted that Regulation (EU) No. 536/2014 does not lay down requirements for Good Manufacturing Practice for active substances of investigational medicinal products. However, if a clinical trial were to be used to support the application for a marketing authorisation, Part II of EudraLex, Volume 4 would need to be considered.

Procedures need to be flexible to provide for changes as knowledge of the process increases and appropriate to the stage of development of the products.

In clinical trials there may be added risk to the subjects compared with patients treated with authorised medicinal products. The application of Good Manufacturing Practice for the manufacture and import of investigational medicinal products is intended to ensure that subjects are not placed at undue risk, and that the results of clinical trials are unaffected by inadequate quality, safety or efficacy arising from unsatisfactory manufacture or import. Equally, it is intended to ensure that there is consistency between batches of the same investigational medicinal product used in the same or different clinical trials, and that changes during the development of an investigational medicinal product are adequately documented and justified.

---

[3] Directive 2001/83/EC of the European Parliament and the Council of 6 November 2001 on the Community code relating to medicinal products for human use (OJ L 311, 28.11.201, p. 67).

The production of investigational medicinal products involves added complexity in comparison with authorised medicinal products by virtue of lack of fixed routines, variety of clinical trial designs and consequent packaging designs. Randomisation and blinding add to that complexity an increased risk of product cross-contamination and mix-up. Furthermore, there may be incomplete knowledge of the potency and toxicity of the product and a lack of full process validation. Moreover, authorised products may be used that have been re-packaged or modified in some way. These challenges require personnel with a thorough understanding of and training in the application of Good Manufacturing Practice to investigational medicinal products. The increased complexity in manufacturing operations requires a highly effective quality system.

For manufacturers to be able to apply and comply with good manufacturing practice for investigational medicinal products, cooperation between manufacturers and sponsors of clinical trials is required. This cooperation should be described in a technical agreement between the sponsor and manufacturer, as referred to in recital 4 of Delegated Regulation (EU) No. 2017/1569.

1   Scope

These guidelines apply to manufacture or import of investigational medicinal products for human use.

For advanced therapy investigational medicinal products, Article 16 of Commission Delegated Regulation (EU) No. 2017/1569 states that the requirements of Good Manufacturing Practice shall be adapted to the specific characteristic of such products in accordance with a risk-based approach, and consistent with good manufacturing requirements applicable to authorised advanced therapy medicinal products. Those adaptations are addressed in the Guidelines on good manufacturing practice for advanced therapy medicinal products[4]. Therefore, these detailed guidelines on Good Manufacturing Practice for investigational medicinal products for human use do not apply to manufacture or import of advanced therapy investigational medicinal products.

Reconstitution of investigational medicinal products is not considered to be manufacturing and is not covered therefore by this guideline.

The reconstitution is understood as the simple process of dissolving or dispersing the investigational medicinal product for administration of the product to a trial subject, or diluting or mixing the investigation medicinal product with some other substance(s) used as a vehicle for the purpose of administering it to a trial subject.

---

[4] Commission guideline on good manufacturing practice for advanced therapy medicinal products, Eudralex Volume 4, Part IV

Reconstitution is not mixing several ingredients, including the active substance, together to produce the investigational medicinal product. An investigational medicinal product must exist before a process can be defined as reconstitution.

The process of reconstitution has to be undertaken as close in time as possible to administration and has to be defined in the clinical trial application dossier and document available at the clinical trial site.

These guidelines do not apply to the processes referred to in Article 61(5) of Regulation (EU) No. 536/2014. Member States should make those processes subject to appropriate and proportionate requirements to ensure subject safety and reliability and robustness of the data generated in the clinical trial.

2 Pharmaceutical Quality System

The pharmaceutical quality system required of the manufacturer according to Article 5 of Commission Delegated Regulation (EU) No. 2017/1569 and designed, set up and verified by the manufacturer should be described in written procedures taking into account EudraLex, Volume 4, Part I, Chapter 1, as applicable to investigational medicinal products.

The product specifications and manufacturing instructions may be changed during development but full control and traceability of the changes should be documented and maintained. Deviations from any pre-defined specifications and instructions should be registered, investigated, and corrective and preventive action measures initiated as appropriate.

The selection, qualification, approval and maintenance of suppliers of starting materials, together with their purchase and acceptance, should be documented as part of the pharmaceutical quality system to ensure the integrity of the supply chain and protect against falsified products. The level of supervision should be proportionate to the risks posed by the individual materials, taking into account their source, manufacturing process, supply chain complexity and the final use to which the material is put in the investigational medicinal product. The supporting evidence for each supplier approval and material approval should be documented and maintained.

2.1 Product specification file

Products specification file, in light of Article 2(3) of Commission Delegated Regulation (EU) No. 2017/1569, brings together and contains all of the essential reference documents to ensure that investigational medicinal products are manufactured according to Good Manufacturing Practice for investigational medicinal products and the clinical trial authorisation. The products specification file is one of the essential elements of pharmaceutical quality system.

Applicable sections of the product specification file should be available at the start of manufacturing of the first batch of investigational medicinal product for a clinical trial.

The product specification file should be continually updated as development of the product proceeds, ensuring appropriate traceability to the previous versions. It should include or refer to at least the following documents:

(i)   Specifications and analytical methods for starting materials, packaging materials, intermediate product, bulk product and finished product;
(ii)   Manufacturing methods;
(iii)   In-process testing and methods;
(iv)   Approved label copy;
(v)   Relevant clinical trial authorisations and amendments thereof, clinical trial protocol and randomisation codes, as appropriate;
(vi)   Relevant technical agreements with contract givers and acceptors, as appropriate;
(vii)   Stability plan and reports;
(viii)   Details of plans and arrangements for reference and retention samples;
(ix)   Storage and transport conditions;
(x)   Details of the supply chain including manufacturing, packaging, labelling and testing sites for the investigational medicinal products, preferably in the format of a comprehensive diagram.

This list of documents is neither exhaustive nor exclusive.

The contents of the product specification file will vary depending on the product and the stage of development.

Where different manufacturing steps are carried out at different locations under the responsibility of different qualified persons, it is acceptable to maintain separate files limited to information of relevance to the activities at the respective locations. The manufacturing site should have access to the necessary documentation of the product specification file, including changes, to enable the relevant activities to be performed.

3   Personnel

The requirements as regards the personnel are defined in Article 6 of Commission Delegated Regulation (EU) No. 2017/1569. The EudraLex, Volume 4, Part I, Chapter 2 should also be taken into account as appropriate.

All personnel involved with the manufacture, import, storage or handling of investigational medicinal products should be appropriately trained in the requirements specific to these types of product.

Even where the number of staff involved in the manufacturing or import of investigational medicinal products is small, there should be, for each batch, separate people responsible for production and quality control.

The qualified person has to fulfil the conditions of qualification set out in Article 49(2) and (3) of Directive 2001/83/EC, as per Article 61(2)(b) of Regulation (EU) No. 536/2014.

The responsibilities of the qualified person are set out in Article 62 of Regulation (EU) No. 536/2015 and further elaborated in Article 12 of Commission Delegated Regulation (EU) No. 2017/1569.

The qualified person who certifies the finished batch of investigational medicinal products for use in the clinical trial should ensure that there are systems in place that meet the requirements of Good Manufacturing Practice, and should have a broad knowledge of pharmaceutical development, clinical trial processes and supply chain of the batch concerned.

4 Premises and Equipment

The toxicity, potency or sensitising potential may not be fully understood for investigational medicinal products and this reinforces the need to minimise all risks of cross-contamination. The design of equipment and premises, inspection/test methods and acceptance limits to be used after cleaning should reflect the nature of these risks and take account of the quality risk management principles detailed in EudraLex, Volume 4, Part I, Chapters 3 and 5.

Consideration should be given to campaign manufacturing, where appropriate. Account should be taken of the solubility of the product in decisions about the choice of cleaning solvent.

A quality risk management process, which includes a potency and toxicological evaluation, should be used to assess and control the cross-contamination risks presented by the investigational medicinal products manufactured. Factors that should be taken into account include:

(i)   facility/equipment design and use;
(ii)   personnel and material flow;
(iii)   microbiological controls;
(iv)   physiochemical characteristics of the active substance;
(v)   process characteristics;
(vi)   cleaning processes;
(vii)   analytical capabilities relative to the relevant limits established from the evaluation of the investigational medicinal products.

Premises and equipment are expected to be qualified in accordance with EudraLex, Volume 4, Annex 15.

5 Documentation

Documentation should be generated and controlled in line with the principles detailed in EudraLex, Volume 4, Part I, Chapter 4. The retention period for instructions and records required to demonstrate compliance with Good Manufacturing Practice should be defined according to the type of document while complying with the requirement of Article 8 of Commission Delegated Regulation (EU) No. 2017/1569, where relevant. In line with Article 8(1) of the above-mentioned Delegated Regulation, the documentation shall be consistent with the Product Specification File. Documents that are part of the Products Specification File shall be retained for the period of at least 5 years, as required by Article 8(3) of the Delegated Regulation.

The sponsor has specific responsibilities for document retention of the clinical trial master file according to Article 58 of Regulation (EU) No. 536/2014 and is required to retain such documentation for at least 25 years after the end of the trial. If the sponsor and the manufacturer are not the same entity, the sponsor has to make appropriate arrangements with the manufacturer to fulfil the sponsor's requirement to retain the clinical trial master file. Arrangement for retention of such documents and the type of documents to be retained should be defined in an agreement between the sponsor and manufacturer.

5.1 Specification and instructions

Specifications for starting materials, immediate packaging materials, intermediate products, bulk products and finished products, manufacturing formulae, and processing and packing instructions should be as comprehensive as possible, given the current state of knowledge. They should be reassessed during development and updated as necessary. Each new version should take into account the latest data, current technology used, regulatory and pharmacopoeial developments, and should allow traceability to the previous document. Any changes should be carried out according to a written procedure, which should address any implications for product quality such as stability and bioequivalence. The approval process for instructions and changes thereof shall include responsible personnel at the manufacturing site.

Rationales for changes should be recorded and the consequences of a change on product quality and on any on-going clinical trials should be investigated and fully documented.

5.2 Order

The manufacturer should retain the order for investigational medicinal products as part of the batch documentation. The order should request the processing and/or packaging of a certain number of units and/or their distribution and be given by or on behalf of the sponsor to the manufacturer. The order should be in writing, though it may be transmitted by electronic means, and be precise enough to avoid any ambiguity. It should be formally authorised by the sponsor or their representative and refer to the product specification file and the relevant clinical trial protocol as appropriate.

5.3 Manufacturing formulae and processing instructions

For every manufacturing operation or supply there should be clear and adequate written instructions and written records, which are prepared using the specific clinical study information detailed in the Product Specification File. Records are particularly important for the preparation of the final version of the documents to be used in routine manufacture once the Marketing Authorisation has been granted.

The relevant information in the Product Specification File should be used to draft the detailed written instructions on processing, packaging, quality control testing and storage, including storage conditions.

5.4 Packaging instructions

Investigational medicinal products are normally packed in an individual way for each subject included in the clinical trial. The number of units to be packaged should be specified prior to the start of the packaging operations, including units necessary for carrying out quality control and any retention samples to be kept. Sufficient reconciliations should take place to ensure that the correct quantity of each product required has been accounted for at each stage of processing.

Procedures should describe the specification, generation, testing, security, distribution, handling and retention of any randomisation code used for packaging investigational medicinal products, as well as a code-break mechanism. Appropriate records should be maintained.

5.5   Batch records

Batch records should be kept in sufficient detail for the sequence of operations to be accurately determined. These records should contain any relevant remarks that justify procedures used and any changes made, enhance knowledge of the product, develop the manufacturing operations and document deviations from predefined requirements.

Batch manufacturing records should be retained by the manufacturer for at least five years after the completion or formal discontinuation of the last clinical trial in which the batch was used, as set out in Article 8(3) of Commission Delegated Regulation (EU) No. 2017/1569.

6   Production

6.1   Packaging materials

Specifications and quality control checks should include measures to guard against unintentional unblinding due to changes in appearance between different batches of packaging materials.

6.2   Manufacturing operations

During development critical parameters should be identified and in-process controls primarily used to control the process. Provisional production parameters and in-process controls may be deduced from prior experience, including that gained from earlier development work. Careful consideration by key personnel is called for in order to formulate the necessary instructions and to adapt them continually to the experience gained in production. Parameters identified and controlled should be justifiable based on knowledge available at the time.

In line with Article 9(3) of Delegated Regulation, the manufacturing process is not to be validated to the extent necessary for routine production but shall be validated in its entirety, as far as is appropriate taking into account the stage of product development. It should be documented in accordance with the requirements detailed in EudraLex, Volume 4, Annex 15. Article 9(3) of Commission Delegated Regulation (EU) No. 2017/1569 also states that the manufacturer shall identify the process steps that safeguard the safety of the subject, and the reliability and robustness of the clinical trial data generated in the clinical study.

To avoid cross-contamination, written cleaning procedures and analytical methods to verify the cleaning process should be available.

For sterile products, the validation of sterilising processes should be of the same standards as for authorised medicinal products, and take account of the principles for the manufacture of sterile medicinal products detailed in EudraLex, Volume 4, Annex 1. Likewise, when required, virus inactivation/removal and removal of other impurities of biological origin should be demonstrated, to assure the safety of biotechnologically derived and biological products by following the scientific principles and techniques defined in the available guidance in this area.

Validation of aseptic processes presents special problems where the batch size is small; in these cases, the number of units filled may be the maximum number filled in production. If practicable, and otherwise consistent with simulating the process, a larger number of units should be filled with media to provide greater confidence in the results obtained. Filling and sealing is often a manual or semi-automated operation presenting great challenges to sterility, so enhanced attention should be given to operator training and validating the aseptic technique of individual operators.

6.3　Modification of comparator products

If a product is modified, data should be available (e.g. stability, comparative dissolution or bioavailability) to demonstrate that these changes do not significantly alter the original quality characteristics of the product.

The expiry date stated for the comparator product in its original packaging might not be applicable to the product where it has been repackaged in a different container that may not offer equivalent protection, or be compatible with the product. A suitable re-test date, taking into account the nature of the product, the characteristics of the container and the storage conditions to which the product may be subjected, should be determined by or on behalf of the sponsor. Such a date should be justified and must not be later than the expiry date of the original package. There should be compatibility of expiry dating and clinical trial duration.

A reference sample of comparator product, which has been repackaged or over-encapsulated for blinding purposes, should be taken at a point representative of the additional processing and retained, because the additional processing step could have an impact on stability or be needed for identification purposes in the event of a quality defect investigation, which would not be covered by the commercial retained sample.

6.4　Blinding operations

Where products are blinded, systems should be in place to ensure that the blind is achieved and maintained while allowing for identification of "blinded" products, when necessary, including batch numbers of the products before the blinding operation. Rapid identification of product should also be possible in an emergency. Where the manufacturer has been delegated the responsibility for generation of randomisation codes, the manufacturer should ensure that unblinding information is available to the appropriate responsible investigator site personnel before investigational medicinal products are supplied.

Where products are blinded, the expiry date assigned should be stated at the expiry of the shortest dated product so that the blinding is maintained.

6.5 Packaging

During packaging of investigational medicinal products, it may be necessary to handle different products on the same packaging line at the same time. The risk of product unintentional mixing (mix-ups) must be minimised by using appropriate procedures and/or specialised equipment as appropriate and relevant staff training. Documentation must be sufficient to demonstrate that appropriate segregation has been maintained during any packaging operations.

Packaging and labelling of investigational medicinal products are likely to be more complex and also more liable to errors that are harder to detect than for authorised medicinal products, particularly when blinded products with a similar appearance are used. Precautions against mislabelling such as reconciliation, line clearance and in-process control checks by appropriately trained staff should accordingly be intensified.

The packaging must ensure that the investigational medicinal product remains in good condition during transport and storage at intermediate destinations. Any opening or tampering of the outer packaging during transport should be readily discernible.

Re-packaging operations may be performed by authorised personnel at a hospital, health centre or clinic that meets the requirements of Article 61(5)(a) of Regulation (EU) No. 536/2014.

6.6 Labelling

Labelling of investigation medicinal products shall comply with the requirements of Articles 66, 67, 68 and 69 of Regulation (EU) No. 536/2014. A list of information that shall appear on the labelling is set out in Annex VI to the said Regulation. The labelling operation should be performed at an authorised manufacturing site that complies with the requirements of Article 61(1) of Regulation (EU) No. 536/2014.

If it becomes necessary to change the expiry date, an additional label should be affixed to the investigational medicinal product. This additional label should state the new expiry date and repeat the batch number and clinical trial reference number. It may be superimposed on the old expiry date, but, for quality control reasons, not on the original batch number.

The re-labelling operation should be performed by appropriately trained staff in accordance with Good Manufacturing Practice principles and specific standard operating procedures, and should be checked by a second person. This additional labelling should be properly documented in the batch records. To avoid mistakes the additional labelling activity should be carried out in an area that is partitioned or separated from other activities. A line clearance at the start and end of activity should be carried out and label reconciliation performed. Any discrepancies observed during reconciliation should be investigated and accounted for before release.

The re-labelling operation may be performed by authorised personnel at a hospital, health centre or clinic that meets the requirements of Article 61(5)(a) of Regulation (EU) No. 536/2014.

7 Quality Control

According to Article 10 of Commission Delegated Regulation (EU) No. 2017/1569, the manufacturer is required to establish and maintain a quality control system placed under the authority of a person who has the requisite qualifications and is independent of production.

As processes may not be standardised or fully validated, testing takes on more importance in ensuring that each batch meets the approved specification at the time of testing.

Quality control of the investigational medicinal product, including comparator product, should be performed in accordance with the information submitted according to Article 25 of Regulation (EU) No. 536/2014, as authorised by the Member State.

Verification of the effectiveness of blinding should be performed and recorded.

Retention periods for samples of investigational medicinal products have to fulfil the requirements of Article 10(4) of Commission Delegated Regulation (EU) No 2017/1569.

Samples are retained to fulfil two purposes: first, to provide a sample for future analytical testing and, second, to provide a specimen of the finished investigational medicinal product that may be used in the investigation of a product quality defect. Samples may therefore fall into two categories:

- Reference sample: a sample of a batch of starting material, packaging material or finished product that is stored for the purpose of being analysed should the need arise. Where stability permits, reference samples from critical intermediate stages, e.g. those requiring analytical testing and release, or intermediates that are transported outside of the manufacturer's control, should be kept.

- Retention sample: a sample of a fully packaged unit from a batch of finished product. It is stored for identification purposes, e.g. presentation, packaging, labelling, package leaflet, batch number, expiry date should the need arise during the shelf-life of the batch concerned.

There may be exceptional circumstances where this requirement can be met without retention of duplicate samples, e.g. where small amounts of a batch are packaged for different markets or in the production of very expensive medicinal products.

For retention samples it is acceptable to store information related to the final packaging as written, photographic or electronic records, if such records provide sufficient information, e.g. examples of packaging, labelling and any accompanying documentation to permit investigations associated with the use of the product. In the case of electronic records, the system should comply with the requirements of EudraLex, Volume 4, Annex 11.

Where reference samples and retention samples are presented identically, i.e. as fully packaged units, the samples may be regarded as interchangeable.

Samples are not expected of an investigational medicinal product that is an unblinded comparator in its original packaging and sourced from the authorised supply chain in the EU, or of a product that holds a Marketing Authorisation granted by a national competent authority in the EU or by the European Commission.

The storage location of samples should be defined in a technical agreement between the sponsor and the manufacturer(s), and should allow timely access by the competent authorities.

Reference samples of finished product should be stored under defined storage conditions in the EU or in a third country where appropriate arrangements have been made by the Union with the exporting country, to ensure that the manufacturer of the investigational medicinal product applies standards of Good Manufacturing Practice at least equivalent to those laid down by the Union. In exceptional circumstances, the reference samples of the finished product may be stored by the manufacturer in another third country, in which case this should be justified and documented in a technical agreement among the sponsor, the importer in the EU and that manufacturer in the third country.

The reference sample should be of sufficient size to perform, on at least two occasions, all critical quality attribute tests as defined in the investigational medicinal product dossier authorised by the Member State. Any exception to this should be justified to, and agreed with, the national competent authority.

8   Release of Batches

Release of investigational medicinal products should not occur until after the qualified person has certified,in line with Article 62(1) of Regulation (EU) No. 536/2014, that the requirements of Article 63(1) and (3) of Regulation (EU) No. 536/2014 and those set out in Article 12 of the Commission Delegated Regulation (EU) No. 2017/1569 are met.

The duties of the qualified person in relation to investigational medicinal products are affected by the different circumstances that can arise and are referred to below:

(i)   Product manufactured within the EU but not subject to an EU Marketing Authorisation: the duties are laid down in Article 62 of Regulation (EU) No. 536/2014 and Article 12(1)(a) of the Delegated Regulation;

(ii)   Product sourced from the open market within the EU in accordance with Article 80(b) of Directive 2001/83/EC and subject to a Marketing Authorisation granted by a competent authority in the EU, regardless of manufacturing origin; the duties are as described above. However, the scope of the certification can be limited to assuring that the products are in accordance with the authorisation of the clinical trial and any subsequent processing carried out by the manufacturer for the purpose of blinding, trial-specific packaging and labelling.

(iii)   Product imported directly from a third country: the duties are laid down in Article 62 of Regulation (EU) No. 536/2014 and Article 12(1)(b) of the Delegated Regulation. Where investigational medicinal products are imported from a third country and they are subject to agreements concluded between the Union and that country, such as a Mutual Recognition Agreement (MRA), equivalent standards of Good Manufacturing Practice apply provided that any such agreement is operational for investigational medicinal products. In the absence of an MRA, the qualified person should determine that equivalent standards of Good Manufacturing Practice apply through knowledge of the quality system employed at the manufacturer. This knowledge is normally acquired through audit of the manufacturer's quality systems. In either case, the qualified person may then certify on the basis of documentation supplied by the manufacturer in the third country and document the rationale for certification.

The information in the product specification file should form the basis for assessment of the suitability for certification and release of a particular batch by the qualified person and should therefore be accessible to them.

Assessment by the qualified person of each batch for certification prior to release should take account of the principles detailed in EudraLex, Volume 4, Annex 16 and may include as appropriate:

(i)   Batch records, including control reports, in-process test reports and release reports demonstrating compliance with the product specification file, the order, protocol and randomisation code. These records should include all deviations or planned changes, and any consequent additional checks and tests, and should be completed and endorsed by the staff authorised to do so according to the quality system;

(ii)   Production conditions;

(iii) Cleaning records;

(iv)   The qualification status of facilities, validation status of processes and methods;

(v)   Examination of finished packs;

(vi)   The results of any analyses or tests performed after importation, where relevant;

(vii) Stability plan and reports;

(viii) The source and verification of conditions of storage and shipment;

(ix)   Audit reports concerning the quality system of the manufacturer;

(x)   Documents certifying that the manufacturer is authorised to manufacture investigational medicinal product for export by the appropriate authorities in the third country;

(xi)   Where relevant, regulatory requirements for Marketing Authorisation, Good Manufacturing Practice standards applicable and any official verification of compliance with Good Manufacturing Practice;

(xii) Verification of the supply chain including manufacturing, packaging, labelling and testing sites for the investigational medicinal products;

(xiii) All factors of which the qualified person is aware that are relevant to the quality of the batch.

The relevance of the above elements is affected by the country of origin of the product, the manufacturer, the status of the product, i.e. with or without a Marketing Authorisation granted by competent authorities in the EU or a third country, and the phase of development of the product.

Where investigational medicinal products are produced and packaged at different sites under the supervision of different qualified persons, sharing of responsibilities among qualified persons in relation to compliance of a batch must be defined in a document formally agreed by all parties.

Where required to support certification, the qualified person has to ensure that investigational medicinal products have been stored and transported under conditions to maintain product quality and supply chain security. Relevant situations may include short expiry date products released prior to final qualified person certification, or where return of investigational medicinal products to an authorised manufacturer for re-labelling and re-packaging remains a possibility.

The qualified person is not required to certify re-packaging or re-labelling carried out pursuant to Article 61(5)(a) of Regulation (EU) No. 536/2014.

Where the manufacturer is delegated by the sponsor to perform the regulatory release. in addition to certification by the qualified person, the arrangements should be defined in an agreement between the sponsor and the manufacturer. Relevant clinical trial authorisation and amendment information should be available for reference in the Product Specification File and the manufacturer should ensure that the necessary clinical trial authorisations are in place prior to shipping product for use in the trial.

After certification by the qualified person, investigational medicinal products should be stored and transported under conditions to maintain product quality and supply chain security.

9 Outsourced Operations

Activities that are outsourced should be defined, agreed and controlled by written contracts between the contract giver and the party to whom the operations are outsourced in accordance with Article 13 of Delegated Regulation and the principles detailed in EudraLex Volume 4, Part I, Chapter 7.

10 Complaints

There should be written procedures describing the actions to be taken upon receipt of a complaint at the manufacturing, storage or importation site. All complaints should be documented and assessed to establish if they represent a potential quality defect or other issue. The procedures should ensure that the sponsor is able to assess the complaints to determine if they justify the reporting of a serious breach, as required by Article 52 of Regulation (EU) No. 536/2014.

The investigation of quality defect should be performed in accordance with the principles detailed in EudraLex, Volume 4, Part I, Chapter 8.

The conclusions of the investigation should be discussed between the manufacturer and the sponsor, if different, in a timely manner. This should involve the qualified person and those responsible for the relevant clinical trial in order to assess any potential impact on the trial, product development and on subjects.

11 Recalls and Returns

11.1 Recalls

Procedures for retrieving investigational medicinal products and documenting this retrieval should be in line with Article 14 of the Delegated Regulation, and be agreed by the sponsor in cooperation with the manufacturer, where different. The manufacturer, investigator and sponsor's representative need to understand their obligations under the retrieval procedure. The procedures for retrieval of investigational medicinal products should be in accordance with the principles detailed in EudraLex, Volume 4, Part I, Chapter 8.

To facilitate recall, a detailed inventory of the shipments made by the manufacturer should be maintained.

11.2 Returns

Returned investigational medicinal products should be clearly identified and stored in an appropriately controlled, dedicated area. Inventory records of returned products should be kept.

11.3 Destruction

The manufacturer or sponsor's representative should destroy investigational medicinal products only with prior written authorisation by the sponsor. The arrangements for destruction of investigational medicinal products have to be described in the protocol. Any arrangement between sponsor and manufacturer in this regard should be defined in their technical agreement.

Destruction of unused investigational medicinal products should be carried out only after reconciliation of delivered, used and recovered products, and after investigation and satisfactory explanation of any discrepancies upon which the reconciliation has been accepted.

Records of destruction operations should be retained, including a dated certificate of destruction or a receipt for destruction to the sponsor. These documents should clearly identify or allow traceability to the batches and/ or patient numbers involved and the actual quantities destroyed.

Glossary of Terms Applicable to these Guidelines

CAMPAIGN MANUFACTURING

Manufacturing a series of batches of the same product in sequence in a given period of time followed by an appropriate (validated) cleaning procedure.

COMPARATOR PRODUCT

An investigational medicinal product used as a reference, including as a placebo, in a clinical trial.

EXPIRY DATE

The date placed on the container/labels of an investigational medicinal product designating the time during which the investigational medicinal product is expected to remain within established shelf-life specifications if stored under defined conditions, and after which it should not be used.

ORDER

The order should request the processing and/or packaging of a certain number of units and/or their shipment and be given by or on behalf of the sponsor to the manufacturer.

RANDOMISATION

The process of assigning trial subjects to treatment or control groups using an element of chance to determine the assignments in order to reduce bias.

RE-TEST DATE

The date when a material should be re-examined to ensure that it is still suitable for use.

SHIPPING

The operation of packaging for and sending of ordered medicinal products for clinical trials.

ANNEX 14 MANUFACTURE OF MEDICINAL PRODUCTS DERIVED FROM HUMAN BLOOD OR PLASMA

Glossary

BLOOD

Blood, as referred to in Directive 2002/98/EC (Art. 3a), means whole blood collected from a donor and processed either for transfusion or for further manufacturing.

BLOOD COMPONENT

A blood component, as referred to in Directive 2002/98/EC (Art. 3b), means a therapeutic constituent of blood (red cells, white cells, platelets and plasma) that can be prepared by various methods.

BLOOD ESTABLISHMENT

A blood establishment, as referred to in Directive 2002/98/EC (Art. 3e), is any structure or body that is responsible for any aspect of the collection and testing of human blood and blood components, whatever their intended purpose, and their processing, storage and distribution when intended for transfusion. Although this definition does not include hospital blood banks, it is understood to include centres where apheresis of plasma is performed.

BLOOD PRODUCTS

A blood product, as referred to in Directive 2002/98/EC (Art. 3c), means any therapeutic product derived from human blood or plasma.

FRACTIONATION, FRACTIONATION PLANT

Fractionation is the manufacturing process in a plant (fractionation plant) during which plasma components are separated/purified by various physical and chemical methods such as precipitation, chromatography.

GOOD PRACTICE GUIDELINES

Good practice guidelines give interpretation on the Community standards and specifications defined for quality systems in blood establishments established in the Annex of Directive 2005/62/EC[1].

MEDICINAL PRODUCTS DERIVED FROM HUMAN BLOOD OR HUMAN PLASMA

Medicinal products derived from human blood or human plasma, as referred to in Directive 2001/83/EC (Art. 1 No. 10), are medicinal products

---

[1] At the time of publication of this Annex adoption of the Good Practice guidelines by the European Commission was still pending.

based on blood constituents which are prepared industrially by public or private establishments.

PLASMA FOR FRACTIONATION

Plasma for fractionation is the liquid part of human blood remaining after separation of the cellular elements from blood collected in a container with an anticoagulant, or separated by continuous filtration or centrifugation of anticoagulated blood in an apheresis procedure; it is intended for the manufacture of plasma-derived medicinal products, in particular albumin, coagulation factors and immunoglobulins of human origin and specified in the European Pharmacopoeia (Ph.Eur.) monograph "Human Plasma for fractionation" (0853).

PLASMA MASTER FILE (PMF)

A Plasma Master File, as referred to in Directive 2001/83/EC (Annex I, Part III, No. 1.1.a), is a stand-alone document, which is separate from the dossier for Marketing Authorisation. It provides all relevant detailed information on the characteristics of the entire human plasma used as a starting material and/or a raw material for the manufacture of sub-/intermediate fractions, constituents of the excipients and active substances, which are part of plasma-derived medicinal products or medical devices.

PROCESSING

According to the terminology of Directive 2005/62/EC, "processing means any step in the preparation of blood component that is carried out between the collection of blood and the issuing of a blood component", e.g. separation and freezing of blood components. In this Annex, processing in addition refers to those operations performed at the blood establishment that are specific to plasma to be used for fractionation.

QUALIFIED PERSON (QP)

The qualified person is the person referred to in Directive 2001/83/EC (Art. 48).

RESPONSIBLE PERSON (RP)

The responsible person is the person referred to in Directive 2002/98/EC (Art. 9).

THIRD COUNTRIES CONTRACT FRACTIONATION PROGRAMME

This is a contract fractionation in a plant of a fractionator/manufacturer in the EU/EEA, using starting material from third countries and manufacturing products not intended for the EU/EEA market.

1   Scope

1.1   The provisions of this Annex apply to medicinal products derived from human blood or plasma, fractionated in or imported into the EU/EEA. The Annex applies also to the starting material (e.g. human plasma) for these products. In line with the conditions set out in Directive 2003/63/EC, the requirements apply also for stable derivatives of human blood or human plasma (e.g. albumin) incorporated into medical devices.

1.2   This Annex defines specific Good Manufacturing Practices (GMP) requirements for processing, storage and transport of human plasma used for fractionation and for the manufacture of medicinal products derived from human blood or plasma.

1.3   The Annex addresses specific provisions for when starting material is imported from third countries and for contract fractionation programmes for third countries.

1.4   The Annex does not apply to blood components intended for transfusion.

2   Principles

2.1   Medicinal products derived from human blood or plasma (and their active substances, which are used as starting materials) must comply with the principles and guidelines of Good Manufacturing Practice (as laid down in Commission Directive 2003/94/EC and the EU Guidelines on GMP published by the European Commission) as well as the relevant marketing authorisation (Directive 2001/83/EC, Art. 46, 51). They are considered to be biological medicinal products and the starting materials include biological substances, such as cells or fluids (including blood or plasma) of human origin (Directive 2001/83/EC, Annex I, Part I, No. 3.2.1.1.b). Certain special features arise from the biological nature of the source material. For example, disease-transmitting agents, especially viruses, may contaminate the source material. The quality and safety of these products rely therefore on the control of source materials and their origin, as well as on the subsequent manufacturing procedures, including infectious marker testing, virus removal and virus inactivation.

2.2   In principle, active substances used as a starting material for medicinal products must comply with the principles and guidelines of Good Manufacturing Practice (see 2.1). For starting materials derived from human blood and plasma, the requirements for the collection and testing defined in Directive 2002/98/EC are to be followed. Collection and testing must be performed in accordance with an appropriate quality system for which standards and specifications are defined in the Annex of Directive 2005/62/

EC and interpreted in the Good Practice guidelines referred to in Article 2 (2) of Directive 2005/62/EC. Furthermore, the requirements of Directive 2005/61/EC on traceability and serious adverse reactions and serious adverse event notifications from the donor to the recipient apply. In addition the monographs of the European Pharmacopoeia are to be observed (Directive 2001/83/EC, Annex 1, Part III, No. 1.1.b).

2.3 Starting material for the manufacture of medicinal products derived from human blood or plasma imported from third countries and intended for use or distribution in the EU/EEA must meet standards that are equivalent to Community Standards and specifications relating to a quality system for blood establishments as set out in Commission Directive 2005/62/EC (Recital 6; Article 2(3)), the traceability and serious adverse reaction and serious adverse event notification requirements as set out in Commission Directive 2005/61/EC (Recital 5; Article 7), and the technical requirements for blood and blood components as set out in Commission Directive 2004/33/EC (Recital 4; point 2.3 of Annex V).

2.4 In the case of third country contract fractionation programmes, the starting material imported from third countries must be in compliance with the quality and safety requirements as laid down in Directive 2002/98/EC and Annex V of Directive 2004/33/EC. The activities conducted within the EU/EEA must fully comply with GMP. Consideration should be given to the Community standards and specifications relating to a quality system for blood establishments set out in Commission Directive 2005/62/EC, the traceability requirements and notification of serious adverse reactions and events set out in Commission Directive 2005/61/EC, and the relevant WHO guidelines and recommendations as listed in the addendum.

2.5 For all subsequent steps after collection and testing (e.g. processing [including separation], freezing, storage and transport to the manufacturer) the requirements of Directive 2001/83/EC apply and must therefore be done in accordance with the principles and guidelines of Good Manufacturing Practice. Normally, these activities would be carried out under the responsibility of a Qualified Person in an establishment with a Manufacturing Authorisation. Where specific processing steps in relation to plasma for fractionation take place in a blood establishment, the specific appointment of a Qualified Person may, however, not be proportionate given the presence and responsibility of a Responsible Person. To address this particular situation and to ensure that the legal responsibilities of the Qualified Person are properly addressed, the fractionation plant/manufacturer should establish a contract, in accordance with Chapter 7 of the GMP Guide, with the blood establishment that defines respective responsibilities and the detailed requirements in order to ensure compliance. The Responsible Person of the blood establishment and the Qualified Person of the fractionation/manufacturing plant (see 3.5) should be involved in drawing up this contract. The Qualified Person should ensure that audits are performed to confirm that the blood establishment complies with the contract.

2.6 Specific requirements for documentation and other arrangements relating to the starting material of plasma-derived medicinal products are defined in the Plasma Master File.

3 Quality Management

3.1 Quality management should govern all stages from donor selection to delivery of the finished product. Reference is made to Directive 2005/61/EC for traceability up to and including the delivery of plasma to the fractionation plant, and to Directive 2005/62/EC for all stages concerning collection and testing of human blood and human plasma to be used for the manufacture of medicinal products.

3.2 Blood or plasma used as source material for the manufacture of medicinal products must be collected by blood establishments and be tested in laboratories that apply quality systems in accordance with Directive 2005/62/EC, authorised by a national competent authority and subject to regular inspections as referred to in Directive 2002/98/EC. Third country contract fractionation programmes have to be notified to the competent EU authority by the manufacturer, as referred to in Directive 2001/83/EC.

3.3 If plasma is imported from third countries, it should be purchased only from approved suppliers (e.g. blood establishments, including external warehouses). They should be named in the specifications for starting materials as defined by the fractionation plant/manufacturer, and be accepted by an EU/EEA competent authority (e.g. following an inspection) and by the Qualified Person of the fractionation plant in the EU/EEA. Certification and release of plasma (plasma for fractionation) as starting material are mentioned in section 6.8.

3.4 Supplier qualification, including audits, should be performed by the fractionation plant/manufacturer of the finished product according to written procedures. Re-qualification of suppliers should be performed at regular intervals taking a risk-based approach into account.

3.5 The fractionation plant/manufacturer of the finished product should establish written contracts with the supplying blood establishments. As a minimum the following key aspects should be addressed:

• definition of duties and respective responsibilities,
• quality system and documentation requirements,
• donor selection criteria and testing,

- requirements for the separation of blood into blood components/plasma,
- freezing of plasma,
- storage and transport of plasma,
- traceability and post donation/collection information (including adverse events).

The test results of all units supplied by the blood establishment should be available to the fractionation plant/manufacturer of the medicinal product. In addition, any fractionation step subcontracted should be defined in a written contract.

3.6   A formal change control system should be in place to plan, evaluate and document all changes that may affect the quality or safety of the products, or traceability. The potential impact of proposed changes should be evaluated. The need for additional testing and validation, especially viral inactivation and removal steps, should be determined.

3.7   An adequate safety strategy should be in place to minimise the risk from infectious agents and emerging infectious agents. This strategy should involve a risk assessment that:

- defines an inventory holding time (internal quarantine time) before processing the plasma, i.e. to remove look back units[2];
- considers all aspects of virus reduction and/or testing for infectious agents or surrogates;
- considers the virus reduction capabilities, the pool size and other relevant aspects of the manufacturing processes.

4   Traceability and Post-collection Measures

4.1   There must be a system in place that enables each donation to be traced, from the donor and the donation via the blood establishment through to the batch of medicinal product, and vice versa.

4.2   Responsibilities for traceability of the product should be defined (there should be no gaps):

- from the donor and the donation in the blood establishment to the fractionation plant (this is the responsibility of the RP at the blood establishment),

---

[2] Plasma units donated by donors during a defined period (as defined on a national/EU basis) before it is found that a donation from a high-risk donor should have been excluded from processing, e.g. due to a positive test result.

- from the fractionation plant to the manufacturer of the medicinal product and any secondary facility, whether a manufacturer of a medicinal product or a medical device (this is the responsibility of the QP).

4.3   Data needed for full traceability must be stored for at least 30 years, according to Article 4 of Directive 2005/61/EC and Article 14 of Directive 2002/98/EC[3].

4.4   The contracts (as mentioned in 3.5) between the blood establishments (including testing laboratories) and the fractionation plant/manufacturer should ensure that traceability and post-collection measures cover the complete chain from the collection of the plasma to all manufacturers responsible for release of the final products.

4.5   The blood establishments should notify the fractionating plant/manufacturer of any event that may affect the quality or safety of the product, including events listed in Annex II, Part A and Annex III, Part A of Directive 2005/61/EC, and other relevant information found subsequent to donor acceptance or release of the plasma, e.g. look back information[4] (post-collection information). Where the fractionation plant/manufacturer is located in a third country, the information should be forwarded to the manufacturer responsible for release in the EU/EEA of any product manufactured from the plasma concerned. In both cases, if relevant for the quality or safety of the final product, this information should be forwarded to the competent authority[5] responsible for the fractionation plant/manufacturer.

4.6   The notification procedure as described in 4.5 also applies when an inspection of a blood establishment by a competent authority leads to a withdrawal of an existing licence/certificate/approval.

4.7   The management of post-collection information should be described in standard operating procedures, taking into account obligations and procedures for informing the competent authorities. Post-collection measures should be available as defined in the "Note for Guidance on Plasma Derived Medicinal Products" in its current version as adopted by the Committee for Medicinal Products for Human Use (CHMP) and published by the European Medicines Agency[6].

---

[3] Both Directives are linked to Article 109 of Directive 2001/83/EC by defining specific rules for medicinal products derived from human blood or plasma.

[4] Information that appears if a subsequent donation from a donor previously found negative for viral markers is found positive for any of the viral markers or any other risk factors that may induce a viral infection.

[5] As referred to in Directive 2001/83/EC.

[6] Current version at date of publication: CPMP/BWP/269/95.

5 Premises and Equipment

5.1 In order to minimise microbiological contamination or the introduction of foreign material into the plasma pool, thawing and pooling of plasma units should be performed in an area conforming at least to the Grade D requirements defined in Annex 1 of the EU GMP Guide. Appropriate clothing should be worn including facemasks and gloves. All other open manipulations during the manufacturing process should be done under conditions conforming to the appropriate requirements of Annex 1 of the EU GMP Guide.

5.2 Environmental monitoring should be performed regularly, especially during the "opening" of plasma containers, and during subsequent thawing and pooling processes in accordance with Annex 1 of the EU GMP Guide. Acceptance limits should be specified.

5.3 In the production of plasma-derived medicinal products, appropriate viral inactivation or removal procedures are used and steps should be taken to prevent cross-contamination of treated with untreated products. Dedicated and distinct premises and equipment should be used for manufacturing steps after viral inactivation treatment.

5.4 To avoid placing routine manufacture at risk of contamination from viruses used during validation studies, the validation of methods for virus reduction should not be conducted in production facilities. Validation should be performed according to the "Note for Guidance on Virus Validation Studies: The Design, Contribution and Interpretation of Studies validating the Inactivation and Removal of Viruses" in its current version as adopted by the Committee for Medicinal Products for Human Use (CHMP) and published by the European Medicines Agency[7].

6 Manufacturing

Starting material

6.1 The starting material should comply with the requirements of all relevant monographs of the European Pharmacopoeia and of the conditions laid down in the respective Marketing Authorisation dossier including the Plasma Master File. These requirements should be defined in the written contract (see 3.5) between the blood establishment and the fractionating plant/manufacturer and controlled through the quality system.

EU GMP GUIDE PART I ANNEX 14 MANUFACTURE OF MEDICINAL PRODUCTS DERIVED FROM HUMAN BLOOD OR PLASMA

---

[7] Current version at date of publication: CHMP/BWP/268/95.

6.2   Starting material for third country contract fractionation programmes should comply with the requirements as specified in 2.4.

6.3   Depending on the type of collection (i.e. either whole blood collection or automated apheresis) different processing steps may be required. All processing steps (e.g. centrifugation and/or separation, sampling, labelling, freezing) should be defined in written procedures.

6.4   Any mix-ups of units and of samples, especially during labelling, as well as any contamination, e.g. when cutting the tube segments/sealing the containers, must be avoided.

6.5   Freezing is a critical step for the recovery of proteins that are labile in plasma, e.g. clotting factors. Freezing should therefore be performed as soon as possible after collection (see the European Pharmacopoeia monograph No. 0853 "*Human Plasma for Fractionation*" and, where relevant, monograph No. 1646 "*Human Plasma pooled and treated for virus inactivation*"), following a validated method.

6.6   The storage and transport of blood or plasma at any stage in the transport chain to the fractionation plant should be defined and recorded. Any deviation from the defined temperature should be notified to the fractionation plant. Qualified equipment and validated procedures should be used.

Certification/release of plasma for fractionation as starting material

6.7   Plasma for fractionation should be released, i.e. from a quarantine status, only through systems and procedures that assure the quality needed for the manufacture of the finished product. It should be distributed to the plasma fractionation plant/manufacturer only after it has been documented by the Responsible Person (or in case of blood/plasma collection in third countries by a person with equivalent responsibilities and qualifications) that the plasma for fractionation does comply with the requirements and specifications defined in the respective written contracts, and that all steps have been performed in accordance with Good Practice and GMP Guidelines, as appropriate.

6.8   On entering the fractionation plant, the plasma units should be released for fractionation under the responsibility of the Qualified Person. The Qualified Person should confirm that the plasma complies with the requirements of all relevant monographs and the conditions laid down in the respective Marketing Authorisation dossier including the Plasma Master File or, in case of plasma to be used for third country contract fractionation programmes, with the requirements as specified in 2.4.

Processing of plasma for fractionation

6.9 The steps used in the fractionation process vary according to product and manufacturer and usually include several fractionation/purification procedures, some of which may contribute to the inactivation and/or removal of potential contamination.

6.10 Requirements for the processes of pooling, pool sampling and fractionation/purification and virus inactivation/removal should be defined and followed thoroughly.

6.11 The methods used in the viral inactivation process should be undertaken with strict adherence to validated procedures and in compliance with the methods used in the virus validation studies. Detailed investigation of failures in virus inactivation procedures should be performed. Adherence to the validated production process is especially important in the virus reduction procedures because any deviation could result in a safety risk for the final product. Procedures should be in place that take this risk into consideration.

6.12 Any reprocessing or reworking may be performed only after a quality risk management exercise has been performed and using processing steps as defined in the relevant Marketing Authorisation.

6.13 A system for clearly segregating/distinguishing between products or intermediates that have undergone a process of virus reduction, from those that have not, should be in place.

6.14 Depending on the outcome of a thorough risk management process (taking into consideration possible differences in epidemiology), production in campaigns including clear segregation and defined validated cleaning procedures should be adopted when plasma/intermediates of different origins are processed at the same plant. The requirement for such measures should be based on the recommendations of the Guideline on Epidemiological Data on Blood Transmissible Infections[8]. The risk management process should consider whether it is necessary to use dedicated equipment in the case of third country contract fractionation programmes.

6.15 For intermediate products intended to be stored, a shelf-life should be defined based on stability data.

6.16 The storage and transport of intermediate and finished medicinal products at any stage of the transport chain should be specified and recorded. Qualified equipment and validated procedures should be used.

---

[8] EMEA/CPMP/BWP/125/04.

EU GMP GUIDE PART I ANNEX 14 MANUFACTURE OF MEDICINAL PRODUCTS DERIVED FROM HUMAN BLOOD OR PLASMA

7 Quality Control

7.1 Testing requirements for viruses or other infectious agents should be considered in the light of knowledge emerging on infectious agents and on the availability of appropriate, validated test methods.

7.2 The first homogeneous plasma pool (e.g. after separation of the cryoprecipitate from the plasma pool) should be tested using validated test methods of suitable sensitivity and specificity, according to the relevant European Pharmacopoeia monographs (e.g. No. 0853).

8 Release of Intermediate and Finished Products

8.1 Only batches derived from plasma pools tested and found negative for virus markers/antibodies and found to be in compliance with the relevant European Pharmacopoeia monographs, including any specific virus cut-off limits, and with the approved specifications (e.g. Plasma Master File), should be released.

8.2 The release of intermediates intended for further in-house processing or delivery to a different site, and the release of finished products, should be performed by the Qualified Person and in accordance with the approved Marketing Authorisation.

8.3 The release of intermediates and final products used in third country contract fractionation programmes should be performed by the Qualified Person on the basis of standards agreed with the contract giver, and in compliance with EU GMP standards. Compliance with relevant European Pharmacopoeia monographs may not be applicable, because these products are not intended for use on the European market.

9 Retention of Plasma Pool Samples

One plasma pool may be used to manufacture more than one batch and/or product. Retention samples and corresponding records from every pool should be kept for at least one year after the expiry date of the finished medicinal product with the longest shelf-life derived from the pool.

10 Disposal of Waste

There should be written procedures for the safe and documented storage and disposal of waste, disposable and rejected items (e.g. contaminated units, units from infected donors, out-of-date blood, plasma, intermediate or finished products).

Addendum

(**A**) Member States should implement the following Directives and guidelines:

(**1**) for collection and testing of blood and blood components:

Directive/Guidelines	Title	Scope
Directive 2002/98/EC of the European Parliament and of the Council	Setting standards of quality and safety for the collection, testing, processing, storage and distribution of human blood and blood components, amending Directive 2001/83/EC	Art. 2 defines standards of quality and safety for the collection and testing of human blood and blood components, whatever their intended purpose, and for their processing, storage and distribution when intended for transfusion
Commission Directive 2004/33/EC	Implementing Directive 2002/98/EC of the European Parliament and of the Council as regards certain technical requirements for blood and blood components	Defines the provision of information to prospective donors and information required from donors (Parts A and B, Annex II), eligibility of donors (Annex III), and storage, transport and distribution conditions for blood and blood components (Annex IV), as well as quality and safety requirements for blood and blood components (Annex V)
Commission Directive 2005/61/EC	Implementing Directive 2002/98/EC of the European Parliament and the Council as regards traceability requirements and notification of serious adverse reactions and events	Defines traceability requirements for blood establishments, donors, blood and blood components, and for the final destination of each unit, whatever the intended purpose. It further defines the reporting requirements in the event of serious adverse events and reactions
Commission Directive 2005/62/EC	Implementing Directive 2002/98/EC of the European Parliament and the Council as regards Community standards and specifications relating to a quality system for blood establishments	Defines the implementation of quality system standards and specifications as referred to in Art. 47 of Directive 2001/83/EC

(2) for collection and regulatory submission of data/information for plasma for fractionation:

Directive/Guidelines	Title	Scope
Directive 2001/83/EC of the European Parliament and the Council	On the Community Code relating to medicinal products for human use	Art. 2 Medicinal products for human use intended to be placed on the market in Member States and either prepared industrially or manufactured by a method involving an industrial process, covering medicinal products derived from human blood or human plasma
Commission Directive 2003/63/EC	Amending Directive 2001/83/EC of the European Parliament and the Council on the Community code relating to medicinal products for human use; Amending the Annex on documentation of medicinal products	
Commission Directive 2003/94/EC	Laying down the principles and guidelines of Good Manufacturing Practice in respect of medicinal products for human use and investigational medicinal products for human use	Art. 1 Principles and guidelines of good manufacturing practice in respect of medicinal products for human use and investigational medicinal products for human use
EU Guidelines on Good Manufacturing Practice	Giving interpretation on the principles and guidelines on GMP	
EMEA/CHMP/ BWP/3794/03 Rev.1, 15 Nov. 2006	Guideline on the Scientific data requirements for a Plasma Master File Revision 1	
EMEA/CHMP/ BWP/548524/2008 EMEA Guideline	Guideline on Epidemiological Data on Blood Transmissible Infections	

(B) Other relevant documents:

Document	Title	Scope
Recommendation No. R (95) 15 (Council of Europe)	Guide to the Preparation, use and quality assurance of blood components	
WHO recommendations for the production, control and regulation of human plasma for fractionation. Annex 4 in: WHO Expert Committee on Biological Standardization. Fifty-sixth report. Geneva: World Health Organization, 2007 (WHO Technical Report Series, No. 941) WHO guidelines on Good Manufacturing Practices for blood establishments	WHO recommendations for the production, control and regulation of human plasma for fractionation	Guidance on the production, control and regulation of human plasma for fractionation

Reference should be made to the latest revisions of these documents for current guidance.

ANNEX 15 QUALIFICATION AND VALIDATION

Principle

This Annex describes the principles of qualification and validation that are applicable to the facilities, equipment, utilities and processes used for the manufacture of medicinal products, and may also be used as supplementary optional guidance for active substances without introduction of additional requirements to EudraLex, Volume 4, Part II. It is a GMP requirement that manufacturers control the critical aspects of their particular operations through qualification and validation over the lifecycle of the product and process. Any planned changes to the facilities, equipment, utilities and processes, which may affect the quality of the product, should be formally documented and the impact on the validated status or control strategy assessed. Computerised systems used for the manufacture of medicinal products should also be validated according to the requirements of Annex 11. The relevant concepts and guidance presented in ICH Q8, Q9, Q10 and Q11 should also be taken into account.

General

A quality risk management approach should be applied throughout the lifecycle of a medicinal product. As part of a quality risk management system, decisions on the scope and extent of qualification and validation should be based on a justified and documented risk assessment of the facilities, equipment, utilities and processes. Retrospective validation is no longer considered an acceptable approach. Data supporting qualification and/or validation studies which were obtained from sources outside of the manufacturers own programmes may be used provided that this approach has been justified and that there is adequate assurance that controls were in place throughout the acquisition of such data.

1   Organising and Planning for Qualification and Validation

1.1   All qualification and validation activities should be planned and take the lifecycle of facilities, equipment, utilities, process and product into consideration.

1.2   Qualification and validation activities should be performed only by suitably trained personnel who follow approved procedures.

1.3   Qualification/validation personnel should report as defined in the pharmaceutical quality system, although this may not necessarily be to a quality management or a quality assurance function. However, there should be appropriate quality oversight over the whole validation lifecycle.

1.4 The key elements of the site qualification and validation programme should be clearly defined and documented in a validation master plan (VMP) or equivalent document.

1.5 The VMP or equivalent document should define the qualification/validation system and include or reference information on at least the following:

(i) Qualification and Validation policy;
(ii) The organisational structure including roles and responsibilities for qualification and validation activities;
(iii) Summary of the facilities, equipment, systems, processes on site, and qualification and validation status;
(iv) Change control and deviation management for qualification and validation;
(v) Guidance on developing acceptance criteria;
(vi) References to existing documents;
(vii) The qualification and validation strategy, including requalification, where applicable.

1.6 For large and complex projects, planning takes on added importance and separate validation plans may enhance clarity.

1.7 A quality risk management approach should be used for qualification and validation activities. In light of increased knowledge and understanding from any changes during the project phase or during commercial production, the risk assessments should be repeated, as required. The way in which risk assessments are used to support qualification and validation activities should be clearly documented.

1.8 Appropriate checks should be incorporated into qualification and validation work to ensure the integrity of all data obtained.

2   Documentation, including VMP

2.1 Good documentation practices are important to support knowledge management throughout the product lifecycle.

2.2 All documents generated during qualification and validation should be approved and authorised by appropriate personnel as defined in the pharmaceutical quality system.

2.3 The interrelationship between documents in complex validation projects should be clearly defined.

2.4 Validation protocols should be prepared that define the critical systems, attributes and parameters, and associated acceptance criteria.

2.5 Qualification documents may be combined together, where appropriate, e.g. installation qualification (IQ) and operational qualification (OQ).

2.6 Where validation protocols and other documentation are supplied by a third party providing validation services, appropriate personnel at the manufacturing site should confirm suitability and compliance with internal procedures before approval. Vendor protocols may be supplemented by additional documentation/test protocols before use.

2.7 Any significant changes to the approved protocol during execution, e.g. acceptance criteria, operating parameters, etc., should be documented as a deviation and be scientifically justified.

2.8 Results that fail to meet the predefined acceptance criteria should be recorded as a deviation and be fully investigated according to local procedures. Any implications for the validation should be discussed in the report.

2.9 The review and conclusions of the validation should be reported and the results obtained summarised against the acceptance criteria. Any subsequent changes to acceptance criteria should be scientifically justified and a final recommendation made as to the outcome of the validation.

2.10 A formal release for the next stage in the qualification and validation process should be authorised by the relevant responsible personnel either as part of the validation report approval or as a separate summary document. Conditional approval to proceed to the next qualification stage can be given where certain acceptance criteria or deviations have not been fully addressed and there is a documented assessment that there is no significant impact on the next activity.

3 Qualification Stages for Equipment, Facilities, Utilities and Systems

3.1 Qualification activities should consider all stages from initial development of the user requirements specification through to the end of use of the equipment, facility, utility or system. The main stages and some suggested criteria (although this depends on individual project circumstances and may be different), which could be included in each stage, are indicated below:

User requirements specification (URS)

3.2 The specification for equipment, facilities, utilities or systems should be defined in a URS and/or a functional specification. The essential elements of quality need to be built in at this stage and any GMP risks mitigated to an acceptable level. The URS should be a point of reference throughout the validation lifecycle.

Design qualification (DQ)

3.3 The next element in the qualification of equipment, facilities, utilities, or systems is DQ where the compliance of the design with GMP should be demonstrated and documented. The requirements of the user requirements specification should be verified during the design qualification.

Factory acceptance testing (FAT)/Site acceptance testing (SAT)

3.4 Equipment, especially if incorporating novel or complex technology, may be evaluated, if applicable, at the vendor prior to delivery.

3.5 Prior to installation, equipment should be confirmed to comply with the URS/functional specification at the vendor site, if applicable.

3.6 Where appropriate and justified, documentation review and some tests could be performed at the FAT or other stages without the need to repeat on site at IQ/OQ, if it can be shown that the functionality is not affected by the transport and installation.

3.7 FAT may be supplemented by the execution of a SAT after the receipt of equipment at the manufacturing site.

Installation qualification (IQ)

3.8 IQ should be performed on equipment, facilities, utilities or systems.

3.9 IQ should include, but is not limited to, the following:

(i) Verification of the correct installation of components, instrumentation, equipment, pipe work and services against the engineering drawings and specifications;

(ii) Verification of the correct installation against predefined criteria;

(iii) Collection and collation of supplier operating and working instructions and maintenance requirements;

(iv)   Calibration of instrumentation;

(v)   Verification of the materials of construction.

Operational qualification (OQ)

3.10   OQ normally follows IQ but, depending on the complexity of the equipment, it may be performed as a combined Installation/Operation Qualification (IOQ).

3.11   OQ should include, but is not limited to, the following:

(i)   Tests that have been developed from the knowledge of processes, systems and equipment to ensure that the system is operating as designed;

(ii)   Tests to confirm upper and lower operating limits and/or "worst case" conditions.

3.12   The completion of a successful OQ should allow the finalisation of standard operating and cleaning procedures, operator training and preventive maintenance requirements.

Performance qualification (PQ)

3.13   PQ should normally follow the successful completion of IQ and OQ. However, it may in some cases be appropriate to perform it in conjunction with OQ or Process Validation.

3.14   PQ should include, but is not limited to, the following:

(i)   Tests, using production materials, qualified substitutes or simulated product proven to have equivalent behaviour under normal operating conditions with worst-case batch sizes. The frequency of sampling used to confirm process control should be justified;

(ii)   Tests should cover the operating range of the intended process, unless documented evidence from the development phases confirming the operational ranges is available.

4   Re-qualification

4.1   Equipment, facilities, utilities and systems should be evaluated at an appropriate frequency to confirm that they remain in a state of control.

4.2 Where re-qualification is necessary and performed at a specific time period, the period should be justified and the criteria for evaluation defined. Furthermore, the possibility of small changes over time should be assessed.

5 Process Validation

General

5.1 The requirements and principles outlined in this section are applicable to the manufacture of all pharmaceutical dosage forms. They cover the initial validation of new processes, subsequent validation of modified processes, site transfers and on-going process verification. It is implicit in this annex that a robust product development process is in place to enable successful Process Validation.

5.2 Section 5 should be used in conjunction with the current EMA guideline on Process Validation:

5.2.1 The guideline on Process Validation is intended to provide guidance on the information and data to be provided in the regulatory submission only. However, GMP requirements for Process Validation continue throughout the lifecycle of the process.

5.2.2 This approach should be applied to link product and process development. It will ensure validation of the commercial manufacturing process and maintenance of the process in a state of control during routine commercial production.

5.3 Manufacturing processes may be developed using a traditional approach or a continuous verification approach. However, irrespective of the approach used, processes must be shown to be robust and ensure consistent product quality before any product is released to the market. Manufacturing processes using the traditional approach should undergo a prospective validation programme, wherever possible, prior to certification of the product. Retrospective validation is no longer an acceptable approach.

5.4 Process Validation of new products should cover all intended marketed strengths and sites of manufacture. Bracketing could be justified for new products based on extensive process knowledge from the development stage, in conjunction with an appropriate on-going verification programme.

5.5 For Process Validation of products that are transferred from one site to another or within the same site, the number of validation batches could be reduced by the use of a bracketing approach. However, existing product knowledge, including the content of the previous validation, should be available. Different strengths, batch sizes and pack sizes/container types may also use a bracketing approach, if justified.

5.6 For the site transfer of legacy products, the manufacturing process and controls must comply with the Marketing Authorisation and meet current standards for Marketing Authorisation for that product type. If necessary, variations to the Marketing Authorisation should be submitted.

5.7 Process Validation should establish whether all quality attributes and process parameters, which are considered important for ensuring the validated state and acceptable product quality, can be consistently met by the process. The basis by which process parameters and quality attributes were identified as being critical or non-critical should be clearly documented, taking into account the results of any risk assessment activities.

5.8 Normally batches manufactured for process validation should be the same size as the intended commercial scale batches and the use of any other batch sizes should be justified or specified in other sections of EudraLex, Volume 4.

5.9 Equipment, facilities, utilities and systems used for Process Validation should be qualified. Test methods should be validated for their intended use.

5.10 For all products, irrespective of the approach used, process knowledge from development studies or other sources should be accessible to the manufacturing site, unless otherwise justified, and be the basis for validation activities.

5.11 For process validation batches, production, development or other site transfer personnel may be involved. Batches should be manufactured only by trained personnel, in accordance with GMP using approved documentation. It is expected that production personnel are involved in the manufacture of validation batches to facilitate product understanding.

5.12 The suppliers of critical starting and packaging materials should be qualified prior to the manufacture of validation batches; otherwise a justification based on the application of quality risk management principles should be documented.

5.13 It is especially important that the underlying process knowledge for the design space justification (if used) and for development of any mathematical models (if used) to confirm a process control strategy should be available.

5.14 Where validation batches are released to the market, this should be predefined. The conditions under which they are produced should fully comply with GMP, the validation acceptance criteria, any continuous process verification criteria (if used) and the Marketing Authorisation or clinical trial authorisation.

5.15 For the process validation of investigational medicinal products (IMP), please refer to Annex 13.

Concurrent validation

5.16 In exceptional circumstances, where there is a strong benefit–risk ratio for the patient, it may be acceptable not to complete a validation programme before routine production starts and concurrent validation could be used. However, the decision to carry out concurrent validation must be justified, documented in the VMP for visibility and approved by authorised personnel.

5.17 Where a concurrent validation approach has been adopted, there should be sufficient data to support a conclusion that any given batch of product is uniform and meets the defined acceptance criteria. The results and conclusion should be formally documented and available to the Qualified Person prior to certification of the batch.

Traditional process validation

5.18 In the traditional approach, a number of batches of the finished product are manufactured under routine conditions to confirm reproducibility.

5.19 The number of batches manufactured and the number of samples taken should be based on quality risk management principles, allow the normal range of variation and trends to be established, and provide sufficient data for evaluation. Each manufacturer must determine and justify the number of batches necessary to demonstrate a high level of assurance that the process is capable of consistently delivering quality product.

5.20 Without prejudice to 5.19, it is generally considered acceptable that a minimum of three consecutive batches manufactured under routine conditions could constitute a validation of the process. An alternative number of batches may be justified, taking into account whether standard methods of manufacture are used and whether similar products or processes are already used at the site. An initial validation exercise with three batches may need to be supplemented, with further data obtained from subsequent batches as part of an on-going process verification exercise.

5.21 A process validation protocol should be prepared that defines the critical process parameters (CPPs), critical quality attributes (CQAs) and associated acceptance criteria, and should be based on development data or documented process knowledge.

5.22   Process Validation protocols should include, but are not limited to the following:

(i)   A short description of the process and a reference to the respective Master Batch Record;
(ii)   Functions and responsibilities;
(iii)   Summary of the CQAs to be investigated;
(iv)   Summary of the CPPs and their associated limits;
(v)   Summary of other (non-critical) attributes and parameters that will be investigated or monitored during the validation activity, and the reasons for their inclusion;
(vi)   List of the equipment/facilities to be used (including measuring/monitoring/recording equipment) together with the calibration status;
(vii)   List of analytical methods and method validation, as appropriate;
(viii)   Proposed in-process controls with acceptance criteria and the reason(s) why each in-process control is selected;
(ix)   Additional testing to be carried out with acceptance criteria;
(x)   Sampling plan and the rationale behind it;
(xi)   Methods for recording and evaluating results;
(xii)   Process for release and certification of batches (if applicable).

Continuous process verification

5.23   For products developed by a quality design approach, where it has been scientifically established during development that the established control strategy provides a high degree of assurance of product quality, then continuous process verification can be used as an alternative to traditional Process Validation.

5.24   The method by which the process will be verified should be defined. There should be a science-based control strategy for the required attributes for incoming materials, critical quality attributes and critical process parameters to confirm product realisation. This should also include regular evaluation of the control strategy. Process Analytical Technology and multivariate statistical process control may be used as tools. Each manufacturer must determine and justify the number of batches necessary to demonstrate a high level of assurance that the process is capable of consistently delivering quality product.

5.25   The general principles laid down in paragraphs 5.1–5.14 above still apply.

Hybrid approach

5.26 A hybrid of the traditional approach and continuous process verification could be used where there is a substantial amount of product and process knowledge and understanding, which has been gained from manufacturing experience and historical batch data.

5.27 This approach may also be used for any validation activities after changes or during on-going process verification, even though the product was initially validated using a traditional approach.

On-going process verification during lifecycle

5.28 Paragraphs 5.28–5.32 are applicable to all three approaches to Process Validation mentioned above, i.e. traditional, continuous and hybrid.

5.29 Manufacturers should monitor product quality to ensure that a state of control is maintained throughout the product lifecycle with the relevant process trends evaluated.

5.30 The extent and frequency of on-going process verification should be reviewed periodically. At any point throughout the product lifecycle, it may be appropriate to modify the requirements taking into account the current level of process understanding and process performance.

5.31 On-going process verification should be conducted under an approved protocol or equivalent documents and a corresponding report should be prepared to document the results obtained. Statistical tools should be used, where appropriate, to support any conclusions with regard to the variability and capability of a given process and ensure a state of control.

5.32 On-going process verification should be used throughout the product lifecycle to support the validated status of the product as documented in the Product Quality Review. Incremental changes over time should also be considered and the need for any additional actions, e.g. enhanced sampling, should be assessed.

6 Verification of Transportation

6.1 Finished medicinal products, investigational medicinal products, bulk product and samples should be transported from manufacturing sites in accordance with the conditions defined in the Marketing Authorisation, the approved label, Product Specification File or as justified by the manufacturer.

6.2   It is recognised that verification of transportation may be challenging due to the variable factors involved; however, transportation routes should be clearly defined. Seasonal and other variations should also be considered during verification of transport.

6.3   A risk assessment should be performed to consider the impact of variables in the transportation process other than those conditions that are continuously controlled or monitored, e.g. delays during transportation, failure of monitoring devices, topping up liquid nitrogen, product susceptibility and any other relevant factors.

6.4   Due to the variable conditions expected during transportation, continuous monitoring and recording of any critical environmental conditions to which the product may be subjected should be performed, unless otherwise justified.

7   Validation of Packaging

7.1   Variation in equipment processing parameters, especially during primary packaging, may have a significant impact on the integrity and correct functioning of the pack, e.g. blister strips, sachets and sterile components; therefore primary and secondary packaging equipment for finished and bulk products should be qualified.

7.2   Qualification of the equipment used for primary packing should be carried out at the minimum and maximum operating ranges defined for the critical process parameters, such as temperature, machine speed and sealing pressure, or for any other factors.

8   Qualification of Utilities

8.1   The quality of steam, water, air, other gases, etc. should be confirmed after installation using the qualification steps described in section 3 above.

8.2   The period and extent of qualification should reflect any seasonal variations, if applicable, and the intended use of the utility.

8.3   A risk assessment should be carried out where there may be direct contact with the product, e.g. heating, ventilation and air-conditioning (HVAC) systems, or indirect contact such as through heat exchangers to mitigate any risks of failure.

9 Validation of Test Methods

9.1 All analytical test methods used in qualification, validation or cleaning exercises should be validated with an appropriate detection and quantification limit, where necessary, as defined in Chapter 6 of EudraLex, Volume 4, Part I.

9.2 Where microbial testing of product is carried out, the method should be validated to confirm that the product does not influence the recovery of microorganisms.

9.3 Where microbial testing of surfaces in clean rooms is carried out, validation should be performed on the test method to confirm that sanitising agents do not influence the recovery of microorganisms.

10 Cleaning Validation

10.1 Cleaning validation should be performed in order to confirm the effectiveness of any cleaning procedure for all product contact equipment. Simulating agents may be used with appropriate scientific justification. Where similar types of equipment are grouped together, a justification of the specific equipment selected for cleaning validation is expected.

10.2 A visual check for cleanliness is an important part of the acceptance criteria for cleaning validation. It is not generally acceptable for this criterion alone to be used. Repeated cleaning and re-testing until acceptable residue results are obtained is not considered an acceptable approach.

10.3 It is recognised that a cleaning validation programme may take some time to complete and validation with verification after each batch may be required for some products, e.g. investigational medicinal products. There should be sufficient data from the verification to support a conclusion that the equipment is clean and available for further use.

10.4 Validation should consider the level of automation in the cleaning process. Where an automatic process is used, the specified normal operating range of the utilities and equipment should be validated.

10.5 For all cleaning processes an assessment should be performed to determine the variable factors that influence cleaning effectiveness and performance, e.g. operators, the level of detail in procedures such as rinsing times, etc. If variable factors have been identified, the worst-case situations should be used as the basis for cleaning validation studies.

10.6 Limits for the carryover of product residues should be based on a toxicological evaluation[1]. The justification for the selected limits should be documented in a risk assessment, which includes all the supporting references. Limits should be established for the removal of any cleaning agents used. Acceptance criteria should consider the potential cumulative effect of multiple items of equipment in the process equipment train.

10.6.1 Therapeutic macromolecules and peptides are known to degrade and denature when exposed to pH extremes and/or heat, and may become pharmacologically inactive. A toxicological evaluation may therefore not be applicable in these circumstances.

10.6.2 If it is not feasible to test for specific product residues, other representative parameters may be selected, e.g. total organic carbon (TOC) and conductivity.

10.7 The risk presented by microbial and endotoxin contamination should be considered during the development of cleaning validation protocols.

10.8 The influence of the time between manufacture and cleaning and the time between cleaning and use should be taken into account to define dirty and clean hold times for the cleaning process.

10.9 Where campaign manufacture is carried out, the impact on the ease of cleaning at the end of the campaign should be considered and the maximum length of a campaign (in time and/or number of batches) should be the basis for cleaning validation exercises.

10.10 Where a worst case product approach is used as a cleaning validation model, a scientific rationale should be provided for the selection of the worst-case product and the impact of new products to the site assessed. Criteria for determining the worst case may include solubility, ability to be cleaned, toxicity and potency.

10.11 Cleaning validation protocols should specify or reference the locations to be sampled and the rationale for the selection of these locations, and define the acceptance criteria.

10.12 Sampling should be carried out by swabbing and/or rinsing or by other means, depending on the production equipment. The sampling materials and method should not influence the result. Recovery should be shown to be possible from all product contact materials sampled in the equipment with all the sampling methods used.

---

[1] See EMA Guideline on setting health based exposure limits for use in risk identification in the manufacture of different medicinal products in shared facilities.

10.13   The cleaning procedure should be performed an appropriate number of times based on a risk assessment and meet the acceptance criteria in order to prove that the cleaning method is validated.

10.14   Where a cleaning process is ineffective or not appropriate for some equipment, dedicated equipment or other appropriate measures should be used for each product as indicated in Chapters 3 and 5 of EudraLex, Volume 4, Part I.

10.15   Where manual cleaning of equipment is performed, it is especially important that the effectiveness of the manual process should be confirmed at a justified frequency.

11 Change Control

11.1   The control of change is an important part of knowledge management and should be handled within the pharmaceutical quality system.

11.2   Written procedures should be in place to describe the actions to be taken if a planned change is proposed to a starting material, product component, process, equipment, premises, product range, method of production or testing, batch size, design space or any other change during the lifecycle that may affect product quality or reproducibility.

11.3   Where design space is used, the impact on changes to the design space should be considered against the registered design space within the Marketing Authorisation and the need for any regulatory actions assessed.

11.4   Quality risk management should be used to evaluate planned changes to determine the potential impact on product quality, pharmaceutical quality systems, documentation, validation, regulatory status, calibration, maintenance and on any other system to avoid unintended consequences and to plan for any necessary process validation, verification or requalification efforts.

11.5   Changes should be authorised and approved by the responsible persons or relevant functional personnel in accordance with the pharmaceutical quality system.

11.6   Supporting data, e.g. copies of documents, should be reviewed to confirm that the impact of the change has been demonstrated prior to final approval.

11.7   Following implementation, and, where appropriate, an evaluation of the effectiveness of change should be carried out to confirm that the change has been successful.

EU GMP GUIDE PART I ANNEX 15 QUALIFICATION AND VALIDATION

12 Glossary

Definitions of terms relating to qualification and validation that are not given in other sections of the current EudraLex, Volume 4, are given below.

BRACKETING APPROACH

A science and risk-based validation approach such that only batches on the extremes of certain predetermined and justified design factors, e.g. strength, batch size and/or pack size, are tested during Process Validation. The design assumes that validation of any intermediate levels is represented by validation of the extremes. Where a range of strengths is to be validated, bracketing could be applicable if the strengths are identical or very closely related in composition, e.g. for a tablet range made with different compression weights of a similar basic granulation or a capsule range made by filling different plug fill weights of the same basic composition into different size capsule shells. Bracketing can be applied to different container sizes or different fills in the same container closure system.

CHANGE CONTROL

A formal system by which qualified representatives of appropriate disciplines review proposed or actual changes that might affect the validated status of facilities, systems, equipment or processes. The intent is to determine the need for action to ensure and document that the system is maintained in a validated state.

CLEANING VALIDATION

Cleaning validation is documented evidence that an approved cleaning procedure will reproducibly remove the previous product or cleaning agents used in the equipment below the scientifically set maximum allowable carryover level.

CLEANING VERIFICATION

The gathering of evidence through chemical analysis, after each batch/campaign, to show that the residues of the previous product or cleaning agents have been reduced below the scientifically set maximum allowable carryover level.

CONCURRENT VALIDATION

Validation carried out in exceptional circumstances, justified on the basis of significant patient benefit, where the validation protocol is executed concurrently with commercialisation of the validation batches.

CONTINUOUS PROCESS VERIFICATION

An alternative approach to process validation, in which manufacturing process performance is continuously monitored and evaluated (ICH Q8).

CONTROL STRATEGY

A planned set of controls derived from current product and process understanding that ensures process performance and product quality. The controls can include parameters and attributes related to drug substance and drug product materials and components, facility and equipment operating conditions, in-process controls, finished product specifications and the associated methods and frequency of monitoring and control (ICH Q10).

CRITICAL PROCESS PARAMETER (CPP)

A process parameter whose variability has an impact on a critical quality attribute and therefore should be monitored or controlled to ensure that the process produces the desired quality (ICH Q8).

CRITICAL QUALITY ATTRIBUTE (CQA)

A physical, chemical, biological or microbiological property or characteristic that should be within an approved limit, range or distribution to ensure the desired product quality (ICH Q8).

DESIGN QUALIFICATION (DQ)

The documented verification that the proposed design of the facilities, systems and equipment is suitable for the intended purpose.

DESIGN SPACE

The multidimensional combination and interaction of input variables, e.g. material attributes, and process parameters that have been demonstrated to provide assurance of quality. Working within the design space is not considered to be a change. Movement out of the design space is considered to be a change and would normally initiate a regulatory post-approval change process. Design space is proposed by the applicant and is subject to regulatory assessment and approval (ICH Q8).

INSTALLATION QUALIFICATION (IQ)

The documented verification that the facilities, systems and equipment, as installed or modified, comply with the approved design and the manufacturer's recommendations.

KNOWLEDGE MANAGEMENT

A systematic approach to acquire, analyse, store and disseminate information (ICH Q10).

LIFECYCLE

All phases in the life of a product, equipment or facility from initial development or use through to discontinuation of use.

ON-GOING PROCESS VERIFICATION (ALSO KNOWN AS CONTINUED PROCESS VERIFICATION)

Documented evidence that the process remains in a state of control during commercial manufacture.

OPERATIONAL QUALIFICATION (OQ)

The documented verification that the facilities, systems and equipment, as installed or modified, perform as intended throughout the anticipated operating ranges.

PERFORMANCE QUALIFICATION (PQ)

The documented verification that systems and equipment can perform effectively and reproducibly based on the approved process method and product specification.

PROCESS VALIDATION

The documented evidence that the process, operated within established parameters, can perform effectively and reproducibly to produce a medicinal product, meeting its predetermined specifications and quality attributes.

PRODUCT REALISATION

Achievement of a product with the quality attributes to meet the needs of patients, healthcare professionals and regulatory authorities, and internal customer requirements (ICH Q10).

PROSPECTIVE VALIDATION

Validation carried out before routine production of products intended for sale.

QUALITY BY DESIGN

A systematic approach that begins with predefined objectives and emphasises product and process understanding and process control, based on sound science and quality risk management.

QUALITY RISK MANAGEMENT

A systematic process for the assessment, control, communication and review of risks to quality across the lifecycle (ICH Q9).

SIMULATED AGENTS

A material that closely approximates the physical and, where practical, the chemical characteristics, e.g. viscosity, particle size, pH, etc., of the product under validation.

STATE OF CONTROL

A condition in which the set of controls consistently provides assurance of acceptable process performance and product quality.

TRADITIONAL APPROACH

A product development approach where set points and operating ranges for process parameters are defined to ensure reproducibility.

WORST CASE

A condition or set of conditions encompassing upper and lower processing limits and circumstances, within standard operating procedures, which pose the greatest chance of product or process failure when compared with ideal conditions. Such conditions do not necessarily induce product or process failure.

USER REQUIREMENTS SPECIFICATION (URS)

The set of owner, user and engineering requirements necessary and sufficient to create a feasible design meeting the intended purpose of the system.

ANNEX 16 CERTIFICATION BY A QUALIFIED PERSON AND BATCH RELEASE

Editor's note The Annex has been revised to reflect the globalisation of the pharmaceutical supply chains and the introduction of new quality control strategies. The revision has been carried out in the light of Directive 2011/62/EU amending Directive 2001/83/EC as regards the prevention of the entry into the legal supply chain of falsified medicinal products. This version also implements ICH Q8, Q9 and Q10 documents, and interpretation documents, such as the manufacturing and importation authorisation (MIA) interpretation document, as applicable. Also, some areas, where the interpretation by Member States has not been consistent, have been clarified.

This Annex came into operation on 15 April 2016.

Scope

This Annex provides guidance on the certification by a Qualified Person (QP) and on batch release within the European Union (EU) of medicinal products for human or veterinary use holding a Marketing Authorisation (MA) or made for export. The principles of this guidance also apply to investigational medicinal products (IMPs) for human use, subject to any difference in the legal provisions and more specific guidance published by the European Commission.

The relevant legislative requirements are provided in Article 51 of Directive 2001/83/EC, as amended, and in Article 55 of Directive 2001/82/EC. Notice is taken of the arrangements referred to in Article 51(2) of Directive 2001/83/EC, as amended, and Article 55(2) of Directive 2001/82/EC, e.g. Mutual Recognition Agreements (MRAs).

This Annex does not address the "Official Control Authority Batch Release" which may be specified for certain blood and immunological products in accordance with Articles 109, 110, 113 and 114 of Directive 2001/83/EC, as amended, and Articles 81 and 82 of Directive 2001/82/EC. However, this Annex does apply to the QP certification and subsequent release of such batches.

The basic arrangements for batch release for a product are defined by its MA. Nothing in this Annex should be taken as overriding those arrangements.

General Principles

The ultimate responsibility for the performance of a medicinal product over its lifetime, its safety, quality and efficacy, lies with the Marketing Authorisation Holder (MAH).

However, the QP is responsible for ensuring that each individual batch has been manufactured and checked in compliance with laws in force in the Member State where certification takes place, in accordance with the requirements of the MA and with Good Manufacturing Practice (GMP).

The process of batch release comprises:

(i)   The checking of the manufacture and testing of the batch in accordance with defined release procedures.

(ii) The certification of the finished product batch performed by a QP signifying that the batch is in compliance with GMP and the requirements of its MA. This represents the quality release of the batch.

(iii) The transfer to saleable stock and/or export of the finished batch of product, which should take into account the certification performed by the QP. If this transfer is performed at a site other than that where certification takes place, then the arrangement should be documented in a written agreement between the sites.

The purpose of controlling batch release is notably to ensure that:

(i)   the batch has been manufactured and checked in accordance with the requirements of its MA;

(ii) the batch has been manufactured and checked in accordance with the principles and guidelines of GMP;

(iii) any other relevant legal requirements are taken into account;

(iv) in the event that a quality defect, as referred to in Chapter 8 of EudraLex, Volume 4, Part I, needs to be investigated or a batch recalled, to ensure that any QPs involved in the certification or confirmation[1] and any relevant records are readily identifiable.

EU GMP GUIDE PART I ANNEX 16 CERTIFICATION BY A QUALIFIED PERSON AND BATCH RELEASE

---

[1] Information required for the confirmation, where QP responsibilities for the batch are being transferred between sites, is presented in Appendix I to this Annex.

1 The Process of Certification

1.1 Each batch of finished product must be certified[2] by a QP within the EU before being released for sale or supply in the EU or for export. Certification can be performed only by a QP of the manufacturer and/or importer, which is described in the MA.

1.2 Any QP involved in the certification, or confirmation of a batch must have detailed knowledge of the steps for which they are taking responsibility. The QPs should be able to prove their continuous training regarding the product type, production processes, technical advances and changes to GMP.

1.3 There may be several sites involved in the various stages of manufacture, importation, testing and storage of a batch before it undergoes certification. Regardless of how many sites are involved, the QP performing certification of the finished product must ensure that all necessary steps have been completed under accepted pharmaceutical quality systems to assure compliance of the batch with GMP, the MA and any other legal obligations in the Member State where certification is taking place.

1.4 For manufacturing steps performed at sites in the EU each manufacturing site must have at least one QP.

1.4.1 Where the site only undertakes partial manufacturing operations in relation to a batch, then a QP at that site must at least confirm that the operations undertaken by the site have been performed in accordance with GMP and the terms of the written agreement detailing the operations for which the site is responsible. If the QP is responsible for providing confirmation of compliance for those operations with the relevant MA, then the QP should have access to the necessary details of the MA.

1.4.2 The QP who performs certification of the finished product batch may assume full responsibility for all stages of manufacture of the batch or this responsibility may be shared with other QPs who have provided confirmation for specified steps in the manufacture and control of a batch. These could be other QPs who are operating under the same manufacturing authorisation (MIA) holder or QPs operating under different MIA holders.

1.4.3 Any sharing of responsibilities among QPs in relation to compliance of a batch must be defined in a document formally agreed by all parties. This document should detail responsibility for

---

[2] The contents of a batch certificate for medicinal products are presented in Appendix II to this Annex.

assessment of the impact any deviation(s) has/have on compliance of the batch with GMP and the MA.

1.5 For medicinal products manufactured outside the EU, physical importation and certification are the final stages of manufacturing that precede the transfer to saleable stock of the batch.

1.5.1 The process of certification as described in Section 1 of this Annex, applies to all medicinal products intended to be released for the EU markets, or for export, irrespective of the complexity of the supply chain and the global locations of manufacturing sites involved.

1.5.2 In accordance with the principles described in Section 1.4 of this Annex, the QP certifying the finished medicinal product batch may take account of the confirmation by, and share defined responsibilities with, other QPs in relation to any manufacturing or importation operations taking place at other sites in the EU and other MIA holders defined in the relevant MA.

1.5.3 Conditions of storage and transport for the batch and the sample, if sent separately, should be taken into account by the QP before certification of a batch.

1.5.4 The QP certifying the finished product is responsible for ensuring that each finished medicinal product batch has been manufactured in accordance with GMP and the MA. Unless an MRA or similar agreement is in place between the EU and the exporting country, the QP is also responsible for ensuring that the finished medicinal product batch has undergone, in a Member State, a full qualitative analysis, a quantitative analysis of at least all the active substances, and all the other tests or checks necessary to ensure that the quality of medicinal products is in accordance with the requirements of the MA.

1.5.5 Sampling of imported product should be fully representative of the batch. Samples may either be taken after arrival in the EU or be taken at the manufacturing site in the third country, in accordance with a technically justified approach, which is documented within the company's quality system. Responsibilities in relation to the sampling should be defined in a written agreement between the sites. Any samples taken outside the EU should be shipped under equivalent transport conditions as the batch that they represent.

1.5.6 Where sampling is performed at a third country manufacturing site, the technical justification should include a formal Quality Risk Management process to identify and manage any risks associated with this approach. This should be fully documented and include at least the following elements:

(i)   Audit of the manufacturing activity including any sampling activity at the third country site and evaluation of subsequent transportation steps of both the batch and samples to ensure that the samples are representative of the imported batch.

(ii)   A comprehensive scientific study, including data to support any conclusions that samples taken in the third country are representative of the batch after importation. This study should at least include:
   • description of the sampling process in the third country;
   • description of the transported conditions of the sample and the imported batch. Any differences should be justified;
   • comparative analysis of samples taken in the third country and samples taken after importation;
   • consideration of the time interval between sampling and importation of the batch and generation of data to support appropriate defined limits.

(iii) Provision for random periodic analysis of samples taken after importation to justify on-going reliance on samples taken in a third country.

(iv)   A review of any unexpected result or confirmed out-of-specification result. These may have implications for reliance on sampling performed at the third-country manufacturing site and should be notified to the Supervisory Authority for the site where certification is performed. Such an occurrence should be regarded as a potential quality defect and investigated in line with the guidance in Chapter 8 of EudraLex, Volume 4, Part I.

1.5.7   Different imported finished product batches may originate from the same bulk product batch. The QPs certifying the different finished product batches may base their decision on the quality control testing of the first imported finished batch, provided that a justification has been documented based on Quality Risk Management principles. This should take into account the provisions of paragraph 1.5.6 in relation to reliance on any samples taken in third countries. Evidence should be available to ensure that the integrity and identity of the imported finished product batch has been established through documented verification of at least the following:

(i)   Relevant requirements for storage of the bulk product prior to packaging have been satisfied;

(ii)   The finished product batch has been stored and transported under the required conditions;

(iii) The consignment has remained secure and there is no evidence of tampering during storage or transportation;

(iv)   Correct identification of the product has been established;

(v)   The sample(s) tested are representative of all finished product batches derived from the bulk batch.

1.6   The QP must personally ensure that the following operational responsibilities are fulfilled prior to certification of a batch for release to market or for export:

(i)   Certification is permitted under the terms of the MIA;

(ii)   Any additional duties and requirements of national legislation are complied with;

(iii) Certification is recorded in a register or equivalent document.

1.7   In addition, the QP has responsibility for ensuring points 1.7.1 to 1.7.21 are secured. These tasks may be delegated to appropriately trained personnel or third parties. It is recognised that the QP will need to rely on the pharmaceutical quality system and the QP should have on-going assurance that this reliance is well founded.

1.7.1   All activities associated with manufacture and testing of the medicinal product have been conducted in accordance with the principles and guidelines of GMP.

1.7.2   The entire supply chain of the active substance and medicinal product up to the stage of certification is documented and available for the QP. This should include the manufacturing sites of the starting materials and packaging materials for the medicinal product, and any other materials deemed critical through a risk assessment of the manufacturing process. The document should preferably be in the format of a comprehensive diagram, where each party, including subcontractors of critical steps such as the sterilisation of components and equipment for aseptic processing, are included.

1.7.3   All audits of sites involved in the manufacture and testing of the medicinal products and in the manufacture of the active substance have been carried out, and the audit reports are available to the QP performing the certification.

1.7.4   All sites of manufacture, analysis and certification are compliant with the terms of the MA for the intended territory.

1.7.5   All manufacturing activities and testing activities are consistent with those described in the MA.

1.7.6   The source and specifications of starting materials and packaging materials used in the batch are compliant with the MA. Supplier quality management systems are in place to that ensure only materials of the required quality have been supplied.

1.7.7   For medicinal products that fall within the scope of Directive 2001/83/EC, as amended, or Directive 2001/82/EC, the active substances have been manufactured in accordance with GMP and, where required, distributed in accordance with Good Distribution Practice (GDP) for Active Substances.

1.7.8   The importation of active substances used in the manufacture of medicinal products for human use should comply with the requirements of Article 46(b) of Directive 2001/83/EC, as amended.

1.7.9   For medicinal products that fall within the scope of Directive 2001/83/EC, as amended, the excipients have been manufactured in accordance with the ascertained GMP referred to in Article 46 (f) of that Directive.

1.7.10 When relevant, the TSE (transmissible spongiform encephalopathy) status of all materials used in batch manufacture is compliant with the terms of the MA.

1.7.11 All records are complete and endorsed by appropriate personnel. All required in-process controls and checks have been made.

1.7.12 All manufacturing and testing processes remain in the validated state. Personnel are trained and qualified as appropriate.

1.7.13 Finished product quality control (QC) test data complies with the Finished Product Specification described in the MA or, where authorised, the Real Time Release Testing programme.

1.7.14 Any regulatory post-marketing commitments relating to manufacture or testing of the product have been addressed. On-going stability data continues to support certification.

1.7.15 The impact of any change to product manufacturing or testing has been evaluated and any additional checks and tests are complete.

1.7.16 All investigations pertaining to the batch being certified (including out-of-specification and out-of-trend investigations) have been completed to a sufficient level to support certification.

1.7.17 Any on-going complaints, investigations or recalls do not negate the conditions for certification of the batch in question.

1.7.18 The required technical agreements are in place.

1.7.19 The self-inspection programme is active and current.

1.7.20 The appropriate arrangements for distribution and shipment are in place.

1.7.21 In the case of medicinal products for human use intended to be placed on the market in the Union, the safety features referred to in Article 54(o) of Directive 2001/83/EC, as amended, have been affixed to the packaging, where appropriate.

1.8 For certain products, special guidance may apply, such as EudraLex, Volume 4, Annex 2: Manufacture of Biological active substances and Medicinal Products for Human Use, and Annex 3: Manufacture of Radiopharmaceuticals.

1.9 In the case of parallel importation and parallel distribution any repackaging operation carried out on a batch that has already been released must be approved by the competent authority of the intended market.

1.9.1 Prior to certification of a repacked batch, the QP should confirm compliance with national requirements for parallel importation and EU rules for parallel distribution.

1.9.2 The QP of the MIA holder, who is named responsible for the certification of the batch in the MA of the repackaged finished product, certifies that the repackaging has been performed in accordance with the relevant authorisation pertaining to the repackaged product and GMP.

1.10 Recording of QP certification.

1.10.1 The certification of a medicinal product is recorded by the QP in a register or equivalent document provided for that purpose. The record should show that each production batch satisfies the provisions of Article 51 of Directive 2001/83/EC, as amended, or Article 55 of Directive 2001/82/EC. The record must be kept up to date as operations are carried out and must remain at the disposal of the agents of the competent authority for the period specified in the provisions of the Member State concerned and in any event for at least five years.

1.10.2 The control report referred to in Article 51 of Directive 2001/83/EC, as amended, or Article 55 of Directive 2001/82/EC, or another proof for release to the market in question, based on an equivalent system, should be made available for the batch in order to be exempted from further controls when entering another Member State.

2   Relying on GMP Assessments by Third Parties, e.g. Audits

In some cases the QP will rely on the correct functioning of the pharmaceutical quality system of sites involved in the manufacture of the product and this may be derived from audits conducted by third parties.

2.1   Relying on assessment by third parties, e.g. audits, should be in accordance with Chapter 7 of the GMP Guide in order to appropriately define, agree and control any outsourced activity.

2.2   Special focus should be given to the approval of audit reports:

(i)   The audit report should address general GMP requirements, such as the quality management system, all relevant production and quality control procedures related to the supplied product, e.g. active substance manufacturing, quality control testing, primary packaging, etc. All audited areas should be accurately described, resulting in a detailed report of the audit.

(ii)   It should be determined whether the manufacture and quality control of the active substance and medicinal product complies with GMP or, in case of manufacture in third countries, GMP at least equivalent to that referred to in Article 46 of Directive 2001/83/EC, as amended, or Article 50 of Directive 2001/82/EC.

(iii)   In case of outsourced activities, compliance with the MA should be verified.

(iv)   The QP should ensure that a written final assessment and approval of third party audit reports have been made. The QP should have access to all documentation that facilitates review of the audit outcome and continued reliance on the outsourced activity.

(v)   Outsourced activities with critical impact on product quality should be defined in accordance with the principles of Quality Risk Management as described in Part III of EudraLex, Volume 4. According to this, the QP should be aware of the outcome of an audit with critical impact on the product quality before certifying the relevant batches.

(vi)   Repeated audits should be performed in accordance with the principles of Quality Risk Management.

3   Handling of Unexpected Deviations

Provided that registered specifications for active substances, excipients, packaging materials and medicinal products are met, a QP may consider confirming compliance or certifying a batch where an unexpected deviation, concerning the manufacturing process and/or the analytical control methods from details contained within the MA and/or GMP, has occurred. The deviation should be thoroughly investigated and the root cause corrected. This may require the submission of a variation to the MA for the continued manufacture of the product.

3.1   The impact of the deviation should be assessed in accordance with a Quality Risk Management process using an appropriate approach, such as described in Part III of the GMP Guide. The Quality Risk Management process should include the following:

(i)   Evaluation of the potential impact of the deviation on quality, safety or efficacy of the batch(es) concerned and conclusion that the impact is negligible;

(ii)   Consideration of the need to include the affected batch(es) in the on-going stability programme;

(iii) In the case of biological medicinal products, consideration that any deviations from the approved process can have an unexpected impact on safety and efficacy.

Taking into account that responsibilities may be shared between more than one QP involved in the manufacture and control of a batch, the QP performing certification of a batch of medicinal product should be aware of and take into consideration any deviations that have the potential to impact compliance with GMP and/or compliance with the MA.

4   The Release of a Batch

4.1   Batches of medicinal products should be released for sale or supply to the market only after certification by a QP as described above. Until a batch has been certified, it should remain at the site of manufacture or be shipped under quarantine to another site that has been approved for that purpose by the relevant Competent Authority.

4.2   Safeguards to ensure that uncertified batches are not transferred to saleable stock should be in place and may be physical in nature, e.g. the use of segregation and labelling, or electronic in nature, e.g. the use of validated computerised systems. When uncertified batches are moved from one authorised site to another, the safeguards to prevent premature release should remain.

4.3   The steps necessary to notify QP certification to the site where the transfer to saleable stock is to take place should be defined within a technical agreement. Such notification by a QP to the site should be formal and unambiguous and should be subject to the requirements of Chapter 4 of EudraLex, Volume 4, Part I.

5   Glossary

Certain words and phrases in this annex are used with the particular meanings defined below. Reference should also be made to the Glossary in the main part of the Guide.

Certification of the finished product batch. The certification in a register or equivalent document by a QP, as defined in Article 51 of Directive 2001/83/EC, as amended, and Article 55 of Directive 2001/82/EC, and represents the quality release of the batch before the batch is released for sale or distribution.

Confirmation (confirm and confirmed have equivalent meanings). A signed statement by a QP that a process or test has been conducted in accordance with GMP and the relevant marketing authorisation or clinical trial authorisation, product specification file and/or technical agreement, as applicable, as agreed in writing with the QP responsible for certifying the finished product batch before release. The QP providing a confirmation takes responsibility for those activities being confirmed

Finished product batch. With reference to the control or test of the finished product, a finished medicinal product batch is described in Annex I, Part I, point 3.2.2.5, of Directive 2001/83/EC and Annex I, Part 2, section E, of Directive 2001/82/EC. In the context of this annex the term in particular denotes the batch of product in its final pack for release to the market.

Importer. The holder of the authorisation required by Article 40(3) of Directive 2001/83/EC, as amended, and Article 44(3) of Directive 2001/82/EC for importing medicinal products from third countries.

Qualified Person (QP). The person defined in Article 48 of Directive 2001/83/EC, as amended, and Article 52 of Directive 2001/82/EC.

Appendix I

Content of the confirmation of the partial manufacturing of a medicinal product

[LETTER HEAD OF MANUFACTURER WHO CARRIED OUT THE MANUFACTURING ACTIVITY]

(1) Name of the product and description of the manufacturing stage (e.g. paracetamol 500 mg tablets, primary packaging into blister packs).
(2) Batch number.
(3) Name and address of the site carrying out the partial manufacturing.

(4) Reference to the Technical Quality Agreement (in accordance with Chapter 7 of the Guide).

(5) Confirmation statement.
I hereby confirm that the manufacturing stages referred to in the Technical Quality Agreement have been carried out in full compliance with the GMP requirements of the EU and the terms described in the Agreement for ensuring compliance with the requirements of the Marketing Authorisation(s) as provided by [Contract Giver/manufacturer certifying and releasing the batch].

(6) Name of the Qualified Person confirming the partial manufacturing.

(7) Signature of Qualified Person confirming the partial manufacturing.

(8) Date of signature.

Appendix II

Content of the Batch Certificate for Medicinal Products
[LETTER HEAD OF THE BATCH CERTIFYING AND RELEASING MANUFACTURER]

(1) Name, strength/potency, dosage form and package size (identical to the text on the finished product package).

(2) Batch number of the finished product.

(3) Name of the destination country/countries of the batch, at least when within the EU.

(4) Certification statement.
I hereby certify that all the manufacturing stages of this batch of finished product have been carried out in full compliance with the GMP requirements of the EU and [when within the EU] with the requirements of the Marketing Authorisation(s) of the destination country/countries.

(5) Name of the Qualified Person certifying the batch.

(6) Signature of the Qualified Person certifying the batch.

(7) Date of signature.

EU GMP GUIDE PART I ANNEX 16 CERTIFICATION BY A QUALIFIED PERSON AND BATCH RELEASE

ANNEX 17 REAL TIME RELEASE TESTING AND PARAMETRIC RELEASE

> **Editor's note:** The previous guideline only focused on the application of Parametric Release for the routine release of terminally sterilised products waiving the performance of a test for sterility on the basis of successful demonstration that predetermined and validated sterilising conditions have been achieved. Moreover, advances in the application of process analytical technology (PAT), quality by design (QbD) and quality risk management (QRM) principles to pharmaceutical development and manufacturing have shown that an appropriate combination of process controls together with timely monitoring and verification of pre-established material attributes provides greater assurance of product quality than finished product testing (conventionally regarded as the end-product testing) alone.
>
> This revision to Annex 17 takes into account changes to other sections of EudraLex, Volume 4, Part I, Chapter 1, Annex 1 and 15, ICH Q8, Q9, Q10 and Q11, QWP Guideline on Real Time Release Testing, and changes in manufacturing and analytical technology.
>
> Deadline for coming into operation: 26 December 2018 [6 months after publication].

1. Principle

1.1   Medicinal products must comply with their approved specifications and subject to compliance with GMP, can normally be released to market by performing a complete set of tests on active substances and/or finished products as defined in the relevant marketing authorization or clinical trial authorization. In specific circumstances, where authorised, based on product knowledge and process understanding, information collected during the manufacturing process can be used instead of end-product testing for batch release. Any separate activities required for this form of batch release should be integrated into the Pharmaceutical Quality System (PQS).

2. Scope

2.1   This document is intended to outline the requirements for application of Real Time Release Testing (RTRT) and parametric release, where the control of critical parameters and relevant material attributes are authorized as an alternative to routine end-product testing of active substances and/ or finished products. A specific aim of this guideline is to incorporate the application of RTRT to any stage in the manufacturing process and to any type of finished products or active substances, including their intermediates.

3. Real Time Release Testing (RTRT)

3.1 Under RTRT, a combination of in-process monitoring and controls may provide, when authorized, substitute for end-product testing as part of the batch release decision.

Interaction with all relevant regulatory authorities prior and during the assessment process preceding regulatory approval is required. The level of interaction will depend on the level of complexity of the RTRT control procedure applied on site.

3.2 When designing the RTRT strategy, the following minimum criteria are expected to be established and met:

(i) Real time measurement and control of relevant in-process material attributes and process parameters should be accurate predictors of the corresponding finished product attributes.

(ii) The valid combination of relevant assessed material attributes and process controls to replace finished product attributes should be established with scientific evidence based on material, product and process knowledge.

(iii) The combined process measurements (process parameters and material attributes) and any other test data generated during the manufacturing process should provide a robust foundation for RTRT and the batch release decision.

3.3 A RTRT strategy should be integrated and controlled through the PQS. This should include or reference information at least of the following:

- quality risk management, including a full process related risk assessment, in accordance with the principles described in EudraLex, Volume 4, Part I, Chapter 1 and Part II, Chapter 2,
- change control program,
- control strategy,
- specific personnel training program,
- qualification and validation policy,
- deviation/CAPA system,
- contingency procedure in case of a process sensor/equipment failure,
- periodic review/assessment program to measure the effectiveness of the RTRT plan for continued assurance of product quality.

3.4 In accordance with the principles described in EudraLex, Volume 4, Part I, Chapter 1, Part II, Chapter 13 and Annex 15, the change control program is an important part of the real time release testing approach. Any change that could potentially impact product manufacturing and testing, or the validated status of facilities, systems, equipment, analytical methods or processes, should be assessed for risk to product quality and impact on reproducibility of the manufacturing process. Any change should be justified by the sound application of quality risk management principles, and fully documented. After change implementation, an evaluation should be undertaken to demonstrate that there are no unintended or deleterious impact on product quality.

3.5 A control strategy should be designed not only to monitor the process, but also to maintain a state of control and ensure that a product of the required quality will be consistently produced. The control strategy should describe and justify the selected in-process controls, material attributes and process parameters which require to be routinely monitored and should be based on product, formulation and process understanding. The control strategy is dynamic and may change throughout the lifecycle of the product requiring the use of a quality risk management approach and of knowledge management. The control strategy should also describe the sampling plan and acceptance/rejection criteria.

3.6 Personnel should be given specific training on RTRT technologies, principles and procedures. Key personnel should demonstrate adequate experience, product and process knowledge and understanding. Successful implementation of RTRT requires input from a cross-functional/multidisciplinary team with relevant experience on specific topics, such as engineering, analytics, chemometric modelling or statistics.

3.7 Important parts of the RTRT strategy are validation and qualification policy, with particular reference to advanced analytical methods. Particular attention should be focused on the qualification, validation and management of in-line and on-line analytical methods, where the sampling probe is placed within the manufacturing equipment.

3.8 Any deviation or process failure should be thoroughly investigated and any adverse trending indicating a change in the state of control should be followed up appropriately.

3.9 Continuous learning through data collection and analysis over the lifecycle of a product is important and should be part of the PQS. With advances in technology, certain data trends, intrinsic to a currently acceptable process, may be observed. Manufacturers should scientifically evaluate the data, in consultation if appropriate, with the regulatory authorities, to determine how or if such trends indicate opportunities to improve quality and/or consistency.

3.10   When RTRT has been approved, this approach should be routinely used for batch release. In the event that the results from RTRT fail or are trending toward failure, a RTRT approach may not be substituted by end-product testing. Any failure should be thoroughly investigated and considered in the batch release decision depending on the results of these investigations, and must comply with the content of the marketing authorisation and GMP requirements. Trends should be followed up appropriately.

3.11   Attributes (e.g. uniformity of content) that are indirectly controlled by approved RTRT should still appear in the Certificate of Analysis for batches. The approved method for end-product testing should be mentioned and the results given as "Complies if tested" with a footnote: "Controlled by approved Real Time Release Testing".

4. Parametric Release and Sterilization

4.1   This section provides guidance on parametric release, which is defined as the release of a batch of terminally sterilised product based on a review of critical process control parameters rather than requiring an end-product testing for sterility.

4.2   An end-product test for sterility is limited in its ability to detect contamination because, first, it utilises only a small number of samples in relation to the overall batch size, and, second, culture media may stimulate growth of only some, but not all, microorganisms. Therefore, an end-product testing for sterility provides only an opportunity to detect major failures in the sterility assurance system (i.e. a failure that results in contamination of a large number of product units and/or in contamination by the specific microorganisms whose growth is supported by the prescribed media). In contrast, data derived from in-process controls (e.g. pre-sterilization product bioburden or environmental monitoring) and by monitoring relevant sterilization parameters can provide more accurate and relevant information to support sterility assurance of the product.

4.3   Parametric release can be applied only to products sterilised in their final container using moist heat, dry heat or ionising radiation (dosimetric release), according to European Pharmacopoeial requirements.

4.4   To utilise this approach, the manufacturer should have a history of acceptable GMP compliance and a robust sterility assurance programme in place to demonstrate consistent process control and process understanding.

4.5   The sterility assurance programme should be documented and include, at least, the identification and monitoring of the critical process parameters, sterilizer cycle development and validation, container/packaging integrity validation, bioburden control, environmental monitoring programme, product segregation plan, equipment, services and facility design, and qualification programme, maintenance and calibration programme, change control programme and personnel training, and incorporate a quality risk management approach.

4.6   Risk management is an essential requirement for parametric release and should focus on mitigating the factors that increase the risk of failure to achieve and maintain sterility in each unit of every batch. If a new product or process is being considered for parametric release, then a risk assessment should be conducted during process development, including an evaluation of production data from existing products if applicable. If an existing product or process is being considered, the risk assessment should include an evaluation of any historical data generated.

4.7   Personnel involved in the parametric release process should have experience in the following areas: microbiology, sterility assurance, engineering, production and sterilization. The qualifications, experience, competency and training of all personnel involved in parametric release should be documented.

4.8   Any proposed change that may impact on sterility assurance should be recorded in the change control system and reviewed by appropriate personnel who are qualified and experienced in sterility assurance.

4.9   A pre-sterilization bioburden-monitoring programme for the product and components should be developed to support parametric release. The bioburden should be performed for each batch. The sampling locations of filled units before sterilization should be based on a worst-case scenario and represent the batch. Any organisms found during bioburden testing should be identified to confirm that they do not form spores, which may be more resistant to the sterilizing process.

4.10   Product bioburden should be minimized by appropriate design of the manufacturing environment and the process by:

- good equipment and facility design to allow effective cleaning, disinfection and sanitisation;
- availability of detailed and effective procedures for cleaning, disinfection and sanitisation;
- use of microbial retentive filters where possible;
- availability of operating practices and procedures that promote personnel hygiene and enforce appropriate garment control;
- appropriate microbiological specifications for raw materials, intermediates and process aids (e.g. gases).

4.11   For aqueous or otherwise microbiologically unstable products, the time lag from dissolving the starting materials, product fluid filtration to sterilization should be defined in order to minimise the development of bioburden and an increase in endotoxins (if applicable).

Sterilization process

4.12   Qualification and validation are critical activities to assure that sterilisation equipment can consistently meet cycle operational parameters and that the monitoring devices provide verification of the sterilization process.

4.13   Periodic requalification of equipment and revalidation of processes should be planned and justified in accordance with the requirements of Annexes 1 and 15.

4.14   Appropriate measurement of critical process parameters during sterilization is a critical requirement in a parametric release programme. The standards used for process measuring devices should be specified and the calibration should be traceable to national or international standards.

4.15   Critical process parameters should be established, defined and undergo periodic re-evaluation. The operating ranges should be developed based on sterilisation process, process capability, calibration tolerance limits and parameter criticality.

4.16   Routine monitoring of the sterilizer should demonstrate that the validated conditions necessary to achieve the specified process are achieved in each cycle. Critical processes should be specifically monitored during the sterilization phase.

4.17   The sterilization record should include all the critical process parameters. The sterilization record should be checked for compliance to specification by at least two independent systems. These systems may consist of two people or a validated computer system plus a person.

4.18   Once parametric release has been approved by the regulatory authorities, decisions for release or rejection of a batch should be based on the approved specifications and the review of critical process control data. Routine checks of the sterilizer, changes, deviations, and unplanned and routine planned maintenance activities should be recorded, assessed and approved before releasing the products to the market. Non-compliance with the specification for parametric release cannot be overruled by a finished product passing the test for sterility.

5 Glossary

CONTROL STRATEGY

A planned set of controls, derived from current product and process understanding that ensures process performance and product quality. The controls can include parameters and attributes related to drug substance and drug product materials and components, facility and equipment operating conditions, in-process controls, finished product specifications, and the associated methods and frequency of monitoring and control.

CRITICAL PROCESS PARAMETERS

A process parameter with variability that has an impact on a critical quality attribute and therefore should be monitored or controlled to ensure the process produces the desired quality [ICH Q8 (R2)].

CRITICAL QUALITY ATTRIBUTES

A physical, chemical, biological or microbiological property or characteristic that should be within an appropriate limit, range, or distribution to ensure the desired product quality [ICH Q8 (R2)].

PARAMETRIC RELEASE

One form of RTRT. Parametric release for terminally sterilised product is based on the review of documentation on process monitoring (e.g. temperature, pressure, time for terminal sterilization) rather than the testing of a sample for a specific attribute (ICH Q8 QampA). (Together with compliance with specific GMP requirements related to parametric release this provides the desired assurance of the quality of the product.) (EMA guideline on Real-Time Release Testing).

REAL TIME RELEASE TESTING (RTRT)

The ability to evaluate and ensure the quality of in-process and/or final product based on process data, which typically include a valid combination of measured material attributes and process controls (ICH Q8).

STATE OF CONTROL

A condition in which the set of controls consistently provides assurance of continued process performance and product quality (ICH Q10).

ANNEX 19 REFERENCE AND RETENTION SAMPLES

1 Scope

1.1 This Annex to the Guide to Good Manufacturing Practice for Medicinal Products ("the GMP Guide") gives guidance on the taking and holding of reference samples of starting materials, packaging materials, or finished products and retention samples of finished products.

1.2 Specific requirements for investigational medicinal products are given in Annex 13 to the Guide.

1.3 This annex also includes guidance on the taking of retention samples for parallel imported/distributed medicinal products.

2 Principle

2.1 Samples are retained to fulfil two purposes: first, to provide a sample for analytical testing and, second, to provide a specimen of the fully finished product. Samples may therefore fall into two categories:

- *Reference sample*: a sample of a batch of starting material, packaging material or finished product that is stored for the purpose of being analysed should the need arise during the shelf-life of the batch concerned. Where stability permits, reference samples from critical intermediate stages (e.g. those requiring analytical testing and release), or intermediates that are transported outside of the manufacturer's control, should be kept.
- *Retention sample*: a sample of a fully packaged unit from a batch of finished product. It is stored for identification purposes, e.g. presentation, packaging, labelling, patient information leaflet, batch number, expiry date, should the need arise during the shelf-life of the batch concerned. There may be exceptional circumstances where this requirement can be met without retention of duplicate samples, e.g. where small amounts of a batch are packaged for different markets or in the production of very expensive medicinal products.

2.2 It is necessary for the manufacturer, importer or site of batch release, as specified under Sections 7 and 8, to keep reference and/or retention samples from each batch of finished product, and for the manufacturer to keep a reference sample from a batch of starting material (subject to certain exceptions – see Section 3.2 below) and/or intermediate product. Each packaging site should keep reference samples of each batch of primary and printed packaging materials. Availability of printed materials as part of the reference and/or retention sample of the finished product can be accepted.

2.3   The reference and/or retention samples serve as a record of the batch of finished product or starting material and can be assessed in the event of, for example, a dosage form quality complaint, a query relating to compliance with the Marketing Authorisation, a labelling/packaging query or a pharmacovigilance report.

2.4   Records of traceability of samples should be maintained and be available for review by competent authorities.

3 Duration of Storage

3.1   Reference and retention samples from each batch of finished product should be retained for at least one year after the expiry date. The reference sample should be contained in its finished primary packaging or in packaging composed of the same material as the primary container in which the product is marketed (for veterinary medicinal products other than immunologicals, see also Annex 4, paragraphs 8 and 9).

3.2   Unless a longer period is required, under the law of the Member State of manufacture, samples of starting materials (other than solvents, gases or water used in the manufacturing process) shall be retained for at least two years after the release of product. That period may be shortened if the period of stability of the material, as indicated in the relevant specification, is shorter. Packaging materials should be retained for the duration of the shelf-life of the finished product concerned.

4 Size of Reference and Retention Samples

4.1   The reference sample should be of sufficient size to permit the carrying out, on at least two occasions, of the full analytical controls on the batch in accordance with the Marketing Authorisation File, which has been assessed and approved by the relevant Competent Authority/Authorities. Where it is necessary to do so, unopened packs should be used when carrying out each set of analytical controls. Any proposed exception to this should be justified to, and agreed with, the relevant competent authority.

4.2   Where applicable, national requirements relating to the size of reference samples and, if necessary, retention samples should be followed.

4.3   Reference samples should be representative of the batch of starting material, intermediate product or finished product from which they are taken. Other samples may also be taken to monitor the most stressed part of a process (e.g. beginning or end of a process). Where a batch is packaged in two, or more, distinct packaging operations, at least one retention sample should be taken from each individual packaging operation. Any proposed exception to this should be justified to, and agreed with, the relevant competent authority.

4.4 It should be ensured that all necessary analytical materials and equipment are still available, or readily obtainable, in order to carry out all tests given in the specification until one year after expiry of the last batch manufactured.

5 Storage Conditions

5.1 Storage of reference samples of finished products and active substances should be in accordance with the current version of the Note for Guidance on Declaration of Storage Conditions for Medicinal Products and Active Substances.

5.2 Storage conditions should be in accordance with the marketing authorisation (e.g. refrigerated storage where relevant).

6 Written Agreements

6.1 Where the marketing authorisation holder is not the same legal entity as the site(s) responsible for batch release within the EEA, the responsibility for taking and storage of reference/retention samples should be defined in a written agreement between the two parties, in accordance with Chapter 7 of the EC Guide to Good Manufacturing Practice. This applies also where any manufacturing or batch release activity is carried out at a site other than that with overall responsibility for the batch on the EEA market, and the arrangements between each different site for the taking and keeping of reference and retention samples should be defined in a written agreement.

6.2 The Qualified Person who certifies a batch for sale should ensure that all relevant reference and retention samples are accessible at all reasonable times. Where necessary, the arrangements for such access should be defined in a written agreement.

6.3 Where more than one site is involved in the manufacture of a finished product, the availability of written agreements is key to controlling the taking and location of reference and retention samples.

7 Reference Samples – General Points

7.1   Reference samples are for the purpose of analysis and, therefore, should be conveniently available to a laboratory with validated methodology. For starting materials used for medicinal products manufactured within the EEA, this is the original site of manufacture of the finished product. For finished products manufactured within the EEA, this is the original site of manufacture.

7.2   For finished products manufactured by a manufacturer in a country outside the EEA:

7.2.1   where an operational Mutual Recognition Agreement (MRA) is in place, the reference samples may be taken and stored at the site of manufacture. This should be covered in a written agreement (as referred to in Section 6 above) between the importer/site of batch release and the manufacturer located outside the EEA;

7.2.2   where an operational MRA is not in place, reference samples of the finished medicinal product should be taken and stored at an authorised manufacturer located within the EEA. These samples should be taken in accordance with written agreement(s) between all the parties concerned. The samples should, preferably, be stored at the location where testing on importation has been performed;

7.2.3   reference samples of starting materials and packaging materials should be kept at the original site at which they were used in the manufacture of the medicinal product.

8 Retention Samples – General Points

8.1   A retention sample should represent a batch of finished products as distributed in the EEA and may need to be examined in order to confirm non-technical attributes for compliance with the Marketing Authorisation or EU legislation. Therefore, retention samples should in all cases be located within the EEA. These should preferably be stored at the site where the Qualified Person (QP) certifying the finished product batch is located.

8.2   In accordance with Section 8.1 above, where an operational MRA is in place and reference samples are retained at a manufacturer located in a country outside the EEA (Section 7.2.2 above), separate retention samples should be kept within the EEA.

8.3   Retention samples should be stored at the premises of an authorised manufacturer in order to permit ready access by the Competent Authority.

8.4　Where more than one manufacturing site within the EEA is involved in the manufacture importation/packaging/testing/batch release, as appropriate for a product, the responsibility for taking and storage of retention samples should be defined in a written agreement(s) between the parties concerned.

9 Reference and Retention Samples for Parallel Imported/Parallel Distributed Products

9.1　Where the secondary packaging is not opened, only the packaging material used needs to be retained, so that there is no, or little, risk of product mix-up.

9.2　Where the secondary packaging is opened, e.g. to replace the carton or patient information leaflet, then one retention sample, per packaging operation, containing the product should be taken, because there is a risk of product mix-up during the assembly process. It is important to be able to identify quickly who is responsible in the event of a mix-up (original manufacturer or parallel import assembler), because it would affect the extent of any resulting recall.

10 Reference and Retention Samples in the Case of Closedown of a Manufacturer

10.1　Where a manufacturer closes down and the Manufacturing Authorisation is surrendered, revoked or ceases to exist, it is probable that many unexpired batches of medicinal products manufactured by that manufacturer remain on the market. In order for those batches to remain on the market, the manufacturer should make detailed arrangements for transfer of reference and retention samples (and relevant GMP documentation) to an authorised storage site. The manufacturer should satisfy the Competent Authority that the arrangements for storage are satisfactory and that the samples can, if necessary, be readily accessed and analysed.

10.2　If the manufacturer is not in a position to make the necessary arrangements this may be delegated to another manufacturer. The Marketing Authorisation Holder (MAH) is responsible for such delegation and for the provision of all necessary information to the Competent Authority. In addition, the MAH should, in relation to the suitability of the proposed arrangements for storage of reference and retention samples, consult with the Competent Authority of each Member State in which any unexpired batch has been placed on the market.

10.3　These requirements apply also in the event of the closedown of a manufacture located outside the EEA. In such instances, the importer has a particular responsibility to ensure that satisfactory arrangements are put in place and that the competent authority/authorities is/are consulted.

GLOSSARY OF TERMS USED IN THE EU GUIDE TO GMP

Note: *Definitions given below apply to the words as used in this guide. They may have different meanings in other contexts.*

AIRLOCK

An enclosed space with two or more doors, which is interposed between two or more rooms, e.g. of differing class of cleanliness, for the purpose of controlling the airflow between those rooms when they need to be entered. An airlock is designed for and used by either people or goods.

BATCH (OR LOT)

A defined quantity of starting material, packaging material or product processed in one process or series of processes so that it could be expected to be homogeneous.

Note: *To complete certain stages of manufacture, it may be necessary to divide a batch into a number of sub-batches, which are later brought together to form a final homogeneous batch. In the case of continuous manufacture, the batch must correspond to a defined fraction of the production, characterised by its intended homogeneity.*

For control of the finished product, the following definition has been given in Annex 1 of Directive 2001/83/EC as amended by Directive 2003/63/EC "For the control of the finished product, a batch of a proprietary medicinal product comprises all the units of a pharmaceutical form which are made from the same initial mass of material and have undergone a single series of manufacturing operations or a single sterilisation operation or, in the case of a continuous production process, all the units manufactured in a given period of time."

BATCH NUMBER (OR LOT NUMBER)

A distinctive combination of numbers and/or letters that specifically identifies a batch.

BIOGENERATOR

A contained system, such as a fermenter, into which biological agents are introduced along with other materials so as to effect their multiplication or their production of other substances by reaction with other materials. Biogenerators are generally fitted with devices for regulation, control, connection, material addition and material withdrawal.

BIOLOGICAL AGENTS

Microorganisms, including genetically engineered microorganisms, cell cultures and endoparasites, whether pathogenic or not.

BULK PRODUCT

Any product that has completed all processing stages up to, but not including, final packaging.

CALIBRATION

The set of operations that establish, under specified conditions, the relationship between values indicated by a measuring instrument or measuring system, or values represented by a material measure, and the corresponding known values of a reference standard.

CELL BANK

Cell bank system: a cell bank system is a system whereby successive batches of a product are manufactured by culture in cells derived from the same master cell bank. A number of containers from the master cell bank are used to prepare a working cell bank. The cell bank system is validated for a passage level or number of population doublings beyond that achieved during routine production.

Master cell bank: a culture of (fully characterised) cells distributed into containers in a single operation, processed together in such a manner as to ensure uniformity and stored in such a manner as to ensure stability. A master cell bank is usually stored at –70°C or lower.

Working cell bank: a culture of cells derived from the master cell bank and intended for use in the preparation of production cell cultures. The working cell bank is usually stored at –70°C or lower.

CELL CULTURE

The result from the in-vitro growth of cells isolated from multicellular organisms.

CLEAN AREA

An area with defined environmental control of particulate and microbial contamination, constructed and used in such a way as to reduce the introduction, generation and retention of contaminants within the area.

> Note: *The different degrees of environmental control are defined in the Supplementary Guidelines for the Manufacture of sterile medicinal products.*

CLEAN/CONTAINED AREA

An area constructed and operated in such a manner as to achieve the aims of both a clean area and a contained area at the same time.

EU GMP GUIDE PART I ANNEX 19 REFERENCE AND RETENTION SAMPLES

CONTAINMENT

The action of confining a biological agent or other entity within a defined space.

Primary containment: a system of containment that prevents the escape of a biological agent into the immediate working environment. It involves the use of closed containers or safety biological cabinets, along with secure operating procedures.

Secondary containment: a system of containment that prevents the escape of a biological agent into the external environment or other working areas. It involves the use of rooms with specially designed air handling, the existence of airlocks and/or sterilisers for the exit of materials and secure operating procedures. In many cases it may add to the effectiveness of primary containment.

CONTAINED AREA

An area constructed and operated in such a manner (and equipped with appropriate air handling and filtration) as to prevent contamination of the external environment by biological agents from within the area.

CONTROLLED AREA

An area constructed and operated in such a manner that some attempt is made to control the introduction of potential contamination (an air supply approximating to Grade D may be appropriate), and the consequences of accidental release of living organisms. The level of control exercised should reflect the nature of the organism employed in the process. At a minimum, the area should be maintained at a pressure negative to the immediate external environment and allow for the efficient removal of small quantities of airborne contaminants.

COMPUTERISED SYSTEM

A system including the input of data, electronic processing and the output of information to be used for either reporting or automatic control.

CROSS-CONTAMINATION

Contamination of a material or of a product with another material or product.

CRUDE PLANT (VEGETABLE DRUG)

Fresh or dried medicinal plant or parts thereof.

CRYOGENIC VESSEL

A container designed to contain liquefied gas at extremely low temperature.

EU GMP Guide Glossary

CYLINDER

A container designed to contain gas at a high pressure.

EXOTIC ORGANISM

A biological agent where either the corresponding disease does not exist in a given country or geographical area, or where the disease is the subject of prophylactic measures or an eradication programme undertaken in the given country or geographical area.

FINISHED PRODUCT

A medicinal product that has undergone all stages of production, including packaging in its final container.

HERBAL MEDICINAL PRODUCT

Medicinal product containing, as active ingredients, exclusively plant material and/or vegetable drug preparations.

INFECTED

Contaminated with extraneous biological agents and therefore capable of spreading infection.

IN-PROCESS CONTROL

Checks performed during production in order to monitor and, if necessary, to adjust the process to ensure that the product conforms its specification. The control of the environment or equipment may also be regarded as a part of in-process control.

INTERMEDIATE PRODUCT

Partly processed material that must undergo further manufacturing steps before it becomes a bulk product.

LIQUIFIABLE GASES

Gases that, at the normal filling temperature and pressure, remain as a liquid in the cylinder.

MANIFOLD

Equipment or apparatus designed to enable one or more gas containers to be filled simultaneously from the same source.

MANUFACTURE

All operations of purchase of materials and products, Production, Quality Control, release, storage, distribution of medicinal products and the related controls.

MANUFACTURER

Holder of a Manufacturing Authorisation as described in Article 40 of Directive 2001/83/EC.

MEDICINAL PLANT

Plant, the whole or part of which is used for medicinal purpose.

MEDICINAL PRODUCT

Any substance or combination of substances presented for treating or preventing disease in human beings or animals. Any substance or combination of substances that may be administered to human beings or animals with a view to making a medical diagnosis or to restoring, correcting or modifying physiological functions in human beings or animals is likewise considered to be a medicinal product.

PACKAGING

All operations, including filling and labelling, that a bulk product has to undergo in order to become a finished product.

> Note: *Sterile filling would not normally be regarded as part of packaging, the bulk product being the filled, but not finally packaged, primary containers.*

PACKAGING MATERIAL

Any material employed in the packaging of a medicinal product, excluding any outer packaging used for transportation or shipment. Packaging materials are referred to as primary or secondary according to whether they are intended to be in direct contact with the product.

PROCEDURES

Description of the operations to be carried out, the precautions to be taken and measures to be applied directly or indirectly related to the manufacture of a medicinal product.

PRODUCTION

All operations involved in the preparation of a medicinal product, from receipt of materials, through processing and packaging, to its completion as a finished product.

QUALIFICATION

Action of proving that any equipment works correctly and actually leads to the expected results. The word *validation* is sometimes widened to incorporate the concept of qualification.

QUALITY CONTROL

See GMP Guide, Chapter 1.

QUARANTINE

The status of starting or packaging materials, intermediate, bulk or finished products isolated physically or by other effective means while awaiting a decision on their release or refusal.

RADIOPHARMACEUTICAL

"Radiopharmaceutical" shall mean any medicinal product that, when ready for use, contains one or more radionuclides (radioactive isotopes) included for a medicinal purpose (Article 1(6) of Directive 2001/83/EC).

RECONCILIATION

A comparison, making due allowance for normal variation, between the amount of product or materials theoretically and actually produced or used.

RECORD

See GMP Guide, Chapter 4.

RECOVERY

The introduction of all or part of previous batches of the required quality into another batch at a defined stage of manufacture.

REPROCESSING

The reworking of all or part of a batch of product of an unacceptable quality from a defined stage of production so that its quality may be rendered acceptable by one or more additional operations.

RETURN

Sending back to the manufacturer or distributor of a medicinal product, which may or may not present a quality defect.

SEED LOT

Seed lot system: a seed lot system is a system according to which successive batches of a product are derived from the same master seed lot at a given passage level. For routine production, a working seed lot is prepared from the master seed lot. The final product is derived from the working seed lot and has not undergone more passages from the master seed lot than the vaccine shown in clinical studies to be satisfactory with respect to safety and efficacy. The origin and the passage history of the master seed lot and the working seed lot are recorded.

Master seed lot: a culture of a microorganism distributed from a single bulk into containers in a single operation in such a manner as to ensure uniformity, to prevent contamination and to ensure stability. A master seed

lot in liquid form is usually stored at or below −70°C. A freeze-dried master seed lot is stored at a temperature known to ensure stability.
Working seed lot: a culture of a microorganism derived from the master seed lot and intended for use in production. Working seed lots are distributed into containers and stored as described above for master seed lots.

SPECIFICATION

See GMP Guide, Chapter 4.

STARTING MATERIAL

Any substance used in the production of a medicinal product, but excluding packaging materials.

STERILITY

Sterility is the absence of living organisms. The conditions of the sterility test are given in the European Pharmacopoeia.

SYSTEM

Used in the sense of a regulated pattern of interacting activities and techniques, which are united to form an organised whole.

VALIDATION

Action of proving, in accordance with the principles of Good Manufacturing Practice, that any procedure, process, equipment, material, activity or system actually leads to the expected results (see also qualification).

PART II: Basic Requirements for Active Substances Used as Starting Materials

1   Introduction

This guideline was published in November 2000 as Annex 18 to the GMP Guide reflecting the EU's agreement to ICH Q7A and has been used by manufacturers and GMP inspectorates on a voluntary basis. Article 46(f) of Directive 2001/83/EC and Article 50(f) of Directive 2001/82/EC, as amended by Directives 2004/27/EC and 2004/28/EC, respectively, place new obligations on Manufacturing Authorisation Holders to use only active substances that have been manufactured in accordance with Good Manufacturing Practice for starting materials. The directives go on to say that the principles of Good Manufacturing Practice for active substances are to be adopted as detailed guidelines. Member States have agreed that the text of former Annex 18 should form the basis of the detailed guidelines to create Part II of the GMP Guide.

1.1   Objective

These guidelines are intended to provide guidance regarding Good Manufacturing Practice (GMP) for the manufacture of active substances under an appropriate system for managing quality. It is also intended to help ensure that active substances meet the requirements for quality and purity that they purport or are represented to possess.

In these guidelines "manufacturing" includes all operations of receipt of materials, production, packaging, re-packaging, labelling, re-labelling, quality control, release, storage and distribution of active substances and the related controls. The term "should" indicates recommendations that are expected to apply unless shown to be inapplicable, modified in any relevant annexes to the GMP Guide or replaced by an alternative demonstrated to provide at least an equivalent level of quality assurance.

The GMP Guide as a whole does not cover safety aspects for the personnel engaged in manufacture, nor aspects of protection of the environment. These controls are inherent responsibilities of the manufacturer and are governed by other parts of the legislation.

These guidelines are not intended to define registration requirements or modify pharmacopoeial requirements, and do not affect the ability of the responsible competent authority to establish specific registration requirements regarding active substances within the context of marketing/manufacturing authorisations. All commitments in registration documents must be met.

1.2 Scope

These guidelines apply to the manufacture of active substances for medicinal products for both human and veterinary use. They apply to the manufacture of sterile active substances only up to the point immediately prior to the active substance being rendered sterile. The sterilisation and aseptic processing of sterile active substances are not covered, but should be performed in accordance with the principles and guidelines of GMP, as laid down in Directive 2003/94/EC and interpreted in the GMP Guide including its Annex 1.

In the case of ectoparasiticides for veterinary use, standards other than these guidelines, which ensure that the material is of appropriate quality, may be used.

These guidelines exclude whole blood and plasma, as Directive 2002/98/EC and the technical requirements supporting that directive lay down the detailed requirements for the collection and testing of blood; however, it does include active substances that are produced using blood or plasma as raw materials.

Finally, these guidelines do not apply to bulk-packaged medicinal products. They apply to all other active starting materials subject to any derogations described in the annexes to the GMP Guide, in particular Annexes 2 to 7 where supplementary guidance for certain types of active substance may be found.

Section 17 gives guidance to parties who, among others, distribute or store an active substance or intermediate. This guidance is expanded in the guideline on the principles of good distribution practices for active substances for medicinal products for human use referred to in Article 47 of Directive 2001/83/EC.

Section 19 contains guidance that applies only to the manufacture of active substances used in the production of investigational medicinal products although it should be noted that its application in this case, although recommended, is not required by Community legislation.

An "Active Substance Starting Material" is a raw material, intermediate or active substance that is used in the production of an active substance and that is incorporated as a significant structural fragment into the structure of the active substance. An Active Substance Starting Material can be an article of commerce, a material purchased from one or more suppliers under contract or commercial agreement or produced in-house. Active Substance Starting Materials normally have defined chemical properties and structure.

The manufacturer should designate and document the rationale for the point at which production of the active substance begins. For synthetic processes, this is known as the point at which "Active Substance Starting Materials" are entered into the process. For other processes (e.g. fermentation, extraction, purification, etc.), this rationale should be established on a case-by-case basis. Table 1 gives guidance on the point at which the Active Substance Starting Material is normally introduced into the process. From this point on, appropriate GMP, as defined in these guidelines, should be applied to these intermediate and/or active substance manufacturing steps. This would include the validation of critical process steps determined to impact the quality of the active substance. However, it should be noted that the fact that a manufacturer chooses to validate a process step does not necessarily define that step as critical. The guidance in this document would normally be applied to the steps shown in grey in Table 1. It does not imply that all steps shown should be completed. The stringency of GMP in active substance manufacturing should increase as the process proceeds from early steps to final steps, purification and packaging. Physical processing of active substances, such as granulation, coating or physical manipulation of particle size (e.g. milling, micronising), should be conducted at least to the standards of these guidelines. These guidelines do not apply to steps prior to the first introduction of the defined "Active Substance Starting Material".

In the remainder of this guideline the term Active Pharmaceutical Ingredient (API) is used repeatedly and should be considered interchangeable with the term "Active Substance". The glossary in section 20 of Part II should be applied only in the context of Part II. Some of the same terms are already defined in Part I of the GMP guide and these should therefore be applied only in the context of Part I.

Table 1 Application of this Guide to API Manufacturing

Type of Manufacturing	Application of this Guide to steps (shown in grey) used in this type of manufacturing				
Chemical Manufacturing	Production of the API Starting Material	Introduction of the API Starting Material into process	Production of Intermediate(s)	Isolation and purification	Physical processing, and packaging
API derived from animal sources	Collection of organ, fluid, or tissue	Cutting, mixing, and/or initial processing	Introduction of the API Starting Material into process	Isolation and purification	Physical processing, and packaging
API extracted from plant sources	Collection of plant	Cutting and initial extraction(s)	Introduction of the API Starting Material into process	Isolation and purification	Physical processing, and packaging
Herbal extracts used as API	Collection of plants	Cutting and initial extraction		Further extraction	Physical processing, and packaging
API consisting of comminuted or powdered herbs	Collection of plants and/or cultivation and harvesting	Cutting/ comminuting			Physical processing, and packaging
Biotechnology: fermentation/ cell culture	Establishment of master cell bank and working cell bank	Maintenance of working cell bank	Cell culture and/or fermentation	Isolation and purification	Physical processing, and packaging
"Classical" Fermentation to produce an API	Establishment of cell bank	Maintenance of the cell bank	Introduction of the cells into fermentation	Isolation and purification	Physical processing, and packaging

Increasing GMP requirements →

2 Quality Management

2.1 Principles

2.10 Quality should be the responsibility of all persons involved in manufacturing.

2.11 Each manufacturer should establish, document and implement an effective system for managing quality that involves the active participation of management and appropriate manufacturing personnel.

2.12 The system for managing quality should encompass the organisational structure, procedures, processes and resources, as well as activities necessary to ensure confidence that the API will meet its intended specifications for quality and purity. All quality-related activities should be defined and documented.

2.13 There should be a quality unit(s) that is independent of production and that fulfils both quality assurance (QA) and quality control (QC) responsibilities. This can be in the form of separate QA and QC units or a single individual or group, depending upon the size and structure of the organization.

2.14 The persons authorised to release intermediates and APIs should be specified.

2.15 All quality-related activities should be recorded at the time they are performed.

2.16 Any deviation from established procedures should be documented and explained. Critical deviations should be investigated, and the investigation and its conclusions should be documented.

2.17 No materials should be released or used before the satisfactory completion of evaluation by the quality unit(s) unless there are appropriate systems in place to allow for such use (e.g. release under quarantine as described in Section 10.20 or the use of raw materials or intermediates pending completion of evaluation).

2.18 Procedures should exist for notifying responsible management in a timely manner of regulatory inspections, serious GMP deficiencies, product defects and related actions (e.g. quality-related complaints, recalls, regulatory actions, etc.).

2.19 To achieve the quality objective reliably there must be a comprehensively designed and correctly implemented quality system incorporating Good Manufacturing Practice, Quality Control and Quality Risk Management.

2.2 Quality risk management

2.20 Quality risk management is a systematic process for the assessment, control, communication and review of risks to the quality of the active substance. It can be applied both proactively and retrospectively.

2.21 The quality risk management system should ensure that:

- the evaluation of the risk to quality is based on scientific knowledge, experience with the process and ultimately links to the protection of the patient through communication with the user of the active substance,
- the level of effort, formality and documentation of the quality risk management process is commensurate with the level of risk.

Examples of the processes and applications of quality risk management can be found, inter alia, in Part III of the GMP guide.

2.3 Responsibilities of the quality unit(s)

2.30 The quality unit(s) should be involved in all quality-related matters.

2.31 The quality unit(s) should review and approve all appropriate quality-related documents.

2.32 The main responsibilities of the independent quality unit(s) should not be delegated. These responsibilities should be described in writing and should include but not necessarily be limited to:

(1) Releasing or rejecting all APIs. Releasing or rejecting intermediates for use outside the control of the manufacturing company;

(2) Establishing a system to release or reject raw materials, intermediates, packaging and labelling materials;

(3) Reviewing completed batch production and laboratory control records of critical process steps before release of the API for distribution;

(4) Making sure that critical deviations are investigated and resolved;

(5) Approving all specifications and master production instructions;

(6) Approving all procedures impacting the quality of intermediates or APIs;

(7) Making sure that internal audits (self-inspections) are performed;

(8) Approving intermediate and API contract manufacturers;

(9) Approving changes that potentially impact intermediate or API quality;

(10) Reviewing and approving validation protocols and reports;

(11) Making sure that quality-related complaints are investigated and resolved;

(12) Making sure that effective systems are used for maintaining and calibrating critical equipment;

(13) Making sure that materials are appropriately tested and the results are reported;

(14) APIs and/or intermediates where appropriate; and

(15) Performing product quality reviews (as defined in Section 2.5).

2.4　Responsibility for production activities

The responsibility for production activities should be described in writing, and should include but not necessarily be limited to:

(1)　Preparing, reviewing, approving and distributing the instructions for the production of intermediates or APIs according to written procedures;

(2)　Producing APIs and, when appropriate, intermediates according to pre-approved instructions;

(3)　Reviewing all production batch records and ensuring that these are completed and signed;

(4)　Making sure that all production deviations are reported and evaluated and that critical deviations are investigated and the conclusions are recorded;

(5)　Making sure that production facilities are clean and when appropriate disinfected;

(6)　Making sure that the necessary calibrations are performed and records kept;

(7)　Making sure that the premises and equipment are maintained and records kept;

(8)　Making sure that validation protocols and reports are reviewed and approved;

(9)　Evaluating proposed changes in product, process or equipment; and

(10) Making sure that new and, when appropriate, modified facilities and equipment are qualified.

2.5　Internal audits (self-inspection)

2.50　In order to verify compliance with the principles of GMP for APIs, regular internal audits should be performed in accordance with an approved schedule.

2.51　Audit findings and corrective actions should be documented and brought to the attention of responsible management of the firm. Agreed corrective actions should be completed in a timely and effective manner.

2.6 Product quality review

2.60 Regular quality reviews of APIs should be conducted with the objective of verifying the consistency of the process. Such reviews should normally be conducted and documented annually and should include at least:

- A review of critical in-process control and critical API test results;
- A review of all batches that failed to meet established specification(s);
- A review of all critical deviations or non-conformances and related investigations;
- A review of any changes carried out to the processes or analytical methods;
- A review of results of the stability monitoring program;
- A review of all quality-related returns, complaints and recalls; and
- A review of adequacy of corrective actions.

2.61 The results of this review should be evaluated and an assessment made of whether corrective action or any revalidation should be undertaken. Reasons for such corrective action should be documented. Agreed corrective actions should be completed in a timely and effective manner.

3 Personnel

3.1 Personnel qualifications

3.10 There should be an adequate number of personnel qualified by appropriate education, training and/or experience to perform and supervise the manufacture of intermediates and APIs.

3.11 The responsibilities of all personnel engaged in the manufacture of intermediates and APIs should be specified in writing.

3.12 Training should be regularly conducted by qualified individuals and should cover, at a minimum, the particular operations that the employee performs and GMP as it relates to the employee's functions. Records of training should be maintained. Training should be periodically assessed.

3.2 Personnel hygiene

3.20 Personnel should practise good sanitation and health habits.

3.21 Personnel should wear clean clothing suitable for the manufacturing activity with which they are involved and this clothing should be changed when appropriate. Additional protective apparel, such as head, face, hand and arm coverings, should be worn when necessary, to protect intermediates and APIs from contamination.

3.22 Personnel should avoid direct contact with intermediates or APIs.

3.23 Smoking, eating, drinking, chewing and the storage of food should be restricted to certain designated areas separate from the manufacturing areas.

3.24 Personnel suffering from an infectious disease or having open lesions on the exposed surface of the body should not engage in activities that could result in compromising the quality of APIs. Any person shown at any time (either by medical examination or by supervisory observation) to have an apparent illness or open lesions should be excluded from activities where the health condition could adversely affect the quality of the APIs, until the condition has been corrected or qualified medical personnel determine that the person's inclusion would not jeopardize the safety or quality of the APIs.

3.3 Consultants

3.30 Consultants advising on the manufacture and control of intermediates or APIs should have sufficient education, training and experience, or any combination thereof, to advise on the subject for which they are retained.

3.31 Records should be maintained stating the name, address, qualifications and type of service provided by these consultants.

4 Buildings and Facilities

4.1 Design and construction

4.10 Buildings and facilities used in the manufacture of intermediates and APIs should be located, designed and constructed to facilitate cleaning, maintenance and operations as appropriate to the type and stage of manufacture. Facilities should also be designed to minimise potential contamination. Where microbiological specifications have been established for the intermediate or API, facilities should also be designed to limit exposure to objectionable microbiological contaminants as appropriate.

4.11 Buildings and facilities should have adequate space for the orderly placement of equipment and materials to prevent mix-ups and contamination.

4.12 Where the equipment itself (e.g. closed or contained systems) provides adequate protection of the material, such equipment can be located outdoors.

4.13 The flow of materials and personnel through the building or facilities should be designed to prevent mix-ups or contamination.

4.14 There should be defined areas or other control systems for the following activities:

- Receipt, identification, sampling and quarantine of incoming materials, pending release or rejection;
- Quarantine before release or rejection of intermediates and APIs;
- Sampling of intermediates and APIs;
- Holding rejected materials before further disposition (e.g. return, reprocessing or destruction);
- Storage of released materials;
- Production operations;
- Packaging and labelling operations; and
- Laboratory operations.

4.15 Adequate, clean washing and toilet facilities should be provided for personnel. These washing facilities should be equipped with hot and cold water as appropriate, soap or detergent, air driers or single service towels. The washing and toilet facilities should be separate from, but easily accessible to, manufacturing areas. Adequate facilities for showering and/ or changing clothes should be provided, when appropriate.

4.16 Laboratory areas/operations should normally be separated from production areas. Some laboratory areas, in particular those used for in-process controls, can be located in production areas, provided that the operations of the production process do not adversely affect the accuracy of the laboratory measurements, and the laboratory and its operations do not adversely affect the production process or intermediate or API.

4.2 Utilities

4.20 All utilities that could impact on product quality (e.g. steam, gases, compressed air, and heating, ventilation and air conditioning) should be qualified and appropriately monitored, and action should be taken when limits are exceeded. Drawings for these utility systems should be available.

4.21 Adequate ventilation, air filtration and exhaust systems should be provided, where appropriate. These systems should be designed and constructed to minimise risks of contamination and cross-contamination and should include equipment for control of air pressure, microorganisms (if appropriate), dust, humidity and temperature, as appropriate to the stage of manufacture. Particular attention should be given to areas where APIs are exposed to the environment.

4.22   If air is re-circulated to production areas, appropriate measures should be taken to control risks of contamination and cross-contamination.

4.23   Permanently installed pipework should be appropriately identified. This can be accomplished by identifying individual lines, documentation, computer control systems or alternative means. Pipework should be located to avoid risks of contamination of the intermediate or API.

4.24   Drains should be of adequate size and should be provided with an air break or a suitable device to prevent back-siphonage, when appropriate.

4.3   Water

4.30   Water used in the manufacture of APIs should be demonstrated to be suitable for its intended use.

4.31   Unless otherwise justified, process water should, at a minimum, meet World Health Organization (WHO) guidelines for drinking (potable) water quality.

4.32   If drinking (potable) water is insufficient to assure API quality, and tighter chemical and/or microbiological water quality specifications are called for, appropriate specifications for physical/chemical attributes, total microbial counts, objectionable organisms and/or endotoxins should be established.

4.33   Where water used in the process is treated by the manufacturer to achieve a defined quality, the treatment process should be validated and monitored with appropriate action limits.

4.34   Where the manufacturer of a non-sterile API either intends or claims that it is suitable for use in further processing to produce a sterile drug (medicinal) product, water used in the final isolation and purification steps should be monitored and controlled for total microbial counts, objectionable organisms and endotoxins.

4.4   Containment

4.40   Dedicated production areas, which can include facilities, air-handling equipment and/or process equipment, should be employed in the production of highly sensitising materials, such as penicillins or cephalosporins.

4.41   Dedicated production areas should also be considered when material of an infectious nature or high pharmacological activity or toxicity is involved (e.g. certain steroids or cytotoxic anti-cancer agents) unless validated inactivation and/or cleaning procedures are established and maintained.

4.42   Appropriate measures should be established and implemented to prevent cross-contamination from personnel, materials, etc. moving from one dedicated area to another.

4.43   Any production activities (including weighing, milling or packaging) of highly toxic non-pharmaceutical materials such as herbicides and pesticides should not be conducted using the buildings and/or equipment being used for the production of APIs. Handling and storage of these highly toxic non-pharmaceutical materials should be separate from APIs.

4.5   Lighting

4.50   Adequate lighting should be provided in all areas to facilitate cleaning, maintenance, and proper operations.

4.6   Sewage and refuse

4.60   Sewage, refuse and other waste (e.g. solids, liquids, or gaseous by-products from manufacturing) in and from buildings and the immediate surrounding area should be disposed of in a safe, timely and sanitary manner. Containers and/or pipes for waste material should be clearly identified.

4.7   Sanitation and maintenance

4.70   Buildings used in the manufacture of intermediates and APIs should be properly maintained and repaired and kept in a clean condition.

4.71   Written procedures should be established, assigning responsibility for sanitation and describing the cleaning schedules, methods, equipment and materials to be used in cleaning buildings and facilities.

4.72   When necessary, written procedures should also be established for the use of suitable rodenticides, insecticides, fungicides, fumigating agents, and cleaning and sanitizing agents to prevent the contamination of equipment, raw materials, packaging/labelling materials, intermediates and APIs.

5 Process Equipment

5.1 Design and construction

5.10 Equipment used in the manufacture of intermediates and APIs should be of appropriate design and adequate size, and suitably located for its intended use, cleaning, sanitization (where appropriate) and maintenance.

5.11 Equipment should be constructed so that surfaces that contact raw materials, intermediates or APIs do not alter the quality of the intermediates and APIs beyond the official or other established specifications.

5.12 Production equipment should be used only within its qualified operating range.

5.13 Major equipment (e.g. reactors, storage containers) and permanently installed processing lines used during the production of an intermediate or API should be appropriately identified.

5.14 Any substances associated with the operation of equipment, such as lubricants, heating fluids or coolants, should not contact intermediates or APIs so as to alter their quality beyond the official or other established specifications. Any deviations from this should be evaluated to ensure that there are no detrimental effects upon the fitness for purpose of the material. Wherever possible, food-grade lubricants and oils should be used.

5.15 Closed or contained equipment should be used whenever appropriate. Where open equipment is used, or equipment is opened, appropriate precautions should be taken to minimize the risk of contamination.

5.16 A set of current drawings should be maintained for equipment and critical installations (e.g. instrumentation and utility systems).

5.2 Equipment maintenance and cleaning

5.20 Schedules and procedures (including assignment of responsibility) should be established for the preventive maintenance of equipment.

5.21 Written procedures should be established for cleaning of equipment and its subsequent release for use in the manufacture of intermediates and APIs. Cleaning procedures should contain sufficient details to enable operators to clean each type of equipment in a reproducible and effective manner. These procedures should include:

- Assignment of responsibility for cleaning of equipment;
- Cleaning schedules, including, where appropriate, sanitising schedules;

- A complete description of the methods and materials, including dilution of cleaning agents used to clean equipment;
- When appropriate, instructions for disassembling and reassembling each article of equipment to ensure proper cleaning;
- Instructions for the removal or obliteration of previous batch identification;
- Instructions for the protection of clean equipment from contamination prior to use;
- Inspection of equipment for cleanliness immediately before use, if practical; and
- Establishing the maximum time that may elapse between the completion of processing and equipment cleaning, when appropriate.

5.22   Equipment and utensils should be cleaned, stored and, where appropriate, sanitized or sterilized to prevent contamination or carry-over of a material that would alter the quality of the intermediate or API beyond the official or other established specifications.

5.23   Where equipment is assigned to continuous production or campaign production of successive batches of the same intermediate or API, equipment should be cleaned at appropriate intervals to prevent build-up and carry-over of contaminants (e.g. degradants or objectionable levels of microorganisms).

5.24   Non-dedicated equipment should be cleaned between production of different materials to prevent cross-contamination.

5.25   Acceptance criteria for residues and the choice of cleaning procedures and cleaning agents should be defined and justified.

5.26   Equipment should be identified as to its contents and its cleanliness status by appropriate means.

5.3   Calibration

5.30   Control, weighing, measuring, monitoring and test equipment that is critical for assuring the quality of intermediates or APIs should be calibrated according to written procedures and an established schedule.

5.31   Equipment calibrations should be performed using standards traceable to certified standards, if they exist.

5.32   Records of these calibrations should be maintained.

5.33   The current calibration status of critical equipment should be known and verifiable.

5.34   Instruments that do not meet calibration criteria should not be used.

5.35   Deviations from approved standards of calibration on critical instruments should be investigated to determine if these could have had an impact on the quality of the intermediate(s) or API(s) manufactured using this equipment since the last successful calibration.

5.4   Computerized systems

5.40   GMP related computerized systems should be validated. The depth and scope of validation depend on the diversity, complexity and criticality of the computerized application.

5.41   Appropriate installation qualification and operational qualification should demonstrate the suitability of computer hardware and software to perform assigned tasks.

5.42   Commercially available software that has been qualified does not require the same level of testing. If an existing system was not validated at the time of installation, a retrospective validation could be conducted if the appropriate documentation is available.

5.43   Computerized systems should have sufficient controls to prevent unauthorized access or changes to data. There should be controls to prevent omissions in data (e.g. system turned off and data not captured). There should be a record of any data change made, the previous entry, who made the change and when the change was made.

5.44   Written procedures should be available for the operation and maintenance of computerized systems.

5.45   Where critical data is being entered manually, there should be an additional check on the accuracy of the entry. This can be done by a second operator or by the system itself.

5.46   Incidents related to computerized systems that could affect the quality of intermediates or APIs, or the reliability of records or test results, should be recorded and investigated.

5.47   Changes to the computerized system should be made according to a change procedure and should be formally authorized, documented and tested. Records should be kept of all changes, including modifications and enhancements made to the hardware, software and any other critical component of the system. These records should demonstrate that the system is maintained in a validated state.

5.48   If system breakdowns or failures would result in the permanent loss of records, a back-up system should be provided. A means of ensuring data protection should be established for all computerized systems.

5.49   Data can be recorded by a second means in addition to the computer system.

6   Documentation and Records

6.1   Documentation system and specifications

6.10   All documents related to the manufacture of intermediates or APIs should be prepared, reviewed, approved and distributed according to written procedures. Such documents can be in paper or electronic form.

6.11   The issuance, revision, superseding and withdrawal of all documents should be controlled with maintenance of revision histories.

6.12   A procedure should be established for retaining all appropriate documents (e.g. development history reports, scale-up reports, technical transfer reports, process validation reports, training records, production records, control records and distribution records). The retention periods for these documents should be specified.

6.13   All production, control and distribution records should be retained for at least 1 year after the expiry date of the batch. For APIs with retest dates, records should be retained for at least 3 years after the batch has been completely distributed.

6.14   When entries are made in records, these should be made indelibly in spaces provided for such entries, directly after performing the activities, and should identify the person making the entry. Corrections to entries should be dated and signed and leave the original entry still readable.

6.15   During the retention period, originals or copies of records should be readily available at the establishment where the activities described in such records occurred. Records that can be promptly retrieved from another location by electronic or other means are acceptable.

6.16   Specifications, instructions, procedures and records can be retained either as originals or as true copies such as photocopies, microfilm, microfiche or other accurate reproductions of the original records. Where reduction techniques such as microfilming or electronic records are used, suitable retrieval equipment and a means of producing a hard copy should be readily available.

6.17 Specifications should be established and documented for raw materials, intermediates where necessary, APIs, and labelling and packaging materials. In addition, specifications may be appropriate for certain other materials, such as process aids, gaskets or other materials used during the production of intermediates or APIs that could critically impact on quality. Acceptance criteria should be established and documented for in-process controls.

6.18 If electronic signatures are used on documents, they should be authenticated and secure.

6.2 Equipment cleaning and use record

6.20 Records of major equipment use, cleaning, sanitization and/or sterilization and maintenance should show the date, time (if appropriate), product and batch number of each batch processed in the equipment, and the person who performed the cleaning and maintenance.

6.21 If equipment is dedicated to manufacturing one intermediate or API, then individual equipment records are not necessary if batches of the intermediate or API follow in traceable sequence. In cases where dedicated equipment is employed, the records of cleaning, maintenance, and use can be part of the batch record or maintained separately.

6.3 Records of raw materials, intermediates, API labelling and packaging materials

6.30 Records should be maintained including:

- The name of the manufacturer, identity and quantity of each shipment of each batch of raw materials, intermediates or labelling and packaging materials for APIs, the name of the supplier; the supplier's control number(s), if known, or other identification number, the number allocated on receipt and the date of receipt;
- The results of any test or examination performed and the conclusions derived from this;
- Records tracing the use of materials;
- Documentation of the examination and review of API labelling and packaging materials for conformity with established specifications; and
- The final decision regarding rejected raw materials, intermediates or API labelling and packaging materials.

6.31 Master (approved) labels should be maintained for comparison to issued labels.

6.4 Master production instructions (master production and control records)

6.40 To ensure uniformity from batch to batch, master production instructions for each intermediate and API should be prepared, dated and signed by one person and independently checked, dated and signed by a person in the quality unit(s).

6.41 Master production instructions should include:

- The name of the intermediate or API being manufactured and an identifying document reference code, if applicable;
- A complete list of raw materials and intermediates designated by names or codes sufficiently specific to identify any special quality characteristics;
- An accurate statement of the quantity or ratio of each raw material or intermediate to be used, including the unit of measure. Where the quantity is not fixed, the calculation for each batch size or rate of production should be included. Variations to quantities should be included where they are justified;
- The production location and major production equipment to be used;
- Detailed production instructions, including the:
  - sequences to be followed,
  - ranges of process parameters to be used,
  - sampling instructions and in-process controls with their acceptance criteria, where appropriate,
  - time limits for completion of individual processing steps and/or the total process, where appropriate, and
  - expected yield ranges at appropriate phases of processing or time;
- Where appropriate, special notations and precautions to be followed, or cross-references to these; and
- The instructions for storage of the intermediate or API to assure its suitability for use, including the labelling and packaging materials and special storage conditions with time limits, where appropriate.

6.5 Batch production records (batch production and control records)

6.50 Batch production records should be prepared for each intermediate and API, and should include complete information relating to the production and control of each batch. The batch production record should be checked before issuance to assure that it is the correct version and a legible accurate reproduction of the appropriate master production instruction. If the batch production record is produced from a separate part of the master document, that document should include a reference to the current master production instruction being used.

6.51   These records should be numbered with a unique batch or identification number, dated and signed when issued. In continuous production, the product code, together with the date and time, can serve as the unique identifier until the final number has been allocated.

6.52   Documentation of completion of each significant step in the batch production records (batch production and control records) should include:

- Dates and, when appropriate, times;
- Identity of major equipment (e.g. reactors, driers, mills, etc.) used;
- Specific identification of each batch, including weights, measures and batch numbers of raw materials, intermediates or any reprocessed materials used during manufacturing;
- Actual results recorded for critical process parameters;
- Any sampling performed;
- Signatures of the persons performing and directly supervising or checking each critical step in the operation;
- In-process and laboratory test results;
- Actual yield at appropriate phases or times;
- Description of packaging and label for intermediate or API;
- Representative label of API or intermediate if made commercially available;
- Any deviation noted, its evaluation, investigation conducted (if appropriate) or reference to that investigation if stored separately; and
- Results of release testing.

6.53   Written procedures should be established and followed for investigating critical deviations or the failure of a batch of intermediate or API to meet specifications. The investigation should extend to other batches that may have been associated with the specific failure or deviation.

6.6   Laboratory control records

6.60   Laboratory control records should include complete data derived from all tests conducted to ensure compliance with established specifications and standards, including examinations and assays, as follows:

- A description of samples received for testing, including the material name or source, batch number or other distinctive code, date sample was taken and, where appropriate, the quantity and date the sample was received for testing;
- A statement of or reference to each test method used;

- A statement of the weight or measure of sample used for each test as described by the method; data on or cross-reference to the preparation and testing of reference standards, reagents and standard solutions;
- A complete record of all raw data generated during each test, in addition to graphs, charts and spectra from laboratory instrumentation, properly identified to show the specific material and batch tested;
- A record of all calculations performed in connection with the test, including, for example, units of measure, conversion factors, and equivalency factors;
- A statement of the test results and how they compare with established acceptance criteria;
- The signature of the person who performed each test and the date(s) the tests were performed; and
- The date and signature of a second person showing that the original records have been reviewed for accuracy, completeness and compliance with established standards.

6.61   Complete records should also be maintained for:

- Any modifications to an established analytical method;
- Periodic calibration of laboratory instruments, apparatus, gauges and recording devices;
- All stability testing performed on APIs; and
- Out-of-specification (OOS) investigations.

6.7 Batch production record review

6.70   Written procedures should be established and followed for the review and approval of batch production and laboratory control records, including packaging and labelling, to determine compliance of the intermediate or API with established specifications before a batch is released or distributed.

6.71   Batch production and laboratory control records of critical process steps should be reviewed and approved by the quality unit(s) before an API batch is released or distributed. Production and laboratory control records of non-critical process steps can be reviewed by qualified production personnel or other units following procedures approved by the quality unit(s).

6.72   All deviation, investigation and OOS reports should be reviewed as part of the batch record review before the batch is released.

6.73   The quality unit(s) can delegate to the production unit the responsibility and authority for release of intermediates, except for those shipped outside the control of the manufacturing company.

7 Materials Management

7.1 General controls

7.10 There should be written procedures describing the receipt, identification, quarantine, storage, handling, sampling, testing, and approval or rejection of materials.

7.11 Manufacturers of intermediates and/or APIs should have a system for evaluating the suppliers of critical materials.

7.12 Materials should be purchased against an agreed specification, from a supplier(s) approved by the quality unit(s).

7.13 If the supplier of a critical material is not the manufacturer of that material, the name and address of that manufacturer should be known by the intermediate and/or API manufacturer.

7.14 Changing the source of supply of critical raw materials should be treated according to Section 13, Change Control.

7.2 Receipt and quarantine

7.20 Upon receipt and before acceptance, each container or grouping of containers of materials should be examined visually for correct labelling (including correlation between the name used by the supplier and the in-house name, if these are different), container damage, broken seals and evidence of tampering or contamination. Materials should be held under quarantine until they have been sampled, examined or tested as appropriate, and released for use.

7.21 Before incoming materials are mixed with existing stocks (e.g. solvents or stocks in silos), they should be identified as correct, tested, if appropriate, and released. Procedures should be available to prevent discharging incoming materials wrongly into the existing stock.

7.22 If bulk deliveries are made in non-dedicated tankers, there should be assurance of no cross-contamination from the tanker. Means of providing this assurance could include one or more of the following:

- certificate of cleaning;
- testing for trace impurities;
- audit of the supplier.

7.23 Large storage containers, and their attendant manifolds, filling and discharge lines should be appropriately identified.

7.24   Each container or grouping of containers (batches) of materials should be assigned and identified with a distinctive code, batch, or receipt number. This number should be used in recording the disposition of each batch. A system should be in place to identify the status of each batch.

7.3 Sampling and testing of incoming production materials

7.30   At least one test to verify the identity of each batch of material should be conducted, with the exception of the materials described below in 7.32. A supplier's Certificate of Analysis can be used in place of performing other tests, provided that the manufacturer has a system in place to evaluate suppliers.

7.31   Supplier approval should include an evaluation that provides adequate evidence (e.g. past quality history) that the manufacturer can consistently provide material meeting specifications. Full analyses should be conducted on at least three batches before reducing in-house testing. However, as a minimum, a full analysis should be performed at appropriate intervals and compared with the Certificates of Analysis. Reliability of Certificates of Analysis should be checked at regular intervals.

7.32   Processing aids, hazardous or highly toxic raw materials, other special materials or materials transferred to another unit within the company's control do not need to be tested if the manufacturer's Certificate of Analysis is obtained, showing that these raw materials conform to established specifications. Visual examination of containers, labels and recording of batch numbers should help in establishing the identity of these materials. The lack of on-site testing for these materials should be justified and documented.

7.33   Samples should be representative of the batch of material from which they are taken. Sampling methods should specify the number of containers to be sampled, which part of the container to sample and the amount of material to be taken from each container. The number of containers to sample and the sample size should be based upon a sampling plan that takes into consideration the criticality of the material, material variability, past quality history of the supplier and the quantity needed for analysis.

7.34   Sampling should be conducted at defined locations and by procedures designed to prevent contamination of the material sampled and contamination of other materials.

7.35   Containers from which samples are withdrawn should be opened carefully and subsequently re-closed. They should be marked to indicate that a sample has been taken.

7.4   Storage

7.40   Materials should be handled and stored in a manner to prevent degradation, contamination and cross-contamination.

7.41   Materials stored in fibre drums, bags or boxes should be stored off the floor and, when appropriate, suitably spaced to permit cleaning and inspection.

7.42   Materials should be stored under conditions and for a period that have no adverse affect on their quality, and should normally be controlled so that the oldest stock is used first.

7.43   Certain materials in suitable containers can be stored outdoors, provided that identifying labels remain legible and containers are appropriately cleaned before opening and use.

7.44   Rejected materials should be identified and controlled under a quarantine system designed to prevent their unauthorised use in manufacturing.

7.5   Re-evaluation

7.50   Materials should be re-evaluated as appropriate to determine their suitability for use (e.g. after prolonged storage or exposure to heat or humidity).

8   Production and In-process Controls

8.1   Production operations

8.10   Raw materials for intermediate and API manufacturing should be weighed or measured under appropriate conditions that do not affect their suitability for use. Weighing and measuring devices should be of suitable accuracy for the intended use.

8.11   If a material is subdivided for later use in production operations, the container receiving the material should be suitable and should be so identified that the following information is available:

- Material name and/or item code;
- Receiving or control number;
- Weight or measure of material in the new container; and
- Re-evaluation or re-test date if appropriate.

8.12   Critical weighing, measuring or subdividing operations should be witnessed or subjected to an equivalent control. Prior to use, production personnel should verify that the materials are those specified in the batch record for the intended intermediate or API.

8.13   Other critical activities should be witnessed or subjected to an equivalent control.

8.14   Actual yields should be compared with expected yields at designated steps in the production process. Expected yields with appropriate ranges should be established based on previous laboratory, pilot scale or manufacturing data. Deviations in yield associated with critical process steps should be investigated to determine their impact or potential impact on the resulting quality of affected batches.

8.15   Any deviation should be documented and explained. Any critical deviation should be investigated.

8.16   The processing status of major units of equipment should be indicated either on the individual units of equipment or by appropriate documentation, computer control systems or alternative means.

8.17   Materials to be reprocessed or reworked should be appropriately controlled to prevent unauthorized use.

8.2   Time limits

8.20   If time limits are specified in the master production instruction (see 6.41), these time limits should be met to ensure the quality of intermediates and APIs. Deviations should be documented and evaluated. Time limits may be inappropriate when processing to a target value (e.g. pH adjustment, hydrogenation, drying to predetermined specification) because completion of reactions or processing steps is determined by in-process sampling and testing.

8.21   Intermediates held for further processing should be stored under appropriate conditions to ensure their suitability for use.

8.3   In-process sampling and controls

8.30   Written procedures should be established to monitor the progress and control the performance of processing steps that cause variability in the quality characteristics of intermediates and APIs. In-process controls and their acceptance criteria should be defined based on the information gained during the development stage or historical data.

8.31   The acceptance criteria and type and extent of testing can depend on the nature of the intermediate or API being manufactured, the reaction or process step being conducted, and the degree to which the process introduces variability into the product's quality. Less stringent in-process controls may be appropriate in early processing steps, whereas tighter controls may be appropriate for later processing steps (e.g. isolation and purification steps).

8.32   Critical in-process controls (and critical process monitoring), including the control points and methods, should be stated in writing and approved by the quality unit(s).

8.33   In-process controls can be performed by qualified production department personnel, and the process adjusted without prior quality unit(s) approval if the adjustments are made within pre-established limits approved by the quality unit(s). All tests and results should be fully documented as part of the batch record.

8.34   Written procedures should describe the sampling methods for in-process materials, intermediates and APIs. Sampling plans and procedures should be based on scientifically sound sampling practices.

8.35   In-process sampling should be conducted using procedures designed to prevent contamination of the sampled material and other intermediates or APIs. Procedures should be established to ensure the integrity of samples after collection.

8.36   Out-of-specification (OOS) investigations are not normally needed for in-process tests that are performed for the purpose of monitoring and/or adjusting the process.

8.4   Blending batches of intermediates or APIs

8.40   For the purpose of this document, blending is defined as the process of combining materials within the same specification to produce a homogeneous intermediate or API. In-process mixing of fractions from single batches (e.g. collecting several centrifuge loads from a single crystallisation batch) or combining fractions from several batches for further processing is considered to be part of the production process and is not considered to be blending.

8.41   Out-of-specification batches should not be blended with other batches for the purpose of meeting specifications. Each batch incorporated into the blend should have been manufactured using an established process and should have been individually tested and found to meet appropriate specifications prior to blending.

8.42 Acceptable blending operations include but are not limited to:

- Blending of small batches to increase batch size;
- Blending of tailings (i.e. relatively small quantities of isolated material) from batches of the same intermediate or API to form a single batch.

8.43 Blending processes should be adequately controlled and documented, and the blended batch should be tested for conformance to established specifications, where appropriate.

8.44 The batch record of the blending process should allow traceability back to the individual batches that make up the blend.

8.45 Where physical attributes of the API are critical (e.g. APIs intended for use in solid oral dosage forms or suspensions), blending operations should be validated to show homogeneity of the combined batch. Validation should include testing of critical attributes (e.g. particle size distribution, bulk density and tap density) that may be affected by the blending process.

8.46 If the blending could adversely affect stability, stability testing of the final blended batches should be performed.

8.47 The expiry or re-test date of the blended batch should be based on the manufacturing date of the oldest tailings or batch in the blend.

8.5 Contamination control

8.50 Residual materials can be carried over into successive batches of the same intermediate or API if there is adequate control. Examples include residue adhering to the wall of a micronizer, residual layer of damp crystals remaining in a centrifuge bowl after discharge, and incomplete discharge of fluids or crystals from a processing vessel upon transfer of the material to the next step in the process. Such carryover should not result in the carryover of degradants or microbial contamination, which may adversely alter the established API impurity profile.

8.51 Production operations should be conducted in a manner that will prevent contamination of intermediates or APIs by other materials.

8.52 Precautions to avoid contamination should be taken when APIs are handled after purification.

9 Packaging and Identification Labelling of APIs and Intermediates

9.1 General

9.10 There should be written procedures describing the receipt, identification, quarantine, sampling, examination and/or testing and release, and handling of packaging and labelling materials.

9.11 Packaging and labelling materials should conform to established specifications. Those that do not comply with such specifications should be rejected to prevent their use in operations for which they are unsuitable.

9.12 Records should be maintained for each shipment of labels and packaging materials showing receipt, examination or testing, and whether accepted or rejected.

9.2 Packaging materials

9.20 Containers should provide adequate protection against deterioration or contamination of the intermediate or API that may occur during transportation and recommended storage.

9.21 Containers should be clean and, where indicated by the nature of the intermediate or API, sanitized to ensure that they are suitable for their intended use. These containers should not be reactive, additive or absorptive so as to alter the quality of the intermediate or API beyond the specified limits.

9.22 If containers are re-used, they should be cleaned in accordance with documented procedures and all previous labels should be removed or defaced.

9.3 Label issuance and control

9.30 Access to the label storage areas should be limited to authorised personnel.

9.31 Procedures should be used to reconcile the quantities of labels issued, used and returned, and to evaluate discrepancies found between the number of containers labelled and the number of labels issued. Such discrepancies should be investigated and the investigation should be approved by the quality unit(s).

9.32 All excess labels bearing batch numbers or other batch-related printing should be destroyed. Returned labels should be maintained and stored in a manner that prevents mix-ups and provides proper identification.

9.33 Obsolete and out-dated labels should be destroyed.

9.34   Printing devices used to print labels for packaging operations should be controlled to ensure that all imprinting conforms to the print specified in the batch production record.

9.35   Printed labels issued for a batch should be carefully examined for proper identity and conformity to specifications in the master production record. The results of this examination should be documented.

9.36   A printed label representative of those used should be included in the batch production record.

9.4   Packaging and labelling operations

9.40   There should be documented procedures designed to ensure that correct packaging materials and labels are used.

9.41   Labelling operations should be designed to prevent mix-ups. There should be physical or spatial separation from operations involving other intermediates or APIs.

9.42   Labels used on containers of intermediates or APIs should indicate the name or identifying code, the batch number of the product and storage conditions, when such information is critical to assure the quality of intermediate or API.

9.43   If the intermediate or API is intended to be transferred outside the control of the manufacturer's material management system, the name and address of the manufacturer, quantity of contents, and special transport conditions and any special legal requirements should also be included on the label. For intermediates or APIs with an expiry date, the expiry date should be indicated on the label and Certificate of Analysis. For intermediates or APIs with a retest date, the retest date should be indicated on the label and/or Certificate of Analysis.

9.44   Packaging and labelling facilities should be inspected immediately before use to ensure that all materials not needed for the next packaging operation have been removed. This examination should be documented in the batch production records, the facility log or other documentation system.

9.45   Packaged and labelled intermediates or APIs should be examined to ensure that containers and packages in the batch have the correct label. This examination should be part of the packaging operation. Results of these examinations should be recorded in the batch production or control records.

9.46   Intermediate or API containers that are transported outside the manufacturer's control should be sealed in a manner such that, if the seal is breached or missing, the recipient will be alerted to the possibility that the contents may have been altered.

10   Storage and Distribution

10.1   Warehousing procedures

10.10   Facilities should be available for the storage of all materials under appropriate conditions (e.g. controlled temperature and humidity when necessary). Records should be maintained of these conditions if they are critical for the maintenance of material characteristics.

10.11   Unless there is an alternative system to prevent the unintentional or unauthorised use of quarantined, rejected, returned or recalled materials, separate storage areas should be assigned for their temporary storage until the decision about their future use has been taken.

10.2   Distribution procedures

10.20   APIs and intermediates should be released for distribution to third parties only after they have been released by the quality unit(s). APIs and intermediates can be transferred under quarantine to another unit under the company's control when authorized by the quality unit(s), and if appropriate controls and documentation are in place.

10.21   APIs and intermediates should be transported in a manner that does not adversely affect their quality.

10.22   Special transport or storage conditions for an API or intermediate should be stated on the label.

10.23   The manufacturer should ensure that the contract acceptor (contractor) for transportation of the API or intermediate knows and follows the appropriate transport and storage conditions.

10.24   A system should be in place by which the distribution of each batch of intermediate and/or API can be readily determined to permit its recall.

11   Laboratory Controls

11.1   General controls

11.10   The independent quality unit(s) should have at its disposal adequate laboratory facilities.

11.11   There should be documented procedures describing sampling, testing, approval or rejection of materials, and recording and storage of laboratory data. Laboratory records should be maintained in accordance with Section 6.6.

11.12   All specifications, sampling plans and test procedures should be scientifically sound and appropriate to ensure that raw materials, intermediates, APIs and labels and packaging materials conform to established standards of quality and/or purity. Specifications and test procedures should be consistent with those included in the registration/filing. There can be specifications in addition to those in the registration/filing. Specifications, sampling plans and test procedures, including changes to them, should be drafted by the appropriate organizational unit, and reviewed and approved by the quality unit(s).

11.13   Appropriate specifications should be established for APIs in accordance with accepted standards and consistent with the manufacturing process. The specifications should include a control of the impurities (e.g. organic impurities, inorganic impurities and residual solvents). If the API has a specification for microbiological purity, appropriate action limits for total microbial counts and objectionable organisms should be established and met. If the API has a specification for endotoxins, appropriate action limits should be established and met.

11.14   Laboratory controls should be followed and documented at the time of performance. Any departures from the above-described procedures should be documented and explained.

11.15   Any OOS result obtained should be investigated and documented according to a procedure. This procedure should require analysis of the data, assessment of whether a significant problem exists, allocation of the tasks for corrective actions and conclusions. Any re-sampling and/or re-testing after OOS results should be performed according to a documented procedure.

11.16   Reagents and standard solutions should be prepared and labelled following written procedures. "Use by" dates should be applied as appropriate for analytical reagents or standard solutions.

11.17   Primary reference standards should be obtained as appropriate for the manufacture of APIs. The source of each primary reference standard should be documented. Records should be maintained of each primary reference standard's storage and use in accordance with the supplier's recommendations. Primary reference standards obtained from an officially recognised source are normally used without testing if stored under conditions consistent with the supplier's recommendations.

11.18   Where a primary reference standard is not available from an officially recognized source, an "in-house primary standard" should be established. Appropriate testing should be performed to establish fully the identity and purity of the primary reference standard. Appropriate documentation of this testing should be maintained.

11.19   Secondary reference standards should be appropriately prepared, identified, tested, approved and stored. The suitability of each batch of secondary reference standard should be determined prior to first use by comparing against a primary reference standard. Each batch of secondary reference standard should be periodically requalified in accordance with a written protocol.

11.2   Testing of intermediates and APIs

11.20   For each batch of intermediate and API, appropriate laboratory tests should be conducted to determine conformance to specifications.

11.21   An impurity profile describing the identified and unidentified impurities present in a typical batch produced by a specific controlled production process should normally be established for each API. The impurity profile should include the identity or some qualitative analytical designation (e.g. retention time), the range of each impurity observed and classification of each identified impurity (e.g. inorganic, organic, solvent). The impurity profile is normally dependent upon the production process and origin of the API. Impurity profiles are normally not necessary for APIs from herbal or animal tissue origin. Biotechnology considerations are covered in ICH Guideline Q6B.

11.22   The impurity profile should be compared at appropriate intervals against either the impurity profile in the regulatory submission or historical data in order to detect changes to the API resulting from modifications in raw materials, equipment operating parameters or the production process.

11.23   Appropriate microbiological tests should be conducted on each batch of intermediate and API where microbial quality is specified.

11.3   Validation of analytical procedures

See Section 12.

11.4   Certificates of analysis

11.40   Authentic Certificates of Analysis should be issued for each batch of intermediate or API on request.

11.41   Information on the name of the intermediate or API, including where appropriate its grade, the batch number and the date of release, should be provided on the Certificate of Analysis. For intermediates or APIs with an expiry date, the expiry date should be provided on the label and Certificate of Analysis. For intermediates or APIs with a re-test date, the re-test date should be indicated on the label and/or Certificate of Analysis.

11.42   The Certificate should list each test performed in accordance with compendial or customer requirements, including the acceptance limits and the numerical results obtained (if test results are numerical).

11.43   Certificates should be dated and signed by authorised personnel of the quality unit(s) and should show the name, address and telephone number of the original manufacturer. Where the analysis has been carried out by a repacker or reprocessor, the Certificate of Analysis should show the name, address and telephone number of the repacker/reprocessor and a reference to the name of the original manufacturer.

11.44   If new Certificates are issued by or on behalf of repackers/reprocessors, agents or brokers, these Certificates should show the name, address and telephone number of the laboratory that performed the analysis. They should also contain a reference to the name and address of the original manufacturer and to the original batch Certificate, a copy of which should be attached.

11.5   Stability monitoring of APIs

11.50   A documented, on-going testing programme should be designed to monitor the stability characteristics of APIs, and the results should be used to confirm appropriate storage conditions and retest or expiry dates.

11.51   The test procedures used in stability testing should be validated and be stability indicating.

11.52   Stability samples should be stored in containers that simulate the market container, e.g. if the API is marketed in bags within fiber drums, stability samples can be packaged in bags of the same material and in smaller-scale drums of similar or identical material composition to the market drums.

11.53   Normally the first three commercial production batches should be placed on the stability-monitoring programme to confirm the retest or expiry date. However, where data from previous studies shows that the API is expected to remain stable for at least two years, fewer than three batches can be used.

11.54　Thereafter, at least one batch per year of API manufactured (unless none is produced that year) should be added to the stability-monitoring programme and tested at least annually to confirm the stability.

11.55　For APIs with short shelf-lives, testing should be done more frequently, e.g. for those biotechnological/biological and other APIs with shelf-lives of one year or less, stability samples should be obtained and should be tested monthly for the first three months, and at three month intervals after that. When data exists confirming that the stability of the API is not compromised, elimination of specific test intervals (e.g. 9 month testing) can be considered.

11.56　Where appropriate, the stability storage conditions should be consistent with the ICH guidelines on stability.

11.6　Expiry and retest dating

11.60　When it is intended to transfer an intermediate outside the control of the manufacturer's material management system, and an expiry or re-test date has been assigned, supporting stability information should be available (e.g. published data, test results).

11.61　An API expiry or retest date should be based on an evaluation of data derived from stability studies. Common practice is to use a retest date, not an expiration date.

11.62　Preliminary API expiry or retest dates can be based on pilot scale batches if: (1) the pilot batches employ a method of manufacture and procedure that simulates the final process to be used on a commercial manufacturing scale; and (2) the quality of the API represents the material to be made on a commercial scale.

11.63　A representative sample should be taken for the purpose of performing a retest.

11.7　Reserve/retention samples

11.70　The packaging and holding of reserve samples are for the purpose of potential future evaluation of the quality of batches of API and not for future stability testing purposes.

11.71　Appropriately identified reserve samples of each API batch should be retained for one year after the expiry date of the batch assigned by the manufacturer, or for three years after distribution of the batch, whichever is the longer. For APIs with re-test dates, similar reserve samples should be retained for three years after the batch is completely distributed by the manufacturer.

11.72 The reserve sample should be stored in the same packaging system in which the API is stored or in one that is equivalent to or more protective than the marketed packaging system. Sufficient quantities should be retained to conduct at least two full compendial analyses or, when there is no pharmacopoeial monograph, two full specification analyses.

12 Validation

12.1 Validation policy

12.10 The company's overall policy, intentions and approach to validation, including the validation of production processes, cleaning procedures, analytical methods, in-process control test procedures, computerized systems, and persons responsible for design, review, approval and documentation of each validation phase, should be documented.

12.11 The critical parameters/attributes should normally be identified during the development stage or from historical data, and the ranges necessary for the reproducible operation should be defined. This should include:

- Defining the API in terms of its critical product attributes;
- Identifying process parameters that could affect the critical quality attributes of the API;
- Determining the range for each critical process parameter expected to be used during routine manufacturing and process control.

12.12 Validation should extend to those operations determined to be critical to the quality and purity of the API.

12.2 Validation documentation

12.20 A written validation protocol should be established that specifies how validation of a particular process will be conducted. The protocol should be reviewed and approved by the quality unit(s) and other designated units.

12.21 The validation protocol should specify critical process steps and acceptance criteria as well as the type of validation to be conducted (e.g. retrospective, prospective, concurrent) and the number of process runs.

12.22 A validation report that cross-references the validation protocol should be prepared, summarising the results obtained, commenting on any deviations observed and drawing the appropriate conclusions, including recommending changes to correct deficiencies.

12.23   Any variations from the validation protocol should be documented with appropriate justification.

12.3   Qualification

12.30   Before starting process validation activities, appropriate qualification of critical equipment and ancillary systems should be completed. Qualification is usually carried out by conducting the following activities, individually or combined:

- Design Qualification (DQ): documented verification that the proposed design of the facilities, equipment, or systems is suitable for the intended purpose;
- Installation Qualification (IQ): documented verification that the equipment or systems, as installed or modified, comply with the approved design, the manufacturer's recommendations and/or user requirements;
- Operational Qualification (OQ): documented verification that the equipment or systems, as installed or modified, perform as intended throughout the anticipated operating ranges;
- Performance Qualification (PQ): documented verification that the equipment and ancillary systems, as connected together, can perform effectively and reproducibly based on the approved process method and specifications.

12.4   Approaches to process validation

12.40   Process Validation (PV) is the documented evidence that the process, operated within established parameters, can perform effectively and reproducibly to produce an intermediate or API meeting its predetermined specifications and quality attributes.

12.41   There are three approaches to validation. Prospective validation is the preferred approach, but there are exceptions where the other approaches can be used. These approaches and their applicability are listed below.

12.42   Prospective validation should normally be performed for all API processes as defined in 12.12. Prospective validation performed on an API process should be completed before the commercial distribution of the final drug product manufactured from that API.

12.43   Concurrent validation can be conducted when data from replicate production runs is unavailable because only a limited number of API batches have been produced, API batches are produced infrequently, or API batches are produced by a validated process that has been modified. Prior to the completion of concurrent validation, batches can be released and used in final drug product for commercial distribution based on thorough monitoring and testing of the API batches.

12.44   An exception can be made for retrospective validation for well-established processes that have been used without significant changes to API quality due to changes in raw materials, equipment, systems, facilities or the production process. This validation approach may be used where:

(1)   Critical quality attributes and critical process parameters have been identified;
(2)   Appropriate in-process acceptance criteria and controls have been established;
(3)   There have not been significant process/product failures attributable to causes other than operator error or equipment failures unrelated to equipment suitability; and,
(4)   Impurity profiles have been established for the existing API.

12.45   Batches selected for retrospective validation should be representative of all batches made during the review period, including any batches that failed to meet specifications, and should be sufficient in number to demonstrate process consistency. Retained samples can be tested to obtain data to retrospectively validate the process.

12.5   Process validation program

12.50   The number of process runs for validation should depend on the complexity of the process or the magnitude of the process change being considered. For prospective and concurrent validation, three consecutive successful production batches should be used as a guide, but there may be situations where additional process runs are warranted to prove consistency of the process (e.g. complex API processes or API processes with prolonged completion times). For retrospective validation, generally data from 10 to 30 consecutive batches should be examined to assess process consistency, but fewer batches can be examined if justified.

12.51   Critical process parameters should be controlled and monitored during process validation studies. Process parameters unrelated to quality, such as variables controlled to minimize energy consumption or equipment use, need not be included in the process validation.

12.52   Process validation should confirm that the impurity profile for each API is within the limits specified. The impurity profile should be comparable to or better than historical data and, where applicable, the profile determined during process development or for batches used for pivotal clinical and toxicological studies.

12.6 Periodic review of validated systems

12.60 Systems and processes should be periodically evaluated to verify that they are still operating in a valid manner. Where no significant changes have been made to the system or process, and a quality review confirms that the system or process is consistently producing material meeting its specifications, there is normally no need for revalidation.

12.7 Cleaning validation

12.70 Cleaning procedures should normally be validated. In general, cleaning validation should be directed to situations or process steps where contamination or carryover of materials poses the greatest risk to API quality, e.g. in early production it may be unnecessary to validate equipment cleaning procedures where residues are removed by subsequent purification steps.

12.71 Validation of cleaning procedures should reflect actual equipment usage patterns. If various APIs or intermediates are manufactured in the same equipment, and the equipment is cleaned using the same process, a representative intermediate or API can be selected for cleaning validation. This selection should be based on the solubility and difficulty of cleaning, and the calculation of residue limits based on potency, toxicity and stability.

12.72 The cleaning validation protocol should describe the equipment to be cleaned, procedures, materials, acceptable cleaning levels, parameters to be monitored and controlled, and analytical methods. The protocol should also indicate the type of samples to be obtained and how they are collected and labelled.

12.73 Sampling should include swabbing, rinsing or alternative methods (e.g. direct extraction), as appropriate, to detect both insoluble and soluble residues. The sampling methods used should be capable of quantitatively measuring levels of residues remaining on the equipment surfaces after cleaning. Swab sampling may be impractical when product contact surfaces are not easily accessible due to equipment design and/or process limitations (e.g. inner surfaces of hoses, transfer pipes, reactor tanks with small ports or handling toxic materials, and small intricate equipment such as micronizers and microfluidizers).

12.74 Validated analytical methods with sensitivity to detect residues or contaminants should be used. The detection limit for each analytical method should be sufficiently sensitive to detect the established acceptable level of the residue or contaminant. The method's attainable recovery level should be established. Residue limits should be practical, achievable, verifiable and based on the most deleterious residue. Limits can be established based on the minimum known pharmacological, toxicological or physiological activity of the API or its most deleterious component.

12.75   Equipment cleaning/sanitization studies should address microbiological and endotoxin contamination for those processes where there is a need to reduce total microbiological count or endotoxins in the API, or other processes where such contamination could be of concern (e.g. non-sterile APIs used to manufacture sterile products).

12.76   Cleaning procedures should be monitored at appropriate intervals after validation to ensure that these procedures are effective when used during routine production. Equipment cleanliness can be monitored by analytical testing and visual examination, where feasible. Visual inspection can allow detection of gross contamination concentrated in small areas which could otherwise go undetected by sampling and/or analysis.

12.8   Validation of analytical methods

12.80   Analytical methods should be validated unless the method employed is included in the relevant pharmacopoeia or other recognised standard reference. The suitability of all testing methods used should none the less be verified under actual conditions of use and documented.

12.81   Methods should be validated to include consideration of characteristics included within the ICH guidelines on validation of analytical methods. The degree of analytical validation performed should reflect the purpose of the analysis and the stage of the API production process.

12.82   Appropriate qualification of analytical equipment should be considered before starting validation of analytical methods.

12.83   Complete records should be maintained of any modification of a validated analytical method. Such records should include the reason for the modification and appropriate data to verify that the modification produces results that are as accurate and reliable as the established method.

13   Change Control

13.10   A formal change control system should be established to evaluate all changes that may affect the production and control of the intermediate or API.

13.11   Written procedures should provide for the identification, documentation, appropriate review and approval of changes in raw materials, specifications, analytical methods, facilities, support systems, equipment (including computer hardware), processing steps, labelling and packaging materials, and computer software.

13.12 Any proposals for GMP relevant changes should be drafted, reviewed and approved by the appropriate organisational units, and reviewed and approved by the quality unit(s).

13.13 The potential impact of the proposed change on the quality of the intermediate or API should be evaluated. A classification procedure may help in determining the level of testing, validation, and documentation needed to justify changes to a validated process. Changes can be classified (e.g. as minor or major) depending on the nature and extent of the changes, and the effects these changes may impart on the process. Scientific judgement should determine what additional testing and validation studies are appropriate to justify a change in a validated process.

13.14 When implementing approved changes, measures should be taken to ensure that all documents affected by the changes are revised.

13.15 After the change has been implemented, there should be an evaluation of the first batches produced or tested under the change.

13.16 The potential for critical changes to affect established retest or expiry dates should be evaluated. If necessary, samples of the intermediate or API produced by the modified process can be placed on an accelerated stability programme and/or can be added to the stability monitoring programme.

13.17 Current dosage form manufacturers should be notified of changes from established production and process control procedures that can impact the quality of the API.

14 Rejection and Re-use of Materials

14.1 Rejection

14.10 Intermediates and APIs failing to meet established specifications should be identified as such and quarantined. These intermediates or APIs can be re-processed or re-worked as described below. The final disposition of rejected materials should be recorded.

14.2 Re-processing

14.20 Introducing an intermediate or API, including one that does not conform to standards or specifications, back into the process and reprocessing by repeating a crystallization step or other appropriate chemical or physical manipulation steps (e.g. distillation, filtration, chromatography, milling) that are part of the established manufacturing process is generally considered acceptable. However, if such reprocessing is used for a majority of batches, such re-processing should be included as part of the standard manufacturing process.

14.21   Continuation of a process step after an in-process control test has shown that the step is incomplete it is considered to be part of the normal process. This is not considered to be reprocessing.

14.22   Introducing unreacted material back into a process and repeating a chemical reaction is considered to be reprocessing unless it is part of the established process. Such reprocessing should be preceded by careful evaluation to ensure that the quality of the intermediate or API is not adversely impacted due to the potential formation of by-products and over-reacted materials.

14.3   Reworking

14.30   Before a decision is taken to rework batches that do not conform to established standards or specifications, an investigation into the reason for non-conformance should be performed.

14.31   Batches that have been reworked should be subjected to appropriate evaluation, testing, stability testing, if warranted, and documentation to show that the reworked product is of equivalent quality to that produced by the original process. Concurrent validation is often the appropriate validation approach for rework procedures. This allows a protocol to define the rework procedure, how it will be carried out and the expected results. If there is only one batch to be reworked, then a report can be written and the batch released once it is found to be acceptable.

14.32   Procedures should provide for comparing the impurity profile of each reworked batch against batches manufactured by the established process. Where routine analytical methods are inadequate to characterize the reworked batch, additional methods should be used.

14.4   Recovery of materials and solvents

14.40   Recovery (e.g. from mother liquor or filtrates) of reactants, intermediates or APIs is considered acceptable, provided that approved procedures exist for the recovery and the recovered materials meet specifications suitable for their intended use.

14.41　Solvents can be recovered and reused in the same processes or different processes, provided that the recovery procedures are controlled and monitored to ensure that solvents meet appropriate standards before re-use or co-mingling with other approved materials.

14.42　Fresh and recovered solvents and reagents can be combined if adequate testing has shown their suitability for all manufacturing processes in which they may be used.

14.43　The use of recovered solvents, mother liquors and other recovered materials should be adequately documented.

14.5　Returns

14.50　Returned intermediates or APIs should be identified as such and quarantined.

14.51　If the conditions under which returned intermediates or APIs have been stored or shipped before or during their return, or the condition of their containers casts doubt on their quality, the returned intermediates or APIs should be reprocessed, reworked or destroyed, as appropriate.

14.52　Records of returned intermediates or APIs should be maintained. For each return, documentation should include:

- Name and address of the consignee;
- Intermediate or API, batch number and quantity returned;
- Reason for return;
- Use or disposal of the returned intermediate or API.

15　Complaints and Recalls

15.10　All quality-related complaints, whether received orally or in writing, should be recorded and investigated according to a written procedure.

15.11　Complaint records should include:

- Name and address of complainant;
- Name (and, where appropriate, title) and phone number of person submitting the complaint;
- Complaint nature (including name and batch number of the API);
- Date complaint is received;
- Action initially taken (including dates and identity of person taking the action);
- Any follow-up action taken;

- Response provided to the originator of complaint (including date response sent); and
- Final decision on intermediate or API batch or lot.

15.12   Records of complaints should be retained in order to evaluate trends, product-related frequencies and severity, with a view to taking additional and, if appropriate, immediate corrective action.

15.13   There should be a written procedure that defines the circumstances under which a recall of an intermediate or API should be considered.

15.14   The recall procedure should designate who should be involved in evaluating the information, how a recall should be initiated, who should be informed about the recall and how the recalled material should be treated.

15.15   In the event of a serious or potentially life-threatening situation, local, national and/or international authorities should be informed and their advice sought.

16   Contract Manufacturers (Including Laboratories)

16.10   All contract manufacturers (including laboratories) should comply with the GMP defined in this Guide. Special consideration should be given to the prevention of cross-contamination and to maintaining traceability.

16.11   Contract manufacturers (including laboratories) should be evaluated by the contract giver to ensure GMP compliance of the specific operations occurring at the contract sites.

16.12   There should be a written and approved contract or formal agreement between the contract giver and the contract acceptor that defines in detail the GMP responsibilities, including the quality measures, of each party.

16.13   The contract should permit the contract giver to audit the contract acceptor's facilities for compliance with GMP.

16.14   Where subcontracting is allowed, the contract acceptor should not pass to a third party any of the work entrusted to them under the contract without the contract giver's prior evaluation and approval of the arrangements.

16.15   Manufacturing and laboratory records should be kept at the site where the activity occurs and be readily available.

16.16   Changes in the process, equipment, test methods, specifications or other contractual requirements should not be made unless the contract giver is informed and approves the changes.

17 Agents, Brokers, Traders, Distributors, Re-packers, and Relabellers

17.1 Applicability

17.10 This section applies to any party other than the original manufacturer who may trade and/or take possession, repack, relabel, manipulate, distribute or store an API or intermediate.

17.11 All agents, brokers, traders, distributors, repackers and relabellers should comply with GMP as defined in this Guide.

17.2 Traceability of distributed APIs and intermediates

17.20 Agents, brokers, traders, distributors, repackers or relabellers should maintain complete traceability of APIs and intermediates that they distribute. Documents that should be retained and available include:

- Identity of original manufacturer;
- Address of original manufacturer;
- Purchase orders;
- Bills of lading (transportation documentation);
- Receipt documents;
- Name or designation of API or intermediate;
- Manufacturer's batch number;
- Transportation and distribution records;
- All authentic Certificates of Analysis, including those of the original manufacturer;
- Retest or expiry date.

17.3 Quality management

17.30 Agents, brokers, traders, distributors, repackers or relabellers should establish, document and implement an effective system of managing quality, as specified in Section 2.

17.4 Repackaging, relabelling and holding of APIs and intermediates

17.40 Repackaging, relabelling and holding of APIs and intermediates should be performed under appropriate GMP controls, as stipulated in this Guide, to avoid mix-ups and loss of API or intermediate identity or purity.

17.41   Repackaging should be conducted under appropriate environmental conditions to avoid contamination and cross-contamination.

17.5   Stability

17.50   Stability studies to justify assigned expiration or retest dates should be conducted if the API or intermediate is repackaged in a different type of container than that used by the API or intermediate manufacturer.

17.6   Transfer of information

17.60   Agents, brokers, distributors, repackers or relabellers should transfer all quality or regulatory information received from an API or intermediate manufacturer to the customer, and from the customer to the API or intermediate manufacturer.

17.61   The agent, broker, trader, distributor, re-packer or re-labeller who supplies the API or intermediate to the customer should provide the name of the original API or intermediate manufacturer and the batch number(s) supplied.

17.62   The agent should also provide the identity of the original API or intermediate manufacturer to regulatory authorities upon request. The original manufacturer can respond to the regulatory authority directly or through its authorized agents, depending on the legal relationship between the authorized agents and the original API or intermediate manufacturer. (In this context "authorized" refers to authorized by the manufacturer.)

17.63   The specific guidance for Certificates of Analysis included in Section 11.4 should be met.

17.7   Handling of complaints and recalls

17.70   Agents, brokers, traders, distributors, repackers or relabellers should maintain records of complaints and recalls, as specified in Section 15, for all complaints and recalls that come to their attention.

17.71   If the situation warrants, the agents, brokers, traders, distributors, repackers or relabellers should review the complaint with the original API or intermediate manufacturer in order to determine whether any further action, either with other customers who may have received this API or intermediate or with the regulatory authority, or both, should be initiated. The investigation into the cause for the complaint or recall should be conducted and documented by the appropriate party.

17.72   Where a complaint is referred to the original API or intermediate manufacturer, the record maintained by the agents, brokers, traders, distributors, repackers or relabellers should include any response received from the original API or intermediate manufacturer (including date and information provided).

17.8   Handling of returns

17.80   Returns should be handled as specified in Section 14.52. The agents, brokers, traders, distributors, re-packers or relabellers should maintain documentation of returned APIs and intermediates.

18   Specific Guidance for APIs Manufactured by Cell Culture/ Fermentation

18.1   General

18.10   Section 18 is intended to address specific controls for APIs or intermediates manufactured by cell culture or fermentation using natural or recombinant organisms, which have not been covered adequately in the previous sections. It is not intended to be a stand-alone Section. In general, the GMP principles in the other sections of this document apply. Note that the principles of fermentation for "classical" processes for production of small molecules and for processes using recombinant and non-recombinant organisms for production of proteins and/or polypeptides are the same, although the degree of control will differ. Where practical, this section will address these differences. In general, the degree of control for biotechnological processes used to produce proteins and polypeptides is greater than that for classical fermentation processes.

18.11   The term "biotechnological process" (biotech) refers to the use of cells or organisms that have been generated or modified by recombinant DNA, hybridoma or other technology to produce APIs. The APIs produced by biotechnological processes normally consist of high molecular weight substances, such as proteins and polypeptides, for which specific guidance is given in this section. Certain APIs of low molecular weight, such as antibiotics, amino acids, vitamins and carbohydrates, can also be produced by recombinant DNA technology. The level of control for these types of APIs is similar to that employed for classical fermentation.

18.12   The term "classical fermentation" refers to processes that use microorganisms existing in nature and/or modified by conventional methods (e.g. irradiation or chemical mutagenesis) to produce APIs. APIs produced by "classical fermentation" are normally low-molecular-weight products such as antibiotics, amino acids, vitamins and carbohydrates.

18.13   Production of APIs or intermediates from cell culture or fermentation involves biological processes such as cultivation of cells or extraction and purification of material from living organisms. Note that there may be additional process steps, such as physicochemical modification, that are part of the manufacturing process. The raw materials used (media, buffer components) may provide the potential for growth of microbiological contaminants. Depending on the source, method of preparation and the intended use of the API or intermediate, control of bioburden, viral contamination and/or endotoxins during manufacturing and monitoring of the process at appropriate stages may be necessary.

18.14   Appropriate controls should be established at all stages of manufacturing to assure intermediate and/or API quality. Although this Guide starts at the cell culture/fermentation step, prior steps (e.g. cell banking) should be performed under appropriate process controls. This Guide covers cell culture/fermentation from the point at which a vial of the cell bank is retrieved for use in manufacturing.

18.15   Appropriate equipment and environmental controls should be used to minimize the risk of contamination. The acceptance criteria for quality of the environment and the frequency of monitoring should depend on the step in production and the production conditions (open, closed or contained systems).

18.16   In general, process controls should take into account:

- Maintenance of the Working Cell Bank (where appropriate);
- Proper inoculation and expansion of the culture;
- Control of the critical operating parameters during fermentation/cell culture;
- Monitoring of the process for cell growth, viability (for most cell culture processes) and productivity where appropriate;
- Harvest and purification procedures that remove cells, cellular debris and media components while protecting the intermediate or API from contamination (particularly of a microbiological nature) and from loss of quality;
- Monitoring of bioburden and, where needed, endotoxin levels at appropriate stages of production; and
- Viral safety concerns as described in ICH Guideline Q5A *Quality of Biotechnological Products: Viral Safety Evaluation of Biotechnology Products Derived from Cell Lines of Human or Animal Origin.*

18.17   Where appropriate, the removal of media components, host cell proteins, other process-related impurities, product-related impurities and contaminants should be demonstrated.

18.2   Cell bank maintenance and record keeping

18.20   Access to cell banks should be limited to authorized personnel.

18.21   Cell banks should be maintained under storage conditions designed to maintain viability and prevent contamination.

18.22   Records of the use of the vials from the cell banks and storage conditions should be maintained.

18.23   Where appropriate, cell banks should be periodically monitored to determine suitability for use.

18.24   See ICH Guideline Q5D *Quality of Biotechnological Products: Derivation and Characterization of Cell Substrates Used for Production of Biotechnological/Biological Products* for a more complete discussion of cell banking.

18.3   Cell culture fermentation

18.30   Where aseptic addition of cell substrates, media, buffers and gases is needed, closed or contained systems should be used where possible. If the inoculation of the initial vessel, or subsequent transfers or additions (media, buffers) are performed in open vessels, there should be controls and procedures in place to minimize the risk of contamination.

18.31   Where the quality of the API can be affected by microbial contamination, manipulations using open vessels should be performed in a biosafety cabinet or similarly controlled environment.

18.32   Personnel should be appropriately gowned and take special precautions handling the cultures.

18.33   Critical operating parameters (e.g. temperature, pH, agitation rates, addition of gases, pressure) should be monitored to ensure consistency with the established process. Cell growth, viability (for most cell culture processes) and, where appropriate, productivity should also be monitored. Critical parameters will vary from one process to another, and for classic fermentation, certain parameters (e.g. cell viability) may not need to be monitored.

18.34   Cell culture equipment should be cleaned and sterilized after use. As appropriate, fermentation equipment should be cleaned and sanitized or sterilized.

18.35   Culture media should be sterilized before use when appropriate to protect the quality of the API.

18.36   There should be appropriate procedures in place to detect contamination and determine the course of action to be taken. This should include procedures to determine the impact of the contamination on the product and those to decontaminate the equipment and return it to a condition for use in subsequent batches. Foreign organisms observed during fermentation processes should be identified as appropriate, and the effect of their presence on product quality should be assessed, if necessary. The results of such assessments should be taken into consideration in the disposition of the material produced.

18.37   Records of contamination events should be maintained.

18.38   Shared (multi-product) equipment may warrant additional testing after cleaning between product campaigns, as appropriate, to minimize the risk of cross-contamination.

18.4   Harvesting, isolation and purification

18.40   Harvesting steps, either to remove cells or cellular components or to collect cellular components after disruption, should be performed in equipment and areas designed to minimize the risk of contamination.

18.41   Harvest and purification procedures that remove or inactivate the producing organism, cellular debris and media components (while minimizing degradation, contamination and loss of quality) should be adequate to ensure that the intermediate or API is recovered with consistent quality.

18.42   All equipment should be properly cleaned and, as appropriate, sanitized after use. Multiple successive batching without cleaning can be used if intermediate or API quality is not compromised.

18.43   If open systems are used, purification should be performed under environmental conditions appropriate for the preservation of product quality.

18.44   Additional controls, such as the use of dedicated chromatography resins or additional testing, may be appropriate if equipment is to be used for multiple products.

18.5   Viral removal/inactivation steps

18.50   See the ICH Guideline Q5A *Quality of Biotechnological Products: Viral Safety Evaluation of Biotechnology Products Derived from Cell Lines of Human or Animal Origin* for more specific information.

18.51 Viral removal and viral inactivation steps are critical processing steps for some processes and should be performed within their validated parameters.

18.52 Appropriate precautions should be taken to prevent potential viral contamination from pre-viral to post-viral removal/inactivation steps. Therefore, open processing should be performed in areas that are separate from other processing activities and have separate air-handling units.

18.53 The same equipment is not normally used for different purification steps. However, if the same equipment is to be used, the equipment should be appropriately cleaned and sanitized before re-use. Appropriate precautions should be taken to prevent potential virus carry-over (e.g. through equipment or environment) from previous steps.

19 APIs for Use in Clinical Trials

19.1 General

19.10 Not all the controls in the previous sections of this Guide are appropriate for the manufacture of a new API for investigational use during its development. Section 19 provides specific guidance unique to these circumstances.

19.11 The controls used in the manufacture of APIs for use in clinical trials should be consistent with the stage of development of the drug product incorporating the API. Process and test procedures should be flexible to provide for changes as knowledge of the process increases and clinical testing of a drug product progresses from pre-clinical stages through clinical stages. Once drug development reaches the stage where the API is produced for use in drug products intended for clinical trials, manufacturers should ensure that APIs are manufactured in suitable facilities using appropriate production and control procedures to ensure the quality of the API.

19.2 Quality

19.20 Appropriate GMP concepts should be applied in the production of APIs for use in clinical trials with a suitable mechanism of approval for each batch.

19.21 A quality unit(s) independent from production should be established for the approval or rejection of each batch of API for use in clinical trials.

19.22   Some of the testing functions commonly performed by the quality unit(s) can be performed within other organizational units.

19.23   Quality measures should include a system for testing of raw materials, packaging materials, intermediates and APIs.

19.24   Process and quality problems should be evaluated.

19.25   Labelling for APIs intended for use in clinical trials should be appropriately controlled and should identify the material as being for investigational use.

19.3   Equipment and facilities

19.30   During all phases of clinical development, including the use of small-scale facilities or laboratories to manufacture batches of APIs for use in clinical trials, procedures should be in place to ensure that equipment is calibrated, clean and suitable for its intended use.

19.31   Procedures for the use of facilities should ensure that materials are handled in a manner that minimizes the risk of contamination and cross-contamination.

19.4   Control of raw materials

19.40   Raw materials used in production of APIs for use in clinical trials should be evaluated by testing, or received with a supplier's analysis and subjected to identity testing. When a material is considered hazardous, a supplier's analysis should suffice.

19.41   In some instances, the suitability of a raw material can be determined before use based on acceptability in small-scale reactions (i.e. use testing) rather than on analytical testing alone.

19.5   Production

19.50   The production of APIs for use in clinical trials should be documented in laboratory notebooks, batch records or by other appropriate means. These documents should include information on the use of production materials, equipment, processing and scientific observations.

19.51   Expected yields can be more variable and less defined than the expected yields used in commercial processes. Investigations into yield variations are not expected.

19.6 Validation

19.60 Process validation for the production of APIs for use in clinical trials is normally inappropriate, where a single API batch is produced or where process changes during API development make batch replication difficult or inexact. The combination of controls, calibration and, where appropriate, equipment qualification assures API quality during this development phase.

19.61 Process validation should be conducted in accordance with Section 12 when batches are produced for commercial use, even when such batches are produced on a pilot or small scale.

19.7 Changes

19.70 Changes are expected during development, as knowledge is gained and the production is scaled up. Every change in the production, specifications or test procedures should be adequately recorded.

19.8 Laboratory controls

19.80 While analytical methods performed to evaluate a batch of API for clinical trials may not yet be validated, they should be scientifically sound.

19.81 A system for retaining reserve samples of all batches should be in place. This system should ensure that a sufficient quantity of each reserve sample is retained for an appropriate length of time after approval, termination or discontinuation of an application.

19.82 Expiry and re-test dating as defined in Section 11.6 apply to existing APIs used in clinical trials. For new APIs, Section 11.6 does not normally apply in early stages of clinical trials.

19.9 Documentation

19.90 A system should be in place to ensure that information gained during the development and the manufacture of APIs for use in clinical trials is documented and available.

19.91 The development and implementation of the analytical methods used to support the release of a batch of API for use in clinical trials should be appropriately documented.

19.92   A system for retaining production and control records and documents should be used. This system should ensure that records and documents are retained for an appropriate length of time after the approval, termination or discontinuation of an application.

20 Glossary

ACCEPTANCE CRITERIA

Numerical limits, ranges or other suitable measures for acceptance of test results.

ACTIVE PHARMACEUTICAL INGREDIENT (API) (OR DRUG SUBSTANCE)

Any substance or mixture of substances intended for use in the manufacture of a drug (medicinal) product which, when used in the production of a drug, becomes an active ingredient of the drug product. Such substances are intended to furnish pharmacological activity or other direct effect in the diagnosis, cure, mitigation, treatment or prevention of disease or to affect the structure and function of the body.

API STARTING MATERIAL

A raw material, intermediate or an API that is used in the production of an API and that is incorporated as a significant structural fragment into the structure of the API. An API Starting Material can be an article of commerce, a material purchased from one or more suppliers under contract or commercial agreement, or produced in-house. API Starting Materials are normally of defined chemical properties and structure.

BATCH (OR LOT)

A specific quantity of material produced in a process or series of processes so that it is expected to be homogeneous within specified limits. In the case of continuous production, a batch may correspond to a defined fraction of the production. The batch size can be defined either by a fixed quantity or by the amount produced in a fixed time interval.

BATCH NUMBER (OR LOT NUMBER)

A unique combination of numbers, letters and/or symbols that identify a batch (or lot) and from which the production and distribution history can be determined.

BIOBURDEN

The level and type (e.g. objectionable or not) of microorganisms that can be present in raw materials, API starting materials, intermediates or APIs.

Bioburden should not be considered contamination unless the levels have been exceeded or defined objectionable organisms have been detected.

CALIBRATION

The demonstration that a particular instrument or device produces results within specified limits by comparison with those produced by a reference or traceable standard over an appropriate range of measurements.

COMPUTER SYSTEM

A group of hardware components and associated software, designed and assembled to perform a specific function or group of functions.

COMPUTERIZED SYSTEM

A process or operation integrated with a computer system.

CONTAMINATION

The undesired introduction of impurities of a chemical or microbiological nature, or of foreign matter, into or on to a raw material, intermediate or API during production, sampling, packaging or re-packaging, storage or transport.

CONTRACT MANUFACTURER

A manufacturer performing some aspect of manufacturing on behalf of the original manufacturer.

CRITICAL

Describes a process step, process condition, test requirement or other relevant parameter or item that must be controlled within predetermined criteria to ensure that the API meets its specification.

CROSS-CONTAMINATION

Contamination of a material or product with another material or product.

DEVIATION

Departure from an approved instruction or established standard.

DRUG (MEDICINAL) PRODUCT

The dosage form in the final immediate packaging intended for marketing (reference Q1A).

DRUG SUBSTANCE

See Active Pharmaceutical Ingredient.

EXPIRY DATE (OR EXPIRATION DATE)

The date placed on the container/labels of an API designating the time during which the API is expected to remain within established shelf-life specifications if stored under defined conditions, and after which it should not be used.

IMPURITY

Any component present in the intermediate or API that is not the desired entity.

IMPURITY PROFILE

A description of the identified and unidentified impurities present in an API.

IN-PROCESS CONTROL (OR PROCESS CONTROL)

Checks performed during production in order to monitor and, if appropriate, to adjust the process and/or to ensure that the intermediate or API conforms to its specifications.

INTERMEDIATE

A material produced during steps of the processing of an API that undergoes further molecular change or purification before it becomes an API. Intermediates may or may not be isolated. (Note: this Guide only addresses those intermediates produced after the point that the company has defined as the point at which the production of the API begins.)

LOT

See Batch.

LOT NUMBER

See Batch Number.

MANUFACTURE

All operations of receipt of materials, production, packaging, re-packaging, labelling, re-labelling, quality control, release, storage and distribution of APIs and related controls.

MATERIAL

A general term used to denote raw materials (starting materials, reagents, solvents), process aids, intermediates, APIs, and packaging and labelling materials.

MOTHER LIQUOR

The residual liquid that remains after the crystallization or isolation processes. A mother liquor may contain unreacted materials, intermediates, levels of the API and/or impurities. It may be used for further processing.

PACKAGING MATERIAL

Any material intended to protect an intermediate or API during storage and transport.

PROCEDURE

A documented description of the operations to be performed, the precautions to be taken and measures to be applied directly or indirectly, related to the manufacture of an intermediate or API.

PROCESS AIDS

Materials, excluding solvents, used as an aid in the manufacture of an intermediate or API that do not themselves participate in a chemical or biological reaction (e.g. filter aid, activated carbon, etc.).

PROCESS CONTROL

See In-process Control.

PRODUCTION

All operations involved in the preparation of an API from receipt of materials through processing and packaging of the API.

QUALIFICATION

Action of proving and documenting that equipment or ancillary systems are properly installed, work correctly and actually lead to the expected results. Qualification is part of validation, but the individual qualification steps alone do not constitute process validation.

QUALITY ASSURANCE (QA)

The sum total of the organised arrangements made with the object of ensuring that all APIs are of the quality required for their intended use and that quality systems are maintained.

QUALITY CONTROL (QC)

Checking or testing that specifications are met.

QUALITY UNIT(S)

An organizational unit independent of production that fulfils both Quality Assurance and Quality Control responsibilities. This can be in the form of separate QA and QC units or a single individual or group, depending upon the size and structure of the organization.

QUARANTINE

The status of materials isolated physically or by other effective means pending a decision on their subsequent approval or rejection.

RAW MATERIAL

A general term used to denote starting materials, reagents and solvents intended for use in the production of intermediates or APIs.

REFERENCE STANDARD, PRIMARY

A substance that has been shown by an extensive set of analytical tests to be authentic material that should be of high purity. This standard can be: (1) obtained from an officially recognised source, (2) prepared by independent synthesis, (3) obtained from existing production material of high purity or (4) prepared by further purification of existing production material.

REFERENCE STANDARD, SECONDARY

A substance of established quality and purity, as shown by comparison to a primary reference standard, used as a reference standard for routine laboratory analysis.

REPROCESSING

Introducing an intermediate or API, including one that does not conform to standards or specifications, back into the process and repeating a crystallization step or other appropriate chemical or physical manipulation steps (e.g. distillation, filtration, chromatography, milling) that are part of the established manufacturing process. Continuation of a process step, after an in-process control test has shown that the step is incomplete, is considered to be part of the normal process and not re-processing.

RETEST DATE

The date when a material should be re-examined to ensure that it is still suitable for use.

REWORKING

Subjecting an intermediate or API that does not conform to standards or specifications to one or more processing steps that are different from the established manufacturing process to obtain acceptable quality intermediate or API (e.g. recrystallizing with a different solvent).

SIGNATURE (SIGNED)

See definition for Signed.

SIGNED (SIGNATURE)

The record of the individual who performed a particular action or review. This record can be initials, full handwritten signature, personal seal, or authenticated and secure electronic signature.

SOLVENT

An inorganic or organic liquid used as a vehicle for the preparation of solutions or suspensions in the manufacture of an intermediate or API.

SPECIFICATION

A list of tests, references to analytical procedures and appropriate acceptance criteria that are numerical limits, ranges or other criteria for the test described. It establishes the set of criteria to which a material should conform to be considered acceptable for its intended use. "Conformance to specification" means that the material, when tested according to the listed analytical procedures, will meet the listed acceptance criteria.

VALIDATION

A documented programme that provides a high degree of assurance that a specific process, method or system will consistently produce a result, meeting predetermined acceptance criteria.

VALIDATION PROTOCOL

A written plan stating how validation will be conducted and defining acceptance criteria, e.g. the protocol for a manufacturing process identifies processing equipment, critical process parameters/operating ranges, product characteristics, sampling, test data to be collected, number of validation runs and acceptable test results.

YIELD, EXPECTED

The quantity of material or the percentage of theoretical yield anticipated at any appropriate phase of production based on previous laboratory, pilot scale or manufacturing data.

YIELD, THEORETICAL

The quantity that would be produced at any appropriate phase of production, based upon the quantity of material to be used, in the absence of any loss or error in actual production.

PART III: GMP-related Documents

Contents of Part III

PART III GMP-RELATED DOCUMENTS

SITE MASTER FILE – EXPLANATORY NOTES ON THE PREPARATION OF A SITE MASTER FILE

These notes are intended to provide guidance on the recommended content of the Site Master File. A requirement for a Site Master File is referred to in Chapter 4 of the GMP Guide.

1   Introduction

1.1   The Site Master File is prepared by the pharmaceutical manufacturer and should contain specific information about the quality management policies and activities of the site, the production and/or quality control of pharmaceutical manufacturing operations carried out at the named site, and any closely integrated operations at adjacent and nearby buildings. If only part of a pharmaceutical operation is carried out on the site, a Site Master File need describe only those operations, e.g. analysis, packaging, etc.

1.2   When submitted to a regulatory authority, the Site Master File should provide clear information on the manufacturer's GMP-related activities that can be useful in general supervision and in the efficient planning and undertaking of GMP inspections.

1.3   A Site Master File should contain adequate information but, as far as possible, not exceed 25–30 pages plus appendices. Simple plans outline drawings or schematic layouts are preferred instead of narratives. The Site Master File, including appendices, should be readable when printed on A4 paper sheets.

1.4   The Site Master File should be a part of documentation belonging to the quality management system of the manufacturer and kept updated accordingly. The Site Master File should have an edition number, the date it becomes effective and the date by which it has to be reviewed. It should be subject to regular review to ensure that it is up to date and representative of current activities. Each Appendix can have an individual effective date, allowing for independent updating.

2   Purpose

The aim of these Explanatory Notes is to guide the manufacturer of medicinal products in the preparation of a Site Master File that is useful to the regulatory authority in planning and conducting GMP inspections.

3   Scope

These Explanatory Notes apply to the preparation and content of the Site Master File.

Manufacturers should refer to regional/national regulatory requirements to establish whether it is mandatory for manufacturers of medicinal products to prepare a Site Master File.

These Explanatory Notes apply for all kind of manufacturing operations such as production, packaging and labelling, testing, re-labelling and re-packaging of all types of medicinal products. The outlines of this guide could also be used in the preparation of a Site Master File or corresponding document by Blood and Tissue Establishments and manufacturers of Active Pharmaceutical Ingredients.

4   Content of Site Master File

Refer to the Annex for the format to be used.

Annex Content of Site Master File

1   General information on the manufacturer

1.1   Contact information on the manufacturer:

- Name and official address of the manufacturer;
- Names and street addresses of the site, buildings and production units located on the site;
- Contact information of the manufacturer including 24 hrs telephone number of the contact personnel in the case of product defects or recalls;
- Identification number of the site such as GPS details, or any other geographical location system, D-U-N-S (Data Universal Numbering System)

---

[1] A D-U-N-S reference is required for Site Master Files submitted to EU/EEA authorities for manufacturing sites located outside the EU/EEA.

Number (a unique identification number provided by Dun & Bradstreet) of the site[1].

1.2   Authorised pharmaceutical manufacturing activities of the site:

- Copy of the valid manufacturing authorisation issued by the relevant Competent Authority in Appendix 1, or, when applicable, reference to the EudraGMP database. If the Competent Authority does not issue manufacturing authorizations, this should be stated;
- Brief description of manufacture, import, export, distribution and other activities as authorized by the relevant Competent Authorities, including foreign authorities with authorized dosage forms/activities, respectively, where not covered by the manufacturing authorization;
- Type of products currently manufactured on-site (list in Appendix 2) where not covered by Appendix 1 or EudraGMP entry;
- List of GMP inspections of the site within the last five years, including dates and name/country of the Competent Authority having performed the inspection. A copy of current GMP certificate (Appendix 3) or reference to the EudraGMP database should be included, if available.

1.3   Any other manufacturing activities carried out on the site:

- Description of non-pharmaceutical activities on-site, if any.

2   Quality management system of the manufacturer

2.1   The quality management system of the manufacturer:
- Brief description of the quality management systems run by the company and reference to the standards used;
- Responsibilities related to the maintaining of quality system including senior management;
- Information of activities for which the site is accredited and certified, including dates and contents of accreditations, and names of accrediting bodies.

2.2   Release procedure of finished products:

- Detailed description of qualification requirements (education and work experience) of the Authorised Person(s)/Qualified Person(s) responsible for batch certification and releasing procedures;
- General description of batch certification and releasing procedure;
- Role of Authorised Person/Qualified Person in quarantine and release of finished products and in assessment of compliance with the Marketing Authorisation;
- The arrangements between Authorised Persons/Qualified Persons when several Authorised Persons/Qualified Persons are involved;

EU GMP PART III SITE MASTER FILE – EXPLANATORY NOTES ON THE PREPARATION OF A SITE MASTER FILE

- Statement on whether the control strategy employs Process Analytical Technology (PAT) and/or Real Time Release or Parametric Release;

2.3   Management of suppliers and contractors:

- A brief summary of the establishment/knowledge of the supply chain and the external audit programme;
- Brief description of the qualification system of contractors, manufacturers of active pharmaceutical ingredients (API) and other critical materials suppliers;
- Measures taken to ensure that products manufactured are compliant with TSE (transmitting spongiform encephalopathy) guidelines;
- Measures adopted where counterfeit/falsified products, bulk products (i.e. unpacked tablets), active pharmaceutical ingredients or excipients are suspected or identified;
- Use of outside scientific, analytical or other technical assistance in relation to manufacture and analysis;
- List of contract manufacturers and laboratories including the addresses and contact information and flow charts of supply chains for outsourced manufacturing and Quality Control activities, e.g. sterilization of primary packaging material for aseptic processes, testing of starting raw materials, etc., should be presented in Appendix 4;
- Brief overview of the responsibility sharing between the contract giver and acceptor with respect to compliance with the Marketing Authorization (where not included under 2.2).

2.4   Quality Risk Management (QRM):

- Brief description of QRM methodologies used by the manufacturer;
- Scope and focus of QRM including brief description of any activities that are performed at the corporate level and those that are performed locally. Any application of the QRM system to assess continuity of supply should be mentioned.

2.5   Product Quality Reviews:

- Brief description of methodologies used.

3 Personnel

- Organisation chart showing the arrangements for quality management, production and quality control positions/titles in Appendix 5, including senior management and Qualified Person(s).
- Number of employees engaged in the quality management, production, quality control, storage and distribution, respectively.

4 Premises and equipment

4.1   Premises:

- Short description of plant, size of the site and list of buildings. If the production for different markets, i.e. for local, EU, USA, etc. takes place in different buildings on the site, the buildings should be listed with destined markets identified (if not identified under 1.1);
- Simple plan or description of manufacturing areas with indication of scale (architectural or engineering drawings are not required);
- Lay-outs and flow charts of the production areas (in Appendix 6) showing the room classification and pressure differentials between adjoining areas and indicating the production activities (i.e. compounding, filling, storage, packaging, etc.) in the rooms;
- Lay-outs of warehouses and storage areas, with special areas for the storage and handling of highly toxic, hazardous and sensitising materials indicated, if applicable;
- Brief description of specific storage conditions if applicable, but not indicated on the lay-outs.

4.1.1   Brief description of heating, ventilation and air-conditioning (HVAC) systems:

- Principles for defining the air supply, temperature, humidity, pressure differentials and air change rates, and policy of air recirculation (%).

4.1.2   Brief description of water systems:

- Quality references of water produced;
- Schematic drawings of the systems in Appendix 7.

4.1.3   Brief description of other relevant utilities, such as steam, compressed air, nitrogen, etc.

4.2   Equipment:

4.2.1   Listing of major production and control laboratory equipment, with critical pieces of equipment identified, should be provided in Appendix 8.

4.2.2   Cleaning and sanitation:

- Brief description of cleaning and sanitation methods of product contact surfaces (i.e. manual cleaning, automatic Clean-in-Place, etc.).

4.2.3   GMP critical computerised systems:

- Description of GMP critical computerised systems (excluding equipment specific Programmable Logic Controllers (PLCs).

5 Documentation

- Description of documentation system (i.e. electronic, manual).
- When documents and records are stored or archived off-site (including pharmacovigilance data, when applicable): list of types of documents/records; name and address of storage site and an estimate of time required retrieving documents from the off-site archive.

6 Production

6.1   Type of products:

- (References to Appendices 1 or 2 can be made);
- Type of products manufactured including:
  - list of dosage forms of both human and veterinary products that are manufactured on the site,
  - list of dosage forms of investigational medicinal products (IMPs) manufactured for any clinical trials on the site and, when different from the commercial manufacturing, information of production areas and personnel;
- Toxic or hazardous substances handled (e.g. with high pharmacological activity and/or with sensitising properties);
- Product types manufactured in a dedicated facility or on a campaign basis, if applicable;
- Process Analytical Technology (PAT) applications, if applicable: general statement of the relevant technology and associated computerized systems.

6.2   Process validation:

- Brief description of general policy for process validation;
- Policy for re-processing or re-working.

6.3   Material management and warehousing:

- Arrangements for the handling of starting materials, packaging materials, bulk and finished products, including sampling, quarantine, release and storage;
- Arrangements for the handling of rejected materials and products.

7 Quality control (QC)

Description of the Quality Control activities carried out on the site in terms of physical, chemical and microbiological and biological testing.

8   Distribution, complaints, product defects and recalls

8.1   Distribution (to the part under the responsibility of the manufacturer):

- Types (wholesale licence holders, manufacturing licence holders, etc.) and locations (EU/EEA, USA, etc.) of the companies to which the products are shipped from the site;
- Description of the system used to verify that each customer/recipient is legally entitled to receive medicinal products from the manufacturer;
- Brief description of the system to ensure appropriate environmental conditions during transit, e.g. temperature monitoring/control;
- Arrangements for product distribution and methods by which product traceability is maintained;
- Measures taken to prevent manufacturers' products falling into the illegal supply chain.

8.2   Complaints, product defects and recalls:

- Brief description of the system for handling complains, product defects and recalls.

9   Self-inspections

Short description of the self inspection system with focus on criteria used for selection of the areas to be covered during planned inspections, practical arrangements and follow-up activities.

Appendix 1   Copy of valid manufacturing authorisation
Appendix 2   List of dosage forms manufactured including the INN names or common name (as available) of active pharmaceutical ingredients (API) used
Appendix 3   Copy of valid GMP Certificate
Appendix 4   List of contract manufacturers and laboratories, including the addresses and contact information, and flow charts of the supply chains for these outsourced activities
Appendix 5   Organisational charts
Appendix 6   Lay outs of production areas including material and personnel flows, general flow charts of manufacturing processes of each product type (dosage form)
Appendix 7   Schematic drawings of water systems
Appendix 8   List of major production and laboratory equipment

QUALITY RISK MANAGEMENT (ICH Q9)

The ICH Q9 document on Quality Risk Management was adopted at step 4 at the ICH Steering Committee meeting on 9 November 2005.

Quality Risk Management can be applied not only in the manufacturing environment, but also in connection with pharmaceutical development and preparation of the quality part of marketing authorisation dossiers. The guideline applies also to the regulatory authorities in the fields of pharmaceutical assessment of the quality part of the marketing authorisation dossier, GMP inspections and the handling of suspected quality defects. Nevertheless, for coherence the text was included within the GMP Guide as Annex 20 in March 2008. Since the creation of Part III of the GMP Guide, it has been recognised that Part III is a more appropriate location for its publication.

As part of the EU implementation of ICH Q9, an amendment to Chapter 1 of the GMP Guide (Quality Management) was published in February 2008, which came into force in July 2008. This amendment incorporated the principles of Quality Risk Management into the chapter.

The text of this document, formerly Annex 20, remains optional and provides examples of the processes and applications of Quality Risk Management.

1 Introduction

Risk management principles are effectively utilized in many areas of business and government, including finance, insurance, occupational safety, public health and pharmacovigilance, and by agencies regulating these industries. Although there are some examples of the use of *quality risk management* in the pharmaceutical industry today, they are limited and do not represent the full contributions that risk management has to offer. In addition, the importance of *quality systems* has been recognised in the pharmaceutical industry and it is becoming evident that Quality Risk Management is a valuable component of an effective quality system.

It is commonly understood that *risk* is defined as the combination of the probability of occurrence of *harm* and the *severity* of that harm. However, achieving a shared understanding of the application of risk management among diverse *stakeholders* is difficult because each stakeholder might perceive different potential harms, place a different probability on each harm occurring and attribute different severities to each harm. In relation to pharmaceuticals, although there are a variety of stakeholders, including patients and medical practitioners as well as government and industry, the protection of the patient by managing the risk to quality should be considered of prime importance.

The manufacturing and use of a drug (medicinal) product, including its components, necessarily entail some degree of risk. The risk to its quality is just one component of the overall risk. It is important to understand that product *quality* should be maintained throughout the *product lifecycle* such that the attributes that are important to the quality of the drug (medicinal) product remain consistent with those used in the clinical studies. An effective Quality Risk Management approach can further ensure the high quality of the drug (medicinal) product to the patient by providing a proactive means to identify and control potential quality issues during development and manufacturing. Additionally, use of Quality Risk Management can improve the decision-making if a quality problem arises. Effective Quality Risk Management can facilitate better and more informed decisions, provide regulators with greater assurance of a company's ability to deal with potential risks, and beneficially affect the extent and level of direct regulatory oversight.

The purpose of this document is to offer a systematic approach to Quality Risk Management. It serves as a foundation or resource document that is independent of, yet supports, other ICH Quality documents and complements existing quality practices, requirements, standards and guidelines within the pharmaceutical industry and regulatory environment. It specifically provides guidance on the principles and some of the tools of Quality Risk Management that can enable more effective and consistent risk-based decisions, both by regulators and by industry, regarding the quality of drug substances and drug (medicinal) products across the product lifecycle. It is not intended to create any new expectations beyond the current regulatory requirements.

It is neither always appropriate nor always necessary to use a formal risk management process (using recognised tools and/or internal procedures, e.g. standard operating procedures). The use of informal risk management processes (using empirical tools and/or internal procedures) can also be considered acceptable. Appropriate use of Quality Risk Management can facilitate but does not obviate industry's obligation to comply with regulatory requirements and does not replace appropriate communications between industry and regulators.

2 Scope

This guideline provides principles and examples of tools for Quality Risk Management that can be applied to different aspects of pharmaceutical quality. These aspects include development, manufacturing, distribution, and the inspection and submission/review processes throughout the lifecycle of drug substances, drug (medicinal) products, biological and biotechnological products (including the use of raw materials, solvents, excipients, packaging and labelling materials in drug [medicinal] products, biological and biotechnological products).

3 Principles of Quality Risk Management

Two primary principles of Quality Risk Management are:

- The evaluation of the risk to quality should be based on scientific knowledge and ultimately link to the protection of the patient.
- The level of effort, formality and documentation of the Quality Risk Management process should be commensurate with the level of risk.

4 General Quality Risk Management Process

Quality risk management is a systematic process for the assessment, control, communication and review of risks to the quality of the drug (medicinal) product across the product lifecycle. A model for quality risk

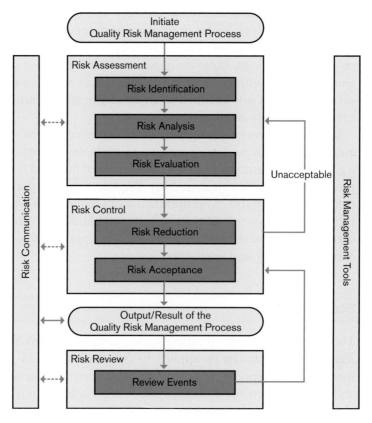

Figure 1 Overview of a typical quality risk management process.

management is outlined in Figure 1. Other models could be used. The emphasis on each component of the framework might differ from case to case, but a robust process will incorporate consideration of all the elements at a level of detail that is commensurate with the specific risk.

Decision nodes are not shown in the diagram above because decisions can occur at any point in the process. These decisions might be to return to the previous step and seek further information, to adjust the risk models or even to terminate the risk management process, based upon information that supports such a decision. Note: "unacceptable" in the flowchart does not refer only to statutory, legislative or regulatory requirements, but also to the need to revisit the risk assessment process.

4.1 Responsibilities

Quality risk management activities are usually, but not always, undertaken by interdisciplinary teams. When teams are formed, they should include experts from the appropriate areas (e.g. quality unit, business development, engineering, regulatory affairs, production operations, sales and marketing, legal, statistics and clinical) in addition to individuals who are knowledgeable about the quality risk management process.
Decision makers should:

- take responsibility for coordinating quality risk management across various functions and departments of their organisation; and
- assure that a quality risk management process is defined, deployed and reviewed, and that adequate resources are available.

4.2 Initiating a quality risk management process

Quality risk management should include systematic processes designed to coordinate, facilitate and improve science-based decision-making with respect to risk. Possible steps used to initiate and plan a Quality Risk Management process might include the following:

- Define the problem and/or risk question, including pertinent assumptions identifying the potential for risk;
- Assemble background information and/or data on the potential hazard, harm or human health impact relevant to the risk assessment;
- Identify a leader and necessary resources;
- Specify a timeline, deliverables and appropriate level of decision-making for the risk management process.

4.3   Risk assessment

Risk assessment consists of the identification of hazards and the analysis and evaluation of risks associated with exposure to those hazards (as defined below). Quality risk assessments begin with a well-defined problem description or risk question. When the risk in question is well defined, an appropriate risk management tool (see examples in Section 5) and the types of information needed to address the risk question will be more readily identifiable. As an aid to clearly defining the risk(s) for risk assessment purposes, three fundamental questions are often helpful:

(1)   What might go wrong?
(2)   What is the likelihood (probability) it will go wrong?
(3)   What are the consequences (severity)?

Risk analysis is the estimation of the risk associated with the identified hazards. It is the qualitative or quantitative process of linking the likelihood of occurrence and severity of harms. In some risk management tools, the ability to detect the harm (detectability) also factors in the estimation of risk.

Risk evaluation compares the identified and analysed risk against given risk criteria. Risk evaluations consider the strength of evidence for all three of the fundamental questions.

In doing an effective risk assessment, the robustness of the dataset is important because it determines the quality of the output. Revealing assumptions and reasonable sources of uncertainty will enhance confidence in this output and/or help identify its limitations. Uncertainty is due to a combination of incomplete knowledge about a process and its expected or unexpected variability. Typical sources of uncertainty include gaps in knowledge gaps in pharmaceutical science and process understanding, sources of harm (e.g. failure modes of a process, sources of variability) and probability of detection of problems.

The output of a risk assessment is either a quantitative estimate of risk or a qualitative description of a range of risk. When risk is expressed quantitatively, a numerical probability is used. Alternatively, risk can be expressed using qualitative descriptors, such as "high", "medium" or "low", which should be defined in as much detail as possible. Sometimes a "risk score" is used to further define descriptors in risk ranking. In quantitative risk assessments, a risk estimate provides the likelihood of a specific consequence, given a set of risk-generating circumstances. Thus, quantitative risk estimation is useful for one particular consequence at a time. Alternatively, some risk management tools use a relative risk measure to combine multiple levels of severity and probability into an overall estimate of relative risk. The intermediate steps within a scoring process can sometimes employ quantitative risk estimation.

4.4   Risk control

Risk control includes decision-making to reduce and/or accept risks. The purpose of risk control is to reduce the risk to an acceptable level. The amount of effort used for risk control should be proportional to the significance of the risk. Decision-makers might use different processes, including benefit–cost analysis, for understanding the optimal level of risk control.

Risk control might focus on the following questions:

- Is the risk above an acceptable level?
- What can be done to reduce or eliminate risks?
- What is the appropriate balance among benefits, risks and resources?
- Are new risks introduced as a result of the identified risks being controlled?

Risk reduction focuses on processes for mitigation or avoidance of quality risk when it exceeds a specified (acceptable) level (see Figure 1). Risk reduction might include actions taken to mitigate the severity and probability of harm. Processes that improve the detectability of hazards and quality risks might also be used as part of a risk control strategy. The implementation of risk reduction measures can introduce new risks into the system or increase the significance of other existing risks. Hence, it might be appropriate to revisit the risk assessment to identify and evaluate any possible change in risk after implementing a risk reduction process.

Risk acceptance is a decision to accept risk. Risk acceptance can be a formal decision to accept the residual risk or it can be a passive decision in which residual risks are not specified. For some types of harms, even the best quality risk management practices might not entirely eliminate risk. In these circumstances, it might be agreed that an appropriate Quality Risk Management strategy has been applied and that quality risk is reduced to a specified (acceptable) level. This (specified) acceptable level will depend on many parameters and should be decided on a case-by-case basis.

4.5   Risk communication

Risk communication is the sharing of information about risk and risk management between the decision-makers and others. Parties can communicate at any stage of the risk management process (see Figure 1, dashed arrows). The output/result of the quality risk management process should be appropriately communicated and documented (see Figure 1, solid arrows). Communications might include those among interested parties, e.g. regulators and industry, industry and the patient, within a company, industry or regulatory authority, etc. The included information might relate to the existence, nature, form, probability, severity, acceptability, control, treatment, detectability or other aspects of risks to quality. Communication need not be carried out for each and every risk acceptance. Between the industry and regulatory authorities, communication concerning quality risk management decisions might be effected through existing channels, as specified in regulations and guidances.

4.6 Risk review

Risk management should be an on-going part of the quality management process. A mechanism to review or monitor events should be implemented.

The output/results of the risk management process should be reviewed to take into account new knowledge and experience. Once a quality risk management process has been initiated, that process should continue to be utilised for events that might impact the original quality risk management decision, whether these events are planned (e.g. results of product review, inspections, audits, change control) or unplanned (e.g. root cause from failure investigations, recall). The frequency of any review should be based upon the level of risk. Risk review might include reconsideration of risk acceptance decisions (section 4.4).

5 Risk Management Methodology

Quality risk management supports a scientific and practical approach to decision-making. It provides documented, transparent and reproducible methods to accomplish steps of the quality risk management, process based on current knowledge about assessing the probability, severity and sometimes detectability of the risk.

Traditionally, risks to quality have been assessed and managed in a variety of informal ways (empirical and/or internal procedures) based on, for example, compilation of observations, trends and other information. Such approaches continue to provide useful information that might support topics such as handling of complaints, quality defects, deviations and allocation of resources.

Additionally, the pharmaceutical industry and regulators can assess and manage risk using recognised risk management tools and/or internal procedures (e.g. standard operating procedures). Below is a non-exhaustive list of some of these tools (further details in Annex 1 and Chapter 8):

- Basic risk management facilitation methods (flowcharts, check sheets etc.);
- Failure Mode Effects Analysis (FMEA);
- Failure Mode, Effects and Criticality Analysis (FMECA);
- Fault Tree Analysis (FTA);

- Hazard Analysis and Critical Control Points (HACCP);
- Hazard Operability Analysis (HAZOP);
- Preliminary Hazard Analysis (PHA);
- Risk ranking and filtering;
- Supporting statistical tools.

It might be appropriate to adapt these tools for use in specific areas pertaining to drug substance and drug (medicinal) product quality. Quality risk management methods and the supporting statistical tools can be used in combination (e.g. Probabilistic Risk Assessment). Combined use provides flexibility that can facilitate the application of quality risk management principles.

The degree of rigor and formality of quality risk management should reflect available knowledge and be commensurate with the complexity and/or criticality of the issue to be addressed.

6 Integration of quality risk management into Industry and Regulatory Operations

Quality risk management is a process that supports science-based and practical decisions when integrated into quality systems (see Annex II). As outlined in the introduction, appropriate use of quality risk management does not obviate industry's obligation to comply with regulatory requirements. However, effective quality risk management can facilitate better and more informed decisions and provide regulators with greater assurance of a company's ability to deal with potential risks, and might affect the extent and level of direct regulatory oversight. In addition, quality risk management can facilitate better use of resources by all parties.

Training of both industry and regulatory personnel in quality risk management processes provides for greater understanding of decision-making processes and builds confidence in quality risk management outcomes.

Quality risk management should be integrated into existing operations and documented appropriately. Annex II provides examples of situations in which the use of the quality risk management process might provide information that could then be used in a variety of pharmaceutical operations. These examples are provided for illustrative purposes only and should not be considered to be a definitive or exhaustive list. These examples are not intended to create any new expectations beyond the requirements laid out in the current regulations.

Examples for industry and regulatory operations (see Annex II):

- Quality management.

Examples for industry operations and activities (see Annex II):

- Development;
- Facility, equipment and utilities;
- Materials management;
- Production;
- Laboratory control and stability testing;
- Packaging and labelling.

Examples for regulatory operations (see Annex II):

- Inspection and assessment activities.

While regulatory decisions will continue to be taken on a regional basis, a common understanding and application of quality risk management principles could facilitate mutual confidence and promote more consistent decisions among regulators on the basis of the same information. This collaboration could be important in the development of policies and guidelines that integrate and support quality risk management practices.

7   Definitions

Decision maker(s): Person(s) with the competence and authority to make appropriate and timely quality risk management decisions.

Detectability: The ability to discover or determine the existence, presence or fact of a hazard.

Harm: Damage to health, including the damage that can occur from loss of product quality or availability.

Hazard: The potential source of harm (ISO/IEC Guide 51).

Product lifecycle: All phases in the life of the product from the initial development through marketing until the product's discontinuation.

Quality: The degree to which a set of inherent properties of a product, system or process fulfils requirements (see ICH Q6A definition specifically for "quality" of drug substance and drug (medicinal) products).

Quality risk management: A systematic process for the assessment, control, communication and review of risks to the quality of the drug (medicinal) product across the product lifecycle.

Quality system: The sum of all aspects of a system that implements quality policy and ensures that quality objectives are met. Requirements: the explicit or implicit needs or expectations of the patients or their surrogates (e.g. health-care professionals, regulators and legislators). In this document, "requirements" refers not only to statutory, legislative, or regulatory requirements, but also to such needs and expectations.

Risk: The combination of the probability of occurrence of harm and the severity of that harm (ISO/IEC Guide 51).

Risk acceptance: The decision to accept risk (ISO Guide 73).

Risk analysis: The estimation of the risk associated with the identified hazards.

Risk assessment: A systematic process of organising information to support a risk decision to be made within a risk management process. It consists of the identification of hazards, and the analysis and evaluation of risks associated with exposure to those hazards.

Risk communication: The sharing of information about risk and risk management between the decision maker and other stakeholders.

Risk control: Actions implementing risk management decisions (ISO Guide 73).

Risk evaluation: The comparison of the estimated risk to given risk criteria using a quantitative or qualitative scale to determine the significance of the risk.

Risk identification: The systematic use of information to identify potential sources of harm (hazards) referring to the risk question or problem description.

Risk management: The systematic application of quality management policies, procedures and practices to the tasks of assessing, controlling, communicating and reviewing risk.

Risk reduction: Actions taken to lessen the probability of occurrence of harm and the severity of that harm.

Risk review: Review or monitoring of output/results of the risk management process considering (if appropriate) new knowledge and experience about the risk.

Severity: A measure of the possible consequences of a hazard.

Stakeholder: Any individual, group or organisation that can affect, be affected by or perceive itself to be affected by a risk. Decision-makers might also be stakeholders. For the purposes of this guideline, the primary stakeholders are the patient, health-care professional, regulatory authority and industry.

Trend: A statistical term referring to the direction or rate of change of a variable(s).

8 References

ICH Q8 Pharmaceutical development.

ISO/IEC Guide 73:2002 – Risk Management – Vocabulary – Guidelines for use in Standards.

ISO/IEC Guide 51:1999 – Safety Aspects – Guideline for their inclusion in standards.

Process Mapping by the American Productivity & Quality Center 2002, ISBN 1928593739.

IEC 61025 – Fault Tree Analysis (FTA).

IEC 60812 Analysis Techniques for system reliability – Procedures for failure mode and effects analysis (FMEA).

Failure Mode and Effect Analysis, FMEA from Theory to Execution, 2nd edn, 2003, D. H. Stamatis, ISBN 0873895983.

Guidelines for Failure Modes and Effects Analysis (FMEA) for Medical Devices, 2003, Dyadem Press, ISBN 0849319102.

The Basics of FMEA, Robin McDermott, Raymond J. Mikulak, Michael R. Beauregard, 1996, ISBN 0527763209.

WHO Technical Report Series No. 908, 2003, Annex 7 *Application of Hazard Analysis and Critical Control Point (HACCP) methodology to pharmaceuticals.*

IEC 61882 – Hazard Operability Analysis (HAZOP).

ISO 14971:2000 – Application of Risk Management to Medical Devices.

ISO 7870:1993 – Control Charts.

ISO 7871:1997 – Cumulative Sum Charts.

ISO 7966:1993 – Acceptance Control Charts.

ISO 8258:1991 – Shewhart Control Charts.

What is Total Quality Control?; The Japanese Way, Kaoru Ishikawa (Translated by David J. Liu, 1985, ISBN 0139524339).

Annex I Risk Management Methods and Tools

The purpose of this annex is to provide a general overview of and references for some of the primary tools that might be used in Quality Risk Management by industry and regulators. The references are included as an aid to gain more knowledge and detail about the particular tool. This is not an exhaustive list. It is important to note that no one tool or set of tools is applicable to every situation in which a Quality Risk Management procedure is used.

I.1   Basic risk management facilitation methods

Some of the simple techniques that are commonly used to structure risk management by organising data and facilitating decision-making are:

- Flowcharts;
- Check sheets;
- Process mapping;
- Cause-and-effect diagrams (also called an Ishikawa diagram or fish bone diagram).

I.2   Failure mode effects analysis (FMEA)

FMEA (see IEC 60812) provides for an evaluation of potential failure modes for processes and their likely effect on outcomes and/or product performance. Once failure modes are established, risk reduction can be used to eliminate, contain, reduce or control the potential failures. FMEA relies on product and process understanding. FMEA methodically breaks down the analysis of complex processes into manageable steps. It is a powerful tool for summarising the important modes of failure, factors causing these failures and the likely effects of these failures.

POTENTIAL AREAS OF USE(S)

FMEA can be used to prioritise risks and monitor the effectiveness of risk control activities.

FMEA can be applied to equipment and facilities and might be used to analyse a manufacturing operation and its effect on product or process. It identifies elements/operations within the system that render it vulnerable. The output/results of FMEA can be used as a basis for design or further analysis or to guide resource deployment.

I.3   Failure mode, effects and criticality analysis

FMEA might be extended to incorporate an investigation of the degree of severity of the consequences, their respective probabilities of occurrence and their detectability, thereby becoming a Failure Mode Effect and Criticality Analysis (FMECA; see IEC 60812). In order for such an analysis to be performed, the product or process specifications should be established. FMECA can identify places where additional preventive actions might be appropriate to minimise risks.

POTENTIAL AREAS OF USE(S)

FMECA application in the pharmaceutical industry should mostly be utilised for failures and risks associated with manufacturing processes; however, it is not limited to this application. The output of an FMECA is a relative risk "score" for each failure mode, which is used to rank the modes on a relative risk basis.

I.4   Fault tree analysis (FTA)

The FTA tool (see IEC 61025) is an approach that assumes failure of the functionality of a product or process. This tool evaluates system (or sub-system) failures one at a time but can combine multiple causes of failure by identifying causal chains. The results are represented pictorially in the form of a tree of fault modes. At each level in the tree, combinations of fault modes are described with logical operators (AND, OR, etc.). FTA relies on the experts' process understanding to identify causal factors.

POTENTIAL AREAS OF USE(S)

FTA can be used to establish the pathway to the root cause of the failure. FTA can be used to investigate complaints or deviations in order to fully understand their root cause and to ensure that intended improvements will fully resolve the issue and not lead to other issues (i.e. solve one problem yet cause a different problem). FTA is an effective tool for evaluating how multiple factors affect a given issue. The output of an FTA includes a visual representation of failure modes. It is useful both for risk assessment and in developing monitoring programmes.

I.5   Hazard analysis and critical control points (HACCP)

HACCP is a systematic, proactive and preventive tool for assuring product quality, reliability and safety (see WHO Technical Report Series No. 908, 2003, Annex 7). It is a structured approach that applies technical and scientific principles to analyse, evaluate, prevent and control the risk or adverse consequence(s) of hazard(s) due to the design, development, production and use of products.

HACCP consists of the following seven steps:

(1) conduct a hazard analysis and identify preventive measures for each step of the process;
(2) determine the critical control points;
(3) establish critical limits;
(4) establish a system to monitor the critical control points;
(5) establish the corrective action to be taken when monitoring indicates that the critical control points are not in a state of control;
(6) establish system to verify that the HACCP system is working effectively;
(7) establish a record-keeping system.

POTENTIAL AREAS OF USE(S)

HACCP might be used to identify and manage risks associated with physical, chemical and biological hazards (including microbiological contamination). HACCP is most useful when product and process understanding is sufficiently comprehensive to support identification of critical control points. The output of a HACCP analysis is risk management information that facilitates monitoring of critical points, not only in the manufacturing process but also in other lifecycle phases.

I.6   Hazard operability analysis (HAZOP)

HAZOP (see IEC 61882) is based on a theory that assumes that risk events are caused by deviations from the design or operating intentions. It is a systematic brainstorming technique for identifying hazards using so-called "guide-words". "Guide-words" (e.g. No, More, Other Than, Part of, etc.) are applied to relevant parameters (e.g. contamination, temperature) to help identify potential deviations from normal use or design intentions. It often uses a team of people with expertise covering the design of the process or product and its application.

POTENTIAL AREAS OF USE(S)

HAZOP can be applied to manufacturing processes, including outsourced production and formulation as well as the upstream suppliers, equipment and facilities for drug substances and drug (medicinal) products. It has also been used primarily in the pharmaceutical industry for evaluating process safety hazards. As is the case with HACCP, the output of a HAZOP analysis is a list of critical operations for risk management. This facilitates regular monitoring of critical points in the manufacturing process.

I.7   Preliminary hazard analysis (PHA)

PHA is a tool of analysis based on applying prior experience or knowledge of a hazard or failure to identify future hazards, hazardous situations and events that might cause harm, as well as to estimate their probability of occurrence for a given activity, facility, product or system. The tool consists of: (1) the identification of the possibilities that the risk event happens, (2) the qualitative evaluation of the extent of possible injury or damage to health that could result, (3) a relative ranking of the hazard using a combination of severity and likelihood of occurrence, and (4) the identification of possible remedial measures.

POTENTIAL AREAS OF USE(S)

PHA might be useful when analysing existing systems or prioritising hazards where circumstances prevent a more extensive technique from being used. It can be used for product, process and facility design, as well as to evaluate the types of hazards for the general product type, then the product class and finally the specific product. PHA is most commonly used early in the development of a project when there is little information on design details or operating procedures; thus, it will often be a precursor to further studies. Typically, hazards identified in the PHA are further assessed with other risk management tools such as those in this section.

I.8   Risk ranking and filtering

Risk ranking and filtering is a tool for comparing and ranking risks. Risk ranking of complex systems typically requires evaluation of multiple diverse quantitative and qualitative factors for each risk. The tool involves breaking down a basic risk question into as many components as needed to capture factors involved in the risk. These factors are combined into a single relative risk score that can then be used for ranking risks. "Filters", in the form of weighting factors or cut-offs for risk scores, can be used to scale or fit the risk ranking to management or policy objectives.

POTENTIAL AREAS OF USE(S)

Risk ranking and filtering can be used to prioritise manufacturing sites for inspection/audit by regulators or industry. Risk-ranking methods are particularly helpful in situations in which the portfolio of risks and the underlying consequences to be managed are diverse and difficult to compare using a single tool. Risk ranking is useful when management needs to evaluate both quantitatively-assessed and qualitatively-assessed risks within the same organisational framework.

I.9 Supporting statistical tools

Statistical tools can support and facilitate Quality Risk Management. They can enable effective data assessment, aid in determining the significance of the data set(s) and facilitate more reliable decision making. A listing of some of the principal statistical tools commonly used in the pharmaceutical industry is provided:

- Control charts, for example:
  - Acceptance control charts (see ISO 7966);
  - Control charts with arithmetic average and warning limits (see ISO 7873);
  - Cumulative sum charts (see ISO 7871);
  - Shewhart control charts (see ISO 8258);
  - Weighted moving average;
- Design of Experiments (DOE);
- Histograms;
- Pareto charts;
- Process capability analysis.

Annex II Potential Applications for Quality Risk Management

This annex is intended to identify potential uses of quality risk management principles and tools by industry and regulators. However, the selection of particular risk management tools is completely dependent upon specific facts and circumstances.

These examples are provided for illustrative purposes and only suggest potential uses of quality risk management. This Annex is not intended to create any new expectations beyond the current regulatory requirements.

II.1   Quality risk management as part of integrated quality management

DOCUMENTATION

To review current interpretations and application of regulatory expectations.

To determine the desirability of and/or develop the content for SOPs, guidelines, etc.

TRAINING AND EDUCATION

To determine the appropriateness of initial and/or on-going training sessions based on education, experience and working habits of staff, as well as on a periodic assessment of previous training (e.g. its effectiveness).

To identify the training, experience, qualifications and physical abilities that allow personnel to perform an operation reliably and with no adverse impact on the quality of the product.

QUALITY DEFECTS

To provide the basis for identifying, evaluating and communicating the potential quality impact of a suspected quality defect, complaint, trend, deviation, investigation, out specification result, etc.

To facilitate risk communications and determine appropriate action to address significant product defects, in conjunction with regulatory authorities (e.g. recall).

AUDITING/INSPECTION

To define the frequency and scope of audits, both internal and external, taking into account factors such as:

• Existing legal requirements;
• Overall compliance status and history of the company or facility;
• Robustness of a company's Quality Risk Management activities;
• Complexity of the site;
• Complexity of the manufacturing process;

- Complexity of the product and its therapeutic significance;
- Number and significance of quality defects (e.g. recall);
- Results of previous audits/inspections;
- Major changes of building, equipment, processes, key personnel;
- Experience with manufacturing of a product (e.g. frequency, volume, number of batches);
- Test results of official control laboratories.

PERIODIC REVIEW

To select, evaluate and interpret trend results of data within the product quality review.

To interpret monitoring data (e.g. to support an assessment of the appropriateness of revalidation or changes in sampling).

CHANGE MANAGEMENT/CHANGE CONTROL

To manage changes based on knowledge and information accumulated in pharmaceutical development and during manufacturing.

To evaluate the impact of the changes on the availability of the final product.

To evaluate the impact on product quality of changes to the facility, equipment, material, manufacturing process or technical transfers.

To determine appropriate actions preceding the implementation of a change, e.g. additional testing, (re)qualification, (re)validation or communication with regulators.

CONTINUAL IMPROVEMENT

To facilitate continual improvement in processes throughout the product lifecycle.

II.2   Quality risk management as part of regulatory operations

INSPECTION AND ASSESSMENT ACTIVITIES

To assist with resource allocation including, for example, inspection planning and frequency, and inspection and assessment intensity (see "Auditing" section in Annex II.1).

To evaluate the significance of, for example, quality defects, potential recalls and inspectional findings.

To determine the appropriateness and type of post-inspection regulatory follow-up.

To evaluate information submitted by industry including pharmaceutical development information.

To evaluate impact of proposed variations or changes.

To identify risks that should be communicated between inspectors and assessors to facilitate better understanding of how risks can be or are controlled (e.g. parametric release, Process Analytical Technology (PAT)).

II.3 Quality risk management as part of development

To design a quality product and its manufacturing process to consistently deliver the intended performance of the product (see ICH Q8).

To enhance knowledge of product performance over a wide range of material attributes (e.g. particle size distribution, moisture content, flow properties), processing options and process parameters.

To assess the critical attributes of raw materials, solvents, Active Pharmaceutical Ingredients (APIs) starting materials, excipients, or packaging materials.

To establish appropriate specifications, identify critical process parameters and establish manufacturing controls (e.g. using information from pharmaceutical development studies regarding the clinical significance of quality attributes and the ability to control them during processing).

To decrease variability of quality attributes:

• reduce product and material defects;
• reduce manufacturing defects.

To assess the need for additional studies (e.g. bioequivalence, stability) relating to scale up and technology transfer.

To make use of the "design space" concept (see ICH Q8).

II.4 Quality risk management for facilities, equipment and utilities

DESIGN OF FACILITY/EQUIPMENT

To determine appropriate zones when designing buildings and facilities, e.g.

• flow of material and personnel;
• minimise contamination;
• pest control measures;
• prevention of mix-ups;
• open versus closed equipment;
• clean rooms versus isolator technologies;
• dedicated or segregated facilities/equipment.

To determine appropriate product contact materials for equipment and containers (e.g. selection of stainless steel grade, gaskets, lubricants).

To determine appropriate utilities (e.g. steam, gases, power source, compressed air, heating, ventilation and air-conditioning (HVAC), water).

EU GMP PART III QUALITY RISK MANAGEMENT (ICH Q9)

To determine appropriate preventive maintenance for associated equipment (e.g. inventory of necessary spare parts).

HYGIENE ASPECTS IN FACILITIES

To protect the product from environmental hazards, including chemical, microbiological and physical hazards (e.g. determining appropriate clothing and gowning, hygiene concerns).

To protect the environment (e.g. personnel, potential for cross-contamination) from hazards related to the product being manufactured.

QUALIFICATION OF FACILITY/EQUIPMENT/UTILITIES

To determine the scope and extent of qualification of facilities, buildings and production equipment and/or laboratory instruments (including proper calibration methods).

CLEANING OF EQUIPMENT AND ENVIRONMENTAL CONTROL

To differentiate efforts and decisions based on the intended use (e.g. multi-purpose versus single-purpose, batch versus continuous production).

To determine acceptable (specified) cleaning validation limits.

CALIBRATION/PREVENTIVE MAINTENANCE

To set appropriate calibration and maintenance schedules.

COMPUTER SYSTEMS AND COMPUTER-CONTROLLED EQUIPMENT

To select the design of computer hardware and software (e.g. modular, structured, fault tolerance).

To determine the extent of validation, e.g.:

- identification of critical performance parameters;
- selection of the requirements and design;
- code review;
- the extent of testing and test methods;
- reliability of electronic records and signatures.

II.5 Quality risk management as part of materials management

ASSESSMENT AND EVALUATION OF SUPPLIERS AND CONTRACT MANUFACTURERS

To provide a comprehensive evaluation of suppliers and contract manufacturers (e.g. auditing, supplier quality agreements).

STARTING MATERIAL

To assess differences and possible quality risks associated with variability in starting materials (e.g. age, route of synthesis).

USE OF MATERIALS

To determine whether it is appropriate to use material under quarantine (e.g. for further internal processing).

To determine appropriateness of re-processing, re-working, use of returned goods.

STORAGE, LOGISTICS AND DISTRIBUTION CONDITIONS

To assess the adequacy of arrangements to ensure maintenance of appropriate storage and transport conditions (e.g. temperature, humidity, container design).

To determine the effect on product quality of discrepancies in storage or transport conditions (e.g. cold chain management) in conjunction with other ICH guidelines.

To maintain infrastructure (e.g. capacity to ensure proper shipping conditions, interim storage, handling of hazardous materials and controlled substances, customs clearance).

To provide information for ensuring the availability of pharmaceuticals (e.g. ranking risks to the supply chain).

II.6   Quality risk management as part of production

VALIDATION

To identify the scope and extent of verification, qualification and validation activities (e.g. analytical methods, processes, equipment and cleaning methods.

To determine the extent for follow-up activities (e.g. sampling, monitoring and re-validation).

To distinguish between critical and non-critical process steps to facilitate design of a validation study.

IN-PROCESS SAMPLING AND TESTING

To evaluate the frequency and extent of in-process control testing (e.g. to justify reduced testing under conditions of proven control).

To evaluate and justify the use of Process Analytical Technologies (PATs) in conjunction with parametric and real-time release.

PRODUCTION PLANNING

To determine appropriate production planning (e.g. dedicated, campaign and concurrent production process sequences).

II.7   Quality risk management as part of laboratory control and stability studies

OUT-OF-SPECIFICATION RESULTS

To identify potential root causes and corrective actions during the investigation of out-of-specification results.

RE-TEST PERIOD/EXPIRATION DATE

To evaluate adequacy of storage and testing of intermediates, excipients and starting materials.

II.8   Quality risk management as part of packaging and labelling

DESIGN OF PACKAGES

To design the secondary package for the protection of primary packaged product (e.g. to ensure product authenticity, label legibility).

SELECTION OF CONTAINER CLOSURE SYSTEM

To determine the critical parameters of the container closure system.

LABEL CONTROLS

To design label control procedures based on the potential for mix-ups involving different product labels, including different versions of the same label.

ICH Q10 NOTE FOR GUIDANCE ON PHARMACEUTICAL QUALITY SYSTEM

The ICH Q10 document on Pharmaceutical Quality System was adopted at Step 4 at the ICH Steering Committee meeting in June 2008.

By virtue of Article 6 of Directive 2003/94/EC and Directive 91/412/EEC, Manufacturing Authorisation holders are already obliged to establish and implement an effective pharmaceutical quality assurance system in order to comply with Good Manufacturing Practice (GMP), and guidance is provided in Chapter 1 of the GMP Guide.

ICH Q10 provides an example of a pharmaceutical quality system designed for the entire product lifecycle and therefore goes beyond current GMP requirements, which, with the exception of the manufacture of investigational medicinal products for human use, do not apply to the development part of the lifecycle. At the time of the EU implementation of ICH Q10 it was also recognised that Chapters 1, 2 and 7 of the GMP Guide should be updated to align with the terminology and concepts utilised in ICH Q10.

The content of ICH Q10 that is additional to the scope of GMP is optional. Its use should facilitate innovation and continual improvement, and strengthen the link between pharmaceutical development and manufacturing activities.

1   Pharmaceutical Quality System

1.1   Introduction

This document establishes a new ICH tripartite guideline describing a model for an effective quality management system for the pharmaceutical industry, referred to as the Pharmaceutical Quality System. Throughout this guideline, the term "pharmaceutical quality system" refers to the ICH Q10 model.

ICH Q10 describes one comprehensive model for an effective pharmaceutical quality system that is based on International Standards Organisation (ISO) quality concepts, and includes applicable Good Manufacturing Practice (GMP) regulations and complements ICH Q8 "Pharmaceutical Development" and ICH Q9 "Quality Risk Management". ICH Q10 is a model for a pharmaceutical quality system that can be implemented throughout the different stages of a product lifecycle. Much of the content of ICH Q10 applicable to manufacturing sites is currently specified by regional GMP requirements. ICH Q10 is not intended to create any new expectations beyond current regulatory requirements. Consequently, the content of ICH Q10 that is additional to current regional GMP requirements is optional.

ICH Q10 demonstrates industry and regulatory authorities' support of an effective pharmaceutical quality system to enhance the quality and availability of medicines around the world in the interest of public health. Implementation of ICH Q10 throughout the product lifecycle should facilitate innovation and continual improvement, and strengthen the link between pharmaceutical development and manufacturing activities.

1.2 Scope

This guideline applies to the systems supporting the development and manufacture of pharmaceutical drug substances (i.e. API) and drug products, including biotechnology and biological products, throughout the product lifecycle.

The elements of ICH Q10 should be applied in a manner that is appropriate and proportionate to each of the product lifecycle stages, recognising the differences among them, and the different goals of each stage (see Section 3).

For the purposes of this guideline, the product lifecycle includes the following technical activities for new and existing products:

- Pharmaceutical development:
  - Drug substance development;
  - Formulation development (including container/closure system);
  - Manufacture of investigational products;
  - Delivery system development (where relevant);
  - Manufacturing process development and scale-up;
  - Analytical method development;
- Technology transfer:
  - New product transfers during development through manufacturing;
  - Transfers within or between manufacturing and testing sites for marketed products;
- Commercial manufacturing:
  - Acquisition and control of materials;
  - Provision of facilities, utilities, and equipment;
  - Production (including packaging and labelling);
  - Quality control and assurance;
  - Release;
  - Storage;
  - Distribution (excluding wholesaler activities);
- Product discontinuation:
  - Retention of documentation;
  - Sample retention;
  - Continued product assessment and reporting.

1.3 Relationship of ICH Q10 to regional GMP requirements, ISO standards and ICH Q7

Regional GMP requirements, the ICH Q7 Guideline, "Good Manufacturing Practice Guide for Active Pharmaceutical Ingredients", and ISO quality management system guidelines form the foundation for ICH Q10. To meet the objectives described below, ICH Q10 augments GMP by describing specific quality system elements and management responsibilities. ICH Q10 provides a harmonised model for a pharmaceutical quality system throughout the lifecycle of a product and is intended for use together with regional GMP requirements.

The regional GMPs do not explicitly address all stages of the product lifecycle (e.g. development). The quality system elements and management responsibilities described in this guideline are intended to encourage the use of science- and risk-based approaches at each lifecycle stage, thereby promoting continual improvement across the entire product lifecycle.

1.4 Relationship of ICH Q10 to regulatory approaches

Regulatory approaches for a specific product or manufacturing facility should be commensurate with the level of product and process understanding, the results of quality risk management and the effectiveness of the pharmaceutical quality system. When implemented, the effectiveness of the pharmaceutical quality system can normally be evaluated during a regulatory inspection at the manufacturing site. Potential opportunities to enhance science- and risk-based regulatory approaches are identified in Annex 1. Regulatory processes will be determined by region.

1.5 ICH Q10 objectives

Implementation of the Q10 model should result in achievement of three main objectives which complement or enhance regional GMP requirements.

1.5.1 ACHIEVE PRODUCT REALISATION

To establish, implement and maintain a system that allows the delivery of products with the quality attributes appropriate to meet the needs of patients, health-care professionals, regulatory authorities (including compliance with approved regulatory filings), and other internal and external customers.

EU GMP PART III ICH Q10 NOTE FOR GUIDANCE ON
PHARMACEUTICAL QUALITY SYSTEM

1.5.2 ESTABLISH AND MAINTAIN A STATE OF CONTROL

To develop and use effective monitoring and control systems for process performance and product quality, thereby providing assurance of continued suitability and capability of processes. Quality risk management can be useful in identifying the monitoring and control systems.

1.5.3 FACILITATE CONTINUAL IMPROVEMENT

To identify and implement appropriate product quality improvements, process improvements, variability reduction, innovations and pharmaceutical quality system enhancements, thereby increasing the ability to fulfil quality needs consistently. Quality risk management can be useful for identifying and prioritising areas for continual improvement.

1.6 Enablers: knowledge management and quality risk management

Use of knowledge management and quality risk management will enable a company to implement ICH Q10 effectively and successfully. These enablers will facilitate achievement of the objectives described in Section 1.5 above by providing the means for science- and risk-based decisions related to product quality.

1.6.1 KNOWLEDGE MANAGEMENT

Product and process knowledge should be managed from development through the commercial life of the product up to and including product discontinuation, e.g. development activities using scientific approaches provide knowledge for product and process understanding. Knowledge management is a systematic approach to acquiring, analysing, storing and disseminating information related to products, manufacturing processes and components. Sources of knowledge include, but are not limited to, prior knowledge (public domain or internally documented), pharmaceutical development studies, technology transfer activities, process validation studies over the product lifecycle, manufacturing experience, innovation, continual improvement and change management activities.

1.6.2 QUALITY RISK MANAGEMENT

Quality risk management is integral to an effective pharmaceutical quality system. It can provide a proactive approach to identifying, scientifically evaluating and controlling potential risks to quality. It facilitates continual improvement of process performance and product quality throughout the product lifecycle. ICH Q9 provides principles and examples of tools for quality risk management that can be applied to different aspects of pharmaceutical quality.

1.7 Design and content considerations

(a) The design, organisation and documentation of the pharmaceutical quality system should be well structured and clear to facilitate common understanding and consistent application.

(b) The elements of ICH Q10 should be applied in a manner that is appropriate and proportionate to each of the product lifecycle stages, recognising the different goals and knowledge available for each stage.

(c) The size and complexity of the company's activities should be taken into consideration when developing a new pharmaceutical quality system or modifying an existing one. The design of the pharmaceutical quality system should incorporate appropriate risk management principles. Although some aspects of the pharmaceutical quality system can be company wide and others site specific, the effectiveness of the pharmaceutical quality system is normally demonstrated at the site level.

(d) The pharmaceutical quality system should include appropriate processes, resources and responsibilities to provide assurance of the quality of outsourced activities and purchased materials as described in Section 2.7.

(e) Management responsibilities, as described in Section 2, should be identified within the pharmaceutical quality system.

(f) The pharmaceutical quality system should include the following elements, as described in Section 3: process performance and product quality monitoring, corrective and preventive action, change management and management review.

(g) Performance indicators, as described in Section 4, should be identified and used to monitor the effectiveness of processes within the pharmaceutical quality system.

1.8 Quality manual

A Quality Manual or equivalent documentation approach should be established and should contain the description of the pharmaceutical quality system. The description should include:

(a) The quality policy (see Section 2);

(b) The scope of the pharmaceutical quality system;

(c) Identification of the pharmaceutical quality system processes, as well as their sequences, linkages and interdependencies. Process maps and flow charts can be useful tools to facilitate depicting pharmaceutical quality system processes in a visual manner;

(d) Management responsibilities within the pharmaceutical quality system (see Section 2).

2   Management Responsibility

Leadership is essential to establish and maintain a company-wide commitment to quality and for the performance of the pharmaceutical quality system.

2.1   Management commitment

(a) Senior management has the ultimate responsibility to ensure that an effective pharmaceutical quality system is in place to achieve the quality objectives, and that roles, responsibilities and authorities are defined, communicated and implemented throughout the company.

(b) Management should:

(1) Participate in the design, implementation, monitoring and maintenance of an effective pharmaceutical quality system;

(2) Demonstrate strong and visible support for the pharmaceutical quality system and ensure its implementation throughout their organisation;

(3) Ensure that a timely and effective communication and escalation process exists to raise quality issues to the appropriate levels of management;

(4) Define individual and collective roles, responsibilities, authorities and interrelationships of all organisational units related to the pharmaceutical quality system. Ensure that these interactions are communicated and understood at all levels of the organisation. An independent quality unit/structure with authority to fulfil certain pharmaceutical quality system responsibilities is required by regional regulations;

(5) Conduct management reviews of process performance and product quality and of the pharmaceutical quality system;

(6) Advocate continual improvement;

(7) Commit appropriate resources.

2.2   Quality policy

(a) Senior management should establish a quality policy that describes the overall intentions and direction of the company related to quality.

(b) The quality policy should include an expectation to comply with applicable regulatory requirements and should facilitate continual improvement of the pharmaceutical quality system.

(c) The quality policy should be communicated to and understood by personnel at all levels in the company.

(d) The quality policy should be reviewed periodically for continuing effectiveness.

2.3 Quality planning

(a) Senior management should ensure that the quality objectives needed to implement the quality policy are defined and communicated.

(b) Quality objectives should be supported by all relevant levels of the company.

(c) Quality objectives should align with the company's strategies and be consistent with the quality policy.

(d) Management should provide the appropriate resources and training to achieve the quality objectives.

(e) Performance indicators that measure progress against quality objectives should be established, monitored, communicated regularly and acted upon as appropriate, as described in Section 4.1 of this document.

2.4 Resource management

(a) Management should determine and provide adequate and appropriate resources (human, financial, materials, facilities and equipment) to implement and maintain the pharmaceutical quality system and continually improve its effectiveness.

(b) Management should ensure that resources are appropriately applied to a specific product, process or site.

2.5 Internal communication

(a) Management should ensure that appropriate communication processes are established and implemented within the organisation.

(b) Communications processes should ensure the flow of appropriate information between all levels of the company.

(c) Communication processes should ensure the appropriate and timely escalation of certain product quality and pharmaceutical quality system issues.

2.6 Management review

(a) Senior management should be responsible for pharmaceutical quality system governance through management review to ensure its continuing suitability and effectiveness.
(b) Management should assess the conclusions of periodic reviews of process performance and product quality and of the pharmaceutical quality system, as described in Sections 3 and 4.

2.7 Management of outsourced activities and purchased materials

The pharmaceutical quality system, including the management responsibilities described in this section, extends to the control and review of any outsourced activities and quality of purchased materials. The pharmaceutical company is ultimately responsible for ensuring that processes are in place to assure the control of outsourced activities and quality of purchased materials. These processes should incorporate quality risk management and include:

(a) Assessing prior to outsourcing operations or selecting material suppliers, the suitability and competence of the other party to carry out the activity or provide the material using a defined supply chain (e.g. audits, material evaluations, qualification);
(b) Defining the responsibilities and communication processes for quality-related activities of the involved parties. For outsourced activities, this should be included in a written agreement between the contract giver and contract acceptor;
(c) Monitoring and review of the performance of the contract acceptor or the quality of the material from the provider, and the identification and implementation of any needed improvements;
(d) Monitoring incoming ingredients and materials to ensure that they are from approved sources using the agreed supply chain.

2.8 Management of change in product ownership

When product ownership changes, (e.g. through acquisitions) management should consider the complexity of this and ensure that:

(a) the ongoing responsibilities are defined for each company involved;
(b) the necessary information is transferred.

3   Continual Improvement of Process Performance and Product Quality

This section describes the lifecycle stage goals and the four specific pharmaceutical quality system elements that augment regional requirements to achieve the ICH Q10 objectives, as defined in Section 1.5. It does not restate all regional GMP requirements.

3.1   Lifecycle stage goals

The goals of each product lifecycle stage are described below.

3.1.1   PHARMACEUTICAL DEVELOPMENT

The goal of pharmaceutical development activities is to design a product and its manufacturing process to consistently deliver the intended performance and meet the needs of patients and healthcare professionals, and regulatory authorities and internal customers' requirements. Approaches to pharmaceutical development are described in ICH Q8. The results of exploratory and clinical development studies, although outside the scope of this guidance, are inputs to pharmaceutical development.

3.1.2   TECHNOLOGY TRANSFER

The goal of technology transfer activities is to transfer product and process knowledge between development and manufacturing, and within or between manufacturing sites to achieve product realisation. This knowledge forms the basis for the manufacturing process, control strategy, process validation approach and on-going continual improvement.

3.1.3   COMMERCIAL MANUFACTURING

The goals of manufacturing activities include achieving product realisation, establishing and maintaining a state of control, and facilitating continual improvement. The pharmaceutical quality system should assure that the desired product quality is routinely met, suitable process performance is achieved, the set of controls are appropriate, improvement opportunities are identified and evaluated, and the body of knowledge is continually expanded.

3.1.4   PRODUCT DISCONTINUATION

The goal of product discontinuation activities is to manage the terminal stage of the product lifecycle effectively. For product discontinuation, a predefined approach should be used to manage activities such as retention of documentation and samples and continued product assessment (e.g. complaint handling and stability) and reporting in accordance with regulatory requirements.

3.2   Pharmaceutical quality system elements

The elements described below might be required in part under regional GMP regulations. However, the Q10 model's intent is to enhance these elements in order to promote the lifecycle approach to product quality. These four elements are:

- Process performance and product quality monitoring system;
- Corrective action and preventive action (CAPA) system;
- Change management system;
- Management review of process performance and product quality.

These elements should be applied in a manner that is appropriate and proportionate to each of the product lifecycle stages, recognising the differences among, and the different goals of, each stage. Throughout the product lifecycle, companies are encouraged to evaluate opportunities for innovative approaches to improve product quality.

Each element is followed by a table of example applications of the element to the stages of the pharmaceutical lifecycle.

3.2.1   PROCESS PERFORMANCE AND PRODUCT QUALITY MONITORING SYSTEM

Pharmaceutical companies should plan and execute a system for the monitoring of process performance and product quality to ensure that a state of control is maintained. An effective monitoring system provides assurance of the continued capability of processes and controls to produce a product of desired quality and to identify areas for continual improvement. The process performance and product quality monitoring system should:

(a) Use quality risk management to establish the control strategy. This can include parameters and attributes related to drug substance and drug product materials and components, facility and equipment operating conditions, in-process controls, finished product specifications, and the associated methods and frequency of monitoring and control. The control strategy should facilitate timely feedback/feed-forward and appropriate corrective action and preventive action;

(b) Provide the tools for measurement and analysis of parameters and attributes identified in the control strategy (e.g. data management and statistical tools);

(c) Analyse parameters and attributes identified in the control strategy to verify continued operation within a state of control;

(d) Identify sources of variation affecting process performance and product quality for potential continual improvement activities to reduce or control variation;

(e) Include feedback on product quality from both internal and external sources, e.g. complaints, product rejections, non-conformances, recalls, deviations, audits, and regulatory inspections and findings;

(f) Provide knowledge to enhance process understanding, enrich the design space (where established) and enable innovative approaches to process validation.

Table 1 Application of process performance and product quality monitoring system throughout the product lifecycle

Pharmaceutical development	Technology transfer	Commercial manufacturing	Product discontinuation
Process and product knowledge generated and process and product monitoring conducted throughout development can be used to establish a control strategy for manufacturing	Monitoring during scale-up activities can provide a preliminary indication of process performance and the successful integration into manufacturing. Knowledge obtained during transfer and scale-up activities can be useful in further developing the control strategy	A well-defined system for process performance and product quality monitoring should be applied to assure performance within a state of control and to identify improvement areas	Once manufacturing ceases, monitoring such as stability testing should continue to completion of the studies. Appropriate action on marketed product should continue to be executed according to regional regulations

3.2.2   CORRECTIVE ACTION AND PREVENTIVE ACTION (CAPA) SYSTEM

The pharmaceutical company should have a system for implementing corrective actions and preventive actions resulting from the investigation of complaints, product rejections, non-conformances, recalls, deviations, audits, regulatory inspections and findings, and trends from process performance and product quality monitoring. A structured approach to the investigation process should be used with the objective of determining the root cause. The level of effort, formality and documentation of the investigation should be commensurate with the level of risk, in line with ICH Q9. CAPA methodology should result in product and process improvements and enhanced product and process understanding.

Table 2 Application of corrective action and preventive action system throughout the product lifecycle

Pharmaceutical development	Technology transfer	Commercial manufacturing	Product discontinuation
Product or process variability is explored. CAPA methodology is useful where corrective actions and preventive actions are incorporated into the iterative design and development process	CAPA can be used as an effective system for feedback, feed-forward and continual improvement	CAPA should be used and the effectiveness of the actions should be evaluated	CAPA should continue after the product is discontinued. The impact on product remaining on the market should be considered as well as other products that might be impacted

3.2.3   CHANGE MANAGEMENT SYSTEM

Innovation, continual improvement, the outputs of process performance and product quality monitoring and CAPA drive change. In order to evaluate, approve and implement these changes properly, a company should have an effective change management system. There is generally a difference in formality of change management processes prior to the initial regulatory submission and after submission, where changes to the regulatory filing might be required under regional requirements.

The change management system ensures that continual improvement is undertaken in a timely and effective manner. It should provide a high degree of assurance that there are no unintended consequences of the change.

The change management system should include the following, as appropriate for the stage of the lifecycle:

(a) Quality risk management should be utilised to evaluate proposed changes. The level of effort and formality of the evaluation should be commensurate with the level of risk;

(b) Proposed changes should be evaluated relative to the marketing authorisation, including design space, where established, and/or current product and process understanding. There should be an assessment to determine whether a change to the regulatory filing is required under regional requirements. As stated in ICH Q8, working within the design space is not considered a change (from a regulatory filing perspective). However, from a pharmaceutical quality system standpoint, all changes should be evaluated by a company's change management system;

(c) Proposed changes should be evaluated by expert teams contributing the appropriate expertise and knowledge from relevant areas (e.g. Pharmaceutical Development, Manufacturing, Quality, Regulatory Affairs and Medical) to ensure that the change is technically justified. Prospective evaluation criteria for a proposed change should be set;

(d) After implementation, an evaluation of the change should be undertaken to confirm the change objectives were achieved and that there was no deleterious impact on product quality.

Table 3 Application of change management system throughout the product lifecycle

Pharmaceutical development	Technology transfer	Commercial manufacturing	Product discontinuation
Change is an inherent part of the development process and should be documented; the formality of the change management process should be consistent with the stage of pharmaceutical development	The change management system should provide management and documentation of adjustments made to the process during technology transfer activities	A formal change management system should be in place for commercial manufacturing. Oversight by the quality unit should provide assurance of appropriate science and risk based assessments	Any changes after product discontinuation should go through an appropriate change management system

3.2.4 MANAGEMENT REVIEW OF PROCESS PERFORMANCE AND PRODUCT QUALITY

Management review should provide assurance that process performance and product quality are managed over the lifecycle. Depending on the size and complexity of the company, management review can be a series of reviews at various levels of management and should include a timely and effective communication and escalation process to raise appropriate quality issues to senior levels of management for review.

(1) The management review system should include:
   (a) The results of regulatory inspections and findings, audits and other assessments, and commitments made to regulatory authorities;
   (b) Periodic quality reviews that can include:
      (i)   Measures of customer satisfaction such as product quality complaints and recalls;
      (ii) Conclusions of process performance and product quality monitoring;
      (iii) The effectiveness of process and product changes including those arising from corrective action and preventive actions;
   (c) Any follow-up actions from previous management reviews.
(2) The management review system should identify appropriate actions, such as:
   (a) Improvements to manufacturing processes and products;
   (b) Provision, training and/or realignment of resources;
   (c) Capture and dissemination of knowledge.

Table 4 Application of management review of process performance and product quality throughout the product lifecycle

Pharmaceutical development	Technology transfer	Commercial manufacturing	Product discontinuation
Aspects of management review can be performed to ensure adequacy of the product and process design	Aspects of management review should be performed to ensure that the developed product and process can be manufactured at a commercial scale	Management review should be a structured system, as described above, and should support continual improvement	Management review should include such items as product stability and product quality complaints

4 Continual Improvement of the Pharmaceutical Quality System

This section describes activities that should be conducted to manage and continually improve the pharmaceutical quality system.

4.1 Management review of the pharmaceutical quality system

Management should have a formal process for reviewing the pharmaceutical quality system on a periodic basis. The review should include:

(a) Measurement of achievement of pharmaceutical quality system objectives;
(b) Assessment of performance indicators that can be used to monitor the effectiveness of processes within the pharmaceutical quality system, such as:
   (1) Complaint, deviation, CAPA and change management processes;
   (2) Feedback on outsourced activities;
   (3) Self-assessment processes including risk assessments, trending and audits;
   (4) External assessments such as regulatory inspections and findings and customer audits.

4.2 Monitoring of internal and external factors impacting the pharmaceutical quality system

Factors monitored by management can include:

(a) Emerging regulations, guidance and quality issues that can impact the Pharmaceutical Quality System;
(b) Innovations that might enhance the pharmaceutical quality system;
(c) Changes in business environment and objectives;
(d) Changes in product ownership.

4.3 Outcomes of management review and monitoring

The outcome of management review of the pharmaceutical quality system and monitoring of internal and external factors can include:

(a) Improvements to the pharmaceutical quality system and related processes;
(b) Allocation or reallocation of resources and/or personnel training;
(c) Revisions to quality policy and quality objectives;
(d) Documentation and timely and effective communication of the results of the management review and actions, including escalation of appropriate issues to senior management.

5 Glossary

ICH and ISO definitions are used in ICH Q10 where they exist. For the purpose of ICH Q10, where the words "requirement", "requirements" or "necessary" appear in an ISO definition, they do not necessarily reflect a regulatory requirement. The source of the definition is identified in parentheses after the definition. Where no appropriate ICH or ISO definition was available, an ICH Q10 definition was developed.

CAPABILITY OF A PROCESS

Ability of a process to realise a product that will fulfil the requirements of that product. The concept of process capability can also be defined in statistical terms (ISO 9000:2005).

CHANGE MANAGEMENT

A systematic approach to proposing, evaluating, approving, implementing and reviewing changes (ICH Q10).

CONTINUAL IMPROVEMENT

Recurring activity to increase the ability to fulfil requirements (ISO 9000:2005).

CONTROL STRATEGY

A planned set of controls, derived from current product and process understanding that assures process performance and product quality. The controls can include parameters and attributes related to drug substance and drug product materials and components, facility and equipment operating conditions, in-process controls, finished product specifications, and the associated methods and frequency of monitoring and control (ICH Q10).

CORRECTIVE ACTION

Action to eliminate the cause of a detected non-conformity or other undesirable situation.

Note: Corrective action is taken to prevent recurrence whereas preventive action is taken to prevent occurrence (ISO 9000:2005).

DESIGN SPACE

The multidimensional combination and interaction of input variables (e.g. material attributes) and process parameters that have been demonstrated to provide assurance of quality (ICH Q8).

ENABLER

A tool or process that provides the means to achieve an objective (ICH Q10).

FEEDBACK/FEED-FORWARD

Feedback: the modification or control of a process or system by its results or effects.

Feed-forward: the modification or control of a process using its anticipated results or effects (*Oxford Dictionary of English* by Oxford University Press, 2003).

Feedback/feed-forward can be applied technically in process control strategies and conceptually in quality management (ICH Q10).

INNOVATION

The introduction of new technologies or methodologies (ICH Q10).

KNOWLEDGE MANAGEMENT

Systematic approach to acquiring, analysing, storing and disseminating information related to products, manufacturing processes and components (ICH Q10).

OUTSOURCED ACTIVITIES

Activities conducted by a contract acceptor under a written agreement with a contract giver (ICH Q10).

PERFORMANCE INDICATORS

Measurable values used to quantify quality objectives to reflect the performance of an organisation, process or system, also known as "performance metrics" in some regions (ICH Q10).

PHARMACEUTICAL QUALITY SYSTEM (PQS)

Management system to direct and control a pharmaceutical company with regard to quality (ICH Q10 based upon ISO 9000:2005).

PREVENTIVE ACTION

Action to eliminate the cause of a potential non-conformity or other undesirable potential situation.

Note: preventive action is taken to prevent occurrence whereas corrective action is taken to prevent recurrence (ISO 9000:2005).

PRODUCT REALISATION

Achievement of a product with the quality attributes appropriate to meet the needs of patients, health-care professionals and regulatory authorities (including compliance with marketing authorisation) and internal customers' requirements (ICH Q10).

QUALITY

The degree to which a set of inherent properties of a product, system or process fulfils requirements (ICH Q9).

QUALITY MANUAL

Document specifying the quality management system of an organisation (ISO 9000:2005).

QUALITY OBJECTIVES

A means of translating the quality policy and strategies into measurable activities (ICH Q10).

QUALITY PLANNING

Part of quality management focused on setting quality objectives and specifying necessary operational processes and related resources to fulfil the quality objectives (ISO 9000:2005).

QUALITY POLICY

Overall intentions and direction of an organisation related to quality as formally expressed by senior management (ISO 9000:2005).

QUALITY RISK MANAGEMENT

A systematic process for the assessment, control, communication and review of risks to the quality of the drug (medicinal) product across the product lifecycle (ICH Q9).

SENIOR MANAGEMENT

Person(s) who direct and control a company or site at the highest levels with the authority and responsibility to mobilise resources within the company or site (ICH Q10 based in part on ISO 9000:2005).

STATE OF CONTROL

A condition in which the set of controls consistently provides assurance of continued process performance and product quality (ICH Q10).

Annex 1 Potential Opportunities to Enhance Science and Risk-based Regulatory Approaches*

Scenario	Potential opportunity
1. Comply with GMPs	Compliance – status quo
2. Demonstrate effective pharmaceutical quality system, including effective use of quality risk management principles (e.g. ICH Q9 and ICH Q10)	Opportunity to: • increase use of risk-based approaches for regulatory inspections
3. Demonstrate product and process understanding, including effective use of quality risk management principles (e.g. ICH Q8 and ICH Q9)	Opportunity to: • facilitate science based pharmaceutical quality assessment • enable innovative approaches to process validation • establish real-time release mechanisms
4. Demonstrate effective pharmaceutical quality system and product and process understanding, including the use of quality risk management principles (e.g. ICH Q8, ICH Q9 and ICH Q10)	Opportunity to: • increase use of risk based approaches for regulatory inspections • facilitate science based pharmaceutical quality assessment • optimise science and risk-based post-approval change processes to maximise benefits from innovation and continual improvement • enable innovative approaches to process validation • establish real-time release mechanisms

*Note: this annex reflects potential opportunities to enhance regulatory approaches. The actual regulatory process will be determined by region.

EU GMP PART III ICH Q10 NOTE FOR GUIDANCE ON PHARMACEUTICAL QUALITY SYSTEM

Annex 2 Diagram of the ICH Q10 Pharmaceutical Quality System Model

This diagram illustrates the major features of the ICH Q10 Pharmaceutical Quality System (PQS) model. The PQS covers the entire lifecycle of a product including pharmaceutical development, technology transfer, commercial manufacturing and product discontinuation, as illustrated by the upper portion of the diagram. The PQS augments regional GMPs as illustrated in the diagram. The diagram also illustrates that regional GMPs apply to the manufacture of investigational products.

The next horizontal bar illustrates the importance of management responsibilities explained in Section 2 to all stages of the product lifecycle. The following horizontal bar lists the PQS elements that serve as the major pillars under the PQS model. These elements should be applied appropriately and proportionally to each lifecycle stage, recognising opportunities to identify areas for continual improvement.

The bottom set of horizontal bars illustrates the enablers – knowledge management and quality risk management – which are applicable throughout the lifecycle stages. These enablers support the PQS goals of achieving product realisation, establishing and maintaining a state of control, and facilitating continual improvement.

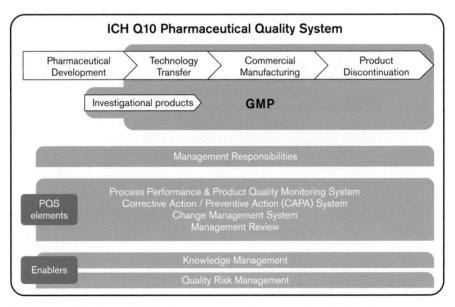

Diagram of the ICH Q10 Pharmaceutical Quality System Model.

MRA BATCH CERTIFICATE

Internationally harmonised requirements for batch certification in the context of Mutual Recognition Agreements, Agreements on Conformity Assessment and Acceptance of Industrial Products and other appropriate arrangements on GMP with the EU

In the framework of Mutual Recognition Agreements (MRAs), the Sectoral Annex on Good Manufacturing Practices (GMP) requires a batch certification scheme for medicinal products covered by the pharmaceutical annex. Batch certification is also required in the Agreements on Conformity Assessment and Acceptance of Industrial Products (ACAA) and other appropriate arrangements on GMP between third countries and the EU.

The internationally harmonised requirements for the content of the batch certificate of a medicinal product are provided in this document.

Each batch of medicinal product transferred between countries that have appropriate arrangements on GMP must be accompanied by a batch certificate issued by the manufacturer in the exporting country. In the framework of MRAs all manufacturing sites must be located in the country issuing the certificate or in another MRA country, if reciprocal arrangements are in force. In the framework of the EU's ACAA with Israel (once in operation) all quality control sites must be located in Israel or the EU.

This certificate will be issued further to a full qualitative and quantitative analysis of all active and other relevant constituents to ensure that the quality of the products complies with the requirements of the marketing authorisation of the importing country. The batch certificate will attest that the batch meets the specifications and has been manufactured in accordance with the marketing authorisation of the importing country, detailing the specifications of the product, the analytical methods referenced and the analytical results obtained, and containing a statement that the batch processing, packaging and quality control records were reviewed and found in conformity with GMP. The batch certificate will be signed by the person responsible for certifying that the batch is suitable for release for sale or supply/export.

The importer/site of batch release of the medicinal product is to receive and maintain the batch certificate issued by the manufacturer of the exporting country. Upon request, it has to be readily available to the staff of the regulatory authorities of the importing country. This certification by the manufacturer on the conformity of each batch is essential to exempt the importer/site of batch release from re-control (for the EU, see Directive 2001/83/EC Art. 51.2 and Directive 2001/82/EC Art. 55.2). Where applicable this batch certificate shall also be used for non-finished medicinal products such as intermediates, bulk or partially packed products.

This certificate may also be used for active pharmaceutical ingredients and investigational medicinal products used in clinical trial authorisations. The terminology may need to be adapted as per the Glossary.

These harmonised requirements have been agreed bilaterally by the EU with the regulatory authorities of the following countries: Australia, Canada, Israel, Japan, New Zealand and Switzerland.

Common part

CONTENT OF THE BATCH CERTIFICATE FOR MEDICINAL PRODUCTS

(Note: For equivalence of terminology refer to the Explanatory Notes and Glossary)

[LETTER HEAD OF EXPORTING MANUFACTURER]

(1) Name of product
(2) Importing country
(3) Marketing Authorisation number or Clinical Trial Authorisation Number
(4) Strength/Potency
(5) Dosage form
(6) Package size and type
(7) Batch number
(8) Date of manufacture
(9) Expiry date
(10) Name, address and Authorisation number of all manufacturing sites and quality control sites
(11) Certificates of GMP Compliance of all sites listed under 10 or, if available, EudraGMP reference numbers
(12) Results of analysis
(13) Comments
(14) Certification statement
(15) Name and position/title of person authorising the batch release
(16) Signature of person authorising the batch release
(17) Date of signature

EXPLANATORY NOTES AND GLOSSARY

(1) **Name of product**
Proprietary, brand or trade or proper name in the importing country, as applicable. For Investigational Medicinal Products (IMPs) the code number as referred to in the clinical trial application.

(2) **Importing Country**

(3) **Marketing Authorisation Number or Clinical Trial Authorisation Number**
The marketing authorisation number of the product in the importing country. For IMPs, the Clinical Trial authorisation number or trial reference to be provided when available.

(4) **Strength/Potency**
Identity (name) and amount per unit dose required for all active ingredients/constituents. IMPs include placebos and the manner in which this information is provided should not unblind the study.

(5) **Dosage form or pharmaceutical form, e.g. tablets, capsules, ointments**

(6) **Package size and type**
This would be the contents of container and vials, bottles, blisters, etc.

(7) **Batch number**
Or Lot number related to the product. Unique combination of numbers, letters or symbols that identifies a batch and from which the production and distribution history can be determined.

(8) **Date of manufacture**
In accordance with national (local) requirements of the importing country.

(9) **Expiry date**
The date placed on the container/label of a product designating the time during which the product is expected to remain within the authorised shelf-life specifications authorised by the importing country, if stored under defined conditions, after which it should not be used.

(10) **Name, address and authorisation number of all manufacturing and quality control sites**
All sites involved in the manufacture including packaging/labelling and quality control of the batch should be listed with name, address and authorisation number. The name and address must correspond to the information provided on the manufacturing authorisation.

(11) **Certificate of GMP Compliance of all sites listed under 10 or, if available, EudraGMP reference number**
Certificate numbers and/or EudraGMP reference numbers should be listed under this item.

EU GMP PART III MRA BATCH CERTIFICATE

(12) Results of analysis

Should include the authorised specifications, all results obtained and refer to the methods used (may refer to a separate certificate of analysis which must be dated, signed and attached).

(13) Comments/remarks

Any additional information that can be of value to the importer and/or inspector verifying the compliance of the batch certificate (e.g. specific storage or transportation conditions).

(14) Certification statement

This statement should cover the fabrication/manufacturing, including packaging/labelling and quality control. The following text should be used: "I hereby certify that the above information is authentic and accurate. This batch of product has been manufactured, including packaging/labelling and quality control, at the above-mentioned site(s) in full compliance with the GMP requirements of the local Regulatory Authority and with the specifications in the Marketing Authorisation of the importing country or product specification file for Investigational Medicinal Products. The batch processing, packaging and analysis records were reviewed and found to be in compliance with GMP".

(15) Name and position/title of person authorising the batch release

Including the name and address, if more than one site is mentioned under item 10.

(16) Signature of person authorising the batch release

(17) Date of signature

GLOSSARY OF EQUIVALENT TERMS USED IN THE CERTIFICATE TEMPLATE (NON-EXHAUSTIVE)

active substances = active pharmaceutical ingredients/constituents
batch = lot
dosage form = pharmaceutical form
manufacturer = fabricator
manufacturing/manufacture = fabrication
manufacturing authorisation = establishment licence
medicinal product = pharmaceutical product = drug product
quality control = testing

TEMPLATE FOR THE "WRITTEN CONFIRMATION" FOR ACTIVE SUBSTANCES EXPORTED TO THE EUROPEAN UNION FOR MEDICINAL PRODUCTS FOR HUMAN USE, IN ACCORDANCE WITH ARTICLE 46B(2)(B) OF DIRECTIVE 2001/83/EC

(1) Directive 2011/62/EU of the European Parliament and of the Council of 8 June 2011 amending Directive 2001/83/EC on the Community code relating to medicinal products for human use, as regards the prevention of the entry into the legal supply chain of falsified medicinal products (OJ L 174, 1.7.2011, p. 74) introduces EU-wide rules for the importation of active substances: according to Article 46b(2) of Directive 2001/83/EC, active substances shall only be imported if, *inter alia*, the active substances are accompanied by a **written confirmation** from the competent authority of the exporting third country which, as regards the plant manufacturing the exported active substance, confirms that the standards of good manufacturing practice and control of the plant are equivalent to those in the Union.

(2) The template for this written confirmation is set out in the Annex below.

ANNEX

Letterhead of the issuing regulatory authority

Written confirmation for active substances exported to the European Union (EU) for medicinal products for human use, in accordance with Article 46b(2)(b) of Directive 2001/83/EC

Confirmation no. (given by the issuing regulatory authority):

....

1. Name and address of site (including building number, where applicable):

....

2. Manufacturer's licence number(s):[3]

....

Regarding the Manufacturing Plant under (1) of the Following Active Substance(s) Exported to the EU for Medicinal Products for Human Use

---

[3] Where the regulatory authority issues a licence for the site. Record "not applicable" in cases where there is no legal framework for issuing a licence.

Active substance(s):[4]	Activity(ies):[5]

The Issuing Regulatory Authority Hereby Confirms That:

The standards of good manufacturing practice (GMP) applicable to this manufacturing plant are at least equivalent to those laid down in the EU (= GMP of WHO/ICH Q7);

The manufacturing plant is subject to regular, strict and transparent controls and to the effective enforcement of good manufacturing practice, including repeated and unannounced inspections, so as to ensure a protection of public health at least equivalent to that in the EU; and

In the event of findings relating to non-compliance, information on such findings is supplied by the exporting third country, without delay to the EU.[6]

Date of inspection of the plant under (1). Name of inspecting authority if different from the issuing regulatory authority:

....

This written confirmation remains valid until:

....

The authenticity of this written confirmation may be verified with the issuing regulatory authority.

This written confirmation is without prejudice to the responsibilities of the manufacturer to ensure the quality of the medicinal product in accordance with Directive 2001/83/EC.

Address of the issuing regulatory authority:

....

Name and function of responsible person:

....

E-mail, Telephone no. and Fax no.:

....

Signature   *Stamp of the authority and date*

---

[4] Identification of the specific active substances through an internationally agreed terminology (preferably international non-proprietary name).

[5] For example, "Chemical synthesis", "Extraction from natural sources", "Biological processes", "Finishing steps".

[6] qdefect@ema.europa.eu.

GUIDELINE ON SETTING HEALTH-BASED EXPOSURE LIMITS FOR USE IN RISK IDENTIFICATION IN THE MANUFACTURE OF DIFFERENT MEDICINAL PRODUCTS IN SHARED FACILITIES

Executive Summary

When different medicinal products are produced in shared facilities, the potential for cross-contamination is a concern. Medicinal products provide a benefit to the intended patient or target animal; however, as a cross-contaminant, they provide no benefit to the patient or target animal and may even pose a risk. Hence, the presence of such contaminants should be managed according to the risk posed which, in turn, is related to levels that can be considered safe for all populations. To this end, health-based limits through the derivation of a safe threshold value should be employed to identify the risks posed. The derivation of such a threshold value (e.g. permitted daily exposure (PDE) or threshold of toxicological concern (TTC) should be the result of a structured scientific evaluation of all available pharmacological and toxicological data, including both non-clinical and clinical data. Deviation from the main approach highlighted in this guideline to derive such safe threshold levels could be accepted if adequately justified.

1 Introduction (Background)

During the manufacture of medicinal products accidental cross-contamination can result from the uncontrolled release of dust, gases, vapours, aerosols, genetic material or organisms from active substances, other starting materials and other products being processed concurrently, as well as from residues on equipment and operators' clothing. Due to the perceived risk, certain classes of medicinal product have previously been required to be manufactured in dedicated or segregated self-contained facilities including: "certain antibiotics, certain hormones, certain cytotoxics and certain highly active drugs". Until now no official guidance has been available in order to assist manufacturers to differentiate between individual products within these specified classes. Chapters 3 and 5 of the GMP guideline have been revised to promote a science and risk-based approach and refer to a "toxicological evaluation" for establishing threshold values for risk identification.

Cleaning is a risk-reducing measure and carry-over limits for cleaning validation studies are widely used in the pharmaceutical industry. A variety of approaches is taken in order to establish these limits and often do not take account of the available pharmacological and toxicological data. Hence, a more scientific case-by-case approach is warranted for risk identification and to support risk reduction measures for all classes of pharmaceutical substances.

The objective of this guideline is to recommend an approach to review and evaluate pharmacological and toxicological data of individual active substances and thus enable determination of threshold levels, as referred to in the GMP guideline. These levels can be used as a risk identification tool and also to justify carry-over limits used in cleaning validation. Although Active Pharmaceutical Ingredients (APIs) are not discussed in Chapters 3 and 5 of the GMP guideline, the general principles outlined in this guideline for the threshold value for risk identification could be applied where required.

Deviation from the main approach highlighted in this guideline to derive safe threshold levels could be accepted if adequately justified.

2   Scope

The scope of the present guideline is to ensure the safety of human patients and target animals exposed to residual active substances via medicinal products, as well as consumers potentially exposed to residual active substances present in food of animal origin as a result of treatment of food-producing animals with veterinary medicinal products in which residual active substances are present.

In doing so, this document aims to recommend an approach for deriving a scientifically based threshold value for individual active substances to be applied for risk identification. The guideline outlines how the data on which the threshold value is derived should be presented in order to achieve a clear and harmonious approach across the pharmaceutical industry.

3   Legal Basis

This guideline should be read in conjunction with:

EudraLex, Volume 4, Good Manufacturing Practice (GMP) Guidelines, Chapters 3 and 5.

Note for Guidance on Impurities: Residual Solvents (CPMP/ICH/283/95 in conjunction with CPMP/ICH/1507/02, CPMP/ICH/1940/00 corr, CPMP/QWP/450/03, EMEA/CVMP/511/03 and CPMP/QWP/8567/99).

VICH GL18(R): Impurities: Residual solvents in new veterinary medicinal products, active substances and excipients (EMA/CVMP/VICH/502/99-Rev.1).

Guideline on the Limits of Genotoxic Impurities (EMEA/CHMP/QWP/251344/2006 and CPMP/SWP/5199/02).

4   Determination of Health-based Exposure Limits

4.1   Calculation of a permitted daily exposure (PDE)

The procedure proposed in this document for determination of health-based exposure limits for a residual active substance is based on the method for establishing the so-called Permitted Daily Exposure (PDE) as described in Appendix 3 of ICH Q3C (R4) "Impurities: Guideline for Residual Solvents" and Appendix 3 of VICH GL 18 on "residual solvents in new veterinary medicinal products, active substances and excipients (Revision)". The PDE represents a substance-specific dose that is unlikely to cause an adverse effect if an individual is exposed at or below this dose every day for a lifetime.

Determination of a PDE involves (i) hazard identification by reviewing all relevant data, (ii) identification of "critical effects", (iii) determination of the no-observed-adverse-effect level (NOAEL) of the findings that are considered to be critical effects, and (iv) use of several adjustment factors to account for various uncertainties. Appendix 3 of the ICH Q3C and of the VICH GL 18 guidelines present the following equation for the derivation of the PDE:

$$ PDE = \frac{NOAEL \times Weight\ Adjustment}{F1 \times F2 \times F3 \times F4 \times F5} $$

In relation to the establishment of health based exposure limits that can be accepted in veterinary medicinal products, it would in principle, be possible to use the PDE approach to establish different limits for different target species. However, this would be highly impractical. Consequently, it is considered pragmatic that PDEs should be derived assuming human exposure. The level of contamination that can be accepted is then calculated from the human PDE, even when the product that will be contaminated is a veterinary medicinal product. This is considered to represent a pragmatic approach and is in line with the approach taken in VICH GL 18, in which human PDEs are used to calculate residual solvent limits applied for veterinary medicinal products.

The derivation of limits will need to take account of the dose to be administered, which will be influenced by the body weight of the species to be treated. In order to facilitate this, the PDE should be calculated on a mg/kg body weight basis (i.e. using a weight adjustment figure of 1) rather than on a per person basis[1].

When the product that may become contaminated with a residual active substance is a veterinary medicinal product for administration to food-producing animals, the carry-over limit applied must take account of both target animal safety considerations and consumer safety considerations. It should therefore be demonstrated, based on worst-case exposure scenarios, that neither the target animal nor the consumer will be exposed to residual active substance levels exceeding the PDE.

Alternative approaches to the NOAEL, such as the Benchmark dose, may also be used.

The use of other approaches to determine health-based exposure limits could be considered acceptable if adequately and scientifically justified.

DATA REQUIREMENTS FOR HAZARD IDENTIFICATION

Hazard identification is the qualitative appraisal of the inherent property of a substance to produce adverse effects. For hazard identification, a review of all available animal and human data should be performed for each compound. Data for hazard identification would include non-clinical pharmacodynamic data, repeat-dose toxicity studies, carcinogenicity studies, *in vitro* and *in vivo* genotoxicity studies, reproductive and developmental toxicity studies as well as clinical data (therapeutic and adverse effects). The availability of data for an active substance will vary depending on the stage of development and indication. If datasets are incomplete, the identified gaps will need to be critically assessed with regard to the impact this might have on deriving a reliable health based exposure limit.

IDENTIFICATION OF CRITICAL EFFECTS

Critical effects would include the most sensitive indicator of an adverse effect seen in non-clinical toxicity studies unless there is clear evidence (e.g. from mechanistic studies, pharmacodynamic data, etc.) that such

---

[1] If the product information for the next medicinal product to be manufactured expresses the daily dose on a per patient basis rather than on a mg/kg bw basis, a standard body weight of 50 kg should be used for human medicinal products. For medicinal products for veterinary use, doses are generally expressed on a mg/kg bw basis. In those instances where this is not the case, a standard body weight of 1 kg should be assumed because this would represent the lower end of animal body weights.

findings are not relevant to humans or the target animal. A critical effect would also include any clinical therapeutic and adverse effect.

ESTABLISHING NOAEL(s)

For all critical effects identified, a NOAEL should be established. The NOAEL is the highest tested dose at which no "critical" effect is observed. If the critical effect is observed in several animal studies, the NOAEL occurring at the lowest dose should be used for calculation of the PDE value. If no NOAEL is obtained, the lowest-observed-adverse-effect level (LOAEL) may be used. A NOAEL based on clinical pharmacodynamic effects should correspond to the highest dose tested that is considered to be therapeutically inefficacious.

APPLICATION OF ADJUSTMENT FACTORS

The PDE is derived by dividing the NOAEL for the critical effect by various adjustment factors (also referred to as safety- uncertainty, assessment or modifying factors) to account for various uncertainties and to allow extrapolation to a reliable and robust no-effect level in the human or target animal population. F1 to F5 address the following sources of uncertainty:

F1: A factor (values between 2 and 12) to account for extrapolation between species;

F2: A factor of 10 to account for variability between individuals;

F3: A factor 10 to account for repeat-dose toxicity studies of short duration, i.e. less than 4 weeks;

F4: A factor (1–10) that may be applied in cases of severe toxicity, e.g. non-genotoxic carcinogenicity, neurotoxicity or teratogenicity;

F5: A variable factor that may be applied if the no-effect level was not established. When only an LOAEL is available, a factor of up to 10 could be used depending on the severity of the toxicity.

The use of additional modifying factors to address residual uncertainties not covered by the above factors may be accepted provided that they are well supported with literature data and an adequate discussion is provided to support their use, e.g. lack of data for reproductive and developmental toxicity (see Section 5.4).

Please refer to Appendix 3 of both the ICH Q3C (R4) and the VICH GL 18 guidelines for further guidance on the choice of adjustment factors F1 and F4. The use and choice of adjustment factors should be justified. A restriction to use of F2 and potentially F5 may be acceptable when deriving a PDE on the basis of human end-points. Deviations from the default values for the adjustment factors presented above can be accepted if adequately and scientifically justified.

SELECTION OF FINAL PDE

If several critical effects have been identified resulting in calculation of more than one PDE value, a decision with respect to the most appropriate PDE to be used for the cleaning validation process should be made with an appropriate justification. Usually, by default, the lowest PDE value will be used.

4.2   Use of clinical data

The aim of determining a health-based exposure limit is to ensure human safety, and consequently it is considered that good quality human clinical data is highly relevant. Unintended pharmacodynamic effects in patients caused by contaminating active substances may constitute a hazard, so clinical pharmacological data should be considered when identifying the critical effect. Consideration should be given to the extent to which the active substance in question has been associated with critical adverse effects in the clinical setting.

If the most critical effect identified to determine a health-based exposure limit is based on pharmacological and/or toxicological effects observed in humans rather than animals, the use of the PDE formula may be inappropriate and a substance-specific assessment of the clinical data may be used for this purpose.

4.3   Extrapolation to other routes of administration

While the PDE value derived for an active substance (contaminant) is generally based on studies applying the intended clinical route of administration, a different route of administration may be applied for the active substance or medicinal product subsequently produced in the shared facility. Changing the route of administration may change the bioavailability; hence, correction factors for route-to-route extrapolation should be applied if there are clear differences (e.g. >40%) in route-specific bioavailability. As bioavailability may vary between species, the correction factors for route-to-route extrapolation should preferably be based on human data or, in the case of veterinary medicinal products, data in the relevant target animal.

In case human or target animal bioavailability data are not available for other routes and it is to be expected that the change in route of administration may result in an increase in systemic exposure for the contaminant (e.g. oral to inhalation), a conservative extrapolation can be performed by assuming 100% bioavailability of the contaminant. For example, in the case of oral-to-inhalation extrapolation, the PDE derived on basis of oral data can be corrected by multiplying with the following correction factor:

Correction factor (oral-to-inhalation): % oral absorption/100% respirable absorption.

In cases where human or target animal bioavailability data is not available for other routes, and it can be expected that the systemic exposure to the contaminant will be lower via the route applied for the contaminated active substance/medicinal product, there is no need to apply a correction factor to the PDE calculation. It is expected that the route-to-route extrapolation will be performed on a case-by-case basis.

5 Specific Considerations

5.1 Active substances with a genotoxic potential

For genotoxic active substances for which there is no discernible threshold, it is considered that any level of exposure carries a risk. However, a predefined level of acceptable risk for non-threshold-related genotoxicants has been established in the EMA Guideline on the Limits of Genotoxic Impurities in the form of the Threshold of Toxicological Concern (TTC) of 1.5 µg/person per day. The TTC represents the genotoxic impurity exposure level associated with a theoretical cancer risk of 1 additional cancer in 100,000 patients when exposed over a lifetime. Given the fact that exposure duration to residual active substances will be much more restricted (e.g. because, in practice, levels of residual active substance carry-over can be expected to diminish on a batch-by-batch basis), limits based on a maximum, exposure to 1.5 µg/person per day in this case would not exceed a theoretical 1×10^{-6} excess cancer risk. Hence, in the case of residual active substances without a threshold, a limit dose of 1.5 µg/person per day may be applied.

When the product that may become contaminated with a residual active substance is a veterinary medicinal product, the same TTC should be used, but expressed on a 'per kg bodyweight' basis (i.e. the TTC is 0.03 µg/kg body weight per day). When the contaminated product is for administration to food-producing animals, the carry-over limit applied must take account of both target animal safety considerations and consumer safety considerations. It should therefore be demonstrated, based on worst-case exposure scenarios, that neither the target animal nor the consumer will be exposed to residual active substance levels exceeding the TTC.

For genotoxic active substances where there is sufficient carcinogenicity data, compound-specific risk assessments to derive acceptable intakes should be applied instead of the TTC-based acceptable intake approach.

For genotoxic pharmaceutical substances with sufficient evidence of a threshold related mechanism, safe exposure levels without appreciable risk of genotoxicity can be established by using the PDE approach.

5.2 Active substances with a highly sensitising potential

Drug-induced immune-mediated hypersensitivity reactions may develop in sensitive individuals. The observed reactions may range from mild cases of contact sensitisation to potentially lethal anaphylactic reactions.

As outlined in Chapter 3, paragraph 3.6 of the GMP guideline, dedicated facilities are required for manufacturing active substances and medicinal products with a high sensitising potential for which scientific data does not support an acceptable level of exposure or the risk associated with the handling the product at the facility cannot be adequately controlled by organisational or technical measures. Classification of an active substance or medicinal product with a high sensitising potential should consider whether the substance shows a high frequency of sensitising occurrence in humans, or a probability of occurrence of a high sensitisation rate in humans based on animal data or other validated tests. Severity of these reactions should also be considered and should be included in a weight of evidence assessment.

5.3 Therapeutic macromolecules and peptides

Therapeutic macromolecules and peptides are known to degrade and denature when exposed to pH extremes and/or heat, and may become pharmacologically inactive. The cleaning of biopharmaceutical manufacturing equipment is typically performed under conditions that expose equipment surfaces to pH extremes and/or heat, which would lead to the degradation and inactivation of protein-based products. In view of this, the determination of health-based exposure limits using PDE limits of the active and intact product may not be required.

Where other potential routes of cross-contamination exist, the risks posed should be considered on a case-by-case basis.

5.4 Lack of animal data on reproductive and developmental toxicity

In order to ensure protection of all populations, the presence of residual active substance should be reduced to a level that will not pose a risk for effects on reproductive and developmental parameters. However, in the early phases of development, non-clinical data to assess the potential of the new active substance to cause reproductive and developmental toxicity may not yet have been generated. Gaps in scientific knowledge may also exist for authorised medicinal products, e.g. the potential for a male-specific drug to cause adverse effects on embryo–fetal development. In these cases, the NOAEL of a subchronic/chronic study may be used in the calculation of a PDE with application of an additional adjustment factor (e.g. 10) if adequately justified. In cases where appropriate data from reproductive and developmental toxicity studies of related compounds are available, a class-specific profile may be used for hazard identification of the contaminant not tested through application of a read across approach.

5.5 Investigational medicinal products

For early development (phase I/II) investigational medicinal products (IMPs) estimation of PDEs may be difficult based on their limited datasets. Where this is apparent, an alternative approach using categorisation into specific default value categories, e.g. based on low/high expected pharmacological potency, low/high toxicity, genotoxicity/carcinogenicity, similar to the tiered TTC approaches proposed by Kroes *et al.* (2004), Munro *et al.* (2008) and Dolan *et al.* (2005)[2], can be considered to derive health-based exposure limits if adequately justified. As most default limits are defined for chronic exposure durations, a higher limit may be justified if a drug substance shares equipment with another that is intended for short-term clinical trials (Bercu and Dolan, 2013)[3]. With the availability of more pharmacological and toxicological data, compound-specific limits

---

[2] Kroes R, Renwick A, Cheeseman M, Kleiner J, Mangelsdorf I, Piersma A, Schilter B, Schatter J, van Schothorst F, Vos JG, Würtzen G. (2004). Structure-based thresholds of toxicological concern (TTC): guidance for application to substances present at low levels in the diet. Fd Chem Toxicol 42, 65–83.
Munro IC, Renwick AG, Danielewska-Nikiel B (2008). The threshold of toxicological concern (TTC) in risk assessment. Toxicol Lett 180, 151–156.
Dolan DG, Naumann BD, Sargent EV, Maier A, Dourson M (2005). Application of the threshold of toxicological concern concept to pharmaceutical manufacturing operations. Regul Toxicol Pharmacol, 43, 1–9.
[3] Bercu JP, Dolan DG, (2013). Application of the threshold of toxicological concern concept when applied to pharmaceutical manufacturing operations intended for short-term clinical trials. Regul Toxicol Pharmacol. 2013; 65(1), 162–167.

should be calculated as described above for the derivation of health-based exposure limits.

6   Reporting of the PDE Determination Strategy

The identification of "critical effects" in the establishment of a PDE, as outlined in section 4, should be based on a comprehensive literature search, including handbook and monographs as well as searches in electronic scientific databases. The search strategy and the results of the search must be clearly documented. Following an expert review, the company should provide a discussion with respect to the critical endpoints of concern and their rationale for the choice of endpoints and dose that are to be used in the derivation of the PDE. The pivotal animal and human studies used for the derivation of the PDE should be sourced to the original reference and reviewed regarding their quality (study design, description of finding, accuracy of the report, etc.). The PDE determination strategy should provide a clear rationale regarding the adjustment factors that were applied in deriving the PDE. Moreover, in order to provide an overview to the GMP inspectors, the initial page of any prepared PDE determination strategy document should be a summary of the assessment process (please see Annex for template example).

7   Implementation

This guideline has been developed as a risk identification tool to facilitate the implementation of a science- and risk-based approach to manufacture of medicinal products using shared manufacturing facilities in accordance with Chapters 3 and 5 of the GMP Guide. To allow manufacturers to adapt accordingly the date of coming into effect will be phased in as follows:

For medicinal products introduced for the first time into shared manufacturing facilities: 6 months from publication of this guideline.

For medicinal products already produced in shared manufacturing facilities the guidance will take effect, or existing arrangements should be scientifically justified, within:

- 1 year of publication of the guideline for manufacturers of products for human use, including those that manufacture human and veterinary medicines using shared manufacturing facilities;
- 2 years after publication of the guideline for manufacturers solely producing products for veterinary use.

8   Definitions

F: Adjustment Factor
GMP: Good Manufacturing Practice
ICH: International Conference on Harmonisation
LOAEL: Lowest Observed Adverse Effect Level
PDE: Permitted Daily Exposure (ADE Allowable Daily Exposure[4])
NOAEL: No Observed Adverse Effect Level
TTC: Threshold of Toxicological Concern
VICH: Veterinary International Conference on Harmonisation

References

Kroes R, Renwick A, Cheeseman M, Kleiner J, Mangelsdorf I, Piersma A, Schilter B, Schatter J, van Schothorst F, Vos JG, Würtzen G (2004). Structure-based thresholds of toxicological concern (TTC): guidance for application to substances present at low levels in the diet. Fd Chem Toxicol 42, 65–83.

Munro IC, Renwick AG, Danielewska-Nikiel B (2008). The threshold of toxicological concern (TTC) in risk assessment. Toxicol Lett 180, 151–156.

Dolan DG, Naumann BD, Sargent EV, Maier A, Dourson M (2005). Application of the threshold of toxicological concern concept to pharmaceutical manufacturing operations. Regul Toxicol Pharmacol, 43, 1–9.

1 Bercu JP, Dolan DG (2013). Application of the threshold of toxicological concern concept when applied to pharmaceutical manufacturing operations intended for short-term clinical trials. Regul Toxicol Pharmacol. 2013; 65(1):162–167.

EU GMP PART III GUIDELINE ON SETTING HEALTH-BASED EXPOSURE LIMITS FOR USE IN RISK IDENTIFICATION

---

[4] PDE and ADE are effectively synonymous.

Annex

PDE determination strategy

Company Name
Company Address
Expert Name and Signature   Date
Assessment Review Date
Chemical Name/s

Hazards identified	YES	NO	UNKNOWN
Genotoxicant			
Reproductive developmental toxicant			
Carcinogen			
Highly sensitizing potential			

Basis for the PDE

Justification for selection of "lead" critical effect used for final PDE calculation NOAEL and applied adjustment factors upon which the PDE is based.

Reference(s)

Publication(s) used to identify the critical effect and dose.

Summary of the Expert CV

GUIDELINES OF 19 MARCH 2015 ON THE FORMALISED RISK ASSESSMENT FOR ASCERTAINING THE APPROPRIATE GOOD MANUFACTURING PRACTICE FOR EXCIPIENTS OF MEDICINAL PRODUCTS FOR HUMAN USE (2015/C 95/02)

Introduction

These guidelines are based on the fifth paragraph of Article 47 of Directive 2001/83/EC[1].

According to the second paragraph of Article 46(f) of Directive 2001/83/EC, the manufacturing authorisation holder is required to ensure that the excipients are suitable for use in medicinal products by ascertaining what the appropriate good manufacturing practice (GMP) is. The appropriate GMP for excipients of medicinal products for human use shall be ascertained on the basis of a formalised risk assessment in accordance with these guidelines. The risk assessment shall take into account requirements under other appropriate quality systems, as well as the source and intended use of the excipients and previous instances of quality defects. The manufacturing authorisation holder shall ensure that the appropriate GMP ascertained is applied. The manufacturing authorisation holder shall document the measures taken.

The excipient risk assessment/risk management procedure should be incorporated in the pharmaceutical quality system of the manufacturing authorisation holder.

Manufacturing authorisation holders should have the risk assessment/management documentation for appropriate GMP for excipients available on site for review by GMP inspectors. Consideration should be given to sharing relevant information from the risk assessment with the excipient manufacturer to facilitate continuous improvement.

A risk assessment as set out in these guidelines should be carried out for excipients for authorised medicinal products for human use by 21 March 2016.

Chapter 1 Scope

1.1　These guidelines apply to the risk assessment for ascertaining the appropriate GMP for excipients for medicinal products for human use. According

---

[1] Directive 2001/83/EC of the European Parliament and of the Council of 6 November 2001 on the Community code relating to medicinal products for human use (OJ L 311, 28.11.2001, p. 67).

to Article 1(3b) of Directive 2001/83/EC, an excipient is any constituent of a medicinal product other than the active substance and the packaging material.

1.2   These guidelines do not cover substances added to stabilise active substances that cannot exist on their own.

Chapter 2 Determination of Appropriate GMP Based on Type and Use of Excipient

2.1   In EudraLex, Volume 4, Guidelines for Good Manufacturing Practice, Medicinal Products for Human and Veterinary Use, Part III: GMP related documents, ICH guideline Q9 on Quality Risk Management (ICH Q9), principles and examples of tools for quality risk management that can be applied to different aspects of pharmaceutical quality, including excipients, can be found.

2.2   These quality risk management principles should be used to assess the risks presented to the quality, safety and function of each excipient and to classify the excipient in question, e.g. as low risk, medium risk or high risk. Quality risk management tools such as those listed in EudraLex, Volume 4, Part III, ICH Q9 (e.g. hazard analysis and critical control points – HACCP) should be used for this purpose.

2.3   For each excipient from each manufacturer used, the manufacturing authorisation holder should identify the risks presented to the quality, safety and function of each excipient from its source – be that animal, mineral, vegetable, synthetic, etc. – through to its incorporation into the finished pharmaceutical dose form. Areas for consideration should include, but are not limited to:

(i)   transmissible spongiform encephalopathy;
(ii)   potential for viral contamination;
(iii)   potential for microbiological or endotoxin/pyrogen contamination;
(iv)   potential, in general, for any impurity originating from the raw materials, e.g. aflatoxins or pesticides, or generated as part of the process and carried over, e.g. residual solvents and catalysts;
(v)   sterility assurance for excipients claimed to be sterile;
(vi)   potential for any impurities carried over from other processes, in the absence of dedicated equipment and/or facilities;
(vii)   environmental control and storage/transportation conditions including cold chain management, if appropriate;
(viii) supply chain complexity;
(ix)   stability of excipient;
(x)   packaging integrity evidence.

2.4   Additionally, with respect to the use and function of each excipient, the manufacturing authorisation holder should consider:

(i)   the pharmaceutical form and use of the medicinal product containing the excipient;

(ii)   the function of the excipient in the formulation, e.g. lubricant in a tablet product or preservative material in a liquid formulation, etc.;

(iii) the proportion of the excipient in the medicinal product composition;

(iv)   daily patient intake of the excipient;

(v)   any known quality defects/fraudulent adulterations, both globally and at a local company level related to the excipient;

(vi)   whether the excipient is a composite;

(vii) known or potential impact on the critical quality attributes of the medicinal product;

(viii) other factors as identified or known to be relevant to assuring patient safety.

2.5   Having established and documented the risk profile of the excipient, the manufacturing authorisation holder should establish and document the elements of EudraLex, Volume 4 that they believe are needed to be in place in order to control and maintain the quality of the excipient, e.g. Annex 1 or/and Annex 2; Part II: Basic Requirements for Active Substances used as Starting Materials.

2.6   These elements will vary depending on the source, the supply chain and the subsequent use of the excipient, but, as a minimum, the following high-level GMP elements should be considered by the manufacturing authorisation holder:

(i)   establishment and implementation of an effective pharmaceutical quality system;

(ii)   sufficient competent and appropriately qualified personnel;

(iii) defined job descriptions for managerial and supervisory staff responsible for manufacturing and quality activities;

(iv)   training programmes for all staff involved in manufacturing and quality activities;

(v)   training programmes related to health, hygiene and clothing identified as necessary to the intended operations;

(vi)   provision and maintenance of premises and equipment appropriate to the intended operations;

(vii) documentation system(s) covering all processes and specifications for the various manufacturing and quality operations;

(viii) systems for coding and identifying starting materials, intermediates and excipients to allow full traceability;

(ix) qualification programme of suppliers;

(x) system for quality control of the excipient and a responsible person independent from production to release the batches;

(xi) retention of records for incoming materials and excipients and retention of samples of excipients for the periods required by EudraLex, Volume 4, Part II;

(xii) systems to ensure that any activity contracted out is subject to a written contract;

(xiii) maintenance of an effective system whereby complaints are reviewed and excipients may be recalled;

(xiv) change management and deviation management system;

(xv) self-inspection programme;

(xvi) environmental control and storage conditions.

Chapter 3 Determination of Excipient Manufacturer's Risk Profile

3.1   After determination of the appropriate GMP, a gap analysis of the required GMP against the activities and capabilities of the excipient manufacturer should be performed.

3.2   Data/evidence to support the gap analysis should be obtained through audit or from information received from the excipient manufacturer.

3.3   Certification of quality systems and/or GMP held by the excipient manufacturer and the standards against which these have been granted should be considered because such certification may fulfil the requirements.

3.4   Any gaps identified between the required GMP and the activities and capabilities of the excipient manufacturer should be documented. Furthermore, the manufacturing authorisation holder should perform a further risk assessment to determine the risk profile, e.g. low risk, medium risk or high risk, for that excipient manufacturer. EudraLex, Volume 4, Part III, ICH Q9 should be used for that purpose. Quality risk management tools such as those listed there – HACCP, etc. – should be used for this.

3.5   The manufacturing authorisation holder should have a series of strategies ranging from acceptance through control to unacceptable for the different risk profiles, and based on these, a control strategy, e.g. audit, document retrieval and testing, should be established.

Chapter 4 Confirmation of Application of Appropriate GMP

4.1   Once the appropriate GMP for the excipient and the risk profile of the excipient manufacturer have been defined, on-going risk review should be performed through mechanisms such as:

(i)   number of defects connected to batches of excipient received;

(ii)   type/severity of such defects;

(iii)   monitoring and trend analysis of excipient quality;

(iv)   loss of relevant quality system and/or GMP certification by excipient manufacturer;

(v)   observation of trends in drug product quality attributes; this will depend on the nature and role of the excipient;

(vi)   observed organisational, procedural or technical/process changes at the excipient manufacturer;

(vii) audit/re-audit of excipient manufacturer;

(viii) questionnaires.

Based on the outcome of the risk review, the established control strategy should be reviewed and revised if needed.

EU GMP PART III GUIDELINES OF 19 MARCH 2015 ON THE FORMALISED RISK ASSESSMENT

Content of the Batch Certificate for Investigational Medicinal Products Referred to in Article 62(1) of Regulation (EU) No 536/2014 and Article 4 of Delegated Regulation 1569/2017

Introduction

This template should be used in conjunction with the Delegated Regulation (EU) No 1569/2017 on Good Manufacturing Practice (GMP) for Investigational Medicinal Products (IMPs) for human use and arrangements for inspections that have as their legal basis the first subparagraph of Article 63(1) of Regulation (EU) No 536/2014 and the detailed Commission guidelines on GMP for IMPs for human use, pursuant to the second subparagraph of Article 63(1) of Regulation (EU) No 536/2014.

Investigational Medicinal Products may not be used in a clinical trial in a member state of the European Union until the completion of the two-step procedure referred to in the "Guideline on the responsibilities of the sponsor with regard to handling and shipping of investigational medicinal products for human use in accordance with Good Clinical Practice and Good Manufacturing Practice".

The first step is the certification of each batch by the Qualified Person of the manufacturer or importer in line with Article 62(1) of Regulation (EU) No 536/2014 to ensure that the provisions of 63(1) and 63(3) of Regulation (EU) No 536/2014 and those set out in Article 12 of the Commission Delegated Regulation (EU) No 1569/2017 have been complied with and documented. The second step is the regulatory release by the sponsor for use in a clinical trial.

In order to facilitate the free movement of IMPs between Member States, a batch certification signed by the Qualified Person should be produced according to Article 62(1) of Regulation 536/2014.

The content of these certificates should be in accordance with the format presented below, with the intention to harmonise the process of certification of batch release. This format may also be used to certify batches destined for use within the Member State of the manufacturer or importer.

[LETTERHEAD OF MANUFACTURER]

Content of the Batch Certificate for Investigational Medicinal Products Referred to in Article 62(1) of Regulation (EU) No 536/2014 and Article 4 of Delegated Regulation 1569/2017

(1) Name(s) of product(s)/product identifier(s) as referred to in the clinical trial application, where applicable

(2) EudraCT No(s) and sponsor protocol code number, when available

(3) Strength
Identity (name) and amount per unit dose for all active substance(s) for each IMP (including placebo). The manner in which this information is provided should ensure that the blinding is maintained.

(4) Dosage form (pharmaceutical form)

(5) Package size (contents of container) and type (e.g. vials, bottles, blisters)

(6) Lot/batch number

(7) Expiry/re-test/use by date

(8) Name and address of manufacturer where the Qualified Person issuing the certificate is located

(9) Manufacturing Authorisation number for the site listed under item 8

(10) Comments/remarks

(11) Any additional information considered relevant by the QP

(12) Certification statement

(13) "I hereby certify that this batch complies with the requirements of Article

(14) 62(1) of Regulation (EU) No 536/2014 and Article 4 of Delegated Regulation 1569/2017"

(15) Name of the QP signing the certificate

(16) Signature

(17) Date of signature

Reflection paper on Good Manufacturing Practice and Marketing Authorisation Holders

1. Introduction and Purpose

This Reflection Paper is focussed on the GMP-related responsibilities that apply to Marketing Authorisation Holder (MAH) companies. While it is recognised that many MAH companies are not directly engaged in the manufacture of medicinal products themselves, the current European Commission (EC) Guide to GMP (hereafter referred to as the 'GMP Guide') refers, in several places, to MAHs and their responsibilities in relation to GMP.

In general, these responsibilities range from responsibilities that relate to outsourcing and technical agreements, to ones that require the MAH to perform certain specific tasks (e.g. evaluating the results of product quality reviews, agreeing irradiation cycles with manufacturers, etc.). These responsibilities are spread over the various chapters and annexes of the GMP Guide, and are quite numerous.

This Reflection Paper seeks to provide clarity as to what the various responsibilities are and what they mean for MAHs at a practical level. In addition to the MAH responsibilities in the GMP Guide, this paper also addresses the various legislative provisions (i.e. in European Directives, Regulations and in other guidelines) which relate to GMP and which concern MAHs. Some of the responsibilities stated in the legislation (e.g. in Directive 2001/83/EC and Regulation (EU) 2019/6) and in applicable guidelines are written in a way that they apply to marketing authorisation applicants, and they are included in this Reflection Paper because those provisions also convey responsibilities upon marketing authorisation holders in the post-authorisation phase.

It should be noted that, as indicated in Annex 16 of the GMP Guide, the ultimate responsibility for the performance of a medicinal product over its lifetime, its safety, quality and efficacy, lies with the MAH. (This does not alter the fact that, also as per Annex 16, the Qualified Person (QP) is responsible for ensuring that each individual batch has been manufactured and checked in compliance with laws in force in the Member State where certification takes place, in accordance with the requirements of the marketing authorisation (MA) and with Good Manufacturing Practice (GMP).) It is also important to note that, while certain activities of an MAH may be delegated to a manufacturer or other party, the MAH retains the responsibilities which are outlined in this paper. The GMP guide also does not provide for *reduced* MAH responsibilities (or for the *delegation* of responsibilities) in situations where the MAH and the manufacturer belong to the same overall group of companies but where the two companies are different legal entities. There is no difference in the responsibilities that apply to the MAH in this situation relative to when the MAH and the manufacturer are from separate and unrelated companies.

It is acknowledged that many MAHs are part of large and complex global organisations which operate shared Pharmaceutical Quality Systems. While tasks pertaining to the MAH responsibilities outlined in this paper may be delegated to other groups or entities within the global organisation, the actual responsibilities of the MAH may not be delegated.

While relevant activities pertaining to the GMP-related responsibilities held by MAHs may be delegated by the MAH to its representative (if there is one) in a member state, none of the responsibilities may be delegated to that person. (Note: The representative of the MAH, commonly known as the local representative, is the person designated by the MAH to represent him in the Member State concerned. (Ref. Part 18a of Article 1 in Directive 2001/83/EC and Article 58 (1) in Regulation (EU) 2019/6).

It is recognised that, while MAHs have a significant role in facilitating GMP and MA compliance, their responsibilities in this area can, in some cases, be difficult to comprehend when reading the GMP Guide or the applicable legislation. Notwithstanding this, such responsibilities are there and may be inferred. This Reflection Paper seeks to provide clarity on these.

In relation to maintaining the supply of medicinal products, the EU medicines legislation, as well as the GMP Guide, place obligations upon the MAH that relate to the supply of its medicinal products and to the maintenance of such supply. This relates to the avoidance of medicines shortages for patients and animals. It is considered that MAHs should also comply with any national requirements that may exist within the EEA in relation to maintaining product supply.

All of the references currently in the GMP Guide (as of April 2019) that relate to MAH responsibilities are discussed in this Reflection Paper. This paper, however, should not be taken to provide an exhaustive list of those references on an ongoing basis. Rather, it sets out the general GMP-related responsibilities and activities of the MAH, and it presents them under a number of different *themes*. These themes are outlined below in Section 5. MAH companies should have a system in place to ensure that they remain up-to-date with current GMP requirements and updates thereafter.

Where possible, the text within each theme provides an explanation of what the various responsibilities may mean at a practical level for MAHs; guidance is also given on what is expected of an MAH when fulfilling that responsibility. It should be noted, however, that this Reflection Paper does not provide guidance on 'how' the various responsibilities might be fulfilled.

Article 111 of Directive 2001/83/EC and Article 123 (1c) Regulation (EU) 2019/6 give powers to member state authorities to inspect the premises of MAH companies; this includes situations in which there are grounds for suspecting non-compliance with the legal requirements laid down in the Directives and Regulations, including with the principles and guidelines of GMP. When such inspections are carried out, this Reflection

Paper may serve as useful guidance for the competent authorities performing the inspections.

2. Scope

The Reflection Paper concerns the responsibilities and activities of MAHs with respect to the European Commission's Guide to GMP (Parts I, II, and its relevant Annexes) for medicines for human and veterinary use. It also covers the responsibilities of MAHs and Sponsors (where the Sponsor is different from the MAH) with regard to the handling of quality defects with investigational medicinal products.

The scope also extends to certain <u>legislative</u> provisions that have relevance to GMP, such as those stated in the GMP Directives 2003/94/EC and 91/412/EC (as amended), as well as relevant articles in Directive 2001/83/EC and Regulation (EU) 2019/6.

When referring to manufacturers and manufacturing sites, the Reflection Paper is referring to any site engaged in manufacturing and related activities (e.g. contract analysis) that are subject to EU GMP requirements. This includes holders of manufacturing and importation authorisations, as well as contract testing facilities e.g. performing batch release testing or ongoing stability testing; this latter refers to annual stability testing.

This Reflection Paper is focussed on the GMP-related responsibilities that apply to all MAH companies, regardless of the authorisation or registration procedure used. This means that it also applies to holders of Registration and Traditional-use Registrations for herbal/homeopathic medicinal products.

FMD: The relevant provisions of the Falsified Medicines Directive 2011/62/EU and the related Delegated Regulations (including the Safety Features Regulation 2016/161) are also within scope of this Reflection Paper. Note that these requirements only apply to medicinal products for human use.

ATMPs: The principles set out in this paper also generally apply to MAHs of ATMPs. However, the specific provisions of Part IV of the GMP Guide are not specifically discussed here, and there are certain specific requirements that apply to ATMPs, as stated in Part IV (such as a 30 year data retention requirement) that differ from what is set out in this Reflection Paper. Note that these requirements only apply to medicinal products for human use.

GDP Responsibilities: While this Reflection Paper is not intended to address the GDP-related responsibilities that may apply to MAHs, it is considered important to highlight here that MAHs do need to understand the type of interfaces that may need to be in place with the wholesalers they employ or engage. For example, current EU GDP guidelines in relation to medicinal products for human use require that medicines wholesalers notify the MAH of certain information, e.g. information concerning falsified products and quality defects (Ref. EU GDP Guidelines, 2013, Sections 6.2 and 6.4). As a result, it is considered that MAHs should have systems in place to accept and act upon such information from the wholesale distribution chain when received. (Note that in relation to veterinary medicinal products, new GDP requirements are expected to be published by January 2022 and these may specify responsibilities for MAHs of veterinary medicinal products.)

The Reflection Paper does not extend to other MAH responsibilities and activities that may be set-out in other official guidance documents and legislation, such as those relating to other GxP areas, pharmacovigilance, etc.

3. How this Reflection Paper sets out the various MAH Responsibilities

In Section 5 of this paper, each GMP requirement that applies to the MAH is outlined, with its key message stated or summarised.

- This is then followed by the exact text that is in the GMP Guide (or in applicable legislation or in other guidelines) on this point. In some cases, the exact text is presented between quotation marks.
- A clear reference to the relevant part of the GMP Guide or the applicable legislation is then stated.
- Where possible, an explanation of what the requirement means at a practical level for the MAH is provided, in italics.

4. The role of the MAH in Facilitating Compliance with GMP and the Marketing Authorisation (MA)

While GMP compliance is the responsibility of the manufacturer, the MAH has a clear role in facilitating GMP compliance. This is reflected in the multiple references to MAH responsibilities that are in the GMP Guide. These responsibilities generally relate to:

- The provision of information by the MAH to competent authorities, manufacturing sites and Qualified Persons;
- The collation of quality-related information from different actors in the manufacturing and distribution chain.

Evidence of GMP Compliance: The applicant has the responsibility to make sure that the manufacturers proposed in a new application for an MA hold a valid Manufacturer's and Import Authorisation (MIA) in the case of sites located in the EEA. In the case of manufacturers located out-side the EEA, there should be a valid proof of authorisation (equivalent to MIA) where one is required, and a valid EU GMP Certificate (or, where an MRA or equivalent applies, evidence of successful GMP inspection in rela-tion to the product category / manufacturing activity of interest). For sites located in EEA, the MIAs and GMP Certificates are publicly accessible on the EudraGMDP database. Note that the validity of GMP certificates for sites which had been inspected more than 3 years prior to when perform-ing the check may be verified with the relevant competent authority.

Abbreviated Version of CTD Module 3/Part 2 of Veterinary Marketing Authorisation dossier: In the introductory chapter to the GMP Guide, it is stated that "Throughout the Guide, it is assumed that the requirements of the Marketing Authorisation relating to the safety, quality and efficacy of the products, are systematically incorporated into all the manufacturing, control and release for sale arrangements of the holder of the Manufac-turing Authorisation." This implies that the MAH has a responsibility to communicate what is registered in the MA to the manufacturing sites. In doing this, MAHs sometimes prepare abbreviated versions of CTD module 3 / Part 2 of the veterinary dossier of the MA for use by the manufacturing sites and QPs; this is considered acceptable; as long as those abbreviated versions are sufficiently comprehensive and are subject to formal change control and oversight activities. It is considered that the provision and use of such abbreviated versions of Module 3/Part 2 should be addressed in a technical agreement between the parties.

Labelling and Product Information: Care should also be taken to ensure that, what is registered in CTD module 1 / Part 1 of the veterinary dos-sier in relation to the approved product labelling (including the package leaflet) and changes to same are communicated to the manufacturer in a timeframe which will enable the manufacturer to ensure that all batches it produces have the correct labelling and product information.

Chapter 7 and MAHs: While Chapter 7 is primarily intended to deal with "the responsibilities of manufacturers towards the Competent Authorities of the Member States with respect to the granting of marketing and man-ufacturing authorisations" (Ref. Chapter 7, Principle), it is also directly relevant to MAHs, as indicated by paragraph 7.3. This states: "Where the marketing authorization holder and the manufacturer are not the same, appropriate arrangements should be in place, taking into account the prin-ciples described in this chapter." (Ref. Chapter 7, Paragraph 7.3).

MA Variations: The need to provide the relevant manufacturing sites with the necessary information about MA variation approval and target implementation dates is considered another important responsibility for the MAH. It is a key activity which enables those sites to ensure that future batches of the product, which may be QP-certified after a certain date, comply with the varied MA. It also facilitates the generation of

Product Quality Reviews in line with Chapter 1 of the EU GMP Guide. This responsibility may be inferred from Chapter 7 of the GMP Guide, in relation to Outsourced Activities, which states:

> "The Contract Giver should provide the Contract Acceptor with all the information and knowledge necessary to carry out the contracted operations correctly in accordance with regulations in force, and the Marketing Authorisation for the product concerned." (Ref. Chapter 7, Paragraph 7.6)

Regulatory Commitments: The management of regulatory commitments (which are often made by MAHs to competent authorities) is another area that can have a significant impact upon MA compliance generally, if it is not under an appropriate level of control by the MAH. This is especially the case in relation to the communication of such commitments to the manufacturing sites by the MAH; thus, the importance of robust communication processes is highlighted in this Reflection Paper. Indeed, the management of regulatory commitments may assume increased importance in the coming years, given that the regulatory environment may move towards greater flexibility in the area of post-approval change management, via ICH Q12, with respect to medicinal products for human use. Such flexibility is likely to rely on the effectiveness of the pharmaceutical quality system that is in place, as this will help assure regulatory compliance in the implementation of such post-approval changes. MAHs may have an important role in this area.

Two-way Communication Systems: MAHs can facilitate compliance by establishing robust two-way communication systems with national competent authorities, manufacturing sites, Qualified Persons (QPs), and any organisations relevant to the monitoring of post-marketing quality (e.g. complaints processing and on-going stability monitoring). Doing so can help ensure that:

- The manufacturing sites and QPs have visibility of what is registered in the marketing authorisation and what, if any, regulatory commitments have been agreed with the competent authorities.
- The MAHs have adequate knowledge of the details of the manufacturing processes, including impurity formation, and their related controls at the finished product and active substance manufacturing sites. Such knowledge can enable MAHs ensure that the active substance and/or finished product specifications reflect those controls, as necessary. This also includes situations where there are Active Substance Master Files (ASMFs) and Certificates of suitability to the monographs of the European Pharmacopoeia (CEPs) in place.
- The MAHs are adequately informed of the change management activities at the manufacturing sites, particularly in relation to changes which

may impact upon Modules 1, 2 and 3 / Parts 1 and 2 of the veterinary dossier, as well as on the contents of ASMFs and CEPs. This can help ensure that the MAHs are involved in regulatory impact assessments for relevant change proposals and that any necessary notifications or variation applications are made to the competent authorities.
- The manufacturing sites are adequately informed by the MAHs of any MA changes which may have an impact on those sites, such as changes to the package leaflet, changes to specifications, etc.

Data integrity: This is another area of relevance to MAHs; it can result in GMP non-compliances if there are not robust control systems to assure the integrity of data pertaining to the MA, which may be used or required by the manufacturers. Thus, it is considered that MAHs should have systems in place to ensure the integrity and reliability of the data that are used to discharge their responsibilities. There should be assurance that product lifecycle data relating to GMP activities, including relevant MA variations, are reliable, complete and accurate. The MAH should also ensure the long term security and archiving of the data upon which the MA relies.

Compliance Management Process: MAHs should be aware of the 'Compliance Management' process that has been put in place within the EEA; this is used in situations where a manufacturing site has been found to be on the border between achieving a minimum level of GMP compliance and serious GMP non-compliance. MAHs should be aware of their ability to facilitate compliance, and may find that their involvement in the remediation of such issues is necessary, in relation to the products for which the MAH has responsibility. More information in this regard is available at (*link – to be inserted when available*).

Non-compliance with MAH Obligations: Based on Article 116 of Directive 2001/83/EC and Article 130 (3) of Regulation (EU) 2019/6, a MA for which the MAH does not fulfil its various obligations may be suspended, revoked or varied by the competent authority. Article 116 of Directive 2001/83/EC states that an authorisation shall be "suspended, revoked, withdrawn or varied where the particulars supporting the application as provided for in Article 8 or Articles 10, 10a, 10b, 10c and 11 are incorrect or have not been amended in accordance with Article 23, or where the controls referred to in Article 112 have not been carried out."

5. Areas of the EC Guide to GMP that relate to MAHs

As noted in the Introduction, there are various references within the GMP guide to MAH-related responsibilities. These span a number of different chapters and annexes, and in this Reflection Paper, they are grouped together under a number of different themes. These are set out below.

While there is some duplication across the different themes, it is considered helpful to consider the responsibilities and activities in this way.

A number of the legislative provisions that exist within EU medicines legislation which concern the GMP-related responsibilities of MAHs are also included within the various themes, where relevant. The themes are:

- Outsourcing and Technical Agreements
- Audits and Qualification Activities
- Communication with Manufacturing Sites (e.g. MA Dossier Information, Variations, Regulatory Commitments, etc.)
- Product Quality Reviews
- Quality Defects, Complaints and Product Recalls
- Maintenance of Supply of Medicinal Products
- Continual Improvement Activities

(Note that FMD-related responsibilities are discussed in Chapter 6.)

5.1. Outsourcing and Technical Agreements

This section discusses the various MAH responsibilities which apply to outsourced activities and technical agreements. (Note that the term 'technical agreement' is considered to mean a document that sets out the responsibilities and tasks/duties of the various parties, as agreed by those parties.) Section 5.2 below, relating to Audits and Qualification, is also relevant here and its contents should be noted.

See also section 5.3 below in relation to the importance of a technical agreement being in place between the MAH and manufacturer when they are different legal entities. That section also addresses communications in relation to situations in which there is an Active Substance Master File (ASMF) or a CEP registered for a MA.

DELEGATION OF ACTIVITIES

As noted earlier in this Reflection Paper, there is no provision within the GMP guide or in applicable legislation for the delegation of responsibilities by an MAH to other parties. However, there may be delegation of the tasks and activities which relate to those responsibilities, and this is relevant to the topic of outsourcing. It is considered that any such delegation should be described in writing and agreed by the relevant parties.

In general terms, it is the responsibility of the MAH to ensure that the person or entity, to whom any task or activity has been delegated, possesses the required competence, information and knowledge to successfully carry out the outsourced activities (Ref: GMP Guide Chapter 7, Paragraphs 7.5 and 7.6). Special attention should be given to situations where tasks have been delegated in a fragmented way - to more than one party – as applying oversight of multiple parties can be a challenge in the life-cycle management of the medicinal product.

DOCUMENTING OUTSOURCED ACTIVITIES

There are obligations to ensure that outsourced activities are described in writing. Chapter 7 of the GMP Guide requires that "any activity that is outsourced should be appropriately defined, agreed and controlled in order to avoid misunderstandings which could result in a product or operation of unsatisfactory quality." (Ref: GMP Guide Chapter 7, Principle).

Chapter 7 of the GMP Guide also states that "Where the marketing authorization holder and the manufacturer are not the same, appropriate arrangements should be in place, taking into account the principles described in this chapter." (Ref. Chapter 7, Paragraph 7.3). In practice there are various scenarios that may apply. For example, the two parties may be different legal entities within the same company group, or they may be unrelated companies. Regardless of such scenarios, it is considered that the arrangements between the parties should be documented in technical agreements.

Where an MAH is engaged in an outsourcing activity, the above means that the MAH should agree in writing what exactly the activity is, and how it will be controlled.

COMPLIANCE WITH THE MARKETING AUTHORISATION

If an outsourced activity is one that may affect compliance with the MA, there should be controls in place which provide assurance that the requirements of the MA are complied with. This also has relevance in relation to activities concerning post-approval changes and their implementation.

The GMP Guide states that "All arrangements for the outsourced activities including any proposed changes in technical or other arrangements should be in accordance with regulations in force, and the Marketing Authorisation for the product concerned, where applicable." (Ref. Chapter 7, Paragraph 7.2)

Chapter 1 of the GMP Guide states that "Where manufacture is outsourced, the technical agreement between MAH and manufacturer should address the respective responsibilities in producing and evaluating the product quality review." (Ref. Chapter 1, Paragraph 1.11). *This means that the manufacturer may be responsible for compiling and evaluating certain elements of the PQR, while the MAH may be responsible for compiling and evaluating other parts of the PQR. (See below and also Section 5.4 for further information in relation to PQRs.) It is noted that PQRs contain information in relation to the MA, in terms of variations, post-approval commitments, etc.*

DOCUMENT RETENTION

There are certain document retention requirements stated in the GMP Guide which are important from the perspective of the MAH, as they support the MA, and also, documentation retention activities may be the subject of outsourcing.

With regard to medicinal products, it is considered that while GMP-related document retention is the responsibility of the manufacturer, the MAH has an interest in this area, given that certain documentation supports information in the Marketing Authorisation. Chapter 4 of the GMP Guide provides useful guidance relating to the storage and retention requirements of documentation. It states that "…the retention period will depend on the business activity which the documentation supports. Critical documentation, including raw data (for example relating to validation or stability), which supports information in the Marketing Authorisation should be retained whilst the authorization remains in force." (Ref. Chapter 4, Paragraph 4.12)

While the above wording in Chapter 4 of the GMP Guide is aimed at the manufacturer and does not convey a direct responsibility on the MAH, it is considered that the MAH should be satisfied with the documentation retention policies and practices that are in place at the manufacturer, given the role of certain documentation in supporting the MA. It is considered that the arrangements in this area should be addressed in a technical agreement or a contract between the parties, whichever may apply.

The above paragraph from Chapter 4 of the GMP Guide goes on to state that:

> "It may be considered acceptable to retire certain documentation (e.g. raw data supporting validation reports or stability reports) where the data has been superseded by a full set of new data. Justification for this should be documented and should take into account the requirements for retention of batch documentation; for example, in the case of process validation data, the accompanying raw data should be retained for a period at least as long as the records for all batches whose release has been supported on the basis of that validation exercise."

Again, the above text is relevant to the MAH, as validation data and reports, and stability reports also, are key elements of the documentation needed to support an MA.

In relation to investigational medicinal products for human use, the GMP Directive 2003/94/EC places a direct responsibility on the MAH with respect to the retention of documentation. In this regard, it requires the batch documentation to:

> "… be retained for at least five years after the completion or formal discontinuation of the last clinical trial in which the batch was used. The sponsor or marketing authorisation holder, if different, shall be responsible for ensuring that records are retained as required for

marketing authorisation in accordance with the Annex I to Directive 2001/83/EC, if required for a subsequent marketing authorisation" (Ref. Directive 2003/94/EC, Article 9).

Please note that this requirement is not stated in Directive 2017/1572 which will replace Directive 2003/94/EC in 2019.

It is considered that record retention responsibilities and activities should be agreed between the manufacturer, MAH or sponsor. The EMA Guideline EMA/202679/2018 (Guideline on the responsibilities of the sponsor with regard to handling and shipping of investigational medicinal products for human use in accordance with Good Clinical Practice and Good Manufacturing Practice) also provides useful information in this regard.

TECHNICAL AGREEMENTS IN RELATION TO PRODUCT QUALITY REVIEWS (PQRS)

Chapter 1 of the GMP Guide states that "Where manufacture is out-sourced, the technical agreement between MAH and manufacturer should address the respective responsibilities in producing and evaluating the product quality review." (Ref. Chapter 1, Paragraph 1.11). *This means that the manufacturer may be responsible for compiling and evaluating certain elements of the PQR, while the MAH may be responsible for com-piling and evaluating other parts of the PQR. (See Section 5.4 below for further information in relation to PQRs.)*

TECHNICAL AGREEMENTS IN RELATION TO THE MANUFACTURE OF BIOLOGICAL ACTIVE SUBSTANCES AND MEDICINAL PRODUCTS FOR HUMAN USE

In relation to the manufacture of biological active substances and medicinal products for human use, there is a responsibility on the MAH to have a technical agreement in place with other parties which describes its respon-sibilities relating to the sourcing of human derived starting materials for biological products. The GMP Guide states that for human tissues and cells used as starting materials for biological medicinal products, "a tech-nical agreement should be in place between the responsible parties (e.g. manufacturers, tissue establishment, Sponsors, MA Holder) which defines the tasks of each party, including the RP [Responsible Person] and Quali-fied Person" (Ref. Annex 2, Paragraph 36(g)).

TECHNICAL AGREEMENTS IN RELATION TO THE USE OF IONISING RADIATION IN THE MANUFACTURE OF MEDICINAL PRODUCTS

In relation to the use of ionising radiation in the manufacture of medicinal products, there are certain responsibilities for the MAH documented in Annex 12 of the GMP Guide.

One is a responsibility for the MAH to agree the design of irradiation cycles with the manufacturer, and another is to agree how and where irradiation cycle records are retained. The Guide states that:

"When the required radiation dose is by design given during more than one exposure or passage through the plant, this should be with the agreement of the holder of the marketing authorisation and occur within a predetermined time period. Unplanned interruptions during irradiation should be notified to the holder of the marketing authorisation if this extends the irradiation process beyond a previously agreed period." (Ref. Annex 12, Paragraph 33).

Annex 12 also states that:

"Process and control records for each irradiation batch should be checked and signed by a nominated responsible person and retained. The method and place of retention should be agreed between the plant operator and the holder of the marketing authorisation." (Ref. Annex 12, Paragraph 44).

Annex 12 also requires the MAH of a product which includes ionising radiation in its processing to refer to the CPMP guidance on "Ionising radiation in the manufacture of medicinal products" (Ref. Annex 12, Note).

Some of the above responsibilities in Annex 12 are quite technical in nature, and they require the MAH to be in a position to understand and to technically assess the design of irradiation cycles.

The direct requirement for the MAH to work with the manufacturer with regard to the design of irradiation cycles is not considered a task that may be delegated by the MAH to the manufacturer of the medicinal product. However, the records retention tasks are considered ones that may be delegated to the manufacturer, and thus may be the subject of outsourcing arrangements.

ARRANGEMENTS IN RELATION TO REFERENCE AND RETENTION SAMPLES

There is an Annex in the GMP Guide that provides guidance in relation to reference and retention samples. This is Annex 19, and it states certain responsibilities for the MAH in this area, mainly in relation to agreeing with the relevant manufacturers the <u>arrangements for the taking and storage of reference and retention samples</u>. (Note that Annex 6 of the GMP Guide provides an exemption to manufacturers of medicinal gases for the need to take and store reference and retention samples of such products, unless such samples are otherwise required.)

In the section titled 'Written Agreements' in Annex 19, the following is stated:

"Where the marketing authorisation holder is not the same legal entity as the site(s) responsible for batch release within the EEA, the responsibility for taking and storage of reference/retention samples should be defined in a written agreement between the two parties in accordance with Chapter 7 of the EC Guide to Good Manufacturing Practice. This applies also where any manufacturing or batch release activity is carried out at a site other than that with overall responsibility for the batch on the EEA market and the arrangements between each different site for the taking and keeping of reference and retention samples should be defined in a written agreement." (Ref. Annex 19, Paragraph 6.1)

Annex 19 also addresses situations involving the closedown of a manufacturer and how reference and retention samples are to be managed. It states that

"If the manufacturer is not in a position to make the necessary arrangements this may be delegated to another manufacturer. The Marketing Authorisation holder (MAH) is responsible for such delegation and for the provision of all necessary information to the Competent Authority. In addition, the MAH should, in relation to the suitability of the proposed arrangements for storage of reference and retention samples, consult with the competent authority of each Member State in which any unexpired batch has been placed on the market." (Ref. Annex 19, Paragraph 10.2)

While the taking and storage of reference and retention samples has often been regarded as purely a manufacturing activity, it is clear from the above that the MAH has responsibilities in this area also.

5.2. Audits & Qualification Activities

There are references to GMP audits within the European medicines legislation which have implications for applicants for MAs as well as for the corresponding MAHs. There is also a need for finished product manufacturers to be suitably qualified in order to be able to verify, for the applicant and the MAH, the GMP compliance status of the active substance manufacturer(s), as required in legislation.

QP DECLARATIONS REGARDING GMP COMPLIANCE STATUS OF THE ACTIVE SUBSTANCE MANUFACTURER

Article 8(3)(ha) of Directive 2001/83/EC, for example, places a legal obligation on the applicant to provide information in the MA application concerning the GMP compliance status of the manufacturer of the active substance, and in this regard, reference is made to audits of that manufacturer. This article requires the applicant to provide "A written confirmation [QP Declaration] that the manufacturer of the medicinal product has verified compliance of the manufacturer of the active substance, with [the] principles and guidelines of good manufacturing practice by conducting audits, in accordance with point (f) of Article 46."

> Article 46 relates to the obligations that are placed upon the holder of the manufacturing authorisation, and sub-point (f) requires the finished product manufacturer "to use only active substances, which have been manufactured in accordance with good manufacturing practice for active substances and distributed in accordance with good distribution practices for active substances."

Article 8(3)(ha) goes on to state that the written confirmation submitted by the applicant "shall contain a reference to the date of the audit and a declaration that the outcome of the audit confirms that the manufacturing complies with the principles and guidelines of good manufacturing practice."

The above means that the MA applicant has a responsibility to confirm that such audits have been carried out prior to the submission of the MA application, and to be satisfied with the GMP compliance status of the manufacturer of the active substance, as determined by the holder of the medicinal product manufacturing authorisation. The above confirmation should be made in the form of a QP Declaration. (Note: The term "Written Confirmation" as used in Article 8(3)(ha) is essentially a reference to the 'QP Declaration'; it is the term used in the European Commission "Guidelines on the details of the various categories of variations" for the QP Declaration.)

In relation to medicinal products for veterinary use, EC Regulation 2019/6 states the following: "The manufacturing processes for the active substance(s) and finished product shall comply with Good Manufacturing Practice (GMP)." (Ref. Article 8 (a) and (b), Annex I item 4.1, and Annex II section I item I.1.4). In parallel, Article 93 (j) of Regulation 2019/06 requires that the holder of a manufacturing authorisation "shall use as starting materials only active substances which have been manufactured in accordance with good manufacturing practice for active substances and distributed in accordance with good distribution practice for active substances". Article 93 (l) requires that the holder of a MA "shall perform audits based on a risk assessment of the manufacturers, distributors and importers from whom the holder of a manufacturing authorisation obtains active substances".

In addition, Eudralex Volume 6 B, Notice to Applicants, states that a declaration(s) from the Qualified Person of the manufacturing authorisation holder is required.

The above means that a QP Declaration based on an audit is also expected for <u>medicinal products for veterinary use</u>.

The above responsibilities to confirm to the competent authority the GMP status of the active substance manufacturer continues into the post-authorisation phase of the medicinal product, and it is the MAH that bears this responsibility. In this regard:

- GMP audits of the manufacturer are again required – such audits are referred to in the guidelines concerning MA variations (Ref. EC Guidelines 2013/C 223/01 and Commission Implementing Regulation (EU) 2021/17 of 8 January 2021).
- In the section dealing with Administrative Changes, the aforementioned guidelines place a responsibility on the MAH to submit a Type 1A variation notification in relation to changes in the date of the audit to verify GMP compliance of the manufacturer of the active substance. This concerns notifying the competent authority of new audits of such sites.
- The MAH is required to provide a "written confirmation from the manufacturer of the finished product stating verification of compliance of the manufacturer of the active substance with principles and guidelines of good manufacturing practices" (Ref. Administrative Change A.8). Note that a variation application is not needed when the information has been otherwise transmitted to the authorities (e.g. through a QP declaration).

The document titled 'Guidance for the template for the qualified person's declaration concerning GMP compliance of active substance manufacture' also addresses the responsibility of the MAH to ensure that a written confirmation of compliance of the manufacturer of the active substance with GMP is provided to the competent authority. This document also indicates that such confirmations of compliance should be based on audits; it states that "Audits of each site for GMP compliance should be undertaken at regular intervals, normally within three years. Justification should be provided if the date since the last audit exceeds this period."

- *Use of the QP declaration template facilitates the provision of the required audit-related information by the MAH.*
- *The audit reports should be readily available and shared with the authorities, if requested.*
- *The above variation (or QP declaration) requirement relates to the fact that the GMP compliance status of the active substance manufacturer is expected to be confirmed by the manufacturer of the finished product and transmitted to the MAH, and that such confirmations (declarations) are based on audits carried out by, or on behalf of, the manufacturer of the finish product, as required by Article 46(f) of Directive 2001/83/EC and Article 93 (l) of Regulation 2019/6.*

The above responsibilities apply to the MA Applicant and then to the MAH after the MA has been granted.

5.3. Communication with Manufacturing Sites and Competent Authorities (e.g. MA Dossier Information, Variations, Regulatory Commitments, etc.)

THE NEED FOR TWO-WAY COMMUNICATION SYSTEMS

As noted earlier in this paper, the introductory chapter to the GMP Guide refers to the need for "the requirements of the Marketing Authorisation, relating to the safety, quality and efficacy of the product", to be "systematically incorporated into all the manufacturing, control and release for sale arrangements of the holder of the Manufacturing Authorisation". *This implies the need for cooperation between the MAH and manufacturer, and the need for <u>two-way communication systems</u> to be in place between them, particularly in relation to what is registered in the MA.*

Likewise, the so called 'GMP Directives' 2003/94/EC and 91/412 require the manufacturer to ensure that "all manufacturing operations for medicinal products subject to a marketing authorisation are carried out in accordance with the information provided in the application for marketing authorisation as accepted by the competent authorities". (Ref. Article 5 of Directives 2003/94/EC and 91/412).

It is reasonable to take the view that manufacturers cannot comply with the GMP requirement for batches to be in line with the relevant MA unless the MAH communicates to them what is registered in the dossier. A similar point is made in the preamble to the forthcoming new GMP Directive 2017/1572. This will replace Directive 2003/94/EC in 2019, when EU regulation 536/2014 on Clinical Trials enters into force, and it states the following:

> "All medicinal products for human use manufactured or imported into the Union, including medicinal products intended for export, should be manufactured in accordance with the principles and guidelines of good manufacturing practice. However, for the manufacturer to be able to comply with those principles and guidelines, cooperation between the manufacturer and the marketing authorisation holder, when they are different legal entities, is necessary. The obligations of the manufacturer and marketing authorisation holder vis-à-vis each other should be defined in a technical agreement between them." (Ref. Directive 2017/1572, Preamble Point 4)

Thus, it is considered important that there is cooperation and communication between the MAH and manufacturer, when they are different legal entities, and that such arrangements be described in a technical agreement between the parties.

SPECIFIC EXAMPLE OF REQUIRED COMMUNICATIONS

Example 1 - The use of ionising radiation in the manufacture of medicinal products

An example which illustrates the need for such communication can be found in Annex 12 to the GMP Guide. This Annex concerns **the use of ionising radiation** in the manufacture of medicinal products.

- It states that the "required dose including justified limits will be stated in the marketing authorisation" (Ref. EU GMP Guide Annex 12, Paragraph 3).
- This implies a need for communication between the MAH and the manufacturer in relation to the strength and limits of the irradiating dose.
- The MAH has a responsibility to ensure that this information is registered in the marketing authorisation, and he is expected to communicate what has been registered with the manufacturer, so that the manufacturer may maintain compliance with the marketing authorisation.

Example 2 - ASMFs and CEPs

Another area of importance in relation to communication processes and responsibilities is where there is an **Active Substance Master File (ASMF)** registered for a marketing authorisation which has both closed and open parts, or where a **Certificate of Suitability to the monographs of the European Pharmacopoeia (CEP)** is registered (or applied for) in the MA. (Note: the information in the CEP replaces those MA dossier sections that normally describe the manufacture and control during manufacture of the active substance (as well as stability data, in cases where the CEP includes a re-test date). Such CEP information will have been evaluated by the European Directorate for the Quality of Medicines (EDQM).)

These approaches are covered by Directive 2001/83/EC and Regulation 2019/6, as follows:

With regard to medicinal products for human use:

"For a well-defined active substance, the active substance manufacturer or the applicant may arrange for the (i) detailed description of the manufacturing process, (ii) quality control during manufacture, and (iii) process validation, to be supplied in a separate document directly to the competent authorities by the manufacturer of the active substance as an Active Substance Master File. In this case, the manufacturer shall, however, provide the applicant with all of the data, which may be necessary for the latter to take responsibility for the medicinal product. The manufacturer shall confirm in writing to the applicant that he shall ensure batch to batch consistency and not modify the manufacturing process or specifications without informing the applicant. Documents and particulars supporting the application for such a change shall be supplied to the competent authorities; these documents and particulars will be also supplied to the applicant when they concern the open part of the active substance master file" (Ref. Directive 2001/83/EC, Annex 1).

"Where the active substance and/or a raw and starting material or excipient(s) are the subject of a monograph of the European Pharmacopoeia, the applicant can apply for a certificate of suitability that, where granted by the European Directorate for the Quality of Medicines, shall be presented in the relevant section of this Module (i.e.

Module 3). Those certificates of suitability of the monograph of the European Pharmacopoeia are deemed to replace the relevant data of the corresponding sections described in this Module. The manufacturer shall give the assurance in writing to the applicant that the manufacturing process has not been modified since the granting of the certificate of suitability by the European Directorate for the Quality of Medicines" (Ref. Directive 2001/83/EC, Annex I)

With regard to medicinal products for veterinary use:

"For a non-biological active substance, the applicant may arrange for the information on active substance in point (2) to be supplied directly to the competent authorities by the manufacturer of the active substance as an Active Substance Master File. In this case, the manufacturer of the active substance shall provide the applicant with all the data (applicant's part of the Active Substance Master File) which may be necessary for the latter to take responsibility for the veterinary medicinal product. A copy of the data provided by the active substance manufacturer to the applicant shall be included in the medicinal product dossier. The manufacturer of the active substance shall confirm in writing to the applicant that he shall ensure batch-to-batch consistency and not modify the manufacturing process or specifications without informing the applicant." (Ref. Regulation 2019/6 Annex II)

"Where a certificate of suitability has been issued by the European Directorate for the Quality of Medicines and HealthCare for a starting material, active substance or excipient, that certificate constitutes the reference to the relevant monograph of the European Pharmacopoeia. Where a certificate of suitability is referred to, the manufacturer shall give an assurance in writing to the applicant that the manufacturing process has not been modified since the granting of the certificate of suitability by the European Directorate for the Quality of Medicines and HealthCare." (Regulation 2019/6 Annex II)

It is important to note that, irrespective of whether an ASMF or a CEP is in place, *the MAH retains his responsibility for ensuring the quality of the active substance. In this regard, the following points should be noted:*

- *The MAH is responsible for ensuring, that it, in conjunction with the finished product manufacturer, has access to all relevant information concerning the current manufacture of the active substance. This requires effective communication processes to be in place between the concerned parties in relation to the manufacture of the active substance. It is expected that the MA applicant/ MAH have access to the open part (or its equivalent) of the ASMF, including when a CEP is used. In the case of an aseptically manufactured active substance, full information on the sterilization step needs to be made available to the finished product manufacturer and should be included in Module 3/Part II of the MA dossier. The MA applicant/MAH should ensure that they have access to all the relevant information.*

- *Such communication processes should also address proposed changes in the manufacturing process or specifications, to enable the MAH to assess the implications of the proposed change on the finished product and to apply for any required variations to the MA, in accordance with the EU Variation Classification Guideline.*
- *In addition, if a CEP for an active substance is registered in an MA, this does not exempt the MAH from the responsibility to have available a declaration of GMP (signed by the Qualified Person) relating to the GMP compliance status of the active substance manufacturer. See the earlier text in this Reflection Paper for information on QP Declarations.*
- *The level of knowledge that the MAH has in relation to the manufacture and control of the active substance should be such that it permits the MAH to take responsibility for the quality of the medicinal product. This should not be less than when there is an ASMF registered in the MA.*

In order for the MAH (or applicant) to be able to fulfil the responsibilities referred to above, it is considered that he should ensure that the above requirements are clearly addressed, and if necessary via a technical agreement between the MAH and the active substance manufacturer.

Example 3 – Documentation reflecting what is registered is the MA

A third example is found in Chapter 4 of the GMP Guide, in relation to **Documentation**. It states that "Documents should be designed, prepared, reviewed, and distributed with care. They should comply with the relevant parts of Product Specification Files, Manufacturing and Marketing Authorisation dossiers, as appropriate. The reproduction of working documents from master documents should not allow any error to be introduced through the reproduction process" (Ref. GMP Guide Chapter 4, Paragraph 4.2).

This implies a responsibility for the MAH to ensure that any documents that it provides to the manufacturing sites relating to what is registered in the MA accurately reflect the relevant parts of the MA.

- Examples of such documents might include the release and shelf-life specifications for the product, information in relation to the registered manufacturing process, copies of the registered artwork for the product packaging, etc.
- It is especially important that documents relating the registered product information intended for the patient or user of the medicine (i.e. labels and leaflets) are in line with the marketing authorisation, and that changes (variations) to these items are communicated to the manufacturing site in a timely manner.

The Effectiveness and Frequency of Communications

It is considered that there should be effective and frequent communications between the MAH and the relevant manufacturing sites. *This is not just in relation to what is registered in the MA, but also, it might concern the results of Product Quality Reviews (PQRs), information about regulatory commitments, proposed changes which may affect Modules 1, 2 and 3 / Parts 1 and 2 of the MA, among other things.*

Documenting Communication Processes – Complexity and Legal Arrangements

How such communication processes and responsibilities may be documented depends on the relationship between the various entities, and on the complexity of the arrangements that may be in place. Complexity in relation to the supply chain is particularly important to consider when determining what communication processes need to be in place – this can relate to the number and type of different manufacturers in the supply chain, the degree of outsourcing that is in place, the geographic spread of the various actors in the supply chain, etc.

In cases where the MAH and the manufacturer are part of the same overall group of companies, it may be sufficient to document, using SOPs, how the actual communication processes are expected to work. This is as long as those SOPs are approved by both parties and as long as they are referred to within the technical agreement between the parties. In other situations, where the MAH and the manufacturer are not part of the same overall group of companies, the communication processes and responsibilities should be documented in technical agreements or in contracts, as they may be more complex and at a higher risk of failing.

The two-way flow of information between the parties is important, especially in the context of proposed changes which may require variation applications or regulatory notifications to the competent authority by the MAH. This is also the case with regard to suspected quality defects and potential recall issues which may have been reported to one or other party, but not to both, and which may need to be reported onwards to the competent authority. See also section 5.5.4 in relation to Quality defects with investigational medicinal products.

Life-cycle Considerations

Communication processes and systems should be maintained with care, extending over the product life-cycle (e.g. during the licensing procedure, commercial manufacture, the fulfilment of regulatory commitments, the submission and implementation of post-approval variations, etc.) or at least up until the end of the relationship between the concerned parties. The MAH should ensure that communication systems are in place which will enable it to keep abreast of all developments, changes and commitments relating to the specific product of concern.

Communications with the Competent Authorities – MA Variations

In relation to manufacturing-related MA variations, the MAH has a responsibility via Directive 2001/83/EC and Regulation 2019/6 to provide the competent authority with information on amendments relative to the information submitted in the dossier. The Directive states that "The marketing authorisation holder shall forthwith provide the national competent authority with any new information which might entail the amendment of the particulars or documents referred to in Article 8(3), Articles 10, 10a, 10b and 11, or Article 32(5), or Annex I" (Ref. Directive 2001/83/EC, Article 23 (2)). Similar provisions are referred to in the Veterinary regulation, Regulation 2019/6, via Article 8(b), 18(1); 18(2) 58 (3), (10), 35, 42 and 43

Some of these articles directly concern GMP-related information, such as Article 8(3) in Directive 2001/83/EC and Article 5 of Regulation 2019/6, which relates to, among other things, a description of the manufacturing method and the control methods employed by the manufacturer.

Communications relating to Product Supply

Robust and timely communications are important in other areas too, not only in ensuring the regulatory compliance status of the product in the marketplace. In relation to ensuring the continued supply of medicinal products for patients and animals, for example, communication processes between MAHs, manufacturers and national competent authorities can play a pivotal role. See Section 5.6 below for further information on this point.

Communications relating to Scientific Advances

Another area in which effective communication processes can be of significant importance is in the maintenance of MAs in line with scientific advances. Article 23 of Directive 2001/83/EC states that, "after an authorisation has been issued, the authorisation holder must, in respect of the methods of manufacture and control provided for in the application, take account of scientific and technical progress and introduce any changes that may be required to enable the medicinal product to be manufactured and checked by means of generally accepted scientific methods." The Veterinary Regulation 2019/6, has similar wording, via Article 58.

The above articles imply a responsibility of the MAH to have communication systems in place with manufacturing sites and other parties which will enable it to keep abreast of scientific and technical progress and advances and to discuss initiatives in this area. This is so that any necessary MA variations can be submitted. This is further discussed in section 5.7 below.

Communicating Changes to CTD Modules 1, 2 and 3 / Parts 1 and 2 of Veterinary Marketing Authorisation dossier to the Manufacturing Sites

As CTD Modules 1, 2 and 3 / Parts 1 and 2 of the MA change over time with the approval of variations and with the introduction of continual improvements, etc., it can be a challenge to retain knowledge at both the MAH and at the manufacturer of what is registered at any one time.

- In this regard, it is expected that the copies of these CTD Modules / Parts 1 and 2 as held by the MAH (and by the manufacturer, if applicable) are continually kept updated (by replacing individual documents or Sections within a Module with the updated versions) as changes are made to those documents or sections within that Module.
- This results in always having up-to-date copies of Modules 1, 2 and 3 / Parts 1 and 2 available as a definitive record of what is registered.
- It can help avoid the need to maintain multiple different documents and document repositories to capture what is registered at any point in time.
- Having such 'live' versions of Modules 1, 2 and 3 / Parts 1 and 2 in place can also facilitate communications between the MAH and the manufacturer in relation to what is registered at any point in time.

5.4. Product Quality Reviews (PQRs)

The area of product quality reviews is a topic that is of a direct relevance to MAHs. This is an area in which the GMP Guide is quite prescriptive, in relation to what is expected of the MAH. Chapter 1 of the Guide addresses this topic; and it states the following:

> "The manufacturer and, where different, marketing authorisation holder should evaluate the results of the review and an assessment made as to whether corrective and preventive action or any revalidation should be undertaken, under the Pharmaceutical Quality System. There should be management procedures for the ongoing management and review of these actions and the effectiveness of these procedures verified during self-inspection. Quality reviews may be grouped by product type, e.g. solid dosage forms, liquid dosage forms, sterile products, etc. where scientifically justified." (Ref. Chapter 1, Paragraph 1.11).

The GMP Guide goes on to state that "Where the marketing authorisation holder is not the manufacturer, there should be a technical agreement in place between the various parties that defines their respective responsibilities in producing the product quality review." (Ref. Chapter 1, Paragraph 1.11).

There are several important points in the above text which are useful to consider.

- *The first is a clear obligation on the MAH, when it is not the product manufacturer, to evaluate the results of the PQR and to make an assessment in relation to the need for corrective and preventive actions (CAPAs), and revalidation activities. The text requires both parties to do the above evaluation and assessment work.*
- *The second is the importance that the GMP Guide places on this PQR evaluation and assessment work by both parties. This is evident from the requirement in Chapter 1 to apply oversight to those activities, and in two different ways –ongoing management review and self-inspection processes.*
- *Lastly, it is clear from the reference to a technical agreement above that each party has responsibilities in relation to PQR activities. In the case of the MAH, the primary responsibility is to perform the PQR evaluation and assessment work that is referred to above.*

Given the importance that the GMP Guide attributes to the involvement of both parties in such work, it is not considered appropriate for the MAH to delegate its evaluation and assessment work to the manufacturer. There are several good and risk-based reasons for this.

- Firstly, there is information to be included and evaluated in PQRs which may be spread across both parties, the MAH and the manufacturer, or primarily held by only one. This includes information concerning complaints (and their investigation), as well as quality-related returns, recalls, MA variations (in terms of their status – submitted, granted or refused), and post-marketing commitments.
- Secondly, there are items to be reviewed in a PQR for which both parties may have had different roles. An example here is the product stability data. The MAH may have outsourced the storage and/or testing of the stability samples to a third party, such as a contract laboratory, which is not the product manufacturer, and the results of the testing may be sent to the MAH, and not directly to the manufacturer by the laboratory. In such a situation, the MAH would have an important role in ensuring that the relevant stability data are included in the PQR and that the data are subject to an adequate review.

The evaluation and assessment of such PQR information by both parties (the MAH and the manufacturer) is important in another way too - it can help mitigate two key risks:

(a) The risk of producing PQRs which are incomplete and which are missing important signals, trends and learnings, and
(b) The risk of placing batches of a product on the market which are non-compliant with the requirements of the MA.

For example, the MAH may have information which the manufacturer may not necessarily have about the required implementation date of a MA variation concerning the package leaflet, submitted to update the leaflet with certain new safety information about the product.

The MAH's evaluation and assessment work on the PQR is beneficial because it has the potential to verify compliance with the variation implementation requirements, not only via a review of the variations section of the PQR, but also via a review of the change control section. The manufacturer's review gives a related opportunity, to review the status of approved product artwork-related MA variations which were listed in the PQR by the MAH.

In order for an MAH to add value in relation to its PQR activities, it is considered that its role in relation to PQRs should be different from thoat of the manufacturer. It is recognised that PQRs are documents that are primarily generated by the product manufacturer, not the MAH. Most of the information and data that needs to be included and reviewed in a PQR is firmly in the realm of GMP, and usually resides at manufacturing sites, not at the MAHs. (This includes information relating to change controls, process deviations, rejected batches, critical in-process controls, etc.)

There are several ways in which MAHs may add value in relation to PQRs:

- *The MAH can ensure that information that it holds which is relevant to the PQR is actually included in the PQR. This applies, for example, to information relating to product complaints, which the MAH may have received directly from the marketplace and which may not have been also been sent directly to the manufacturer, as well as information about product recalls, MA variations and other changes, as well as post-marketing commitments. The manufacturer may have some of the above information, but it may not possess all of it, and the MAH can ensure that the contents of the PQR report in these areas are complete.*
- *The MAH can cross-check the information included in the PQR by the manufacturer against its own records, in order to check whether there are any gaps in the data held by the manufacturer which need to be addressed.*
- *The MAH can review the change control section of the PQR to check that changes with a potential impact on regulatory compliance have been adequately managed.*
- *The MAH can ensure that its evaluation of the results of the PQR is focussed on assessing the MA compliance status of the product during the review period, instead of focussing on areas for which the MAH may not have a high level of competency or expertise, such as in relation to analytical method changes, the adequacy of equipment-related corrective actions, and the qualification status of relevant equipment and utilities, e.g. HVAC (heating, ventilation and air conditioning), water, compressed gases, etc.*

Overall, an MAH's involvement in PQR activities provides tangible benefits, and further information in this regard is presented in Section 5.7 below, in relation to *Continual Improvement Activities*.

Experience has shown that, when MAHs are not involved in the evaluation and assessment of PQR data and reports, those PQRs appear to be at greater risk of not complying with the requirements of Chapter 1 of the GMP Guide, and, more importantly, batches in the marketplace may be at greater risk of having MA non-compliances associated with them.

5.5. Quality Defects, Complaints and Product Recalls

Chapter 8 of the GMP Guide deals with the above topics. In many companies, the management of complaints, quality defects and recalls is performed centrally within the organisation, and Chapter 8 makes provision for this. It states that "the relative roles and responsibilities of the concerned parties should be documented" and that such central management "should not result in delays in the investigation and management of the issue." (Ref. Chapter 8, Paragraph 8.4).

MAH CONTACT PERSON

It is considered that the MAH should be satisfied with the centralised arrangements that are in place for handling quality defects, such as within corporate quality groups or at manufacturing site(s). This includes arrangements regarding the contact persons who may communicate quality defect issues to the competent authorities (and the EMA in the case of products authorised via the Centralised Procedure.) Note that a Qualified Person may be designated by the MAH as the contact person. *It is important to also note that the applicant/MAH is expected to have a dedicated responsible person to serve as a contact person for product defects and recalls in the post-authorisation phase – in this regard, the applicant/MAH is expected to provide information on its contact person in the MA-application form (Ref. MA Application Form in Notice to Applicants Volume 2B, Article 6 of Regulation 726/2004, Annex I to Directive 2001/83/EC, Volume 6B of the Notice to Applicants, and Annex II of Regulation 6/2019.)*

Arrangements for Dealing with Quality Defects and Recalls

Chapter 8 places obligations on the MAH, the manufacturer and other parties to define and agree their respective roles and responsibilities with regard to quality defective medicinal products. In this context, the outsourcing of manufacturing and other activities is of relevance here, as outsourcing is often an activity in which the MAH is directly involved.

Chapter 8 also recognises this, stating that "in case of outsourced activities, a contract should describe the role and responsibilities of the manufacturer, the marketing authorisation holder and/or sponsor and any other relevant third parties in relation to assessment, decision-making, and dissemination of information and implementation of risk-reducing actions relating to a defective product." It clarifies that such contracts "should also address how to contact those responsible at each party for the management of quality defect and recall issues. (Ref. Chapter 8, Principle).

NOTIFICATION OF QUALITY DEFECTS TO COMPETENT AUTHORITIES

There are obligations stated in Chapter 8 which relate to the notification of quality defects to the relevant competent authority, and these are linked with the requirement to notify competent authorities of potential supply restrictions and/or product recall as a consequence of quality defect issues. The MAH often has a direct interest in such notification processes, and it is named in Chapter 8 as a party to such notifications. Chapter 8 states that "Quality defects should be reported in a timely manner by the manufacturer to the marketing authorisation holder/sponsor and all concerned Competent Authorities in cases where the quality defect may result in the recall of the product or in an abnormal restriction in the supply of the product." (Ref. Chapter 8, Paragraph 8.15).

QUALITY DEFECTS WITH INVESTIGATIONAL MEDICINAL PRODUCTS

Chapter 8 also addresses situations in which quality defects may occur in investigational medicinal products, and these can also be of relevance to MAHs. The text here states that "In the case of an investigational medicinal product for which a marketing authorisation has been issued, the manufacturer of the investigational medicinal product should, in cooperation with the sponsor, inform the marketing authorisation holder of any quality defect that could be related to the authorised medicinal product." (Ref. Chapter 8, Paragraph 8.24). This requirement is taken directly from Article 13 of GMP Directive 2003/94/EC for medicinal products and investigational medicinal products for human use, which carries almost identical wording. (Note that there is no equivalent article in the GMP Directive for veterinary medicines.)

POTENTIALLY FALSIFIED MEDICINES & REPORTING REQUIREMENTS

With regard to medicinal products for human use, the Falsified Medicines Directive (FMD), 2011/62/EU, discussed in detail in Section 6, placed specific reporting obligations on manufacturers in relation to products suspected of being falsified. This is relevant to the topic of quality defects, complaints and recalls, as falsified medicines are considered defective medicines and they can lead to recall actions.

In amending Directive 2001/83/EC with the addition of Article 46 (g), the FMD Directive introduced a responsibility for the manufacturer to inform the competent authority and the MAH immediately of information which indicates that a medicinal product within the scope of its manufacturing authorisation is, or is suspected of being, falsified. (This is required irrespective of whether the medicinal product was distributed within the legal supply chain or by illegal means, including illegal sale via information society services.)

The above responsibilities imply that the MAH should have a system in place to receive such quality defect and product falsification reports from manufacturers and it should be able to respond to them in a manner that is appropriate. This is also linked with the requirements of the EU pharmacovigilance legislation, by which the MAH is obliged to have systems in place to deal with adverse reaction reports.

PRODUCT RECALL MANAGEMENT

The management of product recalls is a specific area of importance for the MAH to have robust procedures in. This is because the MAH is usually heavily involved in recall decision making with the national competent authorities and in the coordination of recalls, when they are required. Chapter 8 states that the "effectiveness of the arrangements in place for recalls should be periodically evaluated to confirm that they remain robust and fit for use." It requires such evaluations to "extend to both within office-hour situations as well as out-of-office hour situations" and, when performing such evaluations, it requires consideration to be given "as to whether mock-recall actions should be performed." It also requires such evaluations to be "documented and justified." (Ref. Chapter 8, Paragraph 8.30).

Each of these requirements is applicable to the MAH, given the MAH's role in recall decision making, coordination and management, and it is important that the MAH has systems in place to deal with these activities.

OTHER NOTIFICATION RESPONSIBILITIES

Directive 2001/83/EC also contains provisions in this area that concern the MAH. Article 123 of the Directive, for example, places an obligation upon the MAH to "notify the Member States concerned forthwith of any action taken by the MAH to suspend the marketing of a medicinal product, to withdraw a medicinal product from the market, to request the withdrawal of a marketing authorisation or not to apply for the renewal of a marketing authorisation, together with the reasons for such action." (Ref. Directive 2001/83/EC, Article 123).

Note that, in relation to veterinary medicinal products, Regulation 2019/6 contains a similar (but not identical) provision. It states: "The marketing authorisation holder shall record in the product database the dates when its authorised veterinary medicinal products are placed on the market, information on the availability for each veterinary medicinal product in each relevant Member State and, as applicable, the dates of any suspension or revocation of the marketing authorisations concerned. [...] The marketing authorisation holder shall without delay inform the competent authority which has granted the marketing authorisation or the Commission, as applicable, of any prohibition or restriction imposed by a competent authority or by an authority of a third country and of any other new information which might influence the assessment of the benefits and risks of the veterinary medicinal product concerned, including from the outcome of the signal management process carried out in accordance with Article 81. [...] The marketing authorisation holder shall without delay inform the competent authority which has granted the marketing authorisation, or the Commission, as applicable, of any action which the holder intends to take in order to cease the marketing of a veterinary medicinal product prior to taking such action, together with the reasons for such action.." (Ref. Regulation 2019/6, Articles 58 (6), (10) and (13)).

Article 123 of Directive 2001/83/EC also requires the MAH to declare if such action is based on any of the grounds set out in Article 116 or Article 117(1). These articles relate to situations in which a view is taken by Member States that "the medicinal product is harmful or that it lacks therapeutic efficacy, or that the risk-benefit balance is not favourable, or that its qualitative and quantitative composition is not as declared." They also relate to situations in which "the controls on the medicinal product and/or on the ingredients and the controls at an intermediate stage of the manufacturing process have not been carried out or if some other requirement or obligation relating to the grant of the manufacturing authorisation has not been fulfilled."

5.6. Maintenance of Supply of Medicinal Products

THE MAH'S OBLIGATION TO ENSURE CONTINUED SUPPLY

The EU medicines legislation, as well as the GMP Guide, place obligations upon the MAH that relate to the supply of its medicinal products and to the maintenance of such supply. For example, Article 81 of Directive 2001/83/EC states the following:

> "The holder of a marketing authorisation for a medicinal product and the distributors of the said medicinal product actually placed on the market in a Member State shall, within the limits of their responsibilities, ensure appropriate and continued supplies of that medicinal product to pharmacies and persons authorised to supply medicinal products so that the needs of patients in the Member State in question are covered."

For veterinary medicinal products, Regulation 2019/6 (Article 58 (2)) states the following:

"The marketing authorisation holder shall, within the limits of its responsibilities, ensure appropriate and continued supplies of its veterinary medicinal products."

This directly relates to the avoidance of medicines shortages for patients and animals.

It is considered that MAHs should also comply with any national requirements that may exist within the EEA in relation to maintaining product supply.

REPORTING SUPPLY RESTRICTIONS AND PROBLEMS

In addition, in accordance with Chapter 5 of the GMP Guide, the MAH has a responsibility to report restrictions in supply to the relevant competent authorities. In this regard, the MAH may have to rely upon the manufacturer to notify it of potential supply problems. Chapter 5 states that "The manufacturer should report to the marketing authorisation holder (MAH) any constraints in manufacturing operations which may result in abnormal restriction in the supply. This should be done in a timely manner to facilitate reporting of the restriction in supply by the MAH, to the relevant competent authorities, in accordance with its legal obligations." (Ref. Chapter 5, Paragraph 5.71)

It is useful to consider what actions may be taken by the MAH in order to minimise the impact on patients as a result of potential supply issues with their medicines.

- *At a starting point, it is considered that the MAH should ensure that the communication arrangements between it and the manufacturer on potential supply issues are agreed and clearly documented in a technical agreement between the parties.*
- *Where the two companies are part of the same overall organisation, the specific details in relation to how the communications processes are intended to work at a practical level may be documented in SOPs, as long as those SOPs are approved by both parties and as long as they are referred to within the technical agreement between the parties.*
- *In addition to information from the internal supply chain, alerts on supply problems issued by e.g. wholesalers, pharmacies and hospitals should also be considered by the MAH.*
- *This can help the MAH fulfil its notification obligations to the relevant competent authorities. (Note: The MAH may delegate tasks regarding such notification obligations concerning supply issues to the local affiliate in a member state.)*

There is European legislation in place which governs the notification of supply issues to the competent authorities. If the product ceases to be placed on the market of a Member State, either temporarily or permanently, the MAH is required, via Article 23a of Directive 2001/83/EC, to notify the competent authority of that Member State. The Directive requires that such notifications shall, "other than in exceptional circumstances, be made no less than two months before the interruption in the placing on the market of the product."

The MAH is also required to inform the competent authority of the reasons for such action in accordance with Article 123(2) of the Directive. This article requires the MAH to notify the Member States concerned forthwith "of any action taken by the MAH to suspend the marketing of a medicinal product, to withdraw a medicinal product from the market, to request the withdrawal of a marketing authorisation or not to apply for the renewal of a marketing authorisation, together with the reasons for such action."

Note that, in relation to veterinary medicinal products, Regulation 2019/6 (Article 58(13)) contains a similar (but not identical) provision. It states: "The marketing authorisation holder shall without delay inform the competent authority which has granted the marketing authorisation or the Commission, as applicable, of any action which the holder intends to take in order to cease the marketing of a veterinary medicinal product prior to taking such action, together with the reasons for such action."

POSSIBLE REASONS FOR SUPPLY DISRUPTIONS – COMPLEXITY, OUTSOURCING & OTHER FACTORS

There is a variety of factors that may lead to disruptions of supply chains and product shortages for patients and animals. The globalisation of manufacturing and distribution activities is one such factor; it has contributed to the current situation in which many medicinal products are associated with highly complex supply chains, and this level of complexity gives rise to increased risks of problems arising in those supply chains. These can be difficult to resolve in a timely manner, because coupled with this is the added complexity that extensive outsourcing of manufacturing operations brings. Taken together, they can result in long lead times in manufacturing when crisis situations in the supply of medicines occur.

There are many factors which can lead to product supply issues, and these can be quite diverse, ranging from, for example, a lack of robustness in the supply chain of the active substance, to the poor management of MA transfers between companies, resulting in the correct product artwork not being available in a timely manner following such transfers. The movement of manufacturing processes between two sites can also be a factor if it is not planned and managed adequately, especially where there are tight logistics associated with the manufacturing and supply chain activities.

PREVENTION OF PRODUCT SHORTAGES

It is, therefore, important for MAHs to be proactive in their approach to supply chain management, in order to try and prevent product shortages and to meet the obligation as set out in Article 81 of Directive 2001/83/ EC and Article 58 of Regulation 2019/6. In this regard, it is recommended that MAHs carry out, in line with quality risk management principles, proactive and detailed risk assessments of their manufacturing, regulatory and supply chain processes, and to work to address any identified weaknesses in those areas. A number of useful industry guidance documents on preventing (and reacting to) shortages of medicinal products have been published (e.g. by the ISPE and PDA) and these documents provide useful guidance for MAHs in this area. Note that in addition to proactively preventing shortages, MAHs are encouraged also to have a risk management protocol in place, should a supply disruption occur, to mitigate its impact.

It is worth noting that the ICH Guideline on Quality Risk Management (Q9) refers to product availability risks, and in that context, it links such risks with the potential for patient harm. This is an important point to take account of when working to prevent and mitigate the risks of medicines shortages.

5.7. Continual Improvement Activities

Guidance on the need for continual improvement activities was introduced into the GMP Guide in 2013, when Chapter 1 was revised to align it with the concepts and terminology described in the ICH Q10 tripartite guideline on the *Pharmaceutical Quality System.*

Chapter 1 states that a Pharmaceutical Quality System appropriate for the manufacture of medicinal products should ensure that "Continual improvement is facilitated through the implementation of quality improvements appropriate to the current level of process and product knowledge" (Ref. Chapter 1, Paragraph 1.4(xi)). This is relevant to the MAH in several ways, including PQR activities, where the MAH's involvement in PQRs provides tangible benefits.

For example, the responsibility that the MAH has to evaluate the results of PQRs provides it with process and product knowledge which it may not have had before then. This can help the MAH identify, with its manufacturing site partners, the need for specific continual improvement activities to be initiated.

PQR data can also enable the MAH to identify the need for improvement in its own regulatory affairs processes that operate in conjunction with the manufacturing sites. Examples here include the management of MA variations (relating to CTD Module 3 / Notice to Applicants Part 2) of the MA dossier, the support that the MAH provides manufacturing sites in relation to site change control activities (via the provision of regulatory impact assessments for specific change control proposals), amongst others.

SCIENTIFIC ADVANCES

The concept of continual improvement in medicines manufacturing is related to advances in science. Articles 23 and 58 (3) of Directive 2001/83/EC and Regulation 2019/6, respectively, require MAHs to maintain MAs in line with scientific advances. Article 23 states that, after an authorisation has been issued, "the authorisation holder must, in respect of the methods of manufacture and control" provided for in the marketing authorisation application, take account of "scientific and technical progress and introduce any changes that may be required to enable the medicinal product to be manufactured and checked by means of generally accepted scientific methods". Article 58 (3) of the Veterinary Regulation has similar wording.

- *The above requirements place a responsibility on the MAH to work with the manufacturing sites in order to incorporate generally accepted scientific methods into the registered methods of manufacture and the registered controls.*
- *The MAH also has the responsibility to ensure that any variation applications which may be required in light of the above changes, are submitted to keep the marketing authorisation up-to-date.*
- *This means that, for the manufacturing process, the process description as included in CTD Module 3 / Notice to Applicants Part 2 should be updated, where necessary, to include sufficient details according to current guidelines. In some cases, consideration should also be given to updating the manufacturing process itself.*

It is considered also that, with regard to Article 23 of Directive 2001/83/EC and Article 58 (3) of Regulation 2019/6, a company's internal manufacturing documents which describe the manufacturing process should be kept updated in light of scientific and technical progress and that they contain sufficiently detailed information so as to ensure that key manufacturing details are not lost when site transfers occur.

Regarding updates to the methods of control, the MAH is required to ensure that material and product specifications registered in the MA include tests according to the current pharmacopoeia and quality guidelines, and analytical methods should be able to detect/quantify relevant impurities to ICH and VICH thresholds.

In cases where a Ph. Eur. monograph is revised in line with scientific advances to control an active substance, it can be useful for an MAH to work with the manufacturing sites and consider the need for early testing of the substance in question according to the draft revised monograph, and to submit comments on the draft monograph to the EDQM, if necessary. Such activities involving the MAH and manufacturer could be described in a technical agreement.

OTHER REFERENCES TO CONTINUAL IMPROVEMENT

There are other references to continual improvement in the GMP Guide also which have relevance for the MAH. For example, Chapter 7, on Outsourcing, states that "the Contract Giver should monitor and review the performance of the Contract Acceptor and the identification and implementation of any needed improvement" (Ref. Chapter 7, Paragraph 7.7). *This places a responsibility upon the MAH to perform such review and monitoring activities in cases when it is a contact giver for an outsourced operation involving medicines manufacturing. It is considered that part of this responsibility may be fulfilled through an MAH's evaluation and assessment of the results of PQRs, as PQR data can be indicative of the performance of a manufacturer in the manufacture of a product.*

UPDATING MANUFACTURING PROCESSES IN LINE WITH CHANGES TO THE EU GMP GUIDE

Finally, it is important to note that the MAH has some responsibility in ensuring that updates to the GMP guide are incorporated at manufacturing site level. This is because, in Directive 2001/83/EC, Annex I, it is stated that "the manufacturing process shall comply with the requirements of Directive 91/356/EEC [since replaced in 2003 by Directive 2003/94/EC] laying down the principles and guidelines of GMP for medicinal products for human use and with the principles and guidelines on GMP, published by the Commission in the rules governing medicinal products in the EC, Volume 4." (It is noted that the Veterinary Regulation 2019/6 has similar wording in *Annex I and Annex II*.)

The above relates to the manufacturing process as described in the MA, and as it is the MAH who seeks to register the manufacturing process in the dossier, the above Annex I requirement places an obligation upon the MAH to ensure that the registered manufacturing process is in line with current GMP guidance. This is relevant in the context of continual improvement, because the GMP Guide undergoes periodic improvement activities itself.

6. Falsified Medicines Directive (FMD)-related Responsibilities

In relation to medicinal products for human use, where applicable, the MAH has a number of responsibilities related to the Falsified Medicines Directive (FMD) 2011/62/EU and the related Delegated Regulations (including the Safety Features Regulation 2016/161). One of those responsibilities, as discussed in Section 5.2 of this Reflection Paper (Audits & Qualification Activities), relates to the need to confirm the GMP status of the active substance manufacturer by means of GMP audits. This responsibility is stated in Article 8(ha) of Directive 2001/83/EC, which originated in the FMD Directive.

SAFETY FEATURES

Other FMD-related responsibilities concern safety features on product packaging:

- Commission Delegated Regulation (EU) 2016/161 sets out what is expected of the MAH in relation to the upload to the repositories system of pack serialisation data, as well as responsibilities in relation to the decommissioning of pack serialisation codes.
- Article 33 of this Regulation requires the MAH to ensure that the information of unique identifier and various additional defined data about the medicinal product and its distribution are "uploaded to the repositories system before the medicinal product is released for sale or distribution by the manufacturer, and that it is kept up to date thereafter." (Note that the Q&A Document on the Commission's Website provides additional guidance in this area – see Q&A 4.5.)

It is considered that the QP who certifies batches prior to their release to the market should be satisfied with the arrangements that have been put in place by the MAH for the upload of the safety features data to the repositories system. (In relation to QP responsibilities in this general area, it is useful to note that Annex 16 to the GMP Guide places a responsibility on the QP to ensure that the following point is secured, that:

> "In the case of medicinal products for human use intended to be placed on the market in the Union, the safety features referred to in Article 54(o) of Directive 2001/83/EC, as amended, have been affixed to the packaging, where appropriate." (Ref. Annex 16, Paragraph 1.7.21).
>
> Annex 16 indicates that this task may be delegated to "appropriately trained personnel or third parties", and in this regard, the Annex recognises that the QP will "need to rely on the pharmaceutical quality system" that is in place and it requires the QP to have "on-going assurance that this reliance is well founded". (Ref. Annex 16, Paragraph 1.7.)

It is considered that the transfer of the unique identifier (UI) data from the location where they were generated until their upload to the European Hub is performed in a secure manner and in such as a way that the integrity of data is not compromised.

THE REPOSITORIES SYSTEM & MAH RESPONSIBILITIES

The repositories system is expected to be established and managed by the MAHs (Ref. Paragraph 28 of the preamble text of Delegated Regulation

(EU) 2016/161). Article 32 of the Delegated Regulation sets out the required structure of the repositories system – there should be a central information and data router (known as the European Hub) and repositories which serve the territory of one or multiple Member States. Those repositories are required to be connected to the EU-Hub. The European Medicines Verification Organisation (EMVO) is the organisation representing stakeholders who have taken responsibility for the formation of the European Medicines Verification System (EMVS/EU-Hub).

Each EU Member State is expected to implement a National Medicines Verification System (NMVS) which will be set up and managed by a National Medicines Verification Organisation (NMVO). The MAHs are expected to liaise with both the EMVO and the relevant NMVOs for the concerned products.

Various items of information are required to be uploaded to the repositories system, including:

- The data elements of the unique identifier;
- The coding scheme of the product code;
- The name and the common name of the medicinal product, the pharmaceutical form, the strength, the pack type and the pack size;
- The Member State or Member States where the medicinal product is intended to be placed on the market;
- The name and address of the manufacturer placing the safety features;
- A list of wholesalers who are designated by the MAH, by means of a written contract, to store and distribute the products covered by the marketing authorisation on his behalf.

This and other information is intended to be stored in all of the national or supranational repositories serving the territory of the Member State, or Member States, where the medicinal product bearing the UI is intended to be placed on the market for at least one year after the expiry date of the medicinal product, or five years after the product has been released for sale or distribution, whichever is longer. The same responsibility applies to persons responsible for placing parallel imported or parallel distributed medicinal products onto the market.

SERIALISATION DATA - UPLOADING RESPONSIBILITIES

The MAH may delegate the uploading of the information laid down in Article 33(2) to a third party; such delegation is expected to be documented in a written agreement between both parties. It is important to note that the MAH may subcontract, or delegate, data uploading only to parties which perform the data upload by means of infrastructure, hardware and software, which is physically located within the EEA. Importantly, the MAH remains legally responsible for such tasks, as stated in the document titled

'Safety Features For Medicinal Products For Human Use; Questions And Answers', available on the European Commission's website.

In relation to Contract Manufacturing Organisations (CMOs), these will not be permitted to on-board to the EU-Hub, and it is considered that the relevant MAH needs to ensure that appropriate arrangements are put in place in this regard, in order to ensure the secure upload of the serialisation data.

UNIQUE IDENTIFIER DECOMMISSIONING RESPONSIBILITIES

In relation to decommissioning, which is a term that relates to various pack statuses within the repositories, including the pack status called 'supplied', it is an MAH responsibility according to Article 40 of the Delegated Regulation to ensure the decommissioning of pack codes in the case of a product recall or withdrawal. Article 40 states that "the marketing authorisation holder shall promptly take all the following measures:

(a) ensure the decommissioning of the unique identifier of a medicinal product which is to be recalled or withdrawn, in every national or supranational repository serving the territory of the Member State or Member States in which the recall or the withdrawal is to take place;

(b) ensure the decommissioning of the unique identifier, where known, of a medicinal product which has been stolen, in every national or supranational repository in which information on that product is stored;

(c) indicate in the repositories referred to in points (a) and (b) that that product has been recalled or withdrawn or stolen, where applicable."

The same responsibility applies to persons responsible for placing parallel imported or parallel distributed medicinal products onto the market.

It is worth noting that "decommissioned" as such is not a status in the system; multiple statuses that are different from "active" have been developed in the EMVS by EMVO, such as "RECALLED", "DESTROYED" or "STOLEN". All of these are considered as "decommissioned".

For the above responsibilities to be met by the MAH, it is considered that there should be robust communication systems in place between the MAH and the manufacturer (or other third party) to whom such tasks have been delegated. This is because the various data elements that must be uploaded to the repositories system may be held by the different entities – the manufacturer will likely hold the actual pack serialisation codes per batch, while the MAH may hold the information about the wholesalers which have been designated by it to store and distribute the product, as well as information about the distribution of free medical samples and about product recall actions.

7. Conclusion

The EU Guide to GMP refers in several places to MAH companies and their responsibilities in relation to GMP. Such responsibilities are spread over various chapters and annexes of the Guide, and are quite numerous. There are also various GMP-related responsibilities for MAHs stated in applicable medicines legislation. There appears, however, to be a lack of clarity and understanding as to what these responsibilities actually are in their totality, and what they mean for MAHs, especially at a practical level. Thus, it was considered that it would be of benefit to MAHs (and also to manufacturers, GMP Inspectors and other stakeholders) if these responsibilities were documented in one place and adequately explained. This Reflection Paper seeks to address this.

While it is recognised that many MAH companies are not directly engaged in the manufacture of medicinal products themselves, GMP is an area that has direct relevance for them. Indeed, it is of interest that the GMP Guide states the following: "…the ultimate responsibility for the performance of a medicinal product over its lifetime, its safety, quality and efficacy, lies with the marketing authorisation holder". A significant part of the performance of a medicinal product relates to compliance with the GMP requirements during product manufacturing.

This Reflection Paper sets out what the various responsibilities for MAHs are and it seeks to explain their practical implications. It essentially seeks to present a more complete picture of the regulatory environment with respect to GMP in which the MAH operates. It groups the responsibilities under a number of different *themes*; this is in an effort to illustrate the general areas in which the responsibilities lie, and to provide a holistic view of them. It is intended that this Reflection Paper will provide increased clarity for MAHs in this area, and that it will serve as a useful resource for MAHs when designing (or reviewing) their internal systems as well as their interactions with manufacturing sites.

Overall, this Reflection Paper is intended to be of assistance to MAHs as they work with the product manufacturers and other stakeholders to facilitate compliance of the medicines placed on the market, in terms of GMP and the MA. This ultimately serves the interests of patients and animals, as it contributes to ensuring the availability of high quality, safe and effective medicines.

8. References

The Rules Governing Medicinal Products in the European Union Volume 4 Good Manufacturing Practice Medicinal Products for Human and Veterinary Use https://ec.europa.eu/health/documents/eudralex/vol-4_en

The Rules Governing Medicinal Products in the European Union Volume 2B Presentation and Content of the Dossier (Human Medicinal Products) https://ec.europa.eu/health/sites/default/files/files/eudralex/vol-2/b/update_200805/ctd_05-2008_en.pdf

The Rules Governing Medicinal Products in the European Union Volume 6B Presentation and Content of Application Dossier (Veterinary Medicinal Products)

https://ec.europa.eu/health/sites/default/files/files/eudralex/vol-6/b/nta_volume_6b_2015_.pdf

Directive 2001/83/EC of the European Parliament and of the Council of 6 November 2001 on the Community code relating to medicinal products for human use. (Consolidated version : 16/11/2012) http://eur-lex.europa.eu/legal-content/EN/TXT/PDF/?uri=CELEX:02001L0083-20121116&qid=1472567249742&from=EN

https://ec.europa.eu/health/sites/health/files/files/eudralex/vol-1/dir_2001_83_consol_2012/dir_2001_83_cons_2012_en.pdf

Regulation (EU) 2019/6 of the European Parliament and of the Council of 11 December 2018 on veterinary medicinal products and repealing Directive 2001/82/EC. https://eur-lex.europa.eu/legal-content/EN/TXT/PDF/?uri=CELEX:32019R0006&from=EN

Commission Directive 2003/94/EC of 8 October 2003 laying down the principles and guidelines of good manufacturing practice in respect of medicinal products for human use and investigational medicinal products for human use

http://eur-lex.europa.eu/LexUriServ/LexUriServ.do?uri=OJ:L:2003:262:0022:0026:en:PDF

Directive 1991/412/EEC of 23 July 1991 laying down the principles and guidelines of good manufacturing practice for veterinary medicinal products

https://ec.europa.eu/health//sites/health/files/files/eudralex/vol-5/dir_1991_412/dir_1991_412_en.pdf

Commission Directive (EU) 2017/1572 of 15 September 2017 supplementing Directive 2001/83/EC of the European Parliament and of the Council as regards the principles and guidelines of good manufacturing practice for medicinal products for human use

https://eur-lex.europa.eu/eli/dir/2017/1572/oj

Directive 2011/62/EU of the European Parliament and of the Council of 8 June 2011 amending Directive 2001/83/EC on the Community code relating to medicinal products for human use, as regards the prevention of the entry into the legal supply chain of falsified medicinal products

http://eur-lex.europa.eu/LexUriServ/LexUriServ.do?uri=OJ:L:2011:174:0074:0087:EN:PDF

Commission Delegated Regulation (EU) No 2016/161 of 2 October 2015 supplementing Directive 2001/83/EC of the European Parliament and of the Council by laying down detailed rules for the safety features appearing on the packaging of medicinal products for human use (OJ L 32, 9.2.2016, p. 1-27)

https://ec.europa.eu/health/sites/health/files/files/eudralex/vol-1/reg_2016_161/reg_2016_161_en.pdf

European Medicines Agency: EMA/196292/2014; Guidance for the template for the qualified person's declaration concerning GMP compliance of active substance manufacture "The QP declaration template"

http://www.ema.europa.eu/docs/en_GB/document_library/Regulatory_and_procedural_guideline/2014/06/WC500167852.pdf

ICH Q10, Pharmaceutical Quality System, dated 4 June 2008

http://www.ich.org/fileadmin/Public_Web_Site/ICH_Products/Guidelines/Quality/Q10/Step4/Q10_Guideline.pdf

Final Concept Paper on ICH Q12: Technical and Regulatory Considerations for Pharmaceutical Product Lifecycle Management, dated 28 July 2014, Endorsed by the ICH Steering Committee on 9 September 2014

http://www.ich.org/fileadmin/Public_Web_Site/ICH_Products/Guidelines/Quality/Q12/Q12_Final_Concept_Paper_July_2014.pdf

ICH Q12, Technical and Regulatory Considerations for Pharmaceutical Product Lifecycle Management, adopted 20 November 2019

https://database.ich.org/sites/default/files/Q12_Guideline_Step4_2019_1119.pdf

Veterinary ICH Impurities Guidelines

http://www.vichsec.org/guidelines/pharmaceuticals/pharma-quality/impurities.html

PDA Technical Report No. 68 titled *Risk-based Approach for Prevention and Management of Drug Shortages*, January 2015, available at https://store.pda.org/ProductCatalog/

ISPE Drug Shortages Prevention Plan, A Holistic View from Root Cause to Prevention, October 2014

https://www.ispe.org/sites/default/files/initiatives/drug-shortages/drug-shortages-prevention-plan.pdf

Prevention of Drug Shortages Based on Quality and Manufacturing Issues, Final report by the inter-associations team with representatives from EFPIA / EGA / AESGP / PPTA, ISPE, and PDA, 23/12/2014

https://ispe.org/sites/default/files/initiatives/drug-shortages/prevention-drug-shortages-report-ema.pdf

Guidelines of 5 November 2013 on Good Distribution Practice of medicinal products for human

(Text with EEA relevance) 2013/C 343/01

http://eur-lex.europa.eu/legal-content/EN/TXT/?uri=uriserv:OJ.C_
.2013.343.01.0001.01.ENG&toc=OJ:C:2013:343:TOC
Compliance Management Procedure - *to be inserted once available*

9. List of Abbreviations

ATMP	Advanced Therapy Medicinal Products
ASMF	Active Substance Master File
CTD	Common Technical Document
CAPA	Corrective Actions and Preventive Actions
CEP	Certificate of Suitability to the monographs of the European Pharmacopoeia
CHMP	Committee for Medicinal Products for Human use
CMO	Contract Manufacturing Organisation
EC	European Commission
EDQM	European Directorate for the Quality of Medicines
EMA	European Medicines Agency
EEA	European Economic Area
EMVO	European Medicines Verification Organisation
EMVS	European

EudraGMDP - the name for the Union database referred to in article 111(6) of Directive 2001/83/EC and article 80(6) of Directive 2001/82/EC

EUDRA	European Union Drug Regulatory Authority
FMD	Falsified Medicines Directive (2011/62/EU)
GDP	Good Distribution Practice
GMP	Good Manufacturing Practice
GMDP	Good Manufacturing Practice / Good Distribution Practice
HVAC	Heating, Ventilation and Air Conditioning
ISPE	International Society for Pharmaceutical Engineering
ICH	International Council for Harmonisation of Technical Requirements for Pharmaceuticals for Human Use
MA	Marketing Authorisation
MAA	Marketing Authorisation Application
MAH	Marketing Authorisation Holder
MIA	Manufacturing and Importation Authorisation
NMVS	National Medicines Verification System
NMVO	National Medicines Verification Organisation
PDA	Parenteral Drug Association
PQR	Product Quality Review
QP	Qualified Person

PQS   Pharmaceutical Quality System
QMS   Quality Management System
RH   Registration Holder
RP   Responsible Person
SOP   Standard Operating Procedure
TRH   Traditional-use Registration Holder
UI   Unique Identifier

PART IV: Guidelines on Good Manufacturing Practice Specific to Advanced Therapy Medicinal Products

EU GMP GUIDE PART IV

Editor's note   These Guidelines are specific to ATMPs.
    ATMP manufacturers should comply with these Guidelines and relevant
    paragraphs of Part I of the GMP guide.
    In addition, Annex 2A* of PIC/S GMP also provides further advice on GMP
    standards for advanced therapies, on GMP principles and also specific
    process controls such as those for vectors.
    *PIC/S Annex 2A: https//picscheme.org/docview/2231.

1   Introduction

1.1   Scope

1.10   Compliance with good manufacturing practice (GMP) is mandatory for
all medicinal products that have been granted a marketing authorisation.
Likewise, the manufacture of investigational medicinal products must be
in accordance with GMP. Advanced therapy medicinal products (ATMPs)
that are administered to patients under Article 3(7) of Directive 2001/83/
EC[1] (so-called "hospital exemption") must be manufactured under equivalent quality standards to the manufacturing of advanced therapy medicinal products with a marketing authorisation.

---

[1] Directive 2001/83/EC of the European Parliament and the Council of 6
November 2001 on the Community code relating to medicinal products for
human use, 2001 OJ L 311/67.

1.11   Article 5 of Regulation (EC) No 1394/2007[2] mandates the Commission to draw up guidelines on GMP specific to advanced therapy medicinal products ("ATMPs"). Article 63(1) of Regulation (EU) No 536/2014[3] also empowers the Commission to adopt and publish detailed guidelines on good manufacturing practice applicable to investigational medicinal products.

1.12   These Guidelines develop the GMP requirements that should be applied in the manufacturing of ATMPs that have been granted a marketing authorisation and of ATMPs used in a clinical trial setting. These Guidelines do not apply to medicinal products other than ATMPs. In turn, the detailed guidelines referred to in the second paragraph of Article 47 of Directive 2001/83/EC[4] and Article 63(1) of Regulation (EU) No 536/2014 do not apply to ATMPs, unless specific reference thereto is made in these Guidelines.

1.13   Throughout these Guidelines, the term "ATMP" should be understood as referring to both advanced therapy medicinal products that have been granted a marketing authorisation, and advanced therapy medicinal products that are being tested or used as reference in a clinical trial (i.e. advanced therapy investigational medicinal products). When specific provisions are relevant for only advanced therapy medicinal products that have been granted a marketing authorisation, the term "authorised ATMPs" is used. When specific provisions are only relevant for advanced therapy investigational medicinal products, the term "investigational ATMPs" is used.

1.14   No provision in these Guidelines (including the risk-based approach) can be regarded as derogation to the terms of the marketing authorisation or clinical trial authorisation. It is noted, however, that non-substantial amendments can be made to the procedures and information stated in the investigational medicinal product dossier without the prior agreement of the competent authorities[5]. Throughout this document, the term "clinical trial authorisation" should be understood also to include non-substantial amendments that have been made to the investigational medicinal product dossier.

---

[2] Regulation (EC) No 1394/2007 of the European Parliament and the Council of 13 November 2007 on advanced therapy medicinal products and amending Directive 2001/83/EC and Regulation (EC) No. 726/2004 (OJ L 324, 10.12.2007, p. 121).

[3] Regulation (EU) No 536/2014 of the European Parliament and the Council of 16 April 2014 on clinical trials on medicinal products for human use, and repealing Directive 2001/20/EC (OJ L 158, 27.5.2014, p. 1).

[4] Guidelines published in Volume 4, EudraLex (https://ec.europa.eu/health/documents/eudralex/vol-4_en).

[5] Regulation (EU) No 536/2014.

1.15 These Guidelines do not intend to place any restrain on the development of new concepts of new technologies. While this document describes the standard expectations, alternative approaches may be implemented by manufacturers if it is demonstrated that the alternative approach is capable of meeting the same objective. Any adaptation applied must be compatible with the need to ensure the quality, safety, efficacy and traceability of the product. Additionally, it is stressed that the terms of the marketing/clinical trial authorisation should be complied with.

ROLE OF MARKETING AUTHORISATION HOLDER/SPONSOR

1.16 For the manufacturer to be able to comply with GMP, cooperation between the manufacturer and the marketing authorisation holder (or, in the case of investigational ATMPs, the manufacturer and the sponsor) is necessary.

1.17 The manufacturer should comply with the specifications and instructions provided by the sponsor/marketing authorisation holder. It is the responsibility of the sponsor/marketing authorisation holder to ensure that the specifications/instructions submitted to the manufacturer are in accordance with the terms of the clinical trial authorisation/marketing authorisation. Variations thereto should be notified immediately.

1.18 It is important that marketing authorisation holders/sponsors communicate swiftly to the manufacturer any information that is relevant to the manufacturing process, as well as any information that may have an impact on the quality, safety and efficacy of the medicinal product (e.g. history of cell line). The communication of the relevant information should be exhaustive.

1.19 In turn, manufacturers should inform the marketing authorisation holder/sponsor of any information that is gathered in the context of the manufacturing activities and that is relevant for the quality, safety or efficacy of the medicinal product.

1.20 The obligations of the marketing authorisation/sponsor holder and the manufacturer and vis-à-vis each other should be defined in writing. In the case of investigational products, the agreement between the sponsor and the manufacturer should specifically provide for the sharing of inspection reports and exchange of information on quality issues.

1.2 General principles

1.21 Quality plays a major role in the safety and efficacy profile of ATMPs. It is the responsibility of the ATMP manufacturer to ensure that appropriate measures are put in place to safeguard the quality of the product (so-called "pharmaceutical quality system").

PHARMACEUTICAL QUALITY SYSTEM

1.22 "Pharmaceutical quality system" means the total sum of the arrangements made with the objective of ensuring that medicinal products are of the quality required for their intended use.

1.23 The size of the company and complexity of the activities should be taken into consideration when designing a pharmaceutical quality system. Senior management should be actively involved to ensure the effectiveness of the pharmaceutical quality system. Although some aspects may be company-wide, the effectiveness of the pharmaceutical quality system is normally demonstrated at site level.

1.24 Compliance with Good Manufacturing Practice (GMP) is an essential part of the pharmaceutical quality system. In particular, through the pharmaceutical quality system it should be ensured that:

(i) the personnel are adequately trained and there is clear allocation of responsibilities;

(ii) the premises and equipment are suitable for the intended use and there is appropriate maintenance thereof;

(iii) there is an adequate documentation system that ensures that appropriate specifications are laid down for materials, intermediates, bulk products and the finished product, that the production process is clearly understood and that appropriate records are kept;

(iv) the manufacturing process is adequate to ensure consistent production (appropriate to the relevant stage of development), the quality of the product and the compliance thereof with the relevant specifications;

(v) there is a quality control system, which is operationally independent from production;

(vi) arrangements are in place for the prospective evaluation of planned changes and their approval prior to implementation taking into account regulatory requirements (i.e. variations procedure in the case of authorised ATMPs, or authorisation procedure of a substantial modification of a clinical trial in the case of investigational ATMPs), and for the evaluation of changes implemented;

(vii) quality defects and process deviations are identified as soon as possible, the causes investigated, and appropriate corrective and/or preventive measures are taken; and

(viii) adequate systems are implemented to ensure traceability of the ATMPs and of their starting and critical raw materials.

1.25 A continuous assessment of the effectiveness of the quality assurance system is important. The results of parameters identified as a quality attribute or as critical should be trended and checked to make sure that they are consistent with each other. The manufacturer should conduct self-inspections as part of the pharmaceutical quality system in order to monitor the implementation and respect of good manufacturing practice and to propose any necessary corrective measures and/or preventive actions. Records should be maintained of such self-inspections and any corrective actions subsequently taken.

1.26 In the case of authorised ATMPs, quality reviews should be conducted annually to verify the adequacy and consistency of the existing processes, to highlight any trends and identify opportunities for product and/or process improvements. The extent of the quality reviews should be determined by the volume of the manufactured products and whether there have been changes introduced to the manufacturing process (i.e. the quality review needs to be more extensive when a high number of lots/high product quantity has been produced than in case of low number of lots/low product quantity; the quality review should also be more extensive when changes in the manufacturing process have been introduced during a given year than when no changes have been made). Quality reviews may be grouped by product type where scientifically justified.

1.27 The manufacturer and, when it is a different legal entity, the marketing authorisation holder should evaluate the results of the review and assess whether corrective and/or preventive actions are required.

2 Risk-based Approach

2.1 Introduction

2.10 ATMPs are complex products and risks may differ according to the type of product, nature/characteristics of the starting materials and level of complexity of the manufacturing process. It is also acknowledged that the finished product may entail some degree of variability due to the use of biological materials and/or complex manipulation steps (e.g. cultivation of cells, manipulations that alter the function of the cells, etc.). In addition, the manufacture and testing of autologous ATMPs (and allogeneic products in a donor-matched scenario) pose specific challenges, and the strategies implemented to ensure a high level of quality must be tailored to the constraints of the manufacturing process, limited batch sizes and inherent variability of the starting material.

2.11 ATMPs are at the forefront of scientific innovation and the field is experiencing rapid technological change that also impacts on the manufacturing processes. For instance, new manufacturing models are emerging to address the specific challenges of ATMPs (e.g. decentralised manufacturing for autologous products). Additionally, ATMPs are also often developed in an academic or hospital setting operating under quality systems different to those typically required for the manufacture of conventional medicinal products.

2.12   It follows that, in laying down the GMP requirements applicable to ATMPs, it is necessary to recognise a certain level of flexibility so that the ATMP manufacturer can implement the measures that are most appropriate, having regard for specific characteristics of the manufacturing process and the product. This is particularly important in the case of investigational ATMPs, especially in early phases of clinical trials (phases I and I/II), due to the often incomplete knowledge about the product (e.g. potency), as well as the evolving nature of the routines (in order to adjust the manufacturing process to the increased knowledge of the product).

2.2   Application of the risk-based approach by ATMP manufacturers

2.13   The risk-based approach ("RBA") is applicable to all type of ATMPS. It applies in an equal fashion to all type of settings. The quality, safety and efficacy attributes of the ATMPs and compliance with GMP should be ensured for all ATMPs, regardless of whether they are developed in a hospital or an academic or industrial setting.

2.14   Manufacturers are responsible for the quality of the ATMPs they produce. The risk-based approach permits the manufacturer to design the organisational, technical and structural measures that are put in place to comply with GMP, and thus to ensure quality, according to the specific risks of the product and the manufacturing process. Although the RBA brings flexibility, it also implies that the manufacturer is responsible for putting in place the control/mitigation measures that are necessary to address the specific risks of the product and of the manufacturing process.

2.15   The quality risks associated with an ATMP are highly dependent on the biological characteristics and origin of the cells/tissues, the biological characteristics of the vectors (e.g. replication competence or reverse transcription) and transgenes, the level and characteristics of the expressed protein (for gene therapy products), the properties of other non-cellular components (raw materials, matrices) and the manufacturing process.

2.16   When identifying the control/mitigation measures that are most appropriate in each case, the ATMP manufacturer should consider all the potential risks related to the product or the manufacturing process on the basis of all information available, including an assessment of the potential implications for the quality, safety and efficacy profile of the product, as well as other related risks to human health or the environment. When new information emerges that may affect the risks, an assessment should be made of whether the control strategy (i.e. the totality of the control and mitigation measures applied) continues to be adequate.

2.17   The evaluation of the risks and the effectiveness of the control/mitigation measures should be based on current scientific knowledge and the accumulated experience. Ultimately, this evaluation is linked to the protection of patients.

2.18   The level of effort and documentation should be commensurate with the level of risk. It is not always either appropriate or necessary to use a formal risk management process (using recognized tools and/or internal procedures, e.g. standard operating procedures). The use of informal risk management processes (using empirical tools and/or internal procedures) can also be considered acceptable.

2.19   The application of an risk-based approach can facilitate compliance but does not obviate the manufacturer's obligation to comply with relevant regulatory requirements and to demonstrate that it is able to adequately manage the risks of the product/manufacturing process. It likewise does not replace appropriate communications with the authorities.

INVESTIGATIONAL ATMPs

2.20   The application of GMP to investigational ATMPs is intended to protect the clinical trial subjects and it is also important for the reliability of the results of the clinical trial, in particular by ensuring consistency of the product, that the results of the clinical trial are not affected by unsatisfactory manufacturing and that changes of the product throughout the development are adequately documented.

2.21   It is important to ensure that data obtained from the early phases of a clinical trial can be used in subsequent phases of development. Therefore, a functional quality system should be in place for the manufacturing of investigational ATMPs.

2.22   The quality and safety of the product need to be ensured from the first stages of development. Nevertheless, it is acknowledged that there is a gradual increase in knowledge of the product and that the level of effort in the design and implementation of the strategy to ensure quality will step up gradually. It follows that the manufacturing procedures and control methods are expected to become more detailed and refined during the more advanced phases of the clinical trial.

2.23   While the responsibility for the application of the risk-based approach lies with the manufacturer, it is encouraged that the advice of the competent authorities be sought in connection with the implementation of the risk-based approach for investigational ATMPs and, in particular, regarding early phases of clinical trials. The application of the risk-based approach should be consistent with the terms of the clinical trial authorisation. The description of the manufacturing process and process controls in the clinical trial authorisation application should explain, as appropriate, the quality strategy of the manufacturer when the risk-based approach is applied.

2.24   For aspects that are not specifically covered by the clinical trial authorisation, it is incumbent upon the manufacturer to document the reasons for the approach implemented and to justify that the totality of the measures applied are adequate to ensure the quality of the product. In this regard, it is recalled that alternative approaches to the requirements explained in these Guidelines are acceptable only if they are capable of meeting the same objective.

AUTHORISED ATMPs

2.25   For authorised ATMPs, the application of the risk-based approach should be consistent with the terms of the marketing authorisation. When providing the description of the manufacturing process and process controls in the marketing authorisation application (or, as appropriate, in the context of the submission of a variation), account can be taken of the specific characteristics of the product/manufacturing process to justify adaptation/deviation from standard expectations. Thus, the strategy to address specific limitations that may exist in connection with the manufacturing process, including controls of raw materials and starting materials, manufacturing facilities and equipment, tests and acceptance criteria, process validation, release specifications or stability data, should be agreed as part of the marketing authorisation.

2.26   For aspects that are not specifically covered by the marketing authorisation, it is incumbent upon the manufacturer to document the reasons for the approach implemented when the risk-based approach is applied, and to justify that the totality of the measures applied are adequate to ensure the quality of the product. In this regard, it is recalled that alternative approaches to the requirements explained in these Guidelines are acceptable only if they are capable of meeting the same objective.

2.3   Examples of the application of the risk-based approach

2.27   This section contains a non-exhaustive list of examples to illustrate some of the possibilities and limitations of the risk-based approach.

2.3.1   RBA IN CONNECTION WITH RAW MATERIALS

2.28   The application of the risk-based approach when determining the strategy to ensure the quality of the raw materials is explained in Section 7.2.

2.29   The application of the risk-based approach requires that the manufacturer has a good understanding of the role of the raw material in the manufacturing process and, in particular, of the properties of the raw materials that are key to the manufacturing process and final quality of the product.

2.30   Additionally, it is important to take into account the level of risk of the raw material due to the intrinsic properties thereof (e.g. growth factors versus basic media, culture media containing cytokines versus basal media without cytokines, raw material from animal origin versus autologous plasma, etc.), or the use thereof in the manufacturing process (higher risk if the raw material comes into contact with the starting materials).

2.31   Finally, it needs to be assessed whether the control strategy (e.g. qualification of suppliers, performance of suitable functional testing, etc.) is sufficient to eliminate the risks or mitigate them to an acceptable level.

2.3.2   RBA IN CONNECTION WITH THE TESTING STRATEGY

2.32   It is acknowledged that in some cases it may not be possible to perform the release tests on the active substance or the finished product, for example, due to technical reasons (e.g. it may not be possible to perform the release tests on the combined components of certain combined products, time restrictions (i.e. the product needs to be administered immediately after completion of manufacturing) or when the amount of available product is limited to the clinical dose.

2.33   In these cases, an adequate control strategy should be designed, e.g. consideration can be given to the following options:

2.34   • Testing of key intermediates (instead of the finished product) or in-process controls (instead of batch release testing) if the relevance of the results from these tests to the critical quality attributes of the finished product can be demonstrated.

2.35   • Real-time testing in case of short shelf-life materials/products.

2.36   • Increased reliance on process validation. When the scarcity of materials or the very short shelf-life limits the possibilities for release controls, the limitations should be compensated for by a reinforced process validation (e.g. additional assays, such as potency testing or proliferation assays may be performed after batch release as supporting data for process validation). This may also be relevant for investigational ATMPs: although process validation is not expected for investigational medicinal products (see Section 10.3), it may be important when routine in-process or release testing is limited or not possible.

2.37   It is stressed that the release testing strategy should be performed in accordance with the marketing/clinical trial authorisation.

2.38   The following example may also be considered:

2.39   • The application of the <u>sterility test</u> to the finished product in accordance with the European Pharmacopoeia (Ph.Eur. 2.6.1) may not always be possible due to the scarcity of materials available, or it may not be possible to wait for the final result of the test before the product is released due to short shelf-life or medical need. In these cases, the strategy regarding sterility assurance has to be adapted, e.g. the use of alternative methods for preliminary results, combined with sterility testing of media or intermediate product at subsequent (relevant) time points could be considered.

2.40   The use of validated alternative rapid microbiological methods may also be considered, e.g. sole reliance on alternative microbiological methods according to Ph.Eur. 2.6.27 may be acceptable when this is justified having regard for the specific characteristics of the product and the related risks, and provided that the suitability of the method for the specific product has been demonstrated.

2.41   If the results of the sterility test of the product are not available at release, appropriate mitigation measures should be implemented, including informing the treating physician (see Section 11.3.2):

2.42   • As cells in suspension are not clear solutions, it is acceptable to replace the <u>particulate matter test</u> by an appearance test (e.g. colour), provided that alternative measures are put in place, such as controls of particles from materials (e.g. filtration of raw material solutions) and equipment used during manufacturing, or the verification of the ability of the manufacturing process to produce low particle products with simulated samples (without cells);

2.43   • It may be justified to waive the <u>on-going stability</u> programme for products with shorter shelf-life.

2.3.3   ADDITIONAL CONSIDERATIONS RELEVANT FOR ATMPs THAT ARE NOT SUBJECT TO SUBSTANTIAL MANIPULATION

2.44   Manufacturing processes of ATMPs not involving substantial manipulation of the cells/tissues are typically associated with lower risks than the manufacturing of ATMPs involving complex substantial manipulations. However, it cannot be inferred that processes that are not qualified as "substantial manipulation" are risk free, notably if the processing of the cells entails long exposure of the cells/tissues to the environment. Accordingly, an analysis of the risks of the specific manufacturing process should be performed in order to identify the measures that are necessary to ensure the quality of the product.

2.45   With a view to reduce administrative burden, in the application of the GMP requirements to ATMPs, the manufacturing process of which does not involve substantial manipulation, account may be taken of equivalent standards that are applied by ATMP manufacturers in compliance with other legislative frameworks. For instance, the premises and equipment that have been duly validated to process cells/tissues for transplantation purposes in accordance with standards that can be deemed comparable to those laid down in these Guidelines[6] need not be validated again (for the same type of manufacturing operation).

2.46   However, there are certain elements of GMP that are intended to ensure the quality, safety and efficacy of the ATMPs, which are not specifically addressed under other legislative frameworks and which, therefore, should follow the requirements in these Guidelines, also when the manufacturing process does not involve substantial manipulation. In particular, the requirements on product characterisation (through the setting of adequate specifications), process validation (the expectations for investigational ATMPs are described in Section 10.3), quality controls (in accordance with the terms of the marketing/clinical trial authorisation) and QP certification should be complied with.

2.47   ATMPs manufactured and applied during the same surgical procedure are not exempted from the ATMP Regulation (including therefore GMP compliance).

2.3.4   ADDITIONAL CONSIDERATIONS RELEVANT FOR INVESTIGATIONAL ATMPs

2.48   Although additional adaptations in the application of GMP may be justified in the case of investigational ATMPs, it is stressed that the quality, safety and traceability of the product should also be ensured in a clinical trial setting.

2.49   The following are examples of additional possible adaptations that may be acceptable in the case of investigational ATMPs:

2.50   • Although investigational ATMPs should be manufactured in a facility with air-quality requirements in accordance with the requirements set out in Sections 4.3.2 and 9.5, in the case of investigational ATMPs in

---

[6] For example, validation of premises/equipment used to process cells/tissues under the same surgical procedure derogation provided for under Article 2(2) of Directive 2004/23 or for research purposes is not considered comparable to the standards provided for under this Guideline. Therefore, before the manufacturing of ATMPs in such premises, it is required that the premises and equipment have been validated in accordance with these Guidelines.

very early phase/proof of concept trials, it may be exceptionally possible to manufacture the product in an open system in a critical clean area of Grade A with a background clean area of Grade C if the following (cumulative) conditions are met:

(i) A risk assessment has been performed and demonstrated that the implemented control measures are adequate to ensure manufacture of the product of appropriate quality. In addition, the control strategy should be described in the investigational medicinal product dossier;

(ii) The product is intended to treat a life-threatening condition where no therapeutic alternatives exist;

(iii) The relevant competent authorities agree (agreement of both the assessors of the clinical trial and the inspectors of the site);

2.51 • In early phases of clinical research (clinical trial phases I and I/II) when the manufacturing activity is very low, calibration, maintenance activities, inspection or checking of facilities and equipment should be performed at appropriate intervals, which may be based on a risk analysis. The suitability for use of all equipment should be verified before it is used;

2.52 • The level of formality and detail for the documentation can be adapted to the stage of development. The traceability requirements should, however, be implemented in full;

2.53 • During early phases of clinical development (clinical trial phases I and I/II) specifications can be based on wider acceptance criteria, taking due account of the current knowledge of the risks and as approved by the competent authority that authorises the clinical trial;

2.54 • Possible adaptations regarding qualification of premises and equipment, cleaning validation, process validation and validation of analytical methods are described in Section 10.

3 Personnel

3.1 General principles

3.10 The ATMP manufacturer should have an adequate number of personnel with appropriate qualifications and adequate practical experience relevant to the intended operations.

3.11 All personnel involved in the manufacturing or testing of an ATMP should have a clear understanding of their tasks and responsibilities, including knowledge of the product appropriate to the assigned tasks.

3.2 Training

3.12 All personnel should receive training on the principles of GMP that affect them and receive initial and periodic training relevant to their tasks.

3.13 There should be appropriate (and periodic) training in the requirements specific to the manufacturing, testing and traceability of the product.

3.14 Personnel working in clean areas should be given specific training on aseptic manufacturing, including the basic aspects of microbiology.

3.15 Prior to participating in routine aseptic manufacturing operations, personnel should participate in a successful process simulation test (see Section 9.5.2). Training in the gowning requirements set out in Section 3.3 is also required. The competence of personnel working in Grade A/B areas to comply with the gowning requirements should be reassessed at least annually.

3.16 Microbial monitoring of personnel working in A/B areas should be performed after critical operations and when leaving the A/B area. A system of disqualification of personnel should be established based on the results of the monitoring programme, as well as other parameters that may be relevant. Once disqualified, re-training/re-qualification is required before the operator can be involved in aseptic operations. It is advised that the re-training/re-qualification include participation in a successful process simulation test.

3.17 In addition, there should be appropriate training to prevent the transfer of communicable diseases from biological raw and starting materials to the operators and vice versa. Personnel handling genetically modified organisms ("GMOs") require additional training to prevent cross-contamination risks and potential environmental impacts.

3.18 Cleaning and maintenance personnel should also receive training relevant to the tasks performed, in particular on measures to avoid risks to the product and the environment, and health risks.

3.19 Training can be provided in-house. The effectiveness of training should be periodically assessed. Records of training should be kept.

3.3 Hygiene

3.20 High standards of personal hygiene and cleanliness are essential. Hygiene programmes should be established.

3.21 Eating, drinking, chewing or smoking, as well as the storage of food or personal medication, should be prohibited in the production and storage area.

3.22 Direct contact should be avoided between the operator's hands and the exposed product, as well as with any part of the equipment that comes into contact with the products.

3.23 Every person entering the manufacturing areas should wear clean clothing suitable for the manufacturing activity with which they are involved and this clothing should be changed when appropriate. Additional protective garments appropriate to the operations to be carried out (e.g. head, face, hand and/or arm coverings) should be worn when necessary.

3.24 The clothing and its quality should be appropriate for the process and the grade of the working area. It should be worn in such a way as to protect the operator and the product from the risk of contamination.

3.25 The description of clothing required for clean areas is as follows:

- Grade D: Hair and, where relevant, beard and moustache should be covered. A general protective suit and appropriate shoes or overshoes should be worn. Appropriate measures should be taken to avoid any contamination coming from outside the clean area.
- Grade C: Hair and, where relevant, beard and moustache should be covered. A single or two-piece trouser suit, gathered at the wrists and with high neck and appropriate shoes or overshoes should be worn. They should shed virtually no fibres or particulate matter.
- Grade A/B: Sterile headgear should totally enclose hair and, where relevant, beard and moustache; it should be tucked into the neck of the suit; a sterile facemask and sterile eye coverings[7] should be worn to prevent the shedding of droplets and particles. Appropriate sterilised, non-powdered rubber or plastic gloves and sterilised or disinfected footwear should be worn. Trouser-legs should be tucked inside the footwear and garment sleeves into the gloves. The protective clothing should shed virtually no fibres or particulate matter and retain particles shed by the body.

3.26 Outdoor clothing should not be brought into changing rooms leading to Grade B and C rooms. For every worker in a Grade A/B area, clean (sterilised) protective garments (including facemasks and eye coverings[7]) should

---

[7] Eye coverings are not required when the use thereof impair the ability of the personnel to conduct the assigned task (e.g. visualisation through the microscope).

be provided every time there is an entry into the clean area; the need to exit and re-enter the clean area for a different manufacturing step/different batch should be determined by the risk of the activity. Gloves should be regularly disinfected during operations. Upon exit from a clean area there should be a visual check of the integrity of the garment.

3.27   Clean area clothing should be cleaned and handled in such a way that it does not gather additional contaminants, which can later be shed. When working in a contained area, protective clothing should be discarded before leaving the contained area.

3.28   Wristwatches, make-up and jewellery should not be worn in clean areas.

3.29   Where required to minimise the risk for cross-contamination, restrictions on the movement of all personnel should be applied. In general, personnel (or any other person) should not pass directly from areas where there is exposure to live microorganisms, GMOs, toxins or animals to areas where other products, inactivated products or different organisms are handled. If such passage is unavoidable, appropriate control measures (having regard for the risks) should be applied. When a person moves from one clean room to another clean room (higher to lower grade, or lower to higher grade) appropriate disinfection measures should be applied. The garment requirements required for the relevant grade should be respected.

3.30   Activities in clean areas, especially when aseptic operations are in progress, should be kept to a minimum. Excessive shedding of particles and organisms due to over-vigorous activity should be avoided.

3.31   Only the minimum number of personnel should be present in clean areas. Inspections and controls should be conducted outside the clean areas as far as possible.

3.32   Steps should be taken to ensure that health conditions of the personnel that may be relevant to the quality of the ATMP are declared and that no person affected by an infectious disease that could adversely affect the quality of the product, or with open lesions on the exposed surface of the body, is involved in the manufacture of ATMPs.

3.33   Health monitoring of staff should be proportional to the risks. Where necessary having regard for the specific risks of the product, personnel engaged in production, maintenance, testing and internal controls, and animal care should be vaccinated. Other measures may need to be put in place to protect the personnel according to the known risks of the product and of the materials used in the manufacture thereof.

3.4 Key personnel

3.34 Because of their essential role in the quality system, the person responsible for production, the person responsible for quality control and the Qualified Person (QP) should be appointed by senior management. In case of ATMPs containing or consisting of GMOs, the person responsible for biosafety should also be appointed by senior management.

3.35 The roles and responsibilities of key personnel should be clearly defined and communicated within the organisation.

3.36 As a minimum, the person responsible for production should take responsibility for ensuring that manufacturing is done in accordance with the relevant specifications/instructions, for the qualification and maintenance of the premises and equipment used in manufacturing operations, and to ensure that appropriate validations are done. The responsibilities of the person responsible for quality control are detailed in Section 12.1 and the responsibilities of the QP are explained in Section 11.2.

3.37 Additionally, depending on the size and organisational structure of the company, a separate unit responsible for quality assurance may be established. In this case, the responsibilities of the person responsible for production and the person responsible for quality control are shared with the person responsible for quality assurance.

3.38 The person responsible for production, the person responsible for quality control and, where applicable, the person responsible for quality assurance share some responsibilities regarding the design and implementation of the pharmaceutical quality system and, in particular, concerning training, documentation obligations, process validation, validation of the transport conditions and the reconstitution process (where applicable), control of the manufacturing environment, control of outsourced activities and quality investigations.

3.39 While the duties of key personnel may be delegated to persons with an appropriate qualification, there should be no gaps or unexplained overlaps in the responsibilities of key personnel.

3.40 The same person can perform the role of person responsible for quality control and QP. It is also possible for the QP to be responsible for production. However, responsibility for production and quality control cannot be taken on by the same person. In small organisations, where teams are multi-skilled and trained in both quality control and production activities, it is acceptable that the same person is responsible for both roles (production and quality control) with respect to different batches. For any given batch, the responsibility for production and quality control of the batch must be vested in two different persons. Accordingly, it becomes particularly important that the independence of the quality control activities from the production activities for the same batch be clearly established through appropriate written procedures.

4   Premises

4.1   General principles

4.10   Premises must be suitable for the operations to be carried out. In particular, they should be designed to minimise the opportunity for extraneous contamination, cross-contamination, the risk of errors and, in general, any adverse effect on the quality of products.

4.11   It is important that the following general principles are implemented:

(i)   Premises should be kept clean (disinfection to be applied as appropriate);

(ii)   Premises should be carefully maintained, ensuring that repair and maintenance operations do not present any hazard to the quality of products;

(iii)   Lighting, temperature, humidity and ventilation should be appropriate for the activities performed and should not adversely affect the ATMPs or the functioning of equipment;

(iv)   Appropriate measures to monitor key environmental parameters should be applied;

(v)   Premises should be designed and equipped so as to afford maximum protection against the entry of insects or other animals;

(vi)   Steps should be taken to prevent the entry of unauthorised people. Production, storage and quality control areas should not be used as a transit area by personnel who do not work in them. When such passage is unavoidable, appropriate control measures should be applied;

(vii)   The manufacture of technical poisons, such as pesticides and herbicides, should not be allowed in premises used for the manufacture of ATMPs.

4.12   For production of ATMPs, the premises should be qualified (see Section 10.1).

4.2   Multi-product facility

4.13   Manufacture of ATMPs in a multi-product facility is acceptable when appropriate risk-mitigation measures commensurate with the risks are implemented to prevent mix-ups and cross-contamination. Further explanations can be found in Section 9.4.

4.14 If the manufacturing site produces medicinal products other than ATMPs, based on a risk assessment, the manufacture of ATMPs may need to take place in a dedicated area of the facility.

4.15 Segregated production areas should be used for the manufacturing of ATMPs presenting a risk that cannot be adequately controlled by operational and/or technical measures. Where there are no separate production suites, a thorough cleaning and decontamination procedure of validated effectiveness should take place before any subsequent manufacturing in the same area can occur (segregation in time).

4.16 Special precautions should be taken in the case of manufacturing activities involving infectious viral vectors (e.g. oncolytic viruses); these activities should take place in a segregated area.

Concurrent manufacturing of different batches/products

4.17 Manufacturing activities concerning different starting materials and/or finished products should be separated, either in place or in time.

4.2.1 SEPARATION IN PLACE

4.18 Concurrent production of two different ATMPs/batches in the same area is not acceptable. However, closed and contained systems may be used to separate activities as follows:

4.19 (a) The use of more than one closed isolator (or other closed systems) in the same room at the same time is acceptable, provided that appropriate mitigation measures are taken to avoid cross-contamination or mix-ups of materials, including separated expulsion of the exhausted air from the isolators and regular integrity checks of the isolator.

4.20 When two isolators are used to process different viral vectors within the same room there should be 100% air exhaustion from the room and the facility (i.e. no recirculation). In other cases, air filtration may be acceptable. In addition, in case of concurrent production of viral vectors, it is necessary to provide for closed, separate and unidirectional waste handling;

4.21 (b) The possibility of using more than one biosafety cabinet in the same room is only acceptable if effective technical and organisational measures are implemented to separate the activities (e.g. strict material and personal flows defined, no crossing lines in the use of equipment in the same room, etc.). It is stressed that the simultaneous use of more than one biosafety cabinet entails additional risks and, therefore, it should be demonstrated that the measures implemented are effective to avoid risks to the quality of the product and mix-ups;

4.22 (c) It is acceptable to conduct a manufacturing activity in a clean room which hosts an incubator that is used for a different batch/product if there is separated expulsion of exhausted air from the incubator. Particular attention should be paid to prevent mix-ups;

4.23 (d) The simultaneous incubation/storage of different batches within the same incubator is acceptable only if they are physically separated (e.g. distinct cell cultures in closed vessels). When simultaneous incubation/ storage of different batches takes place as described above, the manufacturer should evaluate the possible risks and implement appropriate measures to avoid mix-ups of materials.

4.24 However, the simultaneous incubation/storage of replication competent vectors/products based on them, or infected material/products based on them with other materials/products is not acceptable;

4.25 (e) Given their lower risk profile, concurrent production of non-viral vectors in separate laminar flow hoods placed in the same room may be acceptable if appropriate measures are implemented to avoid mix-ups.

4.2.2   SEPARATION IN TIME

4.26 The whole manufacturing facility or a self-contained production area may be dedicated to the manufacturing of a specific product on a campaign basis followed by a cleaning process of validated effectiveness (see Section 10.2).

4.3   Production areas

4.3.1   DESIGN AND CONSTRUCTION

4.27 It is recommended that the design of the premises permits the production take place in areas connected in a logical order corresponding to the sequence of the operations and required level of cleanliness. Likewise, the arrangement of the working environment and of the equipment and materials should be adequate to minimise the risk of confusion between different products or their components, to avoid cross-contamination, and to minimise the risk of omission or wrong application of any of the manufacturing or control steps.

4.28 The lay out of the premises should permit the separation of flows of non-sterile and used materials and equipment from those that are sterilised. Where this is not possible, the handling of non-sterile and used materials/equipment should be separated in time and appropriate cleaning measures should be applied.

4.29 Production areas should be effectively ventilated, with air control systems (including temperature and, where necessary, humidity and filtration of air) appropriate to the products handled, the operations undertaken within them and the external environment.

4.30   Air-handling units should be designed, constructed and maintained to prevent the risk of cross-contamination between different areas in the manufacturing site, and may need to be specific for an area. Depending on specific risks of the product, the use of single-pass air systems should be considered.

4.31   In clean areas, all exposed surfaces should be smooth, impervious and unbroken in order to minimize the shedding or accumulation of particles or microorganisms and to permit the repeated application of cleaning agents and disinfectants where used.

4.32   To reduce the accumulation of dust and facilitate the cleaning, there should be no uncleanable recesses and a minimum of projecting ledges, shelves, cupboards and equipment. Doors should be designed to avoid those uncleanable recesses; sliding doors may be undesirable for this reason.

4.33   False ceilings should be sealed to prevent contamination from the space above them.

4.34   Pipes and ducts and other utilities should be installed so that they do not create recesses, unsealed openings and surfaces that are difficult to clean.

4.35   Clean/contained areas should be accessed through an airlock with interlocked doors or by appropriate procedural controls to ensure that both doors are not opened simultaneously. The final stage of the airlock should, in the at-rest state, be the same grade as the area into which it leads.

4.36   Changing rooms should be designed as airlocks and used to provide physical separation of the different stages of changing and to minimize microbial and particulate contamination of protective clothing. They should be flushed effectively with filtered air. The use of separate changing rooms for entering and leaving clean areas is sometimes desirable. In general hand-washing facilities should be provided only in the first stage of the changing rooms.

4.3.2   ASEPTIC ENVIRONMENT

4.37   Premises should be suitable for the intended operations and they should be adequately controlled to ensure an aseptic environment. The measures implemented to ensure an aseptic environment should be adequate having regard to all the specific risks of the product and the manufacturing process. Special attention should be paid when there is no terminal sterilisation of the finished product.

CLEAN AREAS

4.38 A critical clean area is an area where the product is exposed to environmental conditions, and the design thereof should therefore be such as to ensure aseptic conditions. The air in the immediate vicinity of the critical clean area should be adequately controlled also (background clean area). Clean areas should be supplied with air that has passed through filters of an appropriate efficiency. The appropriate level of air classification should be determined with regard to the specific risks, taking into account the nature of the product and the manufacturing process, in particular whether processing takes place in an open or a closed system (see Section 9.5.1).

4.39 The classification of clean rooms/clean air devices should be done according to ISO 14644-1. For qualification, the airborne particles ≥0.5 µm should be measured. This measurement should be performed at rest and in operation. The maximum permitted airborne particle concentration for each grade is as shown in the table.

	Maximum permitted number of particles ≥0.5 µm		
	At rest (per m³)	In operation (per m³)	ISO classification (At rest/in operation)
Grade			
A	3520	3520	5/5
B	3520	352 000	5/7
C	352 000	3520 000	7/8
D	3520 000	Not defined	8

4.40 As part of the qualification of clean rooms, the microbial load of the clean room in operation should be measured. The limits for microbial contamination for each grade are as shown in the table (recommended values).

Grade	Air sample (cfu/m³)	Settle plates (diameter 90 mm) (cfu/4 hours')	Contact plates (diameter 55 mm) (cfu/plate)
A**	<1	<1	<1
B	10	5	5
C	100	50	25
D	200	100	50

'Individual settle plates may be exposed for less than 4 hours. Where settle plates are exposed for less than 4 hours, the limits in the table should still be used. Settle plates should be exposed for the duration of critical operations and changed as required after 4 hours.

**It should be noted that, for Grade A, the expected result should be 0 cfu (colony-forming units) recovered; any recovery of ≥1 cfu should result in an investigation.

4.41   The presence of containers and/or materials liable to generate particles should be minimised in the clean areas.

4.42   Appropriate cleaning/sanitation of clean areas is essential, including the removal of residual cleaning agents/disinfectants. Fumigation may be useful to reduce microbiological contamination in inaccessible places. Where disinfectants are used, the efficacy thereof should be checked. It is also advisable that more than one type be used to avoid the development of resistant strains and to achieve a broader range of bio-decontamination activity. Disinfectants, detergents and cleaning materials used in clean areas of Grades A and B should be sterile.

4.3.3   ENVIRONMENTAL MONITORING

4.43   Environmental monitoring programmes are an important tool by which the effectiveness of contamination control measures can be assessed and specific threats to the purity of the products identified. The environmental monitoring programme should include the following parameters: non-viable/viable contamination, air pressure differentials and, where appropriate, control is required for the process – temperature and relative humidity – and the results should be trended.

4.44   The monitoring locations should be determined with regard to the risks (e.g. at locations posing the highest risk of contamination) and the results obtained during the qualification of the premises.

4.45   The number of samples, volume, frequency of monitoring, alert and action limits should be appropriate, taking into account the risks and overall control strategy for the site. Sampling methods should not pose a risk of contamination to the manufacturing operations.

NON-VIABLE PARTICULATE MONITORING

4.46   Airborne particle monitoring systems should be established to obtain data for assessing potential contamination risks and to ensure an aseptic environment in the clean room. Environmental monitoring is also expected for isolators and biosafety cabinets.

4.47   The degree of environmental control of non-viable particulate and the selection of the monitoring system should be adapted to the specific risks of the product and the manufacturing process (e.g. live organisms). The frequency, sampling volume or duration, alert limits and corrective actions should be established case by case with regard to the risks. It is not necessary for the sample volume to be the same as that used for qualification of the clean room.

4.48 Appropriate alert and actions limits should be defined. With a view to identify potential changes that may be detrimental to the process, the alert limits for Grades B to D should be lower than those specified as action limits and should be based on the area performance.

4.49 The monitoring system should ensure that, when alert limits are exceeded, the event is rapidly identified (e.g. alarm settings). If action limits are exceeded, appropriate corrective actions should be taken. These should be documented.

4.50 The recommended action limits are as shown in the table.

Grade	Recommended maximum limits for particles ≥ 0.5 µm/m³		Recommended maximum limits for particles ≥ 5 µm/m³	
	In operation	At rest	In operation	At rest
A	3 520	3 520	20'	20*
B	352 000	3 520	2 900	29
C	3 520 000	352 000	29 000	2 900
D	Set a limit based on the risk assessment	3 520 000	Set a limit based on the risk assessment	29 000

'Due to the limitations of monitoring equipment, a value of 20 has been retained. Frequent sustained recoveries below that value should also trigger an investigation.

4.51 For grade A areas, particle monitoring should be undertaken for the full duration of critical processing, including equipment assembly, except where duly justified (e.g. contaminants in the process that would damage the particle counter or when this would present a hazard, e.g. live pathogenic organisms). In such cases, monitoring during equipment set-up operations should take place (i.e. prior to exposure of the product to the hazard). Monitoring should also be performed during simulated operations.

4.52 For grade B areas, there should be particle monitoring during critical operations, albeit the monitoring does not need to cover the entire duration of the critical processing. The grade B area should be monitored at an appropriate frequency and with suitable sample size to permit changes in levels of contamination to be identified.

4.53 The monitoring strategy regarding grades C and D should be set with regard to the risks and in particular the nature of the operations conducted.

4.54 When there are no critical operations on-going (i.e. at rest), sampling at appropriate intervals should be conducted. While at rest, the HVAC system should not be interrupted, because this may trigger the need for re-qualification. In the event of an interruption, a risk assessment should be conducted to determine any actions that may be required taking account of the activities performed in the affected areas (e.g. additional monitoring).

4.55 While not required for qualification purposes, the monitoring of the ≥5.0 µm particle concentration in grade A and B areas is required for routine monitoring purposes because it is an important diagnostic tool for early detection of failures. Although the occasional indication of ≥5.0 µm particle counts may be false counts, consecutive or regular counting of low levels is an indicator of a possible contamination and should be investigated. Such events may, for example, be indicative of early failure of the HVAC (heating, ventilation and air-conditioning system) or filling equipment failure or may also be diagnostic of poor practices during machine set-up and routine operation.

VIABLE PARTICLE MONITORING

4.56 Checks to detect the presence of specific microorganisms in the clean room (e.g. yeast, moulds, etc.) should be performed as appropriate. Viable particle monitoring is also expected for isolators and biosafety cabinets.

4.57 Where aseptic operations are performed, monitoring should be frequent using methods such as settle plates, volumetric air and surface sampling (e.g. swabs and contact plates). Rapid microbial monitoring methods should be considered and may be adopted after validation of the premises.

4.58 Continuous monitoring is required during critical operations where the product is exposed to the environment. Surfaces and personnel should be monitored after critical operations. Additional microbiological monitoring may also be required outside production operations depending on the risks.

4.59 The following table shows the recommended maximum limits for microbiological monitoring of clean areas that apply.

Grade	Air sample (cfu/m³)	Settle plates (diameter 90 mm) (cfu/4 hours)*	Contact plates (diameter 55 mm) cfu/plate	Glove print, 5 fingers (cfu/ glove)
A**	<1	<1	<1	<1
B	10	5	5	5
C	100	50	25	–
D	200	100	50	–

*Individual settle plates may be exposed for less than 4 hours. Where settle plates are exposed for less than 4 hours the limits in the table should still be used. Settle plates should be exposed for the duration of critical operations and changed as required after 4 hours.

**It should be noted that for grade A the expected result should be 0 cfu recovered; any recovery of 1 cfu should result in an investigation.

4.60   Appropriate alert and actions limits should be defined. With a view to identifying potential changes that may be detrimental to the process, the alert limits for Grades B to D should be lower than those specified as action limits and should be based on the area performance. If action limits are exceeded, appropriate corrective actions should be taken. These should be documented.

4.61   If microorganisms are detected in a Grade A area, they should be identified to species level and the impact thereof on product quality and the suitability of the premises for the intended operations should be assessed.

AIR PRESSURE

4.62   An essential part of contamination prevention is the adequate separation of areas of operation. To maintain air quality, it is important to achieve a proper airflow from areas of higher cleanliness to adjacent less clean areas. It is fundamental for rooms of higher air cleanliness to have a substantial positive pressure differential relative to adjacent rooms of lower air cleanliness. These pressure cascades should be clearly defined and continuously monitored with appropriate methods (e.g. alarm settings). Adjacent rooms of different grades should have a pressure differential of 10–15 Pa (guidance values).

4.63   However, negative pressure in specific areas may be required in for containment reasons (e.g. when replication-competent vectors or pathogenic bacteria are used). In such cases, the negative pressure areas should be surrounded by a positive pressure clean area of appropriate grade.

4.3.4   DRAINS

4.64   Drains should be of adequate size and have trapped gullies. Drainage systems must be designed so that effluents can be effectively neutralised or decontaminated to minimise the risk of cross-contamination. Open channels should be avoided where possible, but, if necessary, they should be shallow to facilitate cleaning and disinfection. Manufacturers are reminded that, for risks relating to biohazard waste, local regulations should be followed.

4.65   Clean areas of grade A and B should not have sinks or drains installed.

4.4 Storage areas

4.66   Storage areas should be of sufficient capacity to allow orderly storage of the various categories of materials and products: starting and raw materials, packaging materials, intermediate, bulk and finished products, products in quarantine, released, rejected, returned or recalled.

4.67   Storage areas should be clean and dry and maintained within acceptable temperature limits. Where special storage conditions are required (e.g. temperature, humidity), these should be specified and monitored.

4.68   Where quarantine status is ensured by storage in separate areas, these areas should be clearly marked and their access restricted to authorised personnel. Any system replacing the physical quarantine should give equivalent security.

4.69   Separated areas should be provided for the storage of recalled and returned materials/products, unless control of these materials/products is ensured through electronic means. Rejected materials/products should be stored in restricted areas (e.g. locked).

4.70   Highly reactive materials/products should be stored in safe and secure areas.

4.5 Quality control areas

4.71   Quality control laboratories should be designed to suit the operations to be carried out in them. Sufficient space should be given to avoid mix-ups and cross-contamination during testing. There should be adequate suitable storage space for samples and records.

4.72   Quality control laboratories should normally be separated from production areas. However, in-process controls may be carried out within the production area provided that they do not carry any risk for the products. Further details are available in Section 12.1.

4.6 Ancillary areas

4.73   Rest and refreshment rooms should be separate from production, storage and quality control areas. Toilets and washrooms should not directly communicate with production, storage and quality control areas.

4.74   Premises where laboratory animals are kept should be isolated from production, storage and quality control areas with separate entrance and air-handling facilities. Appropriate restrictions of movement of personnel and materials should be put in place.

5 Equipment

5.1 General principles

5.10   Equipment used in production or control operations should be suitable for its intended purpose and should not present any hazard to the product. Parts of production equipment that come into contact with the product should not have unwanted reactive, additive, adsorptive or absorptive properties that may affect the quality of the product. In addition, parts of the equipment that come into contact with cells/tissues should be sterile.

5.11   Major equipment (e.g. reactors, storage containers) and permanently installed processing lines should be appropriately identified to prevent mix-ups.

5.12   The integrity of the equipment's components should be verified as appropriate with regard to the specific risk of the product and the intended manufacturing process (e.g. ensuring structural integrity during freeze and thawing).

5.13   The location and installation of the equipment should be adequate to minimise risks of errors or contamination. Connections that are to be made in aseptic conditions should be performed in a critical clean area of grade A with a background clean area of grade B, unless there is subsequent sterilisation by steam in place or the connection is made by means of a validated sterile system (e.g. sterile tube welders, aseptic connection with a sterile septum).

5.14   Balances and measurement equipment should be of appropriate range and precision to ensure the accuracy of weighing operations.

5.15   Qualification of relevant equipment should be done in accordance with the principles in Section 10.1.

5.16   Defective equipment should, if possible, be removed from production and quality control areas, or at least be clearly labelled as defective.

5.2 Maintenance, cleaning, repair

5.17   Equipment should be adequately maintained:

(i)   Equipment should be calibrated, inspected or checked (as appropriate) at defined intervals to ensure adequate performance. In the case of computerised systems, the checks should include an evaluation of the ability of the system to ensure data integrity. Appropriate records of those checks should be maintained;

(ii)   Air vent filters should be adequately qualified and maintained and should be changed at appropriate intervals (to be set according to the criticality of the filter). Qualification can be done by the manufacturer or the supplier/manufacturer of the filter. When replaced, the filter should be subject to an integrity test.

5.18   Adequate cleaning and storage of the equipment is essential in order to avoid the risk of contamination for the products. Whenever possible, single-use cleaning materials should be used. The cleaning/decontamination procedures applied to multi-use equipment coming into contact with the product should be validated as explained in Section 10.2.

5.19   Repair and maintenance operations should not present any hazard to the quality of the products. As far as possible, maintenance and repair operations should be done outside the clean area. When repair or cleaning operations occur in a clean area, production should not be re-started until it has been verified that the area has been adequately cleaned and that the required environmental status has been re-established.

5.20   Where required to minimise the risk of cross-contamination, restrictions on the movement of equipment should be applied. In general, equipment should not be moved from high-risk areas to other areas, or between high-risk areas (e.g. equipment used for the handling of cells from infected donors or the handling of oncolytic viruses). When this happens, appropriate measures need to be applied to avoid the risk of cross-contamination. The qualification status of the equipment moved should also be reconsidered.

6   Documentation

6.1   General principles

6.10   Good documentation is an essential part of the quality system and is a key element of GMP. The main objective of the system of documentation utilized must be to establish, control, monitor and record all activities that directly or indirectly may affect the quality of the medicinal products. Records required to ensure that traceability should also be kept.

6.11   There are two primary types of documentation relevant for the quality assurance system: specifications/instructions (including, as appropriate, technical requirements, standard operating procedures (SOPs) and contracts) and records/reports.

6.12   Documentation may exist in a variety of forms, including paper-based, electronic, photographic media or video recording.

6.13 Irrespective of the form in which data is kept, suitable controls should be implemented to ensure data integrity, including:

(i) Implementation of measures to protect data against accidental loss or damage, e.g. by methods such as duplication or back-up and transfer to another storage system.

(ii) Implementation of measures to protect the data against tampering or unauthorised manipulation. Physical and/or logical controls should be in place to limit access to computerised systems to authorised persons. Suitable methods of preventing unauthorised entry to the system may include, for example, the use of keys, pass cards, personal codes with passwords, biometrics, or restricted access to computer equipment and data storage areas. The extent of security controls depends on the criticality of the computerised system.

(iii) Implementation of measures to ensure the accuracy, completeness, availability and legibility of documents throughout the retention period.

6.14 The content of documents should be unambiguous.

6.15 Where different manufacturing steps are carried out at different locations under the responsibility of different QPs, it is acceptable to maintain separate files limited to information of relevance to the activities at the respective locations.

6.2 Specifications and instructions

6.16 The specifications for the materials and the finished product and the manufacturing instructions are intended to ensure compliance with the terms of the marketing authorisation/clinical trial authorisation, product consistency (appropriate to the relevant stage of development) and the required level of quality. Therefore, it is important that specifications and instructions are documented appropriately and that they are sufficiently clear and detailed.

6.17 Documents containing specifications and instructions (including changes thereto) should be approved, signed and dated by authorised persons, and the date of entry into operation should be defined. Steps should be taken to ensure that only the current version of a document is used.

6.18 Specifications and instructions should be periodically re-assessed during development and post-authorisation, and be updated as necessary. Each new version should take into account the latest data and current technology used, as well as the terms of the marketing authorisation/clinical trial authorisation. It should also allow traceability to the previous document.

6.19 Rationales for changes should be recorded and the consequences of a change on product quality, safety or efficacy and, where applicable, any on-going non-clinical study or clinical trials should be investigated and documented. It is noted that changes to the manufacturing requirements approved as part of the marketing authorisation must be submitted to the competent authorities (variation procedure)[8], and that substantial modifications in the manufacturing process of an investigational ATMP also require approval by the competent authorities[9].

6.20 As a minimum, the following should be documented:

    (i) Specifications for raw materials, including:
- Description of the raw materials, including reference to designated name and any other information required to avoid risks of error (e.g. use of internal codes). In addition, for raw materials of biological origin, the identification of the species and anatomical environment from which materials originate should also be described;
- For critical raw materials (such as sera, growth factors, enzymes (e.g. trypsin), cytokines), quality requirements to ensure suitability for intended use, as well as acceptance criteria (see Section 7.2). Quality requirements agreed with suppliers should be kept (expectations in the case of investigational ATMPs are explained in Section 7.2);
- Instructions for sampling and testing, as appropriate (see Sections 7.2, 12.2 and 12.3);
- Storage conditions and maximum period of storage;
- Transport conditions and precautions.

    (ii) Specifications for starting materials, including:
- Description of the starting materials, including any relevant information required to avoid risks of error (e.g. use of internal codes). For starting materials of human origin, the identification of the supplier and the anatomical environment from which the cells/tissues/virus originate (or, as appropriate, the identification of the cell line, master cell bank, seed lot) should also be described;
- Quality requirements to ensure suitability for intended use, as well as acceptance criteria (see Section 7.3). Contracts and quality requirements agreed with the suppliers should be kept;

---

[8] Commission Regulation (EC) No 1234/2008 of 24 November 2008, concerning the examination of variations to the terms of marketing authorisations for medicinal products for human use and veterinary medicinal products (OJ L 334, 12.12.2008, p. 7).

[9] The definition of substantial modification is provided for under Article 2.2(13) of the Regulation (EU) No 536/2014.

- Instructions for sampling and testing (see Sections 7.3, 12.2 and 12.3);
- Storage conditions and maximum period of storage;
- Transport conditions and precautions.

(iii) Specifications for intermediate and bulk products should be available where applicable, including release criteria and maximum period of storage.

(iv) Specifications for primary packaging materials, including release criteria.

(v) Where applicable, specifications for other materials that are used in the manufacturing process and that can have a critical impact on quality (e.g. medical devices used in a combined ATMP, materials and consumables that have an inherent biological activity through which they can impact cells, such as monoclonal antibody-coated dishes or beads).

(vi) Batch definition: products generated from different starting materials should be considered as a distinct batch.

(vii) Manufacturing instructions (including description of principal equipment to be used) and in-process controls.

(viii) Specifications for finished products, in particular:
- Name/identification of the product;
- Description of the pharmaceutical form;
- Instructions for sampling and testing (see Sections 12.2 and 12.3);
- Qualitative and quantitative requirements with acceptance limits;
- Storage and transport conditions and precautions. Where applicable, particular attention should be paid to the requirements at cryopreservation stage (e.g. rate of temperature change during freezing or thawing) to ensure the quality of the product;
- The shelf-life.

(ix) Where applicable, the control strategy to address cases when test results for starting materials, intermediates and/or finished product are not available prior to product release (see Section 11.3.2).

(x) Packaging instructions for each product. Particular attention should be paid to ensuring the traceability of the product. It is noted that, for authorised ATMPs, the donation identification code received from the tissue establishment/blood establishment should be included in the outer packaging or, where there is no outer packaging, on the immediate packaging. Other labelling requirements are laid down in Articles 11 and 12 of Regulation (EC) No 1394/2007.

INVESTIGATIONAL ATMPs: THE PRODUCT SPECIFICATION FILE

6.21 In the case of investigational ATMPs, the level of detail of the specifications and instructions should be adapted to the type of product and the stage of development. Given the evolution/refinement of the manufacturing process and quality controls that is typical of investigational products, it is important that the level of documentation is sufficient to enable the identification of the specific characteristics of each batch. It is also noted that a deficient characterisation of the product may hinder the acceptability of the results of the clinical trial for the purposes of obtaining a marketing authorisation.

6.22   In addition to the specifications and instructions, where products are blinded, the Product Specification File should contain appropriate documentation of the system used to ensure the blinding. Such a system should ensure that the blinding is achieved and maintained, while allowing for identification of the product when necessary. The effectiveness of the blinding procedures should be verified.

6.23   A copy of the manufacturing order and a copy of the approved label should also be kept as part of the Product Specification File. As the Product Specification File is typically subject to changes, particular attention should be paid in the manufacturing order to the identification of the version that the manufacturer should adhere to.

6.24   The information contained in the Product Specification File should form the basis for assessment of the suitability for certification and release of a particular batch by the QP and should therefore be accessible to them.

6.3   Records/reports

6.25   Records provide evidence that the relevant specifications/instructions have been complied with. Records should be made or completed at the time each action is taken. Any change to a record should be approved, signed and dated by authorised persons.

6.26   The level of documentation will vary depending on the product and stage of development. The records should enable the entire history of a batch to be traced. Additionally, the records/reports should form the basis for assessment of the suitability for certification and release of a particular batch. As a minimum, the following should be documented:

   (i)   Receipt records for each delivery of raw materials, starting material, bulk, intermediate as well as primary packaging materials. The receipt records should include:
      • name of the material on the delivery note and the containers as well as any "in-house name" and/or internal code if appropriate;
      • supplier's name and manufacturer's name;
      • supplier's batch or reference number;

- total quantity received;
- date of receipt;
- unique receipt number assigned after receipt and any relevant comment.

(ii) A batch processing record should be kept for each batch processed; it should contain the following information:
- name of the product and batch number;
- dates and times of commencement, critical intermediate stages and completion of production;
- quantities and batch number of each starting material;
- quantities and batch number of critical raw materials;
- where applicable, quantities and batch number of other materials that are used in the manufacturing process and that can have a critical impact on quality (e.g. medical devices used in a combined ATMP, materials and consumables that have an inherent biological activity through which they can impact cells, such as monoclonal antibody-coated dishes or beads);
- confirmation that line clearance has been performed prior to starting manufacturing operations;
- identification (e.g. by means of initials or another suitable system) of the operator who performed each significant step and, where appropriate, the person who checked these operations;
- a record of the in-process controls;
- identification of clean room and major equipment used;
- the product yield obtained at relevant stages of manufacture; and
- notes on special problems including details, with signed authorisation for any deviation from the manufacturing instructions.

(iii) Results of release testing.

(iv) Environmental monitoring records.

(v) On-going stability programme in accordance with Section 12.4 (for authorised ATMPs).

(vi) Outcome of self-inspections should be recorded. Reports should contain all the observations made during the inspections and, where applicable, proposals for corrective measures. Statements on the actions subsequently taken should also be recorded.

6.27 Any deviations should be recorded and investigated, and appropriate corrective measures should be taken.

6.4 Other documentation

6.28 There should be appropriate documentation of policies and procedures to be applied by the manufacturer with a view to safeguard the quality of the product, including:

(i)   Qualification of premises and equipment;

(ii)   Validation of manufacturing process (the expectations for investigational ATMPs are described in Section 10.3);

(iii)   Validation of relevant analytical methods;

(iv)   Maintenance and calibration of equipment;

(v)   Cleaning procedures;

(vi)   Environmental monitoring;

(vii)   Investigations into deviations and non-conformances;

(viii) Procedures for handling of quality complaints and recall of products.

6.29   Logbooks should be kept for equipment used for critical manufacturing and testing operations.

6.30   The documentation of the above policies and procedures should be adjusted to the stage of development. The documentation for phase I and I/II clinical trials can be more limited but it is expected that it becomes more comprehensive in later phases of development.

6.31   A Site Master File should be prepared for every site involved in manufacturing of authorised ATMPs. The Site Master File should provide a high-level description of the premises, activities conducted at the site and the quality system implemented[10].

6.5   Retention of documents

6.32   Without prejudice to Section 6.6, batch documentation (i.e. documents in the batch-processing record, results of release testing, as well as, where applicable, any data on product-related deviations) should be kept for one year after expiry of the batch to which it relates, or at least five years after certification of the batch by the QP, whichever is the longest. For investigational medicinal products, the batch documentation must be kept for at least five years after the completion or formal discontinuation of the last clinical trial in which the batch was used.

6.33   It is acceptable that some of the data pertaining to the batch documentation is kept in a separate file, provided that they are readily available and unequivocally linked to the relevant batch.

6.34   Critical documentation, including raw data (e.g. relating to validation or stability) that supports information in the marketing authorisation, should

---

[10] ATMP manufacturers may follow the principles laid down in the Explanatory Notes on the preparation of a Site Master File published in EudraLex, Volume 4 (http://ec.europa.eu/health/files/eudralex/vol4/2011_site_master_file_en.pdf).

be retained while the authorization remains in force. However, it is acceptable to retire certain documentation (e.g. raw data supporting validation reports or stability reports) where the data has been superseded by a full set of new data. Justification for this should be documented and should take into account the requirements for retention of batch documentation.

6.6 Traceability data

6.35 A system that enables the bidirectional tracking of cells/tissues contained in ATMPs from the point of donation, through manufacturing, to the delivery of the finished product to the recipient should be created. Such system, which can be manual or electronic, should be established from the beginning of the manufacture of batches for clinical use.

6.36 In accordance with Article 15 of Regulation 1394/2007, traceability information should also cover raw materials and all substances coming into contact with the cells or tissues. This Section describes the type and amount of data that must be generated and kept by manufacturers of ATMPs.

6.37 The manufacturer should ensure that the following data be retained for a minimum of 30 years after the expiry date of the product, unless a longer period is provided for in the marketing authorisation:

(i)   Donation identification code received from the tissue establishment/blood establishment. For cells and tissues that are not covered by Directive 2004/23/EC[11] or Directive 2002/98/EC[12], such as cell lines or cell banks established outside the EU, information permitting the identification of the donor should be kept.

(ii) Internal code (or other identification system) that is generated by the manufacturer to unequivocally identify the tissues/cells used as starting materials throughout the entire manufacturing process up to the point of batch release. The manufacturer must ensure that the link between the internal code and the donation identification code can always be established. For starting materials not covered by

---

[11] Directive 2004/23 of the European Parliament and the Council of 31 March 2004 on setting standards of quality and safety for the donation, procurement, testing, processing, preservation, storage and distribution of human tissues and cells (OJ L 102, 7.04.2004, p. 48).

[12] Directive 2002/98 of the European Parliament and the Council of 27 January 2003 setting standards of quality and safety for the collection, testing, processing, storage and distribution of human blood and blood components and amending Directive 2001/83/EC (OJ L 33, 8.2.2003, p. 30).

Directive 2004/23/EC or Directive 2002/98/EC, it should be ensured that a link between the internal code and the donor identification can always be established.

(iii) Identification (including batch number) of critical raw materials and other substances that come into contact with the cells or tissues used as starting materials which may have a significant impact on the safety of the finished ATMP (e.g. reagents of biological origin, scaffolds, matrixes). For biological materials, the identification of the supplier, species and anatomical environment from which materials originate should also be described.

(iv) Where applicable, identification (including batch number) of all other active substances that are contained in the ATMPs.

6.38 When xenogeneic cells are used as starting materials for ATMPs, information permitting the identification of the donor animal should be kept for 30 years.

6.39 Traceability data should be kept as auditable documents. It is acceptable that it is kept outside the batch-processing record, provided that they are readily available and unequivocally linked to the relevant medicinal product. The storage system should ensure that traceability data may be accessed rapidly in case of an adverse reaction from the patient.

6.40 By means of a written agreement, the responsibility for the retention of the traceability data may be transferred to the marketing authorisation holder/sponsor.

7 Starting and Raw Materials

7.1 General principles

7.10 The quality of starting and raw materials is a key factor to consider in the production of ATMPs. Particular attention should be paid to avoiding contamination and minimising as much as possible the variability of the starting and raw materials. Specifications related to the product (such as those in Pharmacopoeia monographs, marketing/clinical trial authorisation) will dictate whether and to what stage substances and materials can have a defined level of bioburden or need to be sterile. Prior to introduction in the manufacturing process, the conformity to the relevant requirements should be checked.

7.11 The use of antimicrobials may be necessary to reduce bioburden associated with the procurement of living tissues and cells. However, it is stressed that the use of antimicrobials does not replace the requirement for aseptic manufacturing. When antimicrobials are used, they should be removed as soon as possible, unless the presence thereof in the finished product is specifically foreseen in the marketing authorisation/clinical trials authorisation (e.g. antibiotics that are part of the matrix of the finished product). Additionally, it is important to ensure that antibiotics or antimicrobials do not interfere with the sterility testing, and that they are not present in the finished product (unless specifically foreseen in the marketing authorisation/clinical trial authorisation)[13].

7.2   Raw materials

7.12   Raw materials should be of suitable quality with regard to the intended use. In particular, the growth-promoting properties of culture media should be demonstrated to be suitable for its intended use.

7.13   As far as possible, raw materials used in the manufacturing of ATMPs should take into consideration the *Ph.Eur. 5.2.12 general chapter on raw materials of biological origin for the production of cell-based and gene therapy medicinal products*. Although raw materials should be of pharmaceutical grade, it is acknowledged that, in some cases, only materials of research grade are available. The risks of using research-grade materials should be understood (including the risks to the continuity of supply when larger amounts of product are manufactured). Additionally, the suitability of such raw materials for the intended use should be ensured, including, where appropriate, by means of testing (e.g. functional test, safety test).

7.14   Specifications for raw materials should be set as explained in Section 6.2. In the case of critical raw materials, the specifications should include quality requirements to ensure suitability for the intended use, as well as the acceptance criteria. For authorised ATMPs, these quality requirements should be agreed with the supplier(s) ("agreed specifications"). For investigational ATMPs, the technical specifications for the critical raw materials should be agreed with the suppliers whenever possible. The assessment of whether a specific raw material is critical should be done by the manufacturer (or, as appropriate, the sponsor or marketing authorisation holder) with regard to the specific risks. The decisions taken should be documented. The agreed specifications should cover aspects of the production, testing and control, and other aspects of handling and distribution, as appropriate. The specifications set should be in compliance with the terms of the marketing authorisation or clinical trial authorisation.

---

[13] Ph.Eur., Chapter 2.6.1 on sterility testing describes the use of neutralising substances for products containing antibiotics.

7.15 The ATMP manufacturer should verify compliance of the supplier's materials with the agreed specifications. The level of supervision and further testing by the ATMP manufacturer should be proportionate to the risks posed by the individual materials. Reliance on the certificate of analysis of the supplier is acceptable if all the risks are duly understood and measures are put in place to eliminate the risks or mitigate them to an acceptable level (e.g. qualification of suppliers). For raw materials that are authorised as medicinal products in the EU (e.g. cytokines, human serum albumin, recombinant proteins), the certificate of analysis of the supplier is not required. Where available, the use of authorised medicinal products is encouraged.

7.16 The risk of contamination of raw materials of biological origin during their passage along the supply chain must be assessed, with particular emphasis on viral and microbial safety and Transmissible Spongiform Encephalopathy ("TSE"). Compliance with the latest version of the Note for Guidance on Minimising the Risk of Transmitting Animal Spongiform Encephalopathy (TSE) Agents via Human and Veterinary Medicinal Products is required[14]. Where there is a potential mycoplasma contamination risk associated with a raw material, the ATMP manufacturer should filter the material prior to use (0.1 μm filter), unless the supplier of the raw material has certified that the raw material has been tested and is mycoplasma free.

7.17 The risk of contamination from other materials that come into direct contact with manufacturing equipment or the product (such as media used for process simulation tests and lubricants that may contact the product) should also be taken into account.

7.18 Raw materials in the storage area should be appropriately labelled. Labels for critical raw materials should bear at least the following information:

(i) the designated name of the product and the internal code reference (if applicable);

(ii) a batch number given at receipt;

(iii) storage conditions;

(iv) the status of the contents (e.g. in quarantine, on test, released, rejected);

(v) an expiry date or a date beyond which retesting is necessary.

---

[14] Note for guidance on minimising the risk of transmitting animal spongiform encephalopathy agents via human and veterinary medicinal products (EMA/410/01 rev.3) http://www.ema.europa.eu/docs/en_GB/document_library/Scientific_guideline/2009/09/WC500003700.pdf (updated as appropriately).

7.19 When fully computerised storage systems are used, all the above information need not necessarily be in a legible form on the label. The use of automated systems (e.g. use of barcodes) is permissible.

7.20 Only raw materials that have been released by the person responsible for quality control should be used.

7.21 The ATMP manufacturer should put in place appropriate measures to ensure that critical raw materials can be traced in order to facilitate recall of products if necessary.

7.3 Starting materials

7.22 The donation, procurement and testing of human tissues and cells used as starting materials should be in accordance with Directive 2004/23/EC. For blood-derived cells, compliance with Directive 2002/98/EC regarding donation, procurement and testing is likewise acceptable. The accreditation, designation, authorisation or licensing of the supplier of starting materials, as provided for under the legislation referred to above, should be verified.

7.23 When the cells/tissues used are outside the scope of Directive 2004/23/EC or, as appropriate, Directive 2002/98/EC (e.g. cell lines/cell banks established outside the EU, or cells procured before entry into force thereof), the ATMP manufacturer (or, as appropriate, the sponsor or marketing authorisation holder) should take appropriate steps to ensure the quality, safety and traceability thereof, in accordance with the terms of the marketing authorization/clinical trial authorisation.

7.24 The ATMP manufacturer (or, as appropriate, the sponsor or marketing authorisation holder) should establish quality requirements for the starting materials (specifications), which should be agreed with the supplier(s). These agreed specifications should cover aspects of the production, testing and control, storage, and other aspects of handling and distribution as appropriate. Depending on the product's characteristics, testing in addition to that foreseen in Directive 2004/23/EC (or, as appropriate, Directive 2002/98/EC) may be required. The agreed specifications should be in compliance with the terms of the marketing authorisation or clinical trial authorisation.

7.25 The ATMP manufacturer should verify compliance of the supplier's materials with the agreed specifications. The level of supervision and further testing by the ATMP manufacturer should be proportionate to the risks posed by the individual materials.

7.26 Blood establishments and tissue establishments authorised and supervised in accordance with Directive 2002/98/EC or Directive 2004/23/EC do not require additional audits by the ATMP manufacturer regarding compliance with the requirements on donation, procurement and testing provided for under the national law of the Member State where the blood/tissue establishment is located. It is, however, recommended that the agreement between the ATMP manufacturer and the blood/tissue establishment foresee the possibility for the ATMP manufacturer to audit the blood/tissue establishment. Moreover, if the agreed specifications foresee requirements that imply that the blood/tissue establishment should carry out activities in addition to those authorised and supervised by the competent authority, in accordance with Directive 2002/98/EC or Directive 2004/23/EC (e.g. additional testing), adequate supervision in respect of the additional requirements should be carried out.

7.27 In addition to the specifications for the starting materials, the agreement between the ATMP manufacturer (or, as appropriate, the sponsor or marketing authorisation holder) and the supplier (including blood and tissue establishments) should contain clear provisions about the transfer of information regarding the starting materials, in particular, on tests results performed by the supplier, traceability data and transmission of health donor information, which may become available after the supply of the starting material and may have an impact on the quality or safety of the ATMPs manufactured therefrom.

7.28 The risk of contamination of the starting materials during their passage along the supply chain must be assessed, with particular emphasis on viral and microbial safety and transmissible spongiform encephalopathy (TSE). Compliance with the latest version of the Note for Guidance on Minimising the Risk of Transmitting Animal Spongiform Encephalopathy (TSE) Agents via Human and Veterinary Medicinal Products is required.

7.29 Only starting materials that have been released by the person responsible for quality control should be used.

7.30 Where the results from the test(s) required to release the starting materials take a long time (e.g. sterility test), it may be permissible to process the starting materials before the results of the test(s) are available. The risk of using a potentially failed material and its potential impact on other batches should be clearly assessed and understood. In such cases, the finished product should be released only if the results of these tests are satisfactory, unless appropriate risk mitigation measures are implemented (see also Section 11.3.2).

7.31 Starting materials in the storage area should be appropriately labelled. Labels should bear at least the following information:

(i)   the designated name of the product and the internal code reference (if applicable);

(ii)   a batch number given at receipt;

(iii)   storage conditions;

(iv)   the status of the contents (e.g. in quarantine, on test, released, rejected);

(v)   an expiry date or a date beyond which re-testing is necessary.

7.32   When fully computerised storage systems are used, all the above information need not necessarily be in a legible form on the label. The use of automated systems (e.g. use of barcodes) is permissible.

PROCESSING OF STARTING MATERIALS

7.33   The quality of ATMPs is dependent on the quality of the starting materials. Cells and tissues of human origin must comply with the donation, procurement and testing requirements provided for under Directive 2004/23/EC or, as appropriate, Directive 2002/98/EC. The further processing/manufacturing thereof should take place in a GMP environment.

7.34   However, where steps such as washing or preservation are needed to make the cells/tissues available, this can also take place at the tissue/blood establishment under the requirements of Directive 2004/23/EC or, as appropriate, Directive 2002/98/EC.

7.35   In exceptional cases, it may be acceptable that the manufacture of an ATMP starts from already available cells or tissues, where some initial processing/manufacturing steps have been performed outside the GMP environment, provided that it is impossible to replace such material with GMP-compliant material. The use of cells that have been separated/isolated and preserved outside a GMP environment for the manufacture of an ATMP should remain exceptional and is only possible if a risk analysis is performed to identify the testing requirements necessary to ensure the quality of the starting material. The overall responsibility for the quality – as well as the impact thereof on the safety and efficacy profile of the product – lies with the ATMP manufacturer (and/or, as appropriate, the sponsor or marketing authorisation holder), even if the activities have been outsourced. The release of such cells/tissues for use in the manufacturing process should be done by the person responsible for quality control, after verifying the quality and safety thereof. Additionally, the competent authorities should agree to the control strategy in the context of the assessment of the marketing authorisation application/clinical trial authorisation application.

7.36   In the case of vectors and naked plasmids used as starting materials for the manufacturing of gene therapy medicinal products, the principles of GMP apply from the bank system used to manufacture the vector or plasmid used for gene transfer.

ADDITIONAL CONSIDERATIONS FOR XENOGENEIC CELLS AND TISSUES

7.37 The use of xenogeneic cells/tissues in the manufacture of ATMPs poses additional risks of transmitting known and unknown pathogens to humans, including the potential risk of introducing new infectious diseases. The selection of donor animals must therefore be strictly controlled. Source/donor animals should be healthy and should be specific pathogen free (SPF) and raised in SPF conditions, including health monitoring. The donor/source animal should have been bred in captivity (barrier facility) specifically designed for this purpose. In the manufacture of ATMPs, it is not acceptable to use xenogeneic cells and tissues from wild animals or abattoirs. Similarly, cells and tissues of founder animals should not be used.

7.38 Appropriate measures should be implemented to identify and prevent incidents that negatively affect the health of the source/donor animals or that could negatively impact on the barrier facility or the SPF status of the source/donor animals. In addition to compliance with TSE regulations, other adventitious agents that are of concern (zoonotic diseases, diseases of source animals) should be monitored and recorded. Specialist advice should be obtained in establishing the monitoring programme.

7.39 Instances of ill-health occurring in the herd should be investigated with respect to the suitability of in-contact animals for continued use (in manufacture, as sources of starting and raw materials, in quality control and safety testing). The decisions taken must be documented. A look-back procedure should be in place, which informs the decision-making process on the continued suitability of the biological active substance or medicinal product in which the animal-sourced cells/tissues have been used or incorporated. This decision-making process may include the re-testing of retained samples from previous collections from the same donor animal (where applicable) to establish the last negative donation.

7.40 The withdrawal period of therapeutic agents used to treat source/donor animals must be documented and used to determine the removal of those animals from the programme for defined periods.

8 Seed Lot and Cell Bank System

8.10 It is recommended that the system of master and working seed lots/cell banks be used for allogeneic products that do not require a match between the donor and the patient. However, the establishment of seed lots/cell banks is not mandatory.

8.11 When seed lots and cell banks, including master and working generations, are used, they should be established under appropriate conditions, including compliance with GMP as provided for in these Guidelines. This should include an appropriately controlled environment to protect the seed lot and the cell bank and the personnel handling it. During the establishment of the seed lot and cell bank, no other living or infectious material (e.g. virus, cell lines or cell strains) should be handled simultaneously in the same area.

8.12 The number of generations (doublings, passages) should be consistent with specifications in the marketing authorisation/clinical trial authorisation.

8.13 For stages prior to the master seed or cell bank generation, documentation should be available to support traceability, including issues related to components used during development with potential impact on product safety (e.g. reagents of biological origin) from initial sourcing and genetic development if applicable.

8.14 However, it is acknowledged that comprehensive information may not be available for seed lots and cell banks established in the past (i.e. prior to the entry into force of Regulation 1394/2007). The use of starting materials coming from such seed lots/cell banks can be accepted only in exceptional cases and provided that there is extensive characterisation to compensate for the missing information. Additionally, the competent authorities should agree to the strategy in the context of the assessment of the marketing authorisation application/clinical trial authorisation application.

8.15 Cell bank safety testing and characterisation are important for batch-to-batch consistency and to prevent contamination with adventitious agents. Seed lots and cell banks should be stored and used in such a way as to minimize the risks of contamination (e.g. stored in the vapour phase of liquid nitrogen in sealed containers) or alteration. Control measures for the storage of different seeds/cells in the same area or equipment should prevent mix-up and take account the infectious nature of the materials to prevent cross-contamination.

8.16 Storage containers should be sealed, clearly labelled and kept at an appropriate temperature. A stock inventory must be kept. The storage temperature should be continuously monitored and records retained. Depending on criticality, alarm systems should be considered. Where used, the liquid nitrogen level should also be monitored. Deviation from set limits and corrective and preventive action taken should be recorded.

8.17 After the establishment of cell banks and master and viral seed lots, quarantine and release procedures should be followed. Evidence of the stability and recovery of seeds and banks should be documented and records should be kept in a manner permitting trend evaluation. In the case of investigational ATMPs, a gradual approach is acceptable. Thus, preliminary stability data (e.g. from earlier phases of development or from suitable cell models) should be available before the product is used in a clinical trial, and the stability data should be built up with real-life data as the clinical trial progresses.

8.18   Containers removed from the cryostorage unit can be returned to storage only if it can be documented that adequate conditions have been maintained.

8.19   Access to cell banks should be limited to authorised personnel.

CELL STOCK

8.20   Cell-based products are often generated from a cell stock obtained from a limited number of passages. In contrast with the two-tiered system of master and working cell banks, the number of production runs from a cell stock is limited by the number of aliquots obtained after expansion and does not cover the entire lifecycle of the product. Cell stock changes (including introduction of cells from new donors) should be addressed in the marketing authorisation/clinical trial authorisation and the conditions therein should be complied with.

8.21   It is desirable to split stocks and store the split stocks at different locations so as to minimize the risks of total loss. The controls at such locations should provide the assurances outlined in the preceding paragraphs.

8.22   When cell stocks are used, the handling, storage and release of cells should be done in accordance with the principles outlined above for cell banks.

CELL STOCKS/BANKS AND VIRAL SEED STOCKS ESTABLISHED OUTSIDE OF GMP CONDITIONS PRIOR TO THE ENTRY INTO FORCE OF REGULATION 1394/2007

8.23   The establishment of new cell stocks/banks and viral seed stocks should be done in accordance with GMP. In exceptional and justified cases, it might be possible to accept the use of cell stocks/cell banks and viral seed stocks that were generated prior to the entry into force of Regulation 1394/2007 without full GMP compliance. In these cases, a risk analysis should be conducted to identify the testing requirements necessary to ensure the quality of the starting material. In all cases, the overall responsibility for the quality – as well as the impact thereof on the safety and efficacy profile of the product – lies with the ATMP manufacturer and/or, as appropriate, the sponsor or marketing authorisation holder.

8.24   The use of starting materials from cell stocks/cell banks and viral seed stocks generated prior to the entry into force of Regulation 1394/2007 outside of GMP conditions should be approved by the competent authorities in the context of the assessment of the marketing authorisation application/clinical trial authorisation application.

9   Production

9.1   General principles

9.10   Production operations, including filling, packaging and, as applicable, cryopreservation should follow clearly defined procedures designed to ensure the quality of the product, consistent production (appropriate to the relevant stage of development) and to comply with the requirements set in the relevant manufacturing and marketing/clinical trial authorization.

9.11   In case of investigational ATMPs, the knowledge and understanding of the product may be limited, particularly for early phases of clinical trials (phases I and I/II). It is therefore acknowledged that the manufacturing process (including quality controls) may need to be adapted as the knowledge of the process increases. In the early phases of development, it is critical to carefully control and document the manufacturing process. It is expected that the manufacturing process and quality controls become more refined as development progresses.

9.12   Manufacturing processes and their control strategies should be reviewed regularly and they should be improved as appropriate. Although this is especially relevant during the early phases of clinical trials, it is also important to consider steps necessary to reduce process variability and enhance reproducibility at the different stages of the lifecycle.

9.13   When any new manufacturing formula or manufacturing process is adopted, steps should be taken to demonstrate its suitability. The effects of changes in the production, in relation to the quality of the finished product and consistent production (appropriate to the relevant stage of development), should be considered prior to implementation. Any change to the manufacturing formula or manufacturing method should be managed in accordance with the principles set out in Section 6.2.

9.14   Any deviation from instructions or procedures should be avoided as far as possible. If a deviation occurs, it should be approved in writing by a responsible person (after having assessed the impact thereof on quality, safety and efficacy), with the involvement of the QP as appropriate. Deviations should be investigated with a view to identify the root cause and to implement corrective and preventive measures as appropriate.

9.2   Handling of incoming materials and products

9.15   All handling of materials and products (such as receipt and quarantine, sampling, storage, labelling and packaging) should be done in accordance with written procedures or instructions and recorded as appropriate. The control strategy should be adequate with regard to the risks.

9.16   All incoming materials should be checked to ensure that the consignment corresponds to the order. The specific requirements for raw and starting materials are described in Section 7. For other materials, reliance on the documentation provided by third parties (e.g. supplier) is acceptable provided that all risks are duly understood and appropriate measures are put in place to eliminate the risks or mitigate them to an acceptable level (e.g. qualification of suppliers). Where necessary, identity verification and/or testing should be considered.

9.17   Incoming materials and finished products should be physically or administratively quarantined immediately after receipt or processing, until they have been released for use or distribution.

9.18   Intermediate and bulk products purchased as such should be released by the person responsible for quality control before they can be used in production, after verification of compliance with the relevant specifications.

9.19   All materials and products should be stored under appropriate conditions to ensure the quality and in an orderly fashion to permit batch segregation and stock rotation. Particular attention should be paid to implementing appropriate measures to prevent mix-ups of autologous products and other dedicated products (i.e. products intended for specific patients).

9.20   At all times during processing, all materials, bulk containers, major items of equipment and, where appropriate, rooms used should be labelled or otherwise identified with an indication of the product or material being processed, its strength (where applicable) and batch number. Where applicable, this indication should also mention the stage of production.

9.21   Labels applied to containers, equipment or premises should be clear and unambiguous. It is often helpful, in addition to the wording on the labels, to use colours to indicate status (e.g. quarantined, accepted, rejected, clean). The compatibility of labels with storage or processing conditions (e.g. ultra-low storage temperatures, waterbath) should be verified.

9.22   Containers should be cleaned where necessary. Damage to containers and any other problem that might adversely affect the quality of a material should be investigated, recorded and reported to the person responsible for quality control.

9.3 Utilities

9.3.1 WATER

9.23 Water used in the manufacturing of ATMPs should be of appropriate quality and regular checks should be carried out to verify the absence of contamination (chemical and biological and, as appropriate, from endotoxins).

9.24 Care should be taken in the maintenance of water systems in order to avoid the risk of microbial proliferation. In the case of water for injections generated at the site, special attention should be paid to prevention of microbial growth, e.g. by constant circulation at a temperature above 70°C.

9.25 Water for injections pipes, purified water piping and, where appropriate, other water pipes should be sanitised according to written procedures that detail the action limits for microbiological contamination and the measures to be taken. After any chemical sanitisation of a water system, a validated rinsing procedure should be followed to ensure that the sanitising agent has been effectively removed.

9.26 The use of pre-packaged water for injections compliant with the European Pharmacopeia[15] removes the need for demonstrating the appropriateness of the quality of the water for injections as provided for in the previous paragraphs.

9.3.2 MEDICAL GASES

9.27 Gases used in the production of ATMPs should be of suitable quality.

9.28 Where possible, gases that come into direct contact with the product during processing should be compliant with the European Pharmacopoeia. The use of gases of technical grades should be supported by a risk analysis and their quality described in the clinical trial/marketing authorisation dossier.

9.29 Gases taken into the aseptic work place or that come into contact with the product should be passed through sterilising filters. The integrity of critical gas filters should be confirmed at appropriate intervals which should be scientifically justified. For batches destined for more than one patient, it is generally expected that the critical gas filter filters will be tested prior to batch release. Liquid nitrogen used for storage of cells in closed containers need not be filtered.

---

[15] Monograph 0169.

9.3.3 CLEAN STEAM

9.30 Water used in the manufacture of clean steam should be of appropriate quality. Steam used for sterilisation should be of suitable quality and free from additives at a level that could cause contamination of the product or equipment.

9.4 Prevention of cross-contamination in production

9.31 Before any manufacturing operation starts, steps should be taken to ensure that the work area and equipment are clean and free from any starting materials, products, product residues or documents not required for the current operation. Mix-ups of materials should be prevented; special precautions should be taken to avoid the mixing of autologous materials or other dedicated materials.

9.32 At every stage of production, products and materials should be protected from microbial and other contamination (e.g. pyrogens/endotoxins as well as particulate matter (glass and other visible and subvisible particles)). Appropriate measures should also be put in place to protect the preparation of solutions, buffers and other additions from the risk of contamination (or within the accepted bioburden level foreseen in the marketing authorisation/clinical trial authorisation).

9.33 The risks of cross-contamination should be assessed with regard to the characteristics of the product (e.g. biological characteristics of the starting materials, possibility to withstand purification techniques) and manufacturing process (e.g. the use of processes that provide extraneous microbial contaminants the opportunity to grow). If sterilisation of the finished product is not possible, particular attention should be paid to the manufacturing steps where there is exposure to the environment (e.g. filling).

9.34 In all manufacturing steps that may lead to unwanted formation of aerosols (e.g. centrifugation, working under vacuum, homogenisation, sonication) appropriate mitigation measures should be implemented to avoid cross-contamination. Special precautions should be taken when working with infectious materials.

9.35 Measures to prevent cross-contamination appropriate to the risks identified should be put in place. Measures that can be considered to prevent cross-contamination include, among others:

(i)   Segregated premises;
(ii) Dedicating the whole manufacturing facility or a self-contained production area on a campaign basis (separation in time) followed by a cleaning process of validated effectiveness;

(iii) Use of "closed systems" for processing and material/product transfer between equipment;

(iv) Use of airlocks and pressure cascade to confine potential airborne contaminant within a specified area;

(v) Utilisation of single use disposable technologies;

(vi) Adequate cleaning procedures: the cleaning procedure (technique, number of sanitation steps, etc.) should be adapted to the specific characteristics of the product and the manufacturing process. A risk assessment should be used to determine the cleaning/decontamination procedures that are necessary, including the frequency thereof. As a minimum, there should be appropriate cleaning/decontamination between each batch. The cleaning/decontamination procedures should be validated as explained in Section 10.2;

(vii) Other suitable technical measures, such as the dedication of certain parts of equipment (e.g. filters) to a given type of product with a specific risk profile;

(viii) Other suitable organizational measures, such as keeping specific protective clothing inside areas where products with a high risk of contamination are processed, implementing adequate measures for handling waste, contaminated rinsing water and soiled gowning, or imposing restrictions on the movement of personnel.

9.36 The control strategy is multifaceted and should address all the potential risks, including, therefore, measures at the level of the facilities, equipment and personnel, controls on starting and raw materials, implementation of effective sterilisation and sanitisation procedures, and adequate monitoring systems. The totality of the measures applied should assure the absence of contamination of the products manufactured within the manufacturing site. Sole reliance should not be placed on any terminal process or finished product test.

9.37 The effectiveness of the measures implemented should be reviewed periodically according to set procedures. This assessment should lead to corrective and preventive actions being taken as necessary.

9.38 Accidental spillages, especially of live organisms, must be dealt with quickly and safely. Qualified decontamination measures should be available taking into consideration the organism used in production, as well as the risks attached to the relevant biological materials.

9.5 Aseptic manufacturing

9.5.1 General principles

9.39 The majority of ATMPs cannot be terminally sterilised. In such cases, the manufacturing process should be conducted aseptically (i.e. under conditions which prevent microbial contamination). In particular, this requires that, for any manufacturing activity that may expose the product to a risk of contamination, the following measures should be implemented:

9.40 (a) Manufacturing should take place in clean areas of appropriate environmental cleanliness level. Specifically:

9.41   • production in a closed system, in an isolator, or positive pressure isolators: a background clean area of Grade D is acceptable.

9.42 Isolators should be introduced only after appropriate validation. Validation should take into account all critical factors of isolator technology, e.g. the quality of the air inside and outside (background) the isolator, disinfection regimen of the isolator, the transfer process and the isolator's integrity.

9.43 Monitoring should be carried out routinely and should include frequent leak testing of the isolator and glove/sleeve system. The transfer of materials into and out of the isolator is one of the greatest potential sources of contamination, and appropriate control measures should be put in place.

9.44 When materials are added/withdrawn from the closed system without an aseptic connection (e.g. use of sterile connectors, use of filters), the system can no longer be considered closed.

9.45 In exceptional circumstances and provided that it is duly justified (e.g. manufacturing of the ATMP takes place in the operating theatre and it is not possible to move the production to an outside clean room because the time between the donation and the administration of the product is very short, and the patient is also in the operating theatre waiting for administration of the ATMP), closed systems may be placed in a controlled but non-classified environment. The conditions of the operating theatre where the manufacturing activity takes place should be adequate and sufficient to ensure the quality and safety of the product. It is stressed that this is acceptable only in exceptional cases and that the product should not be exposed at any moment to the environment (e.g. supporting data from leak testing and pressure check of the equipment). Additionally, it should be demonstrated that the expected clinical benefit for the patient outweighs the risks linked to the absence of a classified background.

9.46 • <u>Production in an open system</u>: in general, when the product is exposed to the environment (e.g. working under laminar airflow), a critical clean area of grade A with a background clean area of grade B is required for aseptic preparation and filling.

9.47 The following principles also apply:

• Preparation of solutions that are to be sterile filtered during the process can be done in a clean area of grade C;

- For the manufacturing process of viral vectors, the following considerations apply:
  - The expansion phase before the sterilising filtration can be performed in a critical clean area of grade A with a background clean area of grade C;
  - Sterilising filtration and filling need to be performed in a critical clean area of grade A with a background clean area of grade B, unless a closed system with sterile connectors is used.

9.48   In the case of investigational ATMPs used in very early phase/proof of concept trials, alternative approaches may be possible under the conditions explained in Section 2.3.4.

9.49   • The use of <u>technologies such as processing inside sterile disposable kits, incubation in closed flasks, bags or fermenters</u>[16] in a grade C environment may be acceptable if adequate control measures are implemented to avoid the risk of cross-contamination (e.g. appropriate control of materials, personnel flows and cleanness). Particular attention should be paid if the materials are subsequently moved to a clean area of higher grade.

9.50   (b) Materials, equipment and other articles that are introduced in a clean area should not introduce contamination. To this end, the use of double-ended sterilisers sealed into a wall or other effective procedures (e.g. H_2O_2 locks) should be used.

9.51   Sterilisation of articles and materials elsewhere is acceptable provided that the sterilisation process is validated and there are multiple wrappings (if possible, in numbers equal or above the number of stages of entry to the clean area), and enter through an airlock with the appropriate surface sanitization precautions. Unless culture media is delivered ready-to-use (i.e. already sterilised by the supplier), it is recommended that the media be sterilised *in situ*.

9.52   When sterilisation of articles, materials or equipment is not possible, a strictly controlled process should be implemented to minimise the risks (e.g. treatment of biopsy with antibiotics, sterile filtration of raw materials, appropriate disinfection of materials). The effectiveness of the process should be checked at appropriate intervals.

9.53   (c) Addition of materials or cultures to fermenters and other vessels and sampling should be carried out under carefully controlled conditions to prevent contamination. Care should be taken to ensure that vessels

---

[16] If the closed flasks, bags and fermenters allow for a full isolation of the product from the environment, these would be considered as closed systems and the relevant principles of closed systems would apply.

EU GMP PART IV SECTION 9 PRODUCTION

are correctly connected when addition or sampling takes place. In-line sterilising filters for routine addition of gases, media, acids or alkalis, anti-foaming agents, etc. to bioreactors should be used where possible.

9.54 The conditions for sample collection, additions and transfers involving replication competent vectors or materials from infected donors should prevent the release of viral/infected material.

9.5.2 Aseptic processing validation

9.55 The validation of aseptic processing should include a process simulation test. The aseptic process simulation test is the performance of the manufacturing process using a sterile microbiological growth medium and/ or placebo (e.g. culture media of cells that are demonstrated to support the growth of bacteria) to test whether the manufacturing procedures are adequate to prevent contamination during production. Results and conclusions should be recorded. The process simulation test should follow as closely as possible the routine manufacturing process and it should be conducted in the same locations where the production occurs. The process simulation should focus on all operations carried out by operators involving open process steps. All potential interventions and challenges to the process (e.g. work overnight) should be considered.

9.56 An appropriate simulated model (e.g. use of alternative tools to the manufacturing kit ("mock materials")) may be acceptable provided that this is duly justified.

9.57 Alternative approaches may also be developed for steps that take a long time. The simulation of reduced times for certain activities (e.g. centrifugation, incubation) should be justified with regard to the risks. In some cases, it may also be acceptable to split the process into key stages that are simulated separately provided that the transitions between each stage are also evaluated. When a closed system is used for the manufacture of an ATMP, the process simulation should focus on the steps related to the connections to the closed system.

9.58 In case of manufacturing of various types of ATMPs, consideration can be given to the matrix and/or bracketing approach. Under a bracketing approach, only samples on the extremes of certain design factors would undergo a full process simulation. This approach can be accepted if the handling of different products is similar (same equipment and processing steps). Under a matrix approach, it may be possible to combine media fills for different ATMPs sharing similar processing steps, provided that the worst case is covered by the matrix approach. The use of bracketing and matrixing together should be duly justified.

9.59 Filled containers should be inverted to ensure that the media/placebo touches all parts of the container/closure and should be incubated. The selection of the incubation duration and temperature should be justified and appropriate for the process being simulated and the selected media/placebo.

9.60 All contaminants from the filled containers should be identified. The results should be assessed, in particular in relation to the overall quality of the product and the suitability of the production process. The target should be zero growth. Any growth detected should be investigated. If the growth detected is indicative of potential systemic failure, the potential impact on batches manufactured since the last successful media fill simulation test should be assessed and adequate corrective and preventive actions taken.

9.61 Process simulation test to support initial validation should be performed with three consecutive satisfactory simulation tests per production process.

9.62 Process simulation (one run) should be repeated periodically to provide on-going assurance of the ability of the process and the staff to ensuring aseptic manufacturing. The frequency should be determined based on a risk assessment but should generally not be lower than once every six months (for each production process).

9.63 However, in the case of infrequent production (i.e. if the interval between the production of two batches is more than six months), it is acceptable that the process simulation test is done just before the manufacturing of the next batch, provided that the results of the process simulation test are available prior to the start of production. Nevertheless, in cases of long periods of inactivity (i.e. over one year), the validation prior to restart of production should be done with three runs.

9.64 When considering the frequency of the simulation test, the manufacturer is required to consider also the relevance of the media fill test for the training of operators and their ability to operate in an aseptic environment (see Section 3.2).

9.65 A process simulation should also be conducted in cases when there is any significant change to the process (e.g. modification of HVAC system, equipment, etc.). In this case, three runs are required.

9.5.3 STERILISATION

9.66 The sterilisation processes applied should be suitable with regard to the specific characteristics of the product. In particular, where the sterilisation of the starting materials (e.g. chemical matrixes) and raw materials and excipients is required, it should be ensured that the sterilisation process applied (e.g. heat, irradiation, filtration or chemical inactivation) is effective in terms of removing the contaminants while preserving the activity of starting/raw materials and excipients.

9.67 The sterilisation process(es) applied should be validated. Particular attention should be paid when the adopted sterilisation method is not in accordance with the European Pharmacopoeia. Additional guidance on sterilisation methods can be found in Annex 1 of Part I of the Good Manufacturing Practice Guidelines published in Volume 4 of EudraLex.

9.68 Solutions or liquids that cannot be sterilised in the final container should be filtered through a sterile filter of nominal pore size of 0.22 µm (or less), or with at least equivalent microorganism-retaining properties, into a previously sterilised container.

9.69 The filter should not have a negative impact on the product (e.g. by removing components or by releasing substances into it). The integrity of the sterilising filter should be verified before use, in case it is suspected that the filter may have been damaged by processing, and it should also be confirmed by on-line testing immediately after use by an appropriate method (e.g. bubble point, diffusive flow, water intrusion or pressure hold test). If filter integrity cannot be tested (e.g. small size batches), an alternative approach may be applied, which should be based on a risk assessment. The same filter should not be used for different batches. Additionally, the same filter should not be used for more than one working day, unless such use has been validated.

9.6 Other operating principles

9.70 Critical quality parameters (as identified in the marketing authorisation/clinical trial authorisation) should be monitored at appropriate intervals. When technically possible, continuous monitoring of key process parameters is expected (e.g. in bioreactors). Any deviations should be recorded and investigated, and the measures taken should also be documented.

9.71 Any necessary environmental controls (see Section 4.3.3) should be carried out and recorded.

9.72 Where chromatography equipment is used, a suitable control strategy for matrices, the housings and associated equipment (adapted to the risks) should be implemented when used in campaign manufacture and in multi-product environments. The re-use of the same matrix at different stages of processing is discouraged. Any such re-usage should be supported by appropriate validation data. Acceptance criteria, operating conditions, regeneration methods, lifespan and sanitization or sterilization methods of chromatography columns should be defined.

9.73 Where ionizing radiation is used in the manufacturing of ATMPs, Annex 12 of Part I of the Good Manufacturing Practice Guidelines, published in Volume 4 of EudraLex, should be consulted for further guidance.

9.7 Packaging

9.74 The suitability of primary packaging materials should be ensured with regard to the characteristics of the product and the storage conditions (e.g. products that should be stored at ultra-low temperature). The specifications provided for in the marketing authorisation or the clinical trial authorisation should be complied with.

9.75 The level of documentation regarding the demonstration of suitability of the primary packaging material should be adapted to the phase of development. For production of authorised ATMPs, selection, qualification, approval and maintenance of suppliers of primary packaging materials should be documented.

9.76 ATMPs should be suitably packaged to maintain the quality of the product during storage, handling and shipping. Particular attention should be paid to the closure of containers so as to ensure the integrity and quality of the product. For authorised ATMPs, the closure procedures should be validated and the effectiveness should be verified at appropriate intervals. Validation with surrogate materials is acceptable when materials are scarce.

9.77 Checks should be made to ensure that any electronic code readers, label counters or similar devices are operating correctly. Labels should be compatible with transport and storage conditions (e.g. ultra-low temperatures).

9.78 Prior to product labelling operations, the work area and any equipment used should be clean and free from any product, material or document that is not required for the current operation. Precautions should be taken to avoid mix-ups of products and to protect the product from the risk of contamination.

ADDITIONAL REQUIREMENTS FOR INVESTIGATIONAL ATMPS

9.79 Packaging and labelling of investigational ATMPs are likely to be more complex and more liable to errors, which are also harder to detect than for authorised medicinal products, particularly when "blinded" products with similar appearance are used. Therefore, special precautions should be taken.

9.80 During packaging of investigational ATMPs, it may be necessary to handle different products on the same packaging line at the same time. The risk of product mix-up must be minimised by using appropriate procedures and/or specialised equipment as appropriate and relevant staff training.

9.81   Labelling of investigational ATMPs should comply with the requirements of Regulation (EU) No 536/2014. If it becomes necessary to change the expiry date, an additional label should be affixed to the investigational ATMP. This additional label should state the new expiry date and repeat the batch number. It may be superimposed on the old expiry date, but, for quality control reasons, not on the original batch number.

9.82   Re-packaging and re-labelling operations should be performed by appropriately trained staff in accordance with specific standard operating procedures and checked by a second person.

9.83   Where products are blinded, the blinding system should be described in the Product Specification File (see Section 6.2). Where the manufacturer has been delegated the responsibility for generation of randomisation codes, the manufacturer should enable unblinding information to be available to the appropriate responsible investigator site personnel before investigational medicinal products are supplied. Special precautions should be taken to avoid unintentional unblinding due to changes in appearance between different batches of packaging materials.

9.8   Finished products

9.84   As a general principle, finished products should be held in quarantine until their release under conditions established by the manufacturer in accordance with the terms of the marketing authorisation or the clinical trial authorization. It is acknowledged, however, that, due to the short shelf-life, physical or administrative quarantine of ATMPs may not always be possible. The release of products before completion of all quality control tests is addressed under Section 11.3.2.

9.85   Filled containers of parenteral products should be inspected individually for extraneous contamination or other defects. When the inspection is done visually, it should be done under suitable conditions of illumination and background.

9.86   Any defect detected should be recorded and investigated. The requirements laid down in Section 14.1 are also applicable in case of defects detected at this stage.

9.87   Finished products should be stored under adequate conditions to preserve the quality of the product and to prevent mix-ups. Particular attention should be paid to implementing appropriate measures to prevent mix-ups of autologous products and other dedicated products (i.e. products intended for specific patients).

9.9 Rejected, recovered and returned materials

9.88 Rejected materials should be clearly marked as such and stored separately in restricted areas (e.g. locked). Starting and raw materials should either be returned to the suppliers or removed from the production environment. Whatever action is taken, it should be approved and recorded by authorised personnel.

9.89 The reprocessing of rejected products should be exceptional. For authorised ATMPs, re-processing is permissible only if this possibility is foreseen in the marketing authorisation. In the case of investigational ATMPs, the competent authorities should be informed when, exceptionally, there is re-processing.

9.99 Additionally, the use of re-processed materials is possible only if the quality of the final product is not affected and the specifications are met. The need for additional testing of any finished product that has been re-processed, or into which a re-processed product has been incorporated, should be evaluated by the person responsible for quality control. Records should be kept of the reprocessing. Certification by the QP is required before the product is released.

9.90 Returned products, which have left the control of the manufacturer, should be marked as such and be segregated so that they are not available for further clinical use, unless, without doubt, their quality is satisfactory after they have been critically assessed by the person responsible for quality control.

10 Qualification and Validation

10.1 Qualification of premises and equipment

10.1.1 GENERAL PRINCIPLES

10.10 Premises and equipment used in the manufacture of ATMPs should be qualified. Through the qualification of premises and equipment, it is established that the premises and equipment are adequate for the intended operations.

10.11 Decisions on the scope and extent of the qualification should be based on a risk assessment, which should be documented. The following should be considered when defining the strategy to the qualification of premises and equipment:

10.12 (a) • Clean areas should be qualified in accordance with ISO 14644-1 and re-qualified at appropriate intervals in accordance with ISO

14644-2. In particular, periodic classification testing (in accordance with ISO 14664-1) is expected annually but the frequency can be extended, based on risk assessment, the extent of the monitoring system and data that is consistently in compliance with acceptance limits or levels defined in the monitoring plan;

10.13   (b) • If computerized systems are used, their validation should be proportionate to the impact thereof on the quality of the product[17]. For computerised systems supporting critical processes, provisions should be made to ensure continuity in the event of a system breakdown (e.g. a manual or alternative system);

10.14   (c) • For investigational ATMPs, it is expected that at least the suitability of the air quality system (in accordance with ISO 14644-1 and ISO 14664-2) and the suitability of the premises to adequately control the risk of microbial and nonviable particle contamination is verified. Any other aspect of the premises that is critical with regard to the specific risks of the intended manufacturing process should be qualified (e.g. containment measures when viral replicating vectors are used). Critical equipment should be qualified also.

10.15   Before starting the manufacturing of a new type of ATMP in premises that have already been qualified, the manufacturer should assess if there is a need for re-qualification with regard to the specific risks and characteristics of the new manufacturing process/new product, e.g. if the premises have been qualified for open processing and a closed system is introduced, it can be assumed that the (existing) qualification of the premises covers a worst-case scenario and therefore no re-qualification is needed. In contrast, when the premises have been qualified for a simple manufacturing process and a more complex process is introduced that, for example, may require an additional level of containment, re-qualification is required. Likewise, if there is a significant change in the lay out of the premises, there should be an assessment of whether re-qualification is required.

10.16   Facilities and equipment should be re-evaluated at appropriate intervals to confirm that they remain suitable for the intended operations.

10.1.2   STEPS OF THE QUALIFICATION PROCESS

Setting the user requirement specifications

10.17   The manufacturer or, as appropriate, the sponsor or marketing authorisation holder should define the specifications for the premises and equipment.

---

[17] Principles relevant to the validation of computer equipment are laid down in Annex 11 of Part I of the Good Manufacturing Practice Guidelines, published in Volume 4 of EudraLex.

EU GMP PART IV SECTION 10 QUALIFICATION AND VALIDATION

The user requirement specifications should ensure that the critical quality attributes of the product and the identified risks linked to the manufacturing processes are adequately addressed (e.g. measures to avoid cross-contamination in a multi-product facility). The suitability of the materials of the parts of the equipment that come into contact with the product should be also addressed as part of the user requirement specifications.

Design qualification (DQ)

10.18 The compliance of the user requirement specifications with GMP should be demonstrated and documented.

Verifying compliance with the user requirement specifications

10.19 The manufacturer or, as appropriate, the sponsor or marketing authorisation holder should verify that the premises/equipment comply with the user specifications and are in line with GMP requirements. Typically, this involves the following steps:

10.20 (a) *Installation Qualification (IQ)*: as a minimum, it should be verified that:
  (i)   components, equipment, pipe work and other installations have been installed in conformity with the user specifications,
  (ii)   operating and maintenance instructions are provided (as appropriate), and
  (iii)   instruments are appropriately calibrated and, where applicable, associated alarms are functional.

10.21 (b) *Operational Qualification (OQ)*: the suitability of the premises and equipment to operate as designed (including under "worst-case" conditions) should be tested.

10.22 (c) *Performance Qualification (PQ)*: the suitability of the premises and equipment to operate consistently in accordance with the requirements of the intended manufacturing process (assuming worst-case conditions) should be tested. A test with surrogate materials or simulated product is acceptable.

10.23 Any deviations identified should be addressed before moving to the next qualification step. However, it is acknowledged that, in some cases, it may be appropriate to concurrently perform IQ, OQ and PQ. It may also be acceptable to perform the process validation concurrently with the PQ.

10.24 Where functionality of the equipment is not affected by transport and installation, the documentation review and some tests could be performed at the vendor's site (e.g. through factory acceptance testing), without the need to repeat the relevant elements of IQ/OQ at the manufacturer's site.

10.25   Likewise, when validating several identical pieces of equipment, it is acceptable for the manufacturer to establish a suitable testing strategy based on an evaluation of the risks.

Documentation

10.26   A report should be written summarizing the results and conclusions reached. When qualification documentation is supplied by a third party (e.g. vendor, installers), the ATMP manufacturer or, as appropriate, the sponsor or marketing authorisation holder should assess whether the documentation provided is sufficient, or if additional tests should be performed at the site to confirm suitability of the equipment (e.g. when information gaps exist having regard to the intended manufacturing process, if the equipment is to be used differently to what was intended by the manufacturer of the equipment, etc.)

10.27   Where the qualification of the premises/equipment is outsourced to a third party, the principles laid down in Section 13 also apply.

10.2   Cleaning validation

10.28   The cleaning procedures applied to re-usable tools and parts of equipment that enter into contact with the product should be validated.

10.29   Cleaning validation is the documented evidence that a given cleaning procedure effectively and reproducibly removes contaminants, residues from previous product and cleaning agents below a predefined threshold. There may be more than one way to perform cleaning validation. The objective is to demonstrate that the cleaning process consistently meets the predefined acceptance criteria. The risk of microbial and endotoxin contamination should be duly assessed.

10.30   The following considerations apply when designing the cleaning validation strategy:

- Factors that influence the effectiveness of the cleaning process (e.g. operators, rinsing times, cleaning equipment and amounts of cleaning agents used) should be identified. If variable factors have been identified, the worst-case situations should be used as the basis for cleaning validation studies.
- The influence of the time between manufacture and cleaning, and between cleaning and use, should be taken into account to define dirty and clean hold times for the cleaning process.
- When justified due to the scarcity of the starting materials, simulating agents may be used.

10.31   Cleaning procedures for closely related ATMPs do not need to be individually validated. A single validation study which considers the worst-case scenario is acceptable.

10.32   Cleaning validation should be described in a document, which should cover:

(i)   *Detailed cleaning procedure for each piece of equipment*: grouping approaches[18] are acceptable if appropriately justified (e.g. cleaning of processing vessels of the same design but with different capacity). Where similar types of equipment are grouped together, a justification of the specific equipment selected for cleaning validation is expected. The selection of the equipment should be representative of the worst-case scenario (e.g. the higher capacity vessel);

(ii)   *Sampling procedures*: sampling may be carried out by swabbing and/or rinsing or by other means depending on the production equipment. The sampling materials and method should not influence the result. For swabs, sampling should be from locations identified as "worst case". Recovery should be shown to be possible from all product contact materials sampled in the equipment with all the sampling methods used;

(iii)   *Validated analytical methods to be used*;

(iv)   *Acceptance criteria*, including the scientific rationale for setting the specific limits.

10.33   The cleaning procedure should be performed an appropriate number of times based on a risk assessment, and meet the acceptance criteria in order to prove that the cleaning method is validated (usually three consecutive batches as a minimum). Cleaning validation may be reduced or not required if only disposables are used in the manufacturing process.

10.34   A visual check for cleanliness is an important part of the acceptance criteria for cleaning validation. However, it is not generally acceptable for this criterion alone to be used. Repeated cleaning and re-testing until acceptable residue results are obtained is not considered an acceptable approach either.

APPROACH FOR INVESTIGATIONAL ATMPs

10.35   For investigational ATMPs, cleaning verification is acceptable. In such cases, there should be sufficient data from the verification to support a conclusion that the equipment is clean and available for further use.

---

[18] The design assumes that validation of any intermediate levels is represented by validation of the extremes.

10.3 Process validation

10.36 Process validation is the documented evidence that the manufacturing process can consistently produce a result within specific parameters. Although it is acknowledged that some degree of variability of the finished product due to the characteristics of the starting materials is intrinsic to ATMPs, the aim of the process validation for ATMPs is to demonstrate that the finished product characteristics are within a given range (in compliance with the terms of the marketing authorisation).

10.37 The strategy to process validation should be laid down in a document ("validation protocol"). The protocol should define (and justify as appropriate) the critical process parameters, critical quality attributes and associated acceptance criteria based on development data or documented process knowledge. The approach retained should be justified. As appropriate, the protocol should identify other (non-critical) attributes and parameters that should be investigated or monitored during the validation activity, and the reasons for their inclusion.

10.38 The following should also be specified in the protocol:

(i)   List of the equipment/facilities to be used (including measuring/monitoring/recording equipment) together with the calibration status;

(ii)   List of analytical methods and how they are to be validated, as appropriate;

(iii) Proposed in-process controls with acceptance criteria and the reason(s) why each in-process control is selected;

(iv)   Where required, additional testing to be carried out with acceptance criteria;

(v)   Sampling plan and the rationale behind it;

(vi)   Methods for recording and evaluating results;

(vii) Process for release and certification of batches (if applicable);

(viii) Specifications for the finished product (as provided for in the marketing authorisation).

10.39 It is generally accepted that, as a minimum, three consecutive batches manufactured under routine conditions constitute a validation of the process. An alternative number of batches may be justified taking into account whether standard methods of manufacture are used, whether similar products or processes are already used at the site, the variability of starting material (autologous versus allogeneic), clinical indication (rare disease: only few batches will be produced).

10.40 The limited availability of the cells/tissues, which is typical for most ATMPs, requires the development of pragmatic approaches. The approach to process validation should take into account the quantities of tissue/cells available and focus on gaining maximum experience of the process from each batch processed. Reduced process validation should, where possible, be offset by additional in-process testing to demonstrate consistency of production:

Validation with surrogate materials

10.41   The use of surrogate material may be acceptable when there is shortage of the starting materials (e.g. autologous ATMPs, allogeneic in a matched-donor scenario, allogeneic where there is no expansion of cells to Master Cell Bank). The representativeness of surrogate starting material should be evaluated, including, for example, donor age, use of materials from healthy donors, anatomical source (e.g. femur versus iliac crest) or other different characteristics (e.g. use of representative cell types or use of cells at a higher passage number than that foreseen in the product specifications).

10.42   Where possible, consideration should be given to complementing the use of surrogate materials with samples from the actual starting materials for key aspects of the manufacturing process. For instance, in the case of an ATMP based on modification of autologous cells to treat a genetic disorder, process validation using the autologous cells (affected by the condition) may be limited to those parts of the process that focus on the genetic modification itself. Other aspects could be validated using a representative surrogate cell type.

Concurrent validation approaches

10.43   Due to the limited availability of the starting materials and/or where there is a strong benefit–risk ratio for the patient, a concurrent validation may be acceptable. The decision to carry out concurrent validation should be justified and a protocol should be defined. Regular reviews of data from the manufacture of batches should be subsequently used to confirm that the manufacturing process is able to ensure that the specifications in the marketing authorization have been complied with.

10.44   Where a concurrent validation approach has been adopted, there should be sufficient data to support the conclusion that the batch meets the defined criteria. The results and conclusion should be formally documented and available to the QP prior to the certification of the batch.

Validation strategy for closely related products

10.45   Where the same manufacturing platform is used for a number of closely related products (e.g. genetically modified cells where viral vectors are manufactured according to the same manufacturing process), the extent of validation work for each new product should be based on a justified and documented risk assessment of the process. This should take into account the extent of process knowledge, including existing relevant process validation work, for each significant step in the process. Thus, in so far as the other manufacturing steps remain the same, it may be possible to limit the validation to only the steps that are new to the process.

Investigational ATMPs

10.46 It is not expected that the manufacturing process for investigational ATMPs will be validated, but appropriate monitoring and control measures should be implemented to ensure compliance with the requirements in the clinical trial authorisation. Additionally, it is expected that the aseptic processes (and, where applicable, sterilising processes) have been validated

10.47 Process validation/evaluation data should be collected throughout the development. It is noted that, for the clinical trial to be used in support of a marketing authorisation application, it is important to demonstrate that the manufacturing process of the investigational ATMP ensures consistent production.

10.4   Validation of test methods

10.48 The validation of analytical methods is intended to ensure the suitability of the analytical methods for the intended purpose. Analytical procedures, which are either described in the European Pharmacopoeia or the pharmacopoeia of a Member State, or are linked to a product specific monograph, and are performed according to the monograph, are normally considered as validated. In such cases, the suitability of the validated test for the intended purpose should be verified.

10.49 All analytical methods should be validated at the stage of marketing authorisation application.

Investigational ATMPs

10.50 During clinical development a gradual approach can be applied:

- First-in-man and exploratory clinical trials: sterility and microbial assays should be validated. In addition, other assays that are intended to ensure patient's safety should also be validated (e.g. when retroviral vectors are used, the analytical methods for testing for replication competent retrovirus should be validated).
- Throughout the clinical development, the suitability of analytical methods used to measure critical quality attributes (e.g. inactivation/removal

of virus and/or other impurities of biological origin) should be established but full validation is not required. Potency assays are expected to be validated before pivotal clinical trials.
- Pivotal clinical trials: validation of analytical methods for batch release and stability testing is expected.

10.5 Validation of transport conditions

10.51 Transport conditions may have a crucial impact on the quality of ATMPs. The transport conditions should be defined in writing.

10.52 The adequacy of the defined transport conditions (e.g. temperature, type of container, etc.) should be demonstrated.

10.53 Compliance with the defined transport conditions falls outside the responsibility of the manufacturer (unless such responsibility is assumed by means of contract). Such compliance is outside the scope of GMP.

11 Qualified Person and Batch Release

11.1 General principles

11.10 Each manufacturing site of ATMPs in the EEA must have at least one Qualified Person (QP)[19]. It is not excluded that two or more sites may have the same QP, provided that this does not impair the ability of the QP to provide their services to each of the sites in a continuous fashion.

11.11 Without prejudice to Section 11.5, batches of ATMPs should be released for sale, supply to the market or use in clinical trial only after certification by a QP. Until a batch has been released, it should remain at the site of manufacture or be shipped under quarantine to another authorised site. Safeguards to ensure that uncertified batches are not released should be in place. These safeguards may be physical (via the use of segregation and labelling) or electronic (via the use of computerized systems). When uncertified batches are moved from one authorised site to another, the safeguards to prevent premature release should remain.

---

[19] Article 48(1) of Directive 2001/83/EC on the Community code relating to medicinal products for human use, (OJ L 311, 28.11.2001, p. 67). See also Article 61(2)(b) of Regulation (EU) No 536/2014.

11.2　Qualified Person

11.12　In addition to having the qualification requirements provided for under Article 49 of Directive 2001/83, QPs responsible for ATMPs should have training and experience relevant to the specific characteristics of these products, including cell and tissue biology, biotechnological techniques, cell processing, characterization and potency testing. QPs should have detailed knowledge of the type of ATMP and manufacturing steps for which they are taking responsibility.

11.13　The QP's main responsibility is to verify and certify that each batch produced in the EU has been manufactured and checked in accordance with:

(i)　the requirements of the marketing authorisation/clinical trial authorisation;

(ii)　relevant regulations governing the manufacture of medicinal products, including GMP; and

(iii)　relevant product specifications in the destination country (in the case of exports).

11.14　QPs should have access to:

(i)　the necessary details of the marketing authorisation/clinical trial authorisation to assess if the relevant requirements have been complied with; and

(ii)　relevant data about the entire manufacturing process of the ATMP, including importation activities if any.

IMPORTED ATMPs

11.15　In case of imports of investigational ATMPs from third countries, the QP should ensure that the quality of the batch is in accordance with the terms of the clinical trial authorisation (including compliance with the terms of the Product Specification File) and that it has been manufactured in accordance with quality standards at least equivalent to the GMP requirements applied in the EU[20].

11.16　In case of imports of authorised ATMPs from third countries, the QP should ensure that the quality of the batch is in accordance with the terms of the marketing authorisation, including by means of a full qualitative and quantitative analysis of the active substance(s) as well as any other necessary checks[21]. However, it is acknowledged that for ATMPs it is not

---

[20] Article 62 and 63(3) of Regulation (EU) No 536/2014.
[21] Article 51(1)(b) of Directive 2001/83/EC.

always possible to separate the active substance from the finished product. The re-testing strategy should be in accordance with the terms of the marketing authorisation.

11.17   Additionally, it may be justified to rely on testing performed in the third country in cases where the limited amount of material available (e.g. autologous products) or short shelf-life impedes double release testing. In such cases, the testing in the third country should be conducted in GMP-certified facilities (in the case of authorised ATMPs) or under GMP conditions equivalent to those applicable in the EU (in the case of investigational ATMPs).

11.18   When the QP wishes to rely on testing of samples taken in a third country, transport and storage conditions should be adequate, so as to ensure that the samples taken in the third country are still representative of the batch.

11.19   In all cases, the conditions of storage and transport should be checked before certifying any batch; these conditions must be in accordance with the terms of the marketing authorisation/clinical trials authorisation.

RELYING ON GMP ASSESSMENTS BY THIRD PARTIES, e.g. AUDITS

11.20   In some cases the QP may rely on audits conducted by third parties attesting to the general compliance with GMP in sites involved in the manufacture of the product. In these cases, there should be a clear delimitation of responsibilities and the general requirements in Section 13 also apply.

11.21   The QP should have access to all documentation that facilitates review of the audit outcome and continued reliance on the outsourced activity.

INVOLVEMENT OF MORE THAN ONE QP

11.22   The QP who performs certification of the finished product batch may assume full responsibility for all stages of manufacture of the batch, or this responsibility may be shared with other QPs who have confirmed compliance of specific steps in the manufacture and control of a batch.

11.23   If a site undertakes only partial manufacturing operations, the QP at that site must (as a minimum) confirm that the operations undertaken by the site have been performed in accordance with GMP and the terms of the written agreement detailing the operations for which the site is responsible.

11.24   Where more than one QP is involved in the assessment of one batch, the division of responsibilities among QPs in relation to compliance of the finished batch (including details on the responsibility for assessment of any deviations) should be clearly laid down in writing.

11.25 The QP should have access to any documentation relevant to the task for which they are talking responsibility.

11.3 Batch release

11.3.1 BATCH RELEASE PROCESS

11.26 The process of batch release includes the following steps:

11.27(a) Checking that the manufacture and testing of the batch has been done in accordance with applicable requirements, including that:

(i) all manufacturing steps (including controls and testing) have been done in accordance with the marketing authorisation/clinical trial authorisation;

(ii) the specifications for the raw materials, starting materials (including matrices or devices that are a component of the ATMP) and packaging materials comply with the terms of the marketing authorisation/clinical trial authorisation;

(iii) in case of autologous products (or donor-matched scenario), the match between the origin of the starting material and the recipient has been verified (information on the origin of the cells/tissues should be checked);

(iv) the excipients used in the manufacturing of the finished product are of suitable quality and that they have been manufactured under adequate conditions;

(v) for combined ATMPs, the medical device(s) used comply with the relevant general safety and performance requirements provided for under the EU legislation on medical devices, and are adequate for the use in the combined ATMP;

(vi) where applicable, the viral and microbial safety and TSE status of all materials used in batch manufacture are compliant with the terms of the marketing authorisation/clinical trial authorisation;

(vii) all required in-process controls and checks (including environmental monitoring) have been made and appropriate records exists;

(viii) finished product quality control test data complies with the relevant specifications;

(ix) on-going stability data continues to support certification;

(x) the impact of any deviation to product manufacturing or testing has been evaluated and any additional checks and tests are complete;

(xi) all investigations related to the batch being certified have been completed and support the certification of the batch;

(xii) the self-inspection programme is active;

(xiii) appropriate arrangements for storage and transport exist; and

(xiv) the presence of the safety features referred to in Article 54 of Directive 2001/83/EC have been verified, where applicable[22].

11.28   While the QP has responsibility for ensuring that the above verifications are done, these tasks may be delegated to appropriately trained personnel or third parties.

11.29   In the case of investigational ATMPs, the amount of relevant information available will depend on the stage of development (e.g. medical devices used in an investigational combined ATMP may be in an investigational phase as well and, in such cases, the role of the QP is to ensure that the quality specifications set by the manufacturer are respected). For investigational ATMPs, the assessment of the QP should be based on all available data and information relevant to the quality of the investigational ATMP.

11.30(b)   Certification of the finished product batch by the QP: the QP must certify that each production batch has been manufactured and checked in accordance with the requirements of the marketing authorisation/clinical trial authorisation, and all other relevant regulatory requirements, including GMP.

11.31   The certification should be recorded by the QP in a register or equivalent document provided for that purpose, which must be kept up to date. The register or equivalent document must remain at the disposal of the competent authority for one year after expiry of the batch to which it relates or at least five years after certification of the batch by the QP, whichever is the longest.

11.32   For investigational ATMPs, the certification must be kept for at least five years after the completion or formal discontinuation of the last clinical trial in which the batch was used.

11.33(c)   Assigning the release status to the batch: this is the step that effectively releases the batch for sale, export or (in case of an investigational ATMP) use in a clinical study.

---

[22] ATMPs that contain or consist of tissues or cells are exempted from the safety feature in accordance with Commission delegated Regulation (EU) 2016/161 supplementing Directive 2001/83/EC of the European Parliament and the Council by laying down detailed rules for the safety features appearing on the packaging of medicinal products for human use (OJ L 32, 9.2.2016, p. 1).

11.34 The notification by a QP to the releasing site that certification has taken place should be formal and unambiguous.

ADDITIONAL CONSIDERATIONS FOR INVESTIGATIONAL ATMPs

11.35 Investigational ATMPs should remain under the control of the sponsor until after completion of a two-step procedure: certification by the QP and release by the sponsor for use in a clinical trial. The process of release of the product for use in the clinical site should be agreed between the sponsor and the manufacturer, taking into account the shelf-life of the product. Both steps should be documented as appropriate.

11.36 Transfers of the investigational ATMPs from one trial site to another should remain the exception. When they occur, the QP, in agreement with the sponsor, should establish the specific conditions under which the transfers should take place.

11.3.2 BATCH RELEASE PRIOR TO OBTAINING THE RESULTS OF QUALITY CONTROL TESTS

11.37 Due to a short shelf-life, some ATMPs may have to be released before completion of all quality control tests. In this case, it is possible to organise the procedure for batch certification and release in various stages, for example:

11.38 • Assessment by a designated person(s) of the batch processing records, results from environmental monitoring (where available) and the available analytical results for review in preparation for the initial certification by the QP, which allows release for administration;

11.39 • Assessment of the final analytical tests and other information available for final certification by the QP.

11.40 The delegation of tasks to the designated person(s) and the description of the batch certification and release procedure should be laid down in writing.

11.41 A procedure should be in place to describe the measures to be taken (including liaison with clinical staff) where out-of-specification test results are obtained after the release of the product.

11.42 It is acknowledged that, in the case of ATMPs, out-of-specification products are not always attributable to failures in the manufacturing process (e.g. idiopathic factors of the patient). All instances of out-of-specification products should be investigated and, where a failure in the manufacturing process is identified, the relevant corrective and/or preventive actions taken to prevent recurrence documented. In case of recurrent deviations, the need for changes to the manufacturing process should be assessed.

11.3.3 BATCH RELEASE PROCESS IN CASES OF DECENTRALISED MANUFACTURING

11.43 The manufacturing process is key for the quality, as well as the safety and efficacy, attributes of ATMPs, and it is therefore particularly important to ensure that the manufacturing process and control methods applied are in accordance with the marketing/clinical trial authorisation and that GMP is respected. The process of batch certification and batch release, as well as the role of the QP, is an essential step in this regard.

11.44 There may be cases where manufacturing of the ATMP needs to take place in sites close to the patient (e.g. ATMPs with short shelf-life, clinical advantage of using fresh cells as opposed to freezing the starting materials/finished product, etc.). In such cases, manufacturing of the ATMPs may need to be decentralised to multiple sites so as to reach to patients across the EU ("decentralised manufacturing"). This scenario may occur in the context of both authorised ATMPs and investigational ATMPs.

11.45 The batch certification and release process becomes particularly important in the case of ATMPs manufactured under a decentralised system because manufacturing in multiple sites increases the risk of variability for the product. In particular, through the batch certification and release process, it must be ensured that each batch released at any of the sites has been manufactured and checked in accordance with the requirements of the marketing authorisation/clinical trial authorisation and other relevant regulatory requirements, including compliance with GMP. To this effect, the following aspects should be considered:

11.46 (a) A "central site", which should be established in the EU, should be identified. The central site is responsible for the oversight of the decentralised sites. To this end, the central site assumes, as a minimum, the following tasks:
    (i)   ensuring that those involved in the batch certification and release process are adequately qualified and trained for their tasks, and
    (ii)   performing audits to confirm that the batch certification and release process (as described in SOP) is complied with.

11.47 The marketing authorisation holder/sponsor may be the central site in cases when the marketing authorisation holder/sponsor also assumes the role of manufacturer.

11.48 (b) There should be a written contract/technical agreement between the central site and the decentralised sites establishing the responsibilities of each party, including the responsibility of the QP.

11.49 (c) The steps of the batch certification and release process should be laid down in writing (SOP). The responsibilities of each of the sites/actors involved should be clearly explained. There should be no gaps or unexplained overlaps in the responsibilities of the personnel concerned. The process should also be explained, as appropriate, in the context of the marketing authorisation application/clinical trial authorisation.

11.50 (d) A QP established in the EU should ultimately have responsibility for the batch certification. However, it should be possible for the QP of the central site to rely on data/information that is transmitted to them by qualified and trained personnel at the decentralised sites.

11.51 (e) If a deviation occurs at the decentralised sites, it should be approved in writing by a responsible person (after having assessed the impact thereof on quality, safety and efficacy), with the involvement of the QP as appropriate. Deviations should be investigated with a view to identify the root cause and to implement corrective and preventive measures as appropriate. Any instances of quality defects, deviations or non-conformity should be immediately reported to the central site.

11.4 Handling of unplanned deviations

11.52 As long as the specifications for the finished product are met, a QP may confirm compliance/certify a batch where an unexpected deviation related to the manufacturing process and/or the analytical control methods has occurred provided that:

(i) there is an in-depth assessment of the impact of the deviation that supports a conclusion that the occurrence does not have a negative effect on quality, safety or efficacy of the product; and

(ii) the need for inclusion of the affected batch/batches in the on-going stability programme has been evaluated, where appropriate.

11.5 Administration of out-of-specification products

11.53 Exceptionally, the administration of the cells/tissues that are contained in a cell/tissue-based ATMP that is out of specification may be necessary for the patient. Where the administration of the product is necessary to avoid an immediate significant hazard to the patient, and taking into account the alternative options for the patient and the consequences of not receiving the cells/tissues contained in the product, the supply of the product to the treating physician is justified.

11.54   When the request of the treating physician is received, the manufacturer should provide the treating physician with its evaluation of the risks and notify the physician that the out-of-specification product is being supplied to the physician at their request. The confirmation of the treating physician to accept the product should be recorded by the manufacturer. In a clinical trial setting, the manufacturer should immediately notify the sponsor of such events. In turn, the sponsor should inform the relevant competent authority. For marketed products, the marketing authorisation holder and the supervisory authority for the site of the batch release should be informed.

12   Quality Control

12.1   General principles

12.10   Quality control ("QC") should ensure that the necessary and relevant tests are carried out and that materials are not released for use, nor products released for sale or supply, until their quality has been judged satisfactory. Quality control is not confined to laboratory operations, but must be involved in all decisions that may affect the quality of the product.

12.11   The person responsible for quality control should ensure that the premises and equipment where quality control operations are carried out are appropriate and maintained under suitable conditions and that the personnel working under their responsibility are adequately trained. In-process controls may be carried out within the production area provided that they do not carry any risk for the product.

12.12   The person responsible for quality control supervises all quality control procedures. In particular, it assumes responsibility for the following tasks:

(i)   Approval of specifications, sampling instructions, test methods and other quality control procedures;

(ii)   Approval of conditions for outsourced testing;

(iii)   Control of raw materials, starting materials, medical devices that are used in combined ATMPs, packaging materials, intermediate, bulk and finished products (including approval or rejection thereof). In case of autologous products or allogeneic products in a donor-match scenario, the match between the origin of the starting material and the recipient should be verified (information on the origin of the cells/tissues should be checked);

(iv)   Where, exceptionally, there is release of expired materials for use in the manufacturing process, the person responsible for quality control should ensure the quality thereof through appropriate re-testing;

(v)   Supervision of the control of the reference and/or retention samples of materials and products, as appropriate;

(vi)   Ensuring that all necessary testing is carried out and the associated records are evaluated;

(vii)   Ensuring the monitoring of the stability of the products;

(viii)   Participation in investigations related to the quality of the product.

12.13   Appropriate records in connection with the above-referred activities should be kept. Written procedures should be put in place in connection with the activities listed in (iii) to (vi).

12.14   Quality control personnel should have access to production areas for sampling and investigation as appropriate. All documents that are needed for the assessment of quality control (e.g. description of procedures or records from the manufacturing process and testing) should also be accessible.

12.2 Sampling

12.2.1 GENERAL PRINCIPLES

12.15   Samples should be representative of the batch of materials or products from which they are taken. Bulk containers from which samples have been drawn should be identified. In case of samples of sterile materials or samples that are taken during processing activities, identification of the sample should be done by other appropriate means.

12.16   The sample taking should be done and recorded in accordance with written procedures that describe the method of sampling, including the amount of sample to be taken, precautions to be observed, storage conditions, etc. Containers should bear a label indicating, as a minimum, the content, batch number and date of sampling. When containers are too small, the use of barcodes or other means that permit access to this information should be considered.

12.2.2 RETENTION OF SAMPLES

12.17   Samples are generally retained for analytical purposes should the need arise during the shelf life of the batch concerned (reference samples) and for identification purposes (retention sample of a fully packaged unit from a batch of finished product). The reference sample and the retention sample may be identical in some cases (i.e. a fully packaged unit).

12.18   As a general principle, a reference sample should be of sufficient size to permit the carrying out, on at least two occasions, of the full analytical controls on the batch foreseen in the marketing authorisation/clinical trial authorisation. However, it is acknowledged that this may not always be feasible due to scarcity of the materials or limited size of the batches (e.g. autologous products, allogeneic products in a matched-donor scenario, products for ultra-rare diseases, products for use in first-in-human clinical trial with a very small scale production).

12.19   The retention sample should be contained in its finished primary packaging or in packaging composed of the same material as the primary container in which the product is marketed.

12.20   Samples should normally be stored under the conditions foreseen in the product information. However, for products/materials with a short shelf life, it should be carefully considered if other storage conditions that maximise stability can be used (see below).

12.21   The sampling plan should be documented. The sampling plan should be adapted to the specific characteristics of the product. In designing the sampling strategy, the manufacturer should take into account the risks, the practical limitations that may exist and possible mitigating measures (e.g. increased reliance on in-process testing). The sampling strategy of the manufacturer should be duly justified.

12.22   In particular, the following considerations apply:

12.23   • Samples of raw materials: reference samples of critical raw materials (e.g. cytokines, growth factors, enzymes, sera) are important for investigating possible quality problems with the product. The assessment of whether a specific raw material is critical should be done by the manufacturer (or, as appropriate, by the sponsor or marketing authorisation holder) with regard to the specific risks and possible mitigating measures (e.g. increased QC controls). The decisions taken should be documented. Samples of critical raw materials should be retained during the shelf-life of the relevant raw materials.

12.24   • Samples of the starting materials should generally be kept for two years after the batch release. However, it is acknowledged that the retention of samples may be challenging due to scarcity of the materials. Due to this intrinsic limitation, it is justified not to keep reference samples of the cells/tissues used as starting materials in the case of autologous ATMPs and certain allogeneic ATMPs (matched-donor scenario). In other cases where the scarcity of the materials is also a concern, the sampling strategy may be adapted provided that this is justified and appropriate mitigation measures are implemented.

12.25 • <u>Samples of active substances and intermediate products</u> should generally be kept for two years after the batch release. However, it is acknowledged that, for ATMPs, it is not always possible to separate the sampling of the starting materials, active substance, intermediate and finished product. The considerations regarding scarcity of starting materials apply, adapted as necessary, to the expectations on the retention of samples of active substances and intermediate products.

12.26 • <u>Samples of primary packaging material:</u> samples of primary packaging material should generally be retained for the duration of the shelf-life of the finished product concerned. The retention of samples of primary packaging material may not be necessary in certain cases, with regard to the risks of the materials and/or other relevant consideration (e.g. increased QC controls, primary packaging material is certified as a medical device). A decision not to keep samples of primary packaging materials should be duly justified and documented.

12.27 • <u>A sample of a fully packaged unit</u> (retention sample) should be kept per batch for at least one year after the expiry date. A retention sample is, however, not expected in the case of autologous products or allogeneic products in a matched-donor scenario because the unit produced with the patient's tissues/cells constitutes should be administered to the patient. When it is not possible to keep a retention sample, photographs or copies of the label are acceptable for inclusion in the batch records.

12.28 The retention period of samples of starting materials, active substance and intermediate product should be adapted to the stability and shelf-life of the product and, therefore, shorter periods may be justified. In cases of a short shelf-life, the manufacturer should consider if the retention of the sample under conditions that prolong the shelf-life (such as cryopreservation) is representative for the intended purpose. For instance, cryopreservation of fresh cells may render the sample inadequate for characterisation purposes, but the sample may be adequate for sterility or viral safety controls (the volume of the samples can be reduced according to the intended purpose). When the cryostorage of a sample is considered inadequate for the intended purpose, the manufacturer should consider alternative approaches (e.g. sample of intermediate product such as differentiated cells).

12.3 Testing

12.29 Testing is important to ensure that each batch meets the relevant specifications. In-process controls testing should be performed at appropriate stages of production to control those conditions that are important for the quality of the product.

12.30 Testing of critical raw materials, starting materials and active substance/intermediates/finished products, and stability testing should be performed in accordance with the terms defined in the marketing authorisation/clinical trial authorisation.

12.31 Testing methods should be validated and reference materials should be established (where available) for qualification and routine testing. For investigational ATMPs, the level of validation should be commensurate with the development phase and the criticality of the test results considering the risks for the patient (see Section 10.4).

12.32 The following records should be kept in connection with the tests performed:

(i) Name of the material or product and, where applicable, dosage form;

(ii) Batch number and, where appropriate, the manufacturer and/or supplier;

(iii) References to the relevant specifications and testing procedures;

(iv) Test results, including observations and calculations, and reference to any certificates of analysis;

(v) Dates of testing;

(vi) Initials of the persons who performed the testing (or another suitable identification system);

(vii) Initials of the persons who verified the testing and the calculations, where appropriate (or another suitable identification system);

(viii) A clear statement of approval or rejection (or other status decision) and the dated signature of the responsible person;

(ix) Reference to the equipment used.

12.33 Materials, reagents, culture media and reference standards used for QC tests should be of appropriate quality and used according to instructions. Where necessary, identity verification and/or testing should be considered upon receipt or before use.

TECHNICAL TRANSFER OF TESTING METHODS

12.34 The transfer of testing methods from one laboratory (transferring laboratory) to another laboratory (receiving laboratory) should be described in a detailed protocol.

12.35 The transfer protocol should include, among others, the following parameters:

(i) Identification of the testing to be performed and the relevant test method(s) undergoing transfer;

(ii) Identification of any additional training requirements;

(iii) Identification of standards and samples to be tested;

(iv) Identification of any special transport and storage conditions of test items;

(v) The acceptance criteria.

12.36 Deviations from the protocol should be investigated prior to closure of the technical transfer process. The technical transfer report should document the comparative outcome of the process and identify areas requiring further test method revalidation, if applicable.

12.4 On-going stability programme

12.37 After the marketing authorisation has been granted, a programme should be implemented to verify that, under the relevant storage conditions (as foreseen in the marketing authorisation), the product remains within the specifications during the shelf-life (so-called "on-going stability programme"). The methodology in the on-going stability programme can differ from the approach followed to obtain the stability data submitted in the marketing authorisation application (e.g. different frequency of testing), provided that it is justified.

12.38 The on-going stability studies should generally be performed on the finished product (i.e. as released by the manufacturer). When intermediates can be stored for extended periods of time, consideration should be given to include in the stability programme those batches that have been manufactured from materials stored for longer periods of time. Stability studies on the reconstituted product are performed during product development and need not be monitored on an on-going basis. The use of surrogate materials (i.e. material derived from healthy volunteers) is acceptable in the case of autologous products (or matched-donor scenario) where the batch needs to be administered in its entirety to the patient.

12.39 The number of batches and frequency of testing should be adequate to allow for trend analysis. It is generally expected that at least one batch of the product is included per year in the stability programme, unless none is produced in a given year or a different frequency is otherwise justified. Out-of-specifications and significant atypical trends should be investigated and their possible impact on the batches on the market should be assessed and reported to the competent authorities as appropriate.

13 Outsourced Activities

13.1 General principles

13.10 Activities that are outsourced to a third party (including consultancy work) should be governed by a written contract that establishes the responsibilities of each party. As appropriate, the role and responsibilities in the event of detection of quality defects should be clearly established in the contract, as well as, where applicable, the obligations of each party regarding traceability.

13.2 Obligations of the contract giver

13.11 Prior to outsourcing any activity, the manufacturer or, as appropriate, the sponsor or marketing authorisation holder ("contract giver") should assess the suitability of the contractor ("contract acceptor") to carry out the outsourced activities in accordance with the terms of the marketing authorisation/clinical trial authorisation and other applicable regulations, including compliance with GMP.

13.12 Exceptionally, when the outsourced activity is a highly specialised test (e.g. karyotype test), it is acceptable that the contract acceptor is not GMP certified, provided that it complies with suitable quality standards relevant to the outsourced activity (e.g. ISO) and that this is duly justified.

13.13 The contract giver should provide the contract acceptor with detailed information on the product/manufacturing process, as well as any other data that is necessary to carry out the contracted operations correctly.

13.14 The contract giver should review and assess the records and the results related to the outsourced activities.

13.3 Obligations of the contract acceptor

13.15 The contract acceptor should take all necessary measures (e.g. adequate premises, equipment, trained personnel, etc.) to carry out satisfactorily the outsourced activities. Special consideration should be given to the prevention of cross-contamination and to maintaining traceability.

13.16 The contract acceptor should not introduce changes in the process, premises, equipment, test methods, specifications or any other element related to the outsourced activity without the prior approval of the contract giver.

13.17 All records related to the outsourced activities as well as reference samples should be transferred to the contract giver or, alternatively, the contract giver should be granted access to them.

13.18 Subcontract to a third party is not permissible without the approval of the contract giver.

13.19 The contract acceptor should permit audits/inspections by the contract giver and the competent authorities in connection with the outsourced activities.

14 Quality Defects and Product Recalls

14.1 Quality defects

14.10 A system should be put in place to ensure that all quality-related complaints, whether received orally or in writing, are recorded and that they are thoroughly investigated. Personnel responsible for managing complaint and quality defect investigations should be independent from marketing and sales departments unless otherwise justified. If the QP involved in the certification of the concerned batch(es) does not participate in the investigation, it should be informed in a timely manner.

14.11 Operating procedures should be developed describing the actions to be taken upon the receipt of a complaint, addressing in particular the identification of the potential root cause(s) of the quality defect, the assessment of the risk(s) posed by the quality defect, the need for appropriate corrective or preventive measures, the assessment of the impact that any recall action may have on the availability of the medicinal product to patients, and the internal and external communications that should be made. Where the root cause cannot be ascertained, the most probable reasons should be identified.

14.12 If additional donor (human or animal) health information becomes available after procurement, which affects product quality, an analysis of the risk(s) and the need for corrective or prevented measures is also required.

14.13 When a quality defect is discovered or suspected in a batch, consideration should be given to the need of checking other batches (or, as appropriate, other products) in order to determine if they are also affected.

14.14 Quality defect investigations should include a review of previous quality defect reports or any other relevant information for any indication of specific or recurring problems.

14.15 The priority during an investigation should be to ensure that appropriate risk-management measures are taken to ensure patients safety. All decisions and measures adopted should be documented. The effectiveness of the corrective and/or preventive measures implemented should be monitored.

14.16 Quality defect records should be retained and used to evaluate the possible existence of recurring problems. Competent authorities should be informed in a timely manner in case of a confirmed quality defect (faulty manufacture, product deterioration, detection of falsification, non-compliance with the marketing authorisation or Product Specification File, or any other serious quality problems) with an ATMP that may result in the recall of the product or an abnormal restriction in the supply. Unplanned deviations as described in Section 11.4 should not be notified.

14.17 Where the ATMP is manufactured by an entity that is not the marketing authorisation holder/sponsor, the role and responsibilities of the manufacturer, the marketing authorisation holder/sponsor, and any other relevant third parties in relation to assessment, decision-making, dissemination of information and implementation of risk-reducing actions should be laid down in writing.

ADDITIONAL CONSIDERATIONS FOR INVESTIGATIONAL ATMPs

14.18 Where blinding of investigational medicinal products is required by the protocol of a clinical trial, the manufacturer should implement a procedure for the rapid unblinding of blinded products where this is necessary for a prompt recall. The manufacturer should ensure that the procedure discloses the identity of the blinded product only in so far as it is necessary.

14.2 Product recalls and other risk-reducing actions

14.19 Measures to address quality defects should be proportionate to the risks and the priority should be the protection of patients. Whenever possible, the actions to be taken should be discussed with the concerned competent authorities in advance.

14.20 There should be established written procedures for the recall of products, including how a recall should be initiated, who should be informed in the event of a recall (including relevant authorities and clinical sites) and how the recalled material should be treated. The procedure should foresee the reconciliation between the delivered and the recovered quantities and the recording of the progress until closure. The documented destruction of a defective product at the clinical site is an acceptable alternative to the return of the product. Recalled products should be clearly identified and segregated.

14.21 It should be ensured that recall operations could be initiated promptly and at any time. In certain cases, and with a view to protect public health, it may be necessary to recall products prior to establishing the root cause or the full extent of the quality defect.

14.22 In order to test the robustness of the recall procedure, in the case of authorised ATMPs, consideration should be given to the possibility of performing mock-recall actions. However, it is acknowledged that a mock-recall action may not be appropriate in certain settings (e.g. autologous ATMPs, allogeneic ATMPs in a matched-donor scenario and ATMPs where the time between manufacturing and administration of the product to the patient is very short).

14.23 All concerned competent authorities should be informed prior to the initiation of a recall operation unless urgent action is required to protect public health.

14.24 An action plan should be established for cases where the product cannot be recalled because it has already been administered to the patient(s).

14.25 In addition to recalls, there are other risk-reducing actions that may be considered to manage the risks presented by quality defects, such as the transmission of appropriate information to healthcare professionals.

ADDITIONAL CONSIDERATIONS FOR INVESTIGATIONAL ATMPs

14.26 Procedures for retrieving investigational ATMPs and documenting this retrieval should be agreed by the sponsor in collaboration with the manufacturer, where different. The manufacturer, investigator and sponsor's representative need to understand their obligations under the retrieval procedure. To facilitate recall, a detailed inventory of the shipments made by the manufacturer should be maintained.

15 Environmental Control Measures for ATMPs Containing or Consisting of GMOs

15.10 The handling of ATMPs containing or consisting of genetically modified organisms (GMOs) may pose a risk for the environment, requiring the implementation of additional control measures. As a first step, an assessment of the risks should be performed taking into account the risk of the isolated ATMP, as well as the risk in case of expansion inside a permissive cell host. The risk assessment should result in a categorization of the products as having a negligible, low, moderate or high risk for the environment.

15.11   Containment measures should be established according to the risk of the product that is handled, including measures regarding the design of the premises, organizational and technical measures, and measures regarding the treatment of residues.

15.12   Where replication limited viral vectors are used, measures should be in place to prevent the introduction of wild-type viruses, which may lead to the formation of replication-competent recombinant vectors. The handling of viral vectors should take place in a segregated area and in a biological safety cabinet or an isolator.

15.13   Appropriate decontamination measures should be implemented when personnel or materials move from an area containing GMOs to an area not containing GMOs or between areas containing different GMOs. Unidirectional flows should be considered where possible.

15.14   Emergency plans (adapted to the level of risk) should also be in place covering the actions to be taken in case of accidental release into the environment. The plan should foresee measures/procedures for containment, protection of personnel, cleaning, decontamination and waste management, as well as the notification to the local competent authorities and, where appropriate, the emergency services.

15.15   In the case of authorised ATMPs, the risk assessment, the containment measures and the emergency plan(s) should be part of the Risk Management Plan.

15.16   This Section is without prejudice to the requirements that may be applicable to investigational ATMPs under Directive 2001/18/EC[23] and Directive 2009/41/EC[24].

---

[23] Directive 2001/18/EC of the European Parliament and of Council of 12 March 2001 on the deliberate release into the environment of genetically modified organisms and repealing Council Directive 90/220/EEC, (OJ L 106, 17.4.2001, p. 1).

[24] Directive 2009/41/EC of the European Parliament and of Council of 6 May 2009 on the contained use of genetically modified microorganisms (OJ L 125, 21.5.2009, p. 75).

16 Reconstitution of Product after Batch Release

16.1 Reconstitution activities

16.10 Reconstitution activities can be performed at the administration site (e.g. in hospital pharmacies) outside a GMP environment.

16.11 For the purposes of these Guidelines, the term "reconstitution" covers activities required after batch release and prior to the administration of the ATMP to the patient, and that cannot be considered as a manufacturing step[25]. No activity that entails substantial manipulation can, however, be considered to be reconstitution (e.g. cultivation). Substantial manipulations should be conducted under GMP.

16.12 The following are examples of reconstitution activities relevant for ATMPs. It is stressed that these examples cannot be extrapolated to medicinal products other than ATMPs:
- Thawing, washing, buffer exchange, centrifugation steps necessary to remove preservation solution (e.g. dimethyl sulfoxide [DMSO]), removal of process-related impurities (residual amount of preservation solution, dead cells) including filtering.
- (Re)suspension, dissolution or dilution with solvent/buffer, dispersion;
- Mixing the product with patient's own cells, with an adjuvant and/or with other substances added for the purposes of administration (including matrixes). However, the mixing of a gene therapy vector with autologous cells is a manufacturing activity that should be conducted under GMP;
- Splitting the product and use in separate doses, adaptation of dose (e.g. cell count);
- Loading into delivery systems/surgical devices, transfer to an infusion bag/syringe.

16.13 The above steps can be part of the reconstitution process only if it is appropriately justified that these steps cannot be performed as part of the manufacturing process before batch release without negative impact on the product. Additionally, the above activities can be considered "reconstitution" only when they are carried out at administration site (i.e. it is not acceptable to have these steps outsourced to a third party that is not GMP compliant).

16.2 Obligations of the ATMP manufacturer in connection with reconstitution activities

16.14 The manufacturer or, as appropriate, the sponsor or marketing authorisation holder should describe the reconstitution process, including equipment

---

[25] Grinding and shaping are part of surgical procedures and therefore are neither manufacturing nor reconstitution activities.

to be used and requirements at the site of administration. The instructions should be detailed and clear enough so as to avoid negative impacts on the quality of the product (e.g. when the reconstitution involves thawing, the waiting period at room temperature, the rate of temperature change during thawing, use of a water bath, etc. should be described).

16.15   Likewise, when the reconstitution requires the use of solvents and/or other materials these should be specified or, as appropriate, provided.

16.16   In the case of authorised ATMPs, the manufacturer should validate the reconstitution processes to be followed from the point of batch release to the moment of administration to the patient, i.e. through appropriate studies it should be demonstrated that the specified reconstitution process is sufficiently robust and consistent so that the product can be administered without negative impact on quality/safety/efficacy profile of the ATMP.

16.17   The compliance of the administration site with the defined reconstitution process falls outside the responsibility of the manufacturer and is also outside the scope of GMP.

17   Automated Production of ATMPs

17.1   General principles

17.10   If the output of an automated production system (hereafter referred to as "automated equipment") meets the definition of ATMP, the requirements of the Regulation (EU) No 1394/2007 apply. Accordingly, in the case of authorised ATMPs or ATMPs used in a clinical trial setting, GMP requirements (as laid down in these Guidelines) apply.

17.11   The use of automated equipment may ease compliance with certain GMP requirements and may also bring certain advantages in respect to product's quality. This Section outlines some specific aspects relevant to the use of this technology for the manufacture of ATMPs but, unless stated otherwise, the remaining Sections of these Guidelines are also applicable.

17.2   Automated equipment

17.12   The ATMP manufacturer is responsible for the quality of the ATMP and, therefore, has to ensure the suitability of the automated equipment for the specific intended purpose.

17.13   Although the level of effort to demonstrate suitability may be reduced when the automated equipment is certified for the intended used according to the EU medical device legislation (CE mark), it is stressed that the

CE mark may not be relevant (i.e. automated equipment that does not qualify as medical device) and that, in any case, the CE mark does not suffice to demonstrate suitability as required under these Guidelines.

17.14 Of particular relevance are the following obligations of the ATMP manufacturer:

17.15 Qualification of the equipment: the qualification process as described in Section 10.1 applies. The user requirement specifications should be clear, unambiguous and detailed enough to ensure the suitability of the automated equipment for the intended operations.

17.16 In turn, the amount of information received from the manufacturer of the automated equipment should be sufficient for the ATMP manufacturer to fully understand the functioning of the automated equipment and to identify the steps critical for the quality, safety and efficacy of the product. Additional tests and operating procedures should be developed by the ATMP manufacturer where appropriate (e.g. in case of information gaps in the information provided by the manufacturer of the automated equipment or deviations from the operating instructions supplied).

17.17 The automated equipment should not be used outside the recommendations of its manufacturer/supplier, unless the new operating mode has been fully validated.

17.18 Standard operating procedures (SOPs) should be developed. They should be clear and detailed enough to ensure that the operators understand the manufacturing process and the associated risks. SOPs should also ensure that any deviation can be rapidly identified and that appropriate measures are taken.

17.19 Adequate maintenance: maintenance of the automated equipment to ensure optimal conditions of use and to avoid unintended deviations/ instances of malfunctioning is essential.

17.20 A programme of services/calibration at regular intervals required to ensure that the good performance of the automated equipment should be described by the manufacturer thereof. In turn, the ATMP manufacturer should ensure that the maintenance programme is performed. As appropriate, the split of responsibilities between the manufacturer of the automated equipment and the manufacturer of ATMPs should be laid down in writing.

17.21 Aseptic processing: the automated equipment should be used only under conditions that ensure aseptic processing (e.g. validation of cleaning processes, sterilisation of multiple-use materials that are in contact with the product, adequate checks of the integrity of the equipment, such as by means of pressure-hold test or leak testing, etc.).

17.22   <u>Batch and traceability records</u> should be kept.

17.3   Personnel

17.23   Personnel involved in production should be adequately trained and the associated risks of the process should be duly understood (including risks to the efficacy of the product).

17.4   Premises

17.24   As explained in Section 9.5.1, the room where a closed system is used should be at least of grade D. The transfer of the material into/from the equipment is a critical step and a validated procedure should be put in place to preserve the product from the risk of contamination.

17.25   Section 9.5.1 also explains the conditions under which, exceptionally, closed systems may be placed in a controlled but non-classified environment.

17.5   Production and process validation

17.26   The moment when the manufacturing process starts and finishes should be defined and the role and responsibilities of all actors involved at the different time points should be clearly established.

17.27   Possibilities for in-process controls may be limited by the continuous closed processing. In such cases, continuous monitoring of critical process parameters and other input parameters that affect product quality (as identified in the marketing authorisation/clinical trial authorisation) should be performed if technically possible. When continuous monitoring is not technically possible, monitoring at appropriate intervals with regard to the criticality of the parameter and the risks is required. Data on process parameters should be kept as part of the batch records.

17.28   Validation of aseptic processing by media fill simulation should also be performed. The biannual frequency is recommended but it could be adapted with regard to the risks (see Section 9.5.2).

17.6   Qualified person and batch certification

17.29   Batch certification is a fundamental requirement for all medicinal products, including ATMPs that are manufactured using automated equipment.

Glossary

1. ADVANCED THERAPY MEDICINAL PRODUCT (ATMP)

Gene therapy medicinal products, somatic cell therapy medicinal products and tissue-engineered products as defined in Article 2 of the ATMP Regulation.

2. ANIMALS

Founder animal: animals from which the source/donor animals are initially bred.

Specified pathogen free (SPF): animal materials (e.g. chicken embryos or cell cultures) used for the production or quality control of ATMPs, which are derived from groups (e.g. flocks or herds) of animals free from specified pathogens. Such flocks or herds are defined as animals sharing a common environment and having their own caretakers who have no contact with non-SPF groups.

3. AIRLOCK

An enclosed space with two or more doors, and which is interposed between two or more rooms, e.g. of differing class of cleanliness, for the purpose of controlling the airflow between those rooms when they need to be entered. An airlock is designed for and used by either people or goods.

4. AREA

An "area" is a space. A specific set of rooms within a building associated with the manufacturing of any one product or multiple products that has a common air-handling unit is considered as a single area.

Clean area: an area designed, maintained and controlled to prevent particle and microbiological contamination. Reference for the qualification of the clean rooms and clean air devices can be found in the ISO 14644 series of standards:

- *Critical clean area*: an area where the product is exposed to environmental conditions;
- *Background clean area*: environment in the immediate vicinity of the critical clean area.

Contained area: an area constructed and operated in such a manner (and equipped with appropriate air-handling and filtration) so as to prevent contamination of the external environment by biological agents from within the area.

Segregated area: a segregated area within a manufacturing site requires separate cryostorage, separate production suite with separate HVAC, restrictions on the movement of personnel and equipment (without appropriate decontamination measures) and dedicated equipment reserved solely for the production of one type of product with a specific risk profile.

5. BULK PRODUCT

Any product that has completed all processing stages up to, but not including, final packaging.

6. CAMPAIGNED MANUFACTURE

The manufacture of a series of batches of the same product in sequence in a given period of time followed by strict adherence to pre-established control measures before transfer to another product. Use of the same equipment for distinct products is possible provided that appropriate control measures are applied.

7. CELL BANK

Cell bank system: a cell bank system is a system whereby successive batches of a product are manufactured by culture in cells derived from the same master cell bank. A number of containers from the master cell bank are used to prepare a working cell bank. The cell bank system should be validated for a passage level or number of population doublings beyond that achieved during routine production.

Master cell bank: a culture of (fully characterised) cells distributed into containers in a single operation, processed together in such a manner as to ensure uniformity and stored in such a manner as to ensure stability. The master cell back is used to derive all working cell banks.

Working cell bank: a culture of cells derived from the master cell bank and intended for use in the preparation of production cell cultures.

8. CELL STOCK

Primary cells expanded to a given number of cells to be aliquoted and used as starting material for production of a limited number of lots of a cell-based ATMP.

9. CLEAN ROOM

A room designed, maintained and controlled to prevent particle and microbiological contamination of the products. Such a room is assigned and reproducibly meets an appropriate air cleanliness classification.

10. CLEANING VALIDATION

See Section 10.2.

11. CLEANING VERIFICATION

The gathering of evidence through appropriate analysis after each batch/campaign to show that contaminants, residues of the previous product or cleaning agents have been reduced below a predefined threshold.

12. CLOSED SYSTEM

A process system designed and operated so as to avoid exposure of the product or material to the room environment. Materials may be introduced to a closed system, but the addition must be done in such a way so as to avoid exposure of the product to the room environment (e.g. by means of sterile connectors or fusion systems).

A closed system may need to be opened (e.g. to install a filter or make a connection), but it is returned to a closed state through a sanitization or sterilization step prior to process use.

13. ISOLATOR

A decontaminated unit supplied with Grade A (ISO 5) or higher air quality that provides uncompromised, continuous isolation of its interior from the external environment (i.e. surrounding cleanroom air and personnel).

14. INTERMEDIATE

Partly processed material that must undergo further manufacturing steps before it becomes a bulk product.

16. MANUFACTURING ORDER

Document that contains the request of the sponsor to manufacture a given product. The document should be unambiguous and should refer to the Product Specification File and the relevant clinical trial protocol as appropriate.

17. PRODUCT SPECIFICATION FILE

A file containing, or referring to, files containing the specifications, instructions and other information necessary for the manufacture of an investigational medicinal product and to perform batch certification. The specific content thereof is explained in Section 6.2.

18. QUALIFICATION OF PREMISES AND EQUIPMENT

See Section 10.1.

19. QUALIFICATION OF SUPPLIERS

Process designed to ensure the suitability of suppliers. Qualification of suppliers may be done through various means, e.g. by means of quality questionnaires, audits, etc.).

20. RAW MATERIALS

The definition of "raw materials" is provided in Part IV of the Annex to Directive 2001/83/EC on the Community code relating to medicinal products for human use.

21. ROOM STATUS

At rest: "at-rest" state is the condition where all HVAC systems and installations are functioning but without personnel and with equipment static. The particle limits should be achieved after a short "clean-up period" of approximately 15–20 minutes after completion of operations.

In operation: "in-operation" state is the condition when all equipment and installations are functioning and personnel are working in accordance with the manufacturing procedure.

22. SEED LOT

Seed lot system: a seed lot system is a system according to which successive batches of a product are derived from the same master seed lot at a given passage level. For routine production, a working seed lot is prepared from the master seed lot. The final product is derived from the working seed lot and has not undergone more passages from the master seed lot than what has been shown in clinical studies to be satisfactory with respect to safety and efficacy. The origin and the passage history of the master seed lot and the working seed lot are recorded.

Master seed lot: a culture of a microorganism (virus or bacterium) distributed from a single bulk into containers in a single operation, in such a manner as to ensure uniformity, prevent contamination and ensure stability.

Working seed lot: a culture of a microorganism (virus or bacterium) derived from the master seed lot and intended for use in production.

23. SUBSTANTIAL MANIPULATION

The criterion of substantial manipulation is laid down in Article 2(1) of Regulation (EC) No 1394/2007. Additional guidance on the application thereof can be found in the CAT Reflection paper on classification of advanced therapy medicinal product(s).

24. STARTING MATERIALS

The definition of "starting materials" is provided for in Part IV of the Annex to Directive 2001/83/EC on the Community code relating to medicinal products for human use. http://www.ema.europa.eu/ema/index.jsp?curl=pages/regulation/general/general_content_000296.jsp

Guidance on Manufacture and Importation

UK Guidance on Manufacture

Contents

The Application and Inspection Process: "What to Expect"

Application

Application forms for a manufacturer's licence (MIA), a manufacturer's licence for investigational medicinal products (MIA(IMP)) or a manufacturer's "specials" licence (MS) are available from the Medicines and Healthcare products Regulatory Agency's (MHRA's) website[1]:

An application for a manufacturer's licence or for a manufacturer's "specials" licence should be accompanied by a Site Master File (SMF). This should contain specific and factual information about the production and/or control of the pharmaceutical operations to be carried out. For guidance on what information should be included in the SMF, a worked example for reference purposes can be obtained on request from the GMP Inspectorate.

The MHRA acting as the Licensing Authority will issue a manufacturer's licence or manufacturer's "specials" licence only when it is satisfied, after an inspection of the site, that the information contained in the application is accurate and in compliance with the requirements of the legislation.

When appropriate, the MHRA may refuse to grant the licence or may grant a licence otherwise than as applied for. In such cases the Licensing Authority will notify the applicant of its proposals. The notification will set out the reasons for its proposals and give the applicant a period of not less than 28 days to respond.

Once granted, any changes to the information shown on the licence must be submitted to the Licensing Authority for prior approval. This should be done by submitting a variation application. Variation application forms can be found on the MHRA's website.

Planning

A general Good Manufacturing Practice (GMP) inspection is carried out to assess the degree of conformity to prescribed standards of GMP and to assess compliance with the relevant regulatory requirements, e.g. the licence provisions.

In accordance with the GMP risk-based inspection process, sites will be required to complete a Compliance Report in advance of inspection. Further information and guidance can be found in the section on Risk-based inspections.

Notification

Advance notice of inspection is normally given to a company, unless circumstances require that an unannounced inspection should take place. The timing of the inspection would normally be discussed by telephone with the licence holder and details confirmed in writing. In accordance with the GMP risk-based inspection process, sites will be required to complete a Compliance Report in advance of inspection.

---

[1] https://www.gov.uk/guidance/apply-for-manufacturer-or-wholesaler-of-medicines-licences.

The scope of the inspection may vary depending on the type of inspection and site size. For smaller sites, all regulated activities would normally be inspected at each visit. For large complex sites, all regulated activities would normally be inspected over a period of two years. For an overseas site, the inspection will focus on those activities associated with products licensed for supply in the UK. However, the company will be asked to confirm all products supplied to the EEA and the inspection scope may be extended in consultation with other authorities to ensure adequate coverage of these products. The intent is to minimise as far as possible the number of inspections performed in third countries.

Conduct

The major stages of the inspection process are:

- the introductory or opening meeting;
- the detailed inspection; and
- the summary or closing meeting.

INTRODUCTORY OR OPENING MEETING

The purpose of the meeting is for the inspector to meet with the appropriate key personnel from the company to discuss the arrangements for the inspection. The inspector would typically confirm the purpose and scope of the inspection and areas to be visited, and indicate any documentation that may be required.

SITE INSPECTION

The purpose of the site inspection is to determine the degree of conformity of the operations to requirements of good practice and to assess compliance with the terms and conditions of licences issued under the appropriate legislation or with details submitted in support of an application for a licence.

The inspection schedule is, therefore, determined by the type of inspection planned. The inspection will typically involve visits to operational areas, interviews with key personnel and documentation review. Any observations, recommendations and deficiencies noted during the inspection would normally be discussed with the company representatives at the time.

During inspections of manufacturing operations, samples of starting materials, work in progress and finished products may be taken for testing if an inspector considers that this might assist in the detection of quality deficiencies. Occasionally samples may be taken, when these cannot be obtained from other sources, for routine surveillance purposes.

SUMMARY OR CLOSING MEETING

The purpose of the meeting is for the inspector to provide the company with a verbal summary of the inspection findings and to allow the company to correct any misconceptions at this stage. The inspector would typically summarise the definition and classification of deficiencies they propose to report and the company is encouraged to give an undertaking to resolve the deficiencies and to agree a provisional timetable for corrective action. The inspector would also describe the arrangements for the formal notification of the deficiencies to the company (the post-inspection letter) and what is expected as a response.

The choice of company representatives at the meeting is primarily for the company to decide, but should normally include the senior staff who were present during the inspection, technical management and the QPs.

Definition of deficiencies

All deficiencies are classified as **critical, major** or **other**. A reference to the relevant sections of the GMP legislation or guidelines will be given for those deficiencies classified as critical or major. The definitions used are as per the EU Community Report format:

- **critical deficiency:**
  - a deficiency that has produced, or leads to a significant risk of producing either a product which is harmful to the human or veterinary patient or a product which could result in a harmful residue in a food producing animal;
- **major deficiency:**
  - a non-critical deficiency that has produced, or may produce, a product that does not comply with its marketing authorisation; or
  - that indicates a major deviation from EU GMP; or
  - (within the UK) that indicates a major deviation from the terms of the manufacturing authorisation; or
  - that indicates a failure to carry out satisfactory procedures for release of batches or (within the UK) a failure of the QP to fulfil their legal duties; or
  - a combination of several "other" deficiencies, none of which on their own may be major but which may together represent a major deficiency and should be explained and reported as such;
- **other deficiency:**
  - a deficiency that cannot be classified as either critical or major but that indicates a departure from GMP (a deficiency may be "other" either because it is judged as minor or because there is insufficient information to classify it as major or critical).

Several related major or other deficiencies may be taken together to constitute a critical or major deficiency (respectively) and will be reported as such.

All critical and major deficiencies found will be reported even if remedial action has been taken before the end of the inspection.

Post-inspection letter

A post-inspection letter is sent to provide written confirmation of the deficiencies noted and reported verbally during the closing meeting.

Depending upon the inspection findings and the response from the company during and after the inspection, the inspector may take one of a number of actions ranging from:

- sending a GMP certificate or letter confirming essential compliance with GMP; to
- recommending to IAG for consideration of adverse licensing action against a manufacturer's licence, manufacturer's "specials" licence or marketing authorisation.

Company responses

The inspected site is expected to provide a written response to the post-inspection letter within the required timeframe. The response should consider the context of the deficiency within the overall quality system rather than just the specific issue identified. The response should include proposals for dealing with the deficiencies, together with a timetable for their implementation. It is helpful for the response to be structured as follows:

- restate the deficiency number;
- state the proposed corrective action;
- state the proposed target date for the completion of the corrective action(s);
- include any comment that the company considers appropriate; and
- provide an electronic version via email.

Inspection report

Once the inspector is satisfied that any necessary remedial action has been taken or is in hand and that the site is essentially in compliance with GMP, an inspection report and GMP certificate or close-out letter are finalised.

Risk-based Inspection Programme

Introduction

The MHRA has been incorporating elements of risk management into its inspection programme for a number of years. A formal risk-based inspection programme was implemented on 1 April 2009, and covers all aspects of good practices associated with the inspection of clinical, pre-clinical and quality control laboratories, clinical trials, manufacturers, wholesalers and pharmacovigilance systems. The primary aim of the programme is to enable inspectorate resources to focus on areas that maximise protection of public health while reducing the overall administrative and economic burden to stakeholders.

GMP risk-based inspection programme

The GMP risk-based inspection process commenced for all participating sites on 1 April 2009. Participating sites are those UK sites that hold a manufacturing authorisation (MIA, MS, MIA[IMP]) and third-country sites that are named on a UK marketing authorisation.

Inspections may be conducted on-site, remotely or as a hybrid combination of the two.

Compliance report and interim update

Sites are required to complete a Compliance Report in advance of inspection; this will be prompted by the inspector. A guidance document and example reports are also available to assist completion. The Compliance Report should be returned to the inspector prior to the inspection.

Following a site's first inspection, it is expected that relevant changes affecting the site will be advised to the MHRA on a Compliance Report Interim Assessment.

Risk rating process

Inspectors use the inspection outputs along with a number of other factors to identify a risk rating for the site that equates to a future inspection frequency. As this process is not concluded until the inspection is closed, the risk ratings **will not** be discussed at the closing meeting. However, a copy of the full inspection report, which includes the full risk-rating rationale, is provided to sites once the inspection has been closed.

The issue of a certificate of GMP compliance and/or support of the site on the relevant licence is an indication of meeting the minimum level of GMP compliance. Risk ratings identify the degree of surveillance required within the licensing and inspection programme. There is no intention that sites be rated against each other as a result of risk ratings assigned by the MHRA. Risk ratings can change after inspection, resulting in either increased or decreased risk. Inspection risk ratings will not be published by the MHRA.

There will be no formal process of appeal against risk ratings and future inspection frequency. However, any rating that results in an increased inspection frequency from the previous standard will be peer reviewed before conclusion by a GMP operations manager or a GMP expert inspector. The MHRA does have a formal complaints process if sites wish to log an issue; however, any concerns regarding the inspection process should be raised with the inspector in the first instance.

Conditions for Manufacturer's Licence

The holder of a manufacturer's licence must comply with certain conditions in relation to the manufacture, assembly and importation of medicinal products. These conditions are set out in Regulations 37 to 41 of the Human Medicines Regulations 2012 [SI 2012 No. 1916] ("the Regulations"). They require that the licence holder shall:

- comply with the principles and guidelines for good manufacturing practice set out in the Good Manufacturing Practice Directive, which apply under or by virtue of Regulation B17 of the Regulations;
- use only active starting materials that have been manufactured in accordance with the principles and guidelines for good manufacturing practice for active substances and have been distributed in accordance with the guidelines on good distribution practice for active substances, unless they are for use or used in an exempt medicinal product (special medicinal product);
- verify that:
  - the manufacturer or distributor of an active substance that they have used has complied with the requirements of good manufacturing practice and good distribution practice for active substances by means of an audit performed directly by themselves or by a person acting on their behalf; and
  - where the active substance is imported into Great Britain from an approved country for import or into Northern Ireland from an EEA State, any manufacturers, importers or distributors supplying active substances to the licence holder:
    (i) in the case of a product imported into Great Britain, are registered with the appropriate authority for the registration of such persons in the approved country for import; and
    (ii) in the case of a product imported into Northern Ireland, are registered with the competent authority of a member State in which they are established;
- ensure the authenticity and quality of the active substance;
- ensure:

- that excipients are suitable for use in a medicinal product by ascertaining what the appropriate good manufacturing practice is;
- that the ascertained good manufacturing practice is applied;
- that the suitability of the excipient is ascertained on the basis of a formalised risk assessment as described in the case of a product for sale or supply in Great Britain, in the guidelines that apply under or by virtue of Regulation C17 of the Regulations and, in the case of a product for sale or supply in Northern Ireland, in paragraph 5 of Article 47 of the 2001 Directive, and the assessment takes account of the source requirements under other quality systems, intended use of the excipients and previous instances of quality defects;
- the authenticity and quality of any excipient used is verified; and
- the measures taken under this paragraph are documented by the licence holder;

- maintain such staff, premises, equipment and facilities necessary to conduct the manufacture and assembly of medicinal products in accordance with the requirements of their manufacturer's licence and in the case of a product for sale or supply in Great Britain, the UKMA(GB), UKMA(UK), COR(GB), COR(UK), THR(GB) or THR(UK), or in Northern Ireland, the UKMA(NI), UKMA(UK), COR(NI), COR(UK), THR(NI), THR(UK), EU marketing authorisations or Article 126a authorisations, applying to the medicinal products;
- maintain such staff, premises, equipment and facilities for the handling, control, storage and distribution of the medicinal products manufactured or assembled in accordance with their manufacturer's licence, as necessary to maintain the quality of those medicinal products;
- ensure that any arrangements made for the control, storage and distribution of the medicinal products are adequate to maintain the quality of those products;
- not carry out any manufacture or assembly of medicinal products other than in accordance with their manufacturer's licence and at the premises specified in the licence;
- not use any premises for the handling, control, storage or distribution of medicinal products other than those named on their manufacturer's licence that have been approved by the Licensing Authority for that purpose;
- inform the Licensing Authority before making any material alteration to the premises or facilities used under their manufacturer's licence, or in the operations for which they are used;
- inform the Licensing Authority of any proposed changes to any personnel named in their manufacturer's licence as responsible for quality control, including the person named as the Qualified Person;
- permit the Licensing Authority to carry out inspections, take samples or copies of documentation as necessary to enable the Licensing Authority

to ascertain whether there are any grounds for suspending, revoking or terminating the manufacturer's licence or to verify any statement contained in an application for a licence;

- ensure that any blood or blood component that they import into the UK and use as a starting material or raw material in the manufacture of a medicinal product meets the equivalent standards of quality and safety to those laid down in the Blood Quality and Safety Regulations 2005 or equivalent standards;
- ensure that they have at all times at their disposal the services of at least one Qualified Person who is responsible for carrying out, in relation to the medicinal products being manufactured or assembled, the duties specified in Part 3 of Schedule 7 of the Regulations.

Where the manufacturer's licence holder distributes the medicinal product manufactured or assembled in accordance with the manufacturer's licence they shall:

- comply with the principles of good distribution practice, in the case of a licence holder in GB, published under, or that apply by virtue of, Regulation C17 of the regulations and in the case of a licence holder in Northern Ireland, published by the European Commission in accordance with Article 84 of the 2001 Directive;
- ensure the appropriate and continued supply of the medicinal product that they manufacture or assemble;
- sell only, or offer for sale or supply, the medicinal product in accordance and conformity with a marketing authorisation, in GB, a UKMA(GB), UKMA(UK), a COR(GB), a COR(UK), a THR(GB) or a THR(UK), or, in Northern Ireland, there is a UKMA(NI), UKMA(UK), a COR(NI), a COR(UK), a THR(NI), a THR(UK) and EU marketing authorisation or an Article 126a authorisation, unless it is an exempt medicinal product or is distributed to another Member State where it can be legally used as an unlicensed medicinal product in the Member State concerned;
- distribute only their medicinal products to a holder of a wholesale dealer's licence relating to those products; the holder of an authorisation granted by in the case of a licence holder in Great Britain, the appropriate authority of an approved country for import, in the case of a licence holder in Northern Ireland, the competent authority of another EEA State, which is responsible for authorising the supply of those products by way of wholesale dealing and any person who may lawfully sell those products by retail or who may lawfully supply them in circumstances corresponding to retail sale; or any person who may lawfully administer those products;
- in relation to supply;
  (i) in the case of a licence holder in Great Britain to persons in countries other than approved countries for import, a person who is authorised

or entitled to receive medicinal products for wholesale distribution or supply to the public in accordance with the applicable legal and administrative provisions of the country to which the product is supplied;

(ii) in the case of a licence holder in Northern Ireland to persons in a state other than an EEA State, a person who is authorised or entitled to receive medicinal products for wholesale distribution or supply to the public in accordance with the applicable legal and administrative provisions of the state other than an EEA State concerned;

- where the medicinal product is supplied to a person for retail sale or supply, the manufacturer's licence holder must enclose with the product a document that makes it possible to ascertain the date on which the supply took place, the name and pharmaceutical form of the product supplied, the quantity of product supplied, and the names and addresses of the person or persons from whom the products were supplied and, in the case of a licence holder in Northern Ireland, the batch number of the medicinal products bearing the safety features referred to in point (o) of Article 54 of the 2001 Directive;

- in the case of licence holders in NI, verify the safety features and decommission the unique identifier of that medicinal product in accordance with the requirements laid down in Commission Regulation 2016/161.

The manufacturer's licence holder must immediately inform the competent authority of a Member State and, where applicable, the marketing authorisation holder of medicinal products that come within the scope of their manufacturing authorisation, which the licence holder knows or suspects, or has reasonable grounds for knowing or suspecting, to be falsified.

The Standard Provisions are incorporated into all manufacturer's licences in the form set out in Schedule 4 of the Human Medicines Regulations 2012, i.e. those provisions that may be included in all licences unless an individual licence provides variations to them. They require that the manufacturer's licence holder shall:

- place their quality control system referred to in Article 11(1) of Commission Directive 2003/94/EC under the authority of the head of the Quality Control (QC);

- provide information about the products being manufactured or assembled under their manufacturer's licence and about the operations being conducted in relation to such manufacture or assembly as may be requested by the licensing authority;

- inform the licensing authority of any proposed changes to be made to any personnel, named on their licence, responsible for supervising the production operations, in charge of the animals from which are derived any substances used in the production of the medicinal products being manufactured or assembled, or responsible for the culture of any living tissues used in the manufacture of the medicinal products being manufactured or assembled;

- keep readily available, for inspection by a person authorised by the licensing authority, the batch documentation referred to in Article 9(1) of Commission Directive 2003/94/EC, and permit that person to take copies or make extracts from such documentation;

- keep readily available, for examination by a person authorised by the licensing authority, samples of each batch of finished medicinal product referred to in Article 11(4) of Commission Directive 2003/94/EC;

- withhold any batch of any medicinal product from sale or export so far as may be reasonably practicable for up to six weeks when informed that it does not comply with its licence specifications or with the provisions of the Human Medicines Regulations 2012;

- ensure that any tests for determining conformity with the standards and specifications applying to any particular product used in the manufacture of a medicinal product shall, except so far as the conditions of the product specification for that product otherwise provide, be applied to samples taken from the medicinal product after all manufacturing processes have been completed, or at such earlier stage in the manufacture as may be approved by the licensing authority;

- where the manufacturer's licence relates to the assembly of any medicinal product or class of product, and the licence holder supplies that medicinal product at such a stage of assembly that does not fully comply with the provisions of the product specification that relate to labelling, the licence holder shall communicate the particulars of those provisions to the person to whom that product has been so supplied;

- where the manufacturer's licence relates to the assembly of a medicinal product, and that medicinal product is not manufactured by the licence holder, and particulars as to the name and address of the manufacturer of, or of the person who imports, that medicinal product have been given by the licence holder to the licensing authority, the licence holder shall forthwith notify the Licensing Authority in writing of any changes in such particulars;

- keep readily available for examination by a person authorised by the Licensing Authority durable records of the details of manufacture of any intermediate products held by them that are for use in the manufacture of biological medicinal products for human use and shall be in such form as to ensure that the manufacturer's licence holder has a comprehensive record of all matters that are relevant to an evaluation of the safety, quality and efficacy of any finished biological medicinal product for human use that they manufacture using those intermediate products. The records shall not be destroyed without the consent of the Licensing Authority until the records of the details of manufacture of any finished medicinal products that were or may be manufactured using those intermediate products may be destroyed in accordance with the requirements of these Regulations;

- arrange for animals that are used in the production of any medicinal products to be housed in premises of such a nature, and be managed in such a manner, as to facilitate compliance with the provisions relating to them in the relevant marketing authorisations – in Great Britain, a UK marketing authorisation, certificate of registration or traditional herbal registration, or, in Northern Ireland, a marketing authorisation, Article 126a authorisation, certificate of registration or traditional herbal registration;
- take all reasonable precautions and exercise all due diligence to ensure that any information they provide to the Licensing Authority that is relevant to an evaluation of the safety, quality or efficacy of any medicinal product for human use that they manufacture or assemble, or any starting materials or intermediate products that they hold that are for use in the manufacture of medicinal products, is not false or misleading in any material particular.

The manufacturer's licence holder may use a contract laboratory pursuant to Article 11(2) of Commission Directive 2003/94/EC if operated by a person approved by the Licensing Authority, i.e. if not on the manufacturer's licence a contract laboratory will not be acceptable[1].

A licence holder in Great Britain may manufacture a special medicinal product only for a person in Northern Ireland, and in Northern Ireland may manufacture a special medicinal product only for a person in Great Britain, in response to an order that satisfies the requirements of Regulation 167 of the Regulations.

A licence holder may import such products from, in the case of an import into Great Britain, only a country other than an approved country for import and, in the case of an import into Northern Ireland, only a state other than an EEA State in response to an order that satisfies the requirements of Regulation 167 (supply to fulfil special patient needs), and where the certain conditions are complied with, as follows:

- provide such information as may be requested by the Licensing Authority concerning the type and quantity of any medicinal products that the licence holder imports.
- withhold the batch of imported product from distribution, so far as reasonably practicable, for up to six weeks when told that the strength, quality or purity of a batch of a medicinal product to which the licence relates has been found not to conform with the specification of the medicinal product in question, or those provisions of the Regulations that are applicable to the medicinal product.
- ensure that any tests for determining conformity with the standards and specifications applying to any ingredient used in the manufacture of a

---

[1] A contract laboratory is required to be named on the manufacturer's licence.

medicinal product must, except so far as the conditions of the product specification for that ingredient otherwise provide, be applied to samples taken from the medicinal product after all manufacturing processes have been completed, or at such earlier stage in the manufacture as may be approved by the Licensing Authority,

- take all reasonable precautions and exercise due diligence to ensure that any information provided to the Licensing Authority that is relevant to an evaluation of the safety, quality or efficacy of a medicinal product for human use that is imported from, in the case of an import into Great Britain, a country other than an approved country for import and, in the case of an import into Northern Ireland, a state other than an EEA State, which is handled, stored or distributed under the licence, is not false or misleading in a material particular.

The Standard Provisions also require the holder of a manufacturer's licence relating to the manufacture and assembly of exempt advanced therapy medicinal products to ensure that:

- the immediate packaging of an exempt advanced therapy medicinal product is labelled to show the following particulars:
  - the name of the exempt advanced therapy medicinal product;
  - the expiry date in clear terms including the year and month and, if applicable, the day;
  - a description of the active substance, expressed qualitatively and quantitatively;
  - where the product contains cells or tissues of human or animal origin a statement that the product contains such cells or tissues, and a short description of the cells or tissues and of their specific origin;
  - the pharmaceutical form and the contents by weight, volume or number of doses of the product;
  - a list of excipients, including preservative systems;
  - the method of use, application, administration or implantation and, if appropriate, the route of administration, with space provided for the prescribed dose to be indicated;
  - any special storage precautions;
  - specific precautions relating to the disposal of the unused product or waste derived from the product and, where appropriate, reference to any appropriate collection system;
  - the name and address of the holder of the manufacturer's licence;
  - the manufacturer's licence number;
  - the manufacturer's batch number;
  - the unique donation code referred to in Article 8(2) of Directive 2004/23/EC [assigned by a tissue establishment pursuant to paragraph 1 of Schedule 3A to the Human Fertilisation and Embryology Act 1990, as regards human gametes and embryos; and paragraph 1

of Schedule 2 to the Human Tissue (Quality and Safety for Human Application) Regulations 2007, as regards other human tissues and cells]; and

– where the exempt advanced therapy medicinal product is for autologous use, the unique patient identifier and the words "for autologous use only".

- the package leaflet of the exempt advanced therapy medicinal product shall include the following particulars:
  – the name of the exempt advanced therapy medicinal product;
  – the intended effect of the medicinal product if correctly used, applied, administered or implanted;
  – where the product contains cells or tissues of human or animal origin:
    - a statement that the product contains such cells or tissues, and
    - a short description of the cells or tissues and, where such cells or tissues are of animal origin, their specific origin;
- where the product contains a medical device or an active implantable medical device, a description of that device and, where that device contains cells or tissues of animal origin, their specific origin;
- any necessary instructions for use, including:
  – the posology;
  – the method of use, application, administration or implantation and, if appropriate, the route of administration;
  – a description of symptoms of overdose;
  – action to be taken in the event of overdose, including any emergency procedures;
  – action to be taken if one or more doses have been missed; and
  – a recommendation to consult the doctor or pharmacist for any clarification on the use of the product;
- where adverse reactions are known, a description of those that may occur under recommended conditions of use of the product and, if appropriate, an indication of action to be taken in such a case;
- an instruction that the patient report any adverse reaction not specified in the package leaflet to the doctor or pharmacist;
- the expiry date in clear terms and a warning against using the product after that date;
- any special storage precautions;
- a description of any visible signs of deterioration;
- a complete qualitative and quantitative composition;
- the name and address of the holder of the manufacturer's licence; and
- the date on which the package leaflet was last revised.

The licence holder must keep data to trace the exempt advanced therapy medicinal through the sourcing, manufacturing, packaging, storage, transport and delivery to the establishment where the product is used, for longer than 30 years.

Conditions for Manufacturing Authorisation (IMP)

To comply with the Medicines for Human Use (Clinical Trials) Regulations 2004 [SI 2004 No. 1031] you require a manufacturing authorisation granted by the licensing authority to manufacture (including for export), assemble or import any investigational medicinal product.

This does not apply to the manufacture or assembly of a medicinal product that is manufactured or assembled in accordance with the terms and conditions of a marketing authorisation issued by the licensing authority, or a marketing authorisation issued by EMA or the competent authority of an EEA State in accordance with Directive 2001/83/EC, which is then used in a clinical trial.

The holder of a manufacturing authorisation for investigational medicinal product must comply with the principles and guidelines of good manufacturing practice and the provision of the manufacturing authorisation, and allow the licensing authority access to their premises at any reasonable time. The holder must put and keep in place arrangements that enable the qualified person named on the manufacturing authorisation to carry out their duties, including placing at the Qualified Person's disposal all the necessary facilities.

The holder of a manufacturing authorisation must have at their disposal the services of at least one Qualified Person (QP). Where the manufacturing authorisation relates wholly to the import of an investigational medicinal product into Great Britain from an approved country for import, the named QP must operate and be ordinarily resident in either the UK or an approved country for import. In all other cases the QP must operate and be ordinarily resident in the UK.

Manufacture and assembly

The holder of an authorisation relating to the manufacture or assembly of an investigational medicinal product shall:

- provide and maintain such staff, premises and plant (including technical equipment) as are necessary for the carrying out, in accordance with their authorisation and the product specification, of such stages of the manufacture and assembly of the investigational medicinal products as are undertaken by them;
- not carry out any such manufacture or assembly except at the premises specified in his manufacturing authorisation;
- provide and maintain such staff, premises, equipment and facilities for the handling, storage and distribution of the investigational medicinal products that they handle, store or distribute under their authorisation as are necessary to maintain the quality of the investigational medicinal products;

- not use for such purposes premises other than those specified in the authorisation or that may be approved from time to time by the Licensing Authority and ensure that any arrangements they make with a person for the storage and distribution of the investigational medicinal products are adequate to maintain the quality of those products;
- place the quality control system referred to in Article 11(1) of Commission Directive 2003/94/EC under the authority of the person notified to the Licensing Authority in accordance with paragraph 6(3) of Schedule 6 of the Medicines for Human Use (Clinical Trials) Regulations 2004 as being responsible for quality control;
- provide such information as may be requested by the Licensing Authority for the purposes of the Medicines for Human Use (Clinical Trials) Regulations 2004 or the Human Medicines Regulations 2012 about the products currently being manufactured or assembled under their authorisation, and of the operations being carried out in relation to such manufacture or assembly;
- inform the licensing authority before making any material alteration in the premises or plant used under their authorisation, or in the operations for which they are used, and inform the licensing authority of any change that they propose to make in any personnel named in their authorisation as respectively responsible for supervising the production operations, or responsible for quality control of the investigational medicinal products being manufactured or assembled including the person named as the QP;
- keep readily available for inspection by a person authorised by the Licensing Authority the batch documentation referred to in Article 9(1) of Commission Directive 2003/94/EC and permit the person authorised to take copies or make extracts from such documentation;
- keep readily available for examination by a person authorised by the licensing authority the samples of each batch of bulk formulated products referred to in Article 11(4) of Commission Directive 2003/94/EC;
- ensure that any tests for determining conformity with the standards and specifications applying to any particular product used in the manufacture shall, except so far as the conditions of the product specification for that product otherwise provide, be applied to samples taken from the investigational medicinal product after all manufacturing processes have been completed, or at such earlier stage in the manufacture as may be approved by the Licensing Authority;
- at all times provide and maintain such staff, premises, equipment and facilities as will enable the QP who is at their disposal to carry out their duties.

The holder of an authorisation relating to the manufacture or assembly of an investigational medicinal product may use a contract laboratory pursuant to Article 11(2) of Commission Directive 2003/94/EC if operated by a person approved by the Licensing Authority.

Where the holder of the authorisation has been informed by the Licensing Authority that any batch of any investigational medicinal product to which their authorisation relates has been found not to conform as regards strength, quality or purity with the specification of the relevant product, or the provisions of the Medicines for Human Use (Clinical Trials) Regulations 2004, Human Medicines Regulations 2012 that are applicable to the investigational medicinal product, the holder shall, if so directed, withhold such batch from distribution for use in clinical trials, so far as may be reasonably practicable, for such a period not exceeding six weeks as may be specified by the Licensing Authority.

Where the authorisation relates to the assembly of an investigational medicinal product, and the holder of the authorisation supplies that investigational medicinal product at such a stage of assembly that does not fully comply with the provisions of the product specification that relate to labelling, the holder of that authorisation shall communicate the particulars of those provisions to the person to whom that investigational medicinal product has been so supplied.

Where the manufacturing authorisation relates to the assembly of an investigational medicinal product, where that investigational medicinal product is not manufactured by the holder of the authorisation, and particulars as to the name and address of the manufacturer of, or of the person who imports, that investigational medicinal product had been given by the holder of the authorisation to the licensing authority, the holder of the authorisation shall forthwith notify the licensing authority in writing of any changes in such particulars.

For the purpose of enabling the licensing authority to ascertain whether there are any grounds for suspending, revoking or varying any authorisation or licence granted under the Medicines for Human Use (Clinical Trials) Regulations 2004 or the Human Medicines Regulations 2012, amending the conduct of a clinical trial in accordance with the Medicines for Human Use (Clinical Trials) Regulations 2004 or suspending or terminating any clinical trial, the holder of a manufacturing authorisation relating to the importation of investigational medicinal products shall permit, and provide all necessary facilities to enable, any person duly authorised in writing by the Licensing Authority, on production if required of their credentials, to carry out such inspection or to take such samples or copies, in relation to things belonging to, or any business carried on by, the holder of the authorisation, as such person would have the right to carry out or take under the Human Medicines Regulations 2012 for the purpose of verifying any statement contained in an application for an authorisation or licence.

Importation

The holder of a manufacturing authorisation relating to the importation of an investigational medicinal product shall:

- provide and maintain such staff, premises, equipment and facilities for the handling, storage and distribution of the investigational medicinal products that they handle, store or distribute under their authorisation as are necessary to avoid deterioration of the investigational medicinal products;
- only use for such purposes premises specified in the authorisation or that may be approved from time to time by the Licensing Authority and ensure that any arrangements they make with a person for the storage and distribution of the investigational medicinal products are adequate to maintain the quality of those products;
- provide such information as may be requested by the Licensing Authority concerning the type and quantity of any investigational medicinal products that they import;
- inform the Licensing Authority before making any structural alterations to, or discontinuance of the use of, premises to which their authorisation relates;
- inform the Licensing Authority of changes to the person named as the QP;
- keep readily available for inspection by the Licensing Authority the batch documentation referred to in Article 9(1) of Commission Directive 2003/94/EC and permit the Licensing Authority to take copies or make extracts from such documentation;
- at all times provide and maintain such staff, premises, equipment and facilities as will enable the QP who is at their disposal to carry out their duties.

The holder of a manufacturing authorisation relating to the importation of investigational medicinal products may use a contract laboratory pursuant to Article 11(2) of Commission Directive 2003/94/EC if operated by a person approved by the Licensing Authority.

Where the holder of a manufacturing authorisation relating to the importation of investigational medicinal products has been informed by the Licensing Authority that any batch of any investigational medicinal product to which their authorisation relates has been found not to conform as regards strength, quality or purity with the specification of the relevant product, or the provisions of the Medicines for Human Use (Clinical Trials) Regulations 2004, Human Medicines Regulations 2012 that are applicable to the investigational medicinal product, the holder shall, if so directed, withhold such batch from distribution for use in clinical trials, so far as may be reasonably practicable, for such a period not exceeding six weeks as may be specified by the Licensing Authority.

If the holder of a manufacturing authorisation relating to the importation of investigational medicinal products is not the sponsor of the clinical trial for which the investigational medicinal product is manufactured or assembled, the holder of the manufacturing authorisation shall comply with the provisions of the product specification that relates to the supply of that investigational medicinal product for use in the trial.

For the purpose of enabling the Licensing Authority to ascertain whether there are any grounds for suspending, revoking or varying any authorisation or licence granted under the Medicines for Human Use (Clinical Trials) Regulations 2004 or the Human Medicines Regulations 2012, amending the conduct of a clinical trial in accordance with the Medicines for Human Use (Clinical Trials) Regulations 2004 or suspending or terminating any clinical trial, the holder of a manufacturing authorisation relating to the importation of investigational medicinal products shall permit, and provide all necessary facilities to enable, any person duly authorised in writing by the Licensing Authority, on production if required of their credentials, to carry out such inspection or to take such samples or copies, in relation to things belonging to, or any business carried on by, the holder of the authorisation, as such person would have the right to carry out or take under the Human Medicines Regulations 2012 for the purpose of verifying any statement contained in an application for an authorisation or licence.

Qualified Persons

General

All holders of a manufacturer's licence for licensed products, including for the purposes of import, are required to have available the services of at least one Qualified Person (QP), who must be named on the licence. When considering a nomination, the Licensing Authority (the MHRA) routinely takes into account the assessment of the nominee's eligibility made by the joint assessment panel of The Royal Society of Biology, The Royal Pharmaceutical Society and The Royal Society of Chemistry. Exceptionally, the MHRA will assess a nominee directly if they are not a member of any of these professional bodies.

Regulation 41 of the Human Medicines Regulations 2012 as amended lays down the requirements for QPs in relation to products for human use. Schedule 7, Part 3 defines the duties of the QP; Schedule 7, Parts 1 and 2 define the requirements for eligibility under the permanent and transitional arrangements, respectively. Schedule 2, Part 1 of the Veterinary Medicines Regulations 2013 as amended lays down equivalent requirements in relation to veterinary products. Guidance on the duties of QPs is given in the EU Guide to GMP and, in particular, in its Annex 16. In order to carry out their duties, the QP should be resident in the UK.

By inspection and other means, the Licensing Authority routinely assesses whether or not QPs are fulfilling their duties. In making this assessment, reference is made to the *Code of Practice for Qualified Persons* produced jointly by The Royal Society of Biology, The Royal Pharmaceutical Society and The Royal Society of Chemistry in collaboration with the MHRA and the Veterinary Medicines Directorate. This reference is made whether or not the QP in question is a member of one or more of these bodies (see next section).

All QPs should be guided in fulfilling their duties by the Code of Practice, although the references in Sections 12.1 and 14.2 to the disciplinary machinery of the professional bodies, and in Section 8.3, 9.4, 12.5 and 13.0 to the advice that professional bodies can give, would not be relevant in the case of a QP who is not a member of one of these bodies. The European Industrial Pharmacists Group adopted a similar code[2] in 1995 for the guidance of its members.

Code of Practice for Qualified Persons

1   Introduction

1.1   The concept of the Qualified Person (QP), first established in 1975, is a unique regulatory requirement that applies only within the European Union (EU). The only comparable situation exists within Member States of the European Economic Area with which the EU has reciprocal agreements.

1.2   Each holder of an Authorisation to manufacture products for use in a Clinical Trial, or products subject to Marketing Authorisations, within Member States of the EU, must name a person or persons who are eligible to act in the capacity of QP.

1.3   The requirement for a QP covers both Human and Veterinary Medicinal Products, including any product intended only for export.

1.4   Particular conditions for formal qualifications and practical experience for eligibility to act as a QP are specified in the relevant EU Council Directives (see section 2 below). Ensuring compliance with these conditions is the responsibility of the Competent Authorities of the Member States.

1.5   The primary legal responsibility of the QP is to certify batches of Medicinal Product prior to use in a Clinical Trial (Human Medicinal Products only) or prior to release for sale and placing on the market (Human and

---

[2] European Industrial Pharmacists Group (established June 1966). Code of Practice for Qualified Persons. Available from the Industrial Pharmacists Group of The Royal Pharmaceutical Society.

Veterinary Medicinal Products). However, the wider technical, ethical and professional obligations in terms of patient safety, quality and efficacy must also be considered. Hence this professional Code of Practice is designed to take account of these issues

2   Regulatory basis for the QP

For ease of reference, the key regulatory documents concerning the QP are as follows:

(i)   Directive 2003/94/EC: Principles and Guidelines of Good Manufacturing Practice for Medicinal Products for Human Use – **Article 7.**

(ii) Directive 91/412/EEC: Principles and Guidelines of Good Manufacturing Practice for Veterinary Medicinal Products – **Article 7.**

(iii) Directive 2001/20/EC: Good Clinical Practice in the Conduct of Clinical Trials on Medicinal Products for Human Use – **Article 13.**

(iv) Directive 2001/82/EC: Community Code Relating to Veterinary Medicinal Products – **Title IV** – **Manufacture and Imports** – **Articles 44–57** (note that Articles 44, 50, 51, 53, 54 and 55 have been amended by Directive 2004/28/EC).

(v)   Directive 2001/83/EC: Community Code Relating to Medicinal Products for Human Use – **Title IV** – **Manufacture and Importation** – **Articles 40–53** (note that Articles 46, 47, 49, 50 and 51 have been amended by Directives 2004/27/EC and 2011/62/EC).

(vi) Directive 2011/62/EC: Falsified Medicines Directive.

(vii) EudraLex, Volume 4: Good Manufacturing Practices – in particular:
– Annex 13: Manufacture of Investigational Medicinal Products;
– Annex 16: Certification by a Qualified Person and Batch Release.

3   Purpose of the Code

3.1   It is a requirement that all QPs are subject to a professional code of conduct.

3.2   The purpose of this UK Code of Practice is to provide guidance to QPs on how to comply with the professional code of conduct requirements.

3.3   It aims to provide guidance on how an individual QP can safeguard themselves, aspects that a QP needs to be aware of when working with other QPs named on the same authorisation, and where a QP can obtain support in difficult situations.

3.4   This Code applies to all QPs involved in the manufacture of pharmaceuticals where the QP is:
– employed or providing contract QP services;
– involved in human or veterinary medicines; and
– qualified under the permanent or transitional provisions.

3.5 It should be noted that the Licensing Authority may refer to this Code of Practice in connection with disciplinary proceedings against a QP under Article 52 of Directive 2001/83/EC or Article 56 of Directive 2001/82/EC.

4 Terminology

4.1 The terminology used in this Code of Practice corresponds with that used in the current versions of the EC Directives on Good Manufacturing Practice (GMP) and the Guide to Good Manufacturing Practice.

4.2 Within the EU, the terms Marketing Authorisation, Manufacturer's Authorisation and Clinical Trial Authorisation are generally used and shall henceforth be referred to throughout this Code.

5 General principles

5.1 Pharmaceutical Manufacturers and the Regulatory Authorities of each Member State must ensure that patients are protected and that all medicinal products, whether for sale or supply, meet the appropriate requirements for safety, quality and efficacy.

5.2 The QP performs a unique role on behalf of the patient and the Regulatory Authority when certifying that a batch complies with its predetermined requirements and can be released for sale or supply.

5.3 The QP is responsible for ensuring that each individual batch has been manufactured and checked in compliance with laws in force in the Member State where certification takes place.

5.4 The QP's legal roles and responsibilities apply regardless of where the final product will be sold and/or supplied.

5.5 The QP must understand the requirements of each Authorisation (Manufacturer's, Marketing or Clinical Trial) and ensure that the Pharmaceutical Quality System (PQS) in place is fit for purpose for the activities being performed and types of products involved.

5.6 The QP must use risk-based principles and apply sound knowledge and understanding of the relevant steps of manufacture before certifying any batch for release.

5.7 The QP needs to refer to all applicable guidance and ensure that they are fully conversant with the requirements detailed in Annex 16 of the EU GMP Guide.

5.8 All QPs should ensure that adequate professional indemnity insurance arrangements are in place.

5.9 QPs have a professional duty to decline to certify any batches of product types for which they do not possess the relevant experience and/or knowledge.

5.10 QPs should ensure that this Code of Practice is brought to the attention of senior management and, where practical, the Chief Executive Officer/Site Head so that they are aware of the requirements and expectations detailed within.

6   Practical duties of a Qualified Person

6.1   QPs have duties, some of which may be delegated in line with the above general principles. Before certifying a batch prior to release, the QP should always ensure that all requirements have been met.

Annex 16, Volume 4, EU Guidelines for Good Manufacturing Practice for Medicinal Products for Human and Veterinary Use provides the current guidance on these duties and should be consulted for the details.

6.2   The QP should also recognise the need to consult other experts to reinforce knowledge where required (for example, but not limited to: stability, unusual analytical results, process or equipment changes, potential environmental or microbiological risks, re-labelling, abnormal yields, cross-contamination risks, new technologies).

6.3   The QP should also take account of the nature and size of the operations being performed. For example, in a very small company with a limited range of products, it may be possible for the QP to take direct responsibility for some or all of the duties as detailed in Annex 16. In larger organisations, the QP will typically be dependent upon the knowledge and expertise of colleagues. It is of paramount importance that the QP is assured that the tasks allocated are being performed satisfactorily. Hence the duties of a QP depend upon a team effort.

7   Performance of duties and regulatory compliance

7.1   Each QP has a personal and professional responsibility for being certain that the various checks and tests have been carried out; however, the detail of this work can be the responsibility of others.

Ultimately, the QP must be satisfied either directly or, more usually, by the proper operation of the PQS, that manufacturing, packaging and quality control testing comply with the relevant requirements and that any deviations are controlled and managed effectively. These requirements apply whether the work is carried out on site or at a different site.

Batch certification without such adequate steps may be regarded as professional misconduct.

7.2   The QP depends upon many colleagues for the achievement of quality and regulatory compliance in the manufacture of medicinal products. It is therefore of paramount importance that the QP achieves good working relationships with others.

7.3   The QP should take the necessary steps to inform other functional groups of the legal role and responsibilities of a QP and help them to understand how they can provide effective support.

7.4   Manufacturer's Authorisations include the names of the persons responsible for Production, Quality Control and the name(s) of the QP(s). The duties of these members of staff must be clear in their respective job descriptions and they must have the authority required under the relevant EC Directives.

8 Number and location of Qualified Persons

8.1 The safety of patients is of paramount importance so it is vital that, at each relevant site, there are sufficient QPs available to cover all activities involved, including appropriate measures in place for any shift patterns. This may require a single QP, a team of QPs, a QP providing contract services or a combination thereof.

8.2 The QP should be present at the manufacturing site for a sufficient proportion of the working time to discharge their legal and professional duties. The time spent on site should also allow the QP to fulfil their other duties with respect to the PQS.

8.3 Where there is more than one QP working on the same site, it is an expectation that each QP is sufficiently aware of the activities of the other QP(s). Where any significant discrepancies regarding decision-making are observed, these should be discussed across the QPs. Where significant differences cannot be resolved, these should be brought to the attention of senior management. It may also be advisable for a concerned QP to contact their Professional Body for advice.

8.4 It is expected that QPs will inform senior management if they believe that there are insufficient QPs to perform all the required duties.

8.5 QPs are typically part of the Quality organisation at site. Ideally, the QP or "lead" QP would also be a member of the senior management team.

9 Contracted Qualified Persons

9.1 In a number of cases, especially with smaller companies, a "Contracted" QP provides the service. In such cases, the duties and responsibilities of a "Contracted QP" are the same as those for QPs who are permanently employed by their company.

The term "Contracted QP" is not a formal title and is used only to describe a QP providing an independent service under contract to a company.

9.2 In addition to compliance with the provisions applicable to all QPs including all the practical duties detailed in Annex 16, Contracted QPs should observe the following:

- have a clear written contract, which delineates the duties and responsibilities of the QP – as agreed between the company and the "Contracted QP". Both should sign and retain a copy of the contract;
- be on site for sufficient time to fulfil all legal and professional requirements;

- be readily available to the staff of the company for advice and discussion, be present during regulatory inspections and involved in communications with the inspectors;
- ensure that the company to which the services are provided will allow free access to any people, information, documentation, premises, systems, etc. that are relevant to the decision-making processes when certifying batches; and
- the QP must be informed and aware of any issues arising relating to the PQS that are relevant to a QP, in particular any events that occur when the QP is not on site.

9.3 Particularly for smaller companies, a Contracted QP may agree with the company to personally provide some additional services, e.g. staff training, internal audits and maintenance of authorisations, in addition to performing strictly batch-related QP duties.

9.4 If any doubt exists between the QP and the company concerning the duties and responsibilities of the QP, it is recommended that the QP contact their Professional Body or UK Medicines and Healthcare products Regulatory Agency (MHRA) Inspector for advice.

10 Outsourced activities

10.1 Where products are manufactured and/or packed under contract, there should be a clearly written Quality/Technical Agreement between the contract giver and the contract acceptor; such an agreement should be reviewed by a QP.

10.2 It may be necessary to consider a direct QP/QP agreement in addition to any Quality/Technical Agreement(s) where there is a requirement for clarity on division of responsibilities for QPs, or where there are a number of QPs in the supply chain.

10.3 The provisions in 10.1 apply equally to QC testing of samples under contract. Refer to the MHRA's current guidance on the use of UK standalone contract laboratories for details

11 Continuing professional development

11.1 QPs have a personal and professional duty to ensure that they keep their knowledge and experience up to date.

11.2 This should include all relevant Regulatory aspects, changes to GMP guidelines, regional and international standards and guidelines.

11.3 In addition, it must also include any advances in manufacturing techniques or control technologies relevant to the dosage forms/types of products with which they work.

11.4 Each QP must also ensure that they keep up to date with all changes relating to the PQS, current expectations, recent issues and best working practices.

11.5 Adequate records must be maintained to demonstrate that sufficient continuing professional development (CPD) is being performed, which also complies with any Professional Body requirements.

11.6 Where appropriate, these records need to be submitted to the relevant Professional Body and to be available for review during any Regulatory inspection.

11.7 In the event of a QP undergoing a significant change in job responsibilities in the same company, e.g. introduction of new dosage forms, it is a requirement that the QP undergoes formal training. There should be a plan prepared and approved by senior management detailing the gaps and training required with timelines. Training must be satisfactorily completed and the QP must be named on the relevant company Authorisation prior to performing batch certification.

11.8 In the event that a QP moves company, it is expected that the same approach is taken as 11.7 above and that the QP does not certify any batches until they are familiar with the new PQS and product range.

11.9 If a QP has a break from work and/or temporarily moves away from the QP role, the QP must ensure that they are fully up to date before returning to a QP role and certifying any batch.

12   Professional conduct

12.1 QPs are subject to the overall jurisdiction of the By-laws, Charters and Regulations, Codes of Conduct, Disciplinary Regulations and any general guidelines of their own Professional Body, and should have access to them.

12.2 QPs have duties not only to their employer but also to the MHRA, in particular its Inspection, Enforcement and Standards group. They must ensure that appropriate senior company executives are made fully aware of any manufacturing and/or testing issues that may cast doubt on the certification of batches or may necessitate a product recall.

12.3 If there is any aspect of the PQS that is not in accordance with the Directives and Guidelines for GMP, then the QP has a duty to bring this to the attention of senior management and ensure that appropriate corrective and preventive measures are taken.

12.4 QPs should establish a good working relationship with Regulatory Inspectors and, as far as possible, provide information on request during site inspections.

   Note: there may be situations outside of site inspections where the QP may wish to consult with the local Regulatory Inspector for advice.

12.5 QPs may consult their Professional Body for confidential advice in cases where undue pressures to depart from professional obligations cannot be counterbalanced by reference to this and other relevant guidance, preferably having informed their employer first.

UK GUIDANCE ON MANUFACTURE

Management has a duty to provide appropriate resources, training and expertise within its organisation to ensure that QPs can operate effectively in discharging their responsibilities and that the PQS and communications are not compromised. Those resources may not necessarily reside in a Quality function.

13   Professional bodies

Each Professional Body in the UK has an "Officer" who is a point of contact for QPs. Each Professional Body has made arrangements so that any QP contacting their Professional Body can be directed to an experienced QP to discuss any difficult situations and obtain advice on possible courses of action.

14   Disciplinary procedures

14.1   Article 56 of EU Directive 2001/82/EC and Article 52 of EU Directive 2001/83/EC require that Member States ensure that the duties of QPs are fulfilled, either by means of appropriate administrative measures or by making such persons subject to a Professional Code of Conduct.

Member States may provide for the temporary suspension of such a person upon the commencement of administrative or disciplinary procedures against them for failure to fulfil their obligations.

If it was found that a QP had certified a batch as fit for sale or supply without ensuring that the relevant tests and checks had been performed, this would be a matter for consideration by both the appropriate Professional Body and the MHRA as a matter of professional misconduct.

14.2   The Professional Bodies each have established disciplinary procedures to deal with cases of possible misconduct. One of the powers is to remove the name of an individual (or individuals) from the appropriate register or registers. Where required, the Professional Bodies will work together (e.g. if a person is a member of more than one). In all cases, the Professional Bodies will inform the MHRA of these situations.

14.3   The MHRA has the power to delete the QP's name from any Manufacturer's Authorisation.

Import into the UK

For licensed medicinal products that are imported into the UK, the provisions of paragraphs 12(1)(b) and 12A(1)(b) in Part 3 of Schedule 7 of the Human Medicines Regulations 2012 apply. This includes the full qualitative and quantitative analysis of at least all the active substances and all the other tests or checks necessary to ensure that the quality of the medicinal products is in accordance with the requirements of the marketing authorisation. It is the Qualified Person of the importer who is responsible for ensuring that these requirements are met.

There are currently two exceptions to this requirement: imports from third countries where a relevant Mutual Recognition Agreement (MRA) is in place, and imports to GB from the list of "Approved Countries for Import".

The Trade and Partnership Agreement between the United Kingdom of Great Britain and Northern Ireland and Israel (the UK–Israel Agreement): protocol on conformity assessment

The provisions of the EU–Israel protocol on conformity assessment and acceptance of industrial products (ACAA or CAA) have been incorporated into the UK–Israel agreement. The CAA facilitates mutual recognition of each party's inspectorate results for good manufacturing practice (GMP) for pharmaceuticals. Amendments have been made to the CAA, as expressed in Annex II of the UK–Israel agreement, to remove approximation elements that required Israel to approximate its rules to EU law. **The Protocol includes recognition of batch testing.**

Mutual Recognition Agreements (MRAs)

The UK has MRAs with several third countries. The pharmaceutical or GMP sectors of these MRAs provide benefit to exporters and importers of medicinal products in the UK trading with these countries.

The basis for an MRA concerning medicinal products is equivalence of the principles and guidelines of GMP, the inspection systems and, in most cases, the arrangements for authorising manufacturers between both parties.

Although every imported batch of medicinal product still requires QP certification by the UK importer, the requirement for full qualitative and quantitative analysis is waived and the UK QP can certify on the basis of the manufacturer's batch certificate.

MRAs that include a medicinal products sector are in place between the UK and the following countries:

- Australia
- Canada
- Israel
- Japan
- New Zealand
- Switzerland
- The USA.

The operational status and scope of individual MRAs at any given time may be checked with the MHRA.

List of Approved Countries for Import

Regulation 18A of the Human Medicines Regulations 2012 allows importation of human medicines into Great Britain under a UK wholesale dealer's licence, provided that the UK wholesale dealer confirms that each batch has been certified by a Qualified Person (QP) in a listed country.

The list of approved countries currently comprises the EEA (the 27 Member States of the EU, plus Iceland, Liechtenstein and Norway).

The UK will accept certification by a QP from countries on the list. The list will be reviewed at least every three years.

The UK's acceptance of batch testing done in EEA countries will be reviewed before 31 December 2022. A two-year notice period will be given in the case of changes.

Importing guidance for Investigational Medicinal Products from countries on a list to Great Britain, Pharmaceutical Quality System expectations and Authorisation requirements for IMP importation oversight

1   Introduction

The requirements and procedures for clinical trials in the UK are set out in the Medicines for Human Use (Clinical Trials) Regulations 2004. These regulations require all interventional clinical trials to be ethically approved and authorised by the MHRA. They also include requirements for the application and assessment of each trial, the supply of investigational medicinal products (IMPs), the conduct of clinical trials in accordance with good clinical practice and safety reporting.

Detailed guidance on the manufacture and import of IMPs is described in EudraLex, Volume 4 and EudraLex, Volume 10, including guidance for the issuance of the Qualified Person Declaration for the importation of IMPs manufactured in third countries outside the European Economic Area (EEA).

2   Import of IMPs from an approved country

If you are the Sponsor of a UK clinical trial using IMPs imported into Great Britain from countries on an "approved country for import" list (initially, all EU and EEA countries), you will require a UK Manufacturing and Import Authorisation (MIA(IMP)) holder to put in place an assurance system to check that these IMPs have been certified by a QP in a listed country, before release to the trial.

This assurance system must be overseen by a QP, however the IMPs do not require recertification. The routine tasks relating to verification of QP certification in a listed country may be delegated by the QP named on the UK MIA(IMP) to appropriate personnel operating within their MIA(IMP) quality system. The QP named on the UK MIA(IMP) that is responsible for this verification process may be resident in the UK or a listed country. Any manufacturing activity or importation from a non-listed country must be certified by a QP who is resident in the UK.

A sponsor may perform verification of QP certification in a listed country themselves if they are the holder of a UK MIA(IMP). Alternatively, they may outsource this verification to a third party who holds a UK MIA(IMP).

IMPs coming to Great Britain from Northern Ireland do not require this additional oversight when:

- QP certified IMPs are supplied from the EU/EEA for use at Northern Ireland clinical trial sites and are then onward supplied to Great Britain;
- IMPs are QP certified by a Northern Ireland MIA(IMP) holder.

IMPs coming directly to Great Britain that are not on the approved country for import list will continue to require import and QP certification in the UK by the MIA(IMP) holder as per the existing requirements. Any manufacturing activity or importation from a non-listed country must be certified by a QP named on the UK MIA(IMP) who is resident within the UK.

3   Oversight process

There are two routes for IMPs to be received into Great Britain from a listed country for use in UK clinical trials following QP certification by the listed country MIA(IMP) holder:

- direct to the Great Britain clinical trial site;
- via a Great Britain storage and distribution "hub".

Both require the oversight of a UK MIA(IMP) holder and QP, with systems in place to ensure that:

- IMPs are not made available for use in Great Britain clinical trial sites until appropriate QP certification in a listed country has been verified by the QP named on the UK MIA(IMP);
- IMPs are shipped only to appropriate Great Britain trial sites detailed within the UK trial application;

- up-to-date information and documentation relating to the clinical trial and associated Product Specification File are made available by the sponsor to the QP named on the UK MIA(IMP);
- the clinical trial is authorised by the MHRA before the IMP is made available to the Investigator.

3.1 Written agreements

There should be written agreements that describe the assigned responsibilities and provision of relevant information between the organisations. These include agreements between:

- sponsor and the UK MIA(IMP) holder responsible for the oversight of import from the listed country;
- sponsor and the listed country MIA(IMP) holder;
- UK MIA(IMP) holder and Great Britain storage and distribution hub (if applicable);
- sponsor and Great Britain storage and distribution hub (if applicable).

3.2 Documentation available to the QP named on the UK MIA(IMP)

The QP named on the UK MIA(IMP) should have the following documentation available as part of the oversight process for import of the IMP to Great Britain from listed countries:

- details of the manufacturing and distribution supply chain.
- the UK Clinical Trial Application form, plus amendments. This should be used to confirm the site responsible for final certification of the finished IMP.
- the UK Clinical Trial Application and any amendment approval records (including any post-approval commitment requirements).
- evidence that the certifying site in the listed country is appropriately licensed and holds a current GMP certificate for the IMP dosage form(s) and associated activities (e.g. manufacture, packaging, testing and/or import from a third country).
- details of the approved GB trial sites from the ethics application, plus any updates or amendments.
- details of each shipment of IMP to Great Britain including the addressees' information. This should be verified against the ethics approvals.
- details of any excursions from the stated storage conditions during shipment, along with any decisions taken by the sponsor and certifying QP, and the rationale for those decisions.
- details of the responsibilities described in the written agreement between the sponsor and the listed country MIA(IMP) holder.

This is not an exclusive or exhaustive list because information requirements may vary depending on the responsibilities of each organisation in the supply chain.

Applicable checks should be undertaken for each individual shipment into Great Britain to ensure the above details.

3.3   Acceptable evidence of QP certification

Written evidence should be available to demonstrate that each batch of IMP imported from a listed country has been QP certified for use in the specified UK trial. This should be verified prior to the first shipment of IMP from each batch to the Great Britain trial site(s).

Not all options listed below may be suitable for different supply chain relationships; however, just one of these pieces of evidence is sufficient to satisfy the requirements of the Regulations. Other evidence may be acceptable provided that it confirms that QP certification has taken place for the batch in question.

Batch certification by a QP may be confirmed, using evidence such as:

- batch certificate confirming QP certification in accordance with Article 13.3 of Directive 2001/20/EC;
- statement of certification (ad hoc, confirming certification in accordance with Article 13.3 of Directive 2001/20/EC);
- access to the certifying MIA(IMP) holder's internal systems (e.g. global Enterprise Resource Planning system) that confirms batch certification.

4   Supply of IMP to a GB clinical trial site

Until the QP named on the UK MIA(IMP) confirms that the batch of IMP has been appropriately certified by the listed country QP, the IMP should not be made available for use by the Great Britain trial sites. This may need to include consideration of how and when supplies are made available within an Interactive Response Technology (IRT) system.

This is in addition to the two-step release procedure described in EU GMP Annex 13. Regulatory release of the IMP may be given for some countries at different times, so the sponsor should ensure that the regulatory release is in place for the UK prior to the IMP being made available for use in the trial.

5   Using a GB storage and distribution "hub"

You may use a distribution facility to store IMPs imported from a listed country before supply to GB clinical trial sites. IMPs may be imported to the distribution hub from a listed country before confirming that QP certification has taken place in the listed country, if they are segregated electronically or physically until certification has been confirmed by the QP named on the UK MIA(IMP). Great Britain storage and distribution facilities should be named on the UK MIA(IMP) of the company responsible for oversight of the import.

6   Reference and retention samples

Additional reference and retention samples are not specifically required to be stored within Great Britain, but the storage location should be visible to the QP named on the UK MIA(IMP) and defined in the written agreement with the sponsor. Provision for timely access to the samples by the UK-competent authority should be made within the relevant written agreements.

7   Importing non-investigational medicinal products for use in a clinical trial

If you import authorised or unauthorised products for use in a UK clinical trial in Great Britain that are:

- non-investigational medicinal products;
- unmodified comparators to be labelled in Great Britain prior to QP certification and release to the clinical trial,

importation from a listed country should use a wholesale dealer's licence (WDA(H)). A Responsible Person for import (RPi) may be required. Guidance is available on importation of medicines from an approved country for import and the requirements for an RPi.

Importation from a country that is not a listed country will require a manufacturer's licence.

Obtaining non-investigational medicinal products from Northern Ireland will require a WDA(H), unless you are the sponsor of the clinical trial.

8   MIA(IMP) Authorisation requirements

This section describes how to apply for the required authorised activity for implementing the oversight process on the UK MIA(IMP).

The authorisation should specify "Importation of QP certified IMPs from a country" on the "approved country for import" list as free text within "Other importation activities" in section 2.3 of the licence.

8a   Existing UK MIA(IMP) holders with authorisation for importation from third countries

Procedures should be in place for management of importation and QP certification of IMPs from third countries. It is expected that these systems will be readily adaptable to oversee import of finished IMPs from approved countries. A variation to the MIA(IMP) should also be submitted as described above to add oversight of importation from approved countries.

If the licence holder intends to implement this oversight system, the PQS requirements for the new process (as described in section 9) should be in place by January 2022, or prior to submitting the variation and starting oversight responsibilities.

8b   Existing UK MIA(IMP) holders without authorisation for importation from third countries

A variation to the MIA(IMP) should be submitted to request authorisation for the oversight of importation from approved countries.

The licence holder should have procedures to manage and document the oversight process (as described in section 9) and these should be ready for inspection at the time of application. This inspection may be initially conducted remotely, but this may later require an on-site inspection.

8c   New applications for a UK MIA(IMP) solely for the purposes of the oversight of import of IMPs from approved countries

If no MIA(IMP) is held, then an application for a UK MIA(IMP) will need to be submitted. This may be limited to oversight of IMP import from approved countries.

The PQS should provide a robust mechanism for the oversight process (as described in section 9). An inspection will be performed prior to granting of the licence. This inspection may initially be conducted remotely, but this may later require an on-site inspection.

As the oversight process does not involve any manufacturing, packaging or testing activities, there is no requirement to name a person responsible for production. A person responsible for the overall Quality System (QC), where this person must be a UK resident, and a suitable QP must be named.

9   Expected parts of a PQS to support the oversight process

The PQS, solely for the purposes of the oversight of import of IMPs from approved countries, should include, but is not limited to, the following:

- procedures for the preparation, revision and control of documents (procedures, specifications and records).
- management of Product Specification Files (not all detail in the PSF will be required, but relevant information should be available and maintained up to date).
- training of staff involved in the process, including appropriate experience with IMPs.

- procedures for management of deviations, change control, corrective and preventive action (CAPA), complaints, recall, self-inspection, management review.
- written agreements with relevant parties, including clinical trial sponsor, distribution partners and storage sites as applicable.
- procedures for status control of shipped IMPs. Responsibilities of each party should be defined in technical agreements, and proportionate controls should be in place. If IMPs are shipped directly to the trial site, there should be a robust mechanism to ensure that product is held until notification is provided to the site that the IMP is approved for use.
- formal documentation of any tasks delegated by the QP to appropriate personnel operating within their MIA(IMP) quality system.

There is no requirement to re-certify batches already QP certified in a listed country, or for the QP named on the UK MIA(IMP) to maintain a register of certified batches. Records of all shipments to trial sites in Great Britain using the oversight process should be visible within the PQS and be traceable.

UK Guidance on Certificates of Analysis

In certain circumstances a Certificate of Analysis from a third party may be used as part of a system to ensure the quality of materials. For such a certificate to be considered acceptable the following conditions should apply:

(a) The person responsible for QC in the purchasing company must assure themselves that the organisation issuing the certificate is competent to do so, whether that organisation is part of the supplying company or is independent of it (e.g. is a contract analytical service).

(b) The Certificate must:
   (i)   identify the organisation issuing it. If Certificates are reproduced (e.g. when obtaining starting materials from an Agent, re-packer or re-processor), these Certificates must identify the name and address of the original manufacturer and the original batch Certificate reference number, a copy of which should be attached;
   (ii) be authorised by a person competent to do so, and state their qualifications and position. "Authorisation" may be by signature or acceptable electronic means (please refer to the guidance given on electronic signatures, see paragraph 14 of Annex 11 to the EC Guide to GMP);
   (iii) name the material to which it refers and identify it by a batch number. For materials with an expiry or re-test date, this should be listed on the Certificate;

(iv) state that the material has been tested, by whom and when this was done. In situations where some or all tests have been performed by a contract analytical service, this should be clearly identified, stating the name and address of the laboratory that performed the analysis;

(v) state the specification (e.g. Ph.Eur.) and methods against which, and by which, the tests were performed;

(vi) give the test results obtained, or declare that the results obtained showed compliance with the stated specification.

Possession of a Certificate of Analysis does not eliminate the need to confirm the identity of the material supplied, its supply chain or other relevant factors such as transmissible spongiform encephalopathy status.

Possession of a Certificate of Analysis does not absolve the purchaser from ultimate responsibility for the correctness of the material to which it refers.

The above paragraphs, although particularly relevant to the certification of starting materials, also apply as appropriate to other materials and products.

Note that the Certificate of Analysis described above is not *the Manufacturer's Batch Certificate used within the context of a Mutual Recognition Agreement, Agreements on Conformity Assessment and Acceptance of Industrial Products (ACAA) or other appropriate arrangements on GMP with the European Union* (see Mutual Recognition Agreement section above).

GMP for Starting Materials

(To be read in conjunction with Part II of the EC Guide to GMP.)

From 30 October 2005, manufacturing authorisation holders were required to use as starting materials only active substances that have been manufactured in accordance with GMP.

This includes both total and partial manufacture, including re-packaging or re-labelling activities. Herb active pharmaceutical ingredients (APIs) used as active substances for traditional herbal medicinal products are also required to comply with these requirements.

Legislation gives powers to the MHRA to carry out inspections at the premises of manufacturers of such materials, the marketing authorisation (MA) holder and any laboratories employed by the MA holder. These inspections may be unannounced and may be carried out at the request of an API manufacturer, MHRA or another competent authority. The MHRA has powers to inspect premises, take samples and examine documents.

A report will be provided to the manufacturer or MA holder who has undergone the inspection and, where relevant, a certificate of GMP compliance issued. Certificates issued to UK manufacturers will be entered on an MHRA-GMDP[3] database (and for Northern Ireland into a central Community database), as will any failures in compliance.

In order to ensure the reliability of the supply chain and to respond to the increasing threat of falsified medicines entering the supply chain, legislation also requires that the particulars and documents required for a marketing authorisation now include the written confirmation that the finished product manufacturer has verified that the active substance is manufactured in accordance with good manufacturing practices (GMP) for active substances.

Legislation also provides further obligations on the finished product manufacturer to use only active substances that have not only been manufactured in accordance with GMP for active substances, but which have also been distributed in accordance with good distribution practices (GDP) for active substances, and verify compliance by the manufacturer and distributors of active substances with GMP and GDP by conducting audits at the manufacturing and distribution sites of the manufacturer and distributors of active substances.

The holder of the manufacturing authorisation has to verify such compliance either themselves or through an entity acting on their behalf under a contract.

The primary means by which the MHRA will supervise compliance with the requirement for active substances to be manufactured in accordance with GMP will be through review of audit reports during inspections of manufacturing authorisation holders.

Audits of active substance manufacturers should be performed by suitably trained auditors. During inspections the competence of auditors will be assessed and, if not deemed appropriate, this will be raised as an issue.

The holder of the manufacturing authorisation must also ensure that the excipients are suitable for use in medicinal products by ascertaining what the appropriate GMP is. This shall be ascertained on the basis of a formalised risk assessment in accordance with guidance. Such risk assessment shall take into account requirements under other appropriate quality systems, as well as the source and intended use of the excipients and previous instances of quality defects.

The holder of the manufacturing authorisation must ensure that the appropriate GMP so ascertained is applied and document the measures that have been taken.

The UK legislation requirements also require manufacturers, importers and distributors of active substances to be registered with the MHRA.

---

[3] MHRA-GMDP database: https://cms.mhra.gov.uk/mhra.

GMP for Excipients

(To be read in conjunction with Guidelines on the formalised risk assessment for ascertaining the appropriate good manufacturing practice for excipients of medicinal products for human use.)

Regulation 37(5) of the Human Medicines Regulations provides that:

(5) The licence holder shall ensure that:

(a) excipients are suitable for use in a medicinal product by:
   (i) ascertaining what the appropriate good manufacturing practice is; and
   (ii) ensuring that the ascertained good manufacturing practice is applied;

(b) the suitability of the excipient is ascertained on the basis of a formalised risk assessment as described in the case of a product for sale or supply in Great Britain, in the guidelines that apply under or by virtue of Regulation C17 and, in the case of a product for sale or supply in Northern Ireland, in paragraph 5 of Article 47 of the 2001 Directive;

(c) the assessment under sub-paragraph (b) takes account of:
   (i) the source;
   (ii) requirements under other quality systems;
   (iii) intended use of the excipients; and
   (iv) previous instances of quality defects;

(d) the authenticity and quality of any excipient used are verified; and

(e) the measures taken under this paragraph are documented by the licence holder.

The guidelines on the formalised risk assessment for ascertaining the appropriate GMP for excipients were adopted on 19 March 2015. Risk assessments were required to be carried out for excipients for authorised medicinal products for human use from 21 March 2016.

The Guidelines set out three key areas:

• determination of appropriate GMP based on type and use of excipient;
• determination of Excipient Manufacturer's Risk Profile; and
• confirmation of Application of Appropriate GMP.

MHRA Inspectorate expectations

The excipient risk assessment/risk management procedure should be incorporated in the Manufacturing Import Authorisation holder's PQS.

The Manufacturing Import Authorisation holder should have processes for determining the appropriate level of GMP for the excipients they use and be able to confirm that the excipient manufacturer is applying them.

Importers of medicinal products should have the risk assessment/management documentation available on site.

Whenever it considers that there are grounds for suspecting non-compliance the MHRA may carry out inspections at the premises of manufacturers or importers of excipients.

MHRA GMP Data Integrity Definitions and Guidance for Industry[4]

Introduction

Data integrity is fundamental in a PQS, which ensures that medicines are of the required quality. This document provides MHRA guidance on GMP data integrity expectations for the pharmaceutical industry. This guidance is intended to complement existing EU GMP relating to active substances and dosage forms, and should be read in conjunction with national medicines legislation and the GMP standards published in EudraLex, Volume 4.

The data governance system should be integral to the pharmaceutical quality system described in EU GMP Chapter 1. The effort and resource assigned to data governance should be commensurate with the risk to product quality, and should also be balanced with other quality assurance resource demands. As such, manufacturers and analytical laboratories are not expected to implement a forensic approach to data checking on a routine basis, but instead design and operate a system that provides an acceptable state of control based on the data integrity risk, and that is fully documented with supporting rationale.

Data integrity requirements apply equally to manual (paper) and electronic data. Manufacturers and analytical laboratories should be aware that reverting from automated/computerised to manual/paper-based systems will not in itself remove the need for data integrity controls. This may also constitute a failure to comply with Article 23 of Directive 2001/83/EC, which requires an authorisation holder to take account of scientific and technical progress and enable the medicinal product to be manufactured and checked by means of generally accepted scientific methods.

Establishing data criticality and inherent integrity risk

In addition to an overarching data governance system, which should include relevant policies and staff training in the importance of data integ-

---

[4] MHRA Ref 1.1 March 2015.

rity, consideration should be given to the organisational (e.g. procedures) and technical (e.g. computer system access) controls applied to different areas of the quality system. The degree of effort and resource applied to the organisational and technical control of data lifecycle elements should be commensurate with its criticality in terms of impact to product quality attributes.

Data may be generated by (1) a paper-based record of a manual observation or (2) in terms of equipment, a spectrum of simple machines through to complex highly configurable computerised systems. The inherent risks to data integrity may differ depending upon the degree to which data (or the system generating or using the data) can be configured, and therefore potentially manipulated.

Simple systems (such as pH meters and balances) may only require calibration, whereas complex systems require "validation for intended purpose".

Validation effort increases with system complexity. However, it is common for companies to overlook systems of apparent lower complexity. Within these systems it may be possible to manipulate data or repeat testing to achieve a desired outcome, with limited opportunity of detection when using stand-alone systems with a user-configurable output such as FT-IR or UV spectrophotometers.

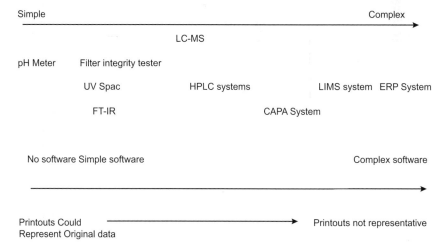

Figure 1 Diagram to illustrate the spectrum of simple machine (left) to complex computerised system (right), and relevance of printouts as 'original data'

Designing systems to assure data quality and integrity

Systems should be designed in a way that encourages compliance with the principles of data integrity. Examples include:

- access to clocks for recording timed events;
- accessibility of batch records at locations where activities take place so that ad-hoc data recording and later transcription to official records are not necessary;
- control over blank paper templates for data recording;
- user access rights that prevent (or audit trail) data amendments;
- automated data capture or printers attached to equipment such as balances;
- proximity of printers to relevant activities;
- access to sampling points (e.g. for water systems);
- access to raw data for staff performing data-checking activities.

The use of scribes to record activity on behalf of another operator should be considered "exceptional", and only take place where:

- the act of recording places the product or activity at risk, e.g. documenting line interventions by sterile operators;
- to accommodate cultural or staff literacy/language limitations, e.g. where an activity is performed by an operator, but witnessed and recorded by a Supervisor or Officer.

In both situations, the supervisory recording must be contemporaneous with the task being performed, and must identify both the person performing the observed task and the person completing the record. The person performing the observed task should countersign the record wherever possible, although it is accepted that this countersigning step will be retrospective. The process for supervisory (scribe) documentation completion should be described in an approved procedure, which should also specify the activities to which the process applies.

In the following definitions, the term 'data' includes **raw data**.

Term	Definition	Expectation / guidance (where relevant)
Data	Information derived or obtained from raw data (e.g. a reported analytical result)	Data must be: A – attributable to the person generating the data L – legible and permanent C – contemporaneous O – original record (or 'true copy') A – accurate

Term	Definition	Expectation / guidance (where relevant)
Raw data	Original records and documentation, retained in the format in which they were originally generated (i.e. paper or electronic), or as a 'true copy'. Raw data must be contemporaneously and accurately recorded by permanent means. In the case of basic electronic equipment which does not store electronic data, or provides only a printed data output (e.g. balance or pH meter), the printout constitutes the raw data.	Raw data must: • Be legible and accessible throughout the data lifecycle. • Permit the full reconstruction of the activities resulting in the generation of the data
Metadata	Metadata is data that describe the attributes of other data, and provide context and meaning. Typically, these are data that describe the structure, data elements, interrelationships and other characteristics of data. It also permits data to be attributable to an individual.	Example: data (bold text) **3.5** and metadata, giving context and meaning, (italic text) are: *sodium chloride batch 1234*, **3.5***mg. J Smith 01/07/14* Metadata forms an integral part of the original record. Without metadata, the data has no meaning.
Data integrity	The extent to which all data are complete, consistent and accurate throughout the data lifecycle.	Data integrity arrangements must ensure that the accuracy, completeness, content and meaning of data is retained throughout the data lifecycle.
Data governance	The sum total of arrangements to ensure that data, irrespective of the format in which it is generated, is recorded, processed, retained and used to ensure a complete, consistent and accurate record throughout the data lifecycle	Data governance should address data ownership throughout the lifecycle, and consider the design, operation and monitoring of processes / systems in order to comply with the principles of data integrity including control over intentional and unintentional changes to information. Data governance systems should include staff training in the importance of data integrity principles and the creation of a working environment that encourages an open reporting culture for errors, omissions and aberrant results. Senior management is responsible for the implementation of systems and procedures to minimise the potential risk to data integrity, and for identifying the residual risk, using the principles of ICH Q9. Contract Givers should perform a similar review as part of their vendor assurance programme.
Data lifecycle	All phases in the life of the data (including raw data) from initial generation and recording through processing (including transformation or migration), use, data retention, archive / retrieval and destruction.	The procedures for destruction of data should consider data criticality and legislative retention requirements. Archival arrangements should be in place for long term retention (in some cases, periods up to 30 years) for records such as batch documents, marketing authorisation application data, traceability data for human-derived starting materials (not an exhaustive list). Additionally, at least 2 years of data must be retrievable in a timely manner for the purposes of regulatory inspection.

UK GUIDANCE ON
MANUFACTURE

Term	Definition	Expectation / guidance (where relevant)
Primary record	The record which takes primacy in cases where data that are collected and retained concurrently by more than one method fail to concur.	In situations where the same information is recorded concurrently by more than one system, the data owner should define which system generates and retains the primary record, in case of discrepancy. The 'primary record' attribute should be defined in the quality system, and should not be changed on a case by case basis.Risk management principles should be used to ensure that the assigned 'primary record' provides the greatest accuracy, completeness, content and meaning. For instance, it is not appropriate for low-resolution or static (printed / manual) data to be designated as a primary record in preference to high resolution or dynamic (electronic) data. All data should be considered when performing a risk based investigation into data anomalies (e.g. out of specification results).
Original record / True Copy:	Original record: Data as the file or format in which it was originally generated, preserving the integrity (accuracy, completeness, content and meaning) of the record, e.g. original paper record of manual observation, or electronic raw data file from a computerised system True Copy: An exact verified copy of an original record.Data may be static (e.g. a 'fixed' record such as paper or pdf) or dynamic (e.g. an electronic record which the user / reviewer can interact with). Example 1: a group of still images (photographs – the static 'paper copy' example) may not provide the full content and meaning of the same event as a recorded moving image (video – the dynamic 'electronic record' example). Example 2: once printed or converted to static pdfs, chromatography records lose the capability of being reprocessed and do not enable more detailed viewing of baselines or any hidden fields. By comparison, the same dynamic electronic records in database format provides the ability to track, trend, and query data, allowing the reviewer (with proper access permissions) to reprocess, view hidden fields, and expand the baseline to view the integration more clearly.	Original records and true copies must preserve the integrity (accuracy, completeness, content and meaning) of the record. Exact (true) copies of original records may be retained in place of the original record (e.g. scan of a paper record), provided that a documented system is in place to verify and record the integrity of the copy. It is conceivable for raw data generated by electronic means to be retained in an acceptable paper or pdf format, where it can be justified that a static record maintains the integrity of the original data. However, the data retention process must be shown to include verified copies of all raw data, metadata, relevant audit trail and result files, software / system configuration settings specific to each analytical run*, and all data processing runs (including methods and audit trails) necessary for reconstruction of a given raw data set. It would also require a documented means to verify that the printed records were an accurate representation. This approach is likely to be onerous in its administration to enable a GMP compliant record. Many electronic records are important to retain in their dynamic (electronic) format, to enable interaction with the data. Data must be retained in a dynamic form where this is critical to its integrity or later verification. This should be justified based on risk. * computerised system configuration settings should be defined, tested, 'locked' and protected from unauthorised access as part of computer system validation. Only those variable settings which relate to an analytical run would be considered as electronic raw data.

Term	Definition	Expectation / guidance (where relevant)
Computer system transactions:	A computer system transaction is a single operation or sequence of operations performed as a single logical 'unit of work'. The operation(s) that make up a transaction may not be saved as a permanent record on durable storage until the user commits the transaction through a deliberate act (e.g. pressing a save button), or until the system forces the saving of data. The metadata (i.e., user name, date, and time) is not captured in the system audit trail until the user commits the transaction. In Manufacturing Execution Systems (MES), an electronic signature is often required by the system in order for the record to be saved and become permanent.	Computer systems should be designed to ensure that the execution of critical operations are recorded contemporaneously by the user and are not combined into a single computer system transaction with other operations. A critical processing step is a parameter that must be within an appropriate limit, range, or distribution to ensure the desired product quality. These should be reflected in the process control strategy. Examples of 'units of work': • Weighing of individual materials Entry of process critical manufacturing / analytical parameters • Verification of the identity of each component or material that will be used in a batch • Verification of the addition of each individual raw material to a batch (e.g. when the sequence of addition is considered critical to process control – see figure 2) • Addition of multiple pre-weighed raw materials to bulk vessel when required as a single manufacturing step (e.g. when the sequence of addition is not considered critical to process control – see figure 3)
Audit Trail	GMP audit trails are metadata that are a record of GMP critical information (for example the change or deletion of GMP relevant data), which permit the reconstruction of GMP activities.	Where computerised systems are used to capture, process, report or store raw data electronically, system design should always provide for the retention of full audit trails to show all changes to the data while retaining previous and original data. It should be possible to associate all changes to data with the persons making those changes, and changes should be time stamped and a reason given. Users should not have the ability to amend or switch off the audit trail. The relevance of data retained in audit trails should be considered by the company to permit robust data review / verification. The items included in audit trail should be those of relevance to permit reconstruction of the process or activity. It is not necessary for audit trail review to include every system activity (e.g. user log on/off, keystrokes etc.), and may be achieved by review of designed and validated system reports.

Term	Definition	Expectation / guidance (where relevant)
		Audit trail review should be part of the routine data review / approval process, usually performed by the operational area which has generated the data (e.g. laboratory). There should be evidence available to confirm that review of the relevant audit trails have taken place. When designing a system for review of audit trails, this may be limited to those with GMP relevance (e.g. relating to data creation, processing, modification and deletion etc). Audit trails may be reviewed as a list of relevant data, or by a validated 'exception reporting' process. QA should also review a sample of relevant audit trails, raw data and metadata as part of self inspection to ensure on-going compliance with the data governance policy / procedures. If no audit trailed system exists a paper based audit trail to demonstrate changes to data will be permitted until a fully audit trailed (integrated system or independent audit software using a validated interface) system becomes available. These hybrid systems are currently permitted, where they achieve equivalence to integrated audit trail described in Annex 11 of the GMP Guide. If such equivalence cannot be demonstrated, it is expected that facilities should upgrade to an audit trailed system by the end of 2017.
Data Review		There should be a procedure which describes the process for the review and approval of data, including raw data. Data review must also include a review of relevant metadata, including audit trail. Data review must be documented. A procedure should describe the actions to be taken if data review identifies an error or omission. This procedure should enable data corrections or clarifications to be made in a GMP compliant manner, providing visibility of the original record, and audit trailed traceability of the correction, using ALCOA principles (see 'data' definition).
Computerised system user access / system administrator roles		Full use should be made of access controls to ensure that people have access only to functionality that is appropriate for their job role, and that actions are attributable to a specific individual. Companies must be able to demonstrate the access levels granted to individual staff members and ensure that historical information regarding user access level is available. Shared logins or generic user access should not be used. Where the computerised system design supports individual user access, this function must be used. This may require the purchase of additional licences.

Term	Definition	Expectation / guidance (where relevant)
		It is acknowledged that some computerised systems support only a single user login or limited numbers of user logins. Where alternative computerised systems have the ability to provide the required number of unique logins, facilities should upgrade to an appropriate system by the end of 2017. Where no suitable alternative computerised system is available, a paper based method of providing traceability will be permitted. The lack of suitability of alternative systems should be justified based on a review of system design, and documented.
		System administrator access should be restricted to the minimum number of people possible taking account of the size and nature of the organisation. The generic system administrator account should not be available for use. Personnel with system administrator access should log in under unique log-ins that allow actions in the audit trail(s) to be attributed to a specific individual.
		System Administrator rights (permitting activities such as data deletion, database amendment or system configuration changes) should not be assigned to individuals with a direct interest in the data (data generation, data review or approval). Where this is unavoidable in the organisational structure, a similar level of control may be achieved by the use of dual user accounts with different privileges. All changes performed under system administrator access must be visible to, and approved within, the quality system.
		The individual should log in using the account with the appropriate access rights for the given task e.g. a laboratory manager performing data checking should not log in as system administrator where a more appropriate level of access exists for that task.
Data retention		Raw data (or a true copy thereof) generated in paper format may be retained for example by scanning, provided that there is a process in place to ensure that the copy is verified to ensure its completeness.
		Data retention may be classified as archive or backup. Data and document retention arrangements should ensure the protection of records from deliberate or inadvertent alteration or loss.
		Secure controls must be in place to ensure the data integrity of the record throughout the retention period, and validated where appropriate.

Term	Definition	Expectation / guidance (where relevant)
		Where data and document retention is contracted to a third party, particular attention should be paid to understanding the ownership and retrieval of data held under this arrangement. The physical location in which the data is held, including impact of any laws applicable to that geographic location should also be considered. The responsibilities of the contract giver and acceptor must be defined in a contract as described in Chapter 7 of the GMP Guide.
• **Archive**	Long term, permanent retention of completed data and relevant metadata in its final form for the purposes of reconstruction of the process or activity.	Archive records should be locked such that they cannot be altered or deleted without detection and audit trail. The archive arrangements must be designed to permit recovery and readability of the data and metadata throughout the required retention period.
• **Backup**	A copy of current (editable) data, metadata and system configuration settings (variable settings which relate to an analytical run) maintained for the purpose of disaster recovery.	A copy of current (editable) data, metadata and system configuration settings (variable settings which relate to an analytical run) maintained for the purpose of disaster recovery.
File structure		File structure has a significant impact on the inherent data integrity risks. The ability to manipulate or delete flat files requires a higher level of logical and procedural control over data generation, review and storage.
• **Flat files:**	A 'flat file' is an individual record which may not carry with it all relevant metadata (e.g. pdf, dat, doc).	Flat files may carry basic metadata relating to file creation and date of last amendment, but may not audit trail the type and sequence of amendments. When creating flat file reports from electronic data, the metadata and audit trails relating to the generation of the raw data may be lost, unless these are retained as a 'true copy'. Consideration also needs to be given to the 'dynamic' nature of the data, where appropriate (see 'true copy' definition) There is an inherently greater data integrity risk with flat files (e.g. when compared to data contained within a relational database), in that these are easier to manipulate and delete as a single file.
• **Relational database:**	A relational database stores different components of associated data and metadata in different places. Each individual record is created and retrieved by compiling the data and metadata for review	This file structure is inherently more secure, as the data is held in a large file format which preserves the relationship between data and metadata. This is more resilient to attempts to selectively delete, amend or recreate data and the metadata trail of actions, compared to a flat file system. Retrieval of information from a relational database requires a database search tool, or the original application which created the record.

Term	Definition	Expectation / guidance (where relevant)
Validation – for intended purpose (See also Annex 15 and GAMP 5)		Computerised systems should comply with the requirements of EU GMP Annex 11 and be validated for their intended purpose. This requires an understanding of the computerised system's function within a process. For this reason, the acceptance of vendor-supplied validation data in isolation of system configuration and intended use is not acceptable. In isolation from the intended process or end user IT infrastructure, vendor testing is likely to be limited to functional verification only, and may not fulfil the requirements for performance qualification. For example - validation of computerised system audit trail • A custom report generated from a relational database may be used as a GMP system audit trail. SOPs should be drafted during OQ to describe the process for audit trail verification, including definition of the data to be reviewed. 'Validation for intended use' would include testing during PQ to confirm that the required data is correctly extracted by the custom report, and presented in a manner which is aligned with the data review process described in the SOP.

Allows for contemporaneous recording of the material addition by the operator and verifier.

Material Additions		
Step	**Instructions**	**Data**
1.	Scan barcode of material ABC123.	ABC123 <Barcode>
2.	Add material ABC123 to the blender.	Operator Signature Verifier Signature

Next Step ➡

Figure 1 Logical design permitting contemporaneous recording of addition of a single material in a manufacturing 'unit of work'. This record is permanently recorded (step 2), with audit trail, before progressing to next 'unit of work'.

Does not allow for contemporaneous recording of the material addition by the operator and verifer.

Material Additions		
Step	**Instructions**	**Data**
1.	Scan barcode of material ABC123.	ABC123 <Barcode>
2.	Add material ABC123 to the blender.	
3.	Scan barcode of material DEF456.	DEF456 <Barcode>
4.	Add material DEF456 to the blender.	
5.	Scan barcode of material GHI789.	GHI789 <Barcode>
6.	Add material GHI789 to the blender.	Operator Signature Verifier Signature

Next Step

Figure 2 Logical design permitting the addition of multiple materials in a manufacturing 'unit of work' before committing the record to durable media. Steps 1, 3 and 5 are contemporaneous entries (bar code), but are not permanently recorded with audit trail until step 6.

Guidance for UK Manufacturer's Licence and Manufacturing Authorisation (for Investigational Medicinal Products) Holders on the Use of UK Stand-Alone Contract Laboratories

Introduction

This section:

- is applicable to all manufacturer's licence holders, i.e. import, export, herbals and specials;
- provides an update and details changes to the June 2010 published guidance;
- outlines the MHRA's criteria for inspection of UK contract laboratories;
- provides guidance[5] as to when a UK contract laboratory must be named on a manufacturer's licence for medicinal products for human use[6] and/ or a manufacturing authorisation for investigational medicinal products;
- provides guidance as to when a UK contract laboratory is not required to be named on a manufacturer's licence or manufacturing authorisation;
- outlines the MHRA's expectations of the manufacturer's licence, manufacturing authorisation holders and UK stand-alone contract laboratories; and
- outlines the inspection process for UK contract laboratories.

It is acknowledged that there are a number of manufacturer's licences and manufacturing authorisation holders that can also offer contract quality control testing to GMP. The inspection of these quality control testing activities is included within the scope of their routine GMP inspections. In this situation, the GMP licence holder who is performing the testing and acts as the contract acceptor should be named as a contract laboratory on the contract giver's GMP licence.

The criteria for inspection have been changed such that any stand-alone contract laboratories that are involved only in microbiological testing of raw materials and/or environmental monitoring (for non-sterile manufacture) will no longer meet the criteria to be inspected. Therefore, these laboratories are no longer required to be named on manufacturer's licences or manufacturing authorisations. Laboratories performing environmental monitoring and/or process simulation (media fill) work for sterile product manufacturers will continue to meet the criteria for inspection.

---

[5] This section is for guidance and it is acknowledged that there may be some specific situations where the actual requirements may vary. In the case of contract laboratories supporting manufacture of biological products, the requirement for inspection will be made on a case-by-case basis, taking into account the guidance on application of GMP described in Annex 2 of the GMP Guide.

[6] Responsibility for veterinary-only licences lies with the Veterinary Medicines Directorate.

Responsibility for oversight of any laboratories involved in raw material testing lies with the manufacturing site using those raw materials and with the certifying Qualified Person to ensure that there is an acceptable level of GMP compliance.

Contract laboratories that no longer meet the criteria for inspection will be removed from any manufacturer's licences or manufacturing authorisations by the licensing office, and the GMP certificates held by these contract laboratories will be allowed to lapse.

Criteria for inspection of contract laboratories by the MHRA

In accordance with the MHRA's risk-based approach to inspections, fee-bearing inspections of stand-alone contract quality control testing laboratories, will be conducted against EU GMP if the laboratory is undertaking the following testing of a medicinal product or an investigational medicinal product for human use:

- microbiological, biological and chemical/physical testing of finished medicinal products including investigational medicinal products, i.e. final testing prior to QP-certification for the purposes of batch release;
- laboratories involved in testing of radiopharmaceutical products (noting that some of the testing is completed post-use);
- stability testing of finished marketed medicinal products;
- environmental monitoring and/or process simulation (media fill) work for sterile product manufacturer; or
- biological testing if it is required to be conducted in accordance with the GMP Guide, as described in Annex 2.

When contract laboratories must be named on manufacturer's licences/manufacturing authorisations

Contract laboratories that meet the criteria for inspection must be named on manufacturer's licences or manufacturing authorisations, irrespective of the quantity or frequency of testing. This also includes any UK stand-alone contract laboratory subcontracted by another stand-alone contract laboratory.

Stand-alone contract laboratories that are testing finished products on import into Great Britain or Northern Ireland from the EU must be named on manufacturer's licences and marketing authorisations.

When contract laboratories should not be named on manufacturer's licences/manufacturing authorisations

Stand-alone contract laboratories that conduct all other testing (e.g. raw material and API testing), or produce data for research where the products are not intended to be released onto the market or used in a clinical trial, do not need to be named on a manufacturing licence or manufacturing authorisations.

MHRA expectations of manufacturer's licence holders, manufacturing authorisation holders and stand-alone contract laboratories

Manufacturer's licence and or manufacturing authorisation holders (contract givers) that wish to use a contract laboratory (contract acceptor) must:

- have a system in place to assess the suitability, competency and GMP compliance of proposed contract laboratories prior to their use, whether the contract laboratory meets the criteria for an MHRA GMP inspection or not;
- ensure that the contract laboratories used, irrespective of their location or whether they meet the criteria for inspection, are visible within the manufacturer's quality management system and listed in their Site Master File;
- update their respective licences/authorisations to name the contract laboratory if the contract laboratory meets the criteria for an MHRA GMP inspection;
- ensure that a written Technical Agreement, which describes the GMP responsibilities of each party, and also refers to the scope of testing and type of tests covered by the agreement, has been put in place;
- have a system of on-going supervision for contract laboratories, including arrangements to periodically formally re-assess compliance, based on risk;
- ensure that contract laboratories meeting the criteria for inspection have a valid GMP certificate in place prior to data generated by the laboratory being used by the contract giver for batch disposition decisions;
- ensure that the stand-alone contract laboratory complies with the approved testing methods.

The presence of a GMP certificate may be used as information to support the use of a contract laboratory; however, the scope of any certificate should be confirmed to be relevant to the work to be performed. The certificate may form part of the contract giver's wider assessment process, but should not be used exclusively as a substitute for a formal assessment by a prospective contract giver.

A laboratory used on an ad-hoc basis to perform specialist testing in support of investigations is not expected to be approved prospectively on the manufacturer's licence and/or manufacturer's authorisation, in order to facilitate timely investigation of unplanned events. Contract givers are encouraged to implement a process by which minimum expectations can be assessed in a timely manner, e.g. by the use of a basic questionnaire and/

or by listing key compliance expectations as part of the written request for analysis, which is then issued to the contract laboratory.

Contract laboratories involved in quality control testing of medicinal products or investigational products for human use must do so in accordance with the marketing authorisation, product specification file and EU GMP.

Inspection process

Inspections of new laboratories are triggered by the submission of a variation to the manufacturer's licence and/or manufacturing authorisation to name the laboratory. Pre-inspection visits are not performed by the MHRA and the laboratory should be ready for inspection when the variation is submitted.

The scope of the inspection of a stand-alone contract laboratory will be to assess their quality system for compliance with EU GMP, along with the specific activities they perform, e.g. chemical/physical analysis, microbiological testing, biological testing.

Within the UK there is no requirement for a stand-alone contract laboratory to hold their own manufacturer's licence or manufacturing authorisation; however, a GMP certificate will be issued to the contract laboratory following a satisfactory inspection outcome.

Confirmation of the compliance status of a stand-alone contract laboratory will be communicated directly to the laboratory on completion of the inspection process. The contract laboratory must notify the contract giver in writing of any data generated prior to receipt of a GMP certificate, and any data generated by the laboratory must not be used by the contract giver for batch disposition purposes until a certificate of GMP compliance has been issued.

Stand-alone contract laboratories details can be accessed via the online MHRA GMDP database. If contract laboratory is in Northern Ireland, then this will in addition be published in the Eudra GMDP database.

GMP non-compliance

GMP non-compliance may be managed via Compliance Escalation or consideration of regulatory action by the Inspection Action Group (IAG).

Compliance Escalation is a non-statutory process to take action in response to repeated poor compliance that does not yet meet the threshold for referral to IAG for the consideration of regulatory action. The main aim of the Compliance Escalation process is to direct companies towards a state of compliance, thus avoiding the need for regulatory action and the potential adverse impact to patient health through lack of availability of medicines.

Actions may include close monitoring of compliance improvement work through additional inspections, meetings and correspondence with company senior management, alerting them to the compliance concerns and clearly outlining the consequences of continued non-compliance. Upon satisfactory conclusion of the remediation work, the company will be returned to the routine risk-based inspection programme; however, referral for consideration of regulatory action may still occur if the required improvements are not achieved in a timely manner.

In the event of serious non-compliance issues, a referral may be made to IAG. The final outcome of the IAG process may result in:

- the laboratory being removed from the licence and/or authorisation;
- the laboratory being issued with a statement of non-compliance with GMP; or
- the laboratory having their GMP certificate either withdrawn or replaced by a conditioned GMP certificate that only allows specific testing to be performed.

These actions may prevent the use of the laboratory for GMP testing until a satisfactory re-inspection has taken place.

Good Laboratory Practice, Good Quality Control Laboratory Practice and Good Manufacturing Practice

The terms Good Laboratory Practice (GLP) and Good Quality Control Laboratory Practice (GQCLP) are generic terms that cause confusion when used to describe the quality control testing of medicinal products. Compliance with the Organisation for Economic Co-operation and Development (OECD) principles of GLP is a regulatory requirement when conducting non-clinical, safety studies of new chemical or biological substances. There is no legal requirement for the quality control testing of medicinal products to be conducted in accordance with the OECD principles of GLP and there is no requirement for laboratories involved in quality control testing of medicinal products to be members of the UK GLP Compliance Monitoring Programme. GQCLP is a term used within the industry and is not a regulatory requirement. This term should not be used within the GMP quality system of a stand-alone laboratory.

Reference

EudraLex, Volume 4 – *Medicinal Products for Human and Veterinary Use: Good Manufacturing Practice*.

Manufacture and Importation of Unlicensed Medicines for Human Use

Introduction

A "medicinal product" is defined by the Human Medicines Regulations 2012 [SI 2012 No. 1916] and Directive 2001/83/EC in Northern Ireland, as amended.

In the UK, to supply a medicinal product (medicine), an authorisation issued by the Licensing Authority is required. However, medicines legislation provides certain exemptions from the need for a marketing authorisation for the supply and use of unlicensed medicines for human use.

Unlicensed medicines may not have been assessed by the Licensing Authority for their quality, safety or efficacy. As such, their use is restricted to the conditions set out in legislation. Regulation 167 of the Human Medicines Regulations 2012 [SI 2012 No. 1916] establishes that unlicensed medicines may be supplied to meet the special clinical needs of patients, which cannot be met by authorised available medicines, in response to a bona fide unsolicited order, formulated in accordance with the specifications of a prescriber and for use by an individual patient under their direct personal responsibility.

Unlicensed medicines may be manufactured in the UK or may be imported into the country.

MHRA Guidance Note 14 provides guidance to importers about the conditions under which they may manufacture, import and supply unlicensed medicinal products and their legal obligations.

Manufacture and supply of unlicensed medicinal products for individual patients ("specials")

In order to manufacture an unlicensed medicine in the UK, commonly referred to as a "special", the manufacturer must hold a Manufacturer's (Specials) Licence issued by MHRA. A "special" may not be advertised and may not be supplied if an equivalent licensed product is available that could meet the patient's clinical needs. Essential records must be kept and serious adverse drug reactions reported to the MHRA. *MHRA Guidance Note 14 The supply of unlicensed medicinal products ("Specials")* provides guidance to manufacturers about the conditions under which they may manufacture and supply "specials" and their legal obligations.

Supply of UK manufactured "specials" can occur only in accordance with Regulation 167 of the Human Medicines Regulations 2012 [SI 2012 No. 1916] as described in the introduction section.

Importation and supply of unlicensed medicinal products for individual patients

To import a human medicine to be used as a special medicinal product in the UK or as an unlicensed medicine in an approved country for import list, the importer must hold the appropriate wholesale dealer's licence or manufacturer's (specials) licence and must comply with its conditions. (For further information on licensing requirements please see MHRA Guidance Notes 5 and 6: *Notes for applicants and holders of a manufacturer's/wholesale dealer's licence or brokering registration.* For additional information on the approved country for import list, please refer to: https://www.gov.uk/government/publications/list-of-approved-countries-for-authorised-human-medicines/list-of-approved-countries.)

Importers of unlicensed medicines must notify the MHRA on each occasion that they intend to import such a product 28 days prior to the importation taking place. Importation may proceed once the MHRA issues a "No Objection" to import letter or 28 days after the date the importer receives written acknowledgement of the requests by the MHRA, a "No Objection (Acknowledgment Letter)", whichever comes first. The MHRA may, within this 28-day period, request additional information objects to importation of the medicinal product. The importer will be notified by the MHRA, in writing, and will not be able to import the product. The MHRA may object and prevent importation because it has concerns about the safety or quality of the product or because it is not satisfied that there is a "special need" for the supply to individual patients.

A "special" may not be advertised and may not be supplied if an equivalent licensed product is available that could meet the patient's clinical needs. Essential records must be kept and serious adverse drug reactions reported to the MHRA. MHRA Guidance Note 14 *The supply of unlicensed medicinal products ("Specials")* provides guidance to manufacturers about the conditions under which they may manufacture and supply "specials" and their legal obligations.

Supply of imported "specials" can occur only in accordance with Regulation 167 of the Human Medicines Regulations 2012 [SI 2012 No. 1916] as described in the introduction section. MHRA Guidance Note 14 provides guidance to importers about the conditions under which they may manufacture, import and supply unlicensed medicinal products and their legal obligations.

Where an unlicensed medicine is imported from a country outside the approved country for import list or, as in the case for Northern Ireland, the EEA, the importer of the medicinal product must also be able to demonstrate compliance with the European Commission's *Notes for guidance on minimising the risk of transmitting animal spongiform encephalopathy agents via medicinal products* and future updates, in accordance with The Unlicensed Medicinal Products for Human Use (Transmissible Spongiform Encephalopathies) (Safety) Regulations 2003 [SI 2003/1680]. (See the MHRA's interim guidance: *Minimising the risk of Transmission of Transmissible Spongiform Encephalopathies via Unlicensed Medicinal Products for Human Use*, available from the MHRA's website www.mhra. gov.uk.)

Notification to MS licence holders due to compliance concerns

The MHRA published guidance to "specials" manufacturers, to provide an interpretation of the good manufacturing practice (GMP) requirements for specials manufacturers[7].

The GMDP Inspectorate has been concerned that some specials manufacturers have not always been receiving written orders, e.g. fax, email, from pharmacists for supply of a "Special" that orders them. This mainly appears to apply to non-sterile specials.

The MHRA has consulted with the General Pharmaceutical Council and the Royal Pharmaceutical Society, and they point to the *Professional Guidance for the Procurement and Supply of Specials* published by the Royal Pharmaceutical Society in December 2015 where, on page 7, the following paragraph can be found:

Pharmacists and their teams agree with the supplier what they require to meet the prescription, this includes strength, formulation and, where relevant, requirements for excipients e.g. sugar-free or alcohol-free formulations, and flavourings. This is based on the pharmacist's understanding of the clinical needs of the patient. Where necessary the agreed formulation is confirmed to the manufacturer in writing.

The General Pharmaceutical Council and the Royal Pharmaceutical Society take the last sentence as requiring a written form of an order to confirm the formulation of the Special required and the General Pharmaceutical Council issued a clarification on this topic through Regulate on 14 April 2016[8].

The MHRA recognises that MS holders have had difficulties in getting some customers to provide written orders and hope that this will clarify the situation and ensure that written orders are received for all Specials supplied.

---

[7] January 2015 https://www.gov.uk/government/publications/guidance-for-specials-manufacturers.

[8] https://www.pharmacyregulation.org/regulate/article/ordering-specials-manufacturers.

GMDP Inspectors will assess the application of this guidance in all future inspections of specials manufacturers to ensure consistency in expectations for placing orders.

For more information around unlicensed medicines please see the section titled "Matters Related to Unlicensed Medicines" in Chapter 10 of this guide.

Contact

For further information about notification of intention to import unlicensed medicines, please contact:

Import Notification System
Medicines & Healthcare products Regulatory Agency (MHRA)
10 South Colonnade
London
E14 4PU
United Kingdom
Telephone: 020 3080 6625
Email: imports@mhra.gov.uk

Manufacture and Supply of Unlicensed Advanced Therapy Medicinal Products for Individual Patients ("Hospital Exemption")

The Advanced Therapy Medicinal Products Regulation (No 1394/2007) came into force on 30 December 2007 (ATMP Regulation).

An Advanced Therapy Medicinal Product (ATMP) is a medicinal product, as defined in Directive 2001/83/EC as amended (the Directive). Specifically, an ATMP is a medicinal product that is:

- a gene therapy medicinal product as defined in Part IV of Annex 1 to Directive 2001/83/EC;
- a somatic cell therapy medicinal product as defined in Part IV of Annex 1 to Directive 2001/83/EC; or
- a tissue-engineered product as defined in Article 2 1 (b) of the ATMP Regulation.

Under the ATMP Regulation, those medicinal products that come within the scope of Directive 2001/83/EC and are categorised as ATMPs are to be regulated under the centralised European procedure. Under this procedure, a centralised European marketing authorisation is granted by the European Commission after assessment by the European Medicines Agency (EMA).

Under Article 3 (7) of 2001/83/EC, there is an exemption from central authorisation for ATMPs that are prepared on a non-routine basis and used within the same Member State in a hospital in accordance with a medical prescription for an individual patient. The exemption was included in the Regulation in recognition of the small scale and developmental nature of activity carried out in some hospitals, which argued for a degree of flexibility over the nature of regulatory requirements. Member States are required to implement this Community requirement for a hospital exemption by putting in place arrangements at a national level to meet the specific requirements set out in the Regulation. The MHRA is responsible for the regulatory arrangements under the exemption in the UK.

The UK's legislation for implementing the Regulation and the requirements that apply under the hospital exemption scheme has been consolidated in the Human Medicines Regulation 2012 [SI 2012/1916; Article 171].

Contact

Contact points for specific enquiries in relation to ATMPs are as follows:

- Manufacturing and exemptions: gmpinspectorate@mhra.gov.uk
- Pre-licensing and scientific guidance: biologicalsandbiotechnology@mhra.gov.uk
- Clinical trials: clintrialhelpline@mhra.gov.uk
- Patient information: patient.information@mhra.gov.uk
- Pharmacovigilance: info@mhra.gov.uk
- Medical device-related aspects of combination ATMPs: info@mhra.gov.uk
- Coordination of UK legislation/guidance: info@mhra.gov.uk
- For queries not covered by other MHRA contact points: info@mhra.gov.uk

UK Guidance on the Manufacture, Importation and Distribution of Active Substances

Contents

Introduction

The Human Medicines Regulations [SI 2012/1916] lay down the rules for the manufacture, import, marketing and supply of medicinal products and ensures the functioning of the internal market for medicinal products while safeguarding a high level of protection of public health in the UK.

The falsification of medicinal products is a global problem, requiring effective and enhanced international coordination and cooperation in order to ensure that anti-falsification strategies are more effective, in particular as regards sale of such products via the internet. To that end, the National Competent Authorities are cooperating closely and supporting on-going work in international fora on this subject.

Active substances are those substances that give a medicinal product its therapeutic effect. They are the Active Pharmaceutical Ingredient (API).

Falsified active substances and active substances that do not comply with applicable requirements of UK national legislation pose serious risks to public health. As such, guidelines are in place for good manufacturing practice and good distribution practice for active substances to minimise the risk to public health associated with falsification.

Registration

To provide a greater level of control, and transparency of supply for active substances, manufacturers, importers and distributors of active substances have to notify the Medicines and Healthcare products Agency (MHRA) of their activities and provide certain details. The MHRA will enter these details into a National Database (MHRA-GMDP database: https://cms.mhra.gov.uk/mhra) after the determination of a successful application for registration. The MHRA may then conduct inspections against the requirements of the relevant good practices before permitting such businesses to start trading. Manufacturers, importers and distributors of active substances will be subject to inspection not only on the basis of suspicions of non-compliance, but also on the basis of risk analysis.

Authorised manufacturers of medicinal products that also manufacture and/or import active substances, either for use in their own products or products manufactured by other companies, are not exempt from the requirement to register.

Persons who are requested to import an active substance from a third country that provides facilities solely for transporting the active substance, or where they are acting as an import agent and imports the active substance solely to the order of another person who holds a certificate of good manufacturing practice issued by the licensing authority, are not required to register.

The registration regime for manufacturers, importers and distributors of active substances will be subject to an application procedure, followed by a determination procedure completed by the MHRA.

The person applying for registration must notify the MHRA immediately of any changes that have taken place as regards the information in the registration form, where such changes may have an impact on quality or safety of the active substances that are manufactured, imported or distributed. These changes shall be treated as incorporated in the application form.

The MHRA must grant or refuse an application for registration within 60 working days, beginning immediately after the day on which a valid application is received.

The MHRA will notify the applicant within 60 days of receipt of a valid application for registration whether they intend to undertake an inspection.

The applicant may not undertake any activity before either:

- 60 days have elapsed and the applicant has not been notified of the Agency's intention to inspect; or
- following inspection the Agency has notified the applicant that they may commence their activities.

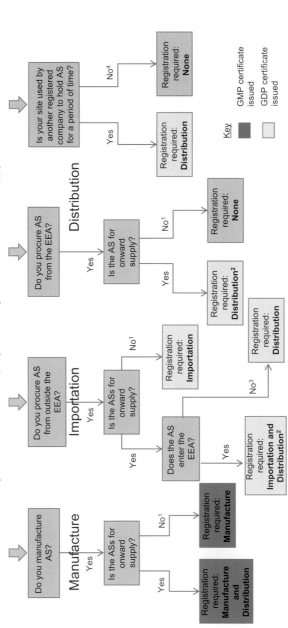

Registration requirements for NI companies involved in the sourcing and supply of an active substance (AS) to be used in the manufacture of human medicines.

This flowchart may be used to determine the appropriate registration required for UK companies.
Where more than one activity is carried out, the company should register for all activities that apply.

Manufacture

Do you manufacture AS?

Yes → Is the ASs for onward supply?

Yes → Registration required: **Manufacture and Distribution**

No[1] → Registration required: **Manufacture**

Importation

Do you procure AS from outside the EEA?

Yes → Is the ASs for onward supply?

Yes → Does the AS enter the EEA?

No[1] → Registration required: **Importation**

Yes → Registration required: **Importation and Distribution[2]**

No[3] →

Registration required: **Distribution**

Distribution

Do you procure AS from the EEA?

Yes → Is the AS for onward supply?

Yes → Registration required: **Distribution[2]**

No[1] → Registration required: **None**

Is your site used by another registered company to hold AS for a period of time?

Yes → Registration required: **Distribution**

No[4] → Registration required: **None**

Key

- GMP certificate issued
- GDP certificate issued

1. Site holds a Manufacturer's Licence and uses the AS in the manufacture of the finished dose form.
2. Where the registration holder contracts out the physical handling of the AS, the company that physically handles the product should be named as a 3rd party site on the registration if they hold the AS and this takes place in the UK.
   In addition, the company should hold its own registration. If the company are based in an approved country for import, they should be registered with the competent authority in that approved country
3. AS is procured from a country other than an approved country for import are supplied directly to customers based in a country other than an approved country for import.
4. AS is not held (stored) for any length of time and the company are simply contracted to transport the AS.

Figure 4.1 Registration requirements for UK companies involved in the sourcing and supply of active substances (ASs) to be used in the manufacture of human medicines.

Registration requirements for GB companies involved in the sourcing and supply of active substance (AS) to be used in the manufacture of human medicines.

This flowchart may be used to determine the appropriate registration required for UK companies.
Where more than one activity is carried out, the company should register for all activities that apply.

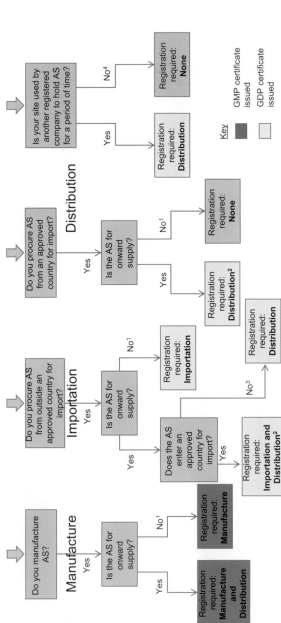

1. Site holds a Manufacturer's Licence and uses the AS in the manufacture of the finished dose form.
2. Where the registration holder contracts out the physical handling of the AS, the company that physically handles the product should be named as a 3rd party site on the registration if they hold the AS and this takes place in the UK.
   In addition, the company should hold its own registration. If the company are based in an approved country for import, they should be registered with the competent authority in that approved country.
3. AS is procured from a country other than an approved country for import are supplied directly to customers based in a country other than an approved country for import.
4. ASs is not held (stored) for any length of time and the company are simply contracted to transport the AS.

Registration requirements for companies involved in the sourcing and supply of active substance (AS) between GB and NI to be used in the manufacture of human medicines.

This flowchart may be used to determine the appropriate registration required for UK companies. Where more than one activity is carried out, the company should register for all activities that apply.

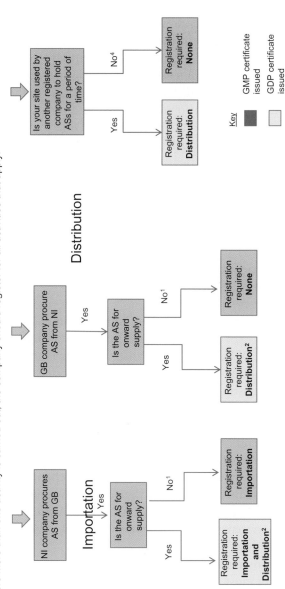

Importation

NI company procures AS from GB

Is the AS for onward supply?

Yes → Registration required: **Importation and Distribution²**

No¹ → Registration required: **Importation**

Distribution

GB company procure AS from NI

Is the AS for onward supply?

Yes → Registration required: **Distribution²**

No¹ → Registration required: **None**

Is your site used by another registered company to hold ASs for a period of time?

Yes → Registration required: **Distribution**

No⁴ → Registration required: **None**

Key

- ▉ GMP certificate issued
- ▢ GDP certificate issued

1. Site holds a Manufacturer's Licence and uses the ASs in the manufacture of the finished dose form.
2. Where the registration holder contracts out the physical handling of the AS, the company that physically handles the product should be named as a 3rd party site on the registration if they hold the ASs and this takes place in the UK.
   In addition, the company should hold its own registration. If the company are based in an approved country for import, they should be registered with the competent authority in that approved country.
3. ASs procured from a country other than an approved country for import are supplied directly to customers based in a country other than an approved country for import.
4. ASs are not held (stored) for any length of time and the company are simply contracted to transport the ASs.

MHRA

UK GUIDANCE ON ACTIVE SUBSTANCES

After inspection the MHRA will prepare a report and communicate that report to the applicant. The applicant will have the opportunity to respond to the report. Within 90 days of an inspection the MHRA shall issue an appropriate good practice certificate to the applicant, indicating that the applicant complies with the requirements of the relevant good practices. Where an applicant is found to be non-compliant with the requisite standards, a statement of non-compliance will be issued by the MHRA.

If after 60 days of the receipt of the application form the MHRA has not notified the applicant of their intention to carry out an inspection, the applicant may commence their business activity and regard themselves as registered. The MHRA will issue a certificate to the applicant and enter the details into the National Database, and for sites in Northern Ireland into the Community Database (EudraGMDP).

The Database, which is publicly available, will enable competent authorities in other countries or other legal entities to establish the bona fides and compliance of manufacturers, importers and distributors of active substances established in the UK. The MHRA will investigate concerns with regard to UK registrations of non-compliance.

Conditions of Registration as a Manufacturer, Importer or Distributor of an Active Substance

A person in the UK may not import, manufacture or distribute an active substance for use in a licensed human medicine unless they are registered with the MHRA in accordance with the Human Medicines Regulations 2012 and the respective conditions of those Regulations are met.

For registration the MHRA must have received a valid registration form from the applicant for import, manufacture or, as the case may be, distribution of the active substance.

Registration holders must submit to the MHRA an annual update of any changes to the information provided in the application or provide a statement that there was no change. Any changes that may have an impact on the quality or safety of the active substance that the registrant is permitted to handle must be notified to the Agency immediately.

An annual compliance report will need to be submitted: by 30 April for the previous year.

For an active substance manufactured in the UK, the registered manufacturer must comply with good manufacturing practice in relation to that active substance.

Where principles and guidelines of good manufacturing practice have been published under, or apply by virtue of, Regulation C17 of the Human

Medicines Regulations 2012 ("the Regulations"), which apply to an active substance manufactured in Great Britain, a manufacturer in Great Britain must comply with those principles and guidelines of good manufacturing practice in relation to that active substance.

Where the Commission has adopted principles and guidelines of good manufacturing practice under the third paragraph of Article 47 of the 2001 Directive, which applies to an active substance manufactured in Northern Ireland, a manufacturer in Northern Ireland must comply with those principles and guidelines of good manufacturing practice in relation to that active substance.

Where principles and guidelines of good distribution practice have been published under, or apply by virtue of, Regulation C17 of the Regulations, which apply to an active substance distributed in Great Britain, a distributor in Great Britain must comply with those principles and guidelines of good distribution practice in relation to that active substance.

Where the Commission has adopted principles and guidelines of good distribution practice under the fourth paragraph of Article 47 of the 2001 Directive, which applies to an active substance distributed in Northern Ireland, a distributor in Northern Ireland must comply with those principles and guidelines of good distribution practice in relation to that active substance.

Where principles and guidelines of good manufacturing practice have been published under, or apply by virtue of, Regulation C17, which apply to an active substance imported into Northern Ireland, and where an active substance is imported into Northern Ireland from a country other than an EEA State so imported:

- the importer must comply with good manufacturing practice and good distribution practice in relation to the active substance;
- the active substances must have been manufactured in accordance with standards that are at least equivalent to good manufacturing practice*; and
- the active substances must be accompanied by a written confirmation from the competent authority of the exporting country of the following:
  - the standards of manufacturing practice applicable to the plant manufacturing the exported active substance are at least equivalent to good manufacturing practice;
  - the manufacturing plant concerned is subject to regular, strict and transparent controls and to the effective enforcement of standards of manufacturing practice at least equivalent to good manufacturing practice, including repeated and unannounced inspections, so as to ensure a protection of public health at least equivalent to that in Northern Ireland; and

   – in the event of findings relating to non-compliance, information on such findings is supplied by the exporting country to the licensing authority without any delay.

Where principles and guidelines of good manufacturing practice have been published under, or apply by virtue of, Regulation C17, which apply to an active substance imported into Great Britain other than from Northern Ireland, and where an active substance is so imported:

- the importer must comply with good manufacturing practice and good distribution practice in relation to the active substance;
- the active substances must have been manufactured in accordance with standards that are at least equivalent to good manufacturing practice*; and
- the active substances must be accompanied by a written confirmation from the competent authority of the exporting country of the following:
  - the standards of manufacturing practice applicable to the plant manufacturing the exported active substance are at least equivalent to good manufacturing practice;
  - the manufacturing plant concerned is subject to regular, strict and transparent controls and to the effective enforcement of standards of manufacturing practice at least equivalent to good manufacturing practice, including repeated and unannounced inspections, so as to ensure a protection of public health at least equivalent to that in Great Britain; and
  - in the event of findings relating to non-compliance, information on such findings is supplied by the exporting country to the licensing authority without any delay.

The criteria mentioned above marked with an "*" do not apply:

- where the country from where the active substance is exported is included in the list referred to in Article 111b of the 2001 Directive (in the case of an import into Northern Ireland) or paragraph (6) (in the case of an import into Great Britain); or
- for a period not exceeding the validity of the certificate of good manufacturing practice, where:
  - in relation to a plant where active substances are manufactured and the competent authority of a Member State or Licensing Authority (in the case of an import into Northern Ireland) or Licensing Authority or an appropriate authority responsible for the licensing of medicinal products in a country included in a list under paragraph (6) (in the case of an import into Great Britain) has found, upon inspection, that a plant complies with the principles and guidelines of good manufacturing practice; and

– the Licensing Authority is of the opinion that it is necessary to waive the requirement to ensure availability of the active substance.

All provisions apply regardless of whether an active substance is intended for export.

GMP for Active Substances

An Active Substance is defined as any substance or mixture of substances intended to be used in the manufacture of a medicinal product and that, when used in its production, becomes an active ingredient of that product intended to exert a pharmacological, immunological or metabolic action, with a view to restoring, correcting or modifying physiological functions or to make a medical diagnosis.

The manufacture of Active Substances should be subject to good manufacturing practice regardless of whether those Active Substances are manufactured in the UK or imported. Where Active Substances are manufactured in third countries it should be ensured that such substances have been manufactured to the required standards of Good Manufacturing Practice (GMP), so as to provide a level of protection of public health equivalent to that provided for by UK law.

A manufacturer or assembler of an Active Substance will have to comply with the principles and guidelines for GMP for Active Substances. Manufacture, in relation to an Active Substance, includes any process carried out in the course of making the substance and the various processes of dividing up, packaging and presentation of the Active Substance. Assemble, in relation to an Active Substance, includes the various processes of dividing up, packaging and presentation of the substance, and assembly has a corresponding meaning. These activities will be the subject of a GMP certificate.

Importers of an Active Substance from a third country have to comply with the guidelines for Good Distribution Practice (GDP) in relation to the Active Substance. This activity will be the subject of a GDP certificate.

Distributors of an Active Substance within the UK that has been sourced from a manufacturer or an importer within the EU will have to comply with the guidelines for GDP for Active Substances. This activity will be the subject of a GDP certificate.

UK GUIDANCE ON ACTIVE SUBSTANCES

GDP for Active Substances

Since March 2015, Guidelines on the principles of GDPs for Active Substances for medicinal products for human use have been published.

The guidelines set out the quality system elements for procuring, importing, holding, supplying or exporting Active Substances. The scope of the guidelines excludes activities consisting of re-packaging, re-labelling or dividing up of Active Substances that are manufacturing activities and as such are subject to the guidelines on GMP of Active Substances. The guidelines, which can be found in Chapter 9 of this Guide, cover:

- Quality system;
- Personnel;
- Documentation;
- Orders;
- Procedures;
- Records;
- Premises and equipment;
- Receipt;
- Storage;
- Deliveries to customers;
- Transfer of information;
- Returns;
- Complaints and recalls; and
- Self-inspections.

Written Confirmation

UK legislation requires importers of active substances for use in the manufacture of authorised medicinal products to obtain written confirmations from competent authorities in third countries that the standards of manufacture of Active Substances at manufacturing sites on their territory are equivalent to EU good manufacturing practice (EU GMP). These confirmations are required before importation of active substances into the UK.

Each shipment of Active Substance received should be accompanied by a written confirmation from the competent authority of the exporting third country, stating that:

- the Active Substance has been manufactured to GMP standards at least equivalent to those laid down in the Human Medicines Regulations;
- the third country manufacturing plant is subject to regular, strict and transparent inspections, and effective enforcement of GMP;
- in the event of non-conformance of the manufacturing site on inspection, such findings will be communicated to the UK without delay.

The European Commission's questions and answers document on this subject can be found on the Commission's website and has been reproduced in Appendix 3 of this guide.

The template for the written confirmation is reproduced here.

The MHRA will generate Written Confirmations for Active Substance manufacturers in Great Britain whether they intend to export Active Substances or not. For a distributor of Active Substances that the site/company did not manufacture, Written Confirmations will not be generated for these activities. If a Written Confirmation is required for a distributor for export activities of an Active Substance not manufactured by that distributor, it may be obtained from the appropriate issuing authority, or directly from the manufacturer.

Importation of Active Substances into Great Britain (England, Wales and Scotland) without a Written Confirmation is accepted from the following list of countries:

- European Economic Area (EEA) countries,
- USA,
- Japan,
- Republic of Korea,
- Brazil,
- Australia,
- Israel,
- Switzerland;

as well as from Northern Ireland.

Northern Ireland will also continue to align with all relevant EU rules relating to the placing on the market of manufactured goods.

TEMPLATE FOR THE 'WRITTEN CONFIRMATION' FOR ACTIVE SUBSTANCES EXPORTED TO THE EUROPEAN UNION FOR MEDICINAL PRODUCTS FOR HUMAN USE, IN ACCORDANCE WITH ARTICLE 46B(2)(B) OF DIRECTIVE 2001/83/EC

(1) Directive 2011/62/EU of the European Parliament and of the Council of 8 June 2011 amending Directive 2001/83/EC on the Community code relating to medicinal products for human use, as regards the prevention of the entry into the legal supply chain of falsified medicinal products (OJ L 174, 1.7.2011, p. 74) introduces EU-wide rules for the importation of active substances: According to Article 46b(2) of Directive 2001/83/EC, active substances shall only be imported if, *inter alia*, the active substances are accompanied by a **written confirmation** from the competent authority of the exporting third country which, as regards the plant manufacturing the exported active substance, confirms that the standards of good manufacturing practice and control of the plant are equivalent to those in the Union.

(2) The template for this written confirmation is set out in the *annex*.

ANNEX

[Letterhead of the issuing regulatory authority]
Written confirmation for active substances exported to the European
Union (EU) for medicinal products for human use, in accordance with
Article 46b(2)(b) of Directive 2001/83/EC

Confirmation no. (given by the issuing regulatory authority):
....

1. Name and address of site (including building number, where applicable):
....

2. Manufacturer's licence number(s):[1]
....

**Regarding the Manufacturing Plant under (1) of the Following Active Sub-
stance(s) Exported to the EU for Medicinal Products for Human Use**

Active Substance(s)[2]	Activity(ies)[3]

The Issuing Regulatory Authority hereby confirms that:
    The standards of good manufacturing practice (GMP) applicable to this
manufacturing plant are at least equivalent to those laid down in the EU
(= GMP of WHO/ICH Q7);
    The manufacturing plant is subject to regular, strict and transparent
controls and to the effective enforcement of good manufacturing practice,
including repeated and unannounced inspections, so as to ensure a protection of public health at least equivalent to that in the EU; and

---

[1] Where the regulatory authority issues a licence for the site. Record 'not applicable' in case where there is no legal framework for issuing of a licence.
[2] Identification of the specific active substances through an internationally
   agreed terminology (preferably international non-proprietary name).
[3] For example, "Chemical synthesis", "Extraction from natural sources", "Biological processes", "Finishing steps".

In the event of findings relating to non-compliance, information on such findings is supplied by the exporting third country without delay to the EU[4].

Date of inspection of the plant under (1).
Name of inspecting authority if different from the issuing regulatory authority:

....

This written confirmation remains valid until:

....

The authenticity of this written confirmation may be verified with the issuing regulatory authority.

This written confirmation is without prejudice to the responsibilities of the manufacturer to ensure the quality of the medicinal product in accordance with Directive 2001/83/EC.

Address of the issuing regulatory authority:

....

Name and function of responsible person:

....

Email, Telephone no., and Fax no.:

....

Signature   Stamp of the authority and date

Written Confirmations for Export to EEA and Northern Ireland of Active Substances Manufactured in Great Britain
1.   Purpose of the Written Confirmation

A Written Confirmation confirms that, for a third country exporting Active Substances to the EEA:

- the standards of Good Manufacturing Practice (GMP) are equivalent to those in the EU/EEA;
- the manufacturing plant is subject to regular inspections (which may be both announced and unannounced);

---

[4] qdefect@ema.europa.eu

- significant non-compliance events would be communicated to the EEA without delay.

A template for the Written Confirmation can be found on the European Commission website.

The requirement for the Written Confirmation is stated in Article 46b(2)(b) of Directive 2001/83/EC.

2. "Third Country" status for Great Britain (England, Wales and Scotland) manufacturers of Active Substances

Great Britain is recognised as a third country for the export of Active Substances for human use to the EEA. Active Substance manufacturers in Northern Ireland will continue to be recognised by the EEA.

A Written Confirmation will then be required for each shipment of Active Substance manufactured in Great Britain that is exported to the EEA and Northern Ireland.

3. Generation of Written Confirmations for Active Substances manufactures in the UK

You will not need to provide any information to the MHRA to allow the Written Confirmation to be generated. All the information required for the Written Confirmations is available within MHRA systems.

Written Confirmations will be generated for Active Substance manufacturers in Great Britain whether they intend to export Active Substances or not.

3.1 Biological products

Manufacture of biological active substance is considered to be partial manufacture of the biological medicinal product. These activities are recorded in section 1.3 of the UK Manufacturing Authorisation (MIA) and the associated GMP certificate issued following a satisfactory inspection "(EU Interpretation of the Union Format for Manufacturer/Importer Authorisation)".

If you hold an MIA that includes manufacture of biological active substance, separate registration as an Active Substance manufacturer is not required. No written confirmation will be issued, because this is already confirmed by the MHRA GMP certificate.

4. Obtaining Written Confirmations for Active Substances manufactured in other third countries

There will be no change to the requirements for obtaining Written Confirmations for importation of Active Substances from other "third countries". You will still need to obtain the Written Confirmations from the issuing authority in that country.

A Written Confirmation will not be required for the supply of Active Substance manufactured in Northern Ireland to Great Britain.

5. Requirements for distributors of Active Substances

If you are a Distributor of Active Substances that you did not manufacture, Written Confirmations will not be generated for your activities. If a Written Confirmation is required for export activities, it can be obtained from the appropriate issuing authority, or directly from the manufacturer.

6. Validity period of a Written Confirmation

A Written Confirmation is valid for the same period as the corresponding GMP certificate. Where required the MHRA will offer an assessment to reissue GMP certificates of Active Substance manufacturing sites in Great Britain, prior to 1 January 2021, to allow generation of Written Confirmations with an appropriate validity period.

Provision of Written Confirmations for Each Shipment of Active Substances Exported to the EEA and Northern Ireland

A "Questions and Answers" document on the EU expectations relating to Written Confirmations is available on the European Commission website. This document identifies how the Written Confirmation should be provided to the customer within the EEA.

8. Companies with confidential GMP certificates

If your company has a confidential GMP certificate due to the nature of the Active Substances manufactured, the Written Confirmation will not be published on the MHRA website. The Written Confirmation will be sent to the contact named on your Active Substance registration.

UK GUIDANCE ON
ACTIVE SUBSTANCES

9.   Requirement for both a GMP certificate and a Written Confirmation

Although similar information is contained in a GMP certificate and a Written Confirmation, both documents serve different purposes:

- UK law requires a GMP certificate to be issued after an inspection;
- EU regulations require a Written Confirmation for any import of Active Substances into the EEA by a third country.

If you export Active Substances made in Great Britain to the EEA or Northern Ireland, you are therefore required to have a valid GMP certificate and a valid Written Confirmation.

10.   Ongoing requirement for Written Confirmations

The need for Written Confirmations is expected to be an interim position. An application will be made to recognise Great Britain's GMP standards for the manufacture of Active Substances in Great Britain as equivalent to those in the EU.

Once a country has been accepted as having equivalent GMP standards, they are added to a "White List" and Written Confirmations are then no longer required.

Short-term Holding of Active Substances

The MHRA has a long-established policy in respect of the licensing of sites undertaking the short-term holding of medicinal products. As with medicinal products, Active Substances should be stored only on premises that are covered by an Active Substance Registration. However, there are certain cases where active substances are held for short periods of time during transportation and prior to onward shipment, e.g. in overnight freight depots. In such instances it has been determined that, as a matter of policy, a site is not required to be registered where:

- Active Substances subject to "ambient" storage temperature requirements remain for less than 36 hours;
- "cold-chain" Active Substances are transported and stored overnight in continuously refrigerated vehicles or in qualified packaging; vehicles must be "in transit" and the active substance is not unloaded at the site (e.g. moved from the vehicle into a fridge or cold store).

As a matter of policy, a site must be registered where:

- ambient storage active substances are held in excess of 36 hours;
- Active Substances requiring refrigeration are placed in a cold store; even when this is for less than 36 hours;
- activities that can be registered, other than storage, are being carried out. This includes the handling of returned goods and where decisions are made regarding suitability for re-sale, as well as the usual activities of picking against orders;
- ownership has been transferred.

Where transportation is performed by a third party and they are holding product, then they require an Active Substance Registration in their own right, naming the relevant sites. Whether the licensed sites require naming as third parties on the supplying registration holder will depend on the nature of the commercial and GDP contracts. In general, if the product is "in transit", the transport site is not required to be named as a third party on the supplier's registration.

Use of Third-party Storage and Distribution Sites

Where an Active Substance registration holder uses a third-party storage and/or distribution provider ("3PL"), the 3PL must have an Active Substance Registration in its own right if it is undertaking activities that can be registered, naming all the sites at which these activities (manufacture, importation or distribution) take place. Any 3PL site that carries out activities that can be registered should be named on the Active Substance Registration of the contract giver.

A Wholesale Dealer's Licence is not relevant to the manufacture, importation or distribution of Active Substances, as a Wholesale Dealer's Licence relates to the procurement, holding or supply of medicinal products (the finished dosage form in the packaging intended for placing on the market). Where a 3PL holds a Wholesale Dealer's Licence, it may give the contract giver some reassurance that the contract acceptor is familiar with the general principles of Good Distribution Practice, because there are a number of parallels between the minimum standards described in Good Distribution Practice for medicinal products and those described for Active Substances; however, this does not lift the requirements of Regulation 45M of the Human Medicines Regulations 2012, as amended, in that the contract giver and contract acceptor both require Active Substance Registrations in their own right.

As required by Section 6.2 of Good Distribution Practice for Active Substances, a contract should be in place between the parties clearly defining responsibilities and the transfer of relevant information. There should be a process of information transfer between the parties that ensures that relevant information is kept up to date across the Active Substance Registrations, such as the range of Active Substances stored/distributed on the contract giver's behalf and the naming of key personnel.

Historically it has been possible for the holder of an Active Substance Registration to use third-party storage and distribution sites located within the European Economic Area (EEA); these sites have never been named on the face of a UK Active Substance Registration, but will hold Active Substance Registrations in their own right in the relevant territory. This MHRA policy continues to be implemented following the UK's exit from the European Union. As with the use of a 3PL in the United Kingdom, there should be a contract in place clearly defining responsibilities and the transfer of information between the contract giver and the contract acceptor.

Segregation of Medicinal Products and Active Substances

Sub-sections 5.1 and 6.7 of Good Distribution Practice for Active Substances require that:

> "Premises and equipment should be suitable and adequate to ensure proper storage, protection from contamination, e.g. narcotics, highly sensitising materials, materials of high pharmacological activity or toxicity, and distribution of active substances. They should be suitably secure to prevent unauthorised access ...

> Active substances should be stored under the conditions specified by the manufacturer, e.g. controlled temperature and humidity when necessary, and in such a manner to prevent contamination and/or mix up ..."

Sub-section 5.5 of Good Distribution Practice for medicinal products requires that:

> "Medicinal products and, if necessary, healthcare products should be stored separately from other products likely to alter them ...

> Medicinal products should be handled and stored in such a manner as to prevent spillage, breakage, contamination and mix-ups ..."

Where a site holds or distributes both medicinal products and Active Substances, there should be adequate segregation of the relevant activities to prevent contamination of one type of product by the other. This is particularly relevant where either the medicinal products or active substances are radioactive materials and other hazardous products, as well as products presenting special safety risks of fire or explosion. Adequate and appropriate security measures should be in place, if necessary restricting personnel who have access to either medicinal product or active substance storage areas if all staff have not received relevant training relating to both product types.

Customer Qualification

Good Distribution Practice for Active Substances requires that supplies of active substances are only made to "... other distributors, manufacturers or to dispensing pharmacies". Key to the supply of an active substance is the definition of an active substance contained in Regulation 8 of the Human Medicines Regulations 2012, as amended:

> "'active substance' means any substance or mixture of substances intended to be used in the manufacture of a medicinal product and that, when used in its production, becomes an active ingredient of that product intended to exert a pharmacological, immunological or metabolic action with a view to restoring, correcting or modifying physiological functions or to make a medical diagnosis;"

One important aspect of this definition is that the substance "...is intended to be used in the manufacture of a medicinal product ..."; in relation to the holding of an Active Substance Registration the medicinal product referred to in this definition is a medicinal product for human use. There is currently no comparable registration regime for active substances intended for the manufacture of veterinary medicinal products, and the controls on active substance manufacture and distribution for veterinary medicinal products are achieved by other means.

It is not uncommon for persons manufacturing and/or distributing active substances to be involved in the supply of substances for other purposes, e.g. foodstuffs, cosmetics or industrial chemicals. It is important for the distributor to establish which of the materials they distribute are subject to controls under UK medicines legislation and those that are subject to different controls, because those materials considered to be Active Substances, rather than falling into some other product type, are subject to particular requirements in legislation and Good Distribution Practice.

In qualifying a customer and their authority to receive a particular substance, the use of "end-user declarations" can be helpful in establishing the legal basis of supply, identifying to what use the customer will be putting the substance they intend procuring. This is particularly relevant to the arena of medicinal products for human use as different controls apply to active substances and excipients. This can help a registration holder focus their resources on the appropriate management of their product portfolio and supplements other customer bona fide checks, such as licence or registration verification against authoritative sources of information.

Annual Reports and Registration Variations

Regulation 45P of the Human Medicines Regulations 2012, as amended, requires that Active Substance Registration Holders must provide the Licensing Authority with an annual report on or before 30 April each year. This report must contain certain information:

- a declaration that the registration holder has an appropriate system in place to ensure compliance with the requirements of Regulations 45N (Registration in relation to Active Substances) and 45O (Requirements for registration as an importer, manufacturer or distributor of an active substance) of the same regulations.
- a description of the system that the registration holder has in place to manage compliance with the regulations.

Regulation 45P then goes on the require that the registration holder must without delay notify the licensing authority of any changes to that system that could affect compliance with the requirements relating to the holding of an Active Substance Registration.

Regulation 45T provides the process for applying for a variation to the scope of an Active Substance Registration. An application for a variation has the effect of changing the scope of the granted Active Substance Registration, e.g. a change in named personnel or the addition or removal of certain active substances manufactured, imported or distributed under the registration. Registration variations should be submitted to the Licensing Authority in a timely manner, and may trigger an inspection dependent on the nature of the change(s) applied for.

From this it can be seen that there is a difference between the scope of an annual report made under Regulation 45P and a registration variation made under Regulation 45T. A registration holder is required to submit an annual report every year, whether or not the scope of the registration changes over time. The processes for the submission of the annual report and submission of a registration variation should be captured in the registration holders quality system, and naturally link in with processes such as change control and deviation management.

There are fees applied to both the submission of an annual report and registration variation, these can be found on the MHRA website[4] (www.gov.uk/mhra). Both annual reports and registration variations are submitted electronically through the MHRA's Process Licensing Portal (https://pclportal.mhra.gov.uk).

The Role of the "Designated Person" for Active Substance Importers and Distributors

Sub-section 3.1 of Good Distribution Practice for Active Substances requires that:

"The distributor should designate a person at each location where distribution activities are performed who should have defined authority and responsibility for ensuring that a quality system is implemented and maintained. The designated person should fulfil his responsibilities personally. The designated person can delegate duties but not responsibilities."

On the face of a UK Active Substance Registration, and within the MHRA Process Licensing Portal, this person is referred to as "Person responsible for Importation, Storage or Distribution Activities".

Within the scope of a Wholesale Dealer's Licence is the "Responsible Person". Sub-section 2.2 of Good Distribution Practice for medicinal products requires that:

"The wholesale distributor must designate a person as responsible person. ...

... The responsible person should fulfil their responsibilities personally and should be continuously contactable. The responsible person may delegate duties but not responsibilities. ...

... The written job description of the responsible person should define their authority to take decisions with regard to their responsibilities. The wholesale distributor should give the responsible person the defined authority, resources and responsibility needed to fulfil their duties. ...

The responsibilities of the responsible person include:

(i) ensuring that a quality management system is implemented and maintained; ..."

UK GUIDANCE ON ACTIVE SUBSTANCES

---

[4] https://www.gov.uk/government/publications/mhra-fees/current-mhra-fees.

In this respect the Designated Person and Responsible Person can be seen to be comparable in their role of ensuring that the compliance of the registration or licence holder with the requirements of legislation and Good Distribution Practice is maintained at an appropriate standard that protects public health.

Although the responsibilities of the Designated Person are less clearly defined in Good Distribution Practice for active substances than those for the Responsible Person in Good Distribution Practice for medicinal products, there are some activities that the MHRA's Good Distribution Practice Inspectorate consider key to the implementation and maintenance of an effective quality system:

- ensuring that importation/distribution activities under the registration are in accordance with the scope of the registration, including the submission of annual reports and applications for registration variations;
- ensuring that roles and responsibilities are clearly defined and understood, and that personnel have received appropriate training and are demonstrably competent;
- ensuring that records are accurate, complete and being generated and maintained contemporaneously;
- ensuring that Active Substances are stored under appropriate conditions and evaluating the impact of departures from the required storage conditions, whether those relate to temperature, humidity, light or other aspects.
- having oversight of customer complaints, particularly those relating to product quality;
- ensuring that Active Substances that are subject to recall action have been withdrawn from the market when required and that relevant information relating to Active Substance quality has been provided to customers and the relevant Competent Authorities;
- ensuring that active substances are sourced only from and supplied to appropriately authorised persons;
- having oversight of activities contracted out to third parties, particularly where those activities can be registered;
- carrying out timely, objective and comprehensive self-inspection activities in assessing the compliance of the registration holder's activities;
- having oversight of changes to or deviations from the company's established operations, particularly where there is potential impact on the importation or distribution of Active Substances, including the application of quality risk management;
- ensuring that the quality system is sufficiently comprehensive in respect of the registration holder's activities and that any other relevant requirements in legislation (e.g. in relation to safety, radioactive substances or Controlled Drugs) have been incorporated into the quality system and are complied with.

As with the Responsible Person, the Designated Person should maintain their competence in and awareness of Good Distribution Practice for Active Substances and the relevant UK legislation by way of on-going training; such training should be documented and demonstrate how relevant learning has been applied to the registration holder's operations. An assessment of the knowledge, awareness and competence of the Designated Person forms part of every inspection of an Active Substance Registration holder; where a Designated Person is not considered to be fulfilling their responsibilities regulatory action may be taken against the registration holder.

For further information on the role and responsibilities of the Responsible Person, please refer to Chapter 8 of this publication.

Legislation on Manufacture and Importation

EU Guidance (Commission Delegated Regulations)

Contents

Commission Directive 2003/94/EC of 8 October 2003 laying down the principles and guidelines of good manufacturing practice in respect of medicinal products for human use and investigational medicinal products for human use

EU GUIDANCE (COMMISSION DELEGATED REGULATIONS)

(Text with EEA relevance)

THE COMMISSION OF THE EUROPEAN COMMUNITIES,

Having regard to the Treaty establishing the European Community,
Having regard to Directive 2001/83/EC of the European Parliament and of the Council of 6 November 2001 on the Community code relating to medicinal products for human use[1], as last amended by Commission Directive 2003/63/EC[2], and in particular Article 47 thereof,
Whereas:

(1) All medicinal products for human use manufactured or imported into the Community, including medicinal products intended for export, are to be manufactured in accordance with the principles and guidelines of good manufacturing practice.

---

[1] OJ L 311, 28.11.2001, p. 67.
[2] OJ L 159, 27.6.2003, p. 46.

(2) Those principles and guidelines are set out in Commission Directive 91/356/EEC of 13 June 1991 laying down the principles and guidelines of good manufacturing practice for medicinal products for human use[3].

(3) Article 13(3) of Directive 2001/20/EC of the European Parliament and of the Council of 4 April 2001 on the approximation of the laws, regulations and administrative provisions of the Member States relating to the implementation of good clinical practice in the conduct of clinical trials on medicinal products for human use[4] requires that detailed guidance be drawn up, in accordance with the guidelines on good manufacturing practice, on the elements to be taken into account when evaluating investigational medicinal products for human use with the object of releasing batches within the Community.

(4) It is therefore necessary to extend and adapt the provisions of Directive 91/356/EEC to cover good manufacturing practice of investigational medicinal products.

(5) Since most of the provisions of Directive 91/356/EEC need to be adjusted, for the sake of clarity that Directive should be replaced.

(6) In order to ensure conformity with the principles and guidelines of good manufacturing practice, it is necessary to lay down detailed provisions on inspections by the competent authorities and on certain obligations of the manufacturer.

(7) All manufacturers should operate an effective quality management system of their manufacturing operations, which requires the implementation of a pharmaceutical quality assurance system.

(8) Principles and guidelines of good manufacturing practice should be set out in relation to quality management, personnel, premises and equipment, documentation, production, quality control, contracting out, complaints and product recall, and self-inspection.

(9) In order to protect the human beings involved in clinical trials and to ensure that investigational medicinal products can be traced, specific provisions on the labelling of those products are necessary.

(10) The measures provided for in this Directive are in accordance with the opinion of the Standing Committee on Medicinal Products for Human Use, set up under Article 121 of Directive 2001/83/EC,

---

[3] OJ L 193, 17.7.1991, p. 30.
[4] OJ L 121, 1.5.2001, p. 34.

HAS ADOPTED THIS DIRECTIVE:

Article 1

Scope

This Directive lays down the principles and guidelines of good manufacturing practice in respect of medicinal products for human use whose manufacture requires the authorisation referred to in Article 40 of Directive 2001/83/EC and in respect of investigational medicinal products for human use whose manufacture requires the authorisation referred to in Article 13 of Directive 2001/20/EC.

Article 2

Definitions

For the purposes of this Directive, the following definitions shall apply:

1 'medicinal product' means any product as defined in Article 1(2) of Directive 2001/83/EC;

2 'investigational medicinal product' means any product as defined in Article 2(d) of Directive 2001/20/EC;

3 'manufacturer' means any person engaged in activities for which the authorisation referred to in Article 40(1) and (3) of Directive 2001/83/EC or the authorisation referred to in Article 13(1) of Directive 2001/20/EC is required;

4 'qualified person' means the person referred to in Article 48 of Directive 2001/83/EC or in Article 13(2) of Directive 2001/20/EC;

5 'pharmaceutical quality assurance' means the total sum of the organised arrangements made with the object of ensuring that medicinal products or investigational medicinal products are of the quality required for their intended use;

6 'good manufacturing practice' means the part of quality assurance which ensures that products are consistently produced and controlled in accordance with the quality standards appropriate to their intended use;

7 'blinding' means the deliberate disguising of the identity of an investigational medicinal product in accordance with the instructions of the sponsor;

8 'unblinding' means the disclosure of the identity of a blinded product.

Article 3

Inspections

1   By means of the repeated inspections referred to in Article 111(1) of Directive 2001/83/EC and by means of the inspections referred to in Article 15(1) of Directive 2001/20/ EC, the Member States shall ensure that manufacturers respect the principles and guidelines of good manufacturing practice laid down by this Directive. Member States shall also take into account the compilation, published by the Commission, of Community procedures on inspections and exchange of information.

2   For the interpretation of the principles and guidelines of good manufacturing practice, the manufacturers and the competent authorities shall take into account the detailed guidelines referred to in the second paragraph of Article 47 of Directive 2001/83/EC, published by the Commission in the 'Guide to good manufacturing practice for medicinal products and for investigational medicinal products'.

Article 4

Conformity with good manufacturing practice

1   The manufacturer shall ensure that manufacturing operations are carried out in accordance with good manufacturing practice and with the manufacturing authorisation. This provision shall also apply to medicinal products intended only for export.

2   For medicinal products and investigational medicinal products imported from third countries, the importer shall ensure that the products have been manufactured in accordance with standards which are at least equivalent to the good manufacturing practice standards laid down by the Community.
    In addition, an importer of medicinal products shall ensure that such products have been manufactured by manufacturers duly authorised to do so. An importer of investigational medicinal products shall ensure that such products have been manufactured by a manufacturer notified to the competent authorities and accepted by them for that purpose.

Article 5

Compliance with marketing authorisation

1   The manufacturer shall ensure that all manufacturing operations for medicinal products subject to a marketing authorisation are carried out in

accordance with the information provided in the application for marketing authorisation as accepted by the competent authorities.

In the case of investigational medicinal products, the manufacturer shall ensure that all manufacturing operations are carried out in accordance with the information provided by the sponsor pursuant to Article 9(2) of Directive 2001/20/EC as accepted by the competent authorities.

2   The manufacturer shall regularly review his manufacturing methods in the light of scientific and technical progress and the development of the investigational medicinal product.

If a variation to the marketing authorisation dossier or an amendment to the request referred to in Article 9(2) of Directive 2001/20/EC is necessary, the application for modification shall be submitted to the competent authorities.

Article 6

Quality assurance system

The manufacturer shall establish and implement an effective pharmaceutical quality assurance system, involving the active participation of the management and personnel of the different departments.

Article 7

Personnel

1   At each manufacturing site, the manufacturer shall have a sufficient number of competent and appropriately qualified personnel at his disposal to achieve the pharmaceutical quality assurance objective.

2   The duties of the managerial and supervisory staff, including the qualified persons, responsible for implementing and operating good manufacturing practice, shall be defined in job descriptions. Their hierarchical relationships shall be defined in an organisation chart. Organisation charts and job descriptions shall be approved in accordance with the manufacturer's internal procedures.

3   The staff referred to in paragraph 2 shall be given sufficient authority to discharge their responsibility correctly.

4   The personnel shall receive initial and ongoing training, the effectiveness of which shall be verified, covering in particular the theory and application of the concept of quality assurance and good manufacturing practice,

and, where appropriate, the particular requirements for the manufacture of investigational medicinal products.

5   Hygiene programmes adapted to the activities to be carried out shall be established and observed. These programmes shall, in particular, include procedures relating to health, hygiene practice and clothing of personnel.

Article 8

Premises and equipment

1   Premises and manufacturing equipment shall be located, designed, constructed, adapted and maintained to suit the intended operations.

2   Premises and manufacturing equipment shall be laid out, designed and operated in such a way as to minimise the risk of error and to permit effective cleaning and maintenance in order to avoid contamination, cross contamination and, in general, any adverse effect on the quality of the product.

3   Premises and equipment to be used for manufacturing operations, which are critical to the quality of the products, shall be subjected to appropriate qualification and validation.

Article 9

Documentation

1   The manufacturer shall establish and maintain a documentation system based upon specifications, manufacturing formulae and processing and packaging instructions, procedures and records covering the various manufacturing operations performed. Documents shall be clear, free from error and kept up to date. Pre-established procedures for general manufacturing operations and conditions shall be kept available, together with specific documents for the manufacture of each batch. That set of documents shall enable the history of the manufacture of each batch and the changes introduced during the development of an investigational medicinal product to be traced.

For a medicinal product, the batch documentation shall be retained for at least one year after the expiry date of the batches to which it relates or at least five years after the certification referred to in Article 51(3) of Directive 2001/83/EC, whichever is the longer period.

For an investigational medicinal product, the batch documentation shall be retained for at least five years after the completion or formal discontinuation of the last clinical trial in which the batch was used. The sponsor or marketing authorisation holder, if different, shall be responsible for ensuring that records are retained as required for marketing authorisation in accordance with the Annex I to Directive 2001/83/EC, if required for a subsequent marketing authorisation.

2   When electronic, photographic or other data processing systems are used instead of written documents, the manufacturer shall first validate the systems by showing that the data will be appropriately stored during the anticipated period of storage. Data stored by those systems shall be made readily available in legible form and shall be provided to the competent authorities at their request. The electronically stored data shall be protected, by methods such as duplication or back-up and transfer on to another storage system, against loss or damage of data, and audit trails shall be maintained.

Article 10

Production

1   The different production operations shall be carried out in accordance with pre-established instructions and procedures and in accordance with good manufacturing practice. Adequate and sufficient resources shall be made available for the inprocess controls. All process deviations and product defects shall be documented and thoroughly investigated.

2   Appropriate technical or organisational measures shall be taken to avoid cross contamination and mix-ups. In the case of investigational medicinal products, particular attention shall be paid to the handling of products during and after any blinding operation.

3   For medicinal products, any new manufacture or important modification of a manufacturing process of a medicinal product shall be validated. Critical phases of manufacturing processes shall be regularly re-validated.

4   For investigational medicinal products, the manufacturing process shall be validated in its entirety in so far as is appropriate, taking into account the stage of product development. At least the critical process steps, such as sterilisation, shall be validated. All steps in the design and development of the manufacturing process shall be fully documented.

Article 11

Quality control

1   The manufacturer shall establish and maintain a quality control system placed under the authority of a person who has the requisite qualifications and is independent of production.

That person shall have at his disposal, or shall have access to, one or more quality control laboratories appropriately staffed and equipped to carry out the necessary examination and testing of the starting materials and packaging materials and the testing of intermediate and finished products.

2   For medicinal products, including those imported from third countries, contract laboratories may be used if authorised in accordance with Article 12 of this Directive and point (b) of Article 20 of Directive 2001/83/EC.

For investigational medicinal products, the sponsor shall ensure that the contract laboratory complies with the content of the request referred to in Article 9(2) of Directive 2001/20/EC, as accepted by the competent authority. When the products are imported from third countries, analytical control shall not be mandatory.

3   During the final control of the finished product before its release for sale or distribution or for use in clinical trials, the quality control system shall take into account, in addition to analytical results, essential information such as the production conditions, the results of in-process controls, the examination of the manufacturing documents and the conformity of the product to its specifications, including the final finished pack.

4   Samples of each batch of finished medicinal product shall be retained for at least one year after the expiry date.

For an investigational medicinal product, sufficient samples of each batch of bulk formulated product and of key packaging components used for each finished product batch shall be retained for at least two years after completion or formal discontinuation of the last clinical trial in which the batch was used, whichever period is the longer.

Unless a longer period is required under the law of the Member State of manufacture, samples of starting materials, other than solvents, gases or water, used in the manufacturing process shall be retained for at least two years after the release of product. That period may be shortened if the period of stability of the material, as indicated in the relevant specification, is shorter. All those samples shall be maintained at the disposal of the competent authorities.

Other conditions may be defined, by agreement with the competent authority, for the sampling and retaining of starting materials and certain products manufactured individually or in small quantities, or when their storage could raise special problems.

Article 12

Work contracted out

1   Any manufacturing operation or operation linked thereto which is carried out under contract shall be the subject of a written contract.

2 The contract shall clearly define the responsibilities of each party and shall define, in particular, the observance of good manufacturing practice to be followed by the contractacceptor and the manner in which the qualified person responsible for certifying each batch is to discharge his responsibilities.

3 The contract-acceptor shall not subcontract any of the work entrusted to him under the contract without written authorisation from the contract-giver.

4 The contract-acceptor shall comply with the principles and guidelines of good manufacturing practice and shall submit to inspections carried out by the competent authorities pursuant to Article 111 of Directive 2001/83/EC and Article 15 of Directive 2001/20/EC.

Article 13

Complaints, product recall and emergency unblinding

1 In the case of medicinal products, the manufacturer shall implement a system for recording and reviewing complaints together with an effective system for recalling, promptly and at any time, medicinal products in the distribution network. Any complaint concerning a defect shall be recorded and investigated by the manufacturer. The manufacturer shall inform the competent authority of any defect that could result in a recall or abnormal restriction on supply and, in so far as is possible, indicate the countries of destination.

Any recall shall be made in accordance with the requirements referred to in Article 123 of Directive 2001/83/EC.

2 In the case of investigational medicinal products, the manufacturer shall, in cooperation with the sponsor, implement a system for recording and reviewing complaints together with an effective system for recalling promptly and at any time investigational medicinal products which have already entered the distribution network. The manufacturer shall record and investigate any complaint concerning a defect and shall inform the competent authority of any defect that could result in a recall or abnormal restriction on supply.

In the case of investigational medicinal products, all trial sites shall be identified and, in so far as is possible, the countries of destination shall be indicated.

In the case of an investigational medicinal product for which a marketing authorisation has been issued, the manufacturer of the investigational medicinal product shall, in cooperation with the sponsor, inform the marketing authorisation holder of any defect that could be related to the authorised medicinal product.

EU GUIDANCE (COMMISSION DELEGATED REGULATIONS)

3 The sponsor shall implement a procedure for the rapid unblinding of blinded products, where this is necessary for a prompt recall as referred to in paragraph 2. The sponsor shall ensure that the procedure discloses the identity of the blinded product only in so far as is necessary.

Article 14

Self-inspection

The manufacturer shall conduct repeated self-inspections as part of the quality assurance system in order to monitor the implementation and respect of good manufacturing practice and to propose any necessary corrective measures. Records shall be maintained of such self-inspections and any corrective action subsequently taken.

Article 15

Labelling

In the case of an investigational medicinal product, labelling shall be such as to ensure protection of the subject and traceability, to enable identification of the product and trial, and to facilitate proper use of the investigational medicinal product.

Article 16

Repeal of Directive 91/356/EEC

Directive 91/356/EEC is repealed.

References to the repealed Directive shall be construed as references to this Directive.

Article 17

Transposition

1 Member States shall bring into force the laws, regulations and administrative provisions necessary to comply with this Directive by 30 April 2004 at the latest. They shall forthwith communicate to the Commission the text of the provisions and correlation table between those provisions and the provisions of this Directive.

When Member States adopt those provisions, they shall contain a reference to this Directive or be accompanied by such a reference on the occasion of their official publication. The Member States shall determine how such reference is to be made.

2   Member States shall communicate to the Commission the text of the main provisions of national law which they adopt in the field covered by this Directive.

Article 18

Entry into force

This Directive shall enter into force on the 20th day following that of its publication in the Official Journal of the European Union.

Article 19

Addressees

This Directive is addressed to the Member States.

Done at Brussels, 8 October 2003.

For the Commission
Erkki LIIKANEN
Member of the Commission

Commission Directive (EU) 2017/1572 of 15 September 2017 supplementing Directive 2001/83/EC of the European Parliament and the Council as regards the principles and guidelines of good manufacturing practice for medicinal products for human use.

> **Editor's note**   Applicable as from the date of entry into application of Regulation (EU) No 536/2014 on Clinical Trials

Article 1

Subject matter

This Directive lays down the principles and guidelines of good manufacturing practice in respect of medicinal products for human use, the manufacture or import of which requires the authorisation referred to in Article 40 of Directive 2001/83/EC.

Article 2

Definitions

For the purposes of this Directive, the following definitions shall apply:

(3) 'manufacturer' means any person engaged in activities for which the authorisation referred to in Article 40(1) and (3) of Directive 2001/83/EC is required;

(4) 'pharmaceutical quality system' means the total sum of the organised arrangements made with the objective of ensuring that medicinal products are of the quality required for their intended use;

(5) 'good manufacturing practice' means the part of the quality assurance that ensures that medicinal products are consistently produced, imported and controlled in accordance with the quality standards appropriate to their intended use.

Article 3

Inspections

1   By means of the repeated inspections referred to in Article 111(1a) of Directive 2001/83/EC, the Member States shall ensure that manufacturers authorised in accordance with Article 40(1) and (3) of Directive 2001/83/EC respect the principles and guidelines of good manufacturing practice laid down by this Directive.

   Member States shall also take into account the compilation, published by the Commission, of Union procedures on inspections and exchange of information.

2   For the interpretation of the principles and guidelines of good manufacturing practice, manufacturers and the competent authorities shall take into account the detailed guidelines referred to in the second paragraph of Article 47 of Directive 2001/83/EC. In the case of advanced therapy medicinal products, the guidelines on good manufacturing practice specific to advanced therapy medicinal products referred to in Article 5 of Regulation (EC) No 1394/2007 on advanced therapy medicinal products shall be taken into account.

3   Member States shall establish and implement in their inspectorates a properly designed quality system that shall be complied with by inspectorates' personnel and management. The quality system shall be updated as appropriate.

Article 4

Conformity with Good Manufacturing Practice

1   The Member States shall ensure that the manufacturing operations are carried out by manufacturers in accordance with good manufacturing practice and the manufacturing authorisation. This provision shall also apply to medicinal products intended only for export.

2   For medicinal products imported from third countries, the Member States shall ensure that the products have been manufactured in accordance with standards that are at least equivalent to the good manufacturing practice standards laid down in the Union, and that such products have been manufactured by manufacturers duly authorised to do so.

Article 5

Compliance with Marketing Authorisation

1   The Member States shall ensure that all manufacturing or import operations for medicinal products subject to a marketing authorisation are carried out by manufacturers in accordance with the information provided in the application for that marketing authorisation.

2   The Member States shall oblige the manufacturer to regularly review their manufacturing methods in light of scientific and technical progress.

If a variation to the marketing authorisation dossier is necessary, the variation shall take place by the arrangements established in accordance with Article 23b of Directive 2001/83/EC.

Article 6

Pharmaceutical Quality System

The Member States shall ensure that the manufacturers establish, implement and maintain an effective pharmaceutical quality system, involving the active participation of the senior management and the personnel of the different departments.

Article 7

Personnel

1 The manufacturer shall be obliged to have at each manufacturing or import site a sufficient number of competent and appropriately qualified personnel at their disposal to achieve the objective of the pharmaceutical quality system.

2 The duties of the managerial and supervisory staff, including the qualified persons referred to in Article 48 of Directive 2001/83/EC, responsible for implementing and operating good manufacturing practice, shall be defined in job descriptions. Their hierarchical relationships shall be defined in an organisation chart. Organisation charts and job descriptions shall be approved in accordance with the manufacturer's internal procedures.

3 The staff referred to in paragraph 2 shall be given sufficient authority to discharge their responsibility correctly.

4 The personnel shall receive initial and on-going training, the effectiveness of which shall be verified, covering in particular the theory and application of the concept of quality assurance and good manufacturing practice.

5 Hygiene programmes adapted to the activities to be carried out shall be established and observed. These programmes shall, in particular, include procedures relating to health, hygiene practice and clothing of personnel.

Article 8

Premises and equipment

1 As regards the premises and manufacturing equipment, the manufacturer shall be obliged to ensure that they are located, designed, constructed, adapted and maintained to suit the intended operations.

2 The Member States shall require that the premises and manufacturing equipment are laid out, designed and operated in such a way as to minimise the risk of error and to permit effective cleaning and maintenance in order to avoid contamination, cross-contamination and, in general, any adverse effect on the quality of the product.

3 Premises and equipment to be used for manufacturing or import operations, which are critical to the quality of the products, shall be subjected to appropriate qualification and validation.

Article 9

Documentation

1   The manufacturer shall be obliged to establish and maintain a documentation system based upon specifications, manufacturing formulae, and processing and packaging instructions, procedures and records covering the various manufacturing operations performed. The documentation system shall ensure data quality and integrity. Documents shall be clear, free from error and kept up to date. Pre-established procedures for general manufacturing operations and conditions shall be kept available, together with specific documents for the manufacture of each batch. That set of documents shall enable the history of the manufacture of each batch to be traced.

 The manufacturer shall be required to retain the batch documentation for at least one year after the expiry date of the batches to which it relates or at least five years after the certification referred to in Article 51(3) of Directive 2001/83/EC, whichever is the longer period.

2   When electronic, photographic or other data-processing systems are used instead of written documents, the manufacturer shall be required to first validate the systems by showing that the data will be appropriately stored during the anticipated period of storage. Data stored by those systems shall be made readily available in legible form and shall be provided to the competent authorities upon request. The electronically stored data shall be protected, by techniques such as duplication or back-up and transfer to another storage system, against unlawful access, loss or damage of data, and audit trails shall be maintained.

Article 10

Production

1   The Member States shall ensure that the manufacturers carry out the different production operations in accordance with pre-established instructions and procedures and in accordance with good manufacturing practice. Adequate and sufficient resources shall be made available by the manufacturer for the in-process controls. All process deviations and product defects shall be documented and thoroughly investigated.

2   The manufacturers shall be required to take appropriate technical and organisational measures to avoid cross-contamination and mix-ups.

3   Any new manufacturing or important modification of a manufacturing process of a medicinal product shall be validated. Critical phases of manufacturing processes shall be regularly revalidated.

Article 11

Quality control

1   The manufacturer shall be obliged to establish and maintain a quality control system placed under the authority of a person who has the requisite qualifications and is independent of production.

   That person shall have at their disposal, or shall have access to, one or more quality control laboratories appropriately staffed and equipped to carry out the necessary examination and testing of starting materials and packaging materials, and the testing of intermediate and finished medicinal products.

2   For medicinal products, including those imported from third countries, contract laboratories may be used if authorised in accordance with Article 12 of this Directive and point (b) of Article 20 of Directive 2001/83/EC.

3   During the final control of the finished medicinal product before its release for sale or distribution, the quality control system shall take into account, in addition to analytical results, essential information such as the production conditions, the results of in-process controls, the examination of the manufacturing documents and the conformity of the product to its specifications, including the final finished pack.

4   Samples of each batch of finished medicinal product shall be retained for at least one year after the expiry date.

   Samples of starting materials, other than solvents, gases or water, used in the manufacturing process shall be retained for at least two years after the release of the product. That period may be shortened if the period of stability of the material, as indicated in the relevant specification, is shorter. All those samples shall be maintained at the disposal of the competent authorities.

   Other conditions may be defined, by agreement with the competent authority, for the sampling and retention of starting materials and certain products manufactured individually or in small quantities, or when their storage could raise special problems.

Article 12

Outsourced operations

1   The Member States shall require that any manufacturing or import operation or operation linked thereto, which is outsourced, is the subject of a written contract.

2   The contract shall clearly define the responsibilities of each party and shall define, in particular, the observance of good manufacturing practice to be followed by the contract acceptor and the manner in which the qualified person referred to in Article 48 of Directive 2001/83/EC responsible for certifying each batch is to discharge their responsibilities.

3   The contract acceptor shall not subcontract any of the work entrusted to him under the contract without written authorisation from the contract giver.

4   The contract acceptor shall comply with the principles and guidelines of good manufacturing practice applicable to the operations concerned laid down in the Union and shall submit to inspections carried out by competent authorities pursuant to Article 111 of Directive 2001/83/EC.

Article 13

Complaints and product recall

1   The Member States shall ensure that manufacturers implement a system for recording and reviewing complaints together with an effective system for recalling, promptly, and at any time, medicinal products in the distribution network. Any complaint concerning a defect shall be recorded and investigated by the manufacturer. The manufacturer shall be required to inform the competent authority and, if applicable, the marketing authorisation holder of any defect that could result in a recall or an abnormal restriction on supply and, in so far as possible, indicate the countries of destination.

2   Any recall shall be made in accordance with the requirements referred to in Article 123 of Directive 2001/83/EC.

Article 14

Self-inspection

The manufacturer shall be required to conduct repeated self-inspections as part of the pharmaceutical quality system in order to monitor the implementation and respect of good manufacturing practice and to propose any necessary corrective measures and/or preventive actions. Records shall be maintained of such self-inspections and any corrective actions subsequently taken.

Article 15

Repeal of Directive 2003/94/EC

Directive 2003/94/EC is repealed with effect from six months after the date of publication in the *Official Journal of the European Union* of the notice referred to in Article 82(3) of Regulation (EU) No 536/2014 or 1 April 2018, whichever is the later.

References to the repealed Directive shall be construed as references to this Directive and to Commission Delegated Regulation (EU) 2017/15691 and read in accordance with the correlation table in the Annex.

Article 16

Transposition

1   Member States shall adopt and publish, by 31 March 2018 at the latest, the laws, regulations and administrative provisions necessary to comply with this Directive. They shall forthwith communicate to the Commission the text of those provisions.

They shall apply those provisions from six months after the date of publication in the *Official Journal of the European Union* of the notice referred to in Article 82(3) of Regulation (EU) No 536/2014 or 1 April 2018, whichever is the later.

When Member States adopt those provisions, they shall contain a reference to this Directive or be accompanied by such a reference on the occasion of their official publication. Member States shall determine how such reference is to be made.

2   Member States shall communicate to the Commission the text of the main provisions of national law that they adopt in the field covered by this Directive.

Article 17

Entry into force

This Directive shall enter into force on the twentieth day following that of its publication in the *Official Journal of the European Union*.

Article 18

Addressees

This Directive is addressed to the Member States.

ANNEX

CORRELATION TABLE

Directive 2003/94/EC	This Directive	Commission Delegated Regulation (EU) 2017/1569 supplementing Regulation (EU) No 536/2014 of the European Parliament and the Council by specifying principles of and guidelines for good manufacturing practice for investigational medicinal products for human use and arrangements for inspections
Article 1	Article 1	Article 1
Article 2	Article 2	Article 2
Article 3	Article 3	–
Article 4	Article 4	Article 3
Article 5	Article 5	Article 4
Article 6	Article 6	Article 5(1)
Article 7	Article 7	Article 6
Article 8	Article 8	Article 7
Article 9	Article 9	Article 8
Article 10	Article 10	Article 9
Article 11	Article 11	Article 10
Article 12	Article 12	Article 13
Article 13	Article 13	Article 14
Article 14	Article 14	Article 15
Article 15	–	–
Article 16	–	–
Article 17	–	–
Article 18	–	–
Article 19	–	–

DIRECTIVE 2013/83/EC, SUPPLEMENT

Commission Delegated Regulation (EU) No 1252/2014 of 28 May 2014 supplementing Directive 2001/83/EC of the European Parliament and of the Council with regard to principles and guidelines of good manufacturing practice for active substances for medicinal products for human use

Article 1

SCOPE

This Regulation lays down the principles and guidelines of good manufacturing practice for active substances of medicinal products for human use, including active substances intended for export.

Article 2

DEFINITIONS

For the purposes of this Regulation, the following definitions shall apply:

(1) "manufacturing" means any total or partial operation of receipt of materials, production, packaging, repackaging, labelling, re-labelling, quality control or release of active substances and the related controls;

(2) "active substance starting material" means any substance from which an active substance is manufactured or extracted;

(3) "active substance intermediate" means a substance that is obtained during the production of an active substance and is intended for further processing;

(4) "raw material" means any substance, reagent or solvent that is intended for use in the production of an active substance and from which the active substance is not directly manufactured or extracted.

Article 3

QUALITY MANAGEMENT

1   Manufacturers of active substances ("the manufacturer") shall establish, document and implement an effective system for managing the quality of those substances during the manufacturing operations performed by them (the "manufacturing process"). The system shall provide for the active participation of the management and manufacturing personnel.

The system shall ensure that the active substances meet the specifications for their quality and purity established in accordance with Article 12(1).

The system shall incorporate quality risk management.

2 The manufacturer shall appoint a quality unit that is independent of the production unit to be responsible for quality assurance and quality control.

3 The manufacturer shall conduct regular internal audits and follow-up on the findings.

Article 4

PERSONNEL

1 The manufacturer shall ensure that there are an adequate number of personnel having the necessary qualifications acquired through education, training or experience to carry out and supervise the manufacturing of active substances.

2 Personnel shall practice good sanitation and hygiene in the manufacturing area. Personnel shall not access the manufacturing area if they:

(a) suffer from an infectious disease or have open lesions or other dermatological conditions on the exposed surface of the body that could negatively affect the quality and purity of the active substance;

(b) wear clothing that is visibly dirty, or does not protect the active substance from potential contamination coming from personnel, or does not protect personnel from exposure to active substances potentially harmful to human health;

(c) at the moment of entering the manufacturing area, are performing activities that could contaminate or otherwise compromise the quality of the active substance.

Article 5

BUILDINGS AND FACILITIES

1 Buildings and facilities used in the manufacturing of active substances shall be located, designed and constructed to suit the intended operations and to facilitate cleaning and maintenance with regard to the type and stage of manufacturing that the buildings and facilities are used for.

Facilities and the flow of material and personnel through the facilities shall be designed to ensure that different substances and materials are kept separate and do not contaminate each other.

2 Buildings shall be properly maintained and repaired and kept in a clean condition.

3 Highly sensitising active substances shall be produced in separate production areas.

EU GUIDANCE (COMMISSION DELEGATED REGULATIONS)

When carrying out production operations, the manufacturer shall assess the need for separate production areas for other active substances with the potential to be harmful to human health because of their potency or their infective or toxic nature. The assessment shall evaluate the risk to human health posed by those active substances by taking account of the active substance potency, toxicity, infectivity and risk-minimisation procedures in place. The assessment shall be documented in writing.

Where the assessment shows a risk of harm to human health, the active substance shall be produced in separate production areas.

Article 6

EQUIPMENT

1   Equipment used in the manufacturing of active substances shall be appropriately designed, sized and located for its intended use, cleaning, maintenance and, where appropriate, sanitisation.

Equipment shall be constructed and operated so that surfaces that come into contact with raw materials, active substance starting materials, active substance intermediates or active substances do not alter the quality of the raw materials, the active substance starting materials, the active substance intermediates or the active substances to the extent that they no longer comply with the specifications established in accordance with Article 12(1).

2   The manufacturer shall establish written procedures for the cleaning of equipment and the subsequent verification of its suitability for use in the manufacturing process.

3   Control, weighing, measuring, monitoring and test equipment that are critical for assuring the quality of the active substance shall be calibrated in accordance with written procedures and an established schedule.

Article 7

DOCUMENTATION AND RECORDS

1   The manufacturer shall establish and maintain a documentation system and written procedures covering the manufacturing process.

All documents in relation to the manufacturing process shall be prepared, reviewed, approved and distributed in accordance with written procedures.

The manufacturer shall maintain records of at least the following elements in relation to the manufacturing process:

(1) equipment cleaning and use;
(2) origins of raw materials, active substance starting materials and active substance intermediates;

(3) controls in relation to raw materials, active substance starting materials and active substance intermediates;

(4) use of raw materials, active substance starting materials and active substance intermediates;

(5) labelling of the active substances and of the packaging materials;

(6) master production instructions;

(7) batch production and control;

(8) laboratory controls.

The issuance, revision, replacement and withdrawal of documents related to the manufacturing process shall be controlled, and records of their revision, replacement and withdrawal shall be kept.

2 All quality-related activities carried out during the manufacturing process shall be recorded at the time they are performed. Any deviation from the written procedures referred to in Article 7(1) shall be documented and explained. Deviations affecting the quality of the active substance or preventing the active substance from meeting the specifications referred to in Article 12(1) shall be investigated, and the investigation and its conclusions shall be documented.

3 After carrying out production and control operations, the manufacturer shall retain all production and control records for at least one year after the expiry date of the batch. For an active substance with re-test dates, the manufacturer shall retain records for at least three years after the complete batch has been placed on the market.

Article 8

MATERIAL MANAGEMENT

1 The manufacturer shall have written procedures in place for ensuring the quality of incoming material covering the following elements:

(1) receipt;

(2) identification;

(3) quarantine;

(4) storage;

(5) handling;

(6) sampling;

(7) testing;

(8) approving;

(9) rejection.

2 The manufacturer shall have a system in place for evaluating suppliers of critical materials.

Article 9

PRODUCTION AND IN-PROCESS CONTROL

1. Production operations shall be subject to controls in order to monitor and adjust the production process or verify that the active substance conforms to the specifications of quality and purity pursuant to Article 12(1). Production operations that are critical to ensure that the active substance meets the quality specifications referred to in Article 12(1) shall be carried out under the visual supervision of qualified personnel or subjected to an equivalent control.

2. Weighing and measuring of raw materials and active substance starting materials shall be accurate and shall be conducted in a manner that does not affect their suitability for use.

3. Production operations, including any operation after purification of the active substance intermediates or the active substance, shall be conducted in a manner that prevents raw materials, active substance starting materials, active substance intermediates and active substances from being contaminated by other materials.

Article 10

PACKAGING AND LABELLING

1. Containers shall provide adequate protection against deterioration or contamination of the active substance from the moment the active substance is packaged to the moment it is used in the manufacturing of medicinal products.

2. Storage, print and use of labels on the packaging of active substances shall be controlled. Labels shall contain the information necessary to assure the quality of the active substance.

Article 11

PLACING ON THE MARKET

An active substance shall be placed on the market only after it has been released for sale by the quality unit.

Article 12

LABORATORY CONTROLS

1. The manufacturer shall establish specifications for the quality and purity of the active substances they manufacture and for the raw materials, active

substance starting materials and active substance intermediates used in that process.

2 Laboratory tests shall be conducted to verify compliance with the specifications referred to in paragraph 1.

The manufacturer shall issue certificates of analysis for each batch of active substance upon the request of:

(a) the competent authorities of a Member State;

(b) manufacturers of active substances supplied directly or indirectly with the active substance for the purpose of further processing, packing, re-packing, labelling or re-labelling the active substance;

(c) distributors and brokers of active substances;

(d) manufacturers of medicinal products supplied directly or indirectly with the active substance.

3 The manufacturer shall monitor the stability of the active substance through stability studies. Dates for the expiry or re-test of active substances shall be set on the basis of an evaluation of data derived from the stability studies. Appropriately identified samples of the active substance shall be retained in accordance with a sampling plan established on the basis of the shelf-life of the active substance.

Article 13

VALIDATION

The manufacturer shall set up and implement a validation policy for those processes and procedures that are critical to ensure that the active substance meets the quality and purity specifications established in accordance with Article 12(1).

Article 14

CHANGE CONTROL

1 The manufacturer shall evaluate the potential impact on the quality of the active substance of any changes to the manufacturing process that may affect the production and control of the active substance before implementing those changes.

2 Changes to the manufacturing process that negatively affect the quality of the active substance shall not be implemented.

3 The manufacturer of an active substance shall notify without delay the manufacturers of medicinal products that they supply with the active sub-

stance of any changes to the manufacturing process that may impact the quality of the active substance.

Article 15

REJECTION AND RETURNS

1 Batches of active substances and active substance intermediates failing to conform to the specifications established in accordance with Article 12(1) shall be rejected, labelled as such and quarantined.

2 The manufacturer who re-processes or re-works rejected batches of an active substance that do not conform to specifications, or recovers raw materials and solvents for re-use in the manufacturing process, shall follow the procedures established in accordance with Article 7(1) and shall perform appropriate controls to ensure that:

(a) the reprocessed or reworked active substance meets the quality specifications established in accordance with Article 12(1);

(b) the recovered raw materials and solvents are suitable for their intended use in the manufacturing process.

3 Returned active substances shall be identified as such and quarantined.

Article 16

COMPLAINTS AND RECALLS

1 The manufacturer shall record and investigate all quality-related complaints.

2 The manufacturer shall establish procedures for the recall of active substances from the market.

3 In the event of the recalled active substance posing a serious threat to public health, the manufacturer shall inform the competent authorities without delay.

Article 17

CONTRACT MANUFACTURING

1 A manufacturing operation or an operation linked thereto that is to be carried out on behalf of the manufacturer of the active substance by another party ("the contract manufacturer") shall be the subject of a written contract. The contract shall clearly define the responsibilities of the contract manufacturer with regard to good manufacturing practice.

2   The manufacturer of the active substance shall control that operations carried out by a contract manufacturer comply with good manufacturing practice.

3   A manufacturing operation or an operation linked thereto that has been entrusted to a contract manufacturer shall not be subcontracted to a third party without the written consent of the manufacturer of the active substance.

Article 18

RE-PACKAGING

Where the active substance is re-packaged by a manufacturer in a container that differs from the original container with regard to its volume, or the material it is made of, or its opaqueness to light, the manufacturer shall conduct stability studies on the active substance and assign an expiration or re-test date for it on the basis of those studies.

Article 19

ENTRY INTO FORCE

This Regulation shall enter into force on the twentieth day following that of its publication in the *Official Journal of the European Union*.

It shall apply from 25 May 2015.

This Regulation shall be binding in its entirety and directly applicable in all Member States.

Commission Delegated Regulation (EU) 2017/1569 of 23 May 2017 supplementing Regulation (EU) No 536/2014 of the European Parliament and of the Council by specifying principles of and the guidelines for Good Manufacturing Practice for investigational medicinal products for human use and arrangements for inspections (see page 12 of this official Journal).

Commission Delegated Regulation (EU) 2017/1569 of 23 May 2017 supplementing Regulation (EU) No 536/2014 of the European Parliament and of the Council by specifying principles of and guidelines for good manufacturing practice for investigational medicinal products for human use and arrangements for inspections

Editor's   Applicable as from the date of entry into application of Regulation (EU)
note   No 536/2014 on Clinical Trials

Chapter I General Provisions

Article 1

SUBJECT MATTER

This Regulation specifies the principles and guidelines of good manufacturing practice for investigational medicinal products for human use, the manufacture or import of which requires an authorisation as referred to in Article 61(1) of Regulation (EU) No 536/2014 and lays down arrangements for inspections of manufacturers in relation to compliance with good manufacturing practice in accordance with Article 63(4) of that Regulation.

Article 2

DEFINITIONS

For the purposes of this Regulation, the following definitions shall apply:

(1) "manufacturer" means any person engaged in activities for which an authorisation is required in accordance with Article 61(1) of Regulation (EU) No 536/2014;

(2) "third country manufacturer" means any person established in a third country and engaged in manufacturing operations in that third country;

(3) "product specification file" means a reference file containing, or referring to files containing, all the information necessary to draft detailed written instructions on processing, packaging, quality control, testing and batch release of an investigational medicinal product and to perform batch certification;

(4) "validation" means action of proving, in accordance with the principles of good manufacturing practice, that any procedure, process, equipment, material, activity or system actually leads to the expected results.

Chapter II Good Manufacturing Practice

Article 3

CONFORMITY WITH GOOD MANUFACTURING PRACTICE

1 The manufacturer shall ensure that manufacturing operations are carried out in accordance with good manufacturing practice for investigational medicinal products specified in this Regulation and subject to an authorisation as referred to in Article 61(1) of Regulation (EU) No 536/2014.

2 When importing an investigational medicinal product, the holder of the authorisation referred to in Article 61(1) of Regulation (EU) No 536/2014 shall ensure that the products have been manufactured by applying quality standards at least equivalent to those laid down by this Regulation and in Regulation (EU) No 536/2014, and that the third country manufacturer is authorised or entitled to, in accordance with the laws of that country, to manufacture those investigational medicinal products in that third country.

Article 4

COMPLIANCE WITH CLINICAL TRIAL AUTHORISATION

1 The manufacturer shall ensure that all manufacturing operations for investigational medicinal products are carried out in accordance with the documentation and information provided by the sponsor pursuant to Article 25 of Regulation (EU) No 536/2014 and as authorised in accordance with the procedure laid down in Chapter II, or if documentation and information was subsequently amended, in Chapter III of above-mentioned Regulation (EU) No 536/2014.

2 The manufacturer shall regularly review their manufacturing methods in the light of scientific and technical progress and experience gained by the sponsor during the development of the investigational medicinal product.

The manufacturer shall inform the sponsor of their reviews of the manufacturing methods.

Where, following a review, an amendment to the clinical trial authorisation is necessary, the application for the amendment shall be submitted in accordance with Article 16 of Regulation (EU) No 536/2014 where the change to the clinical trial is a substantial modification or the amendment shall be carried out in accordance with Article 81(9) of that Regulation where the change to the clinical trial is not a substantial modification.

Article 5

PHARMACEUTICAL QUALITY SYSTEM

1   The manufacturer shall establish, implement and maintain effective organised arrangements to ensure that the investigational medicinal products are of the quality required for their intended use. Those arrangements shall include the establishment of a good manufacturing practice and a quality control.

2   Senior management and personnel from different departments shall participate in the establishment of the pharmaceutical quality system.

Article 6

PERSONNEL

1   At each manufacturing site, the manufacturer shall have a sufficient number of competent and appropriately qualified personnel at their disposal to ensure that the investigational medicinal products are of the quality required for their intended use.

2   The duties of managerial and supervisory staff, including the qualified persons, responsible for implementing and operating good manufacturing practice shall be set out in their job descriptions. Their hierarchical relationships shall be set out in an organisation chart. The organisation chart and the job descriptions shall be approved in accordance with the manufacturer's internal procedures.

3   The staff referred to in paragraph 2 shall be given sufficient authority to discharge their responsibility correctly.

4   The personnel shall receive initial and on-going training covering in particular the following areas:

(a) the theory and application of the concept of pharmaceutical quality;
(b) good manufacturing practice.

The manufacturer shall verify the effectiveness of the training.

5   The manufacturer shall establish hygiene programmes, including procedures relating to health, hygiene practice and clothing of personnel. The programmes shall be adapted to the manufacturing operations to be carried out. The manufacturer shall ensure that the programmes are observed.

Article 7

PREMISES AND EQUIPMENT

1 The manufacturer shall ensure that premises and manufacturing equipment are located, designed, constructed, adapted and maintained to suit the intended operations.

2 The manufacturer shall ensure that the premises and manufacturing equipment are laid out, designed and operated in such a way as to minimise risk of error and permit effective cleaning and maintenance in order to avoid contamination, cross-contamination and any other adverse effect on the quality of the investigational medicinal product.

3 The manufacturer shall ensure that those premises and equipment to be used for manufacturing operations that are critical to the quality of the investigational medicinal products are subjected to appropriate qualification and validation.

Article 8

DOCUMENTATION

1 The manufacturer shall establish and maintain a documentation system recording the following, where appropriate having regard to the activities undertaken:

(a) specifications;
(b) manufacturing formulae;
(c) processing and packaging instructions;
(d) procedures and protocols, including procedures for general manufacturing operations and conditions;
(e) records, in particular covering the various manufacturing operations performed and batch records;
(f) technical agreements;
(g) certificates of analysis.

The documents specific to any investigational medicinal product shall be consistent with the product specification file as relevant.

2 The documentation system shall ensure the data quality and integrity. Documents shall be clear, free from error and kept up to date.

3 The manufacturer shall retain the product specification file and batch documentation for at least five years after the completion or discontinuation of the last clinical trial in which the batch was used.

4   When documentation is stored using electronic, photographic or other data-processing systems, the manufacturer shall first validate the systems to ensure that the data will be appropriately stored during the period of storage laid down in paragraph 3. Data stored by those systems shall be made readily available in readable form.

5   The electronically stored data shall be protected against unlawful access, loss or damage of data by techniques such as duplication, back-up and transfer onto another storage system. Audit trails, meaning records of all relevant changes and deletions in this data, shall be maintained.

6   The documentation shall be provided to competent authority upon request.

Article 9

PRODUCTION

1   The manufacturer shall carry out production operations in accordance with pre-established instructions and procedures.

2   The manufacturer shall ensure that adequate and sufficient resources are made available for the in-process controls and that all process deviations and product defects are documented and thoroughly investigated.

3   The manufacturer shall take appropriate technical or organisational measures to avoid cross-contamination and unintentional mixing of substances. Particular attention shall be paid to the handling of investigational medicinal products during and after any blinding operation.

       The manufacturing process shall be validated in its entirety, as far as is appropriate, taking into account the stage of product development.

       The manufacturer shall identify the process steps that ensure the safety of the subject, such as sterilisation, and the reliability and robustness of the clinical trial data generated in the clinical trial. Those critical process steps shall be validated and regularly re-validated.

       All steps in the design and development of the manufacturing process shall be fully documented.

Article 10

QUALITY CONTROL

1   The manufacturer shall establish and maintain a quality control system under the authority of a person who has the requisite qualifications and is independent of production.

That person shall have access to one or more quality control laboratories appropriately staffed and equipped to carry out the examination and testing of starting materials and packaging materials, and the testing of intermediate and finished investigational medicinal products.

2 The manufacturer shall ensure that the quality control laboratories comply with information provided in the application dossier, referred to in Article 25(1) of Regulation (EU) No 536/2014, as authorised by Member States.

3 When investigational medicinal products are imported from third countries, analytical control in the Union shall not be mandatory.

4 During the final control of the finished investigational medicinal product, and before its release by the manufacturer, the manufacturer shall take into account:

(a) analytical results;
(b) production conditions;
(c) the results of in-process controls;
(d) the examination of the manufacturing documents;
(e) the conformity of the product with its specifications;
(f) the conformity of the product with the clinical trial authorisation;
(g) the examination of the final finished packaging.

Article 11

RETENTION OF SAMPLES USED FOR QUALITY CONTROL

1 The manufacturer shall retain sufficient samples of each batch of bulk formulated product, of key packaging components used for each finished investigational medicinal product batch and of each batch of finished investigational medicinal product for at least two years after the completion or discontinuation of the last clinical trial in which the batch was used.

Samples of starting materials, other than solvents, gases or water, used in the manufacturing process shall be retained by the manufacturer for at least two years after the release of the investigational medicinal product. However, this period may be shortened where the period of stability of the starting material, as indicated in the relevant specification, is shorter.

In all cases samples shall be maintained by the manufacturer at the disposal of the competent authority.

2 Upon application of the manufacturer, the competent authority may grant a derogation from paragraph 1 in relation to the sampling and retention of starting material and for certain products manufactured individually or in small quantities, or when their storage could raise special problems.

Article 12

RESPONSIBILITIES OF THE QUALIFIED PERSON

1   The qualified person referred to in Article 61(2)(b) of Regulation (EU) No 536/2014 shall be responsible for the following:

   (a) where investigational medicinal products are manufactured in the Member State concerned, verifying that each production batch has been manufactured and checked in compliance with the requirements of good manufacturing practice for investigational medicinal products laid down in this Regulation and the information provided pursuant to Article 25 of Regulation (EU) No 536/2014, taking into account the guidelines referred to in Article 63(1) of that Regulation;

   (b) where investigational medicinal products are manufactured in a third country, verifying that each production batch has been manufactured and checked in accordance with quality standards at least equivalent to those laid down in this Regulation and the information provided pursuant to Article 25 of Regulation (EU) No 536/2014, taking into account the guidelines referred to in Article 63(1) of that Regulation.

   The qualified person shall certify in a register or equivalent document provided for that purpose that each production batch complies with the requirements laid down in paragraph 1.

2   The register or equivalent document shall be kept up to date as operations are carried out and shall remain at the disposal of the competent authority for at least five years after the completion of or the formal discontinuation of the last clinical trial in which the product batch was used.

Article 13

OUTSOURCED OPERATIONS

1   Where a manufacturing operation or operation linked thereto is outsourced, the outsourcing shall be the subject of a written contract.

2   The contract shall clearly lay down the responsibilities of each party. It shall lay down an obligation for the party to whom the operations are outsourced to follow good manufacturing practice and set out the manner in which the qualified person responsible for certifying each batch is to discharge their responsibilities.

3   The party to whom the operations are outsourced shall not subcontract any of the operations entrusted to him under the contract without written consent from the contract giver.

4   The party to whom the operations are outsourced shall comply with the principles and guidelines of good manufacturing practice applicable to

the operations concerned and shall submit to inspections carried out by the competent authority pursuant to Article 63(4) of Regulation (EU) No 536/2014.

Article 14

COMPLAINTS, PRODUCT RECALL AND EMERGENCY UNBLINDING

1　The manufacturer shall, in cooperation with the sponsor, implement a system for recording and reviewing complaints together with an effective system for recalling investigational medicinal products that have already entered the distribution network promptly and at any time. The manufacturer shall record and investigate any complaint concerning a defect and shall inform the sponsor and the competent authority of the Member States concerned about any defect that could result in a recall or abnormal restriction on supply.

All trial sites shall be identified and, in so far as possible, the countries of destination shall be indicated.

In the case of an authorised investigational medicinal product, the manufacturer shall, in cooperation with the sponsor, inform the marketing authorisation holder of any defect that could be related to that product.

2　Where blinding of investigational medicinal products is required by the protocol of a clinical trial, the manufacturer in conjunction with the sponsor shall implement a procedure for the rapid unblinding of blinded products, where this is necessary for a prompt recall as referred to in paragraph 1. The manufacturer shall ensure that the procedure discloses the identity of the blinded product only in so far as it is necessary.

Article 15

SELF-INSPECTION BY THE MANUFACTURER

The manufacturer shall conduct regular inspections as part of the pharmaceutical quality system in order to monitor the implementation and respect of good manufacturing practice. They shall take any necessary corrective action and put in place any necessary preventive measures.

The manufacturer shall maintain records of all such inspections and any corrective action or preventive measures subsequently taken.

Article 16

ADVANCED THERAPY INVESTIGATIONAL MEDICINAL PRODUCTS

The good manufacturing principles shall be adapted to the specific characteristics of the advanced therapy medicinal products when used as investigational medicinal products. Investigational medicinal products, which are at the same time advanced therapy medicinal products, shall be manufactured in accordance with the guidelines referred to in Article 5 of Regulation (EC) No 1394/2007.

Chapter III Inspections

Article 17

SUPERVISION BY INSPECTION

1 By means of regular inspections as referred to in Article 63(4) of Regulation (EU) No 536/2014 the Member State shall ensure that holders of an authorisation as referred to in Article 61(1) of that Regulation comply with the principles of good manufacturing practice laid down in this Regulation and take into account the guidelines referred to in the second subparagraph of Article 63(1) of Regulation (EU) No 536/2014.

2 Without prejudice to any arrangements that may have been concluded between the Union and third countries, a competent authority may require a third country manufacturer to submit to an inspection as referred to in Article 63(4) of Regulation (EU) No 536/2014 and this Regulation. This Regulation applies *mutatis mutandis* to such inspections in third countries.

3 Member States shall carry out inspections of third country manufacturers to ensure that investigational medicinal products imported into the Union are manufactured by applying quality standards at least equivalent to those laid down in the Union.

   The Member States are not obliged to routinely inspect third country manufacturers of investigational medicinal products. The necessity of such inspections shall be based on an assessment of risk, but shall take place at least if the Member States have grounds for suspecting that the quality standards applied to the manufacture of the investigational medicinal products imported into the Union are lower than those laid down in this Regulation and in the guidelines referred to in the second subparagraph of Article 63(1) of Regulation (EU) No 536/2014.

4 Inspections may, if necessary, be unannounced.

5 After an inspection, an inspection report shall be drawn up by the inspector. Before the report is adopted by the competent authority, the manufacturer shall be afforded an opportunity to submit comments in relation to the findings of the report.

6 Where the findings of the final report show that the manufacturer complies with the good manufacturing practice for investigational medicinal

products, the competent authority shall, within a period of 90 days of the inspection, issue a certificate of good manufacturing practice to the manufacturer.

7 The competent authority shall enter the certificate of good manufacturing practice that they issue into the Union database referred to in Article 111(6) of Directive 2001/83/EC of the European Parliament and the Council.

8 Where the outcome of the inspection is that the manufacturer does not comply with good manufacturing practice for investigational medicinal products, the competent authority shall enter this information into the Union database referred to in Article 111(6) of Directive 2001/83/EC.

9 The competent authority shall, upon receipt of reasoned request, send the inspection reports referred to in paragraph 5 electronically to the competent authorities of other Member States or to the European Medicines Agency ("the Agency").

10 The competent authority shall enter the information relating to the authorisation referred to in Article 61(1) of Regulation (EU) No 536/2014 in the Union database referred to in Article 111(6) of Directive 2001/83/EC.

Article 18

COOPERATION AND COORDINATION OF INSPECTIONS

The competent authorities shall cooperate with each other and with the Agency in relation to inspections. They shall share information with the Agency on both inspections planned and conducted.

Article 19

RECOGNITION OF INSPECTION CONCLUSIONS

1 The conclusions reached in the inspection report referred to in Article 17(5) shall be valid throughout the Union.

However, in exceptional cases, where a competent authority is unable, for reasons relating to public health, to recognise the conclusions reached following an inspection under Article 63(4) of Regulation (EU) No 536/2014, that competent authority shall forthwith inform the Commission and the Agency. The Agency shall inform the other competent authorities concerned.

2 When the Commission is informed in accordance with the second subparagraph of paragraph 1, it may, after consulting the competent authority that was unable to accept the report, request the inspector who performed

the inspection to perform a new inspection. The inspector may be accompanied by two inspectors from other competent authorities that are not parties to the disagreement.

Article 20

EMPOWERMENTS OF THE INSPECTORS

1   The competent authority shall provide inspectors with suitable means of their identification.

2   Inspectors shall be empowered to:

(a) enter and inspect the premises of the manufacturer and quality control laboratories having carried out checks pursuant to Article 10 for the manufacturer;

(b) take samples, including for independent tests to be carried out by an Official Medicines Control Laboratory or a laboratory designated for that purpose by the Member State; and

(c) examine any documents relating to the object of inspection, make copies of records or printed documents, and print electronic records, and take photographs of the premises and equipment of the manufacturer.

Article 21

COMPETENCE AND OBLIGATIONS OF THE INSPECTORS

1   The competent authority shall ensure that the inspectors possess adequate qualifications, experience and knowledge. In particular, the inspectors shall have the following:

(a) experience and knowledge of the inspection process;

(b) the ability to make professional judgements as to the compliance with the requirements of good manufacturing practice;

(c) ability to apply the principles of quality risk management;

(d) knowledge of current technologies relevant for inspections;

(e) knowledge of the current technologies for the manufacture of the investigational medicinal products.

2   Information acquired as a result of inspections shall remain confidential.

3   The competent authorities shall ensure that inspectors receive the training necessary to maintain or improve their skills. Their training needs shall be assessed regularly by the persons appointed for that task.

4   The competent authority shall document the qualifications, training and experience of each inspector. Those records shall be kept up to date.

Article 22

QUALITY SYSTEM

1 The competent authorities shall establish, implement and comply with a properly designed quality system for their inspectors. The quality system shall be updated as appropriate.

2 Each inspector shall be informed of the standard operating procedures and of their duties, responsibilities and on-going training requirements. Those procedures shall be kept up to date.

Article 23

IMPARTIALITY OF INSPECTORS

The competent authority shall ensure that inspectors are free of any undue influence that could affect their impartiality and judgement.

Inspectors shall be independent, in particular, of:

(a) the sponsor;
(b) the management and personnel of the clinical trial site;
(c) the investigators involved in the clinical trials where the investigational medicinal products manufactured by the inspected manufacturer are used;
(d) the persons financing the clinical trial in which the investigational medicinal product is used;
(e) the manufacturer.

Inspectors shall make an annual declaration of their financial interests in the parties inspected or other links to them. The competent authority shall take the declaration into consideration when assigning inspectors to specific inspections.

Article 24

ACCESS TO PREMISES

The manufacturer shall allow inspectors access to their premises and documentation at all times.

Article 25

SUSPENSION OR REVOCATION OF MANUFACTURING AUTHORISATION

If an inspection reveals that the holder of an authorisation as referred to in Article 61(1) of Regulation (EU) No 536/2014 fails to comply with good manufacturing practice as set out in Union law, the competent authority may, with regard to this manufacturer, suspend manufacture or imports from third countries of investigational medicinal products for human use, or suspend or revoke the authorisation for a category of preparations or all preparation.

Chapter IV Final Provisions

Article 26

TRANSITIONAL PROVISION

The Member States may continue to apply national transposition measures adopted under Commission Directive 2003/94/EC1 to the manufacture of investigational medicinal products used in clinical trials governed by Directive 2001/20/EC of the European Parliament and of the Council in accordance with the transitional provisions laid down in Article 98 of Regulation (EU) No 536/2014.

Article 27

ENTRY INTO FORCE

This Regulation shall enter into force on the twentieth day following that of its publication in the Official Journal of the European Union.

It shall apply from six months after the date of publication in the *Official Journal of the European Union* of the notice referred to in Article 82(3) of Regulation (EU) No 536/2014 or 1 April 2018, whichever is the later.

Commission Directive 2003/94/EC of 8 October 2003 laying down the principles and guidelines of good manufacturing practice in respect of medicinal products for human use and investigational medicinal products for human use (OJ L 262, 14.10.2003, p. 22).

Directive 2001/20/EC of the European Parliament and the Council of 4 April 2001 on the approximation of the laws, regulations and administrative provisions of the Member States relating to the implementation of good clinical practice in the conduct of clinical trials on medicinal products for human use (OJ L 121, 1.5.2001, p. 34).

UK Legislation on Manufacture and Importation

Contents

The Human Medicines Regulations 2012 (SI 2012/1916)

> **Editor's note** These extracts from the Human Medicines Regulations 2012 (SI 2012/1916) as amended are presented for the reader's convenience. Reproduction is with the permission of HMSO and the Queen's Printer for Scotland. For any definitive information reference must be made to the original Regulations.
>
> The numbering and content within this section corresponds with the regulations set out in the published Statutory Instrument (SI 2012/1916).

Citation and commencement

1 (a) These Regulations may be cited as the Human Medicines Regulations 2012.

(b) These Regulations come into force on 14 August 2012.

Medicinal products

2 (1) In these Regulations "medicinal product" means:

(a) any substance or combination of substances presented as having properties of preventing or treating disease in human beings; or

(b) any substance or combination of substances that may be used by or administered to human beings with a view to:

(i) restoring, correcting or modifying a physiological function by exerting a pharmacological, immunological or metabolic action, or

(ii) making a medical diagnosis.

(2) These Regulations do not apply to:

(a) whole human blood; or

(b) any human blood component, other than plasma prepared by a method involving an industrial process.

2A Definition of advanced therapy medicinal product, etc.

(1) In these Regulations, in their application to products for sale or supply in Great Britain only, "advanced therapy medicinal product" means any of the following products:

(a) a gene therapy medicinal product;

(b) a somatic cell therapy medicinal product; or

(c) a tissue-engineered product.

(2) A "gene therapy medicinal product" is a biological medicinal product that has the following characteristics:

(a) it contains an active substance that contains or consists of a recombinant nucleic acid used in or administered to human beings with a view to regulating, repairing, replacing, adding or deleting a genetic sequence; and

(b) its therapeutic, prophylactic or diagnostic effect relates directly to the recombinant nucleic acid sequence it contains, or to the product of genetic expression of this sequence.

(3) A vaccine against infectious diseases is not to be treated as a gene therapy medicinal product.

(4) A "somatic cell medicinal product" is a medicinal product that has the following characteristics:

(a) it contains or consists of cells or tissues that:

(i) have been subject to substantial manipulation so that biological characteristics, physiological functions or structural properties relevant for the intended clinical use have been altered, or

(ii) are not intended to be used for the same essential function in the recipient as in the donor;

(b) it is presented as having properties for, or is used in or administered to human beings with a view to, treating, preventing or diagnosing a disease through the pharmacological, immunological or metabolic action of its cells or tissues.

(5) A "tissue-engineered product" is a medicinal product that:

(a) contains or consists of engineered cells or tissues; and

(b) is presented as having properties for, or is used in or administered to human beings with a view to, regenerating, repairing or replacing a human tissue.

(6) A tissue-engineered product may contain:

(a) cells or tissues of human or animal origin;

(b) viable or non-viable cells or tissues; and

(c) additional substances, including cellular products, biomolecules, biomaterials, chemical sub-stances, scaffolds or matrices.

(7) A product is not a tissue engineered product if it:

(a) contains or consists exclusively of non-viable human or animal cells or tissues;

(b) does not contain any viable cells or tissues; and

(c) does not act principally by pharmacological, immunological or metabolic action.

(8) Cells or tissues are engineered if they:

(a) have been subject to substantial manipulation, so that biological characteristics, physiological functions or structural properties relevant for the intended regeneration, repair or replacement are achieved; or

(b) are not intended to be used for the same essential function in the recipient as in the donor.

(9) The following manipulations are not substantial manipulations for the purposes of paragraphs (4)(a) and (8)(a):

(a) cutting;

(b) grinding;

(c) shaping;

(d) centrifugation;

(e) soaking in antibiotic or antimicrobial solutions;

(f) sterilisation;

(g) irradiation;

(h) cell separation, concentration or purification;

(i) filtering;

(j) lyophilisation;

(k) freezing;

(l) cryopreservation; and

(m) vitrification.

(10) In these Regulations, in their application to products for sale or supply in Great Britain only, "combined advanced therapy medicinal product" means an advanced therapy medicinal product:

(a) that incorporates, as an integral part of the product, one or more medical devices or one or more active implantable medical devices; and

(b) the cellular part of which:

(i) contains viable cells or tissues; or

(ii) contains non-viable cells or tissues that are liable to act upon the human body with action that can be considered as primary to that of the medical devices.

(11) Where an advanced therapy medicinal product contains viable cells or tissues, the pharmacological, immunological or metabolic action of those cells or tissues is to be treated as the principal mode of action of the product.

(12) An advanced therapy medicinal product containing both autologous and allogeneic cells or tissues is to be treated as being for allogeneic use.

(13) A product that falls within the definition of a tissue-engineered product and within the definition of a somatic cell therapy medicinal product is to be treated as a tissue-engineered product.

(14) A product that falls within the definition of:

(a) a somatic cell therapy medicinal product or a tissue engineered product; and

(b) a gene therapy medicinal product,

is to be treated as a gene therapy medicinal product.

General interpretation

8 (1) In these Regulations (unless the context otherwise requires):

"the 2001 Directive" means Directive 2001/83/EC of the European Parliament and of the Council on the Community Code relating to medicinal products for human use;

"the 2018 Regulations" means the Health Service Products (Provision and Disclosure of Information) Regulations 2018;

"active substance" means any substance or mixture of substances intended to be used in the manufacture of a medicinal product and that, when used in its production, becomes an active ingredient of that product intended to exert a pharmacological, immunological or metabolic action with a view to restoring, correcting or modifying physiological functions or to make a medical diagnosis;

"advanced therapy medicinal product" means, in the case of a medicinal product for sale or supply by the holder of a UKMA(NI) or UKMA(UK), a medicinal product described in Article 2(1)(a) of Regulation (EC) No 1394/2007;

"Annex I to the 2001 Directive" means, in relation to UKMA(GB), Annex I to the 2001 Directive, as modified in accordance with Schedule 8B;"

"approved country for batch testing list" means the list published by the licensing authority under paragraph 14(3) of Schedule 7 (obligations of qualified persons) and "approved country for batch testing" means a country included in that list;

"approved country for import list" means the list published by the licensing authority under regulation 18A (approved country for import) and "approved country for import" means a country included in that list;

"Article 126a authorisation" means an authorisation granted by the licensing authority under Part 8 of these Regulations;

"assemble", in relation to a medicinal product or an active substance, includes the various processes of dividing up, packaging and presentation of the product or substance, and "assembly" has a corresponding meaning;

"biological medicinal product" and "biological substance" have the meaning given in the third indent of paragraph 3.2.1.1.(b) of Annex I to the 2001 Directive;

"blood component" means any of the following:

(a) red cells;
(b) white cells;
(c) platelets; and
(d) plasma;

"the British Pharmacopoeia" means the British Pharmacopoeia referred to in regulation 317;

"EU marketing authorisation" means a marketing authorisation granted or renewed by the European Commission under Regulation (EC) No 726/2004;

"European Economic Area" or "EEA" means the European Economic Area created by the EEA agreement;

"excipient" means any constituent of a medicinal product other than the active substance and the packaging material;

"exempt advanced therapy medicinal product" has the meaning given in regulation 171;

"export" means export, or attempt to export, from the UK, whether by land, sea or air;

"falsified medicinal product" means any medicinal product with a false representation of:

(a) its identity, including its packaging and labelling, its name or its composition (other than any unintentional quality defect) as regards any of its ingredients including excipients and the strength of those ingredients;

(b) its source, including its manufacturer, its country of manufacturing, its country of origin or its marketing authorisation holder; or

(c) its history, including the records and documents relating to the distribution channels used;

"the Good Manufacturing Practice Directive" means

(a) in the case of an investigational medicinal product manufactured or assembled in, or imported into, Great Britain:
   (i) Commission Directive 2003/94/EC laying down the principles and guidelines of good manufacturing practice for medicinal products for human use and for investigational medicinal products for human use, as modified by Schedule 2A; or
   (ii) if Regulations have been made under the powers in regulation B17(1), and have come into force, those Regulations;

(b) in the case of an investigational medicinal product manufactured or assembled in, or imported into, Northern Ireland, Commission Directive 2003/94/EC laying down the principles and guidelines of good manufacturing practice for medicinal products for human use and for investigational medicinal products for human use;

"herbal medicinal product" means a medicinal product the only active ingredients of which are herbal substances or herbal preparations (or both);

"herbal preparation" means a preparation obtained by subjecting herbal substances to processes such as extraction, distillation, expression, fractionation, purification, concentration or fermentation, and includes a comminuted or powdered herbal substance, a tincture, an extract, an essential oil, an expressed juice or a processed exudate;

"herbal substance" means a plant or part of a plant, algae, fungi or lichen, or an unprocessed exudate of a plant, defined by the plant part used and the botanical name of the plant, either fresh or dried, but otherwise unprocessed;

"homoeopathic medicinal product" means a medicinal product prepared from homoeopathic stocks in accordance with a homoeopathic manufacturing procedure described by:

(a) the European Pharmacopoeia; or

(b) in the absence of such a description in the European Pharmacopoeia,

   (i) in relation to a certificate of registration or marketing authorisation for a national homoeopathic product in force in Great Britain only, the British Pharmacopoeia, or in an pharmacopoeia used officially in an country that is included in a list published by the licensing authority for this purpose;

   (ii) in relation to a certificate of registration or marketing authorisation for a national homoeopathic product in force in the whole United Kingdom or in Northern Ireland only, in the British Pharmacopoeia or in any pharmacopoeia used officially in an EEA State;

"import" means import, or attempt to import, into the UK, whether by land, sea or air and "imported" is to be construed accordingly;

"inspector" means a person authorised in writing by an enforcement authority for the purposes of Part 16 (enforcement) (and references to "the enforcement authority", in relation to an inspector, are to the enforcement authority by whom the inspector is so authorised);

"intermediate product" means a substance that:

(a) has been manufactured for use in the manufacture of medicinal products; and

(b) is intended for further processing by a manufacturer of such products;

"the licensing authority" has the meaning given by regulation 6(2);

"listed NIMAR product" means a product included in a list maintained in accordance with regulation 167B on the date it is dispatched from Great Britain to Northern Ireland;

"manufacture", in relation to a medicinal product, includes any process carried out in the course of making the product, but does not include dissolving or dispersing the product in, or diluting or mixing it with, a substance used as a vehicle for the purpose of administering it;

"manufacturer's licence" has the meaning given by regulation 17(1);

"marketing authorisation" means:

(a) a UK marketing authorisation; or

(b) an EU marketing authorisation;

"outer packaging" in relation to a medicinal product means any packaging into which the immediate packaging of the medicinal product is placed;

"package" in relation to a medicinal product, includes:

(a) a container of the product;
(b) any box, packet or other article in which one or more containers of the product are or are to be enclosed; and
(c) any box, packet or other article in which a box, packet or other article mentioned in paragraph (b) or this paragraph is or is to be enclosed;

"qualified person", except in relation to the expression "appropriately qualified person", means:

(a) a person who satisfies the requirements specified in Part 1 or 2 of Schedule 7; or
(b) where an application for a licence is made before 30 April 2013, in so far as the application relates to activities in respect of traditional herbal medicinal products, a person who has been engaged in activities in respect of traditional herbal medicinal products equivalent to those in Part 3 of Schedule 7 on or before 30th April 2011 and continues to be so engaged at the time when the application is made;

"Regulation (EC) No 726/2004" means Regulation (EC) No 726/2004 of the European Parliament and the Council of 31 March 2004 laying down Community procedures for the authorisation and supervision of medicinal products for human and veterinary use and establishing a European Medicines Agency as it has effect in EU law;

"Regulation (EC) No 1394/2007" means Regulation (EC) No 1394/2007 of the European Parliament and the Council of 13 November 2007 on advanced therapy medicinal products and amending Directive 2001/83/EC and Regulation (EC) No 726/2004;

"Regulation (EC) No 1234/2008" means Commission Regulation (EC) No 1234/2008 of 24 November 2008 concerning the examination of variations to the terms of marketing authorisations for medicinal products for human use and veterinary medicinal products, as it has effect in EU law;

"the relevant EU provisions" means the provisions of legislation of the European Union relating to medicinal products for human use, except to the extent that any other enactment provides for any function in relation to any such provision to be exercised otherwise than by the licensing authority;

"NIMAR" means Northern Ireland MHRA authorised route;

"special medicinal product" means a product within the meaning of regulation 167 or any equivalent legislation in a country other than the UK;

"UK marketing authorisation" means a marketing authorisation granted by the licensing authority under Part 5 of these Regulations or Chapter 4 of Title III to the 2001 Directive (mutual recognition and decentralised procedure) and:

(a) "UKMA(UK)" means such an authorisation in force in the whole United Kingdom;
(b) "UKMA(GB)" means such an authorisation in force in Great Britain only;
(c) "UKMA(NI)" means such an authorisation in force in Northern Ireland only.

Chapter 1A Good Manufacturing Practice and Good Distribution Practice

Regulations on Good Manufacturing Practice

B17 (1) The Secretary of State may by regulations in respect of Great Britain set out principles and guidelines of good manufacturing practice in respect of medicinal products and investigational medicinal products.

(2) Regulations under paragraph (1) may in particular make provisions as to:

(a) inspections;
(b) compliance with good manufacturing practice and, where relevant, the UK marketing authorisation or EU marketing authorisation;
(c) quality assurance systems;
(d) personnel;
(e) premises and equipment;
(f) documentation;
(g) production;
(h) quality control;
(i) the contracting out of work;
(j) complaints and product recall;
(k) self-inspection.

(3) Subject to any provision made in regulations under paragraph (1), the principles and guidelines set out in the Good Manufacturing Practice Directive have effect in Great Britain on and after IP completion day as they had effect immediately before IP completion day, but subject to the modifications specified in Schedule 2A.

(4) The Secretary of State may by regulations in respect of Great Britain amend or revoke Schedule 2A.

Guidelines on Good Manufacturing Practice and Good Distribution Practice

C17 (1) The licensing authority may publish in relation to the manufacture or assembly of a medicinal product in, or import to, Great Britain:

(a) detailed guidelines of good manufacturing practice in respect of medicinal products, and investigational medicinal products, referred to in Article 46(f) of the 2001 Directive, including guidelines as to the formalised risk assessment for ascertaining the appropriate good manufacturing practice for excipients;

(b) principles and guidelines of good manufacturing practice for active substances, referred to in the first paragraph of point (f) of Article 46 and in Article 46b of that Directive;

(c) principles and guidelines of good distribution practice referred to in the first paragraph of point (f) of Article 46, and Article 84, of that Directive.

(2) Guidelines or principles under paragraph (1) may replace, amend or otherwise modify any guidelines or principles published or adopted by the European Commission under the second, third, fourth or fifth paragraph of Article 47, or Article 84, of the 2001 Directive.

(3) Unless replaced by principles or guidelines published under paragraph (1), principles and guidelines published or adopted by the European Commission under the second, third, fourth or fifth paragraphs of Article 47, or Article 84, of the 2001 Directive, as they applied immediately before IP completion day, continue to apply on and after IP completion day (subject to any amendments or modifications published under paragraph (1)).

(4) Before exercising the power under paragraph (1), the licensing authority must consult such persons as it considers appropriate.

(5) The licensing authority may exercise its power under paragraph (1) only if it considers that it is necessary in order to take account of technical or scientific progress.

(6) If the licensing authority publishes principles and guidelines under paragraph (1), any reference in these Regulations to any principle or guideline adopted under the provisions of the 2001 Directive specified in those paragraphs is instead to be read as a reference to the principle or guideline published under paragraph (1), or that principle or guideline as amended or modified (as the case may be).

Manufacturing of medicinal products

17 (1) A person may not except in accordance with a licence (a "manufacturer's licence"):

(a) manufacture a medicinal product;

(b) assemble a medicinal product;

(c) import a medicinal product into Great Britain from a country other than:

(i) Northern Ireland; or

(ii) an approved country for import,

(d) import a medicinal product into Northern Ireland from a country other than an EEA State; or

(e) possess a medicinal product for the purpose of any activity in sub-paragraphs (a) to (d).

(2) Paragraph (1) is subject to paragraphs (3) to (5).

(3) Paragraph (1) applies in relation to an investigational medicinal product only:

(a) if the product has a marketing authorisation, Article 126a authorisation, certificate of registration or traditional herbal registration; and

(b) to the extent that the manufacture or assembly of the product is in accordance with the terms and conditions of that authorisation, certificate or registration.

(4) In paragraph (3), "marketing authorisation" means:

(a) a marketing authorisation issued by a competent authority in accordance with the 2001 Directive; or

(aa) a UK marketing authorisation; or

(b) an EU marketing authorisation.

(5) Paragraph (1) does not apply to a person who, in connection with the importation of a medicinal product:

(a) provides facilities solely for transporting the product; or

(b) acting as an import agent, imports the medicinal product solely to the order of another person who holds a manufacturer's licence authorising the importation of the product.

(6) Paragraph (1) does not apply to a person who imports a medicinal product for administration to themselves or to any other person who is a member of that person's household.

(7) Paragraph (1) does not apply to imports into Northern Ireland from Great Britain of:

(a) special medicinal products; and

(b) medicinal products that have been released for sale, supply or distribution in an EEA State or the United Kingdom before IP completion day.

(8) For the purposes of paragraph (7) a medicinal product has been released for sale, supply or distribution where, after the stage of manufacturing has taken place, the product is the subject matter of a written or verbal agreement between two or more persons for the transfer of ownership, any other property right, or possession concerning the product, or where the product is the subject matter of an offer to a person to conclude such an agreement.

Application for manufacturer's or wholesale dealer's licence

21 (1) An application for a grant of a licence under this Part must:
 (a) be made to the licensing authority;
 (b) be made in the way and form specified in Schedule 3; and
 (c) contain or be accompanied by the information, documents, samples and other material specified in that Schedule.

 (2) An application must indicate the descriptions of medicinal products in respect of which the licence is required, either by specifying the descriptions of medicinal products in question or by way of an appropriate general classification.

Factors relevant to determination of application for manufacturer's or wholesale dealer's licence

22 (1) In dealing with an application for a manufacturer's licence the licensing authority must in particular take into consideration:
 (a) the operations proposed to be carried out under the licence;
 (b) the premises in which those operations are to be carried out;
 (c) the equipment that is or will be available on those premises for carrying out those operations;
 (d) the qualifications of the persons under whose supervision the operations will be carried out; and
 (e) the arrangements made or to be made for securing the safekeeping and the maintenance of adequate records in respect of, medicinal products manufactured or assembled in pursuance of the licence.

 (2) In dealing with an application for a wholesale dealer's licence the licensing authority must in particular take into consideration:
 (a) the premises on which medicinal products of the descriptions to which the application relates will be stored;
 (b) the equipment that is or will be available for storing medicinal products on those premises;
 (c) the equipment and facilities that are or will be available for distributing medicinal products from those premises; and
 (d) the arrangements made or to be made for securing the safekeeping and the maintenance of adequate records in respect of medicinal products stored on or distributed from those premises.

Grant or refusal of licence

23 (1) Subject to the following provisions of these Regulations, on an application to the licensing authority for a licence under this Part the licensing authority may:

(a) grant a licence containing such provisions as it considers appropriate; or

(b) refuse to grant a licence if, with regard to the provisions of these Regulations, it considers it necessary or appropriate to do so.

(2) The licensing authority must grant or refuse an application for a licence under this Part within the period of 90 days beginning immediately after the day on which it receives the application.

(3) Paragraph (2) applies to an application only if the requirements of Schedule 3 have been met.

(4) If a notice under regulation 30 requires the applicant to provide the licensing authority with information, the information period is not to be counted for the purposes of paragraph (2).

(5) In paragraph (4), the "information period" means the period:

(a) beginning with the day on which the notice is given; and

(b) ending with the day on which the licensing authority receives the information or the applicant shows to the licensing authority's satisfaction that the applicant is unable to provide it.

(6) The licensing authority must give the applicant a notice stating the reasons for its decision in any case where:

(a) the licensing authority refuses to grant an application for a licence; or

(b) the licensing authority grants a licence otherwise than in accordance with the application and the applicant requests a statement of its reasons.

Standard provisions of licences

24 (1) The standard provisions set out in Schedule 4 may be incorporated by the licensing authority in a licence under this Part granted on or after the date on which these Regulations come into force.

(2) The standard provisions may be incorporated in a licence with or without modifications and either generally or in relation to medicinal products of a particular class.

(3) In Schedule 4, in relation to a licence holder in Great Britain, references to the principles and guidelines set out in the Good Manufacturing Practice Directive are to those principles and guidelines as they apply under or by virtue of regulation B17.

Duration of licence

25 A licence granted under this Part remains in force until:

(a) the licence is revoked by the licensing authority; or

(b) the licence is surrendered by the holder.

Certification of manufacturer's licence

31 (1) The licensing authority must issue a certificate in accordance with the following paragraphs of this regulation in relation to a manufacturer's licence relating to the manufacture or assembly of medicinal products if requested to do so by:

    (a) subject to paragraph (5), the holder of the licence;

    (b) a person who intends to export a medicinal product manufactured or assembled by the holder under the licence; or

    (c) the competent authorities of a country other than an EEA State (the United Kingdom) into which a medicinal product manufactured or assembled under the licence is, or is proposed to be, imported.

(2) The certificate must contain:

    (a) information sufficient to identify the holder of the manufacturer's licence;

    (b) details of the medicinal products that may be manufactured or assembled under the licence; and

    (c) any other information concerning the holder, the product or the licence that the licensing authority thinks it appropriate to include, including information relating to clinical trials.

(3) If:

    (a) a request is made:

        (i) under paragraph (1)(a) in relation to the export or the proposed export of a product; or

        (ii) under paragraph (1)(b) or (c); and

    (b) there is a UK marketing authorisation, EU marketing authorisation, Article 126a authorisation or a traditional herbal registration in force for any product to which the licence relates,

    the certificate must be accompanied by the summary of the product characteristics relating to that product.

(4) The licensing authority may restrict the information provided under sub-paragraphs (2)(a) and (b) and paragraph (3) to information relating to the specific medicinal products mentioned in the request made under paragraph (1).

(5) A licence holder who makes a request under paragraph (1) must:

    (a) produce to the licensing authority a UK marketing authorisation, EU marketing authorisation, Article 126a authorisation, certificate of registration or traditional herbal registration in relation to any product to which the certificate is to relate; or

    (b) make a declaration to the licensing authority explaining why no UK marketing authorisation, EU marketing authorisation, Article 126a authorisation, certificate of registration or traditional herbal registration is available.

(6) The licensing authority must have regard to the prevailing administrative arrangements of the World Health Organization when issuing the certificate.

Conditions for manufacturer's licence

36

(1) Regulations 37 to 41 apply to the holder of a manufacturer's licence (referred to in those regulations as "the licence holder") and have effect as if they were provisions of the licence (but the provisions specified in paragraph (2) do not apply to the holder of a manufacturer's licence insofar as the licence relates to the manufacture or assembly of exempt advanced therapy medicinal products).

(2) Those provisions are regulations 37(3), 38, 39(6)(a) and (8), 40 and 41.

(3) The requirements of Part 1 of Schedule 6 apply to the holder of a manufacturer's licence in so far as the licence relates to the manufacture or assembly of exempt advanced therapy medicinal products, and have effect as if they were provisions of the licence.

(4) Where a manufacturer's licence permits the manufacture or assembly of a medicinal product in, or import of a medicinal product into, Northern Ireland, the requirements and obligations contained in a provision of Commission Regulation 2016/161 listed in paragraph (5) have effect as if they were provisions of that licence under this Part.

(5) The provisions mentioned in paragraph (4) are:
   (a) Article 4 (composition of the unique identifier);
   (b) Article 5 (carrier of the unique identifier);
   (c) Article 6 (quality of the printing of the two-dimensional barcode);
   (d) Article 7 (human-readable format);
   (e) Article 10 (verification of the safety features) in so far as it relates to manufacturers;
   (f) Article 11 (verification of the authenticity of the unique identifier) in so far as it relates to manufacturers;
   (g) Article 12 (unique identifiers that have been decommissioned);
   (h) Article 13 (reversing the status of a decommissioned unique identifier) in so far as it relates to manufacturers;
   (i) Article 14 (verification of the two-dimensional barcode);
   (j) Article 15 (record keeping);
   (k) Article 16 (verifications to be performed before removing or replacing the safety features);
   (l) Article 17 (equivalent unique identifier); and
   (m) Article 18 (actions to be taken in case of tampering or suspected falsification).

(6) In distributing a medicinal product in Northern Ireland by way of wholesale dealing, the requirements and obligations contained in a provision of Commission Regulation 2016/161 listed in paragraph (7) shall apply to the holder of a manufacturer's licence and have effect as if they were provisions of the licence.

(7) The provisions mentioned in paragraph (6) are:

    (a) Article 20 (verification of the authenticity of the unique identifier by wholesalers), subject to the exemption contained in Article 21 (derogations from Article 20(b));

    (b) Article 22 (decommissioning of unique identifiers by wholesalers); and

    (c) Article 24 (actions to be taken by wholesalers in case of tampering or suspected falsification).

Manufacturing and assembly

37 (1) This regulation applies in relation to a manufacturer's licence relating to the manufacture or assembly of medicinal products.

    (2) The licence holder must comply with the principles and guidelines for good manufacturing practice set out in the Good Manufacturing Practice Directive which apply under or by virtue of regulation B17.

    (3) Unless paragraph (10) applies, the licence holder shall use active substances as starting materials only if:

        (a) those substances have been manufactured in accordance with good manufacturing practice for active substances; and

        (b) those substances have been distributed in accordance with the guidelines on good distribution practice for active substances.

    (4) The licence holder shall verify:

        (a) that the manufacturer or distributor of an active substance used by the licence holder has complied with the requirements of good manufacturing practice and good distribution practice for active substances by means of audits performed:

            (i) directly by the licence holder; or

            (ii) by a person acting on behalf of the licence holder under a contract;

        (b) that unless the active substance is imported into Great Britain from a country other than an approved country for import or into Northern Ireland from a country other than an EEA State from a third country, any manufacturers, importers or distributors supplying active substances to the licence holder:

            (i) in the case of a product imported into Great Britain, are registered with the appropriate authority for the registration of such persons in the approved country for import; and

(ii) in the case of a product imported into Northern Ireland, are registered with the competent authority of a member State in which they are established; and

(c) the authenticity and quality of the active substance.

(5) The licence holder shall ensure that:

(a) excipients are suitable for use in a medicinal product by:

(i) ascertaining what the appropriate good manufacturing practice is; and

(ii) ensuring that the ascertained good manufacturing practice is applied;

(b) the suitability of the excipient is ascertained on the basis of a formalised risk assessment as described in the case of a product for sale or supply in Great Britain (including a listed NIMAR product for sale or supply from Great Britain to Northern Ireland), in the guidelines that apply under or by virtue of regulation C17 and, in the case of a product for sale or supply in Northern Ireland, in paragraph 5 of Article 47 of the 2001 Directive;

(c) the assessment under sub-paragraph (b) takes account of:

(i) the source;

(ii) requirements under other quality systems;

(iii) intended use of the excipients; and

(iv) previous instances of quality defects;

(d) the authenticity and quality of any excipient used is verified; and

(e) the measures taken under this paragraph are documented by the licence holder.

(6) The licence holder must maintain such staff, premises and equipment as are necessary for the stages of manufacture and assembly of medicinal products undertaken by the licence holder in accordance with:

(a) the manufacturer's licence; and

(b) in the case of a product for sale or supply:

(i) in Great Britain (including a listed NIMAR product for sale or supply from Great Britain to Northern Ireland), the UKMA(GB), UKMA(UK), COR(GB), COR(UK), THR(GB) or THR(UK); or

(ii) in Northern Ireland, the UKMA(NI), UKMA(UK), COR(NI), COR(UK), THR(NI), THR(UK), EU marketing authorisations or Article 126a authorisations, applying to the medicinal products.

(7) The licence holder must not manufacture or assemble medicinal products, or classes of medicinal products, other than those specified in the licence.

(8) The licence holder must not manufacture or assemble medicinal products on premises other than those specified in the licence as approved by the licensing authority for the purpose.

(9) The licence holder must ensure that blood, or blood components, imported into the United Kingdom and used as a starting material or raw material in the manufacture of a medicinal product meet:

(a) the standards of quality and safety specified in the Blood Quality and Safety Regulations 2005; or

(b) equivalent standards.

(10) The requirements in paragraphs (3) to (5) do not apply in relation to the manufacture or assembly of special medicinal product to which regulation 167 (supply to fulfil special needs) applies.

(11) The licence holder must immediately inform the licensing authority and, where applicable, the UK marketing authorisation holder, of medicinal products that come within the scope of manufacturing authorisation, which the licence holder:

(a) knows or suspects; or

(b) has reasonable grounds for knowing or suspecting to be falsified.

Imports from states other than EEA States/countries other than approved countries for import

38 (1) This regulation applies in relation to a manufacturer's licence relating to the import of medicinal products.

(2) The licence holder must comply with the conditions set out in this regulation in relation to the import of medicinal products from:

(a) in the case of an import into Great Britain, a country other than an approved country for import; or

(b) in the case of an import into Northern Ireland, a state other than an EEA State.

(3) The licence holder must:

(a) comply with the principles and guidelines on good manufacturing practice in the Good Manufacturing Practice Directive in so far as they are relevant to the import of medicinal products; and

(b) ensure that active substances have been used as starting materials in the manufacture of medicinal products, other than special medicinal products, imported from, in the case of an import into Great Britain, a country other than an approved country for import and, in the case of an import into Northern Ireland, a state other than an EEA State, only if those substances have been manufactured or assembled in accordance with good manufacturing practice for active substances.

Further requirements for manufacturer's licence

39 (1) This regulation applies in relation to any manufacturer's licence.

(2) The licence holder must maintain such staff, premises, equipment and facilities for the handling, control, storage and distribution of

medicinal products under the licence as are appropriate in order to maintain the quality of the medicinal products.

(3) The licence holder must ensure that any arrangements made for the handling, control, storage and distribution of medicinal products are adequate to maintain the quality of the products.

(4) The licence holder must not handle, control, store or distribute medicinal products on any premises other than those specified in the licence as approved by the licensing authority for the purpose.

(5) The licence holder must inform the licensing authority before making a material alteration to the premises or facilities used under the licence, or to the purposes for which those premises or facilities are used.

(6) The licence holder must inform the licensing authority of any proposed change to:

(a) the qualified person; and

(b) any person named in the licence as having responsibility for quality control.

(7) For the purposes of enabling the licensing authority to determine whether there are grounds for suspending, revoking or varying the licence, the licence holder must permit a person authorised in writing by the licensing authority to do anything that the licensing authority could have done for the purposes of verifying a statement made in an application for a licence.

(8) In distributing a medicinal product by way of wholesale dealing, the licence holder must comply with the following as if they are a holder of a wholesale dealer's licence—

(a) regulations 43(1), (2) and (5), 43ZA and 44(5) and (6), and

(b) regulation 43A, if applicable, where the product is being distributed in NI.

Obligation to provide information relating to control methods

40 (1) This regulation applies in relation to any manufacturer's licence.

(2) The licensing authority may require the licence holder to provide the authority with proof of the control methods employed by the holder in relation to a medicinal product.

Requirements as to qualified persons

41 (1) This regulation applies in relation to any manufacturer's licence.

(2) The licence holder must ensure that there is at the disposal of the holder at all times at least one qualified person who is responsible for carrying out, in relation to medicinal products manufactured, assembled or imported under the licence, the duties specified in Part 3 of Schedule 7.

(3) If the licence holder satisfies the requirements of Part 1 or 2 of Schedule 7, the licence holder may act as a qualified person.

(4) A qualified person may be treated by the licence holder as satisfying the requirements of Part 1 or 2 of Schedule 7 if that person produces evidence that he or she:

   (a) is a member of a body specified in paragraph (5); and

   (b) is regarded by that body as satisfying those requirements.

(5) Those bodies are:

   (a) the Society of Biology;

   (b) the Royal Pharmaceutical Society;

   (c) the Pharmaceutical Society of Northern Ireland;

   (d) the Royal Society of Chemistry; and

   (e) such other body as may be specified by the licensing authority for the purpose of this paragraph.

(6) Where the qualified person changes, the licence holder must give the licensing authority advance notification of:

   (a) that change; and

   (b) the name, address and qualifications of the new qualified person.

(7) The licence holder must not permit any person to act as a qualified person other than the person named in the licence or another person notified to the licensing authority under paragraph (6).

(8) Paragraph (9) applies if the licensing authority thinks, after giving the licence holder and a person acting as a qualified person the opportunity to make representations (orally or in writing), that the person:

   (a) does not satisfy the requirements of Part 1 or 2 of Schedule 7 in relation to qualifications or experience;

   (b) does not satisfy paragraph (b) of the definition of "qualified person" in regulation 8; or

   (c) is failing to carry out the duties referred to in paragraph (2) adequately or at all.

(9) Where this paragraph applies, the licensing authority must notify the licence holder in writing that the person is not permitted to act as a qualified person.

(10) The licence holder must at all times provide and maintain such staff, premises and equipment as are necessary to enable the qualified person to carry out the duties referred to in paragraph (2).

(11) The licence holder is not obliged to meet the requirements of this regulation in relation to any activity under the licence that relates to special medicinal products or, unless conditions attached in accordance with regulation 174(1) provide otherwise, to products authorised on a temporary basis under regulation 174 (supply in response to spread of pathogenic agents, etc.).

Schedule 4 Standard Provisions of Licences

PART 1 Manufacturer's licence relating to manufacture and assembly

1   The provisions of this Part are standard provisions of a manufacturer's licence relating to the manufacture or assembly of medicinal products.

2   The licence holder must place the quality control system referred to in Article 11(1) of the Good Manufacturing Practice Directive under the authority of the person notified to the licensing authority in accordance with paragraph 1(2)(g) of Schedule 3.

3   The licence holder may use a contract laboratory pursuant to Article 11(2) of the Good Manufacturing Practice Directive, if the laboratory is operated by a person approved by the licensing authority.

4   The licence holder must provide such information as may be requested by the licensing authority:

   (a)   about the products currently being manufactured or assembled by the licence holder; and

   (b)   about the operations being carried out in relation to such manufacture or assembly.

5   The licence holder must inform the licensing authority of any change that the licence holder proposes to make to a person named in the licence as:

   (a)   the person whose duty it is to supervise the manufacturing or assembling operations;

   (b)   in charge of the animals from which are derived substances used in the production of the medicinal products being manufactured or assembled; or

   (c)   responsible for the culture of living tissues used in the manufacture of the medicinal products being manufactured or assembled.

6   The licence holder must:

   (a)   keep readily available for inspection by a person authorised by the licensing authority the batch documentation referred to in Article 9(1) of the Good Manufacturing Practice Directive; and

   (b)   permit the authorised person to take copies or make extracts from such documentation.

7   The licence holder must keep readily available for examination by a person authorised by the licensing authority the samples in each batch of finished medicinal product referred to in Article 11(4) of the Good Manufacturing Practice Directive.

8   Where the licence holder has been informed by the licensing authority that the strength, quality or purity of a batch of a medicinal product to which the licence relates has been found not to conform with:

   (a)   the specification for the finished product; or

   (b)   the provisions of these Regulations applicable to the medicinal product.

9 The licence holder must ensure that tests for determining conformity with the standards and specifications applying to a product used in the manufacture of a medicinal product must, except so far as the conditions of the product specification for that product otherwise provide, be applied to samples taken from the medicinal product after all manufacturing processes have been completed, or at such earlier stage of the manufacture as may be approved by the licensing authority.

10 Where the manufacturer's licence relates to the assembly of a medicinal product or class of product, and the licence holder supplies the product at such a stage of assembly that does not fully comply with the provisions of the product specification that relate to labelling, the licence holder must communicate the particulars of those provisions to the person to whom that product has been supplied.

11 Where:
(a) the manufacturer's licence relates to the assembly of a medicinal product;
(b) the medicinal product is not manufactured by the licence holder; and
(c) particulars of the name and address of the manufacturer of the product, or the person who imports the product, have been given by the licence holder to the licensing authority.

12 The licence holder must keep readily available, for examination by a person authorised by the licensing authority, durable records of the details of the manufacture of intermediate products held by the licence holder for use in the manufacture of biological medicinal products, and the records must:
(a) be in such form as to ensure that the licence holder has a comprehensive record of all matters that are relevant to an evaluation of the safety, quality and efficacy of a finished biological medicinal product manufactured using those intermediate products; and
(b) not be destroyed without the consent of the licensing authority until the records of the details of manufacture of finished medicinal products that were or may be manufactured using those intermediate products may be destroyed in accordance with the requirements of these Regulations.

13 Where:
(a) animals are used in the production of medicinal products; and
(b) in the case of a product for sale or supply:
(i) in Great Britain, a UK marketing authorisation, certificate of registration or traditional herbal registration, or
(ii) in Northern Ireland, a marketing authorisation, Article 126a authorisation, certificate of registration or traditional herbal registration,
contains provisions relating to them.

14   The licence holder must take all reasonable precautions and exercise all due diligence to ensure that any information provided to the licensing authority is not false or misleading in any material particular if:

(a)   it relates to a medicinal product that the licence holder manufactures or assembles; or

(b)   it relates to any starting materials or intermediate products held by the licence holder that are for use in the manufacture of medicinal products.

14A   A licence holder:

(a)   in Great Britain may only manufacture a special medicinal product for a person in Northern Ireland, and

(b)   in Northern Ireland may only manufacture a special medicinal product for a person in Great Britain,

in response to an order which satisfies the requirements of regulation 167.

PART 2 Manufacturer's licence relating to the import of medicinal products from a state other than an EEA State/Country other than an Approved Country for Import

15   The provisions of this Part are standard provisions of a manufacturer's licence relating to the import of medicinal products from:

(a)   in the case of an import into Great Britain, a country other than an approved country for import; or

(b)   in the case of an import into Northern Ireland, a state other than an EEA State.

15A   The provisions of this Part are standard provisions of a manufacturer's licence relating to the supply of a listed NIMAR product from Great Britain to Northern Ireland.

16   The licence holder must place the quality control system referred to in Article 11(1) of the Good Manufacturing Practice Directive under the authority of the person notified to the licensing authority in accordance with paragraph 2(2)(h) of Schedule 3.

17   The licence holder may use a contract laboratory pursuant to Article 11(2) of the Good Manufacturing Practice Directive if operated by a person approved by the licensing authority.

18   The licence holder must provide such information as may be requested by the licensing authority concerning the type and quantity of any medicinal products that the licence holder imports.

19   The licence holder must:

(a)   keep readily available for inspection by a person authorised by the licensing authority the batch documentation referred to in Article 9(1) of the Good Manufacturing Practice Directive; and

(b)   permit the person authorised to take copies or make extracts from such documentation.

20 Where the licence holder has been informed by the licensing authority that the strength, quality or purity of a batch of a medicinal product to which the licence relates has been found not to conform with:

(a) the specification of the medicinal product in question; or

(b) those provisions of these Regulations that are applicable to the medicinal product,

21 The licence holder must ensure that any tests for determining conformity with the standards and specifications applying to any ingredient used in the manufacture of a medicinal product must, except so far as the conditions of the product specification for that ingredient otherwise provide, be applied to samples taken from the medicinal product after all manufacturing processes have been completed, or at such earlier stage in the manufacture as may be approved by the licensing authority.

22 (1) Where and in so far as the licence relates to special medicinal products, the licence holder may only import such products from in the case of an import into Great Britain, a country other than an approved country for import and in the case of an import into Northern Ireland, a state other than an EEA State:

(a) in response to an order that satisfies the requirements of regulation 167 (supply to fulfil special patient needs); and

(b) where the conditions set out in sub-paragraphs (2) to (9) are complied with.

(2) No later than 28 days before the day on which each importation of a special medicinal product takes place, the licence holder must give written notice to the licensing authority stating the intention to import the product and stating the following particulars:

(a) the brand name, common name or scientific name of the medicinal product and (if different) any name under which the medicinal product is to be sold or supplied in the United Kingdom;

(b) any trademark or the name of the manufacturer of the medicinal product;

(c) in respect of each active constituent of the medicinal product, any international non-proprietary name or the British approved name or the monograph name, or, where that constituent does not have any of those, the accepted scientific name or any other name descriptive of the true nature of the constituent;

(d) the quantity of medicinal product to be imported, which must not exceed the quantity specified in sub-paragraph (6); and

(e) the name and address of the manufacturer or assembler of the medicinal product in the form in which it is to be imported and, if the person who will supply the medicinal product for importation is not the manufacturer or assembler, the name and address of the supplier.

(3) The licence holder may not import the special medicinal product if, before the end of 28 days beginning immediately after the date on

which the licensing authority sends or gives the licence holder an acknowledgement in writing by the licensing authority that it has received the notice referred to in sub-paragraph (2), the licensing authority has notified the licence holder in writing that the product should not be imported.

(4) The licence holder may import the special medicinal product referred to in the notice where the licence holder has been notified in writing by the licensing authority, before the end of the 28-day period referred to in sub-paragraph (3) that the product may be imported.

(5) Where the licence holder sells or supplies special medicinal products, the licence holder must, in addition to any other records which are required by the provisions of the licence, make and maintain written records relating to:

(a) the batch number of the batch of the product from which the sale or supply was made; and

(b) details of any adverse reaction to the product sold or supplied of which the licence holder becomes aware.

(6) The licence holder must not, on any one occasion, import more than such amount as is sufficient for 25 single administrations, or for 25 courses of treatment where the amount imported is sufficient for a maximum of three months' treatment, and must not, on any one occasion, import more than the quantity notified to the licensing authority under sub-paragraph (2)(d).

(7) The licence holder must not publish any advertisement, catalogue or circular relating to a special medicinal product or make any representations in respect of that product.

(8) The licence holder must inform the licensing authority immediately of any matter coming to the licence holder's attention that might reasonably cause the licensing authority to believe that a special medicinal product imported in accordance with this paragraph can no longer be regarded as a product that can safely be administered to human beings or as a product that is of satisfactory quality for such administration.

(9) The licence holder must cease importing or supplying a special medicinal product if the licence holder receives a notice in writing from the licensing authority directing that, from a date specified in the notice, a particular product or class of products may no longer be imported or supplied.

(10) In this paragraph:

"British approved name" means the name that appears in the current edition of the list prepared by the British Pharmacopoeia Commission under regulation 318 (British Pharmacopoeia: lists of names);

"international non-proprietary name" means a name that has been selected by the World Health Organization as a recommended international non-proprietary name and in respect of which the

Director-General of the World Health Organization has given notice to that effect in the World Health Organization Chronicle; and "monograph name" means the name or approved synonym that appears at the head of a monograph in the current edition of the British Pharmacopoeia, the European Pharmacopoeia or a foreign or international compendium of standards, and "current" in this definition means current at the time the notice is sent to the licensing authority.

23 The licence holder must take all reasonable precautions and exercise due diligence to ensure that any information provided to the licensing authority that is relevant to an evaluation of the safety, quality or efficacy of a medicinal product for human use which is imported from, in the case of an import into Great Britain, a country other than an approved country for import and, in the case of an import into Northern Ireland, a state other than an EEA State, handled, stored or distributed under the licence is not false or misleading in a material particular.

23ZA The licence holder in Great Britain must take all reasonable precautions and exercise due diligence to ensure that any information provided to the licensing authority which is relevant to an evaluation of the safety, quality or efficacy of a product for human use which is supplied from Great Britain into Northern Ireland by virtue of regulation 167A handled, stored or distributed under the licence is not false or misleading in a material particular.

23A A licence holder:

(a) in Great Britain may supply a special medicinal product only to a person in Northern Ireland, and

(b) in Northern Ireland may supply a special medicinal product only to a person in Great Britain,

in response to an order that satisfies the requirements of Regulation 167.

PART 3 Manufacturer's licence relating to exempt advanced therapy medicinal products

24 The provisions of paragraphs 25 to 27 are incorporated as additional standard provisions of a manufacturer's licence relating to the manufacture and assembly of exempt advanced therapy medicinal products.

25 The licence holder must ensure that the immediate packaging of an exempt advanced therapy medicinal product is labelled to show the following particulars:

(a) the name of the exempt advanced therapy medicinal product;

(b) the expiry date in clear terms including the year and month and, if applicable, the day;

(c) a description of the active substance, expressed qualitatively and quantitatively;

(d) where the product contains cells or tissues of human or animal origin:
    (i) a statement that the product contains such cells or tissues; and
    (ii) a short description of the cells or tissues and of their specific origin;

(e) the pharmaceutical form and the contents by weight, volume or number of doses of the product;

(f) a list of excipients, including preservative systems;

(g) the method of use, application, administration or implantation and, if appropriate, the route of administration, with space provided for the prescribed dose to be indicated;

(h) any special storage precautions;

(i) specific precautions relating to the disposal of the unused product or waste derived from the product and, where appropriate, reference to any appropriate collection system;

(j) the name and address of the holder of the manufacturer's licence;

(k) the manufacturer's licence number;

(l) the manufacturer's batch number;

(m) the unique donation code referred to in Article 8(2) of Directive 2004/23/EC [assigned by a tissue establishment pursuant to:
    (a) paragraph 1 of Schedule 3A to the Human Fertilisation and Embryology Act 1990, as regards human gametes and embryos; and
    (b) paragraph 1 of Schedule 2 to the Human Tissue (Quality and Safety for Human Application) Regulations 2007, as regards other human tissues and cells]; and

(n) where the exempt advanced therapy medicinal product is for autologous use, the unique patient identifier and the words "for autologous use only".

26 The licence holder must ensure that the package leaflet of the exempt advanced therapy medicinal product shall include the following particulars:

(a) the name of the exempt advanced therapy medicinal product;

(b) the intended effect of the medicinal product if correctly used, applied, administered or implanted;

(c) where the product contains cells or tissues of human or animal origin:
    (i) a statement that the product contains such cells or tissues; and
    (ii) a short description of the cells or tissues and, where such cells or tissues are of animal origin, their specific origin;

(d) where the product contains a medical device or an active implantable medical device, a description of that device and, where that device contains cells or tissues of animal origin, their specific origin;

(e) any necessary instructions for use, including:
    (i) the posology;
    (ii) the method of use, application, administration or implantation and, if appropriate, the route of administration;
    (iii) a description of symptoms of overdose;
    (iv) action to be taken in the event of overdose, including any emergency procedures;

(v) action to be taken if one or more doses have been missed; and

(vi) a recommendation to consult the doctor or pharmacist for any clarification on the use of the product;

(f) where adverse reactions are known, a description of those that may occur under recommended conditions of use of the product and, if appropriate, an indication of action to be taken in such a case;

(g) an instruction that the patient report any adverse reaction not specified in the package leaflet to the doctor or pharmacist;

(h) the expiry date in clear terms and a warning against using the product after that date;

(i) any special storage precautions;

(j) a description of any visible signs of deterioration;

(k) a complete qualitative and quantitative composition;

(l) the name and address of the holder of the manufacturer's licence; and

(m) the date on which the package leaflet was last revised.

27 The licence holder must keep the data referred to in paragraph 8 of Schedule 6 for such period, being a period of longer than 30 years, as may be specified by the licensing authority.

Schedule 6 Manufacturer's and Wholesale Dealer's Licences for Exempt Advanced Therapy Medicinal Products

PART 1 Manufacturer's licences

1 The requirements in paragraphs 2 to 12 apply to a manufacturer's licence in so far as it relates to the manufacture and assembly of exempt advanced therapy medicinal products.

2 The licence holder must inform the licensing authority of any adverse reaction or suspected adverse reaction of which the holder is aware within the period of 15 days, beginning on the day following the first day on which the holder knew about the reaction.

3 The licence holder must ensure, if using human cells or tissues in an exempt advanced therapy medicinal product, that the donation, procurement and testing of those cells or tissues is in accordance with Directive 2004/23/EC requirements imposed pursuant to:

(a) paragraphs 6 to 9 of Schedule 3A to the Human Fertilisation and Embryology Act 1990, as regards gametes and embryos; and

(b) paragraphs 9 to 12 of Schedule 2 to the Human Tissue (Quality and Safety for Human Application) Regulations 2007, as regards other tissues and cells.

4 The licence holder must ensure that any human tissue or cell component imported into the United Kingdom and used by the holder as a starting material or raw material in the manufacture of an exempt advanced therapy medicinal product shall meet equivalent standards of quality and safety to those imposed pursuant to:

(a) Schedule 3A to the Human Fertilisation and Embryology Act 1990, as regards gametes and embryos; and

(b) Schedule 2 to the Human Tissue (Quality and Safety for Human Application) Regulations 2007, as regards other tissues and cells.

5   The licence holder must ensure that any blood or blood component imported into the United Kingdom and used by the manufacturer's licence holder as a starting material or raw material in the manufacture of an exempt advanced therapy medicinal product meets equivalent standards of quality and safety to those laid down in the Blood Quality and Safety Regulations 2005.

6   Where the holder of a manufacturer's licence distributes by way of wholesale dealing any exempt advanced therapy medicinal product manufactured or assembled pursuant to the licence that person must comply with:

(a) the requirements of paragraphs 15, 16, 18 and 19; and

(b) the guidelines on good distribution practice published by the European Commission in accordance with Article 84 of the 2001 Directive.

7   The licence holder must, at the written request of the licensing authority, set up a risk management system designed to identify, characterise, prevent or minimise risks related to the exempt advanced therapy medicinal product.

8   The licence holder must establish and maintain a system ensuring that the exempt advanced therapy medicinal product and its starting and raw materials, including all substances coming into contact with the cells or tissues that it may contain, can be traced through the sourcing, manufacturing, packaging, storage, transport and delivery to the establishment where the product is used.

9   The licence holder must, subject to paragraph 27 of Schedule 4, keep the data referred to in paragraph 8 for a minimum of 30 years after the expiry date of the exempt advanced therapy medicinal product.

10   The licence holder must secure that the data referred to in paragraph 8 will, in the event that:

(a) the licence is suspended, revoked or withdrawn; or

(b) the licence holder becomes bankrupt or insolvent.

11   The licence holder must, where an exempt advanced therapy medicinal product contains human cells or tissues, ensure that the traceability system established in accordance with paragraph 8 is complementary to and compatible with the requirements imposed pursuant to:

(a) as regards gametes and embryos, Sections 12(3), and 33A to 33D of, and paragraph 1 of Schedule 3A to, the Human Fertilisation and Embryology Act 1990;

(b) as regards blood cells, Regulations 8, 9(e) and 14 of the Blood Safety and Quality Regulations 2005; and

    (c) as regards other cells and tissues, Regulations 13 and 16 of, and paragraph 1 of Schedule 2 to, the Human Tissue (Quality and Safety for Human Application) Regulations 2007.

12   The licence holder must not import or export any exempt advanced therapy medicinal product.

Schedule 7 Qualified Persons

PART 1 Qualification requirements for qualified person

1   A person must satisfy the requirements in paragraphs 2 and 8 or, alternatively, the requirements in paragraphs 7 and 8, of this Schedule before acting as a qualified person (but this is subject to Part 2).

2   The person must have a degree, diploma or other formal qualification that satisfies the requirements of this Part, in one of the following subjects:

    (a) pharmacy;

    (b) medicine;

    (c) veterinary medicine;

    (d) chemistry;

    (e) pharmaceutical chemistry and technology; or

    (f) biology,

3   A qualification satisfies the requirements of this Part if it is awarded on completion of a university course of study, or a course recognised as equivalent by the licensing authority, which:

    (a) satisfies the minimum requirements specified in paragraph 4; and

    (b) extends over a period of at least four years of theoretical and practical study of a subject specified in paragraph 2 (but this is subject to paragraphs 5 and 6).

4 (1) A course should include at least the following core subjects:

    (a) experimental physics;

    (b) general and inorganic chemistry;

    (c) organic chemistry;

    (d) analytical chemistry;

    (e) pharmaceutical chemistry, including analysis of medicinal products;

    (f) general and applied medical biochemistry;

    (g) physiology;

    (h) microbiology;

    (i) pharmacology;

    (j) pharmaceutical technology;

    (k) toxicology; and

    (l) pharmacognosy.

(2) The subjects mentioned in sub-paragraph (1) should be balanced in such a way as to enable the person to fulfil the obligations specified in Part 3 of this Schedule.

5   If the course referred to in paragraph 3 is followed by a period of theoretical and practical training of at least one year, including a training period of at least six months in a pharmacy open to the public and a final examination at university level, the minimum duration of the course is three and a half years.

6   If two university courses, or courses recognised as of university equivalent standard, coexist, one of which extends over four years and the other over three years, the three-year course is to be treated as fulfilling the condition as to the duration of the course in paragraph 3, provided that the licensing authority recognises the formal qualifications gained from each course as being equivalent.

7   If the person's formal qualifications do not satisfy the requirements of this Part, the person may act as a qualified person if the licensing authority is satisfied, on the production of evidence, that the person has adequate knowledge of the subjects specified in paragraph 4(1).

8   (1) The person must (subject to sub-paragraph (2)) have at least two years' practical experience in an undertaking authorised to manufacture medicinal products of:

    (a) qualitative analysis of medicinal products;

    (b) quantitative analysis of active substances; and

    (c) the testing and checking necessary to ensure the quality of medicinal products.

    (2) But:

    (a) if the person has completed a university course lasting at least five years, the minimum period of practical experience under this paragraph is one year; and

    (b) if the person has completed a university course lasting at least six years, the minimum period of practical experience under this paragraph is six months.

PART 2 Qualified persons with long experience

9   (1) This paragraph applies to a person who has acted as a qualified person since the coming into force of Directive 75/319/EEC of 20 May 1975 on the approximation of provisions laid down by law, regulation or administrative action relating to proprietary medicinal products[1].

---

[1] OJ No L 147, 9.6.1975, p. 13, no longer in force.

(2) A person to whom this paragraph applies may continue to act as a qualified person.

10 (1) This paragraph applies to a person who:

(a) holds a degree, diploma or other formal qualification in a scientific discipline awarded on completion of a university course or course recognised as equivalent; and

(b) began the course before 21 May 1975.

(2) A person to whom this paragraph applies may act as a qualified person provided that sub-paragraph (3) (and, where applicable, paragraph 11) is satisfied.

(3) This sub-paragraph is satisfied if, for at least two years before 21 May 1985, the person has carried out one of the following activities in an undertaking authorised to manufacture medicinal products:

(a) production supervision;

(b) qualitative and quantitative analysis of active substances; or

(c) testing and checking, under the direct supervision of the qualified person in respect of the undertaking, to ensure the quality of the medicinal products.

11 If a person to whom paragraph 10 applies acquired the practical experience mentioned in paragraph 10(3) before 21 May 1965, the person must complete a further one year's practical experience of the kind specified in that paragraph immediately before the person may act as a qualified person.

PART 3 Obligations of qualified person

12 In Great Britain, the qualified person is responsible for securing:

(1) (a) that each batch of medicinal products manufactured in the Great Britain, the qualified person has been manufactured and checked in accordance with these Regulations and the requirements of the UK marketing authorisation, certificate of registration or traditional herbal registration or an equivalent authorisation relating to those products; and

(b) in the case of medicinal products imported from a country other than Northern Ireland or a country other than approved country for import, irrespective of whether the products have been manufactured in the United Kingdom or an approved country for import, that each batch has undergone:

(i) a full qualitative analysis;

(ii) a quantitative analysis of all the active substances; and

(iii) all other tests or checks necessary to ensure the quality of medicinal products in accordance with the requirements of the UK marketing authorisation, certificate of registration or traditional herbal registration, or an equivalent authorisation, relating to those products; and

(c) in the case of medicinal products, other than radiopharmaceuticals, that are required to bear safety features pursuant to Article 54a of the 2001 Directive and not intended to be exported to a third country, that the features specified in paragraph 18A of schedule 24 have been affixed on the packaging.

(2) In this paragraph "equivalent authorisation" means, in respect of a medicinal product that does not have a UK marketing authorisation, certificate of registration or traditional herbal registration, such equivalent authorisation or registration granted by an appropriate authority for the licensing of medicinal products in an approved country for import.

12A (1) In Northern Ireland, the qualified person is responsible for securing:

(a) that each batch of medicinal products manufactured in Northern Ireland has been manufactured and checked in accordance with these Regulations and the requirements of the marketing authorisation, Article 126a authorisation, certificate of registration or traditional herbal registration relating to those products; and

(b) in the case of medicinal products imported from a country other than an EEA State, irrespective of whether the products have been manufactured in Northern Ireland or an EEA State, that each batch has undergone:

(i) a full qualitative analysis;

(ii) a quantitative analysis of all the active substances; and

(iii) all other tests or checks necessary to ensure the quality of medicinal products in accordance with the requirements of the marketing authorisation, Article 126a authorisation, certificate of registration or traditional herbal registration relating to those products; and

(c) in the case of medicinal products, other than radiopharmaceuticals, that are required to bear safety features pursuant to Article 54a of the 2001 Directive and not intended to be exported to a country other than an EEA State, that the features specified in paragraph 18A of Schedule 24 have been affixed on the packaging.

(2) This paragraph does not apply in relation to listed NIMAR products in Northern Ireland.

13 (1) This paragraph applies in Northern Ireland where:

(a) a medicinal product that has undergone the controls referred to in paragraph 12A in a member State is imported to Northern Ireland; and

(b) each batch of the product is accompanied by control reports signed by another qualified person in respect of the medicinal product.

(2) Where this paragraph applies, the qualified person is not responsible for carrying out the controls referred to in paragraph 12A.

14 (1) This paragraph applies where:

   (a) medicinal products are imported into Great Britain from a country other than an approved country for import or into Northern Ireland, from a country other than an EEA State; and

   (b) appropriate arrangements have been made, in the case of a product for sale or supply in Great Britain by the licensing authority with the country from which those products are imported and, in the case of a product for sale or supply in Northern Ireland by the European Union with that country, to ensure that:

     (i) the manufacturer of the medicinal products applies standards of good manufacturing practice at least equivalent to those laid down:

       (aa) in the case of a product for sale or supply in Great Britain, in the Good Manufacturing Practice Directive, as supplemented by the guidelines and principles which apply under, or by virtue of, Regulation C17; and

       (bb) in the case of a product for sale or supply in Northern Ireland, by the European Union;

     (ii) the controls referred to in paragraph 12(b) or 12A(b) (as appropriate) have been carried out in that country.

(2) Where this paragraph applies, the qualified person is not responsible for carrying out the controls referred to in paragraph 12 or 12A.

(3) The licensing authority must publish a list of the countries with which it has made appropriate arrangements under sub-paragraph (1)(b) ("approved country for batch testing list").

(4) A country may be included in the approved country for batch testing list subject to any condition or restriction that the licensing authority considers appropriate, including as to categories of medicinal product, and any such condition or restriction must be included in the list.

(5) In order to satisfy itself of the matters specified in sub-paragraphs (1)(b)(i) and (ii), the licensing authority may, in particular, take into account:

   (a) the country's rules for good manufacturing practice;

   (b) the regularity of inspections to verify compliance with good manufacturing practice;

   (c) the effectiveness of enforcement of good manufacturing practice;

   (d) the regularity and rapidity of information provided by that country relating to non-compliant manufacturers;

   (e) any on-site review of that country's regulatory system undertaken by the licensing authority;

   (f) any on-site inspection of a manufacturing site in that country observed by the licensing authority;

   (g) any other relevant documentation available to the licensing authority.

(6) The licensing authority must:
- (a) review any appropriate arrangements it has made under sub-paragraph (1)(b) to determine if that country still satisfies the requirements of sub-paragraphs (1)(b)(i) and (ii), and whether any condition or restriction in those arrangements remains appropriate;
- (b) if it is not so satisfied, remove that country from the approved country for batch testing list or, as the case may be, amend or remove that condition or restriction; and
- (c) undertake such a review at least every three years beginning with the date on which the country is included in that list.

15 (1) The qualified person is responsible for ensuring, in relation to a medicinal product, that documentary evidence is produced that each batch of the product satisfies the requirements of paragraph 12.

(2) The documentary evidence referred to in sub-paragraph (1) must be kept up to date and must be available for inspection by the licensing authority for a period of at least five years.

Prescribed Conditions for Manufacturer's Undertakings for Imported Products

Accompanying material

50 (1) An applicant for the grant of a UK marketing authorisation for a relevant medicinal product must provide:

(1A) An applicant for the grant of a UK marketing authorisation for a relevant medicinal product must provide:
- (a) in the case of an application under the unfettered access route:
  - (i) the material specified in Schedule 8C; and
  - (ii) any material specified in Schedule 8 which is not included in the material specified in Schedule 8C; and
- (b) in all other cases, the material specified in Schedule 8, in relation to the product.

(2) An applicant for the grant of a UK marketing authorisation or parallel import licence for a radionuclide generator must, in addition, provide:
- (a) a general description of the system together with a detailed description of the components of the system which may affect the composition or quality of the daughter nucleide preparation; and
- (b) qualitative and quantitative particulars of the eluate or the sublimate.

(3) The applicant must also, if requested by the licensing authority to do so, provide the licensing authority with material or information that the licensing authority reasonably considers necessary for dealing with the application.

(3A) Paragraph (4) does not apply in respect of an application under the unfettered access route.

(4) If any of the medicinal products to which the application for a UK marketing authorisation relates:

(a) in the case of a UKMA(NI) or a UKMA(UK), is liable to be imported from a country other than an EEA State; or

(b) in the case of a UKMA(GB), is liable to be imported,

the material or information referred to in paragraph (3) may include an undertaking from the manufacturer of the product to comply with the matters set out in Schedule 9.

(5) Material that is submitted under this regulation for the purposes of a UK marketing authorisation must be submitted in accordance with the applicable provisions of Annex I to the 2001 Directive.

(5A) The Secretary of State may by regulations in respect of Great Britain amend Schedule 8B (modifications of Annex I) in relation to a UK MA(GB) for the purpose of further modifying Annex I to the 2001 Directive in order to take account of scientific and technical progress. The Ministers may by regulations amend Schedule 8B (modifications of Annex I) for the purpose of further modifying Annex I to the 2001 Directive in order to take account of scientific and technical progress.

(5B) The licensing authority may publish, for the purposes of applications made pursuant to this regulation:

(a) guidance on the presentation and content of the material specified in Schedule 8;

(b) scientific guidelines relating to the quality, safety and efficacy of medicinal products; and

(c) guidelines describing the active substance manufacturing process and process controls.

(5C) Unless replaced by guidance or guidelines published under the power conferred by paragraph (5B), the following guidance and guidelines continue to apply as they applied immediately before exit day IP completion day (subject to any amendments or variations published under that paragraph):

(a) the guidance published by the European Commission in the rules governing medicinal products in the European Community, Volume 2B, Notice to Applicants, Medicinal Products for human use, Presentation and content of the dossier, Common Technical Document;

(b) the scientific guidelines relating to the quality, safety and efficacy of medicinal products as adopted by the Committee for Medicinal Products for Human Use and published by the EMA and the other pharmaceutical Community guidelines published by the European Commission in the different volumes of the rules governing medicinal products in the European Community; and

(c) guidelines published by the EMA for the purposes of paragraph 3.2.1.2 of Part I of Annex I to the 2001 Directive.

(6) Unless the application is for a parallel import licence this regulation is subject to:

(a) Regulation 50A (requirement for certain applications to include results of paediatric investigation plan);

(b) Regulation 50E (application for paediatric use marketing authorisation);

(c) Regulation 50F (other applications including paediatric indications);

(d) Regulation 50G (applications relating to orphan medicinal products);

(e) Regulation 50H (applications relating to advanced therapy medicinal products);

(f) Regulation 50I (applications relating to conditional marketing authorisations);

(g) Regulation 50J (applications relating to medicinal products containing or consisting of genetically modified organisms);]

(a) Regulation 51 (application for UKMA(NI) relating to generic medicinal products)

  (aa) Regulation 51A (application for UKMA(GB) relating to generic medicinal products);

  (ab) Regulation 51B (application for UKMA(UK) relating to generic medicinal products);

  Regulation 51 (applications relating to generic medicinal products);

(b) Regulation 52 (application for UKMA(NI) relating to certain medicinal products that do not qualify as generic, etc.)

  (ba) Regulation 52A (application for UKMA(GB) relating to certain medicinal products that do not qualify as generic, etc.);

  (bb) Regulation 52B (application for UKMA(UK) relating to certain medicinal products that do not qualify as generic, etc.);

  Regulation 52 (applications relating to certain medicinal products that do not qualify as generic, etc.);

(c) Regulation 53 (application for UKMA(NI) relating to similar biological medicinal products)

  (ca) Regulation 53A (application for UKMA(GB) relating to similar biological medicinal products);

  (cb) Regulation 53B (application for UKMA(UK) relating to similar biological medicinal products);

  Regulation 53 (applications relating to certain biological medicinal products);

(d) Regulation 54 (applications relating to products in well-established medicinal use);

(e) Regulation 55 (applications relating to new combinations of active substances);

(f) Regulation 56 (applications containing information supplied in relation to another medicinal product with consent); and

(g) Schedule 10 (applications relating to national homoeopathic products).

(7) The licensing authority may make appropriate arrangements with any EEA State or the EMA in order to obtain the information it considers necessary to satisfy itself that a product to be imported under a parallel import licence is essentially similar to a product that has been granted a UK marketing authorisation.

(8) If the licensing authority makes arrangements under paragraph (7), it must publish a list of the EEA States or the organisation with which it has made such arrangements.

Schedule 9 Undertakings by Non-EEA Manufacturers

1 The manufacturer must provide and maintain such staff, premises and plant as are necessary for the carrying out in accordance with the UK marketing authorisation of such stages of the manufacture and assembly of the medicinal products to which the authorisation relates as are undertaken by the manufacturer.

2 The manufacturer must provide and maintain such staff, premises, equipment and facilities for the handling, storage and distribution of the medicinal products to which the UK marketing authorisation relates and which the manufacturer handles, stores or distributes as necessary to avoid deterioration of the medicinal products.

3 The manufacturer must provide and maintain a designated quality control department having authority in relation to quality control and being independent of all other departments.

4 The manufacturer must conduct all manufacture and assembly operations in such a way as to ensure that the medicinal products to which the UK marketing authorisation relates conform with the standards of strength, quality and purity applicable to them under the UK marketing authorisation.

5 The manufacturer must maintain an effective pharmaceutical quality assurance system involving the active participation of the management and personnel of the different services involved.

6 Where animals are used in the production of any medicinal product and the UK marketing authorisation contains provisions relating to them, the manufacturer must arrange for the animals to be housed in premises of such a nature and to be managed in such a way as will facilitate compliance with such provisions.

7   The manufacturer must make such adequate and suitable arrangements as are necessary for carrying, out in accordance with the UK marketing authorisation, any tests of the strength, quality or purity of the medicinal products to which the UK marketing authorisation relates.

8   The manufacturer must inform the holder of the UK marketing authorisation of any material alteration in the premises or plant used in connection with the manufacture or assembly of the medicinal products to which the UK marketing authorisation relates or in the operations for which such premises or plant are so used, and of any change since the granting of the relevant UK marketing authorisation in respect of any person:

   (a) responsible for supervising the production operations;
   (b) responsible for quality control of the medicinal products to which the UK marketing authorisation relates;
   (c) in charge of the animals from which are derived any substance used in the production of the medicinal products to which the UK marketing authorisation relates; or
   (d) responsible for the culture of any living tissues used in the manufacture of the medicinal products to which the UK marketing authorisation relates.

9   (1) The manufacturer shall keep readily available for inspection by a person authorised by the licensing authority durable records of:

   (a) the details of manufacture and assembly of each batch of the medicinal product to which the UK marketing authorisation relates; and
   (b) the tests carried out on the product, in such a form that the records will be easily identifiable from the number of the batch, as shown on each container in which the medicinal product is exported from the country where it has been manufactured or assembled.

   (2) The manufacturer shall permit the person authorised to take copies of or make extracts from such records.

   (3) Such records shall not be destroyed for a period of five years from the date of release of the batch concerned, or one year after the expiry date of the batch, whichever is the later.

10 The manufacturer must keep readily available for examination by a person authorised by the licensing authority samples of:

   (a) each batch of finished products for at least a period of one year after their expiry date; and
   (b) starting materials (other than solvents, gases or water) for at least a period of two years after release of the medicinal product of which those materials formed part.

11 (1) The manufacturer must implement a system for recording and reviewing complaints in relation to medicinal products to which a UK marketing authorisation relates, together with an effective system for recalling promptly and at any time the medicinal products in the distribution network.

(2) The manufacturer must record and investigate all complaints described in sub-paragraph (1) and must immediately inform the licensing authority of any defect that could result in a recall from sale, supply or export or in an abnormal restriction on such sale, supply or export.

12 The manufacturer must inform the holder of the UK marketing authorisation of any material change since the day upon which the authorisation was granted in respect of:

(a) the facilities and equipment available at each of the premises of the manufacturer for carrying out any stage of the manufacture or assembly of the medicinal products to which the UK marketing authorisation relates;

(b) the facilities and equipment available at each of the premises of the manufacturer for the storage of the medicinal products to which the UK marketing authorisation relates on, and the distribution of the products from or between, such premises;

(c) any manufacturing operations, not being operations in relation to the medicinal products to which the UK marketing authorisation relates, which are carried on by the manufacturer on or near any of the premises on which medicinal products to which the UK marketing authorisation relates are manufactured or assembled, and the substances or articles in respect of which such operations are carried on;

(d) the arrangements for the identification and storage of materials and ingredients before and during manufacture or assembly of the medicinal products to which the UK marketing authorisation relates and the arrangements for the storage of the products after they have been manufactured or assembled;

(e) the arrangements for ensuring a satisfactory turnover of stocks of medicinal products to which the UK marketing authorisation relates;

(f) the arrangements for maintaining production records and records of analytical and other testing procedures applied in the course of manufacture or assembly of the medicinal products to which the UK marketing authorisation relates; or

(g) the arrangements for keeping reference samples of materials used in the manufacture of the medicinal products to which the UK marketing authorisation relates and reference samples of the medicinal products themselves.

Medicines for Human Use (Clinical Trials) Regulations 2004 [SI 2004 No. 1031]

> **Editor's note** These extracts from the Medicines for Human Use (Clinical Trials) Regulations 2004 [SI 2004 No. 1031] as amended are presented for the reader's convenience. Reproduction is with the permission of HMSO and the Queen's Printer for Scotland. For any definitive information reference must be made to the original Regulations.
>
> The numbering and content within this section corresponds with the regulations set out in the published Statutory Instrument [SI 2004 No. 1031].

Citation and Commencement

1 These Regulations may be cited as the Medicines for Human Use (Clinical Trials) Regulations 2004 and shall come into force on 1 May 2004.

2 Interpretation

 (1) In these Regulations:

 "the 2012 Regulations" means the Human Medicines Regulations 2012;

 "the Act" means the Medicines Act 1968;

 "adult" means a person who has attained the age of 16 years;

 "adverse event" means any untoward medical occurrence in a subject to whom a medicinal product has been administered, including occurrences that are not necessarily caused by or related to that product;

 "adverse reaction" means any untoward and unintended response in a subject to an investigational medicinal product which is related to any dose administered to that subject;

 "assemble", in relation to an investigational medicinal product, means:

 (a) enclosing the product (with or without other medicinal products of the same description) in a container which is labelled before the product is sold or supplied, or used in a clinical trial; or

 (b) where the product (with or without other medicinal products of the same description) is already contained in the container in which it is to be sold or supplied, or used in a clinical trial, labelling the container before the product is sold or supplied, or used in a clinical trial, in that container;

 and "assembly" has a corresponding meaning;

"business", except in Schedule 2, includes a professional practice and includes any activity carried on by a body of persons, whether corporate or unincorporated;

"clinical trial" means any investigation in human subjects, other than a non-interventional trial, intended:

(a) to discover or verify the clinical, pharmacological or other pharmacodynamic effects of one or more medicinal products;

(b) to identify any adverse reactions to one or more such products; or

(c) to study absorption, distribution, metabolism and excretion of one or more such products;

with the object of ascertaining the safety or efficacy of those products;

"Commission Directive 2003/94/EC" means Commission Directive 2003/94/EC laying down the principles and guidelines of good manufacturing practice for medicinal products for human use and for investigational medicinal products for human use;

"Commission Directive 2003/94/EC", other than in Parts 2 and 3 of Schedule 7, means:

(a) in the case of an investigational medicinal product manufactured or assembled in, or imported into, Great Britain:

   (i) Commission Directive 2003/94/EC laying down the principles and guidelines of good manufacturing practice for medicinal products for human use and for investigational medicinal products for human use, as modified by Schedule 2A to the 2012 Regulations; or

   (ii) if Regulations have been made under the powers in regulation B17(1) of the 2012 Regulations, and have come into force, those Regulations;

(b) in the case of an investigational medicinal product manufactured or assembled in, or imported into, Northern Ireland, Commission Directive 2003/94/EC laying down the principles and guidelines of good manufacturing practice for medicinal products for human use and for investigational medicinal products for human use;

"conducting a clinical trial" includes:

(a) administering, or giving directions for the administration of, an investigational medicinal product to a subject for the purposes of that trial;

(b) giving a prescription for an investigational medicinal product for the purposes of that trial;

(c) carrying out any other medical or nursing procedure in relation to that trial; and

(d) carrying out any test or analysis:

   (i) to discover or verify the clinical, pharmacological or other pharmacodynamic effects of the investigational medicinal products administered in the course of the trial;

(ii) to identify any adverse reactions to those products; or

(iii) to study absorption, distribution, metabolism and excretion of those products;

but does not include any activity, undertaken prior to the commencement of the trial, that consists of making such preparations for the trial as are necessary or expedient;

"container", in relation to an investigational medicinal product, means the bottle, jar, box, packet or other receptacle that contains or is to contain it, not being a capsule, cachet or other article in which the product is or is to be administered, and where any such receptacle is or is to be contained in another such receptacle, includes the former but does not include the latter receptacle;

"the Directive" means Directive 2001/20/EC of the European Parliament and of the Council on the approximation of the laws, regulations and administrative provisions of the Member States relating to the implementation of good clinical practice in the conduct of clinical trials on medicinal products for human use;

"Directive 2001/83/EC" means Directive 2001/83/EC of the European Parliament and of the Council on the Community code relating to medicinal products for human use;

"the European Medicines Agency" means the European Medicines Agency established by Regulation (EC) No 726/2004 of the European Parliament and of the Council laying down Community procedures for the authorisation and supervision of medicinal products for human and veterinary use and establishing a European Medicines Agency;

"export" means export to another country from the UK, whether by land, sea or air;

"the GCP Directive" means Commission Directive 2005/28/EC laying down principles and detailed guidelines for good clinical practice as regards investigational medicinal products for human use, as well as the requirements for authorisation of the manufacturing or importation of such products;

"Health and Social Services Board" means a Health and Social Services Board established under the Health and Personal Social Services (Northern Ireland) Order 1972;

"Health Board" means a Health Board established under the National Health Service (Scotland) Act 1978;

"healthcare" means services for or in connection with the prevention, diagnosis or treatment of illness;

"healthcare professional" means:

(a) a doctor,

(b) a dentist,

(c) a nurse,

(d) a pharmacist,

(e) a person registered in the register of optometrists maintained under section 7(a) of [the Opticians Act 1989, or in the register of visiting optometrists from relevant European States maintained under section 8B(1)(a) of that Act];

(f) a person registered in a register established and maintained under article 5 of Health and Social Work Professions Order 2001, other than a social worker registered in Part 16 Health Professions Order 2001;

(g) a registered osteopath as defined by Section 41 of the Osteopaths Act 1993; or

(h) a registered chiropractor as defined by Section 43 of the Chiropractors Act 1994;

"health centre" means a health centre maintained under Section 2 or 3 of the National Health Service Act 1977, Section 36 of the National Health Service (Scotland) Act 1978 or Article 5 of the Health and Personal Social Services (Northern Ireland) Order 1972;

"health service body" means:

(a) a Health Board or Health and Social Services Board;

(b) a Special Health Authority [clinical commissioning group] or Local Health Board established under the National Health Service Act 1977;

(ba) the National Health Service Commissioning Board;

(c) a Special Health Board established under the National Health Service (Scotland) Act 1978;

(ca) Healthcare Improvement Scotland established under the National Health Service (Scotland) Act 1978;

(d) a special health and social services agency established under the Health and Personal Social Services (Special Agencies) (Northern Ireland) Order 1990;

(e) the Dental Practice Board constituted under section 37(1) of the National Health Service Act 1977;

(f) the Scottish Dental Practice Board or the Common Services Agency for the Scottish Health Service established under the National Health Service (Scotland) Act 1978;

(g) the Northern Ireland Central Services Agency for the Health and Social Services established under the Health and Personal Social Services (Northern Ireland) Order 1972;

(h) a National Health Service trust established under the National Health Service and Community Care Act 1990 or the National Health Service (Scotland) Act 1978;

(i) an NHS foundation trust within the meaning of Section 1(1) of the Health and Social Care (Community Health and Standards) Act 2003; or

(j) a Health and Social Services trust established under the Health and Personal Social Services (Northern Ireland) Order 1991;

"hospital" includes a clinic, nursing home or similar institution;

"import", except in regulation 13 and Schedule 13, means import, or attempt to import:

(a) into Great Britain other than from Northern Ireland; or

(b) into Northern Ireland from a country other than an EEA State;

whether by land, sea or air and "imported" is to be construed accordingly;

"investigational medicinal product" means a pharmaceutical form of an active substance or placebo being tested, or to be tested, or used, or to be used, as a reference in a clinical trial, and includes a medicinal product that has a marketing authorisation but is, for the purposes of the trial:

(a) used or assembled (formulated or packaged) in a way different from the form of the product authorised under the authorisation;

(b) used for an indication not included in the summary of product characteristics under the authorisation for that product; or

(c) used to gain further information about the form of that product as authorised under the authorisation;

"investigational medicinal product dossier" means, in relation to an investigational medicinal product, the dossier relating to that product that accompanies a request for authorisation to conduct a trial in which that product is or is to be used, in accordance with paragraph 11 of Schedule 3;

"investigator" means, in relation to a clinical trial, the authorised health professional responsible for the conduct of that trial at a trial site and, if the trial is conducted by a team of authorised health professionals at a trial site, the investigator is the leader responsible for that team;

"investigator's brochure" means a document containing a summary of the clinical and non-clinical data relating to an investigational medicinal product that is relevant to the study of the product in human subjects;

"labelling", in relation to an investigational medicinal product, means affixing to or otherwise displaying on it a notice describing or otherwise relating to the contents, and "label" has a corresponding meaning;

"licensing authority" shall be construed in accordance with Regulation 6 of the 2012 Regulations;

"manufacture", in relation to an investigational medicinal product, includes any process carried out in the course of making the product, but does not include dissolving or dispersing the product in, or diluting it or mixing it with, some other substance used as a vehicle for the purposes of administering it;

"manufacturing authorisation" has the meaning given by regulation 36(1);

"marketing authorisation" means:

(a) a UK marketing authorisation;
(b) an EU marketing authorisation (as defined in the 2012 Regulations); or
(c) an authorisation granted by a regulatory body responsible for licensing medicinal products in a country that is included in the list referred to in regulation 2A(1);

"medicinal product" means a medicinal product within the meaning of Regulation 2(1) of the 2012 Regulations;

"non-interventional trial" means a study of one or more medicinal products that have a marketing authorisation, where the following conditions are met:

(a) the products are prescribed in the usual manner in accordance with the terms of that authorisation;
(b) the assignment of any patient involved in the study to a particular therapeutic strategy is not decided in advance by a protocol but falls within current practice;
(c) the decision to prescribe a particular medicinal product is clearly separated from the decision to include the patient in the study;
(d) no diagnostic or monitoring procedures are applied to the patients included in the study, other than those that are ordinarily applied in the course of the particular therapeutic strategy in question; and
(e) epidemiological methods are to be used for the analysis of the data arising from the study;

"pharmaceutical form of an active substance" includes any substance or article to which these Regulations have effect by virtue of an order under Section 104 or 105 of the Act (which relates to the application of Act to certain articles and substances that are not medicinal products);

"Pharmaceutical Society" in relation to Great Britain means the Royal Pharmaceutical Society of Great Britain, and in relation to Northern Ireland means the Pharmaceutical Society of Northern Ireland;

"the principles and guidelines of good manufacturing practice" means the principles and guidelines of good manufacturing practice set out in Commission Directive 2003/94/EC;

"protocol" means a document that describes the objectives, design, methodology, statistical considerations and organisation of a clinical trial;

"qualified person" means:

(a) a person who as respects qualifications and experience satisfies the requirements of Article 49 or 50 of Directive 2001/83/EC; or

(b) a person who, without satisfying the requirements referred to in paragraph (a):

   (i)   has been engaged in activities equivalent to those to be performed in accordance with Regulation 43(2) in respect of investigational medicinal products for a period of at least six months prior to 1 May 2004;

   (ii)   has, in accordance with paragraph 6(1) of Schedule 6, been named as a qualified person in a valid application for a manufacturing authorisation made prior to 1 May 2006; and

   (iii) is:

      (aa) a member of the Institute of Biology, the Pharmaceutical Society, the Royal Society of Chemistry or such other body as may appear to the licensing authority to be an appropriate body for the purpose of this paragraph; or

      (bb) the holder of a diploma, certificate or other evidence of formal qualifications awarded on completion of a university or other higher education course of study in pharmacy, chemistry, medicine, biology or a related life science, which the licensing authority have stated in a notice in writing to that person to be qualifications sufficient for the purpose of performing the functions of a qualified person;

"sponsor" shall be construed in accordance with Regulation 3;

"subject" means, in relation to a clinical trial, an individual, whether a patient or not, who participates in a clinical trial:

(a) as a recipient of an investigational medicinal product or of some other treatment or product; or

(b) without receiving any treatment or product, as a control;

"third country" means a country or territory outside the European Economic Area;

"trial site" means a hospital, health centre, surgery or other establishment or facility at or from which a clinical trial, or any part of such a trial, is conducted;

"UK marketing authorisation" means:

(a) has the same meaning as "UK marketing authorisation" in the 2012 Regulations (and references to "UKMA(UK)", "UKMA(GB)" and "UKMA(NI)" in these Regulations should be construed in accordance with that definition); and

(b) includes a product licence granted by the licensing authority for the purposes of Section 7 of the Medicines Act 1968;

"unexpected adverse reaction" means an adverse reaction, the nature and severity of which is not consistent with the information about the medicinal product in question set out:

(a) in the case of a product with a marketing authorisation, in the summary of product characteristics (or equivalent document) for that product,

(b) in the case of any other investigational medicinal product, in the investigator's brochure relating to the trial in question.

(2) Any reference in these Regulations to the holder of a manufacturing authorisation shall be construed as a reference to the holder of such an authorisation which is for the time being in force.

(3) Any reference in these Regulations to an application, request or other document that is signed includes a reference to an application, request of other document that is signed with an electronic signature.

13 Supply of investigational medicinal products for the purpose of clinical trials

(1) Subject to paragraphs (3) and (4), no person shall, in the course of a business carried on by him, sell or supply any investigational medicinal product to:

(a) an investigator;

(b) a healthcare professional who is a member of an investigator's team;

(c) a person who provides or is to provide healthcare under the direction or control of a person referred to in sub-paragraphs (a) and (b); or

(d) a subject;

for the purpose of administering that product in a clinical trial, unless the conditions specified in paragraph (2) are satisfied.

(2) The conditions referred to in paragraph (1) are:

(a) the licensing authority has authorised the clinical trial for the purposes of which the product is sold or supplied;

(b) in the case of:

(i) an investigational medicinal product manufactured or assembled in the United Kingdom, the product has been manufactured or assembled:

(aa) in accordance with the terms of a manufacturing authorisation, or

(bb) in the case of assembly only, under the exemption in regulation 37;

(ii) an investigational medicinal product imported into Northern Ireland from an EEA State:

(aa) the product has been manufactured, assembled or imported into an EEA State in accordance with the terms of an authorisation referred to in Article 13 of the Directive granted by a competent authority of an EEA State, and

(bb) the production batch of investigational medicinal products of which the product is a part has been checked and certified by a qualified person pursuant to Article 13(3) and (4) of the Directive;

(iii) an investigational medicinal product imported into Northern Ireland from a country other than an EEA State, the product has been imported into Northern Ireland in accordance with the terms of a manufacturing authorisation;

(iv) an investigational medicinal product imported into Great Britain other than from Northern Ireland, the product has been imported in accordance with the terms of a manufacturing authorisation.

(2A) The condition specified in paragraph (2)(b) does not apply to an investigational medicinal product that has been manufactured or assembled in accordance with the terms of a marketing authorisation or marketing authorisation issued by the competent authority of an EEA State in accordance with Directive 2001/83/EC relating to that product.

(3) ....

(4) The restriction in paragraph (1) shall not apply to:

(a) the sale or supply of a medicinal product in Great Britain in accordance with the terms of a UKMA(GB) or UKMA(UK); and

(b) the sale or supply of a medicinal product in Northern Ireland in accordance with:

(i) the terms of a UKMA(NI) or UKMA(UK); or

(ii) an EU marketing authorisation (as defined in the 2012 Regulations).

Part 6 Manufacture and Importation of Investigational Medicinal Products

36 Requirement for authorisation to manufacture or import investigational medicinal products

(1) Subject to paragraph (2) and Regulation 37, no person shall manufacture, assemble or import any investigational medicinal product except in accordance with an authorisation granted by the licensing authority for the purposes of this regulation ("a manufacturing authorisation").

(2) The restriction in paragraph (1) shall not apply to the manufacture or assembly of a medicinal product to the extent that such manufacture or assembly is in accordance with the terms and conditions of a marketing authorisation or marketing authorisation issued by the competent authority of an EEA State in accordance with Directive 2001/83/EC relating to that product.

37 Exemption for hospitals and health centres

(1) The restriction imposed by regulation 36(1) shall not apply to the assembly of an investigational medicinal product where the conditions specified in paragraph (2) are satisfied.

(2) The conditions referred to in paragraph (1) are that:

(a) the assembly is carried out in:

(i) in a hospital or health centre; and

(ii) by a doctor, a pharmacist or a person acting under the supervision of a pharmacist; and

(b) the investigational medicinal products are assembled exclusively for use in:

(i) that hospital or health centre, or

(ii) any other hospital or health centre that is a trial site for the clinical trial in which the product is to be used.

42   Obligations of manufacturing authorisation holder

The holder of a manufacturing authorisation shall:

(a) comply with the principles and guidelines of good manufacturing practice;

(b) comply with the provisions referred to in regulation 40(3);

(c) allow the licensing authority access to his premises at any reasonable time; and

(d) put and keep in place arrangements that enable the qualified person to carry out their duties, including placing at their disposal all the necessary facilities.

43   Qualified persons

(1) Subject to paragraphs (4) and (5), the holder of a manufacturing authorisation must have at their disposal the services of at least one qualified person:

(a) where the manufacturing authorisation relates wholly to the import of an investigational medicinal product into Great Britain from an approved country for import, who must operate and be ordinarily resident in either the United Kingdom or an approved country for import; or

(b) in any other case, who must operate and be ordinarily resident in the United Kingdom, and who is responsible for carrying out the duties referred to in paragraph 2.

(2) Subject to paragraphs (2A) and (2C), the qualified person is responsible for ensuring that:

(a) in the case of an investigational medicinal product manufactured in Northern Ireland, each production batch has been manufactured and checked in compliance with:

(i)   the requirements of these Regulations;

(ii) the principles and guidelines of good manufacturing practice;

(iii) the product specification, as defined in Part 1 of Schedule 7; and

(iv) the request, particulars and documents submitted to the licensing authority under regulation 17 in respect of the clinical trial in which the product is to be used;

(b) in the case of an investigational medicinal product manufactured in Great Britain, each production batch has been manufactured and checked in compliance with:

(i)   the requirements of these Regulations;

(ii) the principles and guidelines of good manufacturing practice, as modified by Schedule 2A to the 2012 Regulations or any regulations made under the power in regulation B17(1) of those Regulations;

(iii) the product specification, as defined in Part 1 of Schedule 7; and

(iv) the request, particulars and documents submitted to the licensing authority under regulation 17 in respect of the clinical trial in which the product is to be used;

(c) in the case of an investigational medicinal product imported into Northern Ireland from a country other than an EEA State, each production batch has been manufactured and checked in compliance with:

(i) standards of good manufacturing practice at least equivalent to the principles and guidelines of good manufacturing practice;

(ii) the product specification, as defined in Part 1 of Schedule 7; and

(iii) the request, particulars and documents submitted to the licensing authority under regulation 17 in respect of the clinical trial in which the product is to be used;

(d) in the case of an investigational medicinal product imported into Great Britain other than from Northern Ireland, each production batch has been manufactured and checked in compliance with:

(i) standards of good manufacturing practice at least equivalent to the principles and guidelines of good manufacturing practice, as modified by Schedule 2A to the 2012 Regulations or any regulations made under the power in regulation B17(1) of those Regulations;

(ii) the product specification, as defined in Part 1 of Schedule 7; and

(iii) the request, particulars and documents submitted to the licensing authority under regulation 17 in respect of the clinical trial in which the product is to be used.

(2A) The qualified person is not responsible for carrying out the controls in paragraph (2) where:

(a) the product is imported into Great Britain from a country that is included on the list referred to in regulation 43A ("approved country for import"); and

(b) the qualified person ensures that there is appropriate evidence to confirm that each production batch has been certified as provided for in Article 13 of the Directive, or such equivalent certification procedure as applies in the approved country for import.

(2B) The licensing authority must publish guidance on the evidence that it considers to be appropriate for the purposes of paragraph (2A)(b).

(2C)   The qualified person is not responsible for carrying out the controls in paragraph (2) where:

(a) an investigational medicinal product:

(i)   that has a marketing authorisation other than a UKMA(GB), is imported into Northern Ireland as a comparator product; or

(ii) that has a marketing authorisation, or has been approved for marketing in another country, is imported into Great Britain as a comparator product; and

(b) documentation cannot be obtained certifying that each production batch has been manufactured and checked in accordance with standards of good manufacturing practice at least equivalent to those laid down in Commission Directive 2003/94/EC.

(2D)   Where paragraph (2) does not apply by virtue of paragraph (2C), the qualified person is responsible for ensuring that each production batch has undergone all relevant analyses, tests or checks necessary to confirm its quality in accordance with the request, particulars and documents submitted to the licensing authority under regulation 17.

(2E)   The qualified person is responsible for ensuring, in relation to an investigational medicinal product, that documentary evidence is produced that each batch of the product satisfies the provisions of paragraph (2), (2A) or (2D) (as the case may be).

(2F)   The documentary evidence referred to in paragraph (2E) must be:

(a) kept up to date as operations are carried out; and

(b) available for inspection by the licensing authority for a period of at least five years beginning with the date on which the documentary evidence is produced.

(3)   A qualified person shall perform his functions under these Regulations in accordance with the Code of Practice for Qualified Persons in the Pharmaceutical Industry, published jointly by the Institute of Biology, the Royal Pharmaceutical Society of Great Britain and the Royal Society of Chemistry in March 2004.

(4)   If the holder of the authorisation satisfies the requirements as to qualifications and experience specified in paragraph (a) or (b) of the definition of "qualified person" in Regulation 2(1), he may act as the qualified person in accordance with paragraph (2) for the purposes of that authorisation.

(5)   For the purposes of this paragraph, but without prejudice to paragraph (6) below, the holder of the authorisation may regard a person as satisfying the provisions of the said Article 49 or 50, as respects formal qualifications if:

(a) in relation to the obligation in paragraph (1)(a), he is already named as a qualified person in respect of an authorisation issued in an approved country for import; or

(b) he produces evidence that:
   (i) he is a member of:
      (aa) the Institute of Biology,
      (bb) the Pharmaceutical Society,
      (cc) the Royal Society of Chemistry, or
      (dd) such other body as may appear to the licensing authority to be an appropriate body for the purpose of this paragraph; and
   (ii) he is regarded by the body of which he is a member as so satisfying those provisions.

(6) Where, after giving the holder of the authorisation and the person acting as a qualified person the opportunity of making representations to them (orally or in writing), the licensing authority are of the opinion that:

(a) the person so acting does not satisfy:
   (i) the provisions of the said Articles 49 and 50 of Directive 2001/83/EC as respects qualifications and experience; or
   (ii) the requirements as to qualifications and experience specified in paragraph (b) of the definition of "qualified person" in regulation 2(1); or

(b) he is to carry out the duties referred to in paragraph (2) adequately or at all;

and have notified the holder of the authorisation accordingly in writing, the holder of the authorisation shall not permit that person to act as a qualified person.

Part 7 Labelling of Investigational Medicinal Products

46 Labelling

(1) An investigational medicinal product shall be labelled in accordance with Article 15 of Commission Directive 2003/94/EC.

(2) Paragraph (1) shall not apply where the investigational medicinal product is:

(a) for use in a clinical trial with the characteristics specified in the second paragraph of Article 14 of the Directive;

(b) dispensed to a subject in accordance with a prescription given by a healthcare professional; and

(c) labelled in accordance with the requirements of Part 13 of the 2012 Regulations that apply in relation to medicinal products sold or supplied in accordance with a prescription given by a person who is an appropriate practitioner within the meaning of regulation 214(3) to (6) of those Regulations.

SCHEDULE 7 Standard Provisions for Manufacturing Authorisations

Regulation 40(4)

Part 1 Interpretation

In this Schedule:

"Commission Directive 2003/94/EC", in relation to the holder of an authorisation means:

(a) in the case of a holder in Great Britain:

    (i) Commission Directive 2003/94/EC laying down the principles and guidelines of good manufacturing practice for medicinal products for human use and for investigational medicinal products for human use, as modified by Schedule 2A to the 2012 Regulations; or

    (ii) if Regulations have been made under the powers in regulation B17(1) of the 2012 Regulations, and have come into force, those Regulations;

(b) in the case of a holder in Northern Ireland, Commission Directive 2003/94/EC laying down the principles and guidelines of good manufacturing practice for medicinal products for human use and for investigational medicinal products for human use.

"product specification" means:

(a) in the case of an investigational medicinal product manufactured before a request for authorisation to conduct the clinical trial involving those products has been made:

    (i) in the case of an investigational medicinal product manufactured or assembled in Great Britain, in accordance with Regulation 17; or

    (ii) in the case of an investigational medicinal product manufactured or assembled in Northern Ireland, in accordance with regulation 17 or any equivalent provisions in any EEA State;

      the specification for that product provided by the person who is to act as the sponsor of the proposed clinical trial;

(b) in the case of an investigational medicinal product manufactured for the purpose of export, the specification for that product provided by the person to whose order the products are manufactured; or

(c) in any other case, the specification for an investigational medicinal product contained in the investigational medicinal product dossier for that product.

Part 2 Provisions that may be Incorporated in an Authorisation relating to the Manufacture or Assembly of Investigational Medicinal Products

1 The holder of the authorisation shall:

   (a) provide and maintain such staff, premises and plant (including technical equipment) as are necessary for the carrying out, in accordance with his authorisation and the product specification, of such stages of the manufacture and assembly of the investigational medicinal products as are undertaken by them; and

   (b) not carry out any such manufacture or assembly except at the premises specified in their manufacturing authorisation.

2 The holder of the authorisation shall:

   (a) provide and maintain such staff, premises, equipment and facilities for the handling, storage and distribution of the investigational medicinal products which he handles, stores or distributes under his authorisation as are necessary to maintain the quality of the investigational medicinal products;

   (b) not use for such purposes premises other than those specified in the authorisation or which may be approved from time to time by the licensing authority; and

   (c) ensure that any arrangements he makes with a person for the storage and distribution of the investigational medicinal products are adequate to maintain the quality of those products.

3 The holder of the authorisation shall place the quality control system referred to in Article 11(1) of Commission Directive 2003/94/EC under the authority of the person notified to the licensing authority in accordance with paragraph 6(3) of Schedule 6 as being responsible for quality control.

4 The holder of the authorisation may use a contract laboratory pursuant to Article 11(2) of Commission Directive 2003/94/EC if operated by a person approved by the licensing authority.

5 The holder of the authorisation shall provide such information as may be requested by the licensing authority for the purposes of these Regulations or the 2012 Regulations:

   (a) about the products currently being manufactured or assembled under his authorisation; and

   (b) of the operations being carried out in relation to such manufacture or assembly.

6 The holder of the authorisation shall:

   (a) inform the licensing authority before making any material alteration in the premises or plant used under their authorisation, or in the operations for which they are used; and

   (b) inform the licensing authority of any change that they propose to make in any personnel named in their authorisation as, respectively:

(i) responsible for supervising the production operations; or

(ii) responsible for quality control of the investigational medicinal products being manufactured or assembled including the person named as the qualified person for the purposes of Regulation 43 and paragraph 14.

7   The holder of the authorisation shall:

(a) keep readily available for inspection by a person authorised by the licensing authority the batch documentation referred to in Article 9(1) of Commission Directive 2003/94/EC; and

(b) permit the person authorised to take copies or make extracts from such documentation.

8   The holder of the authorisation shall keep readily available for examination by a person authorised by the licensing authority the samples of each batch of bulk formulated products referred to in Article 11(4) of Commission Directive 2003/94/EC

9   Where the holder of the authorisation has been informed by the licensing authority that any batch of any investigational medicinal product to which their authorisation relates has been found not to conform as regards strength, quality or purity with:

(a) the specification of the relevant product; or

(b) the provisions of these Regulations [or the 2012 Regulations] that are applicable to the investigational medicinal product,

they shall, if so directed, withhold such batch from distribution for use in clinical trials, so far as may be reasonably practicable, for such a period not exceeding six weeks as may be specified by the licensing authority.

10   The holder of the authorisation shall ensure that any tests for determining conformity with the standards and specifications applying to any particular product used in the manufacture shall, except so far as the conditions of the product specification for that product otherwise provide, be applied to samples taken from the investigational medicinal product after all manufacturing processes have been completed, or at such earlier stage in the manufacture as may be approved by the licensing authority.

11   Where the authorisation relates to the assembly of an investigational medicinal product, and the holder of the authorisation supplies that investigational medicinal product at such a stage of assembly that does not fully comply with the provisions of the product specification that relate to labelling, that holder of the authorisation shall communicate the particulars of those provisions to the person to whom that investigational medicinal product has been so supplied.

12   Where:

(a) the manufacturing authorisation relates to the assembly of an investigational medicinal product;

(b) that investigational medicinal product is not manufactured by the holder of the authorisation; and

(c) particulars as to the name and address of the manufacturer of, or of the person who imports, that investigational medicinal product had been given by the holder of the authorisation to the licensing authority, the holder of the authorisation shall forthwith notify the licensing authority in writing of any changes in such particulars.

13 The holder of the authorisation, for the purpose of enabling the licensing authority to ascertain whether there are any grounds:

(a) for suspending, revoking or varying any authorisation or licence granted under these Regulations [or Parts 3 to 8 of the 2012 Regulations];

(b) amending the clinical trial authorisation in accordance with regulation 23 or 24; or

(c) suspending or terminating any clinical trial in accordance with Regulation 31;

shall permit, and provide all necessary facilities to enable, any person duly authorised in writing by the licensing authority, on production if required of their credentials, to carry out such inspection or to take such samples or copies, in relation to things belonging to, or any business carried on by, the holder of the authorisation, as such person would have the right to carry out or take under the 2012 Regulations for the purpose of verifying any statement contained in an application for an authorisation or licence.

14 The holder of the authorisation shall at all times provide and maintain such staff, premises, equipment and facilities as will enable the qualified person who is at his disposal pursuant to regulation 43(1) to carry out the duties referred to in regulation 43(2).

Part 3 Provisions that may be Incorporated in an Authorisation relating to the Importation of Investigational Medicinal Products

1 The holder of the authorisation shall:

(a) provide and maintain such staff, premises, equipment and facilities for the handling, storage and distribution of the investigational medicinal products that they handle, store or distribute under their authorisation as are necessary to avoid deterioration of the investigational medicinal products;

(b) not use for such purposes premises other than those specified in the authorisation or which may be approved from time to time by the licensing authority; and

(c) ensure that any arrangements they make with a person for the storage and distribution of the investigational medicinal products are adequate to maintain the quality of those products.

2   The holder of the authorisation may use a contract laboratory pursuant to Article 11(2) of Commission Directive 2003/94/EC if operated by a person approved by the licensing authority.

3   The holder of the authorisation shall provide such information as may be requested by the licensing authority concerning the type and quantity of any investigational medicinal products that they import.

4   The holder of the authorisation shall:

(a) inform the licensing authority before making any structural alterations to, or discontinuance of the use of, premises to which their authorisation relates; and

(b) inform the licensing authority if they change the person named as the qualified person for the purposes of regulation 43 and paragraph 9.

5   The holder of the authorisation shall:

(a) keep readily available, for inspection by a person authorised by the licensing authority, the batch documentation referred to in Article 9(1) of Commission Directive 2003/94/EC; and

(b) permit the person authorised to take copies or make extracts from such documentation.

6   Where the holder of the authorisation has been informed by the licensing authority that any batch of any investigational medicinal product to which their authorisation relates has been found not to conform as regards strength, quality or purity with:

(a) the specification of the relevant product; or

(b) the provisions of these Regulations, the 2012 Regulations or any regulations under the Act that are applicable to the investigational medicinal product,

they shall, if so directed, withhold such batch from distribution for use in clinical trials, so far as may be reasonably practicable, for such a period not exceeding six weeks, as may be specified by the licensing authority.

7   If the holder of the authorisation is not the sponsor of the clinical trial for which the investigational medicinal product is manufactured or assembled, they shall comply with the provisions of the product specification that relates to the supply of that investigational medicinal product for use in the trial.

8   The holder of the authorisation, for the purpose of enabling the licensing authority to ascertain whether there are any grounds:

(a) for suspending, revoking or varying any authorisation or licence granted under these Regulations or Parts 3 to 8 of the 2012 Regulations;

(b) amending the conduct of a clinical trial in accordance with regulation 23 or 24; or

(c) suspending or terminating any clinical trial in accordance with regulation 31;

shall permit, and provide all necessary facilities to enable, any person duly authorised in writing by the licensing authority, on production if required of their credentials, to carry out such inspection or to take such samples or copies, in relation to things belonging to, or any business carried on by, the holder of the authorisation, as such person would have the right to carry out or take under the 2012 Regulations for the purpose of verifying any statement contained in an application for an authorisation or licence.

9   The holder of the authorisation shall at all times provide and maintain such staff, premises, equipment and facilities as will enable the qualified person who is at their disposal pursuant to regulation 43(1) to carry out the duties referred to in regulation 43(2).

UK Legislation on the Manufacture, Importation and Distribution of Active Substances

Contents

The Human Medicines Regulations 2012 (SI 2012/1916)

> **Editor's note** These extracts from the Human Medicines Regulations 2012 [SI 2012/1916] as amended are presented for the reader's convenience. Reproduction is with the permission of HMSO and the Queen's Printer for Scotland. For any definitive information, reference must be made to the original Regulations. The numbering and content within this section correspond with the Regulations set out in the published Statutory Instrument [SI 2012/1916] as amended.

Citation and commencement

1 (1) These Regulations may be cited as the Human Medicines Regulations 2012.

   (2) These Regulations come into force on 14th August 2012.

General interpretation

8 (1) In these Regulations (unless the context otherwise requires):

"active substance" means any substance or mixture of substances intended to be used in the manufacture of a medicinal product and that, when used in its production, becomes an active ingredient of that product intended to exert a pharmacological, immunological or metabolic action with a view to restoring, correcting or modifying physiological functions or to make a medical diagnosis;

"assemble", in relation to a medicinal product or an active substance, includes the various processes of dividing up, packaging and presentation of the product or substance, and "assembly" has a corresponding meaning;

"excipient" means any constituent of a medicinal product other than the active substance and the packaging material;

"export" means export, or attempt to export, from the United Kingdom, whether by land, sea or air;

"falsified medicinal product" means any medicinal product with a false representation of:

(a) its identity, including its packaging and labelling, its name or its composition (other than any unintentional quality defect) as regards any of its ingredients including excipients and the strength of those ingredients;

(b) its source, including its manufacturer, its country of manufacturing, its country of origin or its marketing authorisation holder; or

(c) its history, including the records and documents relating to the distribution channels used;

"import" means import, or attempt to import, into the United Kingdom, whether by land, sea or air; and "imported" is to be construed accordingly:

"the licensing authority" has the meaning given by regulation 6(2).

(8) Subject to regulation C17(6), references in these Regulations to:

(a) good manufacturing practice for active substances relate to the principles and guidelines for good manufacturing practice adopted by the European Commission under the third paragraph of Article 47[1] of the 2001 Directive;

(b) good distribution practice for active substances relate to the guidelines on good distribution practices for active substances adopted by the European Commission under the fourth paragraph of Article 47 of the 2001 Directive.

---

[1] Paragraphs 3 and 4 of Article 47 were substituted by Directive 2011/62/EU of the European Parliament and of the Council (OJ No L 174, 1.7.2011).

Interpretation

A17   In this Part "manufacture", in relation to an active substance, includes any process carried out in the course of making the substance and the various processes of dividing up, packaging, and presentation of the active substance.

Chapter 1A Good Manufacturing Practice and Good Distribution Practice

Guidelines on Good Manufacturing Practice and Good Distribution Practice

C17   (1) The licensing authority may publish in relation to the manufacture or assembly of a medicinal product in, or import to, Great Britain:

(a) detailed guidelines of good manufacturing practice in respect of medicinal products, and investigational medicinal products, referred to in Article 46(f) of the 2001 Directive, including guidelines as to the formalised risk assessment for ascertaining the appropriate good manufacturing practice for excipients;

(b) principles and guidelines of good manufacturing practice for active substances, referred to in the first paragraph of point (f) of Article 46 and in Article 46b of that Directive;

(c) principles and guidelines of good distribution practice referred to in the first paragraph of point (f) of Article 46, and Article 84, of that Directive.

(2) Guidelines or principles under paragraph (1) may replace, amend or otherwise modify any guidelines or principles published or adopted by the European Commission under the second, third, fourth or fifth paragraph of Article 47, or Article 84, of the 2001 Directive.

(3) Unless replaced by principles or guidelines published under paragraph (1), principles and guidelines published or adopted by the European Commission under the second, third, fourth or fifth paragraph of Article 47, or Article 84, of the 2001 Directive, as they applied immediately before IP completion day, continue to apply on and after IP completion day (subject to any amendments or modifications published under paragraph (1)).

(4) Before exercising the power under paragraph (1), the licensing authority must consult such persons as it considers appropriate.

(5) The licensing authority may exercise its power under paragraph (1) only if it considers that it is necessary in order to take account of technical or scientific progress.

(6) If the licensing authority publishes principles and guidelines under paragraph (1), any reference in these Regulations to any principle or guideline adopted under the provisions of the 2001 Directive

specified in those paragraphs is instead to be read as a reference to the principle or guideline published under paragraph (1), or that principle or guideline as amended or modified (as the case may be).

Criteria for importation, manufacture or distribution of active substances

45M   (1) A person may not:
    (a) import;
    (b) manufacture; or
    (c) distribute,
    an active substance unless that person is registered with the licensing authority in accordance with regulation 45N and the requirements in regulation 45O are met.

(2) Paragraph (1) applies in relation to an active substance that is to be used in an investigational medicinal product only:
    (a) if:
        (i) in the case of a product for sale or supply in Great Britain, the product has a UK marketing authorisation, certificate of registration or traditional herbal registration; or
        (ii) in the case of a product for sale or supply in Northern Ireland, the product has a marketing authorisation, Article 126a authorisation, certificate of registration or traditional herbal registration; and,
    (b) to the extent that the manufacture of the active substance is in accordance with the terms and conditions of that authorisation, certificate or registration.

(3) Paragraph (1)(a) does not apply to a person who, in connection with the importation of an active substance:
    (a) provides facilities solely for transporting the active substance; or
    (b) acting as an import agent, imports the active substance solely to the order of another person who holds a certificate of good manufacturing practice issued by the licensing authority.

Registration in relation to active substances

45N   (1) For registration in relation to active substances, the licensing authority must have received a valid registration form from the applicant for import, manufacture or, as the case may be, distribution of the active substance; and
    (a) 60 days have elapsed since receipt and the licensing authority have not notified the applicant that an inspection will be carried out; or

(b) the licensing authority:
- (i) notified the applicant within 60 days of receipt of a registration form that an inspection will be carried out; and
- (ii) within 90 days of that inspection the licensing authority have issued that person with a certificate of good manufacturing practice or, as the case may be, of good distribution practice; and

(c) that person has not instructed the licensing authority to end that person's registration.

(2) The person applying for registration under paragraph (1) must notify the licensing authority of any changes that have taken place as regards the information in the registration form:
- (a) immediately where such changes may have an impact on quality or safety of the active substances that are manufactured, imported or distributed;
- (b) in any other case, on each anniversary of the receipt of the application form by the licensing authority.

(3) For the purpose of paragraph (2), changes that are notified in accordance with that paragraph shall be treated as incorporated in the application form.

(4) Any notification to the licensing authority under paragraph (2) must be accompanied by the appropriate fee in accordance with the Fees Regulations.

(5) A registration form is valid for the purpose of paragraph (1) if:
- (a) it is provided to the licensing authority; and
- (b) is completed in the way and form specified in Schedule 7A.

(6) Paragraph (1) does not apply until 20 October 2013 in relation to a person who had, before 20 August 2013, commenced the activity for which the person would, apart from this provision, need to send a registration form to the licensing authority.

Requirements for registration as an importer, manufacturer or distributor of an active substance

450   (1) Where principles and guidelines of good manufacturing practice have been published under, or apply by virtue of, regulation C17, which apply to an active substance manufactured in Great Britain, a manufacturer in Great Britain must comply with those principles and guidelines of good manufacturing practice in relation to that active substance.

(1A) Where the Commission has adopted principles and guidelines of good manufacturing practice under the third paragraph of

Article 47[2] of the 2001 Directive, which applies to an active substance manufactured in Northern Ireland, a manufacturer in Northern Ireland must comply with those principles and guidelines of good manufacturing practice in relation to that active substance.

(2) Where principles and guidelines of good distribution practice have been published under, or apply by virtue of, regulation C17, which apply to an active substance distributed in Great Britain, a distributor in Great Britain must comply with those principles and guidelines of good distribution practice in relation to that active substance.

(2A) Where the Commission has adopted principles and guidelines of good distribution practice under the fourth paragraph of Article 47 of the 2001 Directive, which applies to an active substance distributed in the Northern Ireland, a distributor in Northern Ireland must comply with those principles and guidelines of good distribution practice in relation to that active substance.

(3) Without prejudice to regulation 37(4) (manufacture and assembly in relation to active substances) and paragraph 9A of Schedule 8 (material to accompany an application for a UK marketing authorisation in relation to an active substance), where principles and guidelines of good manufacturing practice have been published under, or apply by virtue of, regulation C17, which apply to an active substance imported into Northern Ireland and where an active substance is imported into Northern Ireland from a country other than an EEA State so imported:

(a) the importer must comply with good manufacturing practice and good distribution practice in relation to the active substance;

(b) the active substances must have been manufactured in accordance with standards that are at least equivalent to good manufacturing practice; and

(c) the active substances must be accompanied by a written confirmation from the competent authority of the exporting country of the following:

(i) the standards of manufacturing practice applicable to the plant manufacturing the exported active substance are at least equivalent to good manufacturing practice;

(ii) the manufacturing plant concerned is subject to regular, strict and transparent controls and to the effective enforcement of standards of manufacturing practice at least equivalent to good

---

[2] Article 47 was amended by Directive 2011/62/EU of the European Parliament and of the Council (OJ No L 174, 1.7.2011, p. 74).

manufacturing practice, including repeated and unannounced inspections, so as to ensure a protection of public health at least equivalent to that in Northern Ireland; and

(iii) in the event of findings relating to non-compliance, information on such findings is supplied by the exporting country to the licensing authority without any delay.

(3A) Without prejudice to regulation 37(4) (manufacture and assembly in relation to active substances) and paragraph 9A of Schedule 8 (material to accompany an application for a UK marketing authorisation in relation to an active substance), where principles and guidelines of good manufacturing practice have been published under, or apply by virtue of, regulation C17, which apply to an active substance imported into Great Britain other than from Northern Ireland and where an active substance is so imported:

(a) the importer must comply with good manufacturing practice and good distribution practice in relation to the active substance;

(b) the active substances must have been manufactured in accordance with standards that are at least equivalent to good manufacturing practice; and

(c) the active substances must be accompanied by a written confirmation from the competent authority of the exporting country of the following:

(i) the standards of manufacturing practice applicable to the plant manufacturing the exported active substance are at least equivalent to good manufacturing practice;

(ii) the manufacturing plant concerned is subject to regular, strict and transparent controls and to the effective enforcement of standards of manufacturing practice at least equivalent to good manufacturing practice, including repeated and unannounced inspections, so as to ensure a protection of public health at least equivalent to that in Great Britain; and

(iii) in the event of findings relating to non-compliance, information on such findings is supplied by the exporting country to the licensing authority without any delay.

(4) Paragraph (3)(c) or (3A)(c) do not apply:

(a) where the country from where the active substance is exported is included in the list referred to in Article 111b of the 2001 Directive (in the case of an import into Northern Ireland) or paragraph (6) (in the case of an import into Great Britain); or

(b) for a period not exceeding the validity of the certificate of good manufacturing practice, where:

(i) in relation to a plant where active substances are manufactured where the competent authority of a Member State or licensing authority (in the case of an import into Northern Ireland) or licensing authority or an appropriate authority responsible for the licensing of medicinal products in a country included in a list under paragraph (6) (in the case of an import into Great Britain) has found, upon inspection, that a plant complies with the principles and guidelines of good manufacturing practice; and

(ii) the licensing authority is of the opinion that it is necessary to waive the requirement to ensure availability of the active substance.

(5) The criteria in this regulation apply regardless of whether an active substance is intended for export.

(6) The licensing authority may publish a list of countries that it is satisfied have a regulatory framework applicable to active substances exported to Great Britain which is equivalent to the regulatory framework in Great Britain, in that the respective control and enforcement activities in those countries ensure an equivalent level of protection of public health.

(7) Before including a country in the list under paragraph (6), the licensing authority must assess the equivalence referred to in that paragraph by:

(a) reviewing relevant documentation; and

(b) unless the country is included in the approved country for batch testing list, carrying out:

(i) an on-site review of the country's regulatory system; and

(ii) if the licensing authority considers it necessary, an inspection of one or more of that country's manufacturing sites for active substances.

(8) In carrying out an assessment under paragraph (7) the licensing authority must in particular take account of the:

(a) country's rules for good manufacturing practice;

(b) regularity of inspections to verify compliance with good manufacturing practice;

(c) effectiveness of enforcement of good manufacturing practice; and

(d) regularity and rapidity of information provided by that country relating to non-compliant producers of active substances.

(9) The licensing authority must:

(a) review the list under paragraph (6) to determine if a country included in it still satisfies the requirements for inclusion in the list and, if it is not so satisfied, remove that country; and

(b) undertake such a review at least every three years, beginning with the date on which a country is included in the list.

UK LEGISLATION ON
ACTIVE SUBSTANCES

Provision of information

45P   (1) In this regulation:

"R" means a person who is, or has applied to the licensing authority to become, a registered importer, manufacturer or distributor of active substances;

"reporting year" means a period of twelve months ending on 31 March.

(2) On or before the date specified in paragraph (3), R must submit a report to the licensing authority which:

(a) includes a declaration that R has in place an appropriate system to ensure compliance with regulations 45N, 45O and this regulation; and

(b) details the system that R has in place to ensure such compliance.

(3) The date specified for the purposes of this paragraph is:

(a) in relation to any application made before 31 March 2014, the date of the application; and

(b) in relation to each subsequent reporting year, 30 April following the end of that year.

(4) R must without delay notify the licensing authority of any changes to the matters, in respect of which evidence has been supplied in relation to paragraph (2), which might affect compliance with the requirements of this Chapter.

(5) Any report or notification to the licensing authority under paragraph (2) or (4) must be accompanied by the appropriate fee in accordance with the Fees Regulations.

(6) The licensing authority may give a notice to R, requiring R to provide information of a kind specified in the notice within the period specified in the notice.

(7) A notice under paragraph (6) may not be given to R unless it appears to the licensing authority that it is necessary for the licensing authority to consider whether the registration should be varied, suspended or removed from the active substance register.

(8) A notice under paragraph (6) may specify information that the licensing authority thinks necessary for considering whether the registration should be varied, suspended or removed from the active substance register.

Schedule 7A Information to be provided for registration as an importer, manufacturer or distributor of active substances

(1) The name and address of the applicant.

(2) The name and address of the person (if any) making the application on the applicant's behalf.

(3) The address of each of the premises where any operations to which the registration relates are to be carried out.

(4) The address of any premises not mentioned by virtue of the above requirement, where:

    (a) the applicant proposes to keep any living animals, from which substance(s) used in the production of the active substance(s) to which the application relates are to be derived;

    (b) materials of animal origin from which an active substance is to be derived, as mentioned in the above sub-paragraph, are to be kept.

(5) The address of each of the premises where active substances are to be stored, or from which active substances are to be distributed.

(6) The address of each of the premises where any testing associated with the manufacture or assembly of active substances to which the registration relates.

(7) The name, address, qualifications and experience of the person whose duty it will be to supervise any manufacturing operations, and the name and job title of the person to whom they report.

(8) The name, address, qualifications and experience of the person who will have responsibility for the quality control of active substances, and the name and job title of the person to whom they report.

(9) The name, address, qualifications and experience of the person whose duty it will be to supervise any importation, storage or distribution operations, and the name and job title of the person to whom they report.

(10) The name, address and qualifications of the person to be responsible for any animals kept as mentioned in paragraph 4(a).

(11) The name, address and qualifications of the person to be responsible for the culture of any living tissue for use in the manufacture of an active substance.

(12) For each active substance to be manufactured, imported, or distributed:

    (a) the CAS registration number[3] assigned to that active substance by the Chemical Abstracts Service, a division of the American Chemical Society;

    (b) where applicable, the Anatomical Therapeutic Category code[4] assigned to that active substance under the Anatomical Therapeutic Chemical Classification System used for the classification

---

[3] Further information is available from the website of the Chemical Abstracts Service at www.cas.org

[4] Further information is available from the website of the WHO Collaborating Centre for Drug Statistics Methodology at www.whocc.no

of drugs by the World Health Organization's Collaborating Centre for Drug Statistics Methodology;

(c) either:

(i) the International Union of Pure and Applied Chemistry nomenclature, or

(ii) the common name; and

(d) the intended quantities of each active substance to be manufactured, imported or distributed.

(13) Details of the operations to which the registration relates, including a statement of whether they include:

(a) the manufacture of active substances;

(b) the importation of active substances from third countries;

(c) the storage of active substances; or

(d) the distribution of active substances.

(14) A statement of the facilities and equipment available at each of the premises where active substances are to be manufactured, stored or distributed.

(15) A statement as to whether the particular active substances are intended for:

(a) use in a medicinal product with an EU marketing authorisation;

(b) use in a special medicinal product; or

(c) export to a third country.

(16) A separate statement in respect of each of the premises mentioned in the application of:

(a) the manufacturing, storage or distribution operations carried out at those sites, and the specific active substances to which those activities relate; and

(b) the equipment available at those premises for carrying out those activities.

(17) A statement of the authority conferred on the person responsible for quality control to reject unsatisfactory active substances.

(18) A description of the arrangements for the identification and storage of materials before and during the manufacture of active substances.

(19) A description of the arrangements for the identification and storage of active substances.

(20) A description of the arrangements at each of the premises where the applicant proposes to store active substances for ensuring, as far as practicable, the turnover of stocks of active substances.

(21) A description of the arrangements for maintaining:

(a) production records, including records of manufacture and assembly;

(b) records of analytical and other tests used in the course of manufacture or assembly for ensuring compliance of materials used in manufacture, or of active substances, with the specification for such materials or active substances;

(c) records of importation;

(d) records of storage and distribution.

(22) A description of the arrangements for keeping reference samples of:

(a) materials used in the manufacture of active substances; and

(b) active substances.

(23) Where the application relates to active substances intended for use in an advanced therapy medicinal product, an outline of the arrangements for maintaining records to allow traceability containing sufficient detail to enable the linking of an active substance to the advanced therapy medicinal product it was used in the manufacture of and vice versa.

(24) Details of:

(a) any manufacturing, importation, storage or distribution operations, other than those to which the application for registration relates, carried on by the applicant on or near each of the premises; and

(b) the substances or articles to which those operations relate.

Guidance on Good Distribution Practice for Wholesaling, Brokering and Active Substances

EU Guidelines and UK Guidance on Wholesale Distribution

Contents

Introduction

Wholesale distribution of medicinal products is defined as all activities consisting of procuring, holding, supplying, or exporting medicinal products, apart from supplying medicinal products to the public. To ensure the reliability of the supply chain, the Human Medicines Regulations 2012 regulates wholesale distributors. This also includes virtual operations where no physical handling of the products takes place.

Wholesalers of medicines must comply with Chapters 1–9 of the European Commission's Guidelines on Good Distribution Practice of medicinal products for human use. This chapter sets out the guidelines alongside the expectations for UK wholesalers.

Chapter 1 Quality Management

1.1 Principle

Wholesale distributors must maintain a quality system setting out responsibilities, processes and risk management principles in relation to their activities[1]. All distribution activities should be clearly defined and systematically reviewed. All critical steps of distribution processes and significant changes should be justified and where relevant validated. The quality system is the responsibility of the organisation's management and requires their leadership and active participation and should be supported by staff commitment.

1.2 Quality system

The system for managing quality should encompass the organisational structure, procedures, processes and resources, as well as activities necessary to ensure confidence that the product delivered maintains its quality and integrity and remains within the legal supply chain during storage and/or transportation.

The quality system should be fully documented and its effectiveness monitored. All quality system-related activities should be defined and documented. A quality manual or equivalent documentation approach should be established.

A responsible person should be appointed by the management, who should have clearly specified authority and responsibility for ensuring that a quality system is implemented and maintained.

EU GUIDELINES AND UK GUIDANCE ON WHOLESALE DISTRIBUTION PRACTICE

---

[1] Article 80(h) of Directive 2001/83/EC.

The management of the distributor should ensure that all parts of the quality system are adequately resourced with competent personnel, and suitable and sufficient premises, equipment and facilities.

The size, structure and complexity of distributor's activities should be taken into consideration when developing or modifying the quality system.

A change control system should be in place. This system should incorporate quality risk management principles, and be proportionate and effective.

The quality system should ensure that:

(i)   medicinal products are procured, held, supplied or exported in a way that is compliant with the requirements of GDP;
(ii)   management responsibilities are clearly specified;
(iii) products are delivered to the right recipients within a satisfactory time period;
(iv)   records are made contemporaneously;
(v)   deviations from established procedures are documented and investigated;
(vi)   appropriate corrective and preventive actions (commonly known as "CAPA") are taken to correct deviations and prevent them in line with the principles of quality risk management.

1.3   Management of outsourced activities

The quality system should extend to the control and review of any outsourced activities related to the procurement, holding, supply or export of medicinal products. These processes should incorporate quality risk management and include:

(i)   assessing the suitability and competence of the contract acceptor to carry out the activity and checking authorisation status, if required;
(ii)   defining the responsibilities and communication processes for the quality-related activities of the parties involved;
(iii) monitoring and review of the performance of the contract acceptor, and the identification and implementation of any required improvements on a regular basis.

1.4   Management review and monitoring

The management should have a formal process for reviewing the quality system on a periodic basis. The review should include:

(i)   measurement of the achievement of quality system objectives;
(ii)   assessment of performance indicators that can be used to monitor the effectiveness of processes within the quality system, such as

complaints, deviations, CAPA, changes to processes; feedback on outsourced activities; self-assessment processes including risk assessments and audits; and external assessments such as inspections, findings and customer audits;

(iii) emerging regulations, guidance and quality issues that can impact the quality management system;

(iv) innovations that might enhance the quality system;

(v) changes in business environment and objectives.

The outcome of each management review of the quality system should be documented in a timely manner and effectively communicated internally.

1.5   Quality risk management

Quality risk management is a systematic process for the assessment, control, communication and review of risks to the quality of medicinal products. It can be applied both proactively and retrospectively.

Quality risk management should ensure that the evaluation of the risk to quality is based on scientific knowledge, experience with the process, and ultimately links to the protection of the patient. The level of effort, formality and documentation of the process should be commensurate with the level of risk. Examples of the processes and applications of quality risk management can be found in guideline Q9 of the International Conference on Harmonisation (ICH).

UK Guidance on Chapter 1 Quality Management

Introduction

A consistent focus on quality is of prime importance for all wholesale distributors in order to maintain an effective and efficient business that meets customer needs and ensures that product quality is maintained.

Quality management is as much a mind-set as an activity in itself, with the aim of achieving quality processes that permeate throughout all distribution activities, and the ultimate goal of ensuring patient safety.

Quality management system and quality system

A quality system is the sum of all aspects of a system that implements quality policy and ensures that quality objectives are met. This is managed through a quality management system (QMS), which is the system for managing quality and should encompass the organisational structure, procedures, processes and resources, as well as activities necessary to ensure that the product distributed maintains its quality and integrity and remains within the legal supply chain during all wholesale operations.

Examples of QMS application include:

- quality management review;
- establishment of organisational structure, responsibilities matrix and lines of reporting;
- quality planning and strategy.

The quality system is the vehicle by which quality management is delivered and should encompass all GDP operations. The quality system size and complexity should be proportionate to the distribution activities being undertaken and appropriate for the type of organisation. The GDP Guidelines give a detailed breakdown of the areas that should be covered. Additionally, the ICH harmonised guideline Q10 may provide useful information for those designing a quality system.

GDP quality systems should include the following elements:

- quality risk management;
- change management;
- deviation management;
- management of controlled documentation;
- self-inspection;
- control of outsourced activity.

To be fully effective, individual elements of the quality system need to fully integrate both within the organisation's quality system as well as with any integrated third-party systems such as parent companies or subcontractors. To illustrate this, mitigating risk of medicine theft is provided as an example at the end of this section (example 1).

Quality risk management

Quality risk management (QRM) is the identification and control of risks to product quality through the evaluation of the activities that are being performed. Underpinning this is that the evaluation of the risk is based on knowledge and experience of the process and ultimately links to the protection of the patient. The level of effort, formality and documentation of the process should be commensurate with the level of risk. Where a lack of knowledge is associated with an activity, such as a new process, then the lack of knowledge should be incorporated into the risk evaluation.

GDP guidelines refer to ICH Q9 as a useful guidance document on QRM. This includes the principles and concepts of QRM with Annexes I and II identifying various tools and techniques. Deficiency data indicates that QRM has been poorly understood or implemented, so two examples of application are provided at the end of this section (examples 2 and 3). These illustrate two approaches to illustrate the principles of QRM and will not be suitable for all distributors and circumstances. Common weaknesses seen with GDP QRM include:

- the criticality of risk directly correlates with the degree of urgency rather than the appropriate time to address the risk;
- risk assessments are not reviewed;
- QRM is used as an excuse to avoid developing appropriate mitigation;
- QRM is not understood by managers.

Indications of effective QRM includes:

- full integration of QRM principles throughout the quality system;
- QRM being actively used to drive continuous improvement, reduce risks and deviations, and improve understanding of risks;
- QRM processes are easy to understand and apply.

Change management

Change management is a formal process that ensures control is maintained while changes that potentially impact product quality, patient safety or regulatory compliance are carried out. For small or medium-sized wholesalers, change management and change control are often viewed as the same. Companies with more extensive structure or operations may manage these separately, with change management incorporating changes in addition to quality or operational change controls. These could include IT system change management (including software updates), management of changes incorporated within validation studies or changes to commercial terms.

Extensive operational or quality changes may be managed as a project following the same underlying principles of change management, and be supported by individual activities associated with specific change controls.

There should be a clear distinction between what constitutes the use of change control processes and changes that are managed by other means (e.g. a temporary "planned" deviation from established processes).

Change control

Change control is a formal process whereby changes to a process, key personnel, premises or other changes that potentially impact product quality, patient safety or regulatory compliance, are identified, monitored and managed in a controlled way. Changes managed by change control may be permanent or temporary. For temporary changes, these could be managed as a temporary change control or temporary deviation dependent on the design of organisations' quality system.

The level of recorded detail should be in line with the principles of QRM and in accordance with data integrity, and be proportionate to the extent of the change. A register of change controls will enable traceability of all changes and should include both implemented and rejected changes. Change documentation should be raised at the point that a change is first considered, even if the change is not then implemented.

A typical change control process may consist of several stages:

- Submission of a documented change control request to management.
- Assessment of the request by management. This assessment should consider if there is an overall benefit to the organisation. It should include an impact assessment to record associated areas affected by the change, together with identification of potential risks. The assessment should evaluate not only the impact and management following completion of the change (final state) but also how risks are to be managed during the implementation phase of the change.
- Implementation of the change: monitoring of the implementation stages of the change should be carried out and essential stages recorded. Any deviation from the original implementation plan should be documented.
- Review of the change: a review should take place of the effectiveness of the change, including identification of any new risks, and opportunities for improvement in either the specific change or change implementation. This should be recorded.

Deviation management, corrective and preventive actions

Deviation management is the means by which all deviation types are managed. Many wholesalers apply a deviation process to deviations from procedures, with independent processes to address other deviation types such as temperature excursions, service level complaints, complaints relating to outsourced operations, self-inspection observations or validation excursions. It is important that management and the Responsible Person have oversight of all deviation types.

The term "deviation" is most commonly used by wholesalers to refer to an unplanned event not in compliance with their standard operating processes. Deviations can also refer to authorised departure outside the standard operating procedure or normal way of working (but within regulatory requirements) as a temporary measure.

Deviations require a formal process for reporting and assessment. Those deviations that are unplanned also require investigation. It is expected that the level of severity be reflected in the extent of immediate mitigation, documentation, assessment and investigation. Deviations other than very minor ones are likely to be associated with corrective actions and preventive actions, often referred to as CAPA.

Corrective actions are remedial measures taken to address the specific failure. Preventive actions are measures to avoid reoccurrence of the specific failure and, additionally, actions to address existent occurrences of the same failure elsewhere.

Establishment of preventive measures should be a priority where an unplanned event may have a significant impact on public health. The greater the potential impact, the more investigation into root causative effects is required to ensure that a robust preventive action plan is created. A variety of tools can be used to ascertain potential root causes depending on the failure type, and a general description of some of these is available in ICH Q9.

Management of controlled documentation

Good documentation practices including management of controlled documents are an essential element of the quality system and are described in chapter 4 documentation below.

Self-inspection

Self-inspections are the means by which management monitor performance of the quality system and identify opportunities for improvement and deficiencies. It is described in chapter 8 self inspections below.

Control of outsourced activity

The quality system should extend to the control and review of any outsourced activities related to the procurement, holding, supply or export of medicinal products. The relationship between the organisation and person providing activity on behalf of the wholesaler should be described in an agreement as described in chapter 7 outsourced activities below. Control measures should incorporate QRM and include:

- assessing the suitability and competence of the contract acceptor to carry out the activity and include confirmation of authorisation status if required;
- defining the responsibilities and communication processes for the quality-related activities of the parties involved;
- monitoring and review of the performance of the contract acceptor, and the identification and implementation of any required improvements on a regular basis.

Management should monitor the performance of the service provider by means of audit. An audit schedule should be maintained outlining the service provider, service provided, audit scope, and frequency and audit format. The audit should be carried out by competent personnel and, where these are specifically contracted, a vendor assessment of the auditor should be carried out to provide assurance of the competency of the auditor. This is especially important where the activity being audited may not be within the full level of understanding of the wholesaler, e.g. outsourced maintenance of computerised systems may be audited by a contracted auditor with strong experience and knowledge of GDP and computer systems.

Management review and monitoring

Regular review should take place to ensure effectiveness and continual improvement of the QMS.

This review should actively involve company management and key personnel such as the Responsible Person.

The review should incorporate key performance indicators, examples of which include pick accuracy and delivery performance. Performance indicators should be objective and relevant to the organisation's activities, alongside driving continuous improvement.

In very small organisations, the process of review may require taking a step back and objectively reviewing the operational activities and supporting procedures.

Questions to be considered during the management review may include the following:

- is the quality system effective, and does it reflect the current business model?
- has the recall test or test of the business contingency plan identified weaknesses or opportunities, and have they been followed up?
- are activities being carried out in accordance with the principles of QRM, or are there opportunities for improvement with some processes requiring modification?
- has legislation been amended or guidance published that requires that activities need to be reviewed?
- is the business operating effectively, and are the right products getting to the right customers at the right time?
- are improvements needed to address customer complaints?
- are third parties contracted to provide services, and are they complying with their contractual obligations?
- have there been any unforeseen problems or events and has effective CAPA been implemented?

- have planned changes been effective?
- are there staff training issues?

The outcome of each management review should be documented, result in a CAPA plan where necessary and should be effectively communicated to staff.

Example 1 Integration of quality and operational processes to mitigation of risk of theft or diversion of medicine

Whether pilfered for personal use or stolen in bulk for diversion, opportunistic or planned, the theft of medicines and diversion of medicines has a broad impact that increases risk to public health and risks the integrity of the medicine supply chain. The potential impact of theft is widespread and includes:

- diversion into the authorised supply chain of medicines damaged by handling in inadequate conditions;
- delay of essential medicine supply to a patient;
- diversion of medicines to unauthorised consumers;
- loss of good reputation of distributors;
- traumatic for staff.

Considering the amount of UK medicines distributed, the proportion of theft is low; however, the potential risk to an individual patient consuming a stolen medicine is potentially high. Without proper safeguards, distributors may either have medicines stolen or unwittingly procure stock previously stolen. Integration of the quality system and operational practices can mitigate the risk of theft or procurement of stolen medicines. Some measures for consideration are listed below.

Quality management: monitoring of unusual sales patterns, monitoring changes in risk profiles for products supplied and evidence of theft or near misses within deviation reports. Quality risk management incorporates security risks evaluation embedded throughout the quality system.

Personnel: security pre-employment checks, training of drivers in security, development of an open culture that supports reporting and whistle-blowing, restricted personnel access to high-risk areas, and policies in place for management of visitors and control of security passes. Where security awareness within the organisation is low, or where a significant theft has taken place, specialised security consultants may be used, in which case appropriate vetting of these should take place.

Facility and equipment design and maintenance: security measures are built into the design including restriction of vehicular access to loading bay areas, location of high-risk stock within the warehouse, maintenance repair and servicing of buildings, perimeter fences and equipment including shutters and CCTV.

Documentation: stock records safeguarded from unauthorised alteration, including both hard copy and computerised records, stock discrepancies addressed at an appropriate level, records enable clear visibility of discrepancies, including underpicked stock, mislaid stock, and under-delivered stock, and evidence of destroyed stock, including stock for destruction supplied to third countries. Procedures describe how to report medicine theft to the Medicines and Healthcare products Regulatory Agency (MHRA).

Operations: procurement controls include robust authentication of suppliers and customers, incentivisaion of purchasing or sales staff does not conflict with increasing risk of distributing diverted medicines, witness checking for high-risk operations including picking controlled drugs, and control of access and use of security seals.

Complaint management: trending of under-delivered or lost stock.

Returned medicines: control of courier used for reverse logistics, verification that returned stock is genuine and supported by appropriate documentation.

Falsified medicines: clear understanding in all areas of the organisation of standards of operations and how to report suspect medicines and transactions.

Outsourced activities: integration with couriers through written agreements, including immediate reporting to the contract giver of anomalies, assurance of a chain of custody, risk profiling of contractors, monitoring contractor and control of additional subcontracting by the contractor.

Transportation: security features identified as part of user requirement specification, security profiling for high-risk consignments, driver trained in security practices.

Example 2 Application of QRM to GDP transportation risks

This example illustrates some of the QRM considerations and GDP expectations, as it applies to transportation, which remains a significant weakness for many wholesalers, especially those that do not own their own fleet.

Distribution of medicines has inherent risks, and by applying QRM it is possible to identify and define the risks, possibly remove some and create the means to improve detection of risk events, and thereby reduce their impact. It can also help identify what is an acceptable level of risk.

A summary of inherent risks and their criticality assists managers to be mindful of risks in different areas of their organisation, thereby showing consequential change in risk caused by an action, and can also provide a benchmark of current risk level.

Apart from the summary of inherent risks, individual quality risk assessments also feed into risk management. These can be both subject-based assessments, such as evaluation of risks associated with transportation, or incorporated into quality system processes, such as part of evaluation of a change control or a deviation. The latter helps to reduce total risk rather than resolve one issue, but creates a larger risk elsewhere. Quality risk assessments can include the following stages:

- risk assessment;
- risk control;
- risk communication;
- risk review.

RISK ASSESSMENT

An assessment of the transport chain should help identify which parts are associated with greater risk; this can be performed either as a single approach for a route, or by grouping similar routes and transport modes into different transport lanes. For example, one lane may consist of ambient products by air freight to mainland Europe, the next lane include cold chain air freight to Europe, the next lane describe road freight to Europe using own transport, and a fourth describe road transport to Europe using a courier. Each of these lanes will have risk profiles common to all shipments within it but distinct from the other lanes. Separate types of risk should be identified, e.g. high and low product temperature excursions, security breach, damage in transit, and failure to deliver in full and on time.

If high temperature excursion is identified as a potential significant risk, the probability of the excursion, impact of the excursion and the likelihood of detection will be predicted. Probability will be affected by factors such as geographical differences. Initially, the estimate of probability may be subjective based only on experience and knowledge within the organisation. As the model develops and temperature data is accumulated, the objectivity and quality of the estimate of probability will improve. Early subjective probability therefore requires a safety factor to be included in order to mitigate against initial weakness of data and knowledge.

The next stage is to assess the impact of the temperature excursion both on the shipment, and on specific products or product groups.

It is rare to find sound scientific justification for acceptance of a load subject to an excursion and, in the uncommon instances where a supplier or customer contacts the marketing authorisation holder for stability information, it is often not directly comparable to the excursion experienced. The most common presented reason for accepting a consignment with a temperature excursion is purely commercial, which may put patients at risk and undermines any risk management carried out by the company. In some cases, attempts are made to inappropriately apply mean kinetic temperature to underestimate impact rather than develop good control and preventive measures.

Increasing the likelihood of detection provides for earlier excursion warning, may help prevent an excursion and gives greater assurance that temperature conditions have been maintained. In circumstances where each shipment is not monitored for temperature, a very robust validation is required with clearly defined limits of validation and, where these are breached, the whole load is compromised. In practical terms it is normally easier to monitor temperature throughout the load or as monitoring combined with vehicle temperature mapping. Technological advances have provided easy and inexpensive means to relay temperature at receipt or as live data. It is important to ensure appropriate alerts are set in order to highlight potential excursions.

RISK CONTROL

The control of risk involves accepting levels of risk or reducing it to an acceptable level based on sound scientific reasoning. Approaches taken may include avoidance of distributing medicines to specific territories outside the capability of the distributor or outsourcing shipping to couriers better suited for controlled temperature transport. With any risk control measure, the company needs to ensure that potential new risks are identified and any related risk assessment is re-evaluated.

RISK COMMUNICATION

This includes communication of risk information within and outside the organisation. In our transportation example, staff in Customer Services or Finance should not select use of a courier based purely on low price, but should draw from approved couriers where there has been formal quality risk assessment. A written agreement between the supplier and third-party courier provides a route of communication between both parties and can incorporate risk-mitigation measures such as restriction on uncontrolled further sub-contracting, minimum specification of vehicles and drivers used, and prohibition of high-risk activity such as cross-docking in an unauthorised manner.

Where a new fleet is being selected, user requirement specification should incorporate areas of risk such as design criteria and functionality. Good specification design documents support risk communication between different departments, e.g. finance, transportation department, warehousing, quality, fleet supplier.

RISK REVIEW

QRM is dynamic and should adapt as circumstances within or external to the company change. It should be reviewed routinely and after any significant event or deviation.

Example 3 Application of QRM to development of a business continuity plan

The QMS should ensure that business activity is maintained and minimise the impact of unforeseen events. In these circumstances, a disaster contingency or business continuity plan may safeguard the organisation from service disruption as a consequence of internal or external factors. Examples of these factors may include:

- systems failure due to hacking of essential IT system;
- severe weather affecting the distribution chain locally or remotely;
- lack of availability of key personnel including the Responsible Person or a subject matter expert;
- supply disruption from a sole supplier;
- liquidation of 3PL warehouse holding stock;
- changes in operations due to exit from the EEA.

The global COVID pandemic was an example of an external factor with wide-reaching impact to wholesalers that experienced a range of issues. These included:

- cost escalation of operations due to implementation of new processes for hygiene and less efficient process due to separation of shifts and distancing requirements;
- cost fluctuations of medicines due to changes in product availability and increased demand of some lines;
- operational impact due to reduced product flow through the supply chain as a consequence of customers not releasing product or not collecting product due to shielding;
- increased cost to customers;
- uncertainty of financial forecasting;
- staff management including management of furloughs, staff isolating, introduction of homeworking and use of agency contingency staff.

The business continuity plan should be developed and tested in line with QRM principles. The level of detail of the plan may be correlated with the size of the organisation, complexity of operations and complexity of the event at which the contingency is targeted. For wholesalers that distribute medicines that provide an immediate risk to patients if the supply from the wholesaler was interrupted, then the plan should be used to protect continued supply and is likely to be extensive.

A good business continuity plan not only identifies risks, but also assists resource planning if the event occurs, and assists robustness of processes. It can facilitate implementation of approved alternative arrangements of non-critical activities e.g. temporary homeworking arrangement for office staff, while streamlining core critical operations. Business continuity plans provide clear responsibilities and communication channels for all concerned and provide confidence to third parties where they have an involvement in operations.

Where a continuity plan is effective, it may provide competitive advantage to the wholesaler when compared with similar organisations that have not adequately prepared. During the development of the business continuity plan, consideration should be made of those processes critical to public health, e.g. the ability to maintain effectiveness of medicinal product recalls alongside the incident.

The continuity plan should be assessed after closure of the incident, after testing or as a periodic review in order to ascertain effectiveness.

Chapter 2 Personnel

2.1 Principle

The correct distribution of medicinal products relies upon people. For this reason, there must be sufficient competent personnel to carry out all the tasks for which the wholesale distributor is responsible. Individual responsibilities should be clearly understood by the staff and be recorded.

2.2 Responsible Person

The wholesale distributor must designate a person as responsible person. The responsible person should meet the qualifications and all conditions provided for by the legislation of the Member State concerned[2]. A degree in pharmacy is desirable. The responsible person should have appropriate competence and experience as well as knowledge of and training in GDP.

The responsible person should fulfil their responsibilities personally and should be continuously contactable. The responsible person may delegate duties but not responsibilities.

The written job description of the responsible person should define their authority to take decisions with regard to their responsibilities. The wholesale distributor should give the responsible person the defined authority, resources and responsibility needed to fulfil their duties.

The responsible person should carry out their duties in such a way as to ensure that the wholesale distributor can demonstrate GDP compliance and that public service obligations are met.

The responsibilities of the responsible person include:

(i)   ensuring that a quality management system is implemented and maintained;

---

[2] Article 79(b) of Directive 2001/83/EC.

(ii)   focusing on the management of authorised activities and the accuracy and quality of records;

(iii)   ensuring that initial and continuous training programmes are implemented and maintained;

(iv)   coordinating and promptly performing any recall operations for medicinal products;

(v)   ensuring that relevant customer complaints are dealt with effectively;

(vi)   ensuring that suppliers and customers are approved;

(vii)   approving any subcontracted activities which may impact on GDP;

(viii) ensuring that self-inspections are performed at appropriate regular intervals, following a prearranged programme, and necessary corrective measures are put in place;

(ix)   keeping appropriate records of any delegated duties;

(x)   deciding on the final disposition of returned, rejected, recalled or falsified products;

(xi)   approving any returns to saleable stock;

(xii)   ensuring that any additional requirements imposed on certain products by national law are adhered to[3].

2.3   Other personnel

There should be an adequate number of competent personnel involved in all stages of the wholesale distribution activities of medicinal products. The number of personnel required will depend on the volume and scope of activities.

The organisational structure of the wholesale distributor should be set out in an organisation chart. The role, responsibilities and interrelationships of all personnel should be clearly indicated.

The role and responsibilities of employees working in key positions should be set out in written job descriptions, along with any arrangements for deputising.

2.4   Training

All personnel involved in wholesale distribution activities should be trained on the requirements of GDP. They should have the appropriate competence and experience prior to commencing their tasks.

Personnel should receive initial and continuing training relevant to their role, based on written procedures and in accordance with a written training programme. The responsible person should also maintain their competence in GDP through regular training.

---

[3] Article 83 of Directive 2001/83/EC.

In addition, training should include aspects of product identification and avoidance of falsified medicines entering the supply chain.

Personnel dealing with any products which require more stringent handling conditions should receive specific training. Examples of such products include hazardous products, radioactive materials, products presenting special risks of abuse (including narcotic and psychotropic substances) and temperature-sensitive products.

A record of all training should be kept, and the effectiveness of training should be periodically assessed and documented.

2.5 Hygiene

Appropriate procedures relating to personnel hygiene, relevant to the activities being carried out, should be established and observed. Such procedures should cover health, hygiene and clothing.

UK Guidance on Chapter 2 Personnel

Responsible Person

Regulation 45 of the Human Medicines Regulations 2012, as amended, requires that all licensed wholesale dealers should have at their disposal at least one person available as the Responsible Person (RP). The RP should have appropriate competence and experience as well as knowledge of and training in Good Distribution Practice (GDP).

The points below set out the MHRA requirements and expectations for the RP and are designed to help companies and RPs when nominating an RP.

Eligibility requirements

The experience of the RP is expected to be closely aligned to the wholesale distribution activities carried out by the company for which they are nominated. An RP with experience in one type of wholesale business is not automatically eligible to be nominated as an RP on another more complex licence and, where there is a significant change in a business model, an RP may not necessarily remain suitable for that organisation.

Responsibilities of an RP

The RP is responsible for ensuring that the conditions under which the licence was granted have been, and are being, complied with, and ensuring that the quality of medicinal products handled by the licence holder is being maintained in accordance with the requirements of the marketing authorisations applicable to those products. The responsibilities of an RP include:

(i) ensuring that a quality management system is implemented and maintained;

(ii) focusing on the management of authorised activities and the accuracy and quality of records;

(iii) ensuring that initial and continuous training programmes are implemented and maintained;

(iv) coordinating and promptly performing any recall operations for medicinal products;

(v) ensuring that relevant customer complaints are dealt with effectively;

(vi) ensuring that suppliers and customers are approved;

(vii) approving any subcontracted activities that may impact on GDP;

(viii) ensuring that self-inspections are performed at appropriate regular intervals following a prearranged programme and necessary corrective measures are put in place;

(ix) keeping appropriate records of any delegated duties;

(x) deciding on the final disposition of returned, rejected, recalled or falsified products;

(xi) approving any returns to saleable stock;

(xii) ensuring that any additional requirements imposed on certain products by national law are adhered to.

The RP should fulfil their responsibilities personally and should be continuously contactable. The RP should be resident in the UK and proof of identity and address is required as part of the application process.

Where there is more than one RP named on the licence, each is expected to take full responsibility for the role, within the scope of their responsibilities as defined in their job description and agreed with the licence holder. It should be clear within the quality system which of the RPs is primarily accountable for the responsibilities described in GDP; responsibilities may be allocated either by function (e.g. oversight of the training programme) or where a company operates more than one site it may be possible to allocate responsibilities by site, providing full oversight of activities at a particular site or sites.

Contract RPs

The RP does not have to be an employee of the licence holder but must be continuously contactable. Where the RP is not an employee, there should be a written contract between the licence holder and the RP specifying responsibilities, duties, authority and time on site. Where a contract RP provides services from within a contracting company, the contract should be with the specific RP and not the contracting company.

When contracting an RP, the licence holder should carefully consider the competence and knowledge of the RP in relation to the proposed licensed activity. For example, if the primary plan is to export medicines the contract RP must have experience and knowledge of that area of wholesale distribution. As with any outsourced activity, the licence holder should monitor and review the performance of the contract RP.

The contracted RP should also ensure that they have adequate knowledge and experience to carry out the role. The RP must fully understand and have knowledge of the activities being carried out at a site. The RP should conduct a thorough review of operations before committing to a contract to act as RP to assure themselves that GDP will be complied with at the contracted site and any companies that are closely linked to it.

Contracting to be an RP for a company is a serious commitment requiring a high degree of vigilance to ensure that the company has an appropriate awareness of their obligation to comply with GDP and the Human Medicines Regulations.

The contract RP is expected to ensure that they do not over extend themselves and apply to act as RPs or consultants for too many companies.

Obligations of the licence holder

The Human Medicines Regulations 43 to 45 set out the obligations of the licence holder in relation to holding a wholesale dealer's licence. The licence holder is the company to which the licence is issued. The licence holder is ultimately responsible for complying with GDP and the Human Medicines Regulations 2012 through persons employed by the company. The licence holder must have training and awareness of GDP and the Human Medicines Regulations.

It is for the licence holder to appoint a suitable RP who provides it with reassurance that:

- the conditions under which the licence was granted have been, and are being, complied with; and
- ensuring that the quality of medicinal products handled by the licence holder is being maintained in accordance with the requirements of the marketing authorisations applicable to those products.

The licence holder is also responsible for informing the Licensing Authority of any changes in the RP. Any changes must be advised immediately, and no person may act as RP other than those named on the licence or notified to the Licensing Authority.

The licence holder should ensure that there is a process for receiving advice and comment from the RP and recording the consequent action taken as may be necessary.

Knowledge requirements

The RP should have access to relevant pharmaceutical and technical knowledge and advice when it is required, and have personal knowledge of:

- the relevant provisions of the Human Medicines Regulations 2012 and amendments;
- the relevant legislation in the intended market the organisation is supplying to;
- the Guidelines on Good Distribution Practice;
- the conditions of the Wholesale Dealer's Licence for which nominated;
- the products traded under the licence and the conditions necessary for their safe storage and distribution;
- the categories of persons to whom products may be distributed.

The RP should also maintain their competence in GDP through regular training and keep records as evidence.

Experience requirements

The RP must demonstrate they have at least one year's practical experience of the activities authorised on the licence, i.e. procuring, holding, supplying or exporting. The RP must have obtained the technical knowledge of how to qualify suppliers, identify medicinal products, understand storage conditions and temperature control, qualify customers and how to transport medicinal products.

The RP should have at least one year's experience in maintaining a quality management system appropriate to the licence for which nominated.

The RP should be able to demonstrate that they have completed relevant training in GDP.

Assessment of RP knowledge and experience

The knowledge and experience of an RP may be assessed by an inspector when:

- a variation is submitted to name them on a wholesale dealer's licence;
- during an inspection;
- on an ad-hoc basis if non-compliance is established.

If the RP cannot demonstrate the required experience and knowledge or is not adequately carrying out those duties, the Licensing Authority may compulsorily vary the licence to remove the RP or refuse acceptance of the RP on that licence application. These actions may be extended to any other licence on which the RP is named.

Reporting arrangements

To carry out their responsibilities, the RP should:

- have a clear reporting line to the licence holder;
- have the defined authority, resources and responsibility needed to fulfil their duties;
- have access to all areas, sites, stores, staff and records relating to the licensable activities being carried out;
- demonstrate regular review and monitoring of all such areas, sites and staff, etc. or
- have delegated arrangements whereby the RP receives written reports that such delegated actions have been carried out on behalf of the RP in compliance with standard operating procedures and GDP. The RP remains responsible and should have demonstrable oversight of delegated duties;
- focus on the management of licensable activities, the accuracy and quality of records, compliance with standard operating procedures and GDP, the quality of handling and storage equipment and facilities, and the standards achieved;
- keep appropriate records relating to the discharge of the RP's responsibilities.

The delegation of RP duties

Where the licence covers a number of sites, the RP may have a nominated deputy with appropriate reporting and delegating arrangements. However, the RP should be able to demonstrate to the Licensing Authority that the necessary controls and checks are in place. The term "Deputy RP" is not legally recognised but is often used. Only the Responsible Person(s) named on a wholesale dealer's licence has legal responsibility for the organisation's compliance and remains responsible for any duties that have been delegated.

Dispute resolution

Should it prove impossible to resolve a disagreement between the licence holder and the RP, the Licensing Authority should be consulted.

Although a joint referral is clearly to be preferred, either party may approach the Licensing Authority independently. If an RP finds difficulty over performing statutory responsibilities or the activities being carried out under the licence, the Licensing Authority should be consulted in strict confidence.

The Responsible Person Gold Standard

The Human Medicines Regulations 2012 require holders of a Wholesale Dealer's Licence to designate and ensure that there is available at all times at least one person, referred to in the regulations as the "responsible person", who in the opinion of the licensing authority:

(a) has knowledge of the activities to be carried out and of the procedures to be performed under the licence; and

(b) has adequate experience relating to those activities and procedures.

Guidance on the role and responsibilities of the RP is set out in Chapter 2 of the GDP guidelines and these remain the same irrespective of whether the RP is a permanent employee of a company or is an external party working under the terms of a contract.

The RP plays a vital part in ensuring that the quality and the integrity of medicinal products are maintained throughout the distribution chain, and it is essential that they have the right knowledge, demonstrate competence and deploy the right skills so that patients and healthcare professionals have the confidence and trust to use medicines.

In order to facilitate this and to standardise the requirements for individuals operating as, or aspiring to be, an RP, Cogent (the national skills body for the science industries) has, following extensive discussion with pharmaceutical companies and the MHRA, published a "Gold Standard" role profile for the RP.

This sets out an industry-agreed framework that identifies the skills required in four competency areas and includes not only traditional qualifications and technical requirements but also the behavioural skills necessary to do the job to a high standard. The Gold Standard is a competency framework, or role profile, and should be used by:

- the Licence Holder to assist in selection and induction of the RP;
- the RP in identifying the extent to which they fulfil the role and in compiling a training programme;
- the prospective RP in planning their learning and experience to prepare for a future role.

Responsible Person
Medicinal Products

The Human Medicines Regulations require a distributor to designate a Responsible Person(s), named on the applicable licence. Regulation 45 and the EU GDP Guide set out the requirements and the responsibilities.

Where the RP is contracted to a company, the duties remain the same as for those of the permanently employed RP. The responsibilities should be covered in a contract.

Compliance	**The Gold Standard** Job Role skills, knowledge and behaviours
	the individual should understand: • *the role of MHRA in the licensing of medicines and as the competent authority including the risk-based inspection process, the role of the enforcement group, the Inspection Action Group (IAG), and resulting actions that can be taken due to non-compliance* • *the UK regulations in relation to Wholesale Distribution* • *the European Pharmaceutical Directive related to Wholesale Distribution of Medicinal Products* • *Good Distribution Practice (GDP)* • *the importance of a clear reporting line to the wholesale distribution authorisation holder, senior manager and/or CEO* *the individual shall:* • *employ due diligence in the discharge of their duties, maintaining full compliance to procedures and appropriate regulations* • *report to senior management, the Marketing Authorisation holder and the MHRA any suspicious events of which they become aware* *in addition, the individual also has knowledge of:* • *the role of the professional bodies and organisations that regulate those supplying medicinal products to the public e.g. GPhC* • *the role of the Home Office in relation to the handling of Controlled Drugs* • *the role of the Veterinary Medicines Directorate (VMD) in relation to veterinary medicines* • *the role of the European Medicines Agency (EMA) and use of EUDRAGMDP* • *the Falsified Medicines Directive* • *the Principles and Guidelines of Good Manufacturing Practice and how the principles of GDP maintain product quality throughout the distribution chain*
Knowledge	**The Gold Standard** Job Role skills, knowledge and behaviours
	the individual should have: • *the prior relevant knowledge and experience related to the distribution of medicinal products* • *access to pharmaceutical knowledge and advice when it is required* • *knowledge of the products traded under the licence* • *if not a pharmacist or QP, one year's relevant practical and managerial experience of medicinal products*

Supported by MHRA

Responsible Person
Medicinal Products

Technical Competence	**The Gold Standard** Job Role skills, knowledge and behaviours
	the individual is able to perform duties including: **Quality Management** *the individual shall ensure that a quality management system proportionate to the distributor's activities is implemented and maintained including:* • *Quality Risk Management* • *Corrective and Preventative Actions (CAPA) to address deviations* • *Change Control* • *Measurement of performance indicators and management review* **Personnel** *The Responsible Person is required to:* • *understand their own responsibilities* • *carry out all duties in such a way as to ensure that the wholesale distributor can demonstrate GDP compliance* • *define personal and staff roles, responsibilities and accountabilities and record all delegated duties* • *ensure that initial and continuous training programmes are implemented and maintained* • *ensure all personnel are trained in GDP, their own duties, product identification, the risks of falsified medicines and specific training for products requiring more stringent handling* • *maintain training records for self and others and ensure training is periodically assessed* **Premises & Equipment** • *ensure that appropriate standards of GDP are maintained for own premises and contracted storage premises* • *identify medicinal products, legal categories, storage conditions and different Marketing Authorisation types* • *maintain the safety and security of medicinal products within the appropriate environments, including product integrity and product storage* • *use the appropriate systems to segregate, store and distribute medicinal products* • *maintain records for the repair, maintenance, calibration and validation of equipment including computerised systems* • *ensure storage areas are temperature mapped, qualified and validated* **Documentation** *The individual shall focus on:* • *the accuracy and quality of records* • *contemporaneous records* • *records storage* • *maintaining comprehensive written procedures that are understood and followed* • *ensure procedures are valid and version controlled*

EU GUIDELINES AND UK GUIDANCE ON WHOLESALE DISTRIBUTION PRACTICE

Supported by MHRA

cogent | Skills for Science Based Industries

Responsible Person
Medicinal Products

Operations
- carry out due diligence checks and ensure that suppliers and customers are qualified
- ensure all necessary checks are carried out and that medicinal products are authorised for sale
- manage authorised activities to ensure operations do not compromise the quality of medicines and can demonstrate compliance with GDP
- demonstrate the application of activities and provisions in accordance with the wholesale distribution authorisation and of company processes and procedures
- ensure that any additional requirements imposed on certain products by national law are adhered to e.g. specials, unlicensed imports & Controlled Drugs

Complaints, returns, suspected falsified medicinal products and medicinal product recalls
- ensure relevant customer complaints are dealt with effectively, informing the manufacturer and/or marketing authorisation holder of any product quality/product defect issues
- decide on the final disposition of returned, rejected, recalled or falsified products
- approve any returns to saleable stock
- coordinate and promptly perform any recall operations for medicinal products
- co-operate with marketing authorisation holders and national competent authorities in the event of recalls
- have an awareness of the issues surrounding falsified medicines

Outsourced Activities
- approve any subcontracted activities which may impact on GDP

Self-Inspection
- ensure that self-inspections are performed at appropriate regular intervals following a prearranged programme and necessary corrective measures are put in place

Transportation
- apply the appropriate transport requirements and methods for cold chain, ambient and hazardous product
- ensure all transport equipment is appropriately qualified

Brokers
- ensure that transactions are only made with brokers who are registered
- ensure that any broker activities performed are registered

Business Improvement	**The Gold Standard** Job Role skills, knowledge and behaviours
	the individual should: • practise continuous improvement practices and utilise appropriate tools and techniques to solve problems

Supported by MHRA

Responsible Person
Medicinal Products

Functional & Behavioural	The Gold Standard Job Role skills, knowledge and behaviours

	the individual has:
	  • *relevant skills in:*
	    ○ *English (level 2)*
	    ○ *Mathematics (level 2)*
	    ○ *ICT*
	
	the individual can demonstrate relevant personal qualities in:
	  Autonomy
	    ○ *take responsibility for planning and developing courses of action, including responsibility for the work of others*
	    ○ *exercise autonomy and judgement within broad but generally well-defined parameters*
	  • *Management & Leadership*
	    ○ *develop and implement operational plans for their area of responsibility*
	    ○ *manage diversity & discrimination issues*
	    ○ *provide leadership for their team*
	
	  • *Working with others*
	    ○ *ensure effective delegation whilst retaining ownership of the outcome*
	    ○ *develop and maintain productive working relationships with colleagues and stakeholders*
	    ○ *monitor the progress and quality of work within their area of responsibility*
	
	  • *Personal development*
	    ○ *manage their professional development by setting targets and planning how they will be met*
	    ○ *review progress towards targets and establish evidence of achievements*
	
	  • *Communication*
	    ○ *put across ideas in clear and concise manner and present a well-structured case*
	    ○ *communicate complex information to others*
	
	  • *Business*
	    ○ *understands the business environment in which the company operates*
	    ○ *has an appreciation of the industry sector and competitors*
	
	  • *Customers*
	    ○ *understands the customer base and is aware of customer requirements*

For more information on how to achieve the Gold Standard contact us on 01325 740900

Version 2 July 2014

Supported by MHRA   

CHOOSING AN EXTERNAL TRAINING PROVIDER

The licence holder is required to provide an RP with adequate knowledge and experience; learning "on the job" is usual in this industry but experiential training can provide only for some elements of the full package. There is a place for good quality external training, and this should be considered by all licence holders. Before arranging any external training, the licence holder and RP should be fully aware of the collaborative work on the Responsible Person Gold Standard between the GDP Inspectorate and Cogent Skills.

There is, effectively, a hierarchy of RP training provision in the UK. The following shows the range of external training and the extent to which they are recognised by the MHRA.

- Any training provider may offer RP training. Current offerings range from extremely generic courses to targeted courses delivered in the work place. The buyer must verify that the content is accurate and suited to their needs.
- A training provider may align their training with the Responsible Person Gold Standard but without recognition from the MHRA. Once again, there is a range in quality, and the buyer must be wary.
- A list of RP training providers recognised by the MHRA/Cogent Skills is available on the Cogent Skills website[4].

WHAT MAKES A GOOD RP?

RPs may demonstrate their suitability to the licence holder and the inspector as follows:

- knowledge of GDP and the relevant regulations, and application of that knowledge to the organisation's operations;
- industry experience: relevant GDP experience;
- familiarity with the business operations of the licence holder: this can be particularly challenging in a large or complex organisation;
- induction/primary training: role familiarity;
- role definition and place within the organisation: sufficient seniority and influence;
- delegation and training others: the RP is responsible for all GDP activities, even those delegated;
- training records: RP, licence holder and staff;
- continuing development for the RP: as the supply chain continually presents new challenges.

---

[4] Responsible Person in Good Distribution Practice – Consultancy & Courses (cogentskills.solutions).

Knowledge of GDP and the Regulations

There is no real substitute for reading and re-reading the GDP Guidelines and relevant regulations. Many licence holders include the GDP Guidelines within their quality system; this sends the right message to all staff. Reading and understanding the Guidelines should be seen as a clear learning activity and should form part of the RP's training record. Further sources of information are inspectorate blogs and information published on the GOV.UK web site.

Industry experience

It is essential that the RP can demonstrate practical industry experience related to the authorised activities on the licence and GDP, e.g. conducting an effective recall by ensuring that sufficient staff, storage space and written procedures are in place and clearly understood by those involved.

Familiarity with the GDP operations of the licence holder

The RP should familiarise themselves with all aspects of the GDP operations and company structure. Where the RP lacks sufficient oversight or knowledge of the day-to-day operational activities, non-compliance issues can occur. For instance, the licence holder may be conducting GDP activities from an unlicensed site of which the RP is unaware.

Induction/primary training

The induction process is essential when bringing a new RP on board. The licence holder must ensure that the nominated RP has the appropriate knowledge and experience to carry out their duties and provide adequate time at the induction stage.

The nominated RP must ensure that they are fully conversant with all aspects of GDP and the associated regulations; this may take several years before an RP is fully coherent with the roles and responsibilities.

Role definition and place within the organisation

There should be a clear reporting line to the licence holder and the RP should have adequate resources available to ensure the organisation's compliance. Respective responsibilities between the RP and the licence holder should be clearly defined and understood. In the larger organisation, the RP is frequently in the quality department. The position of the RP should always allow sufficient oversight of activities such as the warehouse management system, staff rosters, transport, etc.

Delegation and training others

GDP clearly sets out that all staff should be trained in their role, in GDP, in the identification of medicines and in the avoidance of falsified medicines entering the supply chain. There should be a clear training programme describing these. The RP must ensure that initial and continuous training programmes are implemented and maintained and, although the RP need not conduct all the training themselves, the RP should have sufficient oversight to demonstrate that the trainers, training materials and records are suitable. Licence holders are also expected to undergo training.

Training records

Training records can be paper based or electronic and should include a wide range of learning activities from standard operating procedure (SOP) reading and external training to ad-hoc learning such as shadowing staff. Records should cover all staff; this includes the RP and licence holder. The GDP Inspectorate considers an RP's suitability based on a range of evidence – this would include how they perform their role as well as the range of training they have undertaken.

Continuing development for the RP

Continuing Professional Development (CPD) is a natural progression from initial training. Some professions will require that on-going learning is recorded in the form of CPD, e.g. pharmacists and pharmacy technicians registered with the General Pharmaceutical Council (GPhC). These records can be used as the RP's training record so long as the CPD covers the scope of the role and the records are made available on inspection. Many make use of external training courses – many of these are of a high standard and cover a specific area within GDP. Other external courses are intended to be generally applicable to all RPs and these can still be of use in continuing development.

The Responsible Person (Import)

A wholesale dealer in Great Britain may only import Qualified Person (QP) certified medicines from the European Economic Area (EEA) if certain checks have been made by the 'Responsible Person (import) (RPi)'. Great Britain is England, Wales and Scotland.

Products that do not require RPi oversight

Medicinal products sourced from Northern Ireland for wholesale purposes are out of scope of this guidance. This is permitted under the supervision of an RP.

Products with a UK or Great Britain marketing authorisation that are imported into Great Britain from outside the UK without QP certification from a country on the list will require QP certification under a UK manufacturing and import authorisation before being placed on the market.

Products without a marketing authorisation in the UK, Northern Ireland, Great Britain or a listed country are outside the scope of this guidance. Importation of such products is permitted under the supervision of an RP, with notification to the MHRA of each importation that is for supply to the Great Britain market.

Introduction

The RPi is responsible for implementing a system to confirm products that have been imported into Great Britain from countries on an approved country-for-import list (initially, this will be countries in the EEA):

- that the required QP certification has taken place;
- that the required independent batch release certificate is available for biological products (described on a wholesale dealer's license as "immunologicals and blood products").

The RPi may delegate the activity of checking this certification has taken place but remains responsible for ensuring the effectiveness of these checks.

The RPi is required to implement a system for confirming QP certification and independent batch release certification (for biological products) has taken place when importing into Great Britain the following products from a listed country:

- a UK or Great Britain licensed medicine for use in Great Britain;
- a UK or Great Britain licensed medicine for supply to another third country;
- a Northern Ireland or approved country licensed medicine for supply to fulfil special clinical needs;
- a Northern Ireland or approved country licensed medicine imported as an introduced medicine for supply to another third country;
- a Northern Ireland or approved country licensed medicine for use as a parallel import.

What evidence can be used for QP certification

The RPi should ensure that written evidence is available to demonstrate that each batch of product has been QP certified as required in Article 51 of Directive 2001/83/EC.

Not all options listed below may be suitable for different supply chain relationships; however, just one of these pieces of evidence is sufficient to satisfy the requirements of regulation 45AA of the Human Medicines

Regulations 2012. Other evidence may be acceptable provided it confirms that QP certification has taken place for the batch in question.

EVIDENCE FOR GREAT BRITAIN WHOLESALE DEALERS LICENCE (WDA(H)) HOLDERS IMPORTING A UK, NORTHERN IRELAND, GREAT BRITAIN OR EEA LICENSED MEDICINE FROM A LISTED COUNTRY

Batch certification by a QP may be confirmed using evidence such as:

- batch certificate confirming QP certification in accordance with Article 51 of Directive 2001/83/EC;
- a copy of the "control report" (Appendix II to EU Good Manufacturing Practice Annex 16);
- statement of certification (ad hoc, confirming certification in accordance with Article 51 of Directive 2001/83/EC);
- reference to company internal systems (e.g. global Enterprise Resource Planning system) that shows batch certification;
- confirmation that the final manufacturing step (other than batch certification) of an authorised medicine has been performed by a Manufacturing and Import Authorisation holder in a listed country. A copy of the Marketing Authorisation and technical agreement with the manufacturer should be available to place reliance on this supply chain control;
- for medicines authorised in a listed country, batch certification may be verified by confirming that the medicine has been purchased from an authorised wholesaler after it has been "placed on the market" in the listed country.

WHAT EVIDENCE CAN BE USED FOR INDEPENDENT BATCH RELEASE CERTIFICATION?

Biological products requiring independent batch release certification are listed on the European Directorate for Quality of Medicines website.

Independent batch release may be confirmed using evidence such as:

- a statement from the marketing authorisation holder confirming that a batch certificate has been issued by NIBSC or a Mutual Recognition Agreement partner;
- a copy of the batch certificate issued by NIBSC or a Mutual Recognition Agreement partner;
- confirmation from NIBSC that a batch certificate has been issued. Enquiries should be sent to CPB@nibsc.org.

Batches of QP certified biological medicines that require independent batch release should not be sold or supplied by the importing wholesale dealer in Great Britain until independent batch release certification is also confirmed.

Additional guidance

SUPPLY CHAIN SECURITY

Checks on products imported from a listed country should also ensure that the product is not the subject of a recall or reported as stolen, and is available on the market within the listed country's licensed supply chain. Good Distribution Practice (GDP) requirements for supplier qualification set out in GDP 5.2 must be maintained. The MHRA's supplier verification blog provides additional information. Products that have been certified by a QP but have been diverted to countries not within a listed country or Northern Ireland must be imported by the holder of an MIA and re-certified by a QP.

PRODUCTS IMPORTED FOR PARALLEL IMPORT OR SPECIAL NEED

From 1 January 2022, the RPi should implement a process to confirm the status of the unique identifier for Prescription-Only Medicines, if wholesale dealers are importing products:

- for parallel import;
- for use for special clinical need or introduction.

This is required by the EU's Falsified Medicine Directive. Confirmation of decommissioning may be provided by using evidence such as National Medicines Verification System records from the supplier.

From 1 January 2022, products that are supplied as decommissioned must be decommissioned by the final EEA supplier and not at any other point in the supply chain.

GREAT BRITAIN WDA(H) HOLDERS ACTING AS OR ON BEHALF OF THE UK MARKETING AUTHORISATION HOLDER (MAH)

For Great Britain, WDA(H) holders acting as or on behalf of the UK or Great Britain MAH, the expectation is that products have been certified prior to importation. Shipment to Great Britain under pre-certification quarantine is not acceptable for the WDA(H) importation model.

If supply chains require shipment under quarantine prior to QP certification for technical reasons (e.g. products with very short shelf-life), the MAH should seek further advice from the MHRA by email to GDP. Inspectorate@mhra.gov.uk

Working as an RPi

If you are named as an RPi on a WDA(H), you have an important role in ensuring the safe control of medicines. You have training and an understanding of the industry in order to qualify for the role, where you have the legal responsibility to ensure that batches of authorised medicines imported from countries on a list have been appropriately certified prior to being placed on the Great Britain market.

You will take responsibility for implementing a system for the WDA(H) as a whole. There is no requirement for each site on the WDA(H) to name its own RPi. You do not have to be an employee of the licence holder but must be continuously contactable. Where you are not an employee, there should be a written contract between the licence holder and the RPi specifying responsibilities, duties, authority and time on site.

If you are a contract RPi then you are expected to ensure that you do not over-extend yourself and apply to act as RPi for too many companies.

Becoming an RPi

There are several stages to becoming named as an RPi.

ELIGIBILITY

You must first demonstrate that you are eligible to act as an RPi. This is through a combination of relevant qualifications and experience. It is also expected that you will be a full member of a professional body with a published code of conduct. Once eligibility has been assessed and accepted by the MHRA, you can be named on a register; the register will be maintained by the MHRA and will include all persons eligible to be named as an RPi.

The regulations set out expectations for qualifications, experience and membership of professional bodies.

QUALIFICATIONS

Acceptable qualifications are a diploma, certificate or other evidence of formal qualifications awarded on completion of a university or other higher education course of study in:

- pharmacy;
- chemistry;
- medicine;
- biology; or
- a related life science.

Equivalent qualifications acceptable for RPi candidates include:

- level 5 qualifications from the Chartered Institute of Logistics and Transport;
- a Quality Management System Lead Auditor or Pharmaceutical GMP Lead Auditor qualification awarded by the Chartered Quality Institute.

Other qualifications may also be acceptable. These will be checked during the application process. You can check the suitability of your qualifications by email to GDP.Inspectorate@mhra.gov.uk.

EXPERIENCE

You must be able to demonstrate, e.g. by providing a curriculum vitae (CV), that you have a minimum of 2 years' experience in performing the functions of a responsible person on a WDA(H). Evidence of performing other functions, e.g. a quality assurance role for a pharmaceutical manufacturer, may also be considered equivalent.

PROFESSIONAL BODIES

Acceptable professional body memberships are:

- Royal Society of Biology;
- Royal Pharmaceutical Society;
- Pharmaceutical Society of Northern Ireland;
- Royal Society of Chemistry.

Additional bodies that the licensing authority considers to be equivalent for RPi candidates include:

- the Chartered Institute of Logistics and Transport;
- the Chartered Quality Institute.
- the Organisation for Professionals in Regulatory Affairs.
- Association of Pharmacy Technicians UK (APTUK)

Other professional associations may be acceptable. These will be checked during the application process. You can check the suitability of your professional body membership by email to GDP.Inspectorate@mhra.gov.uk.

You will need to be a "full member" rather than an affiliate or student member of a professional body corresponding to your qualifications and experience. Affiliate membership of a professional body where you do not have a related qualification is not acceptable. You will need to demonstrate continual professional development and comply with the professional code of conduct expected by the professional body

QUALIFIED PERSONS ACTING AS RPI

If you are a person named on the Qualified Persons' register you will also be eligible to act as an RPi. You must still apply to be named on the RPi register. As an alternative to providing evidence of your qualifications and membership of a professional body, you may provide evidence of your QP registration.

SUITABILITY

You must also demonstrate suitability to be named on a specific WDA(H) licence. At the time of application, the MHRA will confirm whether you are named on the register, and check whether your experience is suitable for the proposed licence activity. For example, an eligible RPi without prior experience in parallel importation might not be considered suitable to be named on a WDA(H) where the company are importing licensed products for parallel trade.

APPLYING TO BE NAMED AS AN RPI

RPi applications may be submitted through the MHRA Portal from 1 January 2021.

The Responsible Person (import) (RPi) is described in Regulations 45AA and 45AB of the Human Medicines Regulations 2012 (as amended).

The RPi should be a UK resident. You will need to provide proof of address and identity when you apply.

Chapter 3 Premises and Equipment

3.1 Principle

Wholesale distributors must have suitable and adequate premises, installations and equipment[5], so as to ensure proper storage and distribution of medicinal products. In particular, the premises should be clean, dry and maintained within acceptable temperature limits.

3.2 Premises

The premises should be designed or adapted to ensure that the required storage conditions are maintained. They should be suitably secure, structurally sound and of sufficient capacity to allow safe storage and handling of the medicinal products. Storage areas should be provided with adequate lighting to enable all operations to be carried out accurately and safely.

Where premises are not directly operated by the wholesale distributor, a contract should be in place. The contracted premises should be covered by a separate wholesale distribution authorisation.

Medicinal products should be stored in segregated areas which are clearly marked and have access restricted to authorised personnel. Any system replacing physical segregation, such as electronic segregation based on a computerised system, should provide equivalent security and should be validated.

Products pending a decision as to their disposition or products that have been removed from saleable stock should be segregated either physically or through an equivalent electronic system. This includes, for example, any product suspected of falsification and returned products. Medicinal products received from a third country but not intended for the Union market should also be physically segregated. Any falsified medicinal products, expired products, recalled products and rejected products found in the supply chain should be immediately physically segregated and stored in a dedicated area away from all other medicinal products. The appropriate degree of security should be applied in these areas to ensure that such

---

[5] Article 79(a) of Directive 2001/83/EC.

items remain separate from saleable stock. These areas should be clearly identified.

Special attention should be paid to the storage of products with specific handling instructions as specified in national law. Special storage conditions (and special authorisations) may be required for such products (e.g. narcotics and psychotropic substances).

Radioactive materials and other hazardous products, as well as products presenting special safety risks of fire or explosion (e.g. medicinal gases, combustibles, flammable liquids and solids), should be stored in one or more dedicated areas subject to local legislation and appropriate safety and security measures.

Receiving and dispatch bays should protect products from prevailing weather conditions. There should be adequate separation between the receipt and dispatch and storage areas. Procedures should be in place to maintain control of inbound/outbound goods. Reception areas where deliveries are examined following receipt should be designated and suitably equipped.

Unauthorised access to all areas of the authorised premises should be prevented. Prevention measures would usually include a monitored intruder alarm system and appropriate access control. Visitors should be accompanied.

Premises and storage facilities should be clean and free from litter and dust. Cleaning programmes, instructions and records should be in place. Appropriate cleaning equipment and cleaning agents should be chosen and used so as not to present a source of contamination.

Premises should be designed and equipped so as to afford protection against the entry of insects, rodents or other animals. A preventive pest control programme should be in place.

Rest, wash and refreshment rooms for employees should be adequately separated from the storage areas. The presence of food, drink, smoking material or medicinal products for personal use should be prohibited in the storage areas.

3.2.1 TEMPERATURE AND ENVIRONMENT CONTROL

Suitable equipment and procedures should be in place to check the environment where medicinal products are stored. Environmental factors to be considered include temperature, light, humidity and cleanliness of the premises.

An initial temperature mapping exercise should be carried out on the storage area before use, under representative conditions. Temperature monitoring equipment should be located according to the results of the mapping exercise, ensuring that monitoring devices are positioned in the areas that experience the extremes of fluctuations. The mapping exercise should be repeated according to the results of a risk assessment exercise or whenever significant modifications are made to the facility or the temperature controlling equipment. For small premises of a few square meters which are at room temperature, an assessment of potential risks (e.g. heaters) should be conducted and temperature monitors placed accordingly.

3.3 Equipment

All equipment impacting on storage and distribution of medicinal products should be designed, located and maintained to a standard which suits its intended purpose. Planned maintenance should be in place for key equipment vital to the functionality of the operation.

Equipment used to control or to monitor the environment where the medicinal products are stored should be calibrated at defined intervals based on a risk and reliability assessment.

Calibration of equipment should be traceable to a national or international measurement standard. Appropriate alarm systems should be in place to provide alerts when there are excursions from predefined storage conditions. Alarm levels should be appropriately set and alarms should be regularly tested to ensure adequate functionality.

Equipment repair, maintenance and calibration operations should be carried out in such a way that the integrity of the medicinal products is not compromised.

Adequate records of repair, maintenance and calibration activities for key equipment should be made and the results should be retained. Key equipment would include, for example, cold stores, monitored intruder alarm and access control systems, refrigerators, thermo hygrometers, or other temperature- and humidity recording devices, air handling units and any equipment used in conjunction with the onward supply chain.

3.3.1 COMPUTERISED SYSTEMS

Before a computerised system is brought into use, it should be demonstrated, through appropriate validation or verification studies, that the system is capable of achieving the desired results accurately, consistently and reproducibly.

A written, detailed description of the system should be available (including diagrams where appropriate). This should be kept up to date. The document should describe principles, objectives, security measures, system scope and main features, how the computerised system is used and the way it interacts with other systems.

Data should only be entered into the computerised system or amended by persons authorised to do so.

Data should be secured by physical or electronic means and protected against accidental or unauthorised modifications. Stored data should be checked periodically for accessibility. Data should be protected by backing up at regular intervals. Back up data should be retained for the period stated in national legislation but at least five years at a separate and secure location.

Procedures to be followed if the system fails or breaks down should be defined. This should include systems for the restoration of data.

3.3.2 QUALIFICATION AND VALIDATION

Wholesale distributors should identify what key equipment qualification and/or key process validation is necessary to ensure correct installation and operation. The scope and extent of such qualification and/or validation activities (such as storage, pick and pack processes) should be determined using a documented risk assessment approach.

Equipment and processes should be respectively qualified and/or validated before commencing use and after any significant changes, e.g. repair or maintenance.

Validation and qualification reports should be prepared summarising the results obtained and commenting on any observed deviations. Deviations from established procedures should be documented and further actions decided to correct deviations and avoid their reoccurrence (corrective and preventive actions). The principles of CAPA should be applied where necessary. Evidence of satisfactory validation and acceptance of a process or piece of equipment should be produced and approved by appropriate personnel.

UK Guidance on Chapter 3 Premises and Equipment

Qualification and validation of equipment including computerised systems

The main GDP expectation for qualification and validation of equipment is that the company has identified what equipment is critical to their operations, and that they have a proportionate approach to qualification during installation or following repair or modification in line with quality risk management principles.

A wholesaler may, for example, consider qualification of an uninterrupted power supply generator to power a cold room as being critical and likely to include a high degree of input from external engineers with high impact if it fails, so testing of the system is likely to be extensive to ensure that the unit will operate reliably. Less critical equipment, such as a thermometer, may be considered by the wholesaler to require less extensive qualification, especially where they are of simple design, and multiple thermometers enable some continuous monitoring.

Examples of equipment often deemed most critical include uninterrupted power supply generators, cooling system for cold rooms and electronic staff access systems.

Computerised systems cover a wide range of functions and, as with other equipment, the company should be aware of the most critical systems as well as inherent risks. Factors that may contribute to risk related to software include:

- application (WMS, inventory management, product scanning, premises security);
- design (off-the-shelf, customisable off-the-shelf, bespoke);
- connectivity (customer access portals, networking across company sites, compatibility with other software systems including on-site and with field force);
- maintenance and stability;
- management (in-house, outsourced);
- criticality of data (corruption prevention, protection against unauthorised changes, back-up and restoration functions, archiving).

The extent of qualification or validation for computerised systems should challenge the weakest parts of the system and take account of the greatest risk of system non-compliance or potential failure, rather than simply relying on validation or qualification of the most robust parts of any system.

Temperature control and monitoring

Manufacturers subject their products to stability studies that are used to determine appropriate storage conditions including those for temperature. These conditions are therefore specific for each product, and a licensed wholesale dealer should refer to manufacturers' information when deciding the storage conditions to use.

Following manufacture, some medicinal products can be stored and transported at ambient temperature, whereas others may require lower than ambient temperatures to assure their quality and efficacy.

These are often referred to as "cold chain products" or "fridge lines" and wholesale dealers are expected to store and distribute them in strict accordance with the product labelling requirements as stated in the GDP Guidelines: Chapters 5.5 (Storage) and 9.2 (Transportation) give more information.

Medicinal products experiencing an adverse temperature may undergo physical, chemical or microbiological degradation. In the most serious of cases this may lead to conversion of the medicine to ineffective or harmful forms. The ability to detect these changes may not appear until the medicine has been consumed, and it is therefore essential that appropriate temperature conditions are controlled and monitored throughout each step of the supply chain. This section concerns temperature mapping and the on-going temperature monitoring and control required throughout the wholesale supply chain.

TEMPERATURE MAPPING

Chapter 3.2.1 of the GDP Guidelines states:

"An initial temperature mapping exercise should be carried out on the storage area before use, under representative conditions.

Temperature monitoring equipment should be located according to the results of the mapping exercise, ensuring that monitoring devices are positioned in the areas that experience the extremes of fluctuations.

The mapping exercise should be repeated according to the results of a risk assessment exercise or whenever significant modifications are made to the facility or the temperature controlling equipment.

For small premises of a few square meters which are at room temperature, an assessment of potential risks (e.g. heaters) should be conducted and temperature monitors placed accordingly."

Although the guidelines say that mapping should take place, this should be specific and relevant to your own storage area. The duration of a mapping exercise should be determined based on the variability of the environment and data recorded rather than a standard set period.

Temperature mapping should be carried out to demonstrate, by way of documented evidence, that the chosen storage area is suitable for the storage of temperature-sensitive medicinal products. A mapping exercise of the proposed storage area will also ensure that the company understands their storage area and has identified any potential areas therein that may be unsuitable to store medicines. A mapping exercise will also inform as to where permanent thermometers should be located.

Temperature mapping should be carried out before stock is stored. This might not be possible where a storage area is being reconfigured. In smaller empty storage areas, dummy products could be used to simulate normal operational storage without compromising genuine product, including cold stores and fridges/freezers. In an empty storage area, a mapping exercise should be repeated when fully stocked. Data arising from the exercise should be documented and a risk assessment documented with any hot or cold spots identified. This exercise should then be repeated to take into account seasonal variations.

To temperature map, first look at the area to be used for storage and identify the highest point of storage, not the highest shelf or pallet location. Identify any potential problem areas such as heaters, lighting, windows and doors, loading bays or high storage areas such as mezzanine floors. These areas should be covered in the exercise. Areas such as CD rooms, packing areas, returns and quarantine should be included. When deciding on a storage area, it can be difficult to cool storage areas down as well as heat them up. Calibrated monitoring probes should be used in sufficient numbers dependent on the size of the storage area.

Once the initial mapping exercise is complete, the data should be recorded and risk assessed to determine the most appropriate positions for the permanent monitoring probes and should cover the areas that have the widest temperature fluctuations or indicate areas with any hot or cold spots. A risk assessment would also define and justify the regularity of any future mapping exercises and must also be regularly reviewed, perhaps as part of the self-audit process.

The exercise should be repeated to cover seasonal variations or if the storage area is subsequently reconfigured.

The RP should be party to the whole mapping process and should be fully aware of the mapping exercise findings, risk assessment recommendations and review process. The RP's involvement does not stop at the mapping process, however; the RP should also be able to demonstrate supervision and review of subsequent daily minimum/maximum routine temperature monitoring and recording and should be consulted in the event of any temperature excursions.

Refrigerated and ambient medicinal products: receipt, storage and packing

RECEIPT OF REFRIGERATED PRODUCTS

When cold chain products are received, it is important that they are checked in as a matter of priority and placed in a pharmaceutical refrigerator.

The person responsible for receiving the delivery must also satisfy themselves that the goods have been transported under appropriate conditions (e.g. there has been no direct contact between the products and gel or ice blocks, or if the consignment is warm to the touch).

If it cannot be confirmed that the products have been transported under appropriate conditions and there is concern that their quality may have been compromised, the delivery should be quarantined in a suitable refrigerator while enquiries are made with the supplier.

Until the issue has been clarified, the products in question should be considered as unsuitable and should not be supplied.

If, after enquiries, there is still doubt as to the quality of the medicines received, the delivery should not be accepted and should be returned to the supplier.

STORAGE OF REFRIGERATED PRODUCTS IN A PHARMACEUTICAL REFRIGERATOR

The equipment used for the storage of refrigerated medicinal products should be demonstrably suitable and fit for purpose. Due to the configuration of domestic refrigerators, they are often found to be unsuitable for the storage of pharmaceutical products.

The air within a pharmaceutical refrigerator is typically circulated by a fan, which provides a uniform temperature profile and a rapid temperature pull down after the door has been opened.

Temperature monitoring is recorded by a calibrated electronic min/max thermometer, with an accuracy of ±0.5°C, which can be read without opening the refrigerator door.

Additional benefits are that these refrigerators can be locked and some have the option of either an audio or visual alarm system to alert staff in the event of temperature deviations.

Many refrigerators have glass-fronted doors giving greater visibility of stock levels, aiding stock management and also deterring the storage of non-medicinal products.

When purchasing a new refrigerator, factors to consider might also include how long the unit can maintain the required temperatures if the power is turned off and to what extent the temperature is affected by external ambient temperature variation, e.g. in hot spells.

TEMPERATURE MONITORING IN A REFRIGERATOR

As is applicable for transportation, products stored in a refrigerator should be subject to daily temperature monitoring by a minimum and maximum calibrated device with a supporting appropriate calibration certificate.

Temperature records should identify any temperature deviations and give details of corrective actions taken as a result.

For instances where there has been a temperature deviation, best practice would be to take a further reading later the same day, to ensure that it was a transient deviation, and show that the temperature was now back within prescribed parameters.

The RP should be informed of any deviations.

Temperature records are especially important in the event of a problem with a product and may be required as evidence of appropriate storage. With this in mind, they should be free from alterations or corrections and the person responsible for taking the readings each day should have a trained deputy to cover for absences.

The records should be routinely reviewed and signed off by the RP.

SMALL REFRIGERATORS

It should be demonstrated that refrigerators used to store pharmaceuticals are fit for purpose. In the simplest of cases, a new off-the-shelf refrigerator, installed according to the manufacturer's instructions and temperature monitored with an appropriate device, may be considered appropriately qualified for storing cold chain product that is shown to be unaffected by minor temperature excursions. A refrigerator used for holding more susceptible stock such as biological products will require more extensive qualification.

In addition to temperature mapping and monitoring there should be safeguards to preserve appropriate storage conditions. Some small refrigerators are purported to be medical or pharmaceutical refrigerators but this on its own does not automatically render them suitable for wholesale use. The refrigerator should be capable of restoring the temperature quickly after the door has been opened and without danger of overshooting to extreme cold. This could be assisted by an internal fan and good shelf design that enables an efficient airflow. There should be no internal ice-box and no internal temperature dials capable of being inadvertently knocked and adjusted.

Storage practices for using small refrigerators should include consideration of segregation of stock with different status, e.g. incoming, quarantine, returned and outgoing stock. Sufficient space should be maintained to permit adequate air circulation and product should not be stored in contact with the walls or on the floor of the refrigerator. If the refrigerator is filled to capacity the effect on temperature distribution should be investigated. Where non-refrigerated items are introduced to the refrigerator, such as non-conditioned gel packs, the impact of introducing these items should be assessed regarding the increase in temperature that they cause.

LARGE COMMERCIAL REFRIGERATORS AND WALK-IN COLD ROOMS

Large commercial refrigerators and walk-in cold rooms should be of appropriate design, suitably sited and constructed with appropriate materials. Consideration should be given to protecting entry points from ingress of warm air. The design should ensure that general principles of GDP can be maintained, such as segregation of stock. Condensate from chillers should not be collected inside the unit and there should be a capability of carrying out routine maintenance and service activities as much as possible from outside the unit. The temperature should be monitored with an electronic temperature-recording device that measures load temperature in one or more locations, depending on the size of the unit, and alarms should be fitted to indicate power outages and temperature excursions.

FREEZERS

Most of the problems seen with use of freezers also apply to refrigerators. The same general principles apply to freezers as apply to other cold chain storage units above. Walk-in freezers pose a significant operator health and safety risk, and the impact of ways of working should be reviewed with consideration of risk to causing temperature excursions.

Design considerations

When buying a new freezer, the user should consider what it is to be used for and how they intend using it. This may appear obvious but the use of freezers that are not fit for use and unsuitable operating practices are regularly seen.

The most common use of freezers by wholesalers is for storing and conditioning cold packs for inclusion in passive transport containers. There may also be a need to store frozen medicinal products such as some vaccines, although the range of medicines that require to be stored frozen is small.

The intended use will determine the extent to which a particular freezer design meets your needs, or if any special measures need to be put in place. Consideration should be given to what temperature range you require, with a diversity of freezer models being available that maintain a variety of frozen temperatures. Storage conditions for specific medicines may be found by referring to packaging details or the Summary of Product Characteristics available from the manufacturers' medicines regulatory authority or from the manufacturer.

Considerations of use

Prior to use the freezer should be fully qualified in line with GDP qualification requirements and the exercise documented both for small freezers, in which case qualification may be very simple, and large freezers installed by external specialists. Installation of the freezer should include risk assessment of the impact of the installation, e.g. effect of heat generation by the freezer on the surrounding area. Personnel should be instructed on how to use the freezer, and there should be notification to those staff restricted from using it.

As with all equipment (including freezers and cold packs), don't just rely on qualification data from the marketing brochure or sales rep; make sure qualification fully meets your needs.

Domestic freezers are unlikely to have adequate power to rapidly freeze cold packs from room temperature and may not be suitable for the storage of frozen pharmaceutical products.

Storage of medicines

The range of medicines that require storage in a freezer is small, and the storage equipment most often seen are small freezers holding a small quantity of medicine. There is often a temptation to use the same freezer for other purposes such as conditioning of cold packs. This increases risk to the stored medicines, because high temperature excursions are created either by unconditioned cold packs loaded in bulk or by increased access to the freezer to load or remove the cold packs. It is therefore recommended that freezers used for storing medicines be dedicated in use or otherwise demonstrated to be not adversely affected by freezing cold packs. If the volume of frozen medicines is very small, then the wholesaler should consider whether it is worth either not holding those lines or outsourcing the holding of cold chain medicines to a wholesaler better suited to storing them.

Some companies compromise by using dual refrigerator/freezer units. Although less expensive and with a smaller footprint than separate units, if one unit becomes non-functional then both units are compromised. In addition, if both units are served by a single compressor, the ability of the equipment to maintain temperature in one unit may affect its ability to maintain the other unit. This may be a concern if frozen medicines are stored and the refrigerator is in frequent use, if regular defrosting of the refrigerator occurs or where the thermostat setting for one unit is adjusted.

The majority of frozen medicines require storage in the range of −15°C to −20°C, and the responsibility is on the wholesaler to ensure that they know what frozen temperature is required for a particular product and that the freezer used can maintain this. Requirements to temperature monitor and map freezers for storing medicines or conditioning cold packs are the same as for refrigerators.

Not all frozen medicines require storage at the same frozen temperature.

Conditioning of cold packs

In order for cold packs to perform consistently several points need to be considered. The first is to ensure that the correct type of pack is used because they are designed to maintain different temperatures. This is brought about by the use of different phase change materials, which are materials that change between liquid and solid phases at specific temperatures. One effect of this change in phase is that the pack maintains a stable temperature throughout the change. A pack designed for −15°C may therefore not be suitable for maintaining +5°C.

The packs should be used in accordance with either the manufacturers' instructions or the conditions established through undertaking a qualification exercise. This is because all packs are not the same, e.g. some packs designed to be conditioned within a refrigerator may not be suitable for conditioning within a freezer, and some types are not suitable for multiple freeze/thaw cycles.

CONTROL AND MONITORING OF STORAGE AREAS

Where medicines that may be required in an emergency are stored then contingency measures should be put in place such as linking essential equipment in a large warehouse to a source of emergency power. These emergency measures should be routinely tested, such as the confirmation of restoration of stored data and settings when emergency power supply is activated and after normal power has been resumed. For these products there should be a system in place to ensure that on-call personnel are notified in the event of power failure or temperature alarms being triggered, including notification outside of normal working hours.

BEST PRACTICE

Whatever type of refrigerator or cold store is used, once a mapping exercise has taken place, products should be stored in an orderly fashion on shelves – not directly on the floor of the unit – to ensure air circulation and consistent temperatures throughout and to facilitate cleaning.

Calibrated temperature-monitoring probes should be sited in a central location within the refrigerator and, preferably, between the products.

Probes should not be placed in the door.

The refrigerator should be cleaned regularly (as part of a general cleaning rota) and serviced at least annually.

If the refrigerator is fitted with an audible or visual alarm, this should be routinely tested to confirm correct operation at specified appropriate temperatures.

The stock within the refrigerator should be subject to effective stock rotation based on first expiry, first out (FEFO).

It should not be assumed that the most recent deliveries would have a longer expiry period.

Refrigerators containing medicinal products must not be used for the storage of food and drink or anything that might contaminate the medicinal products.

Calibration of temperature monitoring devices including ambient

In order to have confidence in temperature readings, monitoring devices should be calibrated to demonstrate that they have appropriate accuracy and precision. Temperate storage thermometers should be accurate to ±1°C, and cold chain devices accurate to ±0.5°C. Calibration should extend across the whole of the anticipated working range, so for a temperate storage range of 15–25°C the calibration range may be 10–30°C to allow the thermometer to be used either in assessing temperature excursions or in temperature-mapping exercises. Results of the calibration exercise should be presented in a report or calibration certificate approved by the calibrator and demonstrated to be appropriate for use by the wholesaler. The certificate should include the following details:

- serial number of the calibrated instrument;
- serial numbers of test instruments;
- traceability to national or international calibration standards;
- calibration test method used;
- ISO or equivalent registration details of calibration laboratory;

- date of calibration;
- calibration results;
- unique certificate number;
- approval of results by calibrator.

Where a temperature-monitoring device reads the temperature from a main monitoring unit plus a remote probe, it should be clear from the calibration certificate which part of the device the calibration refers to. Calibration should be carried out annually and, where adjustments are made to the equipment as part of calibration, an assessment of accuracy and precision should be made before and after adjustment. On completion a suitable representative from the wholesaler should approve the calibration indicating its suitability for use.

Short-term Storage of Ambient and Refrigerated Medicinal Products – Requirements for a Wholesale Dealer's Licence

The GDP Guidelines define wholesale distribution as: "all activities consisting of procuring, holding, supplying or exporting medicinal products".

GDP Chapter 9 requires that "provision should be made to minimise the duration of temporary storage while awaiting the next stage of the transportation route".

The Glossary of Terms defines holding as "storing medicinal products". Medicinal products should therefore only be stored on premises that are covered by a wholesale dealer's licence. However, there are certain cases where medicinal products are held for short periods of time during transportation and prior to onward shipment, e.g. in overnight freight depots. In such instances it has been determined that, as a matter of policy, a site is not required to be licensed where:

- ambient products remain for less than 36 hours;
- cold chain products are transported and stored overnight in continuously refrigerated vehicles or in qualified packaging;
- vehicles are in transit and product is not unloaded at the site.

As a matter of policy, a site must be licensed where:

- ambient products are held in excess of 36 hours;
- products requiring refrigeration are placed in a cold store, even when this is for less than 36 hours;
- wholesaling activities other than storage are being carried out. This includes the handling of returned goods and where decisions are made regarding suitability for resale, as well as the usual activities of picking against orders;
- ownership has been transferred.

Where transportation is performed by a third party and they are holding product, then they require a WDA(H) naming the relevant sites. Whether the licensed sites require naming as third parties on the supplying wholesaler's licence will depend on the nature of the commercial and GDP contracts. In general, if the product is "in transit", the transport site is not required to be named as a third party on the supplier's licence.

Chapter 4 Documentation

4.1 Principle

Good documentation constitutes an essential part of the quality system. Written documentation should prevent errors from spoken communication and permits the tracking of relevant operations during the distribution of medicinal products.

4.2 General

Documentation comprises all written procedures, instructions, contracts, records and data, in paper or in electronic form. Documentation should be readily available/retrievable.

With regard to the processing of personal data of employees, complainants or any other natural person, Directive 95/46/EC[6] on the protection of individuals applies to the processing of personal data and to the free movement of such data.

Documentation should be sufficiently comprehensive with respect to the scope of the wholesale distributor's activities and in a language understood by personnel. It should be written in clear, unambiguous language and be free from errors.

Procedure should be approved signed and dated by the responsible person. Documentation should be approved, signed and dated by appropriate authorised persons, as required. It should not be handwritten, although, where necessary, sufficient space should be provided for such entries.

Any alteration made in the documentation should be signed and dated; the alteration should permit the reading of the original information. Where appropriate, the reason for the alteration should be recorded.

Documents should be retained for the period stated in national legislation for at least five years. Personal data should be deleted or anonymised as soon as their storage is no longer necessary for the purpose of distribution activities.

EU GUIDELINES AND UK GUIDANCE ON WHOLESALE DISTRIBUTION PRACTICE

---

[6] OJ L 281, 23.11.1995, p. 31.

Each employee should have ready access to all necessary documentation for the tasks executed.

Attention should be paid to using valid and approved procedures. Documents should have unambiguous content; title, nature and purpose should be clearly stated. Documents should be reviewed regularly and kept up to date. Version control should be applied to procedures. After revision of a document a system should exist to prevent inadvertent use of the superseded version. Superseded or obsolete procedures should be removed from workstations and archived.

Records must be kept either in the form of purchase/sales invoices, delivery slips, or on computer or any other form, for any transaction in medicinal products received, supplied or brokered.

Records must include at least the following information: date; name of the medicinal product; quantity received, supplied or brokered; name and address of the supplier, customer, broker or consignee, as appropriate; and batch number at least for medicinal product bearing the safety features[7].

Records should be made at the time each operation is undertaken.

UK Guidance on Chapter 4 Documentation

Document control

Document control encompasses document lifecycle management and is required for control of quality and operational aspects of an organisation. Documentation must be controlled at all times. There are various levels of control that must be applied in line with the principles of quality risk management. For example, copies of procedures may be provided to third parties as uncontrolled copies of the controlled document or just valid on the day of printing. The system of controlling documents and document templates should be described within a procedure.

The document lifecycle

Quality documents need to follow a lifecycle approach in order to ensure adequate control. The basic stages of the life cycle are as follows:

CREATION

The requirement of the document needs to be clearly identified. Relevant subject matter experts should be involved that ensures not only that it

---

[7] Article 80(e) and Article 82 of Directive 2001/83/EC.

reflects intended use, but also that it is likely to be understood by all users and may assist their buy-in. The use of a standard template helps to ensure that all relevant sections are included, and assists the reader in navigation throughout the document.

REVIEW

The created document should be reviewed prior to approval in order to check technical accuracy, assess its adherence to business objectives and corporate standards for controlled documents, assess any inconsistencies with other documents in the quality system and ensure that its main objective has been met.

APPROVAL

If the draft document is deemed satisfactory, it should be approved by an appropriate authorised person and entered onto the register of controlled documents.

IMPLEMENTATION

The issue date may precede the implementation date to allow time to distribute and train the document, in which it should be clearly stated when the new document takes effect. Documents should be readily accessible to those that are required to use them. All distributed copies should be traceable, including those issued to external parties. It is likely that issuance is aligned with the training programme for major revisions.

USE

The procedure is readily available and in use.

WITHDRAWAL

Notice should be given to all relevant parties when their copy of the document is to be withdrawn. This is likely to align with issuance of a new version. Reconciliation of all circulated copies should take place and followed up where a copy has not been returned.

DESTRUCTION

Documents should be destroyed in line with relevant retention periods. Where more than one retention period exist (e.g. Home Office controlled drug records), the longest required retention period should be adhered to. For GDP records this is generally five years; however, exceptions are in place.

Operating procedures

It is vital that procedures are written with the full involvement of the organisation for which they are intended. This not only ensures that procedures are reflective of the organisation but also enables the organisation to define and develop its own processes. Where procedures intended for other organisations are used, this can often result in inefficiency and non-compliance.

When writing procedures, considerations should be made for all relevant users such as quality personnel, operators and trainers. Documentation should be sufficiently comprehensive with respect to the scope of the wholesale distributor's activities and use a technical level of language understood by personnel. All acronyms and company specific terms should be clearly defined within either the document or a dedicated glossary. Complex processes can be represented by the use of flow charts or visual representations.

Records

The retention and control of records is also an essential aspect of good documentation practice. Records are present in various categories and include;

- financial records, e.g. a purchase order or sales invoice;
- quality records, e.g. deviations and CAPAs;
- employee training and competence records;
- routine monitoring records, i.e. records of equipment maintenance, temperature records and pest control;
- qualification records, i.e. evidence of temperature mapping and transport validation.

Different types of records may need specific considerations to enable full control, for example:

Sales invoices are often a duplicate form also serving as a delivery note by the supplier. There may be a risk that a copy of this used by the accounts department is not maintained as an exact copy, with the consequence that they become contradictory, especially where stock adjustments have been made on one copy.

Where controlled forms have different sections that are managed individually, such as a deviation and associated CAPAs, the individually assigned CAPA forms can become separated from the parent deviation. Records can also become inconsistent, with closure of the deviation being inconsistent with closure of the associated CAPA.

Training records should be available for all members of staff involved and do not often reflect competence of staff. Records should demonstrate briefing of staff that do not have direct GDP responsibilities but could impact GDP operations by their activities, e.g. where they work in a shared warehouse.

Routine monitoring records: the most commonly reviewed monitoring records are temperature-monitoring records. Very often these are reviewed only to confirm that temperatures are in range and not reviewed for trending, which may indicate a system is about to fail. Externally signed maintenance records (e.g. HVAC servicing or pest control) are not always confirmed by the wholesaler, and not always legible or completed to an appropriate standard of recording.

Qualification records are often not correlated with an appropriately defined objective or protocol, which in turn prevents the ability to ascertain if the exercise was successful or not. Reports of externally generated exercises need to be understood by the wholesaler, and approved if appropriate. This is a common problem observed with external calibration of devices.

In order to ensure that records are fully traceable, appropriate logs or registers should be in place. Examples of registers may include a log of procedures, training logs, registers of CAPAs and change control logs. These should be easy to update and maintain in an accurate state.

Restrictions on availability of records

Measures must be in place in order to enable the appropriate control of access to sensitive information, including records and other documents. For permanent staff, this may include limitation to access documents pertinent to their role. Personnel information should be protected in line with General Data Protection Regulation or other similar requirements. Access to commercially sensitive information may need to be restricted for temporary staff and contractors. Patient-specific information associated with orders needs to be restricted for non-relevant staff. The Responsible Person needs to maintain oversight of such information in order to ensure that these supplies are maintained and measures are in place to prevent supply of medicines against falsified redacted prescriptions.

It is vital that the Responsible Person has adequate oversight of the document control process and access to relevant records in order to fulfil their responsibilities.

Data Integrity

In order to trust GDP records, the data needs to be created in line with data integrity (DI) expectations. Data Integrity is the extent to which all data is complete, consistent and accurate throughout the data lifecycle. It is essential that this principle of DI be followed in order to ensure traceability of GDP activities and associated records and other documentation. Failure to meet this requirement has been present in all areas of GxP and, as a result, the MHRA has provided guidance published on the MHRA website that the reader is encouraged to refer to for a complete list of definitions and broader guidance.

Basic concepts

Failure in DI is often caused by weakness in implementation of measures that ensure that DI standards are implemented and maintained, referred to as Data Governance. The MHRA expects that appropriate measures are taken in respect to DI and Data Governance, and it should be clear which data is critical to regulatory compliance and product safety in order to ensure that appropriate resource is applied to the more critical data. For data that is not as important, less effort will be expected along with a rationale as to what data is deemed by the company as being not critical.

Criticality of data

Quality risk management lends itself as a useful tool to determine which data and records are critical to operations and therefore require more robust data governance measures. If GDP activity cannot be reconstructed should specific data be lost, then it can be assumed that the data in question is critical. For equipment that generates data, the extent of qualification in respect to DI should correlate with data criticality. Quality risk management can also be applied to identify which data and records are not critical, such as secondary records, and put in place measures to ensure that critical data does not inadvertently end up on the secondary record. An example of a secondary record is of a customer invoice that gets copied on receipt of stock and retained in the warehouse as evidence of delivery while the original is sent to the accountant. If the warehouse copy is subsequently annotated, e.g. to amend stock quantity booked in, then it is no longer a true copy of the original and therefore both need to be considered as master documents.

If data is transcribed from an instrument or hard copy record onto a computerised system and the original record is considered by the company to be non-critical, then consideration must be made as to how the company considers the original record as not being critical. Appropriate measures of review and approval of the transcribed records must be put in place. Any inconsistency in the computerised record would indicate failure not only in the integrity of the data but also in the governance process concerned with the review and approval of transcription, and any other records approved in the same way including records not related to this event would be circumspect.

ALCOA applied to GDP

A   ATTRIBUTABLE TO THE PERSON GENERATING THE DATA

Any critical data or information recorded for GDP purposes must be attributed to the originator. For hard copy records, entries should be traceable to the person making the record, with initialling and dating being developed as an unconscious habit. Where computerised systems are in use individuals are expected to access systems only by a unique password that can be traced to a level of permission. To guarantee this there should be adequate provision of terminals and a culture of logging out when not using shared devices to prevent work-around arrangements from being developed. A person with administrator access must not use this mode for anything other than maintenance operations and should have a separate user account for daily operations.

Where signatures or names relate to personnel outside of the organisation, e.g. engineer, then the name should be printed in addition to signing and they should also print their job role. For regular contacts, e.g. customers, a signature log may be developed and managed as a controlled document. Where shipments are international and parts of the delivery are outsourced, additional control measures should be put in place to maintain the chain of custody for the delivery from the warehouse to the customer.

L   LEGIBLE AND PERMANENT

Hard copy records are often not legible due to poor training of staff, poor form design and poor process design, and lead to errors in reading and transcription. Simple solutions include provision of clipboards to prevent warehouse and delivery forms being completed on top of non-flat surfaces, leading to poor writing, development of forms that accommodate those with large writing, and training staff in how to record errors and how to use traceable footnotes rather than squeeze notes into a small comments box. Replacement of hard copy with electronic records may improve legibility but may pose other problems such as poor accessibility to records.

The trend towards replacing manual systems with computerised ones has not always been met with appropriate assessment of risk, e.g. there may be emphasis placed on data back-up of records but little attention paid to the ability to restore records. Where computer systems are updated and previous software or hardware is no longer supported, then a quality risk assessment should be carried out and appropriate action undertaken to ensure that records can be retrieved.

The versatility and ease of use of electronic spreadsheets have led to them being very common. They lose the ability to retain original data that is overwritten and entries are normally not attributable to the recorder unless strict document control measures are put in place, including access control and versioning. Other approaches to control spreadsheets include printing in hard copy or pdf form and retaining a log of each approved version.

C CONTEMPORANEOUS

Records should be traceable to the time the activity is carried out in order to reduce the chance of the record being forgotten or traceability of actions lost. Some events are more time critical than others, such as execution of a medicine recall or qualification of a transport lane. In these circumstances recording of events must be consistent, especially where activity spans different time zones or different date formats are in use by the different organisations that are involved.

O ORIGINAL RECORD (OR TRUE COPY)

The original record refers to data as originally generated, preserving the integrity (accuracy, completeness, content and meaning) of the record, e.g. original paper record of manual observation, or electronic raw data file from a computerised system.

A true copy refers to a copy of original information that has been verified as an exact (accurate and complete) copy having all of the same attributes and information as the original. The copy may be verified by dated signature or by a validated electronic signature.

Where hard copy documents are scanned into electronic format for archiving, there must be a process of verification that all records are complete and an accurate representation of the original. Problems can exist where some documents in a bundle are of poor print quality, double-sided or a highlighter has been used. In these cases the electronic records may not be complete or a true copy of the original.

On occasions where documents are provided from third parties, such as copies or translations of customer wholesale dealer's licences, the document must be authenticated as a true copy by reference to an appropriate source such as a regulatory authority. Reliance solely on the word of the third party is not acceptable.

Where copies of originals are made they should be clearly able to be differentiated from the original and prevent mix-up. Possible control measures include use of watermarks, embossing or having original documents on coloured paper with restricted access to the paper.

A ACCURATE

Accuracy of data is essential to GDP, and having good processes to manage errors supports this. Deviation management should ensure that corrections are traceable and approved, and original incorrect data not lost. Processes and systems should be developed that drive accuracy rather than challenge it, and where data is manipulated then there should be defined rules controlling this, e.g. number rounding and conversion of units of measure. A common failure in this respect is in management of stock adjustments where physical stock count and stock records do not match. Stock records need to be managed in an open and honest manner and adjustments not hidden but corrected with appropriate justification and authorisation.

When formulae are used in electronic spreadsheets they are rarely qualified, in which case errors can be introduced without being noticed. The use of check boxes and formulae that detect nonsense values can help reduce errors.

Data governance

Having good quality data and records is not only essential to GDP but also a contributory factor in managing an effective and efficient operation. A fundamental requirement is the development of a quality culture, where all staff can identify weaknesses without feeling intimidated and understand the importance of maintaining accurate records and adherence to procedures.

Good training and level of knowledge is also required, especially for staff in quality assurance roles because they are often responsible for provision of training, design of processes and procedures, evaluation of deviations and creation of quality culture. If they are weak in any of these, then the staff required to make accurate records are at a disadvantage. Training can also be provided specifically in relation to DI so, for example, staff understand the difference between a witness signature and a check signature and the risks to DI associated with a particular process, as well as reviewing records to ensure that data makes sense in addition to confirming all entries are complete.

One of the most common failures in GDP is inadequate control of quality system documents. Where events such as complaints or deviations are recorded in free-vend template forms, these are often not reconciled or reconcilable. This may lead to records being lost or incorrect template versions being used. Good system design with consideration of DI provides the means to ensure that all records are complete with the use of simple solutions, such as use of hard-bound forms or controlled issue of numbered and indexed forms.

Data integrity can be monitored by incorporation into self-inspections or as a single separate horizontal audit to enable best practice to be shared across departments. Monitoring of near misses in addition to full breaches and consideration of opportunities for continuous improvement all add to the data governance tools that can be reviewed during quality management reviews, which in turn lead to further development of a healthy quality culture.

When reviewing data it is important to consider whether the data can be fully relied upon. For example; in an ambient storage warehouse the thermometer indicates a minimum temperature of 58°C and a maximum of 36°C. Potential root causes may include failed calibration history or damage of the thermometer, or low competence of staff using the device. These reasons could indicate unreliability of the records.

Such outlying data as described in the example is easy to spot, but, when faced with data that looks within trend, it is less likely to be challenged; however, the integrity of data can be just as unreliable even though it all appears within the expected range.

GDP COMPUTERISED SYSTEMS

The advance of computerised system and application development has enabled operators to carry out activities at an increasingly fast pace, including flash transactions, sometimes without having sight of stock. The intention to use non-trackable software such as WhatsApp for quality-critical event reporting has been proposed by wholesalers – and refused on the grounds of not being capable of complying with DI requirements; however, the use of computerised systems is encouraged provided that they are appropriately qualified and controlled, especially if they are bespoke to your organisation. The MHRA GxP Data Integrity guidance provides a lot of information on this topic.

The use of robots and electronic audit trails can lead to a false sense of security in relation to data integrity. The simple act of ensuring that stock is delivered to the right address can fail when an electronic proof of delivery signal cannot be picked up either in remote Africa or in mid-Wales and work-arounds are created. Additional problems of maintaining a full audit trail arise when stock changes from one organisation or department to another, e.g. delivery of a consignment through a network of third-party couriers leading to an incomplete document audit trail. Also, some couriers retain their track-and-trace records for only a few weeks before destroying them.

Where records are converted from one form to another, e.g. hard copy supplier invoices converted to pdf, or hard copy temperature records transcribed into an electronic record, then these should be confirmed as being accurate and complete by a person of appropriate seniority. This process should also be assessed for potential failure modes, e.g. when converting hard copy supplier invoices to pdf there may be more than one version of the document (same original but with different annotations on it). Both versions may therefore need to be retained. In addition, some double-sided documents may incorrectly be scanned only single-sided. Copying such documents can be tedious and is often delegated to an office junior, but the implications of not having a complete, accurate and legible set of scanned records will mean that you will not be able to trace activities and will not comply with regulations.

THE USE OF SPREADSHEETS

Spreadsheets are a useful tool for managing and presenting data due to their versatility and ease of use, which has led to wide application within GDP. It is important to note, however, that when data within a spreadsheet cannot be reconstructed elsewhere and is essential to GDP activity when data governance measures must be rigorous. Caution should be taken when number rounding, converting from one unit of measurement to another or from numbers to graphs.

If the spreadsheet has multiple users it may be impossible to ascertain who (Attributable) made an entry, whether entries have been over-written and replaced (permanent), and when the data entries had been made (Contemporaneous). If the spreadsheet is not version controlled and managed as a controlled document, then there may be different versions in use (Original). Where formulae and other functions are used there is potential for these to be corrupted without being detected (Accurate).

Possible ways of gaining appropriate control include restricting the use of spreadsheets only for non-critical data and locking down cells or sheets within it so that write access is restricted. Another potential solution is to use the spreadsheet to create a hard copy version that is version controlled, approved and dated, locked down and managed as the controlled version. In this case it is the approved version that needs to be used as the working document, not the unapproved spreadsheet used to create it. This approach can be useful when data is not entered frequently such as a staff training matrix which may be revised only a few times each year or confirmation of supplier or customer authentication carried out every fortnight.

Where Macros or formulae are used within a spreadsheet these should be defined (e.g. within an operating procedure), tested for accuracy and protected against unauthorised changes. Confirming that these are not corrupted should be part of regular data integrity review.

Some considerations for preparing documentation for a regulatory inspection

Wholesalers have an obligation to ensure that documents are readily available for presentation to a regulatory inspector. Where companies operate over several sites, it may be problematic to have all records available. In these circumstances, the organisation should notify the inspector as soon as possible regarding the notice period for obtaining documents, especially if they are archived off-site.

Where documents are managed electronically, the organisation may need to provide access to the inspector to navigate the documentation system. It may facilitate the inspection to have print facilities for review of electronic documents as hard copy. Some records may be printed prior to the inspection, in which case the inspector should be consulted if they require this. Any printed documents should be clearly legible.

SPECIFIC DOCUMENTATION CONSIDERATIONS – CASE STUDIES

Case Study 1: Export to a third country

When exporting to a third country, several considerations need to be made from a documentation and record keeping perspective. These include the following:

- Procedures and written agreements containing sufficient detail of the export process.
- Evidence of authentication of the customer and their entitlement to receive medicinal products. This may include: copies of the customer's licence, assessment of their financial status, and confirmation against the UK embargo lists of persons and companies.
- Approval of the consignment, which includes: confirmation against UK medicine export restrictions, confirmation of import restrictions into the third country and import licences from the national competent authority.
- A complete documentation chain of custody for the medicinal products from the point of the supplier's authorised storage location to the authorised premises of the customer. This may include: purchase order, instructions to the freight forwarder, customs declarations, sales orders, sales invoices, bill of lading or airway bill, temperature-monitoring records.
- Clear financial records that are consistent with the physical chain of custody.
- Authenticated translations of documentation.

Case Study 2: Temperature mapping exercise

- A clear protocol detailing the methodology and logic behind the mapping exercise.
- The quality of the records enables conclusions to be drawn.
- Written agreements in place for external mapping contractors.
- All externally generated data is provided to the wholesaler.
- Documentation is managed within the document control system.
- Records should be traceable so that it is clear who created individual records and participated in the exercise.
- Names of any external persons involved should be printed in addition to any signatures.

Chapter 5 Operations

5.1 Principle

All actions taken by wholesale distributors should ensure that the identity of the medicinal product is not lost and that the wholesale distribution of medicinal products is performed according to the information on the outer packaging. The wholesale distributor should use all means available to minimise the risk of falsified medicinal products entering the legal supply chain.

All medicinal products distributed in the EU by a wholesale distributor must be covered by a marketing authorisation granted by the EU or by a Member State[8].

Any distributor, other than the marketing authorisation holder, who imports a medicinal product from another Member State must notify the marketing authorisation holder and the competent authority in the Member State to which the medicinal product will be imported of their intention to import that product[9]. All key operations described below should be fully described in the quality system in appropriate documentation.

5.2 Qualification of suppliers

Wholesale distributors must obtain their supplies of medicinal products only from persons who are themselves in possession of a wholesale distribution authorisation, or who are in possession of a manufacturing authorisation which covers the product in question[10].

Wholesale distributors receiving medicinal products from third countries for the purpose of importation, i.e. for the purpose of placing these products on the EU market, must hold a manufacturing authorisation[11].

Where medicinal products are obtained from another wholesale distributor, the receiving wholesale distributor must verify that the supplier complies with the principles and guidelines of good distribution practices and that they hold an authorisation, for example by using the Union database. If the medicinal product is obtained through brokering, the wholesale distributor must verify that the broker is registered and complies with the requirements in Chapter 10[12].

EU GUIDELINES AND UK GUIDANCE ON WHOLESALE DISTRIBUTION PRACTICE

---

[8] Articles 76(1) and (2) of Directive 2001/83/EC.
[9] Article 76(3) of Directive 2001/83/EC.
[10] Article 80(b) of Directive 2001/83/EC.
[11] Article 40, third paragraph of Directive 2001/83/EC.
[12] Article 80, fourth paragraph of Directive 2001/83/EC.

Appropriate qualification and approval of suppliers should be performed prior to any procurement of medicinal products. This should be controlled by a procedure and the results documented and periodically rechecked.

When entering into a new contract with new suppliers the wholesale distributor should carry out "due diligence" checks in order to assess the suitability, competence and reliability of the other party. Attention should be paid to:

(i)   the reputation or reliability of the supplier;
(ii)   offers of medicinal products more likely to be falsified;
(iii) large offers of medicinal products which are generally only available in limited quantities; and
(iv) out-of-range prices.

5.3   Qualification of customers

Wholesale distributors must ensure which they supply medicinal products only to persons who are themselves in possession of a wholesale distribution authorisation or who are authorised or entitled to supply medicinal products to the public.

Checks and periodic rechecks may include: requesting copies of customer's authorisations according to national law, verifying status on an authority website, requesting evidence of qualifications or entitlement according to national legislation.

Wholesale distributors should monitor their transactions and investigate any irregularity in the sales patterns of narcotics, psychotropic substances or other dangerous substances. Unusual sales patterns that may constitute diversion or misuse of medicinal product should be investigated and reported to competent authorities where necessary. Steps should be taken to ensure fulfilment of any public service obligation imposed upon them.

5.4   Receipt of medicinal products

The purpose of the receiving function is to ensure that the arriving consignment is correct, that the medicinal products originate from approved suppliers and that they have not been visibly damaged during transport.

Medicinal products requiring special storage or security measures should be prioritised and, once appropriate checks have been conducted, they should be immediately transferred to appropriate storage facilities.

Batches of medicinal products intended for the EU and EEA countries should not be transferred to saleable stock before assurance has been obtained, in accordance with written procedures, that they are authorised for sale. For batches coming from another Member State, prior to their transfer to saleable stock, the control report referred to in Article 51(1) of Directive 2001/83/EC or another proof of release to the market in question based on an equivalent system should be carefully checked by appropriately trained personnel.

5.5 Storage

Medicinal products and, if necessary, healthcare products should be stored separately from other products likely to alter them and should be protected from the harmful effects of light, temperature, moisture and other external factors. Particular attention should be paid to products requiring specific storage conditions.

Incoming containers of medicinal products should be cleaned, if necessary, before storage.

Warehousing operations must ensure appropriate storage conditions are maintained and allow for appropriate security of stocks.

Stock should be rotated according to the 'first expiry, first out' (FEFO) principle. Exceptions should be documented.

Medicinal products should be handled and stored in such a manner as to prevent spillage, breakage, contamination and mix-ups. Medicinal products should not be stored directly on the floor unless the package is designed to allow such storage (such as for some medicinal gas cylinders).

Medicinal products that are nearing their expiry date/shelf life should be withdrawn immediately from saleable stock either physically or through other equivalent electronic segregation.

Stock inventories should be performed regularly taking into account national legislation requirements. Stock irregularities should be investigated and documented.

5.6 Destruction of obsolete goods

Medicinal products intended for destruction should be appropriately identified, held separately and handled in accordance with a written procedure.

Destruction of medicinal products should be in accordance with national or international requirements for handling, transport and disposal of such products.

Records of all destroyed medicinal products should be retained for a defined period.

5.7 Picking

Controls should be in place to ensure the correct product is picked. The product should have an appropriate remaining shelf-life when it is picked.

5.8 Supply

For all supplies, a document (e.g. delivery note) must be enclosed stating: the date; name and pharmaceutical form of the medicinal product, batch number at least for products bearing the safety features; quantity supplied; name and address of the supplier, name and delivery address of the consignee[13] (actual physical storage premises, if different) and applicable transport and storage conditions. Records should be kept so that the actual location of the product can be known.

5.9 Export to third countries

The export of medicinal products falls within the definition of "wholesale distribution"[14]. A person exporting medicinal products must hold a wholesale distribution authorisation or a manufacturing authorisation. This is also the case if the exporting wholesale distributor is operating from a free zone.

The rules for wholesale distribution apply in their entirety in the case of export of medicinal products. However, where medicinal products are exported, they do not need to be covered by a marketing authorisation of the Union or a Member State[15]. Wholesalers should take the appropriate measures in order to prevent these medicinal products reaching the Union market. Where wholesale distributors supply medicinal products to persons in third countries, they shall ensure that such supplies are only made to persons who are authorised or entitled to receive medicinal products for wholesale distribution or supply to the public in accordance with the applicable legal and administrative provisions of the country concerned.

UK Guidance on Chapter 5 Operations

Qualification of Customers and Suppliers

The qualification and re-qualification of suppliers and customers are fundamental pillars of Good Distribution Practice, and one of the highest risk

---

[13] Article 82 of Directive 2001/83/EC.
[14] Article 1(17) of Directive 2001/83/EC.
[15] Article 85(a) of Directive 2001/83/EC.

areas of Good Distribution Practice (GDP). The MHRA requires organisations to have qualification and re-qualification procedures implemented within their quality management system.

Before commencing wholesale dealing activities with a supplier or customer (trading partners), licensed wholesale dealers must ensure that their proposed trading partners are entitled to trade with them. Checks must demonstrate that trading partners either hold the required manufacturing and wholesale dealer's licence where necessary or that they are entitled to receive medicines for the purpose of retail supply, to a person who may lawfully administer the products or for use in the course of their business.

Qualification of suppliers

Maintaining the integrity of the supply chain is one of the most important aspects of wholesale distribution. A robust, fully documented system to ensure medicines are sourced appropriately must be in place and subjected to regular review. Licensed wholesale dealers must ensure their suppliers are appropriately licensed to supply medicines. The qualification of suppliers requires the following steps to be fully compliant:

- The first step is to verify that supplies of medicinal products come only from persons who are themselves in possession of a wholesale distribution authorisation, or who are in possession of a manufacturing authorisation that covers the product in question.

  Traditionally copies of licences have been requested from suppliers, but this is no longer required because details of a licence of the supplier can be viewed via the MHRA's register of wholesalers. Although the MHRA register is updated regularly, it must not be relied on as a sole means of qualifying suppliers' authority to supply. The information should also be verified by using the MHRAGMDP[16] website because this is updated daily. Currently, the MHRAGMDP website does not contain details of the legal categories of products that can be handled or third-party sites used and must not be relied on as a sole means of qualifying suppliers. When searching for companies, use an asterisk (*) on either side of a name or number to broaden the search.

  One practical way to demonstrate qualification of suppliers could be a printed copy of the appropriate pages, signed and dated as evidence that the checks were made, when and by whom. Evidence held by a company of validation checks should be appropriately traceable to users and include dates of qualification, and retained in line with GDP document retention requirements.

---

[16] https://cms.mhra.gov.uk

Supplies from any other source, such as pharmacies, are not permitted. There remains a persistent misunderstanding that pharmacies can supply a small amount of medicines without a wholesale dealer's licence. This is not the case because the exemption that allows this trade was removed in 2013. Where a pharmacy holds a WDA(H), a company should ensure that they are procuring from the correct legal entity.

- The second step requires that wholesalers verify that any wholesale supplier complies with the principles and guidelines of good distribution practices. To establish GDP compliance, the GDP certificate of the wholesaler should be viewed on the MHRAGMDP website. Certificates when issued are valid for up to 5 years. The date of the certificate expiry should be recorded.

  The MHRA adds conditioning statements to GDP certificates for new applicants and those companies where the inspection outcome indicated a more frequent inspection schedule is required, limiting certificate expiry to 2 years.

  Where certificates have reached expiration dates, further enquiries should be made with those companies to ascertain their compliance status.

- The third step is periodic rechecking of the information obtained and due diligence.

  Wholesalers must be aware of issues that could affect their suppliers' continued authority to supply. Qualification processes must ensure that documented checks are made at least twice a month of the MHRA's list of suspended licence holders and regular checks on the MHRAG-MDP or EudraGMDP website for issued GMP and GDP statements of non-compliance. There should be at minimum annual full re-validation of the information held on suppliers; however, companies should ensure that re-qualification of suppliers is conducted on a risk basis.

  Supporting all of the checks made so far is effective due diligence by the Responsible Person. The MHRA has seen evidence of serious non-compliance pertaining to qualification; quantities of a high-value medicine were stolen and re-introduced into the supply chain. The medicine was sold in an unusually large quantity and purchased by several wholesalers.

  After the event, looking at the evidence available to the purchasers, it was apparent that the company selling the stock had a conditioned GDP certificate, a poor financial history and no previous access to such large volumes of high-value stock.

  When entering into a new contract with new suppliers, the wholesale distributor should carry out "due diligence" checks in order to assess the suitability, competence and reliability of the other party. Questions that should be considered could include:

- checking the financial status of the supplier. How long have they been trading, and do they have an acceptable credit history?
- has an audit been performed of the supplier, or has anyone in your company visited them? If so what was their impression?
- where is the stock coming from and is the product offered a new product for your company?
- is the product being offered available in quantities or volumes that are unusually high or is the price being offered lower than the usual price?
- how transparent is the supply chain of this transaction?
- what will be the method of transportation?
- is the contact managing the business relationship linked to the company they purport to represent? For example, do web domains, IP addresses and phone numbers support claims being made by persons or organisations?
- has there been a recent, rapid change of senior management, or offering of medicines outside of the usual business practices associated with the supplier?

Due diligence checks should be implemented and documented when dealing with a company or transaction that is outside of an established trading pattern.

Organisations must be aware that criminals actively look for weak spots in the supply chain for gain. The MHRA frequently receives reports that companies with wholesale dealer licences are being "cloned". Here, a company uses the licence and address details of a legitimate company but sets up a fake website and bank account that is similar to the real operation. Typically, this fake company will offer some tempting stock and send information using genuine company details but from a different email account. Observed methodologies have included, for example, substituting .com for .co.uk, utilising hyphenation, utilising unrelated email domains and closely mimicking a related website name. The bank account information will be for the fake company. Please take extreme care if your supplier advises that the bank details have changed and your accounts team should be made aware of this practice. Other methods include the purchase of a company and change of ownership, not detectable by routine licence review, and the subsequent supply of high-value medicines.

Any detection of suspicious activity, near misses or active engagement with suspected dishonest actors in the supply chain should be reported to the Licensing Authority.

For companies that are involved in the sourcing of medicines from a third country for export to third countries, then there are different requirements. Companies are obliged to document that checks are made to show that, where the medicinal product is directly received from a third country ("A") for export to a third country ("B"), the supplier of the medicinal product in country A is a person who is authorised or entitled to supply such medicinal products in accordance with the legal and administrative provisions in country A. Any licences obtained should have been translated into English and authenticated by a notary with appropriate due diligence carried out.

If there is no GDP certificate available then other evidence of GDP compliance by the wholesale supplier should be obtained, such as a copy of their last inspection close-out letter confirming GDP compliance. For suppliers from EEA Member States, the same checks should be made on EudraG-MDP and via licences that have been translated. The translated licences should be authenticated as such by a notary.

COMPLIANCE WITH GDP

Licensed wholesale dealers must verify that wholesale suppliers comply with the principles and guidelines of good distribution practices. To establish GDP compliance, the GDP certificate of the wholesaler should be viewed on the relevant website. Certificates when issued are valid for up to five years. The date of the certificate expiry should be recorded. The MHRA adds conditioning statements to GDP certificates for new applicants and those companies where the inspection outcome indicated that a more frequent inspection schedule is required, limiting certificate expiry to two years. If there is no GDP certificate available, then other evidence of GDP compliance by the wholesale supplier should be obtained, such as a copy of the inspection close-out letter confirming GDP compliance.

ROUTINE RE-QUALIFICATION

Licensed wholesale dealers must be aware of issues that could affect their suppliers' continued authority to supply. The following should be carried out:

- Regular checks at least twice a month of the MHRA's list of suspended licence holders.
- Regular checks on MHRAGMDP and EudraGMDP websites for issued GMP and GDP statements of non-compliance.
- A risk-based re-qualification process, conducted at least annually, including a documented full re-qualification of suppliers.

DUE DILIGENCE

When entering into a new contract with new suppliers, the licensed wholesale dealer should carry out "due diligence" checks in order to assess the suitability, competence and reliability of the other party. Questions that should be considered could include, but are not limited to, the following:

- Checking the financial status of the supplier, how long have they been trading and whether they have an acceptable credit history.

- Has an audit been performed of the supplier, or has anyone in your company visited them? If so what was their impression?
- Where is the stock coming from and is the product offered a new product for your company?
- Is the product being offered available in quantities or volumes that are unusually high or is the price being offered lower than the usual price?
- How transparent is the supply chain of this transaction?
- What will be the method of transportation?
- Is the contact managing the business relationship linked to the company they purport to represent? For example, do web domains, IP addresses and phone numbers support claims being made by persons or organisations?
- Is the company directorship consistent with supplied documentation?

Due diligence checks should be implemented and documented when dealing with a company or transaction that is outside of an established trading pattern.

PROCUREMENT FROM THIRD COUNTRIES

For companies that are involved in the sourcing of medicines from a third country for supply to third countries, there are different requirements. Companies are obliged to document that checks are made to show that, where the medicinal product is directly received from a third country ("A") for export to a third country ("B"), the supplier of the medicinal product in country A is a person who is authorised or entitled to supply such medicinal products in accordance with the legal and administrative provisions in country A. Any licences obtained should have been translated into English and authenticated by a notary with appropriate due diligence carried out.

Customer qualification

Licensed wholesale dealers have a key role in guaranteeing medicines are supplied only to authorised organisations, persons entitled to hold medicines and qualified prescribers. For distribution to a wholesale customer, the checks that must be made are similar to the qualification of suppliers, and application of the principles of due diligence and risk based periodic re-qualification applies.

This should include the following:

- The first step is to verify that wholesale recipients of medicinal products are themselves in possession of a wholesale distribution authorisation.

    Traditionally copies of licences have been requested from customers, but this is no longer required as details of a licence of a UK customer can be viewed via the MHRA's register of wholesalers. Although the MHRA register is updated regularly it must not be relied on as a sole means of qualifying customers' authority to receive medicines. The information should also be verified by using the MHRAGMDP website because this is updated daily. Currently the MHRAGMDP website does not contain details of third-party sites used and must not be relied on as a sole means of qualifying customers. When searching for companies use an asterisk (*) on either side of a name or number to broaden the search.

One practical way to demonstrate qualification of customers could be a printed copy of the appropriate pages, signed and dated as evidence that the checks were made, when and by whom. Evidence held by a company of validation checks should be appropriately traceable to users and include dates of qualification and retained in line with GDP document retention requirements.

- The second step requires that wholesalers should verify that any wholesale customer complies with the principles and guidelines of good distribution practices and is entitled to hold the category of medicine they intend to procure. To establish GDP compliance, the GDP certificate of the wholesaler should be viewed on the MHRAGMDP website. Certificates when issued are valid for up to five years. The date of the certificate expiry should be recorded.

The MHRA adds conditioning statements to GDP certificates for new applicants and those companies where the inspection outcome indicated that a more frequent inspection schedule was required, limiting certificate expiry to two years.

Where certificates have reached expiration dates, further enquiries should be made with those companies to ascertain their compliance status.

- The third step is periodic rechecking of the information obtained and due diligence.

Wholesalers must be aware of issues that could affect their customers' continued authority to supply. Qualification processes must ensure that documented checks are made at least twice a month of the MHRA's list of suspended licence holders and regular checks on the MHRAGMDP or EudraGMDP website for issued GMP and GDP statements of non-compliance. There should be at minimum annual full re-validation of the information held on customers; however, companies should ensure that re-qualification of customers is conducted on a risk basis.

Support of all the checks made so far is effective due diligence by the Responsible Person. The MHRA has seen evidence of serious non-compliance pertaining to qualification: quantities of a high value or medicine liable for misuse were stolen and re-introduced in to the supply chain. The medicine was sold in an unusually large quantity and purchased by several wholesalers.

After the event, looking at the evidence available to the purchasers, it was apparent that the company selling the stock had a conditioned GDP certificate, a poor financial history and no previous access to such large volumes of high-value stock.

When entering into a new contract with new customers, the wholesale distributor should carry out "due diligence" checks in order to assess the suitability, competence and reliability of the other party. Questions that should be considered could include the following:

- Checking the financial status of the customer, how long have they been trading and whether they have an acceptable credit history.
- Has an audit been performed of the customer or has anyone in your company visited them? If so what was their impression?
- What will be the method of transportation?
- Is the contact managing the business relationship linked to the company they purport to represent? For example, do web domains, IP addresses and phone numbers support claims being made by persons or organisations?
- Do supply delivery addresses match details provided on documentation that has been validated?

Due diligence checks should be implemented and documented when dealing with a company or a transaction had been identified that is outside of an established trading pattern.

In relation to wholesale distribution of scheduled controlled medicines to other wholesalers, companies must check their customers hold both a wholesale dealer's licence and a Home Office-controlled drugs licence of the appropriate schedule.

For the qualification of a person who may lawfully administer the products then the following registers must be checked prior to supplying:

- Pharmacists and registered pharmacies – General Pharmaceutical Council or Pharmaceutical Society of Northern Ireland website register;
- Doctors – General Medical Council list of registered medical practitioners;
- Dentists – General Dental Council list of registered dental practitioners;
- Paramedics/podiatrists/chiropodists – Health and Care Professions Council (HCPC) website register with listing for POM and local anaesthetic use, if these are the product categories sold;
- Practice nurses – Nursing and Midwifery Council register;
- Hospitals – the CQC in England or equivalents in Wales, Scotland and Northern Ireland.

See Appendix 3 for further information.

SUPPLY TO THIRD COUNTRIES

Licensed wholesale dealers exporting medicinal products to persons in third countries must ensure that such supplies are made only to persons who are authorised or entitled to receive medicinal products for wholesale distribution or supply to the public in accordance with the applicable legal and administrative provisions of the country concerned. As an example, some companies attempt to export products such as Botox to doctors and clinics in the USA. The US Food and Drug Administration (FDA) permits healthcare providers only to obtain and use FDA-approved medications purchased directly from the manufacturer or from wholesale distributors licensed in the USA. In certain circumstances, the FDA may authorise limited importation of medications that are in short supply. Such medications are imported from approved international sources and distributed in the USA through a controlled network, and would not be sold in direct-to-clinic solicitations. UK-licensed versions of FDA-approved drugs are not treated by the FDA as equivalent and must not be sold in the USA to doctors or clinics.

A company must satisfy itself that local legal requirements have been met prior to import. A company should consider and be able to demonstrate knowledge of:

- local legal framework in destination countries;
- any requirements for importation documentation;
- customs, freight or transportation requirements specific to the destination country;
- any paperwork associated with the supply of medicines, including transportation.

Companies should be able to demonstrate delivery to the end location point that they had qualified.

The company should retain copies of the above documentation. Any suspicion of diversion or obtaining medicines by false representation should be reported to the Licensing Authority.

DUE DILIGENCE

Licensed wholesale dealers have an obligation in GDP to monitor their transactions and investigate any irregularity in the sales patterns of narcotics, psychotropic or other dangerous substances. This may include medicines that may not appear to be vulnerable as a finished product, such as antihistamine medicines, including but not limited to cetirizine- and pseudoephedrine-containing products. Unusual sales patterns that may constitute diversion or misuse of medicinal product should be investigated and reported to Licensing Authorities where necessary.

When conducting due diligence checks, a company should never rely on information solely provided by the trader. The following should be considered:

- conducting independent research into the company, by way of review of wider official sources of information, such as Companies House records;
- ensuring that details provided by an organisation match online presence;
- calling numbers or testing contact details obtained independently;
- validating bank details in line with your expectations from experience;
- ensuring that internal training programmes encompass departments that may be approached outside of your direct knowledge, such as finance, and equip staff with mechanisms to report changes to supplier or customer details that you may not be aware of;
- what processes and assessments you have in place to confidently establish the identity of a prospective supplier or customer;
- the types, volumes and prices of products being offered and usual availability as a potential risk;
- ensuring that commercial activities, such as procurement, sales and marketing teams, have appropriate training and regulatory oversight;
- if your risk management processes minimise the prospect of falsified medicines entering the supply chain;
- when re-qualifying suppliers, consider if any significant changes in directorship or ownership have occurred;
- how staff and management can be confident that replies are sent only to approved and valid email addresses;
- how reporting mechanisms from goods in processes generate deviations and integrate into the quality management system;
- how new contact details are reviewed by your company;
- how the company manages trade shows or commercial events and any outputs from these.

The MHRA recognises that determined efforts by unauthorised persons or criminals can be convincing. None the less, there is an expectation that licence holders have appropriate systems to safeguard the supply chain. This may include ensuring that detailed records of collection and delivery activities are made, to assure organisations that actors involved in your supply chain at every step are legitimate, and that activities have been appropriately reviewed, risk assessed and have oversight.

Instances of falsified GDP certificates and wholesale dealer authorisations have been observed throughout the supply chain and organisations must remain vigilant as to risks to patients when dealing with suppliers, customers and brokers.

The MHRA has become aware that certain medicines subject to abuse, including but not limited to diazepam, nitrazepam, zopiclone, codeine linctus, tramadol zolipdem and pseudoephedrine, have been diverted from the regulated supply chain and made available for sale illegitimately. These products are Schedule 4 controlled drugs under the Misuse of Drugs Act. Significant amounts of genuine licensed packs of these products from various manufacturers have been seized and recovered throughout the UK and internationally. Instances of high-value hospital lines being supplied in large quantities represent further risk of diversion and falsification, of which organisations should remain vigilant.

Wholesalers are reminded that they have an obligation in GDP to monitor their transactions and investigate any irregularity in the sales patterns of narcotic, psychotropic or other dangerous substances. Unusual sales patterns that may constitute diversion or misuse of medicinal product should be investigated and reported to competent authorities where necessary. Organisations should establish processes to review transactions and trends on a regular basis to identify what, within their particular business model, is considered unusual or suspicious.

In relation to wholesale distribution of scheduled controlled medicines to other wholesalers, companies must check their customers hold both a wholesale dealer's licence and a Home Office-controlled drugs licence of the appropriate schedule.

For distribution to a wholesale customer, the checks that should be made are similar to the qualification of suppliers outlined in my previous blog. A hard copy of the Home Office licence must be obtained from your customers prior to any supply being made and the validity of this assessed by appropriate staff.

For supplies to pharmacies, hospitals and clinics these organisations are not required to have a Home Office licence because their supplies are for patients. It is particularly important that the usage pattern is considered when fulfilling orders and that order volumes are commensurate with the expected demand of an organisation and their intended market. For example, a retail pharmacy without a WDA(H) would not generally require the same volumes of controlled substances as a specialist hospital unit. There should be procedure in place that sets defined limits to the size of routine orders that can be placed by customers that alert the company Responsible Person to investigate if excessive amounts are ordered.

Other concerns that arise in relation to customer supplies include medical practitioners who request supplies to their home address. The GMC medical register does not include the address of registered doctors so companies should avoid sending products to home addresses. Doctors operating in the independent sector will be working from clinics registered with the CQC in England, Healthcare Inspectorate in Wales, Healthcare Improvement in Scotland and the Regulation and Quality Improvement Authority in Northern Ireland. Medicines should usually be dispatched to these verifiable addresses rather than residential properties. Where medicines are ordered on behalf of a doctor, the medicines should be stored in a verifiable location where those medicines are entitled to be held, or are otherwise licensed by the Home Office.

For wholesale distributors exporting medicinal products to persons in third countries, they must ensure that such supplies are made only to persons who are authorised or entitled to receive medicinal products for wholesale distribution or supply to the public in accordance with the applicable legal and administrative provisions of the country concerned. Wholesalers should be aware that suspicious and unusual transactions may also include export activities and organisations must apply the same vigilance to export orders as to domestic orders.

The principles pertaining to the qualification of suppliers and customers remain consistent with export customers as with any other customer type, and re-qualification should occur on a risk-defined periodic basis.

If licensed wholesale dealers have any concerns pertaining to the procurement or supply of medicines, including unusual sales patter reporting, in the first instance they should email GDP.Inspectorate@mhra.gov.uk. Details of the company and the name and quantities of products that have been ordered in the last six months should be included. This will be dealt with in confidence.

In instances where reporting directly to the Inspectorate may pose a risk to individuals, or you wish to inform the MHRA anonymously of any relevant matters, please contact the whistleblowing section:

Email: whistleblower@mhra.gov.uk.

Any suspicions of fraudulent activity or attempts to impersonate a licence holder should be reported promptly to the Licensing Authority and your local police. Case Referrals, within our Enforcement team, are the responsible team at the MHRA and they will be able to provide support if you need to raise a report:

- Case Referral Centre/Fakemeds Hotline
- Telephone (weekdays 09:00-17:00): 020 3080 6330
- Telephone (out-of-hours emergency): 07795 825 727
- Email: casereferrals@mhra.gov.uk

Parallel Importation

The Human Medicines Regulations 2012 refers to lists of approved countries for:

- importation of medicines under a wholesale dealer's licence;
- batch testing of medicines;
- manufacturing of active substances with regulatory standards equivalent to the UK.

The list of approved countries will enable UK importers and wholesalers to continue to recognise Qualified Person (QP) certification and regulatory standards for active substance manufacture performed in certain countries in the same way as before 1 January 2021. The UK's acceptance of batch testing done in EEA countries will be reviewed before 31 December 2022. A two-year notice period will be given in the case of changes.

The UK Parallel Import Licensing Scheme allows nationally authorised medicinal products from approved countries for authorised human medicines to be marketed in the UK, provided that the imported products have no therapeutic difference from the equivalent UK products. It also allows centrally (European Medicines Agency [EMA]) authorised products to be imported into Great Britain (England, Wales and Scotland) under the same condition. Parallel importation exists in the absence of price harmonisation of pharmaceutical products between UK/GB and from approved countries, i.e. when there are significant price differences between approved countries, and where prices of medicines are not governed by free competition laws, but are generally fixed by local national government.

It involves the transfer of genuine, original branded or generic products, marketed in one approved country for authorised human medicines at a lower price (the source country) to the UK/GB (the country of destination) by a parallel importer, and placed on the market in competition with a therapeutically identical product already marketed there at a higher price by or under licence from the owner of the brand. The scope of the UK Parallel Import scheme is limited to nationally authorised products, i.e. those medicinal products that have been granted a marketing authorisation by a competent authority of an approved country for authorised human medicines.

For GB, only it extends to centrally authorised medicinal products, granted a marketing authorisation by the EMA, which is valid in all approved countries. For Northern Ireland, only the transfer from approved countries of these products is termed "Parallel Distribution". The EMA administers a Parallel Distribution scheme for these types of products. Further information on the EMA parallel distribution scheme can be found on the EMA website and in the section below titled "Parallel Distribution".

Products that are parallel imported from an approved country for authorised human medicines require a Product Licence for Parallel Import (PLPI) granted by the Licensing Authority, the MHRA, following extensive checks to ensure that the imported drug is therapeutically the same as the domestic version. Further information on the PLPI licensing procedure can be found on the MHRA website.

A company intending to import medicines from approved countries for authorised human medicines must ensure their licence allows for such activity and that an RPi is in post.

Parallel importers operating in the UK require a wholesale dealer's licence.

In addition, parallel importers in the UK involved in re-packaging or re-labelling of product must hold a manufacturer's licence (MIA) authorising product assembly and will be inspected regularly for compliance with GMP. Alternatively, re-packaging/re-labelling can be contracted out to another company that already holds such a licence.

Parallel importers are required to have effective recall procedures in place. The MHRA has systems in place to receive and investigate reports of packaging and labelling problems with medicines, including parallel imported products:

https://www.gov.uk/guidance/medicines-apply-for-a-parallel-import-licence.

Parallel distribution

Centrally authorised medicinal products are medicines that have been granted a marketing authorisation by the EMA that is valid in all approved countries and also in Northern Ireland.

The sourcing of centrally authorised medicines (not in the official language of the destination market) from one approved country to another independent of the Marketing Authorisation Holder is termed Parallel Distribution.

The EMA administers a Parallel Distribution scheme whereby holders of a wholesale dealer's licence wishing to import from EEA markets to Northern Ireland must notify the EMA of their intent to import, re-package and distribute the product, and provide the EMA with the latest product information and labelling in the language of the Member State of destination, to be checked for compliance with the marketing authorisation and latest EU legislation on medicinal products. This requirement is set out in Article 76 of Directive 2001/83/EC on the Community code relating to medicinal products for human use.

Similar to Parallel Importation, a company wishing to act as a Parallel Distributor must hold a wholesale dealer's licence. In addition if they intend to carry out the re-packaging/re-labelling themselves, the company will require an MIA or they can contract this activity out to an MIA holder authorised for assembly.

Further information on Parallel Distribution can be found on the EMA website:

http://www.ema.europa.eu/ema/index.jsp?curl=pages/regulation/general/general_content_000067.jspampmid=WC0b01ac0580024594.

Products Imported From Countries on a List

Medicinal products sourced from Northern Ireland for wholesale purposes are out of the scope of this guidance. This is permitted under the supervision of a Responsible Person (RP).

Products with a UK or GB marketing authorisation that are imported into GB from outside the UK without QP certification from a country on the list will require QP certification under a UK manufacturing and import authorisation before being placed on the market.

Products without a marketing authorisation in the UK, Northern Ireland, GB or a listed country are outside the scope of this guidance. Importation of such products is permitted under the supervision of an RP, with notification to the MHRA of each importation that is for supply to the GB market.

Where a company imports products from a country on a list, a Responsible Person for Import (RPi) must be nominated and mechanisms for ensuring the proper authorisation and release of those medicines in the origin market must be implemented.

The RPi is responsible for implementing a system to confirm for products that have been imported into GB from countries on an approved country for import list:

- that the required QP certification has taken place;
- that the required independent batch release certificate is available for biological products (described on a wholesale dealer's license as "immunologicals and blood products").

The RPi is required to implement a system for confirming QP certification and independent batch release certification (for biological products) has taken place when importing into GB the following products from a listed country:

- a UK or GB licensed medicine for use in GB;
- a UK or GB licensed medicine for supply to another third country;
- a Northern Ireland or approved country licensed medicine for supply to fulfil special clinical needs;
- a Northern Ireland or approved country licensed medicine imported as an introduced medicine for supply to another third country;
- a Northern Ireland or approved country licensed medicine for use as a parallel import.

Companies must have appropriate batch specific controls to qualify and ensure that:

- the required QP certification has taken place;

- the required independent batch release certificate is available for biological products (described on a wholesale dealer's license as "immunologicals and blood products");
- where products have originated in the EEA, they have been decommissioned prior to receipt, or otherwise have systems in place to assess the unique identifier for Prescription Only Medicines, if wholesale dealers are importing products, or if medicines are being imported for parallel import, unique clinical need or introduction;
- the product is not the subject of a recall or reported as stolen and is available on the market within the listed country's licensed supply chain.

The RPi should ensure that written evidence is available to demonstrate that each batch of product has been QP certified as required in Article 51 of Directive 2001/83/EC. Documentary evidence of this must be kept by a company.

Not all options listed below may be suitable for different supply chain relationships; however, just one of these pieces of evidence is sufficient to satisfy the requirements of regulation 45AA of the Human Medicines Regulations 2012. Other evidence may be acceptable provided that it confirms that QP certification has taken place for the batch in question:

- Batch certificate confirming QP certification in accordance with Article 51 of Directive 2001/83/EC.
- A copy of the "control report" (Appendix II to EU Good Manufacturing Practice Annex 16).
- Statement of certification (ad hoc, confirming certification in accordance with Article 51 of Directive 2001/83/EC).
- Reference to company internal systems (e.g. global Enterprise Resource Planning system) that shows batch certification.
- Confirmation that the final manufacturing step (other than batch certification) of an authorised medicine has been performed by a Manufacturing and Import Authorisation holder in a listed country. A copy of the Marketing Authorisation and technical agreement with the manufacturer should be available to place reliance on this supply chain control.
- For medicines authorised in a listed country, batch certification may be verified by confirming that the medicine has been purchased from an authorised wholesaler after it has been "placed on the market" in the listed country.

What Evidence Can be Used for Independent Batch Release Certification?

Biological products requiring independent batch release certification are listed on the European Directorate for Quality of Medicines website.

Independent batch release may be confirmed using evidence such as:

- a statement from the marketing authorisation holder confirming that a batch certificate has been issued by the National Institute for Biological Standards (NIBSC) or a Mutual Recognition Agreement partner;
- a copy of the batch certificate issued by the NIBSC or a Mutual Recognition Agreement partner;
- confirmation from the NIBSC that a batch certificate has been issued. Enquiries should be sent to CPB@nibsc.org.

Batches of QP-certified biological medicines that require independent batch release should not be sold or supplied by the importing wholesale dealer in GB until independent batch release certification has also been confirmed.

Processes should be in place to ensure physical or electronic segregation of stock.

Continued Supply

Under the Human Medicines Regulations 2012, the marketing authorisation holder is required to notify the competent authority (the MHRA in the UK) of the date of actual marketing of the medicinal product, taking account of the various presentations authorised, and to notify the competent authority if the product ceases to be placed on the market either temporarily or permanently. Except in exceptional circumstances, the notification must be made no less than two months before the interruption.

Any authorisation that, within three years of granting, is not placed on the market will cease to be valid. In respect of generic medicinal products, the three-year period will start on the grant of the authorisation, or at the end of the period of market exclusivity or patent protection of the reference product, whichever is the later date. If a product is placed on the market after authorisation, but subsequently ceases to be available on the market in the UK for a period of three consecutive years, it will also cease to be valid. In these circumstances the MHRA will, however, when it is aware of the imminent expiry of the three-year period, notify the marketing authorisation holder in advance that their marketing authorisation will cease to be valid. In exceptional circumstances, and on public health grounds, the MHRA may grant an exemption from the invalidation of the marketing authorisation after three years. Whether there are exceptional circumstances and public health grounds for an exemption will be assessed on a case-by-case basis. When assessing such cases, the MHRA will, in particular, consider the implications for patients and public health more generally of a marketing authorisation no longer being valid.

Those provisions are implemented in the UK by Part 5 of the Human Medicines Regulations 2012.

In accordance with the MHRA's interpretation of the expression "placing on the market", the MHRA's view is that a product is "placed on the market" at the first transaction by which the product enters the distribution chain in the UK. The marketing authorisation holder must, therefore, notify the MHRA when a product with a new marketing authorisation is first placed into the distribution chain, rather than the first date it becomes available to individual patients. The MHRA requests that you notify us of this first "placing on the market" within one calendar month. In order to ensure that a marketing authorisation continues to be valid, the marketing authorisation holder must ensure that at least one packaging presentation (e.g. bottle or blister pack) of the product, which can include its own label supplies, authorised under that marketing authorisation is present on the market.

The marketing authorisation holder must report all cessations/interruptions to the MHRA. However, the MHRA does not need to be notified of the following:

(a) normal seasonal changes in manufacturing and/or distribution schedules (such as cold and flu remedies);

(b) short-term temporary interruptions in placing on the market that will not affect normal availability to distributors.

If you are in doubt about whether or not you need to notify an interruption in supply, you should err on the side of caution and report it to the MHRA in the normal way. You must notify the MHRA if any of the presentations authorised under a single marketing authorisation cease to be placed on the market either temporarily or permanently, but, as stated above, the absence of availability of one or more presentations – as long as one presentation of the product authorised under the single marketing authorisation remains on the market – will not invalidate the marketing authorisation. Problems relating to manufacturing or assembly should also be discussed with the appropriate GMP Inspector and issues of availability of medicines relating to suspected or confirmed product defects should be directly notified to, and discussed with, the Defective Medicines Reporting Centre (tel: 020 3080 6574).

The Department of Health and Social Care (DHSC) is responsible for the continuity of supply of medicines and manufacturers have a legal requirement to inform DHSC of any supply problems. DHSC works closely with the Medicines Healthcare products Regulatory Agency (MHRA), NHSE&I, pharmaceutical companies, the wider NHS, wholesalers and others in the supply chain to ensure consistency of supply of medicines.

Under Part 6 of the Health Service Products (Provision and Disclosure of Information) Regulations 2018, manufacturers are legally required to provide information to the DHSC Medicines Supply Team about availability of UK licensed medicines and about discontinuation or anticipated supply shortages. The regulations were introduced in January 2019, superseding previous voluntary arrangements. These requirements ensure that the DHSC Medicines Supply Team have relevant information from manufacturers at the earliest point to help manage supply shortages and mitigate any potential impacts on patients. Marketing authorisation holders are expected to be fully accountable for their supply chain to the UK market and required to understand the potential impact on UK patients should supplies of their products become unavailable. Any Information submitted by companies as outlined in regulation 29(2) of the Health Service Products (Provision and Disclosure of Information) Regulations 2018 is commercially confidential information and treated sensitively by DHSC.

The Human Medicines Regulations 2012 (45)(2), under which the marketing authorisation holder and the distributors of a medicinal product actually placed on the market, shall, within the limits of their responsibilities, ensure appropriate and continued supplies of that medicinal product to pharmacies and persons authorised to supply medicinal products, so that the needs of patients in the UK are covered. Failure by a marketing authorisation holder to comply with this obligation is a criminal offence, unless the marketing authorisation holder took all reasonable precautions and exercised all due diligence to avoid such a failure.

Obtaining medicines for wholesale using prescriptions

The MHRA is aware of a growing use of false NHS and private prescriptions to obtain medicines from Marketing Authorisation Holders (MAHs). Prescriptions are requested by the MAH for a variety of reasons, but mainly to provide evidence that the product is needed for a patient. Typically prescriptions are requested for high-cost medicines not usually seen in dispensing pharmacies. Redacted prescriptions are presented by a pharmacy to the MAH, implying that there is a patient and the product is supplied, but is then wholesaled and not dispensed to a patient.

MAHs have an obligation to ensure appropriate and continued supplies of medicinal product to pharmacies and persons authorised to supply medicinal products so that the needs of UK patients are met, set out in the Human Medicines Regulations 2012. Some MAHs have decided to manage the distribution of specific products by requesting a redacted prescription to ensure that the supply is for a UK patient.

Medicines for wholesale supply cannot under any circumstances be obtained by way of a prescription and doing so is a breach of the conditions of the WDA(H), set out in regulation (43)(2). Companies are reminded that any procurement must be conducted by, and from, holders of WDA(H) from any, and failure to adhere to this is a critical departure from GDP.

Where pharmacies also hold wholesaler authorisations, a clear distinction between pharmacy and wholesale procurement must be maintained.

Storage

Medicinal products and, if necessary, healthcare products should be stored separately from other products likely to alter them, and should be protected from the harmful effects of light, temperature, moisture and other external factors. Particular attention should be paid to products requiring specific storage conditions.

Incoming containers of medicinal products should be cleaned, if necessary, before storage.

Warehousing operations must ensure that appropriate storage conditions are maintained and allow for appropriate security of stocks. There should be a physical or electronic system of segregation in place between wholesale and retail stock, ensuring that products are held within the correct environment in accordance with the labelled conditions.

Stock should be rotated according to the "first expiry, first out" (FEFO) principle. Any exceptions should be confirmed and documented.

Medicinal products should be handled and stored in such a manner as to prevent spillage, breakage, contamination and mix-ups. Medicinal products should not be stored directly on the floor unless the package is designed to allow such storage (such as for some medicinal gas cylinders).

Medicinal products that are nearing their expiry date/shelf-life should be withdrawn immediately from saleable stock either physically or through other equivalent electronic segregation.

Stock inventories should be performed regularly taking into account national legislation requirements. Stock irregularities should be investigated and documented.

Where wholesalers conduct retail operations, electronic or physical segregation should be maintained and an audit trail implemented, demonstrating the procurement of medicines for each specific mechanism, and the final fate of inventory.

The Responsible Person on a WDA(H) must be able to demonstrate that all medicines have been purchased appropriately and in line with GDP.

Whereas it may be appropriate to transfer wholesale inventory to retail stock on some occasions, it is not permitted to move retail products into wholesale remits.

The DHSC have implemented restrictions on goods that can be hoarded. Companies must ensure that processes are implemented to prevent the hoarding and excessive stocking of medicines detailed within a list of medicines published by the DHSC.

Companies can continue to withhold medicines as part of stock management arrangements agreed with MAHs, which is not considered as hoarding.

Companies can also continue to maintain contingency stockpiles built up at the request of the DHSC or Public Health England (PHE).

Destruction of obsolete goods

Medicinal products intended for destruction should be appropriately identified, held separately and handled in accordance with a written procedure.

Destruction of medicinal products should be in accordance with national or international requirements for handling, transport and disposal of such products.

Records of all destroyed medicinal products should be retained for a defined period.

Picking

Controls should be in place to ensure that the correct product is picked. The product should have an appropriate remaining shelf-life when it is picked.

Stock segregation

There should be physical or electronic system of segregation in place between wholesale and retail stock ensuring that products are held within the correct environment in accordance with the product-labelled conditions.

The Responsible Person on a WDA(H) must be able to demonstrate that all medicines have been purchased appropriately and in line with GDP.

The purchasing of medicines from company to company constitutes wholesale distribution, and any company procuring on behalf of another must hold a WDA(H) and be named on a licence as a third-party site. Written agreements defining responsibilities must be in place to properly control the activity.

It is prohibited for Pharmacies to obtain stock using redacted prescriptions for wholesale dealing.

It is a breach of the conditions of the wholesale dealer's licence, set out in regulation 43(2) of the Human Medicines Regulations, to impinge on the ability of the MAH to discharge its obligations that the needs of UK patients are met.

Supply

For all supplies, a document, whether hard or electronic copy (e.g. delivery note) must be enclosed or recorded stating: date; name and pharmaceutical form of the medicinal product, batch number at least for products bearing the safety features; quantity supplied; name and address of the supplier, name and delivery address of the consignee[17] (actual physical storage premises, if different) and applicable transport and storage conditions. Records should be kept so that the actual location of the product can be verified and is traceable.

Companies should be able to demonstrate, where proportionate, by way of risk management, validation and mapping:

- that the goods are transported within label conditions and active or passive shipping solutions are suitable to ensure this;
- that considerations have been taken of extremes of climate;
- the route that medicine will take from despatch to end destination;
- any mitigation strategies employed during transportation to protect the integrity of medicines.

Integration Operational Processes to Mitigation of Risk of Theft or Diversion of Medicine

The theft and diversion of medicines have a broad impact that increases risk to public health and the integrity of the medicine supply chain.

Robust operational practices can mitigate the risk of theft or procurement of stolen medicines. Some measures for consideration are listed below.

Operations undertaken by the company should ensure sufficient measures are in place to mitigate the risk of theft of medicines. The company should consider the following as part of their operations:

Quality management: monitoring of unusual sales patterns, monitoring changes in risk profiles for products supplied and evidence of theft or near misses within deviation reports. Quality risk management incorporates evaluation of security risks embedded throughout the quality system.

Personnel: security pre-employment checks, training of drivers in security, development of an open culture that supports reporting and whistle-blowing, restricted personnel access to high-risk areas and policies in place for management of visitors, control of security passes.

EU GUIDELINES AND UK GUIDANCE ON WHOLESALE DISTRIBUTION PRACTICE

---

[17] Article 82 of Directive 2001/83/EC.

Facility and equipment design and maintenance: security measures are built into the design including restriction of vehicular access to loading bay areas, location of high-risk stock within the warehouse, maintenance repair and servicing of buildings, perimeter fences and equipment including shutters and CCTV.

Documentation: stock records safeguarded from unauthorised alteration including both hard copy and computerised records, stock discrepancies addressed at an appropriate level, records enabling clear visibility of discrepancies, including under-picked stock, mislaid stock, under-delivered stock, and evidence of destroyed stock including stock for destruction supplied to third countries. Procedures describe how to report medicine theft to the MHRA.

Operations: procurement controls include robust authentication of suppliers and customers, incentivisation of purchasing or sales staff not conflicting with increasing risk of distributing diverted medicines, witness checking for high-risk operations including picking controlled drugs. Control of access into high-risk areas and use of consignment security seals.

Standardised packaging of inventory designed to protect and mitigate risk to products from adulteration or theft.

Reporting mechanisms to local police forces and the MHRA.

Complaint management: identifying trends of under-delivered or lost stock.

Returned medicines: control of courier used for reverse logistics; verification that returned stock is genuine and supported by appropriate documentation.

Falsified medicines: clear understanding in all areas of the organisation for standards of operations and how to report suspect medicines and transactions.

Outsourced activities: integration with couriers through written agreements including immediate reporting to the contract giver of anomalies, assurance of a chain of custody, risk profiling of contractors, monitoring contractor and control of additional subcontracting by the contractor.

Transportation: security features identified as part of user requirement specification, security profiling for high-risk consignments, driver trained in security practices.

REPORTING STOLEN AND MISSING MEDICINES TO THE MHRA

Theft of medicines that may pose a significant risk to public health should be reported in a timely manner to the MHRA in addition to any other reporting such as the police or Home Office. This is to enable the MHRA to assess the risk to the public and maintain awareness. For high-risk mislaid stock, it may be better to report this following initial investigation and then later report as found, rather than delay the reporting.

Reports should include:

- the date when the event was first noted;
- products;
- quantities;
- batch numbers (if known);
- details of location;
- contact details;
- police incident number or Home Office reference, where relevant.

Enquiries about potential illegal dealings with medicines should be made to the MHRA Case Referral Centre:

- Tel (weekdays 9am to 5pm): 020 3080 6330
- Tel (out-of-hours emergency) for Case Referral Centre/Fakemeds Hotline: 07795 825 727
- Email: casereferrals@mhra.gov.uk

or via the Yellow Card Scheme:

- Tel: 020 3080 6330 / 020 3080 6701
- Email: fakemeds@mhra.gov.uk

Sourcing and Exporting Medicinal Products – Non-EEA Countries

The GDP guidelines describe the concept that medicinal products may be introduced into the Union that are not intended to be released for free circulation. These are known as introduced medicinal products or products sourced from a country outside of GB for the specific reason of supplying them back to a third country, without entering into the UK supply chain.

"*The provisions applicable to the export of medicinal products from Great Britain and those applicable to the introduction of medicinal products into Great Britain with the sole purpose of exporting them need to be clarified. The provisions applicable to wholesale distributors as well as good distribution practices should apply to all those activities whenever they are performed within Great Britain, including in areas such as free trade zones or free warehouses.*"

UK legislation dictates the need for a wholesale dealer's licence for medicine exported from GB to third countries, and to the sourcing and supply of introduced medicines from and to third countries by way of wholesale.

In the case of wholesale distribution of medicinal products to third countries, GDP provisions pertaining to introduced medicines should apply. Wholesale distributors shall ensure that the medicinal products are obtained only from persons who are authorised or entitled to supply medicinal products in accordance with the applicable legal and administrative provisions of the third country concerned. Where wholesale distributors supply medicinal products to persons in third countries, they shall ensure that such supplies are only made to persons who are authorised or entitled to receive medicinal products for wholesale distribution or supply to the public in accordance with the applicable legal and administrative provisions of the third country concerned.

Introduced medicinal products

For a medicinal product to be an introduced medicinal product, it has to be sourced from a third country by a licensed wholesale dealer and supplied to a third country by the same licensed wholesale dealer. An introduced medicinal product will not have a marketing authorisation for the UK. Such products can be held on a licensed site in a free zone or in a bonded warehouse under an appropriate customs processing procedure.

A medicinal product that is sourced from third country by a licensed wholesale dealer, for the purpose of supply to another legal entity in the UK is not an introduced medicinal product because it will have been freely circulated to that other legal entity within the community when supplied. In such circumstances the activity will be subject to the need for a manufacturer's licence authorising import as required under the Human Medicines Regulations 2012.

When dealing with introduced medicinal products, a licensed wholesale dealer has to ensure that they only source the medicine from a person in the third country who is authorised or entitled to supply medicinal products for wholesale distribution in accordance with the applicable legal and administrative provisions of the third country concerned. A licensed wholesale dealer should also verify that the medicinal products received are not falsified.

A licensed wholesale dealer also has to ensure that they supply the introduced medicinal product only back to a person in the third country who is authorised or entitled to receive medicinal products for wholesale distribution or supply to the public in accordance with the applicable legal and administrative provisions of the third country concerned.

A separate Home Office licence is required for introduced medicines that are also "controlled drugs".

The introduction of a medicinal product can be subdivided into the following categories.

PHYSICAL INTRODUCTION

Introduced medicines are sourced from a third country for the sole purpose of export to a third country. These products by definition will not have a marketing authorisation within GB or the UK. Under the provisions of a wholesale dealer's licence the medicinal product may not be "imported", i.e. the customs procedure code quoted on the C88 document cannot include sole or simultaneous entry into free circulation within GB or the UK. A suitable customs procedure code should be declared.

Generally the site of *holding* these products prior to export will be a registered customs warehouse that is the subject of a wholesale dealer's licence.

Further information in respect of the Union Customs Code (UCC) introduced across GB and the UK on 1 May 2016 may be obtained from HMRC.

FINANCIAL INTRODUCTION

Any trade between two third countries being facilitated and invoiced from GB or the UK will be subject to the Good Distribution Practice Guidelines in accordance with regulation C17 (GDP) in their entirety.

It is necessary for the supplying licensed wholesale dealer to demonstrate full compliance with GDP Guidelines in accordance with regulation C17 GB or the UK.

Companies operating this business model will be required to have a wholesale distribution authorisation authorising the activities of *Procurement* and *Supply* as they are buying and selling the product.

This activity should not be confused with brokering. A broker does not at any time take ownership of the product; a broker will bring a buyer and seller together and typically will receive a commission or fee from one or both parties. Brokers are subject to a registration requirement. They must have a permanent address and contact details in the Member State in which they are registered. Brokers are discussed in more detail elsewhere in this guide. See Chapter 10.

Export to a country not on the approved list

A medicinal product that is exported to a third country will be supplied to the specification of the importing country concerned. This might be a medicinal product that is:

- licensed in the UK and has a national marketing authorisation issued by the MHRA;
- licensed in Northern Ireland and has a national marketing authorisation issued by the competent authority for medicines of the EEA member state concerned;
- an unlicensed medicine manufactured specifically for export by the holder of a manufacturer's licence;
- an introduced product that the same authorised wholesale dealer has sourced from a third country;
- a medicine that is also a "controlled drug" – requiring a separate Home Office licence. (See section titled "Controls on certain medicinal products" earlier in this chapter.)

An unlicensed medicine, known as a "special" manufactured by the holder of a manufacturer's specials licence, cannot be distributed to a third country. This is because, to accord with the Human Medicines Regulations 2012, an unlicensed medicine manufactured for export has to be manufactured by the holder of an Manufacturer/Importers' Authorisation (MIA) and certified prior to release by the Qualified Person named on that manufacturing authorisation.

A licensed wholesale dealer who exports a medicine that is the subject of a GB or UK marketing authorisation to a third country must obtain their supplies of medicinal products only from persons who are themselves in possession of an GB or Northern Ireland wholesale distribution authorisation or a GB or UK manufacturer's authorisation.

They must also verify that the authorised medicinal product they receive is not falsified by checking the safety feature on the outer packaging in accordance with the requirements laid down in the Human Medicines Regulations 2012.

A licensed wholesale dealer also has to ensure that they supply the authorised medicine only to persons in the third country who are authorised or entitled to receive medicinal products for wholesale distribution or supply to the public in accordance with the applicable legal and administrative provisions of the third country concerned.

The definition of wholesale distribution does not depend on whether the distributor is established or operating in specific customs areas, such as in free zones or free warehouses. A wholesale distribution authorisation is required and all obligations related to wholesale distribution activities also apply to these distributors.

A number of companies and their sites that were not previously regulated now require a wholesale distribution authorisation. Parties that may be affected include freight consolidators, freight forwarders and logistics services providers in the air, sea or road transport sector when they are "holding" medicinal products.

Customs-approved warehouse facilities "holding" medicinal products are also required to have a wholesale distribution authorisation.

To clear a medicinal product for export, HMRC will need to know exactly what is being shipped. Medicinal products presented for export should therefore be accompanied by the *commercial invoice* fully detailing the commodity to be exported. Use of "proforma invoices" for export purposes are to be avoided.

Customs documentation must be completed fully and legibly. A false or misleading declaration may lead to a fine or seizure of the item.

The products may be subject to restrictions in the country of destination or there may be trade embargoes or other restrictions preventing certain medicinal products from being exported to certain destinations.

It is the responsibility of the exporter to enquire into import and export regulations (prohibitions, restrictions such as quarantine, pharmaceutical restrictions, etc.) and to find out what documents, if any (commercial invoice, certificate of origin, health certificate, export licence, authorisation for goods subject to quarantine [plant, animal, food products, etc.]) are required in the destination country. See GDP, Chapter 5, Section 5.9:

"Where wholesale distributors supply medicinal products to persons in third countries, they shall ensure that such supplies are only made to persons who are authorised or entitled to receive medicinal products for wholesale distribution or supply to the public in accordance with the applicable legal and administrative provisions of the country concerned."

Export is defined so as to *allow GB goods to leave the customs territory.* It is the responsibility of the exporter (consignor) to ensure that:

- medicinal products remain in the legal supply chain;
- export paperwork is completed correctly;
- proof of export is obtained and retained;
- the Consignee is entitled to receive the medicinal products;
- the product has been stored, handled and shipped in accordance with GDP.

HMRC recommends that exporters should routinely provide their freight agents with the following:

- their UK Economic Operator Registration and Identification (EORI) number.
- details of to whom the goods are to be consigned, their name and address in full.
- a commercial reference that can be incorporated into the Declaration Unique Consignment Reference (DUCR) to assist with the export audit trail.
- details of where the goods are to be exported, i.e. country of final destination.
- shipping or flight details (where known).
- correct value of goods in correct currency code.
- the Commodity Code and a clear and unambiguous description of the goods, their quantity marks and numbers.
- any reference numbers already issued by HMRC, e.g. Inward Processing Relief, Outward Processing relief authorisations or previous declarations should also be provided.

Qualification check in third countries

The MHRA recognises that conducting a qualification check in some third countries can be quite difficult. In the first instance, suppliers and customers in the third countries concerned should be asked to justify their local entitlement and requirements. However, an authorised wholesale dealer should not just accept information from the supplier or customer that they can supply or import medicines, but should take reasonable steps to verify that the information that they have been provided with is valid and accurate. This may involve making additional checks with the regulatory authority for medicines in the country concerned, where possible, and documenting the outcome as evidence. Any licences obtained should have been translated into English and authenticated by a notary with appropriate due diligence carried out. The MHRA's expectation is that an authorised wholesale dealer should have oversight of the export of the introduced medicinal product and have all the appropriate documentation to evidence it. See also section on Qualification of Customers and Suppliers.

Wholesale obligations for exported and introduced medicinal products

For further obligations of licensed wholesale dealers, see Chapter 11 Legislation on Wholesale Distribution. You cannot export medicines on the restricted medicines list that have been put on the market for UK patients to other countries in or outside the EEA.

As of 1 January 2021, you may no longer be able to export branded medicines that have been placed on the UK market to countries in the EEA.

Medicines that cannot be exported from the UK

The DHSC have implemented restrictions on some medicines leaving the UK.

WDA(H) holders must implement effective processes to ensure that medicines periodically defined by the DHSC are not hoarded exported from GB or UK markets and remain available to facilitate UK patient need.

You can continue to export medicines on the restricted medicines list if you, or a company in your group of companies, holds a marketing authorisation for those medicines and have specifically forecast medicines in GB or UK delivery to be exported to meet patient need. The restrictions do not apply.

You can continue to export medicines on the restricted medicines list that are manufactured and intended for markets abroad. The restrictions do not apply.

You can continue to export medicines on the restricted medicines list to:

- ships;
- planes;
- the British, UN and NATO armed forces;

- British citizens abroad;
- British overseas territories and crown dependencies;
- to international humanitarian organisations;
- for clinical trials and other research purposes.

Where companies are actively engaged in export and have orders in place prior to a ban being implemented on a medicine, a final agreed purchase order from an importer must be received before the date of restriction. Open, rolling or frame orders placed by importers before the date of restriction can only be fulfilled if the products have been picked and packed, and transport booked. All orders must be final, evidenced as signed and comply with the above terms.

The restriction for each medicine applies from 00:00am at the start of the date of restriction.

If you export, start hoarding or continue hoarding a medicine on the restricted list it will be considered a breach of regulation 43(2) of the Human Medicines Regulations 2012.

It may lead to regulatory action by the MHRA against the wholesale dealer's licence.

This could include:

- an immediate suspension of the licence or suspension of the supply of certain products under the licence;
- a 28-day notice proposing to vary the licence to restrict or prevent export activity.

Continued breaches could be considered a criminal offence under regulation 34(1), read together with regulation 18(1) of the Human Medicines Regulations 2012.

https://www.gov.uk/government/publications/medicines-that-cannot-be-parallel-exported-from-the-uk

Incoterms®

Incoterms® 2010 rules are internationally accepted standard definitions of trade terms. Incoterms® were developed by the International Chamber of Commerce, Paris, France in 1936 and have been regularly revised to reflect the changes in transportation and documentation. The current version is Incoterms® 2010.

Full information may be obtained from www.iccwbo.org.

There are 11 Incoterms that can be broadly split into subgroups according to which party pays for and arranges the main transport. Each group is discussed briefly below.

The first three groups are applicable to products moved by air, road, rail or sea, or by a combination of transport modes.

BUYER ARRANGES MAIN CARRIAGE – EXW

- EXW – EX Works (… named place).

This Incoterm puts the onus on the customer to complete and pay for the export formalities and for the pre-carriage of the products from the seller's premises to the point of export.

In many cross-border and international transactions this presents practical difficulties. Specifically, the exporter needs to be involved in export-reporting formalities and cannot realistically leave these to the buyer.

BUYER ARRANGES MAIN CARRIAGE – FCA

- FCA – Free Carrier (… named place of delivery).

With this Incoterm the seller has control regarding the transport and customs formalities prior to the goods leaving the Union; the buyer pays for the main transport.

This option crucially gives the seller control over the pre-transport to the point of export and control over the export formalities.

It is the legal responsibility of the declarant to ensure that the goods are accurately declared and presented to HMRC prior to goods leaving the UK. If the exporter is employing a freight agent to declare the goods on their behalf they must ensure they supply them with the appropriate information to submit a legal declaration.

SELLER ARRANGES MAIN CARRIAGE – CPT, CIP, DAT, DAP, DDP

- CPT – Carriage Paid To (… named place of destination);
- CIP – Carriage and Insurance Paid To (… named place of destination);
- DAT – Delivered At Terminal (… named terminal at destination port);
- DAP – Delivered At Place (… named place of destination);
- DDP – Delivered Duty Paid (… named place of destination).

Here the seller has control over the pre-carriage, customs formalities and the main transport mode.

The following two groups are only applicable when transport is via sea freight or by inland waterways.

Buyer arranges main carriage – FAS, FOB

- FAS – Free Alongside Ship (… named port of shipment);
- FOB – Free On Board (… named port of shipment).

Pre-carriage and export formalities by seller the customer pays for the sea freight from the named port of shipment.

Seller arranges main carriage – CFR, CIF

- CFR – Cost and Freight (… named port of destination);
- CIF – Cost Insurance and Freight (… named port of destination).

Pre-carriage and export formalities by seller; seller also pays sea freight to the named destination.

When entering into trade negotiations with potential clients, the selection of the appropriate Incoterm can significantly influence the ability to demonstrate GDP compliance.

Selection of an Incoterm such as ExW or FCA where the buyer pays for the freight does not absolve the seller of their GDP responsibilities with respect to selection of transport conditions.

As the Consignor, the exporter is legally responsible for the information shown on the customs documentation. The definition of export is *to allow Community goods to leave the customs territory of the Union.*

Import of medicinal products

Import is not a function authorised under a wholesale distribution authorisation from countries not named on a list for the purpose of parallel import. For medicinal products that are imported from a non-listed, an Article 40 authorisation (Manufacturer's/Importer's Authorisation [MIA]) is required.

Import is briefly discussed in this section for the sake of completeness and to make a clear distinction of the act of Introduction, a GDP activity executed under a wholesale dealer's licence and Importation, a GMP activity requiring an MIA.

Importation of product manufactured in a third country not on the list for parallel import for use in the UK is a GMP activity. This requires a Manufacturing Licence (typically an MIA but, in particular circumstances, a Manufacturer's Specials licence may be required). Import activity associated with an MIA requires QP release of product.

<u>Transactions where title is passed from EEA company to non-EEA company</u>

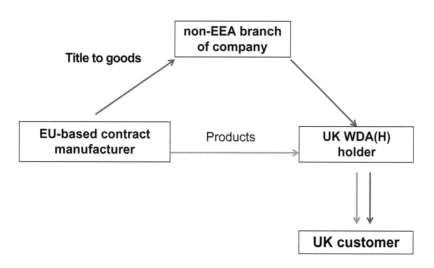

Transactions where title is passed from GB or UK company to non-GB or UK company

In this scenario, licensed medicinal product is manufactured and released within GB or the UK under a Manufacturing Authorisation. The title of the goods is transferred to the *sole UK pre-distribution partner* via a third country while the product physically remains within GB or the UK at suitably licensed premises at all times.

Product transfers directly from the contract manufacturer to the *sole UK pre-distribution partner*. The pre-distributor partner then distributes the products according to their own authorisation.

To accord with regulation 44(1) of the Human Medicines Regulations the holder of a wholesale dealer's licence may not obtain supplies of medicinal products from anyone except:

(a) the holder of a manufacturer's licence or wholesale dealer's licence in relation to products of that description; or

(b) a person who holds an authorisation granted by another country named on a list authorising the manufacture of products of that description or their distribution by way of wholesale dealing.

Therefore these requirements will prohibit the purchasing of medicines from a company in a third country. This transaction is classed as a *fiscal import* from a third country and therefore is not a WDA(H) activity. This business model requires an MIA.

Ensuring that you have the correct authorisations for the intended activity

GDP defines wholesale distribution of medicinal products to mean:

"All activities consisting of procuring, holding, supplying or exporting medicinal products, other than supplying these products to the public."[18]

An authorised wholesale dealer may be authorised to undertake one or more of these activities according to the scope of the granted authorisation. Definitions of these activities are provided in the Annex to EU Guidelines on Good Distribution Practice of Medicinal Products for Human Use (GDP)[19] as below:

HOLDING – storing medicinal products. (*The MHRA apply the interpretation that a site is deemed to be holding when either an ambient product is on site for more than 36 hours or there is active refrigeration taking place regardless of dwell time.*)

---

[18] Article 1(17).
[19] 2013/C 343/01.

EXPORT – to allow GB or UK goods to leave customs territory.

A Home Office licence is required to import or export "controlled drugs". Controlled drugs are named in the Misuse of Drugs legislation, and grouped in schedules. Anyone intending to supply a controlled drug must apply for the relevant schedule licence[20].

Exports and customs procedures

YOUR PRODUCT, YOUR DECLARATION

When exporting a medicinal product, a declaration must be made to HMRC to indicate exactly what is being shipped, who is making the shipment and where the product is ultimately going.

The product should be accompanied by a commercial invoice – proforma invoices are to be avoided as this can, and has, led to misleading customs declarations being completed. A false declaration may result in seizure of the product and may also lead to a fine.

It is the responsibility of the exporter to enquire into the import and export regulations (any prohibitions, restrictions, trade embargoes, etc.) that may be in force in relation to the destination country. The exporter must ensure that certificates of origin, export licences and the like, which may be required in relation to the trade in the particular commodity within the destination country, are applied for and that the correct documentation accompanies the shipment. Copies of this documentation should routinely be retained.

The exporter (consignor) is also responsible for ensuring that:

- medicinal products remain in the legal supply chain;
- export paperwork is correctly completed;
- proof of export is obtained and retained;
- the consignee is entitled to receive the product; and
- the product has been stored, handled and shipped in accordance with GDP.

YOUR FREIGHT FORWARDER OR SHIPPING AGENT IS A KEY PARTNER

It is best practice to routinely provide the freight forwarder, shipping department or freight agent with the following:

- your Economic Operator Registration and Identification (EORI) number;
- details of to whom the goods are to be consigned (name and address in full);
- commercial reference to be incorporated into the Declaration Unique Consignment Reference (DUCR) to assist with export audit trails;
- details of the country of final destination;
- shipping or flight details;

---

[20] https://www.gov.uk/guidance/controlled-drugs-licences-fees-and-returns.

- correct value of goods in the correct currency code;
- the Commodity Code and a clear and unambiguous description of the goods, their quantity, marks and numbers;
- any reference numbers already issued by HMRC – such as any previous declarations made in respect of the product, e.g. the declaration made when the product was "introduced".

While on inspection, upon asking for documentation relating to an export to a third country, the MHRA are frequently presented with invoices that show the Incoterm 'Ex Works'. This generally causes traceability issues at inspection because the consignor may have handed the product over for export to a representative of a company appointed by the consignee. Where this is the case, the consignor generally will be unable to demonstrate GDP compliance or indeed produce any paperwork showing that the product has been exported as claimed. Companies should obtain copies of the documentation (which is interchangeably referred to as the SAD, C88 or export declaration) from their shipping agent and check this for accuracy.

The Incoterm EXW (Ex Works) puts the onus on the consignee to arrange the pre-carriage from the seller's premises to the point of export, and to complete and pay for the export formalities. In most export scenarios this presents practical difficulties. Realistically, for all export transactions the exporter needs to be involved in export-reporting formalities and cannot realistically leave this to the consignee.

A lesser used but more practical Incoterm, when an exporter does not wish to pay for the carriage of the product, is FCA – Free Carrier (named place of delivery). Generally the named place of delivery will be the port through which the product is leaving. With this Incoterm, the seller has control regarding the transport and customs formalities prior to the goods leaving the territory, and the buyer pays for the main transport.

As it is the legal responsibility of the declarant to ensure that the goods are accurately declared when presented to HMRC, using this Incoterm gives the seller the control required. Crucially the seller also takes responsibility for arranging the transport to the point of shipment (or consolidation) and can therefore control where the goods are held and by whom prior to shipment, hence ensuring that the product remains within the legal supply chain and under GDP control up to the point of main transport, which will have been risk assessed according to Chapter 9 of GDP

Both the GDP and GMP inspectorate will be routinely requesting full export documentation at inspection – and this extends to the CHIEF (Customs Handling of Import and Export Freight) entry – bills of lading or airway bills, export licences where applicable, and any certificates of origin that may be required for that particular commodity to be sent to the destination country. For exports we still expect that you can show the same due diligence. As the exporter, the responsibility in ensuring that the information is provided to HMRC rests with you.

Controls on Certain Medicinal Products

Good Distribution Practice (GDP) in accordance with regulation C17 requires the licence holder and/or the RP to consider extra requirements throughout the wholesale process. The RP must ensure that any additional requirements imposed on certain products by national law are adhered to. This will include ensuring that the correct licences are held for the activities undertaken, ensuring that any broker used or any organisation performing outsourced activities is correctly licensed and that customers are entitled to receive the products supplied. Where products are exported, there may be additional national requirements to consider. Supplies made to customers should be monitored to enable any irregularity in the sales patterns of narcotics, psychotropic substances and other dangerous substances to be investigated. Unusual sales patterns may constitute diversion and must be reported to the MHRA.

Some products may present additional risks during storage and transport. These could include cytotoxics, radiopharmaceuticals and flammable products. Special destruction requirements may be imposed by national regulation.

Staff may require additional training for the receipt and handling of hazardous products, radioactive materials and products presenting special risks of abuse, as well as temperature-sensitive products. Handling of temperature-sensitive products is addressed in Chapter 3 – Premises and Equipment.

Transaction arrangements, storage, transport and security measures should all be documented, risk assessed and audited to demonstrate continued suitability and compliance.

GDP frequently refers to "additional requirements imposed on certain products by national law". These medicinal products and substances are subject to additional controls not frequently encountered by the licensed wholesale dealer. Further requirements are in place under GDP for:

- medicinal products derived from blood;
- immunological medicinal products;
- narcotic or psychotropic substances;
- radiopharmaceuticals.

These additional controls are managed by the MHRA or other organisations. Some examples are given below.

Controlled drugs and precursor chemicals

The Home Office Drug & Firearms Licensing Unit is the UK Competent Authority for controlled drug and drug precursor chemical licensing. Licences are needed irrespective of the format of the material, whether finished product (licensed medicine or unlicensed "special"), active substances, starting materials or intermediates, where controlled under the relevant legislation.

"Domestic" Licences are issued to specific "persons" (i.e. companies) at specific premises, covering a single site. They are not transferrable to different corporate entities or premises. If your company operates at a number of sites you need a licence for each one individually. It is your responsibility to ensure that you keep pace with any legislative changes and obtain new licences if needed. You must hold all relevant licences before handling controlled substances.

Prospective licensees must register to use the Drug and Precursor Chemical web application portal and all applications must be submitted electronically. Registration is not automatic and those requesting a user login must be able to show that their business proposals would be lawful and, in principle, have a prospect of success. Prospective licensees looking to handle cannabinoid products should pay particular attention to the Home Office guidance at Cannabis, CBD and other cannabinoids: drug licensing factsheet – GOV.UK (www.gov.uk). Registrations or applications made without a lawful route to market will be rejected.

If a user registration is accepted, it will enable a licensing application to be made, but it is no guarantee that one will succeed. The fees payable are listed here: Drugs licensing – GOV.UK (www.gov.uk).

Import–Export licences are issued for individual consignments and can be sought only after the company has obtained the relevant domestic licence using the process set out above.

Further information is available at:

Drugs licensing – GOV.UK (www.gov.uk);

Precursor chemical licensing – GOV.UK (www.gov.uk).

Use of the mandatory requisition form for Schedule 2 and 3 controlled drugs

On 30 November 2015 legislative provisions came into effect that made it mandatory for specified health and veterinary care professionals, and organisations listed at Regulation 14(4) of the Misuse of Drugs Regulations 2001, to use an approved form for the requisitioning of Schedule 2 and 3 controlled drugs. This change, which the Home Office consulted on in 2011, implemented a final recommendation of the Shipman Inquiry on requisitions[21].

---

[21] https://www.gov.uk/government/publications/circular-0272015-approved-mandatory-requisition-form-and-home-office-approved-wording/circular-0272015-approved-mandatory-requisition-form-and-home-office-approved-wording

Following the introduction of the form, the Home Office has been made aware that activities within the hospital sector, which would normally be governed by provisions under Regulation 14(6), and which were not expected to come within the scope of the new requirement, are now captured as a result of changes in the NHS structures in recent years. This is an unintended consequence of the changes to NHS structures and healthcare delivery since 2011, rather than a result of a regulatory change.

The Home Office circular that introduced the change made it clear that the requirement to use the mandatory form was to be limited to activities undertaken by health and veterinary care practitioners in the community to enable their requisition activities to be monitored. The requirement to use a mandatory form was not expected to extend to the hospital environment, where traditionally supplies of controlled drugs were undertaken by an onsite pharmacy owned by the hospital and under the Regulation 14(6) provisions.

This additional guidance is therefore being issued to explain further how the provisions governing the use of the new mandatory form may be interpreted. This guidance does not impact on the need for a Home Office licence. The guidance should also not be interpreted as a change in Home Office licensing requirements, which these regulatory and procedural requirements relate to but are not necessarily interdependent on:

(1) The use of the form is mandatory when individual health and veterinary care professionals requisition the relevant controlled drugs in the community, including when such drugs are ordered from pharmaceutical wholesalers and community pharmacies.

(2) It is not the intention of the policy on requisitions forms to capture requisition activities for hospital wards, etc. However, as a number of hospital wards now obtain the relevant controlled drugs from other trusts or organisations, and therefore across legal entities, these activities do fall within the scope of Regulation 14(2), and therefore the use of the form is mandatory, unless an exemption applies (e.g. registered pharmacies are completely excluded from the requirement to use a requisition when obtaining the relevant controlled drugs). In order to ensure that the regulatory provisions are complied with, it is the view of the Home Office that the person in charge or acting person in charge of a hospital or care home (excluding hospices) can issue a "bulk" or "global" requisition based on a previous year's orders to a separate legal entity that supplies its wards. Hospital or trust wards can then draw on this "bulk" requisition throughout the year, using the duplicate order forms as happens presently. Hospital or Trust wards therefore do not need to use the mandatory form when obtaining the relevant controlled drugs from another trust or legal entity. Similarly, the person in charge or acting person in charge of an ambulance trust, as defined under the 2001 Regulations, can issue a

"bulk" requisition when obtaining the relevant controlled drugs to be supplied directly to employees of the trust by a separate legal entity. However, those employees, when individually drawing on the "bulk" requisition, must use the mandatory form.

(3) Additionally, pharmaceutical wholesale suppliers (excluding community pharmacies) are exempt under current regulatory provisions from submitting requisitions received for Schedule 2 and 3 controlled drugs to the NHS Business Services Authority (NHSBSA). The only requisition forms that must be submitted to the NHSBSA following the introduction of the mandatory form are those provided by individual healthcare professionals when obtaining the relevant controlled drugs in the community.

The table below provides some examples of how the regulations apply in specific circumstances with reference to Regulations 14(2) and (4). This is only a Home Office view and does not constitute legal advice. Organisations are advised to seek their own independent legal advice where appropriate. This guidance has been developed with the Department of Health and Social Care and the Care Quality Commission.

Supplier	Recipient	Do I need to use the new FP10CDF?	Do I need to submit the FP10 CDF to the NHSBSA
Wholesaler	Practitioners, paramedics and the other professionals and organisations listed in Regulation 14(4)	Yes, all practitioners and the list of healthcare professionals must use the form when they requisition for stocks	No, the Regulation exempts the submission of requisitions received by wholesalers from being sent to the NHSBSA
Wholesaler	Registered pharmacy (including a hospital-registered pharmacy)	No	N/A
Wholesaler	Hospital, care home or ambulance trust without a registered pharmacy **Excludes hospices	Yes, in line with Regulation 14	No, the regulation exempts the submission of requisitions received by wholesalers from being sent to the NHSBSA
Legal entity A	Legal entity B's hospital wards	Yes, person in charge of legal entity B must issue a yearly global requisition to legal entity A. Wards in legal entity B can then draw on this requisition through the year using duplicate order books	No
Legal entity A	Legal entity B's registered pharmacy	No	N/A
Legal entity A	Legal entity B	Yes, if organisation is listed at Regulation 14(4)	No

Controls on strategic goods and drugs usable in execution by lethal injection

The Export Control Organisation (ECO), part of the Department for Business, Innovation and Skills, issues licences for controlling the export of strategic goods. The range of goods and services covered by embargoes and sanctions is extensive, changes from time to time and includes:

- military equipment;
- dual-use goods that can be used for both civil and military purposes;
- products used for torture;
- radioactive sources.

These may apply to medical devices, finished medical products or active substances.

ECO also administers controls on trade in certain goods that could be used for capital punishment, torture or other cruel, inhuman or degrading treatment or punishment. This includes the control on the export of certain drugs usable in execution by lethal injection.

As a result of these controls, exporters need to seek appropriate permission from national export control authorities to export to any destination outside the UK, short- and intermediate-acting barbiturate anaesthetic agents including, but not limited to, the following:

- amobarbital (CAS RN 57-43-2);
- amobarbital sodium salt (CAS RN 64-43-7);
- pentobarbital (CAS RN 76-74-4);
- pentobarbital sodium salt (CAS 57-33-0);
- secobarbital (CAS RN 76-73-3);
- secobarbital sodium salt (CAS RN 309-43-3);
- thiopental (CAS RN 76-75-5);
- thiopental sodium salt (CAS RN 71-73-8), also known as thiopentone sodium.

The control also applies to products containing one or more of the above. These controls are intended to apply to finished products – in other words, those that are packaged for human or veterinary use. It is not intended that they should apply to raw materials or to intermediate products (i.e. products that require further processing to make them suitable for human or veterinary use).

It is the responsibility of a wholesale dealer to ensure that they export responsibly and within the law. ECO provide training for exporters of strategic goods. Further information on training and licensing can be found on the GOV.UK website[22].

---

[22] https://www.gov.uk/controls-on-torture-goods; https://www.gov.uk/government/organisations/export-control-organisation

Control of lisdexamfetamine, tramadol, zaleplon and zopiclone and re-classification of ketamine

On 10 June 2014, the Parliamentary Order controlling and, in the case of ketamine, re-classifying the following drugs, came into force:

- lisdexamfetamine;
- tramadol;
- zaleplon;
- zopiclone;
- medicines containing these substances.

The Order, available on legislation.gov.uk, controls:

- lisdexamfetamine as a Class B drug;
- tramadol as a Class C drug;
- zopiclone and zaleplon as Class C drugs.

The Order also re-classifies ketamine as a Class B drug under the Misuse of Drugs Act 1971.

Companies that possess, supply or produce lisdexamfetamine, tramadol, zaleplon or zopiclone (or medicines containing these substances) need to get the correct licences from the Home Office.

More information on how to apply for a licence, and how much they cost, is available on www.GOV.UK at https://www.gov.uk/controlled-drugs-licences-fees-and-returns or by calling the Duty Compliance Officer on 020 7035 8972.

Companies without the correct licences are at risk of prosecution.

The listed drugs will be scheduled, alongside their control, as follows to ensure that they remain available for use in healthcare:

- Lisdexamfetamine (a drug that converts to dexamfetamine when administered orally and used as second-line treatment for ADHD) will be listed in Schedule 2 alongside dexamfetamine.
- Tramadol will be listed in Schedule 3 but exempted from the safe custody requirements. Full prescription writing requirements under Regulation 15 will apply to its use in healthcare.
- Zopiclone and zaleplon will be listed in Part 1 of Schedule 4 alongside zolpidem.

Ketamine is not being re-scheduled immediately. In line with the Advisory Council on the Misuse of Drugs' (ACMD) advice, the Home Office will carry out a public consultation later this year to assess the impact of re-scheduling ketamine to Schedule 2.

A final decision on the appropriate schedule for ketamine will be made after the consultation. Until then ketamine will remain a Schedule 4, Part 1 drug.

Home Office Circular 008/2014: A change to the Misuse of Drugs Act 1971 – Control of NBOMes, Benzofurans, Lisdexamphetamine, Tramadol, Zopiclone, Zaleplon and Reclassification of Ketamine[23].

Controls and authorisations applying to those handling medicinal products derived from blood

The MHRA is responsible for the controls and authorisations that apply to blood establishments (BEs) and controls that apply to hospital blood banks (HBBs), and sites that collect, test and supply human blood or blood components intended for transfusion. Further information can be obtained from the GOV.UK website[24].

Procurement, storage, distribution and disposal of vaccines

GDP applies to all vaccine wholesale activities. The supply chain in the UK and guidance on who may receive these, how the end-user should store them and how they should be disposed of are further described in *Immunisation against Infectious Disease*, commonly known as the green book. This can be found on the GOV.UK website[25].

In the event of a pandemic there are steps that the Government can take to authorise certain activities, such as allowing wholesalers to amend expiry dates on frozen products when they are removed from frozen to refrigerated status.

Wholesale of radiopharmaceuticals

Many activities will fall under Good Manufacturing Practice Annex 3 as well as GDP. Further guidance from the marketing authorisation must be followed.

Wholesale of veterinary medicinal products

The Veterinary Medicines Regulations 2013 [SI 2013/2033] came into force on 1 October 2013. A wholesaler of veterinary products will usually

---

[23] https://www.gov.uk/government/publications/circular-0082014-changes-to-the-misuse-of-drugs-act-1971

[24] https://www.gov.uk/guidance/blood-authorisations-and-safety-reporting

[25] https://www.gov.uk/government/collections/immunisation-against-infectious-disease-the-green-book#the-green-book

be required to hold a WDA(V). The regulations require that the holder must:

(a) store veterinary medicinal products in accordance with the terms of the marketing authorisation for each product;
(b) comply with the Guidelines on Good Distribution Practice of Medicinal Products for Human Use as if the veterinary medicinal products were authorised human medicinal products;
(c) carry out a detailed stock audit at least once a year; and
(d) supply information and samples to the Secretary of State on demand.

Further information in relation to import and export, the cascade, record keeping, controlled drugs and other veterinary wholesale activities can be found on the GOV.UK website[26].

Sales Representative Samples

Under the legislation on advertising medicines, companies may provide free samples only to persons qualified to prescribe the medicine. Samples may only be supplied in response to a signed and dated request from the prescriber and must be appropriately labelled and accompanied by a copy of the Summary of Product Characteristics (SPC). The company must have adequate procedures for control and accountability for all samples. See Section 6.12 of the MHRA's Blue Guide for details of the legal requirements.

The MHRA is aware that in some cases sales representatives receive samples to fill prescriber requests and that the medicinal products are delivered to them by colleagues or couriers. Either way, the storage and delivery arrangements for these medicinal products must be validated to ensure that the medicinal product will be transported expeditiously under controlled Good Distribution Practice (GDP) conditions and in accordance with labelled storage requirements at all times. It is highly unlikely that samples requiring refrigeration will meet these requirements. With regards to storage it is not acceptable for samples to be stored in the representative's home (on unlicensed premises, which are not GDP compliant), lacking appropriate storage facilities, security and controls to maintain the quality of the medicines and provide an audit trail.

Likewise distribution of samples involving delivery in a representative's vehicle that has no provision for maintaining correct storage conditions is also unacceptable. Temperatures in a car boot in high summer could reach 50°C or go below 0°C in winter. The practice of providing sales representatives with samples of medicinal products that they retain for onward

---

[26] https://www.gov.uk/government/organisations/veterinary-medicines-directorate

distribution is therefore unlikely to be acceptable due to the storage and transport difficulties outlined above. The only reason for which sales representatives may hold samples on a long-term basis is for the purpose of product identification. In this regard procedures must be in place to ensure accountability for any such stock and to ensure no packs are provided to healthcare professionals.

Diverted Medicines

Diversion is the term used for the fraudulent activity where medicines destined for non-GB or -UK markets re-enter the supply chain and are placed back on to the market at a higher price.

The diversion of medicines involves medicinal products being offered at preferential prices and exported to specific markets (normally third countries) outside GB or the UK. Diversion occurs when unscrupulous traders, on receipt of the medicines, re-export the products back to GB or the UK – with the consequence that patients for whom these preferentially priced medicines were intended are denied access to them. Such products appearing on the market are then known as "diverted" from their intended market. This represents not only a corrupt diversion for profit, but such activity also poses the risk of inappropriate or unlicensed use, and the risk that the product may also be compromised due to poor storage and transportation.

As with counterfeit and falsified products, wholesale dealers in particular should maintain a high level of vigilance against the procurement or supply of potentially diverted products. Diverted products may be offered for sale below the established market value, so appropriate checks should be made on the bona fides of the supplier and the origin of the product should be ascertained.

Chapter 6 Complaints, Returns, Suspected Falsified Medicinal Products and Medicinal Product Recalls

6.1 Principle

All complaints, returns, suspected falsified medicinal products and recalls must be recorded and handled carefully according to written procedures. Records should be made available to the competent authorities. An assessment of returned medicinal products should be performed before any approval for resale. A consistent approach by all partners in the supply chain is required in order to be successful in the fight against falsified medicinal products.

6.2   Complaints

Complaints should be recorded with all the original details. A distinction should be made between complaints related to the quality of a medicinal product and those related to distribution. In the event of a complaint about the quality of a medicinal product and a potential product defect, the manufacturer and/or marketing authorisation holder should be informed without delay. Any product distribution complaint should be thoroughly investigated to identify the origin of or reason for the complaint.

A person should be appointed to handle complaints and allocated sufficient support personnel.

If necessary, appropriate follow-up actions (including CAPA) should be taken after investigation and evaluation of the complaint, including where required notification to the national competent authorities.

6.3   Returned medicinal products

Returned products must be handled according to a written, risk-based process taking into account the product concerned, any specific storage requirements and the time elapsed since the medicinal product was originally dispatched. Returns should be conducted in accordance with national law and contractual arrangements between the parties.

Medicinal products which have left the premises of the distributor should only be returned to saleable stock if all of the following are confirmed:

(i)   the medicinal products are in their unopened and undamaged secondary packaging and are in good condition, have not expired and have not been recalled;

(ii) medicinal products returned from a customer not holding a wholesale distribution authorisation or from pharmacies authorised to supply medicinal products to the public should only be returned to saleable stock only if they are returned within an acceptable time limit, for example 10 days;

(iii) it has been demonstrated by the customer that the medicinal products have been transported, stored and handled in compliance with their specific storage requirements;

(iv) they have been examined and assessed by a sufficiently trained and competent person authorised to do so;

(v)   the distributor has reasonable evidence that the product was supplied to that customer (via copies of the original delivery note or by referencing invoice numbers, etc.) and the batch number for products bearing the safety features is known, and that there is no reason to believe that the product has been falsified.

Moreover, for medicinal products requiring specific temperature storage conditions such as low temperature, returns to saleable stock can only be made if there is documented evidence that the product has been stored under the authorised storage conditions throughout the entire time. If any deviation has occurred a risk assessment has to be performed, on which basis the integrity of the product can be demonstrated. The evidence should cover:

(i) delivery to customer;
(ii) examination of the product;
(iii) opening of the transport packaging;
(iv) return of the product to the packaging;
(v) collection and return to the distributor;
(vi) return to the distribution site refrigerator.

Products returned to saleable stock should be placed such that the "first expired, first out" (FEFO) system operates effectively.

Stolen products that have been recovered cannot be returned to saleable stock and sold to customers.

6.4 Falsified medicinal products

Wholesale distributors must immediately inform the competent authority and the marketing authorisation holder of any medicinal products they identify as falsified or suspect to be falsified[27]. A procedure should be in place to this effect. It should be recorded with all the original details and investigated.

Any falsified medicinal products found in the supply chain should immediately be physically segregated and stored in a dedicated area away from all other medicinal products. All relevant activities in relation to such products should be documented and records retained.

6.5 Medicinal product recalls

The effectiveness of the arrangements for product recall should be evaluated regularly (at least annually).

Recall operations should be capable of being initiated promptly and at any time.

The distributor must follow the instructions of a recall message, which should be approved, if required, by the competent authorities.

---

[27] Article 80(i) of Directive 2001/83/EC.

Any recall operation should be recorded at the time it is carried out. Records should be made readily available to the competent authorities.

The distribution records should be readily accessible to the person(s) responsible for the recall, and should contain sufficient information on distributors and directly supplied customers (with addresses, phone and/or fax numbers inside and outside working hours, batch numbers at least for medicinal products bearing safety features as required by legislation and quantities delivered), including those for exported products and medicinal product samples.

The progress of the recall process should be recorded for a final report.

UK Guidance on Chapter 6 Complaints, Returns, Suspected Falsified Medicinal Products and Medicinal Product Recalls

Handling Returns

Returns of refrigerated medicinal products

As a result of the inherent dangers of returning refrigerated products, many licensed wholesale dealers will not consider refrigerated returns for subsequent resale in any event. All such returns are immediately stored in a dedicated and marked area awaiting collection by a licensed disposal company.

In the event of a licensed wholesale dealer accepting a return of a refrigerated product, possibly because of its high monetary value, the product should be returned in accordance with MHRA guidance (below), in an appropriate method of transport, with supporting documentation, such as a returns form. The returns form would normally include the reason for the return, contain details of the product and how it has been stored and should be signed by an authorised and identifiable signatory.

A trained person at the wholesalers should examine the returned product to check for tampering and to confirm that the return has been made in accordance with MHRA guidance. If this examination cannot be undertaken immediately, the product should be stored in a dedicated and marked area in a refrigerator until the checks can be made.

Provided the checks are satisfactory and are documented, the product may then be returned to saleable stock. MHRA guidance on managing returned non-defective (ambient) and refrigerated medicinal products is provided below.

Returns of non-defective medicinal products

Any person acting as a wholesale distributor must hold a wholesale dealer's licence.

Regulation 43(1) of the Human Medicines Regulations 2012[28], as amended, provides that distributors of human medicines must comply with the guidelines for Good Distribution Practice (GDP).

Chapter 6.3 of the GDP Guidelines refers to returned medicinal products, the key elements being that "Medicinal products that have left the premises of the distributor should only be returned to saleable stock if:

(i)   the medicinal products are in their unopened and undamaged secondary packaging and are in good condition, have not expired and have not been recalled;

(ii) medicinal products returned from a customer not holding a wholesale distribution authorisation or from pharmacies authorised to supply medicinal products to the public should only be returned to saleable stock if they are returned within an acceptable time limit, for example 10 days;

(iii) it has been demonstrated by the customer that the medicinal products have been transported, stored and handled in compliance with their specific storage requirements;

(iv) they have been examined and assessed by a sufficiently trained and competent person authorised to do so."

(v)   the distributor has reasonable evidence that the product was supplied to that customer (via copies of the original delivery note or by referencing invoice numbers, etc.) and the batch number for products bearing the safety features is known, and that there is no reason to believe that the product has been falsified."

Definition of licensed and unlicensed sites

The MHRA re-affirm that a licensed site can be interpreted only as being under full GDP control at a licensed wholesale dealer. This applies to all categories of medicines. Medicinal products held in unlicensed storage and distribution sites are not considered to be within the licensed wholesale distribution network.

AMBIENT RETURNS FROM A LICENSED WHOLESALE DEALER'S SITE

The MHRA will adopt a pragmatic approach to the return of non-defective medicinal products for those products returned from a customer operating from a licensed wholesale dealer authorisation (WDA) site.

In such circumstances, the return should be completed as expeditiously as possible and the most expedient and appropriate method of transportation must be used.

The Responsible Person or the authorised person receiving the return must be able to demonstrate evidence of "full knowledge" of the storage of the returned products throughout the period it has been with the customer, including transportation.

---

[28] SI 2012 No. 1916.

AMBIENT RETURNS FROM AN UNLICENSED SITE

For those non-defective ambient medicinal products returned from an unlicensed site, the return should be completed within five days, including transport.

The Responsible Person or the authorised person must be able to demonstrate evidence of "full knowledge" of the storage while at the unlicensed site, including transportation.

REFRIGERATED RETURNS FROM A LICENSED WHOLESALE DEALER'S SITE

The MHRA will adopt a pragmatic approach to the return of non-defective medicinal products for those products returned from a customer operating from a licensed WDA site.

In such circumstances, the return should be completed expeditiously and the most expedient and appropriate method of transportation must be used.

The Responsible Person or the authorised person receiving the return must be able to demonstrate evidence of "full knowledge" of the storage of the returned products throughout the period it has been with the customer, including transportation.

REFRIGERATED RETURNS FROM AN UNLICENSED SITE

For those non-defective refrigerated medicinal products returned from an unlicensed site, the return should be completed within 24 hours, including transport.

The Responsible Person or the authorised person must be able to demonstrate evidence of "full knowledge" of the storage while at the unlicensed site, including transportation.

Falsified Medicines

A "falsified medicinal product" means any medicinal product with a false representation of:

(a) its identity, including its packaging and labelling, its name or its composition (other than any unintentional quality defect) as regards any of its ingredients including excipients and the strength of those ingredients;
(b) its source, including its manufacturer, its country of manufacturing, its country of origin or its marketing authorisation holder; or
(c) its history, including the records and documents relating to the distribution channels used.

The supply of falsified medicines is a global phenomenon and one that the MHRA takes very seriously. Falsified medicines represent a threat to the legitimate UK supply chain and to patient safety. They are fraudulent and may be deliberately misrepresented with respect to identity, composition and/or source. Falsification can apply to both innovator and generic products, prescription and self-medication, as well as to traditional herbal remedies. Falsified medicines may include products with the correct ingredients but fake packaging, with the wrong ingredients, without active ingredients or with insufficient active ingredients, and may even contain harmful or poisonous substances.

The supply and distribution of medicines are tightly controlled.

All licensed wholesalers must comply with good distribution practice (GDP) and there exist strict licensing and regulatory requirements in UK domestic legislation to safeguard patients against potential hazards arising from poor distribution practices, e.g. purchasing suspect or falsified products, failing to establish the "bona fides" of suppliers and purchasers, inadequate record keeping, and so on.

Section 6.4 of GDP is of principal importance to wholesale dealers. This states:

"Wholesale distributors must immediately inform the competent authority and the marketing authorisation holder of any medicinal products they identify as falsified or suspect to be falsified[29] procedure should be in place to this effect. It should be recorded with all the original details and investigated.

Any falsified medicinal products found in the supply chain should immediately be physically segregated and stored in a dedicated area away from all other medicinal products. All relevant activities in relation to such products should be documented and records retained."

Wholesale dealers in particular should maintain a high level of vigilance against the procurement or supply of potentially falsified product. Such product may be offered for sale below the established market price, so rigorous checks should be made on the bona fides of the supplier and the origin of the product. Staff should always be alert to any unusual activities and have a formal mechanism by which they can raise their concerns.

It is known that some wholesalers are themselves developing good practice strategies – such as conducting rigorous physical inspections of packs when grey market purchases are made – and this is encouraged.

Safeguarding examples include the following (this list is not exhaustive):

- what boxes are the stock arriving in – are these unusual in anyway or indicate that maybe they have been stored elsewhere before coming to you?;
- deliveries in taxis/personal cars – ask yourself: under what situation would this be acceptable?;

EU GUIDELINES AND UK GUIDANCE ON WHOLESALE DISTRIBUTION PRACTICE

---

[29] 83/83/EC.

- if you reject the delivery and it is returned to the supplier, where is it being returned to – a different address to where you expect?;
- significant errors in contents of delivery compared with delivery notes;
- large orders becoming unexpectedly available – even if at "normal price"? Why would they become available? Where have these come from? Investigate further to ensure procurement staff are trained to understand indicators of potentially falsified stock.

Any suspicious activity should be reported to:

- **Email:** casereferrals@mhra.gov.uk
- **Telephone:** +44 (0)20 3080 6330

To report suspected counterfeit medicines or medical devices:

- **Email:** fakemeds@mhra.gov.uk
- **Website:** www.mhra.gov.uk
- **Telephone:** +44 (0)20 3080 6701

Reporting Adverse Reactions

An adverse reaction means a response to a medicinal product that is noxious and unintended. A serious adverse reaction is one that results in a person's death, threatens a person's life, results in hospitalisation, persistent or significant disability/incapacity, or results in a congenital abnormality or birth defect.

Wholesalers supplying special medicinal products (unlicensed products) are under an obligation to keep records of any adverse reaction of which they become aware and report any serious adverse reaction to the MHRA; this should be done by submission of a "Yellow Card"[30] report.

Where the product is an exempt advanced therapy medicinal product, the wholesaler is obliged to inform the MHRA of any adverse reaction of which they become aware. All records should be retained for the minimum periods required by UK legislation.

Marketing authorisation, homoeopathic registration and traditional herbal medicinal product licence holders have separate obligations in relation to tracking and reporting adverse reactions.

Product Recall/Withdrawal

Manufacturers, importers and distributors are obliged to inform the MHRA of any suspected quality defect in a medicinal product that could or would result in a recall, or restriction on supply.

---

[30] https://yellowcard.mhra.gov.uk

A defective medicinal product is one that has a quality that does not conform to the requirements of its marketing authorisation or specification or, for some other reason of quality, is potentially hazardous. A defective product may be suspected because of a visible defect or contamination or as a result of tests performed on it, or because it has caused untoward reactions in a patient or for other reasons involving poor manufacturing or distribution practice. Falsified medicines are considered to be defective products.

The Human Medicines Regulations 2012 imposes certain obligations on licence holders with regard to withdrawal and recall from sale. The aim of the Defective Medicines Report Centre (DMRC) within the MHRA is to minimise the hazard to patients arising from the distribution of defective (human) medicinal products by providing an emergency assessment and communications system across the suppliers (manufacturers and distributors), the regulatory authorities and the end-user. The DMRC achieves this by receiving reports of suspected defective (human) medicinal products, monitoring and, as far as is necessary, directing and advising actions by the relevant licence holder(s), and communicating the details of this action with the appropriate urgency and distribution to users of the products. The communication normally used is a "Medicines Recall/Notification".

Immediately a hazard is identified from any source, it will be necessary to evaluate the level of danger and the category of recall, if required. Where the reported defect is a confirmed defect, the DMRC will then take one of the following courses of action and obtain a report from the manufacturer on the nature of the defect, their handling of the defect and action to be taken to prevent its recurrence.

Issue a "Recall"

Under normal circumstances a recall is always required where a defect is confirmed unless the defect is shown to be of a trivial nature and/or there are unlikely to be significant amounts of the affected product remaining in the market.

It is the licence holder's responsibility to recall products from customers, in a manner agreed with the DMRC. The company should provide copies of draft recall letters for agreement with the DMRC. If the company (licence holder) does not agree to a recall voluntarily, the MHRA, as Licensing Authority, may be obliged to take compulsory action.

Issue a "Medicines Recall/Notification"

Recall and withdrawal of product from the market are normally the responsibility of the licence holder. However, where a product has been distributed widely and/or there is a serious risk to health from the defect, the MHRA can opt to issue a Medicines Recall/Notification letter. The Medicines Recall/Notification cascade mechanism ensures rapid communication of safety information; it is not a substitute for, but complementary to, any action taken by the licence holder. The text of the Medicines Recall/Notification should be agreed between the MHRA and the company concerned.

In some cases, where a product has been supplied to a small number of known customers, the MHRA may decide that notification will be adequate and a Medicines Recall/Notification is not needed.

The DMRC may also request companies to insert notification in the professional press in certain cases.

Management of the recall

The company should directly contact wholesalers, hospitals, retail pharmacies and overseas distributors supplied. The DMRC is likely to take the lead in notifying Regional Contacts for NHS Trusts and Provider Units and Health Authorities, special and Government hospitals and overseas regulatory authorities.

The DMRC will liaise with the company and discuss arrangements for the recall, requesting the dates that supply started and ceased, and a copy of any letters sent out by that company concerning the recall. Again, it is desirable that the text of the notices sent via the company and by the DMRC should be mutually agreed.

Management of recall activity by wholesalers

The MHRA expects key personnel, such as the Responsible Person, to keep themselves up to date with medicines safety issues. This can be done, for example, by checking the relevant sections of the MHRA's website daily or alternatively by signing up for relevant MHRA email alerts.

Wholesalers and brokers should retain records of all Medicines Recall/Notification received and/or reviewed, including those notices for which no action is required.

Recall processes should be designed with quality management in mind, e.g. change control and risk management should be applied for significant changes such as a change of Responsible Person or nominated deputy, changes to product handling/storage or changes to transport arrangements. At such times there should be an assessment of whether a test recall should be performed to provide assurance of the on-going effectiveness of the company's processes and identify any weaknesses or areas for improvement.

Chapter 6, section 5 of the GDP Guidelines describes the minimum standards for wholesalers in relation to recall activities.

When the wholesaler receives a Medicines Recall/Notification they should take steps to:

- follow the detail of the recall message;
- identify any affected stock on site or in transit (including that returned from customers);
- identify any customers to whom the affected products have been supplied, including where products may have been supplied as samples;
- directly contact those customers, making them aware of the details of the recall and where necessary providing a mechanism for returning affected stock;
- physically segregate and quarantine any affected product in an area away from other medicinal products, ensuring that such stock does not re-enter the supply chain;
- reconcile the quantities of stock purchased, onsite, sent out and returned;
- keep recall notices open for an appropriate period, so as to capture any affected stock still moving through the supply chain.

All recall activities should be documented at the time they occur and at the conclusion of all recall activities the Responsible Person (or their nominated deputy) should produce a report, making an objective assessment of whether the recall process achieved its objectives and identifying any areas requiring improvement.

Testing the recall process

Section 6.5 of the EU GDP Guidelines requires that "the effectiveness of the arrangements for product recall should be evaluated regularly (at least annually)".

The aim of such an evaluation should be to challenge the internal processes of the licence holder as far as practicable. This is particularly important in organisations where recall activities occur infrequently, e.g. where the product range handled is limited in quantity or scope. Where stock is held on behalf of a licence holder at a third party site, then the recall test should extend to covering activities at the third party site; this will require a degree of liaison between both sites' Responsible Persons.

The test process should be described in the company's quality system in sufficient detail to allow staff to perform the test and to be able to assess the progress of the recall process at each step.

It is expected that as a minimum the test process should mimic a real recall but should stop short of contacting the licence holder's customers. The product and batch selected should be typical of those handled by the company in the previous 12 months and where possible provide a worst-case scenario (e.g. when key staff are absent or for essential medicines when alternative supplies may need to be made available). Correspondence (e.g. emails to staff at a branch level) should, as far as practicable, not indicate that it is being used for test purposes.

The test process should be documented so as to be able to demonstrate that:

- staff can receive information effectively and act on it quickly;
- stock in question can be identified, reconciled and segregated effectively;
- customers supplied with the stock can be identified quickly from records, and their most up-to-date contact details confirmed (including address and telephone details both inside and outside working hours);
- adherence to the company's recall process has taken place;
- the effectiveness of training can be assessed.

For the purposes of a test recall the MHRA does not normally expect licence holders to contact their customers because this could lead to unintended consequences should the customer believe the test recall to be real. Instead, the licence holder should obtain evidence that the contact details (physical address, telephone/fax numbers, email address) they hold for the relevant customers are up to date. Where the licence holder would send a letter/fax/email to their customer with the details of the recall, this should be drafted but not sent.

Where customers are contacted, there should be adequate oversight of the entire test process to ensure that misunderstandings do not occur.

As with all routine recall activities, at the conclusion of test recall activities the Responsible Person should produce a report, making an objective assessment of whether the recall process achieved its objectives and identifying any areas requiring improvement.

It may be possible for a company to use recall activities for non-medicinal products to demonstrate an effective recall process, provided that the process described in the company's quality system covers the handling of both medicinal and non-medicinal products in the same manner and leads to the same outcome.

Follow-up action

The DMRC will monitor the conduct and success of the recall by the manufacturer or distributor. As follow-up action, it may be necessary to consider any or all of the following:

- arrange a visit to the licence holder/manufacturer/distributor;
- arrange a visit to the point of discovery of the defect;
- refer to the Inspectorate to arrange an inspection;

- seek special surveillance of adverse reaction reports;
- refer the matter for adverse licensing and/or enforcement action.

Reporting a suspected defect

Suspected defects can be reported by telephone, email or letter or using our online form:

- **Address:** DMRC, 10 South Colonnade, London E14 4PU, UK
- **Telephone:** +44 (0)20 3080 6574 (08:45–16:45 Monday to Friday)
- **Telephone:** +44 (0)7795 641532 (urgent calls outside working hours, at weekends or on public holidays)
- **Email:** dmrc@mhra.gov.uk
- **Online form:** https://yellowcard.mhra.gov.uk/

Wholesale distributors and pharmacovigilance

The MHRA's Good Distribution Practice (GDP) inspectors have received queries from wholesaler distributors asking in what instances agreements are required between the marketing authorisation holder (MAH) and wholesale distributors for the purposes of fulfilling pharmacovigilance requirements.

If a wholesale distributor could potentially receive safety-related information on behalf of the MAH, or if they are providing a service relating to pharmacovigilance, then they are effectively part of the MAH's pharmacovigilance system. In this situation, contracts or agreements between the MAH and wholesale distributor need to exist, in order for the MAH to ensure that activities performed and services provided by these third parties are in accordance with applicable legislation and guidelines, and in order to ensure that all parties understand and formally agree to the tasks that have been contracted. The terms "contract" and "agreement" are used synonymously.

PROVISIONS IN PUBLISHED GUIDELINES TO CONSIDER

The good pharmacovigilance practices (GVPs) are a set of measures drawn up to facilitate the performance of pharmacovigilance. UK-specific requirements are described in the "Exceptions and modifications to the EU guidance on good pharmacovigilance practices that apply to UK marketing authorisation holders and the licensing authority".

GVP Module VI.2.2 states that "Each marketing authorisation holder shall have in place a system for the collection and recording of all reports of suspected adverse reactions which are brought to its attention". As indicated earlier, wholesale distributors may be a potential source of safety information. Hence, the MAH will need to have a mechanism to collect reports of adverse reactions received by wholesaler distributors.

GVP Module VI.B.7 outlines the reason why agreements between the MAH and wholesale distributors may be required "Where the marketing authorisation holder has set up contractual arrangements with a person or an organisation, explicit procedures and detailed agreements should exist between the marketing authorisation holder and the person/organisation to ensure that the marketing authorisation holder can comply with the reporting obligations. These procedures should in particular specify the processes for exchange of safety information, including timelines and regulatory reporting responsibilities and should avoid duplicate reporting to the competent authorities".

As reports of suspected adverse reactions may be brought to the attention of wholesale distributors, agreements between the MAH and the wholesale distributor support the fulfilment of the collection and recording of these reports by the MAH.

Indeed, section 6.3 of the Good Distribution Practice of medicinal products for human use states "In the event of a complaint about the quality of a medicinal product and a potential product defect, the manufacturer and/or marketing authorisation holder should be informed without delay". Complaints received by wholesale distributors may include reports of suspected adverse drug reactions and should be forwarded to the MAH; the implementation of an agreement between the parties may help facilitate this activity.

FACTORS INFLUENCING WHETHER AN AGREEMENT IS REQUIRED

The MAH needs to assess if the wholesale distributor with which they have engaged is a potential source of safety information (such as reports of adverse reactions, medical enquiries or product quality complaints), and/or are providing pharmacovigilance services on behalf of the MAH, and whether an agreement is required to fulfil pharmacovigilance requirements. Some factors that are likely to result in an agreement being required include:

- if the name and/or contact details of the wholesale distributor appears on product packaging, the patient information leaflet (PIL) or the MAH's website;
- if the MAH does not have a contactable presence in the market where the product is being distributed, which may increase the likelihood of the wholesale distributor becoming a point of contact by a member of the public or healthcare professionals (HCPs);
- if the wholesale distributor is providing services which may increase their interaction with HCPs and the likelihood of receiving safety information, such as actively promoting products via a sales team;
- if the wholesale distributor is performing pharmacovigilance services on behalf of the MAH, e.g. undertaking follow-up of adverse events in their

territory on behalf of the MAH, undertaking local literature searching activities or distributing risk minimisation materials.

The above list is not intended to be exhaustive and the MAH should consider all factors that may result in the wholesale distributor becoming part of the MAH's pharmacovigilance system.

There may be situations when an agreement is not required, e.g. if the wholesale distributor is not in a contractual relationship with the MAH and would not be regarded as a potential source of safety information and thus would not form part of the MAH's pharmacovigilance system.

CONTENT OF AGREEMENTS

If an agreement between the MAH and the wholesale distributor is required, it should contain sufficient detail to ensure that pharmacovigilance requirements are met. It is the responsibility of the MAH to decide what provisions need to be included in these agreements, particularly considering that the content required in agreements may vary depending on the parties involved. Some provisions that the MAH may wish to consider in agreements are outlined below; however, this list is not intended to be exhaustive and the MAH should use their judgement when deciding what information should be included in agreements:

- the roles and responsibilities of each party;
- the types of safety information that should be collected and forwarded to the MAH by the wholesale distributor (e.g. suspected adverse reactions, lack of efficacy reports, product quality complaints, etc.);
- timeframes for the exchange of safety information between parties and case confirmation and/or reconciliation provisions;
- contact details of where the wholesale distributor should send safety information received to;
- how the transfer of outstanding safety information to the MAH will be handled should commercial arrangements be terminated;
- provision for the oversight of the wholesale distributor by the MAH (e.g. in process compliance measures and the right of the MAH to audit the wholesale distributor).

The MAH should consider how to ensure all parties are complying with the terms of the agreements, such as including wholesale distribution partners on the MAH's risk-based audit programme, or implementing routine checks of pharmacovigilance-relevant wholesale distributor activity, such as periodic reconciliation of reports of adverse events between the distributor and the MAH that may identify discrepancies in information exchanged.

EU GUIDELINES AND UK GUIDANCE ON
WHOLESALE DISTRIBUTION PRACTICE

CONCLUSION

In conclusion, when deciding if an agreement between the MAH and the wholesale distributor is required, the MAH needs to consider if the wholesale distributor is a potential source of safety information and/or performance of pharmacovigilance tasks on behalf of the MAH, and implement agreements as appropriate. Provided that the aforementioned factors have been considered, it is anticipated that there may be instances where an agreement between the MAH and the wholesale distributor is not required. The MAH should ensure that, where an agreement is required, these agreements contain sufficient detail and provisions relative to the relationship between the MAH and the partner.

Chapter 7 Outsourced Activities

7.1 Principle

Any activity covered by the GDP guide that is outsourced should be correctly defined, agreed and controlled in order to avoid misunderstandings which could affect the integrity of the product. There must be a written contract between the contract giver and the contract acceptor which clearly establishes the duties of each party.

7.2 Contract giver

The contract giver is responsible for the activities contracted out.

The contract giver is responsible for assessing the competence of the contract acceptor to successfully carry out the work required and for ensuring by means of the contract and through audits that the principles and guidelines of GDP are followed. An audit of the contract acceptor should be performed before commencement of, and whenever there has been a change to, the outsourced activities. The frequency of audit should be defined based on risk, depending on the nature of the outsourced activities. Audits should be permitted at any time.

The contract giver should provide the contract acceptor with all the information necessary to carry out the contracted operations in accordance with the specific product requirements and any other relevant requirements.

7.3 Contract acceptor

The contract acceptor should have adequate premises and equipment, procedures, knowledge and experience, and competent personnel to carry out the work ordered by the contract giver.

The contract acceptor should not pass to a third party any of the work entrusted to him under the contract without the contract giver's prior evaluation and approval of the arrangements and an audit of the third party by the contract giver or the contract acceptor. Arrangements made between the contract acceptor and any third party should ensure that the wholesale distribution information is made available in the same way as between the original contract giver and contract acceptor.

The contract acceptor should refrain from any activity which may adversely affect the quality of the product(s) handled for the contract giver.

The contract acceptor must forward any information that can influence the quality of the product(s) to the contract giver in accordance with the requirement of the contract.

UK Guidance on Chapter 7 Outsourced Activities

Naming of third-party sites on the UK Wholesale Dealer's Licence

Regulation 18(3) of the Human Medicines Regulations 2012, as amended, provides that:

"Distribution of a medicinal product by way of wholesale dealing, or possession for the purpose of such distribution, is not to be taken to be in accordance with a wholesale dealer's licence unless the distribution is carried on, or as the case may be the product held, at premises located in the UK and specified in the licence."

The need for a third-party site to hold a Wholesale Dealer's Licence of their own and be named on another party's licence will rest on the activities being carried out, in particular whether licensable activities (procurement, holding, supply or export) are being undertaken on behalf of the holder of a Wholesale Dealer's Licence. There are instances where such arrangements can be clear cut (e.g. long-term holding) but there are also instances where the need to hold a Wholesale Dealer's Licence and name sites may be less clear (e.g. certain customer or supplier qualification activities or invoicing).

Other exemptions in law or policies operated by the MHRA's Inspectorate may impact on the need for a site to be licensed. One example is the exemption provided for in Regulation 19(4)(b) of the Human Medicines Regulations 2012, in relation to import agents; another example is the policy operated by the MHRA Inspectorate in relation to the short-term holding of ambient storage products (sometimes commonly referred to as the "36-hour rule") This exemption does not apply to cold chain products.

Historically it has been possible for the holder of a Wholesale Dealer's Licence or Manufacturer's licence to use third-party storage and distribution sites located within the European Economic Area (EEA); these sites have never been named on the face of a UK Wholesale Dealer's Licence but will hold Wholesale Distribution Authorisations (WDA(H)) in their own right in the relevant territory. This MHRA policy continues to be implemented following the UK's exit from the European Union.

Clearly the detail of arrangements between the parties involved is key in determining the need for licensing and naming, and responsibilities should be clearly laid out in written agreement(s) signed and dated by key personnel representing both parties. The Responsible Person has a key role in the oversight of outsourced activities, particularly in relation to ensuring compliance with Good Distribution Practice. Even where a licence may not be required or the third-party site needs to be named on the contract giver's licence, the activities are still subject to the requirements of Chapter 7 and Chapter 1 ("Management of Outsourced Activities") of Good Distribution Practice.

Chapter 8 Self-inspections

8.1 Principle

Self-inspections should be conducted in order to monitor implementation and compliance with GDP principles and to propose necessary corrective measures.

8.2 Self-inspections

A self-inspection programme should be implemented covering all aspects of GDP and compliance with the regulations, guidelines and procedures within a defined timeframe. Self-inspections may be divided into several individual self-inspections of limited scope.

Self-inspections should be conducted in an impartial and detailed way by designated competent company personnel. Audits by independent external experts may also be useful but may not be used as a substitute for self-inspection.

All self-inspections should be recorded. Reports should contain all the observations made during the inspection. A copy of the report should be provided to the management and other relevant persons. In the event that irregularities and/or deficiencies are observed, their cause should be determined and the corrective and preventive actions (CAPA) should be documented and followed up.

UK Guidance on Chapter 8 Self-inspections

Self-inspections must be implemented as a key component to maintain compliance with the principles of GDP. The main objective of self-inspections is to perform an impartial assessment of compliance with GDP, and recognise the possible need for corrective actions and provide a means of identifying potential improvements. The self-inspection programme should be reflective of the business model, site-specific operations and the size of the organisation. The self-inspection programme should be conducted in an independent and objective manner.

An annual self-inspection schedule must be implemented as part of the quality management system (QMS). The audit can be conducted as a single exercise or it can be spread throughout the year. The ultimate decision should be made with regard to minimising disruption to operations.

The self-inspection process must be robust enough to identify any symptomatic and sporadic non-compliance with GDP. The self-inspection programme must take into consideration all applicable areas of GDP, the full scope of the QMS, a review of all relevant records, personnel, premises, equipment, computerised systems and compliance with the current legislation. Particular attention should be paid to:

- the documented procedures and their suitability for the specific business model;
- whether QMS outputs are raised contemporaneously and closed within the periods as set out in the organisation's relevant procedures;
- accuracy and availability of records;
- effectiveness of the QMS;
- an audit of transaction records;
- any changes in legislation and impact on the licensable activities.

The scope of the self-inspection programme must extend to assessing any outsourced activities. The review of audit findings of relevant contract acceptors should form part of the self-inspection process.

The observations and outcomes of the self-inspection must be documented. A report containing sufficient level of detail must be made available for review by management and other relevant personnel.

If any areas of non-compliance are identified, investigations must be conducted with the intention of establishing the root cause and implementing appropriate CAPAs. Investigators must consider beyond the initial probable root cause of an incident, and confirm or rule out other plausible potential root causes. It is important to review previous incidents to identify potentially recurring issues. Risk assessments may also be necessary depending on the type of non-compliance identified.

Decisions to implement corrective actions should be based on the observations made during the self-inspection process and the outcomes of any related investigations.

A well-managed self-inspection system

The system supporting investigation activities should be monitored with trending to obtain meaningful information that can be used to drive routine improvements and to ensure that approved timescales are met. This includes scrutiny during the management review of the outcomes of the self-inspection and escalation where needed to ensure that the system remains in control, and an effective means of protecting patients and the integrity of the medicines when things have gone wrong.

Chapter 9 Transportation

9.1 Principle

It is the responsibility of the supplying wholesale distributor to protect medicinal products against breakage, adulteration and theft, and to ensure that temperature conditions are maintained within acceptable limits during transport.

Regardless of the mode of transport, it should be possible to demonstrate that the medicines have not been exposed to conditions that may compromise their quality and integrity. A risk-based approach should be utilised when planning transportation.

9.2 Transportation

The required storage conditions for medicinal products should be maintained during transportation within the defined limits as described by the manufacturers or on the outer packaging.

If a deviation such as temperature excursion or product damage has occurred during transportation, this should be reported to the distributor and recipient of the affected medicinal products. A procedure should also be in place for investigating and handling temperature excursions.

It is the responsibility of the wholesale distributor to ensure that vehicles and equipment used to distribute, store or handle medicinal products are suitable for their use and appropriately equipped to prevent exposure of the products to conditions that could affect their quality and packaging integrity.

There should be written procedures in place for the operation and maintenance of all vehicles and equipment involved in the distribution process, including cleaning and safety precautions.

Risk assessment of delivery routes should be used to determine where temperature controls are required. Equipment used for temperature monitoring during transport within vehicles and/or containers should be maintained and calibrated at regular intervals at least once a year.

Dedicated vehicles and equipment should be used, where possible, when handling medicinal products. Where non-dedicated vehicles and equipment are used, procedures should be in place to ensure that the quality of the medicinal product will not be compromised.

Deliveries should be made to the address stated on the delivery note and into the care or the premises of the consignee. Medicinal products should not be left on alternative premises.

For emergency deliveries outside normal business hours, persons should be designated and written procedures should be available.

Where transportation is performed by a third party, the contract in place should encompass the requirements of Chapter 7. Transportation providers should be made aware, by the wholesale distributor, of the relevant transport conditions applicable to the consignment. Where the transportation route includes unloading and re-loading or transit storage at a transportation hub, particular attention should be paid to temperature monitoring, cleanliness and the security of any intermediate storage facilities.

Provision should be made to minimise the duration of temporary storage while awaiting the next stage of the transportation route.

9.3 Containers, packaging and labelling

Medicinal products should be transported in containers that have no adverse effect on the quality of the products and that offer adequate protection from external influences, including contamination.

Selection of a container and packaging should be based on the storage and transportation requirements of the medicinal products, the space required for the amount of medicines, the anticipated external temperature extremes, the estimated maximum time for transportation including transit storage at customs, the qualification status of the packaging and the validation status of the shipping containers.

Containers should bear labels providing sufficient information on handling and storage requirements and precautions to ensure that the products are properly handled and secured at all times. The containers should enable identification of the contents of the containers and the source.

9.4 Products requiring special conditions

In relation to deliveries containing medicinal products requiring special conditions such as narcotics or psychotropic substances, the wholesale distributor should maintain a safe and secure supply chain for these products in accordance with requirements laid down by the Member States concerned. There should be additional control systems in place for delivery of these products. There should be a protocol to address the occurrence of any theft.

Medicinal products comprising highly active and radioactive materials should be transported in safe, dedicated and secure containers and vehicles. The relevant safety measures should be in accordance with international agreements and national legislation.

For temperature-sensitive products, qualified equipment (e.g. thermal packaging, temperature-controlled containers or temperature-controlled vehicles) should be used to ensure that correct transport conditions are maintained between the manufacturer, wholesale distributor and customer.

If temperature-controlled vehicles are used, the temperature-monitoring equipment used during transport should be maintained and calibrated at regular intervals. Temperature mapping under representative conditions should be carried out and should take into account seasonal variations.

If requested, customers should be provided with information to demonstrate that products have complied with the temperature storage conditions.

If cool packs are used in insulated boxes, they need to be located such that the product does not come in direct contact with the cool pack. Staff must be trained on the procedures for assembly of the insulated boxes (seasonal configurations) and on the re-use of cool packs.

There should be a system in place to control the re-use of cool packs to ensure that incompletely cooled packs are not used in error. There should be adequate physical segregation between frozen and chilled ice packs.

The process for delivery of sensitive products and control of seasonal temperature variations should be described in a written procedure.

UK Guidance on Chapter 9 Transportation

MHRA Expectations in Regard to Control and Monitoring of Temperature During Transportation

After dispatch from a manufacturing facility, the distribution chain for medicinal products can be complex, potentially involving a number of storage locations, wholesalers and modes of transport, before the product finally reaches the patient.

The transportation arrangements from one location to another are regarded as an extension of the storage activities and distributors are expected to treat each journey as unique, with the length and complexity, as well as any seasonal variations, being considered when choosing the packing method and mode of distribution.

Temperature should be monitored and controlled throughout the transportation chain. When planning transport routes, allowances should be made for potential impact on the shipment due to delays or the possibility that the customer may refuse the load and the product needs to be transported back to site. For impact on specific products, the supplier or customer may assess the impact of the temperature excursion on individual medicines in the load or profile them as products with equivalent temperature requirements, physical attributes, formulation and packaging. The acceptable temperature range relates to the labelled conditions for the specific product. MHRA expectations for this are defined below.

With respect to the transport of medicines, the Guidelines on Good Distribution Practice for Medicinal Products clearly require that: "The required storage conditions for medicinal products should be maintained during transportation within the defined limits as described by the manufacturers on the outer packaging. It is the responsibility of the supplying wholesale distributor to ensure that vehicles and equipment used to distribute, store or handle medicinal products are suitable for their use and appropriately equipped to prevent exposure of the products to conditions that could affect their quality and packaging integrity."

This guidance is also applicable to the Manufacturer or Marketing Authorisation Holder and should be adhered to when supplying medicinal products.

Packing of consignments and temperature management during transportation

Before being transported, medicinal products should be appropriately packed in such a way as to ensure that the required temperatures are maintained throughout the journey, to ensure that the medicines are transported in accordance with their labelling requirements in accordance with Chapter 9.3 of the GDP Guidelines.

Phase change materials, stabilised to the correct temperature range according to the packaging instructions, may be added to the packaging to maintain appropriate temperatures throughout the transport. The positioning of these packs within the consignment is extremely important and phase change materials must not be allowed into direct contact with the medicinal products being shipped.

Bespoke packaging with compartments for the phase change materials (also referred to as passive transport systems) is available. It is important to note that these systems will require validating by the wholesaler for the purposes of the transport. Although these systems are often sold with studies indicating the thermal capabilities of these systems, they are not "pre-validated" and there is an expectation that the wholesaler will have verified the systems through their own documented validation programme.

Larger volumes of refrigerated products will generally be shipped via temperature controlled or "active" transport.

Whichever method of transport is used, it is expected that the supplying wholesaler can show that the required temperatures ranges have been maintained.

The implementation of temperature monitoring as a matter of routine for all refrigerated deliveries is considered best practice. Temperatures should be strictly controlled and monitored with calibrated equipment of a suitable sensitivity, to provide temperature data for the entire journey. Some countries require that all imported consignments of medicinal products include a temperature monitor.

Data pertaining to temperature during transport should be retained by the supplying wholesaler for the required five years.

Where transhipment or cross-docking is necessary, daily minimum and maximum temperature monitoring and recording should also be carried out at these locations. The recording devices should be calibrated and the data be available to the supplying wholesaler as part of the route-planning exercise.

Wholesale dealers should review and maintain all temperature records and there should be procedures in place for implementing corrective action in the case of adverse events. Wholesalers should also ensure that consignments are clearly labelled with the required storage and transport conditions to be maintained as stated above.

Mean kinetic temperature (MKT) has been incorrectly applied by wholesalers in attempts to justify temperature excursions caused by lack of control. In the very rare occasions where use of MKT was appropriate, continuous and consistent temperature monitoring was carried out from the point of manufacturer batch release, and supported by appropriate designation of acceptable MKT limits and methodology.

Controlled temperature shipments

Controlled transport is generally referred to in terms of "active" or "passive" systems. In general terms an active system is a temperature-controlled environment such as a mechanical refrigeration system often seen in specialised pharmaceutical delivery vans, refrigerated shipping containers or aircraft holds. A "passive" solution would rely on the use of phase change materials within an insulated box.

Controlled temperature transport is equally applicable to cold chain (generally store between 2°C and 8°C) "ambient" products (which generally have the storage instruction "do not store above 25 or sometimes 30°C"), "Do not refrigerate" products (which it is generally accepted should not be stored or transported below 8°C) or frozen products (for which the temperature range is usually product specific).

Regardless of whether active or passive solutions are utilised, general principals and expectations apply. In general, it should be ensured that the cooling capacity is capable of handling the peak stock level of the time- and temperature-sensitive pharmaceutical products. When packing the load, or loading the vehicle, it is expected that the time for the necessary "conditioning" is known. This conditioning time will vary with the external conditions and should be evaluated as part of the qualification.

For example, during the winter months, the vehicle compartments may need to be warmed to attain the correct loading temperature whereas, in the summer months, the cooler unit will be activated in order to attain and maintain the same target temperature.

When phase change materials are used, it is important that there is a protocol in place for any reconditioning of the material, if indeed it is reusable, and many of these systems are specified as single-use systems.

The general requirements for these systems is that they are:

- capable of maintaining temperatures within a defined temperature range;
- equipped with calibrated temperature-monitoring equipment (either continuous or at a selected (and justifiable) sampling rate such as once every 10 minutes;
- equipped with an alarm system to alert to temperature deviations;
- the sensors are of a calibrated accuracy of $\pm 0.5°$ and can resolve to $0.1°$.
- the sensors are placed according to a mapping study.

The World Health Organization (WHO) estimates that approaching 30% of all pharmaceuticals that are disposed of are directly due to temperature excursions during transport, and that up to 35% of vaccines have reduced efficacy that can be directly attributed to incorrect handling during shipping and transportation.

Qualification/validation/verification studies

It is expected that transport systems will be subject to validation studies to show that the chosen system or systems is or are fit for purpose. The expectation is that sufficient data will be obtained in order that a robust risk assessment for on-going monitoring may be put in place. Typically, these initial studies will be conducted over the course of one full calendar cycle in real delivery scenarios. The object of the exercise is to ascertain: (1) that medicinal products are being transported according to their labelled storage conditions and (2) under what circumstances additional control measures may be required; these circumstances may be predicted in heat waves, or other extreme weather events, the potential for disruption to planned transport lanes due to industrial action; or issues at the border in relation to additional freight checks after changes in border control.

Uncontrolled ambient transport

This is a phrase used to describe a transport system where there are neither active nor passive control measures in place and the environmental conditions are not controlled. Such a transport system can rarely be shown to be GDP compliant where products have specific storage temperature requirements.

Transport providers

During transport, a dedicated temperature-controlled fleet should be utilised or the services of a specialist third-party logistics provider may be contracted. As with uncontrolled ambient transport, it is unlikely that a "general courier service" will be able to provide a GDP compliant service.

GDP guidelines state that, where possible, dedicated vehicles should be used to transport medicinal products; this cannot be achieved by utilising a general courier service (see also Maintaining security during transportation).

Reverse logistics consideration

Some companies operate on a "supplier collects model". This model is only appropriate where the products stay within GB (due to the formalities at the borders, which are the obligation of the wholesaler to fulfil). Where a supplier collection model is in place, provision should be made to facilitate the "reverse logistics" in order that control may be demonstrated in respect of any returned products. Many wholesalers operating on this model find the simplest way to control this aspect is by not accepting returns from their customer. This generally forms part of the transport agreement between the two parties.

Hygiene and contamination

Shipping practices should ensure that the medicinal product does not become contaminated. The majority of measures will be taken during packaging operations, such as control of use of recycled pallets or recycled packing filler and wrapping of product. Some considerations associated with transportation include:

- use of transport hub refrigerators also used to hold raw meat products;
- co-transport of volatile products, e.g. coffee beans, industrial chemicals;
- co-transport with poisons, e.g. pesticides;
- co-transport with active substances, e.g. industrial chemicals, active pharmaceutical ingredients;
- decontamination of shipping containers.

Care should be taken when the load is to be consolidated to inform the shipping company or transport provider of the nature of the product and to avoid the load being consolidated with product that could compromise or cross-contaminate the medicines.

Where possible, dedicated vehicles should be utilised for the transport of medicinal products

Transport lanes

In order to ensure that appropriate transport conditions are applied in the most efficient manner during transportation, some wholesalers apply a transport lane validation approach. This enables knowledge of routes and quality risk management to be applied to proportionate development of controls. In the most basic form, the validation plan approach may consist of palletised shipments between sites within a single company or to a small group of customers being grouped in one transport lane, with the remaining transport chains supplying tote quantities to many customers being grouped in a second lane. More commonly, transport lane validation plans are much more extensive, with lanes developed according to destination territories, transport modes, transportation chains with specific complexities or where a range of medicinal products is especially vulnerable to particular types of risk. The risk-profiling and control measures allocated to each lane will maximise efficiency of management of transportation and monitoring. Transport lane validation is most useful where similar transport chains are used by a wholesaler on a routine basis.

General steps in development of a lane validation approach are provided below, which in practice is likely to vary depending on the organisation and their chosen approach.

STEP 1 DEVELOPMENT OF A VALIDATION PLAN

The aim and development process for the transport lane validation plan should be documented and describe its aim and how it is to be applied. Any individual protocols or route assessments should refer back to this document.

STEP 2 RISK IDENTIFICATION

A variety of approaches to describe risk categories during supply of medicines may be used, such as those associated with medicine type, customer type, geographical regions and transport modes. This can be broad in scope and be further developed at a later stage for higher-risk areas, e.g. if delays are an important consideration for a specific customer, the risk can be broken down to delays at the consolidator, border control, en route for multi-drop shipments, intermodal transfer or be weather related. For this customer, they can be placed into a transport lane where these risks have been previously characterised.

The risks generated as a direct consequence of transportation should be identified, e.g. temperature excursions, delay, mis-delivery, loss including theft, damage due to high humidity, damage due to vibration, compromised associated document trail and compromised chain of custody.

STEP 3 ROUTE PROFILING

The various transport chains are next grouped into transport lanes to reflect similar common characteristics, e.g.

Lane 1 National intra-company distribution of palletised ambient and cold chain medicines using two approved logistics providers.

Lane 2 National inter-company distribution of palletised and non-palletised ambient and cold chain using six logistics providers and one customer-collect transport.

Lane 3 Export to EMEA region within a temperature-controlled container of medicines by sea freight using freight forwarder "X".

Lane 4 Export to EMEA by air freight of medicinal product using freight forwarder "Y".

Alternatively, they may be defined according to common risk profiles. Having assigned transport routes to transport lanes, a review of the routes and risks should be carried out to confirm that they are compatible.

STEP 4 RISK MITIGATION AND MONITORING

Having collated information of different transport chains within a lane, a single mitigation can be developed for each of the risks, e.g. a single packaging qualification representative of all transport chains within a lane to protect against temperature excursions for shipments to a specified geographical region.

The validation plan should be routinely reviewed to confirm validity of the lane criteria and to assess any deviations that may apply to the integrity of the validation.

Advantages of a transport lane validation approach

Transport and packaging qualification and risk assessments can be directed at groups of transport chains rather than for each individual chain, thereby enabling knowledge transfer between lanes and reducing duplication of effort.

The extent of qualification and risk assessment can be reduced for any new transport chain introduced into an established transport lane.

Risks and risk mitigation can be trended easily.

Transport validation plans tend to drive collation of performance data and knowledge of transport chains, resulting in more efficient supply chains.

Maintaining security during transportation

The largest risk of medicine theft in the UK occurs during road transportation. This is due to a number of factors dependent on transportation chain and vehicle type. Routine deliveries can enable thieves to plan thefts, either by the pallet load for vehicles parked overnight in motorway lorry parks or prior to a booked delivery slot, or on a smaller scale for deliveries to pharmacies where multiple deliveries are made and parking may be some way from the delivery point. Selection of vehicle build can mitigate some of these risks, such as use of solid-sided trailers with intrusion sensors or smaller vans that have good quality locks and alarms. Training drivers in practices to minimise security risk not only protects the consignment, but also importantly helps protect the driver.

Safe custody of Controlled Drugs as defined in the Misuse of Drugs Act 1971 should also be considered. For specific guidance on transportation of controlled drugs, please refer to the Home Office.

Other transport modes have vulnerabilities specific to them and different risk profiles apply across geographical areas. The supplying wholesaler should be aware of the risks that apply to them and apply appropriate control measures when planning transport. An example of the application of quality risk management to transportation is provided in MHRA Guidance to Chapter 1.

Examples of some risks applied to transportation

The following are examples of how risks vary across transport modes. It is the responsibility of the supplying wholesaler to develop a good understanding of pertinent risks that apply to their supply chain.

ROAD TRANSPORT
- Relative ease for thieves to track and access vehicles and remove stock.
- Only one driver is normally present.
- There is risk of opportune theft such as the slash-and-grab model in addition to targeted theft.
- Variable operational standards are applied by transport providers and not all are aligned with GDP expectations; it is, however, the responsibility of the wholesaler to select a transport partner who can provide a service that is suitable for the product type.
- Restriction of driver hours leads to forced rest stops, especially from deliveries from mainland Europe, with the consequence that some locations have become theft hotspots for parked vehicles.
- Curtain-sided trailers afford poor temperature control and are more vulnerable to theft.
- Cross-docking poses additional high risks which should be assessed and mitigated.

AIR FREIGHT

Generally, air freight is very secure; however, internal flight transfers within some third countries are vulnerable to theft.

The time spent on the tarmac can provide significant risk of temperature excursions.

Failure to specify hold conditions can lead to damage from low temperature or low air pressure.

See also the IATA Time and Temperature Guidance.

SEA FREIGHT

The relatively long journey time increases risk of an event relevant to the medicine occurring in transit, e.g. temperature excursion duration or medicine recall.

Supply chain delays can extend to days or weeks, e.g. adverse weather, civil unrest, piracy.

Failure to use temperature-controlled shipping containers, commonly known as reefers, leads to vulnerability to exposure of container to heat or cold.

RAIL FREIGHT

Rail freight is not yet commonly used in the UK; however, there has been significant investment in the rail infrastructure for both national and international movements. Some parts of South America are known for risk of hijacking of rail freight. In other countries, it provides a relatively secure service but can be vulnerable to environmental temperature extremes unless temperature-controlled systems are used.

FINAL MILE

Suppliers should be aware of vulnerabilities associated with all stages of their transport chain, including transmodal operations. The final leg of the journey can prove particularly challenging in remote areas or those regions that experience extreme environments. There has been a slow but steady increase in the use of drones to fly medicines to the final destination. These may be convenient, but pose risks of physical damage, theft or weakness in the documented chain of custody.

Other Guidance: United Kingdom Exit From the European Union, and Northern Ireland

The UK's new relationship with the EU

The UK left the EU on 31 January 2020 and moved into a transition period, which ended on 31 December 2020 with the UK and EU agreeing to a Trade and Cooperation Agreement on 24 December 2020.

During the transition period, the UK continued to follow EU legislation and regulations but this changed on 1 January 2021. From 1 January 2021, Northern Ireland (NI) has continued to be aligned to EU legislation and regulations in respect of medicines and medical devices as a requisite of the Ireland/Northern Ireland Protocol and Great Britain (GB) has not.

The Ireland/Northern Ireland Protocol, which came into effect from 1 January 2021, has resulted in changes to regulations regarding medicines in relation to importation requirements and compliance with the Falsified

Medicines Directive. The UK and EU agreed to a phased-in approach of these regulatory requirements until 31 December 2021 to allow time for industry to prepare.

Separate to regulatory differences, under the Protocol, new customs rules and procedures for the movement of all goods from GB to NI apply from 1 January 2021.

As a consequence of the UK leaving the Single Market and Customs Union, the way businesses in GB trade goods with the EU has changed. To export goods to EU businesses now there needs to be compliance with new customs procedures, including UK export declarations and import requirements on entry to EU Member States. For importing medicines into GB from EU Member States new requirements are in place.

The Human Medicines Regulations 2012 refers to lists of approved countries for:

- importation of medicines under a wholesale dealer's licence ("approved country for import list");
- batch testing of medicines ("approved country for batch testing list");
- manufacturing of active substances with regulatory standards equivalent to the UK ("approved country for active substances list").

The UK will accept certification by a Qualified Person and Active Substance manufacture from countries specified in these lists. These lists will initially include EEA countries and other countries with which regulatory equivalence has been confirmed. The lists will be reviewed at least every three years.

The UK's acceptance of batch testing done in EEA countries will be reviewed before 31 December 2022. A two-year notice period will be given in the case of changes.

Approved country for import list

Regulation 18A of the Human Medicines Regulations 2012 will allow importation of human medicines into GB under a UK wholesale dealer's licence from the following countries, provided that the UK wholesale dealer confirms that each batch has been certified by a Qualified Person (QP) in a listed country:

EU countries

- Austria
- Belgium
- Bulgaria
- Croatia
- Republic of Cyprus
- Czech Republic

- Denmark
- Estonia
- Finland
- France
- Germany
- Greece
- Hungary
- Ireland
- Italy
- Latvia
- Lithuania
- Luxembourg
- Malta
- Netherlands
- Poland
- Portugal
- Romania
- Slovakia
- Slovenia
- Spain
- Sweden.

The European Economic Area (EEA)

EU countries, plus Iceland, Liechtenstein and Norway.

Sourcing Medicines for the UK Market

Importing medicines from an EEA State which is on an approved country for import list

Qualified Person (QP) certified medicines from the European Economic Area (EEA) are accepted in Great Britain (England, Wales and Scotland) if certain checks are made. These checks are explained in guidance on acting as a responsible Person for Import.

These medicines will not require re-testing or re-certification by a UK Qualified Person (QP) if imported and checked by a wholesale dealer in Great Britain.

A manufacturer or wholesaler from a country that is on an approved country for import list may only supply a licensed medicine to a wholesaler in GB. The sale and supply to an authorised person (hospital, doctor or retailer) must be from a UK-licensed wholesaler.

Importing UK or Great Britain authorised human medicines from a country on the list for use in Great Britain

If you import a UK or Great Britain authorised medicine from a country on the list, you will need to hold a wholesale dealer's licence that authorises import.

This licence will need to cover the following activities of handling medicinal products:

- 1.1 With "an authorisation" (a UK, Great Britain or Northern Ireland Marketing Authorisation, certificate of registration or traditional herbal registration)

Your licence must authorise wholesale distribution operations, including:

- Products imported from countries on a list;
- Products certified under Article 51 of Directive 2001/83/EC.

You will need a Responsible Person (import).

Importing human medicines from a country on the list for use as a special medicinal product

If you import a medicine from a country on the list, for use as a special medicinal product, you will need to hold a wholesale dealer's licence that authorises import.

IMPORTING MEDICINES LICENSED IN THE LISTED COUNTRY

If the medicine is licensed in the listed country, you will need an RPi.

Your wholesale dealer's licence will need to cover the following activities of handling medicinal products:

- 1.2 Without "an authorisation" (a UK, Great Britain or Northern Ireland Marketing Authorisation, certificate of registration or traditional herbal registration) in GB or EEA and intended for the UK market

This licence will also need to authorise wholesale distribution operations covering:

- products imported from countries on a list;
- products certified under Article 51 of Directive 2001/83/EC.

The current notification of intent to import an unlicensed medicine[31] remains the same.

---

[31] https://www.gov.uk/guidance/import-a-human-medicine

IMPORTING MEDICINES NOT LICENSED IN THE LISTED COUNTRY

If the medicine is not licensed in the UK or a listed country, you will need an ordinary RP and not an RPI.

Your wholesale dealer's licence will need to cover the following activities of handling medicinal products.

- 1.2 Without "an authorisation" (a UK, Great Britain or Northern Ireland Marketing Authorisation, certificate of registration or traditional herbal registration) in GB or EEA and intended for the UK market

Your licence will also need to authorise wholesale distribution operations covering:

- products imported from countries on a list;
- products not certified under Article 51 of Directive 2001/83/EC.

The current notification of intent to import an unlicensed medicine remains the same (https://www.gov.uk/guidance/import-a-human-medicine).

Importing human medicines from a country on the list for export

If you import a medicine from a country on the list, which you will then export, you will need to hold a wholesale dealer's licence that authorises import and export.

"Introduced medicine" is a term used previously for category 1.3 to be clear that a wholesaler could not "import" from a third country because that is a manufacturing activity. A wholesaler could, with the correct customs procedures, "introduce" the product for direct supply to a customer in a third country.

IMPORTING MEDICINES LICENSED IN THE LISTED COUNTRY

If the medicine is licensed in the UK or a listed country, you will need an RPi.

For medicines licensed in the UK: your wholesale dealer's licence will need to cover the following activities of handling medicinal products:

- 1.1 With "an authorisation" (a UK, Great Britain or Northern Ireland Marketing Authorisation, certificate of registration or traditional herbal registration)

Your licence will also need to authorise wholesale distribution operations covering:

- products imported from countries on a list;
- products certified under Article 51 of Directive 2001/83/EC;
- export.

For medicines licensed in a listed country: your wholesale dealer's licence will need to cover the following activities of handling medicinal products:

- 1.3   Without "an authorisation" (a UK, Great Britain or Northern Ireland Marketing Authorisation, certificate of registration or traditional herbal registration) in the UK and not intended for the UK market

Your licence will also need to authorise wholesale distribution operations covering:

- products imported from countries on a list;
- products certified under Article 51 of Directive 2001/83/EC;
- export.

IMPORTING MEDICINES NOT LICENSED IN THE LISTED COUNTRY OR THE UK FOR EXPORT

If the medicine is not the subject of a marketing authorisation in the UK or a listed country then you will need an ordinary RP and not an RPi to import it into Great Britain for export outside the UK.

Your wholesale dealer's licence will need to cover the following activities of handling medicinal products.

- 1.3   Without "an authorisation" (a UK, Great Britain or Northern Ireland Marketing Authorisation, certificate of registration or traditional herbal registration) in the UK and not intended for the UK market

Your licence will also need to authorise wholesale distribution operations covering:

- products imported from countries on a list;
- products not certified under Article 51 of Directive 2001/83/EC;
- export.

Importing medicines from a country on the list for supply to the United Kingdom Parallel Import market

If you import a medicine from a country on the list, for relabelling / repackaging as a parallel import, for supply to the UK Parallel Import market you will need to hold a wholesale dealer's licence that authorises import.

The imported medicine must have the appropriate marketing authorisation in a country on the list for the designated Product Licence Parallel Import (PLPI).

Your licence will need to cover the following activities of handling medicinal products:

- 1.4   With a Marketing Authorisation in EEA member state(s) and intended for the GB Parallel Import market

Your licence will also need to authorise wholesale distribution operations covering:

- products imported from countries on a list;
- products certified under Article 51 of Directive 2001/83/EC.

You will need an RPi if located in Great Britain.

Sourcing a medicine from Northern Ireland to Great Britain

SOURCING FOR WHOLESALE

Medicinal products sourced from Northern Ireland for wholesale purposes are permitted under the supervision of an ordinary RP and not an RPi.

If you hold a WDA with sites in Northern Ireland and Great Britain, an RPi will be required for activities conducted in Great Britain.

PRODUCTS GRANTED AN AUTHORISATION UNDER THE UNFETTERED ACCESS SCHEME

To facilitate unfettered access for Northern Ireland products to the Great Britain market, medicines authorised within Northern Ireland will be granted an authorisation in Great Britain. The product licence numbers will be marked with a "(UA)" suffix on the packaging and summary of product characteristics.

If you source a medicine with a "(UA)" suffix, it may only be purchased from:

- a Northern Ireland manufacturer or wholesaler (a "qualifying business");
- a wholesale dealer in Great Britain.

SOURCING FOR PARALLEL TRADE IN GREAT BRITAIN

If you source a medicine with a marketing authorisation from Northern Ireland for supply to the Great Britain Parallel Import market or for export to a third country, you will need a wholesale dealer's licence. You will need an ordinary RP and not an RPi.

SOURCING BIOLOGICAL MEDICINES

A Northern Ireland manufacturer or wholesaler who supplies a biological medicine to Great Britain will need to confirm that a national batch release certificate has been issued by the National Institute for Biological Standards (NIBSC) for each batch.

Products supplied from the EU to Great Britain

Wholesale dealers in Great Britain that import biological medicines from the EEA will be required to check that each batch has an appropriate NIBSC or Mutual Recognition Agreement certificate before placing on the market in Great Britain. This information can be obtained from the product's Marketing Authorisation Holder.

PRODUCTS SUPPLIED FROM NORTHERN IRELAND TO GREAT BRITAIN

Products supplied from Northern Ireland to Great Britain will require the supplying manufacturer or wholesale dealer in Northern Ireland to confirm that a NIBSC or Mutual Recognition Agreement certificate is available before supplying a GB wholesaler or other authorised person in Great Britain, such as a hospital.

BIOLOGICAL MEDICINES IMPORTED INTO GREAT BRITAIN UNDER A
PARALLEL IMPORT LICENCE

Products placed on the market in Great Britain under a Parallel Import Licence will require a NIBSC certificate. Please follow the guidance above for batches for Great Britain, including the requirement to provide a UK Marketing Information Form and NIBSC certificate in advance of the product being placed on the market.

The Falsified Medicines Directive

The EU Falsified Medicines Directive (2011/62/EU) (FMD) was adopted in 2011 and introduced new harmonised measures to ensure that medicines in the European Union (EU) are safe and that trade in medicines is properly controlled.

The final part of the Directive, the 'safety features' Delegated Regulation (EU) 2016/161 came into force on 9 February 2019, and applies to certain categories of prescription only medicines (POM) and certain named non-prescription medicines.

Following the UK's departure from the EU, the 'safety features' Delegated Regulation (EU) 2016/161 no longer applies in Great Britain (England, Scotland and Wales) but still applies in Northern Ireland.

These safety features are:

- a unique identifier (a 2D data matrix code and human readable information) which will be placed on medical products that can be scanned at fixed points along the supply chain
- tamper evident features (anti-tampering devices) on the pack

The unique identifier comprises:

- a product code which allows the identification of at least:
  - the name of the medicine,
  - the common name
  - the pharmaceutical form
  - the strength, the pack size
  - the pack type

- a serial number which is a numeric or alphanumeric sequence of a maximum of 20 characters randomly generated
- a batch number
- an expiry date

If the member state to which the medicine is being supplied requires it, the unique identifier will also need to include the national reimbursement number. This is not applicable in the UK.

The unique identifier must be printed on the pack in a 2D data-matrix code and be printed in a way in which the information can be read by the human eye.

The choice of tamper-evident feature to be used is for the marketing authorisation holder (MAH) to decide. A European Standard is available with guidance on the types of tamper-evident features which could be considered by MAHs. This is titled 'Tamper verification features for medicinal product packaging EN 16679:2014'.

MAHs are required to place the safety features on the packaging of medicines which fall within the remit of the delegated regulation and upload the data into European Medicines Verification System (EMVS) prior to placing the product on the market.

The 2D barcode is scanned at various points in the supply chain to verify that it is an 'authentic' medicine.

Upon supply to the patient in the EU or Northern Ireland, the unique identifier must be 'decommissioned' via a scan from the FMD system, to prevent any duplication of a legitimate identifier for use on a falsified medicine. This will be checked against data in the national repository, which for Northern Ireland is the UKNI Medicines Verification System (UKNI-MVS) run by SecurMed UK.

Guidance and useful resources

Supply of medicines to GB and NI

Medicines with a marketing authorisation valid only in Great Britain (PLGB) do not require a Unique Identifier. However, we encourage companies to retain the tamper evident device.

Medicines with a marketing authorisation (MA) valid in Northern Ireland (PL and PLNI) require a unique identifier and a tamper evident device on each pack.

Marketing authorisation holders with valid marketing authorisations for Northern Ireland can continue uploading serialisation data into the European Medicines Verification System (EMVS).

A derogation from the delegated regulation is in effect meaning that the unique identifiers on packs with a marketing authorisation valid in NI, supplied by a manufacturer or wholesaler in the EEA do not require de-commissioning when exported to the UK. This supports the flow of products through Great Britain to Northern Ireland. Unique identifiers on these packs should be decommissioned in Northern Ireland as required by EU Delegated Regulation 2016/161.

The above derogation on decommissioning upon export from the EEA is in place until 31st December 2024.

Export of medicines to non-EEA countries

Holders of wholesale dealer authorisations in Great Britain no longer have access to the UKNI MVS and are therefore no longer obliged to decommission packs upon export.

Holders of wholesale dealer authorisations in Northern Ireland continue to have access to the UKNI MVS and should continue to decommission packs upon export to non-EEA countries, including Great Britain, in line with the delegated regulation.

Implementation and enforcement

In accordance with the Northern Ireland Protocol the Northern Ireland market should follow the EU acquis. This is as set out in the draft EU Unilateral Declaration in the Withdrawal Agreement Joint Committee. The UK is committed to meeting the requirements of EU FMD safety features Delegated Regulation in Northern Ireland, and we expect all stakeholders in the supply chain comply with these requirements.

Despite the significant work undertaken to date in the UK and given the complexities associated with setting up the medicines verification system across the EU, it is anticipated issues will arise. It is important that these issues do not compromise confidence in the medicines supply chain. The Government's priority is the continued supply of safe medicines to patients.

For example, several Member States have formally advised those who may receive 'unknown' error messages to dispense anyway. Therefore, the MHRA and DHNI will also be taking a pragmatic, flexible approach to how we enforce the legal requirements, as long as the normal checks are carried out and there is no reason to think that the medicine is falsified. This position will be kept under review.

Error messaging and false alerts

Medicinal products manufactured and released before 9 February 2019 may have had the safety features applied but may not have been uploaded to the repositories system. There are also packs of medicines already on

EU GUIDELINES AND UK GUIDANCE ON
WHOLESALE DISTRIBUTION PRACTICE

the UK market which contain 2D barcodes that do not relate to the FMD safety features due to other international initiatives.

Attempts to verify or verify and decommission these products will trigger system alerts. This situation may continue for a period of time due to the shelf life of medicinal products, in some cases up to five years.

Any instances of suspected falsification (including physical signs of tampering) are to be reported in the usual way via the Yellow Card reporting system.

Where the MAH is notified by the alerting system that a data error has occurred, they are to notify the MHRA if upon further investigation, falsification is suspected.

Further information and explanation of explaining the alert management process may be found on the EMVO website.

Reporting suspected falsified medicines

Any falsified medicines identified should be reported through the Yellow Card reporting system [Report a FAKE or Counterfeit]. For FMD applicable Prescription only Medicines (POM) products containing the Unique Identifier (UI) 2D bar code the following information is needed: A report of an alert for one of these packs should include:

- the alert number in the following format: "GB-xxxxxxxx-xxxx-xxxx-xxxx-xxxxxxxxxxxx" and the following details from the pack itself:
  - GTIN
  - serial number
  - batch id
  - expiry date

Ideally this would be with images of the pack showing all 4 elements in human readable format AND the 2D barcode. The alert could be generated for any of the following codes upon verification or decommissioning;

- NMVS_FE_LOT_03
- NMVS_FE_LOT_12
- NMVS_FE_LOT_13
- NMVS_NC_PC_01
- NMVS_NC_PC_02
- NMVS_NC_PCK_19
- NMVS_NC_PCK_22

For FMD applicable products without a Unique Identifier (UI) 2D bar code from Italy or Greece the following is needed:

- supplier details
- product particulars
- photographs (to include the side where the adhesive stickers / labels should have been present
- date received

Wholesale dealer's licences for sites in Northern Ireland

The MHRA issues WDA(H) for the UK and these reflect the wording as relevant for Great Britain according to the Human Medicines Regulations. For WDA(H) that name sites in Northern Ireland, the licences issued to companies do not reflect the European format and wording, e.g. in GB the category 1.1 states: "with an authorisation" (a UK, Great Britain or Northern Ireland Marketing Authorisation, an Article 126a authorisation, a certificate of registration or traditional herbal registration) and the EEA format states: "1.1 with a Marketing Authorisation in EEA country(s)".

For WDA(H) based in Northern Ireland, they continue to be listed on EUDRAGMDP and as such the functions are mapped on that database to the European format.

EXPORT OF MEDICINES TO APPROVED COUNTRIES FOR IMPORT

According to Article 40(3) of Directive 2001/83/EC and Article 44(3) of Directive 2001/82/EC, the competent authorities of the Union are to ensure that the import of medicinal products into their territory is subject to an authorisation. The authorisation is granted when a number of conditions, as defined in Articles 41 and 42 of Directive 2001/83/EC and Articles 45 and 46 of Directive 2001/82/EC, are fulfilled (e.g. availability of a qualified person within the EU, GMP18 inspection). As of the end of the transition period, medicinal products shipped from GB to the EU will be imported medicinal products, and the requirements for importers apply.

SUPPLIES OF CATEGORY 4 DRUG PRECURSOR CHEMICALS (THESE ARE NOT CONTROLLED DRUGS UNDER THE MISUSE OF DRUGS ACT OR REGULATIONS) FROM GB

Import and export licences are required for companies for the movement of any drug precursor chemicals that are imported or exported to and from Great Britain and, in some cases, Northern Ireland (NI).

For the purposes of drug precursor chemical control, NI will continue to apply EU regulations, while Great Britain will not. This means that NI companies trading with EU Member States will not require import or export licences because this is considered to be "intra-community trade".

However, trade between Great Britain and NI will be subject to licensing in accordance with the requirements in precursor chemical export and import authorisation. This includes "category 4" drug precursor chemicals, namely Medicinal Preparations of ephedrine and pseudoephedrine.

The Drug and Firearms Licensing Unit continues to act as the UK Competent Authority for drug precursor chemical control. Both Great Britain and NI companies should apply to the Drugs and Firearms Licensing Unit of the Home Office for their licences.

International collaboration

Pharmaceutical Inspectorate Co-operation Scheme

The MHRA is a member of the Pharmaceutical Inspectorate Co-operation Scheme (PIC/S), and has contributed to harmonising inspection standards since 1999.

PIC/S and its members continue close international cooperation between pharmaceutical authorities across GMP and GDP areas.

The MHRA maintains membership of the PIC/S Expert Circle on Good Distribution Practice (GDP), which was established in 2013. During this time, the Expert Circle has undertaken training of Inspectors by providing advanced training courses that impart GDP Inspectors with the knowledge and competence to inspect the global supply chain in a harmonised way. The Expert Circle has also developed a number of PIC/S GDP guidance documents, including the PIC/S GDP Guide to which the MHRA contributes.

The MHRA continues to promote the harmonisation of GDP practices and actively works with colleagues to ensure continuing development of regulations.

The goals of the Expert Circle on GDP are to:

- design, develop and implement an advanced training course for GDP Inspectors;
- develop a question and answer document;
- identify, design and develop GDP PIC/S guidance documents.

The MHRA actively contributes to the development of guidance and the identification of emerging regulatory trends.

The Application and Inspection Process: "What to Expect"

Application

To sell or supply medicines to anyone other than the patient using the medicine, you need a wholesale dealer's licence – also known as a wholesale distribution authorisation or WDA(H).

Applicants for a new wholesale dealer's licence or existing licence holders wishing to vary their licence should follow MHRA guidance and instructions, and make their application using the MHRA Process Licensing Portal accessible via the GOV.UK website[32].

The MHRA acting as the licensing authority will issue a wholesale dealer's licence only when it is satisfied, following an inspection of the site(s), that the information contained in the application is accurate and in compliance with the requirements of the legislation.

When appropriate, the MHRA may refuse to grant a wholesale dealer's licence or may grant a wholesale dealer's licence other than as applied for. In such cases the Licensing Authority will notify the applicant of its proposals. The notification will set out the reasons for its proposals and give the applicant a period of not less than 28 days to respond.

APPLY FOR A LICENCE FOR HUMAN OR VETERINARY MEDICINES

The licence applicant must provide the following:

- A separate application for a human medicines wholesale dealer's licence and a veterinary medicines wholesale dealer's licence.
- An application fee (which includes the fee relating to the first inspection).
- Company and site details.
- Nomination of one or more people to be named as Responsible Person (RP) or Responsible Person for import (RPi) for a human medicines wholesale dealer's licence or a wholesale dealer's Qualified Person on a veterinary medicines wholesale dealer's licence. This should be supported with CV, references and identification details for each named person.
- Details of the activities to be carried out and the medicinal products to be wholesaled. For all activities and products included in the application, there must be sufficient provisions on site to support the application.

The licence applicant should also consider if any of the following are required; separate applications are required for each:

- Broker registration;
- Active substance registration.

APPLY TO VARY A LICENCE

The licence holder is required to keep their licence up to date. Any changes to named personnel, sites, activities or categories of products wholesaled require a licence variation. This variation may trigger an inspection, which

---

[32] https://pclportal.mhra.gov.uk/

must take place before the variation can be approved. Wholesale from a new site, new activities or new products may not commence until the replacement licence has been received.

https://www.gov.uk/guidance/apply-for-manufacturer-or-wholesaler-of-medicines-licences.

Inspection

PLANNING

Fee-bearing inspections of licensed wholesale dealers are carried out to assess the degree of compliance with standards of Good Distribution Practice (GDP) and compliance with the provisions of the licence.

Inspections of licensed wholesale dealers are undertaken as part of the risk-based inspection programme, further details of which can be found later in this guide.

NOTIFICATION

Advance notice of inspection is normally given to a company, unless circumstances require that an unannounced inspection should take place. The timing of the inspection would normally be notified in writing by the inspector.

In accordance with the GDP risk-based inspection process, sites will be required to complete a Compliance Report in advance of inspection. Further information and guidance can be found in the risk-based inspections section.

CONDUCT

The major stages of the inspection process are:

- the introductory or opening meeting;
- the detailed site inspection;
- the summary or closing meeting.

Introductory or opening meeting

The purpose of the meeting is for the inspector to meet with the appropriate key personnel from the company to discuss the arrangements for the inspection. The inspector would typically confirm the nature of the business, premises and security arrangements, areas to be visited and any documentation that may be required.

Site inspection

The purpose of the site inspection is to determine the degree of conformity of the operations to the requirements of GDP and to assess compliance with the terms and conditions of licences issued under the appropriate legislation or with details submitted in support of an application for a licence.

The inspection will typically involve visits to goods receipt, storage and dispatch areas (including ambient and refrigerated), returns/quarantine area, interviews with key personnel, and a review of stock movement and quality system documentation including product recalls. Any observations, recommendations and deficiencies noted during the inspection would normally be discussed with the company representatives at the time.

During inspections of manufacturing and wholesale operations, samples of starting materials, work in progress and finished products may be taken for testing if an inspector considers that this might assist in the detection of quality deficiencies. Occasionally, samples may be taken when these cannot be obtained from other sources, for routine surveillance purposes.

The inspection will also assess if the named RP meets the knowledge, experience and responsibility requirements. This will be more noticeable when a person has been newly nominated or if their role has changed substantially.

The licence applicant/licence holder must be prepared to demonstrate that all proposed sites, activities, products and personnel are suitable, within the scope of the licence and accurately reflected on the licence. A table is provided in Appendix 4 to assist the licence holder/applicant in ensuring that they have the correct licence when planning to import or export.

Summary or closing meeting

The purpose of the meeting is for the inspector to provide the company with a verbal summary of the inspection findings and to allow the company to correct, at this stage, any misconceptions. The inspector would typically summarise the definition and classification of deficiencies that they propose to report and the company are encouraged to give an undertaking to resolve the deficiencies and to agree a provisional timetable for corrective action. The inspector would also describe the arrangements for the formal notification of the deficiencies to the company (the post-inspection letter) and what is expected as a response.

Deficiencies are classified as follows:

- Critical deficiency:
  Any departure from Guidelines on GDP resulting in a medicinal product causing a significant risk to the patient and public health. This includes an activity increasing the risk of falsified medicines reaching the patients. A combination of a number of major deficiencies that indicates a serious systems failure. An example of a critical deficiency could be:

  purchase from or supply of medicinal products to a non-authorised person;
  storage of products requiring refrigeration at ambient temperatures;
  rejected or recalled products found in sellable stock.

- Major deficiency: a non-critical deficiency:

    - that indicates a major deviation from GDP; or
    - that has caused or may cause a medicinal product not to comply with its marketing authorisation, in particular its storage and transport conditions; or
    - that indicates a major deviation from the terms and provisions of the wholesale distribution authorisation or a combination of several other deficiencies, none of which on their own may be major, but which may together represent a major deficiency.

- Other deficiency: a deficiency that cannot be classified as either critical or major, but which indicates a departure from guidelines on GDP.

The choice of company representatives at the meeting is primarily for the company to decide, but should normally include the senior staff who were present during the inspection and the RP.

Depending upon the inspection findings and the response from the company during and following the inspection, the inspector may take one of a number of actions ranging from:

- issuing a GDP certificate confirming essential compliance with GDP; to
- referral to the compliance escalation process or the Inspection Action Group (IAG) for consideration for adverse licensing action where serious non-compliance is found.

Further information on the Compliance escalation process and IAG can be found in this publication.

COMPANY RESPONSES

The inspected site is expected to provide a written response (by letter or email) to the post-inspection letter within the required timeframe. The response should consider the context of the deficiency within the overall quality system rather than just the specific issue identified. The response should include proposals for dealing with the deficiencies, together with a timetable for their implementation. The response should be structured as follows:

- restate the deficiency number and the deficiency as written below.
- state the proposed corrective action.
- state the proposed target date for the completion of the corrective action(s).
- include any comment the company considers appropriate.
- provide evidence supporting any corrective action where it is considered appropriate.

INSPECTION REPORT

Once the inspector is satisfied that any necessary remedial action has been taken or is in hand and that the site is essentially in compliance with GDP, an inspection report and GDP certificate are finalised.

Risk-based Inspection Programme

Introduction

The MHRA has been incorporating elements of risk management into its inspection programme for a number of years. A formal risk-based inspection (RBI) programme was implemented on 1 April 2009 and covers all aspects of good practices associated with the inspection of clinical, pre-clinical and quality control laboratories, clinical trials, manufacturers, wholesalers and pharmacovigilance systems. The primary aim of the RBI programme is to enable inspectorate resources to focus on areas that maximise protection of public health while reducing the overall administrative and economic burden to stakeholders.

GDP risk-based inspection programme

The GDP risk-based inspection process commenced for all wholesale dealer's licence holders on 1 April 2009. Inspections may be conducted on-site, remotely or as a hybrid combination of the two.

Compliance report

Sites will be required to complete a Compliance Report in advance of inspection: this will be prompted by the inspector. Guidance to completing the report can be found within the document. The Compliance Report should be returned to your inspector prior to the inspection.

Risk-rating process

Inspectors use the inspection outputs along with a number of other factors to identify a risk rating for the site, which equates to a future inspection frequency. As this process is not concluded until the inspection is closed, the risk ratings *will not* be discussed at the closing meetings. However, a copy of the full inspection report, which includes the full risk rating rationale, is provided to sites once the inspection has been closed.

Issue of a certificate of GDP compliance and/or support of the site on the relevant licence indicates meeting the minimum level of GDP compliance. Risk ratings identify the degree of surveillance required within the licensing and inspection programme. There is no intention that sites be rated against each other as a result of risk ratings assigned by the MHRA. Risk ratings can change following inspection, resulting in either increased or decreased risk. Inspection risk ratings will not be published by the MHRA.

There will be no formal process of appeal against risk ratings and future inspection frequency. However, any rating that results in an increased inspection frequency from the previous standard will be peer reviewed before conclusion by a GDP operations manager. The MHRA does have a formal complaints process if sites wish to log an issue; however, any concerns regarding the inspection process should be raised with the inspector.

Conditions of Holding a Wholesale Dealer's Licence

The holder of a wholesale dealer's licence must comply with certain conditions in relation to the wholesale distribution of medicinal products. These conditions are set out in regulations 43–45 (in the case of a wholesale dealer's licence held in Northern Ireland) or regulations 43 to 45AA (in the case of a wholesale dealer's licence held in GB) of the Human Medicines Regulations 2012 [SI 2012/1916] ("the Regulations"). They require that the licence holder shall:

- comply with the guidelines on Good Distribution Practice[33]; in the case of a licence holder in Great Britain, published under, or that apply by virtue of, regulation C17 of the Regulations and, in the case of a licence holder in Northern Ireland, published by the European Commission in accordance with Article 84 of the 2001 Directive;
- ensure, within the limits of their responsibility as a distributor of medicinal products, that the appropriate and continued supply of such medicinal products to pharmacies and persons who may lawfully sell such products by retail or who may lawfully supply them in circumstances corresponding to retail sale, so that the needs of patients in the UK are met;
- provide and maintain such staff, premises, equipment and facilities for the handling, storage and distribution of the medicinal products under the licence as are necessary to maintain the quality of, and ensure proper distribution of, the medicinal products;
- inform the licensing authority of any proposed structural alteration to, or discontinued use of, premises to which the licence relates or premises that have been approved by the licensing authority;
- inform the licensing authority of any change to the Responsible Person;
- not sell or offer for sale or supply, in the case of a product for sale or supply in GB, if there is a UKMA(GB), UKMA(UK), COR(GB), COR(UK), THR(GB) or THR(UK), or, in Northern Ireland, a UKMA(NI),

---

[33] Guidelines on Good Distribution Practice of Medicinal Products for Human Use (2013/C 343/01) http://eur-lex.europa.eu/LexUriServ/LexUriServ. do?uri=OJ:C:2013:343:0001:0014:EN:PDF

UKMA(UK), COR(NI), COR(UK), THR(NI), THR(UK) and EU marketing authorisation, or an Article 126a authorisation, in force in relation to the product and the sale or supply, or offer for sale or supply, in accordance with that authorisation; this restriction on the holder of a wholesale dealer's licence shall not apply to:

– the sale or supply, or offer for sale or supply, of a special medicinal product in the UK;
– the export from Northern Ireland to an EEA State, or supply for the purposes of such export, of a medicinal product that may be placed on the market in that State without a marketing authorisation, Article 126a authorisation, certificate of registration or traditional herbal registration by virtue of legislation adopted by that State under Article 5(1) of the 2001 Directive;
– the export from GB to an approved country for import, or supply for the purposes of such export, of a medicinal product that may be placed on the market in that country without:
  (i) a marketing authorisation, certificate of registration or traditional herbal registration within the meaning of the 2001 Directive, by virtue of legislation adopted by that country under Article 5(1) of that Directive, where the approved country for import is an EEA State; or
  (ii) such equivalent authorisation, certificate or registration in the approved country for import, under legislation in that country that makes provision that is equivalent to Article 5(1) of the 2001 Directive, where the approved country for import is not an EEA State;
– the sale or supply, or offer for sale or supply, of an unauthorised medicinal product where the Secretary of State has temporarily authorised the distribution of the product under regulation 174; or
– the wholesale distribution of medicinal products:
  (i) from Northern Ireland to a person in a country other than GB or a country other than an EEA State; or
  (ii) from GB to a person in a country other than Northern Ireland or a country other than an approved country for import.

The holder of a wholesale dealer's licence shall:

• keep such documents relating to the sale of medicinal products to which their licence relates as will facilitate the withdrawal or recall from sale of medicinal products in accordance with an emergency plan referred to below;
• have in place an emergency plan that will ensure effective implementation of the recall from the market of any relevant medicinal products where such recall is:
  – ordered by the licensing authority;

- in the case of a licence holder in GB, by an appropriate authority for the licensing of medicinal products in an approved country for import;
- in the case of a licence holder in Northern Ireland, by the competent authority of any EEA State;
- carried out in cooperation with the manufacturer of, or the holder of:
  - in the case of a product for sale or supply in GB, the UKMA(GB) or UKMA(UK), certificate of registration or traditional herbal registration, or
  - in the case of a product for sale or supply in Northern Ireland, the UKMA(NI) or UKMA(UK), EU marketing authorisation, Article 126a authorisation, certificate of registration or traditional herbal registration, for the product;
- keep records, in relation to the receipt, dispatch or brokering of medicinal products, of the date of receipt, the date of despatch, the date of brokering, the name of the medicinal product, the quantity of the product received, dispatched or brokered, the name and address of the person from whom the products were received or to whom they are dispatched, and where the receipt, dispatch or brokering of medicinal products takes places in Northern Ireland, the batch number of medicinal products bearing safety features referred to in point (o) of Article 54 of the 2001 Directive[34].

Where the holder of a wholesale dealer's licence in Northern Ireland imports from another EEA State for which they are not the holder of the marketing authorisation, Article 126a authorisation, certificate of registration or a traditional herbal registration of the product, then they shall notify the holder of that authorisation of their intention to import that product. In the case where the product is the subject of a marketing authorisation granted under Regulation (EC) No 726/2004, the holder of the wholesale dealer's licence shall notify the EMA or, for any other authorisation, they shall notify the Licensing Authority. In both cases they will be required to pay a fee to the EMA in accordance with Article 76(4) of the 2001 Directive[35] or the Licensing Authority, as the case may be, in accordance with the Fees Regulations. These requirements will not apply in relation to the wholesale distribution of medicinal products to a person in a non-EEA country.

Where the licence holder imports into GB a medicinal product, other than for the sole purpose of wholesale distribution of that product to a

---

[34] Point (o) of Article 54 was inserted by Directive 2011/62/EU of the European Parliament and the Council (OJ No L 174, 1.7.2011, p.74).

[35] Article 76(4) was inserted by Directive 2011/62/EU of the European Parliament and the Council (OJ No L 174, 1.7.2011, p.74).

person in a country other than the UK, but is not the holder of a UK marketing authorisation, certificate of registration or traditional herbal registration in respect of that product, they must notify the holder of any authorisation, certificate or registration, granted by an authority in the country from which the product is exported, to sell or supply that product in that country, and the Licensing Authority, of the intention to import that product and pay a fee to the Licensing Authority in accordance with the Fees Regulations.

The licence holder, for the purposes of enabling the Licensing Authority to determine whether there are grounds for suspending, revoking or varying the licence, must permit a person authorised in writing by the Licensing Authority, on production of identification, to carry out any inspection, or to take any samples or copies, which an inspector could carry out or take under Part 16 (enforcement) of the Regulations.

The holder of a wholesale dealer's licence permitting wholesale dealings in Northern Ireland must verify that any medicinal products that they receive which are required by Article 54a of the Directive[36] to bear safety features are not falsified. This does not apply in relation to the distribution of medicinal products received from a third country by a person for supply to a person in a third country. Any verification is carried out by checking the safety features on the outer packaging, in accordance with the requirements laid down in the delegated acts adopted under Article 54a(2) of the 2001 Directive on Medicinal Products that are required to bear safety features pursuant to Article 54a of the 2001 Directive. Before supplying a medicinal product to a person in Northern Ireland who falls within one of the classes specified below, the licence holder must verify the safety features and decommission the unique identifier of that medicinal product in accordance with the requirements laid down in Commission Regulation 2016/161. The classes of person mentioned here are:

- persons authorised or entitled to supply medicinal products to the public who do not operate within a healthcare institution or within a pharmacy;
- persons who receive the product for the purpose of selling, supplying or administering it as a veterinary medicinal product;
- dentists;
- registered optometrists or registered dispensing opticians;
- registered paramedics;
- persons who are members of Her Majesty's armed forces;
- the Police Service of Northern Ireland;

---

[36] Article 54a was inserted by Directive 2011/62/EU of the European Parliament and the Council (OJ No L 174, 1.7.2011, p.74).

- government institutions maintaining stocks of medicinal products for the purposes of civil protection or disaster control;
- universities or other institutions concerned with higher education or research, other than healthcare institutions;
- a prison service;
- persons carrying on the business of a school;
- nursing homes;
- hospices.

The licence holder must maintain a quality system setting out responsibilities, processes and risk management measures in relation to their activities.

The licence holder must also immediately inform the Licensing Authority and, where applicable, the marketing authorisation holder or EU marketing authorisation holder of medicinal products that the licence holder receives or is offered, which the licence holder knows or suspects, or has reasonable grounds for knowing or suspecting, to be falsified.

Where the medicinal product is obtained through brokering, a licence holder in GB must verify that the broker involved fulfils the requirements set out in regulation 45A(1)(b), and a licence holder in Northern Ireland must verify that the broker involved is validly registered with the Licensing Authority or the competent authority of an EEA State.

The licence holder must not obtain supplies of medicinal products from anyone except the holder of a manufacturer's licence or wholesale dealer's licence in relation to products of that description that a person holds an authorisation granted by an approved country for import (in the case of a licence holder in GB) or by an EEA State (in the case of a licence holder in Northern Ireland); where the medicinal product is directly received in the case of a licence holder in GB, from a country that is not an approved country for import ("A"), for export to a country that is not an approved country for import ("B") and, in the case of a licence holder in Northern Ireland, from a state other than an EEA State ("A") for export to another state other than an EEA State ("B"), the supplier of the medicinal product in country A is a person who is authorised or entitled to supply such medicinal products in accordance with the legal and administrative provisions in country A. This does not apply, in the case of a licence holder in GB, to products received from Northern Ireland and, in the case of a licence holder in Northern Ireland, products received from GB.

From 28 October 2013, where the medicinal product is directly received from a non-EEA country for export to a non-EEA country, the licensed wholesale dealer must check that the supplier of the medicinal product in the exporting non-EEA country is authorised or entitled to supply such medicinal products in accordance with the legal and administrative provisions in that country.

The holder of a wholesale dealer's licence must verify that the wholesale dealer who supplies the product complies with the principles and guidelines of good distribution practices, or the manufacturer or importer who supplies the product holds a manufacturing authorisation.

The holder of a wholesale dealer's licence may distribute medicinal products by way of wholesale dealing only to:

- the holder of a wholesale dealer's licence relating to those products;
- the holder of an authorisation granted in the case of a licence holder in GB, the appropriate authority of an approved country for import in the case of a licence holder in Northern Ireland, the competent authority of another EEA State, which is responsible for authorising the supply of those products by way of wholesale dealing;
- the holder of a wholesale dealer's licence relating to those products, the holder of an authorisation granted by the competent authority of another EEA State authorising the supply of those products by way of wholesale dealing, a person who may lawfully sell those products by retail or lawfully supply them in circumstances corresponding to retail sale, or a person who may lawfully administer those products. This does not apply in relation to medicinal products that are distributed by way of wholesale dealing to a person in a non-EEA country;
- in relation to supply in the case of a licence holder in GB to persons in countries other than approved countries for import, a person who is authorised or entitled to receive medicinal products for whole-sale distribution or supply to the public in accordance with the applicable legal and administrative provisions of the country to which the product is supplied and, in the case of a licence holder in Northern Ireland, to persons in a state other than an EEA State, a person who is authorised or entitled to receive medicinal products for wholesale distribution or supply to the public in accordance with the applicable legal and administrative provisions of the state other than the EEA State concerned. This does not apply, in the case of a licence holder in GB, to products supplied to Northern Ireland and, in the case of a licence holder in Northern Ireland, to products supplied to GB.

From 28 October 2013, where the medicinal product is supplied directly to persons in a non-EEA country, the licensed wholesale dealer must check that the person who receives it is authorised or entitled to receive medicinal products for wholesale distribution or supply to the public in accordance with the applicable legal and administrative provisions of the non-EEA country concerned.

Where any medicinal product is supplied to any person who may lawfully sell those products by retail or who may lawfully supply them in circumstances corresponding to retail sale, the licence holder shall enclose with the product a document that makes it possible to ascertain:

- the date on which the supply took place;
- the name and pharmaceutical form of the product supplied;

EU GUIDELINES AND UK GUIDANCE ON WHOLESALE DISTRIBUTION PRACTICE

- the quantity of product supplied;
- the names and addresses of the person or persons from whom the products were supplied to the licence holder; and
- the batch number of the medicinal products bearing the safety features referred to in point (o) of Article 54 of the 2001 Directive in the case of a licence holder in Northern Ireland.

The holder of a wholesale dealer's licence shall keep a record of the information supplied where any medicinal product is supplied to any person who may lawfully sell those products by retail or who may lawfully supply them in circumstances corresponding to retail sale for a minimum period of five years after the date on which it is supplied and ensure, during that period, that that record is available to the licensing authority for inspection.

A licence holder in GB may obtain a medicinal product in respect of which a UKMA(GB) was granted under the unfettered access route only if the product satisfies the definition of qualifying Northern Ireland goods.

The wholesale dealer's licence holder shall at all times have at their disposal the services of a responsible person who, in the opinion of the Licensing Authority, has knowledge of the activities to be carried out and of the procedures to be performed under the licence that is adequate for performing the functions of the RP, and has experience in those procedures and activities that is adequate for those purposes.

The functions of the responsible person shall be to ensure, in relation to medicinal products, that the conditions under which the licence has been granted have been, and are being, complied with and ensuring that the quality of medicinal products handled by the licence holder is being maintained in accordance with the requirements of, in the case of a licence holder in GB, the UK marketing authorisations, certificates of registration or traditional herbal registrations, and, in the case of a licence holder in Northern Ireland, the marketing authorisations, Article 126a authorisations, certificates of registration or traditional herbal registrations, applicable to those products.

The licence holder must notify the licensing authority of any change to the RP, and the name, address, qualifications and experience of the RP. They must not permit any person to act as an RP other than the person named in the licence or another person notified to the licensing authority.

An RPi is required where a licence holder in GB imports a medicinal product from an approved country for import under a wholesale dealer's licence. This requirement does not apply where an unlicensed medicinal product, imported from an approved country for import, for the sole purpose of distribution by way of wholesale dealing as a special medicinal product, or for the sole purpose of wholesale distribution of that product to a person in a country other than an approved country for import. The licence holder must ensure that there is available, at all times, at least one RPi whose name is included in the register established by the Licensing Authority.

An RPi must carry out the functions of an RP unless an RP is performing those functions in respect of the licence, and they must ensure that there is appropriate evidence to confirm that each production batch of a medicine imported from an approved country for import under the licence has been certified as provided for in Article 51 of the 2001 Directive, or such equivalent certification procedure as applies in the approved country for import, and ensure that each production batch of a medicinal product that is subject to the batch testing condition, and that is imported into GB from an approved country for import, has been certified as being in conformity with the approved specifications in the UK marketing authorisation by the appropriate authority, or, where the batch-testing exemption applies, a laboratory in a country that has an agreement with the UK to the effect that the appropriate authority will recognise that certificate in place of the appropriate authority's own examination.

The licence holder must apply to vary the licence if a change is proposed to the RPi and they must not permit any person to act as an RPi other than the person named in the licence.

The standard provisions for wholesale dealer's licences, i.e. those provisions that may be included in all licences unless the licence specifically provides otherwise, in so far as those licences relate to relevant medicinal products, shall be those provisions set out in Part 4 of Schedule 4 of the Regulations.

The licence holder shall not use any premises for the purpose of the handling, storage or distribution of relevant medicinal products other than those specified in their licence or notified to the Licensing Authority by them and approved by the Licensing Authority.

The licence holder shall provide such information as may be requested by the Licensing Authority concerning the type and quantity of any relevant medicinal products which they handle, store or distribute.

Where and in so far as the licence relates to special medicinal products to which regulation 167 of the Regulations apply, which do not have a marketing authorisation and are commonly known as "specials" (refer to MHRA Guidance Note 14), the licence holder shall import such products only from another in the case of an import into GB, an approved country for import and, in the case of an import into Northern Ireland, an EEA State, in response to an order that satisfies the requirements of regulation 167 of the Regulations, and where the following conditions are complied with:

- no later than 28 days prior to each importation of a special medicinal product, the licence holder shall give written notice to the licensing authority stating their intention to import that special medicinal product and stating the following particulars:
- the name of the medicinal product, being the brand name or the common name, or the scientific name, and any name, if different, under which the medicinal product is to be sold or supplied in the UK;

- any trademark or name of the manufacturer of the medicinal product;
- in respect of each active constituent of the medicinal product, any international non-proprietary name or the British approved name or the monograph name or, where that constituent does not have an international non-proprietary name, a British approved name or a monograph name, the accepted scientific name or any other name descriptive of the true nature of that constituent in English;
- the quantity of medicinal product that is to be imported, which shall not exceed more, on any one occasion, than such amount as is sufficient for 25 single administrations, or for 25 courses of treatment where the amount imported is sufficient for a maximum of three months' treatment; and
- the name and address of the manufacturer or assembler of that medicinal product in the form in which it is to be imported and, if the person who will supply that medicinal product for importation is not the manufacturer or assembler, the name and address of such a supplier.
- Subject to the next bullet point below, the licence holder shall not import the special medicinal product if, before the end of 28 days from the date on which the Licensing Authority sends or gives the licence holder an acknowledgement in writing by the Licensing Authority that they have received the notice referred to in the bullet point above, the Licensing Authority have notified them in writing that the product should not be imported.
- The licence holder may import the special medicinal product referred to in the notice where they have been notified in writing by the Licensing Authority, before the end of the 28-day period referred to in the bullet point above, that the special medicinal product may be imported.
- Where the licence holder sells or supplies special medicinal products, they shall, in addition to any other records that they are required to make by the provisions of their licence, make and maintain written records relating to the batch number of the batch of the product from which the sale or supply was made, and details of any adverse reaction to the product so sold or supplied of which they become aware.
- The licence holder shall import no more on any one occasion than such amount as is sufficient for 25 single administrations, or for 25 courses of treatment where the amount imported is sufficient for a maximum of three months' treatment, and on any such occasion shall not import more than the quantity notified to the licensing authority in the notification of intention to import.
- The licence holder shall inform the Licensing Authority forthwith of any matter coming to their attention that might reasonably cause the Licensing Authority to believe that the medicinal product can no longer be regarded either as a product that can safely be administered to human

beings or as a product that is of satisfactory quality for such administration.

- The licence holder shall not issue any advertisement, catalogue or circular relating to the special medicinal product or make any representations in respect of that product.
- The licence holder shall cease importing or supplying a special medicinal product if they have received a notice in writing from the Licensing Authority directing that, as from a date specified in that notice, a particular product or class of products shall no longer be imported or supplied.

A licence holder in GB may supply a special medicinal product only to a person in Northern Ireland, and in Northern Ireland may supply a special medicinal product only to a person in Great Britain in response to an order that satisfies the requirements of regulation 167.

The licence holder shall take all reasonable precautions and exercise all due diligence to ensure that any information they provide to the Licensing Authority, which is relevant to an evaluation of the safety, quality or efficacy of any medicinal product for human use that they handle, store or distribute, is not false or misleading in a material particular.

Where a wholesale dealer's licence relates to exempt advanced therapy medicinal products, the licence holder shall keep the data on the system for the traceability of the advanced therapy medicinal products for such period, being a period of longer than 30 years, as may be specified by the Licensing Authority.

The Standard Provisions also require the holder of a wholesale dealer's licence that relates to exempt advanced therapy medicinal products to obtain supplies of exempt advanced therapy medicinal products only from the holder of a manufacturer's licence in respect of those products or the holder of a wholesale dealer's licence in respect of those products.

The licence holder must:

- distribute an exempt advanced therapy medicinal product by way of wholesale dealing only to the holder of a wholesale dealer's licence in respect of those products, or a person who may lawfully administer those products and solicited the product for an individual patient;
- establish and maintain a system ensuring that the exempt advanced therapy medicinal product and its starting and raw materials, including all substances coming into contact with the cells or tissues that it may contain, can be traced through the sourcing, manufacturing, packaging, storage, transport and delivery to the establishment where the product is used;
- inform the Licensing Authority of any adverse reaction to any exempt advanced therapy medicinal product supplied by the holder of the wholesale dealer's licence of which the holder is aware;

- keep the data for ensuring traceability for a minimum of 30 years after the expiry date of the exempt advanced therapy medicinal product or longer as specified by the Licensing Authority;
- ensure that the data for ensuring traceability will, in the event that the licence is suspended, revoked or withdrawn or the licence holder becomes bankrupt or insolvent, be held available to the Licensing Authority by the holder of a wholesale dealer's licence for the same period that the data has to be kept; and
- not import or export any exempt advanced therapy medicinal product.

Matters Relating to Unlicensed Medicines

Unless exempt, a medicinal product must be the subject of a marketing authorisation before being placed on the market.

Regulation 167 of the Human Medicines Regulations 2012 provides an exemption from the need for a marketing authorisation for a medicinal product that is supplied:

- in response to an unsolicited order;
- manufactured and assembled in accordance with the specification of a person who is a doctor, dentist, nurse independent prescriber, pharmacist independent prescriber or supplementary prescriber;
- for use by a patient for whose treatment that person is directly responsible in order to fulfil the special needs of that patient, and meets the conditions specified in regulation 167(2)–(8).

In the interest of public health the exemption is narrowly drawn because these products, unlike licensed medicinal products, may not have been assessed by the Licensing Authority against the criteria of safety, quality and efficacy.

See MHRA Guidance Note 14 on the supply of unlicensed medicinal products "specials", which contains additional guidance for those who want to manufacture, import, distribute or supply unlicensed medicines for human use for the treatment of an individual patient.

Supply of unlicensed medicines when an equivalent licensed product becomes available

Unlicensed medicines may only be supplied against valid special clinical needs of a patient. This requires that there is no authorised equivalent available on the national market. Supply for reasons of cost, institutional need or convenience is not acceptable and is not a special clinical need.

Examples of inappropriate reasons for supply have included preference for a non-parallel imported product, cost, more convenient presentation and longer shelf-life of the unlicensed product. None of these reasons is acceptable.

Although requests for procurement of unlicensed medicines are not regulated by the MHRA, the supply of unlicensed medicines falls under the Human Medicines Regulations 2012 [SI 2012/1916]. Importers and suppliers must be able to demonstrate compliance with these regulations. This includes supply of unlicensed medicines only to meet valid special clinical needs. Appropriate evidence of supply against such needs should be retained.

https://www.gov.uk/government/publications/supply-unlicensed-medicinal-products-specials.

https://www.gov.uk/guidance/import-a-human-medicine.

Guidelines of 19 March 2015 on Principles of Good Distribution Practice of Active Substances for Medicinal Products for Human Use (2015/C 95/01)

Contents

Introduction

These guidelines are based on the fourth paragraph of Article 47 of Directive 2001/83/EC[1].

They follow the same principles that underlie the guidelines of EudraLex, Volume 4, Part II, Chapter 17, with regard to the distribution

---

[1] Directive 2001/83/EC of the European Parliament and of the Council of 6 November 2001 on the Community code relating to medicinal products for human use (OJ L 311, 28.11.2001, p. 67).

of active substances and the Guidelines of 5 November 2013 on Good Distribution Practice of medicinal products for human use[2].

These guidelines provide stand-alone guidance on Good Distribution Practice (GDP) for importers and distributors of active substances for medicinal products for human use. They complement the rules on distribution set out in the guidelines of EudraLex, Volume 4, Part II, and apply also to distributors of active substances manufactured by themselves.

Any manufacturing activities in relation to active substances, including re-packaging, re-labelling or dividing up, are subject to Commission Delegated Regulation (EU) No 1252/2014[3] and EudraLex, Volume 4, Part II.

Additional requirements apply to the importation of active substances, as laid down in Article 46b of Directive 2001/83/EC.

Distributors of active substances for medicinal products for human use should follow these guidelines as of 21 September 2015.

CHAPTER 1 SCOPE

1.1   These guidelines apply to distribution of active substances, as defined in Article 1(3a) of Directive 2001/83/EC, for medicinal products for human use. According to that provision, an active substance is any substance or mixture of substances intended to be used in the manufacture of a medicinal product and that, when used in its production, becomes an active ingredient of that product intended to exert a pharmacological, immunological or metabolic action with a view to restoring, correcting or modifying physiological functions or to make a medical diagnosis.

1.2   For the purpose of these guidelines, distribution of active substances shall comprise all activities consisting of procuring, importing, holding, supplying or exporting active substances, apart from brokering.

1.3   These guidelines do not apply to intermediates of active substances.

---

[2] OJ C 343, 23.11.2013, p. 1.

[3] Commission Delegated Regulation (EU) No 1252/2014 of 28 May 2014 supplementing Directive 2001/83/EC of the European Parliament and the Council with regard to principles and guidelines of good manufacturing practice for active substances for medicinal products for human use (OJ L 337, 25.11.2014, p. 1).

CHAPTER 2 QUALITY SYSTEM

2.1   Distributors of active substances should develop and maintain a quality system setting out responsibilities, processes and risk management principles. Examples of the processes and applications of quality risk management can be found in EudraLex, Volume 4, Part III: GMP related documents, ICH guideline Q9 on Quality Risk Management (ICH Q9).

2.2   The quality system should be adequately resourced with competent personnel, and suitable and sufficient premises, equipment and facilities. It should ensure that:

    (i)   active substances are procured, imported, held, supplied or exported in a way that is compliant with the requirements of GDP for active substances;

    (ii)   management responsibilities are clearly specified;

    (iii)   active substances are delivered to the right recipients within a satisfactory time period;

    (iv)   records are made contemporaneously;

    (v)   deviations from established procedures are documented and investigated;

    (vi)   appropriate corrective and preventive actions, commonly known as 'CAPA', are taken to correct deviations and prevent them in line with the principles of quality risk management;

    (vii)   changes that may affect the storage and distribution of active substances are evaluated.

2.3   The size, structure and complexity of the distributor's activities should be taken into consideration when developing or modifying the quality system.

CHAPTER 3 PERSONNEL

3.1   The distributor should designate a person at each location where distribution activities are performed who should have defined authority and responsibility for ensuring that a quality system is implemented and maintained. The designated person should fulfil their responsibilities personally. The designated person can delegate duties but not responsibilities.

3.2   The responsibilities of all personnel involved in the distribution of active substances should be specified in writing. The personnel should be trained on the requirements of GDP for active substances. They should have the appropriate competence and experience to ensure that active substances are properly handled, stored and distributed.

3.3 Personnel should receive initial and continuing training relevant to their role, based on written procedures and in accordance with a written training programme.

3.4 A record of all training should be kept, and the effectiveness of training should be periodically assessed and documented.

CHAPTER 4 DOCUMENTATION

4.1 Documentation comprises all written procedures, instructions, contracts, records and data, in paper or in electronic form. Documentation should be readily available or retrievable. All documentation related to compliance of the distributor with these guidelines should be made available on request of competent authorities.

4.2 Documentation should be sufficiently comprehensive with respect to the scope of the distributor's activities and in a language understood by personnel. It should be written in clear, unambiguous language and be free from errors.

4.3 Any alteration made in the documentation should be signed and dated; the alteration should permit the reading of the original information. Where appropriate, the reason for the alteration should be recorded.

4.4 Each employee should have ready access to all necessary documentation for the tasks executed.

Procedures

4.5 Written procedures should describe the distribution activities which affect the quality of the active substances. This could include receipt and checking of deliveries, storage, cleaning and maintenance of the premises (including pest control), recording of the storage conditions, security of stocks on site and of consignments in transit, withdrawal from saleable stock, handling of returned products, recall plans, etc.

4.6 Procedures should be approved, signed and dated by the person responsible for the quality system.

4.7 Attention should be paid to the use of valid and approved procedures. Documents should be reviewed regularly and kept up to date. Version control should be applied to procedures. After revision of a document, a system should exist to prevent inadvertent use of the superseded version. Superseded or obsolete procedures should be removed from workstations and archived.

Records

4.8   Records should be clear, be made at the time each operation is performed and in such a way that all significant activities or events are traceable. Records should be retained for at least 1 year after the expiry date of the active substance batch to which they relate. For active substances with re-test dates, records should be retained for at least 3 years after the batch is completely distributed.

4.9   Records should be kept of each purchase and sale, showing the date of purchase or supply, name of the active substance, batch number and quantity received or supplied, and name and address of the supplier and of the original manufacturer, if not the same, or of the shipping agent and/or the consignee. Records should ensure the traceability of the origin and destination of products, so that all the suppliers of, or those supplied with, an active substance can be identified. Records that should be retained and be available include:

(i)   identity of supplier, original manufacturer, shipping agent and/or consignee;

(ii)   address of supplier, original manufacturer, shipping agent and/or consignee;

(iii)   purchase orders;

(iv)   bills of lading, transportation and distribution records;

(v)   receipt documents;

(vi)   name or designation of active substance;

(vii)   manufacturer's batch number;

(viii)   certificates of analysis, including those of the original manufacturer;

(ix)   re-test or expiry date.

CHAPTER 5 PREMISES AND EQUIPMENT

5.1   Premises and equipment should be suitable and adequate to ensure proper storage, protection from contamination, e.g. narcotics, highly sensitising materials, materials of high pharmacological activity or toxicity, and distribution of active substances. They should be suitably secure to prevent unauthorised access. Monitoring devices that are necessary to guarantee the quality attributes of the active substance should be calibrated according to an approved schedule against certified traceable standards.

CHAPTER 6 OPERATIONS

Orders

6.1 Where active substances are procured from a manufacturer, importer or distributor established in the EU, that manufacturer, importer or distributor should be registered according to Article 52a of Directive 2001/83/EC.

Receipt

6.2 Areas for receiving active substances should protect deliveries from prevailing weather conditions during unloading. The reception area should be separate from the storage area. Deliveries should be examined at receipt in order to check that:

(i)   containers are not damaged;

(ii)   all security seals are present with no sign of tampering;

(iii) correct labelling, including correlation between the name used by the supplier and the in-house name, if these are different;

(iv)   necessary information, such as a certificate of analysis, is available; and

(v)   the active substance and the consignment correspond to the order.

6.3 Active substances with broken seals, damaged packaging, or suspected of possible contamination should be quarantined either physically or using an equivalent electronic system, and the cause of the issue investigated.

6.4 Active substances subject to specific storage measures, e.g. narcotics and products requiring a specific storage temperature or humidity, should be immediately identified and stored in accordance with written instructions and with relevant legislative provisions.

6.5 Where the distributor suspects that an active substance procured or imported by him is falsified, he should segregate it either physically or using an equivalent electronic system and inform the national competent authority of the country in which he is registered.

6.6 Rejected materials should be identified and controlled and quarantined to prevent their unauthorised use in manufacturing and their further distribution. Records of destruction activities should be readily available.

Storage

6.7 Active substances should be stored under the conditions specified by the manufacturer, e.g. controlled temperature and humidity when necessary, and in such a manner as to prevent contamination and/or mix up. The storage conditions should be monitored and records maintained. The records should be reviewed regularly by the person responsible for the quality system.

6.8 When specific storage conditions are required, the storage area should be qualified and operated within the specified limits.

6.9 The storage facilities should be clean and free from litter, dust and pests. Adequate precautions should be taken against spillage or breakage, attack by microorganisms and cross-contamination.

6.10 There should be a system to ensure stock rotation, e.g. "first expiry (re-test date), first out", with regular and frequent checks that the system is operating correctly. Electronic warehouse management systems should be validated.

6.11 Active substances beyond their expiry date should be separated, either physically or using an equivalent electronic system, from approved stock, and not supplied.

6.12 Where storage or transportation of active substances is contracted out, the distributor should ensure that the contract acceptor knows and follows the appropriate storage and transport conditions. There must be a written contract between the contract giver and contract acceptor, which clearly establishes the duties of each party. The contract acceptor should not sub-contract any of the work entrusted to him under the contract without the contract giver's written authorisation.

Deliveries to customers

6.13 Supplies within the EU should be made only by distributors of active substances registered according to Article 52a of Directive 2001/83/EC to other distributors, manufacturers or dispensing pharmacies.

6.14 Active substances should be transported in accordance with the conditions specified by the manufacturer and in a manner that does not adversely affect their quality. Product, batch and container identity should be maintained at all times. All original container labels should remain readable.

6.15 A system should be in place by which the distribution of each batch of active substance can be readily identified to permit its recall.

Transfer of information

6.16 Any information or event that the distributor becomes aware of, which have the potential to cause an interruption to supply, should be notified to relevant customers.

6.17 Distributors should transfer all product quality or regulatory information received from an active substance manufacturer to the customer and from the customer to the active substance manufacturer.

6.18   The distributor who supplies the active substance to the customer should provide the name and address of the original active substance manufacturer and the batch number(s) supplied. A copy of the original certificate of analysis from the manufacturer should be provided to the customer.

6.19   The distributor should also provide the identity of the original active substance manufacturer to competent authorities upon request. The original manufacturer can respond to the competent authority directly or through its authorised agents. (In this context "authorised" refers to authorised by the manufacturer.)

6.20   The specific guidance for certificates of analysis is detailed in Section 11.4 of Part II of EudraLex, Volume 4.

CHAPTER 7 RETURNS, COMPLAINTS AND RECALLS

Returns

7.1   Returned active substances should be identified as such and quarantined pending investigation.

7.2   Active substances which have left the care of the distributor should only be returned to approved stock if all of the following conditions are met:

(i)   The active substance is in the original unopened container(s) with all original security seals present and is in good condition.

(ii)   It is demonstrated that the active substance has been stored and handled under proper conditions. Written information provided by the customer should be available for this purpose.

(iii)   The remaining shelf-life period is acceptable.

(iv)   The active substance has been examined and assessed by a person trained and authorised to do so.

(v)   No loss of information/traceability has occurred.

This assessment should take into account the nature of the active substance, any special storage conditions it requires and the time elapsed since it was supplied. As necessary, and if there is any doubt about the quality of the returned active substance, advice should be sought from the manufacturer.

7.3   Records of returned active substances should be maintained. For each return, documentation should include:

(i)   name and address of the consignee returning the active substances;

(ii)   name or designation of active substance, active substance batch number and quantity returned;

(iii)   reason for return;

(iv)   use or disposal of the returned active substance and records of the assessment performed.

7.4   Only appropriately trained and authorised personnel should release active substances for return to stock. Active substances returned to saleable stock should be placed such that the stock rotation system operates effectively.

Complaints and recalls

7.5   All complaints, whether received orally or in writing, should be recorded and investigated according to a written procedure. In the event of a complaint about the quality of an active substance, the distributor should review the complaint with the original active substance manufacturer in order to determine whether any further action, either with other customers who may have received this active substance or with the competent authority, or both, should be initiated. The investigation into the cause for the complaint should be conducted and documented by the appropriate party.

7.6   Complaint records should include:

(i)   name and address of complainant;

(ii)   name, title, where appropriate, and phone number of person submitting the complaint;

(iii)   complaint nature, including name and batch number of the active substance;

(iv)   date the complaint is received;

(v)   action initially taken, including dates and identity of person taking the action;

(vi)   any follow-up action taken;

(vii)   response provided to the originator of complaint, including date response sent;

(viii)   final decision on active substance batch.

7.7   Records of complaints should be retained in order to evaluate trends, product related frequencies and severity with a view to taking additional and, if appropriate, immediate corrective action. These should be made available during inspections by competent authorities.

7.8   Where a complaint is referred to the original active substance manufacturer, the record maintained by the distributor should include any response received from the original active substance manufacturer, including date and information provided.

7.9   In the event of a serious or potentially life-threatening situation, local, national and/or international authorities should be informed and their advice sought.

7.10   There should be a written procedure that defines the circumstances under which a recall of an active substance should be considered.

7.11   The recall procedure should designate who should be involved in evaluating the information, how a recall should be initiated, who should be informed about the recall and how the recalled material should be treated. The designated person (cf. Section 3.1) should be involved in recalls.

CHAPTER 8 SELF-INSPECTIONS

8.1   The distributor should conduct and record self-inspections in order to monitor the implementation of and compliance with these guidelines. Regular self-inspections should be performed in accordance with an approved schedule.

ANNEX

Glossary of terms applicable to these guidelines

Terms	Definition
Batch	A specific quantity of material produced in a process or series of processes so that it is expected to be homogeneous within specified limits. In the case of continuous production, a batch may correspond to a defined fraction of the production. The batch size can be defined either by a fixed quantity or by the amount produced in a fixed time interval.
Batch number	A unique combination of numbers, letters and/or symbols that identifies a batch (or lot) and from which the production and distribution history can be determined.
Brokering of active substances	All activities in relation to the sale or purchase of active substances that do not include physical handling and that consist of negotiating independently and on behalf of another legal or natural person.
Calibration	The demonstration that a particular instrument or device produces results within specified limits by comparison with those produced by a reference or traceable standard over an appropriate range of measurements.
Consignee	The person to whom the shipment is to be delivered whether by land, sea or air.
Contamination	The undesired introduction of impurities of a chemical or microbiological nature, or of foreign matter, into or onto a raw material, intermediate or active substance during

	production, sampling, packaging or re-packaging, storage or transport.
Distribution of active substances	All activities consisting of procuring, importing, holding, supplying or exporting of active substances, apart from brokering.
Deviation	Departure from an approved instruction or established standard.
Expiry date	The date placed on the container/labels of an active substance designating the time during which the active substance is expected to remain within established shelf-life specifications if stored under defined conditions, and after which it should not be used.
Falsified active substance	Any active substance with a false representation of: (a) its identity, including its packaging and labelling, its name or its components as regards any of the ingredients and the strength of those ingredients; (b) its source, including its manufacturer, its country of manufacture, its country of origin; or (c) its history, including the records and documents relating to the distribution channels used.
Holding	Storing active substances.
Procedure	A documented description of the operations to be performed, the precautions to be taken and measures to be applied directly or indirectly related to the distribution of an active substance.
Procuring	Obtaining, acquiring, purchasing or buying active substances from manufacturers, importers or other distributors.
Quality risk management	A systematic process for the assessment, control, communication and review of risks to the quality of an active substance across the product lifecycle.
Quality system	The sum of all aspects of a system that implements quality policy and ensures that quality objectives are met (ICH Q9).
Quarantine	The status of materials isolated physically or by other effective means pending a decision on the subsequent approval or rejection.
Retest date	The date when a material should be re-examined to ensure that it is still suitable for use.

Supplying	All activities of providing, selling, donating active substances to distributors, pharmacists or manufacturers of medicinal products.
Signed (signature)	The record of the individual who performed a particular action or review. This record can be initials, full handwritten signature, personal seal, or authenticated and secure electronic signature.
Transport (transportation)	Moving active substances between two locations without storing them for unjustified periods of time.
Validation	A documented programme that provides a high degree of assurance that a specific process, method or system will consistently produce a result meeting predetermined acceptance criteria.

EU Guidelines for GDP and UK Guidance on Brokering Medicines

Contents

Introduction

Persons procuring, holding, storing, supplying or exporting medicinal products are required to hold a wholesale distribution authorisation in accordance with the Human Medicines Regulations 2012.

However, the distribution network for medicinal products may involve operators who are not necessarily authorised wholesale distributors. To ensure the reliability of the supply chain, the Human Medicines Regulations 2012 regulates not only wholesale distributors, whether or not they physically handle the medicinal products, but also brokers who are involved in the sale or purchase of medicinal products without selling or purchasing those products themselves, and without owning and physically handling the medicinal products.

Brokers of medicines must comply with Chapter 10 of the European Commission's Guidelines on Good Distribution Practice of medicinal products for human use. This chapter sets out the guidelines alongside the expectations for UK brokers.

Chapter 10 Specific Provisions for Brokers[1]

10.1 Principle

A "broker" is a person involved in activities in relation to the sale or purchase of medicinal products, except for wholesale distribution, that do not include physical handling and that consist of negotiating independently and on behalf of another legal or natural person[2].

Brokers are subject to a registration requirement. They must have a permanent address and contact details in the Member State where they are registered[3]. They must notify the competent authority of any changes to those details without unnecessary delay.

By definition, brokers do not procure, supply or hold medicines. Therefore, requirements for premises, installations and equipment, as set out in Directive 2001/83/EC, do not apply. However, all other rules in Directive 2001/83/EC that apply to wholesale distributors also apply to brokers.

10.2 Quality system

The quality system of a broker should be defined in writing, approved and kept up to date. It should set out responsibilities, processes and risk management in relation to their activities.

The quality system should include an emergency plan which ensures effective recall of medicinal products from the market ordered by the manufacturer or the competent authorities or carried out in cooperation with the manufacturer or marketing authorisation holder for the medicinal product concerned[4]. The competent authorities must be immediately informed of any suspected falsified medicines offered in the supply chain[5].

10.3 Personnel

Any member of personnel involved in the brokering activities should be trained in the applicable EU and national legislation and in the issues concerning falsified medicinal products.

---

[1] Article 85b(3) of Directive 2001/83/EC.
[2] Article 1(17a) of Directive 2001/83/EC.
[3] Article 85b of Directive 2001/83/EC.
[4] Article 80(d) of Directive 2001/83/EC.
[5] Article 85b(1), third paragraph of Directive 2001/83/EC.

10.4   Documentation

The general provisions on documentation in Chapter 4 apply.

In addition, at least the following procedures and instructions, along with the corresponding records of execution, should be in place:

(i)   procedure for complaints handling;

(ii)   procedure for informing competent authorities and marketing authorisation holders of suspected falsified medicinal products;

(iii) procedure for supporting recalls;

(iv) procedure for ensuring that medicinal products brokered have a marketing authorisation;

(v)   procedure for verifying that their supplying wholesale distributors hold a distribution authorisation, their supplying manufacturers or importers hold a manufacturing authorisation and their customers are authorised to supply medicinal products in the Member State concerned;

(vi) records should be kept either in the form of purchase/sales invoices or on computer, or in any other form for any transaction in medicinal products brokered, and should contain at least the following information: date, name of the medicinal product, quantity brokered, name and address of the supplier and the customer, and batch number at least for products bearing the safety features.

Records should be made available to the competent authorities, for inspection purposes, for the period stated in national legislation but at least 5 years.

UK Guidance on Chapter 10 – Specific Provisions for Brokers

Directive 2011/62/EU, known as the Falsified Medicines Directive (FMD), was transposed into UK law on 20 August 2013. It amended Directive 2001/83/EC by including measures aimed at preventing the entry of falsified medicines into the legal supply chain.

To accord with legislation, brokers of medicinal products are required to register their activities with the National competent authority. In the UK, this is the MHRA.

Who can a broker negotiate between?

- the manufacturer and a wholesaler, or
- one wholesaler and another wholesaler, or
- the manufacturer or wholesale dealer with a person who may lawfully sell those products by retail or may lawfully supply them in circumstances corresponding to retail sale or a person who may lawfully administer those products.

- brokers may broker only medicinal products that are the subject of a marketing authorisation granted by the national competent authority.
- brokers must adhere to certain requirements of the registration, including compliance with Chapter 10 of the Guidelines on Good Distribution Practice.

The Human Medicines (Amendments) Regulations 2013, UK Statutory Instruments 2013 No. 1855 Part 2 Regulation 16 "Chapter 3", introduced "Brokering in Medicinal Products" under Regulations 45A to 45L.

Following the changes on 1 January 2021, further amendments to the Regulation have been implemented. The Human Medicines (Amendment, etc.) (EU Exit) Regulations 2020, SI 2020 No. 1488, amended Regulations 45A, 45E and 45F of the Human Medicines Regulations 2012.

Background

A "broker" is a person involved in all activities in relation to the sale or purchase of medicinal products, except for wholesale distribution, that do not include physical handling and that consist of negotiating independently and on behalf of another legal or natural person.

Brokers are subject to a registration requirement. They must have a permanent address and contact details in the UK or approved country where they are registered. They must notify the competent authority of any changes to those details without unnecessary delay.

Brokers do not procure, supply or hold medicines. Therefore, requirements for premises, installations and equipment as set out in legislation do not apply. However, many other rules in legislation that apply to wholesale distributors also apply to brokers.

Brokers based in the UK need to be registered with the MHRA. If a UK wholesaler wishes to engage with a client of an EEA broker they will need to check if that broker is legally entitled to broker in that country, and if their client legally entitled to receive the medicine.

List of approved countries for authorised human medicines – https://www.gov.uk/government/publications/list-of-approved-countries-for-authorised-human-medicines/list-of-approved-countries.

Based on the above definition, the key factors that distinguish the activity of brokering of medicinal products from wholesale distribution include the following:

- Brokering is a financial activity focused only on purchasing and selling. Wholesaling involves a wider range of activities and participation in the supply chain.
- Brokering does not involve taking title for the medicinal products.

- Brokering is limited to negotiation of the relevant financial transactions. It is an intermediary role where the broker acts on behalf of another operator within that supply chain.
- Brokering does not involve the operator physically handling the medicinal products.

Application assessments are normally carried out as a desktop review by nominated MHRA Inspectors. The assessment consists of a review of the broker's quality management system submitted with the application. Once the Inspector is content that the applicant is compliant with GDP and the Human Medicines Regulations 2012, they are entered on to the Register of Brokers.

Some wholesalers may apply for a WDA(H) and broker registration at the same time. If so, both aspects will be looked at on inspection rather than by desktop review.

If an inspection is carried out, a broker will be inspected against Chapter 10 of the GDP Guidelines and regulation 45A of the Human Medicines Regulations 2012.

The requirements for brokers are set out in the Human Medicines Regulations 2012, regulations 45A, 45B, 45E and 45F. Brokers must also comply with GDP Chapter 10.

The Register of Brokers is maintained by the MHRA Data Processing Team and is posted on the MHRA website at the following location: https://www.gov.uk/government/publications/register-of-brokers-authorised-to-deal-in-human-medicines.

How to apply

Brokers apply to be registered through the MHRA Submissions portal: https://www.gov.uk/guidance/medicines-register-as-a-broker.

Once the application has been received, the information is downloaded, processed and passed to the GDP Inspectorate for assessment.

Annually, from 1 April, brokers must submit a declaration confirming compliance with the Regulations. This annual declaration is passed to the GDP Inspectorate for assessment. The annual declaration is requested by the MHRA.

Any changes to the broker registration must be communicated via a variation to the MHRA and significant changes are passed to the GDP Inspectorate for assessment.

Changes passed for assessment would be an issue that potentially affects how the company operates, such as a change in personnel or adding additional sites.

Specific provisions for brokers

Brokers are required to:

- maintain a quality system;
- adhere to some good distribution practice requirements; and
- maintain a sufficient level of documentation relating to transactions carried out, to assist with ensuring full traceability for medicinal products across the supply chain.

Legislation sets out specific provisions with which brokers must comply. These include the following requirements:

- Maintain an emergency plan that ensures effective implementation of any recall from the market ordered by the Competency Authority or carried out in cooperation with the manufacturer or marketing authorisation holder for the medicinal product concerned.
- Keep records either in the form of purchase/sales invoices or on computer, or in any other form, giving for any transaction in medicinal products received, dispatched or brokered at least the following information: date, name of the medicinal product, quantity brokered, name and address of the supplier and consignee, batch number of the medicinal products, at least for products bearing the safety features referred to in point (o) of Article 54 of the Directive[6].
- Keep the records referred to under available to the MHRA, for inspection purposes, for a period of five years.
- Comply with the principles and guidelines of good distribution practice for medicinal products.
- Maintain a quality system setting out responsibilities, processes and risk management measures in relation to their activities.
- Immediately inform the MHRA and, where applicable, the Marketing Authorisation Holder, of medicinal products identified as falsified or suspected to be falsified.

Quality management system (QMS)

When completing the application via the MHRA Submissions portal, there is a requirement to submit the following standard operating procedures for review by the GDP Inspectorate.

---

[6] Point (o) of Article 54 was inserted by Directive 2011/62/EU of the European Parliament and of the Council (OJ No L 174, 1.7.2011, p. 74).

Standard Operating Procedures (SOPs)

The SOPs to be attached are those listed in EU GDP in Chapter 10.4 as follows:

(i) procedure for complaints handling;
(ii) procedure for informing competent authorities and marketing authorisation holders of suspected falsified medicinal products;
(iii) procedure for supporting recalls;
(iv) procedure for ensuring that medicinal products brokered have a marketing authorisation;
(v) procedure for verifying that their supplying wholesale distributors hold a distribution authorisation, their supplying manufacturers, or importers hold a manufacturing authorisation and their customers are authorised to supply medicinal products in the Member State concerned;
(vi) records should be kept either in the form of purchase/sales invoices or on computer, or in any other form for any transaction in medicinal products brokered and should contain at least the following information: date, name of the medicinal product, quantity brokered, name and address of the supplier and the customer and batch number at least for products bearing the safety features.

In addition to the standard operating procedure, a full description of the intending brokering business model should be included in the documentation provided on the Submissions portal. This provides the opportunity for the assessing Inspector to review all submitted documentation and determine if the company is compliant with the proposed business operational model.

The MHRA will inform the company by way of email that they have been approved.

The company do not receive any form of licence; they are added to the Broker Register on the MHRA website.

If a physical inspection is carried out the organisation receives a GDP Broker Certificate of Compliance.

Providing inaccurate information, leads to delaying the approval process. For example,

No procedures

- There is a requirement to provide relevant standard operating procedures as described on the application.

Lack of information

- The information submitted falls extensively short of the requirements for approval.

Lack of clarity on the intended business model

- To ensure I have a clear understanding of your intended business model, would you please confirm that is it your intention to conduct brokering activities as described below.
- A "broker" is a person involved in activities in relation to the sale or purchase of medicinal products, except for wholesale distribution, that "do not include physical handling", and that consist **only** of "negotiating independently" and on behalf of another legal or natural person. Therefore, by definition, brokers do not **procure, supply or hold medicines.**

When applicant really requires a Wholesale Dealer's Licence rather than a Broker registration

- Reference is made to the Responsible Person in several of your procedures and QMS. A Responsible Person is not a requirement of the Broker's registration. The scope of the business model appears to relate to the wholesale distribution of medicinal product.

If an application is incomplete, and a company fails to respond or it becomes clear that a company are not brokers but are wholesalers, they will be invited to withdraw the application by the Inspector, if the invitation to withdraw is not accepted and the company are unsuitable to be registered, the application will be referred the MHRA Inspection Action Group (IAG) for consideration of removal.

Additional UK Guidance

Criteria of broker's registration

A person may not broker a medicinal product unless that product is covered by the licensing authority, or by an appropriate authority responsible for the licensing of medicinal products in an approved country for import, and that person is validly registered as a broker with the Licensing Authority, has a permanent address in the UK and complies with the guidelines on good distribution practice that apply under, or by virtue of, regulation C17 of the Human Medicines Regulations 2012 in so far as those guidelines apply to brokers.

A person may not broker a medicinal product in Northern Ireland unless the product is covered by an authorisation granted under Regulation (EC) No 726/2004, by the Licensing Authority, or by a competent authority of a Member State, and that person is validly registered as a broker with the Licensing Authority or a competent authority of a Member State, except where the person is validly registered with the competent authority of an EEA State, has a permanent address in the UK and complies with the guidelines on good distribution practice published by the European Commission in accordance with Article 84 of the 2001 Directive in so far as those guidelines apply to brokers. Brokers must satisfy all the conditions of brokering and:

- have a permanent address in the UK;
- have an emergency plan that ensures effective implementation of any recall from the market ordered by the in the case of a broker in Great Britain, the Licensing Authority or an appropriate authority responsible for the licensing of medicinal products in an approved country for import, or, in the case of a broker in Northern Ireland, the Licensing Authority or by the competent authority of any EEA State;
- keep records either in the form of purchase/sales invoices or on computer, or in any other form, giving for any transaction in medicinal products brokered at least the following information:
  - date on which the sale or purchase of the product is brokered;
  - name of the medicinal product;
  - quantity brokered;
  - name and address of the supplier or consignee, as appropriate;
  - batch number where the sale or supply of the medicinal product is in Northern Ireland, of the medicinal products at least for products bearing the safety features referred to in point (o) of Article 54 of Directive 2001/83/EC;
- keep the records available to the competent authorities, for inspection purposes, for a period of five years;
- comply with the principles and guidelines of good distribution practice for medicinal products as laid down in Article 84 of Directive 2001/83/EC;
- maintain a quality system setting out responsibilities, processes and risk management measures in relation to their activities.

Where the address at which the plan or records necessary to comply with the provisions of brokering are kept is different from the address notified in accordance with the application, the broker must ensure that the plan or records are kept at an address in the UK and inform the Licensing Authority of the address at which the plan or records are kept.

The broker must provide such information as may be requested by the MHRA concerning the type and quantity of medicinal products brokered within the period specified by the MHRA.

The broker must take all reasonable precautions and exercise all due diligence to ensure that any information provided by that broker to the MHRA is not false or misleading.

For the purposes of enabling the MHRA to determine whether there are grounds for suspending, revoking or varying the registration, the broker must permit a person authorised in writing by the MHRA, on production of identification, to carry out any inspection, or to take any copies, which an inspector may carry out or take under the provisions of the Human Medicines Regulations 2012 [SI 2012/1916].

Provision of Information

Once registered, a broker will have to notify the MHRA of any changes to the details for registration that might affect compliance with the requirements of the legislation in respect of brokering without unnecessary delay. This notification will be subject to a variation procedure. Responsibility for notifying the MHRA of any changes lies with the person responsible for management of the brokering activities.

The person responsible for management of the brokering activities shall be required to submit a report, which shall include:

• a declaration that the broker has in place appropriate systems to ensure compliance with the requirements for brokering;
• provision of the details of the systems that it has in place to ensure such compliance.

An annual compliance report will need to be submitted in relation to any application made before 31 March 2014, the date of the application and, in relation to each subsequent reporting year, by 30 April following the end of that year. The annual compliance report will be subject to a variation procedure so that the broker can change the original details provided.

The broker must without delay notify the Licensing Authority of any changes to the matters in respect of which evidence has been supplied in relation to the compliance report, which might affect compliance with the requirements of brokering.

The broker must immediately inform the MHRA and, in the case of a broker in Great Britain, either the UK marketing authorisation holder or, where applicable, the holder of the licence or authorisation granted by an appropriate authority responsible for the licensing of medicinal products in an approved country for import, or Northern Ireland, either the UK marketing authorisation holder or, where applicable, the EU marketing authorisation holder.

Management of Recall Activity by Brokers

Chapter 10 of the EU GDP Guidelines deals with brokers, and includes the requirement for the broker to have in place "an emergency plan which ensures effective recall of medicinal products from the market". The guidelines go on to specify that brokers should have a written procedure for supporting recalls, alongside an obligation to maintain relevant documentation.

As brokers do not hold or handle stock, the scope of their recall activities are somewhat more limited than wholesalers.

A broker should:

- follow the detail of the recall message;
- identify those persons or companies involved in relevant brokered deals;
- directly contact those customers, making them aware of the details of the recall;
- keep recall notices open for an appropriate period, so as to capture any affected stock still moving through the supply chain.

As with wholesalers, all recall activities should be documented at the time they occur and, at the conclusion of all recall activities, the broker should produce a report, making an objective assessment of whether the recall process achieved its objectives and identifying any areas requiring improvement.

Supply and brokering to countries outside of the UK

Where wholesale stock has been supplied or brokered to countries outside the UK, there are the same obligations to contact the relevant customers to make them aware of the recall. It should be noted that, certainly within approved countries, dependent on the nature of the recall and its impact on product availability and patient health, different countries may take varying levels of action. The wholesaler or broker should confirm with the relevant competent authority the particular terms of a recall in a particular territory.

UK Legislation on Wholesale Distribution

Contents

The Human Medicines Regulations 2012 [SI 2012/1916]

> Editor's These extracts from the Regulations and Standard Provisions of the Human
> note Medicines Regulations 2012 [SI 2012/1916] are presented for the reader's con-
> venience. Reproduction is with the permission of HMSO and the Queen's Printer
> for Scotland. For any definitive information reference must be made to the original
> Regulations. The numbering and content within this section corresponds with the
> regulations set out in the published Statutory Instrument [SI 2012/1916].

Citation and commencement

1 (1) These Regulations may be cited as the Human Medicines Regulations 2012.

   (2) These Regulations come into force on 14th August 2012.

Medicinal products

2 (1) In these Regulations "medicinal product" means:

   (a) any substance or combination of substances presented as having properties of preventing or treating disease in human beings; or

   (b) any substance or combination of substances that may be used by or administered to human beings with a view to:

     (i) restoring, correcting or modifying a physiological function by exerting a pharmacological, immunological or metabolic action; or

     (ii) making a medical diagnosis.

   (2) These Regulations do not apply to:

   (a) whole human blood; or

   (b) any human blood component, other than plasma prepared by a method involving an industrial process.

Definition of advanced therapy medicinal product, etc.

2A (1) In these Regulations, in their application to products for sale or supply in Great Britain only, "advanced therapy medicinal product" means any of the following products:

   (a) a gene therapy medicinal product;

   (b) a somatic cell therapy medicinal product; or

   (c) a tissue engineered product.

   (2) A "gene therapy medicinal product" is a biological medicinal product which has the following characteristics:

   (a) it contains an active substance, which contains or consists of a recombinant nucleic acid used in or administered to human beings with a view to regulating, repairing, replacing, adding or deleting a genetic sequence; and

   (b) its therapeutic, prophylactic or diagnostic effect relates directly to the recombinant nucleic acid sequence it contains, or to the product of genetic expression of this sequence.

   (3) A vaccine against infectious diseases is not to be treated as a gene therapy medicinal product.

   (4) A "somatic cell medicinal product" is a medicinal product which has the following characteristics:

   (a) it contains or consists of cells or tissues that:

      (i) have been subject to substantial manipulation so that biological characteristics, physiological functions or structural properties relevant for the intended clinical use have been altered; or

      (ii) are not intended to be used for the same essential function in the recipient as in the donor; and

  (b) It is presented as having properties for, or is used in or administered to human beings with a view to, treating, preventing or diagnosing a disease through the pharmacological, immunological or metabolic action of its cells or tissues.

(5) A "tissue engineered product" is a medicinal product which:

  (a) contains or consists of engineered cells or tissues; and

  (b) is presented as having properties for, or is used in or administered to human beings with a view to, regenerating, repairing or replacing a human tissue.

(6) A tissue engineered product may contain:

  (a) cells or tissues of human or animal origin;

  (b) viable or non-viable cells or tissues; and

  (c) additional substances, including cellular products, biomolecules, biomaterials, chemical sub-stances, scaffolds or matrices.

(7) A product is not a tissue engineered product if it:

  (a) contains or consists exclusively of non-viable human or animal cells or tissues;

  (b) does not contain any viable cells or tissues; and

  (c) does not act principally by pharmacological, immunological or metabolic action.

(8) Cells or tissues are engineered if they:

  (a) have been subject to substantial manipulation, so that biological characteristics, physiological functions or structural properties relevant for the intended regeneration, repair or replacement are achieved; or

  (b) are not intended to be used for the same essential function in the recipient as in the donor.

(9) The following manipulations are not substantial manipulations for the purposes of paragraphs (4)(a) and (8)(a):

  (a) cutting;

  (b) grinding;

  (c) shaping;

  (d) centrifugation;

  (e) soaking in antibiotic or antimicrobial solutions;

  (f) sterilisation;

  (g) irradiation;

  (h) cell separation, concentration or purification;

  (i) filtering;

  (j) lyophilisation;

    (**k**) freezing;

    (**l**) cryopreservation; and

    (**m**) vitrification.

(**10**) In these Regulations, in their application to products for sale or supply in Great Britain only, "combined advanced therapy medicinal product" means an advanced therapy medicinal product:

    (**a**) which incorporates, as an integral part of the product, one or more medical devices or one or more active implantable medical devices; and

    (**b**) the cellular part of which:

        (**i**) contains viable cells or tissues; or

        (**ii**) contains non-viable cells or tissues which are liable to act upon the human body with action that can be considered as primary to that of the medical devices.

(**11**) Where an advanced therapy medicinal product contains viable cells or tissues, the pharmacological, immunological or metabolic action of those cells or tissues is to be treated as the principal mode of action of the product.

(**12**) An advanced therapy medicinal product containing both autologous and allogeneic cells or tissues is to be treated as being for allogeneic use.

(**13**) A product which falls within the definition of a tissue engineered product and within the definition of a somatic cell therapy medicinal product is to be treated as a tissue engineered product.

(**14**) A product which falls within the definition of:

    (**a**) a somatic cell therapy medicinal product or a tissue engineered product; and

    (**b**) a gene therapy medicinal product,

is to be treated as a gene therapy medicinal product.

General interpretation

8 (**1**) In these Regulations (unless the context otherwise requires):

"the 2001 Directive" means Directive 2001/83/EC of the European Parliament and the Council on the Community Code relating to medicinal products for human use;

"the 2018 Regulations" means the Health Service Products (Provision and Disclosure of Information) Regulations 2018;

"advanced therapy medicinal product" means, in the case of a medicinal product for sale or supply by the holder of a UKMA(NI) or UKMA(UK), a medicinal product described in Article 2(1)(a) of Regulation (EC) No 1394/2007;

"approved country for import list" means the list published by the licensing authority under regulation 18A (approved country for import) and "approved country for import" means a country included in that list;

"Article 126a authorisation" means an authorisation granted by the licensing authority under Part 8 of these Regulations;

"brokering" means all activities in relation to the sale or purchase of medicinal products, except for wholesale distribution, that do not include physical handling and consist of negotiating independently and on behalf of another legal or natural person;

"EU marketing authorisation" means a marketing authorisation granted or renewed by the European Commission under Regulation (EC) No 726/2004;

"European Economic Area" or "EEA" means the European Economic Area created by the EEA agreement;

"exempt advanced therapy medicinal product" has the meaning given in regulation 171;

"export" means export, or attempt to export, from the United Kingdom, whether by land, sea or air;

"falsified medicinal product" means any medicinal product with a false representation of:

(a) its identity, including its packaging and labelling, its name or its composition (other than any unintentional quality defect), as regards any of its ingredients including excipients and the strength of those ingredients;

(b) its source, including its manufacturer, its country of manufacturing, its country of origin or its marketing authorisation holder; or

(c) its history, including the records and documents relating to the distribution channels used;

"herbal medicinal product" means a medicinal product whose only active ingredients are herbal substances or herbal preparations (or both);

"homoeopathic medicinal product" means a medicinal product prepared from homoeopathic stocks in accordance with a homoeopathic manufacturing procedure described by:

(a) the European Pharmacopoeia; or

(b) in the absence of such a description in the European Pharmacopoeia

(i) in relation to a certificate of registration or marketing authorisation for a national homoeopathic product in force in Great Britain only, the British Pharmacopoeia, or in an pharmacopoeia used officially in an country that is included in a list published by the licensing authority for this purpose;

(ii) in relation to a certificate of registration or marketing authorisation for a national homoeopathic product in force in the whole United Kingdom or in Northern Ireland only, in the British Pharmacopoeia or in any pharmacopoeia used officially in an EEA State;

"import" means import, or attempt to import, into the UK, whether by land, sea or air and "imported" is to be construed accordingly;

"inspector" means a person authorised in writing by an enforcement authority for the purposes of Part 16 (enforcement) (and references to "the enforcement authority", in relation to an inspector, are to the enforcement authority by whom the inspector is so authorised);

"the licensing authority" has the meaning given by regulation 6(2);

"listed NIMAR product" means a product included in a list maintained in accordance with regulation 167B on the date it is dispatched from Great Britain to Northern Ireland;

"manufacturer's licence" has the meaning given by regulation 17(1);

"marketing authorisation" means:

(a) a UK marketing authorisation; or

(b) an EU marketing authorisation;

"medicinal product subject to general sale" has the meaning given in regulation 5(1) (classification of medicinal products);

"the relevant EU provisions" means the provisions of legislation of the European Union relating to medicinal products for human use, except to the extent that any other enactment provides for any function in relation to any such provision to be exercised otherwise than by the licensing authority;

"NIMAR" means Northern Ireland MHRA authorised route;

"relevant European State" means an EEA State or Switzerland;

"relevant medicinal product" has the meaning given by regulation 48;

"special medicinal product" means a product within the meaning of regulation 167 or any equivalent legislation in a country other than the UK;

"traditional herbal medicinal product" means a herbal medicinal product to which regulation 125 applies;

"traditional herbal registration" means a traditional herbal registration granted by the licensing authority under these Regulations and:

(a) "THR(UK)" means such a registration in force in the whole United Kingdom;

(b) "THR(GB)" means such a registration in force in Great Britain only;

(c) "THR(NI)" means such a registration in force in Northern Ireland only; "UK marketing authorisation" means a marketing authorisation granted by the licensing authority under Part 5 of these Regulations or Chapter 4 of Title III to the 2001 Directive (mutual recognition and decentralised procedure) and:

   (i) "UKMA(UK)" means such an authorisation in force in the whole United Kingdom;

   (ii) "UKMA(GB)" means such an authorisation in force in Great Britain only;

(iii) "UKMA(NI)" means such an authorisation in force in Northern Ireland only.

"wholesale dealer's licence" has the meaning given by regulation 18(1).

- In these Regulations, references to distribution of a product by way of wholesale dealing are to be construed in accordance with regulations 18(4) and (5).
- In these Regulations, references to selling by retail, or to retail sale, are references to selling a product to a person who buys it otherwise than for a purpose specified in regulation 18(5).
- In these Regulations, references to supplying anything in circumstances corresponding to retail sale are references to supplying it, otherwise than by way of sale, to a person who receives it otherwise than for a purpose specified in regulation 18(5);

Wholesale dealing in medicinal products

18 (1) A person may not except in accordance with a licence (a "wholesale dealer's licence"):

(a) distribute a medicinal product by way of wholesale dealing;

(b) possess a medicinal product for the purpose of such distribution; or

(c) import a medicinal product from an approved country for import into Great Britain for either purpose; or

(d) supply a listed NIMAR product from Great Britain to Northern Ireland.

(2) Paragraph (1):

(a) does not apply:

(i)   to anything done in relation to a medicinal product by the holder of a manufacturer's licence in respect of that product;

(ii) where the product concerned is an investigational medicinal product; or

(iii) if the product is a radiopharmaceutical in which the radionuclide is in the form of a sealed source; and

(b) is subject to regulation 19.

(2A) Paragraph (1)(c) does not apply to imports into Great Britain from an EEA State of medicinal products that have been released for sale, supply or distribution in an EEA State or the United Kingdom before IP completion day.

(2B) For the purposes of paragraph (2A) a medicinal product has been released for sale, supply or distribution where, after the stage of manufacturing has taken place, the product is the subject matter of a written or verbal agreement between two or more persons for the transfer of ownership, any other property right or possession concerning the product, or where the product is the subject matter of an offer to a person to conclude such an agreement.

(3) Distribution of a medicinal product by way of wholesale dealing, or possession for the purpose of such distribution, is not to be taken to be in accordance with a wholesale dealer's licence unless the distribution is carried on, or as the case may be the product held, at premises located in the UK and specified in the licence.

(4) In these Regulations a reference to distributing a product by way of wholesale dealing is a reference to:

(a) selling or supplying it; or

(b) procuring or holding it or exporting it for the purposes of sale or supply, to a person who receives it for a purpose within paragraph (5).

(5) Those purposes are:

(a) selling or supplying the product; or

(b) administering it or causing it to be administered to one or more human beings, in the course of a business carried on by that person.

(6) A wholesale dealer's licence does not authorise the distribution of a medicinal product by way of wholesale dealing, or possession of a medicinal product for the purpose of such distribution, unless:

(a) in the case of a product for sale or supply in Great Britain, a UKMA(GB) or UKMA(UK), certificate of registration or traditional herbal registration is in force in respect of the product, or

(b) in the case of a product for sale or supply in Northern Ireland, a UKMA(NI) or UKMA(UK), EU marketing authorisation, Article 126a authorisation, certificate of registration or traditional herbal registration is in force in respect of the product, or

(c) in the case of a listed NIMAR product, a UKMA(GB) or UKMA(UK) is in force in respect of the product,

but this is subject to the exceptions in regulation 43(6).

(7) In paragraph (6)(b), "marketing authorisation" means:

(a) a marketing authorisation issued by a competent authority of a member State in accordance with the 2001 Directive; or

(b) an EU marketing authorisation.

Approved country for import

18A (1) The licensing authority must:

(a) publish a list of countries from which medicinal products may be imported under a wholesale dealing licence ("approved country for import list"); and

(b) only include in that list a country which is included in the approved country for batch testing list.

(2) In order to determine whether a country should be included in the approved country for import list, the licensing authority may, in particular, take into account:

(a) the country's system for ensuring that each batch of a medicinal product has been manufactured and checked in accordance with the requirements of its legislation and any authorisation in respect of that product;

(b) the country's rules for good distribution practice;

(c) the regularity of inspections to verify compliance with good distribution practice;

(d) the effectiveness of enforcement of good distribution practice;

(e) the regularity and rapidity of information provided by that country relating to non-compliant manufacturers and distributers of medicinal products;

(f) any on-site review of that country's regulatory system undertaken by the licensing authority;

(g) any on-site inspection of a manufacturing site in that country observed by the licensing authority; and

(h) any other relevant documentation available to the licensing authority.

(3) The licensing authority must:

(a) remove a country from the approved country for import list if that country is removed from the approved country for batch testing list;

(b) in any event review the countries it has included in the approved country for import list to determine if it is still satisfied that the country should remain on that list and, if it is not so satisfied, remove that country from the list; and

(c) undertake that review at least every three years beginning with the date on which that country is included in that list.

Exemptions from requirement for wholesale dealer's licence

19 (1) Regulation 18 does not apply to the sale or offer for sale of a medicinal product by way of wholesale dealing, or possession for the purpose of such sale or offer, where paragraph (2) applies and the person selling or offering the product for sale is:

(a) the holder of:

(i) in the case of a product for sale or supply in Great Britain (including a listed NIMAR product for sale or supply from Great Britain to Northern Ireland), a UKMA(GB), a UKMA(UK), a COR(GB), a COR(UK), a THR(GB) or a THR(UK) (an "authorisation") which relates to the product, or

(ii) in the case of a product for sale or supply in Northern Ireland, a UKMA(NI), a UKMA(UK), a COR(NI), a COR(UK), a THR(NI), a THR(UK), an EU marketing authorisation or an Article 126a authorisation (an "authorisation") which relates to the product, including a holder of an authorisation who manufactured or assembled the product; or

(b) a person who is not the holder of an authorisation in relation to the product but manufactured or assembled the product in the United Kingdom to the order of a person who is the holder of an authorisation relating to the product.

(2) This paragraph applies if:

(a) until the sale, the medicinal product has been kept on the premises of the person who manufactured or assembled the product (in this regulation referred to as "authorised premises"); and

(b) those premises are premises authorised for use for manufacture or assembly by that person's manufacturer's licence.

(3) For the purposes of this regulation, a medicinal product is regarded as having been kept on authorised premises at a time when:

(a) it was being moved from one set of authorised premises to another, or from one part of authorised premises to another part; or

(b) it was being moved from authorised premises by way of delivery to a purchaser.

(4) Regulation 18 does not apply to a person who in connection with the importation of a medicinal product:

(a) provides facilities solely for transporting the product; or

(b) acting as an import agent, handles the product where the product is imported solely to the order of another person who intends to sell the product or offer it for sale by way of wholesale dealing or to distribute it in any other way.

(4A) Regulation 18 does not apply in connection with the distribution by way of wholesale dealing of a medicinal product to be used for vaccination or immunisation against coronavirus or influenza virus, where the person distributing the medicinal product:

(a) was supplied with the medicinal product for the purposes of the administration of it under relevant arrangements;

(b) is supplying the medicinal product for the purposes of the administration of it by the person to whom it is being supplied (or by a person employed or engaged by them) under relevant arrangements; and

(c) is authorised by the body making the arrangements to supply the medicinal product as mentioned in sub-paragraph (b) under the relevant arrangements.

(4B) Regulation 18 docs not apply in connection with the distribution by way of wholesale dealing of a medicinal product to be supplied or administered in accordance with a protocol of the type mentioned in regulation 247, where the person distributing the medicinal product:

(a) was supplied with the medicinal product for the purposes of the supply or administration of it to a patient under relevant arrangements;

(b) is supplying the medicinal product for the purposes of the supply or administration of it to a patient by the person to whom it is being supplied (or by a person employed or engaged by them) under relevant arrangements; and

(c) is authorised by the body making the arrangements to supply the medicinal product as mentioned in sub-paragraph (b) under the relevant arrangements.

(4C) In this regulation, "relevant arrangements" means:

(a) arrangements for the provision of services as part of:

    (i) in England, the health service as defined by section 275(1) of the National Health Service Act 2006;

    (ii) in Scotland, the health service as defined by section 108(1) of the National Health Service (Scotland) Act 1978(8);

    (iii) in Wales, the health service as defined by section 206(1) of the National Health Service (Wales) Act 2006(9); and

    (iv) in Northern Ireland, the system of health and social care promoted under section 2(1) of the Health and Social Care (Reform) Act (Northern Ireland)2009(10); or

(b) arrangements for the provision of services (otherwise than as mentioned in sub-paragraph (a)) as part of the medical services of Her Majesty's Forces.

(4D) Paragraphs (4A) to (4C) cease to have effect on 1st April 2022.

(5) .....

(6) Regulation 18 does not apply to a person ("P") who imports a medicinal product into Great Britain from an approved country for import for administration to P or to any other person who is a member of P's household.

Application for manufacturer's or wholesale dealer's licence

21 (1) An application for a grant of a licence under this Part must:

(a) be made to the licensing authority;

(b) be made in the way and form specified in Schedule 3; and

(c) contain or be accompanied by the information, documents, samples and other material specified in that Schedule.

(2) An application must indicate the descriptions of medicinal products in respect of which the licence is required, either by specifying the descriptions of medicinal products in question or by way of an appropriate general classification.

Factors relevant to determination of application for manufacturer's or wholesale dealer's licence

22 (1) In dealing with an application for a manufacturer's licence the licensing authority must in particular take into consideration:

(a) the operations proposed to be carried out under the licence;

(b) the premises in which those operations are to be carried out;

(c) the equipment which is or will be available on those premises for carrying out those operations;

(d) the qualifications of the persons under whose supervision the operations will be carried out; and

(e) the arrangements made or to be made for securing the safekeeping of, and the maintenance of adequate records in respect of, medicinal products manufactured or assembled in pursuance of the licence.

(2) In dealing with an application for a wholesale dealer's licence the licensing authority must in particular take into consideration:

(a) the premises on which medicinal products of the descriptions to which the application relates will be stored;

(b) the equipment which is or will be available for storing medicinal products on those premises;

(c) the equipment and facilities that are or will be available for distributing medicinal products from those premises; and

(d) the arrangements made or to be made for securing the safekeeping of, and the maintenance of adequate records in respect of, medicinal products stored on or distributed from those premises.

Grant or refusal of licence

23 (1) Subject to the following provisions of these Regulations, on an application to the licensing authority for a licence under this Part the licensing authority may:

(a) grant a licence containing such provisions as it considers appropriate; or

(b) refuse to grant a licence if, having regard to the provisions of these Regulations, it considers it necessary or appropriate to do so.

(2) The licensing authority must grant or refuse an application for a licence under this Part within the period of 90 days, beginning immediately after the day on which it receives the application.

(3) Paragraph (2) applies to an application only if the requirements of Schedule 3 have been met.

(4) If a notice under regulation 30 requires the applicant to provide the licensing authority with information, the information period is not to be counted for the purposes of paragraph (2).

(5) In paragraph (4), the "information period" means the period:

    (a) beginning with the day on which the notice is given; and

    (b) ending with the day on which the licensing authority receives the information or the applicant shows to the licensing authority's satisfaction that the applicant is unable to provide it.

(6) The licensing authority must give the applicant a notice stating the reasons for its decision in any case where:

    (a) the licensing authority refuses to grant an application for a licence; or

    (b) the licensing authority grants a licence otherwise than in accordance with the application and the applicant requests a statement of its reasons.

Standard provisions of licences

24 (1) The standard provisions set out in Schedule 4 may be incorporated by the licensing authority in a licence under this Part granted on or after the date on which these Regulations come into force.

(2) The standard provisions may be incorporated in a licence with or without modifications and either generally or in relation to medicinal products of a particular class.

(3) In Schedule 4, in relation to a licence holder in Great Britain, references to the principles and guidelines set out in the Good Manufacturing Practice Directive are to those principles and guidelines as they apply under or by virtue of regulation B17.

Duration of licence

25 A licence granted under this Part remains in force until:

    (a) the licence is revoked by the licensing authority; or

    (b) the licence is surrendered by the holder.

Conditions for wholesale dealer's licence

42 (1) Regulations 43 to 45 (not including regulation 43ZA) (in the case of a wholesale dealer's licence held in Northern Ireland) or regulations 43 to 45AA (including regulation 43ZA) (in the case of a wholesale dealer's licence held in Great Britain) apply to the holder of a wholesale dealer's licence (referred to in those regulations as "the licence holder") and have effect as if they were provisions of the licence (but the provisions specified in paragraph (2) do not apply to the holder of a wholesale dealer's licence in so far as the licence relates to exempt advanced therapy medicinal products).

(2) Those provisions are regulations 43(2) and (8) and 44.

(3) The requirements in Part 2 of Schedule 6 apply to the holder of a wholesale dealer's licence in so far as the licence relates to exempt advanced therapy medicinal products, and have effect as if they were provisions of the licence.

(4) Where a wholesale dealer's licence relates to wholesale dealings in Northern Ireland, the requirements and obligations contained in a provision of Commission Regulation 2016/161 listed in paragraph (5) have effect as if they were provisions of that under this Part.

(5) The provisions mentioned in paragraph (4) are:

(a) Article 10 (verification of the safety features) insofar as it relates to wholesalers;

(b) Article 11 (verification of the authenticity of the unique identifier) insofar as it relates to wholesalers;

(c) Article 12 (unique identifiers which have been decommissioned);

(d) Article 13 (reversing the status of a decommissioned unique identifier) in so far as it relates to wholesalers;

(e) Article 20 (verification of the authenticity of the unique identifier), subject to the exemption contained in Article 21 (derogations from Article 20(b));

(f) Article 22 (decommissioning of unique identifiers); and

(g) Article 24 (actions to be taken in case of tampering or suspected falsification).

(6) Paragraph (4) does not apply in relation to listed NIMAR products in Northern Ireland.

Obligations of licence holder

43 (1) The licence holder must comply with the guidelines on good distribution practice:

(a) in the case of a licence holder in Great Britain, published under, or that apply by virtue of, regulation C17;

(b) in the case of a licence holder in Northern Ireland, published by the European Commission in accordance with Article 84 of the 2001 Directive.

(2) The licence holder must ensure, within the limits of the holder's responsibility, the continued supply of medicinal products to pharmacies, and other persons who may lawfully sell medicinal products by retail or supply them in circumstances corresponding to retail sale, so that the needs of patients in the United Kingdom are met.

(3) The licence holder must provide and maintain such staff, premises, equipment and facilities for the handling, storage and distribution of medicinal products under the licence as are necessary:

(a) to maintain the quality of the products; and

(b) to ensure their proper distribution.

(4) The licence holder must inform the licensing authority of any proposed structural alteration to, or discontinuance of use of, premises to which the licence relates or that have otherwise been approved by the licensing authority.

(5) Subject to paragraph (6), the licence holder must not sell or supply a medicinal product, or offer it for sale or supply, unless:

(a) in the case of a product for sale or supply:

(i) in Great Britain, there is a UKMA(GB), UKMA(UK), a COR(GB), a COR(UK), a THR(GB) or a THR(UK) (an "authorisation"); or

(ii) in Northern Ireland, there is a UKMA(NI), UKMA(UK), a COR(NI), a COR(UK), a THR(NI), a THR(UK), and EU marketing authorisation or an Article 126a authorisation (an "authorisation");

in force in relation to the product; and

(b) the sale or supply, or offer for sale or supply, is in accordance with the authorisation.

(6) The restriction in paragraph (5) does not apply to:

(a) the sale or supply, or offer for sale or supply, of a special medicinal product in the United Kingdom;

(b) the export from Northern Ireland to an EEA State, or supply for the purposes of such export, of a medicinal product which may be placed on the market in that State without a marketing authorisation, Article 126a authorisation, certificate of registration or traditional herbal registration by virtue of legislation adopted by that State under Article 5(1) of the 2001 Directive;

(ba) the export from Great Britain to an approved country for import, or supply for the purposes of such export, of a medicinal product which may be placed on the market in that country without:

(i) a marketing authorisation, certificate of registration or traditional herbal registration within the meaning of the 2001 Directive, by virtue of legislation adopted by that country under Article 5(1) of that Directive, where the approved country for import is an EEA State, or

(ii) such equivalent authorisation, certificate or registration in the approved country for import, under legislation in that country that makes provision that is equivalent to Article 5(1) of the 2001 Directive, where the approved country for import is not an EEA State;

(c) the sale or supply, or offer for sale or supply, of an unauthorised medicinal product where the Secretary of State has temporarily authorised the distribution of the product under regulation 174; or

(d) the wholesale distribution of medicinal products:
  (i) from Northern Ireland to a person in a country other than Great Britain or a country other than an EEA State; or
  (ii) from Great Britain to a person in a country other than Northern Ireland or a country other than an approved country for import.

(7) The licence holder must:
  (a) keep documents relating to the sale or supply of medicinal products under the licence which may facilitate the withdrawal or recall from sale of medicinal products in accordance with paragraph (b);
  (b) maintain an emergency plan to ensure effective implementation of the recall from the market of a medicinal product where recall is:
    (i) ordered by the licensing authority or:
      (aa) in the case of a licence holder in Great Britain, by an appropriate authority for the licensing of medicinal products in an approved country for import;
      (bb) in the case of a licence holder in Northern Ireland, by the competent authority of any EEA State; or
    (ii) carried out in cooperation with the manufacturer of, or the holder of:
      (aa) in the case of a product for sale or supply in Great Britain, the UKMA(GB) or UKMA(UK), certificate of registration or traditional herbal registration; or
      (bb) in the case of a product for sale or supply in Northern Ireland, the UKMA(NI) or UKMA(UK), EU marketing authorisation, Article 126a authorisation, certificate of registration or traditional herbal registration,
    for, the product; and
  (c) keep records in relation to the receipt, dispatch or brokering of medicinal products, of:
    (i) the date of receipt;
    (ii) the date of despatch;
    (iii) the date of brokering;
    (iv) the name of the medicinal product;
    (v) the quantity of the product received, dispatched or brokered;
    (vi) the name and address of the person from whom the products were received or to whom they are dispatched;
    (vii) where the receipt, dispatch or brokering of medicinal products takes places in Northern Ireland, the batch number of medicinal products bearing safety features referred to in point (o) of Article 54[1] of the 2001 Directive.

---

[1] Point (o) of Article 54a was inserted by Directive 2011/62/EU of the European Parliament and the Council (OJ No L 174, 1.7.2011, p. 74).

(8) A licence holder ("L") in Northern Ireland who imports from another EEA State a medicinal product in relation to which L is not the holder of a marketing authorisation, Article 126a authorisation, certificate of registration or a traditional herbal registration shall:

(a) notify the intention to import that product to the holder of the authorisation and:

(i)   in the case of a product which has been granted a marketing authorisation under Regulation (EC) No 726/2004, to the EMA; or

(ii) in any other case, the licensing authority; and

(b) pay a fee to the EMA in accordance with Article 76(4)[2] of the 2001 Directive or the licensing authority as the case may be, in accordance with the Fees Regulations,

but this paragraph does not apply in relation to the wholesale distribution of medicinal products to a person in country other than an EEA State.

(8A) Paragraph (8B) applies to a person ("P") who:

(a) imports into Great Britain a medicinal product, other than for the sole purpose of wholesale distribution of that product to a person in a country other than the United Kingdom; but

(b) is not the holder of a UK marketing authorisation, certificate of registration or traditional herbal registration in respect of that product.

(8B) Where this paragraph applies, P must:

(a) notify:

(i)   the holder of any authorisation, certificate or registration, granted by an authority in the country from which the product is exported, to sell or supply that product in that country; and

(ii) the licensing authority;

of the intention to import that product; and

(b) pay a fee to the licensing authority in accordance with the Fees Regulations.]

(9) For the purposes of enabling the licensing authority to determine whether there are grounds for suspending, revoking or varying the licence, the licence holder must permit a person authorised in writing by the licensing authority, on production of identification, to carry out any inspection, or to take any samples or copies, which an inspector could carry out or take under Part 16 (enforcement).

(10) The holder of a licence permitting wholesale dealings in Northern Ireland ("L") must verify in accordance with paragraph (11) that any medicinal products received by L that are required by

---

[2] Article 76(4) was inserted by Directive 2011/62/EU of the European Parliament and the Council (OJ No L 174, 1.7.2011, p. 74).

Article 54a[3] of the Directive to bear safety features are not falsified, but this paragraph does not apply in relation to the distribution of medicinal products received from a third country by a person to a person in a third country.

(11) Verification under this paragraph is carried out by checking the safety features on the outer packaging, in accordance with the requirements laid down in the delegated acts adopted under Article 54a(2) of the 2001 Directive.

(12) The licence holder must maintain a quality system setting out responsibilities, processes and risk management measures in relation to their activities.

(13) The licence holder must immediately inform the licensing authority and, where applicable, the marketing authorisation holder or EU marketing authorisation holder, of medicinal products which the licence holder receives or is offered which the licence holder:

(a) knows or suspects; or

(b) has reasonable grounds for knowing or suspecting;

to be falsified.

(14) Where the medicinal product is obtained through brokering:

(a) a licence holder in Great Britain must verify that the broker involved fulfils the requirements set out in regulation 45A(1)(b);

(b) a licence holder in Northern Ireland must verify that the broker involved is validly registered with the licensing authority or the competent authority of an EEA State.

(15) In this regulation, as it applies in the case of a product for sale or supply in Northern Ireland "marketing authorisation" means:

(a) a marketing authorisation issued by a competent authority in accordance with the 2001 Directive; or

(b) an EU marketing authorisation.

Obligations of licence holder in Great Britain supplying listed NIMAR products to Northern Ireland

43ZA (1) This regulation applies only to licence holders in Great Britain supplying listed NIMAR products to Northern Ireland.

(2) A licence holder must comply with the guidelines on good distribution practice, published under, or that apply by virtue of, regulation C17.

(3) So that the needs of patients in Northern Ireland are met, the licence holder must ensure, within the limits of the holder's responsibility, the continued supply of listed NIMAR products to—

---

[3] Article 54a was inserted by Directive 2011/62/EU of the European Parliament and the Council (OJ No L 174, 1.7.2011, p. 74).

(a) registered pharmacies in Northern Ireland;

(b) any person who may lawfully sell those products by retail sale or may lawfully supply them in circumstances corresponding to retail sale in Northern Ireland;

(c) any person who may lawfully administer prescription only medicines in Northern Ireland.

(4) The licence holder must provide and maintain such staff, premises, equipment and facilities for the handling, storage and distribution of listed NIMAR products under the licence as are necessary—

(a) to maintain the quality of the products; and

(b) to ensure their proper distribution.

(5) The licence holder must inform the licensing authority of any proposed structural alteration to, or discontinuance of use of, premises to which the licence relates or which have otherwise been approved by the licensing authority.

(6) The licence holder must not sell or supply, or offer for sale or supply, listed NIMAR products to a person in Northern Ireland, unless—

(a) there is a UKMA(UK) or UKMA(GB) in force in relation to that product; and

(b) the sale or supply is in accordance with that authorisation (except for the fact the product will be in Northern Ireland).

(7) The licence holder must—

(a) keep documents relating to the sale or supply of listed NIMAR products under the licence which may facilitate the withdrawal or recall from sale of such products in accordance with paragraph (b);

(b) maintain an emergency plan to ensure effective implementation of the recall from the market of a listed NIMAR product where recall is—

(i) ordered by the licensing authority; or

(ii) carried out in co-operation with the manufacturer of, or the holder of the corresponding UKMA(GB) or UKMA(UK) for the product; and

(c) keep records in relation to the receipt, dispatch or brokering of listed NIMAR products, of—

(i) the date of receipt,

(ii) the date of despatch,

(iii) the date of brokering,

(iv) the name of the listed NIMAR product,

(v) the quantity of the product received, dispatched or brokered,

(vi) the name and address of the person from whom the products were received or to whom they are dispatched; and

(d) provide the records in sub-paragraph (c) to the licensing authority on request.

(8) For the purposes of enabling the licensing authority to determine whether there are grounds for suspending, revoking or varying the licence, the licence holder must permit a person authorised in writing by the licensing authority, on production of identification, to carry out any inspection, or to take any samples or copies, which an inspector could carry out or take under Part 16 (enforcement).

(9) The licence holder must maintain a quality system setting out responsibilities, processes and risk management measures in relation to their activities.

(10) The licence holder must immediately inform the licensing authority of medicinal products which the licence holder receives or is offered which the licence holder—

(a) knows or suspects; or

(b) has reasonable grounds for knowing or suspecting, to be falsified.

(11) Where the listed NIMAR product is obtained through brokering, a licence holder must verify that the broker involved fulfils the requirements set out in regulation 45A(1)(b).

Requirement for wholesale dealers to decommission the unique identifier

43A (1) This regulation applies only to medicinal products that are required to bear safety features pursuant to Article 54a of the 2001 Directive.

(2) Before supplying a medicinal product to a person in Northern Ireland who falls within one of the classes specified in paragraph (3), the licence holder must verify the safety features and decommission the unique identifier of that medicinal product in accordance with the requirements laid down in Commission Regulation 2016/161.

(3) The classes of person mentioned in paragraph (2) are:

(a) persons authorised or entitled to supply medicinal products to the public who do not operate within a healthcare institution or within a pharmacy;

(b) persons who receive the product for the purpose of selling, supplying or administering it as a veterinary medicinal product;

(c) dentists;

(d) registered optometrists or registered dispensing opticians;

(e) registered paramedics;

(f) persons who are members of Her Majesty's armed forces;

(g) the Police Service of Northern Ireland;

(h) government institutions maintaining stocks of medicinal products for the purposes of civil protection or disaster control;

(i) universities or other institutions concerned with higher education or research, other than healthcare institutions;

(j) a prison service;

(k) persons carrying on the business of a school;

(l) nursing homes;

(m) hospices.

Requirement that wholesale dealers to deal only with specified persons

44 (1) ...

(2) The licence holder must not obtain supplies of medicinal products from anyone except:

(a) the holder of a manufacturer's licence or wholesale dealer's licence in relation to products of that description;

(b) the person who holds an authorisation granted by an approved country for import (in the case of a licence holder in Great Britain) or by an EEA State (in the case of a licence holder in Northern Ireland) or

(c) where the medicinal product is directly received:

(i) in the case of a licence holder in Great Britain, from a country that is not an approved country for import ("A"), for export to a country that is not an approved country for import ("B"); and

(ii) in the case of a licence holder in Northern Ireland, from a state other than an EEA State ("A") for export to another state other than an EEA State ("B");

the supplier of the medicinal product in country A is a person who is authorised or entitled to supply such medicinal products in accordance with the legal and administrative provisions in country A.

(d) ...

(3) Where a medicinal product is obtained in accordance with paragraph (2)(a) or (b), the licence holder must verify that:

(a) the wholesale dealer who supplies the product complies with the principles and guidelines of good distribution practices; or

(b) the manufacturer or importer who supplies the product holds a manufacturing authorisation.

(4) ...

(5) The licence holder may distribute medicinal products by way of wholesale dealing only to:

(a) the holder of a wholesale dealer's licence relating to those products;

(b) the holder of an authorisation granted by:

(i) in the case of a licence holder in Great Britain, the appropriate authority of an approved country for import;

(ii) in the case of a licence holder in Northern Ireland, the competent authority of another EEA State;

(iii) that is responsible for authorising the supply of those products by way of wholesale dealing;

(c) a person who may lawfully sell those products by retail or may lawfully supply them in circumstances corresponding to retail sale;

(d) a person who may lawfully administer those products; or

(e) in relation to supply:

    (i) in the case of a licence holder in Great Britain to persons in countries other than approved countries for import, a person who is authorised or entitled to receive medicinal products for wholesale distribution or supply to the public in accordance with the applicable legal and administrative provisions of the country to which the product is supplied;

    (ii) in the case of a licence holder in Northern Ireland to persons in a state other than an EEA State, a person who is authorised or entitled to receive medicinal products for wholesale distribution or supply to the public in accordance with the applicable legal and administrative provisions of the state other than an EEA State concerned.

(6) Where a medicinal product is supplied to a person who is authorised or entitled to supply medicinal products to the public in accordance with paragraph (5)(c) or (e), the licence holder must enclose with the product a document stating the:

(a) date on which the supply took place;

(b) name and pharmaceutical form of the product supplied;

(c) quantity of product supplied;

(d) name and address of the licence holder; and

(e) batch number of the medicinal products bearing the safety features referred to in point (o) of Article 54 of the 2001 Directive, in the case of a licence holder in Northern Ireland.

(7) The licence holder must:

(a) keep a record of information supplied in accordance with paragraph (6) for at least five years beginning immediately after the date on which the information is supplied; and

(b) ensure that the record is available to the licensing authority for inspection.

(8) A licence holder in Great Britain may only obtain a medicinal product in respect of which a UKMA(GB) was granted under the unfettered access route if the product satisfies the definition of qualifying Northern Ireland goods.

(9) Paragraph (2)(c) does not apply to:

(a) in the case of a licence holder in Great Britain, products received from Northern Ireland; and

(b) in the case of a licence holder in Northern Ireland, products received from Great Britain.

(10) Paragraph (5)(e) does not apply to:

(a) in the case of a licence holder in Great Britain, products supplied to Northern Ireland; and

(b) in the case of a licence holder in Northern Ireland, products supplied to Great Britain.

Requirement as to responsible persons

45 (1) Subject to regulation 45AA, the licence holder must ensure that there is available at all times at least one person (referred to in this regulation as the "responsible person") who in the opinion of the licensing authority:

(a) has knowledge of the activities to be carried out and of the procedures to be performed under the licence which is adequate to carry out the functions mentioned in paragraph (2); and

(b) has adequate experience relating to those activities and procedures.

(1A) In respect of licence holder in Great Britain, paragraph (1) is subject to regulation 45AA.

(2) Those functions are:

(a) ensuring that the conditions under which the licence was granted have been, and are being, complied with; and

(b) ensuring that the quality of medicinal products handled by the licence holder is being maintained in accordance with the requirements of:

(i) in the case of a licence holder in Great Britain, the UK marketing authorisations, certificates of registration or traditional herbal registrations, and

(ii) in the case of a licence holder in Northern Ireland, the marketing authorisations, requirements of regulation 167A, Article 126a authorisations, certificates of registration or traditional herbal registrations,

applicable to those products.

(3) The licence holder must notify the licensing authority of:

(a) any change to the responsible person; and

(b) the name, address, qualifications and experience of the responsible person.

(4) The licence holder must not permit any person to act as a responsible person other than the person named in the licence or another person notified to the licensing authority under paragraph (3).

(5) Paragraph (6) applies if, after giving the licence holder and a person acting as a responsible person the opportunity to make representations (orally or in writing), the licensing authority thinks that the person:

(a) does not satisfy the requirements of paragraph (1) in relation to qualifications or experience; or

(b) is failing to carry out the functions referred to in paragraph (2) adequately or at all.

(6) Where this paragraph applies, the licensing authority must notify the licence holder in writing that the person is not permitted to act as a responsible person.

Requirement as to responsible persons where licence holder imports from an approved country for import.

45AA (1) Subject to paragraph (2), this regulation applies to a licence holder in Great Britain where the licence holder imports a medicinal product from an approved country for import under a wholesale dealer's licence.

(2) The requirements of this regulation do not apply where an unlicensed medicinal product falling under paragraph (1) is imported:

(a) from an approved country for import for the sole purpose of distribution by way of wholesale dealing as a special medicinal product; or

(b) for the sole purpose of wholesale distribution of that product to a person in a country other than an approved country for import.

(3) The licence holder must ensure that there is available at all times at least one person (referred to in this regulation as the "responsible person (import)") whose name is included in the register established under regulation 45AB.

(4) A responsible person (import) must:

(a) carry out the functions under regulation 45(2), unless a responsible person under regulation 45 is performing those functions in respect of the licence;

(b) ensure that there is appropriate evidence to confirm that each production batch of a medicine imported from an approved country for import under the licence has been certified as provided for in Article 51 of the 2001 Directive, or such equivalent certification procedure as applies in the approved country for import; and

(c) ensure that each production batch of a medicinal product that is subject to the batch testing condition and that is imported into Great Britain from an approved country for import has been certified as being in conformity with the approved specifications in the UK marketing authorisation by:

(i) the appropriate authority; or

(ii) where the batch testing exemption applies, a laboratory in a country that has an agreement with the United Kingdom to the effect that the appropriate authority will recognise that certificate in place of the appropriate authority's own examination.

(5) The licensing authority must publish guidance on the documentation that it considers to be appropriate evidence for the purposes of paragraph (4)(b).

(6) Guidance published under paragraph (5) may be taken into account by the licensing authority in determining whether it considers there has been a failure to comply with this regulation.

(7) The licence holder must apply to vary the licence if a change is proposed to the responsible person (import).

(8) The licence holder must not permit any person to act as a responsible person (import) other than the person named in the licence.

(9) Paragraph (10) applies if:

(a) the person acting as responsible person (import) in respect of the licence is no longer included in the register under 45AB;

(b) the licensing authority thinks, after giving the licence holder and a person acting as a responsible person (import) the opportunity to make representations (orally or in writing), that the responsible person (import) is failing to carry out the functions referred to in paragraph (4) adequately or at all.

(10) Where this paragraph applies the licensing authority:

(a) must notify the licence holder in writing that the person is not permitted to act as a responsible person (import) in respect of that licence; and

(b) may, subject to regulation 45AB(3)(b), remove that person's name from the register under regulation 45AB.

(11) In this regulation, "unlicensed medicinal product" means a medicinal product in respect of which:

(a) there is no marketing authorisation, within the meaning of the 2001 Directive, in any EEA State in respect of that product, where the product is imported from an approved country for import that is an EEA State; or

(b) there is no licence or authorisation in respect of that product as regards its sale or supply in the approved country for import, where the product is imported from an approved country for import that is not an EEA State.

Register for responsible persons (import)

45AB (1) The licensing authority must maintain a register of persons ("the responsible person (import) register") who may carry out the role of responsible person (import) under regulation 45AA.

(2) The licensing authority may only include a person's name in the responsible person (import) register if that person:

(a) holds:

(i) a diploma, certificate or other evidence of formal qualifications awarded on completion of a university or other higher education course of study in pharmacy, chemistry, medicine, biology or a related life science; or

(ii) such other qualification as the licensing authority is satisfied is equivalent;

(b) is a member of:

(i) the Royal Society of Biology;

(ii) the Royal Pharmaceutical Society;

(iii) the Pharmaceutical Society of Northern Ireland;

(iv) the Royal Society of Chemistry; or

(v) such other body as may be specified by the licensing authority for the purpose of this paragraph; and

(c) has a minimum of 2 years' experience in performing the functions of a responsible person under regulation 45, or in performing such other functions that appear to the licensing authority to be equivalent.

(3) The licensing authority:

(a) may remove a person's name from the responsible person (import) register if it no longer considers that the person satisfies the requirements of paragraph (2); but

(b) it may not exercise that power unless it has given that person the opportunity to make representations to it (orally or in writing).

Schedule 4 Standard provisions of licences

PART 4 WHOLESALE DEALER'S LICENCE
All wholesale dealer's licences

28 The provisions of this Part are standard provisions of a wholesale dealer's licence.

29 The licence holder must not use any premises for the handling, storage or distribution of medicinal products other than those specified in the licence or notified to the licensing authority from time to time and approved by the licensing authority.

30 The licence holder must provide such information as may be requested by the licensing authority concerning the type and quantity of medicinal products which the licence holder handles, stores or distributes.

31 The licence holder must take all reasonable precautions and exercise all due diligence to ensure that any information provided by the licence holder to the licensing authority which is relevant to an evaluation of the safety, quality or efficacy of a medicinal product which the licence holder handles, stores or distributes is not false or misleading.

Wholesale dealer's licence relating to special medicinal products

32   The provisions of paragraphs 33 to 42 are incorporated as additional standard provisions of a wholesale dealer's licence relating to special medicinal products.

33   Where and in so far as the licence relates to special medicinal products, the licence holder may only import such products from, in the case of an import into Great Britain, an approved country for import and, in the case of an import into Northern Ireland, an EEA State:

(a) in response to an order which satisfies the requirements of regulation 167; and

(b) where the conditions set out in paragraphs 34 to 41 are complied with.

34   No later than 28 days prior to each importation of a special medicinal product, the licence holder must give written notice to the licensing authority stating the intention to import the product and stating the following particulars:

(a) the brand name, common name or scientific name of the medicinal product and (if different) any name under which the medicinal product is to be sold or supplied in the United Kingdom;

(b) any trademark or the name of the manufacturer of the medicinal product;

(c) in respect of each active constituent of the medicinal product, any international non-proprietary name or the British approved name or the monograph name, or, where that constituent does not have any of those, the accepted scientific name or any other name descriptive of the true nature of the constituent;

(d) the quantity of medicinal product to be imported, which must not exceed the quantity specified in paragraph 38; and

(e) the name and address of the manufacturer or assembler of the medicinal product in the form in which it is to be imported and, if the person who will supply the medicinal product for importation is not the manufacturer or assembler, the name and address of the supplier.

35   The licence holder may not import the special medicinal product if, before the end of 28 days beginning immediately after the date on which the licensing authority sends or gives the licence holder an acknowledgement in writing by the licensing authority that it has received the notice referred to in paragraph 34, the licensing authority has notified the licence holder in writing that the product should not be imported.

36   The licence holder may import the special medicinal product referred to in the notice where the licence holder has been notified in writing by the licensing authority, before the end of the 28-day period referred to in paragraph 35, that the product may be imported.

37 Where the licence holder sells or supplies special medicinal products, the licence holder must, in addition to any other records which are required by the provisions of the licence, make and maintain written records relating to:

(a) the batch number of the batch of the product from which the sale or supply was made; and

(b) details of any adverse reaction to the product sold or supplied of which the licence holder becomes aware.

38 The licence holder must not, on any one occasion, import more than such amount as is sufficient for 25 single administrations, or for 25 courses of treatment where the amount imported is sufficient for a maximum of three months' treatment, and must not, on any one occasion, import more than the quantity notified to the licensing authority under paragraph 34(d).

39 The licence holder must inform the licensing authority immediately of any matter coming to the licence holder's attention which might reasonably cause the licensing authority to believe that a special medicinal product imported in accordance with this paragraph can no longer be regarded as a product which can safely be administered to human beings or as a product which is of satisfactory quality for such administration.

40 The licence holder must not publish any advertisement, catalogue or circular relating to a special medicinal product or make any representations in respect of that product.

41 The licence holder must cease importing or supplying a special medicinal product if the licence holder receives a notice in writing from the licensing authority directing that, from a date specified in the notice, a particular product or class of products may no longer be imported or supplied.

41A A licence holder:

(a) in Great Britain may only supply a special medicinal product to a person in Northern Ireland; and

(b) in Northern Ireland may only supply a special medicinal product to a person in Great Britain,

in response to an order which satisfies the requirements of regulation 167.

42 In this Part:

"British approved name" means the name which appears in the current edition of the list prepared by the British Pharmacopoeia Commission under regulation 318 (British Pharmacopoeia, lists of names);

"international non-proprietary name" means a name which has been selected by the World Health Organization as a recommended international non-proprietary name and in respect of which the Director-General of the World Health Organization has given notice to that effect in the World Health Organization Chronicle; and

"monograph name" means the name or approved synonym which appears at the head of a monograph in the current edition of the British Pharmacopoeia, the European Pharmacopoeia, or a foreign or international compendium of standards, and "current" in this definition means current at the time the notice is sent to the licensing authority.

Wholesale dealer's licence relating to exempt advanced therapy medicinal products

43   The provisions of paragraph 44 are incorporated as additional standard provisions of a wholesale dealer's licence relating to exempt advanced therapy medicinal products.

44   The licence holder shall keep the data referred to in paragraph 16 of Schedule 6 for such period, being a period of longer than 30 years, as may be specified by the licensing authority.

Schedule 6 Manufacturer's and wholesale dealer's licences for exempt advanced therapy medicinal products

PART 2 WHOLESALE DEALER'S LICENCES

13   The requirements in paragraphs 14 to 20 apply to a wholesale dealer's licence in so far as it relates to exempt advanced therapy medicinal products.

14   The licence holder must obtain supplies of exempt advanced therapy medicinal products only from:

(a) the holder of a manufacturer's licence in respect of those products; or
(b) the holder of a wholesale dealer's licence in respect of those products.

15   The licence holder must distribute an exempt advanced therapy medicinal product by way of wholesale dealing only to:

(a) the holder of a wholesale dealer's licence in respect of those products; or
(b) a person who:
   (i)   may lawfully administer those products; and
   (ii) solicited the product for an individual patient.

16   The licence holder must establish and maintain a system ensuring that the exempt advanced therapy medicinal product and its starting and raw materials, including all substances coming into contact with the cells or tissues it may contain, can be traced through the sourcing, manufacturing,

packaging, storage, transport and delivery to the establishment where the product is used.

17 The licence holder must inform the licensing authority of any adverse reaction to any exempt advanced therapy medicinal product supplied by the holder of the wholesale dealer's licence of which the holder is aware.

18 The licence holder must, subject to paragraph 44 of Schedule 4, keep the data referred to in paragraph 16 for a minimum of 30 years after the expiry date of the exempt advanced therapy medicinal product.

19 The licence holder must secure that the data referred to in paragraph 16 will, in the event that:
(a) the licence is suspended, revoked or withdrawn; or
(b) the licence holder becomes bankrupt or insolvent;
be held available to the licensing authority by the holder of a wholesale dealer's licence for the period described in paragraph 18 or such longer period as may be required pursuant to paragraph 44 of Schedule 4.

20 The licence holder must not import or export any exempt advanced therapy medicinal product.

UK Legislation on Brokering Medicines

Contents

The Human Medicines Regulations 2012 [SI 2012/1916]

Editor's note   These extracts from the Human Medicines Regulations 2012 [SI 2012/1916] are presented for the reader's convenience. Reproduction is with the permission of HMSO and the Queen's Printer for Scotland. For any definitive information reference must be made to the original amending Regulations. The numbering and content within this section corresponds with the regulations set out in the published Statutory Instrument [SI 2012/1916] as amended.

Citation and commencement

1   (1)   These Regulations may be cited as the Human Medicines Regulations 2012.

(2)   These Regulations come into force on 14th August 2012.

General interpretation

8 (1) In these Regulations (unless the context otherwise requires):

"brokering" means all activities in relation to the sale or purchase of medicinal products, except for wholesale distribution, that do not include physical handling and that consist of negotiating independently and on behalf of another legal or natural person;

"falsified medicinal product" means any medicinal product with a false representation of:

(a) its identity, including its packaging and labelling, its name or its composition (other than any unintentional quality defect) as regards any of its ingredients including excipients and the strength of those ingredients;

(b) its source, including its manufacturer, its country of manufacturing, its country of origin or its marketing authorisation holder; or

(c) its history, including the records and documents relating to the distribution channels used.

Brokering in medicinal products

45A (1) A person may not broker a medicinal product in Great Britain unless:

(a) the product is covered by an authorisation granted:

(i) by the licensing authority; or

(ii) by an appropriate authority responsible for the licensing of medicinal products in an approved country for import; and

(b) that person:

(i) is validly registered as a broker with the licensing authority;

(ii) has a permanent address in the United Kingdom; and

(iii) complies with the guidelines on good distribution practice, which apply under, or by virtue of, regulation C17 in so far as those guidelines apply to brokers.

(1A) A person may not broker a medicinal product in Northern Ireland unless:

(a) the product is covered by an authorisation granted:

(i) under Regulation (EC) No 726/2004;

(ii) by the licensing authority; or

(iii) by a competent authority of a member State; and

(b) that person:

(i) is validly registered as a broker with the licensing authority or a competent authority of a member State;

(ii) except where the person is validly registered with the competent authority of an EEA state, has a permanent address in the United Kingdom; and

(iii) complies with the guidelines on good distribution practice published by the European Commission in accordance with Article 84 of the 2001 Directive in so far as those guidelines apply to brokers.

(2) A person is not validly registered for the purpose of paragraph (1)(b) or (1A)(b) if:

(a) the person's permanent address is not entered into a register of brokers kept by a competent authority of a Member State or the licensing authority (as appropriate);

(b) the registration is suspended; or

(c) the person has notified the competent authority of a member State or the licensing authority (as appropriate) to remove that person from the register.

Application for brokering registration

45B (1) The licensing authority may not register a person as a broker unless paragraphs (2) to (7) are complied with.

(2) An application for registration must be made containing:

(a) the name of the person to be registered;

(b) the name under which that person is trading (if different to the name of that person);

(c) that person's:
(i) permanent address in the United Kingdom;
(ii) email address; and
(iii) telephone number;

(d) a statement of whether the medicinal products to be brokered are:
(i) prescription-only medicines;
(ii) pharmacy medicines; or
(iii) medicines subject to general sale;

(e) an indication of the range of medicinal products to be brokered;

(f) evidence that that person can comply with regulations 45A(1)(b) (iii), 45E(3)(a) to (f) and 45F(1); and

(g) any fee payable in connection with the application in accordance with the Fees Regulations.

(3) Where the address at which the emergency plan, documents or record necessary to comply with regulation 45E(3)(b) to (d) are kept is different from the address notified in accordance with sub-paragraph (2) (c)(i), the application must contain:

(a) that address where the plan or records are to be kept;

(b) the name of a person who can provide access to that address for the purpose of regulation 325 (rights of entry); and

    (c) that person's:
      (i) address;
      (ii) email address; and
      (iii) telephone number.
(4) Unless paragraph (6) applies, the application for registration must:
    (a) be in English; and
    (b) be signed by the person seeking a brokering registration.
(5) The pages of the application must be serially numbered.
(6) Where the application is made on behalf of the person seeking a brokering registration by another person ("A"), the application must:
    (a) contain the name and address of A; and
    (b) be signed by A.

Criteria of broker's registration

45E (1) Registration of a broker is conditional on that broker:
    (a) complying with regulation 45A(1); and
    (b) satisfying:
      (i) the criteria in paragraphs (3), (4) and (7), and
      (ii) such other criteria as the licensing authority considers appropriate and notifies the broker of.
(2) The criteria referred to in paragraph (1)(b)(ii) may include (but are not limited to) the criteria specified in paragraphs (5) and (6).
(3) The broker must:
    (a) have a permanent address in the United Kingdom;
    (b) maintain an emergency plan to ensure effective implementation of the recall from the market of a medicinal product where recall is:
      (i) ordered by:
        (aa) in the case of a broker in Great Britain, the licensing authority or by an appropriate authority responsible for the licensing of medicinal products in an approved country for import; or
        (bb) in the case of a broker in Northern Ireland, the licensing authority or by the competent authority of any EEA State; or
      (ii) carried out in cooperation with the manufacturer of, or the holder of the marketing authorisation for, the product;
    (c) keep documents relating to the sale or supply of medicinal products under the licence which may facilitate the withdrawal or recall from sale of medicinal products in accordance with sub-paragraph (b);
    (d) record in relation to the brokering of each medicinal product:
      (i) the name of the medicinal product;
      (ii) the quantity of the product brokered;

(iii) the batch number where the sale or supply of the medicinal product is in Northern Ireland, of the medicinal product bearing the safety features referred to in point (o) of Article 54 of the 2001 Directive;

(iv) the name and address of the:

(aa) supplier; or

(bb) consignee; and

(v) the date on which the sale or purchase of the product is brokered;

(e) maintain a quality system setting out responsibilities, processes and risk management measures in relation to their activities; and

(f) keep the documents or record required by sub-paragraph (c) or (d) available to the licensing authority for a period of five years; and

(g) comply with regulation 45F(1), (2) and (4).

(4) Where the address at which the plan or records necessary to comply with paragraph (3)(b) to (d) are kept is different from the address notified in accordance with regulation 45B(2)(c)(i), the broker must:

(a) ensure that the plan or records are kept at an address in the United Kingdom; and

(b) inform the licensing authority of the address at which the plan or records are kept.

(5) The broker must provide such information as may be requested by the licensing authority concerning the type and quantity of medicinal products brokered within the period specified by the licensing authority.

(6) The broker must take all reasonable precautions and exercise all due diligence to ensure that any information provided by that broker to the licensing authority in accordance with regulation 45F is not false or misleading.

(7) For the purposes of enabling the licensing authority to determine whether there are grounds for suspending, revoking or varying the registration, the broker must permit a person authorised in writing by the licensing authority, on production of identification, to carry out any inspection, or to take any copies, which an inspector may carry out or take under regulations 325 (rights of entry) and 327 (powers of inspection, sampling and seizure).

Provision of information

45F   (1) A broker registered in the UK must immediately inform:

(a) the licensing authority; and

(b) in the case of a broker in:

(i) Great Britain, either:

(aa) the UK marketing authorisation holder; or

(bb) where applicable, the holder of the licence or authorisation granted by an appropriate authority responsible for the licensing of medicinal products in an approved country for import; or

(ii) Northern Ireland; either:

(aa) the UK marketing authorisation holder; or

(bb) where applicable, the EU marketing authorisation holder, of medicinal products that the broker identifies as, suspects to be or has reasonable grounds for knowing or suspecting to be, falsified.

(2) On or before the date specified in paragraph (3), a broker who is, or has applied to the licensing authority to become, a registered broker in the United Kingdom must submit a report to the licensing authority, which:

(a) includes a declaration that the broker has in place an appropriate system to ensure compliance with regulations 45A, 45B and this Regulation; and

(b) details the system that the broker has in place to ensure such compliance.

(3) The date specified for the purposes of this paragraph is:

(a) in relation to any application made before 31 March 2014, the date of the application; and

(b) in relation to each subsequent reporting year, 30 April following the end of that year.

(4) The broker must without delay notify the licensing authority of any changes to the matters in respect of which evidence has been supplied in relation to paragraph (2) that might affect compliance with the requirements of this chapter.

(5) Any report or notification to the licensing authority under paragraph (2) or (4) must be accompanied by the appropriate fee in accordance with the Fees Regulations.

(6) The licensing authority may give a notice to a registered broker requiring that broker to provide information of a kind specified in the notice within the period specified in the notice.

(7) A notice under paragraph (6) may not be given to a registered broker unless it appears to the licensing authority that it is necessary for the licensing authority to consider whether the registration should be varied, suspended or revoked.

(8) A notice under paragraph (6) may specify information that the licensing authority thinks necessary for considering whether the registration should be varied, suspended or revoked.

(9) In paragraph (3)(b), "reporting year" means a period of twelve months ending on 31 March.

Appendices

Appendix 1

Austria

Austrian Medicines and Medical Devices
Agency – Austrian Federal Office for Safety
in Health Care
Traisengasse 5
A-1200 Vienna
Austria
Phone: +43 50 555 36111
Email: BASG-AGESMedizinmarktaufsicht@
ages.at
Website: http://www.basg.gv.at

Belgium

DG Enterprise and Industry – F/2 BREY
10/073
Avenue d'Auderghem 45
B-1049 Brussels
Belgium

Federal Agency for Medicines and Health
Products
Avenue Galilée 5/031210 Brussels
Belgium
Phone: +32 2 528 40 00
Fax: +32 2 528 40 01
Email: welcome@fagg-afmps.be
Website: http://www.fagg-afmps.be/en

Bulgaria

Bulgarian Drug Agency
8, Damyan Gruev Str.
1303 Sofia
Bulgaria
Phone: +359 2 8903 555
Fax: +359 2 8903 434
Email: bda@bda.bg
Website: http://www.bda.bg

Bulgarian Food Safety Agency
15A, Pencho Slaveiko Blvd
1606 Sofia
Bulgaria
Phone: +359 2 915 98 20
Fax: +359 2 954 95 93
Email: cvo@bfsa.bg
Website: http://www.babh.government.bg

Croatia

Croatian Agency for Medicinal Products and
Medical Devices
Ksaverska c.4
10000 Zagreb
Croatia
Phone: +385 1 4884 100
Fax: +385 1 4884 110
Email: halmed@halmed.hr
Website: http://www.halmed.hr

Ministry of Agriculture, Veterinary and Food
Safety Directorate
Planinska Street 2a
10 000 Zagreb
Croatia
Phone: +385 6443 540
Fax: +385 6443 899
Email: veterinarstvo@mps.hr
Website: http://www.veterinarstvo.hr

Cyprus

Pharmaceutical Services – Ministry of Health
7 Larnacos Ave
15 Polyphimou, Stravolos Industrial Area
2033 Nicosia
Cyprus
Phone: +357 22 608 607
Fax: +357 22 339 623
Email: lpanagi@phs.moh.gov.cy
Website: http://www.moh.gov.cy

Czech Republic

State Institute for Drug Control
Srobárova 48
CZ-100 41 Praha 10
Czech Republic
Phone: +420 272 185 111
Fax: +420 271 732 377
Email: posta@sukl.cz
Website: http://www.sukl.eu

Institute for State Control of Veterinary Biologicals and Medicaments
Hudcova Str. 56A
CZ-621 00 Brno-Medlánky
Czech Republic
Phone: +420 541 518 211
Fax: +420 541 210 026
Email: uskvbl@uskvbl.cz
Website: http://www.uskvbl.cz/

Denmark

Danish Medicines Agency
Axel Heides Gade 1
2300 Copenhagen S
Denmark
Phone: +45 44 88 95 95
Fax: +45 44 88 95 99
Email: dkma@dkma.dk
Website(s) http://www.Imst.dk

European Commission

DG Enterprise F2 Pharmaceuticals
Rue de la Loi 200
B-1049 Brussels
Belgium

DG Health and Consumers: Unit D6: Medicinal Products – Quality, Safety and Efficacy;
Rue de la Loi 200
B-1049 Brussels
Belgium
Phone: +32 2 299 11 11
Email: sanco-pharmaceuticals-d6@ec.europa.eu
Website: http://ec.europa.eu/health/human-use/index_en.htm

European Medicines Agency (EMA)
Domenico Scarlattilaan 6
1083 HS Amsterdam
The Netherlands
Phone: +31 (0)88 781 6000
Email: info@ema.europa.eu
Website: http://www.ema.europa.eu/

Estonia

State Agency of Medicines
1 Nooruse Street
EE-50411 Tartu
Estonia
Phone: +372 737 41 40
Fax: +372 737 41 42
Email: info@ravimiamet.ee
Website: http://www. ravimiregister.ravimiamet.ee/en/default.aspx

Finland

Finnish Medicines Agency
PO Box 55
FI-00034 Fimea Helsinki
Finland
Phone: +358 29 522 3341
Fax: +358 29 522 3001
Email: registry@fimea.fi
Website: http://www.fimea.fi/

France

French National Agency for Medicines and Health Products Safety (ANSM)
143–147 bd
Anatole France
FR-93285 Saint Denis Cedex
France
Email: communication.ANSM@ansm.sante.fr
Website: http://www.ansm.sante.fr

Agence Nationale du Médicament Vétérinaire (ANMV)/Agence nationale de sécurité sanitaire de l'alimentation, de l'environnement et du travail (Anses)
14 rue Claude Bourgelat,
Parc d'Activités de la Grande Marche
Javené
CS 70611-35306 Fougères Cedex
France
Phone: +33 (0) 2 99 94 78 71
Email: sylvie.goby@anses.fr
Website: http://www.anses.fr

Germany

Federal Institute for Drugs and Medical Devices (BfArM)
Kurt-Georg-Kiesinger-Allee 3
53175 Bonn
Germany
Phone: +49 (0)228-207-30
Fax: +49 (0)228-207-5207
Email: poststelle@bfarm.de
Website: http://www.bfarm.de

Federal Office of Consumer Protection and Food Safety
Mauerstraße 39–42
D-10117 Berlin
Germany
Phone: +49 30 1 84 44-000
Fax: +49 30 1 84 44-89 999
Email: poststelle@bvl.bund.de
Website: http://www.bvl.bund.de (pharmaceuticals)

Paul-Ehrlich Institut (Federal Institute for Vaccines and Biomedicines)
Paul-Ehrlich-Straße 51–59
63225 Langen
Germany
Phone: +49 6103 77 0
Fax: +49 6103 77 1234
Email: pei@pei.de
Website: http://www.pei.de (vaccines, blood products, sera)

Greece

National Organization for Medicines
Messogion Avenue 284, cholargos

GR-15562 Athens
Greece
Phone: +30 213 2040 384
Fax: +30 213-2040 569
Email: inter.rel@eof.gr
Website: http://www.eof.gr (pharmaceuticals and immunologicals)

Hungary

National Institute of Pharmacy and Nutrition
Zrínyi U. 3
H-1051 Budapest
Hungary
Website: http://www.ogyei.hu/

National Food Chain Safety Office, Directorate of Veterinary Medicinal Products
Szállás utca 8
H-1107 Budapest 10.Pf. 318
Hungary
Phone: +36 1 433 03 30
Fax: +36 1 262 28 39
Email: ati@nebih.gov.hu
Website: http://www.nebih.gov.hu

Iceland

Icelandic Medicines Agency
Vinlandsleid 14
IS-113 Reykjavik
Iceland
Phone: +354 520 2100
Fax: +354 561 2170
Email: ima@ima.is
Website: http://www.ima.is

Ireland

Health Products Regulatory Agency (HPRA)
Kevin O'Malley House
Earlsfort Centre
Earlsfort Terrace
Dublin 2
Ireland
Phone: +353 1 676 4971
Fax: +353 1 676 7836
Email: info@hpra.ie
Website: http://www.hpra.ie

Department of Agriculture and Food
Kildare St
Dublin
Ireland
Phone: +353 1 607 20 00
Fax: +353 1 661 62 63
Email: info@agriculture.gov.ie
Website: http://www.agriculture.gov.ie

Italy

Italian Medicines Agency
Via del Tritone, 181
I-00187 Rome
Italy
Phone: +39 6 5978 401
Fax: +39 6 59944142
Email: forenamefirstletter.surename@aifa.gov.it
Website: http://www.agenziafarmaco.it

Laboratorio di Medicina Veterinaria, Istituto Superiore di Sanità
Viale Regina Elena 299
I-00161 Rome
Italy
Phone: +39 6 49 38 70 76
Fax: +39 6 49 38 70 77

Ministero della Salute, Direzione Generale della Sanità Animale e dei Farmaci Veterinari, Uff. 4
Viale Giorgio Ribotta, 5I-00144 Rome
Italy
Phone: +39 06 59 94 65 84
Fax: +39 06 59 94 69 49
Website: http://www.salute.it

Latvia

State Agency of Medicines
15 Jersikas iela
LV-1003 Riga
Latvia
Phone: +371-7078424
Fax: +371-7078428
Email: info@zva.gov.lv
Website: http://www.zva.gov.lv/

Food and Veterinary Service
Peldu St 30
LV-1050 Riga
Latvia

Phone: +371 67095271
Fax: +371 67095270
Email: nrd@pvd.gov.lv
Website: http://www.pvd.gov.lv

Liechtenstein

Office of Health/Medicinal Products Control Agency
Äulestr 512
FL-9490 Vaduz
Liechtenstein
Fax: +423 236 73 50
Email: pharminfo@llv.li
Website: www.llv.li

Lithuania

State Medicines Control Agency
Žirmūnų str. 139A
LT-09120 Vilnius
Lithuania
Phone: +370 5 263 92 64
Fax: +370 5 263 92 65
Email: vvkt@vvkt.lt
Website: http://www.vvkt.lt

National Food and Veterinary Risk Assessment Institute
J. Kairiukscio str. 10
LT-08409 Vilnius
Lithuania
Phone: +370 5 2780470
Fax: +370 5 2780471
Email: nmvrvi@vet.lt
Website: http://www.nmvrvi.lt

State Food and Veterinary Service
Siesiku str. 19
LT-07170 Vilnius
Lithuania
Email: info@vmvt.lt
Website: http://www.vmvt.lt

Luxembourg

Ministry of Health
Allée Marconi
L-2120 Luxembourg
Luxembourg

Phone: +352 24785593
Fax: +352 24795615
Email: luxdpm@ms.etat.lu
Email: vet marc.schmit@ms.etat.lu
Website: http://www.ms.etat.lu

Malta

Medicines Authority
Sir Temi Zammit Buildings
Malta Life Sciences Park
SGN 3000 San Gwann
Malta
Phone: +356 23439000
Fax: +356 23439161
Email: info.medicinesauthority@gov.mt
Website: www.medicinesauthority.gov.mt

**Veterinary Medicines Section within the
National Veterinary Laboratory of the Veterinary
and Phytosanitary Regulation Department**
Abattoir Square
Albert Town
MRS 1123 Marsa
Malta
Phone: +356 22925375
Email: veterinarymedicine@gov.mt
Website: http://agriculture.gov.mt/en/nvl/Pages/
missionStatement.aspx

The Netherlands

Medicines Evaluation Board
Graadt van Roggenweg 500
NL-3531 AH Utrecht
The Netherlands
Phone: +31 (0) 88 - 224 80 00
Fax: +31 (0) 88 - 224 80 01
Website: http://www.cbg-meb.nl/

Norway

Norwegian Medicines Agency (NOMA)
Postboks 240
Skøyen
0213 Oslo
Norway
Phone: +47 22 89 77 00
Fax: +47 22 89 77 99
Email: post@noma.no
Website: http://www.legemiddelverket.no

Poland

Chief Pharmaceutical Inspectorate
12 Senatorska str.
00-082 Warsaw
Poland
Phone: +48 (22) 831 21 31
Fax: +48 (22) 831 02 44
Email: gif@gif.gov.pl
Website: http://www.gif.gov.pl

**Office for Registration of Medicinal Products,
Medical Devices and Biocidal Products**
Al. Jerozolimskie 181C
02-222 Warsaw
Poland
Phone: +48 22 492 11 00
Fax: +48 22 492 11 09
Website: www.urpl.gov.pl

Portugal

**INFARMED – National Authority of Medicines
and Health Products, IP**
Av. do Brasil 53
P-1749-004 Lisbon
Portugal
Phone: +351 217987100
Fax: +351 217987316
Email: infarmed@infarmed.pt
Website: http://www.infarmed.pt/portal/page/
portal/INFARMED

Food and Veterinary Directorate General
Campo Grande, n.º 50
1349-018 Lisboa
Portugal
Phone: +351 21 323 96 55
Fax: +351 21 346 35 18
Email: dirgeral@dgav.pt
Website: http://www.dgv.pt

Romania

**National Agency for Medicines and Medical
Devices**
48, Av. Sanatescu
011478 Bucharest
Romania
Phone: +4021 317 11 00
Fax: +4021 316 34 97
Website: http://www.anm.ro/en/

Institute for Control of Biological Products and
Veterinary Medicines
Str. Dudului 37, sector 6
060603 Bucharest
Romania
Phone: +40 21 220 21 12
Fax: +40 21 221 31 71
Email: icbmv@icbmv.ro
Website: http://www.icbmv.ro/

Slovakia

State Institute for Drug Control
Kvetná 11
SK-825 08 Bratislava 26
Slovakia
Phone: +421 2 5070 1111
Fax: +421 2 5556 4127
Email: sukl@sukl.sk
Website: http://www.sukl.sk/

Institute for State Control of Veterinary
Biologicals and Medicaments
Biovetská 34
PO Box 52c
SK-949 01 Nitra
Slovakia
Phone: +421 37 6515506
Fax: +421 37 6517915
Email: uskvbl@uskvbl.sk
Website: http://www.uskvbl.sk/

Slovenia

Javna agencija Republike Slovenije za zdravila
in medicinske pripomočke
Ptujska ulica 21
Slovenčeva ulica 22
Sl-1000 Ljubljana
Slovenia
Phone: +386 8 2000 500
Fax: +386 8 2000 557
Email: info@jazmp.si
Website: http://www.jazmp.si

Spain

Spanish Agency of Medicines and Medical Devices
Parque Empresarial Las
Mercedes Edificio 8C
Campezo, 1
E-28022 Madrid

Spain
Phone: +34 91 8225997
Fax: +34 91 8225128
Email: internacional@aemps.es
Website: www.agemed.es

Sweden

Medical Products Agency
Dag Hammarskjölds väg 42/Box 26
SE-751 03 Uppsala
Sweden
Phone: +46 (0) 18 17 46 00
Fax: +46 (0) 18 54 85 66
Email: registrator@mpa.se
Website: www.lakemedelsverket.se

United Kingdom

Medicines and Healthcare products Regulatory
Agency
10 South Colonnade
Canary Wharf
London
E14 4PU
United Kingdom
Phone: +44 (0)20 3080 6000
Fax: +44 (0)203 118 9803
Website: www.mhra.gov.uk

National Institute for Biological Standards and
Control
Blanche Lane
South Mimms
Potters Bar
Hertfordshire
EN6 3QG
United Kingdom
Phone: +44(0) 1707 641000
Fax: +44 (0) 1707 641050
Email: enquiries@nibsc.org
Website: https://www.nibsc.org

Veterinary Medicines Directorate (VMD)
Woodham Lane
New Haw
Addlestone
KT15 3LS
United Kingdom
Phone: +44 1932 33 69 11
Fax: +44 1932 33 66 18
Email: postmaster@vmd.defra.gsi.gov.uk
Website: www.vmd.defra.gov.uk

Appendix 2

The Medicines and Healthcare products Regulatory Agency regulates medicines, medical devices and blood components for transfusion in the UK:
https://www.gov.uk/government/organisations/medicines-and-healthcare-products-regulatory-agency

Register of authorised online sellers of medicines:
http://medicine-seller-register.mhra.gov.uk

The Home Office plays a fundamental role in the security and economic prosperity of the United Kingdom:
https://www.gov.uk/government/organisations/home-office

The UK Border Force is a law enforcement command within the Home Office. It secures the UK border by carrying out immigration and customs controls for people and goods entering the UK:
https://www.gov.uk/government/organisations/border-force

In England the Care Quality Commission monitors, inspects and regulates health and social care services:
http://www.cqc.org.uk

The Regulation and Quality Improvement Authority is responsible for registering and inspecting independent hospitals, clinics and other care services in Northern Ireland:
http://www.rqia.org.uk

Healthcare Improvement Scotland regulates independent specialist clinics and healthcare services in Scotland:
http://www.healthcareimprovementscotland.org

Healthcare Inspectorate Wales is the regulator of independent healthcare in Wales:
http://www.hiw.org.uk

The General Medical Council's register of doctors, including "Licence to practise" information:
http://www.gmc-uk.org/doctors/register/LRMP.asp

The General Pharmaceutical Council's register of pharmacy premises, pharmacists and pharmacy technicians:
http://www.pharmacyregulation.org/registers

The Pharmaceutical Society of Northern Ireland's register of pharmacy premises, pharmacists and pharmacy technicians:
http://www.psni.org.uk/search-register

The Health & Care Professions Council register:
http://www.hpc-uk.org/check-the-register

The Royal College of Veterinary Surgeons' register:
http://www.rcvs.org.uk/registration/check-the-register

The General Dental Council's register:
http://www.gdc-uk.org/Pages/SearchRegisters.aspx

Public Health England's "Green Book" relating to vaccines:
https://www.gov.uk/government/collections/immunisation-against-infectious-disease-the-green-book

UK legislation:
http://www.legislation.gov.uk

European medicines legislation and guidelines:
http://ec.europa.eu/health/documents/eudralex/index_en.htm

European Medicines Agency:
http://www.ema.europa.eu/ema

EudraGMDP database:
http://eudragmdp.ema.europa.eu/inspections/displayWelcome.do

World Health Organization guidelines – distribution:
http://www.who.int/medicines/areas/quality_safety/quality_assurance/distribution/en

World Health Organization "List of globally identified websites of medicines regulatory authorities" (as of November 2012):
http://www.who.int/medicines/areas/quality_safety/regulation_legislation/list_mra_websites_nov2012.pdf?ua=1

Pharmaceutical Inspection Convention and Pharmaceutical Inspection Co-operation Scheme (PIC/S):
http://www.picscheme.org

MHRA-GMDP database relating to manufacturing and wholesale authorisations and certificates:
https://cms.mhra.gov.uk/mhra

Appendix 3

IMPORTATION OF ACTIVE SUBSTANCES FOR MEDICINAL PRODUCTS FOR HUMAN USE

QUESTIONS AND ANSWERS

In June 2016 the Commission published a revised question-and-answer document responding to frequently asked questions in relation to the import of active substances. The revised document is produced here, which includes the addition of Q&A 35 to clarify the requirements in case of importation of active substances released for sale before the expiration date of their written confirmation and minor editing of Q&A 10A and 29A and deletion of Q&A 29B.

The views expressed in this question-and answer-document are not legally binding. Ultimately, only the European Court of Justice can give an authoritative interpretation of Union law.

This documents sets out frequently asked "questions and answers" regarding the new rules for the importation of active substances for medicinal products for human use.

These rules are contained in Articles 46b and 111b of Directive 2001/83/EC.

The "written confirmation" is addressed in Article 46b(2)(b) of Directive 2001/83/EC.

1. QUESTION: WHEN DO THE NEW RULES FOR THE WRITTEN CONFIRMATION APPLY?
Answer: They apply as of 2 July 2013. Any active substance imported into the EU from that date is subject to the rules on the written confirmation.

2. QUESTION: DO THE RULES ON THE WRITTEN CONFIRMATION ALSO APPLY TO ACTIVE SUBSTANCES FOR VETERINARY MEDICINAL PRODUCTS?
Answer: No. The rules apply only to active substances for medicinal products for human use.

2A. QUESTION: DO THE RULES ON THE WRITTEN CONFIRMATION ALSO APPLY TO BLOOD PLASMA?
Answer: No. However, processed derivatives of plasma having a pharmacological, immunological or metabolic action are considered as active substances and written confirmation is thus required.

3. QUESTION: DO THE RULES ON THE WRITTEN CONFIRMATION APPLY TO ACTIVE SUBSTANCES FOR MEDICINAL PRODUCTS INTENDED FOR RESEARCH AND DEVELOPMENT TRIALS?
Answer: Active substances imported to be used in the manufacture of non-authorised medicinal products intended for research and development trials are excluded from the rules.

Active substances imported to be used in the manufacture of authorised medicinal products intended for research and development trials are expected to fulfil the requirements of Directive 2001/83/EC and be accompanied by a written confirmation, unless there is proof that the full amount of the imported API will be used for the manufacture of batches/units of an authorised medicinal product exclusively intended for research and development trials. In the latter case, those batches/units of an authorised medicinal product fall outside the scope of Directive 2001/83/EC and the API used in their manufacture is exempted from the rules on the written confirmation.

4. QUESTION: DO THE RULES ON THE WRITTEN CONFIRMATION APPLY TO ACTIVE SUBSTANCES THAT ARE BROUGHT INTO THE EU WITHOUT BEING IMPORTED ("IN-TRODUCED" ACTIVE SUBSTANCES)? AN EXAMPLE IS THE INTRODUCTION OF AN ACTIVE SUBSTANCE WHICH IS SUBSEQUENTLY EXPORTED.
Answer: No. The rules on the written confirmation only apply to the import of active substances for medicinal products for human use.

5. QUESTION: WHAT IF, AT THE TIME OF EXPORT OF AN ACTIVE SUBSTANCE TO THE EU, IT IS NOT KNOWN WHETHER THE ACTIVE SUBSTANCE IS USED IN A MEDICINAL PRODUCT FOR HUMAN USE OR NOT?
Answer: If the consignment is not accompanied by a written confirmation, the active substance cannot be used in a medicinal product for human use.

6. QUESTION: IS THE WRITTEN CONFIRMATION EXPECTED TO CONFIRM COMPLIANCE WITH EU RULES?
Answer: No. The written confirmation has to confirm compliance with GMP rules "equivalent" to the rules applied in the EU.

7. QUESTION: IN MY NON-EU COUNTRY, THE APPLICABLE STANDARDS FOR MANUFACTURING OF ACTIVE SUBSTANCES ARE THE GOOD MANUFACTURING PRACTICES FOR ACTIVE SUBSTANCES OF THE WORLD HEALTH ORGANIZATION (WHO) – FORTY-FOURTH TECHNICAL REPORT, NO. 957, 2010, ANNEX 2. ARE THESE STANDARDS EQUIVALENT TO THOSE IN THE EU, AS REQUIRED ACCORDING TO EU LEGISLATION?
Answer: Yes.

8. QUESTION: IN MY NON-EU COUNTRY, THE APPLICABLE STANDARDS ARE ICH Q7. ARE THESE STANDARDS EQUIVALENT TO THOSE IN THE EU, AS REQUIRED ACCORDING TO EU LEGISLATION?
Answer: Yes.

9. QUESTION: DOES THE WRITTEN CONFIRMATION HAVE TO BE ISSUED BY A CENTRAL, REGIONAL OR LOCAL AUTHORITY?
Answer: Each non-EU country decides autonomously which body within that country issues the written confirmation. That non-EU country may decide to issue the written confirmation at a central, regional or local level.

10. QUESTION: DO THE RULES APPLY ALSO TO ACTIVE SUBSTANCES CONTAINED IN AN IMPORTED FINISHED MEDICINAL PRODUCT?
Answer: No. Regarding finished medicinal products, the rules for importation of finished medicinal products (importation authorisation and batch release by a qualified person, see Articles 40(3) and 51 of Directive 2001/83/EC) apply. These rules remain unchanged.

10A. QUESTION: IS WRITTEN CONFIRMATION ALSO REQUIRED FOR A STARTING MATERIAL OR AN INTERMEDIATE USED FOR THE PRODUCTION OF AN ACTIVE SUBSTANCE, FOR EXAMPLE BY WAY OF PURIFICATION OR FURTHER SYNTHESIS?
Answer: No. Such starting material or intermediate used for the production of an active substance does not fulfil the definition of Article 1(3a) of Directive 2001/83/EC.

11. QUESTION: IS THE WRITTEN CONFIRMATION ALSO REQUIRED FOR IMPORTED AC-TIVE SUBSTANCES WHICH HAVE ALREADY BEEN MIXED WITH EXCIPIENTS, WITHOUT YET BEING THE FINISHED MEDICINAL PRODUCT?
Answer: No. Such partial manufacturing of the finished product is not included in the rules on the written confirmation.

11A. QUESTION: IS THE WRITTEN CONFIRMATION ALSO REQUIRED WHERE THE FIN-ISHED DOSAGE FORM MANUFACTURED IN THE EU IS DESTINED FOR EXPORTATION ONLY?
Answer: Yes.

12. QUESTION: WHO CHECKS THAT THE IMPORTED ACTIVE SUBSTANCE IS ACCOMPA-NIED BY THE WRITTEN CONFIRMATION?
Answer: This should be checked by the receiving manufacturer of the finished medicinal product. It may also be checked by the importer of the active substance upon its importation.
The verification whether such checks take place depends on the transposing law of the Member State where the active substance is imported. It may be verified:

- by the relevant authority upon importation; and/or
- in the context of an inspection of the importer of the active substance; and/or
- in the context of an inspection of the manufacturer of the medicinal product that uses the imported active substance.

13. QUESTION: HOW CAN I CHECK IF THE WRITTEN CONFIRMATION IS AUTHENTIC?
Answer: You should contact the manufacturer of the active substance or the issuing authority in the non-EU country.

14. QUESTION: IS THE WRITTEN CONFIRMATION SENT TO AN EU REGULATORY AGENCY?
Answer: No. The written confirmation accompanies the imported active substance.

15. QUESTION: DOES THE WRITTEN CONFIRMATION HAVE TO BE SUBMITTED WITH A REQUEST FOR AUTHORISATION OF A MARKETING AUTHORISATION OF A MEDICINAL PRODUCT?
Answer: No.

16. QUESTION: IS THE WRITTEN CONFIRMATION TO BE ISSUED FOR EACH BATCH/CONSIGNMENT?
Answer: No. The written confirmation is issued per manufacturing plant and the active substance(s) manufactured on this site.

17. QUESTION: DOES EACH IMPORTED CONSIGNMENT HAVE TO BE ACCOMPANIED BY THE WRITTEN CONFIRMATION?
Answer: Yes.

18. QUESTION: IS IT ACCEPTABLE THAT THE WRITTEN CONFIRMATION ACCOMPANY-ING THE IMPORTED CONSIGNMENT OF THE ACTIVE SUBSTANCE IS A COPY?
Answer: Yes, provided that the original written confirmation is still valid.

18A. QUESTION: REGARDING THE WRITTEN CONFIRMATION OF "EQUIVALENT" STANDARDS OF GOOD MANUFACTURING PRACTICE, CAN THE ISSUING AUTHOR-ITY OF THE NON-EU COUNTRY BASE ITSELF ON INSPECTION RESULTS FROM EU AUTHORITIES OR OTHER AUTHORITIES APPLYING EQUIVALENT STANDARDS FOR GOOD MANUFACTURING PRACTICE, SUCH AS US FDA?
Answer: Yes. In this case, the written confirmation should indicate which authority has inspected the site.

18B. QUESTION: REGARDING THE WRITTEN CONFIRMATION OF "EQUIVALENT" STANDARDS OF GOOD MANUFACTURING PRACTICE, CAN THE ISSUING AUTHORITY OF THE NON-EU COUNTRY BASE ITSELF ON INSPECTIONS CONDUCTED IN THE PAST?
Answer: Yes. It is not necessary to conduct an inspection specifically for the purpose of issuing the "written confirmation".

19. QUESTION: WHAT IS THE VALIDITY PERIOD OF THE WRITTEN CONFIRMATION?
Answer: The validity of the written confirmation is established by the issuing authority of the non-EU country.

19A. THE WRITTEN CONFIRMATION REFERS TO "UNANNOUNCED INSPECTIONS". DOES THIS MEAN THAT AN UNANNOUNCED INSPECTION HAS TO HAVE BEEN CON-DUCTED?
Answer: No. Rather, the system of supervision as a whole (including different types of inspections, such as unannounced inspections) has to ensure a protection of public health at least equivalent to that in the EU.

20. QUESTION: IF ACTIVE SUBSTANCES ARE MANUFACTURED IN A NON-EU COUNTRY "A", BUT IMPORTED IN THE EU VIA THE NON-EU COUNTRY "B", WHO HAS TO ISSUE THE WRITTEN CONFIRMATION?
Answer: The written confirmation accompanying the imported active substance has to be issued by the non-EU country where the active substance is manufactured (i.e. non-EU country "A").

21. QUESTION: THE TEMPLATE FOR THE WRITTEN CONFIRMATION REFERS TO A "CONFIRMATION NUMBER". DOES THIS NUMBER HAVE TO BE A SEQUENTIAL NUM-BER PER COUNTRY?
Answer: No. This number would be attributed by the issuing authority of the non-EU country.

22. QUESTION: THE TEMPLATE FOR THE WRITTEN CONFIRMATION REFERS TO A "RE-SPONSIBLE PERSON" IN THE ISSUING AUTHORITY. DOES THIS RESPONSIBLE PERSON HAVE TO HAVE A SPECIFIC QUALIFICATION?
Answer: No. The "responsible person" in this context is the person responsible within the adminis-tration for issuing the written confirmation.

23. QUESTION: ACCORDING TO THE TEMPLATE FOR THE WRITTEN CONFIRMATION, INFORMATION OF FINDINGS RELATING TO NON-COMPLIANCE ARE SUPPLIED TO THE EU. TO WHOM SHOULD THIS INFORMATION BE SENT?
Answer: The information should be sent to the European Medicines Agency (qdefect@ema.europa.eu).

24. QUESTION: IS THE WRITTEN CONFIRMATION ALSO REQUIRED WHERE THERE IS A "MUTUAL RECOGNITION AGREEMENT" BETWEEN A NON-EU COUNTRY AND THE EU?
Answer: Yes. The process of a written confirmation is independent of the existence of "mutual rec-ognition agreements".

25. QUESTION: IF A MANUFACTURING PLANT IS LOCATED IN A NON-EU COUNTRY "A", CAN THE WRITTEN CONFIRMATION BE ISSUED BY AN AUTHORITY IN ANOTHER NON-EU COUNTRY (NON-EU COUNTRY "B")?
Answer: No.

26. QUESTION: ARE THERE EXCEPTIONS FROM THE REQUIREMENT OF A WRITTEN CONFIRMATION?
Answer: The Commission publishes a list of countries which, following their request, have been assessed and are considered as having equivalent rules for good manufacturing practices to those in the EU. Active substances manufactured in these countries do not require a written confirmation.
See also Questions 27 and 28.

27. QUESTION: WHERE CAN I FIND THE LIST OF NON-EU COUNTRIES TO WHICH THE REQUIREMENT OF A WRITTEN CONFIRMATION DOES NOT APPLY?
Answer: The list is published in the *Official Journal of the European Union* and also reproduced here: http://ec.europa.eu/health/human-use/quality/index_en.htm.

28. QUESTION: HOW MANY NON-EU COUNTRIES HAVE SO FAR REQUESTED TO BE LISTED?
Answer: A list of non-EU countries which have so far requested to be listed is available here: http://ec.europa.eu/health/human-use/quality/index_en.htm.

29. QUESTION: WHEN IS THE LIST GOING TO BE PUBLISHED BY THE COMMISSION?
Answer: The Commission is going to publish an additional non-EU country on the list once its equivalence assessment has been finalised. The equivalence assessment takes several months from the request from the non-EU country.

29A. QUESTION: HOW DOES A NON-EU COUNTRY REQUEST TO BE LISTED?
Answer: The request is made by way of a letter to the Director-General of DG SANTE. It should contain the relevant information for conducting the "equivalence assessment".
More information on the procedure and the documents to be submitted is available a http://ec.europa.eu/health/human-use/quality/index_en.htm, under the section "Listing of third countries".
The relevant information can also be sent directly to the responsible service within the Commission (sante-pharmaceuticals-b4@ec.europa.eu).

30. QUESTION: DO I NEED A WRITTEN CONFIRMATION, EVEN THOUGH MY MANUFACTURING SITE HAS RECENTLY BEEN INSPECTED BY THE EUROPEAN DIRECTORATE FOR THE QUALITY OF MEDICINES (EDQM) OF THE COUNCIL OF EUROPE?
Answer: Yes. The process of a written confirmation is independent of such inspection activities. See also Question no. 31.

31. QUESTION: DO I NEED A WRITTEN CONFIRMATION, EVEN THOUGH MY MANUFACTURING SITE HAS RECENTLY BEEN INSPECTED BY AN EU MEMBER STATE?
Answer: Yes. The process of a written confirmation is independent of such inspection activities. However, exceptionally, and where necessary to ensure the availability of medicinal products, following inspections by an EU Member State, a Member State may decide to waive the need for a written confirmation for a period not exceeding the validity of the GMP certificate ("waiver").

32. QUESTION: I WOULD LIKE TO BE INSPECTED BY AN EU MEMBER STATE. WHERE DO I "APPLY" FOR SUCH AN INSPECTION?
Answer: You should address through:

- any registered importer of the active substance;
- any holder of a manufacturing authorisation that uses the active substance;
- any holder of a marketing authorisation that lists the active substance manufacturer to the national competent authority of the EU Member State where they are established.

33. QUESTION: WHAT HAPPENS WHEN AN ACTIVE SUBSTANCE MANUFACTURING SITE COVERED BY A WRITTEN CONFIRMATION IS FOUND GMP NON-COMPLIANT FOLLOWING AN INSPECTION BY AN EU MEMBER STATE?

Answer: A statement of GMP non-compliance issued by a EU Member State for a specific site and API supersedes the corresponding written confirmation until the noncompliance is resolved.

34. QUESTION: WHERE CAN I FIND A LIST OF ACTIVE SUBSTANCE MANUFACTURING SITES THAT RECEIVED STATEMENTS OF GMP NON-COMPLIANCE?

Answer: Statements of GMP non-compliance are stored in the EudraGMDP database (http://eudragmdp.eudra.org/inspections/displayWelcome.do) and publicly available.

35. QUESTION: CAN AN API BATCH MANUFACTURED DURING THE PERIOD OF VALIDITY OF A WRITTEN CONFIRMATION BE IMPORTED INTO THE EU ONCE THE WRITTEN CONFIRMATION IS EXPIRED?

Answer: Article 46(b)(2)(b) sets out that active substances can only be imported if manufactured in accordance with EU GMP or equivalent, and accompanied by a written confirmation from the competent authority of the exporting third country certifying, *inter alia*, that (1) the GMP standards applicable to the manufacturing plant are equivalent to those of the EU, and (2) the supervision of the plant compliance with GMP ensures a protection of public health equivalent to that of the EU.

It is legitimate to consider that the guarantees of equivalence provided by the written confirmation apply to any API batch in the scope of the written confirmation which was released for sale within the period of validity of the written confirmation, even if not exported in that time period.

Against this background, it can therefore be considered that the importation into the EU of an API accompanied by an expired WC is acceptable provided that the paperwork accompanying the consignment (1) unequivocally proves that the whole consignment has been manufactured and released for sale by the quality unit before the expiry date of the written confirmation, and (2) provides a solid justification of why a valid written confirmation is not available.

Appendix 4

1. GENERAL

1.1. Question: What are the safety features?
Answer: The safety features consist of two elements placed on the packaging of a medicinal product:

(1) a unique identifier, a unique sequence carried by a two-dimensional barcode allowing the identification and authentication of the individual pack on which it is printed; and
(2) a device allowing the verification of whether the packaging of the medicinal product has been tampered with (anti-tampering device).

1.2. Question: When do the rules on the safety features apply?
Answer: They apply as of 9 February 2019. Belgium, Greece and Italy have the option of deferring the application of the rules by an additional period of up to 6 years.
Belgium has however formally renounced using this option and confirmed the application of the new rules as of 9 February 2019.

1.3. Question: Do the safety features need to be applied on all medicinal products for human use?
Answer: No. The safety features should only be applied on the packaging of the following medicinal products for human use:
(1) medicinal products subject to prescription which are not included in the list set out in Annex I to of Commission Delegated Regulation (EU) 2016/161;
(2) medicinal products not subject to prescription included in the list set out in Annex II of Commission Delegated Regulation (EU) 2016/161.
(3) medicinal products to which Member States have extended the scope of the unique identifier or the anti-tampering device to in accordance with Article 54a(5) of Directive 2001/83/EC.

1.4. Question: Are there exceptions from the requirements for certain medicinal products to bear or not the safety features?
Answer: Yes. The list of categories of medicinal products subject to prescription which shall not bear the safety features are set out in Annex I of Commission Delegated Regulation (EU) 2016/161, while the list of medicinal products not subject to prescription which shall bear the safety features are set out in Annex II of the same Regulation.

1.5. Question: Do the rules on the safety features also apply to veterinary medicinal products?
Answer: No. The rules apply only to medicinal products for human use.

1.6. Question: Do the rules on the safety features apply to medicinal products intended for research and development trials?
Answer: Medicinal products intended for research and development trials and not yet granted a marketing authorisation are excluded from the rules on the safety features.

Authorised medicinal products have to fulfil the requirements of Directive 2001/83/EC and Commission Delegated Regulation (EU) 2016/161 up to the moment it becomes known which batch/unit will be used for research and development trials. In practice, there are two possible situations:

1. The product is manufactured for known use in a clinical trial
    An investigational medicinal product (IMP) that is manufactured in accordance with the marketing authorisation but is packaged for a clinical trial (not in the commercial presentation) is excluded from the rules on the safety features as it is solely manufactured and packed for the use in the clinical trial. The manufacturer would be required to hold a manufacturing and importation authorisation covering IMPs and the IMP certified under that authorisation in accordance with the clinical trial application noting that the clinical trial application must reflect these arrangements.

    Authorised auxiliary medicinal products cannot be manufactured under a manufacturing and importation authorisation covering IMPs and must fulfil the requirements of a marketed pack bearing safety features and decommissioned appropriately (see below).
2. The product is authorised and sourced from the regulated supply chain
    Medicines in their commercial presentations bearing safety features should be decommissioned in accordance with Articles 16 and 25(4)(c) of Commission Delegated Regulation (EU) 2016/161 before use as investigational medicinal products or authorised auxiliary medicinal products.

1.7. Question: Are the safety features required where the medicinal product manufactured in the EU is destined for exportation only?
Answer: No.

1.8. Question: In the case of a medicinal product bearing the safety features is brought into the territory of a Member State in accordance with Article 5(1) of Directive 2001/83/EC, do the rules on the safety features apply?
Answer: When a medicinal product is brought into the territory of a Member State in accordance with Article 5(1) of Directive 2001/83/EC, the rules on the safety features in principle do not apply, unless there is applicable national legislation requiring otherwise.

Member States can however use national legislation to regulate which provisions of Directive 2001/83/EC or of Commission Delegated Regulation (EU) 2016/16 apply to Article 5(1) products brought into their territory. Member States can, for example, require the mandatory verification/decommissioning of Article 5(1) products in accordance with Commission Delegated Regulation (EU) 2016/16.

In the absence of national legislation requiring otherwise, the rules on the safety features do not apply. The "importer" of a medicinal product brought into the territory of a Member State in accordance with Article 5(1) is not required, for example, to (re)place the safety features on its packaging (e.g. through labelling/relabelling operations) or to upload the unique identifiers, if present, into the national repository of the new Member State of destination. The verification of the safety features and decommissioning of the unique identifiers of Article 5(1) products already bearing the safety features are also not mandatory.

Pharmacies, healthcare institutions and other relevant stakeholders in that Member State are nevertheless strongly encouraged to verify the authenticity of and decommission the medicinal product before supplying it to the public.

1.9.　Question: Does an obligation to bear "the safety features" imply an obligation to bear both a unique identifier and an anti-tampering device?
Answer: Yes.

1.10.　Question: Once Commission Delegated Regulation (EU) 2016/161 applies, can manufacturers place the safety features, on a voluntary basis, on medicinal products not required to bear the safety features?
Answer: No. Once Commission Delegated Regulation (EU) 2016/161 applies, manufacturers cannot place the safety features on medicinal products not required to bear the safety features, unless the Member States have extended the scope of application of the unique identifier or of the anti-tampering device to those medicinal products in accordance with Article 54a(5) of Directive 2001/83/EC.

1.11.　Question: Certain medicinal products are currently bearing an anti-tampering device on a voluntary basis. Are those products allowed to maintain the anti-tampering device once Commission Delegated Regulation (EU) 2016/161 applies, if they are not required to bear the safety features?
Answer: Once Commission Delegated Regulation (EU) 2016/161 applies, medicinal products can only bear an anti-tampering device if they are in the scope of Article 54a(1) of Directive 2001/83/EC (i.e. if they are medicinal products subject to prescription or medicinal products listed in Annex II of Commission Delegated Regulation (EU) 2016/161) or if the Member State(s) where they are placed on the market extended the scope of the anti-tampering device to those medicinal products.

1.12.　Question: Would it be possible to place a unique identifier on the packaging of a medicinal product during the 3 years period between the publication of Commission Delegated Regulation (EU) 2016/161 and its application?
Answer: Yes, on a voluntary basis. It is recommended that, whenever possible, unique identifiers are placed on the packaging only once a functional national/supranational repository allowing the storage, verification of the authenticity and decommissioning of those identifiers is in place. Unique identifiers which are placed on medicinal products before such repository is in place are expected to be uploaded in the repository as soon as it becomes operational.

1.13.　Question: Will the mandatory changes to the packaging due to the placing of the unique identifier and of the anti-tampering device require the submission of variations to marketing authorisations?
Answer: The regulatory requirements to be followed to notify the EMA of the placing of the unique identifier and/or the anti-tampering device on centrally authorised products are detailed in an implementation plan developed by the EMA and the European Commission and published in the "product information templates" section of the EMA website: http://www.ema.europa.eu/docs/en_GB/document_library/Other/2016/02/WC500201413.pdf
　The regulatory requirements for nationally authorised products are available on the HMA/CMDh website: http://www.hma.eu/fileadmin/dateien/Human_Medicines/CMD_h_/Falsified_Medicines/CMDh_345_2016_Rev00_02_2016_1.pdf

1.14.　Question: Are there any mandatory specifications for the anti-tampering device?
Answer: In accordance with Article 54(o) of Directive 2001/83/EC and Article 3(2)(b) of Commission Delegated Regulation (EU) 2016/161, an anti-tampering device has to allow the verification of whether the packaging of the medicinal product has been tampered with.
　There are no other mandatory specifications. The standard EN ISO 21976:2020 "Packaging – Tamper verification features for medicinal product packaging" is available for manufacturers to consider.

1.15.   Question: Will the pharmaceutical companies receive any financial support (EU or national) for acquiring the instrumentation for applying the safety features on individual packages?

Answer: No, it is not currently foreseen that pharmaceutical companies will receive any financial support (EU or national) for acquiring the instrumentation for applying the safety features on individual packages.

1.16.   Question: Who shall bear the financial responsibility for the covering the expenses of establishment and implementation of the repository system?

Answer: In accordance with Article 31(1) of Commission Delegated Regulation (EU) 2016/161, the repositories system shall be set up and managed by a non-profit legal entity or non-profit legal entities in the Union by manufacturer and marketing authorisation holders. The costs of the system shall be borne by the manufacturer of medicinal products bearing the safety features in accordance with Article 54a(2)(e) of Directive 2001/83/EC.

1.17.   Question: Are radiopharmaceuticals required to bear the safety features?

Answer: No. All pharmaceutical forms and strengths of radiopharmaceuticals (as defined by Article 1(6) of Directive 2001/83/EC), radionuclide generators (as defined by Article 1(7) of Directive 2001/83/EC), radionuclide precursors (as defined by Article 1(9) of Directive 2001/83/EC) and kits (as defined by Article 1(8) of Directive 2001/83/EC) shall not bear safety features.

The wording of Article 54(o) of Directive 2001/83/EC ("medicinal products other than radiopharmaceuticals") excludes radiopharmaceuticals, as defined by Article 1.6 of the said Directive, from the scope of the safety features. Consequently, any medicinal product fulfilling the definition of radiopharmaceutical shall not bear the safety feature. Since radiopharmaceuticals are outside of the scope of the safety features, their addition to Annex I of Commission Delegated Regulation (EU) 2016/161 is unnecessary.

1.18.   Question: Concerning pandemic-influenza vaccines, the EMA mock-up procedure allows a vaccine to be developed and authorized in advance of a pandemic, containing a strain of flu virus that few people have been exposed to but that could potentially cause a pandemic. These can be modified into pandemic-influenza vaccines in a future pandemic case. After a pandemic has been declared there is an emergency procedure for the final vaccine. Are there exceptions from the requirements for pandemic-influenza vaccines to bear or not the safety features?

Answer: No, as pandemic influenza vaccines are not included in Annex I of Commission Delegated Regulation (EU) 2016/161. Pandemic–influenza vaccines authorised via the mock-up procedure should bear the safety features in accordance with the said Regulation.

1.19.   Question: In case of a bundle of several single packs sold as one unit, should the anti-tampering device and unique identifier be placed on the bundle packaging or on each single pack?

Answer: Whether a manufacturer needs to place the safety features on the bundle packaging or on each single pack within the bundle depends on how the medicinal product is described in its marketing authorisation dossier – regardless of what is the commercial sellable unit.

If, in the marketing authorisation dossier, the product presentation is described as a "multi-pack", the outer packaging as that of the bundle and the single packs as not for individual sale (the text 'can't be sold separately' or equivalent is present on the packs), then both the UI and the ATD need to be placed on the bundle packaging. The outer packaging must include, in addition to the unique identifier and ATD, all applicable labelling requirements as laid down in Article 54 of Directive 2001/83/EC.

If, however, the marketing authorisation dossier of the medicinal product describes the product presentation as a single pack and the text 'can't be sold separately' or equivalent is not present on the packs, then each pack within the bundle needs to be serialised and have an anti-tampering device.

In this case, the bundle packaging should not bear a unique identifier, but it may bear an aggregated code containing the information on all unique identifiers within the bundle.

1.20. Question: If a pack bearing the safety features is lawfully opened (e.g. by parallel traders/ manufacturers replacing the leaflet under the supervision of national competent authorities), can it be resealed (e.g. by applying a new ATD on top of the old, broken ATD)?
Answer: In certain circumstances, based on the assessment of the national competent authority in the destination Member State.

Parallel traders/manufacturers that wish to reseal packages must provide the competent authority in the destination Member State with sufficient information to allow an informed assessment of equivalence of the new anti-tampering device (description, explanation, mock-ups, pictures, etc. of both the original and replacement ATD). The newly placed ATD can only be considered equivalent if, inter alia, it is equally effective in enabling the verification of authenticity of the medicinal product and in providing evidence of tampering.

An anti-tampering device (ATD) placed on top of an older, broken ATD can be considered as effective in providing evidence of tampering as an ATD placed on an intact outer packaging only if:

(a)   The new ATD completely seals the pack and covers any visible sign of the original, broken ATD;
(b)   The replacement of the ATD is conducted in accordance with applicable good manufacturing practice for medicinal products and is subject to supervision by the competent authority; and
(c)   The manufacturer placing the equivalent ATD has verified the authenticity of the unique identifier and the integrity of the ATD on the original pack before breaking the ATD/opening the original pack, in accordance with Article 47a(1)(a) of Directive 2001/83/EC.

1.21. Question: Is it possible for manufacturers/wholesales/parallel traders to market/supply medicinal products with a packaging showing visible signs of opening/intrusion, but where the ATD has been replaced by a new ATD in accordance with Article 47a of Directive 2001/83/EC?
Answer: No. If the pack has been opened lawfully (see Q&A 1.20), the manufacturer placing an equivalent ATD should ensure the pack is perfectly re-sealed and no signs of the original, broken ATD are visible.
It should be noted that Articles 24 and 30 of Commission Delegated Regulation (EU) 2016/161 prohibit wholesalers and persons authorised or entitled to supply who receive a medicinal products having a packaging showing signs of tampering from supplying that product.

1.22. Question: In case of parallel-traded packs, can parallel traders cover or remove the safety features of the original pack?
Answer: Parallel traders covering or removing the existing safety features are required to place equivalent safety features in accordance with Article 47a of Directive 2001/83/EC (see also Q&A 1.20).
The new unique identifier should comply with the requirements of the Member State where the medicine is intended to be placed on the market (Article 17 of Commission Delegated Regulation Regulation (EU) 2016/161).
Furthermore, if the product code and/or batch number of the parallel-traded product change compared to the original product, parallel traders must place a new unique identifier after first decommissioning the original one. Centrally authorised products that are subject to the covering or removing of existing safety features are expected to display the original manufacturer's batch number
When placing an equivalent unique identifier, parallel traders are required to fulfil, inter alia, the obligations laid down in Articles 33, 40 and 42 of Commission Delegated Regulation (EU) 2016/161 concerning the uploading and keeping up to date of the information on the new unique identifier into the repositories system.
In all cases, traceability must be maintained in the repository system in accordance with Article 35(4).

1.23.   Question: Is it possible to place a transparent sticker used as an ATD over the human readable codes or the 2D Data Matrix, even if opening the pack might lead to the human-readable data and/ or 2D barcode being damaged and unreadable?

Answer: It is acceptable to place a transparent sticker, used as an ATD, over the 2D Data Matrix, provided that it does not impact its readability (for example if the sticker is reflective), and the Data Matrix does not contain information intended for the patient or included in accordance with the recommendation in Q&A 2.12 (e.g. content previously included in a QR code).

Concerning the human-readable code, the human-readable batch number and expiry date are relevant information for the patient and should remain readable after the pack is opened. Hence, it is not acceptable to place a transparent sticker, used as an ATD, over the human-readable batch number and expiry date if it risks damaging this information when the pack is opened.

1.24.   Question: In some cases a medicinal product may carry more than one batch number, typically when the product consists of an active component and a solvent. Which batch number(s) should be encoded in the medicines verification system in that case?

Answer: Only the batch number of the active substance needs to be encoded in the medicines verification system.

1.25.   Question: When repackaging or re-labelling a pack for the purpose of using it as authorised investigational medicinal product or authorised auxiliary medicinal product according to Article 16(2) of Commission Delegated Regulation (EU) 2016/161, the unique identifier should be decommissioned. What status of decommissioning should the pack have?

Answer: Until there is a specific status for these medicines in the EMVS system, the pack should be decommissioned as "SUPPLIED" when repackaging or re-labelling for use as an authorised investigational medicinal product or authorised auxiliary medicinal product.

1.26.   Question: During the transitional period, do manufacturers located in the EU/EEA need to place safety features on medicines intended for the Greek or Italian market?

Answer: No. Greece and Italy have decided to defer the entry into application of the safety features in line with Article 2(2)(b) of Directive 2011/62/EU. Medicines produced exclusively for the Greek or Italian market, regardless of their place of manufacture, are therefore not required to bear safety features before the entry into application of the new rules in Greece or Italy.

1.27.   Question: During the transitional period, can manufacturers located in Greece or Italy place unique identifiers on medicines intended for the rest of the EU/EEA? What about uploading data to the EU hub?

Answer: Yes. There are no geographic restrictions on the placing of safety features by manufacturers. Please see Q&A 7.19 regarding data upload.

1.28.   Question: Is there an obligation for direct suppliers to healthcare institutions to offer aggregation services?

Answer: No. The Delegated Regulation does not require hospital suppliers to provide aggregation services. Direct suppliers may however offer the service on a voluntary basis, providing the safeguards outlined in the Expert Group paper on implementation of the Falsified Medicines Directive in the hospital setting[3] are met.

2.   TECHNICAL SPECIFICATIONS OF THE UNIQUE IDENTIFIER

2.1.   Question: Does Commission Delegated Regulation (EU) 2016/161 limit the length of the unique identifier to 50 characters?

Answer: No. Only the length of the product code, one of the data elements of the unique identifier, is limited to 50 characters.

2.2.   Question: Would it be possible to include, on a voluntary basis, a two-dimensional barcode on the packaging of medicinal products for human use not having to bear the safety features if the information carried by the barcode does not serve the purposes of identification and authentication of the medicinal product and does not include a unique identifier?
Answer: Yes, provided that the relevant labelling provisions of Title V of Directive 2001/83/EC are complied with.

   Examples may include two-dimensional barcodes encoding price indications, reimbursement conditions, etc.

2.3.   Is it possible to keep one-dimensional barcodes on the packaging of medicinal products for human use having to bear the safety features, when adding the two-dimensional barcode carrying the unique identifier?
Answer: Yes, provided that the presence of both barcodes does not negatively impact the legibility of the outer packaging. In order to avoid incorrect scanning by end-users, if possible, the barcodes should not be placed in proximity to each other.

2.4.   Question: Is a printing quality of 1.5 according to ISO/IEC 15415 mandatory?
Answer: No. Manufacturers are required to use a printing quality which ensures the accurate readability of the Data Matrix throughout the supply chain until at least one year after the expiry date of the pack or five years after the pack has been released for sale or distribution in accordance with Article 51(3) of Directive 2001/83/EC, whichever is the longer period.

   The use of a printing quality of 1.5 or higher gives a presumption of conformity, i.e. manufactures using a printing quality of 1.5 or higher will be presumed to have fulfilled the requirement mentioned in the first paragraph without need to prove that it is actually the case.

   If a printing quality lower than 1.5 is used, manufacturers may be asked to prove that requirements mentioned in the first paragraph are met.

2.5.   Can manufacturers, on a voluntary basis, place the human readable code on medicinal products with packaging having the sum of the two longest dimensions equal or less than 10 centimetres?
Answer: Yes.

2.6.   Are medicinal products with packaging having the sum of the two longest dimensions equal or less than 10 centimetres exempted from bearing the two-dimensional barcode carrying the unique identifier?
Answer: No, Article 7(2) only provides for an exemption from bearing the unique identifier in human readable format. The unique identifier in machine-readable format – the 2D barcode – is still required.

2.7.   Question: Is it compulsory to print the national reimbursement number in human-readable format?
Answer: The national reimbursement number or other national number should be printed in human readable format only if required by the national competent authorities of the relevant Member State and not printed elsewhere on the packaging. It should be printed adjacent to the two-dimensional barcode if the dimensions of the packaging allow it.

2.8.   Question: Is it compulsory for the human-readable data elements of the unique identifier to be placed adjacent to the two-dimensional barcode?
Answer: Yes, whenever the dimensions of the packaging allow it.

2.9. Question: What is the smallest font size that can be used to print the unique identifier in human-readable format?
Answer: The font size of the unique identifier should be in accordance with the "Guideline on the readability of the labelling and package leaflet of medicinal products for human use" published in Eudralex – Notice to Applicants - Volume 2C (http://ec.europa.eu/health/files/eudralex/vol-2/c/2009_01_12_readability_guideline_final_en.pdf).

2.10. Question: When encoded in the 2D Data Matrix or printed on the packaging in human-readable format, should the data elements of the unique identifier follow the order laid down in Articles 4(b) or 7(1), respectively, of Commission Delegated Regulation (EU) 2016/161?
Answer: No. Manufacturers can choose the order of the data elements provided that all data elements required by national legislation and Article 4(b) (for the 2D Data Matrix) or Article 7 (for the human-readable format) are present.

2.11. Question: Commission Delegated Regulation (EU) 2016/161 does not mention batch number and expiry date as mandatory components of the human readable code. Is it mandatory to print the batch number and the expiry date in a human-readable format and adjacent to the two dimensional barcode?
Answer: Batch number and expiry date are mandatory components of the labelling of all medicinal products – regardless of whether they bear the safety features – and should be printed on the packaging in accordance with Article 54(h) and (m) of Directive 2001/83/EC. There is no obligation to place batch number and expiry date adjacent to the two dimensional barcode.

2.12. Question: Is it allowed to place a QR code on the packaging of a medicinal product bearing the safety features?
Answer: Commission Delegated Regulation (EU) 2016/161 does not prohibit the placing of a QR code as far as it is not used for the purposes of identification and authentication of medicinal products.

Marketing authorisation holders are however encouraged, wherever technically feasible, to exploit the residual storage capacity of the Data Matrix to include the information they would otherwise include in the QR code (see also Q&A 2.16). This would minimise the number of visible barcodes on the packaging and reduce the risk of confusion as regard the barcode to be scanned for verifying the authenticity of the medicinal product.

Furthermore, in order to avoid incorrect scanning by end-users, if possible, the QR code should not be placed in proximity of the Data Matrix.

2.13. Question: Where on the packaging should the unique identifier be placed?
Answer: The Delegated Regulation does not specify where on the outer packaging the safety features should be placed. The placement of the safety features is therefore to be supervised by competent authorities in accordance with current practice for labelling requirements.

2.14. Question: Can the graphics on the containers of the medicinal products be printed separately and the Data Matrix added at the final packaging stage - or are there digital printing technologies where all packaging graphics and the UI can be printed in one step?
Answer: The Delegated Regulation does not specify how the safety features should be applied to the outer packaging. The placement of the safety features is therefore to be supervised by competent authorities in accordance with current practice for labelling requirements. The specifics of the technologies used to apply the UI will be for the individual manufacturer to decide and for them to select the most appropriate model suitable for their needs.

According to Annex 16 of the EU GMP Guidelines paragraph 1.7.21, affixing the UI to the packaging of a medicinal product is the responsibility of the Qualified Person. Any outsourcing of this activity to a third party by the manufacturer of the finished medicinal product must be in accordance with the principles described in Chapter 7 of Part I of the EU GMP Guidelines.

2.15. Question: Upon the medicinal product being supplied to the public, the UI is decommissioned and the package is no longer active in the repository. However, the 2D Data Matrix can still be read-out, for example by a consumer using a smartphone application. Will the possibility to verify the authenticity of the product via the Data Matrix be extended to the end-user (patient)?
Answer: The Delegated Regulation does not provide for verification of the authenticity of the product by the end user. Nevertheless, the verification conducted by the person authorised to supply to the public guarantees that the product is not falsified.

2.16. Question: After the UI data has been encoded, can any residual storage capacity in the Data Matrix be used to store other information?
Answer: The Delegated Regulation states in Article 8 that manufacturers may include information additional to the information contained within the unique identifier in the two-dimensional barcode, where permitted by the competent authority in accordance with article 62 of Title V of the Directive 2001/83/EC. That information should be consistent with the summary of product characteristics, useful for the patient and may not contain promotional elements.
 The amount of residual storage capacity of the Data Matrix after the UI data has been encoded will depend upon the size of the Data Matrix as selected by the individual manufacturers responsible for the placing of the UI on the packaging.

2.17. Question: Do human-readable headers (PC, SN, Lot, EXP, NN) have to be placed adjacent to the respective data elements, on the same line, or is some flexibility possible?
Answer: Human-readable headers are not required to be placed adjacent/on the same line as the respective data element. Headers can be placed in any position which allows the unequivocal identification of the human-readable data element.

2.18. Question: For products bearing the human-readable code, is it acceptable to place data elements in multiple locations across the packaging?
Answer: It depends on the data elements and dimensions of the packaging. The product code and serial number should be placed on the same surface, where space allows, so to facilitate manual decommissioning of the unique identifier. Concerning the other data elements, an effort should be made to place them on the same surface as the product code and serial number. Should the packaging dimensions not allow it, however, it is acceptable to place the other data elements as close to the product code and serial number as possible (e.g. adjacent sides).

2.19. Question: Is it acceptable to use a 2D Data Matrix which is rectangular (rather than square) or printed white on black (rather than black on white)?
Answer: Yes. Manufactures can chose to encode the unique identifier in a 2D Data Matrix which is rectangular and/or printed white on black, provided that it fulfils the technical requirement laid down in Article 5 of Commission Delegated Regulation (EU) 2016/161.

2.20. Question: Is it mandatory to include Application/Data Identifiers as part of the human-readable headers or data elements?
Answer: No. Manufacturers can choose whether to include the Application/Data Identifiers as part of the human-readable headers/data elements.

2.21. Question: Is it acceptable to use stickers to place the unique identifier on the outer/immediate packaging?
Answer: The unique identifier should be printed on the packaging along with all other information required under article 54 of Directive 2001/83/EC, in accordance with Article 5(3) of Commission Delegated Regulation (EU) 2016/161.
Placing the unique identifier by means of stickers can be accepted in the following circumstances:

- No legal and/or technically feasible alternative exists (e.g. safeguard of trademark rights; glass/plastic immediate packaging without outer packaging; etc.); or
- National competent authorities authorise it due to the marketing authorisation, including for parallel import, or to safeguard public health and ensure continued supply.
  In cases where placing the unique identifier by means of stickers is authorised by national competent authorities under the circumstances mentioned above, the following conditions should be met:
- The sticker on which the unique identifier is printed should become one with the outer packaging/immediate packaging, i.e. the sticker should be tamper-evident and it should not be possible to remove it without damaging the packaging or the sticker itself or leaving visible signs;
- The sticker on which the unique identifier is printed should be placed by a manufacturer under GMP conditions; and
- The outer/immediate packaging on which the sticker is placed includes, in addition to the unique identifier, all applicable labelling requirements as laid down in Article 54 of Directive 2001/83/EC. Notwithstanding the above, placing the unique identifier by means of stickers should never be allowed when:
- It impairs readability. Article 56 of Directive 2001/83/EC requires that "the particulars referred to in article 54, 55 and 62 shall be easily legible, clearly comprehensible and indelible"; or
- The sticker on which the unique identifier is printed can be detached from the packaging without damaging the packaging or the sticker itself or leaving visible signs; or
- The sticker on which the unique identifier is printed is intended to be placed on top of an existing sticker, as this could engender confusion and suspicions of tampering.

2.22.   Question: Do human-readable headers (PC, SN, Lot, EXP, NN) have to comply with the provisions of the QRD-template?
Answer: Yes, preferably. According to version 10 of the QRD-template4, the product code, serial number and national reimbursement number in the human readable code should be preceded by the letters "PC", "SN" and "NN". Batch number and expiry date should follow the abbreviations laid out in Appendix IV of the QRD-template5.

2.23.   Question: Are there specific requirements for the characters used in batch and serial numbers?
Answer: No. However, in order to reduce the risk of false alerts due to end-user scanner misconfigurations, manufacturers are strongly encouraged to follow the recommendations below.
   Serial and batch numbers should preferably:
   Contain only uppercase letters;
   Not include special characters (eg. hyphens, question marks, etc.); and
   Avoid the use of the letters "I", "O", "Y" and "Z".

3.   GENERAL PROVISION ON THE VERIFICATION AND DECOMMISSIONING OF THE SAFETY FEATURES

3.1.   Question: How should the unique identifier be decommissioned if the two-dimensional barcode is unreadable or deteriorated?
Answer: The unique identifier in human readable format should be recorded by any suitable method allowing the subsequent manual querying of the repository system in order to verify and decommission the unique identifier.

3.2.   Question: Where the barcode carrying the unique identifier cannot be read, or in case the verification of the unique identifier is temporarily impeded, is it possible to supply the medicinal product to the public?

Answer: Article 30 of Commission Delegated Regulation (EU) 2016/161 prohibits supply to the public if there is reason to believe that the packaging of the medicinal product has been tampered with, or the verification of the safety features of the medicinal product indicates that the product may not be authentic.

In all other cases, the supply of medicinal products to the public is regulated by national legislation.

Without prejudice to national legislation, in the case where it is permanently impossible to read the unique identifier and verify the authenticity of the medicinal product, for example because both the Data Matrix and the human readable code are damaged, it is recommended that the medicinal product is not supplied to the public.

3.3.　Question: Can a medicinal product which cannot be authenticated be returned, and to whom? Who should pay for the return?
Answer: Commission Delegated Regulation (EU) 2016/161 does not change the national provisions in place regulating returns of medicines from persons authorised or entitled to supply medicinal products to the public (e.g. pharmacies and hospitals). The regulation of returns of medicinal products, including their financial aspects, remains a national competence.

3.4.　Question: Is the use of aggregated codes to simultaneously verify the authenticity of or decommission multiple unique identifiers permitted?
Answer: Recital 20 of the Delegated Regulation gives the possibility of giving aggregated codes allowing the simultaneous verification of multiple Unique Identifiers, provided that the requirements of Commission Delegated Regulation (EU) 2016/161 are complied with.

However, since aggregation is not regulated in the Delegated Regulation any action in that sense from manufacturers/wholesalers/parallel traders (or any actor in the supply chain, for the matter) is only voluntary and needs to be agreed upon by the stakeholders.

3.5.　Question: Is it possible to reverse the decommissioned status of a medicinal product that has been physically exported to third countries, when such product is brought back into the EU?
Answer: No. When a medicinal product is physically exported outside of the EU, its unique identifier must be decommissioned in accordance with Article 22(a) of Commission Delegated Regulation (EU) 2016/161. If the exported product is subsequently reimported onto the EU territory (e.g. because it is returned), it is considered an "import" and must be imported by a manufacturing import authorisation (MIA) holder (not a wholesaler) and is subject to the import requirements laid down in Article 51 of Directive 2001/83/EC (batch testing, batch release, etc.). The imported medicinal product should also be given a new unique identifier containing a new batch number and expiry date, if applicable, before it is released for sale and distribution in the EU.

3.6.　Question: Can a medicine with only one of the safety features (either the UI or ATD) that has been released for sale before 9 February 2019 remain on the market?
Answer: Yes, a medicine with either a UI or ATD that has been released for sale before 9 February 2019 and has not been repackaged or re-labelled may remain on the market until its expiry date.

3.7.　Question: Who should verify and decommission medicines with safety features that are to be used in clinical trials as investigational medicinal products or authorised auxiliary medicinal products?
Answer: According to Articles 16, 23 and 25(4)(c) of Commission Delegated Regulation (EU) 2016/161, the unique identifier on medicines in their commercial presentations bearing safety features should be verified and decommissioned either by manufacturers, wholesalers or persons entitled or authorised to supply to the public before use as authorised investigational medicinal products (IMPs) or authorised auxiliary medicinal products.

For medicines repackaged or relabelled for use in clinical trials, the manufacturer holding the manufacturing and importation authorisation covering IMPs should verify and decommission the unique identifier before they repackage or relabel the medicine.

For medicines that are not repackaged or relabelled, the person entitled or authorised to supply to the public who supplies the medicinal product for subsequent use in a clinical trial should verify and decommission the unique identifier.

In some cases, Member States may require wholesalers to verify and decommission unique identifiers on medicines supplied for clinical trials on behalf of certain entitites under Article 23.

4. VERIFICATION OF THE SAFETY FEATURES AND DECOMMISSIONING OF THE UNIQUE IDENTIFIER BY MANUFACTURERS

4.1. Question: Do the records referred to in Article 15 of Commission Delegated Regulation (EU) 2016/161 have to be stored in the repositories system?
Answer: No. The manufacturers can decide how and where to keep the records of every operation he performs with or on the unique identifier.

4.2. Question: Article 18 requires that, in case of suspected falsification or tampering, the manufacturer should inform the competent authorities. Should he also inform the holder of the marketing authorization for the medicinal product?
Answer: Yes, Article 46 of Directive 2001/83/EC requires manufacturers to inform the competent authority and the marketing authorisation holder immediately if they obtain information that medicinal products which come under the scope of their manufacturing authorisation are, or are suspected of being, falsified.

4.3. Question: Articles 18, 24 and 30 of Commission Delegated Regulation (EU) 2016/161 require that manufacturers, wholesalers and persons authorised or entitled to supply medicinal products to the public immediately inform national competent authorities in case of suspected falsification of medicinal products. How should this information be notified by manufacturers?
Answer: It is recommended that manufacturers contact national competent authorities, since the procedure to follow for such notification is a national competence. If they exist, national guidelines should be followed.

4.4. Question: Can a manufacturer use outer packaging carrying a unique identifier which has been placed by a packaging materials provider?
Answer: Yes. Art. 14 of Commission Delegated Regulation (EU) 2016/161 requires that the manufacturer responsible for placing the safety features on the medicinal product verifies that the two-dimensional barcode carrying the unique identifier complies with Articles 5 and 6 of the said Regulation, is readable and contains the correct information before releasing the medicinal product for sale and distribution.

Where pre-printed cartons are used, the outsourcing of the pre-printing of the UI to a packaging material provider should be done in accordance with Chapter 7 of Part I of the EU GMP Guidelines, including the signature of a written agreement among the parties establishing the corresponding responsibilities. The packaging materials provider should be audited and qualified.

The manufacturer releasing the product for sale and distribution (see Q&A 7.13) should verify the capacity of the contracted packaging materials provider to perform the task in accordance with the requirements of the Regulation and in compliance with applicable GMP. Upon receipt of the pre-printed packaging materials, the manufacturer of the finished medicinal product is expected to perform appropriate checks on the quantity and quality of the UIs in line with EU-GMP principles.

4.5. Question: Are manufacturers responsible for ensuring unique identifiers are readable and complete?

Answer: Yes. Manufacturers must check that the 2D barcode is readable and contains the correct information (Article 14 of Commission Delegated Regulation (EU) 2016/161).

Furthermore, manufacturers must work closely with marketing authorisation holders to ensure that all relevant information on unique identifiers has been uploaded correctly to the repository system and corresponds to the information encoded in the unique identifier before they release medicines for sale or distribution (Article 33(2) of Commission Delegated Regulation (EU) 2016/161).

4.6. Question: Can a manufacturer outsource the placing of the safety features on a packaged medicinal product to another manufacturer?

Answer: Yes. The outsourcing of the placing of the safety features on a packaged medicinal product can be contracted to another manufacturer in line with Chapter 7 of Part I of the EU GMP Guidelines, as long as they have a manufacturing authorisation (MIA). The contracting manufacturer must also make a statement confirming compliance with Annex 16 Appendix 1 of the EU GMP Guidelines available to the Qualified Person certifying the final product. The contracted manufacturer must be included in the marketing authorisation.

5. VERIFICATION OF THE SAFETY FEATURES AND DECOMMISSIONING OF THE UNIQUE IDENTIFIER BY WHOLESALERS

5.1. Question: How should the expression "the same legal entity" referred to in Articles 21(b) and 26(3) of Commission Delegated Regulation (EU) 2016/161 be interpreted?

Answer: This expression should be interpreted in accordance with national legislation. As general guidance, and without prejudice to national legislation, a legal entity may be considered the same when, for example, it has the same registration number in the national company registry or, if no national registration is required, the same number for tax purposes (i.e. VAT number).

5.2. Question: Member States may hold stocks of certain medicinal products for the purpose of public health protection. How should the unique identifiers on those products be verified and decommissioned?

Answer: In accordance with Article 23(f) of the Delegated Regulation, Member States may request wholesalers to verify the safety features of and decommission the unique identifier of medicinal products which are supplied to governmental institutions maintaining stocks of medicinal products for the purposes of civil protection and disaster control.

5.3. Question: Articles 18, 24 and 30 of Commission Delegated Regulation (EU) 2016/161 require that manufacturers, wholesalers and persons authorised or entitled to supply medicinal products to the public immediately inform national competent authorities in case of suspected falsification of medicinal products. How should this information be notified by wholesalers?

Answer: It is recommended that wholesalers contact national competent authorities, since the procedure to follow for such notification is a national competence. If they exist, national guidelines should be followed.

5.4.   Question: Articles 20, 21 and 22 require wholesalers to verify the authenticity and/or decommission the unique identifier only. Do wholesalers need to verify the integrity of the anti-tampering device when complying with those Articles?
Answer: No, wholesalers do not need to (but can) verify the integrity of the anti-tampering device when complying with Articles 20, 21 and 22.

5.5.   Question: Article 22(a) requires a wholesaler to verify the authenticity of and decommission the unique identifier of all medicinal products he intends to distribute outside of the Union. Is it necessary to decommission the unique identifier if the medicinal product is sold to a party established outside the EU but that product does not physically leave the wholesaler's premises in the EU?
Answer: No. The purpose of Article 22(a) is to ensure the decommissioning of unique identifiers on packs which leave the EU territory, in order to avoid that those active codes may be harvested by traffickers. In case the medicinal product is sold to a party established outside the EU but physically remains in the wholesaler's premises in the EU, the unique identifier on the product should not be decommissioned. If that medicinal product is subsequently imported (while physically remaining in the EU) by a holder of a manufacturing and import authorisation (a wholesaler cannot import medicinal products), no action from the wholesaler physically holding the product is required with regard to the safety features.

5.6.   Question: Do wholesalers have the obligation to decommissioning the unique identifier of a medicinal product when they sell the product "business-to-business" to a company which buys it for the purpose of research?
Answer: Article 23(g) allows the decommissioning by wholesalers of medicinal products supplied for the purpose of research, except when supplied to healthcare institutions. Although the Article does not explicitly mention that it applies to the supply of products for the purpose of research to companies which are not universities or other higher education establishments, it is desirable to include such a case in the scope of this Article (provided that those companies are not healthcare institutions) in order to guarantee the decommissioning of the unique identifiers on those products.

5.7.   Question: Is wholesale distribution of medicinal products with a damaged/unreadable 2D Data Matrix code allowed, if there is no suspicion of falsification?
Answer: It depends on the human readable code. If the verification of the authenticity of the unique identifier (UI) can be performed using the human readable code, the product can be further distributed.

If the verification of the authenticity of the UI cannot be performed (because the human readable code is damaged or absent), then the wholesaler should not further distribute the product with unreadable codes (Article 24 of Regulation No 2016/161). This requirement is independent of whether the verification was mandatory under Article 20 of Commission Delegated Regulation (EU) 2016/161 or voluntarily performed by wholesalers.

5.8.   Question: Can a wholesaler request another wholesaler to verify the authenticity and decommission the unique identifiers for medicinal products they intend to distribute outside the EU on their behalf?
No. According to Article 22(a), the wholesaler who intends to distribute medicinal products outside the EU must verify their authenticity and decommission the unique identifiers. This obligation cannot be delegated to another wholesaler.

5.9.   Question: During the transition period, can medicinal products destined for the rest of the EU (where safety features are mandatory) be distributed through the territory of Italy or Greece?
Yes. Directive 2001/83/EC and Commission Delegated Regulation (EU) 2016/161 do not prevent the distribution of medicines with safety features to Italy or Greece during the transition period.

5.10. Question: How can a wholesalers be sure that medicines they receive without safety features have been batch released prior to the entry into application of the safety features (9 February 2019)?
According to Commission Delegated Regulation (EU) 2016/161, marketing authorisation holders and manufacturers may only place medicines released before 9 February 2019 on the EU market without safety features. In principle this means that products on the EU market without safety features must have been released before the entry into application of the safety features.

Wholesalers may request that manufacturers include the batch release date in the delivery note of non-serialised medicines in order to confirm that the medicines were released before the safety features became mandatory.

5.11. Question: Should wholesalers be connected to the national repositories or can they be connected to the European hub?
A wholesaler physically holding products and performing activities related to wholesale outlined in Articles 20-23 Commission Delegated Regulation (EU) 2016/161 (such as the verification of returns or decommissioning for export) should be connected to and perform operations in the national repository where the activities take place. A connection to the national system is necessary to ensure that the the audit trail is accurate and complete.

5.12. Question: Is it possible for a wholesaler with multiple locations to use a single NMVO connection and account to verify and decommission medicines?
Answer: No. In order to ensure compliance with Articles 13 and 35(1)(g) of Commission Delegated Regulation (EU) 2016/161, each physical location of the wholesaler must be uniquely identifiable when connecting to the NMVS and performing operations in the system.

5.13. Question: According to Article 20(b) Commission Delegated Regulation (EU) 2016/161, wholesalers must verify medicinal products they do not receive from the manufacturer, marketing authorisation holder or wholesalers designated by the marketing authorisation holder. Is it necessary to verify the unique identifier of medicinal products sent directly from the manufacturer but purchased from a wholesaler who is neither the manufacturer, marketing authorisation holder or designated by the marketing authorisation holder?
Answer: No. The exemption in Article 20(b) refers to the physical transfer of medicines. Even if they have been purchased from a third party, medicines that have been shipped directly from the manufacturer, marketing authorisation holder or a designated wholesaler do not need to be verified in accordance with Article 20(b).

6.   VERIFICATION OF THE SAFETY FEATURES AND DECOMMISSIONING OF THE UNIQUE IDENTIFIER BY PERSONS AUTHORISED OR ENTITLED TO SUPPLY MEDICINAL PRODUCTS TO THE PUBLIC.

6.1. Question: In-patients in a hospital may be administered medicinal products during their stay, the costs of which may be charged to their insurer, which constitutes a sale. In this case, would the hospital (or any other healthcare institution) be allowed to verify the safety features and decommission the unique identifier of those products earlier than the time of supply to the public, in accordance with Article 25(2)?
Answer: Yes. In the case described, the charging of the medicinal products costs to the patient's insurer happens as a consequence of the administration of that product to the patient (regardless of whether the sale takes place before or after the actual administration). Consequently, it is considered that the charging of the cost of the medicinal product to the patient's insurer (or to the patient himself, for the matter) does not preclude hospitals from applying the derogation provided for in Article 25(2).

6.2.　Question: How should the expression "the same legal entity" referred to in Articles 21(b) and 26(3) of Commission Delegated Regulation (EU) 2016/161 be interpreted?

Answer: See Q&A 5.1.

6.3.　Question: Many hospitals and other healthcare institutions supply the contents of packages of a medicinal product to more than one patient. Where only part of a pack of a medicinal product is supplied, when should the decommissioning of the unique identifier be performed?

Answer: The unique identifier should be decommissioned when the packaging is opened for the first time, as required by Article 28 of Commission Delegated Regulation (EU) 2016/161.

6.4.　Question: Does automated dose dispensing require the placing of new safety features on the individual patient doses/packs?

Answer: No. Automated dose dispensing falls in the scope of Article 28 of Commission Delegated Regulation (EU) 2016/161. Consequently, it is not necessary to place new safety features on the individual patient's dose/pack.

6.5.　Question: Is it possible for the wholesaler to scan the unique identifiers (UI) in a consignment before shipping the consignment to a hospital, store the UI information and then, once the hospital received the consignment, decommission the UIs using the stored information following an explicit request by the hospital?

Answer: No, the above process is not in line with the provisions of Commission Delegated Regulation (EU) 2016/161:

− Since the decommissioning would happen through the wholesaler's computer using the wholesaler's log-in ID, the decommissioning operation would be recorded in the system and in the audit trail as an operation performed by the wholesaler, and not by the hospital. This is not acceptable as the audit trail would not reflect the reality of the supply chain, as required by Article 35(1)(g) of the Regulation.

− Articles 23 and 26 of Commission Delegated Regulation (EU) 2016/161 are explicit about those cases where wholesalers are entitled to decommission the safety features on behalf of hospitals. Decommissioning on behalf of hospitals under other circumstances is therefore not allowed.

6.6.　Question: Is it acceptable for hospitals/hospital pharmacies to subcontract their decommissioning obligations to wholesalers?

Answer: No. However, there are possible scenarios, compatible with Commission Delegated Regulation (EU) 2016/161, where wholesalers (including manufactures supplying their own products by wholesale) could facilitate the decommissioning operation of hospitals (illustrative examples only, list not exhaustive):

− Wholesalers could scan the packs in the hospital consignment to acquire the information on the UIs and encode such information into an aggregated code. Decommissioning would then be performed by the hospital by scanning the aggregated code. The only equipment needed for this operation would be a hand-held scanner and a computer (connected to the national repository).

− Wholesalers could acquire the information on the UIs in the hospital consignment and make this information available to the hospital, by secure means. The hospital would then use such information to perform the decommissioning (without having to physically scan the packs).

6.7.　Question: Articles 18, 24 and 30 of Commission Delegated Regulation (EU) 2016/161 require that manufacturers, wholesalers and persons authorised or entitled to supply medicinal products to the public immediately inform national competent authorities in case of suspected falsification of medicinal products. How should this information be notified by persons authorised or entitled to supply medicinal products to the public?

Answer: It is recommended that persons authorised or entitled to supply medicinal products to the public contact national competent authorities, since the procedure to follow for such notification is a national competence. If they exist, national guidelines should be followed.

6.8. Question: For persons authorised or entitled to supply medicinal products to the public operating within a healthcare institution, must the verification of the integrity of the anti-tampering device be done at the same time as the verification and decommissioning of the unique identifier?
Answer: No. Article 25(2) of Commission Delegated Regulation (EU) 2016/161 outlines that verification of the safety features can be done at any time a medicine is in the physical possession of a healthcare institution as long as no sale takes place between delivery to the healthcare institution and supply to the public. Therefore, decommissioning of the UI and verification of the ATD can be done separately before supply to the public.

6.9. Question: Is it possible for a pharmacy chain with multiple locations to use a single NMVO connection and account to verify and decommission medicines in different branches before dispense?
Answer: No. In order to ensure compliance with Articles 13 and 35(1)(g) of Commission Delegated Regulation (EU) 2016/161, each physical location of a pharmacy chain must be uniquely identifiable when connecting to the NMVS and performing operations in the system.

7. ESTABLISHMENT, MANAGEMENT AND ACCESSIBILITY OF THE REPOSITORIES SYSTEM.

7.1. Question: How should the expression "manufacturers of medicinal products bearing the safety features", as used in Commission Delegated Regulation (EU) 2016/161, be interpreted?
Answer: For the purposes of Commission Delegated Regulation (EU) 2016/161, "manufacturer" means the holder of a manufacturing authorisation in accordance with Article 40 of Directive 2001/83/EC. The expression "manufacturers of medicinal products bearing the safety features" encompasses any holder of the said authorisation performing partial or total manufacture of a medicinal product bearing the safety features.

7.2. Question: Article 31 of Commission Delegated Regulation (EU) 2016/161 allows wholesalers and persons authorised or entitled to supply medicinal products to the public to participate in the legal entity/ies setting up and managing the repositories system, at no costs. Can the terms of such participation be regulated by stakeholders, for examples through the statutes of establishment or incorporation of the legal entity/ies?
Answer: Yes, it is possible, provided that the terms do not contradict what is enshrined in legislation. In case of discrepancy, the provisions of Commission Delegated Regulation (EU) 2016/161 and Directive 2001/83/EC prevail.

7.3. Question: What is a supranational repository?
Answer: In practice, a repository serving as "national" repository for more than one Member State.

7.4. Question: How should the expressions "application programming interface" or "graphical user interface" referred to in Articles 32(4) and 35(1) of Commission Delegated Regulation (EU) 2016/161 be interpreted?
Answer: The expression "application programming interface" refers to a software/software interface consisting of a set of programming instructions and standards used by a piece of software to ask another piece of software to perform a task. The programming instructions and standards are set by the software being called upon. In the context of Commission Delegated Regulation (EU) 2016/161,

the expression refers to the programming instructions and standards allowing the software of persons authorised or entitled to supply medicines to the public, wholesalers and national competent authorities to query the repository system.

The expression "graphical user interface" (GUI) refers to a human/computer interface that allows users to interact with software or a database through graphical icons and visual indicators without the need of using complex programming language.

The purpose of Article 35(1)(i) is to ensure that, in case of software failure, wholesalers and persons authorised/entitled to supply medicines to the public have an alternative way to connect to the national medicine verification system to verify the authenticity of/decommission the unique identifier. However, to avoid that wholesalers and persons authorised/entitled to supply medicines to the public rely routinely on the GUI to verify the authenticity of/decommission the unique identifiers on their products, Article 35(1)(i) limits the circumstances in which they are entitled (i.e. have the legal right) to use the GUI to the case of failure of their own software. The use of the GUI in any other circumstance is not prohibited but is subject to the agreement of the national medicine verification organisation owning the GUI. See also Q&A 7.18.

7.5.   Question: Article 33(1), second subparagraph, requires that information referred to in paragraphs 2(a) to 2(d) of that article, with the exception of the serial number, is stored in the hub. Does this mean that the serial number cannot be uploaded to the hub?
Answer: No, the provision only regulates which information is to be stored in the hub.

7.6.   Question: Articles 34(4), 35(4) and 36(n) refer to the linking of the information on unique identifiers removed or covered to the information on the equivalent unique identifiers placed for the purposes of complying with Article 47a of Directive 2001/83/EC. Is the linking required to be at the level of individual unique identifiers? How does the linking work in practice?
Answer: No, it is not necessary to link individual unique identifiers. The link can be made at batch level by linking the list of decommissioned unique identifiers in the "old" batch (the batch to be repacked/relabelled) and the list of new unique identifiers placed on packs in the "new" batch (the repacked batch). The provision does not require the linking to be done at the level of individual unique identifiers, since the number of packs in the batch to be repacked/relabelled (and consequently the number of unique identifiers in that batch) may not correspond to the number of packs (and of unique identifiers) in the new batch – making a one-to-one link between unique identifiers impossible.

7.7.   Question: In Article 35(1)(f), does the upper limit of 300 ms for a repository to respond to queries also apply when multiple repositories are implicated in the query, for example in case of cross-border verification?
Answer: 300 ms is the maximum response time of an individual repository. When the verification/decommissioning operation requires the querying of multiple repositories in the repositories system, for example in case of cross-border verification, the maximum response time is obtained by multiplying the maximum response time of an individual repository (300 ms) by the number of repositories involved in the query – for example, the maximum response time for a query involving national repository A, the hub, and national repository B would be 900 ms.

It should be noted that the system response time does not include the time needed by the query data to move from one repository to the other (which depends from the speed of the internet connection).

7.8.   Question: How will the identity, role and legitimacy of the users of the repository system be verified?
Answer: It is the responsibility of the legal entity establishing and managing a repository to put in place appropriate security procedures ensuring that only verified users, i.e. users whose identity, role and legitimacy has been verified, are granted access to that repository.

7.9.   Question: In Article 38(1), does the sentence "with the exception of the information referred to in Article 33(2)" refer to data access only, or also to data ownership?
Answer: It refers to data access only.

7.10.   Question: In Article 38(1), what is the meaning of "information on the status of the unique identifier"?
Answer: The information on the status of the unique identifier includes whether the unique identifier is active or decommissioned, and in the latter case, the reasons for the decommissioning.

7.11.   Question: What is the purpose of the exceptions laid out to in the second sentence of Article 38(1) concerning access to the information referred to in Article 33(2) and the information on the status of a unique identifier?
Answer: Article 38 of Commission Delegated Regulation (EU) 2016/161 regulates the ownership and the access of the data stored in the repositories system. It lays down the general rule and an exception to that rule. Since the purpose of Article 38 is, inter alia, to protect the confidentiality of data in the repositories system, including commercially confidential data, as required by Article 54a(3)(b) and (c) of Directive 2001/83/EC, the exception should be interpreted narrowly. In particular, the use of the exception should be limited to those cases where access to the data is necessary to perform the verification/decommissioning operations required by Commission Delegated Regulation (EU) 2016/161, as explained in recital 38.

7.12.   Question: Is it possible to have multiple national repositories, multiple supranational repositories or a combination of national and supranational repositories serving the territory of a given Member State?
Answer: No. In accordance with Article 32, paragraphs 1 and 2, the territory of a given Member State should be served by the hub and either a national or a supranational repository connected to the hub.

7.13.   Question: For the purposes of the application of Articles 33 and 48 of Commission Delegated Regulation (EU) 2016/161, what is understood for 'medicinal products that have been released for sale or distribution'?
Answer: The text 'medicinal products that have been released for sale or distribution' refer to products which have been batch released in accordance with Article 51 of Directive 2001/83/EC. According to Annex 16 of the EU Guidelines for Good Manufacturing Practice for Medicinal Products for Human and Veterinary Use "Certification by a Qualified Person (QP) and Batch Release", the process of batch release comprises of:

i.   The checking of the manufacture and testing of the batch in accordance with defined release procedures.
ii.   The certification of the finished product batch performed by a QP signifying that the batch is in compliance with GMP and the requirements of its MA. This represents the quality release of the batch.
iii.   The transfer to saleable stock, and/or export of the finished batch of product which should take into account the certification performed by the QP. If this transfer is performed at a site other than that where certification takes place, then the arrangement should be documented in a written agreement between the sites.

Therefore, medicinal products that have been certified for release by a QP without including the safety features in their packaging before the 9th February 2019, may be placed on the market, distributed and supplied to the public until their expiry date.

7.14.   Question: How should the expression "marketing authorisation holder", as used in Commission Delegated Regulation (EU) 2016/161, be interpreted?
Answer: The term "marketing authorisation holder" is used in Commission Delegated Regulation (EU) 2016/161 to indicate holders of marketing authorisations in the sense of Article 6 of Directive 2001/83/EC.

7.15.   Question: Are parallel importers/distributors required to comply with Article 33(1) and upload the information in Article 33(2) into the repository system? Should they also upload a list of designated wholesalers?
Answer: Parallel traders are obliged to comply with Article 33 and upload in the repositories system in the following two cases:

– If they hold a marketing authorisation in the sense of Article 6 of Directive 2001/83/EC, in which case they may also upload the list of wholesalers they have designated in accordance with Article 20(b) of Commission Delegated Regulation (EU) 2016/161; or
– If they repack/relabel and place new safety features or replace safety features in accordance with Article 47a of Directive 2001/83/EC on the medicinal products they supply. In this case, parallel traders who do not hold a marketing authorisation in the sense of Article 6 of Directive 2001/83/EC may not designate their own wholesalers and should not upload a list of wholesalers into the repository system.

Parallel traders who repack/relabel their products and place new safety features or replace safety features in accordance with Article 47a of Directive 2001/83/EC on the medicinal products they supply have to comply with Articles 33, 40 and 42 of Commission Delegated Regulation (EU) 2016/161 as they are considered the "persons responsible for placing those medicinal products on the market" in that Member State.

7.16.   Question: In accordance with Article 33(1), the information laid down in Article 33(2) must be uploaded in the repositories system before the product is released for sale and distribution. Does this mean that the upload needs to take place before the Qualified Person (QP) performs the batch certification and thus the safety feature information relative to any manufacturing waste should also be uploaded in the system?
Answer: No. The information laid down in Article 33(2) of Commission Delegated Regulation (EU) 2016/161 needs to be present in the system at the time the batch is released for sale and distribution (see Q&A 7.13 for what is understood for released for sale or distribution). It is acceptable to upload that information at such a time that the system is not burdened with information relative to manufacturing waste, i.e. (parts of) manufactured batches that have not been certified, provided that the upload takes place before the medicinal product is transferred to saleable stock.

7.17.   Question: Does Article 37(d) require that a national medicine verification organisation (NMVO) directly alerts the relevant national competent authorities, the EMA and the Commission about a falsification? Is there is a time limit for such alerting?
Answer: The use of the term "provide for" in Article 37(d) of Commission Delegated Regulation (EU) 2016/161 means that an NMVO has to ensure that the national competent authorities, the EMA6 and the Commission7 are informed. The NMVO can fulfil this obligation either directly or by ensuring this task is performed by someone else.
    The NMVO should ensure authorities are informed as soon as it is clear that the alert triggered in accordance with Article 36(b) cannot be explained by technical issues with the repositories system, the data upload, the person performing the verification or similar technical issues.

7.18. Question: Does Article 35(1)(i) of Commission Delegated Regulation (EU) 2016/161 prohibit wholesalers and persons authorised or entitled to supply medicinal products to the public from using the national medicine verification system's graphical use interface (GUI) to verify/decommission the unique identifiers on their products when their own software is not broken?
Answer: No. The use of the GUI by wholesalers and persons authorised/entitled to supply medicines to the public in circumstances other than the failure of their own software is not prohibited but is subject to the agreement of the national medicine verification organisation owning the GUI (in the absence of entitlement, the agreement of the system owner is necessary). See also Q&A 7.4.

7.19. Question: Can a marketing authorisation holder delegate the uploading of the information laid down in Article 33(2) of Commission Delegated Regulation (EU) 2016/161?
Answer: Yes. Marketing authorisation holders (MAHs) may delegate the uploading of the information laid down in Article 33(2) to third parties by means of a written agreement between both parties. Please note that the MAHs can subcontract or delegate data uploading only to parties which perform the data upload by means of infrastructures, hardware and software that are physically located in the EEA. The MAH remains legally responsible for these tasks.

7.20. Question: What is meant by investigation of all potential incidents of falsification flagged in the system in Article 37(d) of Commission Delegated Regulation (EU) 2016/161?
Answer: The purpose of the investigation in Article 37(d) is to rule out that alerts triggered in the system have been caused for technical reasons, such as issues with the repository system, data upload, data quality, incorrect end-user scanning or other similar technical issues.

As outlined in Q&A 7.17, national competent authorities, EMA and the European Commission should be informed as soon as it is clear that alert cannot be explained by technical reasons. On the basis of the information received, an investigation into the falsification incident will be launched by the authorities in line with European and national procedures.

8.   OBLIGATIONS OF MARKETING AUTHORISATION HOLDERS, PARALLEL IMPORTERS AND PARALLEL DISTRIBUTORS.

8.1. Question: Can marketing authorization holders delegate the performing of their obligations under Articles 40 and 41 to a third party?
Answer: Marketing authorisation holders can (but are not obliged to) delegate part of their obligations under Articles 40 and 41 to a third party by means of a written agreement between both parties. However, marketing authorisation holders remain legally responsible for those tasks.

In particular, marketing authorisation holders can delegate the performing of their legal obligation under Article 40(a) and 40(b), as well as the decommissioning task in referred to in Article 41.

8.2. Question: Situations arise where, for the same batch of product, competent authorities from different Member States issue different levels of recall, e.g. patient level vs wholesaler level, or no recall at all. How will Article 40 of Commission Delegated Regulation (EU) 2016/161 work in this type of scenario?
Answer: Article 40 of Commission Delegated Regulation (EU) 2016/161 would not apply to recalls at patient level as the scope of the Delegated Regulation does not extend beyond the supply of the medicinal product to the end consumer. Where a medicinal product is recalled at pharmacy level in a Member State and at wholesale level in another, the marketing authorisation holder should customise the information he needs to provide in the relevant national/supranational repositories in accordance with Article 40(c).

8.3. Question: Certain Member States have national systems managing recalls and withdrawals of medicinal products in place. Would it be possible to interface those national systems with the repositories system for the verification of the safety features?
Answer: Commission Delegated Regulation (EU) 2016/161 does not provide for the connection between the national systems for recalls/withdrawal of medicinal product and the repositories system. Such connections may be considered by the legal entities managing the relevant repositories in the repositories system, on a voluntary basis.

8.4. Question: Are parallel importers/distributors required to comply with Articles 40 and 42 of Commssion Delegated Regulation (EU) 2016/161?
Answer: Parallel traders are obliged to comply with Articles 40 and 42 of Commission Delegated Regulation (EU) 2016/161 in the following two cases:

– If they hold a marketing authorisation in the sense of Article 6 of Directive 2001/83/EC.
– If they repack/relabel and place new safety features or replace safety features in accordance with Article 47a of Directive 2001/83/EC on the medicinal products they supply.

Parallel traders who repack/relabel their products and place new safety features or replace safety features in accordance with Article 47a of Directive 2001/83/EC on the medicinal products they supply have to comply with Articles 33, 40 and 42 of Commission Delegated Regulation (EU) 2016/161 as they are considered the "persons responsible for placing those medicinal products on the market" in that Member State.

8.5. Question: In the case of free samples which are obliged by national law to include in their labelling the sentence "Free sample. Not to be sold", can the obligation to bear the safety features be waived?
Answer: No. Article 41 of Commission Delegated Regulation (EU) 2016/161 requires that marketing authorisation holder intending to supply any of his medicinal products as a free sample shall, where that product bears the safety features, indicate it as a free sample in the repositories system and ensure the decommissioning of its unique identifier before providing it to the persons qualified to prescribe it. Consequently, free samples are in the scope of the Regulation and have to bear the safety features.

8.6. Question: Can marketing authorisation holders upload in the repositories system serial numbers that are never actually used as data elements of unique identifiers?
Answer: No. The purpose of the repository system is to the information on the safety features is contained. Serial numbers that are not actually used as data elements in unique identifiers should not be uploaded and stored in the repositories system as they represent a security risk for the system.

8.7. Question: What are the obligations of operators who supply medicinal products on the ground of Article 126a (Cyprus clause) with regard to the safety features?
Answer: The term "marketing authorisation holder" is used in Commission Delegated Regulation (EU) 2016/161 and in Directive 2001/83/EC to indicate holders of marketing authorisations in the sense of Article 6 of the said Directive. Hence, the term does not apply to operators who distribute medicinal products on the ground of Article 126a. However, in order to handle medicinal products, those legal entities have to have a manufacturing authorisation and/or a wholesale distribution authorisation and/or a parallel import license. They are therefore subject to the obligations laid down in Commission Delegated Regulation (EU) 2016/161 for manufacturers and/or wholesale distributors and/or parallel importers/distributors.

    In addition, should those operators place or replace the safety features in accordance with Article 47a of Directive 2001/83/EC on the medicinal products they supply, they need to comply with

Articles 33, 40 and 42 of Commission Delegated Regulation (EU) 2016/161 as they are the "person responsible for placing those medicinal products on the market" in the Member State for which an authorisations in the sense of Article 126a was granted.

8.8. Question: In the case of replacement of the safety features by parallel traders, can the decommissioning of the original unique identifier be carried out by the wholesaler from whom they receive the product?
Answer: No. The decommissioning of the original unique identifier must be performed by the parallel trader holding the manufacturing authorisation and replacing the safety features (Article 16 of Commission Delegated Regulation (EU) 2016/161).

8.9. Question: Should marketing authorisation holders upload the unique identifiers for products with 2D barcodes released for sale or distribution before 9 February 2019?
Answer: Yes. According to Article 48 of Commission Delegated Regulation (EU) 2016/161, medicines released for sale or distribution before 9 February 2019 without a unique identifier may remain on the EU market until their expiry date, as long as they are not repackaged or relabelled after that date. If they are repackaged or relabelled after 9 February 2019, the manufacturer must place safety features in accordance with Directive 2001/83/EC and Commission Delegated Regulation (EU) 2016/161.

This transitional measure does not apply for products which were released before 9 February 2019 with a unique identifier. The unique identifiers for such products should be uploaded to the system before the entry into application of the new rules (9 February 2019). This should help to avoid alerts for genuine products released before 9 February due to lack of data in the repository.

9. LISTS OF DEROGATIONS AND NOTIFICATIONS TO THE COMMISSION.

9.1. Question: Can marketing authorisation holders submit their proposals for amendments to Annex I of Commission Delegated Regulation (EU) 2016/161 to the Commission?
Answer: Only Member States notifications are taken into account for the purpose of establishing Annex I and II of the Delegated Regulation, in accordance with Article 54a(2)(c) of Directive 2001/83/EC. Concerning Annex I, Member States may inform the Commission of medicinal products which they consider not to be at risk of falsification (Article 54a(4) of Directive 2001/83/EC).

10. TRANSITIONAL MEASURES AND ENTRY INTO FORCE.

10.1. For the purposes of the application of Article 48 of Commission Delegated Regulation (EU) 2016/161, what is understood for 'medicinal products that have been released for sale or distribution'?
Answer: see Q&A 7.13.

11. ANNEX I

11.1. Question: How should the term "Kits" referred to in Annex I to Commission Delegated Regulation (EU) 2016/161 be interpreted?

Answer: The term "kit" is defined in Article 1(8) of Directive 2001/83/EC. It refers to "any preparation to be reconstituted or combined with radionuclides in the final radiopharmaceutical, usually prior to its administration".

11.2.   Question: Are fat emulsions used for parenteral nutrition and having an ATC code beginning with B05BA exempted from bearing the safety features?
Answer: Yes. Fat emulsions having an ATC code beginning with B05BA are included in the category "solutions for parenteral nutrition" listed in Annex I to Commission Delegated Regulation (EU) 2016/161. Such emulsions are therefore exempted from the obligation to bear the safety features.

12.   ANNEX II

12.1.   Question: Are over-the-counter omeprazole products formulated as gastro-resistant tablets in the scope of Annex 2 and therefore required to bear the safety features?
Answer: No. Only over-the-counter medicinal products containing omeprazole 20 or 40 mg formulated as hard gastro-resistant capsules have to bear the safety features, as the two reported incidents of falsification that led to certain omeprazole products being added to Annex II concerned that specific pharmaceutical form of omeprazole.

Index

H